MW00973572

Inside Windows® Server 2003

Inside Windows®
Server 2003

William Boswell

Addison-Wesley

Boston • San Francisco • New York • Toronto
Montreal • London • Munich • Paris • Madrid
Capetown • Sydney • Tokyo • Singapore • Mexico City

The publisher offers discounts on this book when ordered in quantity for bulk purchases and special sales. For more information, please contact:

U.S. Corporate and Government Sales
(800) 382-3419
corpsales@pearsontechgroup.com

For sales outside of the U.S., please contact:

International Sales
(317) 581-3793
international@pearsontechgroup.com

Visit Addison-Wesley on the Web: www.awprofessional.com

Library of Congress Cataloging-in-Publication Data

Boswell, William.
Inside Windows Server 2003 / William Boswell.
p. cm.
Includes index.
ISBN 0-7357-1158-5 (alk. paper)
1. Microsoft Windows Server 2003. 2. Operating systems (Computers) I. Title.
QA76.76.O63B6442 2003
005.4'4769—dc21

2002043779

ISBN 0-7357-1158-5
Text printed on recycled paper
1 2 3 4 5 6 7 8 9 10—CRW—0706050403
First printing, April 2003

This book is dedicated to Christine, who never once complained as the project devoured every last second of my time along with every square inch of horizontal surface in our house. No writer could ask for a more understanding or gracious companion.

Contents

Preface

The release of a new version of an operating system always brings up lots of questions. Is it worth the time and trouble to upgrade? What are the potential problems? How do I prepare for testing and evaluation and maybe for deployment? These decisions are especially complex in this situation because Windows Server 2003 is not a revolutionary change from Windows 2000. Instead, it incorporates hundreds of improvements, large and small, that you'll need to evaluate, both separately and as a whole, to justify an upgrade.

Windows Server 2003 also represents the first time in the history of Microsoft's NT-based product line that the desktop code has been released separately from the server code. By the time Windows Server 2003 products reach the market, XP will have been available for over a year. To deploy Windows Server 2003, then, you'll need to know how to manage a complex mix of Windows Server 2003 and Windows 2000 and NT servers accessed by any one of a half-dozen Windows clients, not to mention a wide variety of third-party clients.

This book is designed to lead you through the complexities of a full Windows Server 2003 deployment in a mixed operating environment. It starts with installing a single server and moves in logical progression through upgrading additional servers, installing hardware, handling name resolution, deploying and integrating Windows Server 2003 DNS, installing and configuring Active Directory, and making Windows Server 2003-based resources available to authorized clients, both on the local network and across the Internet. The release of Windows Server 2003 also represents a milestone because Microsoft has finally gotten truly fanatical about security, so this book pays special attention to the new security features.

Each chapter is constructed to present design principles first, followed by process descriptions that help you identify interoperability issues, and finally the procedures you'll need to install and configure the Windows Server 2003 features covered by the chapter. Each chapter starts off with a list of new features in Windows Server 2003 along with any significant improvements to features carried over from Windows 2000. Experienced Windows 2000 designers and administrators can use this list as a checklist to guide their evaluations.

My approach to presenting process details for Windows Server 2003 features reflects my background as a Naval nuclear power plant operator. In the nuclear program, it's not enough to know how to operate a piece of equipment. You have to know the principles behind each element of the equipment's design, how the equipment integrates into the plant as a whole, and how the equipment will affect plant operations if it fails in a variety of circumstances. I was fortunate because this experience allowed me to see how a team of operators, each with an encyclopedic knowledge of the equipment under his control, can keep complex systems running smoothly and even make the job seem easy. I hope to contribute something to your knowledge of Windows Server 2003 so that you can build the same kind of team in your IT organization.

Who Should Read This Book

Any IT professional who designs, manages, or works with Windows technology should evaluate the features in Windows Server 2003. This book will help you with that evaluation. If you plan on installing one or more of special-function Windows Server 2003, or upgrading to Windows Server 2003 Active Directory, this book will show you how to prepare for the deployment and how to troubleshoot problems that might crop up along the way.

If you have already migrated, or are in the process of migrating, to Windows 2000 and you want to know if Windows Server 2003 has any advantages for you, the New Features checklist at the beginning of each chapter will help guide you to the items you need for your evaluation. At a macro level, I was particularly impressed with the attention to security at all levels, especially IIS, and the improvements to Windows DNS, Active Directory replication, trust relationships between forests, the new Active Directory Migration Tool (ADMT), the integrated Resultant Set of Policies (RSoP) tools for group policy management, and the significant new features in Terminal Services, the Encrypting File System (EFS), Public Key Infrastructure (PKI), and the Distributed File System (Dfs). I would also call to your attention the overall improvement in performance, stability, and memory handling.

It takes time and money to upgrade a large infrastructure, but with Windows Server 2003, you will be rewarded with a system that is fast, handy to manage, and delivers benefits to your users in the form of speed and convenience.

Who This Book Is Not For

I've made the assumption throughout the book that you have experience with Windows NT servers and classic NT domains. If you have an IT background with other operating systems, and you prefer diving into the deep end of the pool when you approach a new subject, I think you'll find sufficient background explanations and references to help guide you through all but the most arcane subject areas. If you are just setting out to learn about Windows and networking technologies, this is not a good place to start.

Because this is a book about Windows Server 2003, if you are primarily concerned with deploying and managing desktops, you may want to check out one of the many books on Windows XP. If you want to know how the server-side features in Windows Server 2003 interoperate with XP and Windows 2000 clients so you can effectively troubleshoot features such as folder redirection, offline files, group policies, resource sharing, name resolution, remote user access, certificate enrollment, EFS, and smart cards, you'll find plenty of details here.

If you are primarily interested in certification on Windows Server 2003, most of the information you need to pass the exams is here, but you may not find it arranged in a way that is conducive to exam preparation. If you want the hands-on experience to go with the paper on the wall, I think you'll benefit from the deployment format of this book as you prepare for the exams.

Because of space limitations, this book does not cover the many new features of Internet Information Services (IIS) 6.0 or all the myriad aspects of Application-mode Terminal Services. It also does not cover the interoperability features for Novell NetWare and Novell Directory Services (NDS), Services for Macintosh (SFM), or Services for UNIX (SFU). Chapter 11, "Understanding Network Access Security and Kerberos," contains details of Windows Server 2003 Kerberos interoperability with UNIX-based MITv5 Kerberos.

Conventions

This book uses the following typographical conventions:

- A new term is set in *italics* the first time it is introduced—for example, Microsoft defines a *site* as an area of reliable, high-speed network communications.
- Paths for files, Active Directory objects, Registry keys and values, and group policy settings are set in fixed font—for example, the Hosts file is located in the `\Windows\System32\Drivers\Etc` folder, and DNS zone configuration information is stored in the Registry under `HKLM | Software| Microsoft| Windows NT | CurrentVersion | DNS Server | Zones`.
- Screen elements that are clicked, selected/deselected, checked/unchecked, opened/closed, or called out for specific attention are set in a fixed-pitch font—for example, click `Add` to open the Add Standalone Snap-In window; or, deselect the `Bridge All Site Links` option to remove global transitive bridging for site links.
- Menu items are set in small caps—for example, right-click the `My Network Places` icon and select PROPERTIES from the flyout menu.

- Names of graphical utilities and command-line utilities with specialized consoles are shown with an initial capital letter—for example, the Certificates console allows you to view your personal certificates, and objects representing disabled domain controllers are removed using Ntdsutil.
- Command-line utilities are set in uppercase when identified by name and in lowercase, fixed font when shown at the command line—for example, you can clear negative responses from the local DNS cache using the IPCONFIG utility as follows: `ipconfig /flushdns`.
- In paths and commands, placeholders are shown in italics—for example, the syntax for the RUNAS command is `runas /u:`*`user@domain.root`* `/smartcard`.

Acknowledgments

The best part of writing a book is the opportunity to work with gifted, passionate professionals. This book would not have been possible without their help and encouragement. I was doubly fortunate because this project was handled by two organizations within Pearson Education: New Riders and Addison-Wesley. I'd like to introduce you to some of the team so I can thank them individually.

The production editor for the majority of the project was Stacia Mellinger at New Riders. Stacia's patience and unswerving devotion to quality was both a challenge and an inspiration. Her hard work, enthusiasm, and good humor made this a tremendously enjoyable project. Stacia turned the project over to Jacquelyn Doucette, production manager at Addison-Wesley. Jacquelyn handled the thousand-and-one final details with an admirable finesse. Tyrrell Albaugh was the production manager who handled all the work caused by the last-minute name change. Thank you all for making this such an enjoyable experience.

The copy editor was Kelli Brooks. Kelli's eye for detail kept the book consistent and readable. Even more, her incredible ability to find meaning within lingo kept the contents pointed at true north no matter how much I swerved about.

The graphics editor was Michael Labonne from New Riders. Mike had the difficult task of taking my sketches and turning them into production-quality diagrams. He found out very quickly why my sixth-grade teacher encouraged me to be a writer instead of an artist.

The acquisition editors were Elise Walter and Jeff Riley from New Riders and Sondra Scott from Addison-Wesley. Jeff crusaded for a Windows Server 2003 title and paved the way for the book you hold in your hands. Elise brought fresh ideas and boundless good cheer to the project, and Sondra stoically stood by the project during the long months as Microsoft slipped its schedules to finalize the product.

The tough job of technical editing fell to two amazing individuals: David Shackelford and Bob Reinsch. Dave and Bob not only brought vast insight and experience to the project, but their insistence on clarity in every paragraph made them diligent advocates for you, the reader. Every writer wishes for peer reviewers of this caliber. There are not enough words to thank Dave and Bob adequately.

Many other folks at New Riders and Addison-Wesley, too numerous to mention, had a hand in making this book an attractive, high-quality product with an affordable price tag. Special thanks to Stephanie Wall from New Riders for all her help, encouragement, and professionalism in the turnover of the project to Addison-Wesley.

I'd like to end by thanking friends who helped out during the two years it took to finish this project. My colleague, Todd Logan, was unfailingly generous with his time, knowledge, and resources. His help was absolutely crucial to the completion of this book. I'm also indebted to Jeremy Moskowitz at Braincore, who freely lent me his expertise in group policy and Active Directory design as I worked through many different scenarios. Todd and Jeremy have a remarkable ability to see the essentials of a problem. They were not shy about pointing out flaws in my reasoning and my research. I appreciate their insight and diligent pursuit of right answers.

About the Author

William Boswell, MCSE, is the principal engineer for the Windows Consulting Group based in Phoenix, Arizona. In addition to training and consulting, Boswell writes the popular "Windows Insider" column for *MCP Magazine* and is a sought-after speaker for conferences such as TechMentor, SANS, and WinConnections. He can be contacted at `bboswell@winconsultants.com`.

About the Technical Reviewers

These reviewers contributed their considerable hands-on expertise to the entire development process for *Inside Windows® Server 2003*. As the book was being written, these dedicated professionals reviewed all the material for technical content, organization, and flow. Their feedback was critical to ensuring that *Inside Windows® Server 2003* fits our reader's need for the highest-quality technical information.

David Shackelford is a network engineer living a wonderful life in Whittier, California. The son of a brilliant programmer and a mother who likes to light firecrackers, David earned a graduate degree studying medieval literature before succumbing to the call of packets and kernels. He earned his MCSE and MCT in 1997 and taught Microsoft networking and operating system classes around the country for the likes of Intel and Hewlett-Packard before settling down to manage a portion of an enterprise network. He currently works for ChoicePoint, Inc., as a lead systems/network engineer and was recently seen teaching Cisco technologies at Biola University. When he's not playing with his sons or brewing beer with his indulgent wife, he reads poetry and tries to talk friends into playing tedious wargames with him.

Bob Reinsch is a trainer and consultant based out of Lawrence, Kansas. He is a graduate of Wichita State University and has been involved with computers since 1977. He is an MCSE, MCT, a Compaq Accredited Systems Engineer and Authorized Compaq Instructor, SAIR/GNU Linux Certified Professional, Certified Technical Trainer, and Authorized Instructor for Real World Security. This is Bob's 18th technical editing effort. Bob can be reached at `bob@piercingblue.com`.

1
Installing and Configuring Windows Server 2003

THE CHAPTERS IN THIS BOOK ARE LAID out roughly in the order you would perform a production Windows Server 2003 deployment. Let's start off with setting up a server. This chapter covers the following topics:

- Feature comparison of the various Windows Server 2003 versions
- Hardware recommendations for Windows Server 2003, Standard and Enterprise Editions
- Comprehensive pre-deployment checklist
- Overview of setup operations to highlight critical decision points
- Detailed steps for a server installation
- Analysis of boot sequence to use for troubleshooting
- Tips for correcting common setup problems

Chapter 2, "Performing Upgrades and Automated Installations," finishes up the deployment topics. Chapter 3, "Adding Hardware," contains information about modifying a system after installation.

Before installing or upgrading production servers, you should read the chapters covering IP-based services in Windows Server 2003, especially name resolution and DNS. If you are deploying servers within a domain, or you plan on upgrading an existing domain, you should get familiar with the requirements of Active Directory (AD) and network access security.

New Features in Windows Server 2003

This chapter covers new features in Windows Server 2003 that relate to setup and post-setup configuration when installing the operating system from CD:

- **New server packaging.** There are four different versions of Windows Server 2003, each with a unique feature set. They are Web Edition, Standard Edition, Enterprise Edition, and Datacenter Edition.
- **New hardware requirements.** Windows Server 2003 requires more memory, faster processors, and more storage capacity.
- **Itanium support.** Separate 64-bit Intel Architecture (IA64) versions of Windows Server 2003, Enterprise and Datacenter Editions, are available. This chapter covers system setup using the Extensible Firmware Interface (EFI) and preparing GUID Partition Table (GPT) disks.
- **NTFS format done during Setup.** Earlier versions of Windows NT/2000 formatted the boot partition as FAT then converted it to NTFS. Formatting the boot partition directly as NTFS reduces Master File Table (MFT) fragmentation and eliminates a restart during Setup.
- **Security settings.** Unlike Windows 2000, Setup in Windows Server 2003 does not install Internet Information Services (IIS) by default. This is good news, because there is no reason to make a server vulnerable to web assaults unless it's necessary to support operations. However, IIS installation still places the Inetpub folder at the root of the boot partition, a serious security deficiency. Always use an unattended installation script when installing IIS to select a different partition for the web folders.
- **Dropped support for legacy software striping and mirroring.** When upgrading from NT, Windows Server 2003 does not convert legacy Fault Tolerant (FT) disk sets to Logical Disk Manager (LDM) striped and mirrored volumes. This is a departure from Windows 2000, which does the conversion automatically. If you have an FT disk set on an NT server, you must back it up then restore from tape following Setup. A Microsoft utility called FTONLINE can recover the disk set following Setup by mounting it in read-only mode so you can back it up.
- **Support for I_2O.** You can install the operating system directly onto I_2O (Intelligent I/O) mass storage devices without loading alternate drivers.
- **System information.** This is a suite of Windows Management Instrumentation (WMI) readouts in a simple-to-use format.
- **Product activation.** Microsoft has incorporated a copy protection scheme into retail versions of Windows Server 2003. Activation links the product identification key of the software with a particular computer to prevent piracy. Volume license versions of Windows Server 2003 do not require activation.

- **Remote desktop.** Windows Server 2003 leverages its integrated Terminal Services by automatically enabling two concurrent sessions by default on all servers. In Windows 2000, this requires a special component selection.
- **Automatic Boot.ini updates.** When new drives are introduced into a server, the Advanced RISC Computing (ARC) path in Boot.ini is updated automatically.

Version Comparisons

There are four different versions of Windows Server 2003. Here is a quick list, followed by a detailed examination of the differences:

- **Standard Edition.** This version is intended for file-and-print services and general purpose application support. It can also act as an Internet gateway and dial-in server.
- **Enterprise Edition.** This version is the upgrade path for Windows 2000 Advanced Server. It has greater memory and processor capacity than Standard Edition, along with support for clustering and advanced certificate services. It is intended for high-end applications and high-availability services. It also supports services that are no longer included in the Standard Edition package.
- **Datacenter Edition.** This version comes as part of a hardware/software package supplied by authorized value-added resellers. It doubles the memory and clustering capacity of Enterprise Edition and contains features that support superior availability. It is intended for large, critical datacenter applications.
- **Web Edition.** This new addition to the Windows server family has been tailored for web services and web hosting applications. It lacks many of the features in the Standard Edition in return for an attractive price and a simple-to-manage platform that is easier to keep secure.

Standard and Web Editions come in 32-bit (IA32) versions only. Enterprise and Datacenter Editions come in both IA32 and IA64 (64-bit) versions. The IA64 version runs only on the Intel Itanium family of processors. There is no Alpha version of Windows Server 2003.

Table 1.1 shows the minimum *recommended* hardware requirements as defined by Microsoft. I emphasize recommended because the minimum requirements published by Microsoft do not yield satisfactory performance in a production environment.

Microsoft also recommends a minimum operating system partition of 1.5GB (2GB for IA64 versions), but my recommendation is to set aside no less than 4GB for the operating system partition. This gives room for application support files and provides sufficient free space for defragmentation.

Table 1.1 Minimum Recommended Hardware Requirements for Windows Server 2003

Hardware Variable	Web Edition	Standard Edition	Enterprise Edition	Datacenter Edition
CPU Speed	550 MHz	550 MHz	733 MHz	733 Mhz
RAM	256 MB	256 MB	256 MB	1 GB
Maximum RAM	2 GB	4 GB	32 GB (64 GB for IA64)	64 GB (512 GB for IA64)
Clusters	N/A	N/A	4 node	8 node
Processor	1 or 2	1 or 2	Up to 8	8 to 32 max (64 for IA64)

The IA32 versions of Enterprise and Datacenter Editions are able to access memory above the 4GB limit imposed by the 32-bit operating system using a set of technologies jointly developed by Microsoft and Intel. See Chapter 3, "Adding Hardware," for a discussion of these extended memory technologies.

Windows Server 2003, Standard Edition

In addition to the features shown in Table 1.1, Windows Server 2003, Standard Edition, has several other significant differences when compared with Windows 2000 Server:

- **Processors.** Standard Edition only supports up to two processors, compared to the four processors supported by Windows 2000. If you have a four-way SQL server currently running on Windows 2000 Server, you must upgrade to Enterprise Edition to get support for all four processors.
- **Memory.** Maximum physical memory is limited to 4GB, just as with Windows 2000 Server, but Standard Edition supports the 4GB Tuning option currently available only in Windows 2000 Advanced and Datacenter Server. This permits you to give an additional 1GB of physical memory to applications running on the server.
- **Network load balancing.** Standard Edition supports Network Load Balance (NLB) clusters. This contrasts to Windows 2000, where you had to pay for Advanced or Datacenter Server to get NLB.
- **Terminal Services.** Standard Edition includes support for Application mode terminal services but it cannot act as a Terminal Server Session Directory in an NLB cluster.
- **Certificate Services.** A Certification Authority (CA) running on Standard Edition can only issue the same certificates issued by Windows 2000 CAs. To get support for newer version 2 certificates and for automatic user enrollment, you must purchase the Enterprise or Datacenter versions. See Chapter 18, "Managing a Public Key Infrastructure," for details.

Windows Server 2003, Enterprise Edition

You pay a premium for the Enterprise Edition if you need any of the following services. The price difference is significant, but as with all Microsoft products, volume discounts are available:

- **IA64 support.** The 64-bit version of Enterprise Edition gives you access to the next generation of Intel processors.
- **Processors.** Enterprise Edition supports up to eight processors in both Symmetric Multiprocessor (SMP) and cache-coherent Non-Uniform Memory Access (ccNUMA) configurations.
- **Memory.** The IA32 version of Enterprise Edition supports up to 32GB of physical memory. This compares to 8GB of RAM supported by Windows 2000 Advanced Server. The IA64 version of Enterprise Edition supports 64GB of physical memory.
- **Clustering.** Enterprise Edition supports 8-node clusters, compared to 2-node clusters in Windows 2000.
- **Hot add memory.** For servers that support this feature, you can add more RAM to a running server. This feature is available in the Datacenter Edition, as well.
- **Metadirectory support.** If you need to consolidate multiple directory services, Microsoft Metadirectory Services (MMS) version 3 is slated for shipment upon release of Windows Server 2003, but it is only supported in the Enterprise Edition. See `www.microsoft.com/windows2000/server/evaluation/news/bulletins/mmsroadmap.asp` for more information.

Windows Server 2003, Datacenter Edition

This product is intended to support high-end applications such as data warehouses, graphic and econometric modeling, and *Online Analytical Processing* (OLAP). In addition to the features in the Enterprise Edition, here are the features supported by Datacenter Edition:

- **IA64 support.** The 64-bit version of Datacenter Edition takes better advantage of the scalable features in IA64 servers, including support for 512GB of physical memory (with supporting chipsets) and 64 processors.
- **Processors.** The IA32 version of Datacenter Edition supports up to 32 processors in both Symmetric Multiprocessor (SMP) and cache-coherent Non-Uniform Memory Access (ccNUMA) configurations.
- **Memory.** The IA32 version of Datacenter Edition supports up to 64GB of physical memory.
- **Clustering.** Datacenter Edition supports 8-node clusters, compared to 4-node clusters in Windows 2000.

You cannot purchase just the Datacenter Edition software. Datacenter Edition comes as a complete package from authorized VARs such as IBM, HP, Groupe Bull, Hitachi, and Unisys, along with Intel stalwarts Dell, Gateway, and NEC. For a full list of partners, go to Microsoft's web site, `www.microsoft.com/servers`, and look under Datacenter Edition.

When you buy a Datacenter Edition system from one of these vendors, you are actually buying a package of hardware, software, and services. Each system is tested before shipment using a Microsoft certification test suite. The VAR provides 7 × 24 support with Microsoft engineers available around the clock for consultation. The partner must provide these services:

- Guaranteed minimum 99.9 percent uptime (which permits about nine hours of downtime in a year)
- Installation and configuration services
- Availability assessments
- 24 × 7 hardware and software support
- Onsite hardware and software support
- Change management service

As you can probably imagine, these platforms and services come with a hefty price tag. In the stratospheric world of high-availability, high-capacity servers, though, a fully equipped Datacenter Edition system can cost much less than a comparable RISC solution.

Windows Server 2003, Web Edition

You may see this version referred to as "Blade Server" because it was designed to work on compact, high-density server farms popular with web service providers.

In addition to a 2GB RAM limitation (virtual memory limit remains at 4GB), Web Edition lacks several of the features commonly associated with Windows servers. It has been stripped down to function as a nimble web platform that can be more easily secured. Here is a quick rundown of the reductions in the feature set:

- **Routing and Remote Access.** Web Edition only supports a single VPN connection intended for management use. It cannot function as a dial-in server or an Internet gateway.
- **Active Directory.** Web Edition cannot be a domain controller. It can join a domain.
- **File-and-print.** Web Edition can accept Windows client connections and it can host a Dfs volume. You can encrypt files on it. It does not support Shadow Copy Restore (Chapter 21, "Recovering from System Failures"). It cannot act as a Remote Installation Services (RIS) server.

- **Certificates.** Web Edition does not support Certificate Services and cannot be a Certification Authority.
- **Terminal services.** Web Edition supports two-session administrative remote access but it cannot function as a full-fledged Application-mode Terminal Server.

Hardware Recommendations

Windows Server 2003 is remarkably adaptable. The same server code can run on a whitebox Pentium 600 and a multiprocessor, multigigahertz powerhouse. The trick is to pick systems that run Windows Server 2003 reliably.

There is an old story that the inventor of chess was offered any gift he desired by a delighted Chinese emperor who had just learned the game. The inventor asked for a simple gift, to have a single grain of rice placed on the first square of a chessboard, then two grains on the second, four on the third, and so on. Using this progression, the emperor would need to put 18,446,744,073,709,551,616 grains of rice on the 64th square to fulfill the request, not to mention filling all the other squares first. As the story goes, the emperor decided it was simpler and cheaper just to execute the inventor. You may make a similar decision concerning your hardware vendor, depending on your Windows Server 2003 installation experiences.

No book could begin to cover the myriad combinations of hardware and software problems that might come up when deploying Windows Server 2003. This chapter contains advice on making basic configuration decisions that can cut down on the number of potential problems, or at least reduce the number to something less than 18,446,744,073,709,551,616.

Hardware Compatibility List

The newest, hottest machines might sell lots of magazines, but I think it's fair to say that system administrators value reliability, interoperability, and high-quality technical support over performance and slick features. This means buying systems and components that are certified to run Windows Server 2003.

Hardware vendors work with Microsoft to test and certify their systems and components. The vendors submit their test results to Microsoft's *Windows Hardware Quality Lab* (WHQL) along with sample hardware and the source code for the drivers. Technicians and engineers check the testing and often rerun the tests to validate the results. Details of this program are available at `www.microsoft.com\hwtest`.

Microsoft maintains a list of certified systems and components in a *Hardware Compatibility List*, or HCL. The most current HCL is available at `www.microsoft.com/hcl`. When checking the HCL, make sure you focus on the server version you plan on running and the expected configuration. Pay particular attention to component versions. You may have a SCSI controller that is only certified when used with a particular system.

If you really want to get into the nuts and bolts of the development and testing process, take a look at `www.microsoft.com\hwdev`. Microsoft's recommendations to hardware vendors for server specification are in the Hardware Design Guide. For the last word on driver development, go to the Open System Resources web site at `www.osr.com`. Here you'll find information from the engineers who teach the engineers at Microsoft.

Support for Certified Hardware

From our perspective as system administrators, the most compelling reason to buy logo-branded hardware is the support commitment that lies behind the logo. If you have a server problem that cannot be resolved by front-line technical support at Microsoft, it will be escalated to a point where support engineers will attempt to replicate your problem using the exact hardware and drivers you are using.

That being said, millions of servers that are not on the HCL run Windows-based server products without a hitch. The key to a satisfactory configuration is getting the vendor's support. If you plan on upgrading an existing system to Windows Server 2003, or you buy a new system that comes with an earlier server version pre-installed, make sure the vendor will work with you during and after the upgrade. This is especially true for older machines that might be unstable or lack the full range of features under Windows Server 2003.

Using Unsupported Hardware

A component or system is considered "supported" if it meets the following conditions:

- It is specifically listed, by make and model, on the HCL.
- A Microsoft-designated driver is used to control the hardware.
- The hardware is used in the configuration under which it was tested.

If you have hardware that is not on the HCL, the Microsoft support representative will put forth a good-faith effort to resolve a problem with the understanding that a satisfactory conclusion is not guaranteed. In my experience, Microsoft technicians lean way over the line to help resolve problems involving unsupported hardware. You are not likely to be denied help with a DNS query failure because you are using an unsupported network card. On the other hand, you are not likely to get the full range of support for an ongoing database corruption problem if you use an unsupported RAID adapter.

No matter where you buy a system, check the vendor's web site to make sure that you have the most current Windows Server 2003 drivers for every component. Look for configuration tips in Microsoft's KnowledgeBase and the Microsoft public newsgroups. A quick search of the Windows server newsgroups is always a good idea. Word of buggy drivers gets out fast. Why go through the same grief as hundreds of other administrators? Better to find new and unique sources of grief.

L2 Cache

If you are upgrading your hardware in preparation for running Windows Server 2003, keep a close eye on the processor's L2 cache specifications. The newer processors have made significant improvements in onboard cache (L1) and bus-attached cache (L2) architecture. The Windows Server 2003 memory management subsystem uses L2 cache extensively, so it is a significant contributor to overall system performance.

In most circumstances, file and print servers can get by with the 256KB cache that comes on standard PIII CPUs. Application servers, however, benefit greatly from larger, bus-speed L2 cache on Xeon processors. The price tag goes up dramatically as you increase cache size, but the performance improvements scale linearly, as well. For example, Dell has released performance numbers for its PowerEdge servers in various L2 configurations. For more information, visit `www.dell.com/us/en/gen/topics/power_ps4q99-L2cache.htm`.

When purchasing IA64 systems, look for Itanium 2 (McKinley) processors with chipsets that support access to all the physical memory the processor can address. The L2 cache in an Itanium 2 processor is relatively puny but the L3 cache can range up to 3MB and runs at full processor speed.

Chipsets, Motherboards, and BIOS

The trade magazines often have bubble charts that show price/performance ratios between many different machines of comparable processor speed. The chipset plays a considerable role in determining a system's place on that bubble chart. Intel is the leading chipset manufacturer. Other leaders include:

- **VIA.** By far the most prolific producer of high-end chipsets for Intel and AMD processors. `www.via.com.tw`.
- **SiS.** The price leader. Mostly specializes in AMD chipsets, although the new DDR (Double Data Rate) chipset looks promising. `www.sis.com.tw`.
- **Micron Technologies**. Known more as a maker of SDRAM and other memory products (including DDR RAM), Micron has made a splash with its new Copperhead DDR chipsets. `www.micron.com`.

The ultimate source for motherboard and chipset comparisons is Tom's Hardware at `www.tomshardware.com`. You can be sure of getting impartial data from Tom and his colleagues without wondering, as I often do, whether a four-page ad for a particular brand of server in a trade magazine had any bearing on its being chosen as a top-rated box. Another good source for hardware news and views is Earthweb's System Optimization Information web site at `www.sysopt.com`.

After you decide on a motherboard vendor, stick with its products for a while. You'll get to know its idiosyncrasies and can make diagnostic decisions should any problems come up.

Make absolutely sure you upgrade the firmware to the latest version. Otherwise, you may encounter problems when trying to implement Windows Server 2003 features.

Memory

If you are specifying hardware for a new server, you should not order less than 512MB of RAM. Adding memory to an older machine is often a hassle, so if you are upgrading an existing NT server, don't order more RAM until you upgrade and evaluate performance. You may find that the server operates just as fast or faster under Windows Server 2003 than it did under NT, thanks to the improvements in the code, thus eliminating the need for more RAM.

If you add more memory to a server to accommodate Windows Server 2003 and you cannot obtain memory that is an exact match to the existing memory, consider removing all existing DIMMs and installing new ones. This ensures that you won't have timing inconsistencies as you cross memory bank boundaries. This can cause subtle instabilities and may even lead to system crashes.

Storage

The drives and drive controllers you use can make as much or more difference in performance and reliability as processor and memory. If a budget battle forces you to pare down your wish list for a server, lean toward improving I/O before upping processor speed.

Your storage decisions are limited only by your pocketbook. In general, you need to decide on drive type, size, RAID configuration, and format.

Drive Type

The drive choice for servers typically boils down to SCSI versus IDE/ATA. Quite a few advances have been made in performance and storage capacity of IDE/ATA drives over the last few years. You can buy 100GB drives at your local Costco or Sam's Club for around $200, and the latest Ultra DMA specification now permits 133 MB/sec burst transfer rates.

SCSI drives deliver faster burst rates (up to 160 MB/s for the current spec, with 320 MB/s waiting in the wings) but the drives are considerably more expensive and high-performance SCSI interface cards cost several hundred dollars.

In spite of the attractive pricing, IDE/ATA drives suffer in performance because only one command can be pending at the bus controller any one time, regardless of the number of devices on the bus. This makes the bus controller a tremendous bottleneck on a busy server. Also, one of the IDE interfaces in a computer is generally given over to a CD-ROM or DVD device. These devices most often use Programmed I/O (PIO) rather than Direct Memory Allocation (DMA). Access to a fast DMA drive is slowed by waiting for PIO transactions if the CD-ROM drive is on the same bus.

For desktops and small servers, fast IDE/ATA controllers and drives deliver acceptable performance, but for real performance you'll be happy you spent the money for SCSI.

If you have the budget and don't mind getting locked into a single vendor for your storage alternatives, take a look at Fibre Channel controllers and drives. The current Fibre Channel specification delivers 100MBps (that's mega*bytes* per second) of full-duplex data transfer, which blows even ultraSCSI into a crumpled garbage pail, with 500MBps coming up real soon now. Also, high-end Fibre Channel controllers support dynamic changes to storage configurations, enabling you to add gigabytes onto a volume just by slipping in a disk and updating the settings.

Drive Size

Give the operating system at least 3GB, with 4GB being preferable. Pay particular attention to the size of the system volume on a system running Application-mode Terminal Services, where user profiles are stored in the system volume by default. It's possible to fill up the system volume very quickly with temporary Internet files and user files saved to their local profile.

If you make the system partition too small, or fill it up with non-system files, you take the chance of fragmenting the NTFS *Master File Table* (MFT). This has a severe impact on performance. Normally, the MFT is protected by a buffer zone of 25 percent of the volume, but the system does not notify you if you puncture this buffer zone, so you won't know you have a problem until you try to defragment the volume and find that your MFT has broken into many pieces.

Windows Server 2003 avoids many of the MFT fragmentation problems in earlier versions because it formats the boot partition directly as NTFS rather than converting the partition after files have been copied to it.

Drive Configuration

Continuity of service is a prime consideration when building a server. For storage, this means using fault tolerant disk subsystems wherever possible. This includes mirroring, RAID 5 striping, or RAID 0+1 stripe/mirroring.

NTFS Versions

Windows Server 2003 uses an updated version of NTFS that changed the record header layout to improve performance. This change renders older imaging and partition utilities inoperable. Make sure you have the most current version of any utility that manipulates the file system.

The NTFS version in Windows Server 2003 is version 3.1. This is the internal version number embedded in the NTFS metadata and it is also the version reported by disk utilities such as FSUTIL. You may see documentation referring to the NTFS version by the same number as the operating system version, 5.2. This is inaccurate but not altogether without precedent. Here are the previous versions of NTFS:

- NT 3.51 – NTFS 1.1
- NT 4.x – NTFS 1.2
- Windows 2000 – NTFS 3.0
- Windows XP – NTFS 3.1

Windows Server 2003 uses a Logical Disk Manager (LDM) subsystem, licensed from Veritas, to control fault tolerant drives. LDM supports RAID 1 mirroring and RAID 5 parity striping. It also supports two configurations that are not fault tolerant: RAID 0 striping and volume spanning. LDM does not support RAID 0+1.

You can mix and match SCSI and IDE drives in the same drive set, although this is not recommended because it generally slows down the array.

One of the most significant changes in Windows Server 2003 compared to Windows 2000 in this area is the total lack of support for legacy fault tolerant (FT) disk sets. Windows 2000 would convert legacy FT disk sets to dynamic disks and incorporate them into the Logical Disk Manager (LDM) database. In Windows Server 2003, you must remove all FT disk sets prior to upgrading. Chapter 2, "Performing Upgrades and Automated Installations," has more information on this requirement. There is a utility called FTONLINE that can recover an FT disk set if you forget to remove it first.

Under most circumstances, you are better off using hardware RAID than LDM. A good RAID controller gives you hot-swap capabilities, hot spares, and dynamic expansion, none of which is provided by LDM. Also, hardware RAID controllers do a much better job of detecting cascading sector failures. Finally, top-of-the-line RAID controllers support RAID 0+1, or mirrored stripe sets. This gives you the best of both worlds: the speed of RAID 0 and the fault tolerance of mirroring. You'll spend more for the drives and enclosures, though.

What's the bottom line? Use hardware RAID if you can afford it and software RAID if money is tight. If you opt for software RAID, you'll get better performance with SCSI compared to IDE because of the multitasking capabilities of the SCSI interface. You'll also get better performance by using multiple SCSI channels for your array rather than putting all devices on the same SCSI bus.

Drive Format

You can install Windows Server 2003 onto a partition that is preformatted with FAT, FAT32, or NTFS. You cannot install Windows Server 2003 onto an HPFS, NetWare, UNIX, or Linux partition.

You'll be happy to know that Windows Server 2003 Setup supports formatting partitions as NTFS as part of Setup without initially formatting them as FAT and then converting. This avoids many of the fragmentation problems in earlier versions. There is also a quick format option that skips the sector scan of a normal formatting to speed up installation.

I recommend using NTFS for all partitions on a server. This gives you security, stability, and scalability. FAT32 has a performance edge over NTFS in terms of raw lookup speed for small partitions, but this does not make up for its fragility and fragmentation problems. You can choose to convert a FAT or FAT32 partition to NTFS during or after Setup. If you format as FAT or FAT32 using Windows Server 2003 Setup, the conversion utility will permit you to change the cluster size.

ERD Commander 2002

The Recovery Console in Windows Server 2003 works similarly to the ERD Commander utility created by the legendary Mark Russinovich and Bryce Cogswell. ERD Commander 2002 sports an Explorer-like interface that adds the ability to change account passwords and perform additional system modifications. You can download an evaluation copy of ERD Commander from `www.sysinternals.com`. The for-cost version includes the ability to edit Registry files and to change the password on accounts in the local *Security Account Manager* (SAM).

Some administrators shy away from NTFS because of the difficulty in booting to a floppy to access files. Windows Server 2003 incorporates a Recovery Console that permits booting to a command prompt and accessing an NTFS drive. Armed with the Recovery Console, you can join Oprah and say goodbye to FAT forever.

Removable Media (CD-RW and DVD-RAM)

Windows Server 2003 supports writing directly to removable read/writable media such as CD-RW and DVD-RAM. The CD writing engine uses file-based technology. This contrasts with packet-based products such as EZ CD Creator from Roxio (`www.roxio.com`), CDRWIN from Goldenhawk Technologies (`www.goldenhawk.com`), and Nero from Ahead Software (`www.nero.com`). (Microsoft licensed portions of the CD writing engine from Roxio. Roxio is a subsidiary of Adaptec, Inc.)

Windows Server 2003 introduces a new image writing API, IMAPI, for interfacing with read/write removable media such as CD-R, CD-RW, and DVD-RAM. You can get more information about this API from `www.microsoft.com/hwdev`. For general information about CD-R technology, visit `www.cdrfaq.org`. It's a great site with well-groomed, current topics.

Windows Server 2003 supports the Joliet extensions to the ISO 9660 standards for CD-ROM, which enabled long filename support. If you have a DVD-RAM, the system can format the disk using FAT32, giving you lots of flexibility in how you use the media. DVDs can also be formatted using UDF 1.5, the industry standard for DVD formatting.

There is no support in Windows Server 2003 for booting into Setup from floppy disks, so you must have a CD-ROM drive that supports the El Torito "no emulation boot" specification.

IA64 Storage Configuration

If you are installing the IA64 version of Windows Server 2003, you must configure the boot drive to use a *GUID Partition Table*, or GPT. The GPT formatting method is part of the *Extensible Firmware Interface* (EFI) specification from Intel. GPT replaces the *Master Boot Record* (MBR) formatting scheme used in classic Intel computers.

Each partition on a GPT boot disk is assigned a Globally Unique Identifier (GUID) and a type designator. There are no hidden partitions or special disk structures, no strange rules for logical drives in extended partitions, no arcane machinations to support hidden OEM utilities.

A GPT disk has a small partition table at the start of the disk with a mirror copy at the end of the disk. Unlike a classic MBR-based partition table, which is limited to four entries, a GPT disk can have 128 partitions. This gives you quite a bit of flexibility in structuring large disks or disk arrays. A typical boot disk will have these partitions:

- **EFI System Partition (ESP).** The ESP contains the files necessary to boot an operating system. If a drive has several partitions containing different operating systems, the EFS keeps a separate folder for each operating system's boot files. The ESP size is set at 1 percent of the physical disk size, with a minimum size of 100MB and a maximum size of 1GB. The ESP is formatted as FAT. A disk can only contain one ESP. ESP partitions cannot be mirrored. The ESP is not shown in the Disk Management console and does not appear as a drive in Explorer.
- **Microsoft Reserved Partition (MSR).** Each boot drive must have one MSR. It stores the Logical Disk Manager (LDM) database should you decide to shift from GPT partitioning to Dynamic disks. The MSR must be the first partition after the ESP. (A non-bootable disk might not have an ESP, in which case the MSR is the first partition.) The MSR size depends on the physical disk capacity. On disks up to 16GB, the MSR is 32MB. On disks over 16GB, the MSR is 128MB. The MSR is formatted as FAT. It is not exposed by Explorer, but it can be seen in the Disk Management console.
- **OEM partition.** Vendors love to ship proprietary diagnostic and setup utilities along with their systems. These utilities are often tucked away in hidden partitions that cause no end of grief for system administrators who want to change the disk partitioning. Using GPT disks, vendors can create their own OEM partition to hold their utilities. Ordinarily, an OEM partition does not appear as a drive in Explorer although it can be seen in the Disk Management console.
- **Microsoft data partition.** This partition type is created by Windows Server 2003 or XP to create general-purpose partitions.

Managing Files Stored in the ESP

The EFI performs its initial bootstrap directly from firmware rather than using boot files on the hard drive. The ESP does not contain copies of Ntldr, Ntdetect.com, or Boot.ini. Here's why:

- The hardware checks performed by Ntdetect.com are not needed because the operating system can obtain this information from firmware.

Viewing the ESP

Ordinarily, you cannot see or change the contents of the ESP from the operating system. You manage the files from the EFI Shell prior to loading the operating system.

However, Windows Server 2003 and XP provide a `/s` switch on the MOUNTVOL utility that redirects a designated drive letter to the EFS partition. The syntax is `mountvol r: /s`. Many of files in the ESP are hidden.

- The boot menu is kept in Non-Volatile RAM (NVRAM), so a separate Boot.ini file is not required. The entries in the boot menu are displayed by the EFI Boot Manager. Windows entries can be changed while Windows Server 2003 is running using the System Properties window or the BOOTCFG utility.
- The secondary bootstrap loader for Windows Server 2003 is called Ia64ldr.efi. It islocated in the ESP in a folder named `\EFI\Microsoft\WINNT50`. A second file in this folder, Fpswa.efi, is the *Floating Point Software Assistance* handler that lists floating-point exceptions needed by the operating system. For more information, see `developer.intel.com/design/itanium/downloads/245415.htm`.

If you have multiple copies of Windows Server 2003 or XP on a machine, each one gets a separate folder in the ESP. For example, the second copy would get the path `\EFI\Microsoft\WINNT50.0` and the third copy would get `\EFI\Microsoft\WINNT50.1`, and so forth.

The EFI Boot Manager stores the path to the operating system partition and the associated secondary bootstrap loader. Here is an example of the menu displayed by the EFI Boot Manager:

```
EFI Boot Manager ver 1.02 [12.36A]
Please select a boot option:
Microsoft Windows Server 2003 Standard Edition
Acpi(PNP0A03,0)/Pci(5|0)/Mac(0003478991556)
EFI Shell [Built-in]
Boot option maintenance menu
```

Each of these entries represents a path, either to boot file or to an operational shell. Following are explanations for these path entries:

- The entry labeled `Acpi(PNP0A03,0)/Pci(5|0)/Mac(0003478991556)` loads the Preboot Execution Environment (PXE), which installs a setup image from a RIS server.
- The `EFI Shell` option loads a command-line environment where you can navigate to various partitions on the drives and run EFI executable files.
- The `Boot Option Maintenance Menu` controls a utility for managing the contents of the boot menu.

The operating system entries, such as `Windows Server 2003, Standard Edition`, entry in the example, represent a compact value in NVRAM that decodes to an entry like this:

```
LoadIdentifier = Microsoft Windows Server 2003, Standard Edition
OsLoadOptions =
EfiOsLoaderFilePath = HardDiskVolume1\EFI\Microsoft\WINNT50\ia64ldr.efi
OsLoaderFilePath = HardDiskVolume2\WINDOWS
```

The individual NVRAM entries are not visible directly from the EFI shell. Microsoft provides a utility in the EFI System Partition called Nvrboot.efi for managing Windows entries in NVRAM. The operation of this utility is covered in Chapter 3, "Adding Hardware."

Backing Up NVRAM

There is no simple way to re-create the operating system path in a Boot Manager entry if you accidentally overwrite an entry in NVRAM or the entry becomes corrupted. For this reason, when Setup creates a Boot Manager entry, it stores a backup copy in a file called Boot0004 stored in the ESP in the same folder as the Ia64ldr.efi file, `\EFI\Microsoft\WINNT50`.

If you have multiple copies of Windows Server 2003 or XP on a machine, the copy of the Boot Manager entry for that instance of Windows is given the next sequential number (`Boot0005`, for example) and stored in the ESP folder that holds the secondary bootstrap loader for that instance.

For example, the Ia64ldr.efi file for the third Windows OS on a machine would be found in `\FFI\Microsoft\WINNT50.1` and the Boot Manager entry stored in that folder would be named `Boot0007`.

If you lose or overwrite the original NVRAM entry for a Windows installation, you can use the Import option of the Nvrboot.efi utility to import the contents of the `Boot000#` file into NVRAM. This creates a new Boot Manager entry and does not overwrite any existing entries.

GPT Drive Sizes

GPT drives can contain 2^{64} logical blocks. A logical block generally contains one sector, or 512 bytes, yielding a capacity of a phenomenal eight zettabytes. (See `physics.nist.gov/cuu/Units/prefixes.html` for a list of scientific notation prefixes.) However, Windows Server 2003 sets a maximum volume size of 16 exabytes, corresponding to the limits of NTFS. This may not seem like much of a limit, but just wait until the next version of Microsoft Office comes out.

MBR Compatibility

A GPT disk cannot be read by standard MBR-based utilities. This can lead to problems for utilities that perform automated processes on unpartitioned drives.

To protect a GPT disk from corruption by these utilities, the GPT specification includes a *protective MBR*. This is an MBR placed at Sector 0 of the disk with a single partition table that spans the entire disk (or the maximum allowable MBR disk size, whichever is smaller). If a utility makes a change to this structure, it will not prevent an IA64 server from accessing volumes on the disk.

Partitioning GPT Disks

GPT disks are partitioned using the EFI firmware on the system or by an IA64 version of Windows Server 2003 or XP. Standard IA32 versions of Windows Server 2003 and XP cannot read or write to a GPT disk. IA64 versions can read and write to an MBR disk but they must boot from a GPT disk. Earlier versions of Windows cannot read, write, or boot from a GPT disk.

Removable media cannot be partitioned as GPT disks. An IA64 system partitions large capacity cartridge drives such as Jaz, Zip, and Orb drives along with magneto-optical disks and superfloppies. A superfloppy disk can have only one partition that can be formatted FAT, FAT32, or NTFS.

Detachable disks, such as Universal Serial Bus (USB) drives or IEEE 1394 drives or SCSI/Fibre Channel drives in a cluster, must be partitioned as MBR disks rather than GPT disks.

Installation Checklist

The vast majority of Windows Server 2003 installations proceed without a hitch. Before you start, however, you should be aware of some common sources of problems. A few precautions taken early can forestall nasty problems later on. This checklist assumes you are doing a clean installation, not an upgrade. See Chapter 2, "Performing Upgrades and Automated Installations," for an upgrade checklist.

Component Configurations

One of the most significant changes in Windows Server 2003 is the use of *Plug and Play (PnP)*. Both Windows Server 2003 and Windows 2000 obtain their PnP information from *Advanced Configuration and Power Interface (ACPI)* in addition to the PnP BIOS. This can lead to resource conflicts and potential incompatibilities. Here are a few preparations you might want to make before installing or upgrading to Windows Server 2003:

- **Firmware.** Make absolutely, positively, completely certain that you are running with the most current firmware versions for your BIOS and all peripherals.
- **ACPI.** If the system has a motherboard that is more than a couple of years old, check to make sure that it is on the HCL. If not, some entries in the ACPI BIOS tables may not be compatible with the Windows Server 2003. For IA64, Microsoft requires that machines conform to the ACPI version 2.0 table requirements. All machines on the HCL meet this requirement.
- **Disable Plug and Play.** It might seem like a contradiction, considering the fact that Windows Server 2003 is a plug-and-play operating system, but you should disable PnP in CMOS before running Setup. Windows Server 2003 prefers to use ACPI rather than the PnP BIOS.
- **Remove UPS Serial Connections.** If you are running a UPS monitoring device such as the UPS support in NT or Windows 2000 or a third-party utility such as PowerChute from APC, you should pull the serial line connection before running Setup. This avoids a long, long stall during device discovery. After Setup has completed, you can reinstall the cable.
- **Disable hardware disk caching.** Only enable hardware disk caching if you have a system specifically designed to support caching under Windows Server 2003. Many incidents involving massive data corruption routinely get traced to unsupported hardware disk caches.

- **Prepare for multimedia devices.** Configuring multimedia devices can be infuriatingly time-consuming. Make sure all multimedia hardware in the system has Windows Server 2003 drivers, and verify that the makes and models match the HCL listing precisely. Double-check the vendor's web site to get the most current drivers. And after all that, you can still count on losing at least one afternoon sweating over a seemingly trivial glitch.
- **Set the boot sequence**. If you plan on running Setup locally at a server, you must boot from the Windows Server 2003 CD. There is no provision for running Setup from floppies. Be sure the boot sequence in CMOS is set to permit booting to the CD before the hard drive.
- **Prepare for dual monitors.** Windows Server 2003 supports using dual monitors. If you have a system with two video cards, PnP will detect both of them. One will be used by BIOS to display the character-based portions of startup. If PnP decides to declare the other adapter as the primary adapter, the graphical display will go to that adapter. So, if you have dual video adapters but only one monitor and the screen goes black during setup, transfer the monitor to the other adapter.
- **Use bus-mastering NICs.** Use only top-quality, bus-mastering PCI NICs. These cards cost only slightly more than their Programmed I/O (PIO) counterparts and perform much, much better. Heavy network users will benefit more from a bus-mastering network adapter than from a faster processor, all other things being equal.
- **Set EFI settings in IA64 servers**. The Extensible Firmware Interface in IA64 systems is used to partition drives and prepare other hardware. Drives must be prepared with GPT (GUID Partition Tables) rather than MBR (Master Boot Records).
- **Use 64-bit PCI cards in IA64 systems.** You will not be able to use legacy 32-bit cards in an IA64 system. Be sure to include in your budget any new peripherals that you might need to purchase, and make absolutely sure the 64-bit card is on the IA64 HCL, not just the IA32 HCL.

Configuring Storage

Perform the following checks to make sure the system is ready to store the Windows Server 2003 system files:

- **Get the most current mass storage drivers**. If the drivers for your SCSI, RAID, or ATA device do not come in Windows Server 2003, or the preinstalled drivers have been upgraded, you should obtain the most current driver and put it on a floppy. When commencing Setup, press `F6`. This will cause Setup to pause a little later and ask you for the mass storage device driver.
- **Remove non-critical devices from SCSI bus**. If you have items like scanners, tape drives, or other peripherals on the same SCSI bus as your mass storage,

you may want to remove them until after Setup has completed. This avoids any potential conflict that might cause Setup to hang.

- **Check SCSI cables.** If you use SCSI drives, Windows Server 2003 demands tighter timing tolerances than classic NT. If you have a SCSI cable that's right on the edge of length spec, you might run into data corruption problems after upgrading.
- **Break software mirrors and legacy FT disk sets.** If you are installing over an existing copy of NT, you must remove all fault tolerant disk sets. If there is data in these disk sets, back them up then restore following Setup. This does not apply to hardware RAID.
- **Use standard disk access.** For IDE/ATA drives, verify that file I/O and disk access is set to `Standard` and not `32-bit` or `Enhanced` in CMOS. Windows Server 2003 does not support the direct INT13 calls used by enhanced interfaces.
- **Removable media drives.** You can install Windows Server 2003 to a removable media drive such as an Iomega Jaz or Castlewood Orb drive. You would not want to do this on a production system, of course, but it makes for a flexible lab environment. If for some reason, you cannot make the removable media bootable, you can boot from a fixed drive and put the system files on the removable media drive.

Configuring Network Adapters

Network connection reliability and performance is often overlooked until after Setup when the machine becomes slow or unstable. Take a couple of minutes to avoid potential problems by taking some precautions:

- **Verify that the NIC is on the HCL.** Microsoft has officially retired several adapters in Windows Server 2003, most notably legacy Token Ring adapters. Still others were dropped because their drivers have caused problems with Windows 2000 or were identified as causing problems during the Windows Server 2003 beta. This includes many inexpensive and so-called "white box" NICs.
- **Resolve potential resource conflicts.** Windows Server 2003 uses PnP to discover and enumerate network adapters. It will attempt to identify legacy adapters and load the correct drivers. If you have a legacy adapter, make sure that you know the resources it uses. These include the following:
  - IRQ
  - I/O base address
  - RAM address. Necessary only if the adapter uses memory addressing. All PC Card network adapters use memory addressing. Windows Server 2003 accommodates 16-bit memory addressing by remapping the onboard RAM to its 32-bit memory space. You should encounter conflicts only if you have multiple network adapters with the same RAM addresses.
  - DMA channels for bus-mastering adapters

For legacy adapters, set aside the IRQ in CMOS so that the PnP manager will not assign that resource to another device.

Always avoid IRQ 9 when selecting resources for a legacy adapter. Windows Server 2003 uses this IRQ for IRQ Steering, a special table in BIOS that lists PCI resources and their interrupts. This table acts as an interrupt router that can be configured by the operating system to point at different interrupt service requests. IRQ Steering cannot be disabled in Windows Server 2003.

- **Shared interrupts.** Shared interrupts may pose a problem depending on your motherboard and chipset. Some machines have no problem at all sharing six or seven devices on the same IRQ. Others are plagued by kernel-mode stop errors and unstable network connections when sharing just two devices on the same interrupt. If Setup hangs during network driver enumeration, this is a sign of a possible problem with resource sharing.

Dual-Boot Considerations

On IA32 systems, the Windows Server 2003 bootstrap loader, Ntldr, can load NT4, Windows 2000, XP, and Windows Server 2003 from any drive or partition. A boot menu stored in Boot.ini defines the path to the boot files for each operating system. On IA64 systems, the EFI bootstrap loader handles multiple operating system selection.

Ntldr can load only *one* alternate operating system thanks to the way the system designates the alternate boot sector. Ntldr stores the alternate boot sector in a file called Bootsect.dos at the root of the boot partition. When you select the alternate OS from the boot menu, Ntldr shifts the processor back to Real mode, loads the boot sector image from Bootsect.dos into memory at `0x700h` (just as if it had been loaded by a standard INT13 call), and then turns control over to the executable code in the image.

If you need to boot more than two operating systems and one of them is not a Windows OS, use a partition manager such as Partition Magic or System Commander. If you want to maintain a multiboot configuration on your machine, you need to take a few issues into account:

- **NTFS version incompatibilities.** Windows Server 2003 Setup converts any existing NTFS volumes to NTFS 3.1. If you dual-boot between Windows Server 2003 and NT4, the NT4 system must be running Service Pack 6a to avoid a crash with kernel-mode stop error `0x0000007d, Inaccessible Boot Device.`

VMWare

If you have a test environment where you need to run Windows and Linux at the same time, you should take a look at the VMWare utility at `www.vmware.com`. A VMWare session can run Linux and any version of Windows inside a virtual machine. You can even simulate adding more drives.

- **Dynamic disks.** Windows Server 2003 includes a Logical Disk Manager (LDM) service that permits dynamically configuring fault-tolerant volumes. Only Windows 2000 and Windows Server 2003 can read the LDM database. You cannot run other operating systems if you plan on using dynamic disks.
- **Separate windows partitions.** Microsoft *strongly* recommends using separate system partitions for each version of 32-bit Windows on a multiple-boot system. The various flavors of Windows have become too similar to keep them on the same partition.
- **NT4 service packs overwrite key system files.** If you install an NT4 or Windows 2000 service pack on a dual-boot machine, it overwrites the Windows Server 2003 version of Ntldr in the root of the boot drive. This prevents Windows Server 2003 from booting. Before applying an alternate service pack, make a copy of Ntldr and Ntdetect.com then copy them back when the service pack has been applied.
- **Disk tools.** You should not run any disk utilities unless they have been certified on Windows Server 2003 or XP. Incompatibilities can cause damage to the operating system files.

Functional Overview of Windows Server 2003 Setup

This topic covers the details of what happens during an installation of Windows Server 2003. It examines the major milestones that occur during Setup to give you a basis for making configuration decisions. Step-by-step instructions are listed in the "Installing Windows Server 2003" section in this chapter.

Windows Server 2003 Setup works like an able seaman docking a ship to a pier. The seaman tosses a light line to shore and uses it to pull over a heavier line. He wraps the heavier line around a winch and uses it to pull across a much heavier line, and then he uses the heavier line to the secure the ship to the pier.

Setup docks Windows Server 2003 to a computer with three separate rounds of file copies performed in two phases, with a third phase for final system configuration:

- **Text phase.** This phase starts with booting from the Windows Server 2003 CD. This phase uses a small set of files to build a miniature session of Windows Server 2003. This session partitions and formats a mass storage device, creates the system folders, mounts a CD, and copies the necessary files to support the next setup phase. Unlike its predecessors, if you elect to format the operating system volume using NTFS, Setup actually formats it using NTFS rather than starting with FAT/FAT32 then converting later on. The system restarts after this phase.

- **Graphic phase.** In this phase, Setup discovers and enumerates the system hardware, obtains configuration information from the user, then copies a final set of files from the CD to get the drivers it needs to finish installing the operating system and configure the services. The system restarts after this phase.
- **Configuration phase.** This phase starts when a user logs on for the first time. A final round of PnP discovery commences that looks for any devices that did not get enumerated during the graphic phase of Setup. The user may be prompted to provide drivers if they are not present. The system also launches a Server Configuration Wizard to walk through any additional settings and the Windows Product Activation Wizard to obtain an activation key. Depending on the nature of the added components and their resource allocations, the system may need to be restarted one final time. Following this third phase, the system is ready for production.

The following sections look at each Setup phase in detail.

Text Setup Phase

This phase begins by booting from the Windows Server 2003 CD. You can also connect to an installation share point and run one of the setup programs: Winnt will start Setup from DOS; Winnt32 will start Setup from NT or Windows 2000. See Chapter 2, "Performing Upgrades and Automated Installations," for details on running Setup from network drives.

Setup Executable Loads

The IA32 Setup CD has a bootable image that conforms to the El Torito non-emulation standards. This image contains the files necessary to create a miniature Windows Server 2003 session that acts as a starting point for the main Setup program. Executable code in the boot image looks for Setupldr.bin, the Windows Server 2003 Setup loader. Setupldr.bin is actually just a copy of the standard Windows Server 2003 secondary bootstrap loader, Ntldr, with a few changes to support installation.

Setupldr.bin orchestrates the text-mode portion of Setup using a script called Txtsetup.sif. This script tells Setup the following:

- Where to find the boot files
- What directories to put on the boot partition
- What files to copy to the system and boot partitions
- What drivers to load initially
- What to do with existing files
- What keys to put in a skeleton Registry built to support the graphic phase of Setup

Initial Hardware Recognition

IA32 machines do not have a hardware recognizer in firmware like an IA64 machine, so Setupldr.bin loads a software-based hardware recognizer called Ntdetect.com. At this point, you see the message `Setup is inspecting your computer's hardware configuration.`

Ntdetect.com finds the hardware information needed by the Windows Server 2003 setup kernel, Ntkrnlmp.exe, and its Hardware Abstraction Layer library, Hal.dll. Setup always uses a multiprocessor kernel and HAL. If it detects that the system has a single processor, it installs a uniprocessor version of the kernel. You can add a second processor later, if the motherboard supports it. Windows Server 2003 will automatically load the multiprocessor kernel files when it detects the additional processor.

ACPI Compatibility Checks

ACPI evolved for a few years before version 2 of the standard was approved in 1999. This means that machines built prior to 1999 used a variety of ACPI features. Windows Server 2003 expects to find ACPI version 2 support on a system, but rather than leave legacy machines behind, Microsoft collected operational information from a variety of platforms and used that information to make corrections in the ACPI feature set.

Now that ACPI has matured, the older *Advanced Power Management* (APM) standard has been more or less abandoned. Again, because of backward compatibility issues, Microsoft maintained support for legacy APM, but only if ACPI is not detected.

Chapter 3, "Adding Hardware," discusses the way that Windows Server 2003 supports legacy ACPI systems. If you have a system that appears to experience ACPI-related problems (inexplicable hangs, crashes, erratic behavior), you can elect to install a Standard PC kernel. Do this at the very beginning of the text mode portion of Setup, when you are prompted to press F6 to install alternate mass storage device driver. Press `F7` to skip the ACPI kernel and install the Standard PC kernel. You cannot shift to the ACPI kernel without re-installing the operating system.

Special Setup Function Keys

A variety of special setup options are available during the first few seconds of the text-mode portion of Setup. You can access the options using these function keys:

- F2. When pressed at the Welcome to Setup window, this launches Automatic System Recovery (ASR), a quick way to recover the operating system from tape. See Chapter 21, "Recovering from System Failures," for details.
- F5. Permits selecting an alternative kernel type. Options include `ACPI`, `Standard PC`, `I486 C-stepping`, and `SGI MP`.
- F6. Permits loading a third-party mass storage device driver that is not on the Windows Server 2003 CD.
- F7. Bypasses ACPI to load a standard PC kernel.
- F10. When pressed at the Welcome to Setup window, this launches the Recovery Console. See Chapter 21, "Recovering from System Failures," for details.

If you press F5 or F6, it takes a while for the system to respond. Wait a few minutes for the menus to appear.

If you want to do an unattended installation, you can change the Txtsetup.inf file to disable ACPI. Here is a standard Txtsetup.inf listing:

```
[ACPIOptions]
ACPIEnable = 2
ACPIBiosDate = 01,01,1999
```

Change the `ACPIEnable` entry from `2` to `0` and reinstall Windows Server 2003.

Drive Letter Assignments

Long, long ago, in a galaxy far, far away, Microsoft decided to use drive letters rather than UNIX-style file system specifiers to identify drive partitions. The intent was to put friendly names on the file system interfaces. There is no doubt that drive letters made file systems easier for users to interact with, but they have become a never-ending source of irritation to system administrators.

The Mount Manager service, MountMgr, is responsible for enumerating drives and assigning drive letters. This enumeration process varies depending on whether you do a fresh install of Windows Server 2003 or an upgrade. Upgrades are covered in Chapter 2, "Performing Upgrades and Automated Installations."

When you do a fresh install of Windows Server 2003, there might already be partitions on the drives that you want to retain, so Setup scans the drives and assigns drive letters to existing partitions. The partitions need not hold recognized file systems. Drive letters can be assigned to HPFS and Linux partitions.

Setup first scans for dynamic disks and uses the drive letters assigned in the LDM database. This assists applications that might reference those drive letters. It separates the partitions into two categories:

- **Hard-linked partitions.** If a disk has been upgraded from a basic to a dynamic disk, the legacy partition table is left in place so the system BIOS can read the table, find the active partition, and load the boot sector from this partition. This is called a *hard-linked partition* because there is no need for the bootstrap code in the MBR to read the LDM database to find the boot partition.
- **Soft-linked partition table.** If a disk has never been partitioned as a basic disk, it has no legacy partition table. Partitions are only defined in the LDM database and are therefore called *soft-linked partitions.*

During the dynamic disk scan, Setup uses the following criteria to assign drive letters:

- **Dynamic disks with hard-linked partitions.** Setup first queries the LDM database to find drive letters assigned to hard-linked partitions. If no letters are assigned, Setup assigns the next available letter.
- **Dynamic disks with soft-linked partitions.** After hard-linked partitions have been given drive letters, Setup queries the LDM database for letters assigned to

volumes in soft-link partitions. It assigns these letters if they do not conflict with hard-linked drive letters. If there is a conflict, or if no drive letters are assigned, it assigns the next available letter.

If logical drive letters must be changed on dynamic disks, Setup writes the new letters to the LDM database. After dynamic disks have been scanned and assigned, Setup turns its attention to basic disks.

Figure 1.1 shows a diagram of drive letter assignments for a system with two drives, one IDE and one SCSI, both configured as basic disks. During the drive scan, the on-board IDE interfaces are scanned before the SCSI interfaces. Ultra-DMA ATA controllers are treated as SCSI interfaces, so they are scanned after the on-board controllers. Drive letters are assigned as follows:

- **Active partitions.** Setup scans the drives looking for primary partitions marked as Active. Assuming that there are no pre-existing dynamic disks, it assigns drive letter C to the first active partition on the first drive in the scan sequence. If a drive does not have an active partition, Setup assigns the next drive letter to the first primary partition on the drive.
- **Extended partitions and removable media drives.** Setup scans the drives again, this time looking for logical drives in extended partitions and removable media drives such as Jaz or Orb drives. It assigns drive letters starting with the next available letter.
- **Primary partitions.** Setup scans the drives again, this time looking for any remaining primary partitions. It assigns drive letters in sequence starting with the next available letter.
- **CD-ROM and DVD drives.** Finally, Setup assigns drive letters to CD-ROM and DVD drives. It assigns letters in sequence so that a CD-ROM drive on IDE controller 0 will get a letter before a CD-ROM drive on IDE controller 1, which itself comes before a CD-ROM drive on a SCSI controller.

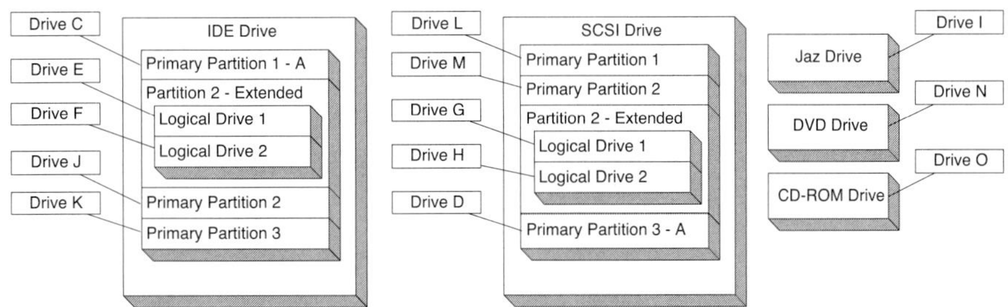

Figure 1.1 Diagram of drive letter assignments for a system with a single IDE drive and SCSI drive. Primary partitions marked A are active.

These drive letter assignments are written to the Registry so they persist between restarts. This makes drive letters "sticky," an important factor when installing applications and creating shortcuts or other OLE connections.

After Setup has completed, you can change drive letters assigned to any of the partitions except for the boot partition and the system partition. This avoids potential conflicts when hard-coded Registry entries expect to see system files at a certain drive letter. Do not attempt to change drive letters using Registry modifications. This works for Windows 2000, but in Windows Server 2003 it causes Windows Product Activation to fail so that it refuses to permit access, forcing you to reinstall the operating system.

Setup Files

Setupldr.bin uses installation files from the boot image to create a miniature version of Windows Server 2003. These files contain video drivers, keyboard drivers, mass storage drivers, and file system drivers. Here are the important drivers and their functions:

- **Atapi.sys.** This is the IDE/EIDE driver. The older Atdisk.sys driver is no longer used. Support for ESDI/WD1003 drives has been dropped.
- **Disk.sys, Class2.sys,** and **Classpnp.sys.** These are mass storage interface drivers and their PnP enumerator.
- **Dmboot.sys, Dmio.sys,** and **Dmload.sys.** This set of drivers supports Logical Disk Manager (LDM).
- **Floppy.sys.** The floppy disk miniport driver.
- **Hardware Abstraction Layer (HAL).** There are several HAL drivers. Setup chooses one based on the type of hardware.
- **I/O extenders.** These are WDM bus drivers that work with the PnP Manager to define data paths in the system. There are extenders for PCMCIA, PCI IDE, Toshiba IDE, VIA IDE, IBM Thinkpad IDE, Intel IDE, and the floppy disk controllers.
- **I2Omp.sys** and **I2Omgmt.sys.** This set of drivers supports the I_2O subsystem. This enables the system to boot from Intelligent Input/Output controllers.
- **I8042prt.sys.** The keyboard driver. This driver virtualizes the 8042 controller BIOS and also controls PS/2 bus mice. If you get garbage onscreen when you type, or experience odd results when using your mouse, this driver might not be compatible with your keyboard, mouse, or PS/2 motherboard interface.
- **Isapnp.sys.** The PnP enumerator for the ISA bus. You may recognize this driver from NT4. It came in the `\Support` directory on the NT4 CD. Multimedia vendors such as Creative Labs used this driver to provide a simpler way to install their ISA sound cards and game boards.
- **Kbdclass.sys** and **Kbdus.dll.** These are the keyboard class driver and the keyboard mapping driver. These two drivers can sometimes cause trouble with cheap

components. If you keep having problems with the Caps Lock key not working properly or the repeat rate being unstable, you may need to upgrade your equipment. The boot image contains a full suite of international keyboard layout DLLs.

- **Ksecdd.sys.** This is the kernel security driver. It works with the I/O drivers to open and read security descriptors on objects.
- **Mountmgr.sys, Ftdisk.sys,** and **Partmgr.sys.** This set of drivers supports basic disk configurations and classic fault tolerant disk sets.
- **National Language Support (NLS).** These files contain locale information for character sets, punctuation, and so forth. For American English installations, Setup loads code pages C_1252.NLS and C_437.NLS. It also loads a primary language file, L_INTL.NLS.
- **Ntdll.dll.** The Windows Server 2003 API function library.
- **Ntfs.sys, Fastfat.sys,** and **Cdfs.sys.** The NT file system driver, FAT file system driver, and CD file system driver. FASTFAT.SYS supports both FAT16 and FAT32. The Windows Server 2003 CD contains other file system drivers, but Setup does not need them at this point.
- **Openhci.sys, Uhcd.sys, Usbd.sys, Usbhub.sys,** and **Hidusb.sys.** The *Universal Serial Bus* (USB) drivers. These work with a set of *Human Interface Device* (HID) drivers to support USB components.
- **Scsiport.sys.** This is the SCSI bus driver. It is accompanied by a slew of miniport drivers for various SCSI boards.
- **Serial.sys** and **Serenum.sys.** The serial bus controller and PnP enumerator. These two drivers work together to find PnP and legacy devices connected to RS232 ports. This search can be a tedious process because the RS232 interface is so slow. For this reason, the standard Boot.ini entry includes a `/fastdetect` switch that delays the serial bus enumeration until after the system has loaded.
- **Setupreg.hiv.** This is a small Registry file with keys to initialize the Windows Server 2003 kernel-mode driver, SETUPDD.SYS. SETUPDD.SYS is the mother driver that loads the other device drivers. You can view the contents of SETUPREG.HIV after installation by loading it into the Registry Editor.
- **Smss.exe.** The Session Manager Subsystem driver. The Session Manager is responsible for loading and initializing system drivers.
- **Vga.sys, Videoprt.sys,** and **Vgaoem.fon.** These are the standard VGA video drivers and one display font.

Choosing a Disk Format

After Setupldr.bin has loaded drivers into memory, it initializes the kernel driver manager, Ntkrlmp.exe. This manager works with the Session Manager, Ssms.exe, to initialize the operating system.

At this point, Setup prompts you to partition the mass storage device and select a format, either NTFS or FAT. You have the option to use a standard format or a quick format. The only difference is that quick format removes the existing file system and creates a new one but does not perform a sector scan. You should only use quick format on a disk that you have already checked using another utility.

Unlike NT and Windows 2000, if you elect to format the operating system partition as NTFS, Setup actually formats it as NTFS rather than formatting it as FAT/FAT32 then converting it later. This avoids MFT fragmentation. If you elect to format as FAT or FAT32 then convert later, the new NTFS conversion retains the same cluster size. In Windows 2000 and NT, conversion always reverts to a 512-byte cluster.

If you specify FAT on a partition that is larger than 2GB (the limit for DOS partitions with 32KB clusters), Setup automatically formats the partition as FAT32. Windows Server 2003 and Windows 2000 will not format a FAT32 partition that is larger than 32GB. If you want to have a boot partition larger than 32GB formatted as FAT32, format the partition with another utility prior to starting Setup. Large boot partitions, especially those formatted using FAT32, are not recommended.

After the boot and system partitions are formatted, the files necessary to support the graphic phase of startup are copied from the CD. The system restarts automatically after the file copy has completed. An entry in Boot.ini tells Ntldr where to find the kernel files so the graphic phase of Setup can commence.

Graphical Setup Phase

Setup reloads when the machine restarts. Like Dorothy leaving drab, old Kansas for colorful Oz, the character-based screens are left behind and the system shifts to Graphic mode.

Quite a bit more happens during this phase of Setup than the character phase, but you get a lot more information onscreen, so it requires less explanation. There are several critical decision points. These concern licensing, naming servers, setting the Administrator password, configuring workgroups and domains, and setting the system time.

Definition of Boot Partition and System Partition

When I use the terms *boot partition* and *system partition*, I try to stay faithful to the way Microsoft uses the terms. You may find their usage to be a little cross-eyed:

- **System partition.** This is the partition that contains the files required to boot Windows. For an Intel platform, these files are Ntldr, Boot.ini, Ntdetect.com, Bootsect.dos, and Ntbootdd.sys (if a SCSI device has no onboard BIOS). The system partition must be flagged as Active (or bootable) in the Master Boot Record. The files must be at the root of the boot drive. Setup assumes that the first IDE drive on the primary IDE controller is the boot drive. If a partition on this drive is not marked Active, Setup will mark it as Active.
- **Boot partition.** This is the partition that contains the files requires to run the operating system. By default in Windows Server 2003, Setup puts these files in a directory called `\Windows`. (In Windows 2000 and NT, the boot files are put in the `\WINNT` folder.) The boot partition can be on any drive. If you put the boot partition somewhere other than the boot drive, Setup prompts you to create a small system partition on the boot drive. This partition can be less than 1MB, just big enough to hold Ntldr, Ntdetect.com, Boot.ini, and Ntbootdd.sys.

Licensing

When you purchase a license for Windows Server 2003, you do not necessarily purchase the license to connect any clients to that server. For this, you need a *Client Access License* (CAL). A CAL is a piece of paper costing between $15 and $40, depending on volume and reseller markup, that gives you legal authorization to connect a client to a Windows Server.

The purchase price of a Windows Server typically includes a pack of five or more CALs, but there are *Stock Keeping Units* (SKUs) that do not include any CALs at all, so you need to read the catalog carefully when you order. Keep those CAL certificates in a safe place. You'll need them if you ever get audited by the *Software Publishers Association* (SPA) or by your corporate auditors.

When you upgrade from Windows 2000 to Windows Server 2003, you must buy CAL upgrades. The license agreement clearly states that the version number of the CAL must match the version number of the server to which the client connects. Here is where you experience the real expense of an upgrade. You might pay only $400 or $500 for the upgrade SKU of a Windows Server 2003, Standard Edition, but the CAL upgrade may cost you $10 to $20 per license.

Windows Server 2003 has two forms of client access licensing: *Per Device* or *Per User* and *Per Server*. Both forms require purchasing a CAL, but the number of CALs you need to buy and how you track them differs.

Per Server Licensing

This licensing method resembles traditional licensing that you might recognize from NetWare or Banyan. Per Server licensing is a concurrent connection license. If you buy a copy of Windows Server 2003 with 25 CALs, for example, you must set the `Per Server` license value to 25 during Setup. The 26th concurrent user will then be denied access. If you get more than 25 users who need to access the server simultaneously, you must purchase additional CALs, then use the License Manager utility to increase the allowable number of licensed connections. Run the utility from the START menu via START | PROGRAMS | ADMINISTRATIVE TOOLS | LICENSE MANAGER.

CALs and Application Servers

It is not necessary to purchase Windows Server 2003 CAL if you are using a server as a platform for a client/server application. If you have a Lotus Notes service running on Windows Server 2003, for example, you do not need a CAL to connect a Notes client to that Notes service. If the user maps a drive to a Windows Server 2003 to run the Notes client executable across the network, however, you do need a CAL. If the application takes advantage of the Windows Server 2003 security subsystem for authenticating connections, you need a CAL as well.

Recovering from a License Lockout

Sometimes users stay connected to a server even though they are no longer using any resources on it. This chews up licensed connections and can cause a *license lockout*, where no further connections are accepted. A user with administrative privileges is permitted to log on during a license lockout to reset the license value or to disconnect users.

If you install a second Windows Server 2003 with Per Server licensing, you must purchase another set of CALs for the same users who connect to the first server to legally connect to the second. Per Server licensing can get to be expensive if you have many servers.

For the most part, Per Server licensing makes sense only when your servers have separate user populations, or at least very little overlap. Otherwise, it is much cheaper to use Per Seat licensing.

Per Device/Per User Licensing

Windows Server 2003 uses a different licensing scheme from any previous version of Windows or NT. Instead of a Per Seat license, the system has a Per Device or Per User license. In classic Per Seat licensing, every device required a Client Access License (CAL). If a developer had five computers in her cubicle, she would need five CALs to stay legal with the licensing agreement.

In Per Device or Per User licensing, the developer with 5 machines would only require a single User CAL. By the same token, if a shift has 10 factory floor workers using handheld PCs to access the network, and workers on each shift use the same handheld PCs, then only 10 Device CALs would need to be purchased.

So, if you have hundreds of PCs and a dozen users, you need to purchase 12 User CALs. If you have hundreds of users and a dozen PCs, you need to purchase 12 Device CALs. If a factory floor worker uses both a handheld PC to take inventory and another walkup workstation to file a time card, then you'll need either two Device CALs or a Device CAL and a User CAL. Granted that keeping track of these CALs can become quite an exercise, but you can save a lot of money if you have many occasional network users.

Any connection that involves a network service, with the exception of anonymous web connections used by nonemployees, requires either a User or Device CAL. This includes using third-party products such as NFS redirectors or ftp services.

You can change from Per Server to Per Device or Per User licensing, but this is a one-time conversion. You cannot go back to Per Server licensing for that particular server. The conversion only makes sense if your organization has grown to the point where purchasing individual licenses for multiple servers doesn't make sense.

Terminal Server Licenses

Unlike NT4, Windows Server 2003 comes with terminal services built right into the operating system. It is exposed by default via the Remote Desktop service. Only administrators can connect to a server via Remote Desktop, though, with a two-connection limit. If you want to allow non-administrative users to access a server using terminal services sessions, you must install Terminal Services to enable the Application Services mode.

Licensing these terminal server sessions can get expensive and time-consuming. In addition to the CAL for the network connection, you must either pay for a Terminal Services CAL or a license of Windows XP Professional. This is because the terminal server session is considered to be just like running a copy of XP. You can get volume discounts for these Terminal Services CALs that can dramatically reduce their cost.

There is an additional subtlety you need to keep in mind when managing TS (Terminal Server) licenses. Licenses are issued to client hardware, not users. When a client makes a remote desktop connection to a Terminal Server, the client is issued a TS CAL that it embeds in its Registry or NVRAM. If you reinstall the operating system, the client will obtain another CAL. When a TS CAL has not been accessed for 120 days, it is returned to the license pool where it can be reused. Windows 2000/XP clients do not consume a license when connecting to a Windows Server 2003 Terminal Server.

Many administrators prefer to use the Citrix MetaFrame product, a multiuser interface that layers on top of Terminal Services. MetaFrame supports a wide variety of features that are not in standard Terminal Services, such as connecting from non-Windows clients, individual application publication, and more manageable server farms. If you plan on deploying MetaFrame on top of Windows Server 2003, you must still pay for the Microsoft Terminal Services CAL in addition to the Citrix server and client licenses.

Tracking Per Seat Licenses

A Licensing Manager service on each server keeps track of everyone who accesses the server in a licensable manner. This includes file services, print services, network authentication, and so forth.

If the License Manager service says that 5,000 different clients have connected at one time or another, you'll need to show an auditor 5,000 CALs. If you have multiple users who access the same computer (in a lab, for example, or a kiosk machine used to file time cards), License Manager will only report the need for a single CAL for the computer.

The License Manager service maintains three files:

- **Cpl.cfg.** This file contains purchase history information. It is located in `\Windows\System32`.
- **Llsuser.lls.** This file contains connection and user information. It is located in `\Windows\System32\Lls`.
- **Llsmap.lls.** This file contains License group information. License groups are used to identify users who access the same machines and do not need independent CALs. The file is located in `\Windows\System32\Lls`.

Keeping track of CALs for Per Seat users at individual servers in a big network can absorb a lot of energy. Windows Server 2003 simplifies this by providing a License Server option. Each site would have a central license server to collect licensing information. The server is primarily intended for tracking Terminal Server licenses, but can collect other license information as well.

Server Naming

One of the decisions you have to make during Setup is what to name the server or desktop. The naming rules come from old NetBIOS standards that go back to the dark ages of the middle 1980s. This is when Microsoft and IBM worked together with other companies to develop PC networking standards. Windows Server 2003 does not use NetBIOS, but the naming restrictions remain. Here they are:

- **Name length.** A computer or username can be no more than 15 characters long. The actual limit is 16, but the operating system inserts a final character, not ordinarily visible from the user interface, that identifies the NetBIOS service using the name. For example, the Workstation service running on a computer named RUMPLESTILTSKIN would have a full NetBIOS name of `RUMPLESTILTSKIN[03]`, where `[03]` is the hex ID for the Workstation service. Shorter names are padded to 15 characters.
- **Flat namespace.** A NetBIOS name must be unique on a network. Two Windows machines in the same broadcast domain and the same IP subnet, or registered with the same WINS server, cannot have the same name. Active Directory also imposes a flat namespace on computer names within a domain. Even though you can build an Active Directory hierarchy with different domain names, you should still implement a naming convention that ensures unique computer names throughout your organization.
- **Special characters**. NetBIOS permits special characters such as spaces, pound signs, percent signs, and so forth. Because Windows Server 2003 also relies on DNS, you should not use any special character not supported by DNS. You may want to avoid underscores if you are concerned about full DNS compatibility, although recent changes to the DNS RFCs permit using an underscore. SQL servers should also avoid underscores due to problems they cause with SQL queries.

Changing Computer Names

You can change the name of a standalone server or a domain member server using the System Properties window in Explorer. In Windows Server 2003, you can change the name of a domain controller using a new NETDOM option called RENAME-COMPUTER. This requires that the domain be running in full Windows Server 2003 functionality level. See Chapter 9, "Deploying Windows Server 2003 Domains," for more information.

Renaming a server requires users to remap their network drives and recreate shortcuts that include the server's name. This is generally a painful experience, for them and for you. You can avoid some of this pain by putting an alias in WINS and DNS.

You can also use the *Distributed File System* (Dfs) to represent your server-based resources as elements in a virtual directory tree. Dfs enables you to rename servers and shares without disturbing user mappings. See Chapter 16, "Managing Shared Resources," for more information.

Managing Administrator Passwords

All Windows Servers have a default account called Administrator. The Administrator account has full privileges on the machine. During Setup, you assign a password to the Administrator account. The password is saved in the local *Security Account Manager* (SAM) database.

When assigning the local Administrator password, make it long, unique, and cryptographically strong. Don't lose the password. If the server is a domain member, you can log on using a domain account, but the Administrator account in the SAM may be your only way to log on locally. If you do forget the Administrator password, or you inherit a server without finding out the password, you can use a utility called ERD Commander from `www.sysinternals.com` to change any password in the SAM. There are two versions of this utility, shareware and for-fee. Only the for-fee version has the capability of changing passwords.

Domains and Workgroups

Windows Server 2003 and classic NT use two terms that are not actually related to each other but often get confused: *domains* and *workgroups*. Here is a definition of each:

- A **domain** is a security entity. Domain members obtain their authentications from special servers called domain controllers.
- A **workgroup** is a resource-location entity. Workgroup members locate each other using special servers called browsers.

If you lived through the Cold War as I did, you'll appreciate the source of the confusion of these two terms. Do you recall Khrushchev or Breshnev? Each man wielded ultimate power in the USSR because he held two positions, the head of the Supreme Soviet and the chairman of the Communist Party. In the same way, a *primary domain controller* (PDC) makes domains and workgroups appear to be the same thing because it holds both the security database and the browsing database.

Using Workgroups

If you install a server that has no need for security affiliations with other machines, you can make it a standalone server that is a member of a workgroup. Clients in the same workgroup on the same IP subnet share the same browser, so they can find the server. Users will be authenticated via the local SAM on the server when they make network connections.

Even if you have a domain, it sometimes makes sense to install standalone servers. For instance, you may have servers in a DMZ that you do not want to communicate secure logon information back through the firewall.

Joining Domains

To avoid relying on a separate authentication database at the server, you need to join it to a domain. It then becomes a *member server* of the domain.

Member servers in an Active Directory domain authenticate users via Kerberos. This provides a highly secure and fast authentication mechanism and one that also contains the authorization information necessary to build a local security context for the user.

Member servers in a classic NT domain authenticate users via NT LanMan Challenge-Response. This requires the server to have a direct line of communication with a backup domain controller.

In classic NT, it was necessary to provide Administrator credentials to join a computer to a domain. In Windows Server 2003 (and Windows 2000), any authenticated user can join a computer to a domain. This is determined by a group policy linked to the Domain Controllers Organizational Unit (OU) in Active Directory. You can change this group policy to restrict who can join computers to a domain.

Dates and Times

One of the final steps taken by Setup is configuring the date and time at the machine. This seemingly trivial operation turns out to be critical for a couple of reasons.

File Timestamps

When you create, modify, or access a file, the file system changes a timestamp attribute in the file record. The timestamp comes from the server clock, not the client clock. The timestamp uses a universal time code. When a client views the timestamp, the time is corrected for the client's time zone. If clients are not synchronized with server times, users will have difficulty sorting through similar files on different servers to see which are the most recent.

Limitation on Authenticated Users Joining Computers to Domains

In Windows Server 2003, members of the Authenticated Users group have the privilege of joining a computer to a domain. There is a limit on this privilege, though. An attribute called `ms-DS-MachineAccountQuota` in the Active Directory Domain object sets the total number of times a non-administrative user can join a computer to a domain. By default, the value for this attribute is set at 10.

When an Authenticated User who is not a Domain Admin joins a computer to the domain, the Computer object in Active Directory is given an additional attribute called `ms-DS-CreatorSID`. When the user tries to join additional computers to the domain, the system counts the number of Computer objects that have the user's SID in the `ms-DS-CreatorSID` attribute. When the user exceeds the `ms-DS-MachineAccountQuota` limit of 10, he gets an "access denied" error. You can use the ADSI Editor in the Resource Kit to change the value for `ms-DS-AccountQuota`. You can also delete the Authenticated Users group from the `Add Computer to a Domain` group policy.

Kerberos Timestamps

Windows Server 2003 uses *tickets* issued by the Kerberos service to control access to the domain and to member servers. Kerberos tickets contain timestamps to thwart bad guys who might copy the tickets and use them later to impersonate a user. If the clock on the client were to get out of synchronization with the domain controllers, the client's Kerberos tickets would be perpetually invalid.

Time Synchronization

Windows Server 2003 keeps time synchronized between domain controllers and domain members using the *Windows Time Service* (WTS). The actual service name is W32Time.

Every Windows 2000, XP, and Windows Server 2003 desktop and server has the W32Time service loaded by default. When a desktop or server joins a Windows Server 2003 domain, the service is enabled so the client can synchronize clocks with its logon server.

W32Time uses RFC-compliant *Simple Network Time Protocol* (SNTP). The time standard for a Windows Server 2003 domain is the PDC Emulator, normally the first domain controller promoted in the domain. The time standard for a Windows Server 2003 forest is the PDC Emulator in the first domain in the forest, also called the *forest root*.

Configuration Phase

Following the completion of the graphical setup phase, the machine restarts. This marks the official end of Setup as a distinct process running on the server. However, from a practical standpoint, a few final nips and tucks need to be done. A user must log on at the console of the server and configure the machine before it can be considered ready for production.

Initial User Logon

After the machine restarts following the graphical installation phase, a Welcome to Windows screen appears prompting the user to press `Ctrl+Alt+Del` to log on. This is known as the *Secure Attention Sequence (SAS)*. The SAS reduces the possibility that a Trojan Horse program could impersonate the logon window and capture the user credentials.

Winlogon

The console logon process is controlled by a service called Winlogon.exe. Winlogon works in concert with the *Local Security Authority* (LSA) to authenticate the user via a set of authentication providers. Kerberos is the primary provider in a Windows Server

2003 domain. An NTLM (NT LanMan Challenge Response) provider and an LM (LanMan Challenge Response) provider are also present for backward compatibility with NT and Windows 9x and for use in standalone machines.

The window that collects the logon credentials comes from the Graphical Identification and Authentication library, Msgina.dll. This is commonly called the GINA. Third-party vendors can replace this library with their own GINA. For example, Novell replaces the GINA window with one that collects NDS, bindery, and scripting options along with the standard Windows logon information.

If the computer was joined to a domain during Setup, the logon window has a drop-down box listing available domain names along with the local computer name. This gives the user the option of logging on to a domain or just to the local SAM.

Final PnP Enumeration

Plug and Play takes advantage of the initial user logon to discover and report any devices that were missed or skipped during Setup. If PnP cannot find drivers, the user is prompted to provide them. Depending on the nature of the devices, the kind of drivers they use, and the resource allocations required to get the devices working, the user may be required to restart the machine.

For example, PnP may not have found drivers for the video adapter so the system installed default VGA drivers. At the first user logon, the user will be prompted to replace the drivers. The system can be told to look at the Windows Update site for replacement drivers. This requires that the machine have an Internet connection, either through dial-up or over a LAN.

This completes the installation overview. It's time to do some real work. Proceed to the next section in this chapter for step-by-step instructions for installing Windows Server 2003 on a new machine.

IA64 Setup Differences

As mentioned earlier, the Extended Firmware Interface (EFI) in an IA64 system boots using a boot menu stored in firmware rather than in a Boot.ini file on the hard drive. Also, the boot drive must contain certain special partitions to hold bootstrap code and special Microsoft data structures.

Windows Server 2003 Setup automatically makes the necessary changes to the firmware boot menu and the drive partitioning if you choose to let it. If you have a drive that came from the vendor with partitioning already in place, you should verify that the drive has the following partitions:

- EFI System Partition (ESP)
- Microsoft Reserved Partition (MSR)
- OEM partition (optional)
- One or more data partitions (optional)

You can use the EFI Shell to verify the partitioning.

EFI Shell

The EFI Shell is one of the options presented in the boot menu. Here is an example boot menu listing:

```
EFI Boot Manager ver 1.02 [12.36A]

Please select a boot option:

Microsoft Windows Server 2003, Standard Edition
Acpi(PNP0A03,0)/Pci(5|0)/Mac(0003478991556)
EFI Shell [Built-in]
Boot option maintenance menu
```

When you select the EFI Shell option, the system launches an operating environment with full access to FAT and FAT32 partitions and a short set of commands for manipulating files and configuring the system.

When the EFI Shell first loads, it lists the available partitions on the drives. You can repeat this list using the `MAP` command from the shell prompt. Here is an example `MAP` listing for a machine with several partitions:

```
Device mapping table

  fs0  : VenHw(Unknown Device:80)/HD(Part1,SigBD1C1A20-685C-01C1-507B-9E5F8078F531)
  fs1  : VenHw(Unknown Device:80)/HD(Part5,Sig1FD4472C-D516-11D5-8473-806D6172696F)
  fs2  : VenHw(Unknown Device:FF)/CDROM(Entry1)
  blk0 : VenHw(Unknown Device:00)
  blk1 : VenHw(Unknown Device:80)
  blk2 : VenHw(Unknown Device:80)/HD(Part1,SigBD1C1A20-685C-01C1-507B-9E5F8078F531)
  blk3 : VenHw(Unknown Device:80)/HD(Part2,Sig1FD44720-D516-11D5-8473-806D6172696F)
  blk4 : VenHw(Unknown Device:FF)
  blk5 : VenHw(Unknown Device:FF)/CDROM(Entry1)
```

The long number in each entry is the GUID assigned to the partition. Each partition is identified with a `blk#` sequence number. Partitions with readable file systems (FAT, FAT32, and Joliet CD-ROM) are also assigned an `fs#` alias.

You can access partition blocks in the EFI shell by entering the block name followed by a colon, such as `blk3:`. This is the same way you would change logical drives at the command prompt of an operating system. You can list the files and folders in each readable partition by running `dir` or `ls` at the prompt.

You can get a partial list of the commands available in the EFI shell by typing `?` at the shell prompt. If you want a full list of the commands, visit the Intel web site at `cedar.intel.com`.

You may notice that you are not prompted for a password prior to entering the EFI Shell. Physical security is the only option for protecting the firmware settings in an IA64 server.

EFI Boot Maintenance Manager

The EFI boot menu has a Boot Maintenance Manager that permits making modifications to the entries in the boot menu. It is not necessary to use this utility to manage Windows Server 2003 boot entries. All Windows Server 2003 boot entries are managed from within the operating system using either System Properties or the `BOOTCFG` command.

You may, however, encounter instances when you want to change the boot order using the Boot Maintenance Manager if you have multiple operating systems. Here are the options:

- **`Boot from a file.`** This option permits you to navigate to a partition, including a CD-ROM or floppy, and launch a boot loader. You can use this option to initiate Setupldr.efi on the Windows Server 2003 CD in preparation for running the Recovery Console. Chapter 21, "Recovering from System Failures," has details.
- **`Add a Boot Option; Delete Boot Option(s).`** This option permits you to change the boot menu itself. Each boot menu item is associated with a partition and a boot loader.
- **`Manage BootNext Setting.`** This option permits you to select which of the Boot Manager options will be launched automatically at boot time.
- **`Set Auto Boot Timeout.`** This option sets the Boot Manager delay interval before launching the option selected by the `BootNext` option. The default timeout is 30 seconds. Using System Properties in Windows Server 2003 to change the boot menu selection timeout also changes this setting in NVRAM.
- **`Console Devices.`** These options define the standard console output, input, and error devices. You can use these options to redirect the console to one of the serial ports. This is similar to the Emergency Management Services (EMS) option in the IA32 version where you can define a serial port in Boot.ini to receive console output.
- **`Cold Reset.`** This restarts the machine using the same POST as if the power switch had been cycled.

Booting Windows Server 2003 Setup Using the EFI Shell

IA32 systems will boot to an El Torito CD-ROM automatically if the boot sequence in CMOS is set to permit this action. An IA64 system does not recognize an El Torito disk. You must initiate Setup manually using the EFI Shell.

Do this by selecting the EFI Shell from the boot menu then changing to the `fs#` alias that represents the CD-ROM. Ordinarily, this would be `fs0` unless there are other operating systems already installed. Launch the setup boot loader, Setupldr.efi, from the root of the CD. Files with an .efi extension contain executable code compatible with the EFI Shell.

The only portion of Windows Server 2003 Setup that looks different on an IA64 machine is the partitioning method for the boot drive. If the boot drive already has an EFI System Partition (ESP), Setup will prompt you of the necessity for a Microsoft Reserved Partition (MSR) and will create one automatically. If the drive has no pre-existing partitions, Setup will create the ESP and MSR partitions, format them, and prompt you to create a partition for the operating system files.

Installing Windows Server 2003

This section contains step-by-step details for installing Windows Server 2003 Server from the Windows Server 2003 CD. The steps assume that you are installing on a fresh drive or a drive that has no data you want to preserve. If you are upgrading an existing server, proceed to Chapter 2, "Performing Upgrades and Automated Installations."

Character Phase Setup

With the Windows Server 2003 CD in the CD-ROM drive, proceed as directed in Procedure 1.1.

Procedure 1.1 Installing Windows Server 2003 on a New Machine

1. Start the machine with the bootable CD in the CD-ROM drive. It's a good idea to initiate Setup using a cold start. Some systems are not good about resetting every bit of hardware with a warm boot.
2. Press a key when prompted. When all drivers have loaded and the Windows Server 2003 Executive has initialized, a Welcome to Setup screen appears (see Figure 1.2).

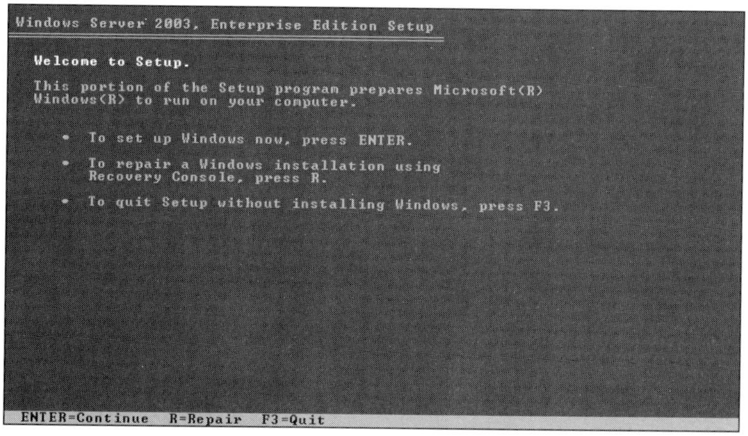

Figure 1.2 Text-mode setup—Welcome to Setup screen.

3. There are three options. The `Recovery Console` option is covered in Chapter 21, "Recovering from System Failures." Press `Enter` to continue with Setup.
4. The Windows Server 2003 Licensing Agreement screen appears. This contains the text of the End User Licensing Agreement (EULA).
5. Press `F8` to agree to the terms of the EULA. A partition management screen appears (see Figure 1.3). If you are installing on a new server, the drives show a status of `Unpartitioned Space`.

   If you have existing partitions that you want to remove, highlight the partition name and press `D`. Setup responds with two confirmation screens to delete the partition. The first confirmation screen appears if the partition is a system partition (flagged `Active` in the Master Boot Record). Press `Enter` to confirm. The second confirmation screen asks you to press `L`.
6. After all partitions have been removed, highlight the `Unpartitioned Space` entry and press `C` to create a partition. If you select a partition other than the active boot partition, Setup prompts you to create a system partition that is bootable. A 1MB partition is sufficient.
7. When you create a partition, Setup prompts you to specify the size of the partition in MB. Give the operating system at least 3GB, with 4GB preferred.
8. When the partition has been created, Setup returns to the partition management screen. Highlight the newly created partition and press `Enter` to install Windows Server 2003 into that partition.

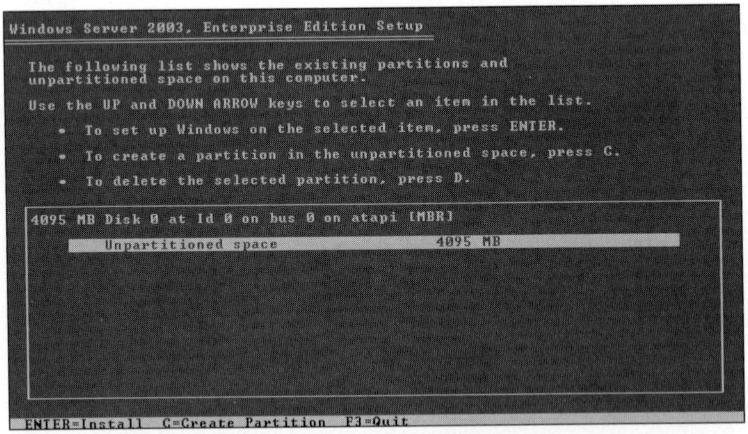

Figure 1.3 Text-mode setup—partition management.

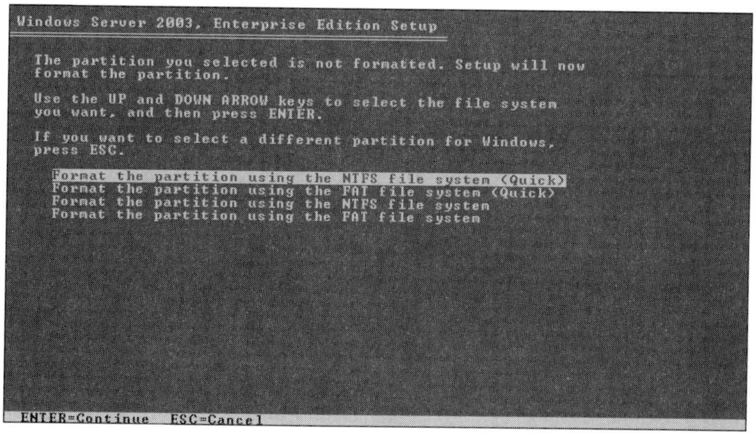

Figure 1.4 Text-mode setup—system partition formatting.

9. Setup now prompts you to format the partition using either NTFS or FAT (see Figure 1.4). You have the option of a standard or fast format. Fast formatting skips a sector scan of the disk.
10. Select a format type and press `Enter`. Setup formats the partition and displays a progress bar.
11. When the format is finished, Setup copies installation files from the CD to the newly formatted partition.
12. When the file copy completes, the system restarts. The graphic phase begins automatically thanks to a pointer in Boot.ini.

Graphic Phase

After restart, the system loads and shifts to Graphic mode and begins Setup again. A Welcome window opens. Follow the steps laid out in Procedure 1.2.

Procedure 1.2 Continuing with the Graphic Mode Portion of Setup

1. Click `Next` at the Welcome window or wait a while for Setup to proceed automatically. The Installing Devices window opens and PnP enumeration begins.

   Give this step lots and lots of time. The machine may seem to hang for many minutes. If you get frustrated and restart, Setup will return to this point and begin the discovery all over again. Don't lose heart.

2. If you make it through the device installation without hangs or errors, the Regional and Language Settings window opens. You have the opportunity here to change the `Locale` and `Keyboard` settings, if necessary.

   `Locale Settings` determine the National Language Support (NLS) files that Setup loads. These files control parameters such as display language, decimal points, monetary units, and such.

   `Keyboard Settings` control key mappings and special keystroke functions.

3. Click `Next`. The Personalize Your Software window opens. Fill in the `Name` and `Organization` fields. These entries are for information only. The name is not used to build any accounts, and the company name you enter does not affect licensing. Setup merely writes the values to the Registry. However, you cannot enter `Administrator` or `Guest`.

Registry Tip: Changing the Registered Owner Name

You should avoid putting actual user names in the Personalize Your Software window. This avoids problems with an old administrator's name appearing in application setups years later. You can change the user information in the Registry:

Key: `HKLM | Software |Microsoft |Windows NT | CurrentVersion`

Value: `RegisteredOwner`

4. Click `Next`. The Product Key window opens. Enter the 25-character product key from the Windows Server 2003 jewel box or other container. If you are using a master license or volume purchase agreement, enter the key associated with the agreement.
5. Click `Next`. The Licensing Modes window opens (see Figure 1.5). Refer to the earlier "Licensing" section in this chapter under the "Functional Overview of Windows Server 2003 Setup" topic for details on making the decision between Per Server and Per Device or Per Client licensing.
6. Click `Next`. The Computer Name and Administrator Password window opens. Refer to the earlier "Managing Administrator Passwords" section in this chapter for advice on selecting server names and passwords.
7. Click `Next`. If you have a modem in the server, the Modem Dialing Information window opens. Enter your area code and any dial-out prefix such as 9 or 19. This information is used to make Registry entries under `HKLM | System | Software | Microsoft | Windows | CurrentVersion | Telephony`.
8. Click `Next`. The Date and Time Settings window opens. Use this window to set the date, time, and time zone. See the earlier "Dates and Times" section in this chapter for details.

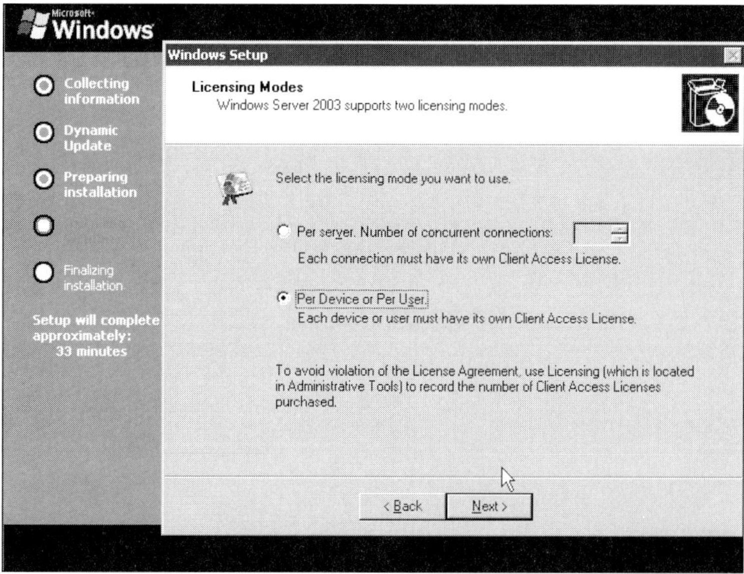

Figure 1.5 Windows Server 2003 Setup—Licensing Modes window.

9. Click `Next`. Setup now performs additional inspections to determine the state of the network and how to configure the network hardware. TCP/IP is always loaded. If Setup discovers SAP broadcasts and accompanying IPX/SPX traffic, for example, it will load the NWLINK transport drivers.

   Note that if you have legacy network adapters that were not configured correctly during the device installation step, the machine may hang at this step. Give Setup lots of time, however, before restarting.

10. After Setup loads the network drivers, the Networking Settings window opens. You have two configuration choices: `Typical Settings` and `Custom Settings` (see Figure 1.6).

    Selecting `Typical Settings` tells Setup to lease an address from DHCP and use the configuration information in the DHCP response packet. If a DHCP server is not available, the TCP/IP driver defaults to a random address from the `169.254.0.0` address space. This is called *Automatic Private IP Addressing.*

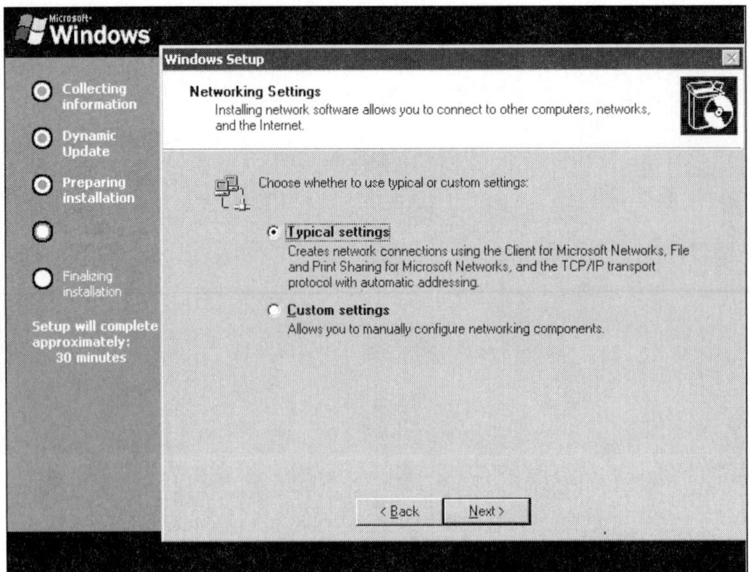

Figure 1.6 Graphic-mode setup—Networking Settings window.

11. Select the `Custom Settings` radio button and click `Next`. The Networking Components window opens (see Figure 1.7). You can use this window to make any special configurations for network services and communication protocols.
12. Double-click `Internet Protocol (TCP/IP)` to open its Properties window. Use this window to enter an IP address, default gateway, and DNS server, along with advanced settings for WINS and security features such as TCP/IP filtering and IPSec.
13. After you have completed entering your configuration settings, click `OK` to close and return to the Networking Settings window.
14. Click `Next`. The Workgroup or Computer Domain window opens (see Figure 1.8). If you want the machine to be in a workgroup, leave the default radio button selected and enter the workgroup name.

    If you want to join the machine to a domain, select the `Yes, Make This Computer A Member Of The Following Domain` and enter the domain name. If you get an `Unable to Locate Domain Controller` error, look for a problem with your WINS or DNS configuration.
15. Click `Next`. Setup begins copying files from the CD.
16. After the file copy is complete, the Performing Final Tasks window opens and Setup begins configuring the services and components you installed.

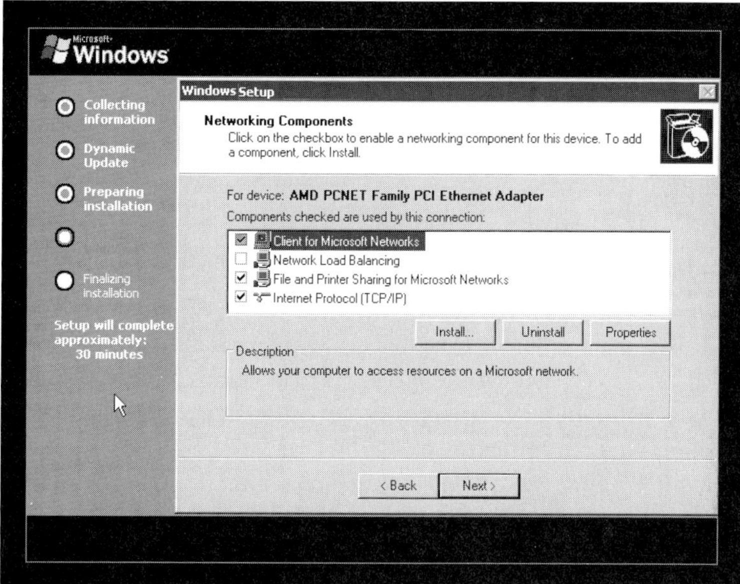

Figure 1.7 Graphic-mode setup—Networking Components window.

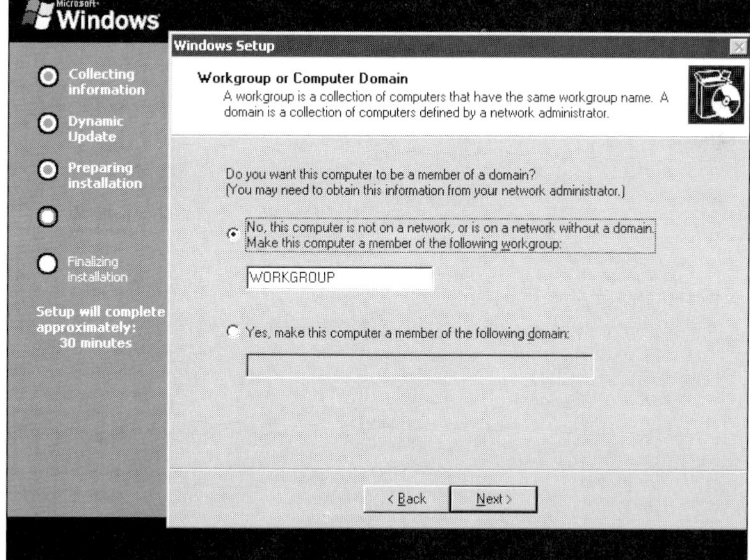

Figure 1.8 Windows Server 2003 Setup—Workgroup or Computer Domain window.

17. After the final tasks have been finished, Setup displays the Completing the Windows Server 2003 Setup Wizard window. The machine restarts automatically if you take no action.

Final Configuration

After restart, the system boots to the Ctrl+Alt+Del logon window. Log on and finish configuring the machine.

When you log on to a Windows Server 2003 or Windows 2000 domain, you are authenticated via Kerberos. Chapter 11, "Understanding Network Access Security and Kerberos," has details of the Kerberos transactions. A service called Userinit.exe sets up your working environment, creates your user profile, and starts the Explorer shell in your security context.

If you are logging on to a newly installed server, the Configure Your Server window opens. This window is controlled by the Server Configuration Wizard, Srvwiz.dll, a component of Mshta.exe, the Internet Explorer repair tool. The Server Configuration Wizard is controlled by a Registry entry under `HKCU | Software | Microsoft | Windows NT | CurrentVersion | Setup | Welcome | Srvwiz`.

The Configuration Wizard consists of a set of Java-based windows that collects features you want to enable, then automates their installation. Figure 1.9 shows an example. The results are logged in `\Windows\Cys.log`.

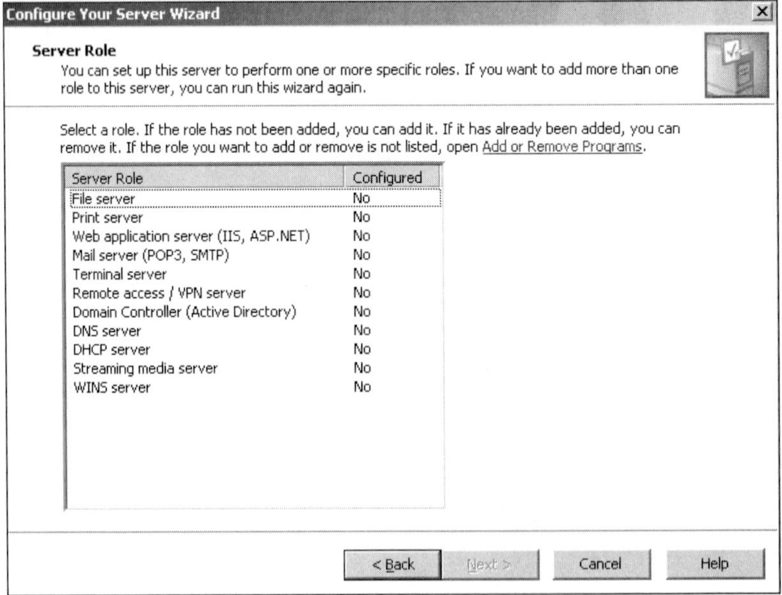

Figure 1.9 Configure Your Server Wizard showing the list of available service control options.

You can close the wizard with the option to not open it again, if you prefer to configure your server manually. Later, if you change your mind and decide that a wizard looks like a pretty good way to configure a server, you can launch it again from the Control Panel using the Configure Your Server applet.

Web Server Configuration Differences

Because Web Server is designed as a platform for IIS, it has a special set of web-based configuration windows that can be used to manage the server.

When you log on for the first time following Setup, the system prompts you to authenticate with web services. This cannot be done if the Administrator account has a blank password because network logons must have a password in Windows Server 2003. Figure 1.10 shows the initial Welcome configuration page.

This window has two navigational bars. The first bar at the top controls access to major administrative areas, such as Status, Network, Disk, Users, and so forth. Each major area has a secondary navigational bar under it that controls access to individual information or configuration pages. Figure 1.11 shows an example of the Interfaces page under Network configuration.

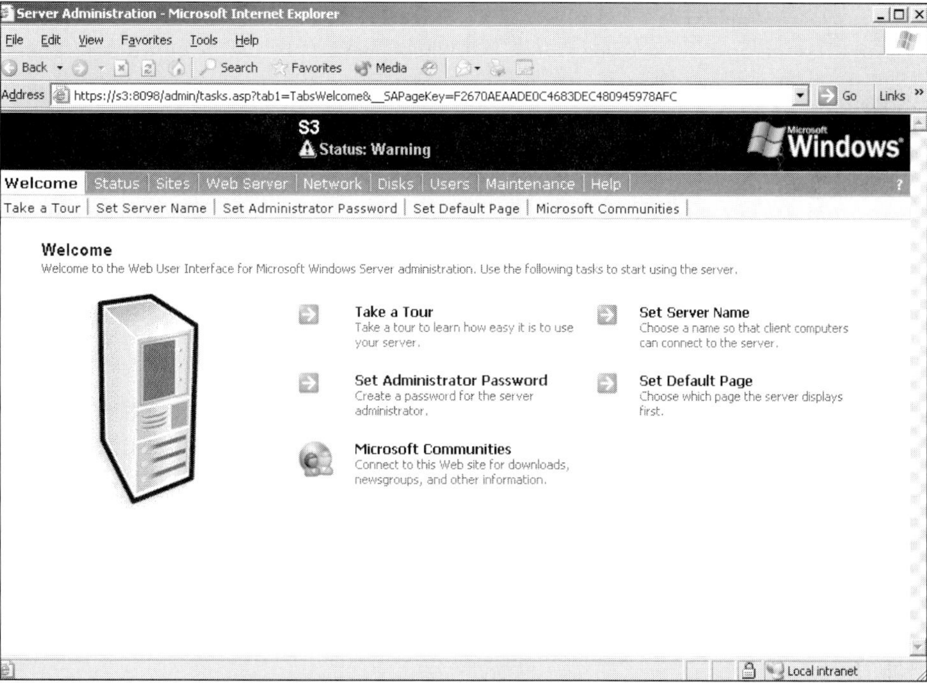

Figure 1.10 Web Server Welcome configuration page.

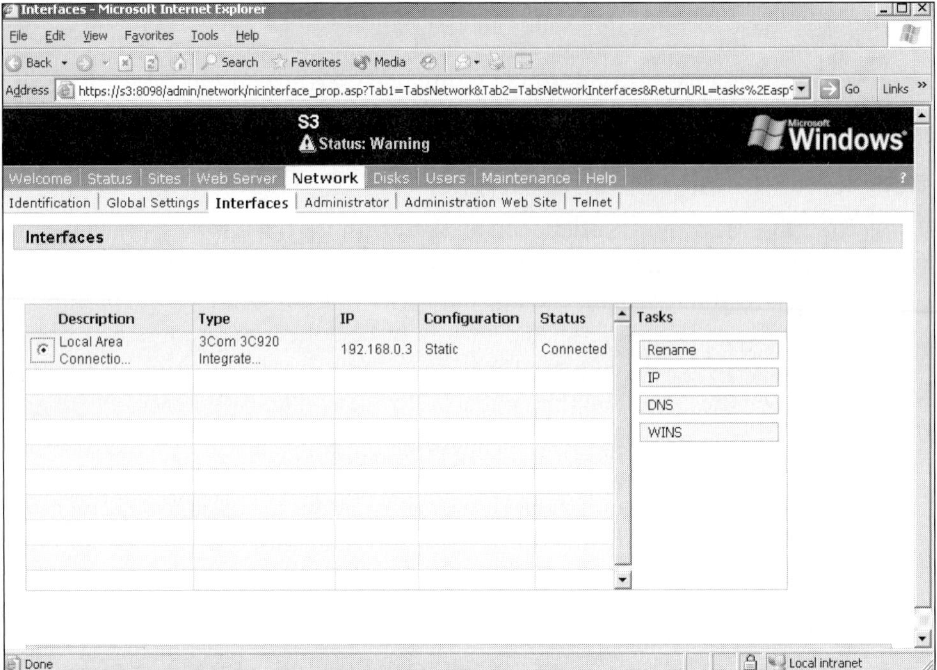

Figure 1.11 Example Web Server configuration page.

Any of the administrative tasks presented in these pages can also be performed using standard Windows Server 2003 MMC-based administration tools. The pages themselves are part of an Administration web site installed at port 8098 on a Web Server. By default, this port requires Secure Sockets Layer (SSL) for access. A non-encrypted port, 8099, exists only to redirect to the SSL port or to give an error message if the SSL port is not used.

Post Setup Configurations

If you have no abnormal indications and the system appears to be functioning normally, you can declare a job well done and give yourself a week off. If Setup did not complete or had significant errors, check the section, "Correcting Common Setup Problems," in this chapter.

You may want to do a few things to tidy up. Here are a few hygiene checks you should perform.

Product Activation

The license agreement accompanying any Microsoft Windows product makes it very clear that the operating system is considered a part of the computer, no different than a chipset or the system BIOS. That's why most retail versions of Windows are called "upgrades," on the assumption that you must have received a Windows operating system with the original hardware. (This is not always the case, of course. It is possible to purchase a server without an operating system, or with an alternative OS such as Linux or NetWare.)

When you install the retail version of Windows Server 2003, you have 30 days to activate the product. This is handled by the *Windows Product Activation (WPA) Wizard*. The executable is called Msoobe.exe, which stands for *MS Out-Of-Box Experience*. WPA has three major components:

- A 25-character product key on the jewel case or other container.
- An Installation ID generated based on the hardware installed in the server at the time of activation. If you are interested in the hardware components that go into the makeup of the Installation ID, a German firm called Fully Licensed has analyzed the WPA process and published a white paper at `www.licenturion.com/xp/fully-licensed-wpa.txt`.
- A Confirmation ID supplied by Microsoft via the Internet, modem, or phone. This number is what "activates" the Windows Server 2003 installation.

If your server does not have direct connection to the Internet but it has a modem, you can use dial-up to one of Microsoft's Product Activation Centers using a number provided in the WPA Wizard. If you do not have a modem, you can call the Product Activation Center directly to obtain a Confirmation ID. There are support centers in each country. Each one is available 7 × 24. The operator does not collect any user information. The operator may ask for a name, but only out of politeness. Microsoft insists that no personal information is recorded.

If you choose to activate via phone, the WPA Wizard displays a window that displays the Installation ID so you can read it to a customer support representative. Figure 1.12 shows an example.

If you reinstall Windows Server 2003 using the same product key on the same machine with the same hardware, you need only validate the existing activation via the Internet or phone or modem. You can perform an unlimited number of validations.

If you do a radical change to your hardware, you will be required to reactivate. The exact nature of the change is something Microsoft will not publish. The retail version of XP is extremely forgiving. If the machine uses the same BIOS, activation will not be triggered.

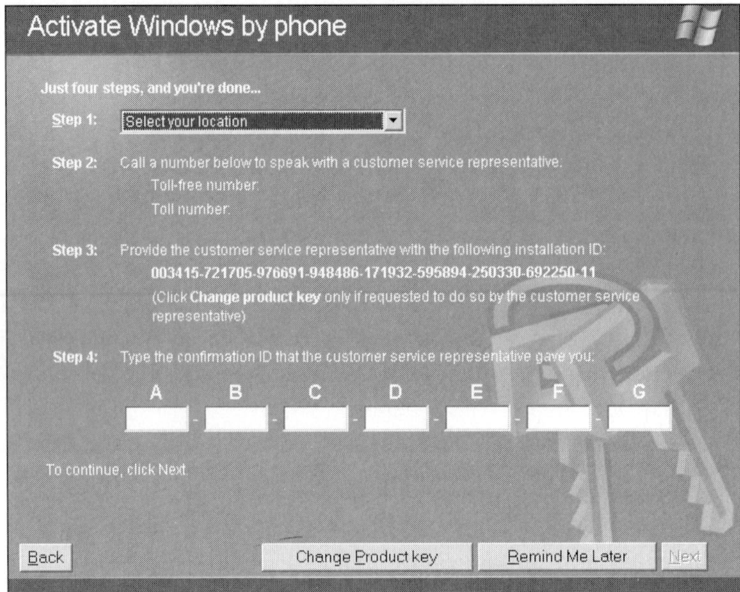

Figure 1.12 Activate Windows screen—phone activation.

WPA only applies to retail versions of the product. The product key you obtain from a Master License Agreement or a Volume Purchase Agreement is not subject to per-instance activation. The minimum number of overall licenses required to qualify for a VPA is relatively modest. Check with your reseller for current requirements.

Event Log Checks

You should check the Event log to make sure no abnormal situations came up during installation and the initial boot. Event logs are stored in the `\Windows\System32\Config` folder along with the Registry hives. You can view the contents of the logs using the Event Viewer console, Eventvwr.msc, or the Event Viewer executable, Eventvwr.exe.

Activation and Registration

Windows Product Activation, as a process, is completely distinct from product registration. Registration lets Microsoft know who you are so you can obtain technical support, product update notifications, and lots of email concerning third-party product information.

Activation does not contain any information that relates a particular user or organization to a particular license of Windows Server 2003. Registration, on the other hand, contains a great deal of information about you and your organization. You do not need to register in order to activate.

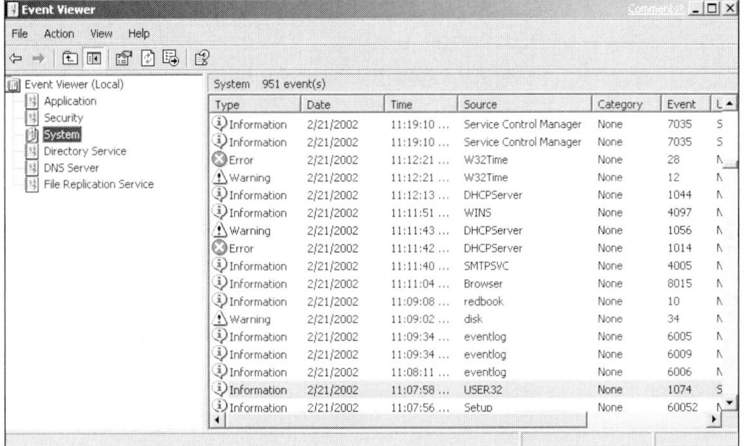

Figure 1.13 Event Viewer console showing typical System log entries after installing Windows Serve 2003.

The Event Viewer console can be opened from the Start menu via START | PROGRAMS | ADMINISTRATIVE TOOLS | EVENT VIEWER. Figure 1.13 shows an example of the Event Viewer console showing the System log. If you are an NT4 administrator, you'll be pleasantly surprised to see that the navigation arrows in the viewer now actually indicate how the cursor will move.

There are several Event logs:

- **Application**. Events from user processes.
- **System**. Events from drivers and Executive processes.
- **Security**. Used only if Auditing is enabled.
- **Directory Services**. Installed only on domain controllers.
- **File Replication Service**. Installed only on domain controllers.
- **DNS**. Installed only on DNS servers.

You should get familiar with the normal Event log entries for your system. Some errors happen all the time and are benign. Others should cause you immediate attention. Each entry in the Event log has a description of the event and many have suggestions for troubleshooting. Figure 1.14 shows what an error looks like in the Event log.

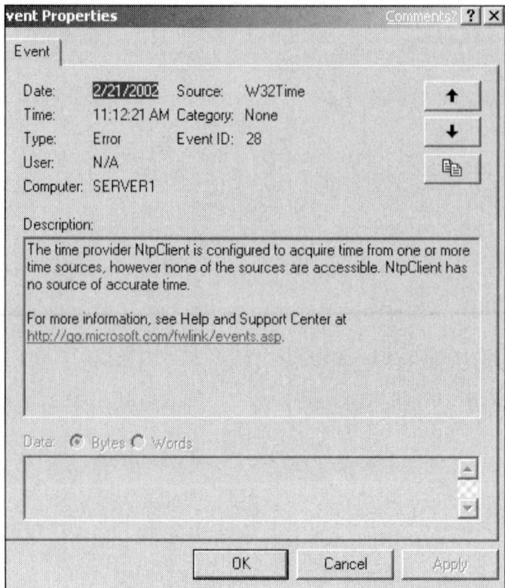

Figure 1.14 Sample Event log entry showing error details.

Move and Configure the Paging File

The paging file holds memory pages that have been swapped out of RAM. The pages are stored in a system file called Pagefile.sys, stored at the root of the system partition. The default minimum size of the paging file is 150 percent of system RAM with a maximum size of 300 percent of RAM.

For small systems with 256MB of RAM, you can get away with keeping the paging file on the system partition. But for large systems with multiple gigabytes of RAM, you should take a few actions to control the file's size and location.

Move the Paging File to Another Disk

You can improve overall system performance by putting the paging file on a fast drive that does not share connections with the operating system drive.

You can have up to 16 paging files as long as each one is on a separate logical drive. You will not get a performance improvement unless the paging files are on separate physical drives, as well.

You should leave a small paging file on the boot partition. This is because the system uses the paging file to hold memory dump information following a kernel-mode stop error (a.k.a. Blue Screen of Death). The memory is dumped first to the paging file and then copied to a dump file following the next restart. That's why the paging file must be at the root of the system partition, because the bugcheck executable has no access to the file system and so must use INT13 calls, which are limited to the root of the boot drive.

The option to dump system memory can force you to set aside very large chunks of disk real estate if you have lots of memory. An alternative is to dump only the operating system memory. This saves considerable disk space and gives Microsoft technical support a more compact file to examine in the event of a crash. Or you can dump just the stack heap if you really want to conserve space (<64KB total). This is outlined in Procedure 1.3.

In most situations, I've found that a stack heap dump gives sufficient information for servers that are not having problems. If you have a server that is crashing frequently, you may need to save a dump of the operating system or even of the entire memory space. At this point, you are probably going to call Microsoft Product Support Services, and they will tell you what sorts of information they need.

Procedure 1.3 Configuring the System to Dump Only the Contents of the Kernel Memory

1. Open the `System` applet in Control Panel.
2. Select the `Advanced` tab.
3. Click `Settings` under `Startup and Recovery`.
4. Under `Write Debugging Information`, select the option to do a `Kernel Memory Dump` or a `Small Memory Dump` (see Figure 1.15).

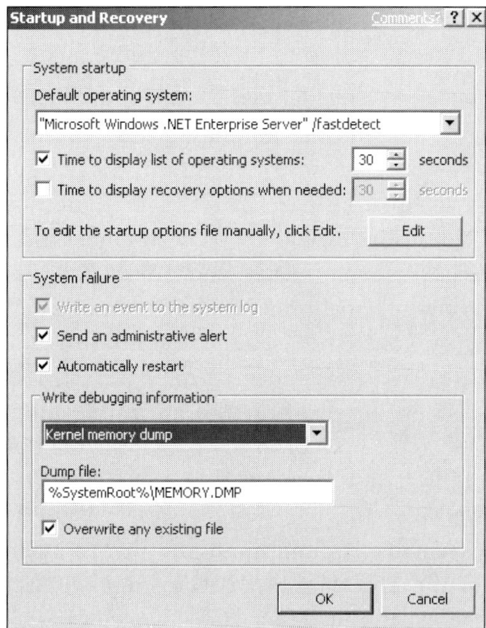

Figure 1.15 Startup and Recovery window showing memory dump options.

Avoid Paging File Fragmentation

The paging file can become fragmented, which hurts performance considerably. Finding pages in a fragmented paging file requires more work. Also, because the paging file is a system file, the disk defragmenter must work around it to defrag the remaining files.

To avoid fragmentation, make sure the drive you select for the paging file is already defragmented, then make the minimum and maximum file sizes the same. This causes the system to lay out the full paging file in a single, contiguous run that won't grow and get fragmented. Be sure to give a generous amount of space. If you are going to run Terminal Services, make the paging file at least double the size of memory up to 4GB.

Functional Description of the Windows Server 2003 Boot Process

Computers are like airplanes: they are most prone to accidents during takeoffs and landings. This topic contains a detailed analysis of the Windows Server 2003 boot process for use in troubleshooting upgrade and setup problems.

What follows is the IA32 boot process. The IA64 boot process is much simpler because EFI locates and launches the secondary bootstrap loader, Ia64ldr.efi, using information stored in Non-Volatile RAM (NVRAM). If you have an IA64 system, skip to the "System Kernel" topic later in this chapter.

Initial Bootstrap

When you turn on any IA32 computer, the system starts out with a *Power On Self Test* (POST). Specific actions during the POST vary from system to system. A short beep at the end indicates a successful completion. For IA64 computers, the POST includes a full system configuration check done by the Extensible Firmware Interface (EFI).

The final step in the POST for IA32 machines is a handoff to an INT13 routine in BIOS that checks for a bootable device. For IA64 machines, the EFI finds the bootstrap loader using information in the boot menu.

Depending on your BIOS settings, the boot routine usually starts at the A: drive followed by the drive determined by the system BIOS to be the boot drive. This is the master drive on the primary IDE interface, if one exists, followed by the SCSI drive designated as the boot drive in the SCSI BIOS. You cannot boot to a SCSI drive if a bootable IDE drive is present. The system loads the Master Boot Record (MBR) from this drive.

There is executable code in the MBR that is just smart enough to scan the partition table at the end of the MBR to find the sector/offset of the active boot partition. If the code cannot find suitable entries in the partition table, it displays the error `Invalid Partition Table`. If the code finds a partition table but cannot locate the start of the active partition, it displays either the error `Error Loading Operating System` or the error `Missing Operating System`.

Secondary Bootstrap

When the executable code in the MBR finds the start of the active partition, it loads the first sector (512 bytes) into memory at location `0x700h`. This is the called the partition boot sector, or more commonly just the boot sector. The boot sector contains executable code designed to find and load a *secondary bootstrap loader*. The executable code in the boot sector cannot read a file system, so the secondary bootstrap loader must be at the root of the boot drive.

On a DOS machine, the secondary bootstrap loader is IO.SYS. On IA32 versions of Windows Server 2003 and XP, Windows 2000, and NT, the secondary bootstrap loader is Ntldr. If Ntldr is missing or will not load, the boot sector code displays error messages such as `A disk read error has occurred` or `Ntldr is missing` or `Ntldr is compressed`. In all these events, the message includes the instructions `Press Ctrl+Alt+Del to restart`.

Ntldr

When Ntldr executes, it initializes the video hardware and puts the screen in 80×25 mode with a black background. It then switches the processor to Protected mode to support 32-bit memory addressing and initializes miniature versions of the NTFS and FAT file system drivers contained in the Ntldr code itself. These file system drivers permit Ntldr to see enough of the drive to load the remaining Windows Server 2003 system files.

Ntldr now locates a file called Boot.ini, which contains the Windows Server 2003 boot menu. See the "Working with Boot.ini" section later in this chapter for details about the entries in Boot.ini. If Ntldr cannot find Boot.ini, it displays the error `Windows Server 2003 could not start because the following file is missing or corrupt: Boot.ini`. If Boot.ini is present but does not contain valid entries, any number of errors can appear. Generally, they indicate a problem with default ARC path.

If there is only one entry in the Boot.ini file, Windows Server 2003 automatically uses that entry with no delay time. If there are multiple entries, the delay time is set to 30 seconds by default.

Ntldr Versions

The Windows Server 2003 version of Ntldr can load Windows 2000 and NT4 boot files, but the opposite is not true. Keep this in mind if you apply a service pack or do an emergency repair on a dual-boot machine. If you overwrite Ntldr, you cannot boot to Windows Server 2003. If you accidentally overwrite Ntldr, you can replace it with a copy from another Windows Server 2003 machine. The same Ntldr is used in Windows Server 2003 and XP.

If you install Windows Server 2003 in addition to an existing operating system such as Windows 9x or DOS, the boot sector from the previous operating system is saved in a file called Bootsect.dos. The alternate operating system becomes a selection in the boot menu.

If you select the alternate operating system from the boot menu, Ntldr loads the contents of Bootsect.dos into memory at file location `700h`, shifts back to Real mode, and turns control over to the executable code in the boot sector image.

You can quickly change the boot menu delay time in both IA32 and IA64 systems using the new BOOTCFG utility in Windows Server 2003. The syntax is `bootcfg /timeout #` where `#` is the number of seconds. You can set the delay time to 0 to avoid the menu entirely.

On IA32 systems, you can manually edit the Boot.ini file to set the timeout value to –1 to disable the countdown timer completely. In this configuration, the system will sit at the boot menu until you make a selection. You can do the same on IA64 systems using the Boot Manager Maintenance utility.

Ntdetect.com

Before Ntldr can execute the kernel image, it needs to know something about the hardware. This is the cue for Ntdetect.com, which gathers the same kind of information on an IA32 machine that EFI delivers from firmware on an IA64 machine.

Don't confuse Ntdetect with the Plug and Play Manager. PnP enumeration happens much further along in the boot process. Ntdetect looks for the following hardware configurations: (The CPU type and FPU type are detected later on by Ntoskrnl.exe and Hal.dll.)

- Machine ID
- Bus/adapter type
- Video
- Keyboard
- Communication port
- Parallel port
- Floppy Drive
- Mouse

Alternative SCSI Driver

If you boot to a SCSI drive, the SCSI interface should have a BIOS that determines the bootable device. If the SCSI adapter does not have a BIOS, or if the BIOS is disabled, the ARC path in Boot.ini will specify the SCSI ID number of the bootable drive. This means Ntldr needs a way to scan the SCSI bus looking for the SCSI ID.

If Setup detects that a SCSI interface does not have a functioning BIOS, it copies the SCSI miniport driver to the root of the boot partition and renames it Ntbootdd.sys. Ntldr loads Ntbootdd.sys and uses the miniport driver to communicate with the drives. The Ntbootdd.sys file must be at the root of the drive because Ntldr must be able to find it using straight INT13 calls.

Ntdetect uses this information to build a data structure in memory that is used later on by the kernel driver to construct the `Hardware` hive in the Registry.

System Kernel

If you select a Windows Server 2003 operating system from the boot menu, the secondary bootstrap loader (Ntldr for IA32 and Ia64ldr for IA64) uses that partition to load the operating system kernel, Ntoskrnl.exe, and its associate Hardware Abstraction Layer library, Hal.dll, along with a video driver, Bootvid.dll. The secondary bootstrap loader puts the images of the kernel files in memory but does not execute them quite yet. First, it searches out and loads the service drivers.

If the secondary bootstrap loader does not find Ntoskrnl.exe, it gives the error `Windows Server 2003 could not start because the following file is missing or corrupt:\<systemroot>\system32\Ntoskrnl.exe`. The most likely cause of this error is an incorrect path in the boot menu entry, although corruption of the file system on the volume can also be the culprit.

If Boot.ini is missing, Ntldr defaults to the drive containing the system partition and searches for a partition containing Ntoskrnl.exe. You'll see this as a "Default" entry in the boot menu.

Initial Service Drivers

The secondary bootstrap loader opens the `System` hive in the Registry and checks the `Select` key to find the `CurrentControlSet`. It then scans the list of `Services` keys in the `CurrentControlSet` looking for devices with a `Start` value of 0, indicating `Service_Boot_Start`, and 1, indicating `Service_System_Start`. It loads these drivers in the order specified by the `Group` value under `Control`, `Service Group Order`.

At this point, the console shows a `Starting Windows Server 2003` message along the bottom of the screen with a progress bar that slides along as the drivers load. When this is complete, the secondary bootstrap loader initializes Ntoskrnl.exe and hands over the driver images now stored in memory.

Kernel Initialization

When Ntoskrnl starts, it initializes Hal.dll and Bootvid.dll. The screen now shifts to graphic mode. Ntoskrnl then initializes the system drivers and uses information from Ntdetect.com (IA32) or EFI (IA64) to create a volatile `Hardware` hive in the Registry. It then calls on the Session Manager, Smss.exe, to do a little preliminary housekeeping.

Session Manager

Session Manager reads its own key in the `System` hive under `HKLM | System | CurrentControlSet | Control | Session Manager` to find entries under `BootExecute`. By default, this includes AUTOCHK, a boot-time version of CHKDSK. Session

Manager also sets up the paging file, Pagefile.sys. After Session Manager finishes its chores, it does the following two things simultaneously:

- Loads the console logon service, Winlogon.exe, to start the authentication verification process. Winlogon starts the Local Security Authority Subsystem, LSASS.EXE, and the print spooler, SPOOLSS.EXE, along with their supporting function libraries.
- Loads the Services Controller, Screg.exe, to finish loading the rest of the devices and services.

In NT, users were often mystified by the long delay between entering their credentials at the logon window and getting to the desktop. In Windows 2000, Microsoft withheld the logon window until the service drivers initialized. In Windows Server 2003, to speed up access to the console, the user is permitted to log on even though many of the services are still being initialized. As long as the user credentials are correct, there's a happy ending. Bring up the violin music. Fade to credits.

If Screg cannot start a device or service, it takes action as defined in the associated Registry key. This runs the gamut from putting a simple message in the Event log to crashing the system with a stop error. If the problem is not catastrophic, Screg displays a console message telling you that a problem occurred and that you should check the Event log. This console message does not always appear, so you should always check the log when you start a server. Histories of abnormal starts should be investigated and the problem isolated and corrected.

Registry Tip: Forcing AUTOCHK to Repair

AUTOCHK normally runs in read-only mode, so it reports problems but does not repair them. You can force AUTOCHK to repair file system problems (similar to running `Chkdsk /f`) by putting a `/p` after the entry in the Registry:

Key: HKLM | System | CurrentControlSet | Control | Session Manager

Value: BootExecute

Data: Autochk * /p

Delaying Initial Console Logon

The Registry entries for the service drivers are stored in a key called the `Control Set`. By default, there are two `Control Set` keys, named `Control Set 1` and `Control Set 2`. As we'll see in Chapter 21, "Recovering from System Failures," one of the actions performed by the Session Manager following a successful logon is to copy the `Control Set` used to boot the system into `Control Set 2` and to declare this the *Last Known Good Control Set*.

It sometimes happens that a problem crops up a little after a successful logon. By that time, it is too late to restart the system using the `Last Known Good Control Set` option. You can avoid this problem by making a quick network connection (not a remote desktop connection) to the server and checking for errors in the System log prior to performing the console logon.

Working with Boot.ini

The IA32 secondary bootstrap loader, Ntldr, relies on Boot.ini to locate the Windows Server 2003 boot partition and the folder containing the boot files. If you encounter strange behavior during restart following an upgrade, or when adding new mass storage hardware, start your investigations with a look at Boot.ini. For details of the contents of a boot menu entry in an IA64 machine, see Chapter 3, "Adding Hardware." Here is an example of a Boot.ini file for a system that also has a DOS partition:

```
[boot loader]
timeout=30
default=multi(0)disk(0)rdisk(0)partition(1)\Windows

[operating systems]
multi(0)disk(0)rdisk(0)partition(1)\Windows="Windows Server 2003, Standard
➥Edition" /fastdetect
c:\= "MS/DOS"
```

The long, inscrutable entry under `[operating systems]` is the *Advanced RISC Computing* path (ARC path). The ARC path is a pointer that leads Ntldr to a Windows Server 2003 partition. ARC syntax uses this convention:

```
controller()disk()rdisk()partition()\systemroot="menu listing"
```

The following subsections explain what each entry means.

controller()—Interface Type

There are three possible entries:

- **`multi()`.** Indicates IDE drives and SCSI drives with an onboard BIOS. The number in parentheses is the ordinal ID of the IDE or SCSI controller. If Windows Server 2003 is installed on a drive connected to the secondary IDE controller, the ARC entry would be `multi(1)`.
- **`scsi()`.** Indicates a SCSI controller with no onboard BIOS or a BIOS that has been disabled. This is a legacy entry from classic NT and no longer used in Windows Server 2003.
- **`signature()`.** Indicates that the drive is not accessible by standard INT13 calls and requires special handling by Ntldr. The number in parentheses is a signature written to the MBR of the disk when it is partitioned during Setup.

System File Attributes and Superhidden Definition

The Boot.ini file attributes are set to `System` and `Read-only` by default. This prevents a casual user from modifying or deleting the file. If you need to modify the contents of Boot.ini, use `Attrib` to toggle the `read-only` attribute.

The remaining system files, such as Ntldr, Ntdetect.com, and Ntbootdd.sys, have both the `System` and `Hidden` attributes set. This is a *superhidden* configuration and keeps the files hidden even if users set the User Interface to show hidden files. Superhidden files are not hidden if you run `DIR /A` from the command line.

If the controller type is `signature()` and the drive is on a SCSI bus with an interface that does not have a BIOS, Ntldr uses the SCSI miniport driver in Ntbootdd.sys to read the drives and find the matching signature.

disk()—SCSI ID

The `disk()` entry was used in conjunction with the `scsi()` controller type to indicate the SCSI ID of the disk where the boot files are located. It is no longer required in Windows Server 2003 because the `signature()` entry identifies the drive uniquely without the SCSI ID. For controller designations of `multi()`, the value for `disk()` is always 0.

rdisk()—Relative Disk Location

The `rdisk()` entry is used in conjunction with `multi()` to indicate the relative disk location. For IDE drives, the relative disk location is determined by the master/slave designation. For example, the slave drive on the first IDE controller would have an ARC designator of `multi(0)disk(0)rdisk(1)`.

For SCSI drives, the relative disk location is determined by the device scan performed by the SCSI BIOS during POST. Generally, the scan order matches the SCSI ID order. If the BIOS reports that there are three drives on the bus, for example, the ARC designator for the third drive would be `multi(0)disk(0)rdisk(2)` regardless of the SCSI ID. If you select a drive other than 0 to be the boot drive, the relative disk locations would change.

For controller designations of `signature()`, the value for `rdisk()` is always 0 because the system uses the MBR signature to find the drive.

partition()—Boot Partition Sequence Number

This is the sequential number of the boot partition. Note that this sequence starts with 1, not 0. See the upcoming sidebar, "Automatic Partition Number Changes," for curious aspects to the numbering sequences.

\systemroot—Windows Server 2003 System Directory

The default system directory in Windows Server 2003 is `\Windows`. That path is used in all examples in this book. A different name can be chosen during Setup. The environment variable `%systemroot%` displays the name of the system directory. You should have only one system root directory on any given partition. Microsoft strongly discourages having multiple Windows installations in the same partition because there are files in locations other than `%systemroot%` that are maintained by the operating system.

"menu listing"—Menu Text

The text in quotation marks is displayed as the menu listing in the boot menu. You can change this text if it helps your users to navigate to the right entry; under normal circumstances, however, users could care less and don't want to see the menu anyway.

ARC Path Examples

Assume, for example, that you have a machine configured with several versions of Windows Server 2003 and NT along with a dual-boot to DOS. The drives and partitions are set up as shown in Table 1.2.

Table 1.2 Example Partition Tables

SCSI ID #	Drive #	Partition #	OS
ID 0	C	1	DOS
ID 0	D	2	NTW 4.0
ID 1	E	1	NTS 4.0
ID 2	F	1	XP Pro
ID 2	G	2	Windows Server 2003 Standard Edition

Automatic Partition Number Changes

There are a few subtleties to the way ARC paths are derived. It is possible to cause a change in the partition numbering without realizing it. Windows Server 2003 anticipates this and changes the ARC paths in Boot.ini automatically. Here's how it works.

A basic Intel IA32 disk can have up to four primary partitions. These primary partitions are numbered sequentially. For example, if you install Windows Server 2003 into the second primary partition, the ARC path entry would be `partition(2)`.

In addition to primary partitions, the drive can have a maximum of one extended partition with as many logical drives as you require. These logical drives also act as partitions in the ARC path. For example, if you install Windows Server 2003 into the second logical drive of an extended partition on a drive that has one other primary partition, the ARC path entry would be `partition(3)`.

When calculating ARC path partitions, Windows Server 2003 counts primary partitions first, then logical drives in an extended partition. This is exactly the opposite of the way drive letters are assigned during Setup, so it may or may not be counterintuitive to you.

Let's say you have a multiple boot machine with a primary partition and a secondary partition with a single logical drive. Windows Server 2003 is installed in the second logical drive. Again, the ARC path entry would be `partition(3)`.

You have a few gigabytes of free space beyond the extended partition. You use it to install another copy of Windows Server 2003 in a new primary partition. (It cannot be an extended partition, because you can only have one on a disk.) The ARC path entry for this instance of Windows Server 2003 would be `partition(2)` because the primary partitions are counted before the logical drives.

You might now expect the `partition()` entry for the first Windows Server 2003 installation to be invalid. It should be `partition(4)`. Windows Server 2003 anticipates this problem and *automatically changes the ARC path* to match the new location of the partition.

This is a new trick in Windows Server 2003, and it doesn't always work, so you may need to change the ARC path manually.

You can modify Boot.ini switches using the new BOOTCFG utility in both the IA32 and IA64 versions of Windows Server 2003. This utility has a variety of features for scripting Boot.ini modifications. In addition, the Help and Support Center exposes a GUI-based utility called the *System Configuration Utility*, or Msconfig, that simplifies making Boot.ini changes.

Here are the ARC paths for each boot partition:

```
multi(0)disk(0)rdisk(0)partition(2)\WINNT="Windows NT Workstation Version 4.0"
multi(0)disk(0)rdisk(1)partition(1)\WINNT="Windows NT Server Version 4.0"
multi(0)disk(0)rdisk(2)partition(1)\WINNT="Windows XP Professional" /fastdetect
multi(0)disk(0)rdisk(2)partition(2)\WINNT="Windows Server 2003 Standard Edition"
➥/fastdetect
c:\="MS/DOS"
```

Boot.ini Switches

Here are the major options and switches used in Boot.ini:

- **`Timeout`.** This determines the pause duration before Ntldr goes to the default partition. The default is 30 seconds.
- **`Default`.** This determines the partition that will be used to boot the system if no action is taken.
- **`[Operating Systems]`.** Lists the bootable partitions by their ARC paths.
- **`/3GB`.** Changes the apportionment of virtual memory to give 3GB to user processors and 1GB to the system. This switch only works on Enterprise and Datacenter Editions.
- **`/bootlog`.** Writes a boot log to a file called Ntbtlog.txt in the `\Windows` directory.
- **`/cmdcons`.** Used in conjunction with loading the Recovery Console.
- **`/fastdetect`.** Skips PnP enumeration of serial interfaces until the graphic portion of the system loads.
- **`/maxmem`.** Used for troubleshooting memory-related problems. This switch limits the amount of real memory the system will use. If you think you have a bad bank of memory, set this value below the second bank. If your problems disappear, replace the memory. You can also use this switch for testing memory-related performance issues.
- **`/pae`** and **`/nopae`.** Configures an Enterprise Edition or Datacenter Edition to use the Physical Address Extensions for accessing memory above 4GB. The `/nopae` switch disables the feature for troubleshooting.
- **`/pcilock`.** Disables most of the automatic resource allocation functions of HAL. This prevents HAL from changing resource allocations made by the PnP BIOS. This is a useful tool for correcting system hangs.
- **`/redirect`.** Used for console redirection in headless servers.
- **`/safeboot:`.** Tells the system to boot in Safe mode. Use in conjunction with these modes: `minimal`, `network`, `dsrepair`. For example /safeboot:minimal. These options correspond to the Safe Mode options listed when you press F8.
- **`/safeboot:minimal(alternateshell)`.** This additional switch permits you to boot to the shell defined in `HKLM | System | CurrentControlSet | Control | Safeboot | AlternateShell`. By default, this is the command shell, CMD.EXE. If

you want to, you can specify another shell here such as PROGMAN.EXE, the original program manager shell.

- `/scsiordinal:x`. Differentiates between identical SCSI controllers. If you add a second controller and boot to a Blue Screen stop, the SCSI driver may be binding to the wrong controller. Set the `x` value to 1 if the Windows Server 2003 files are on the second controller.
- `/sos`. Displays the name of the drivers as they load along with the results of the AUTOCHK scan that is done at each system boot. Think of this switch as "Show Our System."
- `/win95dos` and `/win95`. These switches emulate the dual-boot features in Windows 9x. They are used in conjunction with Bootsect.dos files that contain Windows 95 bootstrap.

An additional set of Boot.ini switches are used for headless server operation and kernel-mode debugging. See Chapter 2, "Performing Upgrades and Automated Installations," for headless server operation and Chapter 21, "Recovering from System Failures," for information on kernel-mode debugging.

Special ARC Paths

Ntldr makes INT13 fixed disk function calls to find the boot drive and files at the root of the boot partition. There are a couple of situations where a standard ARC path is insufficient for Ntldr to use INT13 calls.

No Support for INT13 Extensions

In classic NT, the boot partition could not be larger than 7.8GB and the ending cylinder number could not be greater than 1024. This was due to a limitation in the INT13 function call.

The original INT13 specification assumed a certain set of Cylinder/Head/Sector (CHS) limitations. The CHS limitations have been revised as drive technology supported larger and larger capacities. The PC97 specification included a set of INT13 extensions to accommodate larger drive geometries. Windows 2000 and later support these INT13 extensions, so boot partitions can be larger than 7.8GB.

If you have a system that does not support the INT13 extensions and the boot partition is larger than 7.8GB or lies outside the 1024 cylinder limit, Ntldr needs a different way to find the boot drive.

No SCSI BIOS

A SCSI controller supports INT13 calls via special interfaces in the controller's BIOS. If the SCSI controller does not have a BIOS, or the BIOS has been disabled, Ntldr needs an alternate means of locating the boot drive. Classic NT solved this problem by loading the SCSI miniport driver packaged in Ntbootdd.sys. Ntldr used the miniport driver to scan the SCSI bus. The ARC path entries `scsi()disk()` told Ntldr the ordinal number of the SCSI controller and the SCSI ID of the boot disk.

Because Windows Server 2003 uses Plug and Play, it's possible that the ordinal number assigned to the SCSI controller could change. This would keep Ntldr from finding the boot drive using a classic ARC path. For that reason, Ntldr needs a more reliable means for identifying the boot drive than the SCSI ID.

Signature() Entry

Windows Server 2003 (and Windows 2000) deals with the lack of full INT13 support by using a controller type in the ARC path called `signature()`. Here is an example ARC path using this controller type:

```
signature(ea1aa9c7)disk(0)rdisk(0)partition(1)\WINNT="Microsoft Windows Server
➥2003" /fastdetect
```

The number in the parentheses, `ea1aa9c7`, is a random number written to the MBR of the boot drive during Setup. It is sometimes called a *fault tolerant boot signature*, a holdover term from classic NT.

When Ntldr sees a `signature()` entry in an ARC path, it scans the mass storage devices looking for a drive with an MBR that contains the signature. For IDE drives, it uses standard INT13 calls to do this scan. For SCSI drives, it loads the miniport driver in Ntbootdd.sys. The signature uniquely identifies the boot drive regardless of the SCSI ordinal number.

Signature() Limitations

The `signature()` method of identifying drives in Boot.ini has its drawbacks. If the disk signature is overwritten by a virus or the MBR is corrupted and must be overwritten, Ntldr cannot locate the drive and will give the error `Windows Server 2003 could not start because of a computer disk hardware configuration problem.`

If you encounter this kind of problem, you can correct it as shown in Procedure 1.4.

Procedure 1.4 Correcting Lost Drive Signatures

1. Correct the source of the corruption in the MBR. You can use the Recovery Console to write a new MBR. See Chapter 21, "Recovering from System Failures," for details.
2. Then use a tool like Disk Probe from the Resource Kit to write a new fault tolerant signature to the MBR. Chapter 3, "Adding Hardware," discusses the physical location of the signature. Any 4-byte number will suffice.
3. Create a fault tolerant boot disk using instructions in Chapter 3, "Adding Hardware." Modify the ARC path in Boot.ini to have a `signature()` entry that matches your new fault tolerant signature. Then, boot the system using that boot disk.
4. After the system is up and running, correct the ARC path in the Boot.ini on the boot drive.

Correcting Common Setup Problems

Setting up and configuring a server makes for a long afternoon. Hopefully you're done in time to go home for supper. If not, here are a few hints to help you at least make it home for the evening news.

The first thing to do is look for clues about what happened. Setup leaves behind several records of what it did and how it did it. If you can keep the machine operating for a little while, look for the following files in the `\Windows` folder:

- **Setuplog.txt.** Describes in detail each driver and service that was loaded and each DLL that was registered during the character phase of Setup.
- **Setupact.log.** Describes the file operations that took place during the Graphic phase of Setup.
- **Setuperr.log.** Lists any errors that were reported by any devices or services during Setup. If this log is not zero bytes, Setup offers to display it at the end of the installation.

You can also boot with the `Boot Log` option. This lists the drivers that are loaded by Ntldr and SCREG. To do this, press `F8` at the boot menu and select BOOT LOGGING. This writes an Ntbtlog.txt file to the `\Windows` directory.

Stop *0x0000007b Inaccessible_Boot_Device*

Sometimes the system starts to boot following an installation, but then experiences a kernel-mode stop (Blue Screen of Death) with a bug-check code of `0x0000007b, Inaccessible_Boot_Device`. This problem occurs when the Cylinder/Head/Sector (CHS) configuration reported by BIOS does not match the settings in the Master Boot Record. Frequently, the only way to recover the system is to format the drive and start over. A partition report from Partition Magic or System Commander can help in diagnosing this problem.

System Information

If you are a Windows NT administrator, it may be comforting to know that good, old Winmsd is still available at the `Run` command. In Windows Server 2003, Winmsd launches an alternate executable, Msinfo32.exe from `\Program Files\Common Files\Microsoft Shared\MSInfo`. This executable, in turn, loads the Help and Support Center executables that display system information obtained from Windows Management Instrumentation (WMI). Figure 1.16 shows an example.

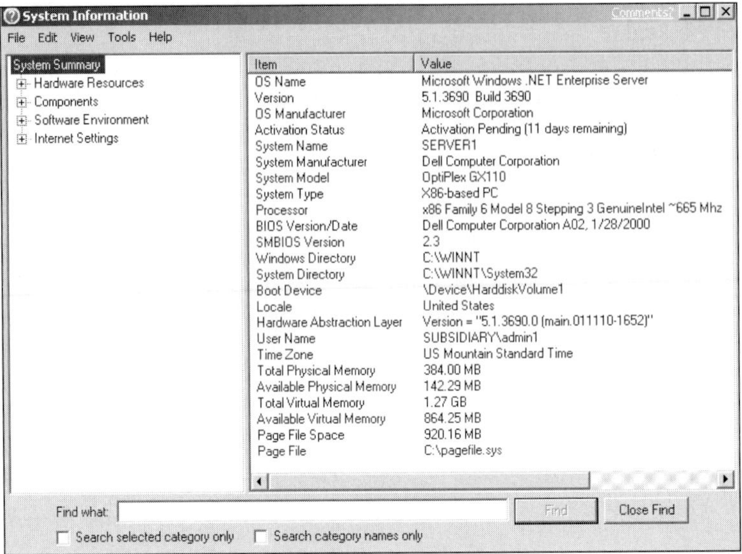

Figure 1.16 System Information display.

An alternate way to get system information, and one that you may like better because it works at the command line, is SYSTEMINFO. Here is an example listing:

```
Host Name:                 SERVER1
OS Name:                   Microsoft Windows Server 2003 Enterprise Edition
OS Version:                5.1.3690 Build 3690
OS Manufacturer:           Microsoft Corporation
OS Configuration:          Primary Domain Controller
OS Build Type:             Uniprocessor Free
Registered Owner:          Admin
Registered Organization:   Company
Product ID:                55039-985-0023054-00576
Original Install Date:     2/21/2002, 11:06:47 AM
System Up Time:            3 Days, 11 Hours, 32 Minutes, 41 Seconds
System Manufacturer:       Dell Computer Corporation
System Model:              OptiPlex GX150
System type:               X86-based PC
Processor(s):              1 Processor(s) Installed.
                           [01]: x86 Family 6 Model 8 Stepping 3 GenuineIntel
                           ➥~665 Mhz
BIOS Version:              DELL   - 7
Windows Directory:         C:\Windows
System Directory:          C:\Windows\System32
Boot Device:               \Device\HarddiskVolume1
System Locale:             en-us;English (United States)
Input Locale:              en-us;English (United States)
Time Zone:                 (GMT-07:00) Arizona
Total Physical Memory:     382 MB
Available Physical Memory: 146 MB
```

```
Virtual Memory: Max Size:  1,302 MB
Virtual Memory: Available: 867 MB
Virtual Memory: In Use:    435 MB
Page File Location(s):     C:\pagefile.sys
Domain:                    company.com
Logon Server:              \\SERVER1
NetWork Card(s):           1 NIC(s) Installed.
                           [01]: 3Com 3C920 Integrated Fast Ethernet Controller
                           ➥(3C905C-TX Compatible)
                                 Connection Name: Local Area Connection
                                 DHCP Enabled:    No
                                 IP address(es)
                                   [01]: 192.168.0.1
```

Setup Hangs

Of all the possible frustrations that can occur during Setup, hangs are the worst because they cause no other overt symptoms. Setup just reaches a point when it seems to be thinking. And it thinks. And it thinks. And it keeps on thinking, like a contestant on *Who Wants to Be a Millionaire*, while you sit in front of the console like Regis Philbin, trying to make pleasant conversation as you glance at your watch.

The first rule for dealing with hangs is to do nothing. Try to wait it out. Delays on the order of hours are not unheard of. The outcome is usually good, and any happy ending is worth waiting for.

If you get a serious hang during the device-detection portion of the Graphic phase, press `Shift+F10` to open a console window and check the contents of Setuplog.txt. If there are entries, you know something is happening. If the progress bar doesn't move for a couple of hours and no further entries are written to the file, you can throw in the towel.

While you're waiting, search the documentation for known incompatibilities. This includes a search of the following:

- Release Notes and Readme files on the Windows Server 2003 CD
- KnowledgeBase listings at `www.microsoft.com/technet`
- Vendor web sites

If you decide to give up and restart, take a few preliminary steps to keep from returning right back to another multi-hour wait. Forget about scientific method. The idea is to get the machine running under Windows Server 2003. You can figure out the precise problem later. Here are some suggestions:

- Go through the pre-installation checklist at the start of this chapter to make sure you didn't miss anything such as firmware upgrades, removing UPS serial line connections, turning off Plug and Play, or setting up legacy components. All of these are notorious sources of hangs.
- Remove the NIC.

- Remove any multimedia boards.
- Disable infrared devices.
- Go through Txtsetup.sif and remark out (semicolon) any unneeded drivers. This requires you to run Setup from a network distribution point.
- If you have two monitor cards, remove one.
- Remove any legacy ISA cards.
- Move PCI cards to different slots.
- If your machine has multiple PCI buses, try moving all the cards to one bus.
- If you have special SCSI components such as scanners or tape drives, take them off the bus.
- If you have any FireWire components, take them off the bus.
- For laptops, take out any PCMCIA cards and remove the unit from its docking station.
- Remove USB components (use a PS/2 keyboard, if a PS/2 connector is available).

Now try Setup again. If it still hangs, double-check the HCL to make sure it lists your system. If so, strip the machine down to hull metal with nothing more than a vanilla VGA card, a keyboard, and a mouse. Disable everything in CMOS that even smells like an advanced option. Then try again. If the system still hangs, try installing Windows Server 2003 on a similar piece of hardware. If you get similar results, it's time to call the vendor.

Some Devices Fail

If you can get the operating system to load but some functions are not available, you may have device malfunctions or resource conflicts. The Device Manager shows these kinds of problems. There are several ways to open Device Manager:

- Open the `Computer Management` console by right-clicking the `My Computer` icon on the desktop and selecting MANAGE from the flyout menu. Expand the tree under SYSTEM TOOLS, DEVICE MANAGER.
- Open the `Device Manager` console by right-clicking the `My Computer` icon, selecting PROPERTIES from the flyout menu, selecting the `Hardware` tab, and then clicking `Device Manager`.
- (My personal favorite) Open the `Run` window, enter `devmgmt.msc`, and press `Enter`.

If a device shows a question mark or a red X, double-click it to view the conflict. Some device failures are more common than others. Some have become downright notorious. See Chapter 3, "Adding Hardware," for details on troubleshooting PnP and hardware problems.

You might need to boot to Safe mode to get to the Device Manager. Press `F8` at the boot menu and then select SAFE MODE from the option list.

Problems Copying Files to the Hard Drive

On occasion, Windows will refuse to recognize a hard drive. If the drive is not listed in Setup's partition manager screen, Ntdetect did not recognize it for some reason. There are several possible causes:

- **Check seating for all cable connectors.** Also make sure the cables are all there—not to mention the drive, if this is a new machine. Boot to DOS and see whether you can see the drive using FDISK.
- **Verify that shadow RAM and write-back cache has been disabled in CMOS.** Hardware caching is a frequent cause of kernel-mode stops and corrupted data. Windows Server 2003 handles all disk caching. You will get better and more reliable performance without a hardware cache unless it is certified to work with Windows Server 2003.
- **Supported disk translations.** Check that drives have not been configured with a special disk manager that is not compatible with Windows Server 2003. Some unique flavors of sector maps are not recognized. If the drive uses a cylinder translation utility such as OnTrack, make sure it is certified to work with Windows Server 2003.
- **IDE recognized in CMOS.** If you have a large IDE drive, make sure that the drive configuration is correct in CMOS.
- **Scan for viruses.** Windows Server 2003 will not install on an infected hard drive. Scan the drive using a DOS or Windows virus detection tool.
- **Check for proper Master Boot Record.** The Master Boot Record might be corrupt. Boot to DOS and run `Fdisk /mbr` to build a new boot record.
- **SCSI terminations.** If you have a SCSI drive, make sure that the SCSI cable is terminated correctly. Even if the drive worked fine under DOS or Windows, it might fail under Windows Server 2003 owing to the different nature of the SCSI driver. Also check to make sure that the SCSI drive you used for Setup is still listed on the SCSI scan that runs during POST.
- **SCSI boot settings.** Make sure that SCSI boot drive settings are correct. You may think you're booting to one drive, but are actually booting to another.
- **Problems with Ultra-DMA ATA interface cards.** If you are using a high-performance ATA mass storage interface, check with the vendor to get the most current driver. This technology changes rapidly. Also, check that you have an 80-wire ribbon connector between the interface card and the drive so that you get full performance.
- **No DriveSpace volumes**. Make sure that the installation volume has not been compressed using DriveSpace or DoubleSpace.

- **No older dynamic partitioning.** Utilities that keep their own hidden partitions or that enable you to dynamically resize partitions may cause Setup to fail. The NTFS version in Windows Server 2003 changed, rendering older utilities inoperable.

Missing or Incorrect CD-ROM Drives

If Setup prompts you over and over and over again to insert the Windows Server 2003 CD-ROM, you know you have an unsupported or misconfigured CD-ROM drive. Use the following list as a starting point to look for problems:

- **Verify supported drive.** Some CD-ROM drives are not supported by Windows Server 2003, especially older drives with proprietary interfaces. Some drives that worked in NT4 were retired and are no longer supported in Windows Server 2003. As with all hardware, check to make sure your CD-ROM drive is on the HCL.
- **Timing problems.** CD-ROM drives that work fine under DOS/Windows or Windows 95/98 sometimes fail to work under Windows Server 2003 because of tighter timing specifications. If you have a SCSI or modified SCSI interface, using the interface BIOS routines to check the device.
- **SCSI terminations.** If you have a SCSI CD-ROM drive, check the device list displayed during the POST scan. If the drive does not appear, check the power connections, ribbon or external cable connections, bus terminations, and possible conflicts with SCSI ID. If the SCSI ID is listed with no name or vendor information, the drive might not be supported by the SCSI BIOS or the drive might be defective.
- **IDE configuration.** If the CD-ROM drive is on an IDE bus that is shared with a hard drive, check for proper master/slave configuration. Check CMOS to make sure the controller interface is enabled.

Missing or Non-Functioning Network Adapters

Network adapters are a common cause of Setup hangs and PnP disasters. Use the following list as a starting point when looking for problems:

- **Incorrect resource allocation.** Use Device Manager to check the resources that have been assigned to the adapter. If there is a conflict, the adapter icon will have either a yellow circle with an exclamation point or a red circle with an X. Double-click on the network adapter to open the Adapter Properties window. Select the `Resources` tab.
- **Improper PCI resource sharing.** PCI adapters rarely have a problem with memory conflicts but they can get I/O base and IRQ conflicts if the system BIOS attempts to share resources or if HAL changes the PCI settings. If this

happens with a legacy adapter, disable PnP in CMOS then assign resources manually. Seriously consider spending a few dollars for a newer adapter.

- **Verify the physical layer.** If the network drivers load but you cannot see the network, you may have a plain old bad adapter (POBA). See whether you can ping the loopback address, `127.0.0.1`. This checks the IP stack down to the NDIS MAC driver, which implies that the Ethernet controller is functioning properly. The problem could then be with the transceiver, the cables and connectors, or the hub or switch. Use known good cable or test the port connection from another computer. Make sure you don't have crossover cable installed—that is, cable that swaps the 1-2 and 3-6 pairs for use in connecting hubs together.
- **Duplex mismatches.** A very common problem when using 10/100Mbps adapters and switches is a mismatch between duplex settings at the adapter and the switch. In full-duplex mode, collision detection is turned off. This permits the port and the NIC to transmit and receive at the same time. If the switch is still in half-duplex mode, however, it will interpret full-duplex transmissions as a collision and reject the frame. The network response turns to molasses and the CRC/alignment check error rate at the switch skyrockets. If you have an autosensing 10/100 NIC, make sure the hub is properly configured. Don't trust the link lights. Try another computer in the same port.

Video Problems

If Setup cannot detect the make and model of the video adapter installed in the machine, it will fall back on standard VGA drivers. Video problems are another common cause of Setup hangs. You may also get kernel-mode stop errors. Check the HCL to see whether the adapter is supported. Use the following list as a starting point when looking for problems:

- **Loss of video sync.** If you change video settings and lose the display as soon as you accept the changes, do nothing. The system returns to its old configuration after 15 seconds. If this does not happen, restart and press `F8` at the boot menu. Select SAFE MODE from the ADVANCED OPTIONS menu. This loads standard VGA drivers and gives you the chance to poke around for a different configuration or driver that works. Avoid the VGA MODE option in the ADVANCED OPTIONS menu. This also loads stock VGA drivers, but does so with persistent Registry entries rather than the transient ones used by Safe mode.
- **Unable to get full range of video options.** Windows Server 2003 relies totally on PnP to discover the video adapter and monitor. If PnP gets the wrong driver, or if the driver on the CD is not recent enough, you may not get the full set of horizontal sweep rates or color densities that the card is advertised to have. Check the vendor's web site for updated drivers.

Online Error Reporting Tools

If you get an error that results in a protection fault or system crash, Windows Server 2003 will collect information about the crash and send it to Microsoft. This is done purely for data collection. It will not result in a call from Product Support Services. See Chapter 3, "Adding Hardware," for the contents of the files sent to Microsoft and the purpose of this online reporting.

Best Practices

Here is a quick checklist of the installation tips in this chapter:

- Verify that the system and all components are on the Hardware Compatibility List.
- Do a clean install, if possible.
- Verify that CPU speed, RAM, and storage meet minimum recommended requirements.
- Get current on all firmware, BIOS, and drivers.
- Use NTFS to format all server partitions.
- Mount disks in all removable media.
- Perform a bare installation first, then install additional services later.
- Use hardware RAID for best performance and fault tolerance.
- Use FDISK to delete all partitions on dynamic disks when doing a clean install. This converts them to basic disks.
- On multiboot machines, install each Windows product into its own partition.
- Purchase Windows Server 2003 and XP using Volume Purchase Agreements to avoid per-instance activation.
- For IA64 systems, ensure that you create the correct GPT partitions in the correct order.
- Remove all unnecessary peripherals if you have Setup problems.
- Improve performance by putting the paging file or files on a separate drive. Leave a small paging file on the boot drive for a stack heap dump (minidump).
- Get disk utilities that are certified to work with NTFS 5.1 and Windows Server 2003/XP.

Moving Forward

Installing a new operating system of any kind is easiest when starting from a clean slate. Upgrades are much more complex. The next chapter covers upgrading to Windows Server 2003 from NT4 and Windows 2000. It also covers automating the installation of Windows Server 2003 using scripts and Remote Installation Service (RIS).

2
Performing Upgrades and Automated Installations

IF YOU'VE EVER MOVED INTO A PREVIOUSLY owned house, you have an idea of the pitfalls of upgrading a server to a new operating system. For houses, minor "settling cracks" turn out to be caused by an infestation of termites. For servers, "occasional" blue screen stop errors turn out to be caused by a RAID driver that is just waiting for the right opportunity to corrupt your data.

For the most part, you'll get a more reliable operating platform by doing a fresh install of the operating system as described in Chapter 1, "Installing and Configuring Windows Server 2003." But, it's one thing to talk about reinstalling the operating system (OS) on every server in your organization and it's quite another thing to spend days and weeks doing the work. If you have a stable server running NT or Windows 2000, you may want to upgrade it to preserve the existing application settings.

This chapter is all about saving time as you deploy Windows Server 2003. It covers upgrading existing servers as well as automating your deployments using scripts, disk images, and a combination of the two. The chapter includes a functional overview of what happens during an NT4 upgrade and a Windows 2000 upgrade along with a step-by-step procedure for upgrading.

New Features in Windows Server 2003

This chapter discusses the following new features in Windows Server 2003 that pertain to automated installations:

- **Setup Manager.** The Setup Manager utility is used to create unattended installation scripts. The updates to the utility in Windows Server 2003 simplify creating a script and permit encrypting the local administrator password. The utility is also valuable for creating Remote Installation Services (RIS) setup scripts and mini-setup scripts to run as part of Sysprep.

- **Sysprep improvements.** Several updates to the Sysprep packaging feature permit modifying a base Sysprep image by installing the original package then making changes and resealing the package. Options exist to manage plug-and-play operations, as well.
- **Remote Installation Services (RIS).** The updates to RIS include support for installing servers with RIS and a richer environment for creating RIS scripts.
- **Headless server operation.** It is now possible, using Windows Server 2003, to deploy the operating system to a machine with no mouse, keyboard, or video adapter. Headless operation also makes it possible to view the startup console and blue screens following a crash, something that is not possible using Remote Desktop or remote control programs.

NT4 Upgrade Functional Overview

When you upgrade to Windows Server 2003 from NT4, you can expect Setup to do the following:

- Retain the computer's Security ID (SID) and domain membership.
- Convert user profiles to Windows Server 2003 format. The profile location remains at `\Winnt\Profiles`, as opposed to the new location in Windows Server 2003 of `\Documents and Settings`. Any new profiles created after an upgrade also go in `\Winnt\Profiles`.
- Retain application and driver settings in the Registry if they are compatible with Windows Server 2003.
- Remove Registry entries for applications or drivers that are deemed incompatible by the upgrade compatibility checker.
- Retain the contents of the SAM and LSA databases on standalone and member servers and desktops. This keeps the local user and group membership intact along with any security settings assigned to those accounts.
- For NT primary domain controllers (PDCs), migrate the contents of the Security Account Manager (SAM) and Security databases into Active Directory. Upgraded backup domain controllers ignore their copy of the SAM and replicate the contents of Active Directory from the upgraded PDC.
- Retain the existing NFTS file security settings and Registry security settings. This means that an upgraded server may lack additional access safeguards normally applied to a new Windows Server 2003.
- Retain the current File Allocation Tables (FAT) partitions, if any. If you prefer, you can convert to NTFS during the upgrade. Unlike previous versions, Windows Server 2003 retains the cluster size assigned to the FAT partition during conversion if the cluster size is equal to or smaller than 4096 bytes.

- Convert any existing NTFS partitions to NTFS 3.1 (compared to version 3.0 in Windows 2000 and version 1.2 in NT4). Existing disk utilities such as defragmentation utilities, imaging utilities, and disk management utilities must be upgraded to versions that are compatible with Windows Server 2003.
- Upgrade network drivers to new Network Device Interface Specifications (NDIS) 5.1 drivers, if available, while retaining current IP and IPX addresses, transport driver settings, drive mappings, printer captures, and remote access configurations. If newer drivers are not available, Setup will prompt for drivers and install without a network if drivers are not provided.
- Upgrade services such as DNS, DHCP, WINS, Internet Explorer (IE), IIS, *Services for Macintosh* (SFM), Certificate Services, and so forth. The upgrades retain existing configuration settings unless those settings are incompatible with Windows Server 2003 features. Management interfaces are upgraded to MMC consoles.

Windows 2000 Upgrade Overview

When you upgrade to Windows Server 2003 from Windows 2000, you can expect Setup to do the following:

- Retain the same user profiles and profile locations while updating the shell to the new look and feel of Windows Server 2003. The shell has only a few changes from its predecessor.
- Retain the same Registry settings for applications and drivers as long as they are compatible.
- Retain the Logical Disk Manager (LDM) database entries for all dynamic disks.
- Retain the NTFS file permissions and Registry permissions assigned by Windows 2000. These settings are somewhat different than the default settings in Windows Server 2003. See Chapter 15, "Managing File Systems," for details.
- Upgrade any existing NTFS 3.0 partitions to NTFS 3.1. The record structure changes a little in NTFS 3.1, making it incompatible with disk and imaging utilities designed for Windows 2000.
- Upgrade Internet Explorer to IE 6.0 along with upgrades to the various media services that interact with IE.
- Upgrade IIS to version 6.0. The primary advantage of the new version is major rework of the underlying services, with improved security and process separation.
- Migrate the network interfaces to NDIS version 5.1. This version supports more robust device management, uses memory more efficiently, and has support for IEEE 802.11b wireless adapters.

Upgrade Paths

Windows Server 2003, Standard and Enterprise Editions do not support upgrading from Windows 9x, Windows ME, or any version of NT Professional (NT4, NT3.51, or NT3.50). The server upgrade paths are as follows.

Upgrading from NT 3.1, NT 3.50, and NT 3.51 requires a two-step process. First, upgrade to NT4, and then you can upgrade to Windows Server 2003.

You can upgrade directly to Windows Server 2003 from any of the following NT4 server versions (all NT4 upgrades require Service Pack 6a):

- **NT4 Server.** This version can be upgraded to Server 2003, Standard Edition or Enterprise Edition. It cannot be upgraded to Web Edition.
- **NT4 Server, Enterprise Edition.** You must upgrade to Windows Server 2003, Enterprise Edition to retain full functionality.
- **NT4 Server, Terminal Services Edition.** If you are running Citrix MetaFrame, you cannot upgrade directly to Windows Server 2003. You must de-install MetaFrame, upgrade, and then install a current version of MetaFrame. Get more information at the Citrix web site, `www.citrix.com`.
- **NT4 Small Business Server.** You can upgrade to Small Business Server Edition of Windows Server 2003 when it becomes available and retain existing services along with the 50-user limit or upgrade to a full version of Windows Server 2003 and BackOffice.

All features in the NT4 Option Pack are incorporated into the core Windows Server 2003 product. The same is true for NT4 Routing and Remote Access Services (RRAS), although the features are implemented differently and dial-up connection management changes significantly. See Chapter 20, "Managing Remote Access and Internet Routing," for details.

Upgrade Preliminaries

The installation prerequisites and checklists in Chapter 1 for clean installs are equally valid for upgrades. If you have incompatible hardware or applications that are not certified to run under Windows Server 2003, you can expect to have problems. Do a thorough inventory of hardware and check the Hardware Compatibility List (HCL) before upgrading. This is especially true for older machines that were built before the *Advanced Configuration and Power Instrumentation* (ACPI) specifications were standardized at version 2.

Backup

It should go without saying that you should get a reliable backup of a server prior to upgrading it. Any number of scenarios can lead to data loss. If you have backups on tape but have not attempted a full restore lately, you should do so before you upgrade. At the very least, recover a file or folder from the latest tape just as a test.

If you use a third-party backup utility or agent, make sure it is compatible with Windows Server 2003. You may want to restore data to the server after you upgrade.

Application Compatibility

When you perform the upgrade, Setup will scan the system looking for potentially incompatible software and drivers. You can get a head start on this check by running the readiness scan from the command line as follows:

```
winnt32 /checkupgradeonly
```

You can also run the readiness scan by inserting the CD, waiting for the Autorun window to open, then selecting `Perform Additional Tasks | Check System Compatibility`.

The scan does the following:

- Contacts Microsoft's Update web site to check for any updates to the compatibility database
- Scans the system looking for incompatible applications or drivers
- Displays the results with an option to save the results to a file

The readiness scan may not catch all incompatible applications. Don't assume that applications that run fine under NT4 will also work under Windows Server 2003. Contact the vendor and do thorough in-house testing. See the "Application Compatibility Checks" topic a little later in this chapter for ways to run older applications on Windows Server 2003.

Free Space

You should have at least 1GB of free space in the operating system partition to upgrade. Add another 400MB to store temporary files if you are upgrading across the network.

Setup determines the necessary free space using entries in a *Setup Information File* (SIF) called Txtsetup.sif located in the `\I386` directory on the product CD. The entries are under the `[DiskSpaceRequirements]` section. The space requirements differ depending on the cluster size in use on the system partition.

Defragment the System Partition

Whether you use NTFS or FAT in your current system partition, it's a good idea to thoroughly defragment before you upgrade. Setup adds quite a few temporary files to the system partition along with swapping just about every file. This tends to promote fragmentation even in the best of circumstances.

If you keep your paging file in the system partition, consider moving it to another drive, if one is available. This helps avoid fragmentation of the system partition.

If you currently run FAT in your system partition and you intend on converting to NTFS, you may want to wait until after the upgrade. This permits you to do the conversion in a controlled evolution. You can also help prevent Master File Table (MFT) fragmentation by using a new feature in the CONVERT utility that uses a temporary space on another drive to hold data during the conversion. See Chapter 15 for details.

Remove NT4 RAID Configurations

Unlike Windows 2000, Windows Server 2003 does not support classic NT fault tolerant disk arrays. (These arrays are also called *FT disk sets* or sometimes *Ftdisk sets*, based on the name of the NT4 driver that controls software-based disk arrays.)

If your NT4 system partition is currently on a mirrored drive, you'll need to break the mirror prior to upgrading. Setup will refuse to start if the system partition is mirrored. After upgrading, you can convert the drives to dynamic disks and mirror them again.

If you have other FT disk sets such as stripe sets, stripe sets with parity, and volume sets, you must back up the data and delete the set before upgrading. You cannot convert the disks in the set to dynamic disks after upgrading. Make sure your backup utility is Windows Server 2003 compliant, or you will not be able to restore the data.

If your Windows 2000 system partition is mirrored, you must first break the mirror prior to upgrading. You can re-mirror after the upgrade. The Logical Disk Manager (LDM) database on the drive is preserved. You do *not* need to revert back to a basic disk (which requires deleting all volumes.)

Remove UPS Serial Line Connections

The Plug-and-Play (PnP) Manager in Windows Server 2003 attempts to enumerate all devices on all buses during the upgrade. If it encounters a UPS device at the end of a serial line connection, it gets very confused. This can cause Setup to hang for hours. Remove the connection from the serial port before upgrading. You do not need to de-install the UPS service. It will be upgraded.

De-Install Virus Scanners

Setup makes extensive changes to the system files along with changes to the partition boot sector. Virus scanners interpret this as an attack and will interfere.

It's a good idea to de-install a virus scanner rather than simply disable it. This ensures that the scanner does not activate and cause system problems following the completion of the upgrade. If the virus scanning application is Windows Server 2003-compatible, you can reinstall it after Setup has completed.

Registry Cleanup

Windows Server 2003 makes extensive changes to the Registry. If you have incompatible Registry entries, they may cause the upgrade to fail or cause erratic performance following the upgrade.

You may want to run a Registry cleanup tool to clear out unused entries prior to upgrading. You can use a commercial Registry cleaner or Microsoft's free utility, Regclean 4.1a, available from `www.microsoft.com/downloads/release.asp?ReleaseID=18924`.

You can compact the Registry hives following Regclean by using tools from Executive Software or the Registry Defragmentation utility at `www.sysinternals.com`.

Drive Letter Assignments

When you upgrade a system, Setup attempts to retain the existing drive letters. It uses two sources of information depending on the disk type:

- **Basic disks.** Drive letters for partitions on basic disks are stored in a Registry key located at `HKLM | System | Mounted Devices`. This includes letters assigned to logical drives in extended partitions. When you upgrade, critical elements from the existing Registry are dumped into a flat file called Migrate.inf, which becomes a script for Windows Server 2003 Setup. The drive list is one of those elements.
- **Dynamic disks.** Dynamic disks are managed by the Logical Disk Manager (LDM) service. This service keeps a database at the end of each dynamic disk that describes the disk configurations (mirrored, striped, RAID 5, and so forth) on all dynamic disks in the machine. This database contains the drive letters assigned to each volume. Setup can read the LDM database and will retain the assigned drive letters.

Hotfixes

Microsoft responds to urgent compatibility issues and new forms of Internet attacks by issuing hotfixes. Often the hotfix is out within hours of the problem identification. This leaves very little time for regression testing, either to the base OS or any applications.

It's possible that a hotfix might be released that causes problems for upgrades to Windows Server 2003. Check Microsoft's web site and Technet to find out if there are any issues with a particular hotfix prior to upgrading. Following the upgrade, you can use Windows Update to automatically download and prepare hotfixes for installation.

Prepare for Possible Service Interruptions

If you are upgrading a server that runs a large number of network support services, you might want to build a temporary server to host at least some of those services until you get a satisfactory upgrade. A minor upgrade glitch might render the server unavailable for a considerable period of time.

Moving these services can require some work because they involve changing IP addresses at the clients, so you may want to configure a standby server with the same name and running the same services but keep it off the wire unless you need it. If you have to use this standby server, you must delete the old server from the domain and join the new server to get a new computer account.

Upgrading an NT4 or Windows 2000 Server

This section describes how to perform an upgrade and takes a detailed look at the upgrade process and what happens to the server. This is meant to help you anticipate potential problems and diagnose any that do occur. The upgrade is divided into two phases:

- **Initial assessment.** In this phase, the Windows Server 2003 installation management utility, Winnt32.exe, asks about your plans for the server and gathers information about the current installation from the Registry. The result of this effort is a *Setup Information File* (SIF) called Winnt.sif that acts as a script for the upgrade.
- **Upgrade implementation.** In this phase, Setup performs the installation based on the Winnt.sif script and the contents of the Registry.

You have the option of running the upgrade from the CD or from a network share. If you upgrade from the CD, only those files necessary to recommence Setup are copied to the hard drive. They are located in a folder called `$win_nt$.~bt`. These are the same files as those used to boot to Setup from the CD. They take about 6MB of storage.

If you upgrade from a network share, Winnt32 copies the Setup files and all the operating system files from the network share to the local hard drive into a folder called `\$win_nt$.~ls`. By default, this folder is located in the system partition. The folder needs just over 300MB of free space in addition to the free space you need for the upgrade.

Initial Assessment Phase

You must have administrator privileges on the server to do an upgrade. If the server is a member of a domain, you should be logged on to the domain rather than the local SAM. This ensures that you have full access to all existing NTFS files and Registry keys. When ready, proceed as shown in Procedure 2.1.

Procedure 2.1 Performing Initial Setup Assessment for NT4 Upgrade

1. Insert the Windows Server 2003 CD in the CD-ROM drive. Autorun initiates Setup.exe. The name is somewhat misleading. Setup merely manages the Windows Server 2003 CD. Winnt32 actually performs the upgrade chores.
2. Click `Install Microsoft Windows Server 2003` to initiate the upgrade. Setup launches Winnt32.exe, the Windows Server 2003 installation management utility. The Welcome to Windows window opens. There are two options, `Upgrade` and `New Installation`:
   - The `Upgrade to Windows Server 2003` option obtains information about the current installation and uses that as a script for installing Windows Server 2003.
   - The `New Installation` option initiates a clean installation as covered in the preceding chapter. If you point the installer at a separate partition, it creates a dual-boot machine.

3. Click `Next`. The License Agreement window opens. You really have no choice other than selecting `I Accept This Agreement`. Winnt32 will not let you proceed if you don't accept the licensing agreement.
4. Click `Next`. The Product Key window opens. Enter the 25-character Product Key from the CD case. Later on, the Windows Product Activation (WPA) service will combine the Product Key with the Installation ID generated based on the server's hardware and submit this information to Microsoft to obtain a Confirmation ID that activates the installation. (WPA is not used for products obtained via Master License and Volume License Agreements.)
5. Click `Next`. If you are connected to the Internet, the Performing Dynamic Update window opens. Click `Yes` to connect to Microsoft's Update web site and download current Setup files. This stage also includes a readiness scan. If incompatible software or drivers are found, Winnt32 reports them to you. You should exit Setup and de-install the applications before continuing.

   If you are not currently connected to the Internet, the Directory of Applications window opens. This gives you the opportunity to connect to the Internet and then view the master application compatibility database at Microsoft.
6. Click `Next`. Winnt32 copies the Windows Server 2003 boot files into a folder named `\$Win_nt$.~bt` at the root of the existing boot partition. Winnt32 also changes Boot.ini to include this folder in the list of available boot options along with a special boot sector, Bootsect.dat, that has executable code for continuing with the next phase of Setup following restart.

Upgrade Implementation Phase

Following restart, Setup proceeds without further user intervention. There are four stages:

- **Device installation.** Setup performs a PnP enumeration and copies the necessary drivers from the CD or the `\$win_nt$.~ls` folder.
- **Networking installation.** Setup performs an additional scan for network devices and protocols and then installs and initializes the appropriate drivers.
- **Component installation.** Setup uses the Winnt.sif script from the original NT4 Registry to select and install components and drivers.
- **Final tasks.** Setup installs the START menu items, registers components, saves final settings, and removes the temporary files.

After Setup finishes the upgrade, the machine restarts one last time and you can log on. The domain affiliation will be the same as before the upgrade, so you can use your normal domain credentials.

Post-Upgrade Checks

After you log on following the upgrade, verify that all services that were operational under NT4 are still operational under Windows Server 2003. Make this check using the Services console. The simplest way to open the console is to enter `Services.msc` from the command line. You can also select it from the menu using START | PROGRAMS | ADMINISTRATIVE TOOLS | SERVICES.

If you disabled any services prior to upgrading, enable and start them now to verify that the new drivers work correctly. Make sure the service is Windows Server 2003 compatible or you may cause the machine to behave erratically.

Verify that services that have already started did so without errors by checking the Event log. Open the Event Viewer from the ADMINISTRATIVE TOOLS menu or enter `Eventvwr.msc` at the command line. You can expect a few warnings but you should not see any critical errors.

Application Compatibility Checks

Now work your way through any applications loaded on the server. If you find one that refuses to run in Windows Server 2003, you can try running it using the Application Compatibility Tool, Apcompat. You must install the tool separately. The installation package, Act20, comes on the Windows Server 2003 CD in `\Support\Tools`. Figure 2.1 shows an example of the Apcompat window.

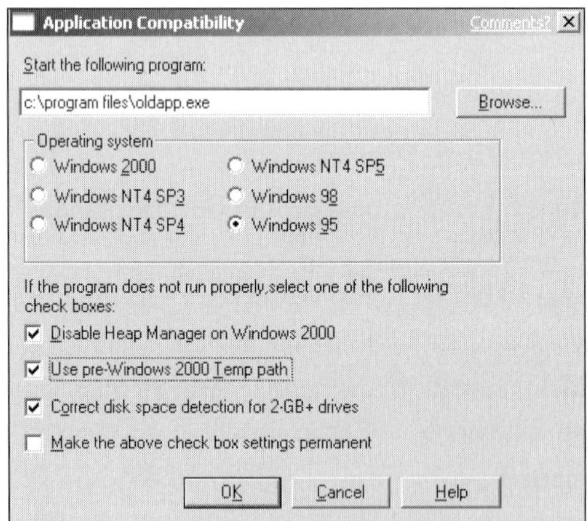

Figure 2.1 Application Compatibility—Used for running applications that demand specific functions from previous operating systems.

If you can find an operating mode that the application likes, you can lock down the Registry settings with the `Make Permanent` option.

Apcompat will help you in situations where the programmer who designed the application hard-coded it to look for a specific version of Windows. It does not permit applications to access hardware (*verboten* in all members of the NT family) nor does it permit the application to run VxDs. Chapter 19, "Managing the User Operating Environment," has additional tips for using more advanced compatibility settings in the Act20 suite of tools.

Security Checks

One of the final actions taken by Setup during a clean install or an upgrade is to apply Registry and NTFS file permissions. The templates for setting these permissions are contained in the `\Windows\Inf` folder. They are as follows:

- **Defltdc.inf.** The standard security settings for a domain controller.
- **Dcfirst.inf.** Additional security settings applied to the first domain controller in a tree.
- **Dcup.inf.** The security settings applied to a domain controller after upgrading from NT4.
- **Dcup5.inf.** The security settings applied to a domain controller after upgrading from Windows 2000.
- **Defltsv.inf.** The standard security settings applied to a server.
- **Dsup.inf.** The security settings applied after upgrading a server to Windows Server 2003 from any previous version.
- **Dsupt.inf.** The security settings applied after upgrading an NT4 Terminal Services Edition server or a Windows 2000 server running Terminal Services in Application mode.

The NTFS and Registry permissions applied by these scripts play a crucial role in controlling access to a server or domain controllers. It is very important that the scripts run to completion. Sometimes a bug or outside incident causes the script to stop. There should be an Event log entry if this happens.

If you peruse the entries in these scripts, you'll also find that the tight lockdowns in Windows Server 2003 are not applied to upgrades. If you want an upgraded server to have the same security settings as a clean install, you can apply the security settings manually. See Chapter 11, "Understanding Network Access Security and Kerberos," for details on the contents of the security templates and how to apply a template to a server.

Automating Windows Server 2003 Deployments

Computers are supposed to be servants, right? So why should we expend countless hours slaving over repetitive installations to get our servants to the point where they can serve? If you have more than one or two servers to install or upgrade, you might want to look into automating the process. There are three general types of automated deployment methods:

- Disk cloning
- Scripted installations
- Remote Installation Services (RIS)

In this section, we'll take a detailed look at each method.

Disk Cloning

Of the three deployment methods, disk cloning is the fastest. It is also the most likely method to cause compatibility problems due to hardware differences between the server where you made the image and the server where you place the image.

Cloning makes sense for desktop deployments where you have many iterations of the same hardware. For servers, I prefer a process that tailors the installation more closely to the underlying platform. Disk cloning is handy, though, for taking snapshots of a server prior to making a change. If the change causes the server to go to the rings of Saturn, you can quickly re-image to recover functionality.

Cloning involves using a disk-imaging package (Microsoft does not provide one) that takes a sector-by-sector snapshot of the contents of the system drive and saves it to a file. You can come back to the same machine at a later time, or to another machine, and apply the image. If the underlying hardware is fairly close to the same, you get an identical copy. If there are subtle differences in the hardware, your copies might start to act in strange and gruesome ways. If you've ever seen Michael Keaton in *Multiplicity*, you have an idea how bad things can get when cloning goes awry.

There are two major disk-imaging products:

- Norton Ghost from Symantec (`www.symantec.com/ghost`)
- DriveImage Pro from PowerQuest (`www.powerquest.com/driveimagepro`)

Both of these products permit you to quickly take an image of a drive, restore the image, and even make changes to parts of the image without disturbing the other parts.

Problems with Disk Imaging

Deployments based on disk imaging start to get complex when you have a variety of server platforms. Thanks to Plug and Play, Windows Server 2003 can forgive certain differences in peripherals, but surprisingly small deltas in critical system components can cause imaged installations to fail or perform erratically. These differences include the CPU model and stepping, firmware revision, chipset, memory configuration, and ACPI (Advanced Configuration and Power Interface) version.

If you change out a major subassembly, though, such as a motherboard, or you place an image on another machine, the Plug and Play Manager may become hopelessly lost and could refuse to recognize the drive interfaces or memory. Be sure to test your cloned configuration on every subset of hardware you have to see whether this is going to be a problem for you.

Disk imaging also causes problems if you use retail versions of Windows Server 2003 that require individual product activation. Because the image has the same Product Key as the master, you will not be able to activate the new server. If you are going to clone servers, be sure to purchase your product using Volume Purchase Agreements that have no activation requirement.

Disk Imaging with Sysprep

You can avoid some of the problems with hardware incompatibilities and product activation hassles by stripping the machine-dependent information out of the Registry prior to imaging the machine. That is the function of *Sysprep*.

Sysprep makes it fast and easy to image a server without SID or compatibility issues. Sysprep has an advantage over the scripted installation methods described later in this chapter because it preserves applications and their Registry settings along with specialized configurations you may want for your servers.

Sysprep is not a panacea for hardware incompatibilities, though. If the target server has a different mass storage device than the server where you ran Sysprep, you can get a kernel-mode stop error after applying the Sysprep image. This is because the operating system cannot locate the boot files thanks to the incompatible mass storage device.

The Sysprep tool is compressed inside the Deploy.cab file located on the Windows Server 2003 CD in the `\Support\Tools` folder. You can extract it from the CAB file directly using Explorer and run it from any folder. Sysprep displays the window shown in Figure 2.2.

You can also run Sysprep from the command line. Run `sysprep /?` for an option list. Here's an example:

```
sysprep -quiet -noreboot -mini -pnp
```

This command runs Sysprep with no prompts, shuts down the system without rebooting after the system has been prepped, initiates a mini-setup at the next restart, and forces a plug-and-play scan of all devices during the mini-setup.

You can use the results of Sysprep to make a drive that can be imaged using Ghost or DriveImage. The image has a full installation of Windows Server 2003 and any applications that were installed on the server but does not have hardware-specific information in the Registry.

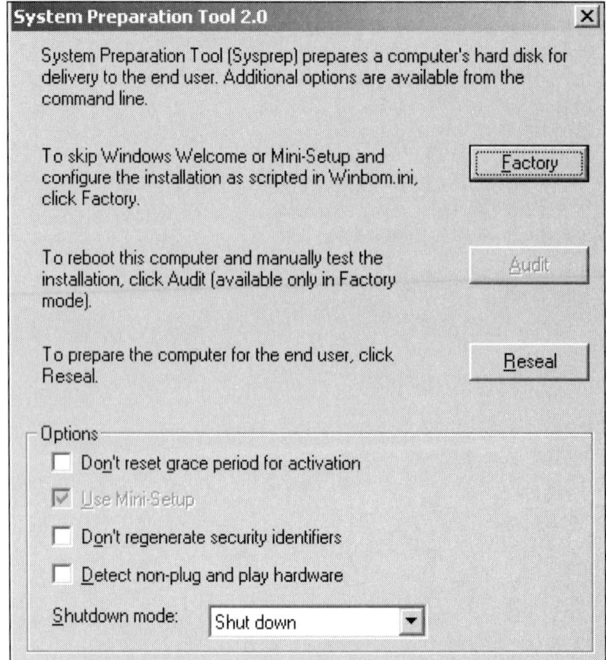

Figure 2.2 System Preparation Tool window showing options.

When you start a server after imaging it with this Sysprep image, a new SID is generated and a mini-setup launches to collect configuration information. You can include a script in your Sysprep deployment image that automates the mini-setup. See "Scripted Installations" later in this chapter.

Auditing a Sysprep Image

You may want to verify that a particular Sysprep image is correct. For example, you may have several images for different server types. You now have the same problem as a chicken farmer: How do you make sure there's a chicken in an egg without breaking the egg and killing the chicken?

You overcome this obstacle by using the `-nosidgen` option. You can install the image to make sure it works then run Sysprep again with the `-nosidgen` option to recreate the image while preserving the configuration files that were generated by the original Sysprep session. You can restart as many times as you like using `-nosidgen`. The `Audit Shutdown` option in the GUI interface performs the same action.

Be sure not to change any files while you are auditing the installation. Sysprep does not scan for file and Registry changes with `-nosidgen`.

Sysprep Factory Options

OEM manufacturers can use Sysprep to create an image that can be cloned onto disks for hundreds of systems. There is a `-factory` option in Sysprep that permits the manufacturer to slipstream changes into the image for a specific model of hardware.

The `-factory` option relies on entries in a Winbom.inf script. You must build this Winbom script manually if you intend on using the `-factory` option. The Ref.chm help file that accompanies Sysprep has a full list of the Winbom.inf options and their syntax. Sysprep looks for the Winbom.inf script on a floppy and, if it exists, incorporates the changes into the image.

The advantage of using the `-factory` option is that the worker on the assembly line (or you, if you build a lot of servers) can have a single master image with floppies that have settings for various different configuration options.

You can add more drivers or make changes to the content of the automated setup after running Sysprep `-factory`. Run Sysprep `-reseal` to prepare the machine for final deployment.

Additional Sysprep Options

If you plan on imaging a domain controller, it is important not to change the server's SID because it uniquely identifies the domain controller in Active Directory. Use the `-nosidgen` option to retain the current SID.

If a server has legacy hardware—that is, hardware that is not Plug and Play—you can use the `-pnp` option to force a full scan for installable devices. Don't use this switch unless you have legacy equipment because it increases the time for the mini-Setup to finish.

Sysprep Limitations

The server you use to build a Sysprep image cannot be a domain controller or a domain member. You can join it to a domain as part of the mini-setup when the imaged machine first starts. You can script this mini-setup to create a hands-off installation.

The server you want to Sysprep cannot have any encrypted files. This is because the SID will change, making obsolete all existing profiles where the encrypted file keys are stored.

You can only run through three Sysprep cycles on a given machine. This prevents avoiding activation by simply running Sysprep when the grace period expires.

The server cannot be a member of a cluster. It cannot be a Certification Authority. Both of these applications require specific information about the machine, its SID, and its hardware. For instance, you would not want someone to be able to take a Sysprep image of a Certification Authority and use it to clone off another server that would pass out counterfeit certificates.

Scripted Installations

When Setup runs in interactive mode, it spends a lot of time asking nosey questions before it gets down to the grunt work of copying files and configuring the system. By scripting your answers to these questions, you can do a fully unattended installation.

Because a server typically has a fixed identity (name, IP address, domain membership, and so forth), installing the operating system with a script is a little more difficult than using scripts to deploy desktops. Still, it's possible to submit identity items as part of the script so that a minimal effort is required to install the server after you get the hardware ready to go.

A scripted installation of a server also ensures that the files are copied from a consistent distribution point. Later on, when you need to install a new service, Windows Server 2003 will go back to that distribution server to find the files. A feature in Windows Server 2003 service packs permits you to *slipstream* a service pack into a distribution point so that you can install a service pack right along with the base operating system. See "Slipstreaming Service Pack Installations" later in this chapter for more information.

Procedure 2.2 shows a quick breakdown of the overall steps for scripting an unattended installation and performing the deployment.

Procedure 2.2 Task List for Setting Up Scripted Installations

1. Create an unattended setup script that automatically answers configuration questions presented by Setup.
2. Copy the Windows Server 2003 installation files and scripts to a folder on a distribution server and share the folder.
3. Build a boot disk that connects a target client to the shared installation directory across the network.
4. Use the unattended setup script to install Windows Server 2003 on the target server.

Creating an Unattended Setup Script

This section covers creating an unattended setup script using the Setup Manager utility, Setupmgr. This utility is compressed inside the Deploy.cab file on the Windows Server 2003 CD in the `\Support\Tools` folder. You can extract the file using Explorer and run it from any folder.

In addition to building the setup script, Setup Manager can automate the creation of a distribution share point to hold the installation files. If you want to take advantage of that option, launch Setup Manager at the console of the server where you want the distribution files to be located. When you're ready, proceed as directed in Procedure 2.3.

Procedure 2.3 Using Setup Manager to Create an Unattended Installation Script

1. Launch Setupmgr. The Setup Manager Wizard starts.
2. Click `Next`. The New or Existing Answer File window opens. Select `Create New`.
3. Click `Next`. The Type of Setup window opens. Select one of the three types of scripted installation:
   - `Unattended Setup` builds a text-based script that contains entries that configure the text and graphical portions of Setup.
   - `Sysprep Setup` builds an INF script that handles the mini-setup that runs the first time a machine starts after having been given a Sysprep image.
   - `Remote Installation Services (RIS)` builds a SIF file for use when deploying a RIS image.
4. Click `Next`. The Product window opens. Select the Windows Server 2003 product or XP product that you are installing. (The unattended setup script used by Windows Server 2003 differs from Windows 2000 and the two should not be mixed.)
5. Click `Next`. The User Interaction window opens (see Figure 2.3). The Fully Automated option scripts the entire installation and should be selected unless you have special requirements.

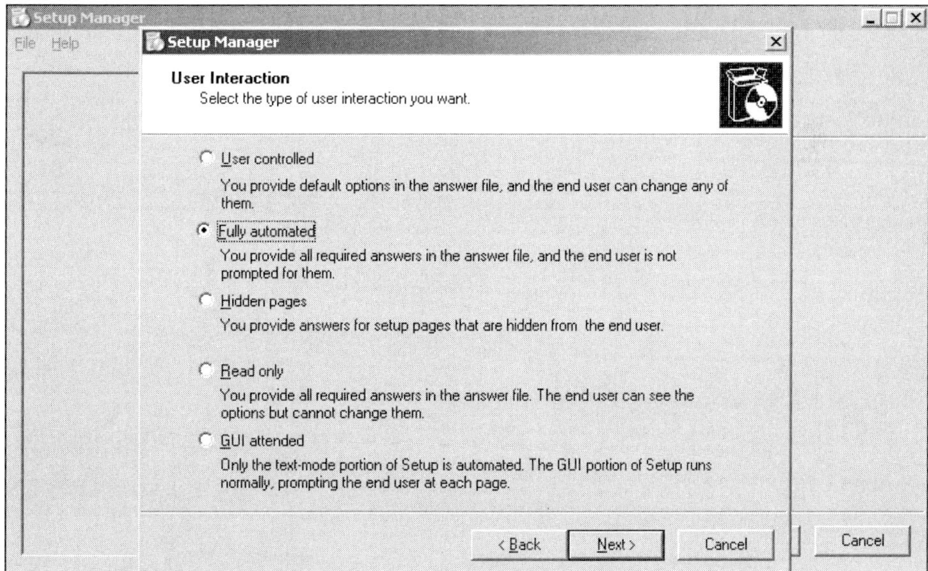

Figure 2.3 Windows Setup Manager Wizard—User Interaction window.

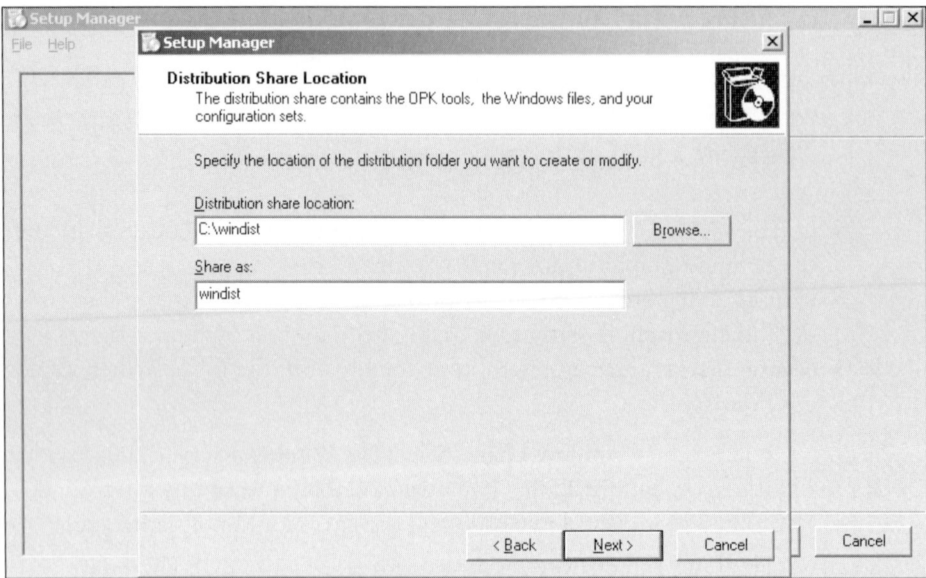

Figure 2.4 Windows Setup Manager Wizard—Distribution Share Location window.

6. Click `Next`. The Distribution Share window opens. Select `Create a New Distribution Share`. This permits you to copy the contents of the CD to a distribution folder and share the folder.
7. Click `Next`. The Location of Setup Files window opens. Select whether to copy the files from the CD or another location. The alternate location option comes in handy when you have slipstreamed various service packs into a network installation point and you want to copy the files from there.
8. Click `Next`. The Distribution Share Location window opens (see Figure 2.4). Enter the path and name of the folder and the share name you want to use. You must do this on the distribution server. The wizard cannot create a share across the network.
9. Click `Next`. The License Agreement window opens. This is your acknowledgement that the automated installations using this script comply with the *End User License Agreement* (EULA). Without an entry here, the unattended installation will stop and prompt for a EULA agreement. Check `I Accept the Terms of the License Agreement.`
10. Click `Next`. The wizard closes and leaves the Setup Manager window open.

Unlike earlier versions of Setup Manager, Windows Server 2003 presents you with a tree of the possible options so that you can quickly pick and choose those that you want to use without spending time stepping through the wizard screens one at a time. See Figure 2.5 for an example.

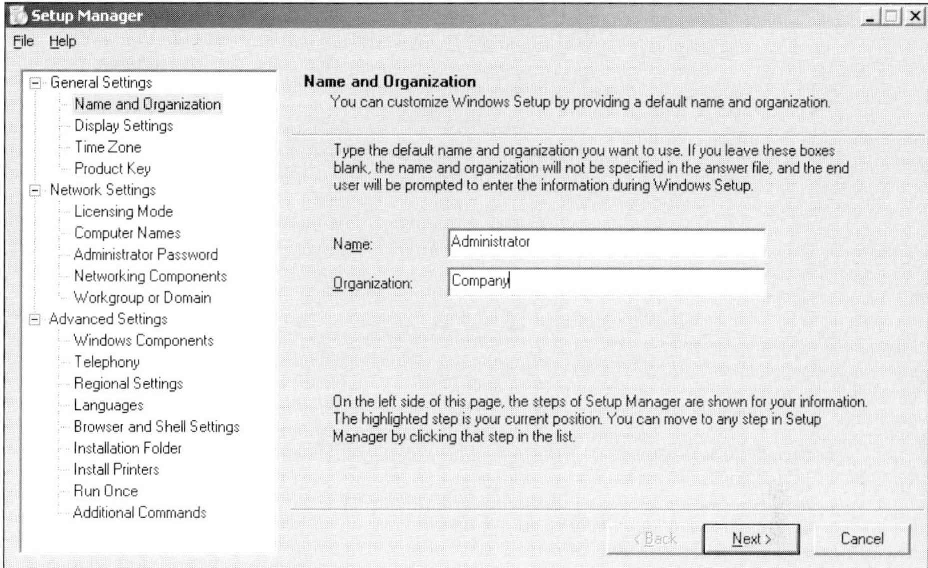

Figure 2.5 Setup Manager main window showing the tree of setup options.

A few of the options require an entry, so the tree doesn't give you truly random access. Some of the options merit special attention:

- The `Computer Names` option permits you to specify a name or to have Setup automatically generate a name. The generated name takes the form of the name you enter in `Personalize This Computer` followed by a dash and then random letters. If you want to specify a name, you must include an Unattended Difference File (UDF) that specifies the name of each server. The server name must be specified on the Winnt or Winnt32 command line when you initiate Setup.
- The `Administrator Password` option (see Figure 2.6) permits you to specify a password for the local Administrator account. Setup Manager puts this password into the installation script. Windows Server 2003 improves security by permitting you to encrypt the password. Without this encryption option, the password is exposed in the script in clear text.
- The `Workgroup or Domain` option permits you to join a domain during Setup. This is generally a worthwhile thing to do, but it again raises the possibility of a security breach because the account you use to join the domain is exposed in clear text. See the sidebar, "Joining Domains During Automated Setup."

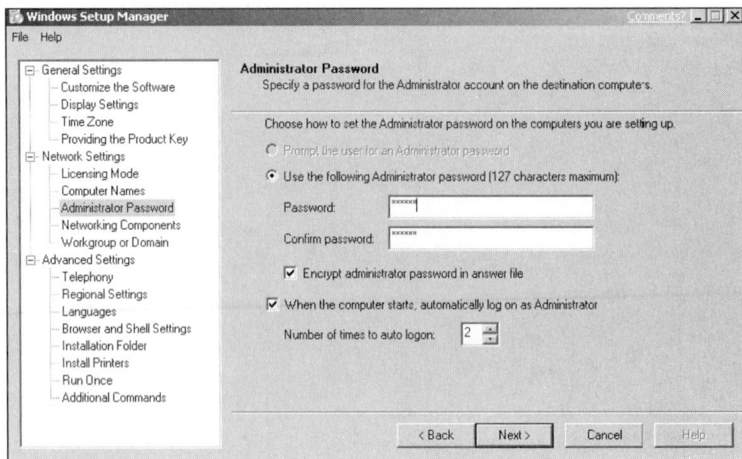

Figure 2.6 Windows Setup Manager Wizard—Administrator Password window.

When you have entered information for the required and optional items, click `Next`. Setup Manager prompts you for the name and path of the unattended setup script. The default name is Unattend.txt.

Put the file in the I386 folder that holds the installation files. If you create the distribution point as part of Setup Manager, it will automatically place the script in the correct location.

Joining Domains During Automated Setup

If you want to join a server to a domain during an unattended setup, the best course of action is first to create a computer account in Active Directory. This can be difficult if you use automatically generated names. You won't know what the name will be.

If you choose to create the account during an unattended setup, one alternative is to protect the installation deployment folder with NTFS permissions that permit users to execute files but not view them.

Another alternative is to create an account with the privilege to join computers to a domain but no other administrative privileges. You can periodically change the password of this account to preserve its security.

A third alternative is to initiate the unattended setup script with a batch file that collects information from the deployment technician.

Windows Server 2003 permits any authenticated user to join a computer to a domain. Don't make the mistake, though, of simply entering a user account into the unattended setup script. Non-administrators can only join a computer to a domain ten times. After that, they are blocked from exercising the privilege.

Example Unattended Setup Script

Here's an example of a setup script created using Setup Manager. The entries highlighted in bold deserve special attention:

```
;SetupMgrTag
[Data]
    AutoPartition=1
    MsDosInitiated="0"
    UnattendedInstall="Yes"

[Unattended]
    UnattendMode=FullUnattended
    OemSkipEula=Yes ;This skips the License Agreement window.
    OemPreinstall=No
    TargetPath=\WINDOWS
    DriverSigningPolicy = ignore ; Add this switch manually
                          to avoid errors with unsigned drivers.

[GuiUnattended]
    AdminPassword=b267df22cb945e3eaad3b435b51404ee36aa83bdcab3c9fdaf321ca42a31c3fc
    EncryptedAdminPassword=Yes ; The encryption uses a two-way cipher of the
    ➥password.
    AutoLogon=Yes ; This option logs on automatically using the Administrator
    ➥credentials.
    AutoLogonCount=1 ; This option limits the number of automatic logons.
    TimeZone=85
    OemSkipWelcome=1

[UserData]
    FullName=Admin ; Do not use Administrator or Guest as an owner name.
    OrgName=Company
    ComputerName=* ; This enables automatic computer naming.

[LicenseFilePrintData]
    AutoMode=PerSeat

[Identification]
    JoinDomain=Company.com
    DomainAdmin=CompAddAccount
    DomainAdminPassword=JabBorE# ;Domain password in clear text. Protect the file
    ➥with NTFS permissions.

[Networking]
    InstallDefaultComponents=Yes
```

Example Unattended Setup Batch File

Setup Manager creates a batch file for initiating the unattended setup. The client maps to the shared distribution folder and executes the batch file. Here is an example:

```
@rem SetupMgrTag
@echo off
rem
rem This is a SAMPLE batch script generated by the Setup Manager Wizard.
rem If this script is moved from the location where it was generated, it may have
➥to be modified.
rem
set AnswerFile=.\unattend.txt
set SetupFiles=\\S1\netsvrdist

\\S1\netsvrdist\winnt32 /s:%SetupFiles% /unattend:%AnswerFile%
```

This batch file uses Winnt32, the 32-bit installation management utility. If you connect to the network share from a DOS client using a network boot disk, you must use the 16-bit installation manager, Winnt. If you do so, you need to add a `/b` switch to the command line, indicating no setup boot disks, and change the word `unattend` to the letter `u` as follows:

```
\\S1\netsrvdist\winnt /b /s:%SetupFiles% /u:%AnswerFile%
```

If you want to specify a local drive for installing Windows Server 2003 other than the default boot drive, use this syntax:

```
set AnswerFile=.\unattend.txt
set SetupFiles=\\S1\netsrvdist
set TargetDrive=c

\\S1\netsrvdist\winnt /s:%SetupFiles% /u:%AnswerFile% /t:%TargetDrive%
```

Unattended Script Customizations

The script generated by Windows Server 2003 Setup Manager includes only the base operating system files and drivers. If you have additional drivers to install, or you want to include applications or other enhancements to the unattended setup, you must add these manually to the distribution share files and the unattended setup script.

A list of all unattended setup script entries and their uses is included in Deploy.chm help file inside the Deploy.cab file on the Windows Server 2003 CD under `\Support\Tools`. It helps to be familiar with the standard Microsoft customization file locations and a few of the more common script entries. Here they are:

- **`$OEM$`**. The top-level folder containing customization files. This folder must be at the root of the distribution point.

- **`$OEM$\Textmode`**. This folder contains drivers and INF scripts for any components that must be loaded as part of the text mode portion of Setup. For example, if you have a RAID controller that needs a driver not included in Windows Server 2003 setup files, you would put the driver and its Oemsetup.inf script here. The same is true for OEM versions of kernel files.
- **`$OEM$\$$`**. This folder contains drivers and files that you want to put in `%systemroot%`. This is generally `C:\Windows`. Examples include component drivers not included in Windows Server 2003. You can have subfolders under `$$`.
- **`$OEM$\$1`**. This folder contains drivers and files that you want to place at the root of the system drive. This would include any drivers required to load before the operating system has fully initialized. You can have subfolders under `$1`.
- **`$OEM$\C,D,`etc**. These folders contain files that you want to put in various logical drives after the system has assigned drive letters. This is especially handy for installing application files. You can define subfolders, as well.

Automating Product Key Entry

If you want to automatically enter the 25-character Product Key as part of the unattended script, you can include it as follows:

```
[UserData]
   ProductID="aaaaa-bbbbb-ccccc-ddddd-eeeee"
```

This is only applicable if you have a Volume Purchase Agreement or a Master License Agreement. Otherwise, you must have a distinct Product Key for each server to successfully activate the installation.

Automating Activation

Speaking of activation, if you are deploying the retail version and you want to activate automatically without bothering the user, you can do so as long as you have an Internet connection. If you have a firewall with an Internet proxy server, you must include proxy entries, as well. The following entries in the unattended script file will initiate the Windows Product Activation automatically:

```
[Unattended]
AutoActivate=Yes
ActivateProxy=Yes

[Proxy]
Proxy_Enable=1
Use_Same_Proxy=1
HTTP_Proxy_Server=proxy-name:80
Proxy_Override=<local>
```

Expanding the System Partition

When you install Windows Server 2003 across the network, Setup first copies the installation files to the local hard drive. This means you need a formatted partition ready to receive the files. The partition must be formatted as FAT or FAT32. To get an acceptable cluster size, you want to keep the size of the FAT partition to the minimum size possible, which is 1.5GB for Windows Server 2003.

You can automatically extend this partition as part of the unattended setup to get more room for the operating system. This can only be done for NTFS partitions, so you must convert the partition, as well. This requires two entries:

```
[Unattended]
ExtendOEMPartition=1
FileSystem=ConvertNTFS
```

If you have a 30GB boot drive, you probably do not want to give the entire drive to the operating system. You can limit the size of the extended partition by specifying the size in megabytes of the final partition. Here's an example:

```
[Unattended]
ExtendOEMPartition=1 2048
FileSystem=ConvertNTFS
```

Running Scripts During Unattended Setup

The easiest way to install applications as part of an unattended setup is to put the application's setup files in a folder under `$OEM$` and then kick off a script or batch file that initiates an unattended setup of the application. Many applications use setup scripts similar in concept, if not form, to Unattend.txt.

Scripts can be included in unattended setups by placing the scripts, batch files, and executables in a folder of your choice under `$OEM$` and then launching the script using a Cmdlines.txt file stored at the root of `$OEM$`.

You must construct the Cmdlines.txt file manually. You must also tell Setup to use it by putting this line in the Unattend.txt file:

```
[UNATTEND]
OEMPREINSTALL = Yes
```

The Cmdlines.txt file must be formatted as follows:

```
[COMMANDS]
  ".\cscript script.vbs"
  ".\batch.cmd"
  ".\app.exe"
```

The script, batch file, or executable launched in Cmdlines.txt must have a short filename. If it has a long filename and you cannot change the name, you can launch it from another batch file with a short name that you can put in Cmdlines.txt.

Because the elements of Cmdlines.txt run before any user logs on, they run in the Local System security context. This means they cannot make network connection to other servers. If you write any information to the Registry, it is written to the Default User profile.

Tailoring Component Installations

In addition to using unattended installation scripts for handling an entire setup, you may want to script specific component installations following Setup. For example, if you want to install IIS, you should always use an unattended setup script so you can designate a location for your web files that are not on the boot drive and to simplify selecting only those web services that you need to support production operations.

The utility that handles the unattended installation of a Windows component is SYSOCMGR. To use this utility, create a text file that contains the component installation settings, then use the file as a parameter of SYOCMGR. Here's an example using a script file called Iis.txt:

```
Sysocmgr /i: %windir%\inf\sysoc.inf /u:c:\iis.txt
```

Here is an example of an unattended setup script that installs only web services and places the web files on the D drive:

```
[Components]
     iis_common = On
     iis_inetmgr = On
     iis_www = On
     iis_ftp = Off
     iis_nntp = Off
     iis_nntp_docs = Off
     iis_pwmgr = Off
     iis_smtp = Off
     iis_smtp_docs = Off
     iis_htmla = Off
     iis_w3samp = Off
     iis_doc_common = Off
     iis_doc_ismcore = Off
     iis_doc_asp = Off
     iis_doc_sdk = Off
     iis_doc_mm = Off

[InternetServer]
     PathFTPRoot=D:\Inetpub\Ftproot
     PathWWWRoot=D:\Inetpub\Wwwroot
```

Slipstreaming Service Pack Installations

In classic NT, getting the operating system installed was only half the work. You then had to install the "second operating system" consisting of a service pack containing hundreds, even thousands, of files containing fixes.

Starting with Windows 2000, Microsoft eased this work quite a bit by making it possible to install the fixed files in the service pack right along with the normal Setup files. You do this by slipstreaming the updates into the distribution folder that holds the regular installation files. To perform this slipstreaming, follow the steps listed in Procedure 2.4.

Procedure 2.4 Slipstreaming Service Pack Files

1. Mount the service pack CD in the CD-ROM drive or copy the contents of the service pack CD to a separate folder.
2. Navigate to the `\I386\Update` folder in the service pack files.
3. Run `update -s:e:\softdistro`, where `e:\softdistro` is the folder containing the Windows Server 2003 distribution files. Note that you point at the folder *above* the I386 folder containing the installation files.

After you have updated the installation files in this manner, running Setup from the distribution point also will install the fixed files.

All service packs are cumulative, so you do not need to retain earlier versions. Update replaces the catalog used by the Windows File Protection system with an updated catalog that has the file signatures for the fixed files. It also puts in place an additional CAB file containing drivers that have been updated or added since the initial release of Windows Server 2003.

You can deploy service packs to installed servers using group policies. See Chapter 12, "Managing Group Policies," for details.

Building a Network Boot Disk

Whether you deploy Windows Server 2003 using Sysprep or a fully scripted installation, if you want to install to a machine that has no operating system installed, you'll need a way to boot from a floppy disk and make network connection to the distribution server holding the installation files.

Building a Windows-based network boot disk isn't simple. Microsoft uses a proprietary open standard for network drivers called the *Network Driver Interface Specification* (NDIS). (You may see the acronym NDIS broken out as Network *Device* Interface Specification. Both are acceptable.)

Bart's Boot Disks

For the ultimate in automating the creation of custom boot disks, I highly recommend visiting Bart's Boot Disks web site at www.nu2.nu/bootdisk. This site has a compilation of CAB files that contain boot files, network files, and configuration files to use for creating boot disks and bootable CD-ROMs.

Real-mode NDIS with TCP/IP support requires a chorus of support files the size of the Mormon Tabernacle Choir.

The Windows Server 2003 CD contains the files required to build a DOS network client but it only provides an eight-year-old installation utility for extracting and configuring the files. You can declare yourself a true Windows networking guru if you memorize the real-mode NDIS files and the contents of the various configuration files to build a boot floppy from scratch.

If you're familiar with NT4, you may know that Microsoft supplied a nifty little utility with NT4 Server called Ncadmin that had a feature for building NDIS boot floppy disks. Microsoft does not include Ncadmin with Windows 2000 or Windows Server 2003. If you need to build an NDIS boot disk, you can get a copy of Ncadmin from an existing NT4 Server CD and use it to build your network boot disks. Ncadmin runs just fine on Windows Server 2003.

If you don't mind spending a few dollars, the major imaging vendors—including Symantec and PowerQuest—provide utilities for building boot disks. These utilities take the real-mode NDIS support files from the Windows Server 2003 CD and the NDIS 2.0 drivers from the network support disk for your adapter and build you a network boot disk. I highly recommend these.

Remote Installation Services

All of the automation techniques we've seen so far require at least some intervention on the part of an administrator. The ultimate automation would be to have a completely hands-off installation where the machine finds its own distribution server, downloads the installation files, installs them, and boots up ready for work. That's the goal of *Remote Installation Services*, or RIS.

RIS combines the hardware-independent flexibility of scripting with the simplicity of imaging. Using RIS, you can build a file-based "image" of a server and deploy that image completely hands-free. It's like getting beer *and* fudge for dinner. Unfortunately, you have to eat your Brussels sprouts first. RIS can be a little complex to set up and manage. You'll be repaid for the work, though.

Functional Overview of RIS

RIS consists of a server component and a client component. The server component is the Remote Installation Services itself, running on a Windows 2000 member server or domain controller.

The RIS service controls access to a set of file-based "images" stored on the server. The image files can come from the installation files on the Server or Professional CD, or they can come from an "image" server or workstation that has been processed using a utility called Riprep. See "Creating RIS Images with Riprep" later in this section for more information.

RIS depends on a variety of services, all of which must be configured just right. This makes it a little complex to do the initial setup. Here is a quick list of the services that require special configuration. I'll discuss how RIS uses each one in detail:

- Pre-boot Execution Environment (PXE)
- DHCP
- Boot Information Negotiation Layer (BINL)
- Client Installation Wizard
- Single Instance Storage (SIS) Groveler
- RIS setup scripts

In addition, because RIS depends on Active Directory, and because changes were made to Active Directory in Windows Server 2003, after you upgrade a domain to Windows Server 2003, you must upgrade the RIS servers to Windows Server 2003 as well.

Pre-Boot Execution Environment

A RIS client must be able to create a small operating environment that has sufficient capacity to download the setup files from a server exactly as a human operator would do. The trick, then, is getting that operating environment delivered to the client. The process that controls this transaction is called the *Pre-boot Execution Environment*, or PXE.

A PXE client knows how to find a server that contains a startup image that the client can download and execute to create an operational environment. It is called *pre-boot* because the PXE client loads before an operating system has a chance to boot.

IA32 class machines built to the PC97 standards or later support PXE booting in BIOS. You often must configure CMOS to enable it and to set the boot order. IA64 machines have a boot menu option to launch PXE.

Even if the computer does not have a PXE boot ROM, many network cards have Ethernet controllers that support PXE if the executable code is available in memory via a boot floppy. PXE adapters must use the PCI bus, which eliminates laptops that use PCMCIA network adapters unless the laptop emulates PCI on the PC Card bus.

The PXE boot floppy is built using the Remote Boot Floppy Generator (RBFG) utility in the `\RemoteInstall\Admin` directory on the RIS server. See the "Creating PXE Boot Disks" section later in this chapter for details.

DHCP

PXE clients use TCP/IP as a transport protocol, so they need an IP address before they can contact a RIS server. You cannot statically map an IP address for a client that lives completely in memory, so it must obtain its address from a DHCP server.

DHCP works a little like getting a beer at a ball game. You don't know the attendant's name, so you shout, "Hey, beer man, what'cha got?" The beer man shouts back an offer and you accept that offer and get a cold one. Here is a typical DHCP transaction:

1. The PXE client broadcasts a DHCP Discovery.
2. A DHCP server answers by broadcasting a DHCP Offer. The offer contains an IP address. At this point, the client has no IP address so the server cannot communicate with it directly.
3. The client broadcasts back a DHCP Request containing the IP address it got from the DHCP Offer packet.
4. The DHCP server unicasts back a DHCP ACK, sealing the deal. In this final ACK, the server includes configuration information such as the IP address of the gateway, the DNS domain suffix, the renewal interval of the address lease, and so forth.

If the DHCP server resides in a different subnet than the client, the intervening routers must be configured to pass DHCP broadcasts via DHCP/BOOTP relaying. As part of the relay, the router is configured with the IP address of one or more DHCP servers. It ferries DHCP broadcasts back and forth between the DHCP server and any clients requesting addresses. Keep this helper function in mind as you read the next section.

During a PXE boot, the client console displays the word `DHCP` with a series of dots during this part of the transaction. When the client gets an IP address, it displays the configuration information and you may see the message change to `BINL` for a few moments as it proceeds to the next stage.

Boot Information Negotiation Layer (BINL)

At this point, the PXE client has an IP address. Now it needs to know the identity of a server hosting a boot image. The PXE client is not very bright, so it uses the same DHCP transaction process to find a RIS server. The RIS server has a special service called the *Boot Information Negotiation Layer*, or BINL, that handles these special DHCP requests. Here's how it works:

1. When a PXE client sends out its initial DHCP Discovery packet, it includes the Globally Unique Identifier (GUID) that is burned into the PXE ROM. If there is no PXE ROM and the client is using a PXE boot disk, the GUID consists of the client's MAC address padded by 20 leading zeros.

2. When a RIS server sees a DHCP Discovery packet with a GUID payload, the BINL service responds with a DHCP Offer of its own. In this offer, the `Client IP` address field is left blank, indicating that this is not an offer of an IP address, and the payload includes a copy of the client's GUID.
3. At first, the client ignores this BINL offer. It is more concerned with getting an IP address. After the new address is bound to the IP stack, the client contacts the BINL server on UDP port 4011 with a second DHCP Request.
4. The server responds with a DHCP ACK that contains the name and path of the boot image. The name of this image is Startrom.com. See the sidebar, "Potential Problems with BINL," for more information.
5. The client now sends a Trivial File Transfer Protocol (TFTP) `GET` request to copy a file called Startrom.com.
6. The server responds by sending the Startrom.com file to the client.

At this point in the transaction, the client displays its IP address and MAC address and you may see a TFTP message flash by before the screen changes to display the Client Installation Wizard, described in the next section.

Client Installation Wizard

At this point, we're nearly finished with the initial transactions. The client executes the Startrom.com image. The image instructs the client to use TFTP to get two more files:

- **Ntldr.** The Windows Server 2003 secondary bootstrap loader.
- **Winnt.sif.** The Windows Server 2003 standard setup script.

Potential Problems with BINL

RIS has a lot of moving parts. It can be frustrating to come up with a configuration where the right clients get their IP and BINL information from the right servers.

Keep the broadcast nature of DHCP transaction in mind and don't forget about the DHCP/BOOTP helpers in the routers. For the most part, if you have one RIS server, it should be running on the DHCP server. This gives you the best chance for reliable packet exchange.

If, on the other hand, you have more than one RIS server, it's important *not* to put RIS on a DHCP server. This is because PXE clients will ignore additional BINL offers they get if the initial offer came from their DHCP server.

If you use DHCP/BOOTP helpers in your routers, the helper needs to include the RIS server in the list of IP addresses. Even then, depending on your router, this might not work. You might need a separate RIS server in each subnet.

Because BINL uses DHCP, the RIS server must be authorized in Active Directory just as you would authorize a regular Windows Server 2003 DHCP server. If the BINL server is not authorized, it will not respond to DHCP Discovery packets and your PXE clients will time out. Authorize the server by loading into a DHCP Manager console then right-clicking the server name and selecting AUTHORIZE from the flyout menu.

Another potential problem with the BINL transaction is the TFTP file transfer. It is possible to use a TFTP `PUT` command to copy files *from* a client *to* the server. This opens the possibility of putting a Trojan Horse file on the server in the form of a replaced Startrom.com file or one of the other support files. Microsoft has acknowledged this possibility, but at the time of this writing it has not published a fix.

The client then prompts to press F12 to begin the *Client Installation Wizard*, or CIW. See the sidebar, "Alternative Startrom Files," for ways to avoid the need to press F12. Figure 2.7 shows the Welcome screen of the CIW.

The job of the CIW is to authenticate the person doing the installation and to display a list of installation images available for downloading. This list is called the *OS Chooser (OSC)*. When the installer selects an image, the CIW downloads the files associated with the image and commences Windows Server 2003 Setup using those files.

The screens displayed by the CIW come from a set of OSC files on the RIS server in the folder `\RemoteInstall\OS Chooser\English`. These OSC files are simply text files based on HTML 2.0 format. You can open one with Notepad to see what it looks like. Because they are text, you can change the display, if you want.

Only a limited number of HTML 2.0 tags are supported in OSC files, so you don't get much leeway for creativity, but it's fairly simple to put additional instructions in existing OSC files or to build OSC files of your own. For example, you can create an OSC file that lets an administrator define the computer name and the target OU before continuing with the automated setup. See the "Customizing CIW Screens" topic later in this chapter for details.

After an initial welcome screen, CIW displays a Login.osc screen to obtain the user's credentials. Figure 2.8 shows an example.

In Windows Server 2003, as with Windows 2000, any authenticated user can perform the installation. Users without administrator credentials are limited to ten installations. You can restrict who can perform installations using group policies. The authentication occurs via BINL (UDP port 4011) and uses NTLM Challenge-Response.

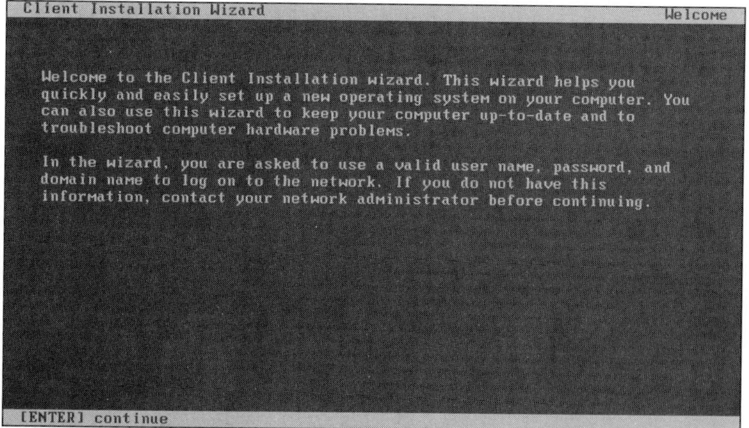

Figure 2.7 RIS Client Installation Wizard—Welcome screen.

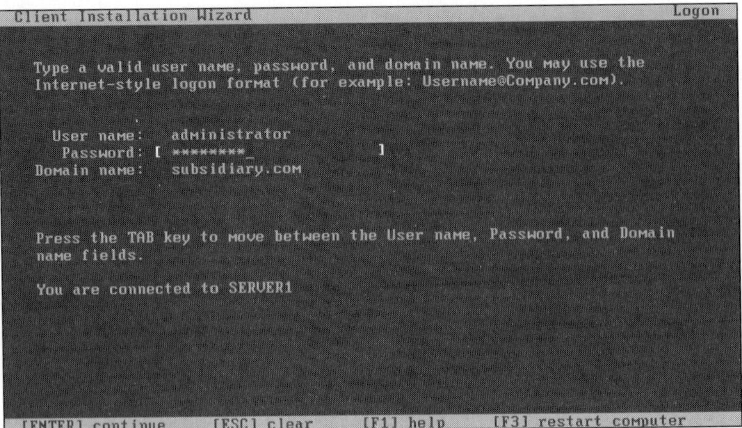

Figure 2.8 RIS Client Installation Wizard—Login screen.

The remaining portions of the CIW consist of walking through a chain of linked OSC files until you get to the Choices.osc screen (see Figure 2.9). This lists the images that are on the RIS server.

When you select an item from the image list, the CIW loads the SIF script for the image from the `\RemoteInstall\Setup\English\Images\WINDOWS\i386\templates` folder. This script defines where to put the files, what name to assign to the machine, and controls other aspects of the installation. If any of these files are missing or incorrectly structured, CIW will give an error.

The final CIW screen, called Install.osc, displays the computer name, its GUID, and the RIS server name. Figure 2.10 shows an example.

In the background, the CIW creates a computer account in Active Directory using this same information. By default, the CIW creates the account in the `Computer` container, but you can change this default location. See "Configuring a RIS Server" later in this chapter.

SIS and the SIS Groveler

The title of this section sounds more like a cheap British romance novel than a technical discussion, but the topic is an important one for RIS.

A RIS server can host multiple images. It might have an image for Windows 2000 Professional, one for XP Professional, another for Windows Server 2003, Standard Edition, and still another for Windows Server 2003, Enterprise Edition. In addition, as we'll see in the "Creating RIS Images with Riprep" section, you can use the Riprep tool to create images of existing servers or desktops, further adding to the number of image files on the server.

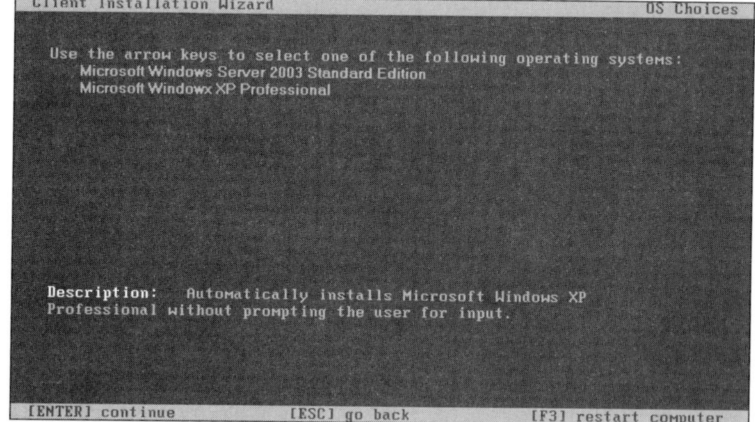

Figure 2.9 RIS Client Installation Wizard—OS Choices screen.

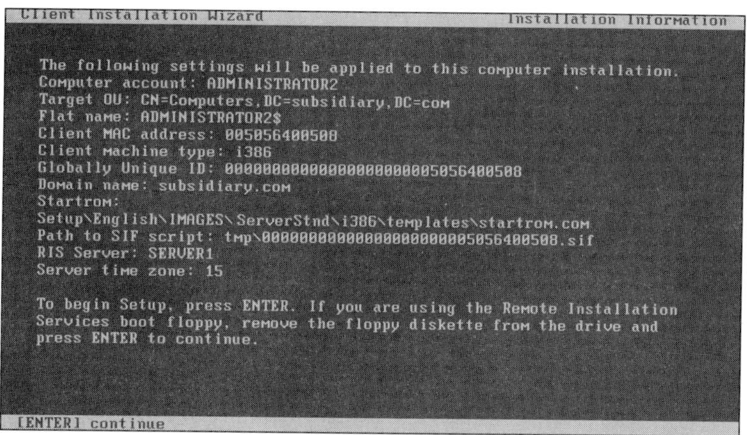

Figure 2.10 RIS Client Installation Wizard—Installation Information screen.

Alternative Startrom Files

The bootstrap image used by RIS client is contained in a file called Startrom.com. This file is located on the RIS server in the folder `\RemoteInstall\OSChooser\I386`. This is the path and filename given by the BINL service to the PXE client.

There are alternative Startrom files in the folder. One of them, Startrom.n12, does not require the installer to press F12. By renaming the original Startrom.com and replacing it with the alternative, the PXE client immediately goes into the Client Installation Wizard (CIW) after it gets the BINL acknowledgement.

If there is only one image at the RIS server, the CIW skips the OS Chooser list and goes right to the Install.osc window. So, with the proper setup, an administrator need only press the `Enter` key to start a RIS-based setup.

The `\RemoteInstall\OS Chooser\I386` folder contains four other alternative Startrom files that are used when installing RIS on a *headless server* (a server without a mouse, keyboard, or video adapter). See section, "Using RIS for Headless Server Installations," later in this chapter for more information.

As you might imagine, these file-based images can consume a lot of disk real estate very quickly. Many of the files are redundant, though, so to reduce the rate of sprawl, Microsoft included a Single Instance Storage (SIS) that shares one copy of a file among the images that use it. The service is called the SIS Groveler, or Grovel.exe.

The SIS Groveler service runs separately from RIS. It maintains a folder called `SIS Common Store` at the root of the partition that holds the RIS files. The folder has the `Hidden` and `System` attributes set, making it a *superhidden* file. You can set group policies that prevent users from viewing superhidden files.

When you install two or more images on a RIS server, the SIS Groveler uses the idle time of the server to analyze the files and find those that are identical. It first catalogs the files by name and takes a *hash* of each file to act as a signature. The hashing algorithm is very sensitive to differences between files. If one bit is different, the signatures will be radically different.

Next, SIS decides which files are identical and compares them byte-by-byte. If the comparison validates that the files are identical, SIS copies the file from the two images to the SIS Common Store. It renames the file to a name that uses a GUID format (making it unique) and makes note of its origins in a database located in the same folder.

Identifying Reparse Points

From a command line, you can determine if a file is real or a reparse point using the Fsutil utility. The syntax is as follows:

```
fsutil reparsepoint query <file_name>
```

Unfortunately, Fsutil does not accept wildcards nor will it report on an entire directory of files. A better tool for this purpose is the *Remote Storage File Analysis* utility, RSDIR, from the Resource Kit. This utility is designed to look for reparse points associated with the Hierarchical Storage Management (HSM) system, but it will also show reparse points created by SIS. Just run RSDIR in a directory to get a listing of the files and their attributes. An example listing looks like this:

```
non-HSM    A------P--Z    0   78716   NA lanma256.bmp
```

The `P` means the file is a reparse point, and the `Z` means it is a sparse file. The logical file size is 78716 bytes, but its actual size is zero.

Finally, SIS replaces the file in the original folders with a *reparse point* of the same name. A reparse point uses a special NTFS record structure to point at a target file or folder. In the Explorer shell, when you view a reparse point, you see the contents of the target file or folder. The replaced files are also configured as *sparse* files, meaning that they report the same file size without actually taking up the space. See Chapter 15 for more information about reparse points and sparse files.

The SIS Groveler calculates how much idle time is available for it to do its work. The initial analysis takes a few hours, so don't expect to see any activity right after you install RIS. If you're in a hurry, you can force SIS to work in the foreground with standard resource sharing until it has analyzed and processed all files. This is done with the GROVCTRL utility. The syntax is `grovctrl f`.

The GROVCTRL utility is not installed by default. You must expand it from the GROVCTRL.EX_ file in the I386 folder on the Windows Server 2003 CD. You can also use it to initiate a volume scan, pause and continue, or stop and start the service.

SIS and File Recovery

It's important to keep the actions of SIS Groveler in mind because they impact your backup and recovery planning. Only backup utilities that use the Windows Server 2003 or Windows 2000 backup API understand reparse points and sparse files. In addition, to ensure proper handling of SIS files, Microsoft included a special filter DLL that exposes function calls that must be used to back up and restore files in the SIS `Common Files` folder. The backup utility must know that this DLL exists and use it when accessing SIS files.

It is also very important to have the SIS Groveler service running before you do a restore of the RIS files on a partition. The service coordinates with the backup DLL to ensure that reparse points are installed correctly. If you are transferring images to another server via tape restore, you can install RIS and then run `Risetup -check` to create the RIS folder structure and start the SIS Groveler.

RIS Setup Scripts

RIS uses a *Setup Information File* (SIF) to control where and how the file-based image is applied to a target drive. This SIF is structured similarly to an unattended setup script with a few different sections that are unique to RIS.

The SIF that controls a particular image is located in the image folder itself under `\RemoteInstall\Setup\English\Images\WINDOWS\i386\templates`. You can use Setup Manager (or Notepad, if you're familiar with the script layout and syntax) to create additional SIF scripts. For instance, you could have one script for computers in the IT department and another script for ordinary users.

The Client Installation Wizard (CIW) lists all the SIF scripts it finds in the templates folder. It uses a short `Description` entry and a `Help` entry in the script to give information about the script's intended use. When the person doing the installation selects the script, it is copied to `\RemoteInstall\tmp` and renamed using the GUID algorithm to ensure it is unique. The client downloads this script along with the setup files and it is used to guide Setup in its chores.

In addition to customizing the contents of the SIF using Setup Manager, you can capture information from the installer with custom windows in CIW. You can define up to 64 variables that can be instantiated in CIW then applied to entries in the SIF.

For example, let's say you want to use RIS to install the retail versions of Windows Server 2003, Standard Edition. This means you cannot include the Product Key in the SIF because it must be different for each installation. You can code a custom OSC file to ask for the Product Key in a CIW window and put the response in an environment variable. Then, in the SIF, set the `ProductID` equal to that environment variable. For example,

```
[UserData]
ProductID = %ProdKey%
```

See the previous section, "Creating an Unattended Setup Script," for details on using Setup Manager. When you use Setup Manager to build a RIS answer file, the wizard displays an option to specify the `Setup Information File Text`. This is where you would set `Description` and `Help` entries for display by the CIW.

Customizing CIW Screens

Because the screens displayed by the CIW during a RIS installation are simply text-based OSC files, they can be tailored to suit your particular needs. The markup language used to construct the OSC files displayed by the CIW is called OSCML, for *OS Chooser Markup Language*.

OSCML is a subset of HTML 2.0. Like HTML, you can define variables using OSCML, but a few have been reserved. See the sidebar, "OSCML Reserved Variables," for a list. Here is an example of how you can use those variables.

By default, when the CIW creates a computer account for a RIS client, it puts the account in the `cn=Computers` container. You can set a different default container as part of the RIS server parameters, but all computer accounts will be created in that OU. Sometimes you want the flexibility of defining where the account will be created.

You could tailor the installation by creating a new OSC file. Call it CHOOSEOU.OSC, although any 8.3 name would be satisfactory. Copy the contents of another OSC for a template. Replace the body with short form that asks for an entry from the user:

```
<FORM ACTION="WARNING">
OU to create computer account: <INPUT NAME="MACHINEOU" MAXLENGTH=255>
</FORM>
```

The user input collected by the `Input` command will be placed in the `Machineou` variable. The form action sends the user to the Warning.osc window after pressing `Enter`. This warns about erasing the hard disk and is displayed just prior to the Install.osc screen where Setup is initiated. You can view the results of Chooseou.osc by modifying Install.osc to display the contents of the `Machineou` variable.

OSCML Reserved Variables

Here is a list of the OSCML variables that have been reserved for a specific use:

- **Language**. Defines the language of the OSC files.
- **Suberror**. Used for error handling.
- **Machineou**. The container where the computer account will be created.
- **Machinename**. The display name of the computer account in Active Directory, such as SERVER1.
- **Netbiosname**. The SAM-Account-Name assigned to the computer. This is the MACHINENAME with a $ suffix, such as SERVER1$.
- **Servername**. The name of the RIS server.
- **Serverdomain**. The domain to which the RIS server belongs.
- **Machinedomain**. The domain the RIS client will attempt to join.
- **Bootfile**. The path to the Startrom.com file at the server.
- **Siffile**. The path to the SIF file. By default, this is the temp file copied from the image template folder.
- **Options**. A variable for holding the results of an Enum command, which lists the SIF files in a given folder.
- **Syspreppath**. The path to the source of a Riprep image.
- **Sysprepdrivers**. The path to Riprep drivers used for PnP.
- **Installpath**. The path to the folder holding the initial installation image files. This is sometimes called the "flat" image.
- **MAC**. The MAC address of the client.
- **GUID**. The GUID of the client. For RBFG clients, there will be 20 zeros and the MAC address.
- **Machinetype**. The client hardware, which would be I386 for an Intel machine.
- **Username, Password, Userdomain**. Used to perform authentication. Password is not stored at server and is overwritten in memory at the client.
- **Timezone**. The server's time zone.

Figure 2.11 shows a custom CIW window that uses several of these variables to display information to the installer.

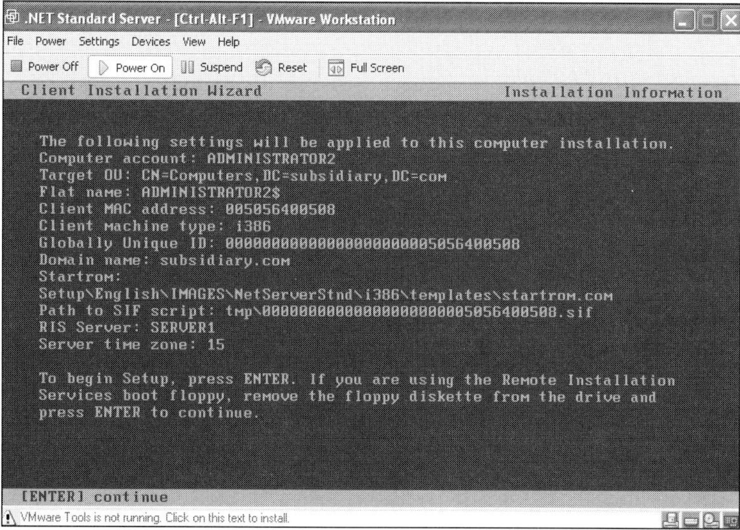

Figure 2.11 RIS Client Installation Wizard—Custom screen using OSCML variables.

You can also check the results of your work at the Install.osc window by going to the domain controller and opening the AD Users & Computers console to verify that the computer account was created in the OU you selected.

Creating RIS Images with Riprep

RIS is a great way to perform a clean install of the operating system, but leaves you with the chore of installing applications. You can avoid this chore by using a utility that comes with RIS called Riprep. The Riprep utility creates an image of an existing server or desktop that is copied to the RIS server and made available as an option in OS Chooser. Like Sysprep, the Riprep image preserves the application files and their Registry settings.

Riprep creates file-based images, not sector-based images such as those created by Ghost or DriveImage. Its primary advantage over the sector-based imaging products (other than its price) is that the resultant image is not as dependent on similar hardware. Riprep images are superior to images created by the other file-based imaging utility, Sysprep, for the same reason. The only hardware dependency in a Riprep image is the Hardware Abstraction Layer (HAL) driver. An image from a machine with an ACPI HAL cannot be installed on a machine with a non-ACPI HAL. Windows Server 2003 can determine a suitable HAL for the client and modify the Riprep image accordingly.

The reason that a Riprep image can be so flexible is that it obtains files from a standard CD-based installation image. This so-called "flat" image contains the additional files that fill in the gaps on a machine that doesn't have similar hardware as the original machine.

Using Riprep

Start by configuring a server or desktop exactly as you'd like it to work. Install any applications you want to run. All files must be on the same partition that holds the Windows system files (`\Windows` or `\Winnt` directory). Riprep can only image the system partition.

Also, by default, RIS takes the entire boot drive as the operating system partition. The target drive for the Riprep image must be at least as big as the source drive. You'll need 2GB for the operating system plus necessary free space. Allot additional space to applications. Don't create an image on a partition that will be too big to fit on your other servers.

When the source machine is ready for Riprep imaging, proceed as directed in Procedure 2.5.

Procedure 2.5 Using Riprep to Image a Windows Server 2003

1. At the server you want to image, map a drive to the `REMINST` share on the RIS server.
2. Navigate to the `\Admin\I386` folder.
3. Run Riprep. The Remote Installation Preparation Wizard opens.
4. Click `Next`. The Server Name window opens. Enter the fully qualified DNS name of the server. (You can use the flat name if you are sure that the DNS resolver will append the correct DNS domain.)
5. Click `Next`. The Folder Name window opens. Enter the folder name where you want to place the files at the RIS server. Do not enter a path. RIS will resolve the path for you.
6. Click `Next`. The Friendly Description and Help Text window opens. Enter a descriptive name for the image that will help someone to select it from the Client Installation Wizard.
7. Click `Next`. The Report System Compatibility window opens. This window reports if elements of the image may not work correctly with RIS. Correct any problems and then start over.
8. Click `Next`. The Stop Services window opens. This window lists the local services that must be stopped while the RIS image is built. The list comes from a Riprep.INF file in the same folder as Riprep.
9. Click `Next`. The Stop Services window shows each service as it stops. If an error is encountered, it will be listed in a Riprep.LOG file in `\RemoteInstall\Setup\English\Images\<Riprep_Image>\i386`.
10. If you have applications open, the Programs or Services Running window opens to prompt you to close them.
11. Click `Next`. The Review Settings window opens. Check the entries to ensure they are correct.
12. Click `Next`. Riprep processes the request and begins copying files to the RIS server. This may take a while depending on your network speed.

Riprep Scripts

When Riprep images a disk, it creates a folder named with the short name of the image. A `Mirror1` subfolder under that main folder contains the installation files. Riprep also creates a `Templates` folder that contains a Riprep.sif file that acts as the mini-setup script for the image.

You can tailor this script to modify the image installation. If you need to make changes to the image files themselves, you must install the image on a machine, change the files, then re-image the machine.

Riprep Requirements

Here is a recap of the Riprep requirements mentioned elsewhere in this section:

- **Only boot partition imaged.** Only the partition with the Windows system files (`\Windows` or `\Winnt`) is included in the image. If you have separate data partitions, you must deal with them in a separate process.
- **Pre-existing flat image.** RIS depends on the installation files in a flat image to perform initial functions on a machine. You cannot Riprep a machine until you create a flat image from the CD of the same operating system.
- **Drive size.** The hard drive of the target machine must be at least as big or bigger than the hard drive of the imaged machine. This is because the image stores a copy of the partition boot sector from the imaged machine. RIS can expand a partition beyond the partition size in the boot sector, but it cannot make it smaller.
- **Matching HAL.** The target machine must use the same HAL as the imaged machine.

Creating PXE Boot Disks

Only machines built to the PC97 standards or later will support PXE booting. If you have an older machine, you can still use RIS as long as the machine contains an Ethernet controller that supports PXE booting or a network adapter with a PXE-compatible Ethernet controller.

You can build a PXE boot disk using the *Remote Boot Floppy Generator* utility, RBFG, in the `\RemoteInstall\Admin\I386` folder. Figure 2.12 shows an example of the RBFG interface. The `Adapters` button opens a window that lists the supported adapters.

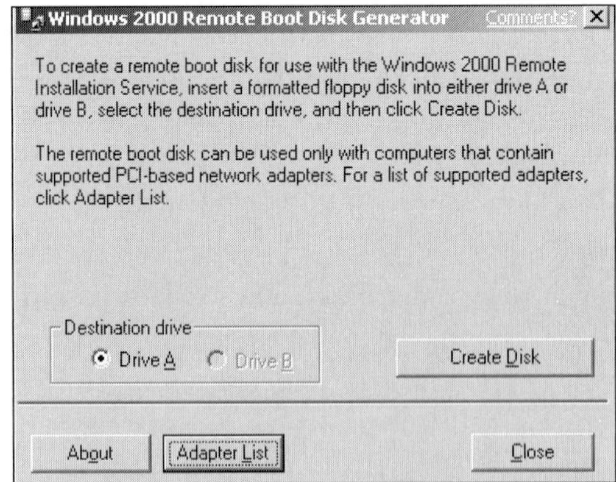

Figure 2.12 Remote Boot Disk Generator main window.

There's only one small caveat to using the PXE boot floppy rather than booting to a true BIOS-based PXE session. The network card has no GUID, so the computer account created by the CIW will only use the MAC address for the GUID padded with 20 leading zeros. This means that if you move the network card to another machine and attempt to do a RIS installation, you will get a "duplicate GUID" error.

If this happens, you must delete the original computer object. If the computer object is still in use by the original computer but you swapped out the network card, you can use the ADSI Editor from the Support Tools to change the `RemoteBoot-GUID` attribute to match the new MAC address. Obtain the MAC address by running `ipconfig /all` from the command line.

RIS Volume Requirements

Like any remote booting service, RIS depends on an image file loaded across the network to the remote boot clients. RIS gets persnickety about the disk volumes that hold the boot image. The following rules apply:

- The volume cannot be the same as that holding the Windows Server 2003 system files.
- The volume must be formatted NTFS.
- You'll need at least 800MB–1000MB of free space.

If you do not meet these requirements, RIS will not work correctly and you'll end up redoing a lot of work.

Installing RIS

To install the RIS driver files, follow the steps given in Procedure 2.6.

Procedure 2.6 Installing Remote Installation Services

1. Select a server to host the RIS boot images. The server itself does not need to be a domain controller, but it must be a member server of a Windows Server 2003 domain.
2. In Control Panel, open `Add/Remove Programs`.
3. Click `Configure Windows`. The Add or Remove Windows Components window opens.
4. Click `Components`. The Windows Server 2003 Components window opens.
5. Select `Remote Installation Services` and click `Next`. The installer does its work and then prompts you to restart. Do so.

This only installs the services and support files on the server. You still need to install and configure a RIS image.

RIS Image Configuration

After installing RIS, to configure a remote installation image, follow the steps given in Procedure 2.7.

Procedure 2.7 Configuring a Remote Installation Services Image

1. Insert a Setup CD for the operating system you want to use for an image. Supported operating systems include Windows 2000 Professional and Server and Advanced Server; XP Professional; and Windows Server 2003, Enterprise Edition.
2. Launch START | PROGRAMS | ADMINISTRATIVE TOOLS | REMOTE INSTALLATION SERVICES SETUP. This starts the Remote Installation Wizard, Risetup.
3. The Welcome window opens. If the server is not a member of a Windows Server 2003 domain, or cannot find the domain controller in DNS, Risetup will fail with an error telling you that the domain could not be located. If the directory configuration for the RIS server is incorrect, the client may not be able to find the RIS, and you will get a similar error.
4. Click `Next`. The Remote Installation Services Options window opens. Select `Add A New OS Image To This Remote Installation Server`.
5. Click `Next`. The Installation Source Files Location window opens. Enter the drive letter of the CD.
6. Click `Next`. The Windows Installation Image Folder Name window opens. Enter the name you want to assign to the image folder on the RIS server. An example is `Adv_Srvr`.

RIS Service Management

If you have existing remote boot clients in your network, or you have another RIS server, you may want to leave the RIS service disabled until you're ready to initiate deployment.

Also, you must stop and start RIS every time you make the slightest change in the image or the RIS configuration. You'll be making lots of changes at first, so it's easier to leave the service disabled until you're ready to use it.

7. Click `Next`. The Friendly Description and Help Text window opens. Enter names that help identify the image from the list in the Client Installation Wizard (CIW).
8. Click `Next`. If you already have images on the RIS server, you'll be asked how you want to deal with the existing CIW screens. Select `Use The Old Client Installation Screens` unless you want to overwrite them.
9. Click `Next`. The Review Settings window opens. If you made a mistake in any of the previous windows, now is the time to change it.
10. Click `Finish`. Risetup now copies files from the Windows Server 2003 Workstation CD to the `RIS` directory. You'll get an informative checklist showing the progress. The last item on the checklist is `Starting the Remote Installation Service`.

Configuring a RIS Server

There is no separate MMC console for managing RIS. All configurations are performed using the computer object in Active Directory. Procedure 2.8 shows how to configure the server.

Procedure 2.8 Configuring a Remote Installation Services Server

1. Load the `AD Users and Computers` console from START | PROGRAMS | ADMINISTRATIVE TOOLS.
2. Find the computer icon for the server running RIS.
3. Right-click the icon and select PROPERTIES from the flyout menu. The Properties window opens.
4. Select the `Remote Install` tab.
5. Click `Advanced Settings`. The Remote Installation Services Properties window opens (see Figure 2.13).
6. In the `New Clients` tab, under `Automatic Computer Naming`, click the combo box under `Generate Client Computer Names Using` (see Figure 2.14). See the sidebar, "Custom Computer Names and RIS," for information about what to select here.
7. Under `Computer Account Location`, select `A Specific Directory Service Location`.

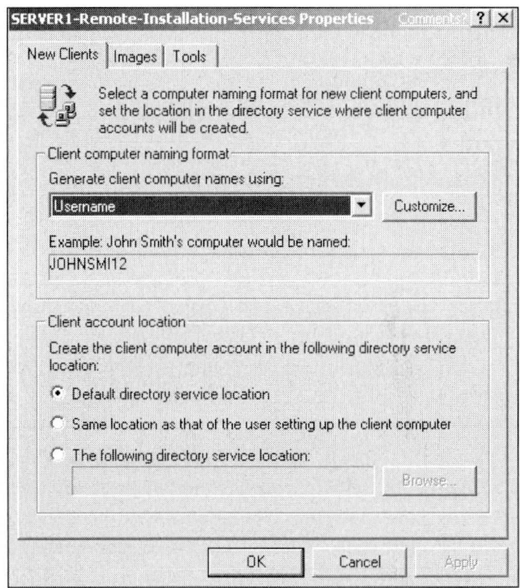

Figure 2.13 Remote Installation Services Properties—Advanced Settings window.

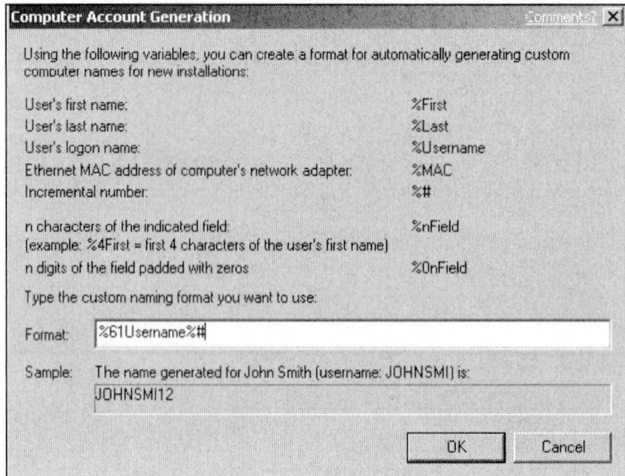

Figure 2.14 Computer Account Generation window.

8. Click `Browse` and select a container where you want the computer objects created by this RIS server to be placed.
9. Select the `OS Images` tab. The list contains the names of images you have configured with Risetup, Riprep, or custom SIF files you have created with Setup Manager.
10. If you want to add a new flat image, put the Windows Server 2003 CD in the CD-ROM drive and click `Add`.
11. Click `OK` to return to the `Remote Install` tab under `Properties`.
12. Click `OK` to save all changes and close the window.
13. Go to a command prompt. Stop and start the BINLSVC service as follows:

```
NET STOP BINLSVC
NET START BINLSVC
```

Custom Computer Names and RIS

RIS has several options for automatically naming computers. Some of these options involve associating a computer name with a username. This is rarely a good idea in large organizations where computers get traded regularly between users. A better choice, if you want automatic naming, is to use the MAC address. This is a clean way to get a unique name that won't change unless you change the network adapter.

The default naming format prefixes the MAC address with the letters `NP`. A character-based prefix is important because some TCP/IP utilities, such as Ping, do not work if the host name starts with a numeral.

Instead of `NP`, you might want to preface the MAC address with two or three letters that designate the workstation's location. Click `Advanced` to change the prefix. Prefixes help sort out workstations on Browse lists. They aren't required for directory browsing because you'll probably put workstations into local containers; until you have completed the transition to Active Directory, however, you should make provision for classic NT browsing.

Controlling Access to RIS Images

You probably don't want users or visitors to accidentally or deliberately image their machines. A machine should not commence a PXE boot unless all other media have failed, but it's a strange universe and all sorts of inexplicable things happen.

You can take several precautions to protect your images from accidental download. First, you can set permission on the images so that only members of a selected group can see them. If there are no images available to OS Chooser, CIW will error out. Procedure 2.9 shows how to set the permissions.

Procedure 2.9 Setting Permissions on RIS Images

1. Load the `AD Users and Computers` console from START | PROGRAMS | ADMINISTRATIVE TOOLS.
2. Find the computer icon for the server running RIS.
3. Right-click the icon and select PROPERTIES from the flyout menu. The Properties window opens.
4. Select the `Remote Install` tab.
5. Click `Advanced Settings`.
6. Select the `Images` tab.
7. Highlight an image and click `Properties`. This opens the Properties window for the SIF file representing the image.
8. Click `Permissions` and then select the `Security` tab.
9. Set the permissions to permit or deny access to the image. Anyone not permitted access to the SIF file will not see the image in the CIW.

You can also restrict a RIS server to distribute images only to computers that have been pre-staged for RIS installation. This permits you to be selective with the machines that can accept an image. For example, you might not want to image a certain class of machine, and by not pre-staging them, you avoid accidental drive erasure.

Pre-staging involves designating a computer object as "managed" in Active Directory. This requires that Active Directory contain a computer object and an associated GUID for each computer that will be given a BINL offer.

The simplest way to pre-stage the computer is to walk through a RIS installation right up to the Install.osc screen, the final information screen where the computer name, RIS server name, and GUID are displayed, using a RIS server in your lab that is configured to distribute images to any client. As part of the Install.osc window, the CIW creates the computer object and populates it with the GUID taken from the PXE network interface. You then stop the machine and deliver it to the deployment team, where it can start the RIS install again on the floor from a RIS server that has been configured to accept requests only from "managed" clients.

As an alternative, you can jot down the GUID from the computer's CMOS, create the computer object, and type the GUID manually into the object's Properties window.

Verifying RIS Server Configurations

The Remote Install properties for a RIS server in Active Directory contain a `Verify Server` button. This button starts Risetup to check the contents of the top-level RIS folders and then starts the RIS-related services BINLSVC and Groveler. It does not verify the contents of the image folders and it does not verify the OSC files. You can perform the same operations by running `Risetup -verify` from the command line.

Controlling RIS with Group Policies

As we'll see in Chapter 12, it's possible to control nearly every facet of system operation with group policies in one way or another. Some group policies make their mark in the Registry. Others, like sinister political operatives, make changes to the security database that controls permissions and privileges on a machine. One group policy controls elements of the Client Installation Wizard. Access the policy as described in Procedure 2.10.

Procedure 2.10 Accessing the Remote Installation Group Policy

1. Open the `AD Users & Computers` console.
2. Right-click the domain icon and select PROPERTIES from the flyout menu. This opens the Properties window.
3. Select the `Group Policy` tab.
4. Double-click the `Default Domain Policy` to open the Group Policy Editor snap-in.
5. Drill down to USER CONFIGURATION | WINDOWS SETTINGS | REMOTE INSTALLATION SERVICES.
6. In the right pane, double-click the `Choice Options` icon. This opens the Choice Options Properties window.

The `Remote Installation` group policy has four options, all of which are applied depending on the location of the user object in Active Directory. Because we've opened the `Default Domain` policy, any user in the domain would be bound by the settings made here. Here are the options:

- **`Automatic Setup.`** This is the default operation of the CWI. The user gets the settings defined in Active Directory for the RIS server. Disabling this policy means that the user will get the Custom Setup window in the CWI.

- **`Custom Setup.`** This option enables showing an additional window in the CWI where the installer can input a computer name and OU. These options override the AD settings for the RIS server.
- **`Restart Setup.`** This option enables the user to commence a RIS transaction using the inputs that were entered prior to loss of connection. This option does *not* affect the graphical portion of Setup. If you proceed beyond the text-mode portion of Setup and you select this option, you will overwrite everything downloaded previously. That is the reason it is disabled by default.
- **`Tools.`** Third parties and Microsoft can develop tools that could run in the real-mode environment of PXE. For example, 3Com has a set of tools for modifying the RIS menus so you can change adapter settings and flash the system BIOS using RIS. Part of enabling those tools involves changing this policy from its default setting of `Disabled` to `Enabled`.

Using RIS for Headless Server Installations

A headless server has no mouse, no keyboard, and no video adapter. It sits in its rack like a leaf on a tree, doing work and producing output without any noticeable external activity other than a flashing LED or two.

Most IT shops have server rooms that conserve space and power by sharing a single Keyboard/Video/Mouse (KVM) among various servers using a KVM switch. There is a long list of vendors who have cunning solutions that pack features and flexibility into their KVM switches.

Still, the ideal would be to need no KVM at all. This is the concept behind headless servers. All server management is done via terminal services sessions (called Remote Desktop in Windows Server 2003) and command-line consoles such as telnet. Windows Server 2003 is designed to facilitate headless operation as much as possible. There is a large number of new command-line utilities that simplify telnet management and boatloads of scripting features.

Still, there's a chicken-and-egg problem to overcome. How do you get the operating system loaded on a headless server? Sure, you can install a video card and connect the server to a KVM switch long enough to run RIS or Sysprep, but there's something aesthetically displeasing about this approach, isn't there? A headless server should be headless from the beginning, a true species and not some guillotined apparition.

Windows Server 2003 supports operating system installation on a headless server via RIS and a suite of features collectively called *Emergency Management Services*, or EMS. One EMS feature is the capability to redirect text-based output from the console during startup and setup to a COM port. You can connect a modem to the COM port (or a port from a classic serial port terminal server) and make Out-of-Band (OOB) connection to the server. Using this OOB connection, you can make your selections in the Client Installation Wizard to kick off the RIS installations.

Configuring RIS for Headless Servers

Recall that a PXE client will initiate a RIS session automatically if there is no media with an operating system. All that's necessary, then, is a way to tell the PXE client to redirect its output to a COM port. This is done using a special Startrom image.

Open the `\RemoteInstall\OS Chooser\I386` folder on a RIS server and look at the files. You'll see four that start with HDLS*, for Headless. HDLSCOM1.COM redirects output to the COM1 port and HDLSCOM2 does the same for COM2. The *.N12 versions permit you to skip pressing F12, which is something you will want to skip because many terminal emulators don't know how to pass F12 on to its peer. Follow the steps in Procedure 2.11 to run Setup on a headless server using RIS.

Procedure 2.11 Using RIS to Run Setup on a Headless Server

1. Connect a null-modem cable between the COM ports of the management computer and the headless server.
2. At the RIS server, rename Startrom.com to another name and rename HDLSCOM1.N12 to Startrom.com.
3. Launch a terminal emulator console on the PC that is connected (logically or physically) to the COM1 port on the server and make the connection.
4. When that's ready, start the server with no operating system on any bootable media. (If you have a server that supports OOB control of the hardware or true Wake-On-LAN, you could do this startup from a distance, as well.)
5. In the console, you should see the server start its PXE boot. Then, when it contacts a DHCP and RIS server, it will bring up the Welcome screen of the CIW. (There's no need to press F12 because of the Startrom version we picked.)
6. Walk through the CIW. When you're ready to start the installation, press `Enter` and watch the fun.

You'll only be able to see the text-based portions of Setup. At some point, like the Apollo astronauts hitting the atmosphere at reentry, you'll lose OOB contact. If everything goes well (meaning that you have configured the RIS setup script correctly and there are no hardware glitches), about 30 to 40 minutes later, Setup should be complete.

All Windows Servers come with a two-session version of Remote Desktop as a standard component of the operating system. You must log on with administrator credentials to use one of these sessions. As soon as Setup has completed and the machine restarts for the final time, you should be able to make a Remote Desktop connection so you can make your final configurations.

Administrative Mode Terminal Services

In Windows 2000, only administrators were given permission to use the two-session Terminal Services connections to manage a server. In Windows Server 2003, access to this feature is controlled by the Remote Desktop Users group. Anyone you put in this group can gain access to a server if he has sufficient privileges.

RIS Summary

If you need a fast, convenient way to deploy large numbers of servers and desktops with diverse hardware specifications, RIS is definitely worth the time to configure. Common problems include the following:

- Failure to authorize the RIS server in Active Directory. Without authorization, the BINL service will not respond to Discovery packets.
- Not running RIS on a server that is in the same broadcast segment as the client or failure to configure DHCP helpers on intervening routers.
- Not installing the proper "flat" image from CD prior to running Riprep.
- Failure to properly back up and restore SIS files.
- Trying to use older PXE clients. The client should be running PXE version .99 or later.
- Trying to image multiple partitions using Riprep.
- Trying to apply a Riprep image to a machine with a smaller hard drive than the original machine.
- Changing the RIS group policy without informing colleagues who might be affected.

Moving Forward

The plan of this book is to move methodically through a complete deployment of Windows Server 2003 in an enterprise. Getting the OS installed on the server is a good start, but there's still a long way to go. We still have TCP/IP support services such as DNS and DHCP to configure, security to set up, Active Directory domains to deploy, shared resources to make available, users to manage, and disasters to plan for.

Before jumping too far ahead, there are a few final touches regarding installation that need attention. The next chapter covers making hardware changes subsequent to the initial installation and troubleshooting problems that might come up along the way.

3
Adding Hardware

BUILDING A PRODUCTION-QUALITY SERVER TAKES TIME. You can automate the installation and testing processes to a large extent, but by the time you're done prepping the RAID array, installing the operating system, partitioning and formatting the data drives, layering on the applications, setting permissions, and verifying that everything works the way your users expect, you've made your way through the better part of a morning.

Even if you take care to anticipate the future needs of the users, the time inevitably comes when you have to add new hardware or update a driver or replace a failed component. You might need a second processor to speed up a slow SQL server or an additional drive to accommodate data growth or a new network adapter with multiple interfaces to speed up a terminal server. Doing this kind of work on a production server requires a little planning. You don't want to interrupt users during working hours, and you sure don't want to create a circumstance where the server doesn't come back online after you've made your changes.

Every piece of hardware has its own idiosyncrasies to which every server reacts in a unique way. It is not possible to cover all the potential perturbations. This chapter introduces the Windows Server 2003 architecture as it pertains to hardware operability then covers the features for installing new devices and troubleshooting them when something goes wrong. It also covers the device management and compatibility features on Intel 64-bit (IA64) platforms and compares them to standard Intel 32-bit platforms (IA32).

New Features in Windows Server 2003

The most significant differences in hardware support come from the IA64 versions of Windows Server 2003. This includes the following:

- New memory architecture to support a larger address space
- Support for 64-bit device architectures such as PCI-X (this support is also included higher-end IA32 systems)
- Improved drive partitioning using GUID Partition Tables (GPT) rather than legacy Master Boot Record (MBR) partitioning
- Application interoperability using the Windows32-on-Windows64 (WOW64) emulator
- Registry and system file interoperability so that 32-bit and 64-bit versions of the same applications don't conflict with each other

Beyond the support for an entirely new platform, the watchwords for hardware support in Windows Server 2003 are sustainability and recoverability:

- **Driver Protection.** A new database has been introduced in Windows Server 2003 that acts as a "bad-boy" list of drivers that are known to cause problems. If you attempt to install a device using one of these drivers, the system prompts you with a warning and refuses to do the installation. The list is kept current via Windows Update. For details, see `www.microsoft.com/hwdev/driver/drv protect.htm`.
- **Windows Update.** This feature was first introduced in Windows 2000 and has been improved in Windows Server 2003. You can choose to automatically download digitally signed updates from Microsoft or you can download them manually to a central server for evaluation and testing prior to internal deployment. The Software Update Service (SUS) from Microsoft automates the download of updates to a central server where they can be deployed after testing.
- **Driver Rollback.** If you upgrade a device driver and the server becomes unstable, you can use Driver Rollback to return to the old driver. This is an improvement over the Last Known Good Configuration gambit, which restores the pre-existing Registry entries but not the drivers themselves.
- **Larger Registry size.** The Registry size in Windows Server 2003 is limited only by the available space on the operating system volume. Previous versions of Windows, including Windows 2000, imposed a Registry size limit (RSL) of about 80 percent of paged pool memory. This change significantly improves the scalability of terminal servers, where each concurrent user has a copy of the user profile loaded in memory.

- **New Registry structure.** Related portions of the Registry (called *cells*) are now kept closer together, with better support for large cells. This improves seek and load times.
- **Improved debugging**. Changes to the kernel and kernel-mode debugging tools have improved the ability of developers to tighten their code. We, as system administrators, benefit because we can use the same tools for troubleshooting.
- **Improved memory usage**. Changes to the way paged pool memory is allocated in Windows Server 2003 greatly conserves memory and makes it possible to handle very large files during backups. Also, the system now allocates identical 4K memory pages by assignment rather than by copying, which prevents applications such as web services from using lots of memory doling out the same information to different users. The total number of contiguous memory pages has been doubled to improve support for terminal servers and applications that require large datasets.
- **Large driver support**. The amount of memory available to a driver has been increased from about 200K in Windows 2000 to 1GB in Windows Server 2003. This improvement is especially good news for video adapter manufacturers.
- **Hot memory addition**. High-availability servers such as Stratus ftServers and the new IBM Summit technology servers give administrators the ability to add memory while a machine is running. Windows Server 2003 supports this feature by dynamically resizing memory when the new RAM is added. This does not work in reverse, however. If memory must be removed for swapping, the server must be shut down.
- **Improved multiprocessor support**. Classic Symmetric Multiprocessor (SMP) servers share their processors on a single bus, which creates bottlenecks. Newer servers use a cache-coherent Non-Uniform Memory Allocation (ccNUMA) scheme for sharing processors. In ccNUMA, processors are married to RAM that is physically situated nearby. These sections of closely allied CPU and RAM connect to each other via a series of crossbars in much the same way that cities in southern California are connected together by freeways. Windows Server 2003 supports ccNUMA architecture by allocating memory calls between "near" memory and "far" memory so that threads and memory stay in the same location.
- **Improved DMA handling**. If you have advanced ATA drives that take advantage of the fast transfer speeds provided by UltraDMA (Direct Memory Access), you'll be happy to know that Windows Server 2003 does a much better job of determining the correct DMA mode for a device than earlier Windows operating systems. Also, Windows Server 2003 dynamically evaluates the DMA performance

of a device and shifts it to PIO (Programmed I/O) operating if it fails DMA too often. This helps maintain support for older CD-ROM devices.

- **Improved Device Removal handling**. Although it is not common to yank components off a running server, you may have servers with removable drives or Universal Serial Bus (USB) peripherals. The proper way to remove a device is to inform the operating system first, but surprise removals are more the rule than the exception. Windows Server 2003 prepares for the surprise removal of drives and drive media by disabling write caching on all removable media drives except IEEE 1394 FireWire.

Functional Description of Windows Server 2003 Architecture

Let's start with a peek behind the curtain to see how Windows Server 2003 is built. This topic focuses on areas of the Windows Server 2003 architecture that affect stability and performance, including memory allocation, legacy application support, memory protection, process protection, I/O handling, and Plug and Play. Each section includes the differences between the IA32 and IA64 versions of Windows Server 2003.

IA32 Memory Management

The IA32 versions of Windows Server 2003 can directly address 2^{32} bytes of memory, or about 4GB. Enterprise and Datacenter Editions can extend this address space. We'll see how that works in a moment.

The 4GB address space is divvied into two 2GB parcels. The upper 2GB is given to the operating system and is called *kernel* memory. The lower 2GB is given to applications and is called *user* memory. This separation of memory prevents badly behaved applications from crashing the system.

Most servers don't have a full 4GB of physical memory, but that doesn't stop Windows Server 2003 from using the entire 4GB address space. An Executive process called the *Virtual Memory Manager* (VMM) makes use of special features in the x86 CPU to map virtual addresses to physical addresses.

VMM acts like a shady real estate dealer who sells the same plot of land several times. It gives each thread its own 4GB of virtual memory, each with the same half-for-the-kernel/half-for-you split. VMM is able to cook the books in this way by shuffling memory into and out of RAM so that processes are completely ignorant of each other.

If VMM had to handle memory in 1-byte chunks, it would be much too slow and require too much overhead. For this reason, it shuffles memory around in 4K *pages*. In addition, Windows Server 2003 supports large memory pages for applications and device drivers that work with large memory images. The size of a large memory page can be set in the Registry, and the default is 4MB.

When a running process needs space in physical memory, VMM looks at the pages owned by other processes and decides which ones have not been used in a while. It moves these pages out of memory and onto disk into one or more paging files. Windows Server 2003 can have up to 16 paging files, each of which must reside on a different logical drive.

The maximum paging file size in Windows Server 2003 is 16TB (that's terabytes). The default paging file size is 150 percent of installed RAM. The paging file size is calculated during Setup and is not resized dynamically if you add memory later. You may want to increase the paging file size if you bump up the memory on a server—if you want to capture the entire contents of memory following a blue screen stop error (bugcheck). See Chapter 21, "Recovering from System Failures," for details.

IA64 Memory Management

The 64-bit (IA64) version of Windows Server 2003 has a theoretical address space of 2^{64} bytes, or 16 exabytes (16 million terabytes). However, the Itanium and McKinley processors use a 44-bit address bus, yielding a 16TB virtual memory limit, if you want to call that a limit.

Physical memory on an Itanium platform is further constrained to 16GB per processor because of limitations in the 460GX chipset. The McKinley processor and its accompanying 870 chipset are much more capable. Along with support for more memory, McKinley has a 400MHz bus that is 128 bits wide, compared to the 266MHz, 64-bit bus in Itanium. Also, the L3 cache in McKinley is integrated into the chip package rather than connected as an add-on, yielding a 32Gbps processing bandwidth compared to the 12Gbps bandwidth in Itanium.

Like the IA32 version of Windows Server 2003, the 16TB addressable memory space in an IA64 system is also divided in half, with 8TB given to user applications and 8TB given to the operating system. This seems generous now, but I'm sure in five or six years we'll be grumbling about how you can't get any *real* computing done with only 8TB of user memory.

The Virtual Memory Manager in the IA64 version of Windows Server 2003 has the same job as the IA32 version; it maps the 16TB virtual address space offered to each process into physical RAM. The pipelined design of the IA64 processor is capable of handling a large number of instructions at each clock tick, so the capability to do memory gymnastics is even more important than in IA32. For this reason, Windows Server 2003 uses 8K memory pages in the IA64 version. IA64 also supports large memory pages.

Windows Server 2003 always requires a paging file, even if you have gigabytes upon gigabytes of RAM. The limit on the total number of paging files is 16, the same as IA32, but the maximum size of the paging file is 512TB. The default paging file size is 150 percent of RAM.

IA32 Legacy Application Support

DOS applications running in a 16-bit memory space are supported on IA32 versions of Windows Server 2003 by a special application called the *NT Virtual DOS Machine*, or Ntvdm.exe. NTVDM is a 32-bit application that builds a virtual, 16-bit environment that emulates the BIOS function calls and memory handling of a standard DOS machine. It also provides a 16-bit command interpreter, COMMAND, that complements the 32-bit interpreter, CMD.

16-bit Windows applications are supported by a *Windows16-on-Windows32* (WOW) subsystem, Wowexe.exe, running inside the virtual DOS machine erected by NTVDM. The WOW subsystem intercepts Win16 function calls and converts them to their Win32 counterparts then passes the result to the Windows subsystem, where the function calls are processed and passed back to Wowexe.

By default, individual 16-bit DOS applications run in separate instances of NTVDM, giving them each a separate memory space. Keep this in mind if you have batch files that launch related DOS applications.

Individual 16-bit Windows applications, on the other hand, all run under a single instance of Wowexec by default. You can elect to run a 16-bit Windows application in its own memory space by modifying the properties of a shortcut to the application. Open the `Properties` for the shortcut, select the `Shortcut` tab, and click `Advanced` to open the Advanced Properties window (see Figure 3.1). Select the `Run In Separate Memory Space` option.

If you elect to run a 16-bit application in its own memory space, then a new instance of NTVDM and Wowexec will be generated for each instance of the application. This consumes resources. Also, if you have 16-bit applications that expect to communicate with each other via a shared memory space, you must run these applications in the same instance of Wowexec.

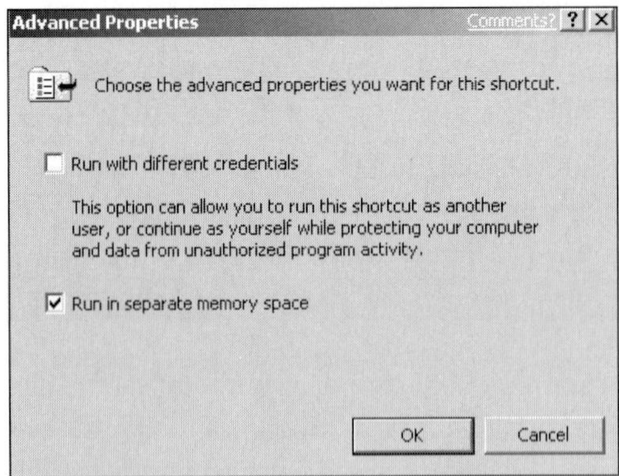

Figure 3.1 Advanced Properties window of a 16-bit application shortcut showing the `Run In Separate Memory Space` option.

IA64 Legacy Application Support

The IA64 version of Windows Server 2003 does not support running 16-bit applications, either DOS apps or 16-bit Windows apps. There is no exception to the "no 16-bit code" rule, but Windows Server 2003 does include a workaround for two setup programs: Microsoft's own Acme installer and the Installshield installer. These setup programs use 16-bit stub code to query for the operating system version. The IA64 version of Windows substitutes a patched 32-bit version of Setup16 for Acme and Setup for Installshield that are called when the installer makes this check. The patch files are located under `\Windows\SysWOW64`.

WOW64

The IA64 version of Windows Server 2003 is happy to support 32-bit applications. A Windows32-on-Windows64 (WOW64) emulator creates a memory environment that simulates the 32-bit addresses and 4K memory pages used by IA32 Windows. WOW64 also intercepts 32-bit function calls and converts them to their 64-bit equivalent for processing by the Windows subsystem.

Unlike the NTVDM/Wowexec pair on an IA32 system, you won't see WOW64 exposed in Task Manager as a separate process. It is implemented as a series of DLLs. The primary work of emulating the operating environment is done by Wow64.dll with Wow64cpu.dll translating the instruction set and Wow64win.dll providing a thunking layer to the kernel side of the Windows subsystem, Win32k.sys. A *thunk* is a function-call conversion. In addition, to aid in troubleshooting, a set of debugging extensions are loaded in Wow64exts.dll.

The chore of providing a full Win32 environment in what is essentially a completely different operating system requires many support services. This means that 32-bit applications running inside the WOW64 emulator consume more than their share of memory and CPU time. For example, consider the two Help and Support Center applications in Windows Server 2003, HelpCtr.exe and HelpSvs.exe. These are among the few applications in the shrink-wrap that have not been ported to native 64-bit versions.

On an IA32 machine, these two applications, taken together, consume about 10MB of memory. On an IA64 system, they combine to take 60MB of actual memory with an overall 82MB virtual memory footprint.

Similar differences exist for all 32-bit applications. In addition, if you run four instances of the same application, the same overhead is added to each instance, making an IA64 server a poor choice for running production terminal services unless the applications run 64-bit code. (The games in the IA64 version have been recompiled as 64-bit code, so you can tell your boss that you are using them for testing.)

Registry Reflection

WOW64 also deals with Registry differences between 32-bit and 64-bit applications. For instance, message queuing and distributed transaction tracking is supported on an IA64 system only for 64-bit applications, so 32-bit applications must not see the associated Registry entries.

To accomplish this and other Registry modifications, IA64 Windows uses a trick stolen from *Snow White and the Seven Dwarves*. It creates a magic mirror that always tells the truth, but only that portion of the truth the viewer wants to hear. Here's how it works.

The Registry on an IA64 machine contains a special key under `HKLM | Software` called `Wow6432Node`. This key contains a replica of the `HKLM | Software` hive with special nips and tucks to accommodate 32-bit applications. WOW64 implements a *Registry reflector* that copies information back and forth between the `HKLM | Software` key and the `HKLM | Software | Wow6432Node` key.

File System Redirection

The folder that holds the operating system files on an IA64 system is named `System32`, just as it is on IA32 systems. Also, most of the operating system files retain the same names even though they have been recompiled as 64-bit applications.

This leaves a 32-bit application with something of a conundrum. If it tries to link to one of the core DLLs in the operating system, it will fail. 32-bit applications cannot use 64-bit DLLs, and vice versa. The system provides a full suite of 32-bit operating system libraries under `\Windows\SysWOW64`, and an application running under WOW64 is redirected to this folder when it makes API calls for support files.

Time will tell how this emulation method fares in production. Microsoft will be forced to implement IA64 service packs that patch both the IA64 code and the IA32 code used by the emulator. Security holes may be found in IA64 applications that cannot be fixed without patching the complementary IA32 files, further complicating hotfixes.

The 32-bit operating system files are stored on the Windows Server 2003 CD in the I386 folder. The 64-bit files are stored in an IA64 folder. The 32-bit files start with W to differentiate them from their 64-bit counterparts. The W is removed when the files are copied to the `\Windows\SysWOW64` folder.

Unsupported Features and Unshipped Applications

A few applications and features are not included in the IA64 versions of Windows Server 2003 that you will find in the IA32 versions. These include the following:

- **Windows Product Activation.** Microsoft feels that the product is not as likely to be pirated.
- **Remote Assistance.** Remote control is available via Remote Desktop, but a user on an IA64 system cannot send an "invitation" for remote assistance.

- **32-bit ActiveX controls.** The 64-bit version of Internet Explorer cannot run 32-bit DLLs and add-ons.
- **Desktop-oriented features.** These include CD burning, Windows Media Player (WMP), Windows Messenger, integrated Zip file handling, and user state migration. You can load WMP and Windows Messenger after initial setup by downloading the latest 32-bit versions from Microsoft's download site.
- **Networking features.** This includes the Network Bridge, support for infrared modems, Internet Connection Sharing, the Home Networking Wizard.
- **Edlin.** A moment of silence, please, for the final passing of this application.

Memory Pools

To prevent user applications from starving the operating system of physical memory, a certain amount of physical memory is set aside for the exclusive use of kernel processes. This memory is allocated in the form of two pools, paged and non-paged:

- **Paged pool memory.** Memory in the paged pool can be swapped to the paging file. The paged pool limit on IA32 systems is 470MB. The limit for IA64 is 128GB. This additional paged pool memory capability helps avoid situations where the system becomes unstable and reports *Out Of Resource* and Remote Procedure Call (RPC) errors when the page pool reaches its limit. Historically, the most common cause of paged pool memory exhaustion has been an overly large Registry, but in both flavors of Windows Server 2003, this is not a problem because the Registry does not consume paged pool memory.
- **Non-paged pool memory.** Memory in the non-paged pool must stay resident in RAM. The system assigns physical memory to the non-paged pool based on the size of the paged pool. The maximum size is 256MB for IA32 versions and 128GB for IA64 versions. Non-paged pool memory is a precious commodity, and developers are encouraged to limit their use of it, but some situations call for keeping memory pages out of the paging file. For instance, the Encrypting File System stores file encryption keys in non-paged pool memory.

You can see the actual and virtual memory used by a process, along with its kernel memory pool allocations, in Task Manager. Select the `Processes` tab then, using VIEW | SELECT COLUMNS from the menu, select the memory elements you want to view. Figure 3.2 shows an example from an IA32 system and Figure 3.3 shows one from an IA64 system.

It is possible for an application or device driver to crash a system by overallocating paged or non-paged pool memory. This can happen in one fell swoop but it is more likely to occur over a period of time as part of a memory leak. Windows Server 2003 improves the resiliency of the operating system against these types of problems by monitoring for inappropriate memory allocations.

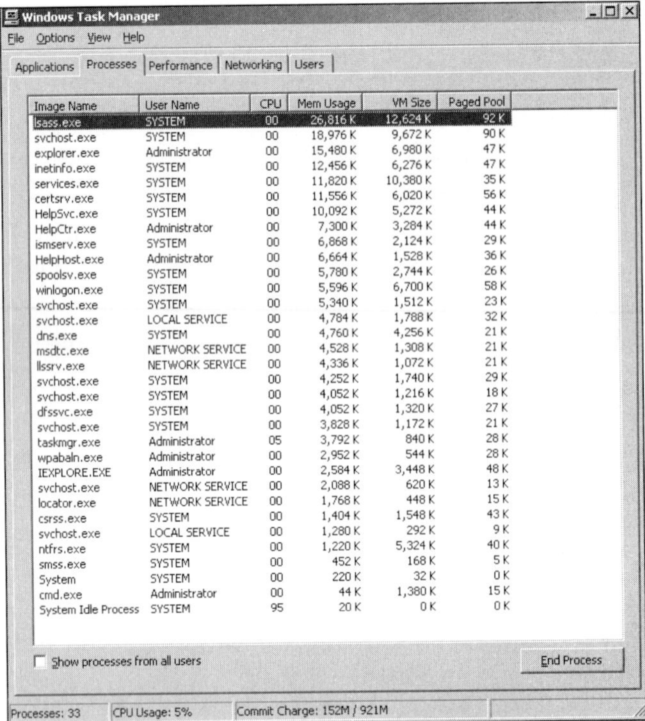

Figure 3.2 Task Manager showing memory allocation for running processes.

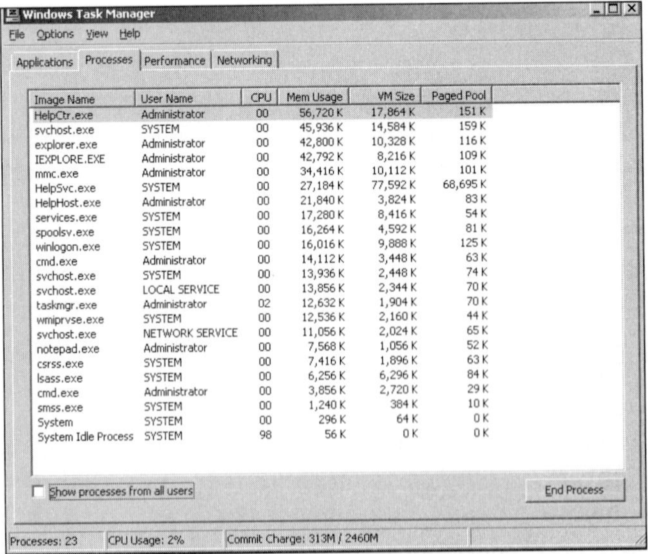

Figure 3.3 Task Manager Processes list showing IA64 memory footprint.

Special IA32 Memory Handling Features

The flat 16TB memory space of IA64 Windows, and its capability to directly address many gigabytes of physical memory, makes it an attractive platform for applications that use large datasets. To take advantage of the additional memory, though, the application must be compiled in native 64-bit code. A 32-bit application running on an IA64 machine is constrained to 2GB. So, until popular applications are released in 64-bit versions, we need ways to extend the memory space available in IA32 systems. This can be done in several ways.

4GB Memory Tuning (4GT)

The 2GB dividing line between user memory and kernel memory is completely arbitrary. The line was drawn at the halfway point to permit the use of a simple "signed bit" algorithm to designate pages as belonging to user space or kernel space.

Although at one time it was unusual to have more than 2GB of physical memory in a server, as of this writing Pricewatch (`www.pricewatch.com`) shows the going price for 512MB DDR DIMMS to be $70, making it a relatively trivial expense to put 4GB of memory in a server. The real limitation nowadays is not the cost of the RAM but the number of DIMM slots on the motherboard and the capacity of the chipset.

If you put 4GB of physical RAM in a server, the operating system does not use more than 1GB of the 2GB set aside for it. If you run an application capable of using more than 2GB of physical memory, the IA32 version of Windows Server 2003 has an option called *4GB Memory Tuning* (4GT) that takes 1GB of virtual memory from the operating system and gives it to user space. This is accomplished by implementing a different page tagging method.

To implement 4GT memory tuning, put a `/3GB` switch on the Advanced RISC Computing (ARC) path that launches the operating system from Boot.ini. The simplest way to do this is to edit the file directly. The BOOTCFG utility does not include an option for installing the `/3GB` switch. Here is a listing that shows the syntax:

```
[boot loader]
timeout=30
default=multi(0)disk(0)rdisk(0)partition(1)\WINDOWS
[operating systems]
multi(0)disk(0)rdisk(0)partition(1)\WINDOWS="Standard Edition" /fastdetect /3GB
```

In Windows 2000, the 4GT option is only supported on Advanced Edition and Datacenter Edition. In Windows Server 2003, it is supported on all IA32 server packages but not on IA64 versions.

There are a few caveats when using 4GT Tuning. For instance, if you run Datacenter Edition and have more than 16GB of physical RAM, you should not use the `/3GB` switch. Also, the `3GB` switch reduces the amount of physical RAM set aside for paged pool memory, and this can cause problems for terminal servers. If you run Exchange 2000, though, you should set the `/3GB` switch even if you have only 1GB of RAM to take advantage of the larger memory images available to files.

Address Windowing Extensions (AWE)

At the end of the *Wizard of Oz*, Dorothy found out that the ruby slippers could have taken her back to Kansas at any time; she just needed to know the trick. You may get the same feeling when I tell you that the Pentium family of processors, starting with Pentium Pro, has always had the capability to access more than 4GB of physical memory. The processor has a 36-bit address range, giving it the capability to access 2^{36} bytes, or 64GB, of physical memory.

Intel has supported this 36-bit addressing capability in a variety of ways. The most current iteration is an Extended Server Memory Architecture that exposes a set of Page Size Extensions using the PSE36 mode of the processor. Windows Server 2003 Advanced and Datacenter Editions make use of this 36-bit memory addressing with an API called *Address Windowing Extensions* (AWE).

Using the AWE API, an application can transfer memory pages above the 4GB limit into the addressable memory area where it can make changes to the pages. This permits applications such as SQL Server that use large datasets to manage them in RAM rather than a slow paging file.

The application must be AWE-aware and capable of making suitable API calls. You should not add more than 4GB of memory to a server unless you are running an AWE-capable application and a version of Windows Server 2003 that can make use of the Physical Address Extensions (PAEs).

Windows Server 2003, Standard Edition, does not support PAE and therefore does not support more than 4GB of physical memory. Windows Server 2003, Enterprise Edition, supports PAE but artificially constrains total memory to 32GB. Windows Server 2003, Datacenter Edition, supports PAE to the full 64GB limit. PAE is not applicable to IA64 systems.

To implement PAE, put a `/pae` switch on the ARC path entry in Boot.ini that launches the operating system. The BOOTCFG utility does not include an option for installing this switch, so edit the file directly. If the server fails to start, the platform does not support PAE. Restart in Safe mode and change the Boot.ini entry back to its original form.

Process Protection

Windows Server 2003 takes advantage of hardware protection elements built into the Intel IA32 and IA64 architecture. Highly privileged operations, those that access physical structures in the computer, can only be initiated by code running in the *Windows Executive* (see Figure 3.4).

The Executive consists of a kernel driver, Ntoskrnl.exe, that links to a function library called the *Hardware Abstraction Layer* (HAL), or Hal.dll, that acts in concert with a long list of system services and drivers. An additional kernel driver in IA32 versions, Ntkrnlpa.exe, supports PAE addressing.

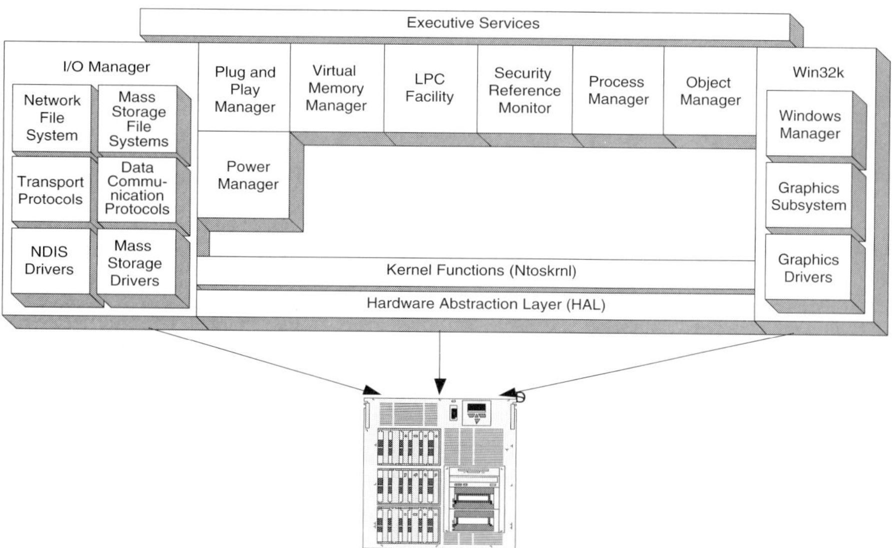

Figure 3.4 Diagram of the Windows Executive.

The kernel version loaded by Setup depends on the nature of the underlying hardware. If the motherboard uses ACPI (Advanced Configuration and Power Interface), Setup loads the ACPI version of the kernel. If the motherboard has no ACPI support, Setup loads a Standard PC kernel. An Itanium server always gets an ACPI kernel. The specification does not permit an IA64 system to operate independently of ACPI.

Setup always uses a multiprocessor kernel during the initial system configuration. If it senses that you have a single processor machine, it will load a uniprocessor version of the kernel for permanent use.

Windows Executive Structure

With the kernel and HAL in place, the remaining Executive services are grouped together based on the processes or data structures they control or use. With a couple of exceptions, these groupings are called Managers.

All Executive services run in kernel mode where they exchange data freely. The IA64 version uses the same Executive structure as the IA32 version. Here is a list of the managers and other service providers in the Windows Server 2003 Executive:

- **Executive Support.** Services that provide pool memory allocation and special queue and thread handling not provided by the kernel driver.
- **Plug and Play (PnP) Manager.** Services that enumerate and define the capabilities of hardware devices.
- **Power Manager.** Services that define hibernate/sleep/wakeup policies for devices.

- **I/O Manager.** Services that control data flows to external storage and network devices. This includes device drivers that communicate directly to hardware without using the kernel or HAL.
- **Object Manager.** Services that control symbolic links and data structures in the object's namespace.
- **Security Reference Monitor.** Services that control access to Windows Server 2003 objects.
- **Process Manager.** Services that provide structured handling for device threads.
- **Configuration Manager.** This service is responsible for the structure and content of the Registry.
- **Local Procedure Call Facility.** A high-level client/server interface between user processes and system services.
- **Virtual Memory Manager.** Services that map virtual memory to physical memory and control contiguous memory allocation.
- **Win32K.** Services that control graphics and window handling. This includes drivers that communicate directly to video and printer hardware without using Ntoskrnl or the HAL.

Windows Server 2003 no longer contains an OS/2 subsystem or a POSIX subsystem. POSIX support comes in a separate Microsoft product called Interix. The cost is somewhere around $80 U.S. For more information, see `www.microsoft.com/windows2000/interix`. (Interix runs on both Windows 2000 and Windows Server 2003.)

Process Separation

Applications are not permitted to make direct use of system services in the Executive. Instead, applications make API calls that are handled by the Windows subsystem. (The Windows subsystem used to be called the Win32 subsystem. Now that there is an IA64 version of Windows, Microsoft chose a more generic term.)

The Windows subsystem consists of a kernel-side component contained in Win32k.sys and a set of user-side components, the *Client/Server Runtime Subsystem* (CSRSS) and Dynamic Link Libraries (DLLs) that translate user-side API calls into kernel-side service calls. Applications in user space are not permitted to run in the privileged memory space of the Executive, or even to talk directly to the Executive services. Unlike political institutions, this separation of executives and workers makes the system highly resistant to crashes and instabilities.

Online Error Reporting

If an application causes a protection fault, the stack and process information is captured by a utility called DrWatson. There are two flavors of DrWatson: Drwatson.exe for 16-bit applications and Drwtsn32.exe for 32-bit applications.

DrWatson saves the failure information in log files under the `All Users` profile in `\Application Data\Microsoft\DrWatson`. (On IA64 systems, there is a space between Dr and Watson in the folder name: `Dr Watson`.)

Additionally, after DrWatson finishes up, an application called Dwwin launches and builds report files in the user's `Temp` directory. This feature uses the Error Reporting Service (ERSvc) to collect information about the state of the machine just prior to the crash, then asks permission to send this information to Microsoft

The information collected by the Error Reporting Service takes the form of XML database files that are packaged up and sent to Microsoft via a secure HTTP connection (Secure Sockets Layer, or SSL). A great deal of information is included in online error reporting, such as the name of every application and driver loaded on the system at the time of the crash. If you have reason for not wanting this information sent outside your company, you should disable error reporting. This can be done in one of several ways:

- Stop error reporting using the Properties window of the Computer icon on the desktop. Select the Advanced tab, click `Error Reporting`, and then select the `Disable Error Reporting` radio button. Figure 3.5 shows the options.
- Disable the ERSvc service using the Services snap-in under Computer Management.
- Enable the Disable Error Reporting group policy for a GPO linked to an Organizational Unit (OU) or container holding the servers you want to configure.

Device Drivers

For the most part, the operating system is protected from hapless user-mode applications, but the same is not true for device drivers. Drivers are capable of running in kernel mode where they have access to all the privileged processes in the Executive. If the driver consumes too much memory or attempts to access memory used by other processes or insists on getting the CPU's attention when it is busy doing something more important, the driver can cause the server to freeze or to throw an exception error, causing a *bugcheck*, otherwise known as a blue screen of death. Chapter 21 has more information about the cause of bugchecks and how to diagnose them.

Hopefully, the number of unexpected crashes caused by inadequately designed device drivers should decline in Windows Server 2003 thanks to a new feature called *Windows Driver Protection*. This feature consists of a database that identifies drivers with known compatibility issues. If you attempt to load one of these drivers, the system will notify you of the compatibility issues and point you at a page of information stored in the Help and Support Center that defines the nature of the incompatibility. The list is refreshed regularly by Microsoft and is downloaded as part of Windows Update.

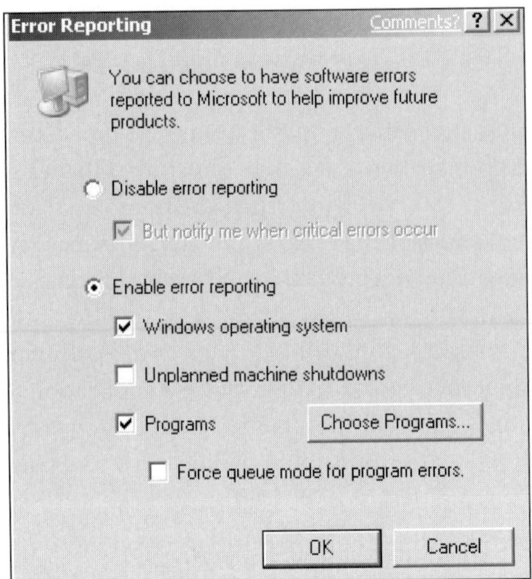

Figure 3.5 `Error Reporting` options displayed as part of System Properties for a server.

You might imagine that a vendor would not appreciate having one of its drivers included on a "bad-boy" list from Microsoft. I expect the Driver Protection program to have a side benefit of making vendors take extra care when coding their drivers. A list of the drivers on the list is available at `www.microsoft.com/hwdev`.

Windows Server 2003 also does a better job of sorting through multiple drivers for the same device as it searches the INF directory, the CD, floppies, and the Windows Update downloads. If multiple drivers are found, they are sorted using the following guidelines:

- Signed drivers are installed ahead of unsigned drivers, even if the signed driver is "compatible," whereas the unsigned driver exactly matches the device.
- Unsigned drivers with NT-specific sections in the INF script are installed ahead of unsigned drivers without NT-specific sections.

I/O Handling

Windows Server 2003 is a multitasking operating system, but not even Bill Gates and Andy Groves can overcome one fundamental limitation of computing: a single CPU can only do one thing at a time. Windows Server 2003 gives the impression of doing many things simultaneously in the same way that a motion picture gives the impression of continuous movement, by running through a series of discrete events very, very quickly.

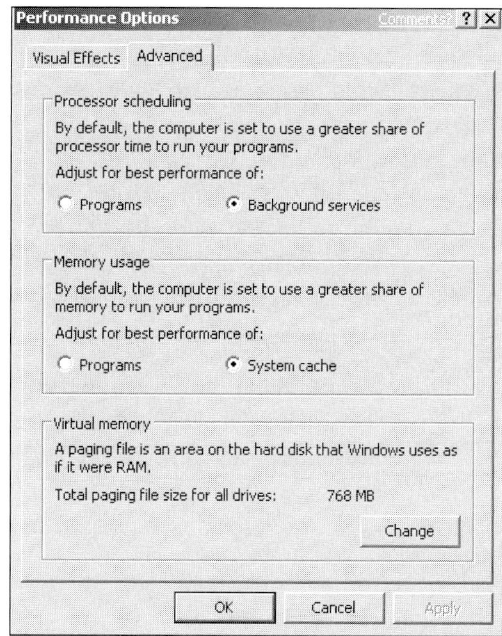

Figure 3.6 System Properties window, `Advanced` tab, showing `Processor Scheduling` and `Memory Usage` options.

Windows Server 2003 uses preemptive multitasking to share CPU cycles between running process threads. Each thread is given the attention of the CPU in its turn, with the amount of time allotted to the thread based on a *quantum timeslice*. This timeslice is short for workstations and long for servers.

You can adjust the time quantum from the UI, but the adjustment is fairly coarse. The setting is in the `Advanced` tab of the System Properties window, which you can open either from the Control Panel or by right-clicking the `My Computer` icon and selecting PROPERTIES from the flyout menu. Figure 3.6 shows an example. The quantum timeslice (also called Processor Scheduling) can be set to favor `Applications` or `Background Services`. The `Application` option sets a shorter time quantum; `Background` sets it longer. You can also set the system to favor system cache or programs when allocating memory.

The Windows Executive uses a trap handler to coordinate activities. The trap handler fields interrupts from two sources: software and hardware. Hardware interrupts are issued by devices that need the attention of the CPU. Software interrupts are issued by applications that have put a placeholder with the CPU to get attention after some other event has occurred.

A thread runs at a certain interrupt request level, or IRQL. For instance, a particular thread might request an IRQL of 7 when it starts. (There are 32 levels of IRQL, with larger numbers having higher priority.) During its quantum timeslice, this thread can only be interrupted by threads having interrupt levels of 8 or higher.

For the most part, software interrupt prioritization lies outside the control of an administrator. However, it is possible to request a certain priority with the `START` command. There are four priority classes—Low, Normal, High, Realtime—and two prioritization levels—Abovenormal and Belownormal. Power users who want a particular application to run at a high priority can launch the application as follows:

```
Start /High /Abovenormal APP.EXE
```

Frankly, I have done lots of fiddling with various IRQL priorities using `START` and I have rarely found it a worthwhile exercise. The performance boost only comes into play when the thread dispatcher is starved of CPU cycles and must begin triage. Not many users let their personal workstations get near this point. Generally, users start closing down other applications instead of figuring out ways to launch apps that hog all the available cycles.

Hardware Interrupts

Devices use hardware interrupts (IRQs) to divert the attention of the CPU when they want something done. Without hardware interrupts, the CPU would be oblivious to the system clock, network adapter, mouse, keyboard, and other peripherals.

Hardware interrupts summon the CPU in the same way that butlers are summoned in an English mansion. A rope in the corner of each room loops through the walls of the mansion and ends up in the pantry, where it is connected to one of many little bells dangling from springs. When someone in the billiard room pulls the rope, the butler hears the bell and looks up to see which spring is shaking. The butler then takes out a 3x5 card labeled Billiard Room and finds instructions on it that say, "Deliver Scotch and cigars to the billiard room." The butler interrupts whatever he was doing (polishing the silver, watching *Masterpiece Theatre*, whatever) and carries out these instructions.

There is a possibility that the interrupt service routines, the instructions associated with an interrupt, could run at an appropriate time if more than one device tries to lay claim to an interrupt. ACPI avoids this problem by building an IRQ routing table that permits multiplexing different devices into the same IRQ. For a nifty little tool that lets you view ACPI elements such as the IRQ routing table, download PCIScope from APSoft at `www.tssc.de`. Figure 3.7 shows a sample of the information displayed by this utility.

The Device Manager console, Devmgmt.msc, can display devices and the resources they have been assigned. This makes it easy to see shared IRQs. From the menu, select VIEW | RESOURCES BY TYPE. Figure 3.8 shows the IRQ resource list. Note the large number of devices multiplexed through IRQ 9.

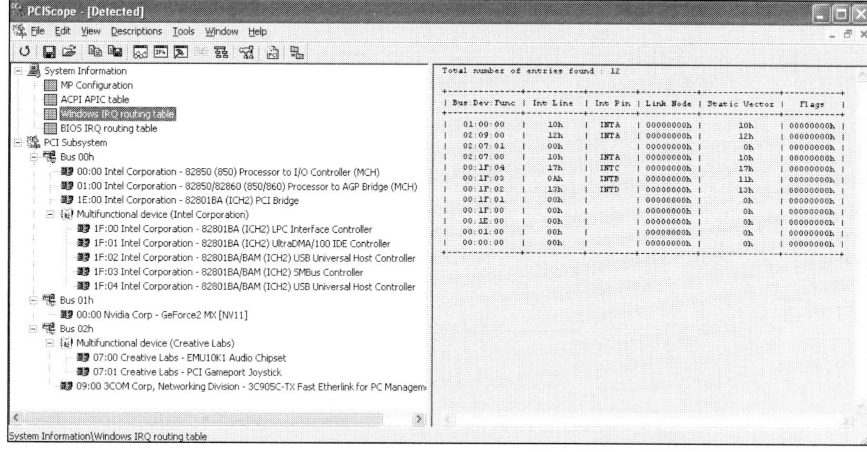

Figure 3.7 PCIScope utility can display the ACPI routing table, BIOS routing table, and PCI header information from each device.

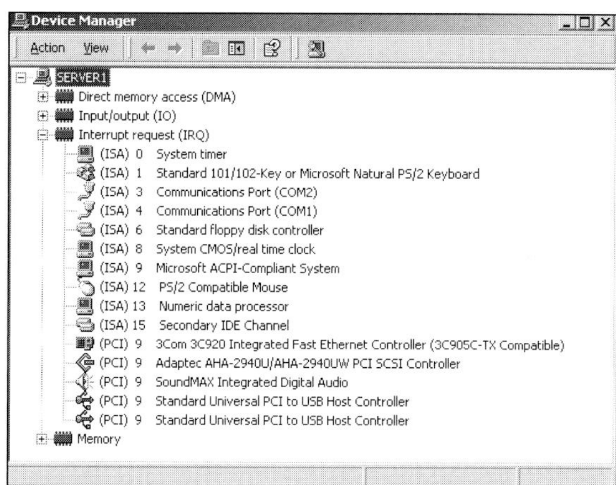

Figure 3.8 IRQ resources assigned in a computer that does not support extended interrupts above 15.

On machines with chipsets that support use of the Advanced Programmable Interrupt Controller (APIC) installed on all modern PCs, Windows Server 2003 can assign IRQs above 15. Figure 3.9 shows the device list on a machine running a Pentium 4 processor with the Intel 850 chipset.

IA64 machines are even more generous with IRQs, forgoing shared IRQs entirely. Figure 3.10 shows the resource list from an HP I2000 workstation.

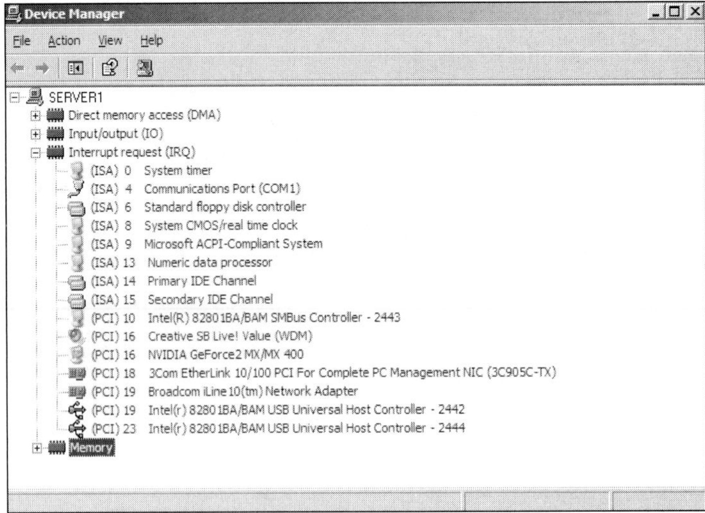

Figure 3.9 IRQ resource assignments on a machine with a chipset that supports IRQs above 15.

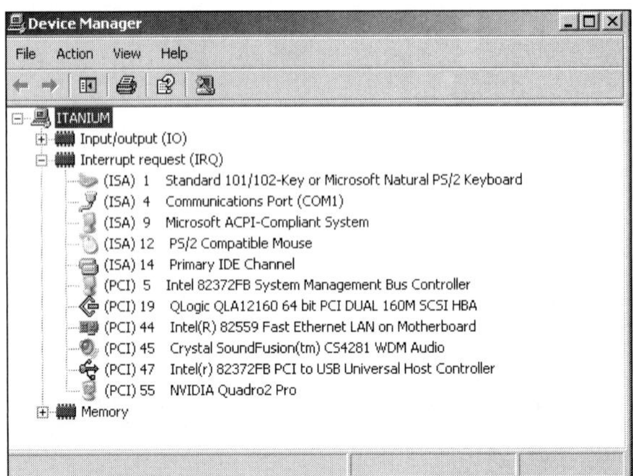

Figure 3.10 Itanium devices sorted by IRQ.

A potential cause of erratic server behavior is improper prioritization of the IRQs assigned to the devices. The CPU is constantly bombarded with hardware interrupt requests, and ACPI is responsible for prioritizing them. One of the considerations that ACPI uses when making its IRQ assignments is the PCI slot that contains the device. For this reason, if you have a device that acts erratically, or does not work at all, put it in another PCI slot. For more information on the PCI specification, see the PCI SIG web site at `www.pcisig.com/tech/index.html`.

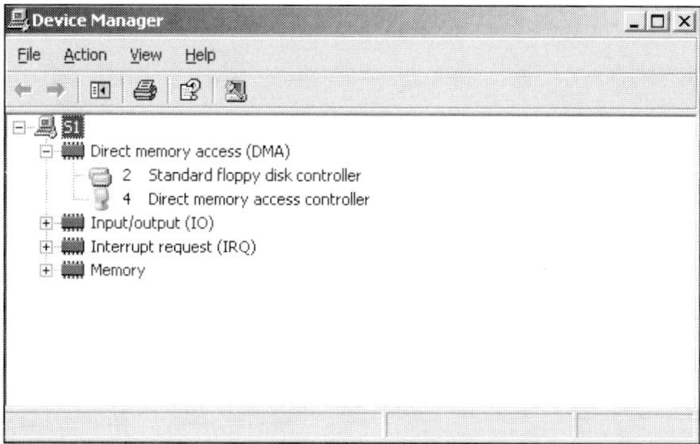

Figure 3.11 DMA assignments to devices on IDE bus.

Direct Memory Access (DMA)

Ordinary data transfers to and from a device and main memory require separate hardware interrupts for each buffer of data. This is called Programmed I/O, or PIO, and it is very inefficient. More advanced devices use Direct Memory Access (DMA) along with bus mastering to transfer data with very little intervention required by the CPU.

Each DMA device is assigned a *channel*, which is essentially an ID used for handling data transfer transactions. DMA channels are negotiated through ACPI. Advanced ATA/IDE controllers use DMA to achieve high data transfer rates with low CPU utilization. Several different DMA versions exist, each with a different transfer rate. Windows Server 2003 uses ACPI plus its own negotiation routines to determine which DMA mode to assign to a device.

Some machines do not support DMA on PCI slots far away from the CPU. If you place a controller card in a server and it does not function, or functions very slowly, you might want to move it to a slot closer to the CPU.

Figure 3.11 shows the DMA assignments to devices on the primary IDE controller bus. Devices can use different DMA versions and a mix of DMA and PIO. These settings are available in the Device Manager console in the Properties window of the IDE controller (primary or secondary).

On IA64 systems, DMA has an even more dramatic impact on performance because of the wider data paths. IA64 machines use a 64-bit PCI bus. In some cases, a device driver might be coded to use 32-bit addresses. Windows Server 2003 responds by double-buffering I/O to the device. This hurts performance. Verify with the vendor that the device meets Microsoft criteria for 64-bit addressing and single-buffer operation.

DMA is enabled by default for DVD and CD-RW drives. The Properties page in Device Manager shows the actual DMA mode.

Overview of Windows Server 2003 Plug and Play

Windows Server 2003 uses the same plug-and-play support introduced in Windows 2000. The Windows Executive has two components that handle PnP services: Plug and Play Manager and Power Manager:

- **Plug and Play Manager.** Discovers PnP devices using a process called *enumeration*. It then loads an appropriate driver and makes Registry entries based on INF scripts written either by Microsoft or the hardware vendor. Plug and Play Manager also allocates resources such as IRQs, I/O ports, and DMA channels based on information gleaned from ACPI.
- **Power Manager.** Handles dynamic interaction with devices to conserve battery life or limit wear and tear on components. Power Manager can be set to spin down a hard drive, for example, after a certain interval of inactivity.

The trick to getting a successful PnP enumeration is having an INF script that calls out the same name as that reported by the device. If PnP Manager cannot match an INF script to the device, it cannot complete the transaction even if the correct driver is available on the machine. Drivers are stored in `\Windows\System32\Drivers`. INF scripts are stored in `\Windows\Inf`.

32-bit drivers cannot be loaded on an IA64 machine. The WOW64 emulator only works in user space, not kernel space. However, the same INF script can be used to load both 32-bit and 64-bit drivers. This enables a vendor to deploy a single script and two sets of drivers. If the vendor wants to load only a 64-bit driver, the .inf extension can be changed to .ia64. This signals the operating system to look only for 64-bit drivers.

Using Device Manager

Before proceeding much further, let's take a look at the MMC console provided by Microsoft for viewing details about the devices loaded on a machine. This is the Device Manager, Devmgmt.msc. In general, if you have hardware problems or want to configure a device, the first place to go is the Device Manager console. There are several ways to open the console:

- Right-click the `My Computer` icon on the desktop and select MANAGE from the flyout menu. Expand the tree under `System Tools | Device Manager`.
- Right-click the `My Computer` icon, select PROPERTIES from the flyout menu, select the `Hardware` tab, then click `Device Manager`.
- My personal favorite is the Run window. I just enter `devmgmt.msc` and press `Enter`.

Figure 3.12 shows an example of the device tree displayed by the Device Manager console.

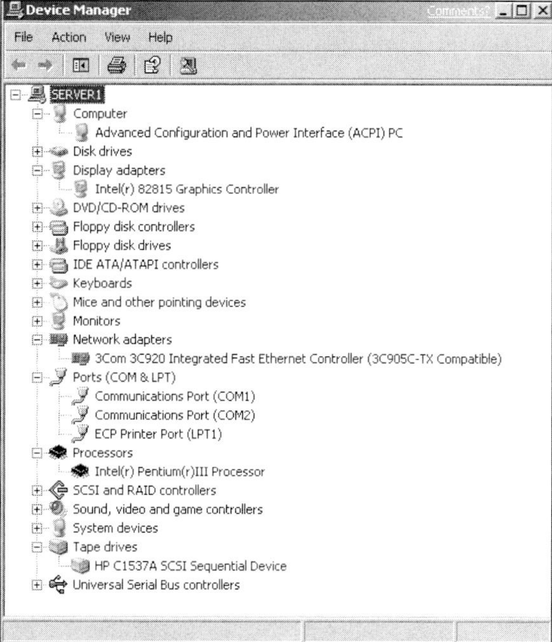

Figure 3.12 Device Manager console showing device tree.

To see the configuration information for a particular device, right-click the `Device` icon and select PROPERTIES from the flyout menu. If `Device Manager` does not list a device that you know is installed in the system, the device might be misconfigured or a legacy device might not be recognized by the PnP Manager. Legacy devices can be installed manually using the Install New Hardware applet in Control Panel.

An exclamation point or question mark next to a device indicates a problem of some sort, usually a resource conflict. A big red X indicates that the problem was severe enough to force disabling of the device.

To assess the problem, open the `Properties` window for the device then select the `Device Status` tab to find the nature of the problem. If the properties indicate a resource conflict, use the Resource view to see what other devices are contending for the same resource.

To clear a conflict, try deleting the device then restarting. This may force PnP Manager to reconsider the resource allocation decision it made the first time. You can also try moving the card to another PCI slot, which forces ACPI to assign different resources.

If a resource conflict persists for a legacy device, try taking manual control of the resource allocation for the device by selecting the `Resources` tab and unchecking the `Use Automatic Settings` option. This option will be dimmed for PCI devices. After you manually allocate resources to a legacy device, restart the machine to see if the error persists or if you caused a problem for another device.

Additional Device Enumeration Tools

Although Device Manager is probably the simplest way to look at the hardware on a machine, it does not give a consolidated view of drivers, resources, and functions. The tool best suited for this type of viewing is the System Information tool, which is most easily launched by entering **WINMSD** at the Run command.

In both Windows 2000 and Windows Server 2003, launching WINMSD immediately launches another utility, Msinfo32. Msinfo32 is located in `\Program Files\Common Files\Microsoft Shared\Msinfo`. WINMSD closes as soon as it opens Msinfo32.

In Windows 2000, Msinfo32 gathers a bit of folder information then launches an MMC console with the `System Information` snap-in. This is the same snap-in used by the Computer Management console in Windows 2000 to display information about the operating system and the hardware.

In Windows Server 2003, there is no `System Information` snap-in. Instead, Msinfo32 launches the Help and Support Center with the focus set on a display of system information gleaned from Windows Management Instrumentation (WMI). Figure 3.13 shows an example.

The Help and Support Center has a more visually friendly display of system information. From the main Support Center window, click `Tools` then `General` then `System Information` then `My Computer Information`. Figure 3.14 shows an example of the information layout.

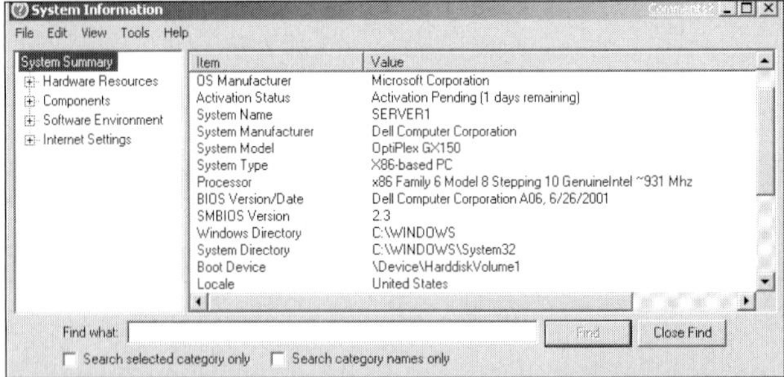

Figure 3.13 System Information listed by the Help and Support Center when launched by Msinfo32 via WINMSD.

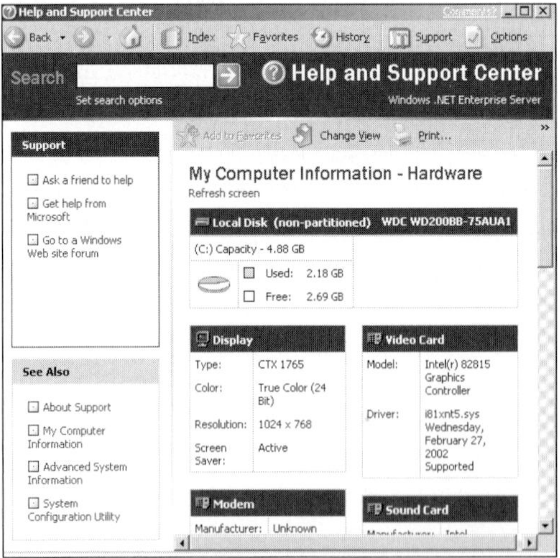

Figure 3.14 Help and Support Services display of system information.

Advanced Configuration and Power Interface (ACPI)

Although Microsoft calls Windows Server 2003, XP, and Windows 2000 "Plug-and-Play" operating systems, they are actually ACPI operating systems. The Advanced Configuration and Power Interface standard defines mechanisms by which devices report their capabilities and resource needs to ACPI, where they are dutifully listed in a set of tables in the volatile memory section of the chip. The operating system reads these tables and makes resource allocation and power management decisions based on the information it finds there.

According to the ACPI 2.0 specification, available at `www.acpi.info`, the following services are provided by the ACPI infrastructure:

- System power management
- Device power management
- Processor power management
- Device and processor performance management
- Plug and Play
- System Events
- Battery management
- Thermal management
- Embedded Controller management
- SMBus Controller management (SMBus is the System Management bus specification promulgated by Intel.)

The ACPI infrastructure on a machine is an intimate part of the machine's operation, so Microsoft chose to incorporate ACPI support directly into the operating system kernel via the Hardware Abstraction Layer (HAL).

As you can see from the list, Windows Server 2003 and XP use ACPI to handle power management as well as plug and play. Don't confuse these power management features with the legacy Advanced Power Management (APM) services that were part of the PC specifications for many years. APM uses function calls in the system BIOS to control the machine's wake-state. Legacy APM function calls are supported only in XP, not in Windows Server 2003 servers.

You can check to see if APM is enabled by clicking the `Power Options` hyperlink in the new `Printers and Other Hardware` section of the new Control Panel interface. If the Power Options window has an `APM` tab, the machine has an APM BIOS. You should only enable APM support if the machine has no other power management options available, indicating that no ACPI functionality has been enabled in the HAL.

Using APMSTAT

There is a utility in the Windows Server 2003 Support Tools called APMSTAT that tests for an APM BIOS on a machine. Here is a sample report using the -v (verbose) switch:

```
C:\Program Files\Resource Kit>apmstat -v
This computer appears to have an APM legal HAL
This machine has an APM bios present that looks OK, and it is
not on the list of machines known to have APM problems.
Check the power applet in the control panel to see if APM is enabled
APM Registry Data Dump
Major = 0001  Minor = 0002
InstallFlags = 0003
Code16Segment = f000  Code16Offset = 56c4  DataSeg = 0040
Signature = APM
Valid = 0001
Detection Log Data:
44 45 54 4c 4f 47 31 00 00 00 00 00 00 00 00 00
 D  E  T  L  O  G  1
```

If APCI is enabled, APMSTAT reports the following :

```
This is an ACPI machine. APM is NOT relevant on this machine.
```

ACPI Compatibility

You should have relatively few problems installing Windows Server 2003 on a new machine that meets the ACPI v2 specification. Older machines built during the time that the ACPI spec was evolving sometimes have problems, ranging from the failure of certain power management features to erratic behavior to periodic freezes and bugchecks.

Microsoft drew a line at 1/1/99 and assumes that any machine built after that date is ACPI 2.0-compliant. Machines that are known exceptions to this rule are listed in the Txtsetup.sif file on the Windows Server 2003 CD under the heading [NWACL], which stands for *Non-Windows ACPI Compliance List*.

Setup determines the ACPI identification of a machine by querying two ACPI tables: the *Fixed ACPI Description Table* (FACP), which contains a string representing the vendor, and the *Root System Description Table* (RSDT), which contains an alphanumeric value assigned by the vendor to represent the machine's make and model. The [NWACL] entry identifies the source of the identification. For example, the Toshiba Portege 3300 and the Fujitsu Sprint are on the NWACL list. Here are the particulars from the [NWACL] section of the Txtsetup.sif file:

```
[ToshibaPortege3300]
AcpiOemId="FACP","TOSHIB"
AcpiOemTableId="FACP","750     "
AcpiOemRevision="<=","FACP",1

[FujitsuSPRINT]
AcpiOemId="RSDT","FUJ   "
AcpiOemTableId="RSDT","SPRINT  "
```

The Txtsetup.sif file also lists machines built prior to 1/1/99 that are known to be ACPI-compliant. These machines are listed under the `[GoodACPIBios]` heading.

There is also a "good but only with some fixes" list included in a file called Biosinfo.inf, also in the `\I386` directory on the Windows Server 2003 CD. This list identifies machines that work only if certain ACPI features are disabled. Here is an example listing:

```
; Workaround for BIOS bug in Dell Dimension 8100, Precision 220,
;and Precision 420 using National PC87364 SuperIO chipsets.
;Parallel port is configured in a way that does not
; work on Win2k or WinXP

[DellNationalPC87364WorkAround]
AddReg=DellNationalPC87364WorkAroundAddReg

[DellNationalPC87364WorkAroundAddReg]
HKLM,SYSTEM\CurrentControlSet\Services\Parport\Parameters,DellNationalPC87364,
0x00010001,1
```

If you have a machine with a motherboard older than 1/1/99 that is not listed on the good-boy list but you think it would be perfectly fine running with the ACPI kernel, you can try changing the `ACPIEnable` option from `ACPIEnable = 2` to `ACPIEnable = 1` in the Txtsetup.sif file. This forces Setup to enable ACPI and load the ACPI kernel. This has the potential to cause the machine to do odd gymnastics, so it is not recommended except for personal experimentation.

Power Management Features

Depending on the ACPI table entries found during Setup, Windows Server 2003 and XP display certain options in the Power Options window opened in Control Panel. Figure 3.15 shows the options for XP running on a laptop. Figure 3.16 shows the options on Windows Server 2003.

After Setup decides on the ACPI configuration for a machine, the entries are hard-wired into the HAL. If you change your mind later on and decide to enable an option in CMOS, you'll need to reinstall the operating system. Keep this in mind when you deploy images.

Windows Driver Model (WDM)

A key benefit to the merging of the corporate and consumer Windows products is the ability to use a single driver throughout the product line. The blueprint for creating those drivers is the *Windows Driver Model*, or WDM. If you are interested in the architecture of WDM drivers or how they are developed, here are a few good references:

- *Programming the Microsoft Windows Driver Model*, by Walter Oney. This is an excellent book for system administrators because it has lucid descriptions of the way the drivers work and the architectural models of the driver internals.

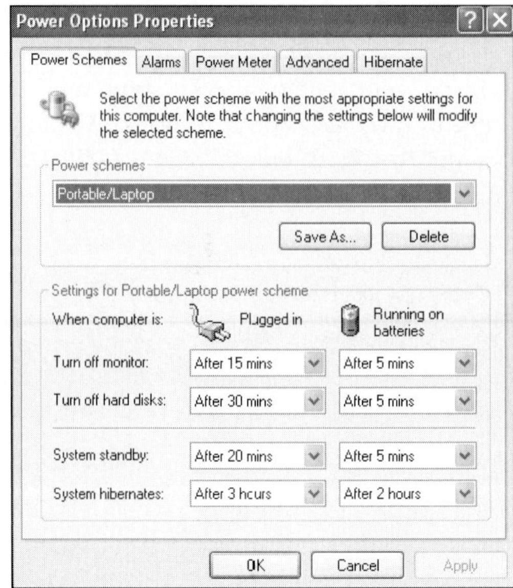

Figure 3.15 Power Options for an XP laptop.

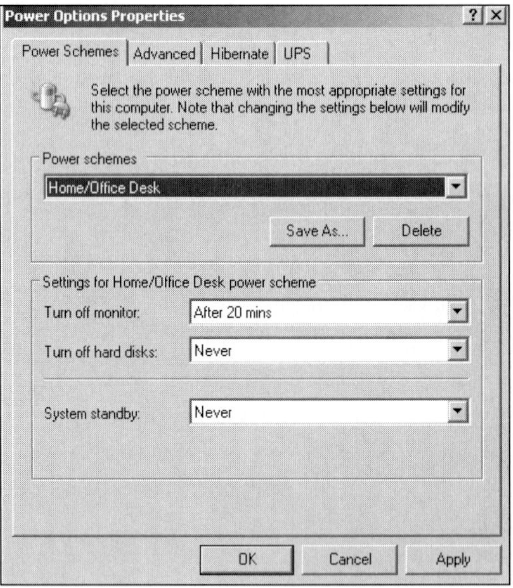

Figure 3.16 Power Options for Windows Server 2003.

- *Developing Windows NT Device Drivers: A Programmer's Handbook*, by Edward Dekker and Joseph Newcomer. This is another excellent resource. You'll get a lot of information if you don't mind sifting through a little complex jargon.
- *Windows NT Device Driver Development*, by Peter Viscarola and Anthony Mason. This is considered the definitive book on NT device drivers. It is geared more for the older NT Driver Model, but has solid coverage of WDM.
- *Windows Server 2003 Driver Development Kit (DDK)*. The documentation in the DDK is terse, but you can't get much more authoritative. The DDK used to be a free download from Microsoft, but now you have to purchase it.

WDM and PnP are inextricably linked in Windows Server 2003, so here is a brief overview just to get the vernacular.

Bus

The WDM view of I/O starts with a bus. A bus is an interface that controls one or more devices. An IDE controller is a bus, for example, because it provides the interface to one or more hard drives. Other buses include the following:

- Personal Computer Interface (PCI) bus
- RS-232 Serial Bus
- Parallel Port
- Advanced Configuration and Power Interface (ACPI)
- Small Computer System Interface (SCSI)
- PC Card (formerly Personal Computer Memory Card International Association, or PCMCIA)
- Universal Serial Bus (USB)
- IEEE 1394 FireWire

Bus Drivers

A bus is controlled by a bus driver. Bus drivers are controlled by the Plug and Play Manager, which communicates with the devices via function calls in the HAL.

A bus driver enumerates devices on its bus and builds a *Physical Device Object* (PDO) for each device it finds. The PDO virtualizes the device, rendering it into a digital form that can respond to commands from the Executive. Other duties of the bus driver include hall monitor, errand boy, receptionist, and gofer. In other words, it does the following:

- Keeps track of events on its bus and reports them to the Plug and Play Manager.
- Responds to I/O request packets (IRPs) from Plug and Play Manager and Power Manager.

- Improves I/O performance by multiplexing bus access requests.
- Performs administrative chores required to keep the devices on the bus running smoothly.

Functional Device Objects

A bus driver generally does not communicate directly to devices on its bus unless the devices use *raw I/O*. Instead, the bus driver virtualizes the physical device objects still further into data constructs called *Functional Device Objects* (FDO). These FDOs are controlled by *function drivers*. The Plug and Play Manager loads one function driver for each device.

Function Drivers

A function driver is implemented as a set of drivers: a *class driver*, a *minidriver*, and one or more *filter drivers*.

- **Class drivers.** Provide basic functionality for a device type, such as a mouse or a scanner or a hard drive. Microsoft usually writes class drivers.
- **Minidrivers.** Determine specific operational functions. Vendors write minidrivers for their hardware.
- **Filter drivers.** Layer above or below the function driver and provide additional services. Microsoft encourages vendors to write filters rather than build entirely new custom minidrivers.

WDM Functional Example

Here is an example of how a device with a WDM driver is enumerated and loaded:

1. Insert a new PC Card SCSI controller with an attached Jaz drive into the PCMCIA slot of a laptop.
2. The PCMCIA driver discovers the new card and creates a Physical Device Object (PDO) for it. It informs Plug and Play Manager about the new PDO.
3. The Plug and Play Manager looks up the correct driver for the new PDO, loads the driver, and passes the PDO over to the SCSI driver.
4. The SCSI driver builds a Functional Device Object (FDO) and attaches it to the driver stack for the PC Card bus.
5. Plug and Play Manager instructs the SCSI driver to enumerate the bus.
6. The SCSI driver enumerates the bus, finds the SCSI drive, and creates a PDO for the drive.
7. Plug and Play Manager looks up the driver for the new PDO, loads the driver, and passes control of the PDO over to the new driver.

8. The disk driver builds an FDO for the drive and attaches the FDO to the device stack for the SCSI bus.
9. The file system drivers in I/O Manager can now communicate with the drive via the SCSI bus interface.

One of the end results of all this PnP discovery, enumeration, and object building is a set of Registry keys under `HKLM | System | CurrentControlSet | Enum`. This is called the Enum tree and is used as a reference for loading services during startup.

This concludes the overview of Windows Server 2003 hardware architecture. It's time to start adding devices.

Installing and Configuring Devices

If your personal work area is anything like mine, you have stacks of PC catalogs sitting on shelves next to your desk. I have thick volumes from Ingram Micro, Tech Data, and Gates Arrow, as well as books from a dozen or so other wholesalers, not to mention mounds of mailers from retailers and hundreds of spam messages every day from resellers and jobbers and manufacturers.

No book could hope to detail the installation steps for all those different components. The installation steps outlined in this topic are intended to give you an idea of how the system reacts when new devices are added and where to find the tools to configure the devices after they are installed. The troubleshooting section at the end of the chapter has hints for diagnosing and correcting problems that might arise.

If you are not running a volume license or master license of Windows Server 2003, you may encounter situations where your repair work initiates the Windows Product Activation. Ordinarily, you would only expect this to happen if you replace an entire motherboard or swap a system drive to another machine (which is essentially the same thing). It can also happen if you change a certain components. See Chapter 1, "Installing and Configuring Windows Server 2003," for more details about the devices included in the WPA evaluation.

This section includes installation steps for the following:

- Using Windows Updates
- Adding or changing CPUs
- Adding IDE hard drives
- Installing SCSI adapters and drives
- Adding removable media drives
- Adding network adapters and configuring bindings
- Using multiple displays

Using Windows Update

Keeping up with changes to applications and drivers is an ongoing problem. Windows Server 2003 enhances the Windows Update feature introduced in Windows 2000 with a simpler interface and better support.

The most common reason for requiring a patch or hotfix is to correct a security vulnerability. There should be a lot fewer of these updates in Windows Server 2003 compared to Windows 2000 and NT, but they won't disappear. There are several ways to analyze for security deficiencies. The simplest to use is the Hfnetchk utility, branded by Microsoft as the Baseline Security Analyzer.

If you want to refresh the drivers for a particular server, the simplest thing to do is run Windows Update from the Help and Support Center (HSC). The main HSC page has a hyperlink to the Windows Update site, `v4.windowsupdate.microsoft.com`, which is displayed within the HSC frame. The first time you touch the site, you'll be prompted to download an ActiveX control for managing updates.

The Update site walks you through scanning for new drivers based on the devices loaded on your machine. If you want to download drivers for another user's system, follow Procedure 3.1.

Procedure 3.1 Using Windows Update to Obtain Drivers for Another System

1. In the Windows Update window in HSC, click `Personalize Windows Update`.
2. Select the option `Display The Link To The Windows Update Catalog`.
3. Click `Save Settings`.
4. Under `See Also` in the left frame, click `Windows Update Catalog`.
5. In the main window, click `Find Driver Updates for Hardware Devices`. This opens a page with links to various device types. Figure 3.17 shows an example.

You can use this procedure to download drivers to a central location on your network where desktop administrators or users can obtain them.

If you want your servers to download updates automatically, you can configure this option in the System Properties window. Select the `Automatic Updates` tab (see Figure 3.18).

All in all, Windows Update is a simple way to keep up with fixes, especially security updates, but there is no guarantee that a particular suite of updates won't make a server unstable. I would advise doing a manual scan and selection rather than automatically doing a wholesale download.

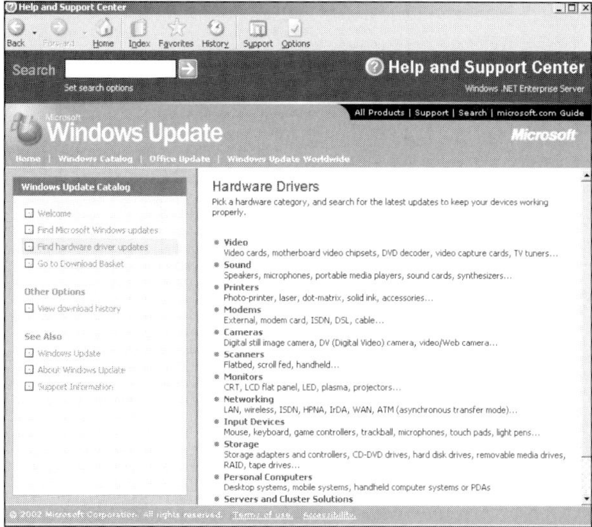

Figure 3.17 Hardware Drivers page at the Windows Update Catalog site.

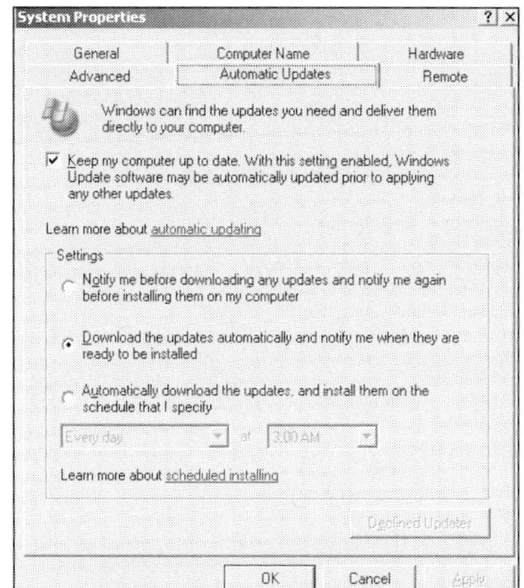

Figure 3.18 System Properties window showing the `Automatic Updates` tab and the configuration settings.

Software Update Services (SUS)

In July of 2002, Microsoft released a new service that permits centralized distribution of hotfixes and security updates from a server internal to an organization rather than going directly to the Microsoft Update site. Software Update Services (SUS) is included in Windows Server 2003.

Using SUS has several advantages:

- You can evaluate each update to ensure that it does not cause problems prior to installing it on a production server or servers.
- You can deploy updates to servers that are not connected to the Internet.
- You can standardize your servers by specifying only those updates that should be installed. By doing this specification at the SUS server, you centrally manage your update deployment process.
- Updates can be targeted to servers via group policies.

Microsoft is continually refining SUS. Check for the latest updates and procedures at `www.microsoft.com`.

Security Updates

You should be able to keep up with security patches using either Windows Update or Software Update Services (SUS). However, you may find yourself in a situation where you want to install a particular update or hotfix individually on a server for testing or evaluation. You can do this by executing the hotfix at the console of the server.

If you want to avoid multiple reboots when locally installing more than one hotfix, use the QCHAIN utility available as a download from Microsoft.

Adding or Changing CPUs

Adding a second CPU in prior versions of Windows NT and Windows 2000 was a chore because Setup would install a uniprocessor kernel if it discovered a single processor in a machine. This was done even if the motherboard supported multiple processors.

In Windows Server 2003, all you need to do to add a second processor is put the cartridge in the machine according to the manufacturer's instructions and start up again. The system detects the additional processor and swaps out the uniprocessor system drivers with their multiprocessor equivalents.

You can verify that the system sees the second processor by opening Task Manager. The Performance window will show graphs for each processor. If the second processor is not seen, make sure it is fully seated and that no changes are required in CMOS. Also, make sure the voltage regulators or other motherboard devices are in place and firmly seated.

The situation is not so simple if you want to change the type of kernel that was loaded by Setup. If you initially install Windows Server 2003 with the ACPI kernel and later discover that the system is unstable and you want to shift to the Standard PC kernel, you must reinstall Windows Server 2003 completely.

The reason for this is that the two different kernels store Registry information differently in `HKLM | Hardware`. The settings are not interoperable. If you disable ACPI support in CMOS on a machine that is running the ACPI kernel, the machine will bugcheck (crash with a Blue Screen of Death).

Adding IDE Hard Drives

The most difficult part of adding a new IDE drive is getting the right master/slave jumper combinations on the devices. If the new drive displays in CMOS with the correct size and drive geometry, Windows Server 2003 should have no problem finding it using the existing IDE bus drivers. You can see the new drive using the `Disk Management` snap-in in the Computer Management console. Open the `Computer Management` console via START | PROGRAMS | ADMINISTRATIVE TOOLS | COMPUTER MANAGEMENT. See Chapter 14, "Configuring Data Storage," for the steps to configure a new disk and allocate its storage space.

If you add another drive on the same IDE controller with the intention of striping the drives with RAID 0, you will not get a performance improvement. An IDE interface can write to only one device at a time. Put the devices on separate controllers or use an ATA/IDE RAID controller. The same applies to mirroring drives, because you can slow down the operating system by forcing it to mirror between IDE drives on the same controller.

If you install ATA devices that use UltraDMA (UDMA), make sure the system detects the correct DMA setting for the device. This is displayed in the Properties window of the IDE controller in Device Manager. Select the `Advanced Settings` tab. The `Device Type` is generally locked to `Auto Detection`, so you will need to work with your vendor to figure out why the system is not seeing the correct UDMA version.

Installing SCSI Adapters and Drives

You can improve server I/O performance considerably by changing from IDE to SCSI. Part of this is due to the faster SCSI bus, although ATA100 and UltraDMA 5 close this gap considerably. More importantly, SCSI uses asynchronous communication so the interface can multiplex data packets to several devices. IDE/ATA controllers can only talk to one device at a time. SCSI also consumes fewer CPU cycles per megabyte transferred, so it is more efficient and therefore gives faster overall throughput.

When you install a SCSI adapter and start the machine, Plug and Play Manager detects the new adapter and loads the appropriate drivers. If PnP recognizes that new hardware has been added but does not find drivers, you will need to supply Windows Server 2003 or Windows 2000 drivers.

If the adapter hosts the drive where you want to install the operating system, and there are no drivers for the adapter in the miniature version of Windows Server 2003 loaded by Setup, you can press F6 at the beginning of the text-based portion of Setup and load the driver.

Placing a new drive in an IA64 machine that already has an operating system installed requires no action in firmware. When you use the Disk Management console in the operating system to partition the drive, the proper GPT-based data partitions are created.

If you replace the boot drive in an IA64 machine and you intend to install Windows Server 2003, you still need to take no action in firmware. Chapter 1 discusses how to use the Extensible Firmware Interface (EFI) shell to navigate to the Windows Server 2003 CD to start the operating system installation. Setup will create the necessary EFI System Partition, Microsoft Reserved Partition, and a generic data partition for the operating system.

When installing new devices on the SCSI bus, pay particular attention to SCSI IDs and terminations. Ninety percent of all SCSI problems originate from these two issues. Modern SCSI adapters are good at determining the active terminations used by devices on the bus, but it is still a good idea to mark each device clearly as to whether it has active termination enabled or disabled.

If you add a drive that changes the scan order of the bus containing the boot drive, you may end up unable to boot the machine. This is true even if the SCSI BIOS is set to boot from the correct drive. The problem occurs because the ARC path in Boot.ini references the bus devices in the order they are scanned by the SCSI controller. For instance, here is a sample ARC path:

```
multi(0)disk(0)rdisk(0)partition(1)\WINDOWS="Standard Edition" /fastdetect
```

If you change the scan order so that the boot drive is now the second (`rdisk(1)`) or third (`rdisk(2)`) drive, NTLDR will not be able to find the boot partition and you will get an `Unable to Locate Ntoskrnl.exe` error.

You should always low-level format new SCSI drives prior to placing them in service. This ensures that the translation table on the SCSI interface matches that used by the device. This is especially true if the drive is part of a RAID array. Some very subtle failures can occur if a drive is not matched to its controller. Low-level formatting can take quite a while, so include a couple of extra hours into your estimates for adding or replacing SCSI drives.

You can simplify analyzing problems with SCSI drives by selecting drives that support S.M.A.R.T. technology. Get details at `www.pcguide.com/ref/hdd/perf/qual/ featuresSMART-c.html` and at `www.storagereview.com/guide2000/ref/hdd/perf/qual/featuresSMART.html`.

Using EFI Disk Utilities

Windows Server 2003 Setup places several disk utilities in an `MSUtil` folder on the EFI System Partition. You can use these utilities to create and manage drive partitions, although this is generally simpler to do from within the operating system itself rather than from the EFI shell.

These EFI-based disk utilities give you a lot of control over the disk partitioning, but that control comes at a price. You can very easily destroy one or all partitions on a disk. Chapter 2, "Performing Upgrades and Automated Installations," describes the use of the EFI Shell environment. Be very sure to use the `map` command in the shell to verify partition block numbers and mount aliases prior to using any of the utilities described here.

Diskpart.efi.

This utility operates in a similar fashion to the DISKPART utility in Windows Server 2003. You can use it to create new EFI System Partitions, new Microsoft Reserved Partitions, and new data partitions prior to installing the operating system. This is not required, because Setup is able to prepare a new drive, but the steps are included here in the event that you need to prepare a disk in a system that does not yet have an operating system loaded.

When using Diskpart.efi to create a partition, it will create the GUID automatically but you'll need to give the partition a friendly name. You'll need to specify the partition size in megabytes. For instance, `size=1024` would create a 1GB partition. Follow Procedure 3.2.

```
CmdCreate arguments:
SelectedDisk = 0
Name=PARTITION_NAME
TypeGuid = EBD0A0A2-B9E5-4433
TypeName = MSDATA
Requested OffsetInBlocks = 0
Requested SizeInMegabytes = 1024
Attributes = 0
Resulting Size In Blocks = 2097152
Resulting Size In Bytes = 1073741824
```

Procedure 3.2 Using EFI DISKPART to Create a New Data Partition

1. Boot to the EFI shell.
2. Change directory to `fs0:\MSUtil`.
3. Run `DISKPART`.
4. Enter `List` to see a list of the manageable drives in the machine.
5. Enter `Select #` where `#` is the ID number of the drive shown in the `List` command.
6. Enter `Symbols` to get a list of the partition types. There are three options: `MSRES` (Microsoft Reserved), `EFISYS` (EFI System), and `MSDATA`. You'll be using the `MSDATA` option when creating the partition.
7. Enter `Create name=partition_name type=msdata size=1024 ver`. The `ver` option gives a verbose listing of the result. Here is an example listing of a successful partition creation:

You can also use DISKPART to wipe a disk using the `Clean` command then prepare a new GUID Partition Table using the `New GPT` command. This results in a loss of all data on the drive, of course, so only use this option if you want to refresh a drive from another machine. For SCSI drives, you should use low-level formatting to accomplish this task and sync the translation tables between the controller and the drive at the same time.

Fdisk.efi

This utility has one function. It creates an EFI System Partition on a blank disk. If you use it on a disk with existing partitions, you will lose those partitions and any data they contain.

Format.efi

This utility is intended solely to format the EFI System Partition created by Fdisk.efi. The only available format options are FAT and FAT32. Before using FORMAT, you must first mount the partition created by FDISK. Use the `Mount` command for this—for example, `mount blk4 fs8`.

After the partition is mounted, do a quick format using the `Format` command as follows: `format fs8 /fs:fat /q`.

Nvrboot.efi

If you accidentally overwrite or delete the boot menu entry in NVRAM that points at the Windows Server 2003 operating system partition, you can use Nvrboot.efi to recover the original boot menu entry. You can also use this utility as an alternative to the EFI Boot Menu Management utility to modify the entries in the boot menu.

If you want to modify the contents of the boot menu entries themselves, Nvrboot only works with entries installed by Windows products. Other entries, such as the EFI Shell entry and the PXE boot entry, can only be managed by the Boot Menu Management utility.

Nvrboot has these options:

- **`Display.`** This option shows the full NVRAM entry for the boot item.
- **`Modify.`** This option permits you to change the `LoadIdentifier` and `OsLoadOptions` variables in the entry. The two load paths cannot be modified.
- **`Export.`** This option permits you to make a backup copy of one or all NVRAM options. This is a terrific way to keep a copy of the entries on-hand in case something goes wrong. You can put a copy of the exported file on a floppy then copy the file back from the floppy in the event that the NVRAM entries are overwritten.
- **`Import.`** This option permits you to import one or more NVRAM entries from a file into NVRAM.

- `Copy.` Use this option to make a copy of an entry prior to making changes to the main entry.
- `Erase.` Use this option to delete an entry you no longer want displayed on the boot menu. Use caution. The system will permit you to erase all entries by entering an asterisk (*).

Adding Removable Media Drives

Windows Server 2003 has a new service called the *Removable Storage Manager* (RSM). The RSM service simplifies managing removable media if you have large CD-ROM jukeboxes or a robotic tape library, but it can make simple interfaces such as small CD disc changers more difficult to handle.

In classic NT, each disk in a jukebox or disc changer got a separate drive letter. This caused much frustration when configuring big CD libraries because there aren't enough letters to accommodate a 100-disc library. RSM solves this problem by assigning a single drive letter to the device itself and manipulating the CDs in the background.

But for small 4x and 6x CD changers, the separate drive letters actually added to the convenience of using the product. A user who wants a particular CD can go to a drive letter and find it. Higher-end changers cache the CD contents so that the drives can be browsed quickly without causing the changer to move them around. This is not possible with RSM. Each disk must be mounted by name using the RSM `Mount` command. This requires that you know the logical media ID assigned to the CD by RSM. This information is available in the `RSM` snap-in within the Computer Management console.

Removable media drives come in three general types:

- Fast oversized floppy disk drives: Zip, Sony, and so on
- Slow undersized hard disk drives: Jaz, Shark, and so on
- Fussy plastic burners: CD-R and CD-RW drives and magneto-optical drives

Most of these drives have parallel port and SCSI models. All major vendors have models with Windows 2000 drivers, which should work with Windows Server 2003. The Plug and Play Manager detects the drive during enumeration and loads the appropriate driver. It then turns control over to RSM. The drive is presented in Explorer with an icon that represents a removable media drive.

If you have a SCSI removable media drive, be sure to select a SCSI ID for it that doesn't conflict with other devices on the bus. Also, remember that the results of the SCSI bus scan determine the relative disk location for the ARC path in Boot.ini. If the removable storage device has a SCSI ID lower than that of the primary drive, it inserts itself into the scan list ahead of the boot drive and you get an `Unable to Locate Ntoskrl.exe` error.

Media in removable media drives cannot be partitioned. This includes LS120/240 superfloppies, DVD-RAM drives, Castlewood Orb drives, and other removable media drives with large capacities.

Drive letter assignments can become a challenge when you have removable media drives on a server. During initial Setup, drives and drive partitions are scanned in this order:

- System partition on the boot drive is assigned drive C.
- Boot partition, if in a different partition, is assigned drive D.
- Logical drives in extended partitions and removable media drives come next.
- Basic partitions on fixed drives come last.

This scan order means that removable media drives will get letters ahead of partitions on fixed drives, which you may not prefer. You can change the drive letter after Setup has completed.

If you install a removable media drive after initial setup, it will not disturb the existing drive letters. It adopts the next available drive letter starting from the top of the alphabet. For example, if you have three existing partitions lettered E, F, and M, the removable media drive will take drive letter G.

If you have two or more removable media drives, you can sometimes cause problems because they can swap drive letters if you disable and reinstall them.

If you have a network drive that uses the first letter after the existing hard drives, the removable media drive steps on the network drive and takes the letter. LanMan Server attempts to use the letter then displays an error saying `The Local Device Name Is Already In Use`. You should configure the system to break this network connection and remake it using another letter.

Adding Network Adapters

Even if you disregard all the other features in PnP, the way it simplifies adding and configuring network adapters makes it worth the price of admission.

When selecting server adapters, stick to high-end models from reputable manufacturers. Microsoft has dropped support for many desktop-quality and whitebox network adapters. Also, you may get performance improvements if the adapter supports *Network Driver Interface Specification* (NDIS) 5.0 offload capabilities. See `www.microsoft.com/hwdev/tech/network/taskoffload.asp` for more information.

The *NDIS* drivers that support Windows networking have a well-deserved reputation for being difficult to interface with. PnP, coupled with a properly prepared INF and a driver written by someone who really knows how to code a WDM device driver, makes installing a new network adapter a brief and event-free operation.

Plug and Play Manager discovers the new device during bus enumeration after you start the machine. If you have a server that permits hot-swapping of PCI adapters and a network adapter that is hot-swap enabled, PnP will see the device as soon as you release the software lock on the PCI bus.

PnP assigns resources to the device based on information it obtains from ACPI, which obtained the information from the PCI header of the device. PnP will also discover legacy network adapters, although these are becoming rare and should be avoided. If resources claimed by a legacy device conflicts with a PnP device, the PnP Manager will attempt to assign a different resource to the PnP device. Errors in the Event log will warn you of these sorts of conflicts.

By default, new network interfaces are configured to use Dynamic Host Configuration Protocol (DHCP). To change the TCP/IP settings to static mappings, or to install additional transports, clients, or network services, open the `Properties` of the connection from the Network Connections windows.

If you do not have a DHCP server, the new interface will obtain a network address using *Automatic Private IP Addressing*, or APIPA. This mechanism assigns an address from the `169.254.0.0/16` address space. Microsoft owns this address space and has assigned it for this purpose.

An APIPA client selects a random address from the 65,535 it has available in this space, then pings the address to see if some other client got there first. It makes three attempts before giving up and putting an error on the console. After the client has obtained an address via APIPA, it continues to look for a DHCP server once every five minutes.

If you configure two LAN interfaces to talk to the same network segment, you will get a `Duplicate Computer Name` error. This is because the second adapter will attempt to register its NetBIOS name after the first adapter has already laid claim to it. When installing multiple adapters, you should use either different IP subnets or the `Network Bridge` option.

Diagnosing Network Problems

The Windows Server 2003 Task Manager has an additional tab for monitoring network interface traffic. This provides a quick-and-dirty check on interface performance.

The interface status (available from the Interface icon in the Notification Area or from the Network Connections window) has a Repair option that gets a new IP address from the DHCP server (if applicable) and performs other routines designed to fix network communications.

Hidden Network Adapters

If you have previously uninstalled a network adapter on a server, you may get an error message when you attempt to reinstall another adapter. This is because the interface has not been completely removed from the system but might be hidden from the Device Manager. Open the Device Manager console via Devmgmt.msc and show the hidden devices via View | Show Hidden Devices. Then remove the outdated network device.

When problems get trickier, one handy way to get a quick look at all the network settings for a server is to use the Network Diagnostics window in Help and Support Center. This support page uses WMI parameters to show you the current status of the network interfaces on a server.

There is also a valuable command-line tool, NETDIAG, that performs the same checks and reports them to the console. This is handy for creating scripts and batch files that can take periodic system snapshots.

A new switch was added to the `Netsh` command in Windows Server 2003 that also helps in troubleshooting. It is the `-diag` switch. Using it in conjunction with `-diag show`, you can get a quick listing of current settings and statistics for all network interfaces and network services such as DHCP and WINS.

Using Multiple Displays

If you are a CAD operator or graphic designer, you probably either have a big 21-inch monitor or dual monitors, or both. Both Windows 2000 and Windows Server 2003 support dual displays, but Windows Server 2003 and XP also support DualView adapters, which permit putting different portions of the same image on the two screens.

Only a limited number of vendors produce DualView-compatible adapters. On desktops, the Matrox "G" line includes its Dual Head technology, which can deliver full-frame DVD in one monitor and business graphics in the other, just in case you want to watch *Shrek* while you do spreadsheets. On laptops, Trident Microsystems and SiS are the major suppliers of DualView video controllers.

If you are shopping around for a second video adapter to put in a system that already has an Accelerated Graphics Port (AGP) adapter, be cautious about using the same model PCI adapter because the drivers are different but might have the same name.

You can use the same steps to configure a system with two video adapters or one with a single, DualView adapter and two monitors. The monitors are configured in Display Properties, which is most easily accessed by right-clicking anywhere on the desktop and selecting PROPERTIES from the flyout menu. The `Settings` tab shows the two monitors.

The `Primary` display determines which monitor will display the START menu and status bar. This does not make changes to the underlying system BIOS, so you may see the other monitor display the POST results and initial text phase portion of the Windows boot sequence.

The default orientation puts the logical monitors side by side. You can move the display monitors to change that orientation. You can select different resolutions and refresh rates, but this might cause images to become distorted as you move them between monitors.

Troubleshooting New Devices

When you install a new device, you take the chance that a stable machine will suddenly cease to function or become erratic. Basic diagnostic procedures always apply. If possible, undo what you just did and see if the problem goes away. If not, begin analyzing what changes were made and correlate them to the symptoms you're seeing. This section contains some common tools to help you diagnose problems caused by adding components.

Device Driver Update and Rollback

The easiest way to update a driver is by using the Device Manager console. Obtain the Windows Server 2003/XP or Windows 2000 driver and the associated INF setup script and proceed as directed in Procedure 3.3.

Procedure 3.3 Device Driver Update

1. Right-click the device icon and select `Update Driver`. This launches the Hardware Update Wizard.
2. Select the `Install from a List or Specific Location` option.
3. Click `Next`. The Please Choose Your Search window opens. Select the `Don't Search` option.
4. Click `Next`. The Select Network Adapter window opens. (This will vary, of course, depending on the device you are updating.)
5. Click `Have Disk`. A browse window opens. Navigate to the location of the driver and the associated INF setup script.
6. Select the INF script corresponding to the device. The system displays the strings in the INF. Verify that they match the device you are updating.
7. Click `Next` to install the drivers.
8. Click `Finish` to close the wizard.

At this point, the Properties window for the device should show the new version information. If the machine becomes unstable or crashes at this point, you can boot to Safe mode then roll back the device to the old driver until you figure out what happened. Follow Procedure 3.4.

Procedure 3.4 Device Driver Rollback

1. Open the `Properties` window for the device.
2. Select the Driver tab (see Figure 3.19).

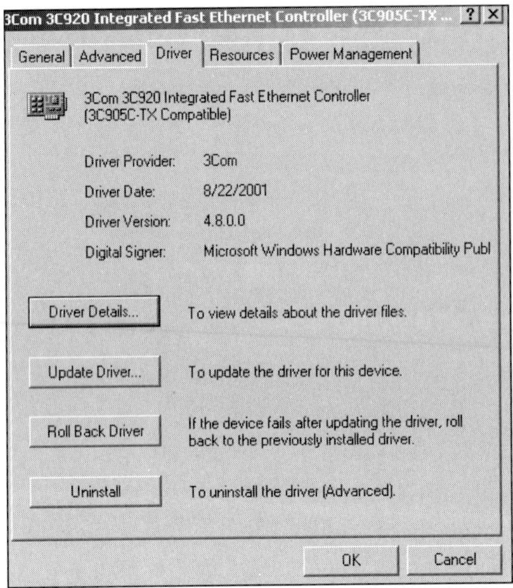

Figure 3.19 Device Driver properties showing `Roll Back Driver` option.

3. Click `Roll Back Driver`.
4. The system asks if you're sure. Click `OK` to complete the job.

The system obtains the old driver out of the driver library and reinstalls it. The Properties window refreshes with the old version number.

Building a Windows Server 2003 Boot Disk

It is very common when adding new mass storage devices or interfaces that the machine refuses to boot. This occurs generally because the additional drive or interface changed the ARC path to the Windows Server 2003 boot partition. Other reasons for failure to boot include the following:

- The Windows Server 2003 system files at the root of the boot partition have been corrupted or deleted.
- The boot sector has been corrupted by a virus.
- A user ran SYS against the C drive in an attempt to make the machine dual-boot.
- The primary drive in a mirrored set has failed (software RAID only).
- The Ntbootdd.sys driver has been deleted or corrupted on a system with a SCSI interface that has no BIOS.

In all these situations, the core Windows Server 2003 files in the `\Windows` directory are probably just fine; all you need to do is bypass the corrupted files and disk structures at the beginning of the boot drive. You can do this on IA32 machines by booting to a floppy that contains the same Windows Server 2003 system files found at the root of the boot disk. This is called a *fault tolerant boot disk*.

It is not necessary, nor is it possible, to use a fault tolerant boot disk on an IA64 machine. Use the EFI shell to select a boot partition. See Chapter 1 for details.

When building a fault tolerant boot disk, it's important to use a floppy that has been formatting on a machine running Windows Server 2003 or XP. These system files are capable of booting earlier versions of NT-based operating systems, but the opposite is not true. You cannot boot Windows Server 2003 using a fault tolerant disk built on a Windows 2000 server.

To configure a fault tolerant boot disk in Windows Server 2003, follow Procedure 3.5.

Procedure 3.5 Creating a Fault Tolerant Boot Floppy Disk

1. Use the ATTRIB utility to remove the read-only and hidden attributes from the following system files at the root of the boot drive:

```
Ntldr
Ntdetect.com
Boot.ini
Ntbootdd.sys (if present)
```

2. Insert a blank floppy disk into the floppy disk drive and format it. You can use the `Quick Format` option if you're sure that there are no disk defects.
3. When format is complete, copy the files listed in Step 1 to the floppy.
4. Open `Notepad` and use it to edit the Boot.ini file on the floppy disk.
5. Change the `Time Setting` entry to `-1`. This disables the countdown timer. (You do not have to do this, but I find it helpful to keep the counter from ticking down when I'm troubleshooting.)
6. Save the changes and close `Notepad`.
7. Restart the computer and boot from the fault tolerant boot floppy disk.
8. When the BOOT menu appears, highlight the entry representing the partition containing the Windows Server 2003 system files and press `Enter` to finish the boot.

The ARC path in Boot.ini tells NTLDR where to find the Windows Server 2003 boot files on the hard drive. The remainder of the boot process should proceed normally. At this point, the floppy disk is no longer needed. Remove it from the drive.

Keep a copy of the fault tolerant boot disk handy for booting workstations and servers in the field. If the boot partition has more than 7.8GB, or a non-standard geometry, or is on a SCSI drive with an interface that has no BIOS, the ARC path will have a `signature()` entry. The number in the parentheses is a unique ID written to the Master Boot Record (MBR) of the boot drive. The Boot.ini for this machine will not work on another machine. Clearly label the boot floppy disk and keep it in safe place.

Resolving SCSI Problems

If Plug and Play Manager does not recognize the controller or the disks on the controller, or you get data corruption or a significant number of errors in the Event log relating to the SCSI devices on that interface, the most likely causes are improper termination or excessive cable length. The following can cause improper termination:

- Mixing active and passive terminations.
- Mixing cable types, which can cause impedance matching and timing problems.
- Having too many terminations, such as having the SCSI controller in the middle of the bus with active termination enabled on the controller and terminators at either end of the cable.
- Forgetting to attach the resistor pack.
- Attaching a resistor pack when active termination is enabled.
- Thinking that you have enabled active termination on a device but actually putting the jumper on the wrong pins.
- Thinking that you have disabled active termination on a device but actually removing the jumper from the wrong pins.

The cable and terminator configuration might have worked in NT4, but Windows Server 2003 puts much greater demand on the hard disk interface to boost performance. Weaklings break down quickly. Replace the interface with one on the HCL. If it is built into the motherboard, get a PCI adapter and disable the motherboard interface.

If you already have a SCSI adapter and you add a second one of the exact make and model, you may need to disable the BIOS on the second adapter to keep it from squabbling with the first adapter. This does not affect Windows Server 2003 functionality; if you put an installation of Windows Server 2003 on a disk connected to the second adapter, however, Setup will copy the SCSI miniport driver to the root of the partition and name it Ntbootdd.sys so that NTLDR can use the driver to scan the SCSI bus.

Primary Drive Failure

If you have mirrored drives and the primary drive fails, you can use the fault tolerant boot floppy disk to boot from the mirrored partition. If the mirrored drive is the second disk on a SCSI chain, for example, the ARC path would be `multi(0)disk(0)rdisk(1)partition(1)\WINNT)`.

Setup will also use a `signature()` controller ID in the ARC path in Boot.ini to identify the drive. The parameter in the parentheses of `signature()` is a special signature in the Master Boot Record placed there by Setup.

You may get an `Unable to Locate Operating System` error after adding a second SCSI controller. You can thank PCI for that. In most cases, the SCSI adapter with the lowest IOBase address is assumed to be the boot host adapter. In PnP systems, the PCI slot closest to the CPU normally gets the lowest IOBase address. Therefore, if you installed the second adapter in a slot closer to the CPU (lower number), you changed your active drive designation. Try swapping PCI slots. Plug and Play Manager assigns component identifiers based on their PCI slot; therefore, by swapping slots, you'll force a new PnP enumeration.

Correcting Non-PnP System Hangs

If the system hangs while NTDETECT is running, you probably have a problem with the motherboard or memory or hard drive interface. The function of NTDETECT is to recognize hardware. If it cannot do its job, it stalls.

You cannot resolve this error until you know what component is causing the hang. There are a couple of ways to find this out. One way is to press `F8` at the BOOT menu and select the `Boot Logging` option. This writes a Boot log to the hard drive; if you can't get booted, however, you cannot read the log.

The second alternative is to use a debug version of Ntdetect.COM called Ntdetect.chk. The Ntdetect.chk file is located on the Windows Server 2003 CD in the `\Support\Debug\I386` directory. Use Ntdetect.chk as instructed in Procedure 3.6

Procedure 3.6 Using Ntdetect.chk

1. Make a fault tolerant boot floppy using Windows Server 2003.
2. Copy Ntdetect.chk onto the duplicate disk.
3. Rename Ntdetect.com to Ntdetect.old.
4. Rename Ntdetect.chk to Ntdetect.com.
5. Reboot using the disk with the renamed Ntdetect.chk.

The debug version of NTDETECT works just like the regular version except that it displays what it detects as each component is encountered. When the system hangs, the last component on the screen is the one causing the problem. Look for IRQ or IOBase conflicts.

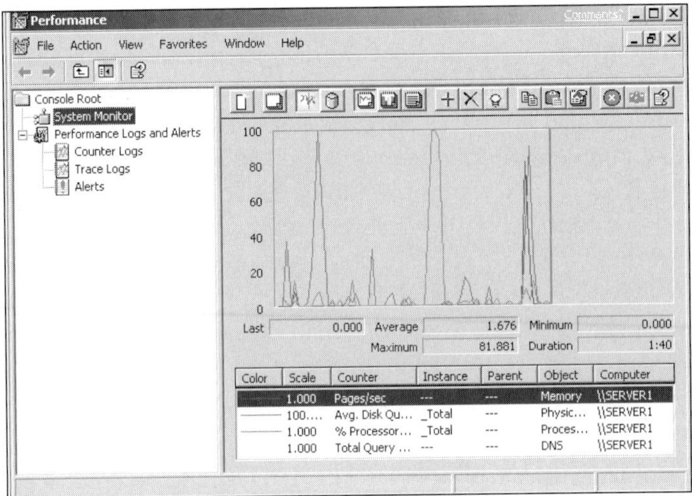

Figure 3.20 Performance Monitor console.

Tracking Kernel Memory Use

You should try to keep long-term statistics for kernel memory use on your servers so that you can spot abnormal trends. The most convenient tool for doing this is Performance Monitor. Open the `Performance Monitor` console using START | PROGRAMS | ADMINISTRATIVE TOOLS | PERFORMANCE. Figure 3.20 shows an example.

The Performance Monitor console contains two snap-ins. The `System Monitor` snap-in is an ActiveX control designed to display performance counters in graphical format. The `Performance Logs and Alerts` snap-in is designed to collect performance statistics and write them to a log or send alerts to a console or Event log. Logs are the best way to collect long-term performance statistics. Configure a log to collect kernel memory statistics by following the steps shown in Procedure 3.7.

Procedure 3.7 Configuring Performance Monitor to Collect Kernel Memory Statistics

1. Expand the tree under `Performance Logs and Alerts` and highlight `Counter Logs`.
2. Right-click a blank area in the right pane and select NEW LOG SETTINGS from the flyout menu. The New Log Settings window opens.
3. Enter a name for the log, such as `Long-Term kernel Memory Use`.
4. Click `OK`. A management window opens for the log. The window name matches the log name you assigned in Step 3.
5. Click `Add`. The Select Counters window opens.

6. Under `Performance Object`, select `Memory` from the drop-down box.
7. Select the `All Counters` radio button. Long-term performance data collection involves taking snapshots at infrequent intervals, such as once an hour, so collecting all available counters will not be too much of a burden on the server.
8. Click `Add` to add the counters to the log, and then click `Close` to return to the main log management window.
9. Set the `Sample Data Every` value to `1 Hour`.
10. Select the `Log Files` tab. The default location of the log is a folder called `\Perflog` at the root of the system partition. You can change this location using the `Browse` button.
11. The default filename uses the name you assigned to the log plus a six-digit number. If you stipulate a `Log File Size Limit` at the bottom of the window, a log fills up, then closes, and another begins filling.
12. Click `OK` to save the selections and return to the Performance Monitor console.

Collect statistics for a few days, then view the contents of the log using the `System Monitor` snap-in. To do this, select the log as the source for the chart by following the steps shown in Procedure 3.8.

Procedure 3.8 Charting Performance Monitor Logs

1. Highlight the `System Monitor` icon. An empty chart appears in the right pane.
2. Right-click the chart and select PROPERTIES from the flyout menu. The Properties window opens.
3. Select the `Source` tab.
4. Select the `Log File` radio button.
5. Click `Browse` to open the Select Log File navigation tool. The focus is set automatically to the `\Perflog` folder.
6. Double-click the name of the counter log you configured to select it and return to the System Monitor Properties window.
7. Click `OK` to save the selections, close the window, and return to the main Performance window. Nothing happens quite yet.
8. Right-click the right pane again and this time select ADD COUNTERS from the flyout menu. The Add Counters window opens.
9. Select the `All Counters` radio button, and then click `Add` followed by `Close`. This adds all the counters to the chart. If that makes the chart too busy, you can delete counter entries.

The chart shows the statistics you collected in the log. Up to 100 data points can be displayed. Press `Ctrl+H` to turn on highlighting so that any counter you select in the lower part of the window turns into a white line in the chart.

Moving Forward

Now that we have the Windows Server 2003 operating system installed on a few servers, it's time to do something useful with them. You can't use a server, though, unless you can find it, so the next two chapters cover name resolution and service location.

4 Managing NetBIOS Name Resolution

Although Windows Server 2003 is unquestionably a TCP/IP product, a few vestiges of its NetBIOS ancestors still lurk in the shadows. These vestiges make their appearance when you try to resolve a computer name or service name into an IP address when mapping network drives or using other features of Windows networking.

For example, consider the domain configuration shown in Figure 4.1. If the Windows client cannot determine the IP addresses corresponding to the domains and their domain controllers, the client cannot authenticate itself or any of its users. If it cannot resolve the names of servers, it cannot connect users to network resources. Name resolution, therefore, is a vital task. You should focus your attention on designing a solid name resolution infrastructure before beginning an enterprise deployment of Windows Server 2003.

This chapter concentrates on classic NetBIOS name resolution to support down-level clients and applications that rely on NetBIOS name resolution. Chapter 5, "Managing DNS," covers DNS name resolution. Windows Server 2003 can use either or both methods, depending on the situation and configuration.

Because name resolution is integrated into network protocols, the chapter starts with an overview of Windows Server 2003 networking with a focus on the addresses and ports used for name resolution. The focus then shifts to implementation and covers the following topics:

- Network diagnostic utilities
- Resolving NetBIOS names using broadcasts, Lmhosts, and WINS
- Installing WINS
- Configuring and managing WINS replication
- Disabling NetBIOS name resolution

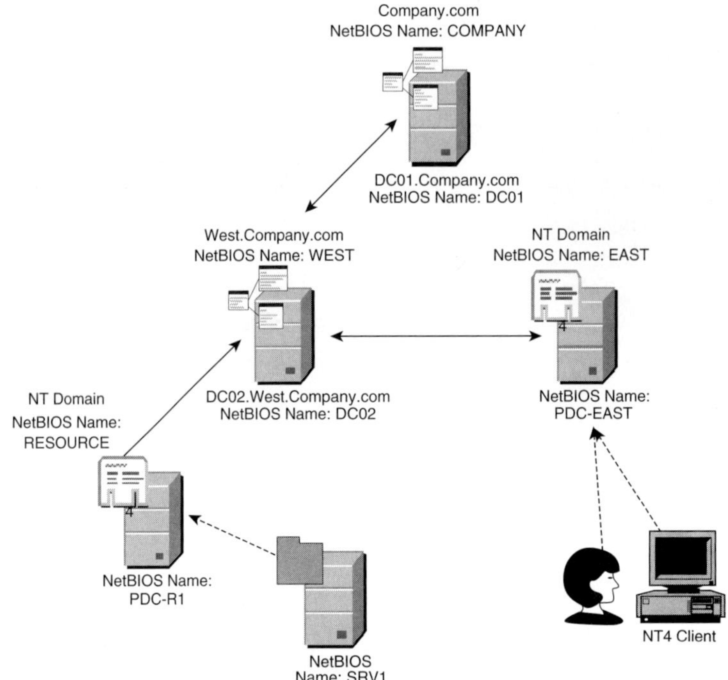

Figure 4.1 Sample network configuration for analyzing classic name resolution.

New Features in Windows Server 2003

No enhanced classic name resolution features have been included in Windows Server 2003 compared to Windows 2000. The WINS MMC console has been improved to simplify selecting, sorting, and listing database entries.

Overview of Windows Server 2003 Networking

This topic covers the methods used by Windows Server 2003 to determine the proper address and port at each Network layer. It uses the standard Open System Interconnection (OSI) model as a road map (see Figure 4.2). Windows networking doesn't precisely follow OSI, but the structure is close enough to permit parallels.

Data Link Layer

In the OSI model, the data link layer defines methods for packaging data to be transmitted over physical media. The OSI data link layer is divided by IEEE 802.1 into a *Media Access Control* (MAC) layer and a *Logical Link Control* (LLC) layer.

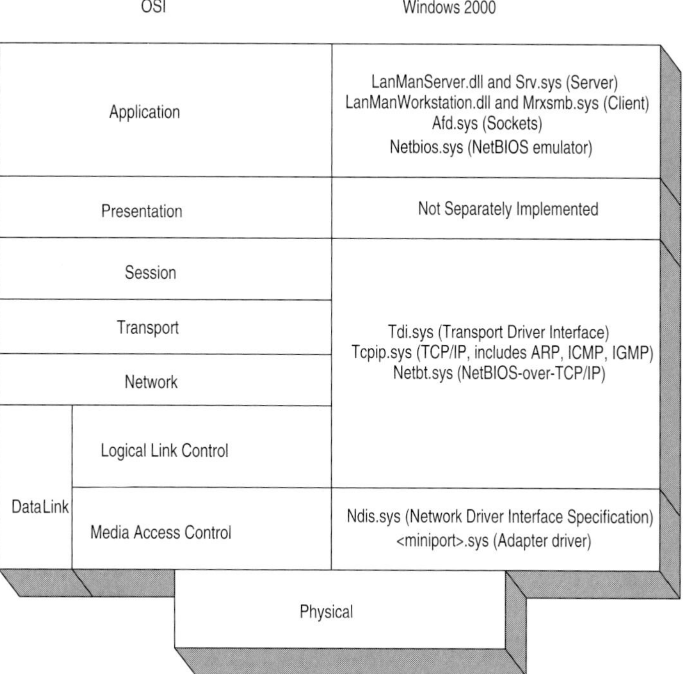

Figure 4.2 Diagram of OSI layers and Windows Server 2003 network drivers.

Windows networking does not implement separate MAC and LLC drivers. Instead, the network transport drivers handle LLC, whereas MAC duties are handled by the *Network Driver Interface Specification* driver (NDIS), Ndis.sys, along with a set of miniport and filter drivers written by vendors. Adapter miniport drivers come in the form of SYS drivers stored under `\Windows\Drivers`. A driver is installed with the help of an associated INF file located in `\Windows\Inf`. The network INF files are prefixed with NET*.

The NDIS and adapter miniport drivers work with the controller chip on the adapter to frame data for transmission. The transmission method depends on the physical media. It could be Ethernet, Token Ring, IEEE 802.11b wireless, or some other communication method.

A transmission frame requires a MAC address to identify the destination interface. NDIS cannot discover this address. A higher-level protocol must supply it.

MAC Address Components

The MAC address is branded into the adapter's ROM. It consists of a unique six-octet number. The first three octets identify the manufacturer. (For example, the machine I'm using has a NetGear adapter branded with 00A0CC for the manufacturer's ID.) Most major manufacturers have several MAC IDs assigned to them. The final three octets of the MAC address are assigned in sequence by the manufacturer.

Network and Transport Layers

A little further up the OSI stack is the Network layer, responsible for traffic management, and the Transport layer, responsible for connection management. In TCP/IP, Network layer functions are assigned to the *Internet Protocol* (IP) and Transport layer functions are assigned to either the *Transport Control Protocol* (TCP) or the *User Datagram Protocol* (UDP). Windows Server 2003 uses a single driver, Tcpip.sys, to implement both protocols.

Addressing at the Network layer takes the form of an IP address, a 32-bit number normally shown in dotted-decimal notation, such as `10.1.50.233`. Every IP packet must contain the IP address of the destination host unless it is a broadcast or multicast packet. A key responsibility of Tcpip.sys is to determine the IP address associated with a packet's destination.

Addressing at the Transport layer takes the form of a port number. Many TCP/IP network applications have well-known port numbers. For example, FTP uses TCP port 21 and HTTP uses TCP port 80. RFC 1700, "Assigned Numbers," lists these port numbers.

The combination of an IP address and a port number is called a *socket*. A high-level application provides a socket number that the Tcpip.sys driver parses into its component parts when constructing datagrams and packets.

Some high-level applications do not use TCP or UDP. These so-called *raw IP* applications communicate directly to the IP layer. Windows Server 2003 supports raw IP applications as long as they use standard API calls where the host identification can be extracted. A respected member of the Internet community, Steve Gibson, has voiced concerns over this raw IP support because of the potential for Denial-of-Service and spoofing exploits. Read a summary of Mr. Gibson's white paper at `grc.com/dos/xpsummary.htm`.

Session Layer

The OSI Session layer is responsible for handling connection-oriented communications. This works in a similar fashion to human communication. You and I make eye contact, we shake hands, and we maintain each other's attention while we alternately speak and listen.

IPv6 Support in Windows Server 2003

The standard 32-bit IP address space is becoming a deployment barrier thanks to the limited number of networks and hosts it can support. Its 128-bit replacement, IPv6, has been in standards track for several years but is making slow inroads. Legacy hardware must be upgraded to support it, and the proliferation of Network Address Translation (NAT) has taken away the urgency to upgrade. IPv6 is described in RFC 2460, "Internet Protocol, Version 6 (IPv6) Specification."

If you want to enable IPv6 support in Windows Server 2003, do so by running `ipv6 install` at a command prompt or by clicking install in the interface properties window. This makes no changes to the UI tools. All IPv6 protocol management is performed using the `ipv6` utility. The IPv4 and IPv6 address spaces can coexist on the same machine.

Rather than create a separate driver for session management, the TCP/IP stack gives responsibility to the TCP protocol to implement Session layer functionality. TCP assigns a session number to a connection, sequences the datagrams exchanged across the connection, and guarantees delivery of those datagrams. High-level applications usually obtain session support by calling upon TCP, but they are also free to use their own session-control methods.

Sessionless applications resemble dysfunctional relationships where one computer listens only as long as the other computer has something interesting to say. When it is not necessary to build a session, high-level applications use the UDP protocol. UDP is capable of packaging data into a single datagram and does not guarantee delivery of that datagram. Applications typically use UDP for broadcasts/multicasts and brief messages. DNS, for example, uses UDP.

Presentation Layer

Presentation layer functionality, such as encryption and data translation, is not implemented as a distinct set of drivers in Windows Server 2003. Applications must provide this service, if they require it.

Application Layer

At the top of the OSI model sits the Application layer. This is where the Windows Server 2003 network services live. An example is the LAN Manager Workstation service and its complementary file system driver, Mrxsmb.sys. The workstation service communicates with the LAN Manager Server service and its file system driver, Srv.sys.

Network applications can use any method they desire for identifying their peers. Windows networking components such as LAN Manager Workstation and LAN Manager Server use computer names. These names are often called NetBIOS names because the underlying command protocol, Server Message Block (SMB), has its roots in NetBIOS. See section, "SMB and NetBIOS Names," for more information.

A NetBIOS name consists of 15 characters and a 1-byte service identifier. If the actual name has fewer than 15 characters, the name is padded to 15 bytes before appending the service identifier. For example, the Messenger service on computer `SVR3` would identify itself in an SMB message as `SVR3 <03>`. The number in angle brackets is the service ID.

NetBIOS Name Restrictions

NetBIOS names are often called *flat names* because they have no hierarchical structure. Flat names must be unique within a Windows domain. Also, flat names must be unique regardless of their domain or workgroup affiliation if the hosts share the same network segment. For example, a computer in the `LOX` domain with an IP address of `10.1.1.1/16` cannot have the same name as a computer in the `BAGEL` domain with the IP address `10.1.1.2/16`. This is not true of TCP/IP host names. DNS is perfectly happy saying, "This is my brother Darrell and this is my other brother Darrell."

> **NetBIOS Scope Options**
> Quite a while back, Microsoft and IBM tried to introduce a form of hierarchical domain naming called *scope options* into NetBIOS, but these scopes were clumsy to use and never really caught on. The design simulated DNS naming hierarchies in a very limited way, but was too convoluted to be effective.

NetBIOS names can contain any ANSI character, including spaces, with the following exceptions: `/\[]":;|<>+=,?*`. Acceptable NetBIOS names include the following:

```
MYSUPERCOMPUTER
MY   COMPUTER
MY#1COMPUTER
MY_COMPUTER
MY-COMPUTER
MY!COMPUTER
```

Some characters are permitted in NetBIOS names but not included in standard DNS naming. See RFC 952, "DOD Internet Host Table Specification," and RFC 1123, "Requirements for Internet Hosts—Application and Support," for more information. Because Windows Server 2003 computers live in both the TCP/IP world and the NetBIOS world, you may want to avoid characters not supported by DNS. A commonly used character in Windows names, the underscore, is now part of the official DNS character set but not universally recognized thanks to older DNS servers.

SMB and NetBIOS Names

NetBIOS is a high-level network interface. It got its name because it was originally implemented in hardware. A NetBIOS application builds a data structure called a *Network Control Block* (NCB) then initiates a BIOS function call to send the NCB contents to a network adapter. Windows Server 2003 supports NetBIOS applications using a NetBIOS emulator, which traps the BIOS calls and converts them to network function calls.

NetBIOS applications are becoming very rare. SMB applications such as LanMan Workstation and LanMan Server use NetBIOS naming but are not NetBIOS applications. The reason for the similar nomenclature lies in their shared history. IBM co-developed NetBIOS with Sytek and it became a *de facto* standard for PC network interfaces. At the same time, IBM and Microsoft were working with 3Com to develop the network command language that eventually became SMB. Early versions of SMB applications used NetBIOS as a network interface with NETBEUI (NetBIOS Extended User Interface) as a transport protocol.

Beginning with NT Advanced Server (and versions of OS/2 LAN Manager and Warp from IBM), SMB matured into a transport-independent command language. Because SMB and NetBIOS grew up together, backward compatibility required that a few NetBIOS conventions be retained in SMB. This includes NetBIOS naming and NetBIOS name resolution.

NetBIOS Services

The final byte in a NetBIOS computer name designates a service such as Browser, Domain Controller, and so forth. The combination of the computer name in the first 15 bytes and the service ID in the 16th byte forms a unique identifier, similar to the way an IP address and TCP/UDP port number combine to form a unique socket. Figure 4.3 shows a list of the NetBIOS record types managed by a WINS server. See the "Installing WINS" topic in this chapter for information on using the WINS console.

The combination of NetBIOS name and service identifiers are classified into NetBIOS name types. The Netbt.sys driver uses NetBIOS name types to handle name registration. Here are the registration handling methods:

- **Unique.** The associated name/service combination can use only one IP address. If another computer tries to register the same name/service combination with a different IP address, it will be challenged. If one Windows Server 2003 computer named BORIS is already on the network, for example, a second computer named BORIS will not be permitted to register the same NetBIOS service.
- **Group.** Multiple computers can use the associated name/service combination. The Netbt.sys driver uses the Group type to define multicast groups. An SMB message directed at a multicast group in network `10.1.0.0`, for example, would use an IP multicast address of `10.1.255.255`. Multicasting reduces the processing load on computers in the network because only members of the multicast group need to examine the packet.

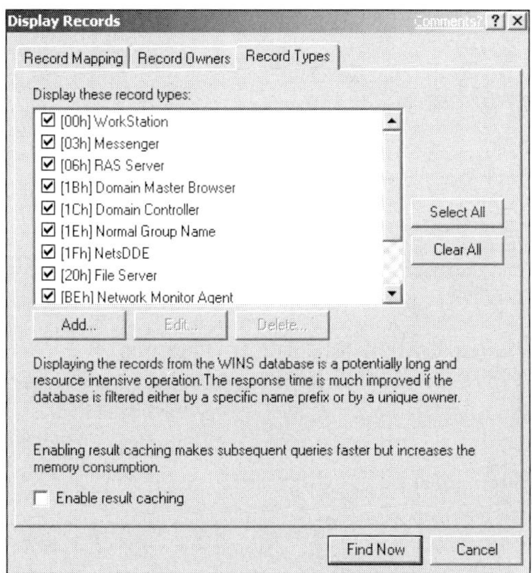

Figure 4.3 WINS console showing NetBIOS record types managed by a WINS server.

- **Multihomed.** This name/service combination must be unique, but can be associated with multiple IP addresses. The Netbt.sys driver uses the Multihomed type to designate services registered by a machine with multiple network adapters. The computer's name/service combination is registered with the IP address of each adapter.
- **Internet.** This special group designation identifies primary and backup domain controllers. A primary domain controller (PDC) normally replicates with its backup domain controllers (BDCs) using multicasts for efficiency. Some routers block multicast packets. This is where WINS takes over. The WINS server takes the multicast replication packets and directs them as unicast packets directly to the IP addresses of BDCs in its database. These unicast packets make it through intervening routers to their respective BDCs.

Name Resolution and Network Services

Table 4.1 lists the addresses, ports, and names used at each layer of the OSI model as it is implemented in Windows Server 2003. Processes running at each layer communicate with their peer processes at other stations using these addresses, ports, and names.

Let's now work our way down the OSI stack to see how each layer resolves the NetBIOS name into an address that can be used to communicate with its peer layer on another machine.

Table 4.1 Addresses and Names Used at Each Windows Server 2003 Network Layer

Layer	Protocol	Name or Address
Application	SMB	NetBIOS name
Transport	TCP or UDP	Port number
Network	IP	IP address
Data link	NDIS	MAC address

Multihomed NetBIOS Registrations and Single Adapters

The *Multihomed* NetBIOS name type is not assigned to name/service combinations originating from a computer with multiple IP addresses bound to the same adapter. Only the first IP address bound to the adapter is registered with WINS, but an SMB connection can be made to any IP address in the binding list. This contrasts to NT, where an SMB connection could only be made to the top address in the binding list.

Application Layer and Server Message Block (SMB)

Windows client redirectors and servers use the SMB protocol to communicate with each other. There are a variety of SMB dialects representing different maturity states of the protocol. One of the first actions in an SMB transaction is a negotiation between the parties to agree on a common dialect. Windows Server 2003 uses the NT LM 0.12 dialect.

A few years ago, Microsoft rechristened SMB as the *Common Internet File System* (CIFS). The new name is purely market positioning. The CIFS/SMB dialect used by Windows Server 2003 is the same dialect used by all versions of NT since 3.51.

In the absence of a locator mechanism such as WINS or DNS, SMB applications can use broadcasts to find each other. This works something like a CB radio. When the Workstation service on one station wants to communicate with the Server service on another station, for example, the Workstation service puts out a broadcast that essentially says, "Breaker on that Ethernet. This here's the Workstation service on PRO1 looking for that Server service on SVR13. Come on back, SRV13 Server service." When the Server service on SVR13 gets this message, it returns a response such as, "You got that SRV13 Server service, good buddy. Come on back." The two services agree on a dialect, assign a unique ID to the session, and begin communications.

When a Windows computer that is a member of a domain establishes SMB communication with a domain controller, it also establishes a secure *Remote Procedure Call* (RPC) session. This RPC session uses SMB but is capable of encrypting the traffic used to carry sensitive information between a client and a server. This includes authentication information.

The computer password is stored in the local Security Account Manager (SAM) of the client and in Active Directory. If a domain member cannot resolve the domain controller name into an IP address, it cannot build a secure RPC channel and users cannot get authenticated in the domain.

Transport Layer

SMB is a session-oriented protocol. Peer SMB applications running on two stations must establish a link with each other prior to exchanging SMB messages. For this reason, SMB traffic is always carried in TCP datagrams.

SMB and System Integration

SMB is the *lingua franca* for a variety of network operating systems, not just Windows Server 2003. It is used by all versions of Windows, from Windows for Workgroups through Windows 9x and classic NT. OS/2 Warp uses SMB because Warp and NT share a common ancestor in OS/2 LAN Manager. SMB is also used by Samba, a UNIX port of SMB. There are Samba implementations for NetWare and VMS, as well.

Different SMB applications can talk to each other, although you might not get full functionality. It's like a conversation between a Portuguese merchant and an Italian tourist. The general ideas might get across just fine, but there may be problems with the details of the transaction. SMB applications on non-Windows platforms most commonly have problems with authentication.

The well-known port for SMB traffic is TCP port 139. This port is used by the NetBIOS-over-TCP helper, Netbt.sys, which essentially "tunnels" SMB into TCP. Windows Server 2003 and Windows 2000 computers can use TCP directly to carry SMB commands. This "direct hosting" of SMB occurs over TCP port 445. Windows computers capable of direct SMB communication will always use TCP port 445 to exchange traffic with each other while falling back on classic TCP port 139 to exchange traffic with downlevel clients. See "Disabling NetBIOS-over-TCP/IP Name Resolution" at the end of this chapter for more information about the benefits of using direct hosting of SMB exclusively.

Windows computers can also exchange sessionless traffic. Examples include name resolution/registration transactions and NetBIOS broadcasts. Because these messages do not require sessions and are generally quite small, they use UDP. Windows uses UDP port 137 for NetBIOS name resolution/registration and UDP port 138 for NetBIOS broadcasts and unidirectional traffic. For example, when you use the `net send` command to pop up a message on a user's console, the message goes out over UDP port 138.

A TCP-based service places a "listen" on a TCP port then waits for connections to that port. You can get a list of the active TCP ports on a server using the NETSTAT utility with the syntax `netstat -a`. If a port is listed in the Services file located at `C:\Windows\System32\drivers\etc`, the registered port name is used in place of the port number. You can get a full list of ports from `www.iana.org`.

A new feature in the NETSTAT utility in Windows Server 2003 is the ability to list the process that owns each port. This helps identify rogue processes and acts as a troubleshooting aid. Here is a sample listing:

```
C:\>netstat -ao

Active Connections

  Proto  Local Address          Foreign Address         State          PID
  TCP    LAPTOP:http            LAPTOP.company.com:0    LISTENING      1420
  TCP    LAPTOP:epmap           LAPTOP.company.com:0    LISTENING      976
  TCP    LAPTOP:https           LAPTOP.company.com:0    LISTENING      1420
  TCP    LAPTOP:microsoft-ds    LAPTOP.company.com:0    LISTENING      4
```

You can get a mapping of PIDs (process IDs) to service names using Task Manager or the new TASKLIST utility in Windows Server 2003. Here is a sample listing using the `/svc` switch to show the individual services under each process executable:

```
svchost.exe                  976 RpcSs
svchost.exe                 1000 AudioSrv, Browser, CryptSvc, Dhcp, dmserver,
                                 ERSvc, EventSystem, helpsvc, lanmanserver,
                                 lanmanworkstation, Messenger, Netman, Nla,
                                 RasMan, Schedule, seclogon, SENS,
                                 ShellHWDetection, srservice, TapiSrv,
                                 TermService, Themes, TrkWks, uploadmgr,
                                 W32Time, winmgmt, WmdmPmSp, wuauserv, WZCSVC
```

```
svchost.exe                1164 Dnscache
svchost.exe                1188 LmHosts, RemoteRegistry, SSDPSRV, WebClient
spoolsv.exe                1280 Spooler
inetinfo.exe               1420 IISADMIN, W3SVC
```

Another great utility for seeing TCP port usage is the FPORt tool from Foundstone (www.foundstone.com). Here is a sample listing:

```
D:\>fport
FPort v2.0 - TCP/IP Process to Port Mapper
Copyright 2000 by Foundstone, Inc.
http://www.foundstone.com

Pid   Process            Port  Proto Path
1420  inetinfo       ->  80    TCP   C:\WINDOWS\System32\inetsrv\inetinfo.exe
976   svchost        ->  135   TCP   C:\WINDOWS\system32\svchost.exe
4     System         ->  139   TCP
1420  inetinfo       ->  443   TCP   C:\WINDOWS\System32\inetsrv\inetinfo.exe
4     System         ->  445   TCP
1000  svchost        ->  1025  TCP   C:\WINDOWS\System32\svchost.exe
1420  inetinfo       ->  1027  TCP   C:\WINDOWS\System32\inetsrv\inetinfo.exe
```

Network Layer

The IP protocol takes UDP and TCP datagrams and packages them for delivery to the NDIS driver waiting at the MAC layer. IP can also carry so-called raw IP traffic from applications that bypass TCP and UDP.

The Tcpip.sys driver is responsible for determining the IP address of the destination based on the NetBIOS name in the SMB message. Tcpip.sys can either use its own internal DNS resolver or it can rely on the NetBIOS-over-TCP/IP helper, Netbt.sys, to resolve the address using NetBIOS name resolution. In brief, Tcpip.sys has the following tools at its disposal:

- **Lmhosts.** This file contains a set of entries consisting of IP addresses and their corresponding NetBIOS computer names.
- **Hosts.** This file contains a set of entries consisting of IP addresses and their corresponding DNS host names.
- **Broadcasts.** This method uses UDP datagrams sent as IP multicasts that request a response from the station having the destination name in the datagram. A response to this datagram contains the station's IP address.
- **WINS.** This is a central database containing flat NetBIOS names, service IDs, and IP addresses.

Restricting SMB Traffic Through Firewalls

If you want to restrict SMB communications from outside the local network, configure your firewall or TCP/IP filter to block traffic over TCP port 139 and UDP ports 138 and 137. If you want to block SMB traffic from Windows Server 2003, XP, and Windows 2000, also block TCP port 445.

- **NetBIOS name cache.** When a NetBIOS name is resolved, it is cached to speed up subsequent lookups.
- **DNS.** This is a central database containing hierarchical host names and IP addresses.
- **DNS resolver cache.** When a DNS name is resolved, it is cached to speed up subsequent lookups.

A simple way to remember the order in which TCP/IP uses these tools is the phrase "Can We Buy Large Hard Drives?" The first letters are keys for cache, WINS, Broadcast, Lmhosts, Hosts, and DNS.

Media Access Control Layer

By the time the original SMB message arrives at the network adapter, it has been sliced and diced and nearly fully digested. Just one thing is lacking. The NDIS drivers at the MAC layer don't know diddly about NetBIOS names, TCP/UDP ports, or IP addresses. Down here in the basement of the OSI stack, only one thing counts, and that is the MAC address associated with the physical device. Tcpip.sys must provide a MAC address to the NDIS driver so NDIS can build a transmission frame. For this purpose, Tcpip.sys uses the *Address Resolution Protocol*, or ARP.

ARP works by broadcasting the destination stations' IP address then waiting for a response. All network interfaces on the subnet hear the broadcast, but only the station with the matching IP address responds. The response contains the station's MAC address.

Tcpip.sys plucks the MAC address out of the ARP response and gives it to NDIS. The NDIS drivers use the MAC address to build the header of the transmission frame. Tcpip.sys caches the IP address/MAC address pair so it doesn't need to do another ARP broadcast for a while. A cache entry times out after 10 minutes if it is used and after 2 minutes if it is not used.

ARP broadcasts succeed even in routed environments. IP routers are programmed to act on ARP requests for IP addresses in their network range. The router responds by returning the MAC address of the router interface associated with the network number in the IP address. This fools the originating station into thinking that it is talking to the destination station. The router then repackages the packet and sends it either to the destination network (if it is in the routing table) or to its own gateway for further processing.

Internet Control Management Protocol (ICMP)

Another Network layer protocol implemented by Tcpip.sys is the *Internet Control Management Protocol* (ICMP).

The most familiar use of ICMP is in diagnostic programs such as Ping and Tracert. When you ping a host, for example, the result is a series of ICMP Echo Request and ICMP Echo Reply transactions.

ICMP is also used to communicate network connection problems between physical layer entities. For example, if an IP packet exceeds the *Maximum Transmission Unit* (MTU) value for a router interface, the router discards the packet and sends back an ICMP message with the correct MTU.

You can view the MAC address returned from a host as part of an arp transaction in a couple of ways. One way is to first ping the host then display the contents of the arp cache using the arp utility with this syntax: arp -c. A better way is to use the new GETMAC utility in Windows Server 2003. Here is an example listing:

```
D:\>getmac /s 192.168.0.1

Physical Address    Transport Name
=================== ==========================================================
00-02-3A-2A-3C-DC   \Device\Tcpip_{CDB02354-574F-4FEE-8CFF-AFBCE6CC1511}
```

You can see the MAC address associated with the network adapters in your machine by opening a command prompt and entering `ipconfig /all`. This also shows the IP information associated with the interfaces. Here is an example:

```
C:\>Ipconfig /all

Windows Server 2003 IP Configuration

        Host Name . . . . . . . . . . . . : PRO1
        Primary DNS Suffix  . . . . . . . : Company.com
        Node Type . . . . . . . . . . . . : Hybrid
        IP Routing Enabled. . . . . . . . : No
        WINS Proxy Enabled. . . . . . . . : No

Ethernet adapter Local Area Connection 2:

        Connection-specific DNS Suffix  . : Company.com
        Description . . . . . . . . . . . : NETGEAR FA310TX Fast Ethernet
➥Adapter (NGRPCI)
        Physical Address. . . . . . . . . : 00-A0-CC-AA-AA-AA
        DHCP Enabled. . . . . . . . . . . : No
        IP Address. . . . . . . . . . . . : 10.1.200.1
        Subnet Mask . . . . . . . . . . . : 255.255.0.0
        Default Gateway . . . . . . . . . : 10.1.1.254
        DNS Servers . . . . . . . . . . . : 10.1.1.1
```

Network Diagnostic Utilities

Before examining network name resolution in detail, we need to take a look at a few network diagnostic utilities in Windows Server 2003 and the Resource Kit. (They are also available in Windows 2000.) These tools are useful for displaying the contents of the many name caches and to modify their contents. They are IPCONFIG, NETSTAT, TRACERT, PATHPING, NBTSTAT, and NETDIAG.

IPCONFIG

The IP parameters for an interface are set and configured using the Network and Dial-up Connection window. You can view these settings from the command line using IPCONFIG. Run `ipconfig /all` to display detailed information for each interface.

Here is an example:

```
Ethernet adapter :
    Host Name: . . . . . . . . . . . . . : PRO1.company.com
        Description . . . . . . . . . . . : NETGEAR FA310TX Fast Ethernet
        ➥Adapter (NGRPCI).
        Physical Address. . . . . . . . . : 08-00-09-AA-AA-AA
        DHCP Enabled. . . . . . . . . . . : Yes
        IP Address. . . . . . . . . . . . : 10.1.60.1
        Subnet Mask . . . . . . . . . . . : 255.255.0.0
        Default Gateway . . . . . . . . . : 10.1.254.254
        Primary WINS Server . . . . . . . : 10.1.100.254
        Secondary WINS Server . . . . . . : 10.1.100.253
        Lease Obtained. . . . . . . . . . : Saturday, December 16, 2001 3:35:06 AM
        Lease Expires . . . . . . . . . . : Sunday, December 24, 2001 3:35:06 AM
```

Here are the switches associated with IPCONFIG and their functions:

- **`Ipconfig /release.`** If an adapter is configured for DHCP, this option releases the currently leased address. Use this switch to force the client to give up an address that you want to assign to another client.
- **`Ipconfig /renew.`** If the adapter is configured for DHCP, this option sends a renewal request to the DHCP server that initially leased the address. Under most circumstances, the client will obtain the address that it had previously leased. Use this option to download a new DHCP configuration packet.
- **`Ipconfig /displaydns.`** This option shows the records in the local DNS cache.
- **`Ipconfig /flushdns.`** This option clears the local DNS cache.
- **`Ipconfig /registerdns.`** This option registers the client with Dynamic DNS.
- **`Ipconfig /showclassid.`** This option lists the allowable DHCP class IDs for the adapter.
- **`Ipconfig /setclassid.`** This option modifies the DHCP class ID.

Netstat

This utility displays data collected from interfaces configured for TCP/IP. Here are the switches and what they display:

- **`Netstat -a.`** Displays the various TCP and UDP sessions established on an interface. Use this switch when you want a quick check for potential teardrop attacks or other possible problems that could cause a server to accumulate excessive TCP listens and sessions:

```
TCP    DC01:3269        DC01.subsidiary.com:0      LISTENING
TCP    DC01:6548        DC01.subsidiary.com:0      LISTENING
TCP    DC01:nbsession   DC01.subsidiary.com:0      LISTENING
TCP    DC01:389         DC01.subsidiary.com:1065   ESTABLISHED
TCP    DC01:389         DC01.subsidiary.com:1095   ESTABLISHED
TCP    DC01:389         DC01.subsidiary.com:1103 ESTABLISHED
```

Graphical IP Configuration

You may prefer a graphical representation of an interface's IP configuration, such as that used by Winipcfg in Windows 9x. You can get such a display by right-clicking the connection icon in the system tray and selecting STATUS from the flyout menu. This opens the Status window for the connection. Then select the `Support` tab to show the IP configuration information. Figure 4.4 shows an example. You can renew and release DHCP addresses using this window.

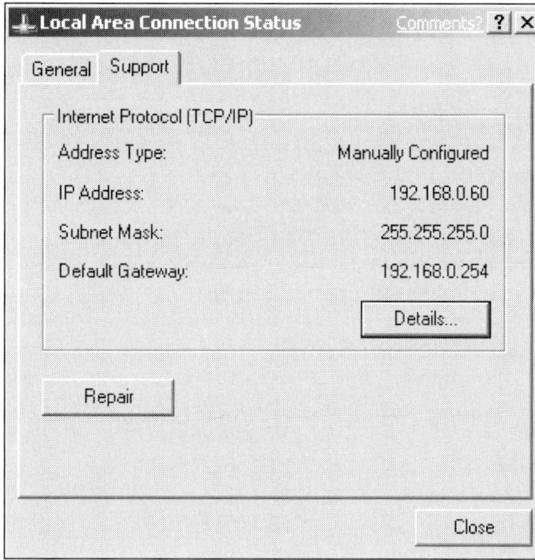

Figure 4.4 Local Area Connection Status window showing IP connection information.

If you do not see a connection icon in the system tray, enable the `Show Icon In Taskbar Notification Area When Connected` option in the properties for the connection.

- **`Netstat -e.`** Displays Ethernet statistics including problem packets:

```
Interface Statistics
                               Received       Sent
Bytes                           870327        9569847
Unicast packets                 6729          10074
Non-unicast packets             2345          725
Discards                         0            0
Errors                           0            2
Unknown protocols                0
```

- **`Netstat -n.`** Displays local addresses and port numbers for the various sessions and listens:

```
Active Connections
  Proto  Local Address          Foreign Address        State
  TCP    10.1.100.1:445         10.1.1.1:1160          ESTABLISHED
  TCP    10.1.100.1:445         10.2.1.1:1313          ESTABLISHED
  TCP    10.1.100.1:445         10.3.1.2:1047          ESTABLISHED
  TCP    10.1.100.1:2261        10.1.1.254:3389        ESTABLISHED
```

- **`Netstat -p [tcp] [udp] [ip]`.** Similar to `-n`, but lists by host name. The list includes protocol represented by `p`. The example is for `Netstat -p tcp` (The `microsoft-ds` entry corresponds to TCP port 445):

```
Proto  Local Address              Foreign Address        State
TCP    srv1:microsoft-ds          DC01:1160              ESTABLISHED
TCP    srv1:microsoft-ds          DC02:1313              ESTABLISHED
TCP    srv1:microsoft-ds          DC03:1047              ESTABLISHED
TCP    srv1:2261                  NT401:3389             ESTABLISHED
```

- **`Netstat -r`.** Displays the contents of the local routing table. The listing also includes the active ports:

```
===========================================================================
Interface List
0x1 ................ Internal loopback interface for 127.0.0.0 network
0x2 ................ Internal RAS Server interface for dial in clients
0x3 ...08 00 09 aa aa aa ...... NETGEAR FA310TX Adapter (NGRPCI)
===========================================================================
===========================================================================
Active Routes:
Network Destination        Netmask          Gateway       Interface  Metric
10.1.0.0                   255.255.0.0      10.1.30.1     10.1.30.1    1
10.1.30.1                  255.255.255.255  127.0.0.1     127.0.0.1    1
10.255.255.255             255.255.255.255  10.1.30.1     10.1.30.1    1
127.0.0.0                  255.0.0.0        127.0.0.1     127.0.0.1    1
127.0.0.1                  255.255.255.255  127.0.0.1     127.0.0.1    1
224.0.0.0                  224.0.0.0        10.1.30.1     10.1.30.1    1
255.255.255.255            255.255.255.255  10.1.30.1     10.1.30.1    1
==============================================================================
```

- **`Netstat -s`.** Displays statistics for each protocol. Use the `-p` switch to select a particular protocol:

```
TCP Statistics
  Active Opens                        = 1103
  Passive Opens                       = 1204
  Failed Connection Attempts          = 1
  Reset Connections                   = 34
  Current Connections                 = 22
  Segments Received                   = 23942
  Segments Sent                       = 27209
  Segments Retransmitted              = 134
```

Tracert

This utility is similar to the UNIX `traceroute`. It reports the IP address and name of each interface between the client and the target. If Ping fails, Tracert can tell you where the responses have stopped.

Tracert works by sending out a series of ICMP Echo Requests to the destination host, similar to Ping, except that Tracert controls the *Time-To-Live* (TTL) value in the ICMP packet to get a response from each intervening router.

Tracert sends the first ICMP Echo Request with a TTL of 1, so the first router responds but the second times out with a `TTL Exceeded in Transit` error. The next ICMP has a TTL of 2, then 3, and so forth until the ultimate host finally responds. Each request is repeated three times and the output is presented as a series of router names and IP addresses. By default, Tracert does a reverse DNS query to get the name associated with each IP address. Here is a sample Tracert report:

```
C:\Documents and Settings\Admin>tracert www.google.com
Tracing route to www.google.com [216.239.35.100]
over a maximum of 30 hops:
  1     1 ms     1 ms    <1 ms  192.168.0.254
  2    13 ms    12 ms    12 ms  12.48.12.1
  3    16 ms    58 ms    77 ms  12.0.121.81
  4    21 ms    29 ms    15 ms  c1-pos4-1.phnxaz1.home.net [24.7.76.173]
  5    21 ms    19 ms    19 ms  c1-pos2-0.sndgca1.home.net [24.7.65.134]
  6    25 ms    57 ms    23 ms  c1-pos1-0.anhmca1.home.net [24.7.64.69]
  7    23 ms    26 ms    25 ms  c1-pos1-0.lsanca1.home.net [24.7.65.169]
  8    30 ms    26 ms    25 ms  c1-pos2-0.snbbca1.home.net [24.7.65.174]
  9    31 ms    29 ms    30 ms  c2-pos3-0.snjsca1.home.net [24.7.64.49]
 10    30 ms    32 ms    32 ms  above-athome.sjc2.above.net [208.185.175.133]
 11    32 ms    36 ms    31 ms  core4-core3-oc48.sjc2.above.net [208.184.102.198]
 12    32 ms    64 ms    32 ms  core2-sjc2-oc48.sjc3.above.net [208.184.233.50]
 13    31 ms    31 ms    63 ms  main1colo56-core2-oc48.sjc3.above.net
 ➥[208.185.175.198]
 14    31 ms    31 ms    32 ms  sjni1-gige-2-1.google.com [216.239.47.18]
 15    38 ms    75 ms    40 ms  192.168.254.86
 16    38 ms    30 ms    40 ms  www.google.com [216.239.35.100]
Trace complete.
```

Here are the Tracert switches:

- **`Tracert -d.`** Turns off host name lookups. This significantly speeds up traces. Highly recommended.
- **`Tracert -h.`** Increases the maximum hop count. The default is 30.
- **`Tracert -j host-list.`** This option is used to force Tracert to use a specific router via source routing.
- **`Tracert -w.`** Increases the maximum timeout.

Pathping

Tracert can take a long time to produce a listing because it waits for the Echo Response from the final host. You'll get a faster trace using Pathping. This utility sends out a series of ICMP Echo Requests with incremented TTLs, just as Tracert does, but it displays the intermediate host address immediately then waits until the ultimate host is contacted before calculating statistics. The calculation takes a long time and you can abort it with Ctrl+C.

Nbtstat

When a Windows TCP/IP client resolves a NetBIOS name, it caches the results in a NetBIOS Name Cache table. By default, the entry stays in the cache for 600 seconds (10 minutes). You can view and manipulate the contents of the NetBIOS Name Cache using Nbtstat. Here are the Nbtstat switches and their functions. The switches are case sensitive:

- **`Nbtstat -c.`** Displays the contents of the local name cache. Use this switch when you want to verify that a computer has cached the correct IP address for a target host.

  The following code listing shows a sample name cache. The Type column is the 2-byte hex ID of the NetBIOS service. The first three entries were pre-loaded from a local Lmhosts file, which gives them a life of 60 seconds rather than the default 600 seconds:

  ```
  Node IpAddress: [10.1.1.10] Scope Id: []
                NetBIOS Remote Cache Name Table
  Name                   Type            Host Address    Life [sec]
  ------------------------------------------------------------
  DC02                <03>  UNIQUE      10.1.1.20          60
  DC02                <00>  UNIQUE      10.1.1.20          60
  DC02                <20>  UNIQUE      10.1.1.20          60
  NTS01               <00>  UNIQUE      10.1.1.101         600
  ```

- **`Nbtstat - a.`** Displays the name cache on a remote computer given its NetBIOS name. This option also displays the MAC address of the remote network adapter. Example syntax: `Nbtstat -a dc01`.

- **`Nbtstat -A.`** Displays the name cache on a remote machine given its IP address. Also displays the MAC address of the remote network adapter. Example syntax: `Nbtstat -A 10.1.1.1`.

- **`Nbtstat -n.`** Displays the NetBIOS names associated with the local computer. This includes the computer name with all services, the locally logged-on user with all services, the workgroup or domain of the computer, and any browser services running:

  ```
  Node IpAddress: [10.1.10.3] Scope Id: []
              NetBIOS Local Name Table
  Name                        Type         Status
  ---------------------------------------------------
  PRO1                <00>    UNIQUE      Registered
  PRO1                <03>    UNIQUE      Registered
  PRO1                <20>    UNIQUE      Registered
  COMPANY             <00>    GROUP       Registered
  COMPANY             <1E>    GROUP       Registered
  ..__MSBROWSE__.     <01>    GROUP       Registered
  ```

- **`Nbtstat -r.`** Lists the names in the name cache and how they were resolved. This is handy when you are trying to determine whether a computer used broadcasts or WINS to get an IP address:

```
    NetBIOS Names Resolution and Registration Statistics
    ----------------------------------------------------

    Resolved By Broadcast     = 2
    Resolved By Name Server   = 5
    Registered By Broadcast   = 32
    Registered By Name Server = 8

    NetBIOS Names Resolved By Broadcast
---------------------------------------------
           DC01        <00>
            DC01        <00>
```

- **`Nbtstat -R.`** Purges the name cache and loads the preload (`#PRE`) items out of the Lmhosts file. See "Resolving NetBIOS Names Using Lmhosts" later in the chapter.

- **`Nbtstat -S.`** Displays the current sessions on the local machine showing the IP addresses of the connected machines. This is very useful when you want a quick display of the services that have active connections:

```
NetBIOS Connection Table
Local Name               State     In/Out  Remote Host       Input   Output
---------------------------------------------------------------------------
PRO1             <03>    Listening
PRO1                     Connected   In     10.1.100.3         2KB      3KB
ADMINISTRATOR     <03>    Listening
```

- **`Nbtstat -s.`** Same as `-S`, but with the name of the connected machine rather than the IP address:

```
NetBIOS Connection Table
Local Name               State     In/Out  Remote Host       Input   Output
---------------------------------------------------------------------------
PRO1            <03>     Listening
PRO1                     Connected   In      SRV1            2KB      3KB
ADMINISTRATOR   <03>      Listening
```

- **`Nbtstat -RR.`** Releases the name registration in WINS and then reregisters. Introduced in NT4 SP4, this switch is extremely useful for correcting WINS errors. A bad record can be deleted manually from WINS, and then the client can be reregistered with this option.

If you discover during all this pinging and tracing and name cache scanning that everyone else in the area is working fine and only this machine is having problems, try opening the Network Connections window and checking the status of the connection icon. If it has a big X on it, the interface has lost communication with the network. Check the Event log to see whether there is some reason for the failure.

Registry Tip: Location of NetBIOS Cache Control Keys

The Registry key that contains the configuration parameters such as cache timeouts and broadcast counts is located in `HKLM | System | CurrentControlSet | Services | NETBT`.

Netdiag

This utility does a comprehensive set of tests on just about every network function. The report is too long to read inside a console or to reproduce here. Pipe the output to a file for review.

If you have a network problem that goes beyond a simple connectivity glitch, Netdiag is the first place to turn. It will either point right to the source of the trouble or give you a good set of clues to start troubleshooting. It may take a while to sort through the report, but the root cause should be buried in there somewhere.

Netsh

The Network Shell utility is the primary unified command-line management tool for all network interfaces and basic TCP/IP services with the exception of DNS. A new parameter in Windows Server 2003, called Diag, gives lots of good information about the state of each interface. The syntax for a full test is `netsh> diag show test`.

Resolving NetBIOS Names Using Broadcasts

Broadcasting was the earliest method used by Microsoft to resolve names into IP addresses. Resolving names by broadcasting is like getting help from a neighbor in a small town. You lean your head out a screen door and yell, "John Henry, when y'all get a second, come on over here and give me a hand. Y'hear?"

For this kind of broadcast-based name calling to work, though, there can be only one John Henry in town. And when a Windows computer broadcasts for a computer named SRV1, there should only be one server on the wire with that name. For this reason, Windows computers also use broadcasts to *register* their names. This ensures uniqueness. Broadcast registration works as described in Procedure 4.1.

Procedure 4.1 Functional Sequence for NetBIOS Name Resolution Using Broadcasts

1. When a Windows computer named PRO1 is booted and comes onto the network, it first checks to make sure that no other computer is using its name. It does this by sending out a *NetBIOS Name Registration* broadcast. This application layer broadcast is placed into an IP multicast packet at the Network layer and directed at the client's subnet.

   For example, a client with the IP address `10.1.3.150`, subnet `255.255.0.0`, would send out a name registration multicast addressed to `10.1.255.255`. Stations that are in the multicast space but not in network `10.1.0.0` ignore the multicast.

2. If another computer with the name PRO1 hears the multicast, it sends back a challenge saying, in effect, "Back off. I'm using that name, and here's my IP address to prove it."
3. The newcomer doesn't meekly retreat in the face of this challenge, however. It verifies the identity of the challenger by sending out an ARP broadcast containing the challenger's IP address. If the ARP gets no response, the newcomer uses the name anyway. If the ARP gets a response, the newcomer gives up, refuses to bind network services to the adapter, and informs the user of the duplicate name. It also puts a warning in the Event log.
4. If the newcomer is satisfied that its name is unique, it binds the application layer protocols such as Workstation, Server, and Browser to the TCP/IP stack and initializes the network drivers.
5. When the network applications can see the network, the SMB redirector—LanMan Workstation in the case of Windows Server 2003—prepares to communicate with a server—call it SRV1. LanMan Workstation builds an SMB message destined for SRV1 and sends it to the Tcpip.sys driver.
6. When Tcpip.sys gets the SMB message, it uses Netbt.sys to send out a *NetBIOS Name Resolution* multicast looking for the IP address of the destination server. Netbt.sys sends out the multicast every half-second for three tries and then gives up if it does not get a response.
7. If SRV1 hears the multicast, it responds with an acknowledgement that contains its IP address. The acknowledgement is sent directly back to the client because SRV1 learned the client's NetBIOS name, IP address, and MAC address from the name resolution multicast.
8. Tcpip.sys nabs the IP address from the name resolution response and sends out an ARP to confirm the address. When it is confirmed, Netbt.sys caches the name and IP address of the server in a *NetBIOS name table* where it can be used in subsequent transactions.

This small-town method of shouting out names and waiting for responses doesn't work very well in the bright lights and big city of a routed TCP/IP network, where routers and Layer 3 switches and intelligent bridges are configured to stop broadcasts and multicasts. The next two topics cover how to use Lmhosts and WINS to handle name resolution and registration in a routed environment.

Resolving NetBIOS Names Using Lmhosts

In the early days of NetBIOS, Microsoft borrowed an idea from UNIX for resolving host names using a static lookup file. UNIX hosts were resolved using a Hosts file, and because the Microsoft team was working on OS/2 LAN Manager at the time, the NetBIOS name lookup table was called Lmhosts. Neither filename has an extension.

TCP/IP-Related File Locations

The `\Windows\System32\Drivers\etc` folder holds a sample Lmhosts file called Lmhosts.sam. You can either rename this file to Lmhosts and modify the contents or you can create a new file called Lmhosts.

The directory holding Lmhosts is defined by the following Registry entry:

Key: `HKLM | SYSTEM | CurrentControlSet | Services | Tcpip | Parameters`

Value: `DataBasePath`

The `\Windows\System32\Drivers\etc` directory holds these other TCP/IP-related files:

- **Hosts.** Used to provide TCP/IP host name lookups.
- **Services.** Contains well-known TCP and UDP ports and their uses.
- **Protocol.** Contains the list of IP protocols used on the computer in accordance with RFC 1060.
- **Networks.** Contains a quick lookup of network names and their corresponding gateway IP addresses.
- **Quotes.** Supports the ever-popular Quote of the Day protocol. The default entries lean rather heavily on George Bernard Shaw and Charles Dickens, but you're free to add more.

Configuring Lmhosts

The idea behind Lmhosts is to have a place where Netbt.sys can resolve a name without broadcasting. The file is a plain ASCII text file consisting of IP addresses and host names. Here is an example listing three servers, two of which are domain controllers in a domain called `COMPANY`:

```
# Lmhosts file for Domain COMPANY
10.1.1.10       DC01            #PRE     #DOM:COMPANY
10.1.1.20       DC02            #PRE     #DOM:COMPANY
10.1.1.30       PRO3            #PRE
10.1.1.100      PRO4            #PRE

#BEGIN_ALTERNATE
#INCLUDE        \\PRO3\PUBLIC\ETC\Lmhosts
#INCLUDE        \\DC02\PUBLIC\ETC\Lmhosts
#END_ALTERNATE
```

The pound sign (#) has two functions:

- Precedes a standard Lmhosts parameter such as `#PRE`, `#DOM`, and `#INCLUDE`
- If not followed by a recognized parameter, indicates a remark, such as that used in the first line

Here are the standard Lmhosts parameters. The name must be uppercase, otherwise the entry is considered a remark:

- **`#PRE`.** This parameter tells the system to load the associated entry into the NetBIOS name cache at boot time. This speeds up initial name lookups.
- **`#DOM`.** This parameter flags the entry as a domain controller with the name after the colon being the domain name. If you use Lmhosts in a domain environment, this switch is a necessity because it tells the local client where to go to get authenticated.

- **#INCLUDE.** Tells Tcpip.sys to load the Lmhosts file from another computer. The `#INCLUDE` option enables you to maintain a single, central Lmhosts file that can be referenced by other workstations in a workgroup. The entry uses a UNC name, such as `\\SRV1\Public`, where `Public` is a share name. There is a subtle Catch-22 at work here. The UNC path contains a NetBIOS name, so you must make sure the local Lmhosts file has an entry for that name.
- **#BEGIN_ALTERNATE** and **#END_ALTERNATE.** Use these statements to bracket multiple entries under a single `#INCLUDE` statement. If you have only one `#INCLUDE` statement, you do not need bracketing statements.

Using Lmhosts

Lmhosts should be used only as a last resort. Those little static mappings become ticking bombs that follow you around like the crocodile that chased Captain Hook in *Peter Pan*. One day, you'll forget they're out there and *snap*.

That being said, there are some common uses for Lmhosts. For instance, some administrators use Lmhosts to resolve names over dial-up connections. There is an option to use WINS over dial-up, but very often it is ineffective or takes too long to work. A quick-and-dirty Lmhosts entry at the dial-up client can contain entries for domain controllers and servers associated with persistent client mappings.

Rather than using Lmhosts to resolve a name in a mapped drive, however, you may want to consider just entering the IP address of the server in the UNC path. For instance, instead of mapping to `\\Srv1\Users\LLuthor` and using an Lmhosts entry to resolve `\\Srv1` to `10.1.1.43`, you could enter a UNC name of `\\10.1.1.43\Users\LLuthor`. If you change a server's IP address, users must remap, but this is often easier than talking them through reconfiguring an Lmhosts file.

Resolving NetBIOS Names Using WINS

The venerable *Windows Internet Name Service* (WINS) is an alternative to statically mapping names and IP addresses in Lmhosts. WINS maintains a database of NetBIOS names and IP address mappings that WINS clients use to register their own NetBIOS services and to find the IP addresses of the services running on other WINS clients.

WINS is based on protocols and services defined in RFC 1001, "Protocol Standard For A NetBIOS Service On A TCP/UDP Transport: Concepts And Methods," and RFC 1002, "Protocol Standard For A NetBIOS Service On A TCP/UDP Transport: Detailed Specifications." These are public standards but, in practice, Microsoft WINS is the only commercial NetBIOS name service.

> **Resolving Names over Dial-Up Connections**
> The Routing and Remote Access Services (RRAS) service in Windows Server 2003 can be configured to permit broadcast-based name resolution across a dial-in connection. This eliminates the need for Lmhosts files and special mapping procedures on dial-in clients, at least in small networks. For routed networks where the target host lies on the other side of a router, you may still need an Lmhosts file.

WINS is, without a doubt, the single most pernicious cause of weird, inexplicable behavior in a classic NT network. Managing WINS in a large network is one of the most complex duties of a classic NT administrator. Thankfully, the need for WINS is diminishing thanks to Dynamic DNS.

This section provides an overview of installing, configuring, and troubleshooting WINS on Windows Server 2003.

WINS Functional Overview

WINS works like a bridal registry, where happy couples go to Nordstrom's or Wal-Mart and *register* their wedding plans so their friends can go to the store and *resolve* their gift-buying decisions. With WINS, clients go to a WINS server to *register* their NetBIOS names and services so that other WINS clients can query WINS to *resolve* NetBIOS names and services into IP addresses. Let's look at registration first.

Name Registration Using WINS

Here is a typical sequence of events when a client registers itself with its WINS server:

1. When the WINS client comes up on the network, it sends a *name registration request* to its WINS server. The client sends a separate registration request for each of its SMB-based services. For example, if the client is running the Server, Workstation, and Messenger services, it would submit three registration requests to WINS.

   If the client has multiple network adapters (also known as a *multihomed* WINS client), it submits registration requests for each service on each adapter.

2. If the WINS database at the server contains no other records that use the name or IP address that the client is requesting, the WINS server returns a *positive name registration response* and adds the records to its database along with a *renewal interval* after which the registration expires. The client must renew the registration within this period. By default, the renewal interval is six days.

3. If the WINS database at the server contains a record with the same name but different IP address, the WINS server tells the client to wait for a short time (five minutes) while it sends a *name query request* to the client that already has the registration. If the existing client responds, the WINS server sends a *negative name registration response* to the requesting client.

   If an existing client does not respond to the name query request, the WINS server returns a positive response to the requesting client and modifies the records in the database. It also starts a new renewal interval.

4. At the halfway point of the renewal interval, the client sends a renewal request to the WINS server for each registered service. The server responds and the renewal interval clock is reset.

5. If the WINS client goes off the network using a standard shutdown process, it sends a *name release* to its WINS server.
6. The server marks the associated records as released and assigns an *extinction interval* to the record. During the extinction interval, the released record is not replicated. The owner server is free to reassign the name or address to another client, but replication partners are not. This interval simplifies reregistration when the client comes back online.

In short, the name registration cycle for a WINS client consists of the following:

- A registration request followed by a registration response informing the client that it owns the name
- A period of active status during which the client periodically renews its registration
- A release request followed by a release response telling the client that it no longer owns the name
- A period of released status during which the client can be reregistered quickly

Selective Domain Responses

It sometimes happens that you want to decommission a particular NetBIOS domain. This can happen during domain consolidation or migration from an NT domain to a Windows Server 2003 domain. When the domain is removed from the system, it leaves lingering records in WINS. You can elect to filter out a domain from the list of records that will be returned by a WINS server. The server returns a No-ACK rather than a useless resource record.

Name Registration Failure Handling

The WINS name registration process includes the following several features for handling common failure modes:

- **Failure to reregister.** If a client releases a registration and does not subsequently reregister, the server waits until the end of the extinction interval and then assigns a status of *tombstoned* to the record. Tombstoned records are replicated so that other WINS servers know that the name and IP address are available should another client attempt to register using them. An extinction timeout interval is assigned to the tombstoned record. The default interval is six days. After this interval, the record is removed from the database during scavenging.
- **Failure to renew.** If a client does not renew a registration within the renewal period, the record is assigned a status of *released*. The server assigns an extinction interval to the record after which it is tombstoned.

- **Failure to release.** If a client does not release a registration within the renewal period, the record is released automatically. The server assigns an extinction interval to the record, after which it is tombstoned.
- **Unable to contact primary WINS server.** If the primary WINS server is unavailable when the client attempts to renew a registration, the client can renew with its secondary WINS server, if one has been configured. This can lead to an awkward situation where the primary server has an active record and the secondary server has a released record. To prevent this, if the client releases a registration to a WINS server that is not the owner, the record is immediately tombstoned.
- **Client crash.** The WINS server has no way of knowing whether a client goes offline abnormally until the end of the renewal interval. The client record stays active and the server continues to hand out the client's IP address in response to query requests. If a client gets the address for a crashed client and attempts to use it, the connection attempt will fail. The client reports this failure to the WINS server, which checks the status of the client using a name query request. If the WINS server gets no reply, it releases the record with an extinction interval.

In a small network with one WINS server, this relatively simple sequence of events is sufficient to maintain database integrity, ensure name uniqueness, and give rapid response to lookup queries. In a big network with several WINS servers configured to replicate with each other, the situation becomes much more complex. Details are in "Functional Description of WINS Replication" later in the chapter. First, let's see how name resolution works.

Name Resolution Using WINS

When a WINS client needs to resolve a NetBIOS name associated with a service, the Netbt.sys driver sends a *name lookup query* to the WINS server. If the name contains a dot or is longer than 16 characters, Tcpip.sys considers it a DNS host name and uses the DNS resolver, not Netbt, to resolve the name.

When a WINS server receives a lookup query, it locates the record in the Jet database that contains the name registrations. If the record exists and if it is marked *active*, the WINS server returns a *name lookup response* with the IP address.

If a client is configured to use two WINS servers, a primary and a secondary, the client will query the secondary server if the primary server is unavailable.

Client Name Resolution Options

A Windows client can be configured to register and resolve NetBIOS names in one of two ways, broadcast or WINS. There are several combinations of these two methods. The combination used by a client is determined by its NetBIOS node type. There are four node types:

- **b-node (broadcast).** The Netbt driver uses IP multicasts to register and resolve names. If there is a router, L3 switch, or intelligent bridge between the client and server, the name registration is only heard on the local subnet. This results in user complaints such as, "I'm looking in My Network Places and I can see the servers in my building but I can't see the servers in Building 303." b-node is the default node type if WINS is not enabled.
- **p-node (point-to-point).** This method uses WINS exclusively. If a p-node client cannot find its WINS server, all registrations and resolutions fail.
- **m-node (mixed).** This method avoids the complete reliance on WINS by first using broadcasts to resolve a name on a local subnet and contacting the WINS server if the broadcast fails.
- **h-node (hybrid).** This method is not defined in RFC 1001 or 1002. Microsoft introduced it to reduce the broadcast traffic produced by m-node clients. An h-node client contacts WINS first and then falls back on local broadcasts only if the WINS query fails. This is the default node type if WINS is enabled.

Choosing a node type is a matter of balancing convenience, fault tolerance, and operational stability. b-node is generally a poor choice in all but the smallest networks. If you have a Windows server, you should configure it as a WINS server.

m-node is inadvisable for pretty much the same reason. Why broadcast if you have a WINS server? You may find situations, though, where an organization has slow WAN links and a single remote WINS server. If the majority of resources used by clients are local to their subnet, you can change the node type from h-node to m-node to increase the speed of local resource access.

The real choice for node type, in most cases, is between p-node and h-node. Here you have to weigh your alternatives. h-node seems like the rational alternative; in practice, however, h-node clients frequently generate broadcasts even when a WINS server is available. Also, h-node clients exhibit a tendency to hang a long time at logoff because they insist on deregistering both with WINS and by broadcast.

p-node clients, on the other hand, generate no broadcast traffic and break off the wire cleanly after they deregister at the WINS server, which takes a negligible amount of time. The problem with p-node is that you lose all NetBIOS name resolution if the WINS server goes down or is otherwise unavailable.

If you have a secondary WINS server and you can respond quickly if a server goes unavailable, you should choose p-node. If you have only one WINS server and want to maintain service continuity if the server goes down, opt for h-node.

Functional Description of WINS Replication

It is theoretically possible to handle NetBIOS name resolution for an entire global enterprise with a single WINS server equipped with only moderately powerful hardware (Pentium 400, 64MB RAM, 10MB NIC). Such a server can handle thousands of registrations a minute, enough to support a client community of 30,000 or so nodes.

Issues of fault tolerance and WAN traffic must also be considered. Generally, you should distribute WINS servers to each major office or LAN installation. If you have hundreds of small networks, such as a retail business, however, you do not need a WINS server in each location. Set up regional WINS servers and use the WAN for name registration/resolution.

Each WINS server maintains a database of the registration records requested by its clients. The server is said to be the *owner* of those records. A WINS server can replicate its database entries to other WINS servers that are configured as its replication partners. The servers each maintain a single database with records identified by owner. When a new replication partner is added, its database records are merged with the existing entries.

WINS uses two replication modes, somewhat reminiscent of Dr. Doolittle—a Push mode and a Pull mode:

- **Push mode.** When accumulated changes reach a preset level, the WINS server contacts its replication partners and sends them the updates. *Push replication is event driven.*
- **Pull mode.** A particular WINS server's replication partners periodically poll for updates. *Pull replication is time driven.*

Name registrations in the WINS databases of both partners are replicated to each other as they accumulate and at intervals throughout the day. WINS clients can use either these servers or both of them with one configured as a primary and the other as a secondary.

Registry Tip: Configuring the Netbt Node Type

You can set the Netbt node type in one of two ways. If you use DHCP, set scope option 44, `WINS/NBNS Servers`, to point at one or more WINS servers and then set scope option 46, `WINS/NBT Node Type`, for the desired node type. See Chapter 5 for details on configuring DHCP.

For non-DHCP clients, configure the node type locally in the Registry as follows:

Key: `HKLM | System | CurrentControlSet | NETBT | Parameters`

Value: `Type`

Data: 1=b-node, 2=p-node, 4=m-node, 8=h-node

The default is b-node if the client does not have a WINS server configured for an interface and h-node if it does.

Registry Tip: WINS Database Parameters

The WINS database is named Wins.mdb. It is a Jet database, similar to that used by Access but with a different and incompatible format. The database and its support files are located in `\Windows\System32\Wins`.

The WINS database location and other WINS parameters are controlled by Registry keys under `HKLM | System | CurrentControlSet | Services | WINS`. The `Partners` key under `WINS` contains the IP address and control parameters for replication partners, if any.

WINS uses TCP/UDP port 42 for replication. This port was originally designated for Home Name Server (a kind of super Hosts file) that was abandoned in favor of DNS.

Only updated records are replicated between replication partners. This minimizes network traffic. Each record has a version ID that increments when the record is updated. In push replication, the server sends records with a version ID higher than the last batch that was sent to that particular partner. In pull replication, the pull partner sends a replication request containing the highest version ID it has received from that partner. The partner then sends updates with a higher version ID.

If you have a slow or expensive WAN link, you can use pull replication and set the replication interval relatively long. There are other possible combination of pushes and pulls, but for the most part they exist only for certification exam scenarios.

When you set up replication between multiple WINS servers, try to create a defined replication topology. You can use a ring, similar to Active Directory replication, where each WINS server replicates to the server on either side. Or, you can use a hub-and-spoke, where all WINS servers replicate to a central master, which then distributes the updates to the other servers. Most large organizations opt for hub-and-spoke because it is easier to manage and limits the number of hops required to replicate a change to the other WINS servers. Or, you can set up a meshed topology where all servers replicate to each other. This last option gives you the fastest convergence, but is the most prone to database anomalies. Regardless of the topology, be careful not to set yourself up for replication loops.

Managing WINS

Let's get to work installing and configuring a WINS server. You'll need the Windows Server 2003 CD. You can run WINS on any of the server versions, even Web Server.

If you do not presently use WINS on your network and you are deploying only modern Windows machines (Windows Server 2003, XP, and Windows 2000), you may be able to avoid WINS entirely. Windows Server 2003 clients use DNS for resolving host names and NetBIOS names. Also, you may encounter applications that depend on NetBIOS name resolution and to support these applications in a routed environment, you will need WINS. An example is Exchange 5.5, which uses flat names to communicate between Exchange servers.

Installing WINS

If you have an existing WINS infrastructure in place, you can upgrade the existing NT4 WINS servers to Windows Server 2003 (or Windows 2000). This automatically upgrades the WINS database while preserving the current configuration settings and database mappings.

When you upgrade, Setup runs a Jetconv utility to convert the Jet databases to the new format. This conversion does not always proceed smoothly. If the existing Jet databases are corrupt or unstable, the upgrade could fail. If the Jet upgrade fails for either or both of the WINS and DHCP databases, follow the steps listed in Procedure 4.2.

Procedure 4.2 Recovering from Failed Jet Database Conversion

1. Stop the service if it has started.
2. Restore the old database from tape.
3. Run Jetpack.exe on the database to compact it and reindex.
4. Start the service again. This starts the Jet conversion automatically.

If the conversion still fails, the database is probably corrupt. The best course of action is to delete the databases and recreate them from scratch.

If a particular WINS server is also a domain controller, you should consider transferring WINS to another server unless you are ready to migrate your domain to Active Directory at the same time that you upgrade WINS.

To install and configure WINS on Windows Server 2003, proceed as directed in Procedure 4.3.

Procedure 4.3 Installing WINS on Windows Server 2003

1. From Control Panel, double-click the `Add/Remove Programs` applet. The Add/Remove Programs window opens.
2. Click `Add/Remove Windows Components`. The Windows Components Wizard starts.
3. Highlight `Networking Services` and click `Details`.
4. Select the `Windows Internet Name Service (WINS)` option and click `OK` to return to the main window.
5. Click `Next` to accept the change and proceed with the installation.
6. When the drivers finish loading, the wizard displays a completion window. Click `Finish` to close the wizard and return to the Add/Remove Programs window.
7. Click `Close`. The service starts automatically. There is no need to restart.

WINS is configured and managed from an MMC console, Winsmgmt.msc. Open the console using START | PROGRAMS | ADMINISTRATIVE SERVICES | WINS. There's nothing to configure at the moment because no clients are using the server. Let's set up a few clients and then come back to see how the WINS console works.

Configuring WINS Clients

Any Windows network client can be directed at a Windows Server 2003 WINS server. If the client uses DHCP, see the sidebar, "Registry Tip: Configuring the Netbt Node Type," for configuration information. If the client is statically mapped, you must configure it locally. Configure WINS at a Windows Server 2003 client as directed in Procedure 4.4.

Procedure 4.4 Configuring a WINS Client

1. Right-click `My Network Places` and select PROPERTIES from the flyout menu. The Network and Dial-up Connections window opens.
2. Right-click `Local Area Connection` and select PROPERTIES from the flyout menu. The Local Area Connection Properties window opens.
3. Double-click the `Internet Protocols (TCP/IP)` entry. The Internet Protocol (TCP/IP) Properties window opens.
4. Click `Advanced`. The Advanced TCP/IP Settings window opens.
5. Select the `WINS` tab (see Figure 4.5). Ensure that the `Enable NetBIOS over TCP/IP` option is selected. If you disable this option, the client will not use WINS, even if you configure it with the address of a WINS server.

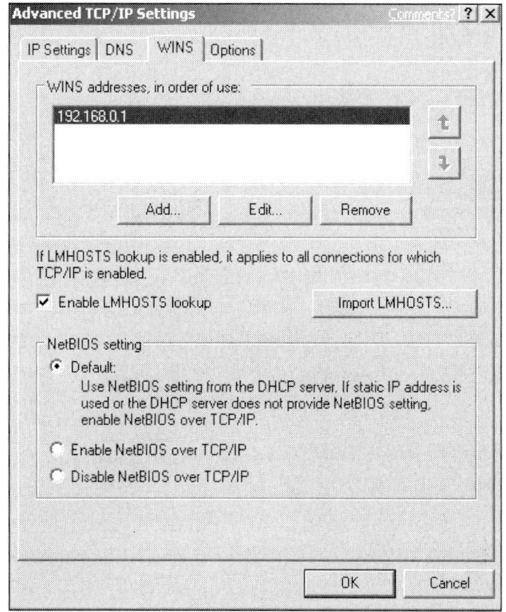

Figure 4.5 Advanced TCP/IP Settings window—`WINS` tab.

6. Click `Add`. The TCP/IP WINS Server window opens. Enter the IP address of a WINS server and click `Add` to save the change and return to the Advanced TCP/IP Settings window. You can add the address of a backup WINS server, if there is one. The WINS client queries the backup server if the primary server is unavailable.
7. Click `OK` to save the changes and return to the Internet Protocol (TCP/IP) Properties window.
8. Click `OK` to close the window and return to the Local Area Connection Properties window.
9. Click `OK` to close the window.
10. Open a command prompt.
11. Enter `Nbtstat -RR` to register the client with the WINS server.

Repeat this for the remainder of your statically mapped clients. Then, go back to the WINS server to check the registration listings and to manage the records.

Managing WINS Records

After a Windows client has been configured to use a WINS server, the name registration and resolution process happens automatically. You can see the results by opening the WINS console using START | PROGRAMS | ADMINISTRATIVE SERVICES | WINS.

If you are an NT administrator accustomed to the standard WINS management executable, you'll find that the WINS console operates much differently. The right pane consists of a tree that you can populate with WINS servers in your organization. You can manage classic NT WINS servers using this console. Figure 4.6 shows an example with several WINS servers.

Under each server is an Active Registrations node and a Replication Partners node. Right-click `Active Registrations` for a server and select DISPLAY RECORDS from the flyout menu. In the Display Records window, select the `Record Owners` tab (see Figure 4.7). This displays a list of the server's replication partners. Each server is listed as an `Owner`, meaning that it owns certain records in the WINS database.

Many new WINS administrators find this business of "ownership" a little confusing. When a client registers at a WINS server, that server is said to "own" the record. The record owner is responsible for replicating this information to its replication partners.

When you browse down the list of servers in the WINS console and look at the contents of the individual WINS databases, you see records owned by that server plus records it obtained from its replication partners and stored in its WINS database. Ideally, the database at each server matches those of its replication partners. This is only the case if the server regularly receives updates from the record owners.

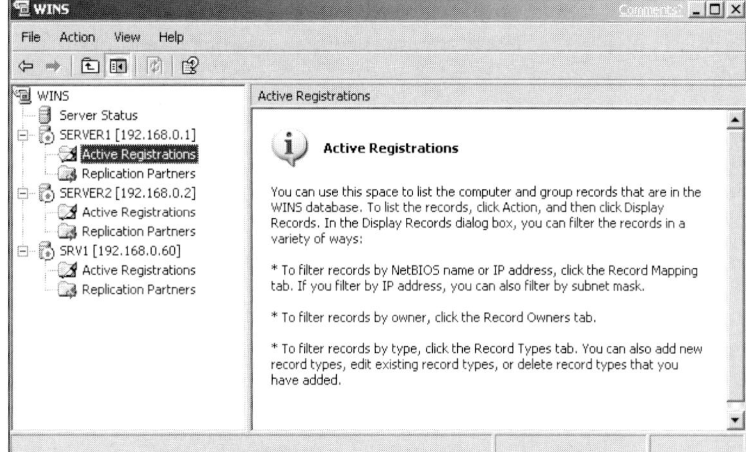

Figure 4.6 WINS console with several servers loaded and ready to be managed.

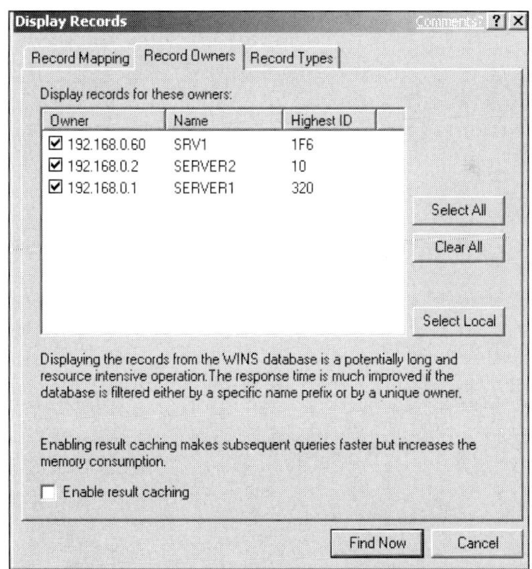

Figure 4.7 WINS console—Display Records window, `Record Owners` tab showing list of replication partners with records in the server's database.

Click `Find Now` in the Display Records window to list the records owned by the servers you selected. The left pane populates with records (see Figure 4.8).

Viewing WINS Record Properties

To view the contents of a WINS record, right-click the record icon in the right pane of the console window and select PROPERTIES from the flyout menu to open the Properties window for the record. Figure 4.9 shows an example.

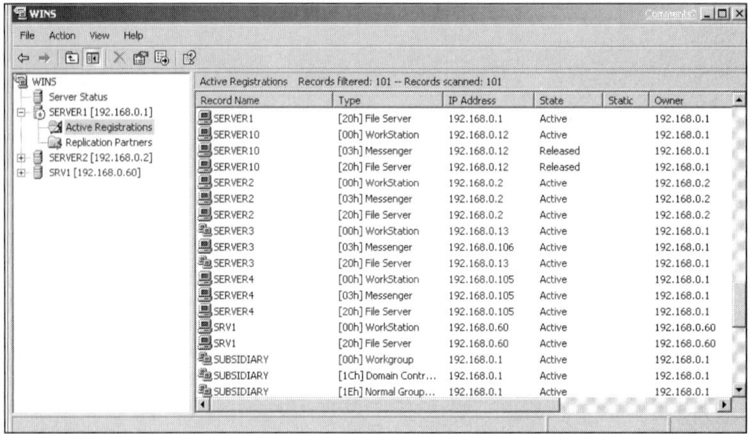

Figure 4.8 WINS console showing a list of client registrations from all owners at a selected WINS server.

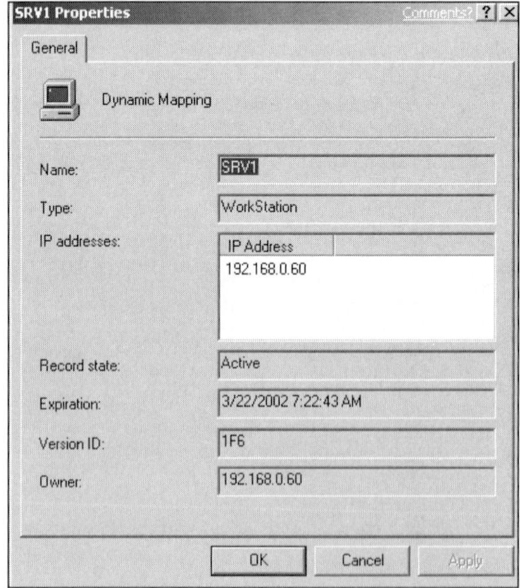

Figure 4.9 Properties of a WINS record.

The `Type` entry shows the service that was registered. This corresponds to the service ID at the end of the NetBIOS name.

The `Record State` can be one of the following:

- **Active.** The WINS client is online with a current record in the WINS database.
- **Released.** The WINS client has notified the server that it is going offline or the record has expired without being renewed.
- **Tombstoned.** The expiration timeout period has elapsed and the client has not renewed the registration.

The `Expiration` date is determined by the default extinction timeout, which is six days, by default.

The `Version ID` is the sequential number assigned to the record by the record owner. A WINS server maintains a counter, much like the wheel of numbers in a Baskin-Robbins. Each time a record is changed, the version number is updated with the next number from the counter. This is how replication partners update each other. The server tells its partner, "I already have record number 3A7 from you. Give me 3A8 and higher."

Statically Mapping WINS Records

If you have UNIX servers or other IP-based hosts that do not use NetBIOS name registration, you can store their names and IP addresses in WINS using static mapping. This is the equivalent of adding a host record to DNS, and it helps legacy Windows clients who use WINS but not DNS to resolve names. You can also use static mapping to show Windows hosts in another network. Add a static mapping as directed in Procedure 4.5.

Procedure 4.5 Adding a Static WINS Mapping

1. Open the `WINS` console and expand the tree to `Active Registrations`.
2. Right-click `Active Registrations` and select NEW STATIC MAPPING from the flyout menu. The New Static Mapping window opens. Figure 4.10 shows an example.
3. Enter the name and IP address of the server. Leave the `NetBIOS Scope` field blank. Leave the `Type` entry at `Unique`.
4. Click `OK` to save the entry and return to the main WINS console.
5. The Active Registrations list now shows three listings for the host: File Server, Workstation, and Messenger. This is standard for all static registrations.

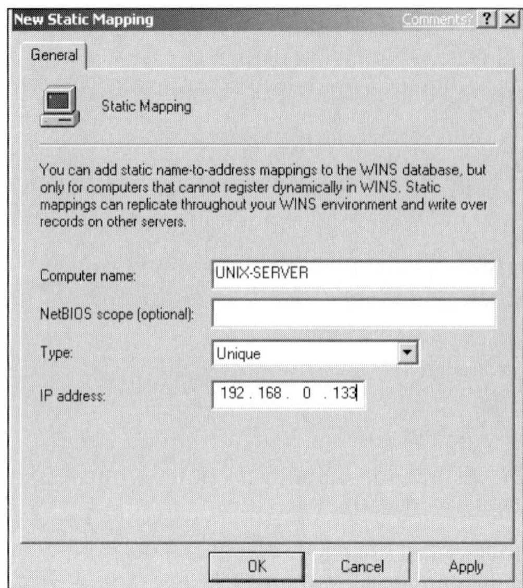

Figure 4.10 New Static Mapping window showing sample server entry.

6. From a WINS client, verify that you can make a network connection to the new host using the flat NetBIOS name. The connection will succeed if the host has SMB resources available.

Deleting Records

A WINS database tends to accumulate clutter. It is not unusual to see many duplicate records and tombstoned entries and records for defunct workgroups and static client mappings. To delete a particular entry, right-click the entry and select DELETE from the flyout menu. A Delete Record window opens (see Figure 4.11). Here are the available options:

- **`Delete the Record Only from This Server.`** This option is appropriate when an incorrect record or records exists only at one server. For instance, a server may have been experiencing replication problems. You have fixed the problem, but not before the database accumulated a few dozen bad entries. Use this option to delete those entries.
- **`Replicate Deletion of the Record to Other Servers (Tombstone).`** This option does not delete the record immediately, but rather it marks the record for deletion by giving it a tombstoned status. This tombstoned record is replicated, informing all the other servers that this record is no longer valid. At the end of the extinction interval, it is deleted.

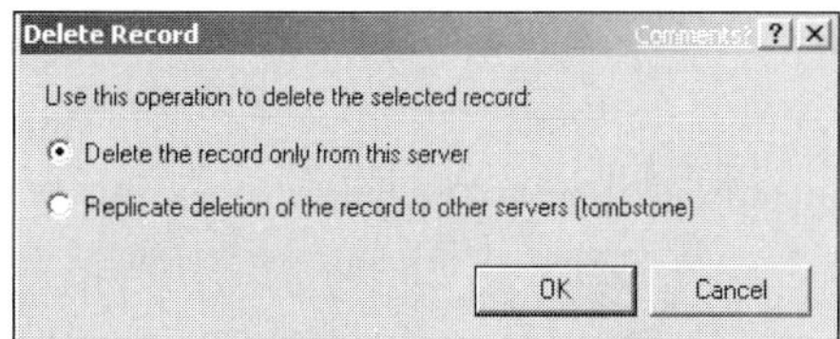

Figure 4.11 Delete Record window for selecting the deletion option from a WINS database.

Configuring WINS Replication

Before you configure WINS replication, you should have a diagram of the replication topology you plan to use. With this diagram in hand, use the steps shown in Procedure 4.6 to configure replication.

Procedure 4.6 Configuring WINS Replication

1. Open the `WINS` console from START | PROGRAMS | ADMINISTRATIVE TOOLS | WINS.
2. Right-click `Replication Partners` and select NEW REPLICATION PARTNER from the flyout menu. The New Replication Partner window opens.
3. Enter the IP address of the WINS server that you want to use as a replication partner. Enter the server's NetBIOS name only if it is on the same network segment.
4. Click `OK` to save the change.
5. At the replication partner, perform the same steps to establish the first server as a replication partner.
6. When the replication succeeds, records from the partners will appear in the respective databases and the name will appear in the `Display Owners` tab in the Display Records window.
7. Right-click the icon for the replication partner and select PROPERTIES from the flyout menu. The Properties window opens.
8. Select the `Advanced` tab (see Figure 4.12). The default replication configuration is Push/Pull. The default replication interval is 30 minutes. You can change this for expensive WAN links.
9. Under both `Pull Replication` and `Push Replication`, select the `Use Persistent Connection for Replication` option. This option avoids a problem in classic WINS where the connection would only be made long enough to replicate. This limited the number of long-term connections across a WAN, but it added to the replication delay. With modern data communications equipment, it makes sense to improve performance by using persistent connections.

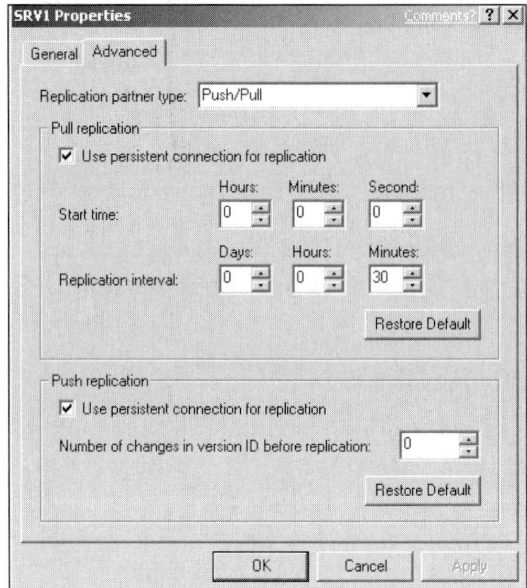

Figure 4.12 Replication Partner Properties window—`Advanced` tab showing partner type, replication interval, and persistent connection.

10. Under `Push Replication`, leave the `Number of Changes in Version ID Before Replication` set to 0 so that changes propagate as soon as they are made.
11. After you have finished configuring replication at both partners, check the System log using the Event Viewer to verify that replication has completed.

See the next section for steps to manage replication after you have verified that the databases have replicated.

Managing the WINS Database

In addition to configuring options for viewing records and controlling replication, a set of features associated with the WINS service itself controls database and record handling. These are accessed by right-clicking the server icon in the WINS console and selecting PROPERTIES from the flyout menu. The Properties window opens for the server with the focus set to the `General` tab (see Figure 4.13).

The `Automatically Update Statistics Every` option is selected by default. It refreshes a set of WINS server statistics that can be viewed by right-clicking the server icon and selecting DISPLAY SERVER STATISTICS. This opens a WINS Server Statistics window that lists replication information for all replication partners.

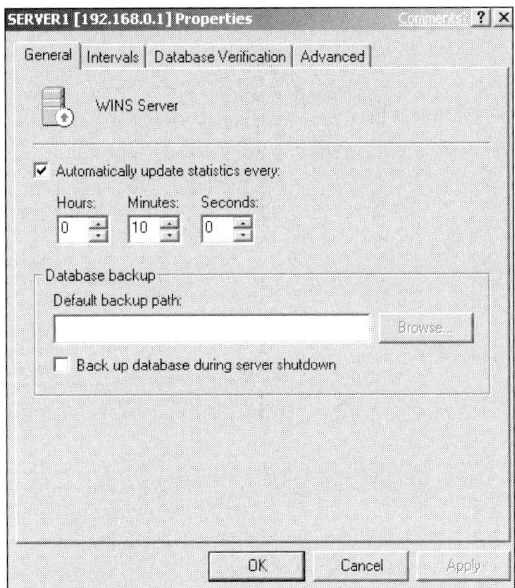

Figure 4.13 WINS Server Properties window—`General` tab.

The `Back Up Database During Server Shutdown` option is not selected by default. This option closes down the Jet database engine and then makes a copy of the Wins.mdb file any time the server shuts down. If you are performing normal backups, you do not need to enable this feature. Make sure the backup utility is certified for use on Windows Server 2003 so that it can capture a copy while the database is open.

Setting Renewal and Extinction Intervals

Select the `Intervals` tab (see Figure 4.14). There are four interval settings controllable in this window. Under most circumstances, the default settings deliver optimized results. Changing the values without first analyzing their interrelation can seriously affect database consistency. The following list details the four interval settings:

- **`Renewal Interval`.** This is the interval during which a client must renew its registrations. Clients ordinarily renew halfway through the renewal interval. The renewal interval also determines the periodic scavenging frequency for the server. During scavenging, the system deletes tombstoned entries and compacts the database. Frequent scavenging is good preventative medicine and improves performance. You can manually initiate scavenging by right-clicking the icon for the WINS server in the WINS console and selecting SCAVENGE DATABASE from the flyout menu.

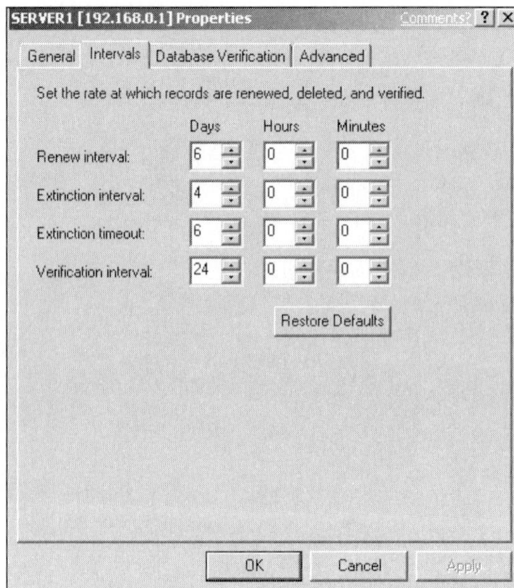

Figure 4.14 WINS Server Properties window—`Intervals` tab.

- **`Extinction Interval`.** This value is assigned to a released record. During the extinction interval, the record owner does not replicate the record. It is waiting for the client to reregister. After the extinction interval, if the client has not reregistered, the record is tombstoned.
- **`Extinction Timeout`.** This value is assigned to a tombstoned record. If a client does not claim the name or IP address associated with the record by the end of the extinction timeout, the record is removed at the scavenging.
- **`Verification Interval`.** This value is assigned to a replicated record. During scavenging, if the record age exceeds the verification interval, the server queries its replication partner to determine whether the record is still valid. If not, it is deleted. If so, the record gets a fresh timestamp and a new verification interval. The default verification interval is 24 days.

Ensuring Database Consistency

Select the `Database Verification` tab (see Figure 4.15). This window exposes to the UI a feature that was available in classic WINS only by making manual Registry entries. A database consistency check consists of copying the contents of the database at a replication partner and verifying that it matches the local database.

The `Begin Verifying At` option sets the start time for the verification check. The default is 2 A.M.

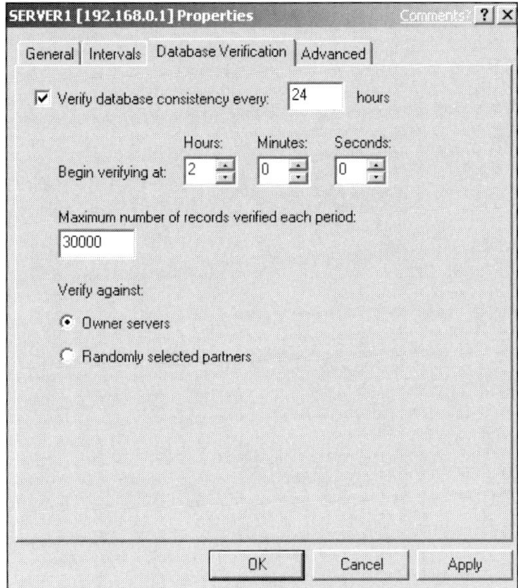

Figure 4.15 WINS Server Properties window—`Database Verification` tab.

This check is enabled by default and should be left enabled unless you have a very large WINS database that consumes too much time to verify every night. In that case, select the `Randomly Selected Partners` option to do a portion of the database verifications each night.

Controlling Log and Database Location and Burst Handling

Select the `Advanced` tab (see Figure 4.16). This tab contains three options.

The `Log Detailed Events to Windows Event Log` results in a log entry whenever just about anything occurs in the WINS database. The window warns you that this will fill up the log quickly and it isn't kidding. Use this option for diagnostic purposes only.

The `Enable Burst Handling` option controls the way the WINS service handles multiple registration requests. When you first put a WINS server online in a large network and point many thousands of clients at it, the database can get overwhelmed with building new records. Ordinarily, the system starts dropping requests if the request queue gets full. With Burst Handling enabled, the clients are given a positive registration response with a short renewal interval—five minutes. This is equivalent to the WINS server saying, "Come back when Daddy isn't busy." If the server gets really busy, it starts assigning longer and longer renewal intervals.

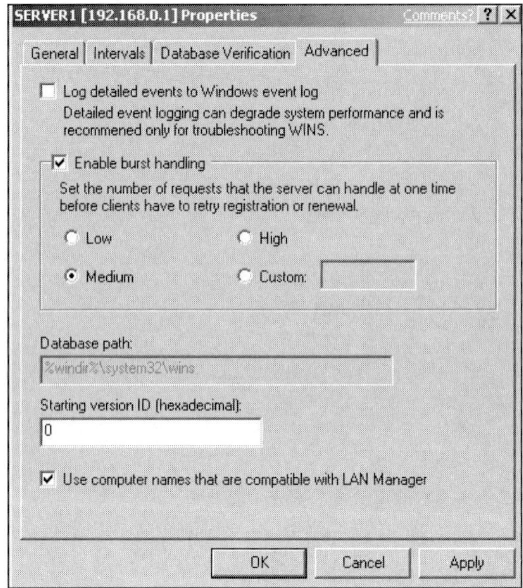

Figure 4.16 WINS Server Properties window—`Advanced` tab.

The four radio buttons control the `BurstQueSize` value in `HKLM | System | CurrentControlSet | Services | WINS | Parameters`. Following are the presets. The values represent the number of pending registration requests that haven't yet been fulfilled:

`Low`	300
`Medium`	500
`High`	1,000

If you have a dedicated WINS server with lots of horsepower and a fast hard drive, you can push `Custom` up to 2,500.

The `Database Path` option is useful if you want to change the location of the WINS database to get it out of the system partition and onto a faster drive or a volume with more space. Stop the service before moving the database. Be sure to move the log files as well.

Setting Default WINS Console Properties

A few options affect the WINS console itself. In the WINS console, right-click the `WINS` icon at the top of the tree and select PROPERTIES from the flyout menu. The WINS Properties window opens.

Using this window, you can elect to display the servers by `Name` or by `IP Address`.

The `Show DNS Names for WINS Servers` option displays the fully qualified DNS name for the server rather than the flat NetBIOS name. This option is a little misleading because the fully qualified name is pulled from the DNS suffix entry in System properties rather than the TCP/IP properties. If the WINS server has not been joined to a domain, it's likely that the DNS suffix is blank.

To check the DNS suffix setting, open the `System` icon in Control Panel and select the `Network Identification` tab. If the `Full Computer Name` entry does not have a DNS suffix, click `Properties`, and then click `More` to add one. You must restart the machine after saving the entry.

Selecting the `Validate Cache of WINS Servers at Startup` option causes WINS to query the list of WINS servers you have loaded into the console. If one or more are offline, the system displays a console message and makes an Event log entry.

Do's and Don'ts of WINS

When managing a large WINS installation, a bit of advice from my grandfather, an old-time New Mexico cowboy, is appropriate. Granddad was fond of saying, "Don't get in front of the herd, don't make any sudden moves, and remember that you can always shoot the troublemaker." Here is how that advice applies in the context of wrangling WINS:

- **Don't put a WINS server in every LAN segment.** WINS replication has a well-deserved reputation for skittishness. WINS clients can find a name server through many intervening routers. Install servers in strategic locations and use the WAN to route registrations and queries.
- **Don't set up independent WINS servers.** WINS replication in an organization needs to be carefully coordinated. Working around authority figures is a prized American right, and is even laudable at times; but in the case of WINS, it can cause real problems.
- **Map your replication topology carefully.** Be especially watchful for replication circularities.
- **Check database statistics regularly.** Don't wait for a database corruption problem to catch you off-guard. The new Jet database engine in Windows Server 2003 is much less likely to corrupt a WINS database than its predecessors; the possibility still exists, however, and you should be watchful.
- **Avoid using WINS proxies.** Proxies are used to support Windows clients who do not have a Microsoft IP stack. A WINS proxy listens for address resolution broadcasts from non-WINS clients and forwards them to a WINS server on behalf of the client. When the resolution returns from the WINS server, the proxy forwards it to the client. WINS proxies are very slow, have a limited cache, and crash often. If you have older Windows 3.x machines, upgrade the operating system instead of deploying WINS proxies.

- **When all else fails, delete and start over.** If a particular WINS server seems to be causing problems, your best course of action is to stop the WINS service, delete the files in `\Windows\System32\Wins`, and then start all over again. This is especially true if the server has replication partners. It's better to repopulate a local WINS database and recreate any static mappings than to pollute an entire WINS infrastructure.

Disabling NetBIOS-over-TCP/IP Name Resolution

After you have completed the transition to Windows Server 2003 and Windows 2000 servers and desktops, you can disable NetBIOS-over-TCP/IP name resolution and use DNS exclusively. Windows Server 2003 and Windows 2000 computers exchange SMB traffic over TCP port 445. Eliminating NetBIOS-over-TCP/IP name resolution results in a substantial reduction in network traffic.

Practically speaking, you cannot get rid of NetBIOS-over-TCP/IP name resolution completely until you've purged all downlevel Windows clients and servers from your network. Classic services such as Browser and Messenger rely on Netbt services to function. When you're ready to make the transition, proceed as shown in Procedure 4.7.

Procedure 4.7 Disabling NetBIOS-over-TCP/IP Name Resolution

1. Open the Network and Dial-up Connections window by right-clicking `My Network Places` and selecting PROPERTIES.
2. Right-click the `Local Area Connection` icon and select PROPERTIES from the flyout menu. The Local Area Connection Properties window opens.
3. Highlight `Internet Protocol (TCP/IP)` and click `Properties`. The Internet Protocol (TCP/IP) Properties window opens.
4. Click `Advanced`. The Advanced TCP/IP Settings window opens.
5. Select the `WINS` tab.
6. Select the `Disable NetBIOS over TCP/IP` radio button. Note that this setting can also be distributed by DHCP clients.
7. Click `OK` to save the change and return to the Internet Protocol (TCP/IP) Properties window.
8. Click `OK` to return to the Local Area Connection Properties window.
9. Click `OK` to save all changes and close the window.

Changing NetBIOS Options in the Registry

The NetBIOS options configured at the UI can also be changed in the Registry as follows:

Key: `HKLM | SYSTEM | CurrentControlSet | Services | NETBT | Parameters | Interfaces | Tcpip_{classid}`

Value: `NetbiosOptions`

Data: `0` – DHCP selected; `1` – enabled; `2` – disabled

Moving Forward

This chapter covered classic NT name resolution using broadcasts, Lmhosts, and WINS. The next chapter leaves the classic NT/NetBIOS world behind and moves on to the name resolution using Dynamic DNS. The next chapter also covers how to use DHCP to proxy downlevel clients into Dynamic DNS.

5 Managing DNS

THE PRECEDING CHAPTER COVERED THE CLASSIC NT mechanisms for resolving computer names into IP addresses. Windows Server 2003 can use those methods, but the preferred name resolution method is the *Domain Name System*, or DNS.

DNS is a tremendously important component of modern Windows. It is not an exaggeration to say that three out of every four problems with Active Directory or Kerberos have their root cause in a DNS configuration error of one form or another. A slew of other features, big and small, also depend on DNS to function correctly.

This chapter covers the operation of Windows Server 2003 DNS, how to design a DNS architecture, and how to perform specific configuration steps. It includes best practices gleaned from many production deployments of Windows DNS, especially in mixed environments of Windows and non-Windows DNS servers.

New Features in Windows Server 2003

Windows Server 2003 includes the following new DNS features that are not in Windows 2000:

- **Application naming contexts.** If you use Active Directory Integrated zones, you can configure DNS to store the resource records in separate Active Directory naming contexts rather than putting them all in the Domain naming context. This simplifies zone replication in a large forest. An executable called Dnsadddp.exe runs each time a domain controller is booted. This application is responsible for creating the DNS application partitions if they do not already exist. See Chapter 7, "Managing Active Directory Replication," for more information on DNS naming contexts and replication.

- **DNS stub zones.** This feature simplifies zone delegation. A stub zone contains the Start of Authority (SOA) and Name Server (NS) records associated with a child zone along with the A records for the name servers. The stub zone then periodically checks the child zone and pulls updates if the NS records have changed. This eliminates the need to manually update delegation records.
- **Conditional forwarding.** This feature permits a name server to select a forwarder based on the domain specified in a client query rather than forwarding all out-of-zone queries to a single DNS server.
- **IPv6 host records.** An IPv6 host address uses a 128-bit address space in contrast to the 32-bit address space used in IPv4. Windows Server 2003 DNS supports the AAAA host resource record that contains IPv6 addresses. This feature is based on RFC 1886, "DNS Extensions to Support IP Version 6." Windows Server 2003 does not include support for the newly proposed A6 resource record type and the proposed restructuring of the IPv6 reverse lookup zone outlined in RFC 2874, "DNS Extensions to Support IPv6 Address Aggregation and Renumbering."
- **DNS extensions.** The current DNS implementation uses UDP for exchanging information between name servers and clients. The standard UDP datagram is limited to 512 octets. Many new and proposed DNS features require more than 512 octets. Currently, this requires a setup and teardown of a TCP session when delivering large resource records, adding overhead and complexity. Windows Server 2003 permits a client and name server to negotiate a larger datagram size, if possible. This feature is based on RFC 2671, "Extension Mechanisms for DNS (EDNS0)."
- **Reverse lookup zone subnetting**. In Windows Server 2003, if you use non-standard subnet masking, you can specify the subnet mask as part of the reverse lookup zone name. This enables the system to apportion Pointer (PTR) records to the correct subnet.

If you are an NT administrator, you'll find many improvements in Windows Server 2003 that were carried over from Windows 2000. These include the following:

- **Notification-driven zone transfers.** Standard DNS requires secondary name servers to poll a master name server for updates. Windows 2000 and Windows Server 2003 incorporate notification features that let a master name server inform its secondaries when an update has occurred. The secondaries then replicate immediately, greatly shortening convergence times. This feature is based on RFC 1996, "A Mechanism for Prompt Notification of Zone Changes."
- **Incremental zone transfers.** Standard DNS replication transfers the entire contents of a zone file from a master name server to its secondaries for every update. Windows 2000 and Windows Server 2003 permit a secondary name server to request only those changes that have occurred since the last zone transfer. This

significantly reduces replication traffic, making it possible to locate secondary name servers at the end of slow network connections. This feature is based on RFC 1995, "Incremental Zone Transfer In DNS."

- **Service locator records.** Many services need a way to "publish" their existence so that clients can find them. Windows 2000 and Windows Server 2003 support the *service locator*, or SRV, resource record. The SRV record specifies a service name, its protocol (TCP or UDP), its port number, and the server or servers where it can be found. This feature is based on RFC 2782, "A DNS RR for specifying the location of services (DNS SRV)."
- **Active Directory Integrated zones.** DNS resource records can be stored in the Active Directory and updated by any domain controller running DNS. This eliminates the bottleneck of a single primary master server in standard DNS. This feature is proprietary to Windows 2000 and Windows Server 2003.
- **Negative query caching.** All DNS clients cache query results to minimize load on the name servers and reduce network traffic. Windows 2000 and Windows Server 2003 both support caching of negative query responses. This prevents a client from repeatedly querying for a record that does not exist. This feature is based on RFC 2308, "Negative Caching of DNS Queries (DNS NCACHE)."
- **Secure DNS Updates.** Dynamic DNS Updates can be limited exclusively to trusted clients. This helps prevent attacks designed to populate a zone with false resource records that could send users or user data to unsecured locations. There are two primary Standards Track RFCs that describe how to perform secure DNS Updates: RFC 2535, "Domain Name System Security Extensions," and RFC 2930, "Secret Key Establishment for DNS." Windows 2000 does not support these RFCs at all and Windows Server 2003 only provides basic support. Secure DNS Updates in Windows Server 2003 continue to use the proprietary method introduced in Windows 2000.

Overview of DNS Domain Structure

Before getting too far into DNS domains, let's deal with the ongoing confusion between Microsoft's use of the word *domain* and the way the term is used in DNS.

Prior to introducing Active Directory, a Microsoft "domain" was completely different than a DNS domain. A DNS domain defines a namespace, such as `Company.com`. Resource records for hosts within this namespace are stored in a zone file, often simply called a zone. In classic Windows, a domain defines a security structure. Account records for users, groups, and computers within this security structure are stored in the `SAM` hive in the Registry.

With the advent of Active Directory, the two territories described by the term *domain* became synonymous. The security structure defined by the account records in Active Directory conforms to a namespace defined by DNS.

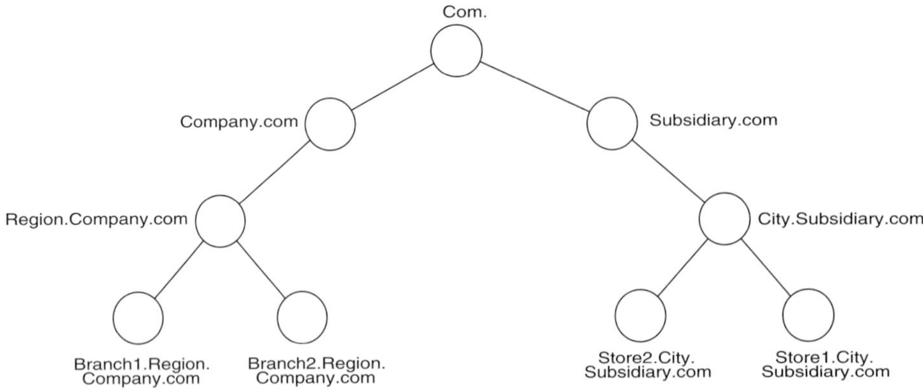

Figure 5.1 Example DNS namespace.

The namespace of a DNS domain describes a relationship between hosts. If a host named Srv1 is in the domain Company.com, its *fully qualified domain name*, or FQDN, would be `srv1.company.com`. Another host, Srv2, in the same domain would have an FQDN of `srv2.company.com`.

Domains can be joined into a hierarchy based on a contiguous namespace. A DNS domain named `branch.company.com` would be a child of the domain `company.com`. Figure 5.1 shows an example DNS hierarchy with several child domains.

The top domain, or *root*, in a DNS hierarchy is identified by a trailing dot (.) at the end of the FQDN. This dot serves the same purpose as the leading slash in a file system path. It defines the top of the tree. A *DNS resolver* parses the FQDN starting at the leftmost element of the name and ending at the root next to the dot at the right side of the FQDN.

The trailing dot at the end of a FQDN is not generally shown in DNS documentation, and Windows DNS tools add it automatically, so it's easy to forget it's there. When troubleshooting, though, it's a good idea to add the trailing dot just to be on the safe side.

Public DNS Namespace

The domain at the top of a DNS namespace is the *root domain*. For public DNS domains, the root domain is also called the *top-level domain,* or TLD.

The organization responsible for registering names in the public Internet namespace is the Internet Corporation for Assigned Names and Numbers, or ICANN. Its web site is `www.icann.org`.

ICANN has contracted with Network Solutions, doing business as Verisign Global Registry Services, to manage the name servers for the largest of the top-level domains: `com`, `net`, and `org`. The Verisign web site is `www.verisign-grs.com`.

Table 5.1 New Top Level Domains and Their Sponsors

TLD Name	Sponsor	URL
aero	Societe Internationale de Telecommunications Aeronautiques SC (SITA)	www.sita.com
biz	Neulevel, Inc.	www.neulevel.biz
coop	National Cooperative Business Association	www.cooperative.org
info	Afilias, LLC	www.afilias.info
museum	Museum Domain Management Assoc	musedoma.museum
name	Global Name Registry	www.theglobalname.org
pro	RegistryPro, Ltd	www.registrypro.com

In early 2001, Verisign migrated the name servers for its three TLDs to 64-bit servers located at key nodes in the Internet, both in the continental U.S. and overseas. As of this writing, there are 12 Verisign TLD servers, named a.gtld-servers.net through m.gtld-servers.net.

The remaining standard TLDs—mil, gov, and edu—are hosted on servers managed by Network Solutions but the zones are controlled by other ICANN designees. The TLD servers for these zones are a.root-servers.net through m.root-servers.net plus a few additional servers for the .mil namespace. The a.root-servers.net server gives referrals to the new Verisign TLD servers.

ICANN has approved seven new TLDs to help differentiate the crowded com and org namespace. Table 5.1 lists the TLD names and the agencies or companies that sponsor them:

ICANN is also responsible for country code TLDs, abbreviated ccTLDs. For example, a web site in Norway would have an FQDN ending in NO, such as www.sol.no. The two-letter country designations follow the ISO 3166 standards. For information about the registrar for a particular ccTLD, see www.iana.org/cctld/cctld-whois.htm.

Private DNS Namespace

You are not constrained to using a public TLD as a root domain in your private network. You can define your own root domain for internal use. For a while, a proposal circulated around the Internet to designate the .local designator as the reserved root domain for private DNS namespaces. This recommendation did not catch on.

In general, you are free to use virtually any combination of letters for the root of your private namespace that have not already been taken by ICANN. Many organizations maintain a private DNS namespace with the same root domain name as their public namespace. This requires maintaining two DNS servers with different zones.

Hosts File

Before a client goes to the trouble to make a DNS query to resolve a host name into an IP address, it first consults a local file called Hosts. Here is an example Hosts file. The pound sign (#) denotes a comment:

```
10.1.1.1    dc01.company.com           #domain controller in Company
10.1.1.2    dc02.company.com           #another domain controller in Company
10.3.1.27   srv1.branch1.company.com   #general purpose server in branch office
10.2.1.12   web7.subsidiary.com        #web server in affiliate domain
```

The host name specified by a TCP/IP application must exactly match the entry in the Hosts file to get a successful lookup. For example, using the preceding Hosts file, a ping to `dc01` would not succeed, but a ping to `dc01.company.com` would succeed. If the name is not in the Hosts file, the client then uses DNS to resolve the name.

Primary and Secondary Name Servers

A conventional DNS server stores its resource records in a zone file. Windows-based DNS servers give zone files a .DNS extension. For example, the zone file for the `company.com` zone would be `company.com.dns`. The zone files are stored in the `\Windows\System32\DNS` folder. A zone can also be integrated into Active Directory, in which case the resource records are stored as objects in the AD database.

Refer to Figure 5.2. In a standard DNS architecture, only one name server has a read/write copy of a zone file. That server is called the *primary name server*. All zone changes must be funneled to this server.

For fault tolerance and performance, it is a good idea to install one or more *secondary name servers*. A secondary name server hosts a read-only copy of the zone file. The secondary servers pull copies of the zone from primary name servers or from other secondary servers.

A name server that simply caches the results of queries so it can pass the information along to its clients is called a *caching-only name server*.

This reliance on a single primary name server is a weakness of classic DNS. As we'll see, Active Directory Integrated zones overcome this weakness by making any domain controller running DNS a primary name server for its zones.

> **Registry Tip: Hosts File Location**
>
> The Hosts file is located in `\Windows\System32\Drivers\Etc` folder along with other TCP/IP-related files such as Lmhosts, Protocols, Networks, and Services. This directory is specified by the following Registry value:
>
> Key: `HKLM | SYSTEM | CurrentControlSet | Services | TCPIP | Parameters`
>
> Value: `DataBasePath`
>
> Data: `\Windows\System32\Drivers\Etc\`

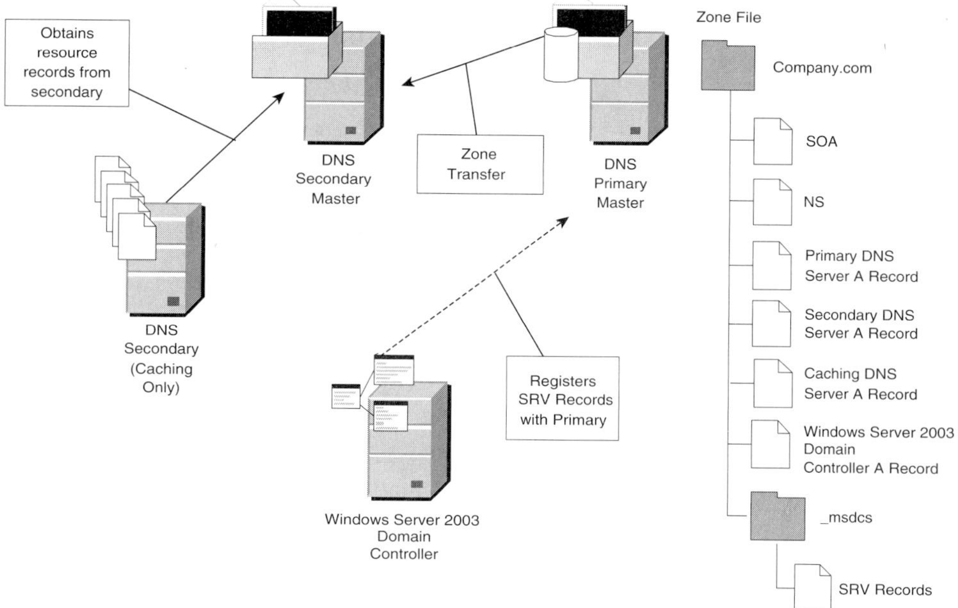

Figure 5.2 Example DNS Server Architecture.

Resource Records

A zone file contains a set of *resource records*. Each record contains specific information about a host or service in the DNS domain. RFC 1183, "New DNS RR Definitions," defines more than a dozen DNS record types. Only a few are used with any frequency.

When a DNS client needs information from a name server, it queries for a resource record. For example, if a client needs the IP address corresponding to a server named `srv1.company.com`, it sends the DNS server a request for the `A`, or Host, record for that server. The DNS server responds by finding the `A` record in the zone and then copying the contents of the record into a DNS reply, which it sends back to the client.

So, DNS is nothing more than an exchange of resource records between clients and servers. The trick to making your DNS structure work correctly is making sure that the clients can find the right DNS servers and the servers have the right information in their zone files.

Authoritative Query Responses

When a DNS server is presented with a query for a resource record, it responds differently depending on whether or not it hosts a copy of the zone containing that resource record.

A DNS server that hosts a copy of a zone file is said to be *authoritative* for that zone. When tracing a DNS query, the buck always stops at an authoritative server for the zone specified in the query.

When a query arrives for a resource record within a name server's zone of authority, the server performs an *authoritative lookup*. Here is how it handles that lookup:

- If the server finds the requested record in its zone file, it responds with a copy of the record contents.
- If the server has recently done a lookup on the same record, it responds with a cached copy of the record. This is much faster than doing a file lookup from disk.
- If the server cannot find the requested record, it returns a `Record Not Found` response to the client.

Non-Authoritative Query Responses

If a DNS server does not have a copy of the zone file for a requested zone, it has three alternatives when handling the query:

- Query other name servers until the record is found, then return a copy to the requestor.
- Respond with a referral to a name server further up the tree that might have a copy of the record.
- Respond with a cached copy of the record that was stored following a previous lookup.

All three methods result in a *non-authoritative reply*. The choice of which method to use, #1 or #2, is based in large part on a *search type* flag included in the client query. The flag has two possible states:

- **Recursive.** This tells the DNS server to respond with a copy of the requested resource record no matter what. If the server has to consult with other DNS servers to find the record, so be it. A recursive query is like a Spartan mother sending her son into battle saying, "Come back carrying your shield or lying on it."
- **Iterative.** This request permits the DNS server to return a referral to another DNS server that is likely to have a copy of the record rather than chase down the referral itself. An iterative search puts the workload on the client to follow up on the referral.

DNS clients typically set the recursive flag in their queries on the assumption that the DNS server has more capacity for handling the search. Recursive queries from thousands of clients can put a great deal of load on a DNS server, so it is not uncommon to find servers configured to reject recursive queries. For example, the Verisign TLD servers are configured to reject recursive queries. See "Configuring Advanced DNS Server Parameters" for the steps to disable recursive queries on a Windows Server 2003 running DNS.

If your ISP maintains a name server that permits recursive queries, or you find an open name server at another ISP, it is good etiquette to get permission prior to sending recursive queries to the server.

DNS servers typically use iterative queries when they search on behalf of their clients. The server has the resources to handle referrals, so it doesn't make sense to put unnecessary burden on upstream DNS servers. Windows Server 2003 running DNS will default to iterative queries. There are no adjustment parameters to change this default.

Root Hints

DNS servers within a contiguous namespace can use a simple referral mechanism to find entries in each other's zones. For example, a DNS server in `branch.region.company.com` that gets a request for an `A` record for `srv1.company.com` can go right to a name server at the root of the `company.com` namespace to begin its iterative search if it knows the identity of the name servers at the root domain. An administrator can include these names in the configuration for the name server.

When a DNS server gets a query for a resource record for a server on the Internet, it needs a way to find the TLD servers that host the root of the public domains. The DNS server finds these TLD servers using a special file called *root hints*. Figure 5.3 shows the root hints stored on a Windows Server 2003 running DNS.

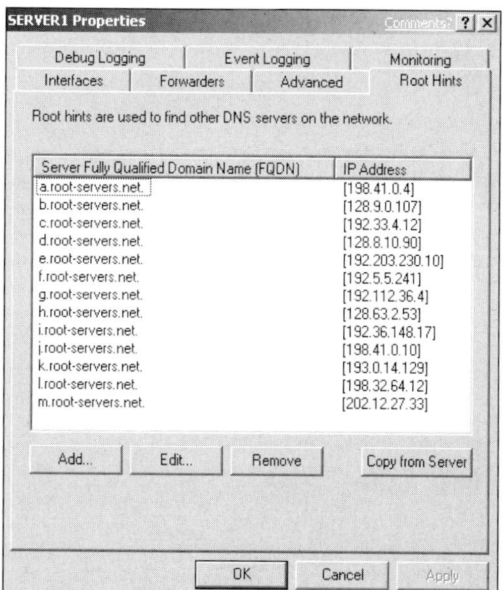

Figure 5.3 Standard root hints for a Windows Server 2003 running DNS.

Root hints are contained in a text file that lists the names and IP addresses of the name servers at the root of the DNS namespace. Windows DNS servers store their root hints in a file called Cache.dns located in `\Windows\System32\DNS`. This root hints file contains the older TLD servers, not the new Verisign TLD servers. For an interim period, the `a.root-servers.net` TLD server will give referrals to the new TLD servers.

DNS Client Resolvers

The client service responsible for querying DNS and handling the responses is called a *resolver*. In Windows, the DNS resolver is part of the main TCP/IP driver.

When an application first specifies the name of a particular server, the resolver first looks in its Hosts file. If the resolver does not find an entry in the Hosts file, it then goes to DNS. Like a good *Jeopardy* contestant, the resolver always submits its DNS requests in the form of a question, a *DNS Query*.

When the resolver gets a response to its query, it caches the results in memory to speed up subsequent queries for the same record. DNS servers that search out records on behalf of their clients also cache the results.

A name cache can get very large if the entries are never removed. Also, an entry might change but the server would not find out because it only looks in its cache. To prevent these problems, a DNS resource record contains a *Time-To-Live* (TTL) setting that specifies how long to cache the entry.

Negative Caching

Starting with Windows 2000, Microsoft included support for RFC 2308, "Negative Caching of DNS Queries." This permits a client to cache negative responses along with the resource records it receives. The idea behind negative caching is to prevent sending repeated queries to a name server that has already admitted that it cannot find the record. If you're the parent of a two-year-old, you can understand the value of negative caching.

Unfortunately, negative caching can interfere with troubleshooting. For instance, let's say you forgot to put a host record for a new server into DNS. You start getting calls that folks cannot find the new server. You realize your mistake and create the host record. The phone calls continue to come in from those who have already tried to contact the server because their DNS client cached the negative response.

Root Server Selection

Root hints include multiple servers, so the local DNS server must decide which one to use for root queries. It does this by trying each root server in turn during the normal course of handling queries.

When the DNS server sends these queries, it measures the *round-trip time* (RTT) of the responses. After it has collected RTT data on all the root servers, it picks the one with the shortest RTT and uses it for subsequent queries. This is done on the assumption that the TLD server with the shortest RTT is closest to the DNS server.

If the RTT for the selected server degrades, the DNS server polls again to reevaluate the RTTs and may select a new root server based on the result of the evaluation.

You can clear these negative responses out of the local DNS cache using the IPCONFIG utility as follows:

```
ipconfig /flushdns
```

Unfortunately, this command must be issued at the client.

Servers also cache query results, including negative responses. If you want to clear out the DNS cache of a server, use the DNSCMD utility with this syntax:

```
dnscmd /clearcache
```

When you clear the cache, the client or server must accumulate entries again. This may hurt performance for a short while.

NetBIOS Resolution Versus DNS Resolution

A modern Windows client (Windows Server 2003, XP, or Windows 2000) uses NetBIOS name resolution to support SMB-based network application such as LanMan Workstation and LanMan Server. (SMB stands for Server Message Block, the command language used in Windows networking.)

For example, if you map a drive to a share point on a server, the flat server name in the UNC path is resolved to an IP address using NetBIOS name resolution. If the name contains a dot (.) or is longer than 16 characters, the client uses DNS name resolution. With the default h-node configuration, a modern Windows client uses the following sequence for NetBIOS name resolution:

1. NetBIOS name cache
2. WINS query
3. Lmhosts file
4. Broadcast
5. Hosts file
6. DNS

For Windows Sockets-based applications, all Windows clients use DNS name resolution (Hosts then DNS) as the primary means of resolving names to IP addresses. A modern Windows client will initiate NetBIOS name resolution in parallel, so if there is a disparity between the flat name in WINS and the hierarchical name in DNS, you can end up with a tricky problem to troubleshoot.

Flat names cannot be submitted to a DNS server. If you ping a flat host name, such as `svr1`, the DNS resolver takes the following action:

- If the name does not have an embedded dot and is shorter than 16 characters (a flat name), the client appends the DNS suffix for the computer onto the name and sends it to DNS.

- If the name has an embedded dot and does not have a trailing dot, the resolver appends a trailing dot and sends the result to DNS. If the query fails to return a host record, the resolver appends the entire domain suffix and tries again.
- If the first DNS suffix fails to get a host record from DNS, the resolver appends any alternative DNS suffixes that have been configured for the interface.
- If all secondary suffixes fail, the resolver gives up.

Functional Description of DNS Query Handling

It's important to have a fairly good idea of how DNS queries are handled before starting to architect your name resolution system (or change an existing system that is functioning properly). This topic contains step-by-step descriptions of DNS queries using several scenarios:

- A query handled by an authoritative server
- A query handled by a non-authoritative server
- A reverse-lookup query

Knowing how DNS queries are handled helps when designing a DNS system and when integrating Windows Server 2003 name services into an existing DNS infrastructure.

Queries Handled by Authoritative Servers

Assume, for example, that a user at a Windows Server 2003 computer in the `company.com` domain pings a server called `srv1`. Procedure 5.1 shows what happens from the point of view of DNS.

Procedure 5.1 Functional Description of Query Handling by an Authoritative Name Server

1. Tcpip.sys needs the IP address of `srv1` so it can build an ICMP packet. To get this address, Tcpip.sys uses its internal DNS resolver. The remainder of this discussion refers to this resolver as if it were a separate service.
2. The resolver fires off a query to its associated DNS server. The query contains the following:
   - The fully qualified DNS name of the target computer—in this case, `srv1.company.com`.
   - The resource record type being requested. It's doing a simple host name lookup, so the query is for an `A` record.
   - The resource record class being requested. This is nearly always the IN, or Internet, class. Other classes are used only in very limited circumstances.

DNS Packet Contents

It can be instructive to view the contents of the DNS messages involved in a name query transaction. The Network Monitor service that comes with Windows Server 2003 is a great tool for capturing and examining packets going to and from the local network interface. Figure 5.4 shows a captured packet containing the response to a Host query (A record) from an authoritative DNS server. The following are the key items to examine:

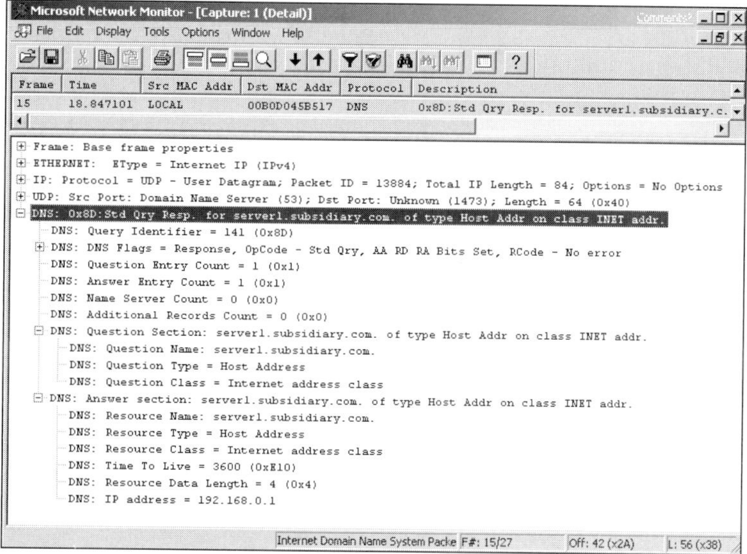

Figure 5.4 Captured packet showing DNS standard query response.

- **UDP entry.** Indicates that DNS query uses UDP port 53. This is the well-known port for DNS.
- **DNS flags.** The server indicates that it is authoritative for the domain, it supports recursive queries, and there was no error in the response.
- **DNS question section.** This contains a copy of the original DNS query asking for a host record for `dc01.company.com`.
- **DNS answer section.** The response contains the A record information for `dc01.company.com`, including its IP address and the default TTL value from the SOA record.

If you have a DNS server inside a firewall and you need to send queries to a TLD root server or some other public name server, you must either enable UDP port 53 at the firewall or configure your DNS server to use Network Address Translation (NAT) or a proxy to access the Internet. Windows Server 2003 running DNS answers a DNS query on the same interface that receives the query, so enabling UDP port 53 is adequate to support DNS queries and their responses.

3. When the DNS server receives the query, it parses the host name to find the DNS domain, `company.com`. In this instance, the DNS server is authoritative for the requested zone, so it does a zone lookup to find the requested resource record.
4. When the DNS server finds the A record for `srv1`, it sends the entire contents of the record back to the client in the form of a *DNS Query Response*. If the A record does

not contain a TTL value, the DNS server inserts the minimum TTL value from the `SOA` record for the zone. The default TTL is one hour, or 3,600 seconds.

If the DNS server cannot find the requested record, it returns a `Record Not Found` response. An authoritative DNS server does not consult another DNS server when it cannot resolve a query within its zone of authority. When the resolver gets a `Record Not Found` response from an authoritative name server, it returns an error to the application without attempting further lookups.

5. Now that the resolver has obtained the IP address, Tcpip.sys has some work to do. It uses the IP address from the `A` record to build an IP packet, then it uses *Address Resolution Protocol* (ARP) to find the MAC address associated with the IP address. Tcpip.sys then hands over the packet and the MAC address to the NDIS (Network Driver Interface Specification) driver, which works with the adapter driver to build a transmission frame that is sent to the target server.
6. Tcpip.sys also hands the `A` record over to the *DNS Resolver Cache* service. The Resolver Cache holds onto the `A` record for the time period specified in the TTL.

Queries Handled by Non-Authoritative Servers

Consider the situation if the user, instead of trying to access a file on a server on the internal network, tries to access a file on an external network such as the Internet. For example, the user opens a browser and points it at `www.roswellnm.org`. (I was born in Roswell. My friends say that explains a lot about me.) In this trace, let's skip the OSI Layer 7 details and get right to the DNS query (see Procedure 5.2).

Procedure 5.2 Functional Description of Query Handling by Non-Authoritative Name Server

1. The DNS resolver sends off a recursive query to its DNS server asking for an `A` record for `www.roswellnm.org`. A recursive query tells the DNS server to do all the work in resolving the address.
2. The local DNS server in the `company.com` DNS domain has no zone file for `roswellnm.org`. The recursive query tells the server to refer the request to another DNS server, but which one? This is where the root hints in the Cache.dns file come into play.
3. After consulting the root hints file, the DNS server fires off an iterative query to a top-level domain (TLD) server saying, in effect, "Give me an `A` record for `www.roswellnm.org` or tell me the name of a server that can help me."
4. In every likelihood, the TLD root server does not have an `A` record for `www.roswellnm.org`. However, the TLD server is authoritative for the domain `.org`. That means it has name server (`NS`) records pointing at servers that host the zone for `.org`.

5. The root server consults its NS records and discovers several name servers for roswellnm.org. It returns the NS and A records for each of these name servers. Here's one example: dns1.interland.net at IP address 64.224.20.132.

Trace Names

If you're wondering where I got the specific names and addresses in this trace, skip ahead to the section in this chapter on Nslookup, "Examining Zones with Nslookup."

6. The company.com DNS server now sends an iterative query to dns1.interland.net asking for an A record for www.roswellnm.org. The resolver at the client is still waiting patiently.
7. The DNS service on dns1.interland.net is authoritative for roswellnm.org. It does a zone file lookup and finds an A record for www with the IP address 209.35.62.148.
8. When the company.com DNS server receives the A record for www.roswellnm.org in answer to its query, it forwards the record to the client that originally sent the query. It also caches a copy in case another client sends a similar query. The aging time is determined by the TTL value in the A record.

The key point to remember about the actions of the non-authoritative server is that the root hints file is used to find the name and IP address of a root server. Without root hints or a forwarder, the query would have failed.

Reverse Lookup Queries

A standard DNS zone is called a *forward lookup zone* because it searches by the name of the record until it either finds the entry or reaches the end of the zone. But what if a user knows the IP address of a host and wants the associated name? An example of this kind of reverse lookup occurs when you use ping with the -a switch. This tells ping to display the host name along with the ICMP Echo Reply, like this:

```
E:\>ping -a 10.1.1.254
Pinging router.company.com [10.1.1.254] with 32 bytes of data:
Reply from 10.1.1.254: bytes=32 time<10ms TTL=128
```

This seems simple enough, but it turns out to be something of an exercise. DNS forward lookup zones are structured around host names, not IP addresses. Extracting a host name based on an IP address from a forward lookup zone would require an incredibly expensive scan that could encompass all the millions of zones scattered on DNS servers all over the planet.

DNS avoids this impossible situation by creating a separate zone file based on IP addresses. This is called a *reverse lookup zone*. Figure 5.5 shows an example reverse lookup zone displayed in the Windows Server 2003 DNS console.

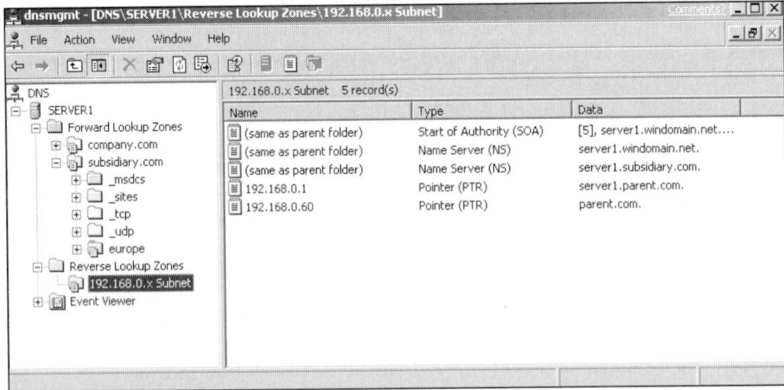

Figure 5.5 DNS console showing a reverse lookup zone.

Structure of a Reverse Lookup Zone

A reverse lookup zone is built using one record type, the PTR record. A PTR record contains the octets from the host ID in reverse order. The following listing contains examples of zone entries from a reverse lookup zone for the 10.1.0.0 network:

```
; Database file 1.10.in-addr.arpa.dns for 1.10.in-addr.arpa zone.
; Zone version:  8
;  Zone records
1.1          PTR    dc01
21.1         PTR    srv12
254.1         PTR    router01
```

Note that the network address `10.1.0.0` is reversed to make `1.10`. If the network address were `222.100.93.0`, the start of the zone file name would be `93.100.222`.

This reversal is necessary because the dotted-decimal notation used by IP addresses puts the most significant octet to the far *left*, whereas the referral mechanism used by DNS assumes that the most significant field is at the far *right*. Following the DNS referral method to its logical conclusion, if the inverted IP addresses form a contiguous tree, there would need to be 255 root domains with 255 separate primary name servers, one each for the 255 available addresses in the upper octet of the dotted-decimal IP address format.

The top of this reverse lookup namespace needs a root, so the *Advanced Research Project Administration* (ARPA), which was in charge of the Internet at the time DNS was devised, created an artificial root with the name `in-addr.arpa`. With the `in-addr.arpa` root in place, a single TLD server can own the whole reverse lookup zone with 255 nodes at the second level, a paltry number compared to the kazillions of second-level domains in the `.com` namespace.

What this means to you as a DNS administrator is that you must build a reverse lookup zone rooted at `in-addr.arpa` for every IP network in your organization. The name for each of these zones would start with the reverse of its network ID followed by the suffix `in-addr.arpa`. For example, the network ID `209.12.73.0` would have a reverse lookup zone of `73.12.209.in-addr.arpa`. Typically, you would use the primary name server for the root domain of your organization as the primary server for the reverse lookup zones.

Reverse Lookup Process

Procedure 5.3 shows how DNS handles a reverse lookup request. Assume, for example, that a user in the `company.com` domain, address `10.1.0.0`, uses `ping -a` to find the host name for `209.12.73.4`.

Procedure 5.3 Functional Description of Reverse Lookup Query

1. The resolver sends its DNS server a reverse lookup query, called a *Domain Name Pointer* request, for `4.73.12.209.in-addr.arpa`.
2. The DNS server is not authoritative for the `73.12.209.in-addr.arpa` zone, so it refers the query to one of the TLD servers.
3. The TLD server does not have a zone file for `73.12.209.in-addr.arpa`, but it has an `NS` record for the name server that holds the zone for `209.in-addr.arpa`. It returns a referral containing the `NS` and `A` records for that name server.
4. The `company.com` DNS server now sends its `PTR` query to the name server in the referral. This server does not have a zone file for `73.12.209.in-addr.arpa` either, but it returns the `NS` and `A` records for a name server holding the zone for `12.209.in-addr.arpa`.
5. The `company.com` DNS server now sends the `PTR` query to the name server in the referral. This server *does* hold the zone file for `73.12.209.in-addr.arpa`. It returns the contents of the `PTR` record for `4` along with the associated `A` record, which contains the host name, `www.newmexico.com`.

Many DNS administrators don't create reverse lookup zones on the theory that they aren't used often enough to make them worth the trouble. I recommend creating reverse lookup zones so you have all DNS tools at your disposal.

Designing DNS Domains

Now that you know the components of DNS and how they function, you're ready to design your own DNS system. Like all distributed network functions, your major goals are unbroken continuity of service, fast performance, minimum network traffic across the WAN, strong security, and a reasonably small need for administrative attention.

We've already seen how primary and secondary DNS servers can be distributed to provide fault tolerance. This section covers these additional DNS features:

- Zone replication
- Using forwarders
- Deploying into an existing DNS infrastructure
- WINS forwarding
- Dynamic zone updates
- Automated database scavenging
- Active Directory integration
- Secure DNS Updates

We'll take a look at each of these features from the viewpoint of fitting them into the design architecture. Then we'll see how to configure them using the DNS Management console.

Zone Replication

A secondary name server obtains a copy of a zone file either from the primary name server or another secondary via a mechanism called a *zone transfer.*

Classic DNS zone transfers require the secondary server to poll its feeder server at regular intervals and copy the entire zone file if a change occurred. This method has a couple of weaknesses. First, polling mechanisms are an inefficient use of bandwidth. Second, copying an entire zone file takes an inordinate amount of bandwidth and CPU time.

Windows 2000 and Windows Server 2003 incorporate two RFC-based provisions, *update notification* and *incremental zone transfers*, designed to improve classic DNS zone transfers. In addition, zone information can be stored in Active Directory, eliminating the need for specialized zone transfer mechanisms entirely.

Update Notification

In a standard zone transfer, the secondary name server polls its master periodically to see whether the zone has changed. The polling interval is set by a Refresh Interval in the *Start of Authority* (`SOA`) record. Figure 5.6 shows an example `SOA` record.

When a secondary server reaches the end of its refresh interval, it asks its master for a copy of its `SOA` record. This record contains a serial number, which is a sequence number incremented each time the zone is updated. If the serial number in the `SOA` record held by the secondary is lower than the serial number in the `SOA` record polled from the master, the secondary initiates a zone transfer.

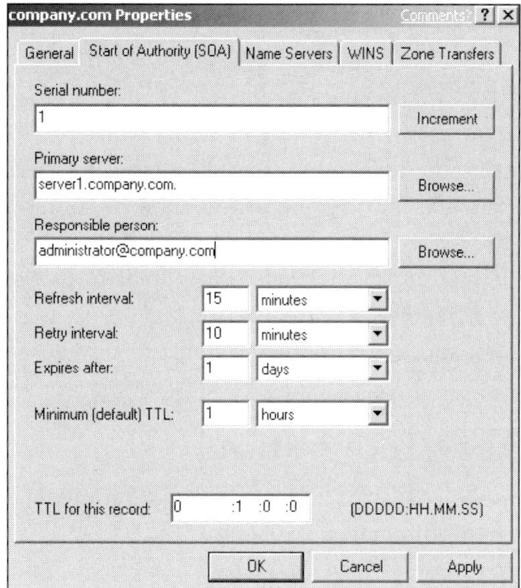

Figure 5.6 Zone Properties window showing `Start of Authority (SOA)` tab. The Refresh interval determines the polling time between zone transfers.

Windows Server 2003 and Windows 2000 DNS implements the provisions of RFC 1996, "A Mechanism for Prompt Notification of Zone Changes." This RFC defines a new DNS opcode (operations code, one of the commands understood by DNS servers and clients) called *DNS Notify*. Procedure 5.4 shows how it works.

Procedure 5.4 Functional Description of Standard Polled Zone Transfer

1. When an update is made to the zone at the master name server, the server sends out a DNS Notify message to its secondary name servers. It must be configured with the IP addresses of these servers.
2. The secondary name servers respond to the DNS Notify message by returning a standard update request for the `SOA` record.
3. From this point forward, the zone transfer proceeds in a traditional fashion.

Notification Differences from NT4

NT4 DNS implemented the DNS Notify opcode, but the administrator was required to manually initiate the notification by selecting Update Server Data File from the zone's Property menu. This was required because NT4 DNS used standard zone transfers, which copied the entire zone file.

Windows Server 2003 and Windows 2000 support incremental zone transfers, so notification is done automatically and the updates are copied as quickly as the secondaries can pull them down.

Incremental Zone Transfers

A standard DNS zone transfer involves copying the entire zone file from the primary name server to its secondaries and from secondary to secondary in a tiered structure. Windows Server 2003 and Windows 2000 avoid this sometimes lengthy file transfer by implementing the provisions of RFC 1995, "Incremental Zone Transfer in DNS."

In an incremental transfer, the secondary server supplies the serial number from its copy of the SOA record when it requests a zone transfer. The master server sends only those updates that have been made subsequent to that serial number.

If a Windows Server 2003 or Windows 2000 name server is a secondary to a master that does not support incremental transfers, it falls back to using full zone transfers.

Active Directory Integration

In addition to the two RFC-compliant zone transfer methods, Windows Server 2003 DNS zone can be integrated into Active Directory. This eliminates the need for conventional zone transfers because Active Directory is replicated using its own multiple-master replication scheme.

Active Directory integration also makes it possible for any Windows Server 2003 or Windows 2000 domain controller that is running DNS to update the zone.

The DNS service requires very little overhead, so you can easily deploy DNS on every domain controller. In terms of performance, bandwidth utilization, and manageability, integrating DNS into Active Directory is a win. There are a few caveats, however:

- **No ASCII zone files.** Resource records are stored in Active Directory as objects. If you want a text file to use as a fallback, you can maintain at least one standard secondary name server. Windows Server 2003 and Windows 2000 DNS will provide zone updates to the secondary and the secondary can save these in a regular text file.
- **Relies on Active Directory availability.** Clients need DNS to find domain controllers. Hosting DNS on the same server that hosts Active Directory means you have multiple failures if the server goes down or is otherwise unavailable. You can minimize this risk by including at least two DNS servers in the TCP/IP configuration for the clients. Also, remember that the domain controller is also a DNS client, so make sure it points at itself for DNS lookups.
- **A Windows DNS server must be the primary name server.** This may cause discomfort for DNS administrators who currently run UNIX or NetWare DNS and are hesitant about cutting over to Windows.

Using Forwarders

When a DNS server gets a query for a record in another zone that it does not have in cache, it checks its root hints to find a root server and then uses iterative queries to "walk the tree" until it finds a name server that has the record. This process is detailed in the earlier section in this chapter, "Functional Description of DNS Query Handling."

There is an alternative to doing all that grunt work, and that is to check with another server that might have already done the grunt work first. This is called forwarding. The server being referenced by your DNS server is called a *forwarder*. Figure 5.7 shows an example DNS configuration that incorporates forwarders.

The primary name server in the figure is configured to use a forwarder in two situations:

- When the server receives queries for hosts in the `subsidiary.com` zone, it forwards those queries to one or more name servers in the subsidiary.com DNS domain. This is called *conditional forwarding* and is a new feature in Windows Server 2003.
- When the server receives queries for hosts outside its own zone and not in `subsidiary.com`, it forwards those queries to a name server maintained by an ISP.

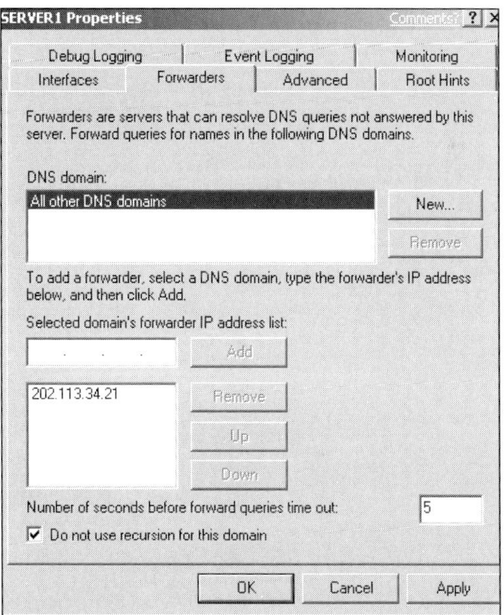

Figure 5.7 DNS configuration using standard forwarding and conditional forwarding.

In the second case, if the primary name server also has a functional set of root hints for the Internet top-level domain servers, it waits a while and then sends a query to one of those servers as well. It's betting that the forwarder will come through with the requested record before it has to do an iterative walk through the Internet to find a name server for the requested domain.

A server configured to use a forwarder exclusively for out-of-zone lookups is called a *slave server*. A slave server depends completely on its forwarder. If the forwarder cannot find the record, the slave sends a `No Record` response back to the client. A Windows Server 2003 or Windows 2000 DNS server can be made into a slave server by selecting the `Do Not Use Recursion for This Domain` option in the Forwarders configuration in the server properties window.

Conditional Forwarding

Windows Server 2003 introduces a new feature that simplifies integrating DNS with name servers in other domains. Rather than designating a single server to use as a forwarder, you can designate separate forwarders for individual domains. This is configured as part of the DNS server properties in the DNS console. Figure 5.8 shows the configuration.

Here's an example of how to use conditional forwarding. Let's say that you have an extranet connection to a vendor that is used for sharing database access and the occasional file transfer. The vendor's DNS domain name is `vendor.com`. The IP address of the vendor's DNS server is `192.168.0.30`. Your clients have access to this server for purposes of submitting DNS queries.

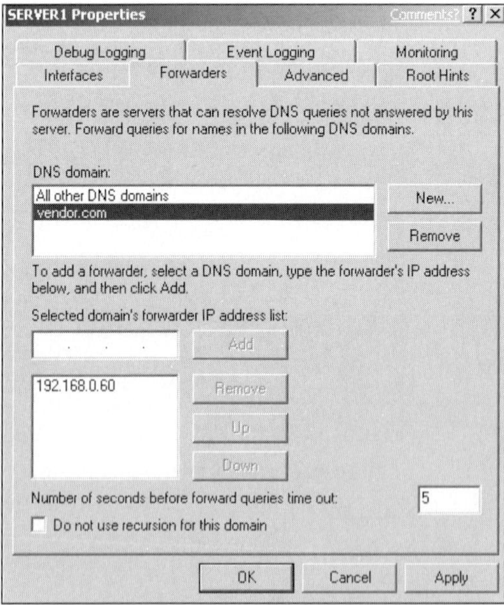

Figure 5.8 DNS server properties showing conditional forwarder configuration.

Windows 2000 and Root Zones

Windows 2000 caused a bit of grief for administrators trying to configure forwarders and root hints for their DNS servers. In Windows 2000, a newly installed DNS server was automatically configured with a root domain, indicated by a folder with a dot (.) at the top of the namespace. This root domain tells a DNS server that it sits at the top of the entire DNS namespace and whatever domains it hosts are top-level domains.

This is absurd, of course. No private server can be a TLD server. At best, it can be the root server for its own domain. But as long as that root zone exists, a Windows server cannot be convinced it is anything other than the once and future king, wielder of the sacred sword, master of the Elvish rings, and so on. This means the server will not accept root hints and cannot be configured to use forwarders.

This "feature" of Windows 2000 forced administrators to delete the root zone so that they could correctly configure their DNS infrastructure. In Windows Server 2003, the root zone is not installed by default.

You can configure conditional forwarding at your DNS server so that all requests for resource records in the `vendor.com` domain are sent to `192.168.0.30`. Your DNS server sends an iterative request to the target DNS server and forwards the response back to the clients.

Stub Zones

Windows Server 2003 supports a special type of zone configuration called a *stub zone*. A stub zone is used in place of delegation records when configuring a parent DNS server to send referrals to delegated DNS servers in a child domain.

A stub zone contains the `SOA` record and `NS` (Name Server) records for a child zone along with the `A` records (also called *glue* records) corresponding to the name servers in the child zone. The stub zone server periodically updates its copy of the resource records. This simplifies delegation management.

Here's an example. Let's say you are the administrator of the `company.com` zone. You want to delegate the `branch.company.com` zone to another DNS server in your organization that is managed by another administrator.

Ordinarily, you would accomplish this by creating delegation records in the `company.com` zone that point at the name servers in `branch.company.com`. If the administrator responsible for `branch.company.com` adds or removes a name server, you would need to add and remove delegation records in `company.com`.

With stub zones, instead of creating delegation records, you create a stub zone on the `company.com` DNS server that points at `branch.company.com`. When you initially create the stub zone, it copies the `SOA`, `NS`, and glue records from the DNS server in `branch.company.com`.

When the `company.com` DNS server gets requests for resource records in `branch.company.com`, it uses name servers in the target domain to resolve the requests recursively. This speeds up subsequent requests because the stub zone server builds up a cache of resource records from the target zone.

If the administrator for `branch.company.com` adds or removes a name server, the stub zone on your DNS server picks up the changes automatically. This relieves you of the responsibility for manually updating your delegation records.

Deploying Windows DNS into an Existing Infrastructure

Many DNS administrators tend to be leery about trusting Windows DNS. If you currently use BIND or Lucent QIP or NetWare 5.x for your DNS services, you do not need to change to Windows Server 2003 simply to accommodate Active Directory.The non-Windows DNS server must support RFC 2052,"A DNS RR for Specifying the Location of Services (DNS SRV)." In addition, it should support RFC 2136, "Dynamic DNS."

As we'll see when we get to Active Directory design, Windows Server 2003 depends on DNS to provide the structure for the new generation of Windows domains. You may find it difficult to combine the namespace you want for Active Directory with your existing DNS namespace.You may need to create a separate namespace for Active Directory that is hosted on Windows DNS servers rather than BIND servers. Figure 5.9 shows an example of how such a split namespace can be achieved.

The example contains the following configuration features:

- The zone for the Active Directory domain is hosted on a Windows Server 2003 running DNS to take advantage of secure dynamic updates.

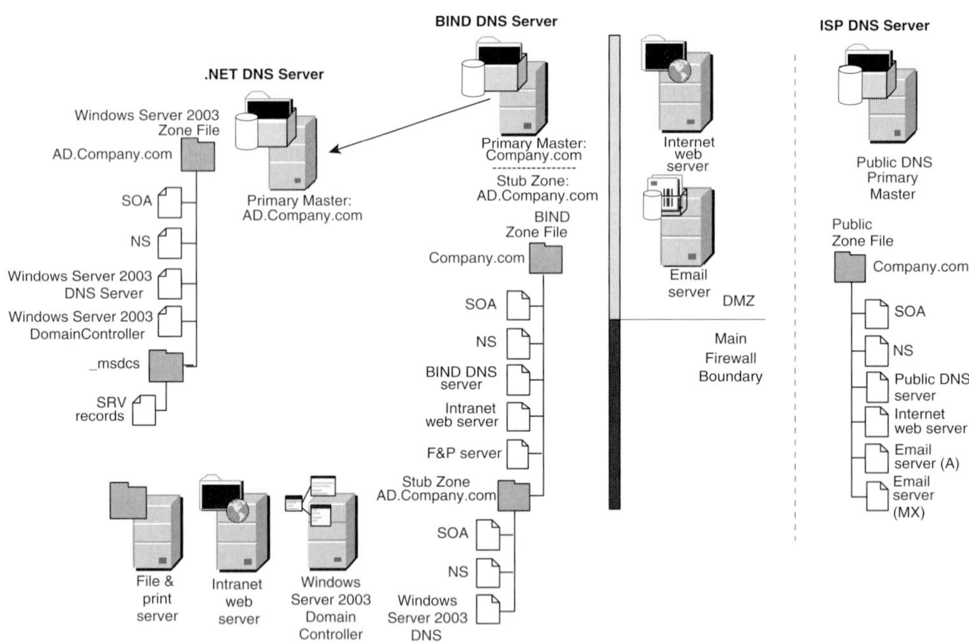

Figure 5.9 DNS configuration showing a split namespace for private and public zones with same name.

- The main corporate zone is hosted on a BIND server, which has a stub to the Windows zone rather than delegation records. UNIX clients in the organization obtain resource records from the Active Directory domain via referrals through the stub zone.
- The Windows Server 2003 running DNS uses the BIND server as a forwarder. This permits Windows clients to obtain resource records from the main corporate zone.
- The BIND server forwards out-of-zone traffic to a DNS server at an ISP. This permits both UNIX and Windows clients to resolve Internet names.
- The BIND server is configured as a slave to the ISP forwarder so that it does not use root hints to get records directly from the Internet TLDs. This minimizes traffic through the firewall.
- The ISP name server hosts the primary zone for the public corporate domain. This permits Internet users to resolve addresses for servers in the corporate DMZ without giving access through the firewall to the internal DNS server.

Most organizations use a hybrid of this basic configuration. For instance, an organization might want to maintain its own public DNS server in the DMZ. Or, the administrators might want the Windows DNS server to forward directly to the ISP name server and eliminate a potential single point of failure at the BIND server.

Whatever configuration you choose, if you use Windows DNS servers, make sure that Windows clients (this includes member servers and domain controllers) point at Windows DNS servers. This ensures that they see the `SRV` records they need to support access to vital domain controller services such as LDAP and Kerberos.

WINS Forwarding

While we're on the subject of forwarding, let's take a look at a form of forwarder that has been around since NT4 DNS.

Windows servers occupy a special place because they are both TCP/IP hosts with hierarchical host name and SMB-based servers with flat NetBIOS names. In the SMB world, the servers happily register their names and services with WINS with little or no administrative intervention. In the DNS world, someone must create records for the servers in the correct zone so non-Windows clients can find them.

Rather than maintain two databases, NT4 introduced a couple of proprietary resource records, the `WINS` record and the `WINS-R` record. These records pointed a Windows DNS server at one or more WINS servers. This enabled the server to forward DNS requests for Windows servers to WINS.

Dynamic Updates

Properly configured secondary servers improve reliability and reduce WAN traffic—two of the major goals for your DNS design. Another goal is to reduce administrative work, and that's where dynamic updates come into play.

Windows 2000 and Windows Server 2003 support dynamic zone updates as described in RFC 2136, "Dynamic Updates in the Domain Name System." This RFC defines a new opcode called *DNS Update* that can be used to add records to a zone automatically. A DNS Update message contains the type of record to add (for example, an `A` record for a host name or an `SRV` record for a domain controller service), the name of the zone where the record should be added, and any prerequisite records that must or must not be present. As a minimum, modern Windows clients register an `A` (host) record and a `PTR` (reverse lookup pointer) record with their DNS server.

Dynamic DNS clients (Windows Server 2003, XP, and Windows 2000) register their `A` and `PTR` records at boot time then refresh them every 24 hours. These dynamic updates are performed by the DHCP Client service. Do not disable this service, even if you use static IP addressing on your servers. Domain controllers refresh their DNS records every hour. This is controlled by the Netlogon service.

Non-RFC 2136 clients such as downlevel Windows clients can register their `A` and `PTR` records by proxy through Dynamic Host Configuration Protocol (DHCP). See "Configuring DHCP to Support DNS," near the end of this chapter for details.

You can force dynamic registration at Windows Server 2003, XP, and Windows 2000 clients using IPCONFIG as follows:

```
ipconfig /registerdns
```

Certain stipulations apply when dynamically registering a resource record:

- When a client attempts to register a record that does not already exist, the DNS server adds the new record updates to the zone.
- If a record exists with a different name but the same IP address, the new record is added and the old record is left in place.
- If a record exists with the same host name but different IP address, the original record is overwritten with the new address value.

Although the primary DNS server has the only read/write copy of the zone file, the DNS client can be configured to point at any authoritative server for the zone. The secondary servers pass the DNS Update messages from the clients up to the primary master. The primary name server notifies its secondaries of the change, and the secondaries pull an incremental zone transfer.

If the client is configured to point at a non-authoritative server such as a caching-only server, the dynamic updates are not passed on to the authoritative server and the client is not registered.

Dynamic Updates and Domain Controllers

An Active Directory domain controller (Windows Server 2003 or Windows 2000) automatically registers its `A` and `PTR` records along with its service locator (`SRV`) records via the Netlogon service. The records are refreshed each time the service starts (usually at boot time) and hourly thereafter.

If you make a change to a domain controller and you want to update DNS immediately, stop and start the Netlogon service. The domain controller continues to perform Kerberos authentications with Netlogon turned off but downlevel clients (Windows 9x and NT) cannot authenticate.

If a domain controller cannot find its DNS server or the DNS server does not accept dynamic updates, you will see errors in the Event log. These errors are common in a BIND Domain Name System (DNS) infrastructure where dynamic updates have been disabled at the name server.

If you want to avoid Event log errors and a constant drone of invalid request traffic to your BIND servers, you can disable automatic `SRV` record renewal by making a Registry change:

Key: `HKEY_LOCAL_MACHINE\SYSTEM\CurrentControlSet\Services\NetLogon\Parameters`

Value: `DnsRegisterARecords`

Data: `0x0 (REG.DWORD)`

You will also need to delete the Netlogon.dnb file from the `C:\Windows\System32\Config` folder. This file contains records for automatic updating.

You can also control automatic DNS updates from clients and domain controllers using group policies. It is still necessary to delete the Netlogon.dnb file manually.

Record Scavenging

Dynamic registration carries the risk that your nice, clean DNS zone might start to look like something best described as an aftermath. To avoid this, use scavenging to clean out old and unused records.

Scavenging is not enabled by default. It can be enabled for a particular zone or for every zone on a DNS server. Scavenging only applies to primary zones and Active Directory Integrated zones. Secondary zones are read-only. If you scavenge the master zone, the secondary zones get cleaned up during the zone transfers.

Because scavenging works by including an aging value in the dynamically registered resource records, it changes the format of the zone file, making it incompatible with non-Windows name servers. Zone transfers are unaffected because the DNS service filters out the aging value, but you cannot take a copy of the .DNS file for the zone and load it onto an NT4 or BIND name server.

Scavenging uses two intervals, the *non-refresh interval* and the *refresh interval*, to determine when a particular record should be removed from the zone file. Both intervals are set for seven days by default. Here is how they work.

When a resource record is first dynamically created, DNS assigns an aging value based on the seven-day non-refresh interval. During this seven-day interval, DNS does not accept refreshes to the record. This prevents the system from being overwhelmed every morning with refreshes from thousands of machines as they are turned on.

After the initial, seven-day non-refresh interval, the record is free to be refreshed. DNS clients refresh their records at boot time and every 24 hours, if they are left on. The refresh interval lasts for another seven days. At the end of the seven-day refresh interval, if the aging value has not been refreshed, the record will be removed during scavenging.

Scavenging can be initiated manually from the PROPERTIES menu of the zone icon or by scheduling it to run periodically as part of the DNS server properties (see "Configuring Scavenging" later in this chapter).

If a user goes on vacation for more than two weeks and leaves her machine off, the DNS registration for her A and PTR records will age out and periodic scavenging will remove them from the zone. This is not a catastrophe. The user does not lose any security privileges or functionality. When the user starts up the machine after coming back from vacation and logs on, the system will re-register with DNS and build a new resource record.

DNS Security

A primary goal of DNS design is security. DNS security has several facets:

- Limit the number of administrators who can make changes to the zone.
- Prevent exposing the contents of your zones to unauthorized individuals.
- Avoid potential abuse of the dynamic record registration mechanism.

Limit Administrative Access

You can control the security settings for accessing a DNS server. By default, Domain Admins, Enterprise Admins, DNS Admins, and the Administrators groups have full control. You can remove some of these groups to limit access to just members of the DNS Admins group or you can create another group for this purpose.

The DNS Admins group is created in Active Directory by default when you install DNS. The Administrator account is a member of the group. The group is given Full Control rights over any DNS server in the domain as well as Full Control rights over the DNS zone information in Active Directory for Active Directory Integrated zones.

If you define a separate group for DNS administration, be sure that you don't put the group in an OU where someone with administrator privileges can change the group membership. This defeats the purpose of the security group. Also remove the

DNS Admins group from the access control list, because anyone with administrator rights in Active Directory can control the membership of this group.

When setting security configuration for a DNS server, be sure to leave the Authenticated Users group on the access control list with the special rights they are assigned by default. This permits DNS clients to read the contents of a DNS server.

Prevent Unauthorized Zone Transfers

DNS servers make particularly enticing targets for intruders. They hold the IP address of every host in your network, and that kind of information can be damaging in the wrong hands. For instructions on adding or removing a server from the list of authorized servers, see the upcoming section, "Enabling Zone Transfers and Update Notifications."

One consequence of locking down zone transfers is that you cannot use tools like Nslookup to view the contents of the zone file. This is because these tools use the same zone file transfer opcodes that a secondary server uses. This is not true for the DNSCMD utility that is installed when you install DNS on a server. If you have administrative privileges for a DNS server, you can use DNSCMD to dump the contents of a zone file.

Secure Dynamic Updates

One of the most important security measures you can take regarding dynamic updates is to control the computers that are permitted to register resource records. Without adequate controls, someone could accidentally or maliciously poison your zone file with false or misleading records. Or, they could stage a denial of service attack by registering thousands and thousands of bogus resource records.

The current Standards Track documents for controlling DNS Update security are RFC 2535, "Domain Name System Security Extensions," and RFC 2930, "Secret Key Establishment for DNS." These and other supporting RFCs combine to form the DNSSec documentation. Windows Server 2003 does not implement DNSSec transactions, but it does support the new resource record types involved in those transactions.

Windows Server 2003 permits you to restrict dynamic DNS Updates so that only authenticated computers in a domain can update their DNS information. To get this security, you must integrate the zone into Active Directory. A default group, DNS Admins, has read/write access to these DNS objects. Figure 5.10 shows an example access control list.

For instructions on configuring a secure update zone, see the "Managing Dynamic DNS" section later in this chapter.

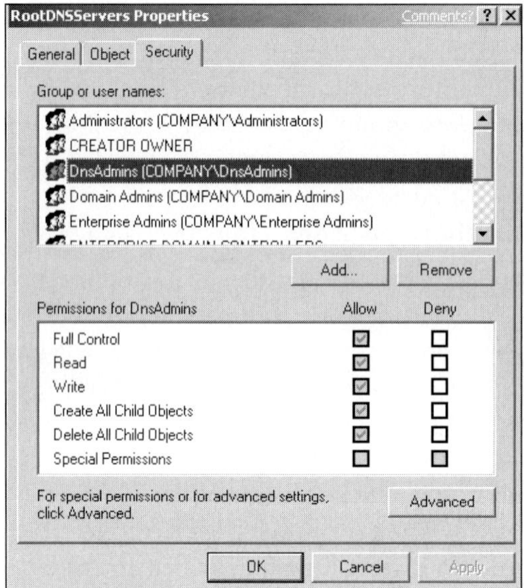

Figure 5.10 Access control list for Active Directory Integrated DNS zone showing DNS Admins group.

Configuring DNS Clients

It's about time to install DNS, but first let's configure a few DNS clients so that they will be ready to use the server after it is in operation. Windows Server 2003 clients need two pieces of information about DNS:

- The IP address of the DNS server or servers to which they will send queries.
- The default domain name to use when sending queries. (This is also called the DNS Suffix.)

The IP address information is configured in TCP/IP Properties. The DNS Suffix information is configured in two places: the TCP/IP Properties for the network interface and System Properties for the computer. These entries are stored in separate places in the Registry.

Configuring DNS Information in TCP/IP Properties

When you have the information you need to configure a client's DNS settings, proceed as shown in Procedure 5.5.

Using Multiple DNS Servers

You can configure a client to query multiple DNS servers. If the first server on the list does not respond, the resolver consults the next server. If the first server responds authoritatively with a `Record Not Found` error, the client does not consult additional servers.

Procedure 5.5 Configuring DNS Information for TCP/IP Interface Properties

1. Right-click `My Network Places` and select PROPERTIES from the flyout menu. The Network and Dial-up Connections window opens.
2. Right-click the `Local Connection` icon and select PROPERTIES from the flyout menu. The Local Connection Properties window opens.
3. Double-click the `Internet Protocol (TCP/IP)` entry to open its Properties window.
4. Click `Advanced`. The Advanced TCP/IP Settings window opens.
5. Select the `DNS` tab.
6. Under `DNS Server Addresses`, click `Add`. The TCP/IP DNS Server window opens.
7. Enter the IP address of the DNS server and click `Add` to add it to the list. You can add several servers to the list.
8. Leave the `DNS Suffix for This Connection` field blank. Do not select the `Use This Connection's DNS Suffix in DNS Registration` option. Wait for the next section to configure these settings in `System Properties`.
9. Click `OK` to retain the change and close the window.
10. Click `OK` to return to the TCP/IP Properties window.
11. Click `OK` to close the window and update the Registry with the changes.

Configuring DNS Information in System Properties

The DNS Suffix information in System Properties is used as the primary suffix for building FQDNs and is used to register the computer in Dynamic DNS. You will get the best results by putting suffix information here rather than in TCP/IP Properties. View and modify the DNS Suffix information in System Properties as described in Procedure 5.6. A system restart is required if you make changes.

Procedure 5.6 Configuring DNS Information in the System Properties Window

1. Right-click `My Computer` and select PROPERTIES from the flyout menu. The System Properties window opens.
2. Select the `Network Identification` tab.
3. Click `Properties`. The Identification Changes window opens.
4. Click `More`. The DNS Suffix and NetBIOS Computer Name window opens.
5. Enter the DNS domain name. Be sure to check the `Change Primary DNS Suffix when Domain Membership Changes` option. This ensures that the server's DNS domain matches its Active Directory domain.
6. Click `OK` to save the change.

7. Click OK to return to the System Properties window. The system prompts you that the change requires a restart.
8. Click OK, and then OK again to close the System Properties window. The system prompts again to restart. Do so.

After you complete configuring a client, use `ipconfig /all` to double-check your work.

Installing and Configuring DNS Servers

If you have existing NT4 or Windows 2000 DNS servers, you can upgrade them to Windows Server 2003 and preserve your existing server configuration and zone files. If you decide to upgrade, start with the primary DNS server, then upgrade the secondary servers.

Here's a quick checklist to use as a roadmap for your DNS deployment:

- Lay out your DNS domain namespace so you know which zones you need. DNS names affect nearly every aspect of your system, so spend sufficient time with this step so that everyone agrees on the naming conventions.
- Decide how you will integrate Windows DNS into your existing DNS infrastructure. If you use WINS, you also need to decide if you will use WINS forwarding.
- Decide how you will resolve Internet addresses. This can be with root hints by using a forwarder, or a combination of both.
- Decide how you will provide name services for public zones. You can get DNS services from your ISP, place a DNS server in your DMZ, or open a conduit in your firewall for DNS query traffic.
- Decide if you need to support name resolution behind the firewall for outside DNS domains. This includes extranets and network connections from subsidiaries, affiliates, or other trusted organizations. You can use conditional forwarding or stub zones to resolve addresses for these connections.
- Define the locations where you will need DNS servers. Remember that you want to maximize availability and minimize WAN traffic.
- Decide whether you will use standard DNS primary and secondary servers or Active Directory Integrated zones. If you use Active Directory Integrated zones, you must place domain controllers in strategic locations to support name resolution as well as LDAP and Kerberos lookups.
- Decide if you will support dynamic resource record updates. If so, consider integrating your zones into Active Directory so you can take advantage of secure updates.

- Decide how you will configure your DNS servers for special features such as round-robin, netmask prioritization, and name checking.

After you've made your design assessments, use the step-by-step instructions in this section for configuring your servers.

Installing the DNS Service

When you're ready to install the DNS service on Windows Server 2003, follow Procedure 5.7. You'll need the Windows Server 2003 CD-ROM.

Procedure 5.7 Installing DNS Drivers

1. From Control Panel, open the `Add/Remove Programs` applet.
2. Click `Add/Remove Windows Components`. The Windows Components Wizard starts with the focus set to the Windows Components window.
3. Highlight `Networking Services` and click `Details`. The Networking Services window opens.
4. Select `Domain Name System (DNS)` and click `OK` to save the change and return to the Windows Components window.
5. Click `Next`. The Configuring Components window opens and the drivers begin loading. When the drivers have loaded and the configuration is complete, the wizard displays a successful completion window.
6. Click `Finish` to close the window and return to the Add/Remove Programs window.
7. Close the `Add/Remove Programs` window.

At this point, you can begin configuring your zones. There is no need to restart.

Creating a Forward Lookup Zone

The first forward lookup zone you create should be for the root of your DNS namespace. In the `Company` public namespace used in these examples, the first zone would be for the `company.com` DNS domain. Follow the steps in Procedure 5.8.

DNS Boot Information

The DNS service starts automatically at boot time. You can start and stop the service using the DNS console or from the command line using `net stop dns` and `net start dns`.

If the DNS service is configured as a standard primary or secondary, it initializes the zone based on Registry entries located at `HKLM | Software| Microsoft| Windows NT | CurrentVersion | DNS Server | Zones`. This is a change from Windows 2000, where the zone information was stored as part of the DNS service key.

Each zone has a separate key with values that define the name of the database file, whether it allows dynamic updates, and whether updates must be from secure clients.

Procedure 5.8 Creating a Forward Lookup Zone

1. From the START menu, select START | PROGRAMS | ADMINISTRATIVE TOOLS | DNS. The DNS console opens. The DNS tree shows the local server and two empty branches for forward and reverse lookup zones.
2. Right-click the `Forward Lookup Zone` icon and select NEW ZONE from the flyout menu. This starts the New Zone Wizard.
3. Click `Next`. The Zone Type window opens (see Figure 5.11). Leave the default selection at `Primary Zone`. If you want to create a standard primary zone, uncheck the `Store The Zone In Active Directory` option.

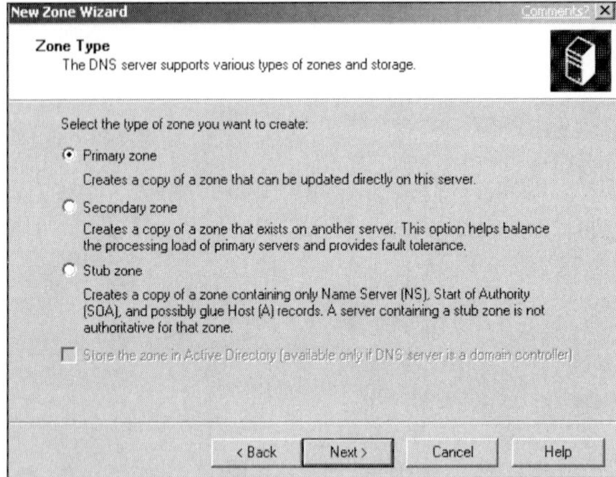

Figure 5.11 New Zone Wizard—Zone Type window showing default selection of `Primary Zone`.

4. Click `Next`. The Zone Name window opens. Enter the name of the zone.
5. Click `Next`. The Zone File window opens. The zone filename should match the zone name with a .DNS extension. If you have an existing zone file, you can import it at this point with the `Use This Existing File` option.
6. Click `Next`. The Dynamic Update window opens. Select your update option. The `Allow Only Secure Dynamic Updates` option will only be available for Active Directory Integrated zones.
7. Click `Next`. The wizard displays a completion window.
8. Click `Finish` to complete the configuration and close the window. The new zone appears as a folder under the `Forward Lookup Zones` icon in the left pane of the window. When that zone icon is highlighted, the associated resource records are displayed in the right pane (see Figure 5.12).

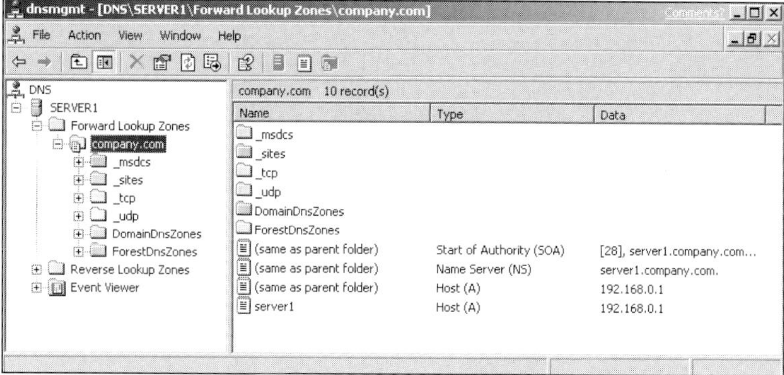

Figure 5.12 DNS console showing new forward lookup zone.

Creating a Reverse Lookup Zone

The forward lookup zone handles standard queries such as `A` record and `SRV` record requests. The reverse lookup zone will handle those few queries where the client knows the IP address and wants a host name. You can get by without creating reverse lookup zones, but they come in very handy for troubleshooting (and I highly recommend installing them). To create a reverse lookup zone, follow Procedure 5.9.

Procedure 5.9 Creating a Reverse Lookup Zone

1. Right-click the `Reverse Lookup Zone` icon and select NEW ZONE from the flyout menu. This starts the New Zone Wizard.
2. Click `Next`. The Zone Type window opens. Leave the default selection at `Primary Zone`. If you want to create a standard primary zone, uncheck the `Store The Zone In Active Directory` option.
3. Click `Next`. The Reverse Lookup Zone window opens (see Figure 5.13). Under `Network ID`, enter the network portion of the subnet the zone will service. The examples in this book use the 10.x networks with a 16-bit subnet mask, so the entry shows 10.1 with the last two octets empty. Each unique number in the second octet requires a separate reverse lookup zone.
4. Click `Next`. The Zone File window opens. Leave the default setting. The zone filename should match the zone name with a .DNS extension. If you have an existing zone file, you can import it at this point with the `Use This Existing File` option.
5. Click `Next`. The Dynamic Update window opens. Select your update option. The `Allow Only Secure Dynamic Updates` option will only be available for Active Directory Integrated zones.

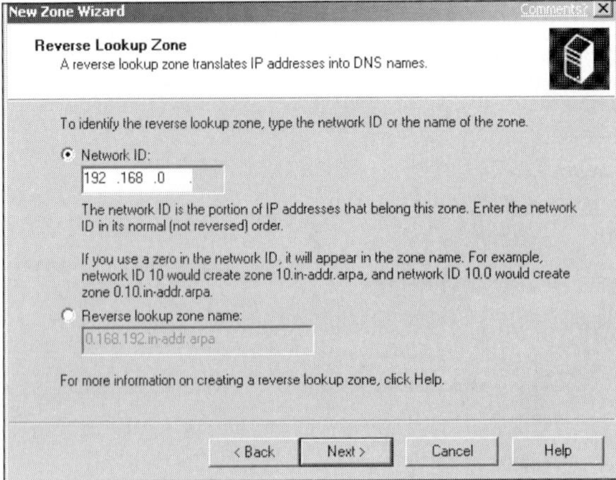

Figure 5.13 New Zone Wizard—Reverse Lookup Zone window.

6. Click `Next`. The wizard displays a completion window.
7. Click `Finish` to close the window and return to the DNS console.

After the reverse lookup zones are in place, create a few test host records to make sure the associated `PTR` records are created successfully. Then, test the zone from a client by pinging the test records and the DNS server.

Configuring Hierarchical Zones

After you have installed your first DNS server and created the first zone, you can configure additional zones to build a hierarchical DNS namespace. For example, you could start with a `company.com` zone and then configure separate zones for each continent, such as `na.company.com` and `eu.company.com` and so forth.

If you use separate zones, you need to configure the name servers to resolve queries between the zones. Plan your configuration around these two situations:

- Queries from DNS clients in a child zone for records in its parent zone. This requires configuring the root hints file.
- Queries from DNS clients in a parent zone for records in a child zone. This requires configuring delegation.

Configuring Root Hints

Queries from DNS clients in a child zone for records in its parent zone are resolved by configuring root hints on the DNS server in the child zone to include an authoritative server or servers in the parent zone.

Start by installing DNS on two servers and creating the zones. The objective of the following steps is to make it possible for a user in the child domain to resolve an address in the parent domain by querying only the DNS server in the child domain. Follow Procedure 5.10.

Procedure 5.10 Configuring Root Hints

1. Open the `DNS` console.
2. Right-click the `DNS server` icon and select PROPERTIES from the flyout menu. The Properties window opens.
3. Select the `Root Hints` tab.
4. Click `Add`. The Create New Record window opens.
5. Enter the fully qualified DNS name of the root server, with or without the trailing dot, under `Server Name`.
6. Enter the IP address of the server under `Server IP Addresses` and then click `Add` to put it on the list. If the server has multiple IP addresses, you can add each of them to the list. If you prefer that the queries use one of the addresses preferentially, use the `Up` and `Down` buttons to adjust the search list.
7. Click `OK` to retain the changes and return to the Properties window. Make sure that the root server is at the top of the list.
8. Click `OK` to save the changes and close the window.
9. Test the configuration by pinging a host in the parent domain from a client in the child domain. The ping may take a while, but eventually it will succeed.

Configuring Delegation

The preceding section showed how to get a successful query for a host in a domain higher in the DNS namespace. Getting a successful query for a host lower in the namespace takes a bit more work. Assume, for example, that you are in the `company.com` DNS domain and you want to ping a server called `srv1` in the `branch1.company.com` DNS domain.

For ping to succeed, the DNS server in the `company.com` domain must find an `A` record for the server. But the `company.com` DNS server only has a copy of the `company.com` zone file. It must obtain the resource record from a name server in the `branch1.company.com` domain. This is called *delegation*.

Updating Root Hints

The root hints that come with Windows Server 2003 reflect the legacy name servers maintained by Network Solutions and not the new TLD servers maintained by Verisign (doing business as Network Solutions). You can update your root hints manually using information obtained from Verisign Global Registry Services, `www.verisign-grs.com/dns/ dnsfaq.html`.

As described in the topic, "Stub Zones," earlier in this chapter, the simplest way to delegate with a Windows Server 2003 running DNS is to configure a stub zone on the DNS server in the parent zone to point at one or more name servers in the child zone. The stub zone replicates the `SOA`, `NS`, and glue records from the child zone automatically. This requires zone transfer authorization in the child zone, and if you lack this authorization, you must use standard delegation as described in this section.

DNS servers, like military brass, always delegate down, not up. Therefore, when configuring delegation in your DNS namespace, start at the root and work your way down as shown in Procedure 5.11.

Procedure 5.11 Configuring Delegations

1. Open the `DNS` console.
2. Right-click the zone name and select NEW DELEGATION from the flyout menu. This starts the New Delegation Wizard.
3. Click `Next`. The Delegated Domain Name window opens.
4. Enter the flat name of the child domain under `Delegated Domain`. The fully qualified name is built automatically.
5. Click `Next`. The Name Servers window opens.
6. Click `Add`. The New Resource Record window opens.
7. Under `Server Name`, enter the fully qualified name of an authoritative server for the child zone. See the sidebar, "Lame Delegations," for the reason it is so important to select an authoritative server.
8. Under `IP Address`, enter the IP address of the name server in the child domain, and then click `Add` to put it on the list.
9. Click `OK` to retain the changes and return to the Name Servers window. The server appears on the Server Name list.
10. Click `Next`. The wizard displays a completion window.
11. Click `Finish` to save the changes and close the wizard.

Lame Delegations

A common error when configuring delegation is specifying a server that is not authoritative for the specified domain. This results in what is called a *lame delegation.*

A lame delegation is a ticking time bomb. The system appears to work just fine until one day when the non-authoritative server returns the wrong record out of its cache. The DNS server in the parent domain forwards the faulty response to the querying client and puts it in its own cache where other clients get it.

Remember how you felt when you found out your parents weren't infallible? Well, DNS clients who get faulty responses from lame delegations feel the same way. Make sure that you always delegate to an authoritative server.

The DNS tree in the left pane of the DNS console shows the child domain listed under the parent. The right pane shows an `NS` record for the child domain name server. Test the delegation by pinging a host in the child domain from a DNS client in the parent domain. The ping should succeed nearly immediately. A packet trace shows the referral to the child domain.

Configuring Secondary DNS Servers

This section covers the configuration steps for a secondary DNS server. Secondary servers have a local read-only copy of a zone file that is pulled from a master name server. Secondary servers are authoritative for their zones, but cannot make changes to the zone. This section also covers the steps necessary to configure a master name server to accept zone transfer requests from a secondary and to notify the secondary when zone updates have occurred.

The initial service installation for a secondary DNS server is the same as for a primary server. Only the zone configuration steps differ. Load the service drivers using the steps in "Installing and Configuring DNS Servers," earlier in this chapter, and then return here.

Enabling Zone Transfers and Update Notifications

A secondary server cannot pull a zone until zone transfers and notifications are enabled at the master name server. To enable these options, follow Procedure 5.12.

Procedure 5.12 Enabling Zone Transfers and Notifications

1. Open the `DNS` console.
2. Right-click the zone icon and select PROPERTIES from flyout menu. The Properties window opens.

3. Select the `Zone Transfers` tab. Select the `Allow Zone Transfers` option. There are three notification options:
   - **`To Any Server`.** This is self-explanatory and not recommended. This permits any server or user to pull a zone from your name server. A comprehensive list of host names and IP addresses is not something that you want in unauthorized hands.
   - **`Only to Servers Listed in the Name Servers Tab`.** This option limits zone transfers to servers with `NS` records in the zone file. This is the preferred option because it does not involve keeping two lists of servers (actually three lists, because you must also maintain a notification list). If you delegate to untrusted domains, however, you may not want to select this option because it permits administrators of the delegated name server to pull a zone.
   - **`Only to the Following Servers`.** This option gives you the most control over zone transfers by identifying each authorized secondary individually. This does not prevent an intruder from spoofing the IP address of a secondary so that it can initiate a zone transfer, but it's better than leaving the door wide open.
4. Click `Notify`. The Notify window opens. Update notification is enabled by default in Windows Server 2003. This ensures that the zone files on the secondary name servers are kept current. You have the option in this window of automatically notifying servers in the `NS` list or specifying servers. If you chose the `Only to the Following Servers` option in the previous window, you must also individually select secondary servers for notification.
5. Click `OK` to save the notification settings and return to the Properties window.
6. Click `OK` to save the zone transfer settings and return to the DNS console.
7. Close the `DNS` console.

Test both the zone transfer setting and update notification by adding a test record at the primary. After refreshing the DNS console at the secondary, the record appears on the list. If this does not occur, check the IP addresses and notification settings.

Configuring a Secondary DNS Server

An authoritative secondary name server maintains a local copy of the zone. It uses root hints or a forwarder to handle queries that are outside of the zone.

If you have configured a master name server to do zone transfers only with selected secondaries, you must first add the IP address for this server to the list. You should also include the new secondary on the list of secondary servers to notify for updates. To configure the secondary server, look at Procedure 5.13.

Procedure 5.13 Configuring a Secondary Server

1. Open the `DNS` console.
2. Right-click the `Forward Lookup Zone` icon and select NEW ZONE from the flyout menu. The New Zone Wizard starts.
3. Click `Next`. The Zone Type window opens. Select `Secondary Zone`.
4. Click `Next`. The Zone Name window opens. Enter the FQDN name of the zone you are going to transfer to this server. For example, enter `company.com`.
5. Click `Next`. The Master DNS Servers window opens.
6. Enter the IP address of the master name server that you designated for use by this secondary and click `Add` to add it to the list. You can pull zones from several masters.
7. Click `Next`. The wizard displays a completion window.
8. Click `Finish` to close the wizard and return to the DNS console. The zone is transferred automatically.
9. Verify that you got the zone file records by refreshing the tree. If you get a big red X with a `Zone Not Loaded` error, press `F5` to refresh again. If the red X persists, you possibly forgot to enable zone transfers at the master server and add the secondary to the zone transfer list.

After the secondary server is operational, configure clients to use it and verify by pinging hosts inside and outside the zone. If pings outside the zone do not work, check your root hints at the primary and secondary.

Integrating DNS Zones into Active Directory

When a zone is integrated into the Directory, the ASCII zone file is abandoned and Directory objects are created for each resource record. You must run DNS on a domain controller to get access to the Directory Integrated zone. You can only integrate a primary zone. When you meet the conditions for an integrating zone and are ready to migrate a primary zone to an Active Directory Integrated zone, do as directed in Procedure 5.14.

Procedure 5.14 Integrating a Primary Zone into Active Directory

1. Open the `DNS` console.
2. Right-click the zone that you want to integrate into the directory and select PROPERTIES from the flyout menu. The Properties window opens.
3. At the `General` tab, adjacent to the `Type` entry, click `Change`. The Change Zone Type window opens (see Figure 5.14).

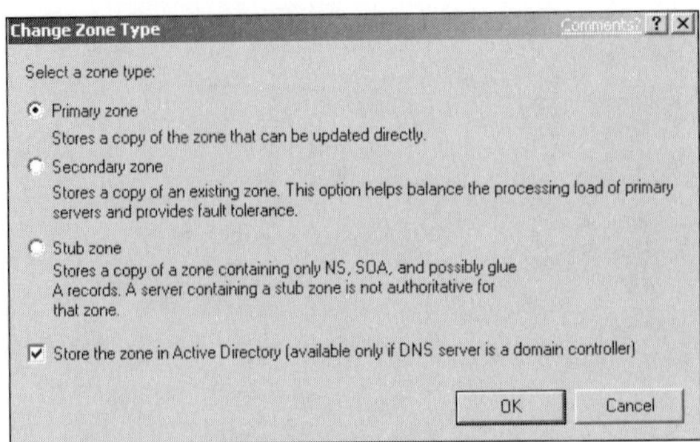

Figure 5.14 Change Zone Type window showing selection for `Active Directory Integrated zone`.

4. Select the `Store The Zone In Active Directory` option. Click `OK` to make the change. A confirmation window appears.
5. Click `OK` to confirm and return to the Properties window. The `Type` now shows `Active Directory Integrated`.
6. Click `OK` to save the change, close the window, and return to the DNS console.

Verify that the zone entries were transferred to the Directory by following Procedure 5.15.

Procedure 5.15 Verifying Resource Record Integration

1. Open the `AD Users and Computers` console via START | PROGRAMS | ADMINISTRATIVE TOOLS | ACTIVE DIRECTORY USERS AND COMPUTERS.
2. From the CONSOLE menu, select VIEW | ADVANCED VIEW. This exposes the System folder, among other items.
3. Expand the tree to `System | MicrosoftDNS`. The zone file displays as a folder containing dnsNode objects. Each of these objects represents a resource record. Figure 5.15 shows an example.

The dnsNode objects are not manageable as resource records from the AD Users and Computers console. DNS zone management is still done from the DNS console or by using the DNSCMD utility.

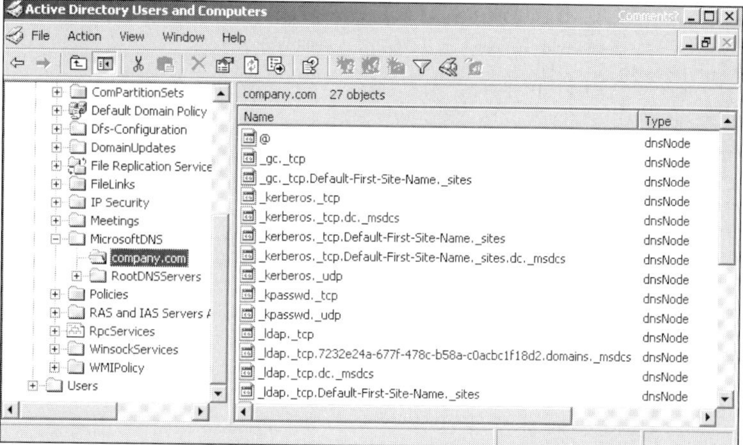

Figure 5.15 AD Users and Computers console showing contents of *company.com* zone under MicrosoftDNS container.

Configuring a Caching-Only Server

Caching-only servers are used to speed up query response by collecting a large number of cached records in response to client lookups. A caching-only server does not have a copy of a zone file and is therefore not authoritative. It obtains resource records from other DNS servers on behalf of clients.

The name cache is kept in memory, so make sure that the machine has lots of RAM. You can see the amount of memory used by DNS via the Task Manager window. Select the `Processes` tab and look for `dns.exe`. Get a baseline value then see how much it goes up as time goes by.

If you want to flush the cache, you can stop and start the DNS service or use the DNSCMD utility. The syntax is `dnscmd /clearcache`. Purging defeats the purpose of a caching-only server, however; so if you find yourself purging frequently to maintain performance, consider getting more memory.

A caching-only server does not pull zone transfers, so there is no need to add it to the list of secondaries at the master DNS server.

The initial DNS service installation is the same as for a primary DNS server. Only the configuration steps differ (see Procedure 5.16). Load the service drivers using the steps in "Installing and Configuring DNS Servers," earlier in this chapter, and then return here to configure the service.

Procedure 5.16 Configuring a Caching-Only Server

1. Open the `DNS` console.
2. Right-click the server icon and select PROPERTIES from the flyout menu. The Properties window opens.
3. Select the `Root Hints` tab.
4. Delete the TLD root servers from the list (if they are there) using the `Remove` button.
5. Click `Add`. The New Resource Record window opens with the `Name Server (NS)` tab showing.
6. Enter the FQDN of the master name server and its IP address. Click `Add` to add the IP address to the list. You can configure multiple name servers. They do not need to be in the same zone.
7. Click `OK` to save the entries and return to the Properties window.
8. Click `OK` to save the list and return to the DNS console.
9. Close the console.

Verify that the caching-only server works by pinging a remote server name from a client that is configured to use the server for DNS. Ping several host names to stock up the cache and then try the same names from another desktop. The response time should be much quicker.

Configuring a DNS Server to Use a Forwarder

A DNS server can be configured to send an out-of-zone query to another on the chance that the server has already located the record and has it in cache. If the bet fails and the record is not available, the forwarding server walks the tree to find the record on its own.

Before configuring a server to send queries to a forwarder, it is considered good manners to inform the administrator. A forwarding server has the potential for sending many thousands of queries to the forwarder.

The example steps assume that you are configuring an existing DNS server inside a firewall and using a forwarder outside the firewall to resolve Internet addresses. Configure the forwarding option as shown in Procedure 5.17.

Procedure 5.17 Configuring a DNS Server to Use a Forwarder

1. Open the `DNS` console.
2. Right-click the server name and select PROPERTIES from the flyout menu. The Properties window opens.

3. Select the `Forwarders` tab.
4. Select the `Enable Forwarders` option.
5. Enter the IP address of the forwarder and click `Add` to add it to the list.
6. Leave the `Forward Time-Out (seconds)` option set for five seconds. The forwarder should answer out of its cache, which doesn't take very long. If the forwarder takes longer than five seconds to respond, it is probably doing a search.
7. Click `OK` to save the settings and return to the DNS console.
8. Stop and start the DNS service by right-clicking the server icon and selecting ALL TASKS | RESTART from the flyout menu.

Verify that the forwarder works by pinging an Internet host name from a DNS client. The ping succeeds after a short time delay. If the ping does not succeed, check the IP addresses to make sure that you are pointed at the correct server.

Managing Dynamic DNS

Keeping a traditional DNS zone updated with new resource records requires lots of manual work. A large network with thousands of servers needs a full-time administrator just to manage DNS. With Dynamic DNS, clients and servers can register their `A` records automatically at boot time. Application servers can register `SRV` and other specialized records. Outdated records can be scavenged periodically to prevent clutter. It's a fairly automated process. Dynamic DNS probably won't do away with the need for full-time DNS management in a big network, but it should help rescue the administrator from a little of the tedium.

This topic covers how to enable Dynamic DNS in Windows Server 2003, how to configure security so that only trusted clients can register their resource records, and how to maintain the zone to prevent accumulating outdated records.

Configuring a Dynamic Zone

After you have installed and configured a Windows Server 2003 running DNS, enable Dynamic DNS for a particular zone as shown in Procedure 5.18.

Procedure 5.18 Configuring a Dynamic Zone

1. Open the `DNS` console.
2. Right-click the zone that you want to configure for Dynamic DNS and select PROPERTIES from the flyout menu. The Properties window opens.
3. In the `Allow Dynamic Updates` drop-down box, select `Yes`.

4. Click OK to save the change and return to the DNS console.
5. Verify that dynamic registration works by opening a command prompt at a Windows Server 2003 client that is configured to use this DNS server and entering `ipconfig /registerdns`. The host record is added to the zone file automatically. You may need to refresh the console to see it.

You must configure the reverse lookup zones for dynamic updates, as well. If you fail to do this, DNS will add A records but not PTR records when new clients come online.

Managing Dynamic DNS Security

If you enable Dynamic DNS with no security options, it is possible that a computer can come online with the same name as a host that is already in the zone and overwrite the A record. This has the potential to be very disruptive. Imagine that your company post office has the name MAIN-PO. A user could bring a workstation online called MAIN-PO and DNS would obediently overwrite the A record of the post office. If it is a malicious user doing this, you have a real problem.

The only way to avoid this behavior is to integrate the zone into Active Directory and require that Dynamic DNS clients be members of the domain. This avoids overwrite problems because two computers are not permitted to have the same name in an Active Directory domain.

After a zone has been integrated into the Directory, the resource records are protected by Active Directory object security. DNS clients that are not domain members cannot dynamically register their host records. Figure 5.16 shows a System log error from the DNSAPI service on a Windows Server 2003 DNS client that has attempted to register a host record when it is not a member of the domain.

The disadvantage to this security method is that not all your desktops might be running a modern Windows client. They might not even be running Windows. You can dynamically register DHCP clients using Windows Server 2003 or Windows 2000 DHCP. See "Configuring DHCP to Support DNS" for details.

Disabling DNS on an Interface

If you do not Directory Integrate a dynamic zone, you can at least take steps to prevent outsiders from registering records on your server. If you have a DNS server with two network interfaces, for example, one connected to the public network and the other connected to the local network, you can disable DNS (and Dynamic DNS registrations) on the public interface. Do this by completing the steps in Procedure 5.19.

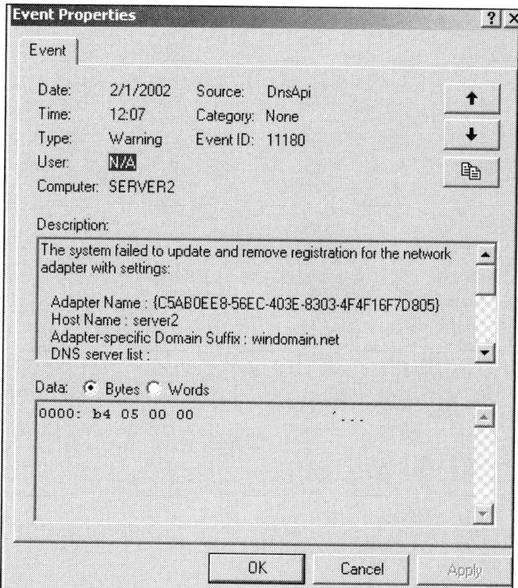

Figure 5.16 Event Properties from System log showing rejected registration attempt by client that is not a domain member.

Procedure 5.19 Disabling DNS on an Interface

1. Open the `DNS` console.
2. Right-click the server icon and select PROPERTIES from the flyout menu. The Properties window opens with the `Interfaces` tab selected.
3. Under `Listen On`, select the `Only the Following IP Addresses` option.
4. Use the `Remove` button to delete all but the private interface.
5. Click `OK` to save the new settings and return to the DNS console.
6. Close the console.

Registry Tip: Dynamic Updates

The `Listen On` option sets the following Registry value:

Key: `HKLM | System | CurrentControlSet | Services | TcpIp | Parameters | Interfaces | {GUID}`

Value: `DisableDynamicUpdate`

Data: `0x1` disables updates; `0x0` enables updates

Configuring Scavenging

Dynamically registered records can become obsolete when machines crash or come on and off the network at infrequent intervals, as laptops are prone to do. When scavenging is enabled, DNS applies an aging value to dynamically registered resource records. Scavenging removes records that have not been refreshed for more than 14 days.

If you enable scavenging, the format of the zone file changes to allow room for the aging value. This is a proprietary change, so you cannot move the zone file to a non-Windows Server 2003 name server. A standard secondary can pull a zone because the DNS server will filter out the aging records.

Scavenging can be enabled for a single zone or for all zones on the server. Enable scavenging for a zone as follows in Procedure 5.20.

Procedure 5.20 Configuring Scavenging

1. Open the `DNS` console.
2. Right-click the zone icon and select PROPERTIES from the flyout menu. The Properties window opens.
3. At the `General` tab, click `Aging`. The Zone Aging/Scavenging Properties window opens.
4. Select the `Scavenge Stale Resource Records` option.
5. Leave the default seven-day values for `No-Refresh Interval` and `Refresh Interval`.
6. Click `OK` to save the settings. A warning message appears informing you that the zone file record format will be changed.
7. Click `Yes` to acknowledge the warning and apply the change.
8. At the Properties window, click `OK` to save the changes and close the window.

From this point forward, any new dynamic registrations are assigned an aging value. Old records will be purged when scavenge runs. Set scavenging to run periodically as follows in Procedure 5.21.

Procedure 5.21 Setting Periodic Scavenging

1. Right-click the server icon and select PROPERTIES from the flyout menu. The Properties window opens.
2. Select the `Advanced` tab (see Figure 5.17).
3. Select the `Enable Automatic Scavenging of Stale Records` option.

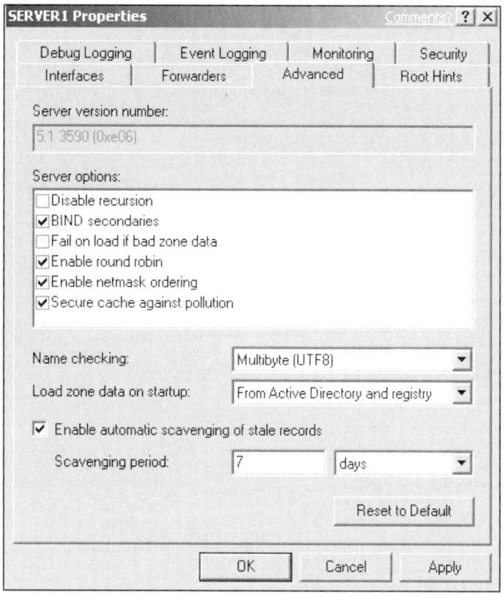

Figure 5.17 DNS Server Properties window—`Advanced` tab showing automatic scavenging enabled.

4. Leave the `Scavenging Period` set for the default of seven days.
5. Click `OK` to save the settings and close the window.

You should arrange to check the status of the zone file periodically to make sure that scavenge is working. If you see many old records that should have been scavenged, try scavenging them manually. If that succeeds, check your periodic scavenging settings. If it does not succeed, make sure that you have correctly configured scavenging to work for the zone.

WINS Forwarding

Although WINS forwarding is not strictly a Dynamic DNS feature, it is covered here because it provides essentially the same service.

In NT4 DNS, Microsoft introduced a couple of new DNS resource records, WINS and WINS-R, that contain the IP address of a WINS server to use in the event that a host address cannot be located in the local zone file. This record is added and configured using a special properties page in the zone properties. Access the page by right-clicking the zone icon and selecting PROPERTIES from the flyout menu and then selecting the `WINS` tab. A similar page for the WINS-R record is present in the Properties window for a reverse lookup zone. Figure 5.18 shows an example.

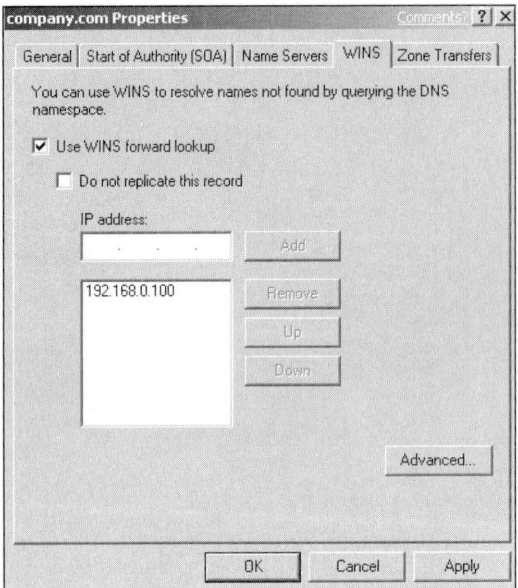

Figure 5.18 Zone Properties window showing the `WINS` tab.

The `Use WINS Forward Lookup` option is disabled by default. When selected, it creates a WINS resource record. A Windows Server 2003 running DNS recognizes this WINS record and uses it to locate a WINS server to use for forwarding.

If you elect to use WINS forwarding, add the IP address of at least one WINS server to the list by entering the IP address and clicking `Add`. You can specify more than one WINS server for fault tolerance.

The `Do No Replicate This Record` option is not selected by default. It prevents replicating the WINS record to DNS servers that do not recognize the record type.

Configuring Advanced DNS Server Parameters

Several DNS server options are collected under the `Advanced` tab in the DNS server Properties window. Several of these options are covered elsewhere in the chapter. This topic covers the remaining options. The advanced options access these options as shown in Procedure 5.22.

Procedure 5.22 Accessing Advanced Server Parameters

1. Open the `DNS` console.
2. Right-click the server icon and select PROPERTIES from the flyout menu. The Properties window opens.
3. Select the `Advanced` tab.

The following options are available in this window:

- **`Disable Recursion.`** By default, a Windows Server 2003 running DNS and Windows 2000 DNS server accepts recursive queries. This enables the server to do DNS searches on behalf of clients and is the preferred configuration. Select the `Disable Recursion` option if you want the server to accept only iterative queries.
- **`BIND Secondaries.`** By default, a Windows Server 2003 running DNS and Windows 2000 DNS server does a zone transfer by copying multiple records in compressed format. If you have secondary name servers running BIND versions earlier than 4.9.4, select the `BIND Secondaries` option.
- **`Fail On Load if Bad Zone Data.`** See the sidebar, "Starting DNS from a BIND Boot File."
- **`Enable Round Robin.`** If multiple `A` records exist for a host, DNS returns just one of them. It evens out the load using round-robin if this option is selected.
- **`Enable Netmask Ordering.`** If a zone file has multiple resource records that fit a particular query, this option causes the DNS server to sort the responses so that the records in the same subnet as the querying client are listed first. If this option is not checked, the responses are ordered as they appear in the zone file. This option overrides round-robin.
- **`Secure Cache Against Pollution.`** All name servers cache query results to speed subsequent queries for the same record. One possible attack method is to use indirection to get an improper record in the cache where it can then send users to an unsecured site. If a user browses the Internet to `www.company.com` and the user's name server has an alias for `www.company.com` that points at `www.competitor.com`, for example, the `A` record for `www.competitor.com` would be added to the local name server cache. Returning a record from one DNS domain in response to a query for a record in another DNS domain can result in *cache pollution*. The `Secure Cache Against Pollution` prevents this problem by caching only query results that match the root domain of the query.
- **`Name Checking.`** By default, Microsoft's DNS permits any ANSI character to be used in a DNS host name. This includes special characters not included in standard DNS names as defined by RFC 1123, "Requirements for Internet Hosts—Application and Support." If you have non-Microsoft name servers, or expect to interface with non-Microsoft name servers, select the `Strict RFC (ANSI)` option. If you have only Microsoft DNS and you want to enable Unicode host names, select the `Multibyte (UTF8)` option.
- **`Enable Automatic Scavenging of Stale Records.`** See the "Configuring Scavenging" steps in Procedure 5.20.

Starting DNS from a BIND Boot File

Windows Server 2003 supports file-based booting like that used by BIND. If you need to boot a Windows Server 2003 running DNS using a boot file from a BIND server, copy the file to `\Windows\System32\DNS` and then configure the boot method as shown in Procedure 5.23. (The `\Windows\System32\DNS\Samples` directory contains a boot file you can use for a template.)

Procedure 5.23 Starting DNS from a BIND File

1. Open the DNS console.
2. Right-click the DNS server icon and select PROPERTIES from the flyout menu. The Properties window opens.
3. Select the Advanced tab.
4. Under Load Zone Data on Startup, select From File.
5. Click OK to save the changes and close the window.
6. Close the console.

If the BIND file contains data that is not permitted in Microsoft DNS zone files, such as giving an alias (CNAME) record the same name as the host, the DNS service will ignore the bad records, log them to the Event log, and continue to load the zone file. If you would prefer to abort the zone file load in case of an error, proceed as directed in Procedure 5.24.

Procedure 5.24 Setting the Fail on Load if Bad Zone option

1. Open the DNS console.
2. Right-click the DNS server icon and select PROPERTIES from the flyout menu. The Properties window opens.
3. Select the Advanced tab.
4. Under Server Options, select Fail on Load if Bad Zone Data.
5. Click OK to save the changes and close the window.
6. Close the console.

Examining Zones with Nslookup

When you run into problems with DNS, the Nslookup utility is the tool of choice for tracking down problems. Nslookup enables you to perform selective zone transfers so that you can examine resource records in the zone. You can also use Nslookup to verify that a DNS server exists, find out what zone it manages, verify that the DNS server has a particular resource record, and browse the resource records as if you were browsing a directory.

Nslookup has two modes: Interactive and Non-Interactive. If you run Nslookup and specify parameters on the command line, you run the utility in Non-Interactive mode. To see the IP address for `www.guam.net` and the name servers that are authoritative for the zone that holds the `A` record, for example, issue the `Nslookup` command followed by the name of the server as follows:

```
C:\>nslookup www.guam.net c.root-servers.net.
4.33.192.in-addr.arpa    nameserver = NS.PSI.NET
NS.PSI.NET        internet address = 192.33.4.10
Name:     www.guam.net
Served by:
- NS.GUAM.net
          198.81.233.2
          GUAM.net
```

To use the Interactive mode, just enter `Nslookup` with no parameters.

When you enter Interactive mode, you get a listing of the default name server followed by a command prompt, >:

```
U:\>nslookup
Default Server:  dns1.primenet.net
Address:  206.165.5.10
>
```

From the command prompt, enter a question mark (`?`) to see the list of Nslookup commands.

If you want to see the default settings for Nslookup, use `set all`. (You cannot just type `set` like a DOS command. This makes Nslookup think that you are querying for a server named `set`.) For example,

```
> set all
Default Server:  dns1.primenet.net
Address:  206.165.5.10
Set options:
  nodebug        defname        search         recurse
  nod2           novc           noignoretc     port=53
  querytype=A    class=IN       timeout=2      retry=3
  root=a.root-servers.net.            domain=company.com
  srchlist=company.com
```

The following sections cover the most common Nslookup interactive commands and `Set` parameters.

server

Use this command to change the name of the DNS server that fields the Nslookup queries. Be sure to use FQDNs with a trailing dot. For example, if your default name server is `dns1.company.com` but you want to troubleshoot another DNS server, `dns02.company.com`, you would enter the following:

```
> server dns02.company.com.
Default server: dns02.company.com
Address: 10.5.1.10
```

lserver

The `lserver` command works like `server`, but always uses the default name server. This enables you to escape from a dead end when you use the `server` command to get onto a name server that is not authoritative and cannot resolve another server name. If you use `server` to change to a name server that has no zone file, you won't be able to use the `server` command to go to another server because it cannot resolve the new host name. The `lserver` command gets you back to your home DNS server by using the original server to resolve the name.

root

This command works like the `server` command to change the default DNS server, but it selects the name from the top of the server list in the CACHE.DNS file. This is usually a public TLD root server. If the server is a private root server, the file would contain one or more internal name servers.

ls

This command lists the resource records in a particular zone. In essence, `ls` does a zone transfer of the selected record type. You can limit the scope of the transfer by specifying a record type using the `-t` switch. Here is an example showing the host records (`A` records) in the `company.com` zone:

```
> ls -t a company.com.
[dc01.company.com]
 company.com.                  A       10.1.1.1
 gc._msdcs.company.com.        A       10.1.1.1
 dns01.branch1.company.com.    A       10.3.1.1
 dc01.company.com.             A       10.1.1.1
 nt30.company.com.             A      10.1.1.201
```

If you specify `any` as the record type, or use the `-d` switch with `ls`, Nslookup returns the entire zone file. Use caution: This can be quite an extensive list on some name servers. Use the indirection pipe (>) to save the output of `ls` to a file.

You may be thinking that `ls` represents a security problem. You would be correct. Because `ls` works by performing a zone transfer, you can block it by controlling the servers that are allowed to pull a zone transfer. See "Enabling Zone Transfers and Update Notifications" earlier in this chapter for details.

set [no]debug

When `debug` is set, the report from an interactive command includes debugging information. This debugging information shows the results of a query including intermediate name servers included in the search. The following example is the result of a recursive query for `roswellnm.org`:

```
> set debug
> roswellnm.org.
```

```
Server:  proxy7.az.farlap.com
Address:  24.1.208.35

------------
Got answer:
    HEADER:
        opcode = QUERY, id = 2, rcode = NOERROR
        header flags:  response, auth. answer, want recursion, recursion avail.
        questions = 1,  answers = 1,  authority records = 3,  additional = 3

    QUESTIONS:
        roswellnm.org, type = A, class = IN
    ANSWERS:
    ->  roswellnm.org
        internet address = 209.35.62.148
        ttl = 900 (15 mins)
    AUTHORITY RECORDS:
    ->  roswellnm.org
        nameserver = dns1.interland.net
        ttl = 0 (0 secs)
    ADDITIONAL RECORDS:
    ->  dns1.interland.net
        internet address = 64.224.20.132
        ttl = 900 (15 mins)
------------
Name:    roswellnm.org
Address:  209.35.62.148
```

The `debug` option is especially useful for locating improper referrals caused by incorrect delegations.

Set [no]d2

Set this parameter if you aren't satisfied knowing the results of the query and you also need to know the exact format of the query itself. Here is the additional `d2` information from a `roswellnm.org` lookup:

```
> set d2
> roswellnm.org.
;truncated to show differences from standard debug listing
------------
SendRequest(), len 32
    HEADER:
        opcode = QUERY, id = 10, rcode = NOERROR
        header flags:  query, want recursion
        questions = 1,  answers = 0,  authority records = 0,  additional = 0

    QUESTIONS:
        Roswellnm.org, type = A, class = IN
```

set [no]defname

You may have noticed a trailing period at the end of each server name in the example lookups. The trailing dot tells Nslookup that the name is fully qualified. If you do not include the period, Nslookup appends the default domain name for the client. If you have a hard time remembering to include the trailing period, you can use `set nodefname` to tell Nslookup not to append the domain name.

set [no]recurse

If you want Nslookup queries to emulate a DNS server rather than a DNS client, queries should be configured as iterative and not recursive. Use this switch to change the query type as needed.

set querytype

You can limit or change the scope of a query by setting a certain record type. If you want to query for the `MX` records on a name server, for example, give the following command:

```
> set type=mx
> roswellnm.org.
Server:  proxy7.az.farlap.com
Address:  24.1.208.35

Non-authoritative answer:
roswellnm.org   MX preference = 5, mail exchanger = mail.roswellnm.org

roswellnm.org   nameserver = DNS1.INTERLAND.NET
mail.roswellnm.org      internet address = 209.35.103.30
DNS1.INTERLAND.NET       internet address = 64.224.20.132
```

Command-Line Management of DNS

The DNS Management console provides a GUI interface for working with DNS servers. You can use the console to connect to any Windows 2000 or Windows Server 2003 running DNS in your organization. If you prefer to work from a command line, you should get familiar with the DNSCMD utility.

You can do virtually any action with DNSCMD that you can do from the DNS Management console. This includes adding and deleting resource records, listing the contents of zones, resetting the DNS service, Directory Integrating a zone, scavenging old dynamic records, and clearing the DNS cache. Armed with a little time and some scripting tools, you can tailor a set of utilities that can do just about any operation that needs doing.

DNSCMD comes with command-line help for options and syntax. The online help contains extensive examples. It's a tool worth learning if you are going to manage a number of DNS servers.

Configuring DHCP to Support DNS

If you have downlevel clients that you want to register in DNS, you can take advantage of the DHCP proxy features for Dynamic DNS registration. This proxy makes it possible to move large numbers of desktops and servers over to DNS-enabled name resolution very quickly.

The DHCP proxy feature was structured using the provisions of Internet Draft draft-ietf-dhc-dhcp-dns-10.txt, "Interaction Between DHCP and DNS." This draft outlines the use of a new DHCP option called `Client FQDN`, option 81. This option includes a new message format that a client can use to inform the DHCP server of its FQDN. The DHCP server uses this information to send a DNS Update message to the DNS server on behalf of the client.

Important: If you plan on using DHCP to proxy DNS updates, be sure to use Active Directory Integrated zones with Secure Dynamic Updates enabled. This protects the zone records from accidental or deliberate overwrites. Do not install DHCP on a domain controller. The DHCP service runs in the LocalSystem security context, and therefore has full privileges on the machine. This permits a DHCP client to update any record in DNS, with potentially disastrous results.

Installing DHCP

Before installing DHCP, you should inventory your current IP address assignments and ensure that you know the hosts that have static addresses. Windows Server 2003 DHCP, along with NT4 SP4, will use ICMP to verify that an address is free before leasing it, but that verification is not comprehensive. When you are ready to install DHCP and set aside addresses to lease, follow Procedure 5.25.

Procedure 5.25 Installing DHCP Service Drivers

1. From Control Panel, open the `Add/Remove Programs` applet.
2. Click `Add/Remove Windows Components`. The Windows Components Wizard starts with the focus set to the Windows Components window.
3. Highlight `Networking Services` and click `Details`. The Networking Services window opens.
4. Select `Dynamic Host Configuration Protocol (DHCP)` and click `OK` to save the change and return to the Windows Components window.
5. Click `Next`. The Configuring Components window opens and the drivers begin loading. When the drivers have loaded and the configuration is complete, the wizard displays a successful completion window.
6. Click `Finish` to close the window and return to the Add/Remove Programs window.
7. Close the `Add/Remove Programs` window.

At this point, you can begin configuring the service. There is no need to restart.

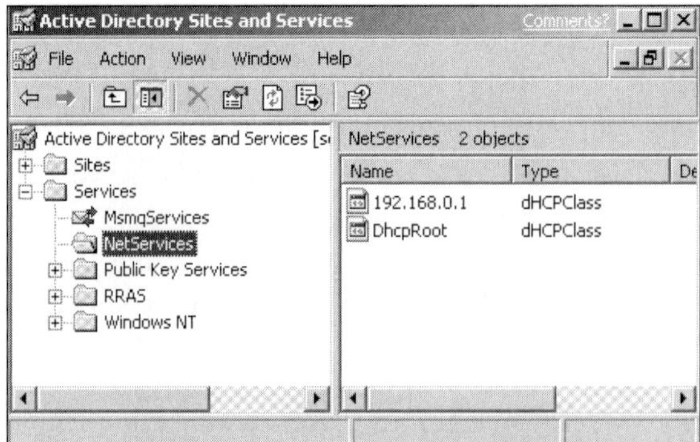

Figure 5.19 AD Sites and Services console showing authorized DHCP server.

Authorizing a DHCP Server

After the service drivers have been loaded, open the `DHCP` console. The server icon shows a red down arrow, meaning that the service has not started. If you are installing the service on a domain controller or domain member server, the status in the right pane will show `Not Authorized`. If you are installing in a workgroup, press `F5` to refresh the console. The server status should change to `Running`.

Windows Server 2003 DHCP has a feature that attempts to prevent rogue DHCP servers from coming on the wire and leasing improper IP addresses. This feature requires a DHCP server to be *authorized*. An authorized DHCP server has a DHCPClass object in Active Directory. This object can be viewed using the AD Sites and Services console. It is stored under `Services | NetServices`. Figure 5.19 shows an example.

Authorize a DHCP server by right-clicking the server icon in the right pane and selecting AUTHORIZE from the flyout menu. The DHCP object is added to the directory automatically. Then, refresh the console by pressing `F5`. The server status changes to `Running`. Figure 5.20 shows an operational DHCP scope with leased addresses.

Verify that the server is issuing addresses by renewing an existing DHCP client. If you are in a routed network that uses DHCP helpers, you need to configure the BOOTP relay agents at your routers to point at the new DHCP server. After you have verified basic operability, take the server out of production by deactivating the scope while you configure the scope options.

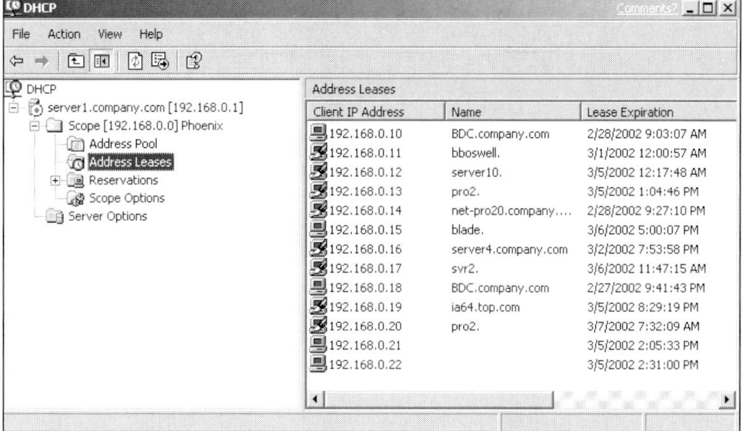

Figure 5.20 DHCP console showing authorized DHCP server that has leased addresses.

Configuring Scope Options

While the scope is deactivated, select the scope options that you want to include in the DHCP ACK packet that is returned to the clients along with their leased address. The list of scope options does not include the new option 81, `FQDN Client` option. This option is configured separately as part of scope properties. It is covered in the next section. At this point, you need to configure options for DNS server(s), a DNS domain name, and a default gateway. You may have other options you want to include, but these are the basics. To configure scope options, follow the steps in Procedure 5.26.

Procedure 5.26 Configuring Scope Options

1. Right-click the server icon and select NEW SCOPE from the flyout menu. The New Scope Wizard starts.
2. Click `Next`. The Scope Name window opens. Give the scope a name and description that can help you identify it when it displays in the console.
3. Click `Next`. The IP Address Range window opens (see Figure 5.21). Enter an address range and subnet mask for the scope. The example shows the private network of `10.1.0.0` with a 24-bit subnet mask.
4. Click `Next`. The Add Exclusions window opens. If you have addresses within the scope that are already assigned to hosts or need to be set aside for static assignment, exclude them here.

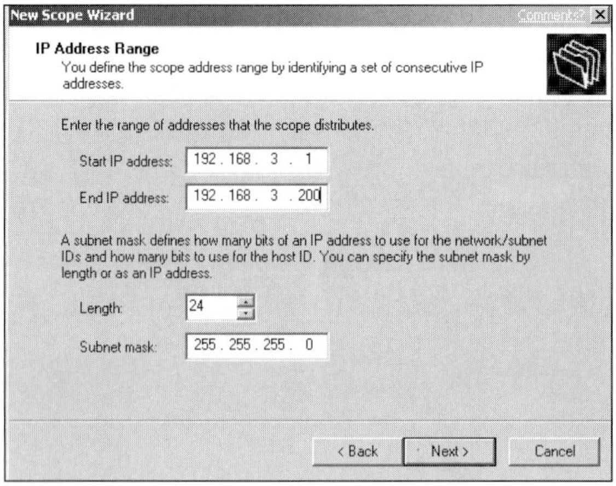

Figure 5.21 New Scope Wizard—IP Address Range window.

5. Click Next. The Lease Duration window opens. The new default lease duration is eight days, up from three days in NT4. This gives enough time for a user to go on a week's vacation and still get the old address back. If you have a shortage of addresses, you can cut the lease duration back to eight hours.
6. Click Next. The Configure Your DHCP Options window opens. Let's skip the rest of the wizard and configure the options from the DHCP console. It's faster. Select `No, I Will Configure These Options Later`.
7. Click Next. The wizard displays a completion window.
8. Click Finish to close the wizard and return to the DHCP console. The console now shows the new scope with its address pool and exclusions.
9. Right-click the Scope Options window and select NEW SCOPE OPTIONS from the flyout menu. The Scope Options window opens.
10. Select `Option 006 DNS Servers`. Enter the FQDN of the DNS server that you want to use for this scope and click Resolve to get its IP address. (I prefer this method because it quickly validates that the DNS configuration is correct.)
11. Select `Option 015 DNS Domain Name`. Enter the DNS domain name (same as DNS Suffix) you want to distribute to clients in this scope. This name must exist as a DNS zone on the server selected in option 006.
12. Select other options you want to include in the configuration packet. Typical entries are `Option 003 Router`, `Option 046 WINS/NBNS Servers`, and `046 WINT/NBT Node Type`.
13. Click OK to set the options and close the window.
14. Right-click the Scope icon and select Active. This permits the DHCP service to respond to DHCP requests and makes the address pool in the scope available. The status of the scope changes to Active in the right pane of the console.

When a DHCP client leases an address, it gets a configuration packet containing the IP address of one or more DNS servers. The client registers its newly leased address, both the `A` and `PTR` records, with the DNS server. You can verify this by checking the DNS console to see whether new addresses appear as Windows Server 2003 DHCP clients get their DHCP configuration packets.

DNS Update Proxy Configuration

If a DHCP client is not running Windows Server 2003 or some other client that supports Dynamic DNS Updates, it will not register its leased DHCP address in DNS. This limits the effectiveness of DNS as a name repository in a peer networking environment, at least if you want to get away from running WINS.

You can configure the DHCP server to act as a DNS update proxy for downlevel clients. Open the server Properties window and select the `DNS` tab. Figure 5.22 shows an example.

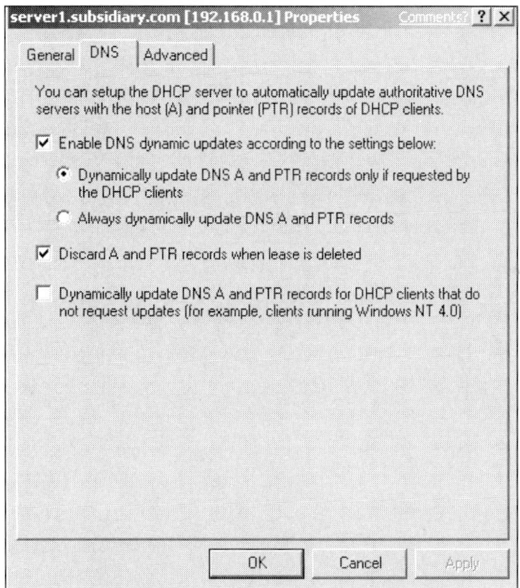

Figure 5.22 DHCP server Properties window showing the `DNS` tab.

Dynamic Client Icons

If you highlight the `Address Leases` icon and look at the list of active DHCP clients, you will notice that the icons for dynamically registered clients have fountain pen emblems.

The `Automatically Update DHCP Client Information in DNS` selection enables option 81, `Client FQDN`, for all addresses in the scope. The remaining options are dimmed if this is deselected. Here is a list of the functions for the various configuration options:

- **`Update DNS Only if DHCP Client Requests`.** This is the preferred option. If the client has selected the `Register This Connection's Addresses in DNS` option under `TCP/IP Properties`, the client takes responsibility for updating DNS and the DHCP server bows out.
- **`Always Update DNS`.** This option overrides the `Register This Connection's Addresses in DNS` setting at the client and uses the FQDN message from the client to register. If this option is selected, a flag is toggled in the option 81 message to the client telling it not to update DNS.
- **`Discard Forward (Name-to-Address) Lookups When Lease Expires`.** This option is selected by default. It removes the `A` record when the lease expires. The DNS scavenger does this, too, but it's better to keep the zone tidy day-by-day.
- **`Enable Updates for DNS Clients That Do Not Support Dynamic Updates`.** This option is not set by default. It provides a way for downlevel clients to dynamically register their resource records. If you are prepared to have a couple of thousand resource records appear in your zone file during tomorrow morning's logon, select this option.

If you select the last option that registers downlevel clients by proxy, you'll see the icons appear as dynamic registration icons (fountain pen emblems) as the clients renew their leases. As clients renew their leases, they renew their Dynamic DNS registrations, as well.

Moving Forward

This chapter covers a lot of ground, but it's worth taking time to get a solid understanding of DNS before proceeding. A reliable and fully functional DNS infrastructure is crucial to the success of Active Directory deployment.

Still, I'm sure you're impatient to get past the introductory acts. You want to see the star of the show. So put your hands together, ladies and gentlemen, for Active Directory.

6 Understanding Active Directory Services

CLASSIC NT HAS MANY ECCENTRICITIES—big and small—that limit its scalability and functionality. Many of these eccentricities stem from NT's clumsy, flat-file, Registry-based account management system. What is lacking in classic NT is a true *directory service* capable of handling the management chores for a network containing hundreds of thousands, if not millions, of users, computers, groups, printers, shared folders, network appliances, and so forth.

The hallmark of modern Windows is an enterprise-class directory service called Active Directory. We're going to spend the next six chapters learning to configure, deploy, manage, and fix Active Directory. The purpose of this chapter is to introduce you to the components of Active Directory and how they fit together. We'll also take an initial look at the tools provided by Microsoft to access and modify the contents of Active Directory.

New Features in Windows Server 2003

Microsoft has done quite a bit of tuning on Active Directory in Windows Server 2003 to improve scalability and speed and to correct a couple of key deficiencies. Some of these updates might not make much sense until you read further, but here is a synopsis to use for reference. The first three features require having Windows Server 2003 on every domain controller:

- **Site scalability.** The calculations for determining replication topology between sites have been streamlined. This corrects a problem where large organizations with hundreds of sites might experience replication failure because the topology calculations cannot be completed in the time allotted to them.

- **Backlink attribute replication.** Group members are now replicated as discrete entities instead of replicating the entire group membership list as a single unit. This corrects a problem where membership changes made to the same group on different domain controllers in the same replication interval overwrite each other.
- **Federations.** A new trust type called Forest was added to simplify transitive trust relationships between root domains in different forests. Using Forest trusts, it is possible to build a *federation* of independent Active Directory forests. This feature does not implement true "prune and graft" in Active Directory, but it goes a long way toward simplifying operations within affiliated organizations.
- **Simplified domain logon.** Universal group membership can be cached at non-global catalog servers. This permits users to log on even if connectivity to a global catalog server is lost. This enhancement is coupled with a feature in XP where the domain\name result of cracking a User Principal Name (UPN) is cached locally. This permits a user at an XP desktop to log on with the format `user@company.com` even if a global catalog server is not available.
- **Application naming contexts.** Windows Server 2003 introduces the capability to create new naming contexts to hold DNS record objects for Active Directory Integrated zones. One naming context holds domain zone records and one holds the _msdcs records used throughout a forest. These naming contexts make it possible to target replication of DNS zones only to domain controllers that are running DNS.
- **Eliminate piling onto new domain controllers.** There is potential for a problem when an NT4 primary domain controller (PDC) is upgraded to Windows Server 2003. In this circumstance, all existing Windows 2000 and XP desktops will use the newly promoted PDC as a logon server. In Windows Server 2003, domain controllers can be configured to respond to modern Windows clients as if they were still classic NT domain controllers until sufficient domain controllers are available to handle local authentication. This feature is also available in Windows 2000 SP2 and later.
- **DNS diagnostics.** Proper DNS configuration is critical for proper Active Directory operation. The Domain Controller promotion utility now performs a suite of DNS diagnostics to ensure that a suitable DNS server is available to register the service locator resource records associated with a Windows domain controller.

- **Fewer global catalog rebuilds.** Adding or removing an attribute from the Global Catalog no longer requires a complete synchronization cycle. This minimizes the replication traffic caused by adding an attribute to the GC.
- **Management console enhancements.** The Active Directory Users and Computers console now permits drag-and-drop move operations and modifying properties on multiple objects at the same time. There is also the capability of creating and storing custom LDAP queries to simplify managing large numbers of objects. The new MMC 2.0 console includes scripting support that can eliminate the need to use the console entirely.
- **Real-time LDAP.** Support was added for RFC 2589, "LDAPv3: Extensions for Dynamic Directory Services." This permits putting time-sensitive information in Active Directory, such as a user's current location. Dynamic entries automatically time out and are deleted if they are not refreshed.
- **Enhanced LDAP security.** Support was added for digest authentication as described in RFC 2829, "Authentication Methods for LDAP." This makes it easier to integrate Active Directory into non-Windows environments. Support was also added for RFC 2830, "LDAPv3: Extension for Transport Layer Security." This permits using secure connections when sending LDAP (Lightweight Directory Access Protocol) queries to a domain controller.
- **Schema enhancements.** The ability was added to associate an auxiliary schema class to individual objects rather than to an entire class of objects. This association can be dynamic, making it possible to temporarily assign new attributes to a specific object or objects. Attributes and object classes can also be declared defunct to simplify recovering from programming errors.
- **LDAP query enhancements.** The LDAP search mechanism was expanded to permit searching for individual entries in a multivalued Distinguished Name (DN) attribute. This is called an *Attribute Scoped Query*, or ASQ. For example, an ASQ could be used to quickly list every group to which a specific user belongs. Support was also added for Virtual List Views, a new LDAP control that permits large data sets to be viewed in order instead of paging through a random set of information. This change permits Windows Server 2003 to show alphabetically sorted lists of users and groups in pick lists.
- **Interoperability.** Support was added for RFC 2798, "Definition of the inetOrgPerson LDAP Object Class." This enhances interoperability with Netscape and NetWare directory services, both of which use the inetOrgPerson object class to create User objects.

- **Speedier domain controller promotions.** The capability was added for using a tape backup of the Active Directory database to populate the database on a new domain controller. This greatly simplifies domain controller deployments in situations where it is not practical to ship an entire server.
- **Scalability.** The maximum number of objects that can be stored in Active Directory was increased to over one billion.

Limitations of Classic NT Security

The first questions you may ask when hunkering down to study Active Directory is, "What is it?" and "Why have it?" This section answers the second question. The remainder of the chapter answers the first.

Account administration in a classic NT network is hampered by many limitations. The most important of these limitations are the following:

- Restricted SAM size
- Multiple logon IDs
- Single point of failure at the primary domain controller
- Poor operational performance
- Poor replication performance
- Lack of management granularity
- The fact that security databases differ between servers and domain controllers
- Nontransitive trust relationships

I'm going to discuss each of these limitations to show exactly how they hinder classic NT operations. This also helps to understand why certain decisions were made in the design of Active Directory.

Restricted Account Database Size

Security accounts in classic NT are stored in the Security Account Manager database, called the SAM for short. The SAM is a flat-file database consisting of a set of Groups and a set of Users. Computer accounts are also included in the SAM as a special form of user account.

SAM Database Structure

Ordinarily, you cannot view the contents of the SAM database because the Registry only permits access by the System account. If you want to take a peek inside, you can set the Registry permissions to give your account or the Administrators group Read access. Actual data is encrypted and stored in binary format, but you can view the structure. Figure 6.1 shows an example.

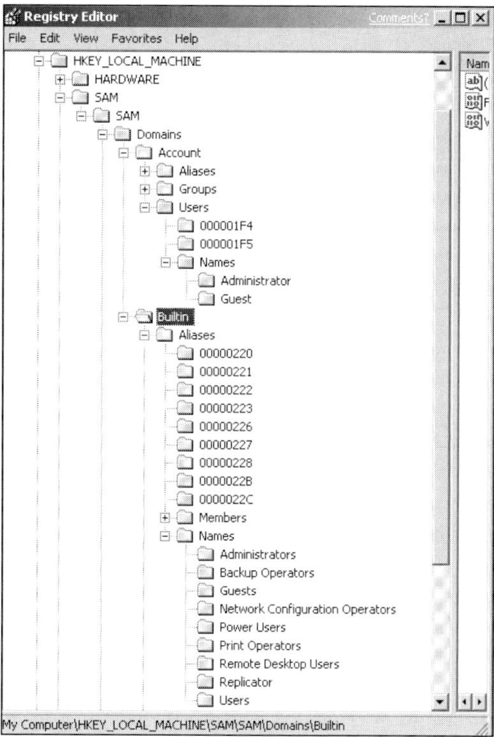

Figure 6.1 SAM database viewed by the Registry Editor after changing security permissions.

The total number of users, computers, and groups in classic NT is limited because the SAM cannot grow above a certain size. This is due to restrictions on overall Registry size called the *Registry size limit* (RSL). The RSL permits the Registry to grow to a maximum of 80 percent of paged pool memory. Paged pool memory has a ceiling of 192MB in NT and 470MB in Windows 2000 and Windows Server 2003.

Memory Pool Registry Settings

Memory used by the kernel in all Windows server products is divided between non-paged pool memory and paged pool memory. You can view settings for the memory pools in the following Registry key:

```
HKLM | System | CurrentControlSet | Control | Session Manager | Memory Management
```

The default values are zero, indicating that the system calculates them dynamically. You should not change any values without specific direction from Microsoft Product Support Services.

In modern Windows, the RSL is adjusted automatically when the Registry is about to exceed the current RSL setting. The RSL can also be adjusted from the User Interface (UI) using the Computer Management console as follows:

1. Launch the Computer Management console by entering COMPMGMT.MSC from the Run window.
2. Right-click the Computer Management icon and select PROPERTIES from the flyout menu.
3. Select the Advanced tab.
4. Click Performance Options.
5. Under Virtual Memory, click Change. This opens the Virtual Memory window.
6. Put a new value in the Maximum Registry Size field.

The SAM is only one component of the Registry, so its size is restricted still further. A classic SAM has enough room for about 40,000 users if you count the groups you'll need to manage them. Practical limits on replication and user management reduces this number considerably, although I know of at least one company that has in excess of 60,000 users in a single classic NT domain.

Single Point of Failure

The PDC is the only server that has read/write access to the SAM in a classic NT domain. If the PDC crashes or the telecommunications link to it goes down, you cannot make any changes to the domain constituents. You cannot add new users to a group. You cannot join computers to the domain. Users can still log on via a backup domain controller (BDC) but they cannot change their passwords.

To correct this problem, an administrator must promote a BDC to PDC somewhere in the domain. If the promoted BDC doesn't have the horsepower of the original PDC, worldwide performance suffers. A worse situation occurs if the WAN connection that connects the PDC to the rest of the domain goes down. In this situation, you don't dare promote a BDC because when the WAN connection returns, you'll have two PDCs with slightly different security database contents. This forces you to make a Solomon-like decision to keep one PDC and kill the other. In short, you have the makings of a real disaster.

Poor Operational Performance

The single PDC in a classic NT domain also imposes practical limits on daily operations. Assume, for example, that you are an administrator of a global NT network with 30,000 users. You are stationed in Omaha but the PDC for the master security domain is in Boston. You open User Manager for Domains to add a new user. User Manager pulls the account database from the SAM on the PDC, not a local BDC. Depending on the speed of the intervening WAN links, it can take a long, long time to scan through a big SAM. Administrators in large NT domains learn to use command-line utilities to avoid this irritation.

Poor Replication Performance

The hub-and-spoke replication model of classic NT imposes operational limits beyond the problem with limited SAM size. A large network with many BDCs imposes a great deal of load on the PDC to keep the databases replicated. By default, replication occurs when 200 updates accumulate every seven minutes or at a random interval between one and seven minutes. If you don't want to wait for replication to carry an update to a remote BDC, you must use Server Manager to force replication. This means opening still another tool and waiting another period of time.

SAM Database Differs Between Servers and Domain Controllers

The SAM database has a different structure on a classic domain controller than on a regular server. For this reason, a classic NT server cannot be promoted directly to domain controller or demoted from a domain controller down to a server. You must reinstall the operating system completely to change the server's security role.

Lack of Management Granularity

A major weakness in the flat-file SAM structure is its inability to support hierarchical management. Administrators wield supreme power in a domain. A few BuiltIn groups such as Account Admins and Server Operators have specially tailored privileges, but there is no provision for localizing admin rights or creating new groups with a different set of limited rights. Third-party tools are available to overcome this lack of management granularity, but they carry their own replication and management baggage along with a hefty price tag.

Nontransitive Trust Relationships

Of all the limitations in classic NT, the ugliest is the inability to link domains together seamlessly while maintaining separate administrative roles.

Classic domains are linked by *trust relationships.* Domain controllers in trust-*ing* domains perform *pass-through authentications* to check the credentials of users from trust-*ed* domains. These trust relationships are based on entries in the NT Security database called *LSA Secrets.* (LSA stands for Local Security Authority.) A pair of LSA Secrets, one in each SAM database, links the two domains together.

Classic trust relationships can only operate in one direction. You can add complementary pairs of trusts to get the appearance of two-way authentication, but the two trusts operate independently.

Worse yet, classic trusts cannot extend beyond the two domains that form the trust endpoints. For instance, if Domain A trusts Domain B and Domain B trusts Domain C, then Domain A does not trust Domain C, or vice versa. This forces large NT systems to have many interlocking trusts. You know when you walk into the operations center of a big NT shop because there's butcher paper on the walls with circles and arrows going everywhere.

Multiple Logon IDs

In an ideal universe, a single network logon account would provide access to all server-based applications. In the past, application designers have been reluctant to base their authentication services on the classic NT logon mechanism. Part of this reluctance was due to the inscrutable set of security APIs that Microsoft provided. Designers were also put off by the inflexible nature of the SAM.

This means trying to achieve true single sign-on under NT has been very difficult. This forces users to memorize passwords for many different applications as well as their network logon. Because users often select the same password for different applications, the entire security system becomes as secure as the most vulnerable interface.

Improvements Made by Active Directory

Now that I've listed the litany of sins in classic NT, let's take a quick look at what Active Directory does to resolve them:

- The Active Directory account database in Windows Server 2003 can hold a billion objects. This resolves scalability concerns.
- Multiple domain controllers can host read/write copies of Active Directory, eliminating the problems with a single point of failure and poor operational performance.
- The Active Directory replication engine can be tuned to make best use of available bandwidth. This reduces WAN traffic.
- A modern Windows server (Windows 2000 or Windows Server 2003) can be promoted to a domain controller and demoted back to a member server without the need to reinstall the operating system.
- Active Directory can be configured with as many branches as needed to localize and compartmentalize administrative functions.
- Active Directory domains still use "trusts" as an operational model but the trusts now give full, two-way access to resources and are fully transitive between domains.
- The presence of a truly world-class directory service in Windows has sparked renewed interest among application developers in achieving single sign-on. Microsoft has helped encourage this interest by simplifying the security access methods and greatly expanding the access interfaces.

So, now we know what we're leaving behind. Let's move on to see what we're getting. The next section describes what goes into a directory service.

Directory Service Components

A directory service compiles information about objects of interest in the world and dispenses that information when given a suitably formulated request. The Yellow Pages are a kind of directory service. A library card catalog is another.

People like to have their information classified for easy retrieval. For instance, the Yellow Pages has categories like "Theaters—Movies" and "Restaurants—Outrageously Overpriced." A library card catalog classifies items into "Books—Fiction," "Books—Nonfiction," "Periodicals," and so forth.

Information needs to be readily accessible, as well. People want one-stop shopping. At the same time, you don't want all the information at a single location. This produces bottlenecks, single points of failure, and turf hassles. For this reason, the information in a directory service needs to be distributed among many sources. Each source of information is responsible for maintaining its little piece of the distributed database.

Information needs to follow rules to make it consistent and reliable. Yellow Pages ads contain a limited set of information about businesses in a community. You would not go to the Yellow Pages to look up the current stock price of a company.

A network directory service has entries for users and groups, workstations and servers, policies and scripts, printers and queues, switches and routers, and just about anything else that relates to computing. The attributes for these entries have something to do with their relationship to network services. For example, authentication credentials can be stored in a directory service so users can log on from anywhere the directory service is available. On the other hand, you would not expect to see a user's cologne preference in the directory service.

A directory service is not a general-purpose database. You would not implement a directory service to manage a point-of-sale system in a chain of video stores. But you would consider implementing a directory service to manage the salespeople who log on at the point-of-sale terminals.

Finally, a directory service needs management tools. Administrators need some way to add information to the directory, remove outdated information, and make use of the information that remains. These tools need to be global in scope, straightforward to operate, and aid in diagnosing any problems that might arise.

So let's get down to some basic questions. How does a directory service work? Why does it work that way? How does it break? How is it fixed? And most important, how does it make my job easier so I don't spend all my spare time managing the service that's supposed to be helping me manage the network?

Brief History of Directory Services

There's an old saying that you can't get to where you're going unless you know where you've been. Before analyzing Active Directory, let's start with a look at the history of directory services in general. This is not an academic exercise. It's important to understand the reason behind the decisions made when directory services were formulated and who made those decisions.

ITU-T

The directory service story starts with a smallish document called X.500, "Data Networks and Open System Communications—Directory." The cast of characters in this story includes a group of standards bodies and vendors from all over the world.

First and foremost is the *International Telecommunication Union* (ITU). The ITU is a United Nations agency that acts as a forum for governments that want to achieve consensus on global telecom issues. The ITU membership includes manufacturers and service providers from over 130 countries.

The branch of the ITU specifically tasked with making directory service recommendations is the Telecommunication Standardization Sector, or ITU-T. The ITU-T was formerly called the *Comité Consultatif International Téléphonique et Télégraphique* (CCITT).

The ITU-T issues recommendations in many areas, from broadcast requirements and measuring equipment to faxing. These recommendations are grouped into lettered series. For example, the V series covers data communication over telephone networks and includes such famous standards such as V.34, "Wideband Analog Modem Communication," and V.90, "Connecting Analog to Digital Modems."

The X series of recommendations, which includes the X.500 recommendations for directory services, covers a variety of data network and open system communication technologies, such as X.25 packet-switched networks and X.400 messaging systems. For a complete listing of ITU recommendations, see `www.itu.int/publications/telecom.htm`.

ISO

The ITU-T does not set standards; it only makes recommendations. Getting an international standard approved requires the consent of the *International Organization for Standardization* (ISO).

Source of the ISO Name

You may wonder why the initials ISO do not match the name, International Organization for Standardization. Actually, the letters are not initials at all. They come from the Greek word *isos*, meaning equal. These letters were used to avoid the hodgepodge of acronyms that would have resulted if the various member countries translated International Organization for Standardization into their own language with their own initials.

Unlike the ITU, whose membership comes from industry vendors, ISO members come from national standards bodies. The U.S. member is the *American National Standards Institute* (ANSI). The ISO web site is located at `www.iso.ch`. The `ch` indicates that the site is in Switzerland, just in case you are not up on your ISO 3166 two-letter country codes.

The ISO is responsible for standardization in just about every area, from the quality standards of ISO 9000 to the standard paper sizes of ISO 216. In the networking industry, it is most famous for ISO 7498, "Information Technology—Open System Interconnection—Basic Reference Model," better known as the OSI Network Model.

ISO standards that affect data communication technology are often jointly published with the ITU-T. For example, the ISO standard that parallels the ITU-T X.500 recommendations for directory services is ISO 9594, "Information Technology—Open Systems Interconnection—The Directory." Because the ISO issues standards and the ITU-T issues recommendations, it is actually a misnomer to refer to the *X.500 Standard*, but this is commonly done because the two documents are identical.

IEC

The ISO is the senior standards body in the world, but it certainly is not the only one. Many agencies dip their spoons in the standards soup bowl and they sometimes slosh on each other. In the data communications field, there is overlap between standards published by the ISO and standards published by the *International Electrotechnical Commission* (IEC).

The IEC deals with international standardization for electronics, magnetics, electromagnetics, electroacoustics, telecommunication, and energy production/distribution. They promulgate terminology, symbols, measurement standards, performance standards, dependability, design, development, safety, and environmental standards. The U.S. member of the IEC is also ANSI. The ISO and IEC joined with the ITU in publishing the directory service standards. The IEC web site is located at `www.iec.ch`.

ANSI

In the United States, there is one senior standards body, ANSI. You are probably most familiar with ANSI for its work to standardize character-based data formats, although there are ANSI standards for just about anything. I used to work in the nuclear industry, where even the ballpoint pens were built to conform to an ANSI standard. The ANSI web site is `www.ansi.org`.

IETF

In a country where millions of people call television talk shows to give advice to total strangers about their sex lives, it should come as no surprise that many advisory bodies are eager to give input to ANSI. An advisory body with a great deal of influence over implementation of the X.500 standard is the *Internet Engineering Task Force* (IETF). Its web site is located at `www.ietf.org`.

The IETF is an amalgam of vendors, developers, researchers, designers, and architects of all stripes who have an interest in the workings of the Internet. Special working groups within the IETF ride herd on Internet workings in collaborative effort called the *Internet Standards Process*, a unique and somewhat lengthy operation that consists of thrashing a good idea mercilessly until it breaks into pieces that can be easily digested by the collective organism.

Request For Comments (RFC)

The Internet Standards Process is facilitated by documents called *Request for Comments* (RFCs) and *Internet Drafts*. To give you an idea of how long it takes to assimilate new ideas into Internet standards, out of the hundreds and hundreds of standards-track RFCs listed in RFC 2700, "Internet Official Protocol Standards," there are only 59 standards. The rest of the documents squirm somewhere in the approval process.

Copies of RFCs, Standards, Standards Track documents, Internet Drafts, and other working papers can be found at the IETF site and at various mirrored sites around the Internet. I prefer the search engine at the Internet Engineering Standards Repository, `www.normos.org`.

The IETF can bypass ISO/IEC standards and ITU recommendations if they deem it necessary to get useful protocols out into the world. An example of this is the *Lightweight Directory Access Protocol* (LDAP). LDAP is a pared-down version of the X.500 directory service that forms the basis of Active Directory, Netscape Directory Services, and other products.

There is no LDAP standard from ISO and no LDAP recommendation from the ITU. LDAP is purely an Internet concoction. Active Directory implements the most current version of LDAP, version 3, as documented in RFC 2251, "Lightweight Directory Access Protocol v3." This RFC expands and augments the original LDAP Standards Track document, RFC 1777, "Lightweight Directory Access Protocol." There is a long list of RFCs that expand various LDAP features.

Although LDAP is not precisely an X.500 implementation, a great deal of the design basis of LDAP comes from X.500. So before going through LDAP in detail, let's take a quick look at its parent.

X.500 Overview

A directory service is a distributed store of information about the users of a computer system and the infrastructure that supports that system.

The goal of X.500 was to cut through the babble of competing information repositories to define a single place where users from all nations could go to locate each other, learn about each other, discover common likes and dislikes, and eventually communicate freely to find a path to universal peace and brotherhood and the dawning of the Age of Aquarius. The key features of an X.500 directory service are as follows:

- The information is distributed among many different servers.
- Users can submit queries to any server to find information anywhere in the system.
- Servers can find information on other servers because they share common knowledge about each other.

X.500 Components

The magic of X.500 comes from the flexible way it compartmentalizes and distributes information. This flexibility comes at the cost of complexity, though—not the least of which is a thicket of nomenclature rife with obscure computing jargon and Three Letter Acronyms (TLAs). These X.500 acronyms crop up quite a bit in Active Directory documentation, so it pays to give them a Quick Run Through (QRT). Refer to Figure 6.2 for a roadmap. Here are the X/500 TLAs:

- Information in an X.500 Directory is stored in a *Directory Information Base* (DIB).
- The DIB is divided into pieces that are structured into a hierarchy called a *Directory Information Tree* (DIT).

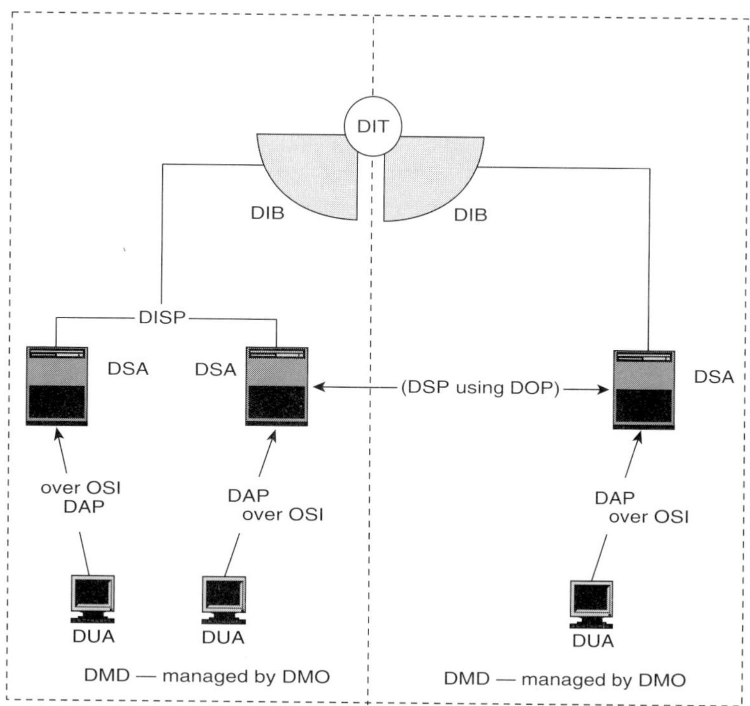

Figure 6.2 X.500 components and their communication protocols.

- Each piece of the DIB is stored on a server called a *Directory Service Agent* (DSA).
- A user who needs information from Active Directory submits queries via an application interface called a *Directory User Agent* (DUA).
- A DUA communicates with a DSA using the *Directory Access Protocol* (DAP).
- One DSA communicates with another using the *Directory System Protocol* (DSP).
- Administrative information exchanged between DSAs is controlled via policies defined by the *Directory Operational Binding Management Protocol* (DOP).
- A single *Directory Management Organization* (DMO) takes charge of a *Directory Management Domain* (DMD) that contains one or more DSAs.
- Information held by one DSA is replicated to other DSAs in the same DMD using the *Directory Information Shadowing Protocol* (DISP).

DAP, DSP, DISP, and all other high-level communication protocols in X.500 use OSI networking as defined in ITU Recommendation X.200/OSI-EIU Standard 7498.

X.500 Transaction Example

Here's an example of how these X.500 components tie together (see Figure 6.3). Let's say that the secondhand car dealers in America get together and decide to form an association. They want a directory service to store information about vehicles available for sale at each member's showroom.

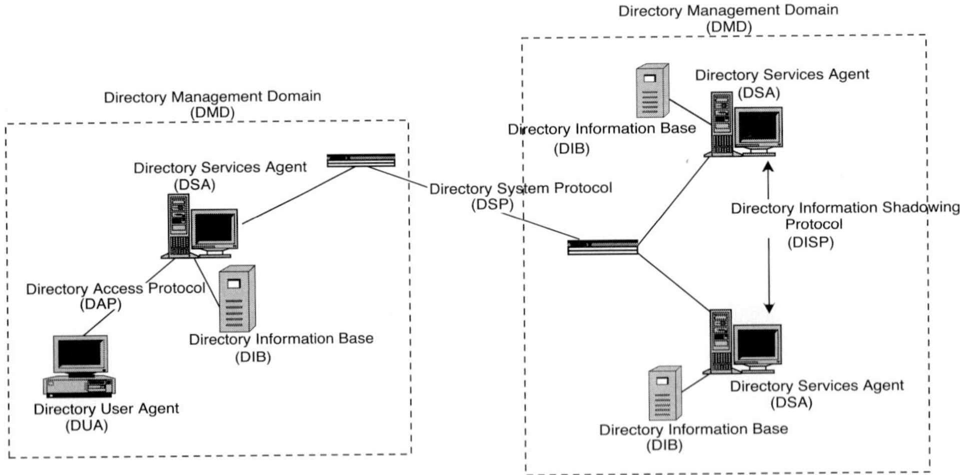

Figure 6.3 Diagram of an example X.500 communication scheme.

The DIB for this dealership directory service includes makes, models, years, vehicle identification numbers, and unbeatable prices. Each dealer is assigned a DMO that controls a DMD. The DIB in each DMD is hosted by at least one DSA, which exchanges administrative information with DSAs in other DMDs using DOP. Dealerships in the same region have individual DSAs that replicate their copy of the DIB between each other via DISP. The pieces of the DIB are joined into a single DIT, the root of which is hosted by a DSA at headquarters.

Why go through all this trouble? Well, if a customer at a dealership in Kankakee wants a cherry-colored Cherokee, the salesperson can sit at a DUA and submit a query to a local DSA via DAP. The DSA would check its copy of the local DIB and if it failed to locate a record, it would use DSP to query other DSAs until it either found a match or exhausted all possibilities. The DUA could then be programmed to suggest alternatives, like a cream-colored Chevelle in Chicago.

The important point to remember about this transaction is that there is no central repository of information. Each local DSA holds its own copy of the DIB. Referral mechanisms are used to distribute queries around the system.

Why LDAP Instead of X.500?

Several pedigreed X.500 directory services are commercially available, but few have achieved widespread popularity. The problem with pristine X.500 implementations is the overhead represented by all those protocols. When you get an army of DUAs all talking DAP to DSAs that refer queries to other DSAs using DSP while at the same time mirroring their DIBs to other DSAs in their DMD via DISP, my friend, you've got a whole D★ lot to go wrong.

In the early 90s, a few bright folks at the University of Michigan wanted to build a directory service to handle their 100,000+ students, staff, and faculty. They gave up on the complexities of X.500 and came up with a scheme that retained the X.500 directory structure but gave it a streamlined access protocol based on standard TCP/IP instead of ISO. They also came up with a pared-down referral mechanism, a more flexible security model, and no fixed replication protocol. They called the result the *Lightweight Directory Access Protocol*, or LDAP. The rest, as they say, is history. The Blue and Maize folks no longer control LDAP development. The current repository of LDAP knowledge is at `www.openldap.org`.

Active Directory and LDAP

When Microsoft decided to replace the clumsy Registry-based account management system in classic NT with a true directory service, rather than devise a proprietary directory service of their own, they chose to adopt LDAP. Even more importantly, from our perspective as administrators, Microsoft chose to deliver their LDAP directory service using two proven technologies.

Extensible Storage Engine (ESE)

At its heart, a directory service database is made up of tables with rows representing objects of interest and columns representing attributes of those objects. What sets different databases apart is the way the tables are managed. This table manager is often called a *database engine*.

The LDAP standards do not stipulate a particular table management technology. For the Active Directory table manager, Microsoft used a revved-up version of the *Extensible Storage Engine* (ESE) first introduced with Exchange. Microsoft chose ESE over the SQL Server database engine because a SQL engine does not work efficiently with the object-oriented structure of an LDAP directory. The ESE engine, on the other hand, was primarily designed as an object-oriented database.

DNS-Based Locator System

Users cannot take advantage of the information in a directory service if they cannot find the servers hosting the information. Microsoft chose to build its LDAP directory service around the *Domain Name System* (DNS). When an LDAP client needs to find a server hosting a directory service, it does so by querying DNS. This enabled Microsoft to use new features in DNS to simplify the search.

For example, Microsoft took advantage of the relatively new service locator (SRV) record type to put pointers in DNS to indicate the names of servers hosting LDAP and Kerberos services. SRV records have a relatively complex structure, but Microsoft was able to avoid typographical errors by registering them automatically using Dynamic DNS.

LDAP Information Model

A directory service may be a bit fancier than the database you use to tally the overtime pay you've lost since taking your salaried administrator position a few years back, but the principles of operation are pretty much the same.

Object-Oriented Database

In X.500 terminology, the directory service database is called a *Directory Information Base* (DIB). If you think of an old-style library card catalog system as a kind of directory service, one of those big oak cabinets with rows of drawers would be a DIB.

The X.500 directory service structure was developed at a time when object-oriented databases represented leading-edge technology. If your only exposure to database technology has been more modern relational databases, the design constraints of an object database can look a little strange.

In an object-oriented database, each record (object) occupies a unique position in a hierarchical namespace. The object's name and path traces its origins to the top of the namespace, in much the same way that a Daughter of the American Revolution traces her forebears back to the Mayflower. A file system is an example of an object-oriented database.

Object databases consist of big, structured sequential files connected by a set of indexes that are themselves nothing more than big, structured sequential files. This underlying database technology is called *Indexed Sequential Access Method*, or ISAM. You'll see this term in the Event log and other reports.

The ESE database engine exposes the flat ISAM structure as a hierarchy of objects. In addition, Microsoft makes extensive use of COM technology by representing Active Directory objects as COM objects via the *Active Directory Services Interface* (ADSI).

Classes and Attributes

A directory service contains information about specific types of objects, such as User objects, Computer objects, and so forth. These are called object *classes*. A class is a bundle of *attributes* with a name. Figure 6.4 shows how attributes and classes are related.

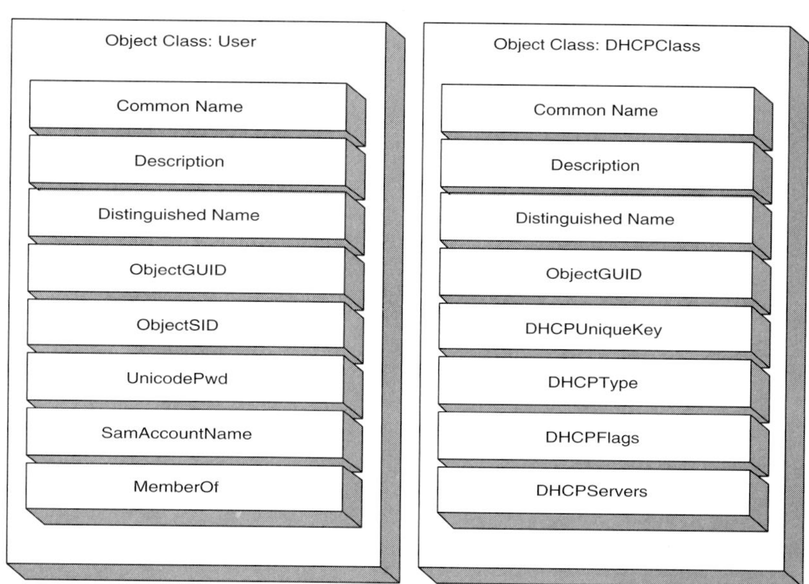

Figure 6.4 Classes and attributes in a directory service.

Attributes and Properties

Attributes are also often called *properties*. There is a difference between these two terms, but it is so subtle that most reference manuals, including this one, use them interchangeably.

The attributes associated with a particular object class differentiate it from other object classes. For example, *User* objects have different attributes than *Computer* objects or *IP Security* objects. Using a library card catalog as an example, different card formats represent different classes of items. A certain card format is used to record entries for `Books`. Another format is used for `Tapes`. The card format for `Books` would have spaces for `Title`, `Author`, `ISBN`, and so forth. A card for `Tapes` would have spaces for those entries plus additional spaces for `Read-By` and `Play-Time`.

An object class, then, is really nothing more than a bundle of attributes with a name. RFC 2256, "A Summary of the X.500(96) User Schema for use with LDAPv3," defines 21 classes and 55 attributes for use in a standard LDAP directory service. Active Directory adds quite a few more for a total of about 200 object classes and 1500 attributes.

Classes also define the scope of a directory service database. You would not expect to find cards in a library card catalog representing Off-The-Road Vehicles or Double-Meat Hamburgers. Microsoft engineers defined the initial scope of Active Directory by including a certain set of object classes and attributes. This list can be extended by other applications or by administrators. For example, your organization could create attributes and classes for storing badge numbers and social security numbers in Active Directory.

Class Inheritance

Directory service designers strive to limit complexity by defining the minimum number of classes and attributes necessary to describe the objects of interest that need to be stored in the directory service database.

For example, in a library card catalog, it would be a mistake to create a class called Somewhat-Less-Than-Riveting-Early-20th-Century-American-Novels, even though it seems like quite a few objects would fit that class. In relation to the overall scope of a library, this classification would be too narrow. It would be better to have an attribute called Boring with a Boolean value. You could assign this attribute to the Book class so that objects derived from that class would get a Boring attribute that could be given a value of Yes or No or left empty. You could also assign the Boring attribute to the Periodical, Tape, and Video classes, as well.

A directory can have hundreds of classes and many hundreds of attributes. If the attributes for each class had to be separately defined, the sheer number of perturbations would make the directory look less like a tree and more like an example of German expressionism.

Fortunately, attributes associated with a particular class often overlap those of other classes. For example, the attribute list for the Mailbox class includes all the attributes associated with the Mail-Recipient class with one addition, the Delivery-Mechanism attribute. So, instead of separately defining all the attributes in Mailbox class, LDAP allows the class to be defined as a child of the Mail-Recipient class. This permits it to *inherit* the attributes of its parent. The designer need only stipulate the new additional attribute or attributes that make the subordinate class unique.

Attributes flow down the hierarchy of object classes like genes in a family tree. Figure 6.5 shows an example of class inheritance for the Computer object class.

All LDAP classes derive from a class called *Top*. This makes it possible to define certain attributes that every class would have in common. For example, every class needs a *Common-Name* attribute. The attribute is assigned to Top and the rest of the classes inherit it.

Think of Top as a director who never actually appears on camera but leaves a distinctive mark on the production. Top is an Abstract class, one of three class types in LDAP. They are as follows:

- **Abstract.** Classes that exist solely to derive other object classes. There are 14 abstract classes in the Active Directory. Examples include Top, Device, Person, and Security Object.
- **Structural.** Classes that have objects in Active Directory. Examples include User, Group, and Computer.
- **Auxiliary.** Used to extend the definition of an Abstract class for specialized purposes. There are only six of these classes in Active Directory: Mail-Recipient, Dynamic-Object, MS-MMS Object, Sam-Domain, Sam-Domain-Base, and Security-Principal.

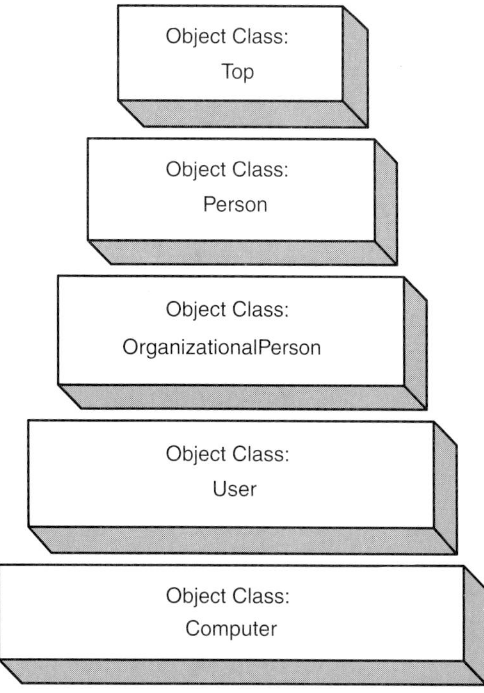

Figure 6.5 Inheritance diagram for the Computer object class.

These three class types act like assembly line robots designed to produce things called "objects." The Structural classes are the tools and dies that stamp and shape the objects. The Abstract classes are the mill workers and pattern makers that build the tools and dies. The Auxiliary classes act like a custom shop at the end of the line where special versions of standard objects are turned out.

Object Instances

Each object in Active Directory is derived from a specific object class. Another way of saying this is that an object represents an *instance* of a class. Each instance of an object class differs from another instance by having different values for its attributes.

Remember the movie *Elephant Man*? In a great scene, the lead character, John Merrick, stands in front of a curious mob and exclaims, "I am not an elephant. I am a human being." Had Mr. Merrick been a directory services designer, he could have clarified his point by adding, "I am an instance of the Human Being class, not the Elephant class. And the only difference between you and me is a relatively minor attribute of mine that has a different value from yours. So lay off, will you?"

Defining suitable attributes for an object class can be slippery. Subtle differences may force a designer to create a new class. If you were designing a library card catalog, you might start out by defining a class called Tape with an attribute called Type that has two permitted values, Audio and Video. This decision forces you to define attributes for the Tape class that fully defines both audiotapes and videotapes. After months of agonizing, you might decide that the properties of audio and video tapes are so different that they warrant creating two classes, AudioTape and VideoTape, each with their own unique attribute sets. There are many instances in Active Directory and LDAP where two object classes differ by only one or two attributes.

Schema

A database schema defines the content and structure of the database. In a library card catalog, the schema would be a set of procedures and rules set down by the librarian. "Books go on green cards," she tells you. "Videos go on red cards. File the cards alphabetically by Title in this cabinet and by Subject in that cabinet." So on and so on. The schema for an LDAP directory service defines these items:

- The attributes associated with each object class
- The permissible object classes
- The parent-child relationship of object classes, which in turn determines attribute inheritance
- The data type associated with each attribute
- The physical representation of the object in the user interface

The schema can take the form of an external table that acts as data dictionary or an internal table that is structured using the same rules as the database itself. Active Directory uses an internal schema. Many of the design constraints we'll see in the next chapter stem from the necessity to keep a consistent schema throughout all the servers that host a copy of the directory database.

Later in this chapter, we'll see how to modify the Active Directory schema to add new attributes and object classes that can be used by applications to support network operations.

LDAP Information Model Summary

Here are the important information model concepts to carry forward with you when you start designing an Active Directory system for your own organization:

- LDAP uses an object-oriented database. The database engine for Active Directory is the Extensible Storage Engine, or ESE.
- An object class defines a unique set of attributes for a particular type of object.
- Object classes inherit attributes from their parents. This permits the designer to identify only the new attributes for a new object class.
- Each object is an instance of an object class. The attributes for the object are assigned values that describe that particular object.
- A schema defines the content and structure of the LDAP database. In the case of Active Directory, the schema is contained within the directory itself.
- The directory schema must be consistent on every server hosting a copy of the database.

LDAP Namespace Structure

A directory service has two major features. First, it distributes its information base among many different servers. Second, users can access directory information by querying any of those servers. Making this work requires defining a *namespace* in which each object's location can be quickly determined.

Common Names

As we saw in the last section, information in an LDAP database comes in the form of objects. Objects have attributes that describe them. For example, the User object for Tom Jones would have attributes such as Tom's logon name, his password, his phone number, his email address, his department, and so forth.

When an LDAP client needs to locate information about an object, it submits a query that contains the object's distinguished name (DN) and the attributes the client wants to see. A search for information about Tom Jones could be phrased in a couple of ways:

- You could search for attributes in Tom's User object. "Give me the Department attribute for `cn=Tom Jones,cn=Users,dc=Company,dc=com`."
- You could search for attributes that end up including Tom's object. "Give me all User objects with a Department attribute equal to `Finance`."

In either case, LDAP can find Tom's object because the name assigned to the object describes its place in the LDAP namespace.

Figure 6.6 shows a portion of the LDAP namespace in Active Directory. With one exception, each folder represents a Container object, which in turn holds other objects. The exception is the domain controllers object, which is an Organizational Unit (OU). Domain controllers are placed in an OU so that they can have discrete group policies. Generic Container objects cannot be linked to group policies.

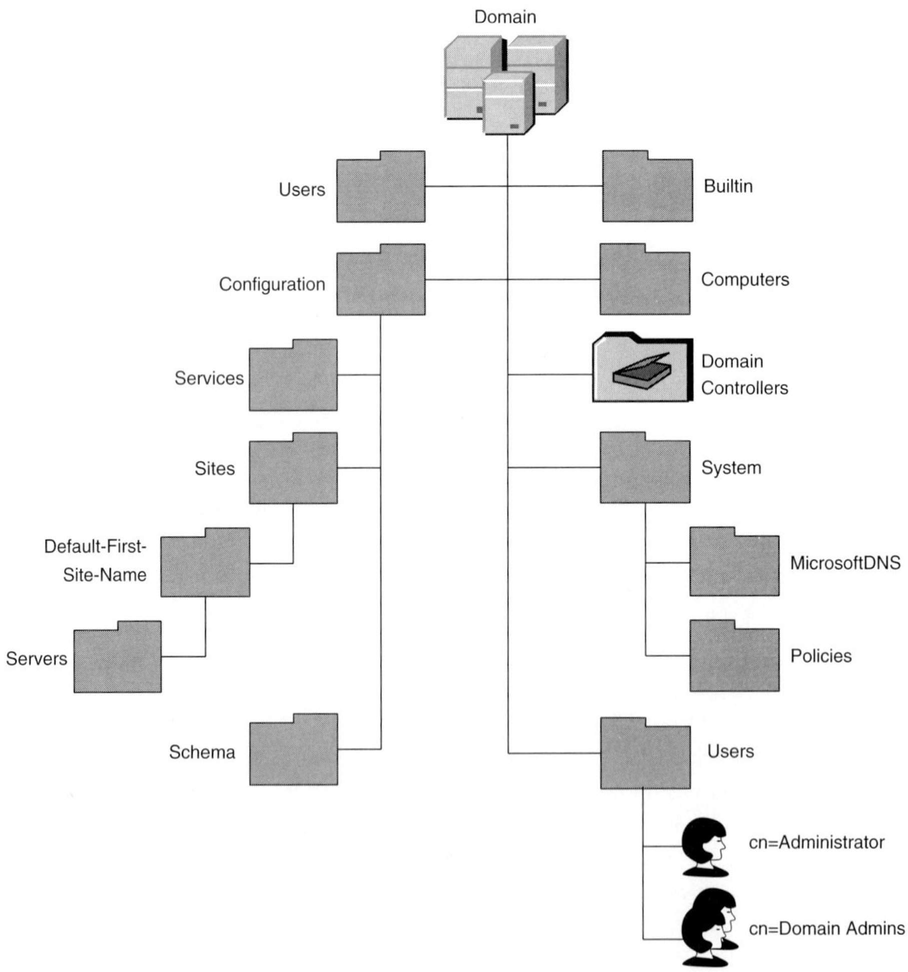

Figure 6.6 Example LDAP directory hierarchy.

The User objects in the diagram have designators that start with CN, meaning *Common Name*. The CN designator applies to all but a few object types. Active Directory only uses two other object designators (although LDAP defines several). They are as follows:

- **Domain Component (DC).** DC objects represent the top of an LDAP tree that uses DNS to define its namespace. Active Directory is an example of such an LDAP tree. The designator for an Active Directory domain with the DNS name Company.com would be `dc=Company,dc=com`.
- **Organizational Unit (OU).** OU objects act as containers that hold other objects. They provide structure to the LDAP namespace. OUs are the only general-purpose container available to administrators in Active Directory. An example OU name would be `ou=Accounting`.

Distinguished Names

A name that includes an object's entire path to the root of the LDAP namespace is called its *distinguished name*, or DN. An example DN for a user named CSantana whose object is stored in the `cn=Users` container in a domain named `Company.com` would be `cn=CSantana,cn=Users,dc=Company,dc=com`.

An identifying characteristic of LDAP distinguished names is their little-endian path syntax. As you read from left to right, you travel up the directory tree. This contrasts to file system paths, which run down the tree as you read from left to right.

Relative Distinguished Names

An object name without a path, or a partial path, is called a *relative distinguished name*, or RDN. The common name `cn=CSantana` is an example of an RDN. So is `cn=CSantana,cn=Users`. The RDN serves the same purpose as a path fragment in a filename. It is a convenient navigational shortcut.

Two objects can have the same RDN, but LDAP has a rule that no two objects can have the same DN. This makes sense if you think of the object-oriented nature of the database. Two objects with the same DN would try to occupy the same row in the database table. *C'est impossible*, as we say in southern New Mexico.

Case Sensitivity of LDAP Names

Distinguished names in Active Directory are not case sensitive. In most instances, the case you specify when you enter a value is retained in the object's attribute. This is similar to the way Windows treats filenames. Feel free to mix cases based on your corporate standards or personal aesthetic.

Typeful Names

The combination of an object's name and its LDAP designator is called a *typeful* name. Examples include `cn=Administrator` and `cn=Administrator,cn=Users,dc=Company,dc=com`.

Some applications can parse for delimiters such as periods or semicolons between the elements of a distinguished name. For example, an application may permit you to enter `Administrator.Users.Company.com` rather than the full typeful name. This is called *typeless* naming. When entering typeless names, it is important to place the delimiters properly.

The console-based tools provided by Microsoft use a GUI to navigate the LDAP namespace, so you don't need to worry about interpreting typeful or typeless names right away. But if you want to use many of the support tools that come on the Windows Server 2003 CD or in the Resource Kit, or you want to use scripts to manage Active Directory, you'll need to use typeful naming. After you get the hang of it, rattling off a long typeful name becomes second nature.

Directory Information Tree

In LDAP, as in X.500, the servers that host copies of the information base are called *Directory Service Agents*, or DSAs. A DSA can host all or part of the information base. The portions of the information base form a hierarchy called a *Directory Information Tree*, or DIT. Figure 6.7 shows an example.

The top of the DIT is occupied by a single object. The class of this object is not defined by the LDAP specification. In Active Directory, the object must come from the object class *DomainDNS*. Because Active Directory uses DNS to structure its namespace, the DomainDNS object is given a DC designator. For example, the object at the top of the tree in Figure 6.7 would have the distinguished name `dc=Company,dc=com`.

Typeless Names and Delimiters

If you write scripts and you need to allow for periods in object names, precede the period with a backslash. This tells the parser that the period is a special character, not a delimiter. For example, if your user names look like `tom.collins`, a typeless name in a script would look like this: `tom\.collins.Users.Company.com`. The same is true for user names that have embedded commas and periods, such as `Winston H. Borntothepurple, Jr.` An ADSI query for this name would look like this: `winston h\. borntothepurple\, jr\.`

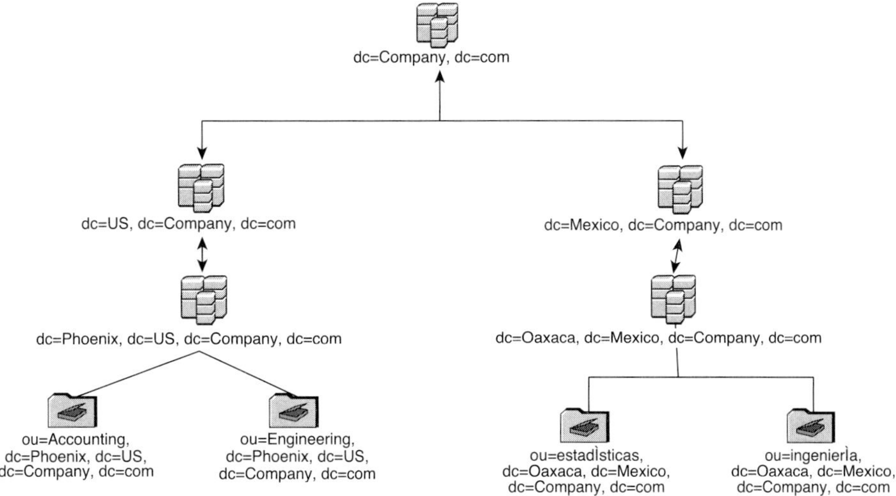

Figure 6.7 Directory Information Tree.

> **Active Directory and DNS Roots**
> Active Directory cannot be rooted at the very top of a DNS namespace. The assumption is that many different Active Directory namespaces could share the same root. For this reason, the DomainDNS object at the top of the tree must always have at least two domain component designators.

An LDAP tree contains branches formed by containers underneath the root container. These containers hold objects that have some relation to each other as defined by the namespace. For instance, in Active Directory, the default container for User objects is `cn=Users`. For Computer objects, it is `cn=Computers`. Information about group policies, DNS, Remote Access Services, and so forth go in `cn=System`. As we'll see when we discuss Active Directory design in Chapter 8, "Designing Windows Server 2003 Domains," administrators have the ability to create Organizational Units (OUs) to contain objects that have similar management or configuration requirements.

Naming Contexts

As the number of objects in a DIT grows, the database may get too large to store efficiently on one DSA. Also, an organization might want to use bandwidth more effectively by using a DSA in New York to store information about users in North America and another DSA in Amsterdam to store information about users in Europe.

Naming Contexts and Partitions

X.501, "Information Technology—Open Systems Interconnection—The Directory: Models," defines the term naming context as, "A subtree of entries held in a single master DSA." It goes on to describe the process of dividing a tree into multiple naming contexts as *partitioning.*

Novell chose to adopt the term *partition* to define separate pieces of the directory database. In their seminal book, *Understanding and Deploying LDAP Directory Services*, Tim Howe, Mark Smith, and Gordon Good use the term *partition* in favor of naming context, although they describe both as meaning the same thing. Microsoft uses the two terms interchangeably.

The tools that come with the Windows Server 2003 CD and in the Resource Kit favor the term *naming context.* That is the term I use throughout this book.

Here is where the distributed nature of an LDAP database comes into play. The Directory Information Base can be separated into parts called *naming contexts*, or NCs. In Active Directory, each domain represents a separate naming context. Domain controllers in the same domain each have a read/write replica of that Domain naming context. Configuration and Schema objects are stored in their own naming contexts, as are DNS Record objects when using Active Directory Integrated DNS zones.

When a client submits a query for information about a particular object, the system must determine which DSA hosts the naming context that contains that particular object. It does this using the object's distinguished name and knowledge about the directory topology.

If a DSA cannot respond to a query using information in the naming contexts it hosts, it sends the client a *referral* to a DSA hosting the next higher or lower naming context in the tree (depending on the distinguished name of the object in the search). The client then submits the request to a DSA hosting the naming context in the referral. This DSA either responds with the information being requested or a referral to another DSA. This is called *walking the tree.*

DSAs that host copies of the same naming context must replicate changes to each other. It's important to keep this in mind as you work with Active Directory servers. If you have separate domains, then clients in one domain must walk the tree to get access to Active Directory objects in another domain. If the domain controllers for the domains are in different locations in the WAN, this can slow performance. Many of the architectural decisions you'll make as you design your system focus on the location, accessibility, and reliability of naming contexts.

LDAP Searches

From a client's perspective, LDAP operates like a well-run department store. In a department store, you can sidle up to the fragrance counter and ask, "How much is the Chanel No. 5?" and be sure of getting an immediate reply, especially if you already have your credit card in hand. The same is true of LDAP. When a search request is submitted to a DSA that hosts a copy of the naming context containing the objects involved in the search, the DSA can answer the request immediately.

But in a department store, what if you ask the fragrance associate, "Where can I find a size 16 chambray shirt that looks like a Tommy Hilfiger design but doesn't cost so darn much?" The associate probably doesn't know, but gives you directions to the Menswear department. You make your way there and ask your question to an associate standing near the slacks. The associate may not know the answer, but gives you directions to the Bargain Menswear department in the basement behind last year's Christmas decorations. You proceed to that area and ask an associate your question again. This time you're either handed a shirt or given an excuse why one isn't available.

LDAP uses a similar system of referrals to point clients at the DSA that hosts the naming context containing the requested information. These referrals virtually guarantee the success of any lookup so long as the object exists inside the scope of the information base.

The key point to remember is that LDAP referrals put the burden of searching on the clients. This contrasts to X.500, where all the messy search work is handed over to the DSAs. LDAP is Wal-Mart to the Nordstroms of X.500.

RootDSE

When LDAP clients need information from a DSA, they must first *bind* to the directory service. This authenticates the client and establishes a session for the connection. The client then submits queries for objects and attributes within the directory. This means the client needs to know the security requirements of the DSA along with the structure of the directory service it hosts.

DSAs "advertise" this information by constructing a special object called *RootDSE*. The RootDSE object acts like a signpost at a rural intersection. It points the way to various important features in the directory service and gives useful information about the service. LDAP clients use this information to select an authentication mechanism and configure their searches.

Each DSA constructs its own copy of RootDSE. The information is not replicated between DSAs. RootDSE is like the eye above the pyramid on the back of a dollar bill. It sits apart from the structure but knows all about it. You'll be seeing more about RootDSE later in this book in topics that cover scripting. Querying RootDSE for information about Active Directory rather than hard-coding that information into your scripts is a convenient way to make your scripts portable.

LDAP Namespace Structure Summary

Here are the highlights of what you need to remember about the LDAP namespace structure to help you design and administer Active Directory:

- An object's full path in the LDAP namespace is called its distinguished name. All DNs must be unique.

- The Directory Information Tree, or DIT, is a distributed LDAP database that can be hosted by more than one server.
- The DIT is divided into separate units called naming contexts. A domain controller can host more than one naming context.
- Active Directory uses separate naming contexts to store information about domains in the same DIT.
- When LDAP clients search for an object, LDAP servers refer the clients to servers that host the naming context containing that object. They do this using shared knowledge about the system topology.
- Each DSA creates a RootDSE object that describes the content, controls, and security requirements of the directory service. Clients use this information to select an authentication method and to help formulate their search requests.

Active Directory Namespace Structure

At this point, we know enough about a generic LDAP directory service to begin applying the terms and concepts to Active Directory.

Let's start with what we need to store in Active Directory. You can classify the required information into three general categories:

- **Information about network security entities.** This includes users, computers, and groups along with applications such as group policies, DNS, RAS, COM and so forth.
- **Information about the Active Directory mechanisms.** This includes replication, network services, permissions, and user interface displays.
- **Information about the Active Directory schema.** This includes objects that define the classes and attributes in Active Directory.

Microsoft had to devise a way to structure this information in a way that was compatible with LDAP while retaining backward compatibility with classic NT. In classic NT, information about security entities is stored in the SAM and SECURITY databases in the Registry. Microsoft calls the contents of the SAM database a domain. Because the only way to control access to the SAM is to control access to the entries in the SAM, a domain defines a security boundary as well as a management boundary.

The SAM databases in classic NT domains cannot be combined. To get a common security boundary, the domains must be knitted together using *trust relationships*. When one domain trusts another, members of the trust-*ed* domain can be used as security entities in the trust-*ing* domain. The underlying authentication mechanism, NT LanMan Challenge Response, supports this trust relationship by permitting pass-through authentication of users from trusted domains.

Domains

LDAP gave Microsoft the freedom to construct just about any namespace it chose. There is no naming restriction other than at the top of the namespace, where the distinguished name of the root object needs to correspond to a DNS domain name.

Janis Joplin had it right, though, that freedom's just another word for nothing left to lose, and Microsoft had a lot to lose if it designed Active Directory in such a way as to not be compatible with classic NT. For this reason, Microsoft chose to structure Active Directory around the classic concepts of domains and trust relationships.

In Active Directory, a *domain* defines a separate namespace, a separate security structure, a separate management structure, and a separate naming context. The Active Directory database is hosted on *domain controllers*. Users and computers are *members* of a domain. Group policies are contained within a particular domain, even if they impact users in other domains.

Active Directory Naming Contexts

Active Directory is capable of holding a billion objects. This is enough to hold account, computer, mailboxes, and group memberships for every person in the western hemisphere. A big Active Directory database is like an NBA center, though. He may be the key to winning, but only if he doesn't have to move too fast or too often.

The Active Directory database, Ntds.dit, can grow very quickly. The DIT for a domain with 150,000 objects could be well over 2GB depending on the number of groups and the length of the group membership. A DIT this size can be difficult to replicate and manage. Also, it does not make sense to replicate information about users in one continent to domain controllers on other continents unless those users regularly share information.

Domain Naming Contexts

LDAP permits breaking up a directory into separate naming contexts. Managing the interfaces between these naming contexts can get a little tricky, though. To get maximum performance, it is often necessary to generate local caches containing references to objects in other naming contexts. Riding herd on these external reference caches to make sure they reflect the most current information takes some doing.

Microsoft chose to avoid many of the complexities involved with naming contexts by eliminating the ability to create ad hoc naming contexts. As an Active Directory administrator, you have only two places where you can create a naming context (see Figure 6.8):

- At a domain boundary
- By creating a special Application naming context (a new feature in Windows Server 2003)

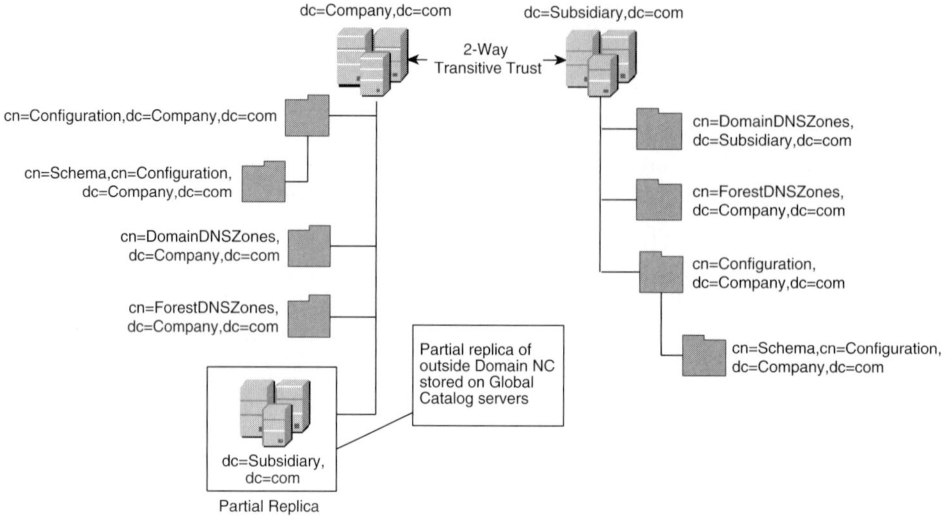

Figure 6.8 Active Directory forest showing naming contexts.

The Application naming context has only limited utility (it is currently used only to support DNS), so the only real option to break apart a big DIT is to create separate domains. In addition to the Domain naming context, each Active Directory implementation contains two other naming contexts: Configuration and Schema. Every domain controller in the forest gets a replica of these two naming contexts. The Schema replica is read-only except for the domain controller selected as the Schema Operations Master.

Schema Naming Contexts

The Schema naming context holds ClassSchema and AttributeSchema objects that represent the various classes and attributes in Active Directory. If this sounds like a circular definition, it's meant to be. Unlike some directory services that load the schema in a separate file, the Active Directory schema is completely self-referential.

Every domain controller in a forest hosts a read-only copy of the Schema naming context. Only one domain controller, the Schema Role Master, can make changes to the schema.

The Schema container object is an instance of the Directory Management Domain (DMD) class. This is a holdover from Exchange, which uses X.500 terminology to define the information store. Because the Schema object represents a naming context boundary, it also contains replication control attributes similar to those in the Configuration object and the Domain-DNS object.

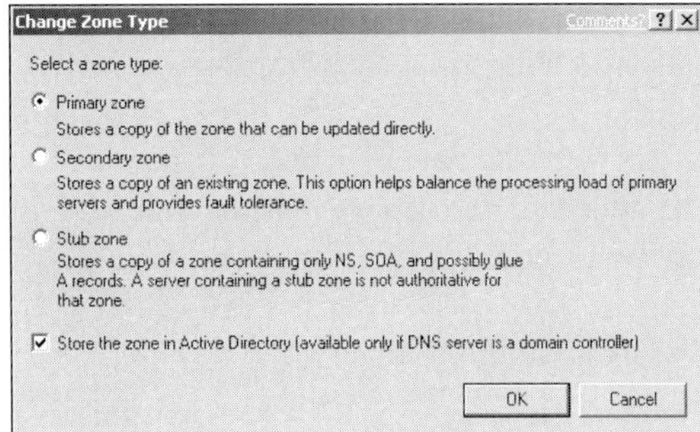

Figure 6.9 DNS zone properties—Change Zone Type window showing Active Directory Integration option.

If you search through the objects in the Schema container, you'll come across a special object called Aggregate. This lone instance of the LDAP SubSchema class has attributes called AttributeTypes and ObjectClasses that lists the names of all classes and attributes in Active Directory. LDAP clients query for the contents of this object to discover the structure of the directory. This helps them formulate queries.

Application Naming Contexts

A new feature in Windows Server 2003 is the ability to create additional naming contexts that can be placed on specific domain controllers. Microsoft uses this feature to store DNS resource records for Active Directory Integrated zones.

You elect to Active Directory Integrate a zone using the Properties of the zone in the DNS console. The General tab displays the zone type. Click Change to open the Change Zone Type window that lists your options. Figure 6.9 offers an example.

If you elect to integrate a zone into Active Directory, the resource records are copied from the existing text-based zone file into Active Directory as discrete DNSzone objects. In Windows 2000, these objects are stored in a MicrosoftDNS container in cn=System,dc=<domain>,dc=<root>. This gave limited flexibility to administrators who wanted to deploy Active Directory Integrated DNS in large, multidomain forests.

The application naming contexts added by Windows Server 2003 gives this additional flexibility. When you Active Directory Integrate a zone on a DNS domain controller running Windows Server 2003, the domain controller creates two additional naming contexts:

- **DomainDNSZones.** A replica of this naming context is placed on domain controllers running the DNS service. Each domain gets a separate DomainDNSZones NC.

- **ForestDNSZones.** A replica of this naming context is placed on domain controllers running DNS throughout the forest.

When you elect to Active Directory Integrate a zone, a new entry called `Replication` is added to the `General` tab in the zone Properties window. Click the `Change` button next to this entry to open the Change Zone Replication Scope window (see Figure 6.10).

This window gives you the following replication options:

- **`All DNS servers in the forest.`** If you select this option, the zone records are placed in the ForestDNSZones naming context. This is the broadest scope and involves the most replication traffic.
- **`All DNS servers in the domain.`** This option places the resource records in the DomainDNSZones naming context for the domain of the DNS server. For instance, if you create stub zone on a DNS server in `Company.com` that points at Branch.Company.com, the records in the stub zone would be placed in `cn=DomainDNSZones,dc=Company,dc=com`.
- **`All domain controllers in the domain.`** This option places the zone records in the Domain naming context under `cn=MicrosoftDNS,cn=System,dc=<domain>, dc=<root>`. This is the same container used by Windows 2000, so select this option when you have Windows 2000 DNS server hosting Active Directory Integrated zones.
- **`All domain controllers specified in the scope of the application directory partition.`** This option permits you to select a specific application naming context.

If you have a single domain, there is nothing to be gained by using the separate naming context to store DNS records. Select the `All domain controllers in the domain` option.

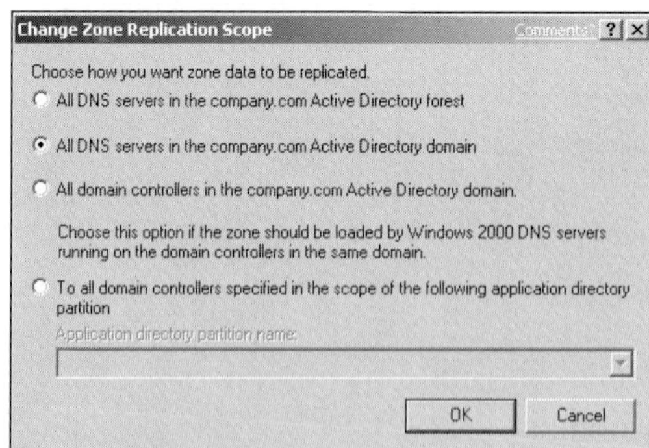

Figure 6.10 Change Zone Replication Scope window.

If you have a multidomain forest, use the `All DNS servers in the domain` option when you want to limit the scope of replication to a particular domain. This is typical for most domain-based zones.

All domain controllers in a forest need `SRV` and `CNAME` records from the zone representing the forest root domain. Under normal circumstances, DNS servers in the other domains would obtain these records recursively from the DNS servers in the root domain. You can speed this process up a little by setting the replication scope of the root domain to `All DNS servers in the forest.`

If this seems like too many records to replicate globally, you can create a new zone just for the resource records that require forest-wide scope. These records are stored in the forest root zone under `_msdcs`. For example, if the forest root domain were `Company.com`, you could create a new zone called `_msdcs.company.com`. The records would be extracted from the `company.com` zone and placed in this new zone. Set the replication scope for the `_msdcs.company.com` zone to `All DNS servers in the forest.`

Configuration Naming Context

The Configuration naming context holds information about parameters that control the services that support Active Directory. Every domain controller in a forest hosts a read/write copy of the Configuration naming context. It holds eight top-level containers. Here is a brief description of their purpose and content.

Display Specifiers

This container holds objects that alter the viewable attributes for other object classes. This is called *shadowing*. For example, the *User-Display* object shadows the User class. Display Specifiers provide *localization* and *context menu* functions.

Localization is the task of producing foreign language versions of an application. Rather than translate the contents of each attribute for each AD object into French, Italian, German, Spanish, Cyrillic, Kanji, Szechwan, Arabic, Korean, Hebrew, Thai, and so on, the system looks to see which country code was used during installation and filters the output through the appropriate Display Specifier.

Display Specifiers also define separate context menus, property pages, and icons based on whether or not the user accessing the object has administrator privileges. For example, when you right-click an object, the flyout menu that appears comes from a context menu associated with that object class. The Display Specifier filters the menu to display only those items you are permitted to perform.

Sorting Through Display Specifiers

When you view the contents of the DisplaySpecifiers container in Active Directory, you'll see a container with a number. This is the *code page* for the *National Language Group* in hex. The United States English code page is number 1033, which corresponds to 409 hex. The code pages for FIGS countries are French, 1036; Italian, 1040; German, 1031; and Spanish, 1034.

Extended Rights

Directory objects are also Windows security objects. This makes it possible to assign permissions to the object itself as well as any of the properties associated with the object. A User object can have many properties. Selecting precisely which properties to assign access rights to get a particular result can get tedious.

Extended Rights control access to objects by consolidating sets of property permissions into a single entity. For example, an extended right called Membership grants the ability to modify the membership of a single group, selected groups, every group in a container, or every group in a container and its subordinate containers.

Like the Display Specifiers mentioned previously, each Extended Rights object is associated with a structural object that it controls. For example, the *Personal-Information* and *Public-Information* objects are associated with both User and Contact classes.

There are over 50 Extended Rights objects covering a wide assortment of management operations, such as changing passwords, changing domain configurations, resetting user lockouts, and managing BackOffice services.

Lost and Found Config

This container holds objects that get orphaned during database replication. For instance, if a container is deleted during the same replication cycle that an object was created in the container, the object is sent to Lost and Found. Both the Domain and Configuration naming contexts have a Lost and Found container. The Schema naming context does not need one because Schema objects can never be deleted. See Chapter 7, "Managing Active Directory Replication," for more information.

Partitions

This container holds the cross-reference objects that list other domains in the forest. Domain controllers use the contents of this container to build referrals to other domains.

The Partitions container is extremely important for maintaining the integrity of a forest. It would be very bad to have objects representing invalid naming contexts in this container. For this reason, only one domain controller in a forest is permitted to update the contents of this container.

Physical Locations

This container holds Physical Location DN objects associated with Directory Enabled Networking (DEN). For example, a DEN-aware router can place a locator object in this container. Because DEN makes use of standard LDAP functionality, this is the only object class in Active Directory that uses the Location attribute.

The DEN initiative has developed a set of policies for controlling network parameters affecting Quality of Service (QoS), IP Security (IPSec), and other core networking functions. All leading routing and infrastructure vendors have pledged support for DEN, and many have allied themselves with both Microsoft and Novell for the Directory part of DEN. Visit the web site of your favorite vendor to see its DEN-aware products and find out its plans for Active Directory integration.

Services

This container is exposed in the AD Sites and Services console by selecting VIEW | SHOW SERVICES option from the menu. Think of the contents of the Services container as a kind of enterprise-wide Registry. Distributed applications put objects into this container where they can be seen by other servers running the same application.

A disadvantage to this container is that it is replicated to every domain controller in the forest. You may have applications that only need their objects to be seen at selected domain controllers. For this reason, Microsoft included the ability to create a separate Application naming context that can be placed on individual domain controllers of your choice.

Sites

The Sites container is also exposed in the AD Sites and Services console. The objects in this container control Active Directory replication and other site-specific functions. Sites are used to control replication between domain controllers.

Well-Known Security Principals

The object-based security used by classic NT and Windows Server 2003 assigns a unique Security Identifier (SID) to every security principal. There is a set of well-known SIDs that represents special-purpose groups. This includes groups like Interactive, which designates users who are logged on at the console of a machine; Network, which designates users who have logged on to the domain; and Everyone, which designates every user. This container holds the names and SIDs of these groups.

Active Directory Trees and Forests

Recall that domains represent security boundaries for users as well as management boundaries for administrators. Users in one domain cannot access resources in another domain unless some provision is made to support a secure connection. If you have separate domains, you need a way to connect them into a single security structure. Classic NT uses Master domains and Resource domains for this purpose. Active Directory uses trees and forests.

Trees

Active Directory uses DNS domains to define its namespace. As we've seen, a standard LDAP hierarchy conforms to a contiguous namespace called a Directory Information Tree. An Active Directory namespace that follows a contiguous namespace is also called a *tree* (see Figure 6.11).

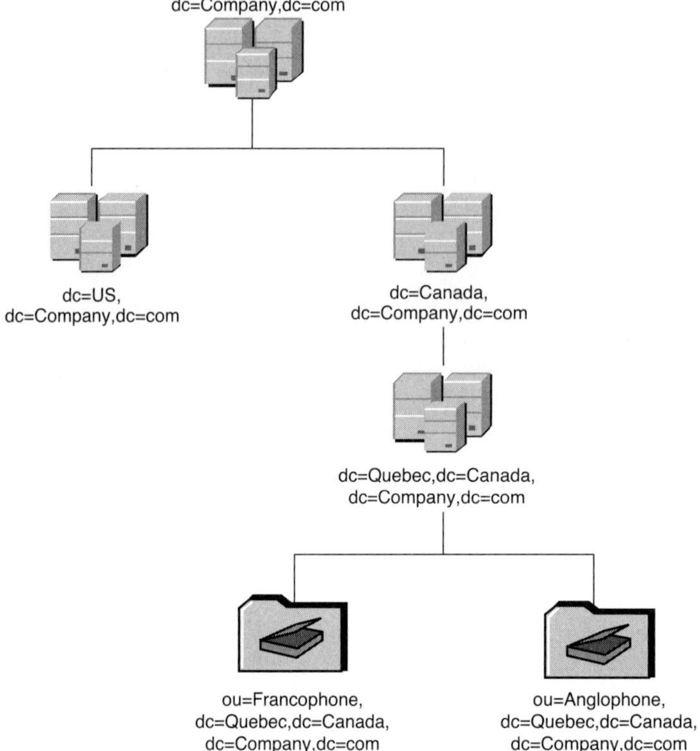

Figure 6.11 Active Directory tree.

Figure 6.11 shows the way an Active Directory tree coincides with a standard DNS namespace. In this diagram, a root domain called `Company.com` has two child domains, one for the `US` and one for `Canada`. The `Canada` domain has a child domain of its own for `Quebec`. The `Quebec` domain has Organizational Units (OUs) that divide objects depending on language. The `US` domain has OUs that divide objects depending on geography. Both represent acceptable uses of OU containers.

From an LDAP perspective, this tree structure looks pretty standard. If a client in the `Quebec` domain queries LDAP for information about a server in the `US` domain, the client will get a chain of referrals that walks the tree up to root and then down to a domain controller in the `US` domain.

Recall that each of these domains represents the contents of a naming context. The naming context for a domain is hosted on a domain controller in that domain. When a query walks the tree, it moves from one domain controller to another. If the domain controllers are in different locations in a WAN, the transaction may take a while to complete.

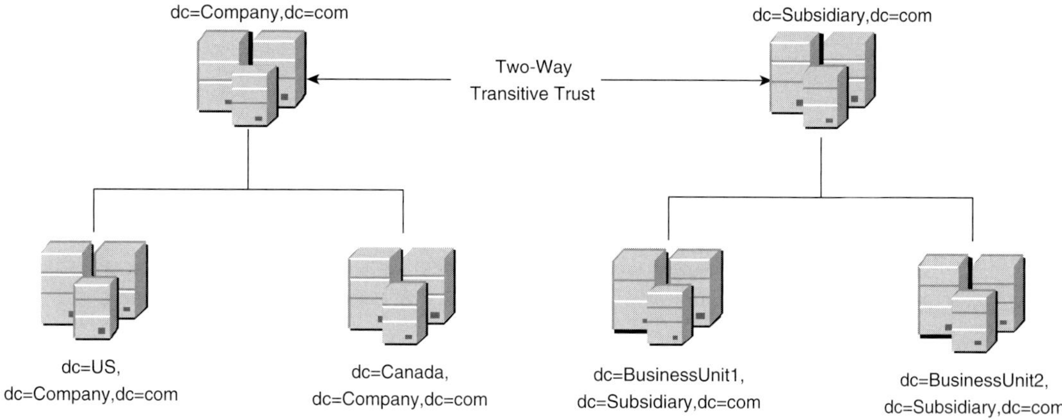

Figure 6.12 Active Directory forest.

Forests

Not every organization is fortunate enough to have a clean tree structure. Many companies have business units that are virtually autonomous fiefdoms with their own DNS root domains and independent administrative staffs and even separate lunchrooms. Many universities, too, have colleges with separate IT staffs and campuses that maintain their own infrastructures.

To accommodate these and other untree-like business structures, Microsoft tweaked the LDAP standard just a bit to develop a second structure called a *forest*. See Figure 6.12 for an example.

Domains in an Active Directory forest do not need to follow a contiguous namespace. A secure connection between the root domains forms a conduit that permits access by users in one domain to resources in the other domains.

Global Catalog

In a standard LDAP search involving multiple naming contexts hosted by multiple servers, the servers pass referrals to the client, and the clients walk the tree to get information from the various servers. This process of query and referral consumes time and bandwidth. And if one of those domain controllers is at the wrong end of a 56K line oversubscribed with users downloading MP3s, the search might take a while.

Active Directory speeds up searches and reduces WAN traffic by aggregating the contents of the various Domain naming contexts into a structure called a *Global Catalog*, or GC.

Global Catalog Structure

Because the GC contains a copy of every Domain naming context in a forest, it holds a copy of every object. In a big organization, this could make the database very large. It would not make sense to use separate domains to get separate naming contexts only to roll them up again into a GC that must be available at each location.

To reduce GC size and replication traffic, only a small number of commonly used attributes are stored in it. The list of attributes included in the GC is determined by the *Partial Attribute Set,* or PAS. The PAS contains only 200 or so out of the 1700 attributes in the Active Directory schema. Further, the partial naming contexts hosted by a GC server are read-only, so the GC server need only concern itself with replicating updates from a domain controller hosting a full copy of the naming context.

The Global Catalog is not a separate entity. A domain controller does not have a separate DIT file for a GC. Rather, the GC is really just a name for a domain controller function. The function is controlled by a flag in Active Directory. With the flag set to FALSE, a domain controller hosts only the standard three naming contexts—its own Domain NC, the Configuration NC, and the Schema NC. With the flag set to TRUE, the domain controller adds a partial replica for the other naming contexts in the forest. These naming contexts are stored in Ntds.dit right along with the three standard naming contexts.

Global Catalog Function

A Global Catalog server differentiates itself from a standard domain controller by listening for LDAP queries on a second port. The standard LDAP wire protocol uses TCP/UDP port 389. Global Catalog servers listen on this port but they also listen and respond on TCP/UDP port 3268. Here are the three possibilities for handling a search submitted to a GC on port 3268:

- If the GC server receives a search request involving an attribute or attributes in the Partial Attribute Set (PAS), it responds to the request with a dataset containing the requested objects and attributes.
- If the GC server receives a search request involving an attribute or attributes that are not in the PAS but the objects are in its own domain, it responds to the request with a dataset containing the requested objects and attributes. It obtains this information from the full copy of its Domain naming context.
- If the GC server receives a search request involving an attribute or attributes that are not in the PAS and for objects in another domain, it responds to the request with a referral to the other domain. The LDAP client follows up on the referral and completes the search by walking the tree.

Global Catalog servers play a crucial role in the operation of Active Directory in an enterprise. If you have a multidomain forest, it is very important that all users be able to reach a GC server. In the next few chapters, we'll come back to the operation of the GC and the role it plays in authentication and access control.

Global Catalogs and Naming Context Locations

Just as a recap, take a look at the forest in Figure 6.12. The forest contains six different domains. Let's say that a domain controller in the `Canada` domain is configured to be both a Global Catalog server and a DNS server for an Active Directory Integrated DNS zone. This server would host the following naming contexts:

- A full, read/write copy of `dc=Canada,dc=Company,dc=com`
- A full, read/write copy of `cn=Configuration,dc=Company,dc=com`
- A full, read-only copy of `cn=Schema,cn=Configuration,dc=Company,dc=com`
- A full, read/write copy of `cn=ForestDNSZones,dc=Company,dc=com`
- A full, read/write copy of `cn=DomainDNSZones,dc=Canada,dc=Company,dc=com`
- A partial, read-only copy of the remaining domain naming contexts

Active Directory Trust Relationships

Creating trees and forests requires a way to pipe secure transactions between the various domains. Like classic NT, this pipe is called a trust relationship.

Classic NT trusts have always reminded me of the Dr. Seuss story *The Zax*. In this story, a North-going Zax meets a South-going Zax in the prairies of Prax. They stand nose to nose, unwilling to move out of each other's way. One Zax says, "I'm a North-Going Zax and I always go north. Get out of my way, now, and let me go forth!" To which the other Zax replies, "You're in MY way! And I ask you to move, and let me go south in my south-going groove."

A classic one-way NT trust behaves exactly the same way. The rights implicit in the trust only flow in one direction and cannot flow from one domain to another. A big NT system based on interlocking trusts between many different resource and master domains can begin to look a little like a Dr. Seuss drawing, as well.

Transitive Kerberos Trusts

The picture gets a little neater with Active Directory. When two Active Directory domains trust each other, users and groups and computers from one domain can seamlessly access resources in the other domain. The trust flows both ways.

In addition, Active Directory trusts are transitive, meaning that they flow from one domain to another if domains are chained together. For example, if five Active Directory domains trust each other, users from one domain can access resources in any of the other four domains, assuming that they have been granted access permissions.

The magic that makes this work comes from the Kerberos authentication mechanism that underlies the trust relationships. See Chapter 12, "Managing Group Policies," for more information about how Kerberos works and how it supports transitive trusts.

Trust Types

Active Directory domains have several ways they can trust each other, or trust down-level NT domains, depending on the structure you want to build. There are six types of trust relationships, illustrated in Figure 6.13:

- **Parent/Child trusts.** This style of trust exists between two Active Directory domains that share a contiguous DNS namespace and belong to the same forest.
- **Tree Root trusts.** This style of trust exists between root domains in the same forest that do not share a common DNS namespace.
- **Shortcut trusts.** This style of trust exists between two domains in different trees within the same forest. It is used to expedite Kerberos transactions between the domains. With a shortcut trust in place, a client can obtain a Kerberos ticket directly from the trusted domain without walking the tree.

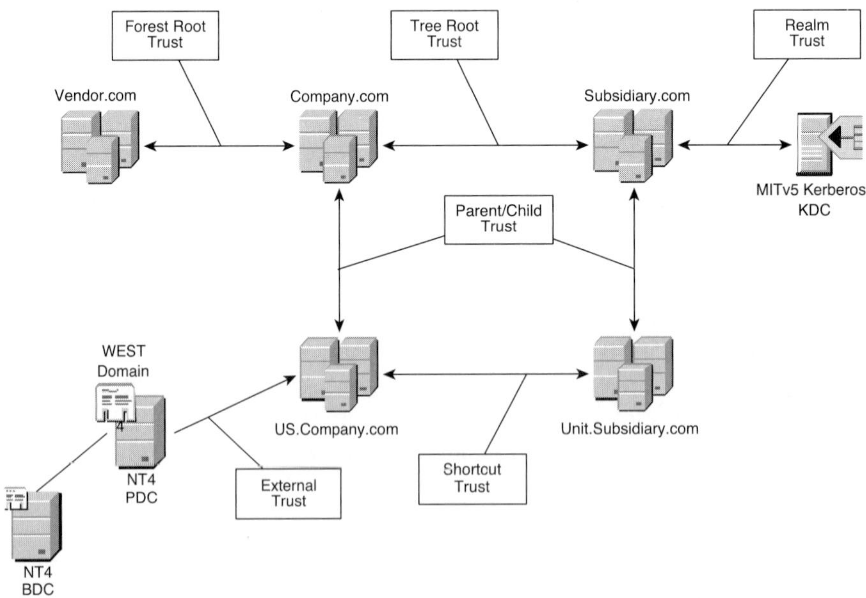

Figure 6.13 Diagram of various Active Directory trust options in Windows Server 2003.

- **External trusts.** This style of trust exists between an Active Directory domain and a downlevel NT4 domain. You can also create an external trust to a Samba domain. An External trust resembles a classic NT trust. It is one-way and non-transitive, meaning it cannot link an entire forest to a downlevel domain. LDAP searches and Kerberos authentications do not cross the trust boundary.
- **Kerberos realm trusts.** This style of trust exists between an Active Directory domain and an MIT v5 Kerberos realm. (MIT stands for Massachusetts Institute of Technology, where Kerberos originated.) The trust can be made transitive and two-way.
- **Forest trusts.** This style of trust exists between two Active Directory forests. It can be made transitive and two-way. The forests do not share a common Schema or Configuration naming context. This trust type forms a *federation* of forests. It is used to join two organizations that have existing Active Directory deployments and do not want to migrate accounts into a single forest. This trust type is a new feature in Windows Server 2003 and requires all domains in the forests and the forests themselves to be running at full Windows Server 2003 functionality (no legacy domain controllers.) You must be a member of the Incoming Forest Trust Builders group to create a Forest trust.

The new Forest Trust type should not be considered a panacea for organizational restructurings. Because the two forests do not share a common Configuration or Schema naming context, they cannot share applications that require a common configuration. A principal example is Exchange 2000, which places critical information into the Configuration naming context. A federation of forests cannot be placed into a single Exchange organization, so users cannot see a common Global Address List (GAL) or use common distribution lists.

Establishing Parent/Child and Tree Root Trusts

Parent/Child trusts and Tree Root trusts can only be formed when a domain is created. There are no tools for consolidating domains (grafting) or prying them apart (pruning) after the forest is in place. Every domain controller in a forest hosts an identical copy of the Schema naming context. There are no tools to coordinate and consolidate two sets of schemas.

I'm going to repeat this point in a different way because it's important to remember. New domains can only be added to a forest when the first domain controller is promoted in that domain. After you create a forest, the constituent domains cannot be removed without demoting every domain controller in the domain, essentially losing all Active Directory information for that domain.

External and Realm trusts do not rely on the Schema or Configuration naming contexts, so they can be created and broken while leaving the end-point domains intact. If you break the trust, users in the trusted domain lose access to resources in the other domains. If you make the trust again, the users regain access.

Establishing Forest Trusts

Forest trusts are a bit more complex to configure than the standard Windows 2000 trust types. Although the trust itself is two-way and transitive, you can select the domains in each forest that participate in the trust. For example, consider the diagram in Figure 6.14. This diagram shows two forests in a federation connected by a Forest trust. Each forest has domains connected by Parent/Child trusts.

In a fully transitive configuration, users in the `US.Company.com` and `Canada.Company.com` domains would be able to access resources in the `PacRim.Subsidiary.com` and `Europe.Subsidiary.com` domains and vice-versa. However, you may not want to enable fully transitive resource access. Using the Properties window for the trust, you can select which domains will participate in the Forest trust and in which direction the trust will be effective.

Using this feature, you can target trusts in the federation. For example, you can configure the Forest trust so that users in `PacRim.Subsidiary.com` can access resources in `US.Company.com` but not in `Canada.Company.com`.

You must be a member of the Incoming Forest Trust Builders group to create a Forest trust to another domain. This new Builtin group permits a root domain administrator to grant permissions for an administrator in another root domain to create a trust without giving that administrator full domain administrative privileges.

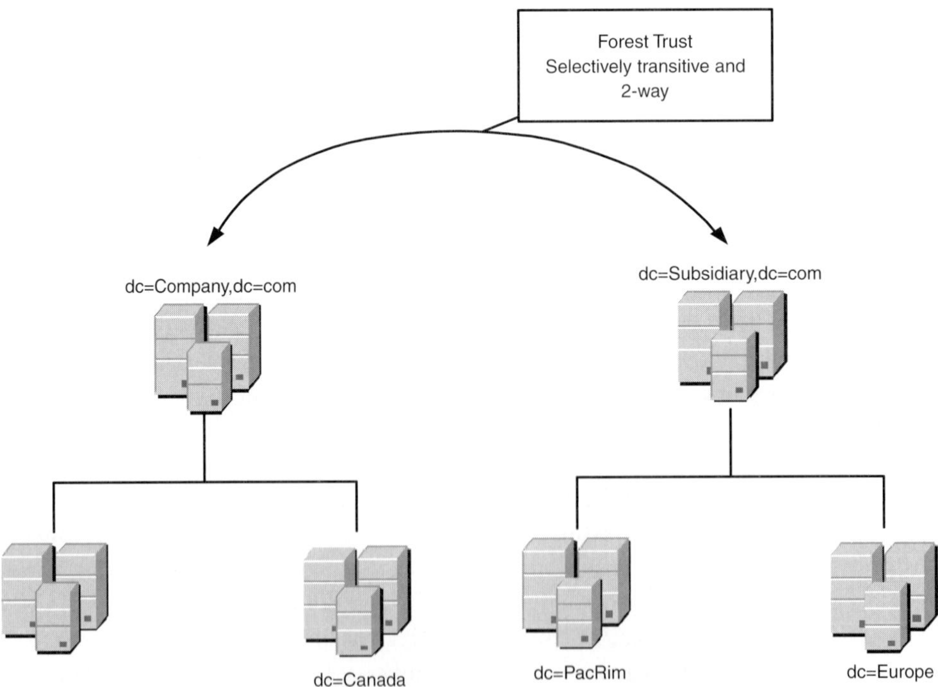

Figure 6.14 Federation of two Active Directory forests.

Object Migration Between Domains and Forests

You cannot build or break Parent/Child and Tree Root trusts after they are formed, so the only way to change your forest structure is to migrate objects between domains. Microsoft provides a utility for performing these object migrations called the *Active Directory Migration Tool*, or ADMT.

Moving user, computer, and group accounts between domains involves issues of security and accessibility. Both classic NT and modern Windows servers use Security IDs (SIDs) to identify users. These SIDs are placed on access control lists (ACLs) to control access to resources. ADMT performs a complex set of functions designed to preserve the original SIDs so that users retain access to their resources. The new version in Windows Server 2003 also preserves passwords and the original user profiles. There are a variety of third-party tools that can help with object migration between domains and forests. See Chapter 9, "Deploying Windows Server 2003 Domains," for details.

Sysvol

There's more to being a domain controller than simply hosting the Active Directory database. The domain controller is also responsible for distributing the files associated with group policies. Group policies are used to centrally manage member servers, desktops, and users. They are covered in detail in Chapter 12, "Managing Group Policies."

Active Directory domain controllers must also support downlevel clients by providing a place to obtain classic scripts and system policies contained in Config.pol or Ntconfig.pol files. In an NT domain, these files are stored in the Netlogon share, physically located at `C:\Winnt\System32\Repl\Import\Scripts`.

Sysvol Files

To meet its dual responsibilities of supporting modern group policies and classic system policies and scripts, Active Directory domain controllers host a special folder called Sysvol. The location of the folder is determined during Dcpromo. Sysvol must be on an NTFS volume because folders within Sysvol use reparse points, which are only supported by NTFS.

Sysvol contains a folder with the name `Domain` that holds the group policy files in a folder called `Policies` and classic scripts in a folder called `Scripts`. The `Scripts` folder is shared as Netlogon to support downlevel clients. Modern scripts that are distributed as part of group policies are stored as part of a particular group policy under the `Policies` folder.

Clients access Sysvol via a special *fault tolerant share* with the Universal Naming Convention (UNC) path of `\\`*<domain_name>*`\Sysvol`. For example, you can do a directory of `\\company.com\Sysvol` from any client in the `Company.com` domain. Accessing fault tolerant shares requires that the Dfsclient service be running on the client.

File Replication and Sysvol

The contents of Sysvol are replicated to every domain controller in a domain. It is important that the contents stay in sync. Otherwise, users will get different group policies, system policies, and classic scripts when they log on to different domain controllers.

A service called the *File Replication Service*, or FRS, is responsible for synchronizing the contents of Sysvol between domain controllers. (The actual service name is Ntfrs, which you may see in Event log entries.) FRS replicates an entire file when any changes are made to the file. To prevent race conditions that could occur if the file were locked, the file is first copied to a `Staging` folder then replicated to the other domain controllers.

Locating Active Directory Services

Active Directory clients use DNS to locate domain controllers. They do this by querying for Service Locator (SRV) records that point at LDAP, Kerberos, and Global Catalog ports on the servers. Refer to RFC 2052, "A DNS RR for Specifying the Location of Services." (RR stands for Resource Record.)

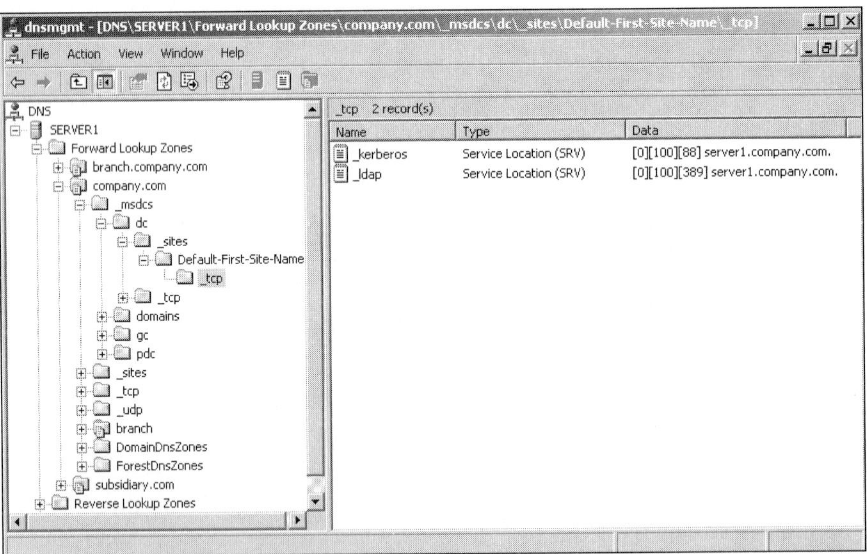

Figure 6.15 DNS console showing SRV records for the `Company.com` domain.

SRV Records for Active Directory

Figure 6.15 shows a DNS zone table for the Company.com domain. The zone table contains the SRV records registered by the first domain controller in a Windows Server 2003 domain.

Here are the SRV records in a standard zone table format:

```
_kerberos._tcp.phoenix._sites.dc._msdcs       600     SRV     0 100 88
➥dc-01.company.com._
 kerberos._tcp.phoenix._sites                 600     SRV     0 100 88
➥dc-01.company.com.
_kerberos._tcp.dc._msdcs                      600     SRV     0 100 88
➥dc-01.company.com.
_kerberos._tcp                                600     SRV     0 100 88
➥dc-01.company.com.
_kerberos._udp                                600     SRV     0 100 88
➥dc-01.company.com.
_kpasswd._tcp                                 600     SRV     0 100 464
➥dc-01.company.com.
_kpasswd._udp                                 600     SRV     0 100 464
➥dc-01.company.com.
_ldap._tcp.phoenix._sites.gc._msdcs           600     SRV     0 100 3268
➥dc-01.company.com.
_gc._tcp.phoenix._sites                       600     SRV     0 100 3268
➥dc-01.company.com.
_ldap._tcp.gc._msdcs                          600     SRV     0 100 3268
➥dc-01.company.com.
_gc._tcp                                      600     SRV     0 100 3268
➥dc-01.company.com.
_ldap._tcp.phoenix._sites.dc._msdcs           600     SRV     0 100 389
➥dc-01.company.com.
_ldap._tcp.phoenix._sites                     600     SRV     0 100 389
➥dc-01.company.com._
 ldap._tcp.dc._msdcs                          600     SRV     0 100 389
➥dc-01.company.com.
ldap._tcp.{guid of domain}.domains._msdcs     600     SRV     0 100 389
➥dc-01.company.com.
_ldap._tcp                                    600     SRV     0 100 389
➥dc-01.company.com.
_ldap._tcp.pdc._msdcs                         600     SRV     0 100 389
➥dc-01.company.com.
 dc-01                                        1200    A     10.1.1.1
 gc._msdcs                                    600     A     10.1.1.1
 {GUID of DC invocation}._msdcs                  600     CNAME
➥dc-01.company.com.
```

Format of SRV Record Names

The leading underscores in SRV record names are there to avoid collision with other records by the same name. The naming format is specified in RFC 2052, "SRV Record Format and Use."

Windows DNS reverses the SRV record names to display them as a hierarchy of folders. Here are the functions of the SRV records based on their groupings in the DNS console:

- **_MSDCS.** This heading collects SRV records based on their status as domain controllers, domain invocations, global catalog servers, and primary domain controllers. Domain controllers and global catalog servers are broken down by site. This tells Active Directory clients very quickly where to find local services. Domain invocations support replication. Each domain controller gets a GUID that it uses when invoking replication. The PDC entry contains the SRV record for the domain controller assigned to be the PDC Emulator, a domain controller that acts as the PDC to downlevel NT BDCs.
- **_SITES.** A site represents an area of high-speed connectivity associated with one or more distinct IP subnets. By indexing domain controllers based on their site affiliation, clients can look in _SITES to find local services rather than sending their LDAP lookups across the WAN. Standard LDAP queries use port 389. Global Catalog queries use port 3268.
- **_TCP.** This heading collects all domain controllers in the DNS zone. The _TCP grouping acts as a catchall for clients that cannot find their specific site or that need to find a domain controller elsewhere in the network if none of those with local SRV records respond.
- **_UDP.** Kerberos v5 permits clients to use connectionless services to get tickets and change passwords. This is done via UDP ports that correspond to the TCP ports for the same services, UDP port 88 for ticketing and UDP 464 for password changes.

Operational Description of SRV Record Queries

When a user initiates a process that requires an Active Directory lookup, the AD client process sends a query to DNS for SRV records corresponding to server advertising LDAP ports. The first query is for SRV records in the client's local site. This ensures that LDAP searches do not go to domain controllers elsewhere in the WAN. If there are no domain controllers in the client's site, it asks for all SRV records regardless of site.

Registry Tip: Site Name Cache

Clients cache their site information in the following Registry location:

```
Key:    HKLM | System | CurrentControlSet | Services | Netlogon | Parameters
Value:  DynamicSiteName
Data:   Flat name of the last domain controller authenticating the client—
for example, dc-01
```

DNS returns all SRV records that meet the query conditions. If there are five domain controllers in a site, DNS returns five SRV records accompanied by the Host record containing the IP address of the server in each SRV record. This is different than standard DNS operation, where it would normally return a single record in a round-robin selection process.

When the client receives the SRV records, it performs a quick LDAP ping to all of them by sending out a bind query to UDP port 389. The first domain controller to respond is selected as the primary LDAP server by the client. Here are details of the transaction:

1. When the operating system loads, the network client locates a domain controller by querying DNS for SRV records. The client in the diagram sends a query for `_kerberos._tcp.Phoenix._sites.dc._msdcs.Company.com`. Notice that the scope of this query is limited to domain controllers from the same site and domain. The client stores the site name in the Registry under `HKLM | System | CurrentControlSet | Services | Netlogon | Parameters | DynamicSiteName`.
2. When the DNS server receives this query, it returns all SRV records that meet the query criteria, sorting them by priority and weight.
3. When the network client receives the SRV records, it fires off an LDAP ping (a single UDP packet) over port 389 to every domain controller on the list. It sends these pings in rapid succession, every one-tenth of a second.
4. When a domain controller gets the LDAP ping, it returns an LDAP response. The client designates the first domain controller to respond as the logon server and proceeds to authenticate via Kerberos.

At this point, the client behaves like a lonely kid who has finally found a friend. It hounds the domain controller with all subsequent LDAP requests, Kerberos authentication requests, and group policy downloads.

You can determine the identity of the domain controller that authenticated a member Windows Server 2003 using the SYSTEMINFO utility. Here is a partial listing showing the logon server information:

```
Virtual Memory: Max Size:  1,733 MB
Virtual Memory: Available: 1,344 MB
Virtual Memory: In Use:    389 MB
Page File Location(s):     C:\pagefile.sys
Domain:                    company.com
Logon Server:              \\DC01.company.com
Hotfix(s):                   0 Hotfix(s) Installed
```

If the client is in a forest, the domain controllers generate referrals to other domains. Clients use SRV records for those domains to locate domain controllers that host copies of the target Domain naming contexts.

Site Coverage

You cannot configure a preferred domain controller for a client. If you have a large LAN and you want to compartmentalize your clients based on their area of a campus LAN or MAN (metropolitan area network), you must structure your replication topology around multiple sites. This is true even if your WAN interties meet the requirements for a high-speed connection that would not normally require separate sites.

Domain controllers automatically register their SRV records using their site name. They also return referrals to clients to ensure that clients use a local domain controller for authentication and LDAP queries. This "localization" feature is possible because each site is associated with one or more IP networks connected by Site Links. A domain controller can read the IP address of a client and determine the site it should designate when making DNS requests for SRV records.

Here's how this works. Let's say that the client is a laptop. The user shuts down the laptop, flies to Houston, and connects to the network again:

1. The client gets a local address from Dynamic Host Configuration Protocol (DHCP). It remembers that it is in the Phoenix site and queries DNS for domain controllers in that site.
2. DNS returns the requested SRV records and the client sends LDAP pings to the domain controllers in Phoenix.
3. A domain controller in Phoenix examines the client's IP address and sees that the client is in the Houston site. It knows this by comparing the IP address to the IP Subnet objects in Active Directory.
4. The domain controller responds with a referral telling the client to query DNS for the Houston site.
5. The client responds by repeating the DNS query for SRV records from the Houston site. In this way, the client automatically adjusts to changes in location.

Clients cache their site information in the following Registry location:

```
Key:   HKLM | System | CurrentControlSet | Services | Netlogon | Parameters
Value: DynamicSiteName
Data:  Flat name of domain controller authenticating the client—for example,
dc1
```

This site localization feature herds clients toward local domain controllers for authentication and LDAP queries. If you have a location that does not have a domain controller, you should still create a site for the location. This populates DNS with SRV records for the next site upstream so that clients authenticate at the closest domain controllers.

Compatibility Settings

For backward compatibility, certain Active Directory features are disabled while domain controllers running something other than Windows Server 2003 are in operation.

A Windows Server 2003 domain faces two compatibility challenges (at least with other Windows servers):

- Operation with downlevel NT domain controllers
- Operation with Windows 2000 domain controllers

Each of these challenges requires a different compatibility setting.

Operation with Downlevel NT Domain Controllers

Active Directory domain controllers can coexist with NT4 Domain Controllers in the same domain. This is called *Windows 2000 Mixed*. In Mixed, a Windows Server 2003 domain controller designated as the PDC Emulator uses classic LMRepl (LanMan Replication) to deliver selected Active Directory updates to downlevel BDCs.

In Mixed, certain advanced features in Active Directory are disabled because they are incompatible with classic NT4. Here is a list:

- **Universal groups.** This group type can have members from any domain in a forest and can be placed on access control lists anywhere in a forest.
- **Global group nesting.** In Native, Global groups from different domains can be nested together and nested into Universal groups.
- **Local access to Domain Local groups.** In Native, Domain Local groups from Active Directory can be placed on access control lists on member servers and desktops.
- **Downlevel clients can participate in transitive authentication.** After a domain is running in Native, the domain controllers can proxy NTLM authentication requests from downlevel clients to give them access to domains that they would not be able to access in a standard NT master/resource domain structure.

After you have upgraded or decommissioned all NT4 BDCs, you can get these advanced features by shifting the domain to *Windows 2000 Native*. This stops replication from the PDC Emulator to any remaining NT4 BDCs. After a domain has been shifted to Windows 2000 Native, it cannot be shifted back to Windows 2000 Mixed.

Functional Levels

Several new Windows Server 2003 features are incompatible with Windows 2000. Here is a quick list:

- The calculations for determining replication topology between sites have been streamlined. This corrects a problem where large organizations with hundreds of sites might experience replication failure because the topology calculations could not be completed in the time allotted to them.
- Group members are now replicated as discrete entities instead of replicating the entire group membership list as a single unit. This corrects a problem where membership changes made to the same group on different domain controllers in the same replication interval would overwrite each other.
- A new trust type has been added to simplify transitive trust relationships between domains that are not in the same forest.
- Support has been added for the inetOrgPerson object class, which is used on other commercial LDAP directory services to represent users. inetOrgPerson objects can be given a SID and used as security principals for logon and put on access control lists.
- Domain controllers can be renamed in a Windows Server 2003 domain. Domains themselves can be renamed in a Windows Server 2003 forest. This permits restructuring a forest by changing parent/child relationships between domains.
- Schema objects can be declared defunct so that the parameters can be reused in another Schema object. A Schema object cannot be deleted nor can the Common Name (CN) be changed.
- Changes made to elements of the Global Catalog, such as adding an attribute to the GC or taking one away, do not now require a full rebuild and replication of the GC.

As long as Windows Server 2003 domain controllers coexist with Windows 2000 Domain Controllers, these features are disabled. When all Windows 2000 Domain Controllers have been upgraded to Windows Server 2003 or demoted to standard servers, the domains and the forest can be shifted to full Windows Server 2003 functionality. This is a one-time operation and cannot be reversed. See Chapter 9, "Deploying Windows Server 2003 Domains," for the prerequisites and steps to change functional levels.

Client Compatibility

Windows Server 2003 Active Directory domains are compatible with any and all Windows clients as well as the Microsoft DOS client and the most current versions of Samba.

The opposite is also true. Windows Server 2003 and XP can operate in any Windows domain environment: classic workgroups, classic NT, Windows 2000 Active Directory, and of course, Windows Server 2003 Active Directory. (The sole exception is XP Home Edition, which cannot join a domain of any form.)

One subtle problem that arose in Windows 2000 was fixed in Windows Server 2003 and in Windows 2000 SP2. When Kerberos-based Windows clients operate in downlevel domains, they happily use NTLM Challenge-Response for their authentication. This means they can log on to classic backup domain controllers (BDCs) and participate in pass-through authentication.

Piling On

When the domain is upgraded to Active Directory, however, a Kerberos-based client changes a flag in its security database to disable NTLM Challenge-Response and use only Kerberos. This means that if you have deployed a few thousand Windows 2000 or XP desktops in your NT domain, as soon as you upgrade the PDC, all those desktops will scurry to that one machine to authenticate. Microsoft calls this behavior "piling on."

In addition, after a client has authenticated with an Active Directory domain controller, it behaves like a teenager who has finally gotten up the gumption and money to move out of the house. It sets a flag in its local security database and thereafter will only authenticate with Active Directory domain controllers. If only classic BDCs are available, the client logs users on using cached credentials rather than deign to use a classic BDC. This can cause operational difficulties if you have large numbers of desktops and member servers that have already been upgraded to Windows 2000 or XP or Windows Server 2003 when you do the upgrade of the PDC. If the clients are in Guam and your PDC is in Galveston, the morning logons in Guam are going to be exceedingly slow.

To avoid this problem, Windows Server 2003 includes a feature that keeps an Active Directory domain controller pretending that it is still a downlevel domain controller to its clients. After you have installed enough Windows Server 2003 Domain Controllers to handle the logon requests, you can pull up the curtain and turn on the footlights and let the clients switch to Kerberos authentication.

The feature consists of a Registry entry that makes a newly promoted Windows Server 2003 domain controller pretend to be classic NT4 domain controller. Here is the entry:

```
Key:    HKLM | System | CurrentControlSet | Services | Netlogon | Parameters
Value:  NT4Emulator
Data:    1 (REG_DWORD)
```

It is important that you put this entry in place on all NT domain controllers *before* you upgrade them. The domain controller will still register its SRV records, but when the modern Windows clients go to authenticate, the domain controller will only respond with an NTLM authentication sequence.

Special NT4 Emulator Considerations

During the time that you have the `NT4Emulator` switch in place, your XP and Windows 2000 desktops will continue to use NTLMv2 authentication rather than Kerberos. This imposes the following limitations:

- Clients do not download or implement group policies.
- You cannot use Active Directory management tools such as AD Users and Computers or AD Sites and Services from the client because it has not authenticated using Kerberos and therefore cannot gain LDAP access to Active Directory.
- You cannot promote a member server to a domain controller because it cannot make LDAP connection to an existing domain controller.
- If the `NT4Emulator` switch is set on domain controllers in the root domain of the forest, you cannot create a new domain in the forest because the new domain controller cannot make LDAP connection to an existing domain controller in the root domain.

You can avoid these limitations on a case-by-case basis by permitting the client to ignore the `NT4Emulator` behavior of a domain controller and to log on using Kerberos. Do this by putting an entry into the Registry at the client:

```
Key:    HKLM | System | CurrentControlSet | Services | Netlogon | Parameters
Value:  NeutralizeNT4Emulator
Data:    1 (REG_DWORD)
```

After putting this entry in place, log off and back on again. The desktop finds the Windows Server 2003 domain controller and uses Kerberos to authenticate. You can verify that this occurs using the Kerbtray utility from the Resource Kit.

When you have sufficient Windows Server 2003 domain controllers deployed to handle the expected volume of Kerberos authentications and group policy deliveries, flip the `NT4Emulator` switch to 0 in the Registry of each domain controller and restart it. This enables the domain controller to authenticate using Kerberos as well as NTLMv2. Be sure you flip the switch on all domain controllers to avoid confusion.

Active Directory Namespace Highlights

Here is a summary of the key points to remember about how the Active Directory namespace is structured. These points become critical design elements when the time comes to deploy Active Directory in your organization:

- The Active Directory database is divided into separate replication units called naming contexts. There are four types of naming contexts: Domains, Configuration, Schema, and Application.
- Active Directory domains form separate security and management units as well as separate naming contexts.

- Every domain controller in a forest has a replica of the Configuration and Schema naming context. This ensures that the domain controllers share the same knowledge about Active Directory topology, operation, and object management.
- Separate Active Directory domains can be connected together into a common security structure. If the domains share a contiguous DNS namespace, they form a tree. If they do not share a contiguous namespace, they form a forest.
- Active Directory uses trust relationships between domains to form trees, forests, and secure connections to external domains, forests, and MIT Kerberos realms. A trust can also be used to create a shortcut between domains in the same forest.
- Trust relationships between Kerberos-based Windows domains can be made transitive and two-way. Trusts to downlevel domains are one-way and non-transitive.
- Active Directory improves the performance of deep LDAP searches (searches that include multiple domains) by aggregating a partial replica of all Domain naming contexts into a Global Catalog. Any domain controller can host a copy of the GC.
- Active Directory clients use SRV records in DNS to locate Active Directory services on domain controllers. Clients preferentially use domain controllers from their local network to reduce WAN traffic and improve performance.
- Windows Server 2003 maintains backward compatibility to both classic NT4 domains and Windows 2000 domains.
- All domains in a forest and the forest itself must be shifted to Windows Server 2003 Functional Level to get access to all new Active Directory features.

Active Directory Schema

When discussing directory service structure and operation up to this point, I've used general terms that are applicable to just about any LDAP implementation. It's now time to spend a while looking at specific features in Active Directory. You may find this information to be a little too much detail for helping you manage day-to-day operations in Windows Server 2003. However, it's good to know some of the important functional and operational details of the directory service to help you create reliable domain designs and to troubleshoot problems that arise.

As a quick review, the object-oriented LDAP database that comprises Active Directory is structured around a set of object classes and their associated attributes. Individual objects are instances of specific object classes. The schema defines the available object classes, their associated attributes, the data types and permitted ranges for those attributes, and the rules for arranging and managing objects within the Active Directory database.

Schema Functional Operation

To visualize how the schema works, consider a simple, paper-based directory. Every month or so I get a catalog from Land's End, the clothing retailer. This catalog is a database of sorts, similar to a directory service except that it guides the user to a garment instead of a network entity. Consider this:

- The schema for this directory defines a set of object classes with the scope "Garments Sold by Land's End." These classes represent objects of interest to garment purchasers, such as Sweaters, Suits, Blazers, Accessories, and so forth.
- The schema also defines the available attributes that can be associated with the object classes, such as Size, Color, Inseam-Length, and Price, along with more subtle attributes specific to the directory itself, such as Picture-Of-Garment.
- The schema has *content rules* that define what attributes can be associated with a class. Some attributes, like Size and Color, might be associated with nearly every class. An attribute like Inseam-Length, however, might only be associated with classes like Slacks and Jeans, not Sport-Coats or Shoes.
- Some garment classes have attributes that are nearly identical. For example, the attributes that define the Polo-Shirts class differ only slightly from the attributes that define the Sport-Shirts class. The Polo-Shirts class derives from the Sport-Shirts class and inherits the attributes associated with its parent. The new attributes are then just tacked on to the new class.
- Class inheritance makes it important to have *structure rules* that keep the directory aligned with the real world. For example, a structure rule prevents placing an object from the Bathrobe class under a container from the Shoe class.
- A particular garment is an *instance* of its garment class. For example, an instance of the Blazer class would be the solid red blazer with green plaid lining that I gave my brother for Christmas last year. (The snide thank you note I received in return came from the Hallmark directory service as an instance of the Ungrateful-Sibling class.)
- The Land's End schema has *syntax rules* that define the values that can be associated with an attribute. For example, the Size attribute must have whole integer values while the Shoe-Size attribute can have real number (fractional) values.
- Because the garment classes and their attributes can change, the Land's End directory is *extensible*. For example, a new attribute called Number-Of-Sleeve-Buttons can be added and the Blazers class modified to include that attribute.
- For flexibility, certain special object classes can be *dynamically assigned* to a specific object. This makes it possible to create special bundles of attributes for a certain object like a Rad-Phat T-shirt object without altering all other instances of the T-shirt class.

I know this was a long example, so here are the key terms and concepts:

- **Object Classes.** Define the objects that can appear in Active Directory and their associated attributes.
- **Class Derivations.** Define a method for building new object classes out of existing object classes.
- **Object Attributes.** Define the available attributes. This includes extended attributes that govern actions that can be taken on object classes.
- **Structure Rules.** Determine possible tree arrangements.
- **Syntax Rules.** Determine the type of value an attribute is capable of storing.
- **Content Rules.** Determine the attributes that can be associated with a given class.
- **Extensible schema.** Additions can be made to the list of available classes and attributes.
- **Dynamic class assignments.** Certain classes can be dynamically assigned to a specific object rather than an entire class of objects.

Object Classes and Class Derivations

An object class is nothing more than a bundle of attributes with a name. The User class, for example, has certain attributes that, taken together, make it distinct from the Organizational-Unit class or the Server class. The X.500/9594 standard as modified by RFC 2256, "A Summary of the X.500(96) User Schema for use with LDAPv3," defines 21 classes and 55 attributes in a standard LDAP directory schema.

The Active Directory schema extends this list quite a bit, out to nearly 200 classes and just under 1700 attributes. If you want a complete list, check out the Windows Server 2003 Platform SDK or look at the MSDN web site, `msdn.microsoft.com`.

Standard LDAP Classes and Attributes in Active Directory

The Active Directory schema includes all RFC 2256 classes, except for Alias and Strong-Authentication-User, and all attributes, except for Aliased-Object-Name. The exclusion of Alias was deliberate. Aliases are a notorious source of performance difficulties and integrity problems in directory services. In addition, most of the object classes that would normally be given aliases are required to have unique names in Active Directory. This includes Users, Computers, and Groups.

Windows .NET includes the inetOrgPerson class as defined in RFC 2798, "Definition of the inetOrgPerson Object Class." This makes Active Directory more compatible with Netscape Directory Services and Novell Directory Services, both of which derive their User class from inetOrgPerson.

Schema Rules

It's not enough to define schema components in terms of objects, actions, and relationships. Laws and customs are also necessary to avoid anarchy. These take the form of *schema rules*. Directory service designers build certain rules into the schema that determine how classes and attributes are used, what kind of values they can have, and what relationship they have to each other. These rules fall into three categories:

- Structure Rules
- Content Rules
- Syntax Rules

Structure Rules

Frank Lloyd Wright established the design paradigm for twentieth century architecture by declaring that form should always follow function. He was a building architect rather than directory services architect, of course, but Active Directory is as much of a monument to form and function as a prairie house, and it is the *structure rules* that accomplish this.

There is really only one structure rule in Active Directory: Each object class has only certain classes that can be directly above it, called *Possible Superiors*. This structure rule is very important because classes inherit attributes from their parents. Structure rules prevent putting a User class object under a totally unrelated container class, like IPSEC-Base or NTDS Settings.

Content Rules

Every object class has certain attributes with values that cannot be left blank when an object is instantiated. These are called *must-contain attributes*. For example, every instance of the User class must have a value for the Common-Name attribute. Other attributes are optional and are designated *may-contain attributes*.

An important design principle of Active Directory is that only attributes with values are stored in the database. This greatly reduces the size and complexity of the database. Because attributes can be added after an object is created and then later removed if they are set to null, the database engine must constantly pack and repack the data. This is done by a garbage collection service that runs every 12 hours.

Syntax Rules

Attributes store data. Data must have a data type to define the storage requirements. Real numbers have a different form from integers, which are different from long integers, which are different from character strings.

An attribute can have only one data type. It cannot hold a string when associated with one object class and an integer when associated with another. The syntax rules in the schema define the permissible values types and ranges for the attributes.

Schema Definition Objects

Individual objects are always instances of an object class. Achieving this design principle involves using a template that defines the attributes, schema rules, and class hierarchy for the objects within an object class. The same applies for attributes, which require a template to define the syntax rules. This suite of templates makes up the schema definitions for a directory service information store.

Some directory services put the schema definitions into a separate file that is loaded at boot time or whenever the schema requires changing. In contrast, the Active Directory schema is self-referential. That is to say, all class definitions, attribute definitions, and schema rules are part of the schema itself. An appropriate title for an Active Directory schema self-help book would be *Everything I Need to Know I Learned from Myself.*

The Active Directory schema contains two schema object classes, ClassSchema and AttributeSchema. Objects derived from these classes act like patterns in a lathe to turn out other objects. The schema objects are stored in the directory in the `cn=Schema,cn=Configuration,dc=<domain_name>,dc=<domain_root>` container.

In addition to ClassSchema and ClassAttribute classes, the Schema container holds a class called SubSchema with one instance, an object called Aggregate. The distinguished name of this object is `cn=aggregate,cn=schema,cn=configuration,dc=company,dc=com`. The purpose of Aggregate is to provide a single point for LDAP clients to discover information about the Active Directory schema. Without this object, clients would be forced to perform expensive scans of the entire Schema container.

Identifying Objects

We've completed the overview of the schema structure, function, and rules. Before moving forward, let's look at how Active Directory uniquely identifies objects. This information is crucial to understanding the more advanced Active Directory tools. Here is a brief attribute listing for a sample User object made using the LDIFDE utility. The unique identifiers are highlighted:

```
C:\>ldifde -d cn=bgates,cn=users,dc=dotnet,dc=com -f con
Connecting to "DC01.Company.com"
Logging in as current user using SSPI
Exporting directory to file con
Searching for entries...
Writing out entries.dn: CN=bgates,CN=Users,DC=dotnet,DC=com
changetype: add
objectClass: top
objectClass: person
objectClass: organizationalPerson
objectClass: user
cn: bgates
distinguishedName: CN=bgates,CN=Users,DC=dotnet,DC=com
instanceType: 4
whenCreated: 20020812134034.0Z
```

```
whenChanged: 20020812134034.0Z
uSNCreated: 13772
uSNChanged: 13774
name: bgates
objectGUID:: 7swJ8PXwqkWu8N2Qv+jQ+Q==
userAccountControl: 512
badPwdCount: 0
codePage: 0
countryCode: 0
badPasswordTime: 0
lastLogoff: 0
lastLogon: 0
pwdLastSet: 126736332347481024
primaryGroupID: 513
objectSid:: AQUAAAAAAAUVAAAAdbl1VBUlr0cWwOoyVQQAAA==
accountExpires: 0
logonCount: 0
sAMAccountName: bgates
userPrincipalName: bgates@dotnet.com
sAMAccountType: 805306368
objectCategory: CN=Person,CN=Schema,CN=Configuration,DC=dotnet,DC=com
```

Distinguished Name

Because LDAP uses an object-oriented database, it is important that each object has a unique path in the namespace, similar to the way that a filename and path must be unique in a file system.

The Distinguished Name (DN) attribute of an object defines the LDAP path all the way to the root of the namespace; therefore, the DN must be unique. If you move an object to a different container in Active Directory, in reality, you are simply changing the DN.

Globally Unique Identifier (GUID)

In classic Exchange, Microsoft used the DN as the unique database row identifier for objects in the directory service store. This unfortunate engineering decision created a configuration problem for Exchange. When an object is moved, its DN changes, but a unique row identifier in a database cannot ever change. For this reason, in Exchange 5.5 and earlier, mailbox recipients cannot be moved but must be freshly created and then linked to a User account in the SAM.

To avoid that problem in Active Directory, Microsoft used a different unique row identifier called the *Globally Unique Identifier*, or GUID . A GUID is created using an algorithm that virtually guarantees its uniqueness within a system.

Using a GUID permits you to move objects at will between containers in Active Directory without changing the unique row numbers for the objects, thereby maintaining internal referential integrity in the database. Keep this behavior in mind, because you'll see it at work when we discuss the role of the Infrastructure Master in keeping track of group members from other domains.

Other Uses for GUIDs

Microsoft uses the GUID algorithm in a variety of different circumstances. You will see them in designators used to identify COM objects and OLE registrations. Group policies use the GUID algorithm to create a unique folder name for each policy. The operating system identifies hardware using GUIDs during Plug-and-Play enumeration. GUIDs also go by the names *Universally Unique Identifier* (UUID) and *Class ID* (CLSID).

Security Identifier (SID)

Three classes of Active Director objects can be placed on the access control lists (ACLs) used to protect security objects. These object classes are User, Computer, and Group. Together, they are termed *security principals*.

A security principal is assigned a unique number called a *Security Identifier*, or SID. This is exactly the same SID used by NT to identify users, groups, and computers. A SID for a security principal is made up of the SID of the security principal's domain and a unique suffix, called a Relative ID, or RID. The series of RIDs for security principals that can be created by an administrator start at decimal 1000. For example, the first User account created following the creation of a domain would be given RID 1000. The next object, call it a group, would be RID 1001, and so forth.

The combination of a domain SID and a RID form a unique number within a domain and within a forest. The pool of RIDs is maintained by a specially designated Windows Server 2003 domain controller called a RID Master.

SAM Account Name

In an NT domain, every object in the SAM must have a unique name. This is true for computers, users, and groups. A unique name guarantees that the object will have a unique NetBIOS presence in the network as well as a one-to-one correspondence between the logon name (in the case of users and computers) and the SID used to control resource access.

The same restriction is left in place in Windows 2000 and Windows Server 2003. Every user, computer, and group in a domain must have a unique name. This attribute is called `SAMAccountName`, although you might hear it called *logon name* or *flat name*. When you create a new security principal, regardless of the container where you place the object, it must have a unique flat name in the domain.

User Principal Name (UPN) and Service Principal Name (SPN)

Just as unique flat names identify security principals in NetBIOS, User Principal Names (UPNs) identify security principals within the hierarchical LDAP namespace in Active Directory. A UPN takes the form `User@Company.com`.

Unique UPNs ensure that users can log on with their UPN rather than the classic *`domain\username`* construct. The Global Catalog is used to "crack" the UPN into its constituent parts.

To assure uniqueness, when a security principal is created, the system refers to the Global Catalog to verify that the UPN has not already been used. If a GC server is not available, the system displays an error message prompting the administrator to wait until a GC is available so that uniqueness can be verified.

In a Parent/Child trust configuration, the UPN suffix of the root domain is assigned to every security principal. In a Tree Root trust configuration, you must manually assign a common UPN suffix. This is done using the Properties window of the domain tree in the AD Domains and Trusts console.

Object Identifier (OID)

In addition to the attributes that assure uniqueness of a particular object, Active Directory needs a way to assure that objects of the same class all come from the same Schema object. This is done by assigning a unique Object Identifier, or *Object Identifier* (OID) to each object in the Schema naming context. ISO defines the structure and distribution of OIDs in `ISO/IEC 8824:1990`, "Information Technology—Open Systems Interconnection—Specification of Abstract Syntax Notation One (ASN.1)."

ASN.1 provides a mechanism for standards bodies in various countries to enumerate standard data items so that they do not conflict with one other. ASN.1 governs more than just directory services classes and attributes. For example, OIDs are used extensively in SNMP to build hierarchies of Management Information Base (MIB) numbers. They are also assigned to many items associated with the Internet. If you're interested in the list of organizations that assign OID numbers and their hierarchy, it is available at `ftp.isi.edu/in-notes/iana/assignments/enterprise-numbers`.

If you ever need to create a new attribute or object class in Active Directory, you must have a unique OID. There are a couple of ways to get one. The first is to apply to ANSI for your own numerical series. This costs a few thousand dollars and takes a while to process. The other is to use the OIDGEN utility from the Resource Kit. This will generate a Class and an Attribute OID out of Microsoft's address space. The disadvantage to using OIDGEN is that the resultant number is very, very, very long. Here is an example:

```
C:\>oidgen
Attribute Base OID:
1.2.840.113556.1.4.7000.233.180672.443844.62.26102.2020485.1873967.207938
    Class Base OID:
1.2.840.113556.1.5.7000.111.180672.443844.62.199519.642990.1996505.1182366
```

Finding OID Hierarchy Information

Many thanks to Harald Alvestrand, who made good use of a long winter in Trondheim, Norway, to build a hyperlinked tree showing many of the common OID registrations. His information is now slightly out of date but the structure is still valid and very instructive. Visit his web site at `www.alvestrand.no/objectid`.

Active Directory Support Files

The ESE engine used by Active Directory is based on Microsoft's Jet database technology. Jet uses a b-tree file structure with transaction logs to ensure recoverability in the event of a system or drive failure.

When you promote a server to a domain controller, you select where to put the Active Directory files. The default path is in the boot partition under `\Windows\NTDS`. Generally, it is a good idea to put them on a separate volume from the operating system files to improve performance.

The following list contains the Active Directory support files and their functions:

- **Ntds.dit.** This is the main AD database. NTDS stands for *NT Directory Services*. The DIT stands for *Directory Information Tree*. The Ntds.dit file on a particular domain controller contains all naming contexts hosted by that domain controller, including the Configuration and Schema naming contexts. A Global Catalog server stores the partial naming context replicas in the Ntds.dit right along with the full Domain naming context for its domain.
- **Edb.log.** This is a transaction log. Any changes made to objects in Active Directory are first saved to a transaction log. During lulls in CPU activity, the database engine commits the transactions into the main Ntds.dit database. This ensures that the database can be recovered in the event of a system crash. Entries that have not been committed to Ntds.dit are kept in memory to improve performance. Transaction log files used by the ESE engine are always 10MB.
- **Edbxxxxx.log.** These are auxiliary transaction logs used to store changes if the main Edb.log file gets full before it can be flushed to Ntds.dit. The xxxxx stands for a sequential number in hex. When the Edb.log file fills up, an Edbtemp.log file is opened. The original Edb.log file is renamed to Edb00001.log, and Edbtemp.log is renamed to Edb.log file, and the process starts over again. ESENT uses circular logging. Excess log files are deleted after they have been committed. You may see more than one Edbxxxxx.log file if a busy domain controller has many updates pending.
- **Edb.chk.** This is a *checkpoint file*. It is used by the transaction logging system to mark the point at which updates are transferred from the log files to Ntds.dit. As transactions are committed, the checkpoint moves forward in the Edb.chk file. If the system terminates abnormally, the pointer tells the system how far along a given set of commits had progressed before the termination.
- **Res1.log** and **Res2.log.** These are reserve log files. If the hard drive fills to capacity just as the system is attempting to create an Edbxxxxx.log file, the space reserved by the Res log files is used. The system then puts a dire warning on the screen prompting you to take action to free up disk space quickly before Active Directory gets corrupted. You should never let a volume containing Active Directory files get even close to being full. File fragmentation is a big

performance thief, and fragmentation increases exponentially as free space diminishes. Also, you may run into problems as you run out of drive space with online database defragmentation (compaction). This can cause Active Directory to stop working if the indexes cannot be rebuilt.

- **Temp.edb.** This is a scratch pad used to store information about in-progress transactions and to hold pages pulled out of Ntds.dit during compaction.
- **Schema.ini.** This file is used to initialize the Ntds.dit during the initial promotion of a domain controller. It is not used after that has been accomplished.

Active Directory Utilities

We've now seen all the components in Active Directory. Over the next few chapters, we'll see how to use those components to build a reliable, useful structure. First, though, let's take a look at the tools of the trade for Active Directory. You get some of these tools when you promote Windows Server 2003 to a domain controller. Others come from the support tools on the Windows Server 2003 CD. Others require purchasing the Resource Kit. I'll identify the origin as I discuss the tools.

Standard Active Directory Management Consoles

Windows Server 2003 comes with three standard MMC-based consoles for viewing and managing Active Directory objects. MMC console files have an .msc extension. The management consoles can be differentiated by the naming context they are used to manage:

- **AD Users and Computers.** This console is used to manage the contents of a Domain naming context. The console name is Dsa.msc.
- **AD Sites and Services.** This console is used to manage the Sites and Services containers inside the Configuration naming context. The console filename is Dssite.msc.
- **AD Domains and Trusts.** This console is used to manage the contents of the Partitions container inside the Configuration naming context. It uses the CrossRef objects in the Partitions container to identify domains in the forest in their assigned hierarchy. The console filename is Domain.msc.

These consoles can all be launched from the Start button at Windows Server 2003 using START | PROGRAMS | ADMINISTRATIVE TOOLS | <CONSOLE NAME>. You can also launch them by entering the name of the MMC console file, such as Dssite.msc, in a Run window or on the command line. Specific instructions for using these AD management consoles are contained in the remaining Active Directory chapters. The most important thing to note at this time, as you get familiar with them, is that virtually all functionality is available from a right-click of the mouse. Very few features require operations from the menu.

Virtual List Views

If you have experience with Windows 2000, you may notice a difference in the way Windows Server 2003 displays pick lists that are built as a result of LDAP searches.

In Windows 2000, the results of the search were delivered to the client in increments of 1500 ordered sequentially as matches were found in the directory. This made pick lists difficult to manage because the items were not sorted.

In Windows Server 2003, search results are fully collected and sorted at the server then delivered in increments stipulated by the client. This means that pick lists are automatically sorted alphabetically, making it easier to locate a particular item.

Schema Console

Microsoft makes it fairly difficult to get access to the Schema naming context. It does not include a standard MMC console for managing the schema. You must create a custom console that contains the Schema snap-in. A snap-in is a *Dynamic Link Library* (DLL) that is loaded by the MMC executable. After you have associated one or more snap-ins with a console, you can save the console with a unique name that has an .msc extension.

Before you can create a custom MMC console for schema management, you must have access to the Schema snap-in. This snap-in is part of the administrative tools but is not registered by default. This prevents casual monkeying around with the schema. To register the Schema snap-in, open a command console, navigate to `C:\Windows\System32`, and run `regsvr32 schmmgmt.dll`.

After the Schema snap-in is registered, create a custom MMC console for it as directed in Procedure 6.1.

Procedure 6.1 Creating a Custom Schema Management Console

1. From the Run window, type **`mmc`** and click `OK`. This opens an empty MMC console.
2. From the CONSOLE menu, select FILE | ADD/REMOVE SNAP-IN. The Add/Remove Snap-in window opens.
3. Click `Add`. The Add Standalone Snap-in window opens.
4. Double-click `Active Directory Schema` and then click `Close`.
5. Click `OK` to save the change and return to the MMC window. The `Active Directory Schema` tree will appear under the `Console Root` folder.
6. Save the file with a name like Schema.msc. The system will put the file in your personal profile. Save it to the \Windows\System32 folder if you want other administrators to use it.

Figure 6.16 Properties window for the `attributeSchema` object used to create the `SamAccountName` attribute.

When you expand the Schema tree, you'll see the objects that make up the classes and attributes of the schema. You can double-click to see the properties for one of these objects. Figure 6.16 shows an example of the properties for the SamAccountName attribute, which holds a user's logon name.

There is a list of options that affect how this attribute will be used in Active Directory:

- **`Allow This Attribute To Be Shown In Advanced View`**. Each AD console has an ADVANCED VIEW option. This prevents cluttering the interface with options that are only used occasionally. (It also confounds administrators who are trying to perform an operation and don't know that the option is hidden in a normal view. This is called a *feature*.)
- **`Attribute Is Active`**. Some attributes are not required for system operation and can be disabled to prevent them from getting values.
- **`Index This Attribute In Active Directory`**. Like any database, performance improves when you search for indexed attributes. Indexing consumes disk space and processor time, though, and an attribute must be unique to make the index worthwhile. Only the most commonly searched attributes are selected for indexing.

- `Ambiguous Name Resolution (ANR)`. ANR permits searching for partial matches. An ANR search for a `SamAccountName` of "gh" would return "ghawn," "ghaskell," "ghowell," and so forth. ANR searches put quite a strain on the database engine, so only nine attributes are selected to use it by default. If you design an application with an attribute that would benefit from ANR searching, you can use this option to add it to the ANR set.
- `Replicate This Attribute To The Global Catalog`. This setting determines if an attribute should be included in the Global Catalog. Only commonly searched attributes are included to minimize GC size and replication load. In Windows 2000, adding or removing an attribute from the GC required a full GC rebuild and replication. This had the potential for creating significant traffic. Windows Server 2003 permits modifying the contents of the GC without forcing a full rebuild.
- `Attribute Is Copied When Duplicating A User`. With this option selected, the value for the attribute would be carried over to a new User object with the Copy function. The `SamAccountName` must be unique in a domain, so this option is disabled for this attribute.
- `Index This Attribute For Containerized Searches In The Active Directory`. The search routines provided in the LDAP API and with Microsoft ADSI permits searching a container rather than the entire directory. You can select this option to improve lookup times for container searches.

The schema can only be modified at one domain controller, the one designated as a *Schema Operations Master*. This ensures the integrity of the schema by preventing potentially conflicting changes from being made at two different domain controllers during the same replication interval.

You can identify the Schema Operations Master by right-clicking `Active Directory Schema` and selecting OPERATIONS MASTER from the flyout menu.

You do not need to be at the console of the Schema Operations Master server to view and modify the schema. You can put the focus of the Schema console on this server by right-clicking `Active Directory Schema` and selecting CHANGE DOMAIN CONTROLLER.

Search Flags

Several of the attribute property options listed in the Schema Manager control a value called `SearchFlags`. This value controls the following actions (values are additive):

1 = Index this attribute

2 = Index this attribute and its container

4 = Add to ANR set (must have indexing set)

8 = Keep the attribute when deleting the object and creating a tombstone

16 = Copy the attribute's value when creating a new copy of an object

Of these settings, only number "8" cannot be controlled from the Schema Manager snap-in. You can use the ADSI Edit console (covered in the next section) to change the value.

Registry Requirements for Schema Modifications

Windows 2000 had a security measure that required a special `Schema Updated Allowed` parameter in the Registry of the machine where you ran the Schema console. This requirement has been removed in Windows Server 2003.

You must be a member of the Schema Admins group to modify any part of the schema. By default, the Administrator account is a member of this group. The Schema Admins group has a set of special permissions for the Schema container. These include the following:

- Change Schema Master
- Manage Replication Topology
- Replicating Directory Changes
- Replication Synchronization
- Update Schema Cache

You should not make changes to the schema unless you are very familiar with its structure and what you want to accomplish. New schema objects cannot be deleted. Changes to existing objects can cause problems that could force reinstalling Active Directory from scratch or recovering from a backup tape.

General-Purpose Active Directory Tools

The standard AD management consoles provide a feature-rich interface for accessing and modifying Active Directory objects and attributes. They also hide a lot of the gears and pulleys that go together to make Active Directory work.

We're now going to take a look at a few tools that take us behind the glitzy façade of those fancy AD management consoles. We're going to see the real world that underlies Active Directory. If you've ever seen *The Matrix*, you have an idea of what we're in for. I have just one question before we start:

Do you want to take the red pill or the blue pill?

ADSI Edit

The first set of general-purpose tools we'll look at come in the suite of Support Tools on the Windows Server 2003 CD. Install the support tools by double-clicking the `\Support\Tools\2000RKST.MSI` icon and walking through the installation wizard.

After the tools are installed, open a Run window and enter **`adsiedit.msc`**. This is the console filename for the ADSI Editor. When the ADSI Edit console opens, you see icons representing the three standard naming contexts for a domain controller: `Domain NC`, `Configuration Container`, and `Schema`. (It cannot display the Application naming contexts.) See Figure 6.17 for an example.

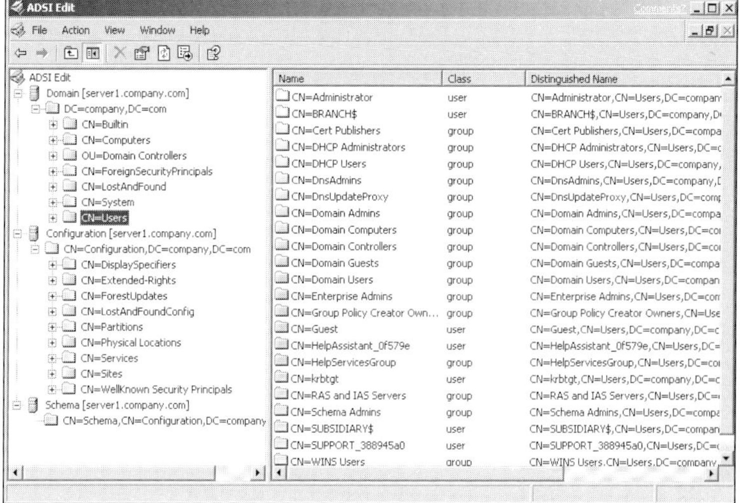

Figure 6.17 ADSI Edit console showing the three standard naming contexts for a domain controller.

Selecting Alternative Domain Controllers for ADSI Edit

If you do not see any naming contexts when you open ADSI Edit, or you want to view a naming context on another domain controller, proceed as follows:

1. Right-click the `ADSI Edit` icon and select CONNECT TO from the flyout menu. The Connection window opens.
2. Under `Computer`, select the `Select or Type a Domain or Server` radio button.
3. In the combo box, type the fully qualified DNS name of a domain controller. When you make this entry, the `Path` entry automatically changes.
4. Click `Advanced`. The Advanced window opens (see Figure 6.18).

The options in this window are used as follows:

- **Credentials.** If you are connecting to Active Directory in another domain, or you are currently logged on using an account that does not have administrator privileges, you can specify a set of administrator credentials.
- **Port Number.** If this field is left blank, ADSI Editor uses well-known TCP port 389 for LDAP. You can specify a different port if you are browsing a non-standard implementation. You could also use this option to browse the Global Catalog through TCP port 3268, but it is more convenient to use the Protocol feature.
- **Protocol.** Select whether you want to browse Active Directory (port 389) or the Global Catalog (port 3268).

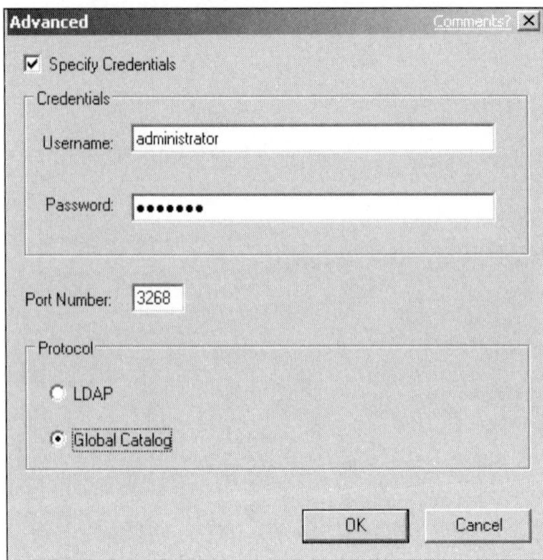

Figure 6.18 ADSI Editor Advanced window showing alternative credentials, specific port number, and protocol selection.

5. Click `OK` to save the changes and return to the Connections window.
6. Click `OK` to save the changes and return to the main ADSI Edit console. The display refreshes to show the new settings, if you made any changes.

Using ADSI Edit to View and Modify AD Objects

Use the steps in Procedure 6.2 to view and modify information about Active Directory objects.

Procedure 6.2 Using the ADSI Editor to View AD Objects

1. Expand the tree to show the top of the naming context you want to view. You can open several Domain naming contexts from several domain controllers at the same time, making ADSI Edit a handy way to view a big enterprise.
2. You can view the attributes associated with any object in any naming context. For example, expand the Domain NC tree to show the list of objects under `cn=Users` and then right-click `cn=Administrator` and select PROPERTIES from the flyout menu. The Properties window opens (see Figure 6.19).

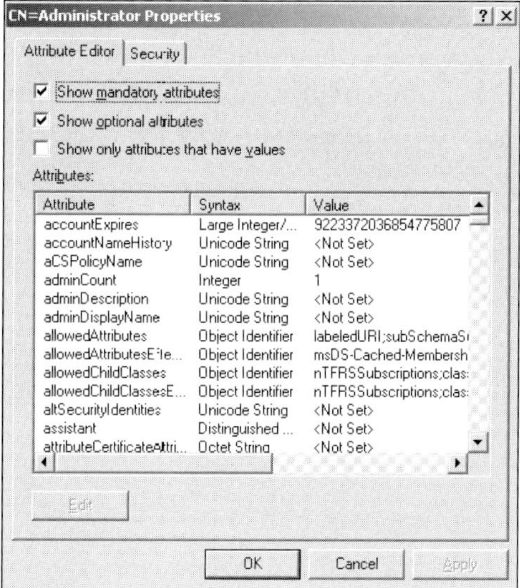

Figure 6.19 Properties for distinguished name `cn=Administrator,cn=Users,dc=Company,dc=com`.

3. The `Show Mandatory Attributes` and `Show Optional Attributes` options are checked by default. Select the `Show Only Attributes That Have Values` option to eliminate extraneous information in the window.
4. Scroll down through the window to view the various attributes and their values.
5. To change a value, double-click it. ADSI Edit will select the appropriate low-level editor to modify the attribute.

Think of ADSI Edit as a kind of super Regedit for Active Directory. All the same caveats apply. You can turn a perfectly tuned domain into sad, twisted carnage with a few mouse clicks. You can also perform miraculous surgery that solves seemingly intractable problems.

LDAP Browser

ADSI Edit is built from the ground up as a tool to manage Active Directory naming contexts. The Support Tools also includes a generic LDAP tool that is capable of accessing any RFC-compliant LDAP directory service. This tool is a true executable, not an MMC snap-in. It is called the LDAP Browser, or Ldp.exe.

LDP is a little less convenient to use than ADSI Edit, and it requires you to know a little more about how to use LDAP. But it's well worth the effort to learn. LDP provides a lot more information with a single mouse click than ADSI Edit. Also, some LDAP operations are hidden by ADSI Editor but exposed by LDP.

Installing LDP

When you use LDP, you must walk through a few steps to bind (authenticate) and set up to view the directory tree. Procedure 6.3 demonstrates how it works.

Procedure 6.3 Binding with LDP

1. At a client in a domain, open the Run window and enter `LDP`. This opens the LDP window.
2. Select CONNECTION | BIND to open the Bind window.
3. Enter administrator credentials in the domain or forest.
4. Click `OK`. The attributes associated with the RootDSE object appear in the right pane. These attributes show the structure and content of the directory on the server. (LDP will bind to your logon server. You can use the `Connect` option to select another server.)
5. From the menu, select VIEW | TREE. This opens the Tree View window.
6. Under `BaseDN`, enter the distinguished name of the container you want to browse. For example, you can enter `dc=Company,dc=com` to start at the top of the Domain naming context for the `Company` domain. You can also specify a container lower in Active Directory. For example, you could select the Users container by entering `cn=Users,dc=Company,dc=com`. The interface is not case sensitive.
7. Click `OK`. The left pane of the window now shows the root of the container you entered. Click the + sign or double-click the name to expand the tree. This generates an LDAP query that enumerates the child objects in the container, which are listed in the tree in the left pane. It also generates a query for the attributes associated with the domain object. These are listed in the right pane (see Figure 6.20).

Searching for a Specific Attribute

LDP is also a convenient place to search the directory for specific instances of an attribute (see Procedure 6.4).

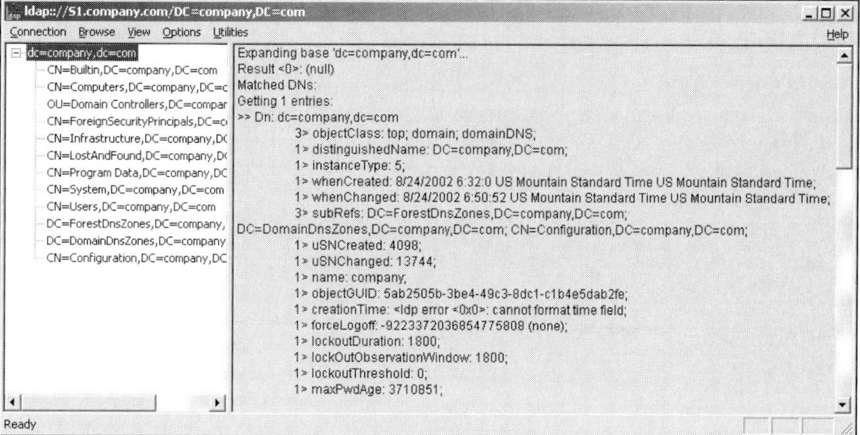

Figure 6.20 LDP window showing tree view of `Company.com` domain.

Procedure 6.4 Searching with LDP

1. Select BROWSE | SEARCH from the main menu to open a search window.
2. In `Base DN`, enter the distinguished name of the container you want to search. You can enter the DN of the root domain of a tree if you want to search the entire tree, but this might take a while if you have a large enterprise with several child domains.
3. In `Filter`, enter the search criteria. The syntax is a little tricky. LDAP expects to see Boolean operators such as `&` (AND) and `|` (OR) at the beginning of the search string. For example, if you want to find all Users who are in the Finance department, you would enter `(&(objectclass=user)(department=finance))`. The entry is not case-sensitive.
4. If you want to search just the object you entered the DN for, select Base. If you want to search the base object and any objects directly under it, select `One Level`. If you want to search all containers under the base container, select `Subtree`. LDP cannot search an entire forest. You must select a base DN at the root of each tree in the forest and run the search multiple times.

LDP Search Wildcards

LDP only accepts wildcards at the middle and end of a filter option. You can search for `department=fin*` or for `department=fin*ce` but not for `department=*ance`.

You can do many fancy tricks with LDP. You can get a quick view of the security descriptor for an object. You can view the replication metadata associated with all the properties of an object (something we'll cover in more detail in Chapter 7, "Managing Active Directory Replication"). It's well worth your time to learn the ins and outs of LDP. You'll also learn a lot about LDAP and Active Directory at the same time. You'll be glad you took the red pill.

DCDIAG

This tool comes in the Resource Kit. It is an invaluable diagnostic utility for examining and troubleshooting a variety of Active Directory operations. You'll find that these tests give great information about the current state of your Active Directory domains, trusts, and replication status. Enter **dcdiag /?** to get a list of the tests that are performed. Every element of Active Directory operation is tested. This utility is highly recommended.

DS Tools

Windows Server 2003 expands the number of command-line tools available for administering Active Directory with a set of DS tools. Here is a list:

- **Dsadd.** Creates an object of a specified class. A wide variety of attributes can be given values at the same time. For example, here are the attributes for `dsadd user`:

```
dsadd user <UserDN> [-samid <SAMName>] [-upn <UPN>] [-fn <FirstName>]
  [-mi <Initial>] [-ln <LastName>] [-display <DisplayName>]
  [-empid <EmployeeID>] [-pwd {<Password> | *}] [-desc <Description>]
  [-memberof <Group ...>] [-office <Office>] [-tel <Phone#>]
  [-email <Email>] [-hometel <HomePhone#>] [-pager <Pager#>]
  [-mobile <CellPhone#>] [-fax <Fax#>] [-iptel <IPPhone#>]
  [-webpg <WebPage>] [-title <Title>] [-dept <Department>]
  [-company <Company>] [-mgr <Manager>] [-hmdir <HomeDir>]
  [-hmdrv <DriveLtr:>] [-profile <ProfilePath>] [-loscr <ScriptPath>]
  [-mustchpwd {yes | no}] [-canchpwd {yes | no}]
  [-reversiblepwd {yes | no}] [-pwdneverexpires {yes | no}]
  [-acctexpires <NumDays>] [-disabled {yes | no}]
  [{-s <Server> | -d <Domain>}] [-u <UserName>]
  [-p {<Password> | *}] [-q] [{-uc | -uco | -uci}]
```

- **Dsmod.** Modifies selected attributes of an existing object.
- **Dsrm.** Removes an object or container. Use caution. You can accidentally remove an entire branch of the tree and force yourself into a tape restore to recover.
- **Dsmove.** Moves an object to a new container. The container must be in the same naming context.
- **Dsquery.** Finds objects that match a specified search criteria.
- **Dsget.** Views selected properties from a specified object.

Bulk Imports and Exports

You may find yourself in a situation where you want to dump information out of Active Directory into a flat file for searching. Or you may need to create large numbers of objects and you want to simplify your work by importing information from a flat file. A standard Windows domain controller has a couple of utilities that help with this kind of bulk object processing. First, we need to take a look at the format for exchanging LDAP information.

LDAP Data Interchange Format (LDIF)

RFC 2849, "The LDAP Data Interchange Format (LDIF)—Technical Specification" defines a standard structure for exchanging LDAP information. The following example shows the LDIF format for the attributes of the Administrator account in the `Company.com` domain:

```
dn: CN=Administrator,CN=Users,DC=company,DC=com
memberOf: CN=Group Policy Admins,CN=Users,DC=company,DC=com
memberOf: CN=Enterprise Admins,CN=Users,DC=company,DC=com
memberOf: CN=Schema Admins,CN=Users,DC=company,DC=com
memberOf: CN=Administrators,CN=Builtin,DC=company,DC=com
memberOf: CN=Domain Admins,CN=Users,DC=company,DC=com
accountExpires: 9223372036854775807
adminCount: 1
badPasswordTime: 125693193676075896
badPwdCount: 0
codePage: 0
cn: Administrator
countryCode: 0
description: Built-in account for administering the computer/domain
isCriticalSystemObject: TRUE
lastLogoff: 0
lastLogon: 125693891796993128
logonCount: 109
distinguishedName: CN=Administrator,CN=Users,DC=company,DC=com
objectCategory: CN=Person,CN=Schema,CN=Configuration,DC=company,DC=com
objectClass: user
objectGUID:: gLgtb/ju0hGcKADAT1NqTQ==
objectSid:: AQUAAAAAAAUVAAAAoF4uDLI/DAf7Cwgn9AEAAA==
primaryGroupID: 513
pwdLastSet: 125681556744344992
name: Administrator
sAMAccountName: Administrator
sAMAccountType: 805306368
userAccountControl: 66048
uSNChanged: 1532
uSNCreated: 1410
whenChanged: 19990410040835.0Z
whenCreated: 19990410034956.0Z
```

There are a few items of note with this example:

- LDIF files use simple ASCII characters. If you have high-order Unicode values in some of the attributes, they might not survive the translation.
- Long integers that represent time and dates will be represented in decimal format and, as such, will not survive reimport. These items are discarded and created afresh when an entry is imported and a new object created.
- Octet strings are converted to Base64 format. This is indicated by a double-colon after the attribute name. *ObjectGUID* is an example. These values withstand a reimport. For the most part, though, this syntax is used for values that are unique for an object so the imported values would be ignored.
- The attributes conform to the Active Directory schema for the forest where they were obtained. Attempting to import these values into a foreign directory service can result in compatibility issues. At the very least, you'll need to change the distinguished names, because it is unlikely that the foreign directory service would use the same namespace.

The LDIF standard includes several command verbs that are used to determine what to do with a particular record. These verbs permit adding, modifying, replacing, or deleting an entire object or individual attributes of an object. They also permit modifying the directory schema. Active Directory permits LDIF to add and modify object classes and attributes, but it does not permit them be deleted. After a class or attribute has been added to the schema, it's there to stay.

LDIF and Active Directory Schema Upgrades

Lest you think that LDIF is one of those obscure programmer toys that reasonable system administrators should avoid like it was oozing with plague, consider this: When you upgrade the first Windows 2000 domain controller in a domain to Windows Server 2003, new objects are added and old objects modified to support changes in the new operating system version. In addition, the Active Directory schema must be modified to support the new features in Windows Server 2003. How does Microsoft install these schema updates? With LDIF files, that's how.

Check the Windows Server 2003 CD in the `\I386` folder. Look for a series of files with an LDF extension. These contain the LDIF entries that modify Active Directory contents and the schema. The CD includes an uncompressed executable called Schupgr.exe. This executable loads the changes from the LDF files into Active Directory.

One last feature of this upgrade method is important to note. The last step in each LDF file modifies an attribute of the Schema container called ObjectVersion. This is how Windows keeps track of the LDF files applied by Windows updates. Installing Windows Server 2003 upgrades the schema to version number 30. Installing Exchange also modifies the schema but does not change the schema version number.

LDIFDE

A Windows domain controller comes with a command-line tool for importing and exporting LDIF files, LDIFDE. Run **`ldifde`** with no switches to get a list of parameters.

LDIFDE simplifies importing and exporting large numbers of records to and from Active Directory, but it also comes in handy for making quick checks of directory entries without opening up a pesky MMC snap-in. Use the `-f con` switch to direct the output to the console. For example:

- To know the group membership of a user, use `Ldifde -d cn=username,cn=Users, dc=company,dc=com -f con`.
- To check the entries in a trusted domain, use `Ldifde -s alb-dc-01.office. company.com -d dc=Office,dc=Company,dc=com -f con`.
- To find all the printers in an organizational unit, use `Ldifde -d ou=Phoenix, dc=Company,dc=com -r "(objectclass=printers)" -f con`.

You can use LDIFDE to dump a file of information about a user and then modify the settings and the username and import that file as a new user. To do this, use the `-m` option to remove the SAM-specific information from the dump file.

You can also use LDIFDE to modify attributes of existing objects, but you need to know a little trick. After you've created an LDIF file consisting of entries you want to modify, you must put a dash on the first blank line at the end of the entries and then a blank line after that. Here's an example showing how to change the `Description` attribute for a user named Avguser:

```
dn: CN=avguser,OU=Phoenix,DC=company,DC=com
changetype: modify
replace: Description
Description: Wazula
-

```

Without that dash, you'll get an error similar to the following:

```
Failed on line 4.  The last token starts with 'W'. The change-modify entry is
missing the terminator '-'.
```

CSVDE

Working with the LDIF format can get a little tedious because it sorts attributes vertically rather than horizontally. If you prefer a more standard spreadsheet layout, use the CSVDE utility. The switches for CSVDE are the same as for LDIFDE.

Here's an example of using CSVDE. Let's say you are the administrator for a school district and you want to add 5000 new students into Active Directory. Your student list may be in a mainframe or AS400 application or a UNIX application of one form or another or a SQL database. You can write a little JCL (Job Control Language) routine or do a quick SQL query to output the student list to a delimited file. Import the delimited file into a spreadsheet and massage it until you get the required data for Active Directory. (Do a `csvde -f output.ldf` to see the column headings and data types.) Then use `csvde -i` to import the spreadsheet contents into Active Directory.

Reimporting LDIF Dumps

If you do an LDIFDE or CSVDE export, many of the attributes for user and group objects are owned by the system and cannot be reimported. Here's a trick. Run the export with the `-m` switch. This enables SAM Logic, which is another way of saying that the export skips the attributes that are owned by the system. This gives you a template to use when building your import files or spreadsheets.

Other LDAP Tools

Because Active Directory is an RFC-compliant implementation of LDAP, you can use virtually any LDAP tool for browsing objects and collecting information. Here are a few sources of LDAP tools and related information:

- **OpenLDAP** (`www.openldap.org`). If you are an open source kind of person, you should take a look at the latest wares from that community. These toolkits are not for the fainthearted, and there are no compiled packages to play with, but it's worth a peek if you want to build your own administration tools to replace those clumsy MMC snap-ins.
- **Novell** (`www.novell.com/products/nds/ldap.html`). NetWare 5 boogies on IP and so does NDS. Novell is putting lots of calories into doing the "Internet thing" right. Also take a look at `developer.novell.com` for LDAP and X.500 tools that might be useful in a mixed network.

Moving Forward

This chapter covered the structure and operation of Active Directory. The next five chapters describe how to design, deploy, and manage Active Directory-based domains, how to manage replication between domain controllers, and how to repair and recover Active Directory in the event of a problem.

7 Managing Active Directory Replication

ALL DOMAIN CONTROLLERS (DCs) HOST A read/write copy of Active Directory. This simple statement opens a world of complexity. Keeping dozens or hundreds of replicas of the Active Directory database consistent and secure in the face of uncertain network conditions requires a good deal of ingenuity on the part of the developers and design savvy on the part of system administrators.

You need a detailed knowledge of replication operation before you can design an effective Active Directory architecture. Without making allowance for replication, you'll end up with domain controllers that never get in sync, clients that authenticate indiscriminately throughout the network, poor LDAP (Lightweight Directory Access Protocol) search performance, logon failures, and possibly even database corruption.

New Features in Windows Server 2003

Here are the Windows Server 2003 features that have the most dramatic influence on replication:

- **Scalable site architectures.** The algorithm used by the Knowledge Consistency Checker (KCC) to calculate inter-site topology was streamlined. This resolves a problem in Windows 2000 where large organizations with many sites are forced to configure connections manually because the KCC cannot finish its calculations.
- **Group membership replication.** Linked values, such as group members, now replicate as discrete entities rather than replicating the entire attribute. This resolves a problem in Windows 2000 where updates made to the same group membership during the same replication interval conflict and overwrite each other.

- **Application naming contexts.** A new type of naming context called an Application naming context that holds application-specific objects. Windows Server 2003 uses this type of naming context to hold DNS zone objects.
- **Global Catalog rebuilds minimized.** Adding or removing an attribute from the Global Catalog (GC) no longer requires a complete synchronization cycle. This minimizes the replication traffic caused by adding an attribute to the GC.
- **Schema enhancements.** The ability was added to associate an auxiliary schema class to individual objects rather than to an entire class of objects. This association can be dynamic, making it possible to temporarily assign new attributes to a specific object or objects.

Replication Overview

It helps to manage Active Directory replication if you have a road map of how the domain controllers connect to each other and what information they exchange. In this section, we'll take a look at what Active Directory components get replicated, where the replication traffic goes, how that traffic is managed, and what happens when conflicting updates collide with each other.

Replication and Naming Contexts

Domain controllers are like hard-working parents. They can only give what they have. Each domain controller has at least three naming context replicas:

- **Configuration.** All domain controllers in a forest have a read/write copy of this naming context.
- **Schema.** All domain controllers in a forest have a read-only copy of this naming context.
- **Domain.** Each domain controller in a domain has a read/write copy of that domain's naming context.

In addition, Global Catalog servers host partial naming contexts for domains other than their own. You can also create Application naming contexts for holding DNS zone objects and place those naming contexts on domain controllers running DNS. Figure 7.1 shows a three-domain forest and the naming contexts that would be found on a Global Catalog server in one of those domains.

As you build a mental image of replication, keep in mind that each naming context constitutes a separate replication unit. Domain controllers must propagate changes made to their replica of a naming context out to other domain controllers hosting a replica of the same naming context.

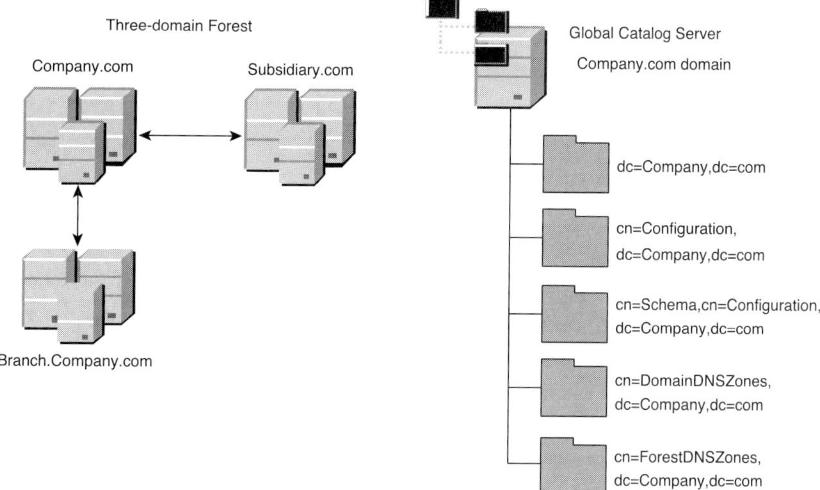

Figure 7.1 Diagram of three-domain forest and the naming contexts hosted by a GC in the root domain.

Connections

Domain controllers replicate with specific partners. These partners are defined by Connection objects in Active Directory. The map of domain controllers and their connections is called a *topology*.

The service responsible for handling replication between two domain controllers is the *Directory Replication Agent*, or DRA. The DRA depends on the Connection objects in the topology map to determine which partners to contact when replicating updates to a naming context.

Connection objects define inbound replication paths. Domain controllers *pull* updates from their partners. When a domain controller needs to update its copy of a naming context, the DRA sends a replication request to its partners. The DRAs on the partners respond by assembling a replication packet containing updates to the naming context then delivering the packet to the requesting partner.

This replication packet varies in size depending on the memory in the domain controller. The packet size is 1/100 of the amount of RAM. For this reason, it is advantageous to add memory to a DC. A heavily loaded DC would also benefit from a second processor.

Watching domain controllers select their partners is like watching teenagers pick seats in the cafeteria at lunchtime. The DRA prefers to use a single Connection object to define the end points for all the naming contexts hosted by a domain controller. For this reason, domain controllers prefer to replicate with other domain controllers in their own domain. If necessary, a domain controller will replicate its Configuration and Schema naming contexts with one partner and its Domain naming context with another partner, but only if no other options are available.

Global Catalog servers have a special challenge when selecting replication partners. GC servers need a partial replica of every Domain naming context. They can replicate the partial naming context replicas from another GC or directly from domain controllers in the source domain. Keep this behavior in mind as you lay out your architecture. Make sure that GC servers can link to other GC servers to prevent a server from snaking out links to multiple domain controllers in other domains.

Property Replication

It would be a tall order to replicate the entire contents of a naming context each time a domain controller updates its partners. It's more efficient to replicate only the items that change.

The Exchange directory service from which Active Directory was derived takes the approach of replicating an entire object when any property of that object changes. This makes for a simple replication mechanism, because the DRA simply copies an entire row out of the table holding the object's information. Replicating entire objects abuses the network with unnecessary traffic, though, and complicates the collision handling mechanism if conflicting changes are made in the same replication interval.

The Active Directory engine replicates individual properties rather than entire objects. This conserves bandwidth at the expense of a little added complexity. It's more difficult to ensure database consistency with lots of individual properties flying around the network.

To help control property replication, each property contains a set of information that defines when the property was last modified, where the modification originated, and how many total revisions have been applied to the property. This is called the *property metadata*. The metadata is stored right along with the property's primary value, such as Name or CN or Department. See the "Property Metadata" section later in this chapter.

Sites

Replication reliability is heavily dependent on the underlying infrastructure. If a network link is slow or unreliable, the replication connections using that link will fail.

Microsoft defines a *site* as an area of reliable, high-speed network communications. Replication within a site is called *intra-site*. Replication between sites is called *inter-site*.

Deciding where to create sites and how to define and provision the links between those sites constitutes a critical part of laying out the Active Directory architecture.

Measuring Link Performance

Unlike classic NT, Windows Server 2003 dynamically measures link performance to determine if a slow or fast link exists. The calculation goes like this:

1. Ping a server with 0 bytes of data and time the round trip. If the time is less than 10ms, it's a fast link.
2. Ping the same server with 4KB of data and time the round trip.
3. Calculate the delta between the 4KB round trip and the 0KB round trip. This results in the time necessary to move 4KB of data.
4. Repeat 3 times and get an average 4KB transfer time.
5. Convert to bits-per-second and compare to benchmark. The default benchmark is 500Kbps.

A site is usually a LAN or MAN. It can also be a campus network if you have sufficient bandwidth between buildings. You should have at least 500Kbps of bandwidth to support full speed replication within a site. See the "Measuring Link Performance" sidebar. Even if the links are fast, though, if they regularly become oversubscribed or demonstrate long periods of high latency, you may experience replication problems if you do not define separate sites.

Sites are also used to limit network traffic caused by LDAP searches and Kerberos authentication. Details of this localization are in the "Localizing Active Directory Access" topic.

Replication Frequency

Active Directory uses a *loosely coupled replication mechanism*. This means an interval of some duration exists between the time a modification is made to a property in one replica and the time the modified property appears in all replicas. During this interval, an LDAP query to one domain controller could produce a different result than the same query submitted to another domain controller. Keep this behavior in mind when troubleshooting problems.

The time it takes for a modified property to replicate to all domain controllers is called *convergence time*. Ideally, changes would propagate nearly instantaneously so that convergence time would be zero. That ideal cannot be obtained in a practical network. Convergence time is always a compromise between low network traffic and fast update propagation. Active Directory uses two methods for controlling convergence time: notification and polling.

Notification

When a domain controller modifies a property in one of its naming contexts, it notifies its replication partners within a site that a change has been made. The partners then pull a copy of the changed property and apply it to their naming context replica. Those domain controllers, in turn, notify their own replication partners and the change propagates in stages around the site.

Urgent Replication

Three items are replicated immediately, regardless of the notification interval setting. These are

- Account lock-outs
- Changes to LSA secrets
- Changes to the RID Manager

Urgent changes are only replicated quickly within a site. Because inter-site replication partners do not use notification, they cannot propagate urgent replication packets. This can affect lockout handling because the user who entered the wrong password several times might be in a different site than the administrator who needs to reset the lockout.

You might expect password changes to also be replicated urgently, but they are handled using a different mechanism. Password changes are sent directly to the PDC Emulator using a secure channel rather than standard replication. The PDC Emulator acts as a second-check for all denied passwords.

Short notification intervals will propagate changes more quickly than long intervals, but generate more traffic to carry the same amount of information. (Each replication packet is smaller.) The default notification interval is 15 seconds.

Notification is only used between domain controllers in the same site. Replication between bridgehead servers in different sites uses polling only, not notification. This permits the system to accumulate sufficient changes (more than 50KB) to warrant compression.

Polling

Domain controllers periodically query their replication partners to see if any changes have occurred. Shorter polling intervals reduce convergence time.

The polling interval between domain controllers in the same site is set to 1 hour. This intra-site polling is not intended to propagate changes. It simply acts as a status check to ensure that the replication partner is available in the event that no Active Directory changes are made during that hour.

The default polling interval between domain controllers in different sites is set to 180 minutes, or 3 hours. This is a long time to wait for updates to propagate. You can set it to a shorter interval.

Keep these replication intervals in mind. You'll use the numbers over and over as you set up your sites and configure replication parameters. They also affect daily operation. For example, a Help Desk technician responsible for changing group members needs to remember that a change made to a user's group membership could take three hours (or longer) to replicate to the site containing the user who was just added to the group.

Urgent replication items are propagated between sites using the normal polling frequency. You can enable notification between sites but this is not recommended. See "Controlling Replication Parameters" for details.

Replication Methods

Most communication between network entities uses an application-layer protocol. For instance, when a Windows network client copies a file from a Windows server, it uses the Server Message Block (SMB) protocol. When an Internet email client wants to send a message to a post office, it uses Simple Mail Transport Protocol (SMTP). Active Directory replication can use one of two high-level protocols.

Remote Procedure Calls

The primary protocol used by Active Directory replication is the *Remote Procedure Call*, or RPC. RPC transactions are simple to code and have a robust set of tools for creating and managing a connection. RPCs are especially attractive for Active Directory replication because they have a straightforward encryption methodology. Encryption is an essential component of replication. You do not want someone with a packet sniffer to view sensitive directory information as it transits the network.

In an RPC transaction, an RPC client issues a function call to the complementary RPC server without much regard for the state of the intervening network. This greatly simplifies the way applications are coded. On the other hand, the application can get impatient if it waits too long for a response. This can cause a loss of connection if the client gives up.

Here's the bottom line: RPCs make for a great data communication tool but they are finicky over wide area connections. For this reason, Active Directory uses two forms of RPC: a high-speed form for use in a local network and a low-speed form for use across a WAN. The low-speed form has higher latency (longer timeouts) and will suffer through multiple connection losses before giving up.

SMTP

Active Directory can also use Simple Mail Transport Protocol (SMTP) for transferring replication packets. SMTP is a robust protocol, well suited for use across uncertain network connections. SMTP also permits asynchronous communication, making it possible to transfer replication packets in bulk.

Unfortunately, SMTP has a couple of serious drawbacks when it comes to Active Directory replication. The first is structural. SMTP transfers messages in clear text. For this reason, the system automatically encrypts SMTP messages using a proprietary form of secure messaging. This form of encryption uses certificates, so you must have a Certification Authority. Encryption puts a significant load on a server, so ensure that the bridgeheads are especially fast with multiple processors to share the workload.

The second drawback of using SMTP is a limitation of the File Replication Service (FRS). Recall that FRS is used to sync the contents of Sysvol between domain controllers. FRS can only use RPCs to carry replication traffic. In addition, FRS uses the same replication topology (including the same connection options) as those specified for Active Directory replication, so you cannot specify one transport for Active Directory replication and another for FRS.

Because of this limitation, SMTP cannot be used to replicate the contents of a Domain naming context because the contents of Sysvol cannot be kept in sync. SMTP can be used for all other naming contexts, including the Configuration, Schema, and Application naming contexts and the partial naming contexts that make up the Global Catalog.

If you have a remote location with a slow, unreliable connection that calls for the queuing capabilities of SMTP, you'll need to create a separate domain for that location.

Replication Topology

Domain controllers know each other's location and the connections between them. The LDAP term for this topology information is *knowledge*. The service responsible for tailoring the replication topology is the *Knowledge Consistency Checker*, or KCC.

The KCC treats the domain controller topology like a game of K*Nex. Every 15 minutes, it surveys the domain controllers in the domain and decides where to place Connection objects so that each domain controller gets its updates in a reasonable amount of time. The KCC on a bridgehead server includes the bridgehead servers in other sites in its calculations.

The KCC makes its decisions based on a spanning tree algorithm. One of the improvements made in Windows Server 2003 is a streamlining of this algorithm that enables the KCC to handle more sites and larger topologies. In Windows 2000, there was a limit of approximately 100 sites and domain controllers before an administrator would be forced to intervene and create manual connections. Using Windows Server 2003, a much larger number of sites and domain controllers are supported. Microsoft has not specified a limit.

Intra-Site Topology

If you're an Exchange administrator, you'll be pleased with the changes made to the KCC in Windows Server 2003.

When it comes to selecting replication partners, the Exchange directory service behaves like a sailor on a 24-hour pass. It creates point-to-point replication connections between every domain controllers in a site. The Active Directory KCC is much more discriminating. It selects a limited number of partners to structure a tightly controlled topology. For intra-site replication, the KCC builds a replica ring. See Figure 7.2 for an example.

When constructing a replica ring, the KCC follows a 3-hop rule: no domain controller is more than 3 hops from any other domain controller. Recall that a domain controller can wait up to 15 seconds to notify its replication partners following a change to one of its naming contexts. By limiting the hop count, the KCC ensures that changes converge quickly.

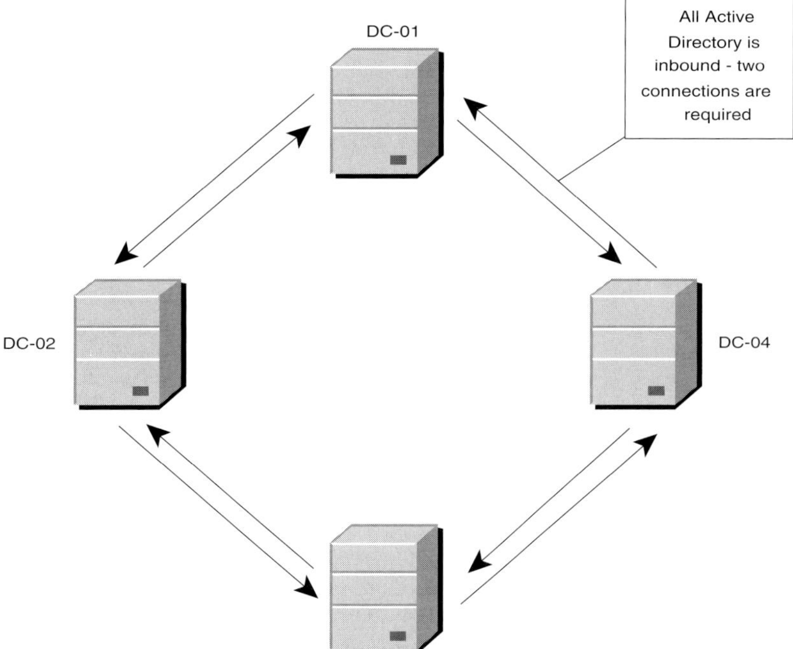

Figure 7.2 Simple replication ring.

Replica Ring Formation

When a new domain controller is promoted, the KCC on that domain controller gets a copy of Active Directory in much the same way that aliens invading Earth get the name and location of the White House. They land furtively and use a slimy tendril to suck the brains out of an innocent human being who wasn't doing them any harm at all. (Excuse the emotion. I was born and raised in Roswell, where we're a little sensitive about this sort of treatment.)

During a domain controller promotion, the Active Directory Promotion Wizard creates a connection to an existing domain controller then uses that connection to pull a full copy of Active Directory. When the next KCC on the existing domain controller runs (sometime in the next 15 minutes), it sees the new connection and builds a complementary connection to the new domain controller. They are now full-fledged replication partners.

The KCCs on the other domain controllers take note of these changes and proceed to break and make their own connections to insert the new domain controller into the replica ring. This happens without any administrative intervention.

If the ring gets more than six domain controllers, such as that in Figure 7.3, the KCC running on each domain controller realizes that there are more than three hops in the ring. It sets to work building *optimizing connections* between domain controllers to reduce the hop count. Remember that the domain controllers share common knowledge about connections, so they eventually work out a mutually agreeable topology.

Replica Ring Repair

If a domain controller does not respond to a replication request, the DRA wakes up the KCC. The KCC takes over and builds new connections to bypass the failed domain controller, like a heart muscle healing itself after a heart attack.

The DRA keeps trying to contact the lost domain controller. When the domain controller comes back online again, the KCC sets to work restructuring the connections to reintroduce it back into the ring.

Under normal circumstances, all this repair work happens automatically. The only time an administrator should need to do any manual configuration is in the event that the KCC is unable to find a suitable replication partner due to a Domain Name System (DNS) failure. This generally occurs when a failed domain controller is also the DNS server for a site. If you always specify multiple DNS servers in your TCP/IP configuration, you should avoid this problem.

Inter-Site Topology

The replication picture changes considerably when the domain controllers are in different sites. Let's consider for a moment what would happen if there were such thing as inter-site replication. Figure 7.4 shows what this would look like.

In this configuration, the Directory Replication Agents running on the domain controllers have no way of knowing that the intervening network connections are slow and prone to oversubscription and potential failure. They blithely replicate as fast and as often as they would for normal network connections.

That's when trouble begins. The high-speed RPC connections begin to fail when the WAN links become oversubscribed and latency increases. The symptoms of RPC failures include persistent differences between replicas, DRA and KCC errors in the Event log, and eventually fatal RPC end-point errors when the connections fail repeatedly.

Active Directory avoids this carnage by building connections between sites that use special, low-speed RPCs. For this reason, inter-site replication uses an entirely different topology. See Figure 7.5 for an example.

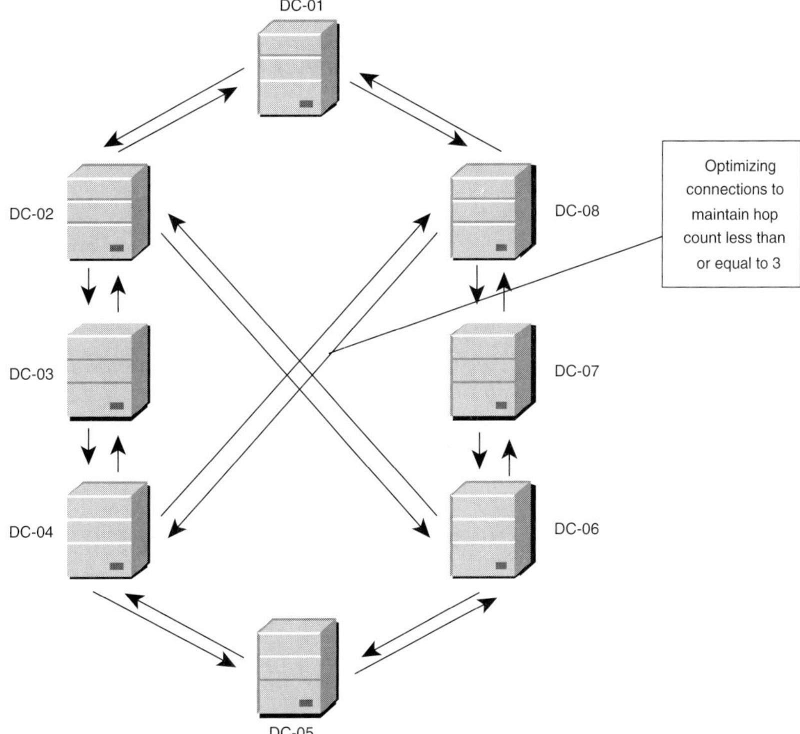

Figure 7.3 Meshed replication ring.

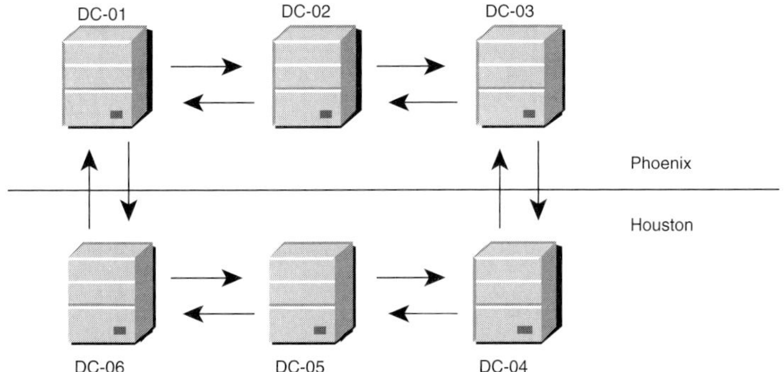

Figure 7.4 Replica ring without special site configurations.

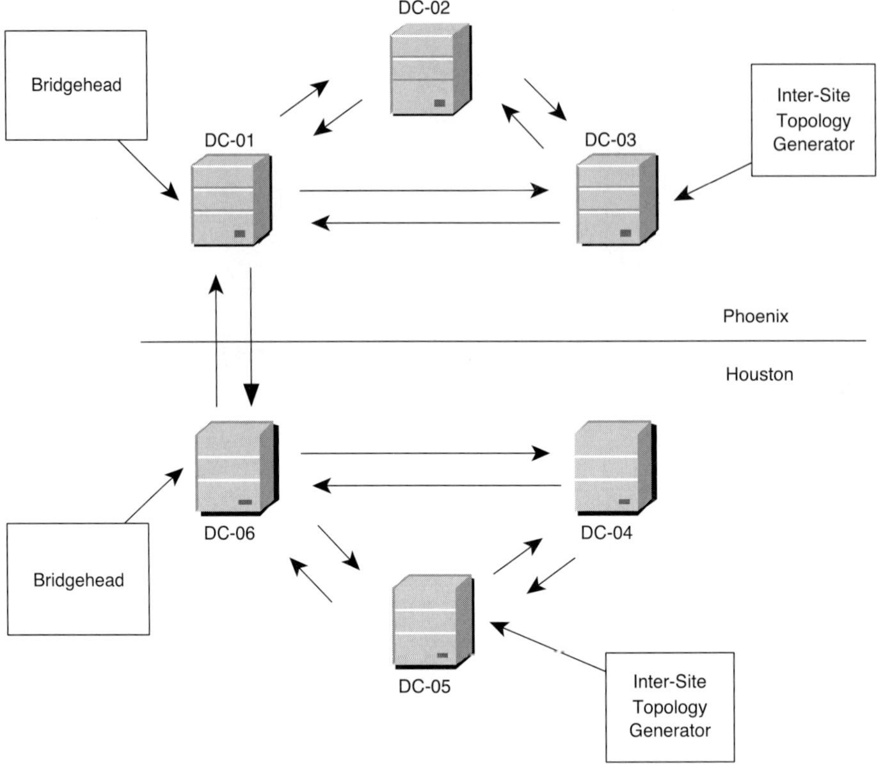

Figure 7.5 Inter-site replication topology.

Inter-Site Replication Compared to Intra-Site Replication

Several features differentiate inter-site replication topology from its intra-site cousin:

- Replication between sites occurs only between two domain controllers, called *bridgeheads*.
- Notification is disabled between bridgehead servers. Replication is controlled solely by polling. The default inter-site polling interval is 180 minutes (3 hours).
- Replication packets between sites are compressed to conserve bandwidth. Compression puts more of a CPU load on the domain controller, so bridgeheads should be capable machines with sufficient speed and processors to handle their duties.

Bridgehead Server Selection

The KCC selects a server to act as the bridgehead for a site. It makes this decision using the following criteria:

- It looks to see if an administrator has selected any preferred bridgehead servers. If so, it uses these as a selection pool.
- If there are no preferred bridgehead servers, any domain controller in the site is a candidate.
- The KCC lines up the candidates in order of their Globally unique Identifier (GUID). The domain controller with the highest GUID wins.

Inter-Site Topology Generator

The bridgehead selection is something of a secret in that domain controllers in other sites don't know the results until they are told, something like waiting for the College of Cardinals to select a pope.

Rather than watching for the color of the smoke from the chimney of the Sistine Chapel, the sites wait for a Connection object between the bridgeheads to appear in the Configuration naming context. This Connection object is created by a domain controller designated as the *Inter-Site Topology Generator*, or ISTG.

There is only one ISTG in a site. It is selected using the same criteria as the bridgehead server—that is, the domain controller with the highest GUID. For this reason, the ISTG is often a bridgehead server, but it doesn't have to be. For instance, the ISTG might not be on the list of preferred bridgehead servers.

Identifying the Bridgehead Server and ISTG

You can identify the server designated as the bridgehead for a site using the REPADMIN utility with the following syntax:

```
C:\>repadmin /bridgeheads /verbose
Gathering topology from site Phoenix (s1.company.com):
Bridgeheads for site Phoenix (s1.company.com):
Source Site   Local Bridge       Trns     Fail. Time   #    Status
Houston             S1            RPC       (never)    0    Operation
➥completed successfully.

Naming Context   Attempt Time          Success Time         #Fail  Last Result
subsidiary       2002-02-07  08:53:01   2002-02-07 08:53:01    0    Operation
➥completed successfully.
Configuration    2002-02-07  09:04:42   2002-02-07 09:04:42    0    Operation
➥completed successfully.
Schema            2002-02-07  08:49:19   2002-02-07 08:49:19    0    Operation
➥completed successfully.
```

You can identify the ISTG for a site by opening the Properties window for the NTDS Site Settings object in the AD Sites and Services console.

The ISTG runs as a separate function from the KCC because one site can have more than one bridgehead if there are multiple domains. Each of these bridgeheads has a copy of the Schema and Configuration naming contexts and may have a copy of the Global Catalog partial naming contexts, as well. Inter-site replication would turn into anarchy if all those bridgeheads made independent decisions about where to create Connection objects.

Inter-Site Topology Highlights

If you're experiencing a little anarchy of your own right now in trying to construct a mental picture of all this, here are some highlights (refer to Figure 7.5)

- There is only one ISTG per site. It creates the Connection objects that define the replication path between bridgeheads in different sites.
- There is one bridgehead server for each Domain naming context in each site. One Domain bridgehead server is designated as the bridgehead for the Configuration and Schema naming contexts. Another bridgehead will be responsible for the DomainDNSZones and ForestDNSZones naming contexts if the Configuration and Schema bridgehead is not a DNS server.
- The KCC selects the bridgehead by picking the domain controller with the highest GUID from a list of candidate domain controllers. If an administrator has selected preferred bridgehead servers, they become the only candidates.
- If you create an Application naming context and designate domain controllers in different sites to host a replica, each site will have a bridgehead for this naming context. This may or may not be the same bridgehead used by another naming context.

Failure of a Bridgehead or ISTG

If a bridgehead fails, its partners in other sites will be unable to complete replication transactions. The Directory Replication Agents on the bridgehead's local replication partners will notice that the bridgehead has stopped responding. They snitch to the KCC, which sets to work selecting a replacement. The KCC waits a period of time (two hours by default) before transferring responsibility to the new bridgehead

If an administrator has selected a set of preferred bridgehead servers and none of these servers is available, the KCC will not select a replacement bridgehead and inter-site replication will fail. For this reason, it is very important that you select multiple preferred bridgehead servers for each Domain naming context.

If a failed bridgehead comes back on line, it does not reassume its old responsibilities. It gets in line as a candidate for replacing the new bridgehead should the new bridgehead ever fail.

Detecting an ISTG failure is a little trickier. The ISTG is like an emeritus professor; it only shows up at ceremonial occasions and funerals. To make sure everyone knows it's still alive, the ISTG periodically updates an attribute called InterSiteTopologyGenerator in its NTDS Settings object. By default, it does this update every 30 minutes. The update replicates to the rest of the domain controllers so they know the ISTG is on the line. If an hour passes without this attribute being updated, the KCC on the other domain controllers select a new ISTG using the highest GUID rule.

Site Objects in Active Directory

Active Directory stores the objects that control replication under the Sites container in the Configuration naming context. Because every domain controller hosts a copy of the Configuration naming context, every domain controller has the same information about site names, locations, and connections. This is how the KCC services on separate domain controllers all come to the same conclusion about replication topology. They all work from the same crib sheet.

Figure 7.6 shows how Active Directory objects represent the various components of a replication topology. Here is a list of the objects and their functions:

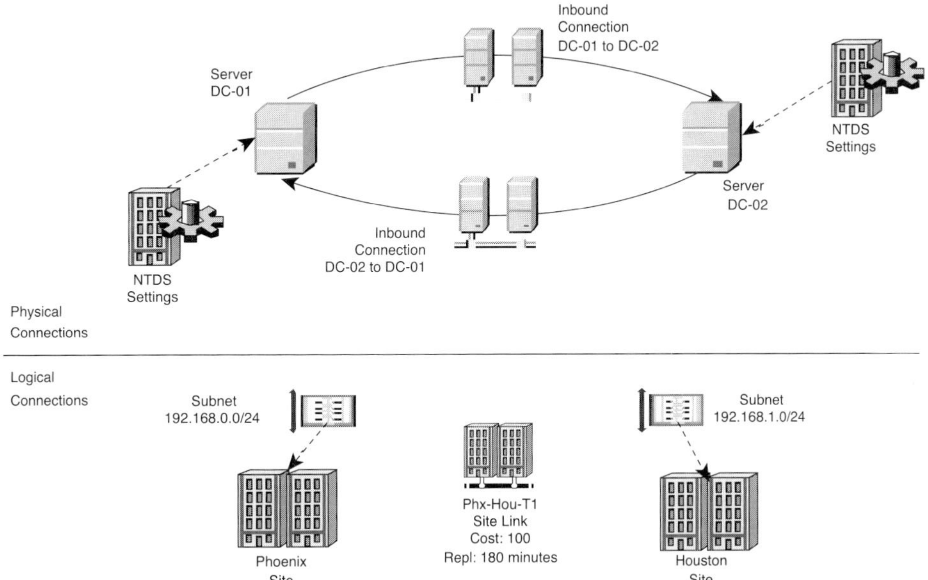

Figure 7.6 Active Directory objects representing replication topology.

- **Site.** This object acts as a placeholder for the objects underneath.
- **<sitename>**. This object represents a specific site. The object contains a Site-Object-BL attribute that points to a Subnet object such as 10.3.20.0/24. Every site must be linked to at least one Subnet object.
- **Subnet.** This object contains a Site-Object attribute that points at the linked Site object. A site can be linked to more than one subnet, but a subnet can be linked to only one site.
- **<servername>.** This object represents a specific server. It contains attributes that define the DNS host name of the server and its Globally Unique Identifier (GUID). This information is included in each property that is changed on the server and acts as a marker when the changed properties are replicated to other servers.
- **NTDS Settings.** This object lists the naming contexts hosted by the associated domain controller. For example, a Global Catalog server in domain DomA in a two-domain forest with DomB would have these entries:

```
hasMasterNCs: CN=Schema,CN=Configuration,DC=DomA,DC=com
hasMasterNCs: CN=Configuration,DC=DomA,DC=com
hasMasterNCs: DC=DomB,DC=com
hasPartialReplicaNCs: DC=DomB,DC=com
```

- **NTDS Site Settings.** This object has an attribute called Schedule that determines the default replication schedule for the Connection objects in the site. It also has an Inter-site-Topology-Generator attribute that identifies the ISTG for the site.
- **Site Link.** This object contains a Site-List attribute that shows the sites that act as end-points for the link. The system defines a default Site Link object called Default-IP-Site-Link.
- **Connection.** This object defines parameters for inbound replication to the domain controller. It has a From-Server attribute that identifies the replication partner. A Transport-Type attribute specifies the transport used by the connection. A Schedule attribute defines how often to poll for updates. By default, a Connection object uses the schedule defined by its parent NTDS Site Settings object.

The "Configuring Inter-site Replication" section later in this chapter describes how these objects are used when configuring sites and inter-site replication.

Replication Topology Summary

Here are the important points to remember when you begin detailing your Active Directory site architecture:

- Active Directory is divided into separate naming contexts. Each naming context forms a discrete replication unit.

- Only changed properties are replicated, not entire objects. Properties contain special metadata information used to validate database consistency and control replication traffic.
- Sites define areas of reliable, high-speed network communication. A high-speed link is 500Kbps or faster.
- Domain controllers replicate from specific partners. Connection objects in Active Directory define replication partners. All replication is inbound across the connection.
- The KCC is responsible for mapping out replication topology by creating Connection objects between domain controllers in the same site. The ISTG creates Connection objects between bridgehead servers in different sites.
- Intra-site topology uses a ring with sufficient meshed connections to maintain a hop count of 3 or fewer. Inter-site replication uses bridgeheads.
- Within a site, domain controllers notify their partners when updates are pending. The default notification interval is 15 seconds. Between sites, bridgeheads wait for polling. The default polling interval is 3 hours.
- There are three replication transports: high-speed RPCs used within a site, low-speed RPCs used between sites, and SMTP that can be used between domains. SMTP requires IPSec and a Microsoft Certificate Authority.

Detailed Replication Transaction Descriptions

Now that we have a general idea of how replication works, let's examine details of the replication transactions themselves. This information helps to diagnose replication problems. It also helps to make critical architectural decisions such as where to place specific domain controllers and how to select the proper inter-site polling frequency.

Multiple-master replication raises several challenges:

- **Data consistency**. It is important that the replicas of each naming context match exactly on every domain controller after all updates have converged.
- **Redundant updates**. Domain controllers should not waste time replicating updates that they have already received from the same replication partner.
- **Circulating updates**. Domain controllers should not waste bandwidth by replicating updates from one partner when they have already received the update from another partner.
- **Update collisions.** There is a good possibility that changes could be made to the same property or object on different domain controllers during the same replication interval. These potentially conflicting changes will eventually collide as they propagate around the system. Domain controllers must handle these collisions consistently to avoid database corruption.

Property Metadata

Active Directory deals with the challenges of multi-master replication by embedding replication control information into each property. This information is called *property metadata*. The metadata information is saved along with the property's primary value each time the property is modified. This is called an *atomic transaction*, meaning that if one value isn't written, none of them are written.

You can view the property metadata for an object in one of several ways. The simplest is to use the REPADMIN utility. This utility is available on all domain controllers. You'll need to know the distinguished name (DN) of the object you want to view. For instance, the DN for the Sites object in the Company.com domain would be: `cn=Sites,cn=Configuration,dc=Company,dc=com`. Here is the REPADMIN syntax and a sample listing. The property in bold was updated after the object was initially created:

```
repadmin /showmeta cn=sites,cn=configuration,dc=company,dc=com
10 entries.
Loc.USN    Originating DSA   Org.USN   Org.Time/Date         Ver  Attribute
=======    ===============   =======   =============         ===  =========
   1165    Phoenix\DC-01        1165    2002-02-23 17:48.40    1   objectClass
   1165    Phoenix\DC-01        1165    2002-02-23 17:48.40    1   cn
   2765    Phoenix\DC-02        2843    2002-02-24 18:14.10    3   description
   1165    Phoenix\DC-01        1165    2002-02-23 17:48.40    1   instanceType
   1165    Phoenix\DC-01        1165    2002-02-23 17:48.40    1   whenCreated
   1165    Phoenix\DC-01        1165    2002-02-23 17:48.40    1   showInAdvancedViewOnly
   1165    Phoenix\DC-01        1165    2002-02-23 17:48.40    1   nTSecurityDescriptor
   1165    Phoenix\DC-01        1165    2002-02-23 17:48.40    1   name
   1165    Phoenix\DC-01        1165    2002-02-23 17:48.40    1   systemFlags
   1165    Phoenix\DC-01        1165    2002-02-23 17:48.40    1   objectCategory
```

The column headings in the listing are abbreviations for the property metadata entries. Here is a description of their function:

- **Local Update Sequence Number (USN).** A USN is a sequential number assigned to a property when it is created or modified. Each domain controller maintains a USN counter. Each time any property on any object is modified, the next available USN is obtained from the counter and stored in the property metadata. The USN is a 64-bit number, big enough for a domain controller to allot 10,000 USNs per second for 66 million years.
- **Originating DSA**. DSA is the LDAP term for a server that hosts a copy of the Directory database. An Active Directory domain controller is an LDAP DSA. The REPADMIN listing identifies the DSA by its site and computer name, but the actual value is the server's Globally Unique Identifier (GUID). You may see a bare GUID if the server where you run REPADMIN cannot resolve the name and site of the originating server.
- **Originating USN**. This is the USN assigned to the property in the replica hosted by the originating DSA. Note that in the example, with one exception, the Local and Originating USNs match. This indicates that the object was

created on domain controller DC-01. The Description property was modified on domain controller DC-02. Note that a domain controller updates the Local USN value when a property is modified for any reason: a direct change or a replicated change.

- **Originating Time/Date.** This is a timestamp indicating when the property was modified at the originating DSA. This information is used as a tiebreaker in case a property is changed at two different domain controllers in the same replication interval.
- **Property Version Number (PVN).** The PVN is a sequential number that identifies how many times a property has been modified.

The PVN is the key value that determines whether two replicas are internally consistent. The entire replication system is geared to ensure that properties with the same PVN have the same primary value. This is how Active Directory resolves the data integrity challenge. The next few sections detail how property metadata values help control redundant replication requests, prevent circulating updates, and manage collisions.

Example Replication Transactions

The next few examples use a three-node replication ring in a single domain and single site as shown in Figure 7.7. The Global Catalog status does not matter because there is only one domain.

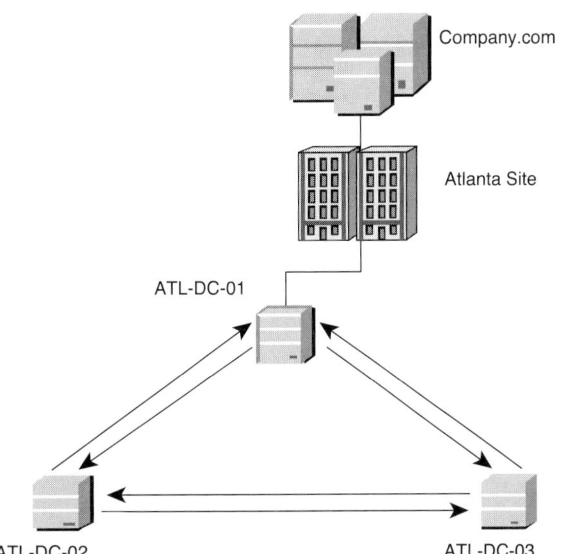

Figure 7.7 Three-node replication ring with all domain controllers in the same domain and site.

The example traces a change to a property for a user object with the common name `cn=Al Bondigas`. Here are a few of the property metadata values for the `cn=Al_Bondigas` object. The listing was taken by running REPADMIN on domain controller DC-01. The USN and PVN values for the Title property, shown in bold, are different because it was updated after Al's user object was created:

```
Loc. USN   Originating DSA    Org.USN   Org.Time/Date                  PVN   Attribute
=======    ===============    ====      =============                  ===   =========
   1416    Atlanta\DC-01      1416      2002-022002-02-01 01:20.50     1     objectClass
   1416    Atlanta\DC-01      1416      2002-022002-02-01 01:20.50     1     cn
   1416    Atlanta\DC-01      1416      2002-022002-02-01 01:20.50     1     description
   14D3    Atlanta\DC-01      14D3      2002-022002-02-02 12:14.31     2     title
   1416    Atlanta\DC-01      1416      2002-022002-02-01 01:20.50     1     department
```

Use of Update Sequence Number (USN)

The *Local USN* value prevents redundant replication requests. The system uses the Local USN as a high water mark to filter out all but the most current updates between replication partners. Procedure 7.2 shows how it works.

Procedure 7.2 Replication Trace Showing USN Operation

1. This series of examples modifies the Description property of the `cn=Al Bondigas` object. Here is the property metadata on DC-01:

   ```
   Loc. USN   Originating DSA    Org.USN   Org.Time/Date          PVN   Attribute Name
   =======    ===============    ====      =============          ===   =========
   1416       Atlanta\DC-01      1416      2002-02-01 01:20.50    1     description
   ```

   Here is the property metadata on DC-02:

   ```
   Loc. USN   Originating DSA    Org.USN   Org.Time/Date          PVN   Attribute
   =======    ===============    ====      =============          ===   =========
   2F5        Atlanta\DC-01      1416      2002-02-01 01:20.50    1     description
   ```

   Note the difference in the *Local USN* values. When a domain controller applies a change to a property, it includes the next available USN value from its own USN counter.

2. Now let's modify the Description attribute for Al's object on DC-01. Here is the metadata for the modified attribute:

   ```
   Loc. USN   Originating DSA    Org.USN   Org.Time/Date          PVN   Attribute
   =======    ===============    ====      =============          ===   =========
   15B1       Atlanta\DC-01      15B1      2002-02-21 02:35.33    2     description
   ```

   Note that the PVN was incremented by one.

3. DC-01 notifies DC-02 of the change and DC-02 pulls a replication packet. Here is the property metadata after DC-02 applies the update:

```
Loc.USN   Originating DSA     Org.USN   Org.Time/Date          PVN   Attribute
=======   ===============     ====      =============          ===   =========
3AC       Atlanta\DC-01       15B1      2002-02-21 02:35.33    2     description
```

   The Local USN value reflects the state of the USN counter on DC-02 when the update arrived.

4. When DC-02 received the update from DC-01, it took note of the USN assigned by DC-01. It put this in a *USN Table*. It uses entries in the USN Table to request only new updates from its partners. Let's see how this works by looking at another replication event, this one for the `Department` property.

   Here is the property metadata from DC-01 prior to any changes:

```
Loc.USN   Originating DSA     Org.USN   Org.Time/Date          PVN   Attribute
=======   ===============     ====      =============          ===   =========
1416      Atlanta\DC-01       1416      2002-02-01 01:20.50    1     department
```

   Note that the PVN is 1 and the Local USN matches the Originating USN. This indicates that the object was created on DC-01.

5. Now let's modify the Department attribute at DC-01. The new metadata listing looks like this:

```
Loc.USN   Originating DSA     Org.USN   Org.Time/Date          PVN   Attribute
=======   ===============     ====      =============          ===   =========
15B2      Atlanta\DC-01       15B2      2002-02-21 02:37.15    2     department
```

   Note that the PVN has incremented to 2.

6. DC-01 notifies DC-02 of the change and DC-02 pulls a replication packet but it also includes a stipulation. It refers to its USN Table and includes the last USN it got from DC-01, `15B1`. It says, in effect, "Only send updates you haven't already sent me."

7. DC-01 receives the request with the high water mark USN. It sifts through the queued updates and filters out the update to the `Description` property because its USN, `15B1`, is equal to the high water mark USN submitted by DC-02. This leaves the update to the `Department` property with USN `15B2`. DC-01 packages the update and sends it to DC-02.

8. DC-02 applies the change. The metadata listing after the update looks like this:

```
Loc.USN   Originating DSA     Org.USN   Org.Time/Date          PVN   Attribute
=======   ===============     ====      =============          ===   =========
3AD       Atlanta\DC-01       15B2      2002-02-21 02:37.15    2     department
```

If you get impatient working through process traces, I really don't blame you. Here are the important points to remember so far:

- When a property is modified, its PVN is incremented and the domain controller applies the next available USN.
- When a domain controller obtains updates, it stores the USN applied by its replication partner in a USN Table.
- When a domain controller requests updates, it includes the last USN it got from its replication partner. This high water mark USN prevents getting redundant updates.

Use of Up-To-Dateness Vector

The circular nature of directory replication makes it possible for updates to propagate back to domain controllers that have already received the update. Unchecked, these updates keep circulating and circulating, the packets getting bigger and bigger, until the entire network hemorrhages in an Ebola virus of unchecked replication traffic.

Positive feedback calls for a dampener of some sort. In this case, the feedback dampener is called the *Up-to-Dateness Vector,* or UTD Vector. It works like this.

The property metadata includes the identity of the originating server. When a domain controller receives a replication packet, it takes note of the originating server and the USN assigned by that server and stores this information in the UTD Vector table. The UTD Vector table contains the GUID and high USN for every domain controller that has ever originated an update.

A domain controller includes its copy of the UTD Vector along with the high water mark USN in each replication request. In effect, it says, "Give me the most recent updates and also don't bother giving me any updates that I've gotten from another source." Procedure 7.3 is an example of how this works.

Procedure 7.3 Replication Trace Showing UTD Vector Operation

1. Recall from the previous example that the Description attribute modified at DC-01 looks like this:

```
Loc. USN   Originating DSA    Org.USN   Org.Time/Date        PVN  Attribute
=======    ===============    ====      =============        ===  =========
15B1       Atlanta\DC-01      15B1      2002-02-21 02:35.33  2    description
```

   The metadata for this property at DC-02 looks like this:

```
Loc.USN   Originating DSA    Org.USN   Org.Time/Date         PVN   Attribute
=======   ===============    ====      =============         ===   =========
3AC       Atlanta\DC-01      15B1      2002-02-21 02:35.33   2     description
```

When DC-02 applied the update, it also improved the UTD Vector entry for DC-01 to reflect the `15B1` USN.

2. Now consider what happens when DC-02 replicates the updated `Description` property to DC-03. Here is the property metadata at DC-03 before and after the update:

   Before:

```
Loc.USN   Originating DSA   Org.USN   Org.Time/Date         Ver   Attribute
=======   ===============   ====      =============         ===   =========
101       Atlanta\DC-01     1416      2002-02-01 01:20.50   1     description
```

   After:

```
Loc.USN   Originating DSA   Org.USN   Org.Time/Date         Ver   Attribute
=======   ===============   ====      =============         ===   =========
1B9       Atlanta\DC-01     15B1      2002-02-21 02:35.33   2     description
```

3. When DC-03 applies the update, it improves the UTD Vector entry for DC-01 to show the `15B1` USN value.
4. Within five minutes after applying the update, DC-03 notifies DC-01 that it has a pending update. DC-01 then requests a replication packet.
5. Now, as the carnival magician says, watch the cards, not my hands. Ordinarily, DC-03 would include the update to the Description property in the replication packet. But DC-01 also included a copy of its UTD Vector, which shows an entry for itself of `15B2`, the latest USN it assigned to an update in its own replica (the `Department` property described in the last trace).
6. DC-03 sifts through the pending updates and sees that DC-01 was the originating server for the `Description` property with USN `15B1`. This USN is lower than the `15B2` value in the UTD Vector, so DC-03 filters the update from the replication packet. The feedback loop is broken. Civilization is saved. Cut to commercial.

The UTD Vector is a critical component in preventing replication storms. Remember these important points:

- The UTD Vector is a combination of the GUID of the originating server and the USN applied by that server.
- A domain controller includes a copy of the UTD Vector with every replication request.
- When a domain controller receives a replication request, it filters out any updates with USNs equal or lower than the entries on the UTD Vector submitted by the replication partner.

Replication Collision Handling

So far, we've seen how property metadata ensures data consistency and controls unnecessary replication. We now need to address the final challenge of multi-master replication: how to deal with conflicting changes made on different domain controllers. These are called *collisions*. Several situations can cause a collision:

- **Simultaneous modifications.** The same property is modified on different domain controllers.
- **Identical DNs.** Objects with the same common name are created in the same container on different domain controllers.
- **Object moved.** An object's property is modified on one domain controller while the object is moved to a different container on another domain controller.
- **Object deleted.** An object's property is modified on one domain controller while the object is deleted on another domain controller.
- **Container deleted.** An object's property is modified on one domain controller while the container holding the object is deleted on another domain controller.

We'll take a detailed look at how Active Directory deals with each of these situations. First, though, we need to see what happens to deleted objects.

Deleted Object Handling

Objects deleted from Active Directory are not immediately removed from the database. This is because the system relies on replication to inform replication partners of changes, and it cannot very well replicate the absence of an object.

Instead, a deleted object is treated like a disgraced officer. It is stripped of most of its attributes and moved to a hidden container called *Deleted Objects*. The object cannot be "undeleted."

Following the object deletion, the domain controller notifies its replication partners. The partners pull a replication packet with an update that, essentially, changes the distinguished name of the object to move it to the Deleted Objects container. The replication partners perform this object move and strip the attributes.

The Deleted Objects container is not revealed in the Active Directory management consoles. Nor does it appear in the ADSI Edit tool. See the sidebar, "Viewing Deleted Objects," for a way to browse the deleted objects in a given naming context.

Viewing Deleted Objects

Microsoft deliberately obfuscates the Deleted Objects container because there is really nothing to be gained by viewing its contents. During an incident analysis, you may want to make certain that an object was deleted and when it the deletion occurred. The tool to use for viewing the Deleted Objects container is the LDAP Browser, Ldp.exe, from the Support Tools:

1. Bind to the domain.
2. From the menu, select BROWSE | SEARCH. This opens a Search window.
3. In the Base DN field, enter the following information (substituting your own domain name). The angle braces are important:

   ```
   <WKGUID=18E2EA80684F11D2B9AA00C04F79F805,DC=domain,DC=root>
   ```

4. Click `Options` then `Controls`. This opens a Controls window.
5. In the `Object Identifier` field, enter the following value:

   ```
   1.2.840.113556.1.4.417
   ```

6. Clear the check for `Value`.
7. Set `Control Type` to `Server`.
8. Clear the check for `Critical`.
9. Select the `Check In >>` option.
10. Click OK to save the change and close the window.
11. Under `Search Call Type`, select `Extended`.
12. Clear the check for `Attributes Only`.
13. Clear the check for `Chase Referrals`.
14. Select the `Display Results` option.
15. Click `OK` to save the changes and close the window.
16. Under `Scope`, select the `Subtree` option.
17. Click `Run`. The results of the search displays in the right pane. These are the objects in the Deleted Objects container.

Garbage Collection

Objects in the Deleted Objects container are called *tombstones*. Tombstones remain in the Deleted Objects container for 60 days. This is often called the *tombstone interval*.

When the tombstone interval expires for a given object, the object is eligible for complete removal from the database. The removal is performed by the *garbage collection* process. Garbage collection runs every 12 hours. When garbage collection runs, it removes any expired tombstones then packs the database and re-indexes. Without doing this periodically, performance would degrade.

Garbage collection compacts the database but leaves the physical size of the Ntds.dit file the same. The only way to recover physical disk space is to run offline defragmentation.

A 60-day tombstone interval may seem like a long time, but it is long for a purpose. It is essential that the presence of deleted objects not cause database corruption following a tape restore of Active Directory.

Consider what would happen if the tombstone interval were 1 day instead of 60. Let's say a domain controller fails. You are unable to find a viable tape newer than three days old—not an uncommon occurrence. You decide to use the tape because you know that the domain controller will update the older Active Directory copy by pulling changes from its replication partners.

Unfortunately, the tape is older than our hypothetical 1-day tombstone interval. This means that objects deleted since the tape backup may have been expunged from the directory database on other domain controllers. When you restore from the older tape, the objects would be in their original containers and there would be no information to the contrary in the databases of the replication partners. This would leave the objects in their original locations, corrupting the directory because it would now be different than its peers.

The 60-day interval gives you lots of leeway in doing a tape restore; but always keep in mind that any copy of Active Directory, whether it comes from tape or a disk image or wherever, becomes useless 61 days after it was obtained.

Armed with this information about deleted object handling, we can proceed to see how Active Directory handles replication collisions.

Simultaneous Modification

Consider this situation. The Chief Executive Officer wants her title to appear when people search "that Active Directory thing that you folks installed:"

- The CEO calls the Help Desk. The technician handling the call is happy to help and changes the Title attribute of the CEO's user object to "CEO."
- A system administrator gets a call from the CEO's Administrative Assistant asking for a favor. "Please change the boss' title, would you?" The administrator obliges by changing the Title attribute of the CEO's user object to "Chief Executive Officer."

The Help Desk technician and the system administrator are logged on to different domain controllers. They make their changes during the same replication interval. This means that the modified attributes have the same PVN but contain different information.

Offline Defragmentation

There is no advantage to offline defragmentation other than reducing the physical size of the Ntds.dit file. You should size your storage to handle the largest possible size of Ntds.dit and its support files, so there is really no need to ever run offline defragmentation.

Within the next 15 seconds, the changes begin to circulate around to the other domain controllers. Because the updates have the same PVN, the other domain controllers must decide which one to retain.

They start by using the timestamp applied by the originating domain controller as a tiebreaker. If one update were saved a few seconds after the other, it would be retained.

If the updates were saved at exactly the same time, the domain controllers apply an ultimate tiebreaker: a comparison of the GUID of the originating domain controller. The highest GUID wins. Sure, it's arbitrary, but at least it's consistent—something like parental discipline.

Identical Distinguished Names

Here's another situation. A new user joins the company. Your internal procedures require that an HR representative with special directory permissions create the user object in Active Directory and set the correct parameters. This particular user is a VIP, though, and someone expedites the process by calling an Operations administrator directly.

The HR representative and the Operations administrator both create a user object with the same name in the same container during the same replication interval. Objects cannot have the same distinguished names in Active Directory. When the new objects begin to replicate around the network, the other domain controllers are faced with a decision. Which object should be retained and which should be discarded?

There's a possibility that information about a user could be lost if one object simply overwrites another, so both objects must be retained. One object is renamed to give it a different distinguished name. Each domain controller must rename the same object the same way so that the directory replicas remain consistent.

The tiebreaker once again is timestamp followed by GUID. If the objects were created at different times, the domain controllers retain the name on the object with the later timestamp. The object with the earlier timestamp is renamed. If the timestamps match, the object created on the server with the higher GUID retains its name.

The losing object gets a new name using this process:

- Keep the original name as a prefix
- Append a reserved character, an asterisk (*)
- Append the GUID of the originating domain controller

The resultant name would look like this:

```
cn=Jane Jones*2FAC1234-31F8-11B4-A222-08002B34C003
```

The only warning you get about this action is an entry in the Event log. When you discover the problem, you must examine both objects to decide which one to keep and which to delete.

Notification of Collision Results

When Active Directory errors occur, such as a replication collision, the system logs a warning in the Event log and goes on about its business. You may want to install a utility that sends you an email or a page when critical errors or warnings occur.

An example of such a utility is LogCaster from RippleTech, Inc., at `www.rippletech.com`. This utility can be configured to look for specific events and send SNMP traps, pages, cell phone messages, and emails.

A similar product called Event Log Monitor can be evaluated and purchased at Sunbelt Software at `www.sunbeltsoftware.com`.

Moved Objects

Here's another situation that can cause a collision. You make a change to an object's property while, at the same time, another administrator on another domain controller moves the object to a different container. When the property update arrives at the domain controller where the object was moved, the directory engine has a dilemma. The distinguished name of the object has changed, but the DN associated with the property for that object has not.

Active Directory resolves this problem easily because the GUID of the object does not change when the DN changes. The directory just does a lookup for the object GUID, finds the new DN, and updates the property in the correct location.

Deleted Objects

The next collision situation could occur in this fashion. A Facilities staffer makes a change to the Telephone attribute for a user. At same time, the user's manager fires the user and insists that a network administrator delete the user's object. (In a true production environment, you would disable a user account for a period of time rather than delete it. You don't want to lose the user's Security Identifier (SID) until you're sure the user will never return.)

Recall that when an object is deleted, the object is moved to the Deleted Objects container. It is also stripped of all but a few properties. If an update for one of those stripped properties arrives after the object has been deleted, the system ignores the update.

Deleted Containers

This collision scenario involves deleting an entire container on one domain controller while an object has been moved to the container on another domain controller.

For instance, let's say that a friend of yours, Andy, calls you up to say that he's been promoted to manager of the company's branch office. "Do what you folks do to get me their computer stuff in the branch office, okay?" he says to you. What he wants is to be put in the Branch OU so he can get their desktop configuration and group policies. You're happy to do it and you move the object.

At the same time, the CEO walks into another administrator's office and says, "We're destaffing the branch office. Do whatever you computer people do to remove their network access. They won't be back." The administrator obliges the CEO by deleting the entire Branch OU.

An object move changes several properties of an object, including the object's distinguished name. If the updates to Andy's object arrive at a domain controller after the Branch OU has been deleted, Active Directory has a problem. Ordinarily, the system would move Andy's object to the target OU in its new location, but in this case that is the Deleted Objects container and the system doesn't know if you really wanted to delete the object. So instead, it moves the object to a hidden container called *Lost & Found*.

Unlike the Deleted Objects container, Lost & Found can be viewed from the AD Users and Computers console by enabling the `Advanced` view options. The user object remains enabled so the user can still log on. You may be unaware that there's a problem unless the user complains that the desktop doesn't show the expected result from inheriting group policies.

You can move an object out of the Lost & Found container to another container. You can also decide to delete it.

Windows Time Service

Proper time synchronization is critical for railroads, airports, blind dates, and Active Directory domains. Proper collision management requires consistent timestamps, so it's important that domain controller clocks stay in sync with each other. Also, the Kerberos authentication system uses timestamps to ensure that bad guys don't hijack authentication tickets and replay them at a later time.

The service responsible for time synchronization is the *Windows Time Service*, or WTS. The actual service name for WTS is *Win32Time*, part of the Services.exe suite.

WTS uses a standard implementation of the Simple Network Time Protocol (SNTP) as promulgated in RFC 2030, "Simple Network Time Protocol (SNTP) Version 4 for IPv4, IPv6 and OSI." Every Windows 2000 and Windows Server 2003 domain controller is an SNTP time server.

SNTP uses a hierarchical approach to distributing time updates. The PDC Emulator acts as the time standard for a domain. (See Chapter 8, "Designing Windows Server 2003 Domains," for a description of Flexible Single Master Operators such as the PDC Emulator.) In a forest, the PDC Emulators in each domain sync their clocks with the PDC Emulator in the root domain. The root domain is the first domain created in the forest.

Registry Tip: Windows Time Service

The Registry settings for the Windows Time Service are stored as follows:

```
Key:        HKLM | SYSTEM | CurrentControlSet | Services | W32TIME | Parameters
Value/Data: LocalNTP / 0
Value/Data: Period / SpecialSkew
Value/Data: Type / NT5DS
```

You can enable logging for the W32TIME, which is a big help when trying to diagnose time synchronization problems:

```
Key:    HKLM | System | CurrentControlSet | Services | W32Time | Config
Value:  FileLogName
Data:   <path and name of log file>
Value:  FileLogEntries
Data:    0-109 (enter this as shown)
```

Stop and restart the service to initialize the file and start logging. Remove the entries to stop logging.

NET TIME and WIN32TM

Windows Server 2003 has two command-line tools for managing WTS: NET TIME and W32TM. Of the two, W32TM has more options for setting and viewing SNTP parameters.

For example, if you want to know the time source for a particular client, type

```
w32tm -source -v
```

This prints out a verbose listing that shows how WTS on the server discovered its time sources and what sources it discovered. By default, modern Windows clients use a domain controller for a time standard.

You can also use `net time /querysntp` to show the time source for a client, but this will show `time.windows.net`, a time server on the Internet maintained by Microsoft. Member computers ignore this SNTP time source entry in favor of their logon server. Domain controllers ignore this SNTP time source entry in favor of the PDC Emulator in their domain. The PDC Emulators in each domain look to the PDC Emulator in the root domain.

If you want to synchronize the PDC Emulator in the root domain with a time standard, you can type:

```
net time /setsntp:<time_standard>
```

The most commonly used time servers in the U.S. are maintained by the National Institute of Standards and Technology (NIST). Go to `www.boulder.nist.gov/timefreq/service/time-servers.html` for a list of the servers and their IP addresses. You'll need to open UDP port 123 through your firewall to use SNTP.

You can use this same procedure if you have a standalone server or desktop at home that you want to keep synchronized with an Internet time standard. If you want to resynchronize a client, type

```
w32tm -once
```

This does a one-time resync to the NTP time standard for the client. You can also type

```
net time /domain:<domain_name> /set
```

Both of these options require you to have *Change Local Time* permission at the client. You can verify that you have this permission using the WHOAMI utility from the Resource Kit. Enter `whoami /all` to see your permissions and the groups you belong to by name and SID. Ordinary users are not granted permissions to change the local system time.

If you have laptop users who experience time synchronization problems because they are off the network for long periods of time, you can give them permission to change the local time with a group policy. The policy is located in `Computer Configuration | Windows Settings | Local Policies | User Rights Assignments | Change The System Time`. Create a security group for your laptop users and add that group to the policy.

You should not manually set the time on a domain controller. If you do, it puts incorrect timestamps on the updates it makes to Active Directory properties until it syncs again with the PDC Emulator. This can cause integrity problems when the objects are replicated. Always change time by synchronizing the domain controller with the time standard server. The easiest way to do this is by using the `NET TIME` command as follows:

```
net time \\local_computer_name /set
```

The `NET TIME` command cannot be used to connect to a non-Windows server because it uses SMB (Server Message Block) to handle the transaction. If you want to set a server to an outside time source, use the following syntax (the example shows the time standard server from the National Institute of Standards and Technology):

```
net time /setsntp:nist1.datum.com
```

The `net time /setsntp` option updates the Registry with the names or IP addresses of SNTP time servers. The target time server is checked when the server boots. If you use `net time` or `net time /set`, the `/setsntp` switch has no effect.

Designing Site Architectures

Any design involves applying available features with adequate safeguards for failures. When laying out sites for your organization, keep the following guidelines in mind:

- Minimize convergence time without swamping WAN links.
- Localize client access to domain controllers for authentication and Active Directory services. This includes Global Catalog queries.
- Prepare for possible failure of bridgehead servers.
- Prepare for possible loss of WAN links.
- Ensure that all naming contexts have a replication path through each site.

The site plan depends on the network infrastructure. Begin with an evaluation of that infrastructure. Figure 7.8 shows a typical WAN layout for a medium-sized organization. The company has four offices scattered around the Southwest. They could just as easily be offices in the same city or overseas. The issue is not distance but the speed and reliability of the connections.

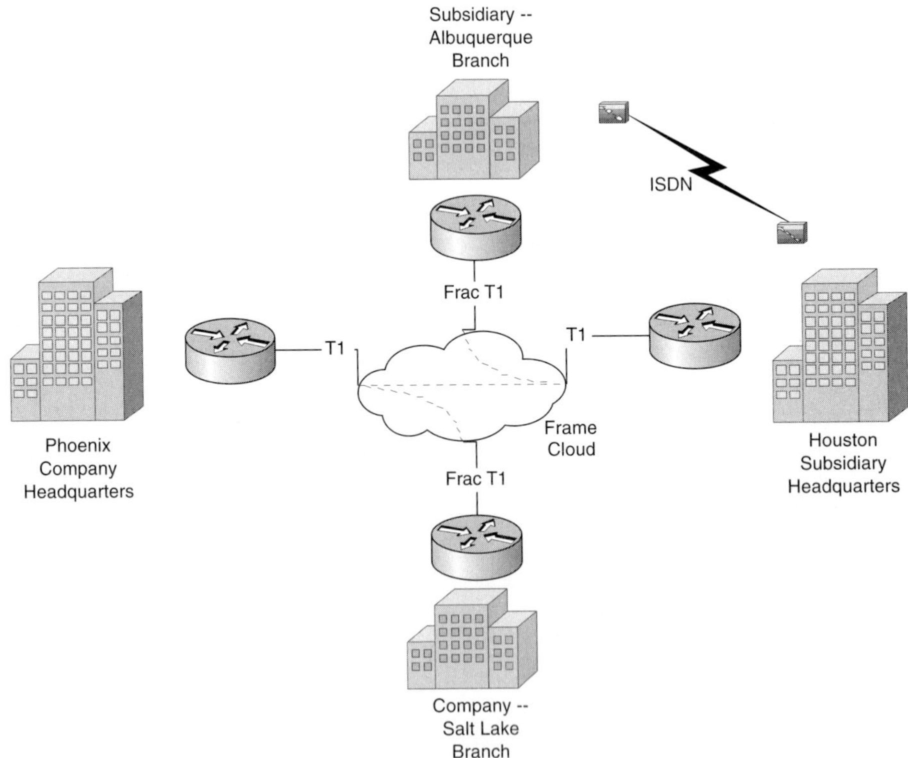

Figure 7.8 WAN layout for offices in four cities.

Here are the key aspects of the infrastructure that affect site design:

- Connections between offices use WAN links of various speeds. Some links, like the ISDN line, are expensive if used continually. This requires costing out the site links to ensure replication takes place over an appropriate path.
- The network links, with the exception of the ISDN line, can handle respectable volumes of traffic. This makes it possible to use short inter-site polling frequencies.
- The forest contains two domains. You must ensure that domain controllers from both domains can obtain updates from partners in the same domain. You must also ensure that Global Catalog servers can obtain updates from other GC servers.
- All locations are well connected, so there is no need to use SMTP or to set special replication schedules.

Figure 7.9 shows a provisional site plan for the infrastructure shown in Figure 7.8.

In the example, each office is assigned a site. You might be tempted to put offices connected by high-speed links in the same site to minimize convergence time, but you have a secondary objective to localize client access. Using separate sites ensures that clients in each office authenticate on local domain controllers. Even if the offices were connected by DS-3 or SONET links, you would want to define separate sites in view of the objective to minimize the impact of a lost link.

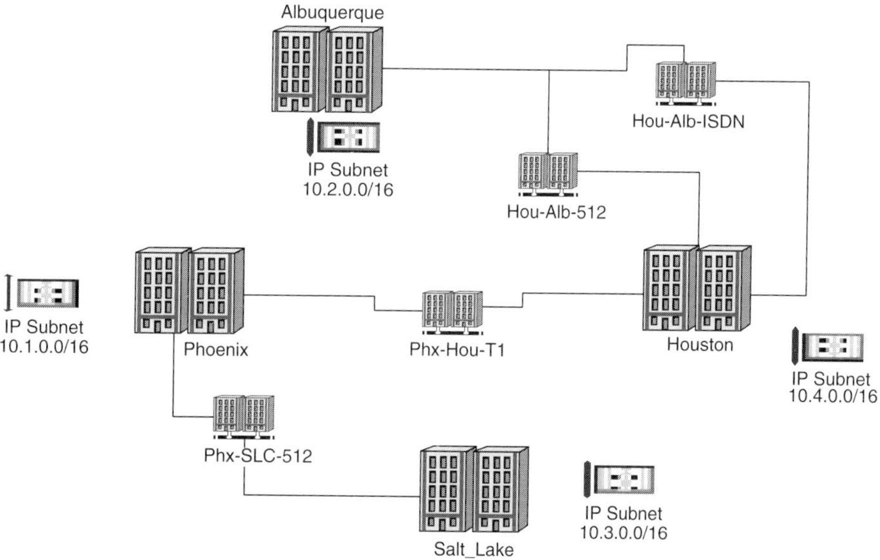

Figure 7.9 Site plan showing replication connections corresponding to WAN layout in Figure 7.8.

The IP Subnet objects use the IP addresses assigned to each office by the routing infrastructure. This permits domain controllers to guide a client to the correct site based on the client's IP address.

The Site Link objects mimic the underlying network infrastructure only to the extent necessary to define the inter-office topology. There is no need to create Site Links for every routing path. Site links do not tell Active Directory how to route individual replication packets. They simply define the underlying connection lines. The primary concern is to tell the ISTG about available paths to the other sites so it can create appropriate Connection objects between the bridgeheads.

The Site Link names include the names of the end-points so that you can tell at a glance where the link goes. This works like rural highway names in the Midwest. For example, in Cincinnati, the Carmel-Tabasco road connects the town of Carmel to the town of Tabasco.

You can also include the connection type in the name to differentiate multiple links between the same sites. For example, the primary connection between the Houston office and the Albuquerque office is a frame relay PVC with a Committed Information Rate (CIR) of 512Kbps, so the name would be Hou_Alb_512.

The link costs reflect the speed of the underlying WAN links. The costs tell the bridgeheads where to pull replication. In the example, the bridgehead in Albuquerque would replicate from the Phoenix bridgehead through the bridgehead in Houston. It uses this path rather than pulling directly from Phoenix using the ISDN line because the cost on the Site Link to Houston is lower than that of Phoenix. In the example, costs are assigned as follows:

- The fastest connection is given a cost of 5. This gives some headroom for the future if a faster link is installed.
- The remaining links costs are in ratio to the fastest link. For instance, the 512Kbps links are 1/3 of a full T-1, so the costs are 3*5 or 15. The cost of the ISDN link is 60 (1/12 of a full T-1, or 12*5).

The polling frequency assigned to each fast link is set to 15 minutes. This is the minimum replication interval and yields the fastest convergence. The polling frequency for the ISDN line is set to 30 minutes to reduce the load on the slow link.

The plan designates preferred bridgehead servers. This is not a required step. The KCC will select bridgeheads automatically. Designating a set of preferred bridgeheads is desirable when you want to ensure that the job is given to the most capable machines. It is important that you clearly label your preferred bridgeheads so that the operations staff does not inadvertently take them out of service and stop replication from a site.

> **Site Link Bridge**
> The KCC in each site assumes that it can obtain a naming context from a remote site by way of an intervening site. This transitive site replication is called *bridging*. The IP Transport has a property called Bridge All Site Links that puts all site links into one big bridge. This leaves the bridgehead free to pull replication from the least cost connection regardless of the costs of the upstream connections.
>
> If you have a large network with many different routes and several domains, certain route combinations might be preferable. In that case, you can disable the `Bridge All Site Links` option and define specific Site Link Bridges. This is only required if you experience severe replication delays caused by inappropriate routes selected by the bridgeheads.

Finally, the plan has to designate the location of domain controllers and Global Catalog servers. Here is a set of guidelines:

- Small offices with a few users are not given a local domain controller. The office is still defined as a site so that clients authenticate to the domain controllers in the closest office.
- Slightly larger sites are given a local domain controller that is not configured as a Global Catalog server. The domain controller is configured to cache Global Catalog information so that a cut WAN link does not prevent users from authenticating.
- Large sites are given both a DC and a GC. This ensures that sufficient domain controllers are available for handling peak authentication requests. It also maintains link continuity between sites containing different domains. In practice, you could make each domain controller a GC if you have fast, reliable servers.

You should configure the sites in Active Directory before deploying controllers in the various sites. This permits the system to place the domain controllers in the correct site as they are promoted. Otherwise, you must move the server to the correct site manually.

Configuring Inter-site Replication

After you have a plan in place that defines your sites, IP subnets, site links, costs, and bridgeheads, you can proceed to create the objects in Active Directory. Here is the general course of action:

- Rename the Default-First-Site-Name object
- Create new Site objects
- Create Subnet objects
- Create Site Link objects
- Designate bridgehead servers

After completing this work, the KCC should handle any changes you make to the distribution of domain controllers and Global Catalog servers in the network with no further intervention.

Rename the Default-First-Site-Name Site

The name for the first site is a little long and clumsy for most uses. The steps to rename it are listed in Procedure 7.4.

Procedure 7.4 Renaming the Default-First-Site-Name Object

1. Open the `AD Sites and Services` console.
2. Right-click the `Default-First-Site-Name` object and select RENAME from the flyout menu. The object name gets a bounding box and a blue background.
3. Change the name to the name of the site in your site plan and press `Enter`. The example shows a new name of `Phoenix`.
4. Leave the console open. You need it to perform the next steps.

The name change is registered with DNS automatically. Verify using the DNS console that the name change took effect. This ensures that the site references used by the Active Directory clients are correct. If the DNS server is offline when you change the name, or if you lose network connection while the change is replicating, the new site name will be registered as soon as connection to DNS is re-established. You may need to delete the old site name manually from the zone table.

Create New Sites

After you rename the first site, create site objects for the remaining sites in your plan. Do this using the AD Sites and Services console as shown in Procedure 7.5.

Procedure 7.5 Creating a New Site Object

1. Right-click the `Sites` object and select NEW SITE from the flyout menu. The New Object – (Site) window appears (see Figure 7.10).
2. Under `Name`, enter the name of the site. The example uses a site name of `Houston`.
3. Under `Link Name`, highlight `DefaultIPSiteLink`. This is only a placeholder. You'll be creating specific links a little later.
4. Click `OK` to create the `Site` object.

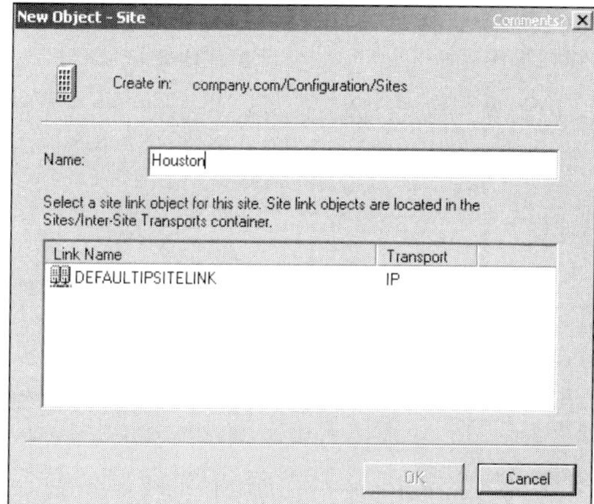

Figure 7.10 New Object — (Site) window.

When you create the Site object, the system automatically creates a Server container and two Settings objects, `Licensing Site Settings` and `NTDS Site Settings`. The system also adds several SRV records to DNS that point at the new domain controller. These records are grouped under the `_msdcs` and `_sites` headings.

Create IP Subnets

Active Directory uses subnets to differentiate between sites. Create Subnet objects for each subnet in your network as shown in Procedure 7.6.

Procedure 7.6 Creating a Subnet Object

1. Right-click the `Subnets` object and select New Subnet from the flyout menu. The New Object – (Subnet) window appears (see Figure 7.11).
2. Under `Name`, enter the subnet address and the number of bits in the subnet mask. The example uses a private 10-space network, 10.1.1.0, with a 24-bit mask corresponding to 255.255.255.0.
3. Select a Site object to associate with the Subnet object. The example uses the Phoenix site. If you have more than one subnet in a Site, you can create multiple Subnet objects and associate them with the same site.
4. Click `OK` to create the subnet object and return to the main console window.

Use the same procedure to create Subnet objects for all the subnets in your network.

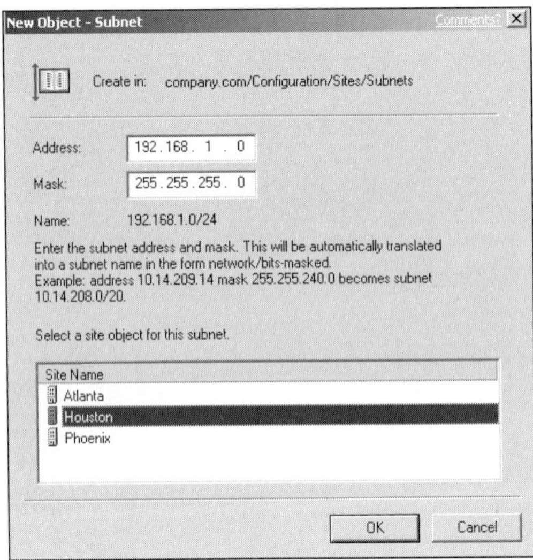

Figure 7.11 New Object — (Subnet) window showing subnet for the Phoenix site.

Create Site Links

You are now ready to create and configure the necessary Site Link objects to describe your network infrastructure. Follow the steps in Procedure 7.7.

Procedure 7.7 Creating and Configuring Site Link Objects

1. Expand the tree to find the `IP` object under `Sites | Inter-Site Transports`.
2. Right-click the `IP` object and select NEW SITE LINK from the flyout menu. The New Object – (Site Link) window appears (see Figure 7.12).
3. Under `Name`, enter a name for the Site Link object.
4. Select two sites and click `Add` to put them in the `Sites In This Link` list. You must have at least two sites associated with a Site Link.
5. Click `OK` to create the object.
6. Open the Properties window for the new Site Link object (see Figure 7.13).
7. Enter a `Description` for the link. You might want to include the type of connection, the bandwidth, and any helpful information that helps you isolate problems should you have trouble with the link.

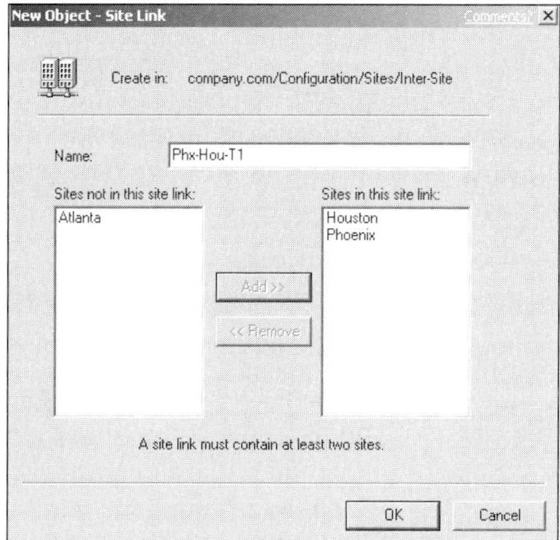

Figure 7.12 New Object — (Site Link) window.

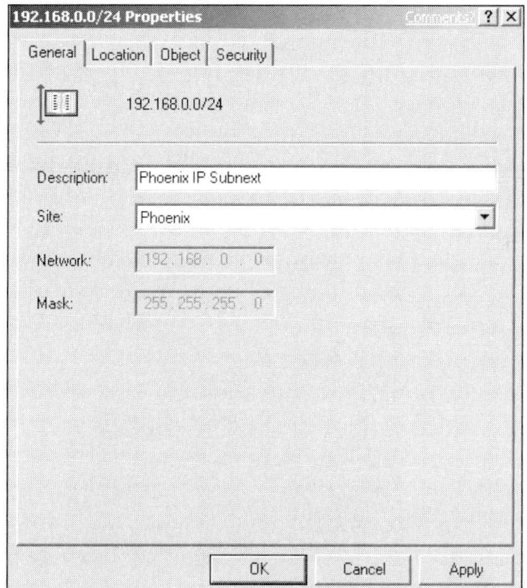

Figure 7.13 Site Link Properties for the Phoenix to Houston link showing description, cost, and interval.

8. Assign a `Cost` to the link. This is the highest-speed link in the example network, so it gets a cost of 1. For the 512K links to the branch offices, assign a cost of 20. For the emergency ISDN line, assign a cost of 100. Keep the options to a minimum. The KCC uses these numbers to build a spanning tree map. If you use too many values, you'll confuse matters rather than help them.
9. Shorten the default `Replication` interval unless the link is especially slow or heavily subscribed. The shortest interval that the system accepts is 15 minutes. If you enter a shorter interval, the change is accepted, but the interval is set to 15.
10. Click `Change Schedule`. The Schedule window opens for the link (see Figure 7.14).
11. If the connection is up at certain times, clear the blue for the intervals where it is not available. Use this option if you have a slow link that experiences peak traffic at certain times and you don't want to add replication traffic to the mix. When you play games with replication intervals, keep in mind that you're affecting latency.
12. Click `OK` to save the change and return to the Properties window.
13. Click `OK` to save the changes and return to the console.
14. Close the console.

Now create Site Link objects for the remaining connections between sites.

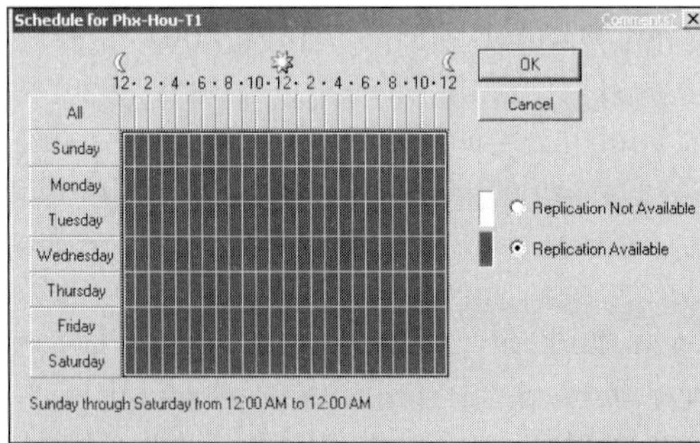

Figure 7.14 Schedule window for the Phoenix to Houston Site Link showing that replication is available 7x24.

Designating Bridgehead Servers

The KCC may select a bridgehead that is not the most capable domain controller in a site. Or it may select a bridgehead that is not a Global Catalog server, which would require the system to create additional connections to handle GC replication between sites.

You can reduce the complexity of inter-site replication and improve performance by selecting preferred bridgehead servers. It is important to designate multiple preferred bridgeheads so that the failure of a single server does not cause a failure of inter-site replication. Procedure 7.8 designates a Bridgehead server.

Procedure 7.8 Designating a Bridgehead Server

1. Open the `AD Sites and Services` console.
2. Expand the tree to show the Server object representing the domain controller you want to use for a bridgehead server.
3. Right-click the Server object and select PROPERTIES from the flyout menu. The Properties window opens (see Figure 7.15).
4. Select the IP transport and click `Add` to move it to the bridgehead side of the window.
5. Click `OK` to save the change.

The `Computer` field indicates the Computer object associated with the Server object used to control replication. The two names should always be the same.

Bridgehead Servers and Firewalls

Another common reason for designating specific Bridgehead servers is to configure replication through a firewall. By assigning the servers that handle inter-site replication, you can configure the firewall to pass traffic only from those servers.

You can designate the port used by the bridgehead server. This helps to configure replication through the firewall. This option requires a Registry entry:

```
Key:    HKLM | System | CurrentControlSet | Services | NTDS | Parameters
Value:  TCP/IP Port
Data:   <port number>
```

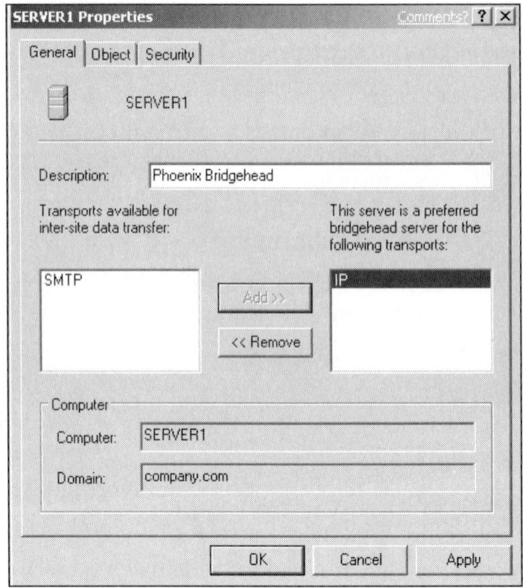

Figure 7.15 Properties window for server showing transports that have been added to the bridgehead list.

Creating Site Link Bridge Objects

You may find after laying out the Site Links and running the system in production a while that the bridgeheads need a bit more information about your network to lay their replication plans effectively. This involves creating specific Site Link Bridge objects to describe preferred routes. Follow the steps in Procedure 7.9 to disable global site link bridging and to build Site Link Bridge objects.

Procedure 7.9 Building a Site Link Bridge Object

1. Open the `AD Sites and Services` console.
2. Right-click the `IP` object and select PROPERTIES from the flyout menu. The IP Properties window opens (see Figure 7.16).
3. Deselect the `Bridge All Site Links` option. This removes the global transitive bridging for site links.
4. Right-click the `IP` object and select NEW SITE LINK BRIDGE from the flyout menu. The New Object – (Site Link Bridge) window appears (see Figure 7.17).
5. Select the links you want to define for the preferred route and click `Add` to put them on the list.

6. Click `OK` to save the changes and return to the console. The `Site Link Bridge` object is added to the list of IP link objects.
7. Monitor your Event log and Connection object status carefully over the next few hours to see how the KCC reacts to the change.

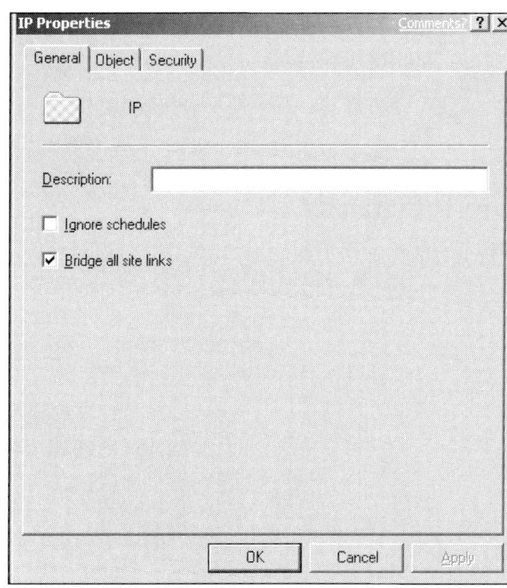

Figure 7.16 IP Properties window showing the global bridging option.

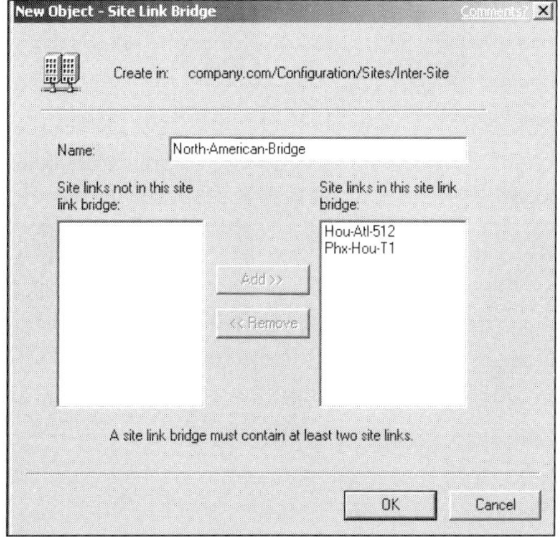

Figure 7.17 New Object — (Site Link Bridge) window.

Only a few more items to take care of, then the job is complete. One of those items is making sure that efficient use is made of the domain controllers when it comes to propagating replication traffic. To do that, we may need Bridgehead servers.

Controlling Replication Parameters

The default replication intervals set by the NTDS Site Settings object support most operations. This topic covers ways to adjust the default replication intervals if you want to tune your system. It also shows how to force replication if you want to hurry the process along.

Setting Replication Intervals

Within a site, domain controllers send out replication announcements within five minutes after receiving an update. This does not apply to replication between sites. Replication between sites is controlled solely by fixed polling schedules.

Changing Notification Parameters

When a domain controller updates its copy of a naming context, it notifies its replication partners so they can pull a copy of the update. The default notification interval is five minutes. The domain controller sends a notification to one partner then waits 30 seconds before sending a notification to the next partner.

The Registry values that control these notification intervals are stored in two values under `HKLM | System || CurrentControlSet | NTDS | Parameters:`

- `Replicator notify pause after modify (secs) - 300 secs`
- `Replicator notify pause between DSAs (secs) - 30 secs`

If you want a shorter notification interval, you can reduce the `Replicator Notify Pause After Modify` interval, but keep an eye on utilization levels.

In addition to update notifications, domain controllers replicate with their partners at fixed intervals. The purpose for this fixed schedule is to check for broken connections. The fixed replication interval is set by an attribute in the Connection object.

Changing Inter-Site Polling Frequency and Schedule

The default inter-site polling frequency is a 15-minute window every three hours. The interval is set by an attribute of the Site Link. You can change this interval using the AD Sites and Service console. See Figure 7.18 for an example. The minimum interval is 15 minutes.

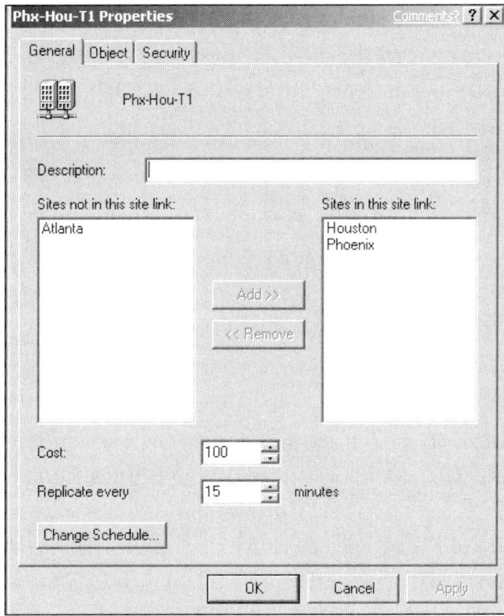

Figure 7.18 Site Link object properties showing replication interval.

The default inter-site polling schedule is set to permit replication at any time. You can change the schedule to permit replication only during specific time periods. For example, you may want to delay replication until after working hours.

The interval is set by another attribute of the Site Link. If you click `Change Schedule`, a Schedule window opens to show the replication schedule. It's possible to set up schedules that put a particular site in a replication "shadow." This occurs when the schedules for intervening connections have no overlap. If you have scheduling problems, you can override all schedules using the `Ignore Schedules` option in the Properties window of the IP or SMTP transport object.

Forcing Replication

If you want a particular update to replicate sooner than the default interval, you can force replication. One way to do this is by using the AD Sites and Services console as described in Procedure 7.10.

Procedure 7.10 Forcing Replication with the AD Sites and Services Console

1. Expand the tree to the server to which you want to replicate. Remember that connections represent inbound data flows.
2. Find the `NTDS Settings` object and its associated `Connection` objects under the server icon.
3. Right-click the connection from the replication partner and select REPLICATE NOW from the flyout menu. You get a message indicating that the replication commenced. If the link is broken, you get a message saying that the RPC connection is unavailable. If the connection is an inter-site connection, the replication request will be queued.

You can check the Event log to verify that replication is complete. Alternatively, you can check the properties of a target object to verify that they changed. Replication does not occur immediately, so wait a few minutes before checking.

If you prefer command-line tools, you can force replication using REPADMIN with this syntax:

```
repadmin /syncall <DSA> <NC>
```

`<DSA>` is the fully qualified domain name of the server to which you want to replicate. `<NC>` is the distinguished name of the naming context you want to replicate. For example:

```
repadmin /syncall dc-01.company.com dc=company,dc=com
```

Diagnosing RPC Problems

Intra-site replication takes place over secure RPC connections. A failed RPC connection can result in Event log errors such as `There are no more endpoints available from the RPC Endpoint Mapper.`

This is generally caused by network hardware failure, either a bad switch port or bad router table or a failed network adapter. It could also be caused by another RPC application that decided to interfere with the RPC Endpoint Mapper and the TCP ports it uses. The Microsoft RPC Runtime service selects TCP ports above 1024 at random to make its connections. If another process steps on one of those ports, you will get replication errors.

Another possible cause of an RPC failure is a failure of the RPC Locator service. This service uses TCP port 135 to reach out to an RPC server. Sometimes a rogue application uses TCP port 135 and steps on the Locator service. More often, though, losing this port is the result of a zealous firewall administrator.

If you think you are getting a failure of the RPC Locator service, try using the Rpcping utilities from the Resource Kit. These were originally designed for Exchange, but they are just as useful for Active Directory.

There are two components to RPC tracing using Rpcping. At the server, you start the *RPC Listener* by running RpingS32. From the client, generate RPC traffic by running Rpings and specifying the fully qualified DNS name of the server. If you get a response, you know the RPC Locator service is working at the client end and the RPC Runtime is properly configured at the server.

If Rpcping fails, check your network connections and configurations. Try restarting the server. You may have a problem with the network adapter driver, so always make sure you have the most current driver.

Special Replication Operations

After you set up your sites and deploy your domain controllers, there shouldn't be much else to do but bask in a job well done. One or two things may crop up, though, that demand your attention.

Manually Creating Connections

Given enough time, the KCC will create an intra-site replication topology that converges changes as rapidly as possible. The ISTG will do the same for inter-site replication.

If a domain controller goes down, it may take a while for the KCC to recognize the problem and begin work to heal the replication ring. If the KCC or ISTG fails to respond in time to forestall an emergency, you can intervene and create a connection manually.

When you build a manual connection, you interfere with the automatic operation of the KCC. This isn't necessarily a bad thing. The network will not melt down if you make a mistake. But you may find that a domain controller gets into unexpected replication difficulties caused by your actions. Consider all manual interventions carefully before proceeding.

Moving Server Objects Between Sites

You may be part of a central IT group that builds new servers for remote locations and then ships them for installation by a local tech or an outsourcing agent. During the domain controller promotion, the local IP address of the server defines its site affiliation. This site may not be correct for the ultimate destination.

If you change the IP network of a domain controller, or build a new site that is assigned the IP network of an existing domain controller, you need to move the Server object for the domain controller to a new Site container along with the NTDS Settings object and the Connection objects. This is done using the AD Sites and Services console. Drag and drop the server object onto the Server container under the target site.

After moving a Server object, give the KCC lots of time to set up the new replication topology and change the replication transport from high-speed RPC to low-speed RPC. If you try to force replication before the KCC does its work, you'll get an error. Wait at least a half hour (two KCC intervals) then try again. If it still fails, check the Event log. You may see an error such as the one in Figure 7.19.

If you get a connection error, make sure you didn't accidentally associate the site with the wrong IP address. Check DNS to ensure that the SRV records are in their proper places and that the server is configured to point at a functioning DNS server. Also, if this is the first domain controller in the new site, it will become both the bridgehead and the ISTG, which will take a while to configure automatically.

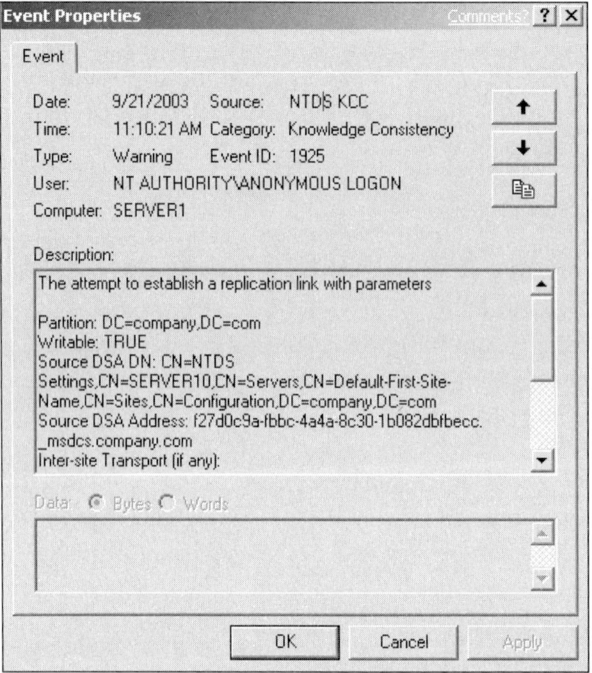

Figure 7.19 Event Log entry showing failure of the KCC to build a connection.

Manually Controlling Replication Topology

When the KCC builds a connection, it selects two end-point domain controllers and places a Connection object into the NTDS Settings container for those servers. Connection objects always represent inbound data flows. You cannot change the inbound target of a Connection object, but you can change its replication partner.

When building manual connections, make absolutely sure that you don't inadvertently put the domain controller into a loop or place the end-point at a domain controller in the forest that does not communicate directly with other domain controllers holding replicas of the same naming contexts.

Also, the KCC will not delete manual connections when new domain controllers are added to the replica ring or other domain controllers are taken out or fail. You'll need to change the topology by hand after you take manual control of the connections.

You have two choices when manually controlling replication topology: you can select a new replication partner for a given connection or you can build a new Connection object.

Selecting a New Replication Partner

When you are ready to select a new replication partner, follow Procedure 7.11.

Procedure 7.11 Selecting a New Replication Partner

1. Open the `AD Sites and Services` console.
2. Expand the tree to find the target server and highlight its `NTDS Settings` icon.
3. Double-click the `Connection` object from the domain controller you want to change. This opens the Properties window for the connection (see Figure 7.20).

   The `Replicate From` field contains the name of the replication partner, the partner's site, and the domains that are replicated from that partner. In the example, the target server is in the Subsidiary.com domain and is not a Global Catalog server, so it does not replicate any other naming contexts.
4. In the `Replicate From` field, click `Change`. The Find Domain Controllers window opens. If you have an extensive forest, this list might be fairly long.
5. Double-click the domain controller that you want to be the server's new replication partner. This closes the window and returns you to the Properties window. The new replication partner is listed in the `Server` field.
6. Click `OK` to save the changes and close the window. The DRA sees the change and begins replication from the new partner. If this is an inter-site connection, it may take a while for replication to occur.

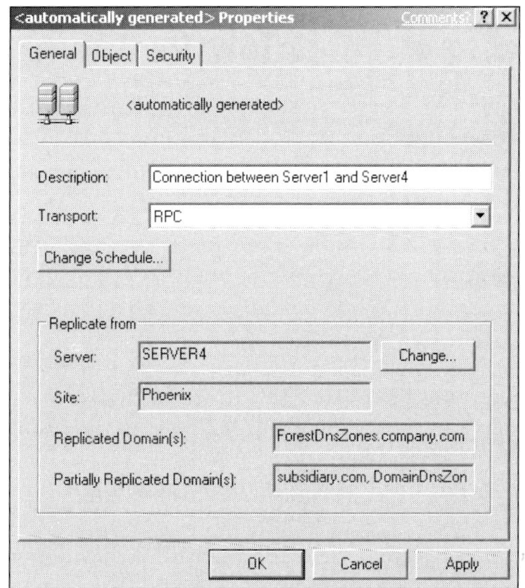

Figure 7.20 Properties window for `<automatically generated>` connection showing its replication partner.

Building New Connections

When you are ready to create a new connection between domain controllers, do as directed in Procedure 7.12.

Procedure 7.12 Building a New Connection Object

1. Open the `AD Sites and Services` console.
2. Expand the tree to show the contents of the `NTDS Settings` container under the server for which you want to build a connection. There should already be at least one `Connection` object designated `<automatically generated>`. This was built by the KCC.
3. Right-click the `NTDS Settings` object and select NEW NT DS CONNECTION from the flyout menu. The Find Domain Controllers window opens.
4. Select the domain controller from which you want to build a connection. Remember that Connection objects always represent inbound data flows.
5. Click `OK`. The New Object – (Connection) window opens. The name of the domain controller you selected is inserted in the `Name` field.
6. Click `OK` to save the change and return to the console. The new Connection object appears on the list. You should keep an eye on the Event log to make sure the DRA sees the new connection and replicates across it. You may need to enable Active Directory diagnostics to do this. See the next section.

Troubleshooting Replication Problems

Active Directory replication involves a series of complex transactions. If one of these transactions fails, the problems it causes tend to be . . . well . . . complex. In general, replication problems are caused by unstable server hardware, poor network connections, and DNS errors.

The symptoms usually are a series of Error Log messages about failed replication. The logged message tells you the cause of the failure, but it doesn't necessarily tell you the cause of the problem. Several tools are available to help you get more information. They include the following:

- Special diagnostic traces that put more information in the Event log
- Command-line replication administration utility, REPADMIN
- Graphical Replication Monitor utility, Replmon

Also watch for problems with other services that depend on Active Directory. This includes services that have service accounts that must authenticate in the domain.

Directory Diagnostics Traces

One tool for tracing replication problems is hidden in the Registry. A variety of Diagnostics settings under `HKLM | System | CurrentControlSet | Services | NTDS | Diagnostics` dump information into the Event log. Three possible settings exist for each diagnostic trace (in addition to 0 for disabled):

1. Minimum reporting
3. Moderate reporting
5. Full reporting

Full reporting gives the most information but can fill up the Directory Services log quickly in a production environment. This doesn't hurt anything, but you may miss an important piece of data.

The contents of an Event log can be exported to a CSV or TXT tab-delimited file and then imported into a database or spreadsheet. From the Event Log menu, select File | Save As and then select the file type and location for the export.

An Export menu option also exists, but it has the same functions as Save As. In addition, you can use a tool in the Resource Kit, called Dumpel, for the three standard logs—application, security, and system. As of this writing, Dumpel does not work with the Directory Services log or the File Replication log.

Using the Command-Line Replication Administrator, REPADMIN

Microsoft supplies a command-line Resource Kit utility, called the Replication Administrator, or REPADMIN, for managing the inner workings of replication. A graphical tool, Replmon, shows much of the same information. For details, see the section "Using the Graphical Replication Monitor, Replmon" later in this chapter.

The online help (`repadmin /?`) shows the syntax for options and switches. What follows is a brief rundown of the nomenclature, in case the terms are unfamiliar:

- DSA is X.500 terminology for Directory Services Agent. An Active Directory domain controller is a DSA.
- When entering the name of a DSA, use the fully qualified DNS name. For example, enter `dc-01.branch.company.com`.
- GUID stands for Globally Unique Identifier. This is an octet string that is assigned to a domain controller. A domain controller actually has two GUIDs: an object GUID and an invocation GUID. The object GUID designates the DSA itself. The invocation GUID designates Active Directory replica hosted by that DSA.
- The naming context designates one of the Directory partitions hosted by the DSA. Only GC servers host copies of all domain naming contexts, and those are read-only.
- Object DN designates the LDAP distinguished name of the object you want to list.

In some respects, the functions in the Replication Administrator duplicate those in the AD Sites and Services console. For example, if you want to know whether a domain controller is configured as a Global Catalog server, you can open the console, navigate to the NTDS Settings object for that server, and check the properties. Or, you can open a command prompt and type `repadmin /options`.

Standard REPADMIN Functions

The AD Sites and Services console lacks many of the details available in REPADMIN. The following are a few of the questions that REPADMIN can answer:

- What is the status of knowledge consistency for this replication ring?

```
repadmin /kcc
Consistency check on local host successful.
```

- What was the result of the last replication event from each replication partner? (This listing shows the results for the Schema naming context at the DC-01 DSA.)

```
repadmin /showreps

Phoenix\DC-01
DSA Options : IS_GC
objectGuid  : 61d9fcd2-1172-11d3-b902-00c04f536a4d
invocationID: 61d9fcd2-1172-11d3-b902-00c04f536a4d

==== INBOUND NEIGHBORS ======================================
CN=Schema,CN=Configuration,DC=company,DC=com

Phoenix\DC-02
    DEL:604ba650-124d-11d3-b903-00c04f536a4d via RPC
        objectGuid: 85e37932-124d-11d3-b903-00c04f536a4d
        Last attempt @ 2002-02-26 19:53.35 failed, result 1722:
            The RPC server is unavailable.
        Last success @ 2002-02-25 17:45.37.
        27 consecutive failure(s).
Phoenix\DC-03 via RPC
        objectGuid: ce87aef1-1232-11d3-b903-00c04f536a4d
        Last attempt @ 2002-02-26 19:53.35 was successful.
Atlanta\DC-04 via IP
        objectGuid: fba7a044-1176-11d3-b903-00c04f536a4d
        Last attempt @ 2002-02-26 19:53.35 was successful.

==== OUTBOUND NEIGHBORS FOR CHANGE NOTIFICATIONS ============

CN=Schema,CN=Configuration,DC=company,DC=com
    Phoenix\DC-05 via RPC
        objectGuid: fba7a044-1176-11d3-b903-00c04f536a4d
```

Without a connection, the system can report only the GUID of the failed replication partner, not its name. You can interrogate the domain controllers to find their GUIDs and then figure out which one failed. A glance at the Event log is helpful because it lists the GUIDs in the context of the server that caused the error. The `showreps` listing for a site with many domain controllers can be difficult to interpret. If you want to look at just the failures, use the `/unreplicated` switch.

Expert REPADMIN Functions

Windows Server 2003 includes many additional functions that can be performed by REPADMIN. To see the instructions for these functions, run `repadmin /experthelp`. Here is an example listing:

```
Expert Help
 /add <Naming Context> <Dest DC> <Source DC> [/asyncrep] [/syncdisable]
    [/dsadn:<Source DC DN>] [/transportdn:<Transport DN>] [/mail]
    [/async] [/readonly]
 /mod <Naming Context> <Dest DC> <Source GUID>
    [/readonly] [/srcdsaaddr:<dns address>]
    [/transportdn:<Transport DN>]
    [+nbrflagoption] [-nbrflagoption]
 /delete <Naming Context> <Dest DC> [<Source DC Address>] [/localonly]
    [/nosource] [/async]
 /removelingeringobjects <Dest DC> <Source DC GUID> <NC> [/ADVISORY_MODE]
 /addrepsto <Naming Context> <DC> <Reps-To DC> <Reps-To DC GUID>
 /updrepsto <Naming Context> <DC> <Reps-To DC> <Reps-To DC GUID>
 /delrepsto <Naming Context> <DC> <Reps-To DC> <Reps-To DC GUID>

 /options [DC] [{+|-}IS_GC] [{+|-}DISABLE_INBOUND_REPL]
     [{+|-}DISABLE_OUTBOUND_REPL] [{+|-}DISABLE_NTDSCONN_XLATE]

 /siteoptions [DC] [/site:<Site>] [{+|-}IS_AUTO_TOPOLOGY_DISABLED]
     [{+|-}IS_TOPL_CLEANUP_DISABLED] [{+|-}IS_TOPL_MIN_HOPS_DISABLED]
     [{+|-}IS_TOPL_DETECT_STALE_DISABLED]
     [{+|-}IS_INTER_SITE_AUTO_TOPOLOGY_DISABLED]
     [{+|-}IS_GROUP_CACHING_ENABLED] [{+|-}FORCE_KCC_WHISTLER_BEHAVIOR]

 /testhook [DC] [{+|-}lockqueue] [{+|-}link_cleaner]
  [{+rpctime:<call_name>,<ip or hostname>,<seconds_to_run>|-rpctime}]
   [{+rpcsync:<call_name>,<ip or hostname>|-rpcsync}]

nbrflagoptions:
  SYNC_ON_STARTUP DO_SCHEDULED_SYNCS TWO_WAY_SYNC
  NEVER_SYNCED IGNORE_CHANGE_NOTIFICATIONS DISABLE_SCHEDULED_SYNC
  COMPRESS_CHANGES NO_CHANGE_NOTIFICATIONS
```

There are two important options in these expert features. The first is the ability to remove so-called *lingering objects* from a replica of Active Directory. A lingering object can appear following the restoration of the Active Directory database, especially if the tape is older than the garbage collection tombstone interval of 60 days.

The second option that warrants your attention is the ability to disable compression on inter-site replication. This is done with the `-compress changes` option. If a bridgehead server has multiple replication partners, as you might have in a hub-and-spoke arrangement, the processor(s) on the bridgehead may become swamped with compression requests for the replication packets. If you have sufficiently fast WAN connections, you can significantly reduce the CPU load on the bridgehead by disabling compression.

Using the Graphical Replication Monitor, Replmon

In addition to the command-line tool, REPADMIN, the Support Tools includes a graphical replication management tool called *Replication Monitor*, or Replmon.

Replmon puts a lot of information on the screen in a highly useful format. To open the Replication Monitor and select a domain controller to monitor, follow Procedure 7.13.

Procedure 7.13 Configuring Replmon

1. Open the Replication Monitor from the Support Tools menu. Although it is not an MMC console, it has the same look-and-feel.
2. When the main window opens, right-click `Monitored Servers` and select ADD MONITORED SERVERS from the flyout menu. The `Add Monitored Server Wizard` starts.
3. Select the `Search The Directory For The Server To Add` option. After a brief pause while the server does a Directory lookup, the name of the server's domain is inserted into the drop-down box field.
4. Click `Next`. The Add Server To Monitor window opens. The top pane shows the list of available sites in the forest. Select a server by expanding the tree and double-clicking a server icon. You can also select the `Enter The Name Of The Server` option at the bottom of the window and enter the name of the server you want to monitor. You can enter the flat name.

   If you are going to monitor a server in another domain and you are not logged on with administrative rights in that domain, select the `Use Alternate Credentials` option, click `Change`, and enter suitable credentials in the target domain.
5. Click `Finish`. The server is added to the main Replication Monitor window. Expand the tree to show the naming contexts (see Figure 7.21 for an example). Highlight one of the servers in the tree to view the replication log for that connection.

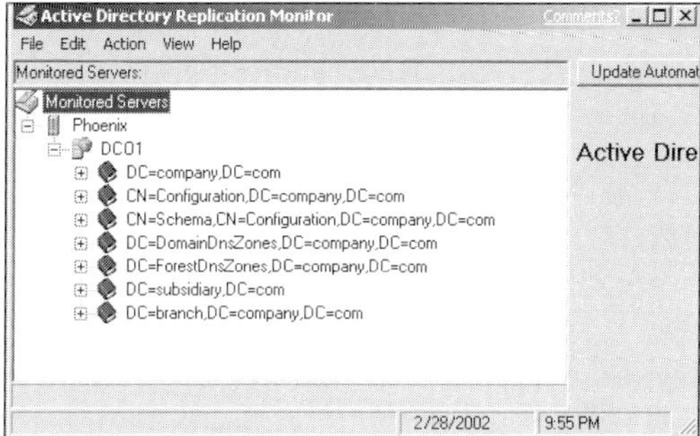

Figure 7.21 Replication Monitor (Replmon) main window showing naming contexts on server DC-01.

The following is a quick rundown of the information shown on the main Replication Monitor window, as shown in Figure 7.21:

- **Naming Contexts.** Each naming context hosted by the server is listed. If the server is a Global Catalog server, the list includes every domain in the forest. If the server is a standard domain controller, the list includes the domain naming context and the Schema and Configuration naming context from the root domain.
- **Replication partners.** The tree under each naming context lists the inbound replication partners for that naming context. The names are listed by site and then by flat name. In the example, DC-01 has four replication partners for the Schema and Configuration naming contexts.
- **Server icons.** The double-server icon with a link indicates an intra-site replication partner. A server icon that looks as though it is talking on a futuristic phone represents an intra-site connection. A miniature PC indicates the local server.
- **Log entries.** The right pane lists the replication history for the connection. New entries are added to the end.

Registry Tip: Replication Monitor Settings

The Replication Monitor parameters are stored in the following location:

```
Key:    HKCU | Software | VB and VBA Program Settings | Active Directory
        ➥Replication Monitor | Settings
Values: View Menu Options
```

Replmon View Options

After you configure Replmon to monitor a domain controller, set viewing options by selecting VIEW | OPTIONS from the menu. The Active Directory Replication Monitor Options window opens with the focus set to the `General` tab. See Figure 7.22 for a sample of this window.

Most of the options in this window are self-explanatory. Some that might be a little obscure include the following:

- **Show Retired Replication Partners.** These are server objects that were tombstoned but not yet deleted by the ESENT database engine. They are usually deleted over time. The NTDSUTIL utility has an option for cleaning up metadata that can delete these old entries.
- **Show Transitive Replication Partners and Extended Data.** This option enables Replmon to show USN and metadata information from servers outside the local site that are multiplexed on the same Site Link.
- **Notify When Replication Fails After This Number Of Attempts.** This option, coupled with the `Notification Options` entry in the next field, can be used to send email if a connection fails to replicate. Set the attempt number at 3-5 to account for a couple of missed attempts that might happen in the ordinary course of operations.
- **Log Files.** This changes the default path for the log files. The default location is the Resource Kit directory.
- **Enable Debug Logging.** This option is for debugging Replmon, not for debugging replication. Debug Logging writes a great deal of information about the Replmon application to the Application log. This fills the Event log very quickly, so only use this option during troubleshooting.

Replmon Connection Properties

You can view a great deal of information about a particular replication connection by opening the Properties window for the connection. Figure 7.23 shows an example. The `General` tab shows the connection type and information about the connection itself. The important statistics are the last three lines, which show whether replication attempts failed and the associated error message.

The `Update Sequence Numbers` tab shows the current USN received from each replication partner. This option requires you to select the `Show Transitive Replication Partners and Extended Data` option in the VIEW options menu.

The `Flags` tab lists the configuration settings for the replication connection. The flags shown in the example are standard for an inter-site connection.

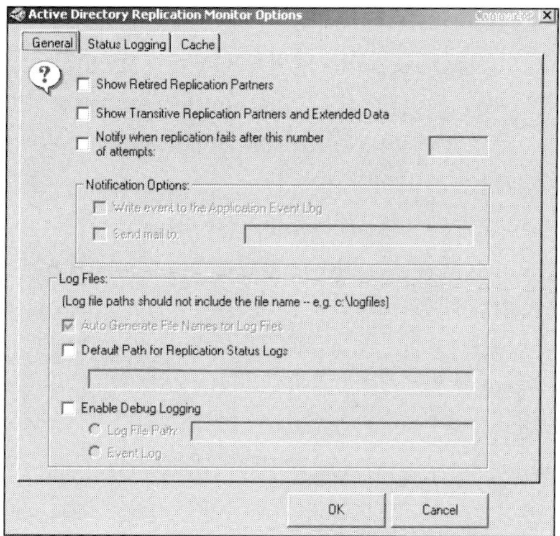

Figure 7.22 Active Directory Replication Monitor Options window.

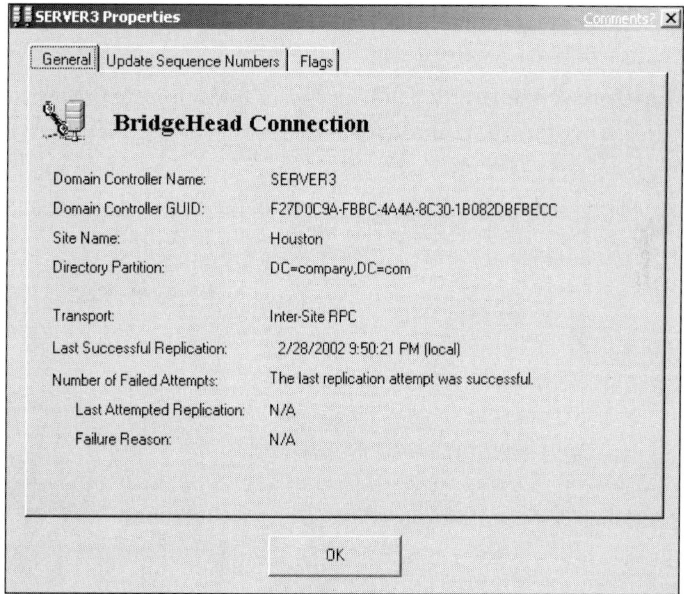

Figure 7.23 Replication Connection Properties window—`General` tab.

Replmon Replica Synchronization Options

Right-click a Naming Context icon and select SYNCHRONIZE THIS DIRECTORY PARTITION WITH ALL SERVERS. This opens a window of the same name. Figure 7.24 shows an example. This list of options enables you to override the default replication behavior in a variety of ways:

- **Disable Transitive Replication.** By default, all inter-site replication uses the same default Site Link, and the KCC is free to build connections between domain controllers regardless of their site affiliation. If you are troubleshooting problems with replication loops or failed replication to a particular server, you can disable transitive replication when initiating a replication event to see if it succeeds.
- **Push Mode.** By default, the DRA "pulls" updates from a replication partner. This selection enables Push mode for a single replication transaction.
- **Cross Site Boundaries.** This option enables you to directly initiate an inter-site replication, but it is effective only for RPC connections. The default inter-site connection transport is IP. You can use the Properties window for a connection to change the transport to RPC and then select this option. If you change the transport for a connection, the connection status changes to a static connection that requires manual control.
- **Skip Initial Topology Check.** This speeds up replication across a slow network with many domain controllers. It takes the chance that a server or link is down.

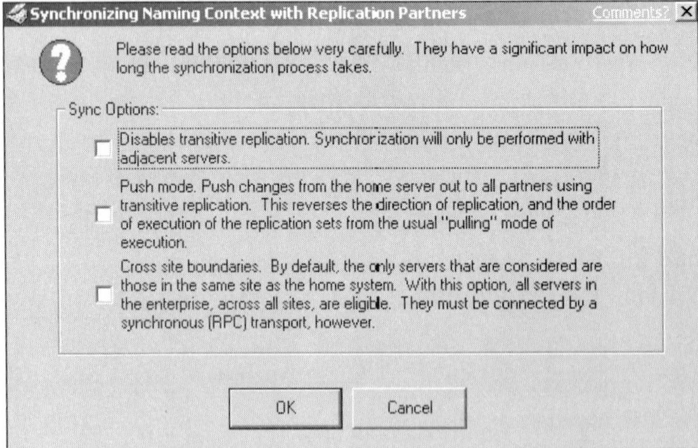

Figure 7.24 Synchronizing Naming Context with Replication Partners window.

- **Generate Fatal Error On Unreachable Server.** Not enabled.
- **Disable All Synchronization.** Not enabled.
- **Return Server DN.** Not enabled.

Replmon Server Property Menu Selections

When you right-click the server icon in Replication Monitor, a flyout (PROPERTIES) menu appears. Several of the options in this menu can give you highly useful information about replication in particular and the domain controller status in general:

- **Generate Status Report.** Select this option to get a comprehensive report on the domain controller's Active Directory configuration. The list of items in the report is selected from a Report Options window that opens prior to running the report. Figure 7.25 shows an example.
- **Show Group Policy Status.** Lists all the Group Policy objects for the domain and whether the object was synced. Use this information if users on some domain controllers are getting policies and other users aren't.
- **Show Trust Relationships.** This option shows the same information as the AD Domains and Trusts window, but much more conveniently.

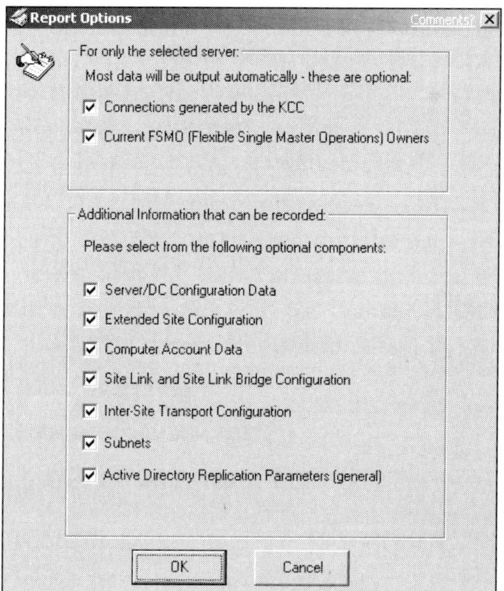

Figure 7.25 Report Options window for Replmon server status report.

- **Display Metadata Properties.** When you select this option, you are prompted to enter a set of alternate credentials, if necessary, and then the distinguished name of an object whose replication data you want to view. This is equivalent to `repadmin/showmeta`. Metadata information is invaluable when trying to isolate a problem with a corrupt property or corrupt user object. By comparing the metadata on various replicas, you can discover whether you have a corruption problem and how extensive the problem has become.

Server Properties

Right-click the server icon in the Replmon window and open the Properties window. The tabs in this window give you an update of the server's replication status:

- **Server Flags.** Lists special domain controller options including GC status, KDC status, and W32Time status.
- **FSMO Roles.** The window lists all the FSMO role masters by name and site with a `Query` button for each to verify that the server is still online. Figure 7.26 shows an example.
- **Inbound Replication Connections.** This window answers the who, why, and how for each inbound replication connection. Figure 7.27 shows an example.

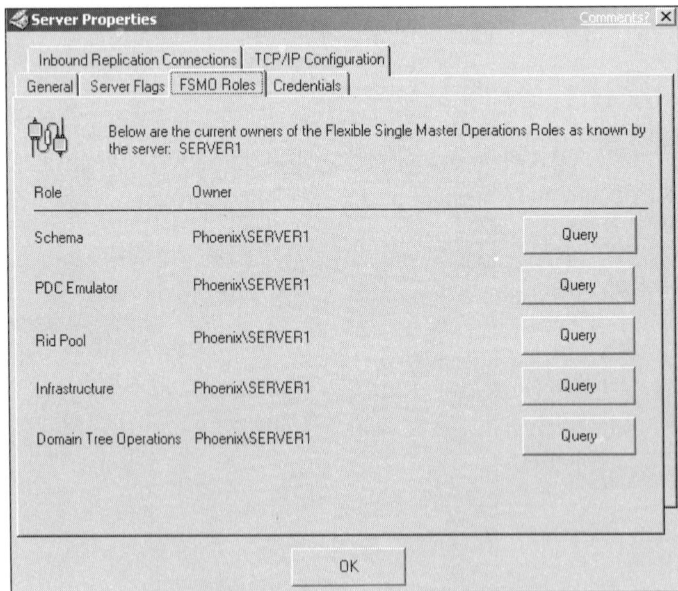

Figure 7.26 Replmon Server Properties window—FSMO Roles window.

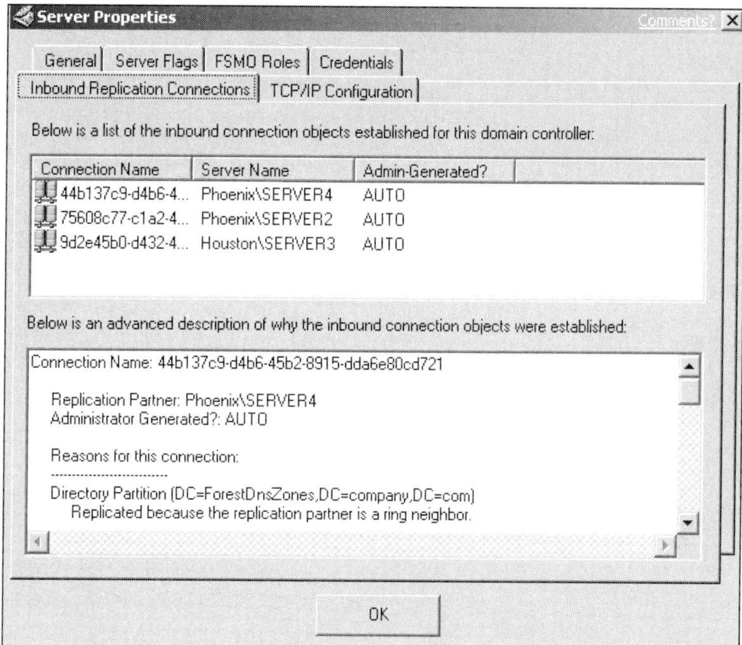

Figure 7.27 Replmon Server Properties window—Inbound Replication Connections.

Moving Forward

At this point, we have enough information about Active Directory operation and replication to begin our design work. In the next chapter, we'll see how to lay out a directory that makes best use of the features in Active Directory.

8 Designing Windows Server 2003 Domains

THE LAST FEW CHAPTERS HAVE EXAMINED THE critical components of DNS and Active Directory. We now know how a directory service improves operations compared to classic NT. Now it's time to get out the proverbial blank sheet of paper and start laying out an architectural plan.

Active Directory is a complex piece of technology. Many of the decisions you make regarding directory design have wide-ranging implications. Generally, the design should start with evaluating the technical merits of each available feature with an eye towards improving your current operations. If you do your homework and account for most of the variables, you'll end up with a design that is technologically sound. Good designs don't necessarily translate into deployable designs, though, generally because of issues at the eighth layer of the OSI model—the political layer.

This chapter addresses both the technical and the political issues involved in Active Directory design. I'll identify compromises that many administrators have had to make in their Active Directory designs and the best way to avoid problems caused by those compromises. I'll also outline the best practices that have emerged over the last couple of years as Active Directory has matured.

You have three major concerns when laying out the general structure of an Active Directory forest:

- Number and name of domains
- Upper Organizational Unit structure
- Local Organizational Unit structure

The end result of this initial design assessment is a sketch that defines how your domain or domains should look, the DNS zones that will support the domain namespace, and the layout of the management organization defined by Organizational Units.

When that's done, you can define the location of your DNS servers, domain controllers, Global Catalog servers, and Flexible Single Master Operations servers (covered in detail later in this chapter).

New Features in Windows Server 2003

Only a few of the new Windows Server 2003 features have a direct impact on Active Directory architecture. Those that do, however, give a lot more flexibility to your designs than was available in Windows 2000. Here are those features:

- **Rename capabilities.** Domains now can be renamed and their parent/child relationships changed. This helps restructure a forest following a reorganization within a company. Domains cannot be dynamically split off to form their own forests, however, nor can domains from one forest be merged as a unit into another forest. Domain controllers can be renamed as well.
- **Federations.** A new trust type called Forest trust supports transitive trust relationships between domains in separate forests. Microsoft calls this a federation. The ability to form a federation greatly simplifies Active Directory operations in an organization such as a conglomerate or a university where entities are constantly being added and removed.
- **Improved security.** Support was added for digest authentication as described in RFC 2829, "Authentication Methods for LDAP." This makes it easier to integrate Active Directory into non-Windows environments.
- **Schema flexibility.** Schema components can now be declared "defunct," making it possible to trim away object classes and attributes that were added by an application but are no longer needed.
- **Interoperability.** Support was added for the InetOrgPerson class as defined in RFC 2798, "Definition of the inetOrgPerson LDAP Object Class." This enhances interoperability with Netscape and NetWare directory services, both of which use the inetOrgPerson object class to create user objects.
- **Scalability.** The maximum number of objects that can be stored in Active Directory was increased to over a billion.

Design Objectives

I'm as much of a hardware/software geek as the next administrator. I admire innovative technology packed with cutting edge ideas. But networks don't exist just for administrators. We just tend the farm. Somebody else eats the crop. Like it or not, networks exist for users.

Every administrator has war stories about impatient users who babble and scream when faced with even the most trivial network operation. Map a drive? Forget it. Connect to a printer? Out of the question. Users demand simple, reliable, high-performance access to network resources. If a resource is more than two clicks away or requires learning anything that remotely smacks of jargon, the resource might as well be in the Far Magellanic Clouds. If your Active Directory design doesn't create a simpler and more reliable environment for your users, it will fail.

So, proper domain design should make resource access as intuitive as possible. Fine. But there is more to good design than simplicity. From the perspective of a system administrator, domain designs must meet a host of objectives. Here are some of the major ones:

- **Security.** The methods and protocols used to control access to resources must be strong enough to protect millions or billions of dollars of data and hardware. The design must make it as difficult as possible to gain unauthorized access and as simple as possible to gain authorized access. It must support auditing so that abuse is discovered early before extensive damage is done. And it must do this security checking as fast and unobtrusively as possible.
- **Stability.** No network operating system is acceptable that presents network resources in an unpredictable manner or demonstrates oddball behavior when called on to do its chores. Network resources should operate in the same way every minute of every day.
- **Reliability.** A good design avoids single points of failure. Because full redundancy is hard to achieve, the design must also incorporate straightforward failure contingency plans that have a high probability of successful execution.
- **Manageability.** After a domain is in place, it should not take a platoon of system engineers working around the clock to keep it working. Ideally, a few administrators in a central location should be able to manage all system resources.
- **Interoperability.** No administrator can avoid running a mix of hardware and multiple operating systems. A good design should minimize friction when information transits from one system to another.
- **Recoverability.** Active Directory is a database, and no database is safe from corruption, bugs, and bad karma. A good design expects directory problems, monitors for them proactively, and makes allowances for repair with a minimum of service disruption.
- **Efficiency.** Directory service operations take a toll on infrastructure such as communication links and server hardware. Your Active Directory design should minimize infrastructure costs and make the unavoidable costs so incontestable that only the most miserly executive would dare slash them out of the budget.

In addition, there are less definable but equally compelling design influences generally grouped under headings such as *ooomph*, *juice*, *pull*, and *politics*. These influences can take an otherwise elegant design and mash it up beyond all recognition if you aren't careful. The foremost source of initial design compromises when laying out an Active Directory structure is the domain name. Let's address that issue first.

DNS and Active Directory Namespaces

As we saw in Chapter 6, "Understanding Active Directory Services," an Active Directory domain must be rooted in a DNS domain name. Figure 8.1 shows a DNS domain namespace and a corresponding Active Directory tree.

There's no question that deploying and managing Active Directory is simpler if you use Windows Server 2003 name servers. However, if you have an existing third-party DNS platform, it's not likely that you can shift to Windows Server 2003 overnight. You may not even want to shift at all. Because DNS is such a critical element in Active Directory design and operation, you must decide how you will integrate Windows Server 2003 into your current DNS infrastructure. Here are three popular configurations:

- Forget about Windows DNS completely and use third-party name servers to host the zone for the Active Directory domain.
- Create a separate DNS domain for Active Directory, host the zone on Windows Server 2003 name servers, and forward queries for records in other zones to a third-party name server.
- Use your current public DNS domain to root the Active Directory domain and create a split public/private zone with the private zone hosted by Windows Server 2003 name servers.

The next few sections examine these options in detail.

Active Directory and Third-Party Name Servers

You do not need to run Windows Server 2003 DNS to support Active Directory, but your DNS servers must run a version of DNS that supports the Service Locator (SRV) resource record type as defined in RFC 2782, "A DNS RR for Specifying the Location of Services (DNS SRV)."

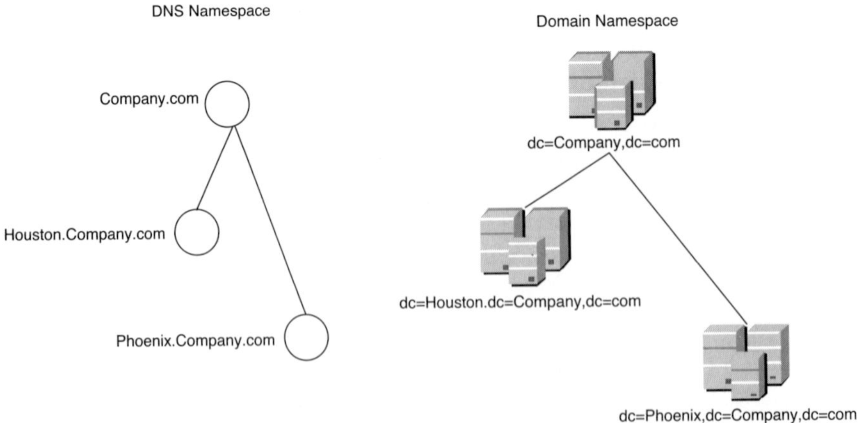

Figure 8.1 DNS Namespace and Active Directory tree.

Active Directory domain controllers use SRV records to publish their Lightweight Directory Access Protocol (LDAP) and Kerberos services. The format for these records is specified in RFC 2052, "SRV Record Format and Use." Name servers running BIND 8.1.2 and later support SRV records—so do servers running the most current version of Lucent QIP or NetWare 5.x DNS.

Because SRV records have a complex format, and Active Directory uses a lot of them, it is helpful to use a DNS platform that supports dynamic record registration as defined in RFC 2136, "Dynamic Updates in the Domain Name System (DNS UPDATE)."

If your DNS platform uses only static zones, or you don't want to enable dynamic updates, you must manually enter the SRV records in their proper format. The Domain Controller Promotion Wizard creates a file called Netlogon.dns in the `C:\Windows\System32\Config` folder. This file contains the SRV records that Netlogon attempted to register with DNS. You can import this file into a third-party name server, but your job doesn't stop there. You must remember to manually update the zone for any subsequent changes such as promoting or demoting domain controllers, creating new site objects, or changing a domain controller's site affiliation.

Separate Windows Domain and Windows-Based Zone

You may decide that your current DNS name is unsuitable for Active Directory. Or you may be unable to convince management to host Active Directory resource records on your current name servers. If so, you can create a separate DNS domain and root Active Directory in that namespace. Host the zone for the new domain on a Windows name server and use the existing name server as a forwarder. This configuration is shown in Figure 8.2.

In this configuration, your Windows clients point at the Windows name servers. When the clients request a record in an outside zone, the Windows name server forwards the request to the original name server. For Internet records, the Windows server can use root hints to sent iterative requests to the Verisign Top Level Domain (TLD) servers.

Public Domain with Split Public/Private Zone

This option is commonly used by organizations that want to retain their current, registered DNS domain name as their Active Directory domain name. For instance, the International Widget Company may prefer to use its registered Widget.com name rather than Widget.net or Widget.local or some other private namespace. Figure 8.3 shows this configuration.

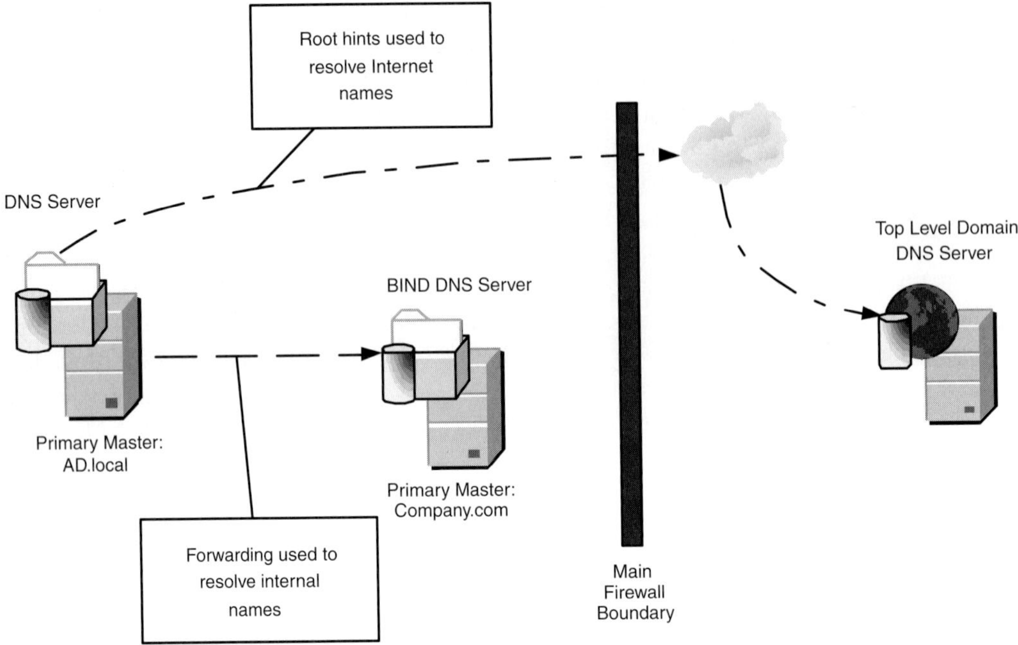

Figure 8.2 Windows Server 2003 DNS running with third-party forwarder.

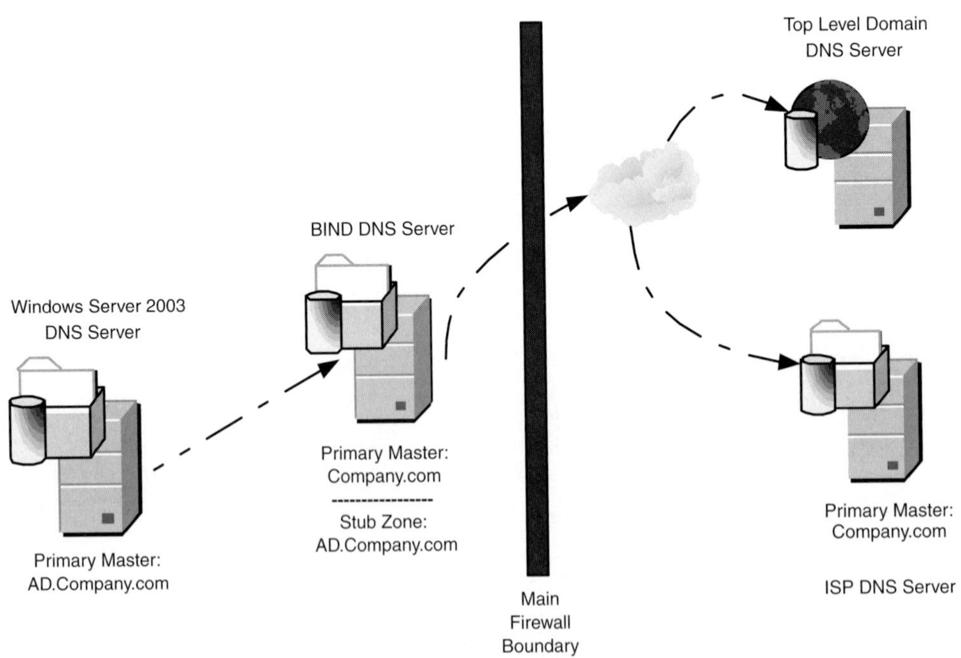

Figure 8.3 Public DNS domain name with split public/private zones.

This configuration uses separate zones for the public namespace and the private namespace. The private zone is hosted on a name server inside the firewall. The public zone is hosted on a name server in the DMZ or on an ISP's name server. In either case, clients point at the name server inside the firewall. This name server uses the outside name server as a forwarder or uses root hints to resolve addresses outside its zone of authority. You get the most flexibility for Active Directory by hosting the private zone on a Windows name server.

If you use this split configuration or one similar to it, keep in mind that Active Directory clients cannot access the private name server while they are outside the firewall. The client can only authenticate when connected through the firewall using a dial-up connection, a Virtual Private Network (VPN), or some other form of protected connection. Clients can use the Logon Using Dial-Up Connection option at the initial logon window to establish their credentials at logon. For Windows 2000/XP clients, this initiates a Kerberos-based logon that significantly speeds up subsequent access to member servers.

Root Domain Name

"What's in a name?" asked Juliet as she gazed at the heavens and dreamt of her Romeo. Names turn out to be critically important, in computing and love. Don't pay the price that Romeo and Juliet paid by ignoring names as you design your domains.

Windows clients live in two worlds: a hierarchical world where the only name that really matters is the fully qualified DNS domain name and a flat world where the NetBIOS name has ultimate significance. Your domain design must support both these naming structures.

When you promote the first domain controller in an Active Directory domain, the Domain Controller Promotion Wizard (Dcpromo) generates a flat NetBIOS name from the left-most element of the fully qualified DNS name. For example, the `Company.com` DNS name yields the flat name `COMPANY`. It's theoretically possible to designate a flat name during the domain controller promotion that does not match the leftmost element in the DNS name. This can cause confusion among users, who may wonder what name to use in any given circumstance.

If you want to retain your current NT domain name as your Active Directory domain name, you must select a DNS domain name that uses the flat name as the lowest domain constituent. For example, the NT domain called `COMPANY` could have a DNS name of `Company.com`, `Company.net`, `Company.local`, or `Company.Enterprise.ParentDomain.com`.

Domain Name Restrictions Caused by Flat Names

To retain your current NT domain name as the flat name for your Active Directory domain, you must upgrade the existing PDC. You cannot create a parallel Active Directory domain with the same flat name because this causes a NetBIOS name conflict.

For example, let's say you have an existing NT domain named COMPANY. If you try to promote a new Windows Server 2003 domain controller and root Active Directory in a DNS domain called `Company.com`, the Domain Controller Promotion Wizard attempts to register the flat name COMPANY it derived from `Company.com`. When it does this registration, it gets a notification from the PDC of COMPANY (or from WINS) declaring that the COMPANY domain name already exists. The promotion wizard will suggest COMPANY0. You should not accept this or any other alternative that results in a flat name that does not match the lowest DNS domain.

If you don't like your current NT domain name and you want your Active Directory domain to have a different flat name, you must set up a new Active Directory domain and migrate objects into the that domain from the existing NT domain. The next chapter contains details on object migration.

Suggestions for Resolving Name Disputes

The pairing of Active Directory and DNS in many organizations is as star-crossed as Romeo and Juliet's relationship. Large organizations often have a multitude of highly competitive IT groups who may have fractured the DNS namespace into many zones that forward and delegate in ways that would give a chess champion a headache.

The DNS namespace for a university, for example, might have separate domains for Academic Services, Administration, Alumni, Biology, Chemistry, Physics, Fine Arts, Physical Education, Facilities, Math-Physics, Humanities, Bookstore, Student Union, and Library with subdomains under each for Undergrads, Grads, Law, Medical, and Hospital, not to mention more branches for outlying campuses and extended campuses and minicampuses and walk-in learning centers and on and on and on.

If you are an administrator in a department or office that exists in a DNS subdomain, you may be wondering how to handle your Active Directory design. To avoid the inevitable bureaucratic decision process, you may be tempted to root your Active Directory forest in your current DNS subdomain and proceed with your deployment. Here is why that would be a mistake.

Let's say your DNS subdomain is Humanities.EastCampus.BigUniversity.edu. Your current NT domain name is PLATO. When you migrate to Active Directory, you want to change the domain's flat name because Plato has been exposed as an intellectual despot who wreaked carnage on centuries of western thought. You decide to create a Windows Server 2003 domain rooted in your DNS subdomain with the flat name HUMANITIES. This has two unfortunate consequences:

- The domain's flat name must be unique in a forest to preserve backward compatibility. There are other Humanities departments at other campuses and they would not like you preempting the name.

- By rooting your Active Directory domain at Humanities.EastCampus.Big University.edu, you form a new forest. When the rest of the university eventually migrates to Active Directory, you'll be forced to migrate objects from your forest to their forest or to form a transitive Forest Trust. The second option limits your ability to share resources and makes comprehensive domain management much more difficult.

Your best option is to meet with IT staff from the various campuses and decide how to move forward together with a DNS namespace that supports a unified Active Directory design and deployment. If you are absolutely stymied by bureaucracy and inertia, you can proceed with your own forest but be prepared to do lots of work in the future to heal the breach.

Domain Design Strategies

In Active Directory, as with classic NT, a *domain* defines a discrete security and administrative unit. It also defines a replication boundary, as each domain forms a separate naming context within the Active Directory database.

As you doodle your initial designs, start by looking for ways to use a single Active Directory domain. Do this even if you have a strong feeling that a single domain will not be feasible in your organization due to political turmoil. A single domain has several advantages:

- **Easier navigation.** Users look at network structures with all the fear and suspicion of medieval serfs gaping up at a comet. The simpler you make it for them to find resources, the more likely your design has of being successfully implemented.
- **Simpler DNS configuration.** If you have multiple domains in complex parent/child configurations, the resulting DNS zone referrals get a little tricky to configure. DNS causes the majority of Active Directory problems, so it makes sense to avoid complexity when possible.
- **Simpler replication topology.** Managing replication is much more straightforward in a single domain because you are not mixing different domain naming contexts and Global Catalog servers into your replication topology.

Name Lengths

When deciding what to name your domains, keep the names short and simple. Abbreviate where possible. Users will get irritated if their UPN is `user@Albuquerque.NewMexico.UnitedStates.NorthAmerica.Company.com`.

Keep Organizational Unit names short, as well. A distinguished name cannot be longer than 255 characters. This includes the typeful designators such as `DC=`, `CN=`, and `OU=`.

- **Eliminate separate Global Catalog servers.** With a single domain, you eliminate the reliance on separate Global Catalog servers because you can enable the Global Catalog on every domain controller.
- **Simpler security implementation.** It's true that transitive Kerberos trusts make it possible to seamlessly access resources in other domains, but just because a feature is transparent doesn't mean it's simple to manage. An administrator's worst nightmare is trying to resolve a problem with file and directory access permissions by sifting through the membership list for hundreds of groups in separate domains.

Reasons for Using Multiple Domains

You may also encounter sizeable resistance to a single domain on the part of administrators who want an autonomous domain no matter what. I group these objections under *political restrictions*. This is not because I think they are any less important than the technical reasons. They aren't. The stability and performance of an information system has a lot more to do with people than it does with technology. It's just that political design restrictions tend to change considerably during the approval process, so you may be able to apply them less rigorously than the technical restrictions.

There are only a few technical restrictions in Active Directory that may require you to use multiple domains. These include database size, performance restrictions, the need to have unique password policies, and the presence of sites that require Simple Mail Transport Protocol (SMTP) replication.

Database Size Restrictions

The more objects you pack into a single domain, the larger you make the Active Directory database, Ntds.dit, and the more changes you have to replicate between domain controllers. Active Directory can accommodate one billion objects, so you have lots of overhead to play with, but an extremely large database needs more powerful servers to handle authentications and LDAP requests. There comes a point, such as with the Roman Empire, where size affects durability.

An Active Directory database for 100,000 users, their computers, and the groups necessary to manage them would be about 1.5GB. If you add in the additional directory overhead of Exchange 2000, you might touch 2GB. Extrapolating upward, an organization with half a million users would have an Ntds.dit file of 10GB, which is certainly within the capability of an average mirrored or RAID 5 array.

These aren't huge databases by today's standards, so the decision to split into separate domains doesn't really boil down to the number of users and computers and groups. You should be more concerned with replication traffic and acceptable authentication performance.

The vast majority of Windows domains contain fewer than 10,000 users, not enough to make Active Directory breathe hard. The toughest job for the designer of such a system is convincing management not to put additional services on the domain controllers such as messaging or database management. In general, domain controllers work fine when given DNS, DHCP (Dynamic Host Configuration Protocol), and WINS (Windows Internet Name Service) duties, but resist the urge to ladle on other chores. You don't want an application failure to force you into restarting or rebuilding a domain controller.

Only truly gargantuan organizations with many hundreds of thousands of users and computers need to consider dividing their operations into separate domains. Microsoft has not published hard and fast rules about maximum practical database size, so if you are in one of those super-sized organizations, you'll need to work closely with Microsoft Consulting Services to structure your domain.

Performance Restrictions

Most companies deploying Active Directory opt to use separate domains for their overseas operations to reduce the need to replicate across expensive WAN links. This generally means having a Europe domain, a Pacific Rim domain, a South America domain (unless a solid link is available), an Asia domain for China and India, and an Africa domain.

To get acceptable authentication performance, you'll need to size your domain controllers based on the user population in a particular site. If you have a few hundred users in a site who all log on at about the same time in the morning, you can easily get by with a 1U rackmount server with a single Xeon processor, 256MB of memory, a 100Mbps network card, and mirrored drives to hold the Active Directory files. Such a server costs less than $4,000 from top-tier vendors.

If you have several thousand users authenticating in the morning at the same site, you can spread out the load by installing several smaller domain controllers or beef up a few domain controllers with dual processors, multiple network adapters, and separate mirrored spindles for the Active Directory and Sysvol files.

Password Policy Restrictions

Three sets of policies affect attributes of the Domain object in Active Directory and cannot be modified by group policies in subordinate containers like OUs. They are as follows:

- **Password policies.** These include maximum and minimum password age, minimum password length, password history, complexity requirements, and reversible password storage.
- **Account lockout policies.** These include the number of bad attempts that trigger a lockout, lockout duration, and reset interval.
- **Kerberos policies.** These include service and user ticket lifetimes, ticket renewal interval, and permissible clock skew.

If these policies must have different settings within the same organization, you'll need to create separate domains. This might happen if you are working on a contract and the client wants you to have certain security restrictions that are different than those in your organization.

SMTP Replication Restrictions

You may have a site or sites in remote, forsaken corners of the world like Tierra del Fuego or Hobbs, New Mexico. The network links to these sites might not be able to maintain stable data communications. If you attempt to construct a standard inter-site low-speed RPC connection over these links, the connections may fail often enough to prompt the bridgeheads to give up.

If this happens, you can use Simple Mail Transport Protocol (SMTP) as the transport for replication to the remote site.

SMTP is well suited for transporting replication packets over unreliable connections, but it has limitations when it comes to security. The RPCs used for inter- and intra-site replication encrypt traffic, but SMTP traffic is transferred in the clear. To avoid potential compromise of secure Active Directory information, the messages are encrypted using a form of secure messaging. This requires a Domain Controller certificate at the bridgehead servers on either side of the connection. To get this certificate, you'll need a Microsoft Certification Authority.

Another limitation when using SMTP lies with the File Replication Service, or FRS. This service replicates the content of Sysvol, which contains group policy template files and the files used for classic system policies and scripting. FRS cannot use SMTP. This means that group policy container objects in Active Directory will not stay in sync with group policy files in Sysvol. For this reason, you cannot use SMTP to connect bridgeheads in the same domain.

Political Restrictions

A single domain should work for all but the largest and most geographically diverse organizations. As we get further into the operation of authentication, rights delegation, group management, and group policies, you'll see that it is entirely possible to build a single domain with Organizational Units to define management and administrative boundaries.

Still, a good single-domain design can fracture during the approval process, usually because of balkanization rather than any engineering limitations. System administrators and their managers may view domain consolidation with suspicion. Depending on your personal force of will and your backing from management, you may end up with more domains than you really need.

Try not to let local administrators carry their independence too far at the expense of reliability and performance. Large numbers of domains, especially when they each comprise a separate tree in the forest, complicate replication and domain controller placement.

If you are a local administrator facing an initiative by central IT to consolidate domains, try to rein in your suspicions. You can get wide operational latitude in an OU and still share the benefits of a single Active Directory structure.

Figure 8.4 shows an example of a forest where global regions have been compartmentalized into separate domains and large offices have been made into domains rather than OUs. The company has separate business units that also insisted on being in separate domains.

Administratively, this structure becomes unwieldy because it forces you to manage many different Domain naming contexts with many possible variations of OUs and group policies. If your organization has no central IT staff whatsoever, this structure might work for you. Otherwise, you should try to avoid proliferating separate domains below major geographical areas.

Multiple Domains and Groups

If you decide that you must have multiple domains, you need to consider the impact of security groups very early in your design cycle. Chapter 12, "Managing Group Policies," takes a detailed look at security group functionality, but let's take a sneak preview right here to find out what we need to know for domain design. Here are the important elements to watch out for:

- There are three different group types in Active Directory and their membership and application scopes differ. You must be in Native to get maximum flexibility.
- The security subsystem uses groups to determine access authorization. If you do not plan correctly, users might be unable to reach certain resources, or you might be unable to lock them out.

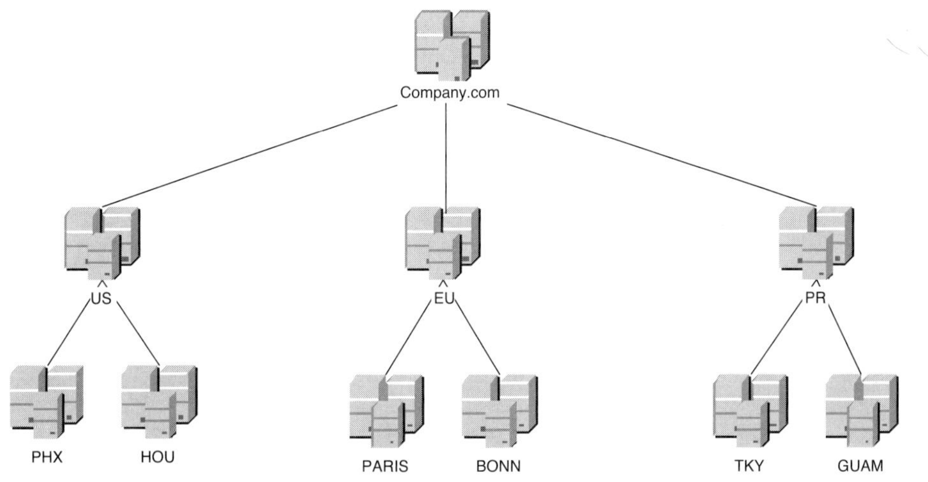

Figure 8.4 Upper directory containers using multiple domains.

- Membership lists for the various group types are stored differently in the Global Catalog. This makes access to a GC a highly important element of your Active Directory design.

Group Classifications

Active Directory recognizes three classes of security groups: Domain Local, Global, and Universal. A fourth type, Machine Local, is only present in the local SAM of a member computer.

Groups are differentiated by their scope of membership and scope of use:

- **Domain Local.** This group type can have members from any domain in the forest. It can only be assigned to access control lists (ACLs) within its own domain.
- **Global.** This group type can have members only from its own domain. It can be assigned to ACLs anywhere in the forest.
- **Universal.** This group type can have members from any domain in the forest. It can be assigned to ACLs anywhere in the forest.

Group Nesting

Groups can be nested in other groups—that is, one group can be a member of another group. Nesting rules restrict which group type can be a member of another group type. The nesting rules vary depending on whether the domain is Mixed or Native. Here are the nesting rules:

- In Mixed, Domain Local groups cannot nest within other groups. In Native, Domain Local groups can nest in other Domain Local groups in the same domain but not in any another group type. Domain Local groups can never nest in groups in other domains.
- In Mixed and Native, Global groups can nest in Domain Local groups. In Native, Global groups can nest in other Global groups and Universal groups.
- Universal groups can only be created and used in Native. They can nest into Domain Local, Global, and other Universal groups. If you have users from several domains in a Universal group, you can still nest the Universal group into a Global group as long as the two are in the same domain.

A user's group membership helps determine which resources the user is authorized to touch. The group nesting rules determine how hard a user's logon server has to work to determine the user's group membership.

Groups and Authorization

When a user logs on, the Local Security Authority Subsystem (LSASS) at the logon server constructs a *Privilege Access Certificate*, or PAC, for the user. The PAC contains the user's Security ID (SID), a batch of security policies (password length, password history, logon time restrictions, and so forth), the SID of every group to which the user belongs, and the SID of *any groups to which those groups belong*.

I emphasized the last part of that sentence because the way groups nest together has an impact on how you design your domains and lay out your security structures. Here's an example.

Let's say that the security descriptor for a particular folder has an access control list (ACL) containing entries for two groups. Group A has `Deny All` permissions. This means that every member of group A is denied access. Group B has `Full Control` permissions. This means that every member of group B can create, read, write, modify, and change the security descriptor of files in the folder.

If you nest group B into group A, all members of group B are suddenly denied access. The most restrictive permission has precedence.

To make this nesting trick work, LSASS must chase down all cascading group memberships so that the user's PAC contains every applicable SID. This brings us to the final distinction between security groups.

A Group object has an attribute called `Member`. This attribute contains the distinguished name (DN) of each group member. When you add a user or another group to the membership list of a group, you add the user or group's DN to the Member attribute. The Active Directory stores the `Member` attribute for a group differently depending on the group type:

- A standard domain controller holds the Member attribute for all Group objects in its domain: Domain Local, Global, and Universal.
- The Global Catalog stores the Member attribute for Universal groups from all domains in a forest.
- The Global Catalog does not store the Member attribute for Domain Local and Global groups.

Microsoft chose to exclude Domain Local and Global group membership from the GC to conserve replication bandwidth. The reasoning goes like this:

- Universal groups can be nested into groups in other domains. Those groups can be placed on ACLs in any domain. For this reason, the LSASS must chase down cascading group memberships for Universal groups. To avoid walking the tree each time a domain controller performs this search, the Universal group `Member` attribute is included in the Global Catalog.
- Domain Local groups cannot be nested into groups in other domains. When the LSASS assembles a PAC, it does not need to chase down any cascading group memberships in other domains because there cannot be any. It can get all the information it needs from the local Domain naming context. Therefore, it is not necessary to store Domain Local group membership in the Global Catalog.
- Global groups can be nested into Domain Local and Universal groups in other domains. Domain Local groups cannot be placed on ACLs outside their own

domain, so there is no need to chase down those cascading memberships. Universal group membership is already included in the Global Catalog. So, for Global groups, the LSASS can get all the information it needs from searching the local Domain naming context. It is not necessary to store Global group membership in the Global Catalog.

Summary of Groups and Active Directory Design

As you can see, group interaction in a multi-domain forest can get complex. The complexity grows if you decide to use Exchange 2000 as your messaging platform because security groups control access to public folders. Also, Exchange makes use of a second group type called the Distribution group to create email distribution lists without security credentials.

Here are key points to keep in mind regarding groups when you lay out your Active Directory design:

- Changing the membership of a Universal group results in a replication event to every Global Catalog server in the forest. If you define different domains for large geographical areas such as North America, Europe, Pac-Rim and so forth, you will incur additional communication traffic if the Universal group members change frequently. For this reason, Microsoft recommends putting users in Global groups and nesting Global groups into Universal groups.
- Universal groups and the advanced nesting rules for Global groups are only available in Native, so your design should make the transition from classic NT as simple and quick as possible.
- The user's logon server must be able to determine the user's Universal group membership to properly construct the user's Privilege Access Certificate. To prepare for a potential loss of a GC server, you should either configure multiple GC servers in a site or configure a standard DC to cache the GC contents.

If you use multiple domains, it's imperative that you develop a set of standards for your operations and administration staff to define the group types to create for various situations. Otherwise, you'll soon have a mishmash of group types that makes chasing down resource access permissions very difficult.

Designing Trusts in Multiple Domain Forests

If you must have more than one domain, you need to decide how you will structure the trusts between the domains. You have several choices depending on how you plan on doing business over the next few years:

- **Tree.** You'll get the most straightforward structure by confining your domains to a contiguous namespace, forming a tree. Individual domains in the tree trust each other using a Parent/Child trust. This simplifies your LDAP searches and makes scripting more straightforward, as well. It also simplifies user management, because individual objects can be quickly and easily moved between OUs.

- **Forest.** If you cannot configure your DNS namespace to accommodate a single, contiguous tree, your next most effective solution is a forest of trees. Conglomerates and universities often select this structure because they have a diverse, decentralized IT organization. Each business unit or college gets its own top-level domain with its own DNS root. The root domains trust each other using a Tree Root trust. The child domains participate in the trust thanks to transitive, two-way Kerberos authentication.
- **Federation.** If you cannot convince your colleagues to merge their separate domains into a single forest, you can achieve something approaching a single security entity using a Forest trust between the root domains in each forest. This trust type supports transitive two-way Kerberos authentication, which simplifies user access to resources. A Forest trust is *not* a replacement for a true Tree Root trust. The two forests represent completely separate administrative entities and you cannot easily move objects between them. You also cannot write simple scripts to manage the two forests. The Forest trust is most advantageous in situations where you must quickly build a security structure then wait a while before consolidating the objects into a single forest.
- **Mixed Domains.** If you have downlevel NT domains, Samba domains, or MIT Kerberos v5 realms that you want to integrate into your Active Directory architecture, you can form External trusts or Realm trusts. You can also form External trusts to Active Directory forests with which you cannot form a Forest trust. Realm trusts can be two-way and transitive. External trusts are always one-way and intransitive.

Configuring Logons for Multiple Domains

If you have a single global domain, users can travel from Phoenix to Seoul, sit down at a workstation, press Ctrl-Alt-Del, and log on with their standard credentials. The local domain controller in Seoul has a replica of the same Domain naming context as the domain controller in Phoenix.

If you have multiple domains, though, you need to train your traveling users to use one of two approaches:

- Select their home domain from the Winlogon pick list. This requires users to remember their home domains, which might be something of a feat for a user who scarcely remembers a password. Also, the standard Winlogon window doesn't show the domain pick list by default. You have to click the `Options` button.
- Log on using their UPN (User Principal Name). An example would be `tjones@company.com`. As soon as the Winlogon window sees an @ sign in the user name, the Domain pick list is dimmed.

The system behaves exactly the same whether the user logs on using a UPN or a flat name with a domain. The user authenticates using Kerberos in an Active Directory domain and NTLM Challenge-Response in an NT domain. Using the UPN does not cause a client to "seek out" an Active Directory domain controller in a mixed-mode domain. The only difference is that the UPN logon requires a lookup at a Global Catalog server to "crack" the string into its component parts of username and domain. When you create a Parent/Child domain trust using a contiguous DNS namespace, the child domain is automatically configured to use the UPN of the root domain in the tree. The same is not true for forests where the domains or domain trees occupy a discontiguous DNS namespace.

You can use a UPN logon to your advantage in a Discontiguous forest by assigning a custom UPN Suffix that all users in a forest can use so they don't need to know their home domain. If you select flat names that correspond to the users' email mailboxes, the logon names and email names would be the same. This is nowhere near a single sign-on solution, but it simplifies the user experience with two of the major systems that require authentication.

By assigning a custom UPN Suffix, you can have a universal logon structure to simplify training. However, you must be sure to keep the flat names unique in the various domains. If you attempt to assign a flat name that already exists in another domain, the domain controller will query a Global Catalog server to verify that the name is unique. If a GC server is not available, you will not be permitted to create the potentially non-unique name. Assign a custom UPN Suffix using the AD Domains and Trusts console as described in Procedure 8.1.

Resetting UPNs with Scripts

If you look at the Account tab in a user's properties, you'll see a `User Logon Name` field that combines the user's flat logon name and the UPN Suffix. For any new users you create, you can select the new UPN Suffix from a pick list in the New User window.

For existing users, though, you'll need to change the UPN to use the new suffix. This can be done quickly using Active Directory Services Interface (ADSI) in a script. Here is an example script that resets the UPN suffix to `@BigCompany.com` for users in an OU called `Phoenix` in the Company domain. A production script would include error checking and possibly a check to see if the current UPN were already correct to avoid unnecessary updates:

```
set OU = GetObject("LDAP://ou=Phoenix,dc=Company,dc=com")
OU.filter = Array("User")

NewUPNSuffix = "@BigCompany.com"

For Each User in OU
     Wscript.echo "Current UPN: " & User.UserPrincipalName
     Wscript.echo "Current logon name: " & User.SamAccountName
     User.UserPrincipalName = user.SamAccountName & NewUPNSuffix
     User.Setinfo
     Wscript.echo "New UPN: " & User.UserPrincipalName
Next
```

Procedure 8.1 Assigning Custom UPN Suffixes

1. Right-click the AD Domains and Trusts icon and select PROPERTIES from the flyout menu. The Properties window opens as shown in Figure 8.5.

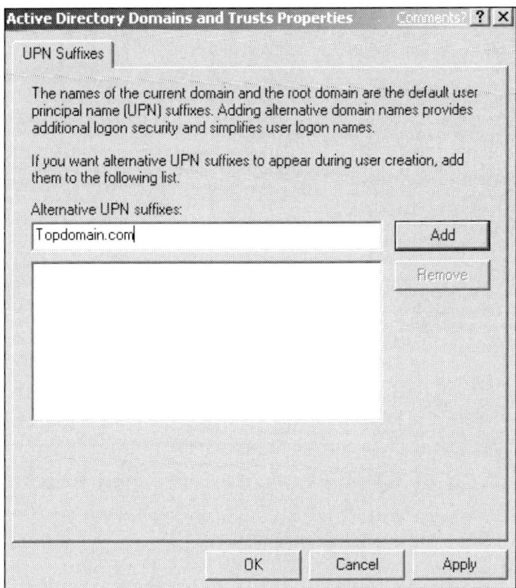

Figure 8.5 AD Domains and Trusts Properties window showing `UPN Suffixes` tab.

2. There is only one tab in the Properties window, UPN Suffixes. Enter the suffix in the `Alternative UPN Suffixes` field and click `Add`.
3. Click `OK` to save the change and close the window.

Strategies for OU Design

Figure 8.6 shows the default structure of a Domain naming context. The standard containers in a domain have the advantage of simplicity, but that's about it. Using them is acceptable for small organizations but they fall short of the mark if you want to compartmentalize management or group policies. If you start off using the standard containers, you'll know it's time to tailor a new design when administrators start pointing fingers at each other when directory objects or rights "mysteriously" change or when users from one department complain that they want a different desktop than users in another department.

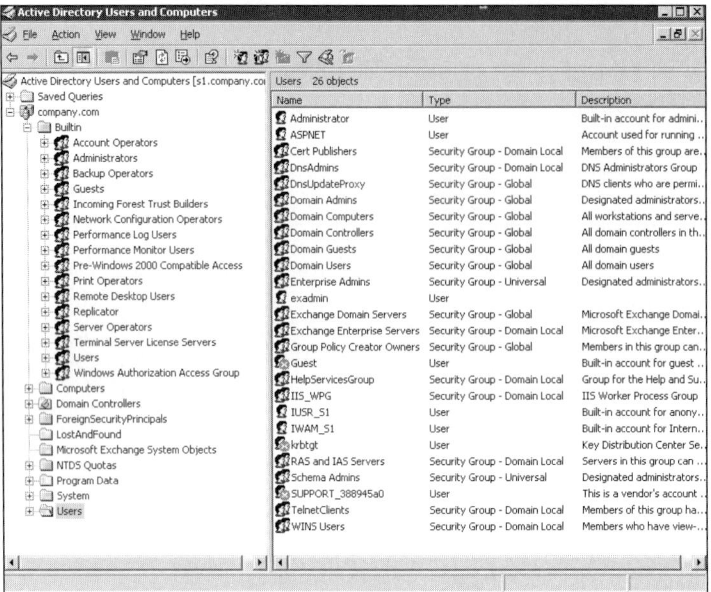

Figure 8.6 Default containers for a new Windows Server 2003 Domain naming context.

Both of these problems, lack of management granularity and inability to target specific group policies, can be solved by aggregating Active Directory objects into separate containers then assigning different rights and policies to those containers. The only general-purpose container at your disposal in Active Directory is the *Organizational Unit* (OU). The more generalized Container class is available only to the system. The Country, Organization, and Locality classes defined by LDAP are present in the Active Directory schema but are not exposed by the standard tools.

You should consider several factors as you decide where to place OUs:

- OUs represent separate management units because permissions on the OU and its child objects can be delegated.
- OUs represent separate user configuration units because group policies can be linked to them.
- OUs act as a sorting tool when constructing LDAP queries. In essence, they help keep the directory tidy, not a trivial thing when you have thousands upon thousands of objects to manage.

OU Placement

The OU container is intended to facilitate management based on the functional boundaries within an organization. Before putting in a call to HR to get the most current org charts, though, consider who uses the directory.

Users never interact with the Active Directory unless you show them how to perform searches. Even then, most searches deal with the entire forest rather than distinct domains or OUs. The only people who care about the AD structure are administrators. So, when you lay out your OUs, you want to match the operation of your IT staff, not the users. If you build it, they will come.

Management Divisions

Figure 8.7 shows the IT organization for a company with two business lines. The primary business line carries the company's principal name, Company, Inc. The second business line is a wholly owned company named Subsidiary Corp. These two business lines share common offices in a couple of cities. Other than the fact that their employees eat lunch in the same cafeteria and bank at the same credit union, they are completely separate operating entities.

This separation applies to the IT departments, as well, and with a vengeance. Not only do the Company and Subsidiary IT departments have their own staff and budgets, their administrators pride themselves on managing their systems a thousand times better than those dunderheads on the other side of the basement. The company also maintains a small corporate IT group, but those folks are forced to do five-year return-on-investment projections and distribute hefty reports in Lotus Notes instead of centrally managing technology deployments.

Administrative Functions

If you try to design the OU structure based solely on the IT organization chart, you're destined to spend many, many days in long and arduous meetings getting one ephemeral consensus after another, all of which evaporates like a mist in the morning when your plan gets to upper management.

Organizational charts don't reveal functional hierarchies, regional hierarchies, and business-line cross-matrix hierarchies that affect the way the IT department really runs. Even modern, forward-thinking companies dedicated to empowerment and individual ownership have some sort of hierarchical relationship among groups, if only to determine who gets first dibs on the parking spaces.

So, don't design in a closed office. Get out and interview people, even if you've known them for years. Determine how your IT organization divides its management duties, either vertically by business unit or horizontally by region, then put on your detective hat and search out all the administrators and their managers and see how they interact on a day-to-day basis.

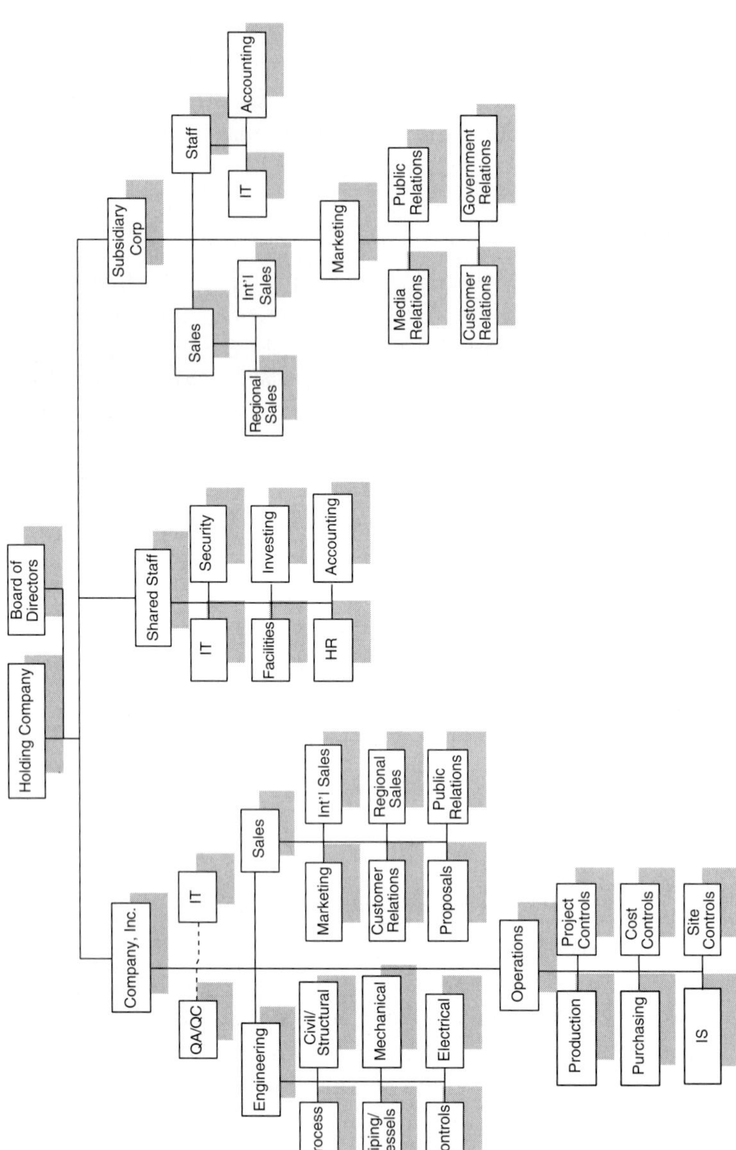

Figure 8.7 Example IT organization for moderate-sized company.

While you're sleuthing, don't just look for people with job titles that say *Administrator*. Look for hidden lines of responsibility. You'll find power users and department gurus outside of the formal IT structure who have wide-ranging administrative responsibilities. You may find corporate IT staffers matrixed into local organizations with a variety of administrative rights. And you are bound to find a few consultants who have administrative or management duties that are integral to daily operations but not officially recognized by management. In short, find anyone who might need or want administrative privileges in the domain or domains you are designing.

After you outline the true IT administrative hierarchy, find out how the staff members interact with each other. Define their administrative privileges then separate them into groups based on the privileges they exercise and who they administer.

Upper Level OUs

With all the information you collected about the IT administrative structure laid out in front of you, sketch two OU layers:

- An upper layer that defines IT staff administrative boundaries. For example, an oil company like Conoco might define two top-layer OUs, Upstream and Downstream, to separate the business units with autonomous IT staff.
- A second layer that defines objects requiring the same group policies or with specialized management needs. For example, you may outsource your desktop support so you would want to create a separate OUs for computer objects with permissions delegated to the outsource group.

Use the upper OUs layer to delegate administrative permissions. For instance, you might give the local administrators Full Control rights over their own OUs but no rights on any other OUs. This compartmentalizes system administration.

Use the lower layer or layers to distribute group policies (more on this in a moment) and separate out departments that need administrative permissions on their own equipment, groups, or users. Often managers are willing to trust a central IT group for managing equipment but splinter off user and group management to their own department personnel.

It doesn't take a Wharton MBA to figure out that you want to push management responsibility as low in the organization as possible. Design to achieve centralized control of the directory structure with localized control of directory objects. In a nutshell, this means that a few top-level administrators can create or modify OUs at the root of the domain, whereas local administrators can create, modify, delete, and change permissions for objects in those OUs.

Decentralized Operations

Figure 8.8 shows the top-level OUs structure for a domain that encompasses a good chunk of the western United States, Mexico, and a bit of Central America. The company has two business lines; a wholly owned subsidiary shares facilities in two of the company offices and has separate facilities in two remote cities.

The company has several departments with quasi-independent computing staff. The HR department, for example, insists that the confidential nature of the data on their servers and local hard drives (they still don't quite trust the network) makes it imperative that only members of their own administrative staff manage their resources.

The upper container structure for this domain divides along geographic lines because each office has its own IT staff. Departments with independent computing staff get separate containers under their office. This permits local IT personnel to administer the subordinate containers instead of relying on a central IT group. The Salt_Lake OU is an example of the opposite situation. The local IT staff would be perfectly content being in the Phoenix OU, but the Phoenix staff didn't want them to have administrative rights.

The design puts nearly all the OUs at or near the top of the directory. No performance penalty accrues for having a wide directory structure. In fact, the opposite is true. You should avoid going too deep with your OU structure. The indexing and caching features in the Active Directory engine can handle 10 levels with ease. Going deeper is possible but not recommended. If you are having trouble maintaining a shallow container structure, you might want to consult with Microsoft field engineers to determine an optimal configuration for your situation.

Centralized Operations

The OU structure in the previous example would change radically if the company had an omnipotent central IT department with closely bound office staff subject to frequent audits and performance appraisals. In such a case, you could eliminate an entire upper stratum of the directory. Figure 8.9 shows an example.

The container layout for a highly centralized IT organization distributes management rights among autonomous groups in the central IT organization. These containers hold the users, groups, computers, printers, and shared folders controlled by that group regardless of the office where they are located. The directory is replicated everywhere, so a container such as `User Support` can hold user objects from Phoenix, Houston, and Mexico City. Notice that the administrators in the Subsidiary business unit didn't trust the central IT group and insisted on having a separate namespace joined to the forest with a Tree Root trust.

Display Specifiers and Localization

Special filter objects called Display Specifiers in the Active Directory schema handle translation of the object contents. Display Specifiers look to see what language group was selected when a particular workstation or server is installed and they filter the object contents accordingly. Thanks to Display Specifiers, the fields and options for directory objects in the example would be displayed in Spanish for the Mexico City staff.

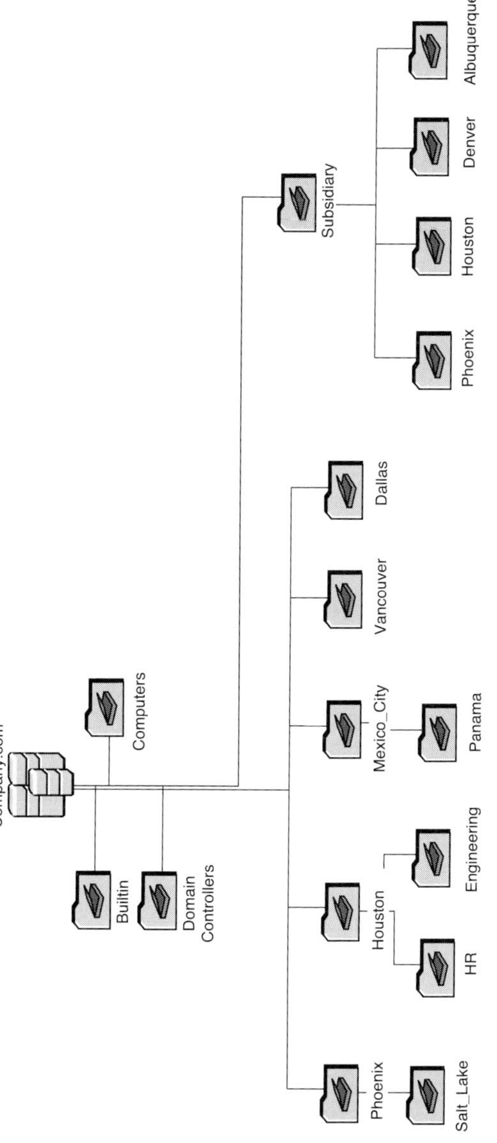

Figure 8.8 Upper container structure for North American company with two business lines and a single domain.

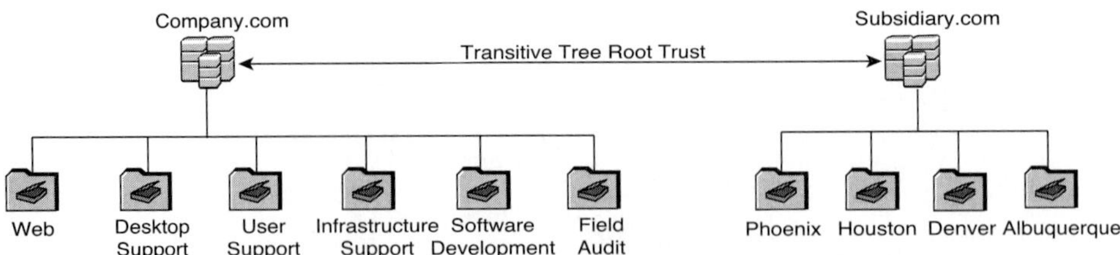

Figure 8.9 Upper containers for highly centralized IT organization with subsidiary business line configured as a peer domain in a forest.

Lower Level OUs

The rules for OU placement at lower levels of the domain are based more on user and computer management than delegating administrative privileges. This involves manipulating the user experience in one way or another. The tools most suited for this purpose are *group policies*.

Chapter 12, "Managing Group Policies," covers group policies in detail. Here is what we need to know at this point to aid in making design decisions. Group policies are a set of instructions that modern Windows clients (Windows 2000 and XP) download from their logon server and apply to their local Registry and security databases. There are 13 different policy types in Windows Server 2003. The operations supported by these policy engines are as follows:

- Registry updates (known as Administrative Templates)
- Security updates
- Logon/Logoff scripts
- Software distribution
- Folder redirection
- Disk quota management
- Wireless network management
- Restricted software selection
- Public key distribution
- IPSec policy management
- Internet Explorer management
- Remote Installation Services management
- Quality of Service (QoS) management

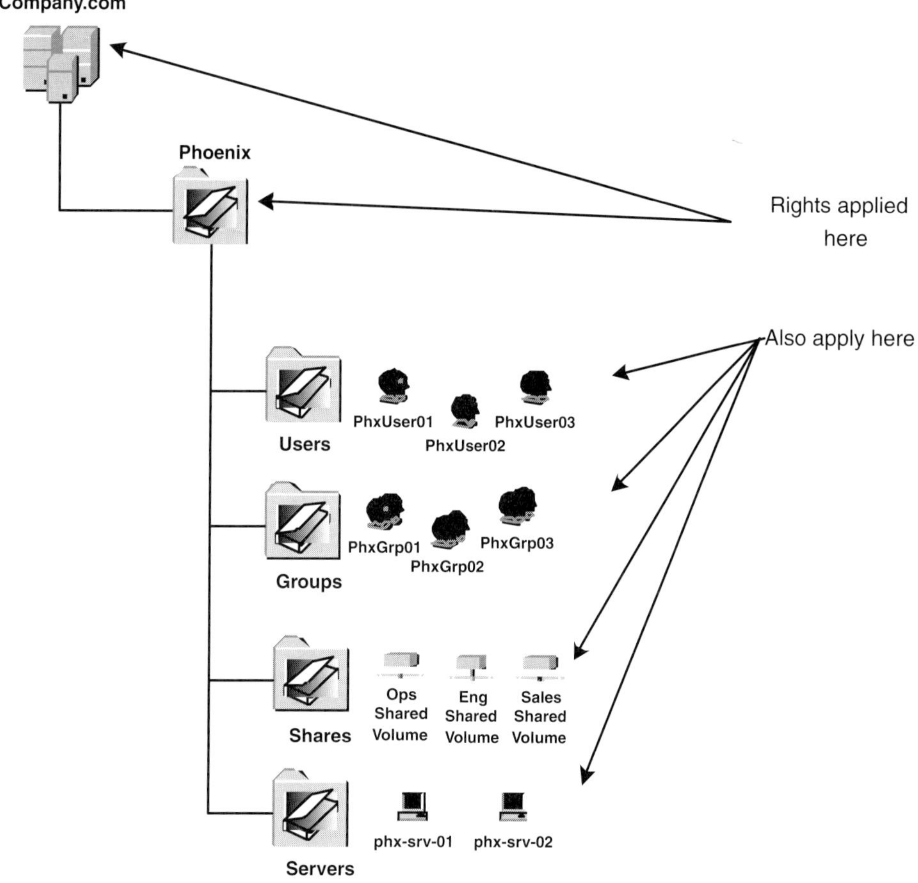

Figure 8.10 Domain and OU structure showing inherited group policies and the RSoP.

Group Policy Links

Group policies are linked to containers in Active Directory. This is how clients determine which policies affect them. Group policies can be linked to the following containers, listed in order of least precedence to highest:

- Sites
- Domains
- Organizational Units

Policies flow down the Active Directory tree. In other words, users and computers inherit policies linked to their parent OUs and to any superior OUs, then the domain, then their local site.

The list of policies that apply to a particular user or computer is called a *Resultant Set of Policies*, or RSoP. Windows Server 2003 includes a new feature that displays the RSoP for a user or computer. Figure 8.10 shows how policies inherit in a tree and what an RSoP display looks like.

Here's a rule of thumb: The closer a group policy object sits in relation to a user or computer in the Active Directory tree, the higher the precedence of the policies in the group policy object. For instance, a "Hide The 'My Computer' Icon" policy linked directly to the OU holding a user object will override a "Don't Hide The 'My Computer' Icon" policy linked to an OU higher in the tree.

As we'll see in Chapter 12, "Managing Group Policies," you can block policy inheritance at a particular OU so that objects below that point don't experience the effects of policies linked to sites, domains, and other OUs higher in the tree. You can also override a policy block so that administrators in subordinate OUs cannot stop their users from getting policies dictated by central IT management.

Group Policy Components

Group policies have two distinct components that work together to deliver the policy instructions to the client for processing.

- **Group Policy Container (GPC).** The GPC is an Active Directory object that defines a policy name, the client-side extension used to process the policy, where the instructions for the policy resides, and what container the policy is linked to. The GPC is located in the cn=Policies,cn=System,dc=<domain_name>,dc=<root> container in the Domain naming context. You can use the AD Users and Computers in Advanced View to see this container. Figure 8.11 shows an example of a policy that contains a software distribution policy, which puts additional information into Active Directory.

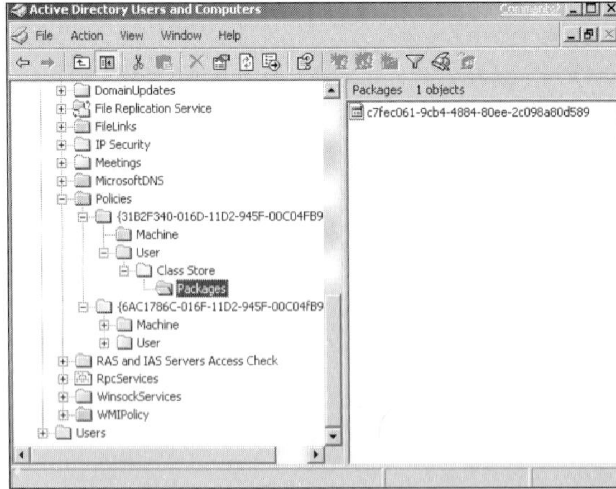

Figure 8.11 AD Users and Computers showing Policies container.

- **Group Policy Template (GPT).** The GPT is a set of instructions associated with a particular group policy. For example, a Logon policy would have a GPT consisting of a script. An Administrative Template (Registry) policy would have a GPT consisting of an entry in a file called Registry.pol. Clients download these GPT files and process them locally. The GPT files for a particular policy are located in the \Windows\Sysvol\Sysvol\<domain_name>\<policy_name> folder. The Sysvol contents are replicated among domain controllers via the *File Replication Service*, or FRS.

These two group policy components, taken together, are called a *Group Policy Object*, or GPO. Microsoft's use of the term GPO was unfortunate because you typically think of objects as being entries in Active Directory, whereas the GPO is an umbrella term for a directory object and a set of template files.

When you create a new group policy, you link it to an OU, domain, or site. The next time computers in that container start up, or users in that container log on, they download the policy. Administrative Template policies are applied in a volatile fashion so they do not tattoo the Registry like NT System Policies.

Group Policy Tools

Group policies are created and configured using the Group Policy Editor (GPE). You open the GPE by opening the Properties window for the container where you want to link the policy then selecting the Group Policy tab. Figure 8.12 shows the default group policies linked to the Domain container.

When you add or change a policy in the GPE, the system immediately creates or updates the associated GPC object and GPT files. There is no "Are you sure you want to do this?" warning.

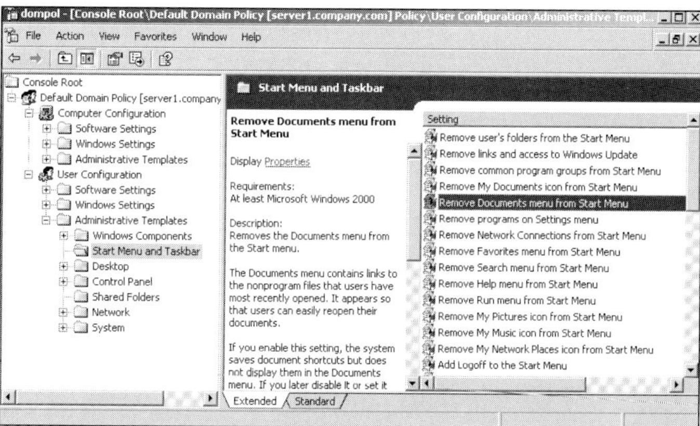

Figure 8.12 Group Policy Editor showing the Default Domain policies.

Group Policies and OU Design

You will find yourself using policies extensively to control users and computers in an Active Directory domain, so it's important to take them into account when you lay out the lower OU levels. For example, the Sales manager might want every desktop in her department nailed down tight so that the salespeople focus on their quotas instead of fooling with their PCs. On the other hand, the field construction superintendent might consider even mild desktop restrictions to be too confining.

Figure 8.13 shows an example OU design based around applying group policies. All designs are different, but here is the basis for the design decisions in the example:

- **Users.** This container holds the accounts for all users in the Phoenix office except for HR and field personnel, who attach to the network via a WAN link to the Phoenix LAN. Putting all users in a single container makes it possible to delegate administrative control of the container as well as define group policies. The subordinate container for Sales accommodates a request for a different group policy. In theory, each department could have its own OU with policies tailored for its specific needs.

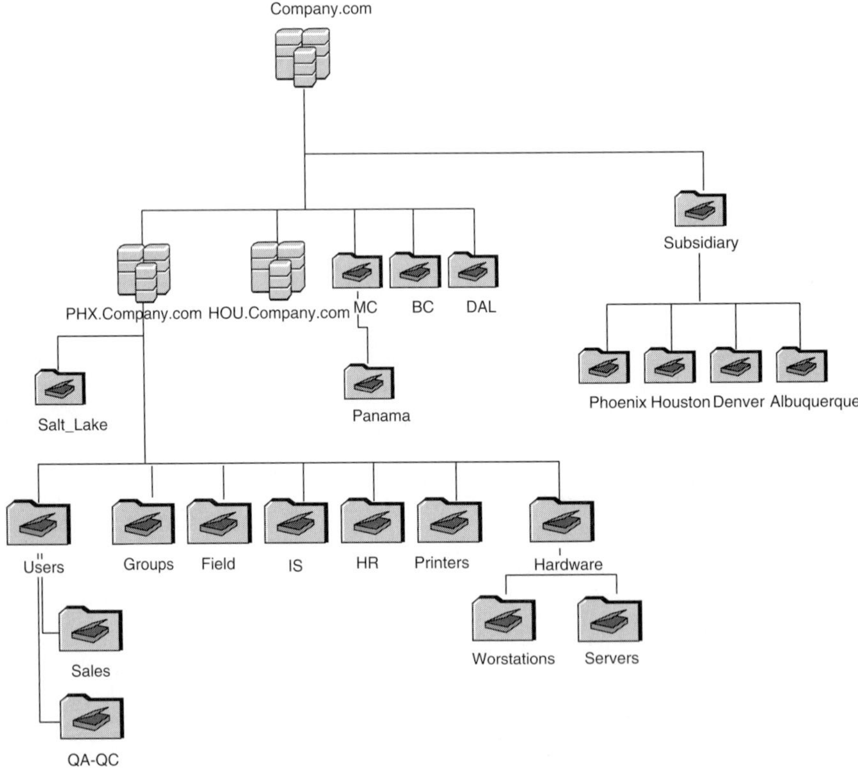

Figure 8.13 Lower-level container structure for single domain in a multiple-domain directory.

- `Groups.` You cannot assign group policies to groups, only users and computers, but this container reflects a certain tidiness on my part. I like keeping group objects in a separate container to make them easy to find. There is no performance penalty for putting groups in different containers from their members.
- `Field.` This container provides a place to put objects for remote locations such as job sites and temporary quarters. The separate container accomplishes two things. First, group policies for field personnel are usually much less restrictive than office policies. Second, field operations often have local technicians who are not full-fledged administrators. The separate container provides a way to assign them limited administrative rights over their users and machines.
- `IS` and `HR`. These containers provide discrete management units that satisfy the need for autonomy on the part of the staff. The danger, of course, is that the department administrators in the HR container will somehow bollix up their part of the directory and no one from the main IT group will be able to rescue them.
- `Printers` and `Shared_Folders`. These containers place items that users search for near the top of the container structure. The fewer containers a user has to negotiate to find a shared item in the directory, the more likely they are to use it. If you don't make directory access drop-dead simple, you'll never wean users away from browsing.
- `Hardware.` This container puts Computer objects into two separate containers, one for workstations and one for servers, where they can be managed as distinct units. The desktop administrators or break/fix technicians can be given admin rights over the Workstation container, whereas only network administrators have rights over the Server container. There is no operational advantage to putting Computer objects in the same container as their users. It's much easier to find objects in a container that isn't cluttered with different object classes.

After you draw out the lower-level design, start getting input from your colleagues, administrators in other parts of the organization, and management. Plan on this stage taking a while, even in a small organization. You might want to set up a small lab environment so that you can walk through typical operations.

Simplified OU Structure

If you work in a smaller organization, or you are a consultant with a practice that focuses on small and medium-sized companies, you may find the design in Figure 8.13 to be a bit too much. Figure 8.14 shows a directory for a smaller organization.

When IT staff is limited, local department gurus and power users tend to take on more administrative duties. For this reason, the design in Figure 8.14 divides the lower containers along functional lines. A group in each OU can be assigned management rights for the OU and you or a central administrator can modify the group memberships based on requests from the department managers.

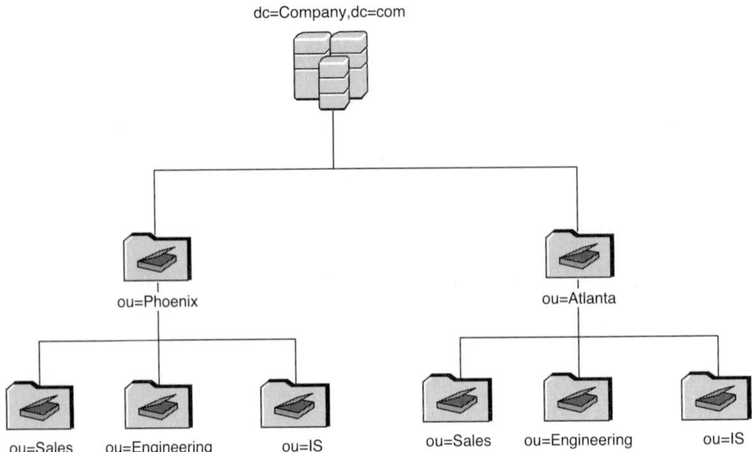

Figure 8.14 Directory design for a small company.

Whatever design method you choose, leave yourself room for changes and don't be afraid to shake up the design quite a bit in response to changes in the IT work processes. As long as you can avoid splitting off a new domain and you don't get too creative with your policies, you can make changes without affecting users.

This just about takes care of the design preparations. Now you need to attend to a few housekeeping chores involving the placement of special-purpose servers.

Flexible Single Master Operations

In a multiple-master replication environment, any domain controller can theoretically change any object in Active Directory. As we saw in the last chapter, Active Directory has special features to handle conflicting updates performed during the same replication interval.

Certain Active Directory functions just cannot be shared without causing potential data consistency problems. These special functions are called *Flexible Single Master Operations*, or FSMOs (pronounced FizzMohs). The domain controller assigned a particular FSMO is called a *role master.* Here are the five FSMOs and the MMC console you would use to view and set the role master:

- PDC Emulator—AD Users and Computers
- RID Master—AD Users and Computers
- Infrastructure Master—AD Users and Computers
- Domain Naming Master—AD Domains and Trusts
- Schema Master—Custom console containing the Schema snap-in

Identifying FSMOs

You can find the identity of a FSMO by right-clicking the top icon in the associated MMC console and selecting OPERATIONS MASTER from the flyout menu. This opens an Operations Master window with tabbed entries for each FSMO controlled by that MMC console.

The FSMO role masters are flagged in Active Directory by an attribute called `FSMORoleOwner`. This attribute is assigned to the object that controls the function requiring single-master operation. The `FSMORoleOwner` attribute is linked to the following objects:

- PDC Emulator—`Domain` container
- RID Master—RID Manager$ object in `cn=System,dc=<domain>,dc=<root>`
- Infrastructure Master—`Infrastructure` container under `dc=<domain>,dc=<root>`
- Schema Master—`Schema` container
- Domain Naming Master—`Partitions` container under `cn=Configuration,dc=<domain>,dc=<root>`

You can use a batch file in Resource Kit called Dumpfsmos.cmd to list the FSMOs. This batch file uses the NTDSUTIL utility to enumerate the FSMO roles. The syntax is `dumpfsmos <dc_name>`.

PDC Emulator

Active Directory supports the presence of downlevel NTbackup Domain Controllers (BDCs). To make this trick work, Active Directory fools the BDCs into thinking that a Windows Server 2003 domain controller is an NT Primary Domain Controller (PDC). This is necessary because BDCs will only replicate from a PDC. This special domain controller is the *PDC Emulator* role master.

The PDC Emulator packages up Active Directory updates that affect objects shared by the classic SAM and replicates those updates to the downlevel BDCs using LanMan Replication. While in Mixed, objects representing security principals (users, computers, and groups) can only be created by the PDC Emulator.

After all domain controllers have been removed from operation, the domain can be shifted to Native. When this is done, the LanMan Replication service is stopped and the downlevel BDCs no longer get updates. They remain active, however, getting older and older and further and further out of date, a little like 1960s rock bands.

You cannot promote a classic NT BDC to PDC after you have begun upgrading your domain to Active Directory. You can, however, transfer the PDC Emulator role to another Windows Server 2003 domain controller (or a Windows 2000 domain controller if you are still running in Functionality Level 0). From the perspective of the downlevel BDCs, this looks as if a BDC has been promoted. They shift their allegiances to the new PDC Emulator and begin replicating from that server.

Windows 9x and NT clients that are members of a domain know that the only domain controller with write permissions on the domain SAM is the PDC. Therefore, when these clients need to change a password, they communicate directly to the PDC. In modern Windows, any domain controller can update a user's password but the downlevel clients don't know this. The PDC Emulator gives the downlevel clients a place to go when they want to change passwords or make any other change involving the classic SAM.

Updating Logon Processes for Downlevel Clients

The DSCLIENT patch on the Windows Server 2003 CD modifies the behavior of a downlevel Windows 9x client so that it can change a password on any domain controller, not just the PDC Emulator. The Active Directory update for NT4, available as a download from the Microsoft web site, does the same for NT4 clients.

This patch also changes the authentication mechanism for Windows 9x/ME clients to use NLTM Challenge-Response version 2 rather than LanMan Challenge-Response. Classic NT clients running SP3 or later already use NTLM v2. The AD client patch does not permit any downlevel client to use Kerberos.

In addition to its duties as housemaid to the downlevel BDCs, Microsoft decided to throw additional single master operations onto the PDC Emulator. For example, as we saw in Chapter 7, "Managing Active Directory Replication," the PDC Emulator is also the primary time standard for other domain controllers in a domain. There are three additional duties assigned to the PDC Emulator.

Final Validation for Password Changes

When a user changes a password, or an administrator resets a password for a user, the update is replicated to the PDC Emulator on a "best effort" basis. This means that schedules on intervening inter-site links are ignored.

The domain controllers in a domain use the PDC Emulator as a "last court of appeals" for invalid passwords. If a user enters an incorrect password, the local DC checks with the PDC emulator to see if the password has been changed and the user's password is actually valid. If so, the user is given access. This feature prevents calls to the Help Desk following a password change.

Preferred Group Policy Location

Group policies consist of two components: a Group Policy Container (GPC) in Active Directory and a Group Policy Template (GPT) in `\Windows\Sysvol\Sysvol\<domain_name>`. If these two components get out of sync, a user will either try to get a policy when the GPT is not yet in Sysvol or will miss a policy in Sysvol because the GPC hasn't yet replicated to the logon server.

To avoid this problem and other inconsistencies that might arise from multi-master replication, when you open the Group Policy Editor, the focus of the tool is set to the PDC Emulator. This ensures that all administrators in the domain make their group policy modifications on the same machine, reducing the likelihood of synchronization problems.

Disabling Invalid Password Checking

The double-check of invalid passwords puts a strain on the PDC Emulator and the WAN links leading to it. You may want to disable invalid password checks when the local domain controller is in a different site than the PDC Emulator. You can do this with a Registry update on the local domain controller:

```
Key:   HKLM\CurrentControlSet\Services\Netlogon\Parameters
Value: AvoidPDConWAN
Data:  1
```

If the PDC Emulator is not available (either because it is down or the WAN link is cut), you'll be prompted to pick another domain controller or to wait until the PDC Emulator is available again. If you are fairly confident that your modification won't conflict with changes made by other administrators, you can select another domain controller.

Keep this behavior in mind as you update your group policies. If you are several slow hops away from the PDC Emulator, it may take you a while to get your screen refreshed.

Domain Master Browser

Windows is a little like the Beverly Hillbillies in some respects. You can dress it up and put it in a fancy setting, but at some point or another you're going to end up with lye soap cookin' out by the cement pond.

An example of this unsophisticated behavior is *browsing*. I don't know of a single Windows feature that has caused more administrative headaches than browsing.

Modern Windows does not need browsing. You can publish your printer resources in Active Directory. You can use the Distributed File System (Dfs) to abstract your share points away from their home servers. But for some reason, users find it comforting to open My Network Places and scratch around looking for resources.

Windows Server 2003 provides backward compatibility for browsing. Windows Server 2003 and XP desktops participate in browse elections on an equal footing with NT4 servers and workstations. If they win the election, they become the Subnet Master Browsers.

In a routed enterprise, browsing depends on a single server, a Domain Master Browser, to aggregate the subnet browser databases and distribute a comprehensive server list. In a classic NT domain, the PDC acts as the Domain Master Browser. In an Active Directory domain, the PDC Emulator takes on this chore.

WINS plays an important role in browsing by publishing the IP address of the Domain Master Browser and any Subnet Master Browsers. It's important that the PDC Emulator be a WINS client so it will register the appropriate browser records.

RID Master

All security objects have a SID. The SID is a combination of the SID of the domain and a sequential number called the *Relative ID*, or RID. In a classic NT domain, security principals added after initial installation get RIDs starting with 1000. Here is an example of a few SIDs from a domain:

```
PhxUser1:   S-1-5-21-515967899-764733703-1708537768-1000
XP-WKS-01$: S-1-5-21-515967899-764733703-1708537768-1001
PhxAdmins:  S-1-5-21-515967899-764733703-1708537768-1002
PhxUser2:    S-1-5-21-515967899-764733703-1708537768-1003
```

Notice that the last four digits, the RID for each SID, are in sequence. In a native-mode domain where any domain controller can create a security principal, the RIDs may not be in sequence, but they must be unique. For this reason, only one domain controller can hold the RID pool. This is the *RID Master.* The available RIDs are stored in an attribute called `RIDAllocationPool`.

While in Mixed, the RID Master and PDC Emulator stay in constant touch because only the PDC Emulator can create security principals. In Native, the RID Master slices hunks from the RID list and passes them out to the domain controllers when they request it.

There is one RID Master per domain. By default, the RID Master and the PDC Emulator roles are held by the same domain controller. You can transfer the RID Master role to another domain controller, but it is important that it remain available as long as you are in Mixed. Continuous service is not as critical in Native because each domain controller has a big slice of the RID pie, but you would not be able to promote new domain controllers without the RID Master.

Infrastructure Master

When you add a user to a group, the user's distinguished name (DN) is added to the `Member` attribute for the group. The User object has a corresponding `MemberOf` attribute that contains the distinguished names of the groups to which the user belongs.

This pair of attributes, `Member` and `MemberOf`, are examples of *linked attributes.* In a pair of linked attributes, the primary attribute is termed a *forward link* and the other attribute is a *back-link*. In the example, the `Member` attribute is the forward link and the `MemberOf` attribute is a back-link. Only the forward link can be modified directly. The back-link is calculated.

There are many instances of linked attributes in Active Directory. Another example is the `Manager` attribute, a forward link that identifies a user's manager, and the `Reports` attribute, a back-link that lists the users who report to a single manager.

When a forward link is changed, for example, when a new user is added to a group, the user DN is replicated to all domain controllers hosting a replica of the affected naming context. When a domain controller applies the update, it recalculates the back-link attribute for the affected user object.

If you think this process has the potential to get a little messy and complicated, you're right. Maintaining referential integrity between linked attributes is one of the more complex processes in a directory service.

The linked `Member` and `MemberOf` attributes play an important role in Active Directory security because groups, as security principals, are used to protect objects. Users who are members of a group get the access permissions assigned to the object. When a user logs on, the system does a search for any groups that have the user's DN in their `Member` attribute. It resolves these group names into SIDs and adds them to the *Privilege Access Certificate* (PAC) for the user. The security subsystem on a member server uses the PAC to construct a local access token for the user.

If the user's distinguished name changes, the system must update all the group objects that have the user as a member. This must be done as quickly as possible so the user doesn't "fly under the radar" and get inappropriate access permissions.

Updates to the `Member` attribute for group objects in the same domain as the user with the changed name happen immediately because the domain controller holds both the user object and the group object. But when a user is a member of a group in another domain, the update can take a while. A domain controller in the remote domain must be informed about the name change so it can change the `Member` attribute for any affected groups in that domain.

The job of quickly disseminating these name changes falls to the *Infrastructure Master.*

Domain Naming Master

When you create a new domain in an existing forest, the other domain controllers need to know that the new domain exists because the domain represents a separate naming context. The Directory Service Agent's (DSA's) shared knowledge about each other's naming contexts is one of the principal foundations of LDAP.

Active Directory stores pointers to other domains in a special `CrossRef` object located in a `Partitions` container in the Configuration naming context. This object contains attributes that describe the distinguished name, DNS name, the flat name, and the name of the Domain naming context along with the kind of trust relationship that binds the domain to the forest.

If two administrators were to create new domains with identical names during the same replication interval, the standard collision management algorithms would fail to prevent a snarl of incorrect links, references, and replication connections. For this reason, only one computer in a forest can make changes to the `Partitions` container, and that is the *Domain Naming Master.*

By default, the Domain Naming Master is the first domain controller promoted in a forest. You can transfer this role to any domain controller in any domain, although it's best to put it on a domain controller in the root domain so there is no question about which group of administrators can have access to the server.

Schema Master

The objects in the Schema naming context define the very structure and identity of Active Directory for a forest. Objects can only be added, modified, or removed from the schema under strictly controlled circumstances. Only one domain controller in a forest can update the schema, and that is the *Schema Master.*

Chapter 6, "Understanding Active Directory Services," discussed the requirements to modify the schema manually. This permits you to add attributes and object classes to support in-house applications for departments such as Human Resources or Facilities. Client/server applications such as Exchange 2000 also make changes to the schema. Newer network management applications can take advantage of features in Active Directory and they often make schema changes.

When you install an application that modifies the schema, you do not need to be at the console of the Schema Master, but the Schema Master must be online and available before the schema updates can be applied. Also, you must be a member of the Schema Admins group.

The role master for a FSMO can be transferred to another domain controller or seized if the original domain controller has crashed and cannot be revived. The procedures for these actions are in Chapter 10, "Active Directory Maintenance."

Role Master Location

If you take no actions to transfer FSMO roles, the first domain controller you promote will have all the roles, making it a significant risk as a single point of failure. Here is a set of recommendations for placing FSMO role masters:

- **PDC Emulator and RID Master.** Keep these two FSMOs on the same domain controller. Use a fast, reliable machine that is well connected to your WAN. Remember that all other domain controllers in the domain check invalid passwords by querying the PDC Emulator for a second opinion.
- **Infrastructure Master.** Move this FSMO to a domain controller that is *not* a Global Catalog server. Make sure the server is well connected because it is responsible for updating the other domain controllers with name cross-reference changes.
- **Domain Naming Master.** Move this FSMO to a domain controller that is also a Global Catalog server. This server does not need to be fast but it must be available when you create a new domain.
- **Schema Master.** Microsoft recommends putting the FSMO on the same domain controller assigned as Domain Naming Master, but this is not an absolute requirement. The schema rarely needs updating, but you want to maintain tight security on the Schema Master. All servers share a copy of the schema, so the Schema Master does not need to be a GC.

Domain Controller Placement

You should avoid making every Windows Server 2003 into a domain controller. This hurts performance by taking CPU cycles for replication and directory management. It also makes the replication topology unnecessarily complex.

The initial number of domain controllers depends primarily on fault tolerance. You should *always* have at least two domain controllers in a domain to ensure that you have a full copy of Active Directory ready for action in case either server should fail. I recommend having three so that you can do maintenance on one server while the other two are up and ready for work.

Reliability and performance then become the primary criteria for selecting domain controllers. Plan on putting at least two domain controllers in every large office (1000+ users) to get acceptable performance during morning logon and for fault tolerance.

Put at least one domain controller in every office where you do not want users authenticating over the WAN. If you have a solid, fast network infrastructure, you might be able to draw the line at 50 users. If your infrastructure is slow or prone to failure, you might want to reduce the number to 10.

If you do not have a domain controller in an office with member servers, a network WAN failure will eventually cut the users off from their local servers. This is because the Kerberos tickets eventually expire (10-hour default lifetime). You don't want to put the production floor of a factory down because some construction worker put a backhoe through the communication link to your domain controller. In these instances, you'll need a local domain controller.

Global Catalog Servers

Global Catalog servers are a vital component of your Active Directory architecture. The Windows authentication system relies on the Global Catalog to obtain Universal group membership. Client/server applications like Exchange 2000 rely on the GC for information. Many LDAP queries take a lot longer if the client is forced to walk the tree rather than query the GC.

If a site has no GC server available, users will only be allowed to log on to the domain if a local domain controller has been configured to cache the GC information. Otherwise, they will get an error saying that no GC server can be contacted and logon has been denied. This restriction does not apply to administrators.

Designating a domain controller as a GC server can significantly increase the hardware requirements for the server in a big network. If you have 200,000 users in your forest but only 20,000 or so in any one domain, the GC servers in each domain will have a fairly hefty Ntds.dit file to handle. You must size your server hardware accordingly.

Place at least one GC in every large office. Smaller offices can either have a GC or a standard domain controller configured to cache GC information.

If you have only one domain, you should enable the Global Catalog on every server. This ensures that a client can send a query to port 3268 on any server and get a response. There is no additional overhead or performance decrement for taking this action.

DNS Secondaries

The stability and reliability of a Windows Server 2003 domain absolutely depends on the stability and reliability of the dynamic DNS system that provides name resolution services for that domain. It does no good to put a domain controller in a branch office to achieve fault tolerance without placing a dynamic DNS secondary for the zone in the same office.

The most straightforward way to distribute DNS services in conjunction with Active Directory is to use Active Directory Integrated zones (see Chapter 5, "Managing DNS," for details). This places the DNS records directly into Active Directory where every domain controller can reach them. All you need to do is install DNS on a domain controller and that's that. It will see the integrated zones and display them automatically. And thanks to the multiple-master nature of Active Directory, every domain controller running DNS can make changes to the zone.

A few caveats apply when using Active Directory Integrated DNS zones. Foremost is the requirement that the DNS servers must also be domain controllers. You can, if you want, create standard secondaries that pull a copy of the zone from an Active Directory Integrated primary. As with standard DNS, this secondary copy will be read-only. You should always have at least one standard secondary DNS server so you can quickly recover a zone should there be a problem with Active Directory replication. You do not need to point any clients at this server. It's just there as an online backup.

If a domain controller is running DNS, you should always configure the TCP/IP properties to point at another DNS server for name resolution. Pointing a domain controller at itself can result in a Catch-22 situation where the domain controller cannot replicate changes because it cannot find the IP address of its replication partners and it cannot update its copy of the zone to get those IP addresses because of the replication failure. You could also encounter problems during boot in which the Active Directory services start before DNS starts.

Moving Forward

At this point, your design needs to be reviewed and affirmed by just about everyone in the company. When you schedule these design review meetings, take a tip from Arlo Guthrie in "Alice's Restaurant." Come prepared with lots of pictures that have circles and arrows and a paragraph on the back explaining what each one of them means. I have also had good luck by supplying lots of Krispy Kreme donuts and espresso. Caffeine, sugar, and saturated fats always speeds up the approval process.

It's time to begin deploying Windows Server 2003 domains. The next chapter covers installation details for upgrading existing classic NT or Windows 2000 domain controllers and promoting new Windows Server 2003 domain controllers. It also covers shifting from Mixed, Functionality Level 0 to Native, Functionality Level 1 and migrating users, computers, and groups between domains.

9 Deploying Windows Server 2003 Domains

THE TIME FOR TALK IS OVER. You've assayed the alternatives, written the reports, drawn the drawings, met the meetings, consumed carloads of coffee, parlayed plans, fought fights, arrived at agreements, and now you're ready to do the deed and deploy an Active Directory domain. This chapter covers the following scenarios:

- Upgrading a classic NT4 domain to Windows Server 2003
- Upgrading a Windows 2000 domain to Windows Server 2003
- Migrating from an NT4 or Windows 2000 domain to a Windows Server 2003 domain

In general, organizations make the decision to migrate rather than upgrade when they want to change the structure of their domains during the cutover. The most common circumstances are the following:

- **Domain name changes**. When you do a direct upgrade, you must retain the original NetBIOS flat name as the leftmost element of the new Domain Naming System (DNS) name, such as `BRANCH` becoming `Branch.Company.com`. Otherwise, you must create a new Windows Server 2003 domain with a new flat name and migrate your users and groups and computers to that new domain.
- **Collapsing account domains**. If you currently have a multiple-master domain configuration and you want to end up with a single Active Directory domain, your best course of action is migrate the contents of the various NT domains into a new Windows Server 2003 domain.
- **Collapsing resource domains**. Ordinarily, resource domains contain just computer accounts, not users and groups. Migrating these computers out of the NT resource domain into a new Windows Server 2003 domain is not

simply a matter of changing the domain affiliation, though. You need to make sure that access permissions assigned to resources are preserved, along with user profiles and other critical structures.

- **Restructuring Windows 2000 domains.** The new Forest trust feature in Windows Server 2003 gives additional flexibility to inter-forest resource sharing. This may encourage your organization to redefine your domain plans to create separate forests rather than separate domains within the same forest. This could happen if you plan on dividing the business in the near future.

Of these reasons, the one that most often causes administrators to retool their cutover strategy is the need to change domain names. Many organizations have a DNS infrastructure with naming conventions that do not accommodate the exiting NT domain names.

For example, the administrators in a university might want to use the existing DNS root name, `University.edu`, as the Active Directory root domain with child domain names such as `Undergrad.University.edu`, `Grad.University.edu`, `Law.University.edu`, and so forth. If the resultant flat names, `UNDERGRAD` and `GRAD` and `LAW`, do not correspond to existing NT domain names, the administrators will be forced to create new Windows Server 2003 domains and migrate users from the existing NT domains.

This chapter describes several upgrade and migration roadmaps designed with these key elements in mind:

- Keeping user accounts intact
- Maintaining appropriate access to network resources
- Minimizing disruption of user activities
- Obtaining a viable management hierarchy for domain and forest-related objects and processes

New Features in Windows Server 2003

Windows Server 2003 includes several new features and tools for handling domain deployments and improving interoperability. They are as follows:

- **Active Directory Migration Tool (ADMT) improvements.** The new version of ADMT supports password migration, retains access to user profiles, and greatly simplifies re-permissioning of member servers and desktops.
- **Functional levels.** While NT and Windows 2000 domain controllers remain operational, many new Windows Server 2003 features must be kept disabled. The new features are phased into operation using a set of *functional levels*. Two of these functional levels mimic the Mixed and Native operation of Windows 2000. The remaining two functional levels enable Windows Server 2003 features first in a domain then in the forest.

- **Application naming contexts.** This feature was mentioned in Chapter 5, "Managing DNS," but it bears repeating here. A Windows Server 2003 domain controller is capable of storing Active Directory Integrated DNS zone records in separate Application naming contexts. This gives much more flexibility to the design of Windows-based DNS in a large enterprise.
- **Domain controller overload prevention.** Windows 2000 and XP desktops prefer to do their logons at Active Directory-based domain controllers. This can cause problems early in a deployment when the number of desktops may be out of proportion to the number of new domain controllers. A special Registry entry can be enabled at the Windows Server 2003 domain controllers so that they emulate classic backup domain controllers (BDCs) until a sufficient number have been deployed to support the desktops.
- **Domain controller promotion using backup tapes.** If you have a large domain with a massive Active Directory database, it can take a while to promote a domain controller across a slow Wide Area Network (WAN) link. This new feature permits using a copy of Active Directory restored from backup tape or backup file as the source for the initial build of the AD database on a newly promoted domain controller.
- **New schema.** Windows Server 2003 makes roughly 400 changes to the base schema in Windows 2000. These changes must be in place prior to upgrading a Windows 2000 domain controller to Windows Server 2003. A new utility called ADPREP upgrades the schema and installs new attributes and containers in the Domain naming context to support the upgrade.
- **New domain operations.** A Windows Server 2003 forest can be restructured by changing the names of the domains and their parent/child relationships. You can also rename domain controllers within a domain, although you cannot move a domain controller between domains without first demoting it.

Preparing for an NT Domain Upgrade

Figure 9.1 shows a fairly simple classic NT domain configuration consisting of a single account domain with a primary domain controller (PDC) in the main office and BDCs in the outlying areas to handle local logons. Member servers in this domain validate user credentials via pass-through authentication to their respective BDCs.

In this configuration, an upgrade starts by having a little conversation with the PDC that goes something like a scene out of *The Sopranos*:

> You sit down in front of the server and say, "You took an oath, PDC, but you broke it. First you got slow, then you stopped talking to the BDCs, and now I hear you're leaking information to the password crackers."
>
> "I tried to keep you out of harm's way. I really did," PDC says back, bezel lights flashing mournfully.

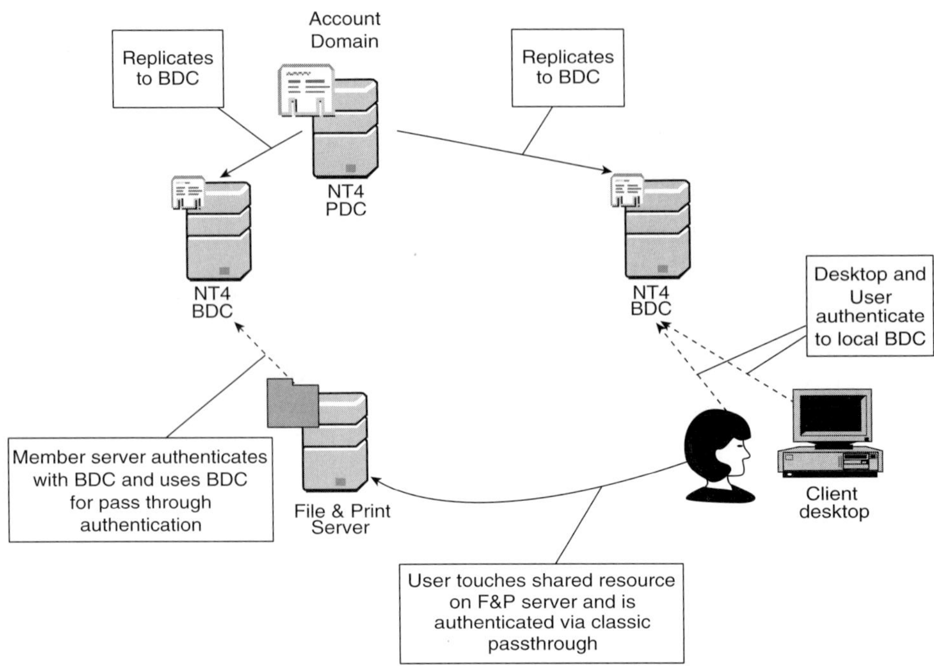

Figure 9.1 Single domain with multiple BDCs to handle logon in remote locations.

> "It's too late," you say. "We're going to have to make some changes." You reach inside your jacket and pull out a copy of the Windows Server 2003 CD.
>
> "Okay," it replies, "only just . . . just . . . not in the console, okay? Leave me my eyes."

You slide open the CD-ROM caddy, put in the disk, and when the splash screen asks you if you want to upgrade, you give a final little salute with your eyebrows and click `Yes`. About an hour later, the job is done. You light a candle for the old PDC and start configuring Active Directory parameters.

It takes a good bit of planning to get to this point, so let's back up a little and start with a checklist of the upgrade prerequisites. Then, we'll trace through what you can expect to happen when you upgrade the PDC and how to proceed when upgrading the remaining domain controllers and shifting the domain and forest functional levels to Windows Server 2003.

DNS

Before you upgrade, you must have a DNS infrastructure deployed that supports service locator (SRV) records and, hopefully, dynamic registrations. The second item is not an absolute requirement, but it saves you from manually importing long lists of SRV records. As discussed in Chapter 5, "Managing DNS," you do not need Windows Server 2003 running DNS or even Windows 2000 DNS servers to support Active

Directory. Any version of BIND starting with 8.1.3 will do very nicely, and this includes the latest versions of Lucent QIP.

If you are currently running Windows 2000 DNS servers, and they are not domain controllers, you may want to upgrade them to Windows Server 2003 running DNS to get support for conditional forwarding and stub zones.

If you have not yet decided on the DNS name of your Active Directory domain, it's time to get everyone around a table so you can come to a consensus. Unlike Windows 2000, Windows Server 2003 will let you change a domain name after it has been deployed, but the change is not simple and it is better to avoid the work, if possible.

Remember that if you are upgrading an existing NT domain, the leftmost element of the fully qualified DNS name must match the current flat NetBIOS domain name. Also, if you are installing a separate Windows Server 2003 domain, the leftmost element of the domain name cannot match the existing flat name of any domain, server, or user. This will cause *duplicate name* errors when you attempt to promote the first domain controller in the new domain.

Configure the TCP/IP properties of your NT domain controllers to point at the dynamic DNS servers before doing the upgrade. This ensures that the servers will register their SRV records during the domain controller promotion phase that follows the upgrade. Also make sure that your clients point at these same DNS servers so they can find the SRV records and use them to locate the newly promoted domain controllers.

Domain Controller Requirements

Your existing NT PDC might date back to the origins of NT4 in the dark ages of the middle 1990s when Pentium 90 servers were considered state of the art and you had to fight to get approval for mirrored 2GB SCSI drives to hold the operating system.

Chapter 1, "Installing and Configuring Windows Server 2003," lists the minimum recommended hardware requirements for Windows Server 2003, including CPU speed, system memory, L2 cache, I/O performance, disk capacity, and network connections. A domain controller should be sized for I/O performance and reliability rather than raw CPU speed. If you have fewer than ten thousand users and the domain controller handles only a few hundred users logging on concurrently in the morning, then you can get by with a single-processor server, 600MHz or higher, with 256MB of RAM and dual mirrored drives for the operating system along with dual mirrored drives for the Active Directory database files. You can find such machines in a 1U form factor from major vendors for less than $3000.

If you have tens of thousands of users in the domain and thousands who authenticate in one location in the morning, and you have lots of group policies to deploy to those users, you need more than one domain controller and each of them needs multiple processors and lots of memory.

You must be running Service Pack 6a to upgrade any NT server to Windows Server 2003, including domain controllers.

Purge Lmhosts and Hosts Files

Before upgrading an NT domain controller, check for the presence of Hosts and Lmhosts files. Entries in these files might cause name resolution problems after the server has been upgraded to Windows Server 2003. It's easy to forget that you have these files. They lie there quietly, like a Stephen King character lurking under a bridge, waiting . . . to . . . pounce.

You should find the files in `\WINNT\System32\Drivers\Etc` unless someone has changed the Registry setting for the default location. This Registry setting is `HKLM | System | CurrentControlSet | Services | TCPIP | Parameters | DataBasePath`.

You must have at least one NTFS volume on the domain controller to hold Sysvol. If an NT4 domain controller you plan on upgrading has only FAT partitions, it's best to convert the partitions to NTFS prior to doing the upgrade. That way, if something goes wrong, you aren't trying to diagnose two problems, the upgrade and the file system conversion.

Always put the Active Directory database files on a separate set of mirrored drives. Most of the I/O involving Active Directory is read rather than write, so mirroring improves performance. If you have hundreds and hundreds of users authenticating on a domain controller at the same time in the morning, and therefore pulling their group policies from Sysvol on that domain controller, you might want to put Sysvol on a separate set of mirrored drives, as well.

Application Compatibility Considerations

Even if your existing server hardware is capable of supporting a full-fledged Windows Server 2003 domain controller, you might not want to do a direct upgrade because of incompatible applications running on the server, or a Registry that resembles an old bulletin board with layers and layers of entries that no one has ever seen fit to remove, or an operating system volume choked with old management software and analytical tools you've experimented with over the years.

A domain controller can act as a file-and-print server and even run small applications such as TCP/IP support services, but it should not be used for heavy-duty client/server applications. This is not so much a limitation of the operating system as it is a logistical decision. If you are running a mail server and you need to shut it down to do maintenance on the information store, you don't want that evolution to affect the authentication services provided by a domain controller.

Leapfrog Upgrade

If you want to do a direct upgrade of your domain, you cannot simply place Windows Server 2003 on the wire and promote it to be a domain controller in that domain. You must always upgrade the existing PDC, then you can introduce as many new Windows Server 2003 domain controllers as you like. If your PDC is a little wheezy, the workaround is to leapfrog the upgrade (see Figure 9.2).

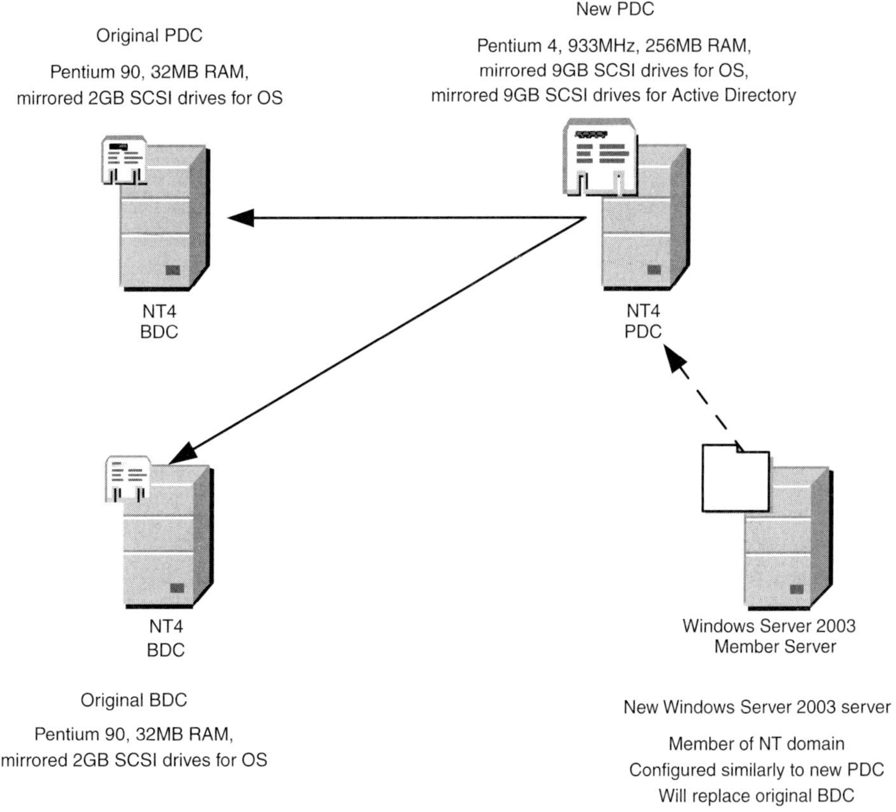

Figure 9.2 Leapfrogging a PDC to introduce a new server for upgrading.

First, spec out the hardware for a server that is adequate for your domain controller needs. Do a test installation of Windows Server 2003 on this server just to make sure you have no compatibility issues. Make sure you test all the SCSI channels and drives that you will eventually use to store Active Directory files.

Now, wipe the operating system drive on the new server and install NT4 as a BDC in your existing NT domain. Make sure you verify that you get steady replication between this server and the PDC. Leave the new server on the wire for a day or two to check for complications prior to upgrading.

Promote the new server to PDC with User Manager. This automatically demotes the existing PDC to a BDC. Again, let the system bake for a couple of days to make sure everything works as you would expect.

When you're ready to upgrade the domain, start by upgrading the new PDC to Windows Server 2003. You already know the hardware works with Windows Server 2003, so the upgrade should proceed without complication barring any pre-existing corruption in the Security Account Manager (SAM) or a power failure during the upgrade.

After the upgrade, you can either upgrade or replace the existing BDCs in the domain. The example in the diagram shows a Windows Server 2003 member server waiting in the wings to take over for the old BDC.

Upromote and NT Domain Controllers

If you are running applications on NT domain controllers, it is often impractical to upgrade the server to a Windows Server 2003 domain controller. You have the option following the upgrade to leave the server as a member server rather than complete the Domain Controller Promotion Wizard (Dcpromo) to upgrade to a Windows Server 2003 domain controller.

If you prefer, you can demote the NT BDC to a standard member server prior to the upgrade. This can be done using a third-party tool called Upromote from Algin Technologies. Using Upromote, you can demote a classic NT BDC to a member server, and you can also promote a standard server to a BDC. This gives you quite a bit of flexibility.

Use caution when changing the status of a domain controller if you have added domain local groups to access control lists (ACLs) on files and Registry keys on the server. Standard member servers do not recognize domain local groups, and you could cause users to lose access to files.

Protect the SAM

Upgrades can go sour for a variety of reasons:

- Hardware incompatibilities with Windows Server 2003 that prevent upgrading the operating system
- Hardware failures during the operating system upgrade or domain controller promotion
- SAM or Local Security Authority (LSA) corruption that prevents migrating accounts and policies to Active Directory
- Inadequate DNS and Windows Internet Name Service (WINS) preparation

In all of these potential failure scenarios, your prime concern is protecting the account database. The PDC has the only read-write copy of the `SAM` and `Security` Registry hives. This is where the accounts and account policies are stored along with trust relationship information. If the upgrade fails and the PDC cannot be recovered, users can still log on to the domain via the BDCs but you cannot change passwords, group memberships, or user privileges.

You can speed up recovery by making an image of the operating system partition just prior to starting the upgrade using imaging tools such as Ghost from Symantec or DriveImage from PowerQuest. Or, you can do a standard tape backup using Ntbackup or, better yet, a backup utility with an emergency restore feature.

Another potential problem is corruption of the `SAM` and `Security` hives that doesn't come to light until after the promotion. If the corrupted entries get replicated to the BDCs, you could cause users to lose access to the domain. To prepare for this type of failure, many organizations use an offline BDC as an insurance policy. Here's how it works.

Install NT Server as a BDC on a spare machine. It does not need to be a server-class machine. All you want is a live copy of the `SAM` and `Security` hives. After you've verified that the BDC is functioning properly, take it offline. If the `SAM` or `Security` hives should become corrupted during the upgrade or in the days just following the upgrade, you can take the following actions to recover:

1. Take the Windows Server 2003 domain controllers and NT4 BDCs offline.
2. Put the offline BDC back on the wire.
3. Promote the BDC to PDC using Server Manager.
4. Verify in WINS that the server is listed as the PDC for the domain. Delete other domain controller listings, if necessary.
5. Put the NT4 BDCs back on the wire one at a time and force replication. Check the Event log to verify that they were able to find the new PDC and replicate from it.
6. Restore the original PDC from tape or image.
7. When you put the original PDC back on the wire, it will see that another server is now the PDC and will not start Netlogon.
8. Demote the original PDC to a BDC then promote it to PDC to return the system to status quo ante.

After you've restored full functionality to the network, you can assess what went wrong and start over again. You'll need to wipe and reinstall any new Windows Server 2003 domain controllers you introduced into the system.

The offline BDC is only good insurance for a few days. As time goes by, the passwords and group memberships it holds get more and more out of date. One of the first things you should do after you complete the upgrade of the PDC and each BDC is to get a good backup so that you can keep the system running on Windows Server 2003 domain controllers rather than roll back completely to NT4 should a disaster occur.

Functional Levels

When you promote an NT PDC to Windows Server 2003, the domain functional level is set to Windows 2000 Mixed. This retains compatibility with NT4 domain controllers. The following new features are available in Windows 2000 Mixed functional level:

- Discrete Application naming contexts for Active Directory integrated DNS zones
- Ability to save queries in AD Users and Computers
- A new Trust Wizard that simplifies trust creation

Windows 2000 Native functional level disables replication to NT4 BDCs and enables the following features:

- Universal groups
- Global group nesting
- Policy-based remote access permissions
- Per-user remote access addressing and routing
- Universal group membership caching
- Transitive cross-domain resource access for downlevel clients and member servers
- Retaining SID History for migrated security principals

Shifting a domain to Windows 2000 Native functional level does *not* prevent downlevel clients from operating. A Windows 9x/ME or NT4 desktop can authenticate to the domain and access resources just as it would do in an NT domain. Make sure you're running the most current service packs on the NT desktops, though, to avoid compatibility issues with the older NTLMv1 authentication. You should also seriously consider upgrading any member servers and desktops that are running NT 3.51 so you can use NTLMv2.

When all Windows 2000 domain controllers have been upgraded or decommissioned, you can shift the domain functional level to Windows Server 2003. This enables the following features:

- Renaming domain controllers
- Updates to the logon timestamp
- Full security principal treatment for InetOrgPerson objects
- Kerberos Key Distribution Center (KDC) key version numbers

When all domains have been shifted to Windows Server 2003 functional level, you can shift the forest functional level to Windows Server 2003. This enables the following features:

- Restructuring forests by renaming domains to change parent/child hierarchies
- Creating transitive trusts between forests
- Special schema operations, including disabling schema objects, creating dynamic auxiliary classes, and modifying the characteristics of the inetOrgPerson class
- Individual group member replication, part of an overall change to the way linked values are replicated
- Modified Global Catalog (GC) replication
- Improved replication topology management

If a domain has only Windows Server 2003 and NT domain controllers, you can set the functional level to Interim. This enables discrete group membership replication.

The shift to Windows Server 2003 functional level for the domain is done using AD Users and Computers. Right-click the top of the tree and select RAISE DOMAIN FUNCTIONAL LEVEL from the flyout menu. This opens a Raise Domain Functional window as shown in Figure 9.3.

The shift to Windows Server 2003 functional level for the domain uses the AD Domains and Trusts console. Right-click the top of the tree and select RAISE FOREST FUNCTIONAL LEVEL from the flyout menu. Figure 9.4 shows the Raise Forest Functional Level window.

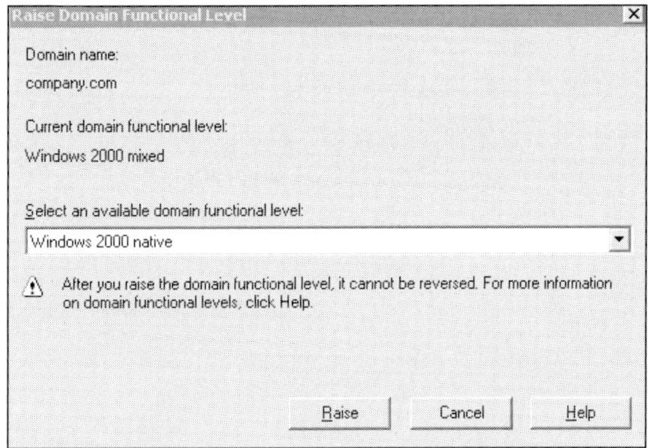

Figure 9.3 Raise Domain Functional Level window showing current functional level and the next available level.

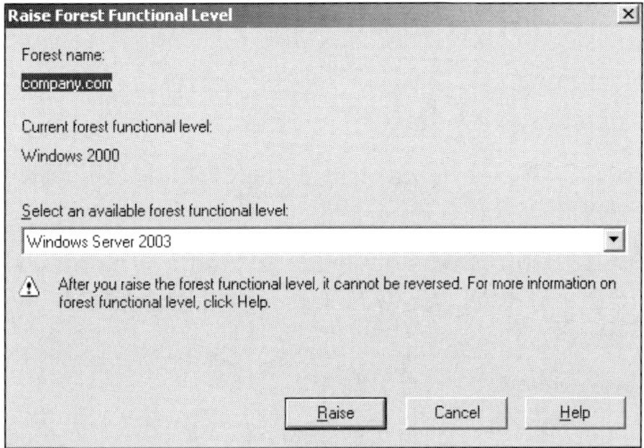

Figure 9.4 Raise Forest Functional Level window showing current forest functional level and the next available level.

New BDCs in Mixed

While running in Windows 2000 Mixed functional level, you can introduce a new classic NT BDC into the domain, but you must first create the computer account using AD Users and Computers. When creating the new object, select the `Allow Pre-Windows 2000 Backup Domain Controllers To Use This Account` option. Figure 9.5 shows an example.

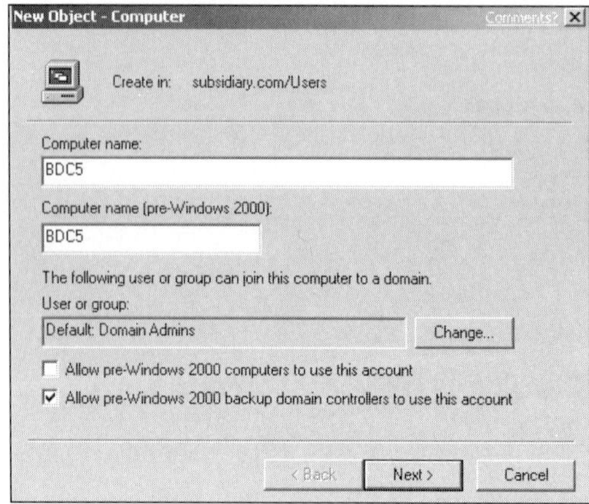

Figure 9.5 Computer object in Active Directory created for classic BDC.

Mixed Domains and Group Policies

A Windows desktop running Windows 2000 or XP could find itself in one of the following situations regarding access to domain controllers for authentication and group policy access:

- Strictly NT4 domain
- Windows 2000 Mixed domain with NT4 and Windows 2000 domain controllers
- Windows 2000 Mixed domain with NT4 and Windows Server 2003 domain controllers
- Windows 2000 Mixed domain with NT4 and Windows 2000 and Windows Server 2003 domain controllers
- Windows 2000 Native domain with strictly Windows 2000 domain controllers or with a mix of Windows 2000 and Windows Server 2003 domain controllers
- Windows Server 2003 functional level with strictly Windows Server 2003 domain controllers

In a purely NT domain, group policies are not available from the domain so Windows 2000 and XP desktops use local policies stored in template files on the local drive and classic system policies downloaded from their logon server in the form of Ntconfig.pol files. In an Active Directory domain, modern Windows clients do not download or process classic system policies.

The situation gets more complex in the other scenarios where group policies from Windows 2000, XP, and Server 2003 get mixed together. It is worth spending a little time to understand how policies are created and modified so you can avoid situations where group policy objects contain policy files that lack crucial settings.

Preferential Logon

Microsoft designed Windows 2000 and XP clients to "seek out" Active Directory domain controllers in preference to classic NT BDCs. Each time a modern Windows desktop starts up, it queries DNS to see if this is the day when an Active Directory domain controller has finally registered SRV records in its zone. If it gets back a negative reply from DNS, it heaves a sigh and falls back on classic NT LanMan (NTLM) authentication with a classic BDC.

If DNS returns SRV records pointing at Active Directory-based domain controllers, Windows 2000 and XP clients happily go to them to authenticate. This ensures that the modern clients get group policies at logon.

After a modern client has a taste of logging on using Active Directory, it does not go back to classic BDCs. If no AD-based domain controllers are available, the clients use cached credentials (and cached group policies) rather than ask a BDC for authentication.

Piling On

Stop a moment and count up the number of modern Windows desktops you have running in your NT4 domain. Do they number 20 percent of your fleet? 40 percent? All of them? Where are they located? All your offices in the U.S.? Overseas? Oil platforms in the Gulf? Military outposts in Diego Garcia? Are they connected to the main network by WAN links? Satellites? Virtual private networks over broadband?

Imagine that you upgrade your PDC this evening. You start at 6:00 p.m. after the last user has left the office and you finish up a couple of hours later. You go home feeling very pleased with yourself. The next morning, here's what happens. All those modern Windows desktops in your network, situated throughout the world, wake up to find SRV records in DNS. They clap their hands like little kids who find presents under the tree from Santa; then they converge on that single, new Windows Server 2003 domain controller with their logon requests.

NT4Emulator

You may want to avoid this onslaught by delaying support for Kerberos authentication and group policy deployment for a while until you have sufficient Windows Server 2003 domain controllers to handle the demand. You can do this by setting a Registry entry that makes a newly promoted Windows Server 2003 domain controller pretend to be classic NT4 domain controller. Here is the entry:

```
Key:    HKLM | System | CurrentControlSet | Services | Netlogon | Parameters
Value:  NT4Emulator
Data:    1 (REG_DWORD)
```

It is important that you put this entry in place on all NT domain controllers *before* you upgrade them. The domain controller will still register its SRV records, but when the modern Windows clients go to authenticate, the domain controller will only respond with an NTLM authentication sequence. If you wait until after the upgrade, when the clients have already logged on with Kerberos and reset their local LSA configuration, it's too late. You've released the troubles from Pandora's box and you won't be able to put them back again.

NeutralizeNT4Emulator

During the time that you have the NT4Emulator switch in place, your XP and Windows 2000 desktops will continue to use NTLMv2 authentication rather than Kerberos. This means you will not be able to use MMC-based Active Directory management tools, which require Kerberos to support Lightweight Directory Access Protocol (LDAP) binding. Also, you cannot promote a server to domain controller or introduce another domain into the forest because the servers cannot bind to LDAP on the existing domain controller.

You can force an individual desktop or server to bypass the NT4Emulator behavior of the domain controller and perform a Kerberos logon by putting this entry into the Registry at the desktop:

```
Key:    HKLM | System | CurrentControlSet | Services | Netlogon | Parameters
Value:  NeutralizeNT4Emulator
Data:    1 (REG_DWORD)
```

After putting this entry in place, log off then back on again. The desktop will find the Windows Server 2003 domain controller and use Kerberos to authenticate and the MMC-based consoles will start functioning. You can toggle `NeutralizeNT4Emulator` off if you want to stop using the desktop for management.

When you have sufficient Windows Server 2003 domain controllers deployed to handle the expected volume of Kerberos authentications and group policy deliveries, flip the `NT4Emulator` switch to 0 in the Registry of each domain controller and restart it.

XP Policy Placement

To understand how XP desktops will get XP-related group policies in a mixed environment of Windows 2000 and Windows Server 2003 domain controllers, we need to review how group policies are constructed.

When you create a new Group Policy Object, the Group Policy Editor creates two sets of items:

- A Group Policy Container (GPC) object in Active Directory
- One or more Group Policy Template (GPT) files in Sysvol

Both of these sets of items are created at the PDC Emulator, regardless of where you actually run the Group Policy Editor. This ensures that two administrators don't step on each other's policies because of synchronization differences.

Now, when you first open the Group Policy Editor, it needs to know what Registry-based policy options to display under the Administrative Templates icon. It obtains this list of policy settings from ADM files stored in the `\WINNT\Inf` folder on Windows 2000 machines and the `\Windows\Inf` folder on Windows Server 2003 or XP machines.

Here's where things get interesting. Refer to Figure 9.6, which shows a domain running at Windows 2000 Native functional level with both Windows 2000 and Windows Server 2003 domain controllers in operation. Let's say that Bob, working at a Windows 2000 desktop, creates a new Group Policy Object (GPO) using the AD Users and Computers console utility that comes as part of the Windows 2000 Adminpak.msi toolkit.

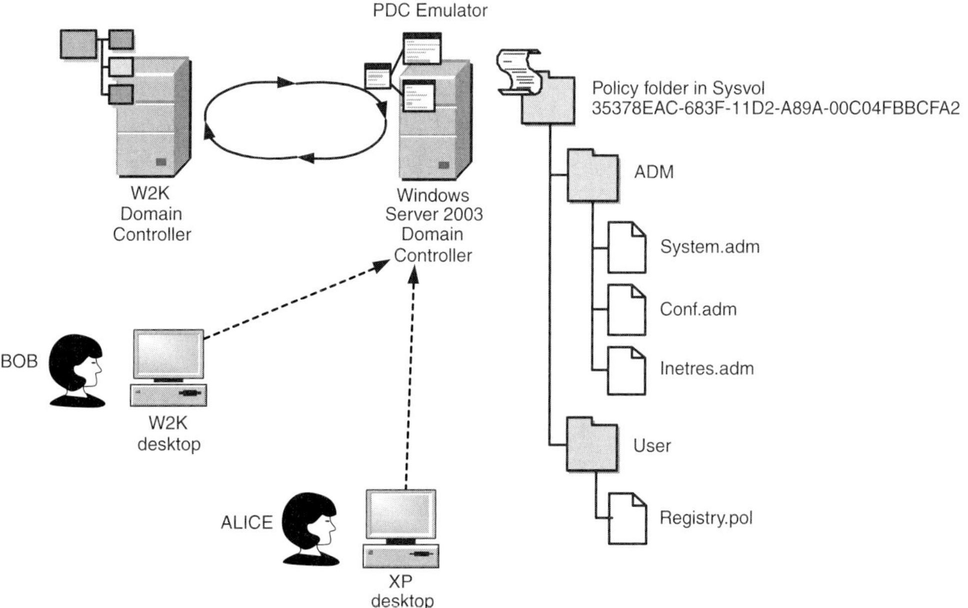

Figure 9.6 Deploying XP-based policies in mixed Windows 2000 and Windows Server 2003 domain.

The Administrative Template settings in the GPO created by Bob come from ADM files on Bob's Windows 2000 desktop and therefore have no XP policy settings. If Alice modifies the GPO from her XP desktop, the ADM files on her desktop have timestamps later than the Windows 2000 ADM files and overwrite the files in the ADM folder under the policy folder in Sysvol. The GPO now contains XP policy settings. If Bob installs a service pack on his Windows 2000 desktop then modifies the GPO, the timestamp on the ADM files could be later than those from Alice's XP desktop, and the XP policy settings disappear.

If Chester modifies the GPO from a server running Windows Server 2003, the timestamp on the ADM files might be later than the Windows 2000 service pack files and the policy settings would change again. To avoid this constant changing of group policies, you should adopt the following operating procedures:

- Only create new group policies from clients that have the most current ADM files.
- Always put the latest service packs on the machines used to update group policies.
- Do not change the content of existing ADM files because that will change the timestamp and potentially overwrite existing ADM files. Instead, create custom ADM files.

You may never encounter this problem, but if you do, you can spend a while thinking how much more difficult this is going to be when Longhorn, the next version of Windows, comes on the market in 2004.

Support for Classic NT4 RAS Access

As described in Chapter 20, "Managing Remote Access and Internet Routing," when a user dials into a Windows remote access server, the server authenticates the user using one of a variety of methods. The default method, at least for Windows clients, is Microsoft's proprietary Challenge Handshake Authentication Protocol, version 2, or MS-CHAPv2. This protocol is used in classic NT RAS and Windows 2000 RRAS, as well.

MS-CHAPv2 authentication requires the remote access server to make a secure connection to a domain controller so it can obtain a copy of the user's NT password hash. The RRAS service in Windows Server 2003 and Windows 2000 is capable of making this connection using the Kerberos credentials belonging to the underlying computer account. Classic NT4 RAS servers are not so fortunate. They know nothing about Kerberos.

In NT, RAS servers create secure connections to NT4 domain controllers using what is called a *null session*. A null session is a special connection type where the entity requesting the connection provides no credentials. An NT4 domain controller is coded to create a local thread for this null session. It assigns access permissions to the thread using an access token containing the Everyone group and the Network group. The Everyone group in NT has permission to execute certain function calls designed to set up a secure connection.

In Windows Server 2003 and Windows 2000, null session connections to Active Directory are not permitted. Therefore, under normal circumstances, a classic NT4 RAS server that is a member of an Active Directory-based domain cannot authenticate dial-in users.

If upgrading your NT4 RAS servers to Windows Server 2003 or Windows 2000 is not an option for some reason, you can elect to retain classic RAS authentication by selecting the `Retain Pre-Windows 2000 Compatible Access` option during the domain controller promotion. This option, in Windows Server 2003, puts the Everyone group and the Anonymous Logon group into a group called *Pre-Windows 2000 Compatible Access (PW2CA)*. The PW2CA group has sufficient permissions in Active Directory to retrieve a user's credentials and verify a user's dial-in permissions.

Windows 2000 adds only the Everyone group to the Pre-Windows 2000 Compatible Access group. This is not sufficient in Windows Server 2003 because the Everyone group is not assigned to null sessions. For more information on the specific permissions assigned to the Pre-Windows 2000 Compatible Access group, see Chapter 20, Managing Remote Access and Internet Routing."

After you have upgraded your NT4 RAS servers, you can return security to normal by removing the Everyone group and Anonymous Logon group from the Pre-Windows 2000 Compatible Access group. *You must restart all domain controllers before the change takes effect.*

Supporting Classic Scripts and Policies

Classic NT logon scripts are identified by entries in each user's account in the SAM. For example, if you want user Rdangerfield to run a logon script called Logon.cmd each time he authenticates on the domain, you must enter the name `logon.cmd` into the `Scripts` field of the user's profile.

When a Windows user has a logon script defined in his account, the Windows network client looks for the script in a share called Netlogon at the domain controller that authenticates the user. The script must reside in that share. If it does not, the network client skips the script and continues on with the network logon.

Classic system policies are also stored in the Netlogon share. These policy files, Config.pol for Windows 9x/ME clients and Ntconfig.pol for NT-based clients, are downloaded by downlevel Windows client whenever they authenticate onto the domain.

In Windows Server 2003, the Netlogon share points at `\Windows\Sysvol\domain\Scripts`. Because the contents of Sysvol are kept in sync on all domain controllers by the File Replication Service, clients can log on at any Windows Server 2003 domain controller and be assured of finding their logon scripts and system policies.

The same is not true of clients that log on at classic BDCs in a Mixed domain. There is no service in Windows Server 2003 to replicate the contents of the Netlogon share to downlevel BDCs. Classic NT has such a service, Lmrepl, but it is not supported on either Windows Server 2003 or Windows 2000.

If you have downlevel BDCs and you use logon scripts or system policies, you must create a "bridge" between a Windows Server 2003 domain controller and the downlevel BDCs. This is done by configuring one of the BDCs as the Lmrepl export server. Configure the other BDCs to pull their updates from the `$Repl` share on this server. The `$Repl` share points at `\WINNT\System32\Repl\Export`.

Next, set up an automated copy utility such as Robocopy from the Resource Kit to keep the contents of the `$Repl` share in sync with the Netlogon share at the Windows Server 2003 domain controller. Using this workaround, you can continue to use classic system policies and logon scripts for your downlevel clients.

Placement of Flexible Single Master Operations (FSMO) Servers

When you upgrade the PDC in the first account domain, it will hold all five FSMO roles. These are as follows:

- PDC Emulator
- RID Master
- Infrastructure Master
- Schema Master
- Domain Naming Master

As you deploy your new Windows Server 2003 domain controllers, it is important to ensure that these FSMOs are assigned to appropriate domain controllers.

In Windows 2000 Mixed functional level, the PDC Emulator and RID Master roles should always be hosted by the same domain controller because the PDC Emulator is the only domain controller that can create and modify user, group, and computer objects. After shifting the functional level to Windows 2000 Native, you can split the roles between domain controllers, but this is not recommended.

Another important duty of the PDC Emulator is to act as a "court of last resort" for password verification. If an administrator resets a user's password, the change is communicated immediately to the PDC Emulator, where it is written to its replica of Active Directory. If the user submits a bad password to any domain controller in the domain, the domain controller consults the PDC Emulator before denying access to the user. For this reason, make sure the PDC Emulator is at a well-connected location in your WAN.

If you have multiple domains in a forest, it is important that the Infrastructure Master in each domain be assigned to a domain controller that is not a Global Catalog server. The Infrastructure Master is responsible for verifying that names on phantom records representing security principals in other domains in the forest match the names in the Global Catalog. Domain controllers hosting the Global Catalog do not have phantom records so they must not be assigned as Infrastructure Master.

There is only one Schema Master and one Domain Naming Master for an entire forest. Microsoft recommends assigning these roles to the same domain controller to simplify management. The Domain Naming Master must be assigned to a Global Catalog server to get access to all Domain naming contexts.

Unsupported Domain Operations

The following operations are not supported by Windows Server 2003 or Windows 2000:

- **Breaking trusts.** You cannot break a Domain trust or a Tree Root trust to form an independent forest. If you want to pull apart domains into separate forests, you must create new forests and migrate security principals between them.
- **Moving Domain Controllers Between Domains.** There is no utility for moving a domain controller between domains. You must demote it to a standard server, join it to the new domain, and then promote it to a domain controller in the new domain.

Additional Deployment Issues

Here are some additional checklist items for upgrading a classic PDC:

- **SAM and LSA databases.** All user, group, and computer accounts are copied from the SAM into Active Directory. LSA secrets for trust relationships, computer account passwords, and so forth are copied into Active Directory, as well. Security information in LSA, such as User Rights and Policy Rights, are transferred to the Security Editor database where they are implemented as domain and domain controller group policies.
- **Classic trust relationships.** Any classic NT trust relationships that exist between the domain you are about to upgrade and other domains are converted to External trusts. This includes one-way trusts from resource domains and two-way trusts between account domains.
- **Access permissions.** User and Group SIDs do not change, so all access permissions remain intact. Users and groups from other NT domains can still be recognized via the External trust.
- **Allotted time for the upgrade.** The Netlogon service is disabled at the PDC from the time you start the operating system upgrade until you complete the domain controller promotion and restart the server. During this time, the server cannot authenticate users or accept changes to elements of the SAM or LSA, nor can it replicate to BDCs.

- **Privileges required to perform the upgrade.** You need full `Administrator` privileges in the NT domain to perform the upgrade. Be absolutely sure you know the password of the Administrator account in case something goes wrong and other accounts get locked out.
- **Storage preparation.** You need at least 1GB of free space in the operating system partition to upgrade an NT server to Windows Server 2003. You'll need another partition, preferably on another spindle, to store the Active Directory database files. The required size of this partition depends on the expected size of the Ntds.dit file that holds the database. A mirrored 9GB drive is adequate for anything less than a quarter million users. All partitions should be formatted with NTFS and defragmented thoroughly.
- **Browsing.** The classic NT PDC is also the Domain Master Browser (DMB). During the relatively lengthy upgrade, a browse election may occur during which one of the BDCs will obtain control of the browse database, but the PDC will remain registered in WINS as the DMB. As soon as the server restarts for the final time as a full-fledged domain controller, it forces another browse election, takes back the copy of the browse database, and takes over once again as DMB.

In-Place Upgrade of an NT4 Domain

At this point, you should have a clear roadmap of your deployment plans. You should know which classic domain controllers you are going to upgrade and in what order. All the prerequisites should be complete. You have brewed a big pot of coffee, and you're ready to begin.

Figure 9.7 shows a classic NT multiple-master domain with a single resource domain. In a production network, there could be many resource domains with interlocking trusts to several account domains. The configuration in the diagram shows a user in the second account domain who accesses a shared resource on a server in the resource domain.

The server cannot validate the user directly because there is no trust between the resource domain and the user's account domain. Classic NT domains are not transitive. The user must either log on using credentials from the first account domain or present an alternate set of credentials when mapping to the resource.

The following examples describe how to upgrade this multiple master NT configuration to a single Windows Server 2003 forest. The administrators in this example have decided to retain the same domain structure in Active Directory as they now use in NT. The "Migrating from NT and Windows 2000 Domains to Windows Server 2003" section discusses how to collapse the classic domains into a single domain.

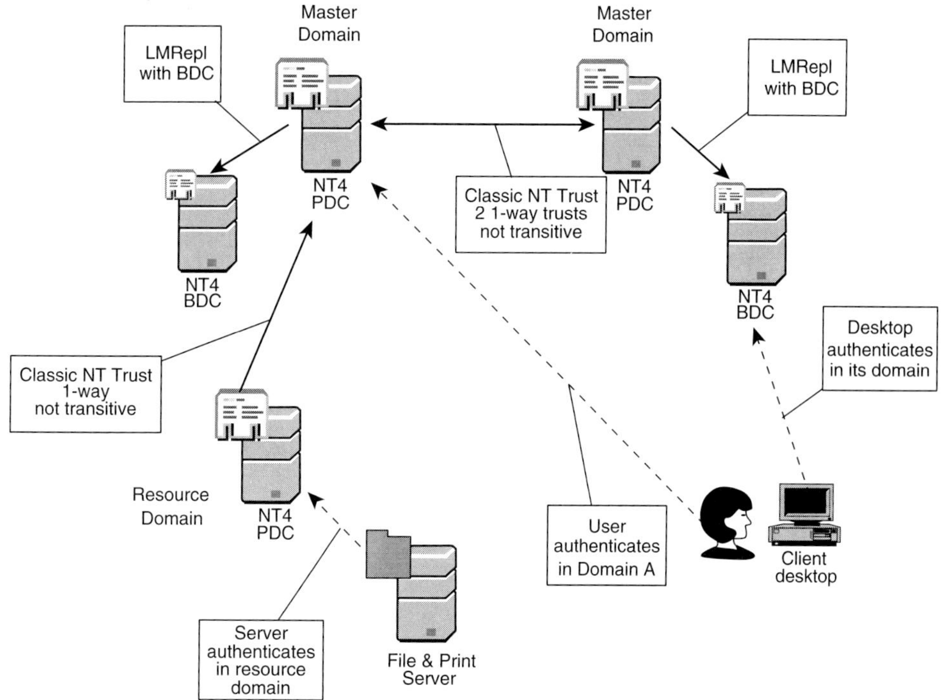

Figure 9.7 Classic NT multiple master domain.

Here is the order of events:

1. Install a placeholder domain to act as the root domain of the forest.
2. Upgrade the PDC of the first account domain.
3. Upgrade the BDCs in the first account domain.
4. Shift the functional level of the first account domain to Windows Server 2003.
5. Upgrade the PDC and BDCs of the resource domains under the first account domain or migrate all the users and computers to the newly created Windows Server 2003 domain.
6. Shift the functional level of any upgraded resource domains to Windows Server 2003.
7. Upgrade the PDC and BDCs of the second and subsequent account domains and shift the functional level to Windows Server 2003.
8. Shift the forest functional level to Windows Server 2003.

Install a Placeholder Domain

If you have several NT account domains that you plan on preserving after the upgrade to Windows Server 2003 and Active Directory, you should strongly consider installing a placeholder domain to act as the root domain of the forest. This is sometimes called an *empty root* because it has no production user accounts. Figure 9.8 shows an example.

The empty root clearly defines who manages the forest you're building. Both the Configuration naming context and the Schema naming context are considered a part of the root domain even though all domain controllers have a replica of them.

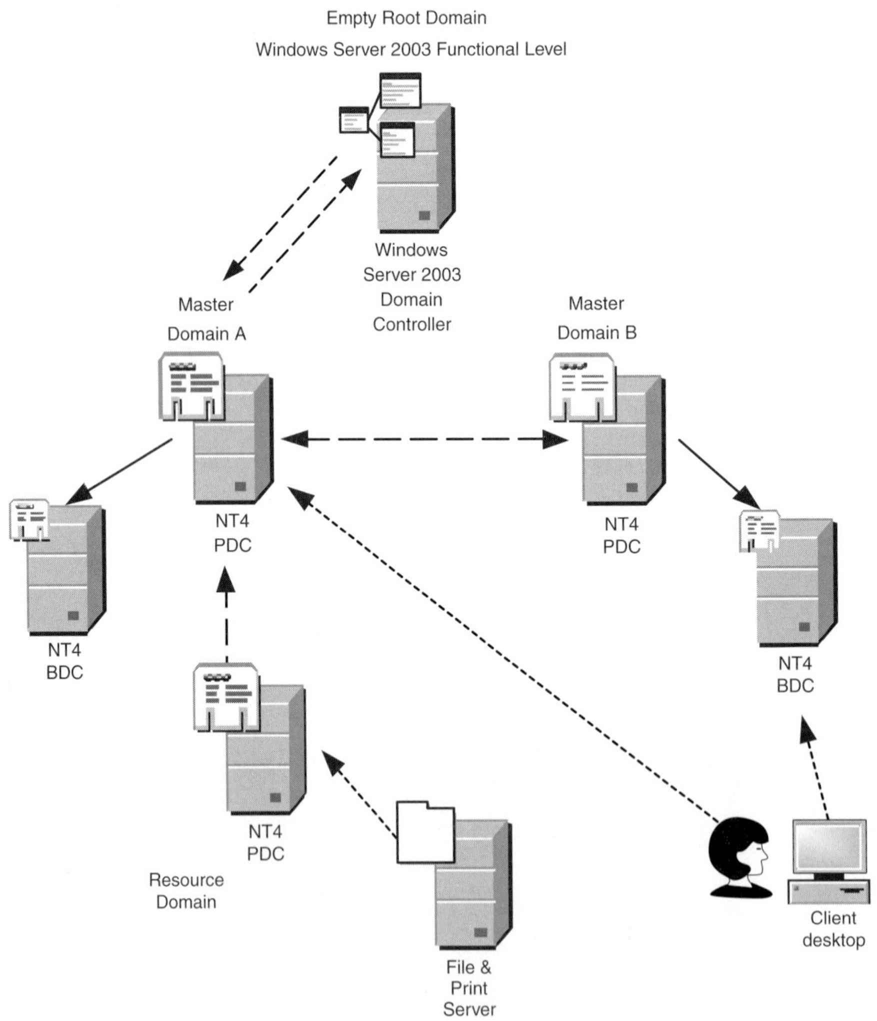

Figure 9.8 NT domain upgrade beginning with new Windows Server 2003 domain acting as placeholder above existing NT account domains.

Domain Controller Promotion and the Local SAM

When promoting Windows Server 2003 to a domain controller, the SAM hive in the Registry is deleted and replaced with a standard hive containing the Administrator account, a disabled Guest account, and the standard Builtin groups for a server, except that the Power Users group is included rather than the Server Operators group.

If you have been using a server for file-and-print duties and it has local groups or user accounts, be sure to replace the access control list (ACL) entries for these accounts on the data files and printers prior to promoting the server to a domain controller.

Domain administrators in the empty root have control over these forest-wide naming contexts, whereas domain administrators in the child domains are free to manage their own naming contexts but have no forest-wide authority. Without a placeholder root, the first account domain to be upgraded would become the root domain of the forest, and the administrators in that domain would have extensive authority.

Because the placeholder domain has no preexisting NT4 or Windows 2000 domain controllers, it is simple to install. Obtain at least two servers that meet your specification for domain controllers and install Windows Server 2003 on them. These servers can also act as DNS servers with Active Directory integrated zones and DNS Application naming contexts. Later on, you can place these DNS naming contexts on selected domain controllers in other domains to create a separate DNS replication topology.

Using a placeholder domain also simplifies initial installation. Creating the first domain controller in the placeholder domain, and the forest, requires simply running Dcpromo on Windows Server 2003. The domain functional level can be shifted to Windows Server 2003 as soon as the new domain controller is operational.

Use the steps in Procedure 9.1 to promote a server running Windows Server 2003 to a domain controller and initialize the first domain in a forest. Make sure the server is configured to point at the DNS server you have designated to host the Active Directory zone.

Procedure 9.1 Promoting the First Windows Server 2003 Domain Controller

1. Launch `Dcpromo` from the Run window. The Active Directory Installation Wizard starts.
2. Click `Next`. The Domain Controller Type window opens. Select `Domain Controller For A New Domain`. Keep in mind that this action will delete the existing `SAM` and `Security` hives in the Registry (see Figure 9.9).
3. Click `Next`. The Create New Domain window opens. Select `Domain In A New Forest`. This designates the new placeholder domain as the root domain in the forest.
4. Click `Next`. The New Domain Name window opens. Enter the fully qualified DNS name you've selected for the placeholder domain (see Figure 9.10).

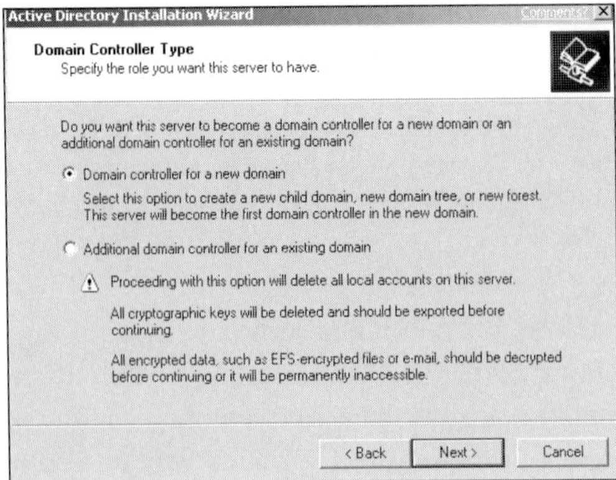

Figure 9.9 Dcpromo—Domain Controller Type window.

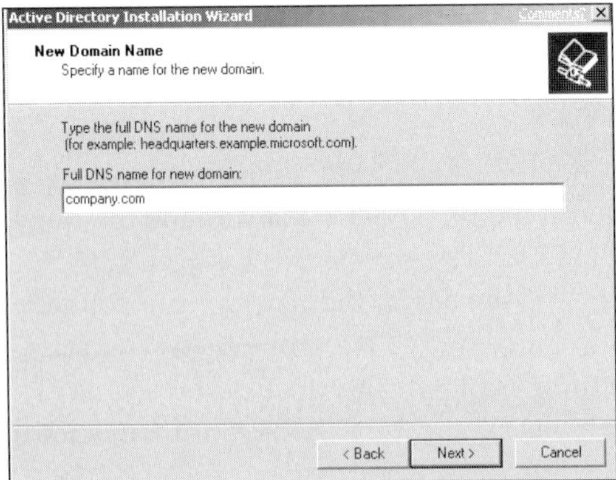

Figure 9.10 Dcpromo—New Domain Name window.

5. Click `Next`. The wizard queries WINS and broadcasts to verify that no other domain or NetBIOS entity has registered the flat name that corresponds to the DNS name you entered.
6. If no name collision occurs, the NetBIOS Domain Name window opens and displays the flat name for the new domain.
7. Click `Next`. The Database and Log Folders window opens. Enter the path to the volume you've prepared to hold the Active Directory files (see Figure 9.11).

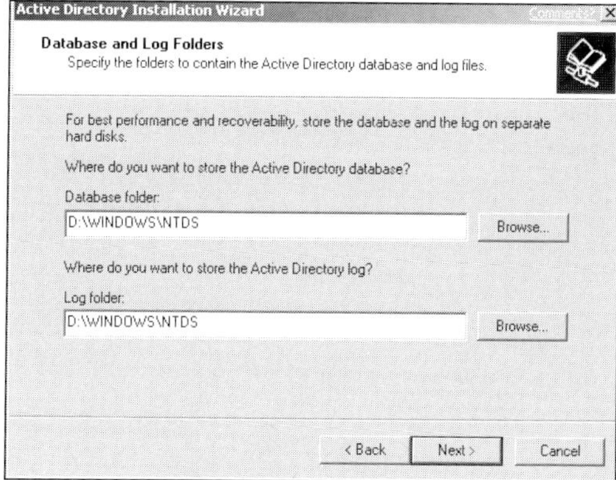

Figure 9.11 Dcpromo—Database and Log Folders window.

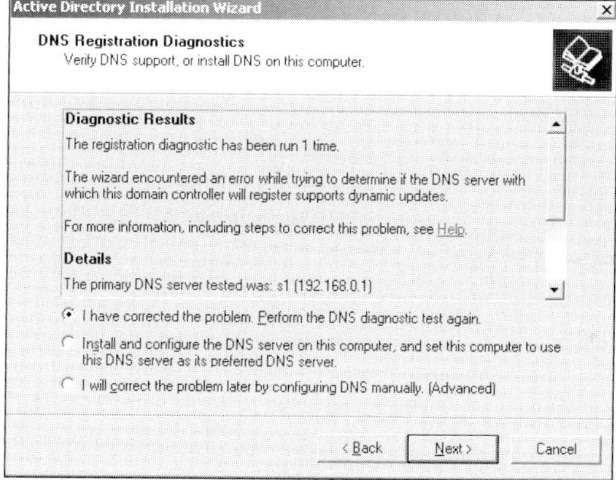

Figure 9.12 DNS Registration Diagnostics window.

8. Click `Next`. The Shared System Volume window opens. Enter the path to the volume you've prepared to hold the Sysvol folder. This can be the same volume that holds the Active Directory database files.
9. Click `Next`. The DNS Registration Diagnostics window opens (see Figure 9.12). The DNS analysis tool reports the results of a diagnostic check. If the DNS server is available and the zone is present and configured for dynamic update, the analysis tool reports a success. Otherwise, the error is reported and followup actions are suggested.
10. Click `Next`. The Permissions window opens (see Figure 9.13). If you no longer have NT4 RAS servers on the network, select `Permissions Compatible Only With Windows 2000 or Windows Server 2003 Operating System`.

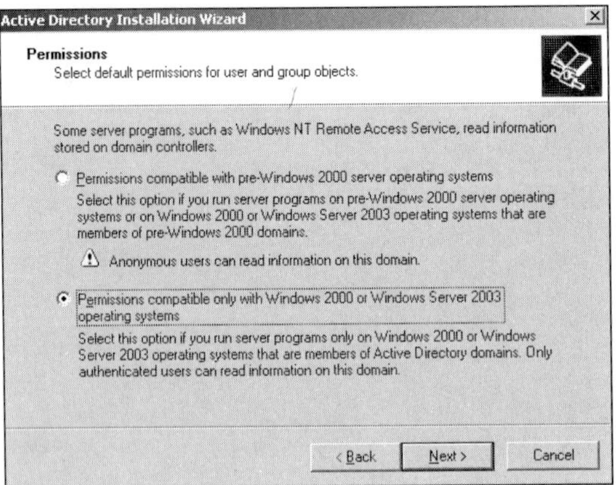

Figure 9.13 Dcpromo—Permissions window.

11. Click `Next`. The Directory Services Restore Mode Administrator Password window opens. Enter the password to be assigned to the Administrator account in the new SAM that will be installed on the server. This account provides access when Active Directory is not available.
12. Click `Next`. A summary window opens.
13. Click `Next`. The wizard begins installing the directory service. This takes between three and five minutes depending on the speed of your server. When installing new domain controllers in an existing domain, allow sufficient time for the Active Directory contents to replicate to the new domain controller.

When the promotion has completed, the machine restarts. When you log on following the restart, use the Administrator account you defined during the promotion.

Before proceeding, make sure that the SRV records for the domain were registered correctly in the DNS zone. This registration is performed by Netlogon. It takes a few minutes to complete, so check back with the DNS server five minutes after you are able to log on at the console of the server. If the SRV records fail to appear, resolve the problem immediately. If the problem were an incorrect DNS configuration at the domain controller, you can register the DNS records manually by starting and stopping Netlogon.

Troubleshoot Promotion Problems

The most common cause of promotion problems is improper DNS configuration. If you get an inexplicable failure during promotion, check your DNS setup carefully. There are many subtle ways that DNS can derail a promotion. Other potential sources of problems are the following:

- Corrupt `SAM` or `Security` hives
- Registry corruption or improper Registry settings involving critical services
- Running out of memory or drive space during the promotion (could be due to massive fragmentation rather than actual drive space limitations)
- Network connection problems
- Driver or file corruption

During Dcpromo, the `Configuring Active Directory` window gives a running report of the actions taken by the promotion wizard. The wizard writes a full report to Dcpromoui.log located in `\Windows\Debug`. Another log file, Dcpromo.log, describes the gory details of each API call and error reports, if any.

Table 9.1 shows a typical sequence of events during a domain controller promotion as logged by the AD Installation Wizard in Dcpromo.log. Check this list if you have a failure and you want to see what a successful promotion looks like.

Add More Domain Controllers

You do not want to operate for an extended period with Active Directory files hosted on a single domain controller. This tempts Murphy. Promote a second domain controller as soon as the first one is operating satisfactorily.

The only difference between promoting a second domain controller and promoting the first one is the selection of a domain type at the start of Dcpromo. The `Select Additional Domain Controller For An Existing Domain` option tells the wizard to replicate the contents of Active Directory from the existing domain controller.

If you want to avoid the tedious replication of a large Active Directory database across a slow WAN link, you can opt to populate the database on the new domain controller from a restored copy of the database from another domain controller.

To use this option, first run a system state backup at an existing domain controller then restore the backup tape or file to a temporary folder at the server you are going to promote. Be sure to give the temporary folder lots of elbow room. It needs to hold at least 300MB at a minimum, not including the size of the Ntds.dit file, because Ntbackup will only let you restore the entire system state, not just the Active Directory files inside the system state.

Table 9.1 Dcpromo.log Entries for a Successful Domain Controller Promotion

Action	Explanation
Path validation	Paths to Active Directory database, logs, and Sysvol checked and created, if necessary.
Domain creation	Verifies that domain flat name is unique.
Promotion begins	Netlogon is stopped and target folders created. Sysvol configured for replication.
Active Directory Installation	Credentials verified to have sufficient privileges for domain creation. Active Directory files created. Schema naming context created and populated. Configuration naming context created and populated. Domain naming context created and populated.
Account creation	User, group, and computer accounts moved from SAM to Active Directory. Original domain SID assigned to new domain.
Security settings	LSA policies copied and prepared. Windows Time Service initialized. Netlogon configured. LSA policies initialized.
Registry security	Domain controller (DC) promotion security template applied to Registry.
File security	DC promotion security template applied to system files and folders.
Cleanup	Upgrade temp files and old Netlogon information removed.
Success	Wizard is informed of the successful completion of the promotion.

To get the option for using a local copy of the AD files, launch `Dcpromo` with the `/adv` switch: `dcpromo /adv`. In this advanced mode, when you elect to create an additional domain controller for an existing domain, the wizard presents an additional window called Copying Domain Information that permits you to point at a backup file. Figure 9.14 shows an example. Point the wizard at the temporary folder where you restored the system state files.

If the AD source files came from a Global Catalog server, Dcpromo queries if you want the new domain controller to be a GC, as well. You can say `No` and the wizard will only import the naming context for the source domain plus the Configuration and Schema naming contexts.

When the promotion is complete, verify that the Knowledge Consistency Checker (KCC) establishes connections to other domain controllers in the site. Use AD Sites and Services to view the Connection objects and verify replication. See Chapter 7, "Managing Active Directory Replication," for details.

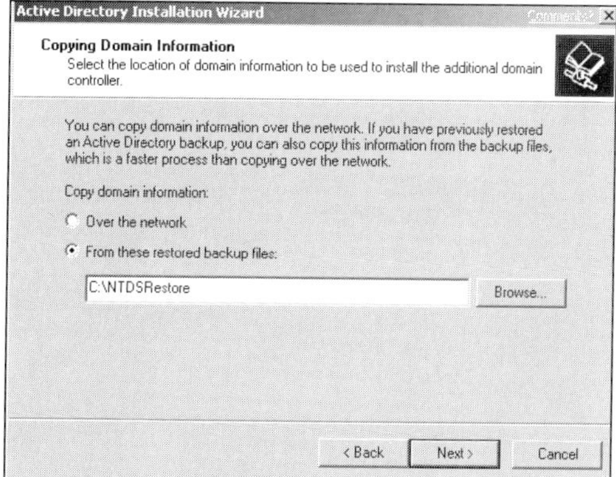

Figure 9.14 Active Directory Installation Wizard—Advanced Options—Copying Domain Information window showing the option for using a backup file to populate the Active Directory database.

If you want, you can create an external trust to one or all of the NT account domains. This is not required for the forest deployment, but it can be reassuring to know that administrators in the account domains can view resources in the root domain. Any External trusts you create between the root domain and the NT domains will be converted to Domain trusts when the account domain is upgraded.

Set Domain Controller Roles

The first domain controller in a domain is a Global Catalog server, by default. When configuring an empty root domain, configure the second server to be a Global Catalog server, as well. This ensures fault tolerance. If you choose to leave one of the servers as a standard domain controller, it is very important to transfer the Infrastructure Master role to that server.

Use the AD Sites and Services console to configure a domain controller as a GC. Open the `Properties` window for the NTDS Settings object under the server. Check the `Global Catalog` option. Figure 9.15 shows an example.

Give the server a while to replicate the contents of the Global Catalog from another GC server or to collect the partial naming context replicas from domain controllers in the various domains in the forest. You can follow the result of this replication in the Event log.

You can verify the identity of the Global Catalog servers in a forest using Replmon. Right-click a server and select SHOW GLOBAL CATALOG SERVERS IN ENTERPRISE from the flyout menu. You can also configure the ADSI Editor (Adsiedit.msc) from the Support Tools to query just port 3268, the port used for handling LDAP queries sent to a GC. If the server responds to queries on this port, you know it is a GC server.

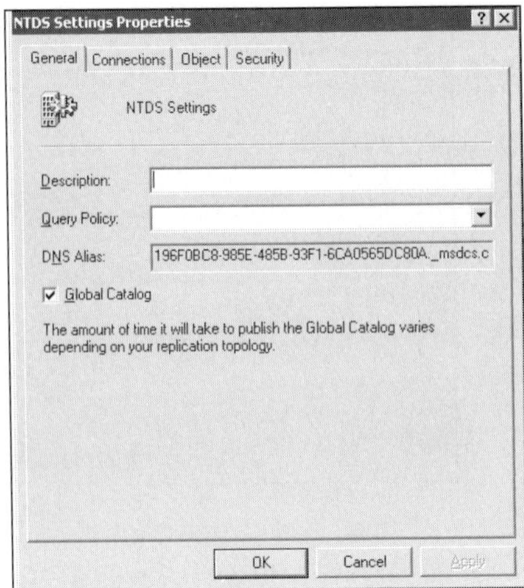

Figure 9.15 NTDS Settings object for a newly promoted domain controller showing the Global Catalog setting.

You can leave the remaining FSMOs with the first domain controller unless you have some other reason to transfer them. For example, the second server might have a faster processor or dual processors, making it a better choice for PDC Emulator. You should transfer the RID Master along with the PDC Emulator. This is not strictly required, especially when operating at a Windows Server 2003 functional level, but it makes recovery a little less complicated when you do not split the PDC Emulator and RID Master roles between servers.

If the server is the first server in a site, it will become the Inter-site Topology Generator (ISTG) and the bridgehead server to the connected sites. Use AD Sites and Services to ensure that the domain controller establishes connection to its fellow bridgeheads and that it replicates according to the schedule and frequency you have assigned to the site links.

Shift Root Domain Functional Level to Windows Server 2003

By default, the functional level of a new Windows Server 2003 domain is set to Windows 2000 Mixed. There is no need to retain a low functional level in the placeholder domain, so before proceeding to the upgrade of the NT domains, shift the root domain functional level to Windows Server 2003.

Use the AD Users and Computers console to shift domain functional levels. Right-click the top of the tree and select Raise Domain Functional Level from the flyout menu. This opens a window that permits you to select either `Windows 2000 Native` or `Windows Server 2003` functional level. Figure 9.16 shows an example.

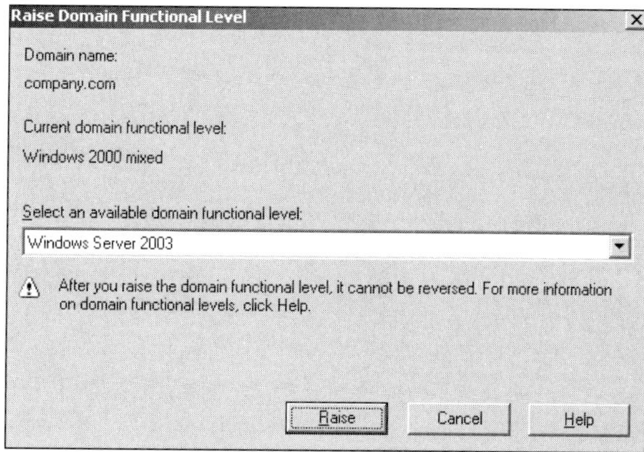

Figure 9.16 Using the Raise Domain Functional Level window to set a domain to Windows Server 2003 functional level.

After shifting the Domain functional level to Windows Server 2003, you must restart the domain controllers to gain full access to the new Windows Server 2003 features.

Active Directory Integrated DNS Zones

You can choose to move forward with the account domain upgrades, but you may want to pause for a while and reconfigure your DNS infrastructure. When you promoted the domain controllers in the root domain, they registered their SRV records with a preexisting DNS server. If you prefer to use Active Directory integrated zones, you can install DNS onto the new domain controllers and configure them to be the primary DNS servers for the Active Directory zone.

Be careful to configure the TCP/IP settings for one DC to point at the other DC as its primary DNS server. This avoids problems where a failure of replication causes a failure to update DNS records when then solidifies the inability to replicate. See Chapter 5, "Managing DNS," for details on installing DNS and changing zone types.

In Windows 2000 Mixed or Native functional level, the resource records for an Active Directory integrated DNS zone are stored in the Domain naming context. This is satisfactory if you have a single domain in your forest, but it can cause problems when you have multiple domains with domain controllers that reside in geographically remote locations. Clients need access to SRV records representing servers throughout the forest.

In Windows 2000, you could provide local access to forest-wide SRV records by creating a separate primary zone for the forest-related SRV records in _msdcs and placing secondary copies of this zone on DNS servers in the various domains.

Windows Server 2003 handles the problem more elegantly. When you shift a domain functional level to Windows Server 2003, you can put the DNS resource records in their own naming contexts rather than into the Domain naming context. Windows Server 2003 creates two naming contexts for this purpose, one for domain-related SRV records and one for forest-related records. You can see these new naming contexts using the Replication Monitor utility from the Support Tools. Figure 9.17 shows an example. You can view the contents of the naming contexts using the LDAP Browser, Ldp, which also comes in the Support Tools.

Upgrade the PDC in the First Account Domain

After the placeholder domain is in place, you're ready to upgrade the first account domain. Figure 9.18 shows the result of this stage. The first step is to upgrade the PDC. A domain controller upgrade has two stages. First, the operating system is upgraded, followed by an automatic launch of Dcpromo to create the Active Directory domain. During the promotion, you will join the domain to the forest root in the placeholder domain.

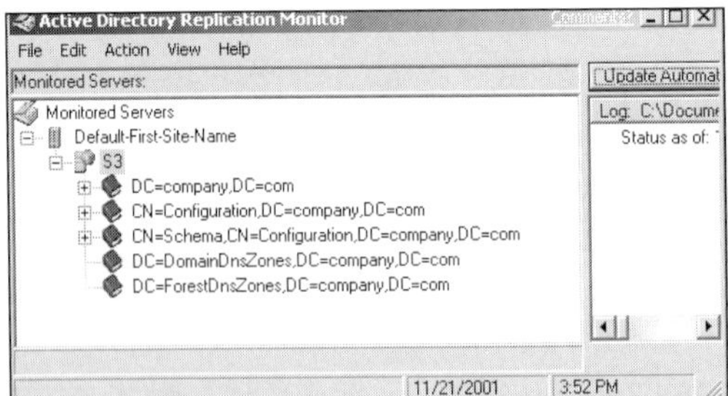

Figure 9.17 Replication Monitor showing the new DNS naming contexts created when a domain is shifted to Windows Server 2003 functional level.

If you do not use a master license or volume license copy of Windows Server 2003, you must activate the server following installation. You have thirty days to do the activation, but the system will kvetch at you regularly until you comply, so you might as well get it out of the way as soon as you upgrade.

When the prerequisites have been met and your disaster recovery actions have been taken, follow Procedure 9.2.

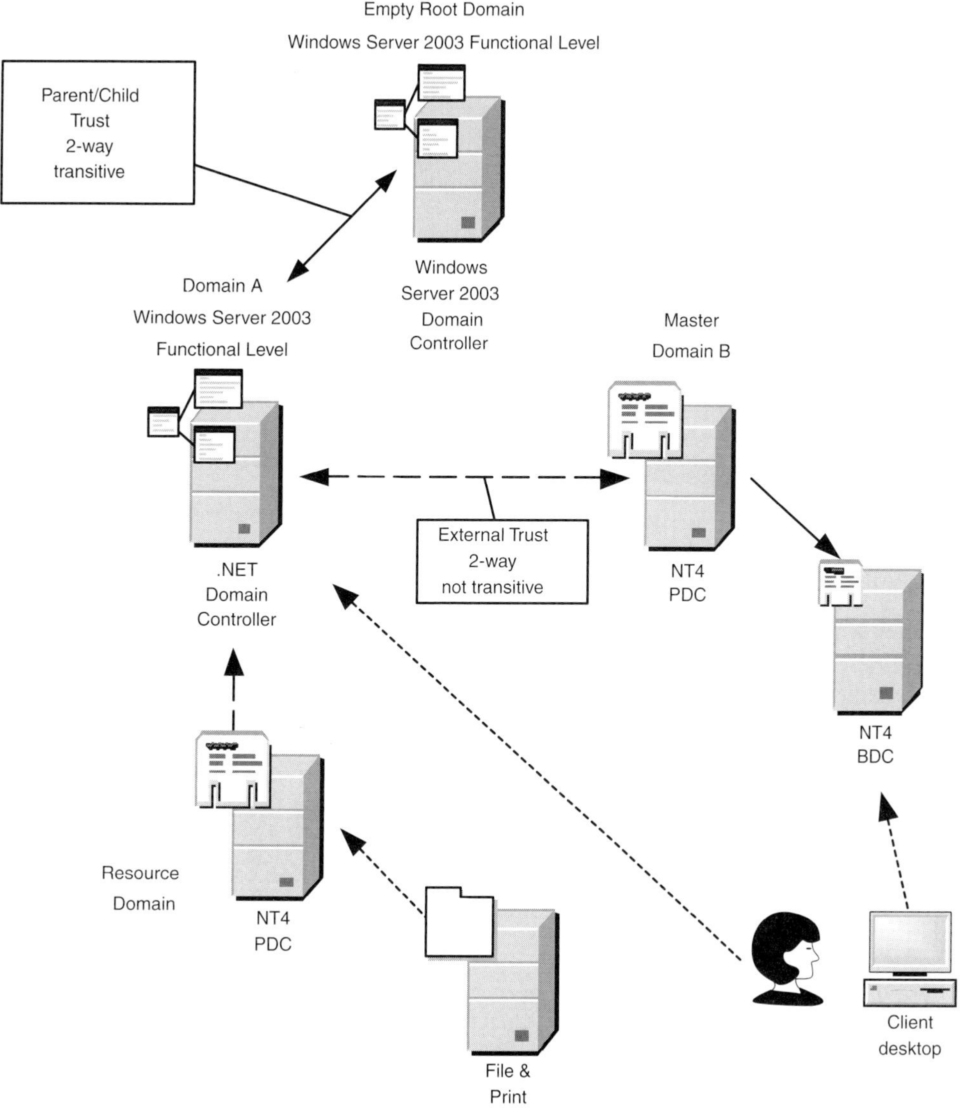

Figure 9.18 NT domain following upgrade of first account domain PDC.

Procedure 9.2 Upgrading an Account Domain PDC

1. Insert the Windows Server 2003 CD or initiate `Winnt32` from a network drive. This launches the upgrade wizard.
2. When prompted, accept the End User Licensing Agreement (EULA) and enter the 25-character Product Key. The remaining portions of the operating system upgrade proceed without further user input.
3. Following the final restart after the network operating system upgrade, the Active Directory Installation Wizard, Dcpromo, launches automatically. At this point, the classic `SAM` and `Security` hives are still intact but the server does respond to logon requests. Users can still log on to the domain via the BDCs.
4. Before commencing Dcpromo, open a command prompt and verify using Nslookup that the server can see its DNS server and that the DNS server hosts the zone that will form the Active Directory domain.
5. In the Dcpromo wizard, click `Next`. The Create New Domain window opens. Select `Child Domain In An Existing Tree`. This prepares the domain to join the forest rooted at the placeholder domain.
6. Click `Next`. The Network Credentials window opens. Enter the name and password of an account with administrator privileges in the root domain along with the fully qualified DNS name of the root domain.
7. Click `Next`. The Child Domain Installation window opens. Under `Parent Domain`, enter the fully qualified DNS name of the parent. In this example, the parent is the root domain of the forest. Under `Child Domain`, enter the flat name of the NT domain you are upgrading.
8. Click `Next`. The Database and Log Folders window opens. Enter the path to the Active Directory files and the log files. This should be a separate spindle than the operating system.
9. Click `Next`. The Shared System Volume window opens. Enter the path for the Sysvol folder. This can be on the same spindle as the Active Directory files if the server will not be heavily loaded during morning logons. The volume must be formatted as NTFS.
10. Click `Next`. The DNS Registration Diagnostics window opens. This presents a report of the DNS connectivity for the server. If it was able to find a DNS server that hosts the specified zone and the zone can be dynamically updated, the wizard reports a success. Otherwise, it points you in the direction of the problem and gives you a chance to fix it before proceeding.
11. Click `Next`. The Permissions window opens. If you have no legacy NT4 RAS servers in production, select `Permissions Compatible Only With Windows 2000 or Windows Server 2003 Operating Systems`.

12. Click `Next`. The Directory Services Restore Mode Administrator Password window opens. Enter the password that you will use to access the server when Active Directory is not available. This password is assigned to the Administrator account in a new SAM installed at the completion of the promotion.
13. Click `Next`. A summary window opens.
14. Click `Finish`. The wizard begins the promotion.

Following the promotion, the server restarts to finalize the settings. The next section contains a set of verification checks you should perform to make sure everything went well.

Post-Upgrade Verifications

Following the upgrade and promotion of the PDC, perform a quick set of checks to make sure critical services installed during the upgrade work as expected. This includes the following:

- **Account Replication to BDCs**. Make sure that the upgraded PDC, which is now a Windows Server 2003 PDC Emulator, is able to replicate to its down-level BDCs. You cannot verify this directly by running User Manager from the BDCs because User Manager always points at the PDC. Verify replication by running Server Manager at the BDC, highlighting the BDC name on the list, and selecting COMPUTER | SYNCHRONIZE WITH PRIMARY DOMAIN CONTROLLER from the menu. This starts a replication cycle. Check the Event log to verify that the replication occurred.
- **DNS record verification.** Make absolutely sure that the SRV records for the new domain are registered in DNS. This registration is performed by Netlogon. It takes a few minutes to complete, so check back with the DNS server five minutes after you are able to log on at the console of the server. If the SRV records fail to appear, resolve the problem immediately. You can stop and start Netlogon to reregister the SRV records. By default, the server will refresh its registration once per hour.
- **User authentication**. Log on at a variety of client desktops to ensure that you can get authenticated. Some forms of SAM corruption cause a situation where Windows 98 users can logon but NT users cannot. This is due to a failure to import the NT password hash during the Active Directory promotion.
- **Group policies.** Log on from XP and Windows 2000 desktops to verify that you get Kerberos authentication and that you get group policies from the newly upgraded PDC. This can be verified quickly using the Kerbtray utility from the Resource Kit.

- **Profile settings.** Verify that users get their roaming profiles and home directories as specified in their user accounts.
- **Dial-in verification.** Test at least one dial-in user to verify that the account works to permit dial-in and that the RAS server is able to check the user's credentials.
- **Computer authentication.** Restart at least one of each type of NT-based client to ensure that computer accounts were copied successfully to Active Directory. If you have thousands of computers, you may want to check that the total number of computers present after the upgrade matches the total before the upgrade.
- **Trust authentication.** Log on at a desktop in a resource domain using an account in the newly upgraded domain to ensure that the trust is still in place. If you have a two-way trust between account domains, do this for accounts in both domains. Also, use the AD Domains and Trusts console to check the presence of each trust.
- **Logon script and system policy verification.** Check to make sure that the existing logon scripts and system policies were migrated to the `\WINNT\Sysvol\Domain\Scripts` folder. (The system folder is not renamed during an upgrade.) Put the alternate copy method in place to refresh the Netlogon share at the BDCs, and then log on at various clients to ensure that they get the logon scripts.
- **Share point verification.** Verify that any pre-existing shares are still in place. This includes the administrative (dollar-sign) shares. The simplest way to do this is using the `NET SHARE` command.
- **Application verification.** If the server was running special applications prior to the upgrade, make sure those applications are still functioning. This includes items such as backup agents (or the backup application itself), antivirus agents, web sites, and Simple Network Management Protocol (SNMP) agents.

Upgrade Account Domain BDCs

You can operate for a while in Windows 2000 Mixed, but to get the benefit of the new Active Directory features in Windows Server 2003, you need to shift the domain functional level to Windows Server 2003. This means getting the classic BDCs off the wire, either by upgrading them or decommissioning them. Figure 9.19 shows the configuration following this stage.

If the servers acting as BDCs have suitable hardware for Windows Server 2003 and are relatively free of legacy applications, you can upgrade them to Windows Server 2003 domain controllers in the same way that you did the PDC upgrade. The only real difference is the source of the files for creating the local replica of Active Directory. The BDCs do not convert their local `SAM` and `Security` hives. They copy the contents of Active Directory from an existing domain controller.

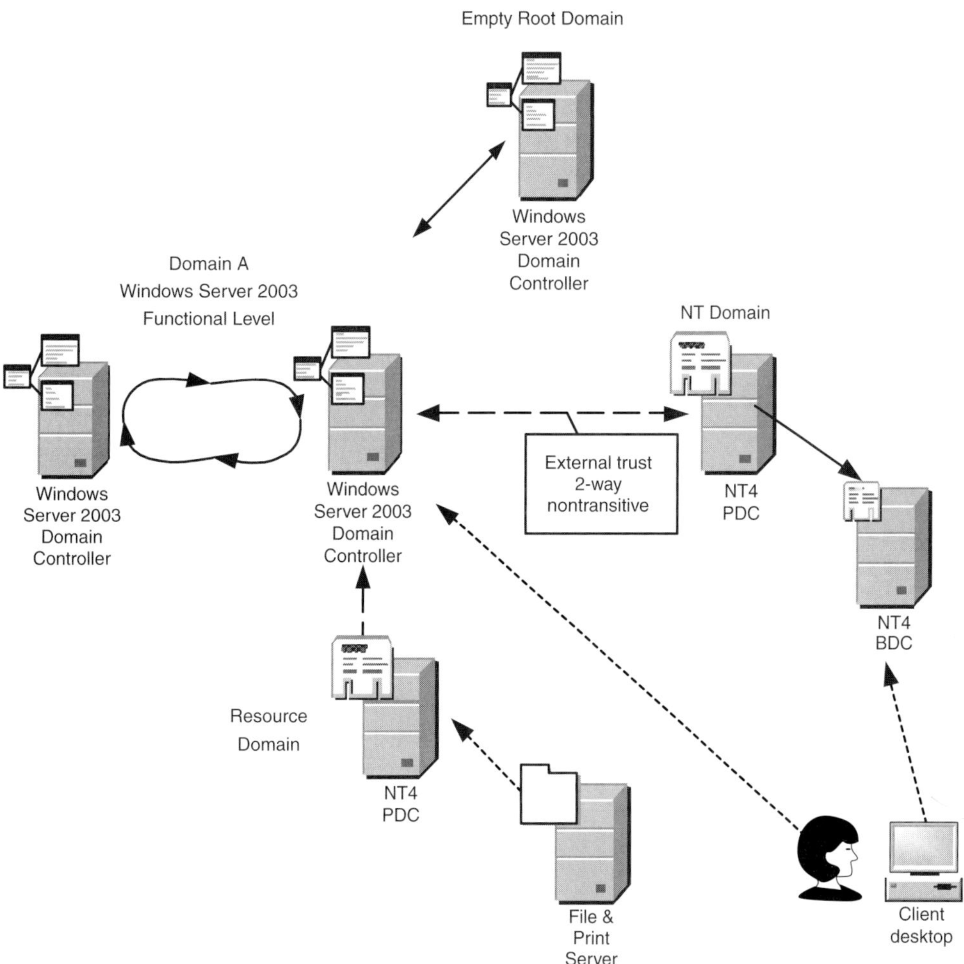

Figure 9.19 Mixed NT and Windows Server 2003 domains following upgrade of remaining BDCs in first account domain.

If the BDC is in the same location as the PDC, the upgrade and promotion should not take long. The Active Directory database is not large or complex at this stage of the deployment because of the backwards compatibility with existing BDCs. If you have several thousand users, you can use backup files as described in the placeholder domain upgrade.

You can also build new Windows Server 2003 domain controllers in the same site as the newly upgraded PDC then ship them out to the remote locations. When the domain controller arrives at the remote site, have a local administrator put the server on the wire and configure the TCP/IP settings. At that point, move the server to the correct site based on its new subnet.

Following the BDC upgrade, ensure that the newly promoted Windows Server 2003 domain controller replicates correctly with the other domain controllers. If this is the first domain controller in its site, verify that it acts as the bridgehead server and consider configuring it as a Global Catalog server. Also verify that it has connections to bridgeheads in the other sites as defined by the site link objects.

Upgrade Resource Domains

You've now finished the first stage of the upgrade and you need to decide what to do with the resource domains, as shown in Figure 9.20. You can upgrade them, in which case they are controlled by domain admins similar to the management processes used by classic NT, or you can migrate the computer accounts to the newly upgraded Windows Server 2003 domain and leave the resource domains behind.

If you decide to retain separate domains, it is important to shift the functional level to Windows 2000 Native as soon as possible. This permits downlevel clients to access resources in the other domains via transitive Kerberos trusts on the intervening domains.

Upgrade Remaining Master Account Domains

At this point, you've completed the migration of an entire classic NT domain, including the account domain and all resource domains. Now you need to upgrade the remaining account domains and join them to the Windows Server 2003 forest.

Follow the same procedure for upgrading the remaining account domains as you did for upgrading the first one. The DNS domain name you select for the domain must be contiguous with the root domain. Be sure to verify user access to resources and replication between domain controllers, especially if the domain controllers are in different sites. Don't make the mistake of assuming that inter-site replication will just work all by itself. Sure, often it does, but you cannot be sure until you check.

You should also be careful to verify the transitive trust relationships that are created between the domains (see Procedure 9.3). Use the Trust Wizard in the AD Domains and Trusts console for this purpose.

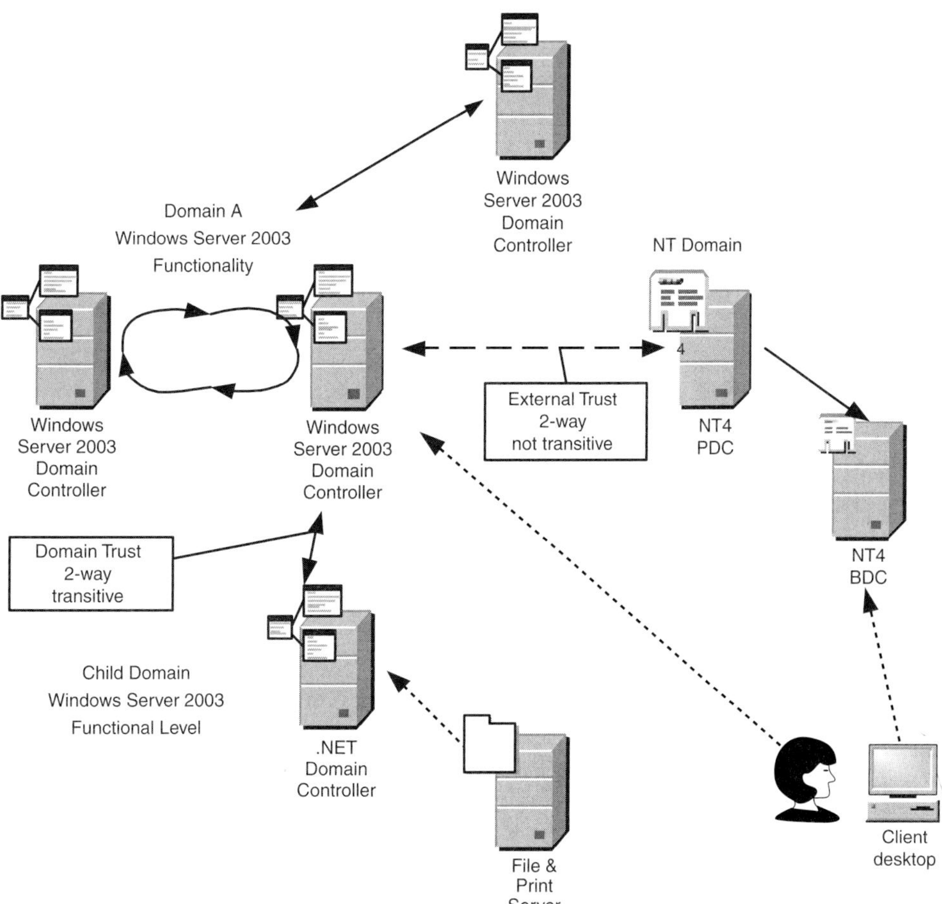

Figure 9.20 Mixed NT and Windows Server 2003 domains following upgrade of domaincontrollers in the resource domain.

Procedure 9.3 Verifying Transitive Trust Accessibility

1. Open the `AD Domains and Trusts` console at one of the domain controllers.
2. Open the `Properties` window for one of the domains. Select the `Trusts` tab (see Figure 9.21).

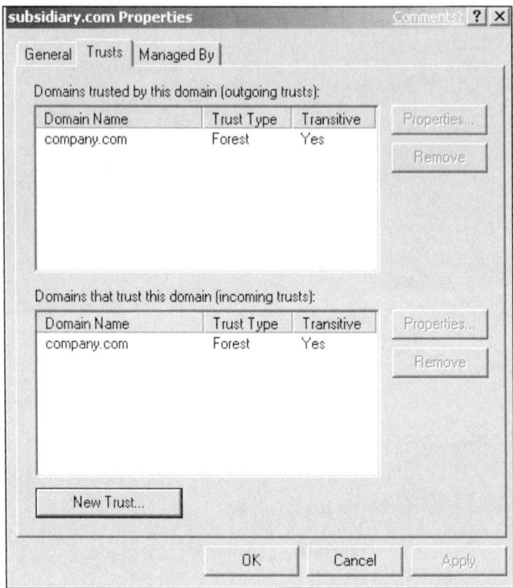

Figure 9.21 Properties window for showing Tree Root trust.

3. Highlight the trust and click `Properties`.
4. In the Properties window, click `Validate`. You'll be prompted for credentials in the remote domain.

If the validation is successful, it means the secret account that the two domains share is accessible and they both know the password. If it fails, you may need to reset the trust. When these checks show that you have full functionality in the resource domain, promote the remaining domain controllers.

Shift the Forest Functional Level to Windows Server 2003

When all downlevel domain controllers have been purged, you're ready to shift the forest functional level to Windows Server 2003. This opens up many additional features, primarily the ability to replicate discrete group members rather than the entire membership list. It also lets the Inter-Site Topology Generators (ISTG) and KCCs in each site use a streamlined spanning tree calculation to keep track of replication topology, increasing the scalability of the forest.

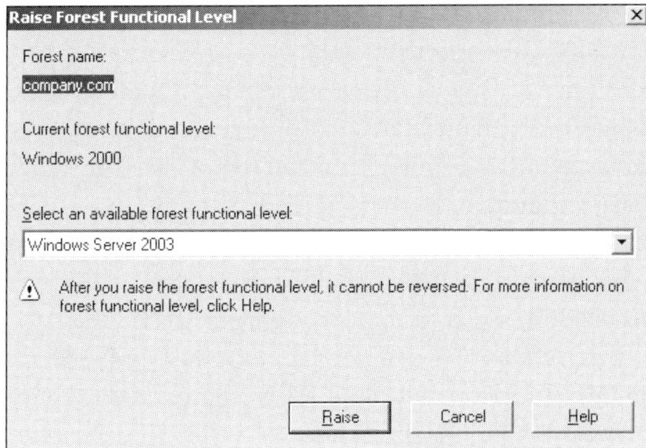

Figure 9.22 Raise Forest Functional Level window showing selection of Windows Server 2003.

Shift the forest functional level using the AD Domains and Trusts console. Right-click the top of the tree and select RAISE FOREST FUNCTIONAL LEVEL from the flyout menu. This opens the Raise Forest Functional Level window shown in Figure 9.22.

Click `Raise` to implement the change. You will not be offered the option as long as any domains in the forest operate at any functional level other than Windows Server 2003. You must restart all domain controllers in all domains in the forest to implement the change completely.

After you shift the forest functional level to Windows Server 2003, you are officially FINISHED with the deployment! The final step is to use your favorite search engine to look for a great vacation spot.

In-Place Upgrade of a Windows 2000 Forest

If you are in the fortunate position of having already finished your Windows 2000 deployment, the upgrade to Windows Server 2003 should not involve too much work. Servers that are suitable for Windows 2000 domain controllers should be adequate for Windows Server 2003, although you should think about upgrading hardware if you have a server skating near the minimums. Microsoft recommends a 550MHz processor, 256MB of RAM, 4GB of storage for the operating system, and sufficient space on the data drives to hold the Active Directory database files.

The Active Directory database in Windows Server 2003 is somewhat larger than Windows 2000, but not enough to make a difference for storage calculations. If you are within 20 percent of filling the drive containing your current Active Directory files, you should be thinking about getting larger drives, whether or not you choose to upgrade.

If you have multiple domain controllers in a site, you can do the upgrade during working hours, assuming that you have no other applications running on the server. Use caution not to disable the site bridgehead server, the sole Global Catalog server, or any FSMO role master during working hours.

Probably the most exciting Active Directory feature in Windows Server 2003 is the ability create transitive, Kerberos-based trusts between two forests. To see how this works, the examples in this topic walk through an upgrade of two Windows 2000 forests with domains that share an External trust such as that shown in Figure 9.23.

In this diagram, users in the two domains share access to resources in their respective domains. A typical example is an extranet connection between a manufacturer and a vendor. Another example is a hospital on a university campus where the doctors are also members of the faculty and therefore need access to the main campus domain.

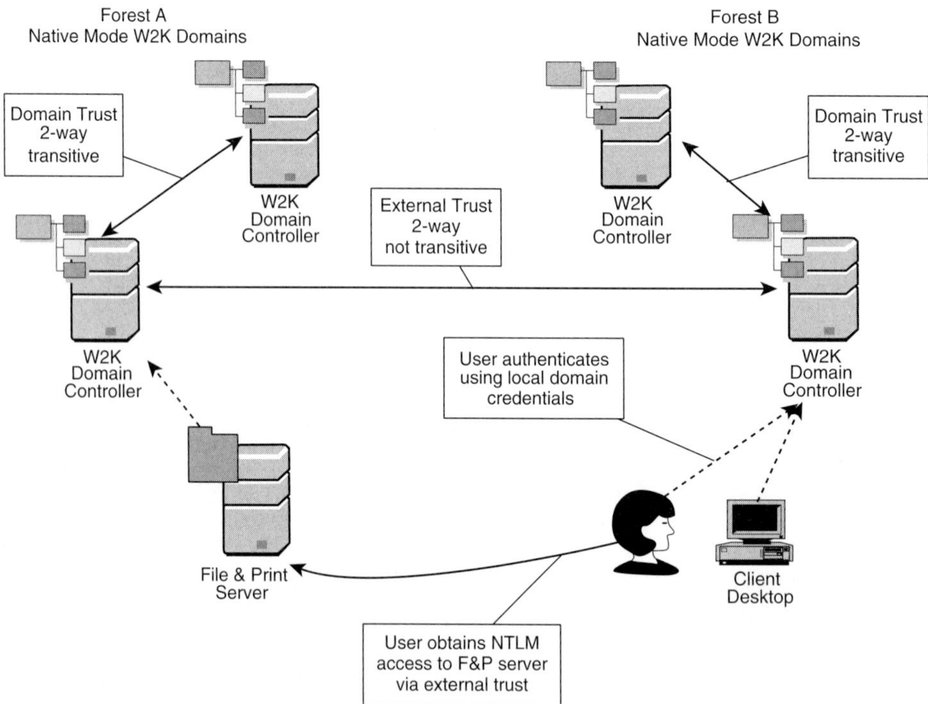

Figure 9.23 Windows 2000 forests with domains connected by an External trust.

The domain hosting the servers and the domain hosting the users have been configured with a two-way External trust. This mimics a classic NT trust in that it is really two, one-way trusts that use NTLM authentication, not Kerberos, so they are not transitive. This is why the domains trust each other directly and do not use trusts between the root domains.

Upgrading the domains and forests in this configuration to Windows Server 2003 involves these major stages:

1. Upgrade the schema and prepare the domains for upgrade.
2. Upgrade the domain controllers in the root domains and shift the domain functional level to Windows Server 2003.
3. Upgrade the domain controllers in the child domains and shift the domain functional level to Windows Server 2003.
4. Shift the forest functional level to Windows Server 2003.
5. Replace the External trust between the child domains with a Forest trust between the root domains.

Schema Upgrade

Before you can upgrade a Windows 2000 domain controller to Windows Server 2003, or introduce a Windows Server 2003 domain controller into a Windows 2000 domain, you must first upgrade the Windows 2000 schema. Windows Server 2003 makes over 400 changes to the schema, including new classes and attributes, changes to indexing, and changes to the attributes published in the Global Catalog. This last item requires a rebuild of the Global Catalog, which is then replicated to every GC server in the forest.

In addition to big changes in the schema, Windows Server 2003 requires a few nips and tucks in the domains, as well. These changes support inter-forest connections and help to track domain updates.

The utility that performs these schema and domain updates is called ADPREP. It is located in compressed form in the `\I386` folder on the Windows Server 2003 CD.

The simplest way to install ADPREP is to run `winnt32 /checkupgradeonly` from the Windows Server 2003 CD. This extracts ADPREP to the `\WINNT\System32` folder and copies over 11 LDIF files, numbered Sch14.ldf through Sch24.ldf, that hold the new schema entries.

The number assigned to these Sch##.ldf files correspond to schema version numbers. The Windows 2000 schema is version 13, which is why the Sch##.ldf files start at 14. Exchange 2000 also upgrades the schema, but it uses a separate set of LDAP Data Interchange Format (LDIF) files that do not change the schema version number.

The ADPREP utility has two switches, both of which must be run prior to upgrading a Windows 2000 domain controller to Windows Server 2003 or installing a new Windows Server 2003 domain controller in an existing Windows 2000 domain:

- **`adprep /forestprep`.** This switch performs the schema upgrade. It calls another utility, SCHUPGR, and feeds it the Sch##.ldf files in sequence. The `/forestprep` switch also updates Active Directory permissions and makes changes to the display specifiers to support the new classes.
- **`adprep /domainprep`.** This switch applies new attributes to the Domain object that are used for maintaining trust quotas. It also adds a new container under `System` for tracking domain updates.

You must be running Windows 2000 SP2 or later on all domain controllers in the forest prior to updating the schema. You must have administrator rights in the root domain of the forest along with membership in the Schema Admins group.

Run `adprep /forestprep` at the Schema role master for the Windows 2000 forest. You can identify this server using the DUMPFSMOS command script from the Resource Kit. The syntax is `dumpfsmos` *<dc_name>*.

The `/domainprep` switch must be run on the Infrastructure role master in each domain. You must have administrator rights in the domain. No changes are made to the schema. The `/domainprep` switch simply adds support for inter-forest trust quotas and adds a new container under the System container to track updates.

Upgrade Windows 2000 Root Domains

After the ADPREP changes have propagated to all domain controllers in the forest, you can begin upgrading the domain controllers in the root domains. Figure 9.24 shows the end result. Unlike upgrading an NT domain controller, the operating system and the directory service are upgraded at the same time in Windows 2000. The process can take quite a while, well over an hour in some cases, depending on the processor speed and any Registry translations that might need to be done.

You have the option of simply promoting a Windows Server 2003 member server as a domain controller rather than upgrading the existing domain controllers. If you decide to use this route, you must transfer all five FSMO roles to the new domain controllers prior to decommissioning the Windows 2000 DCs.

DUMPFSMOS

The DUMPFSMOS command script uses the Ntdsutil utility in batch form as follows:

```
ntdsutil roles Connections "Connect to server %1" Quit "select Operation Target"
"List roles for connected server" Quit Quit Quit
```

Actually, Ntdsutil only needs enough of each word to make an unambiguous entry, so the script could be abbreviated as follows:

```
Ntdsutil r c "co t s %1" q "sel o t" "l r f c s" q q q
```

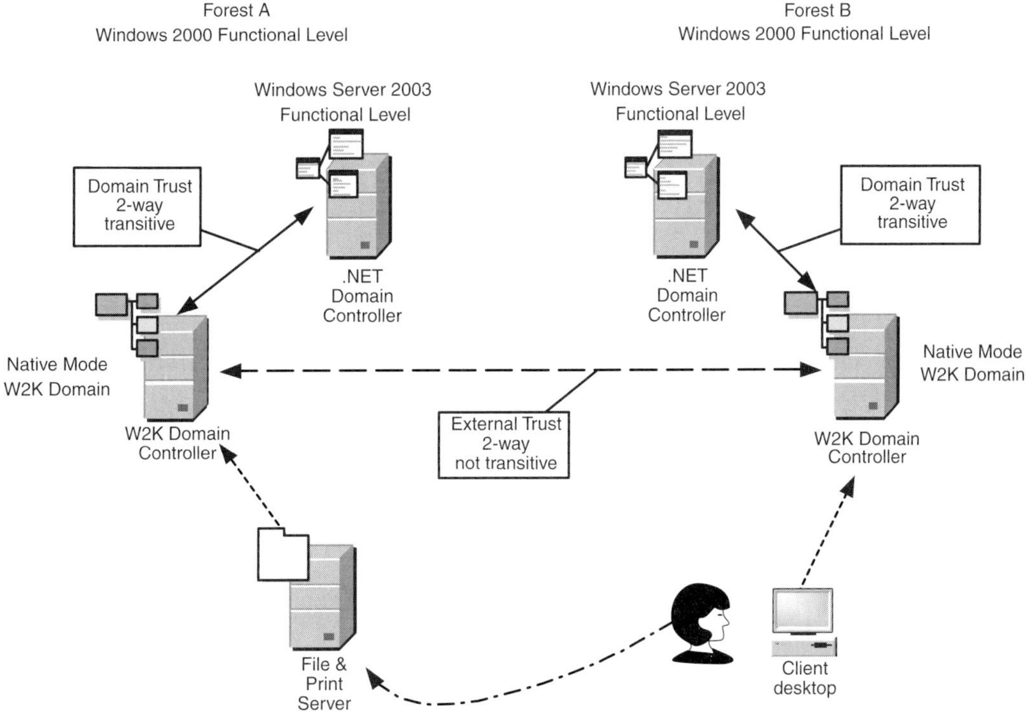

Figure 9.24 Windows 2000 forests following upgrade of root domains to Windows Server 2003.

If you decide to upgrade, it is a good idea to start with the PDC Emulator. This is not a requirement, but the PDC Emulator is the default server for editing group policies as well as the time standard and the Domain Master Browser, so you might as well get it out of the way first.

As soon as you finish upgrading all domain controllers in the root domain, shift the domain to Windows Server 2003 functional level. Verify that the trust relationship to the child domains remains intact. Verify that administrators can still log on to the root domain and retain their enterprise privileges in the child domains.

Upgrading Child Domains

Now that the root domains have been upgraded, you're ready to start upgrading the child domains. Remember that you must prepare the domain with `adprep /domainprep` before upgrading the first domain controller. Figure 9.25 shows the final configuration with the forest functional level set at Windows Server 2003.

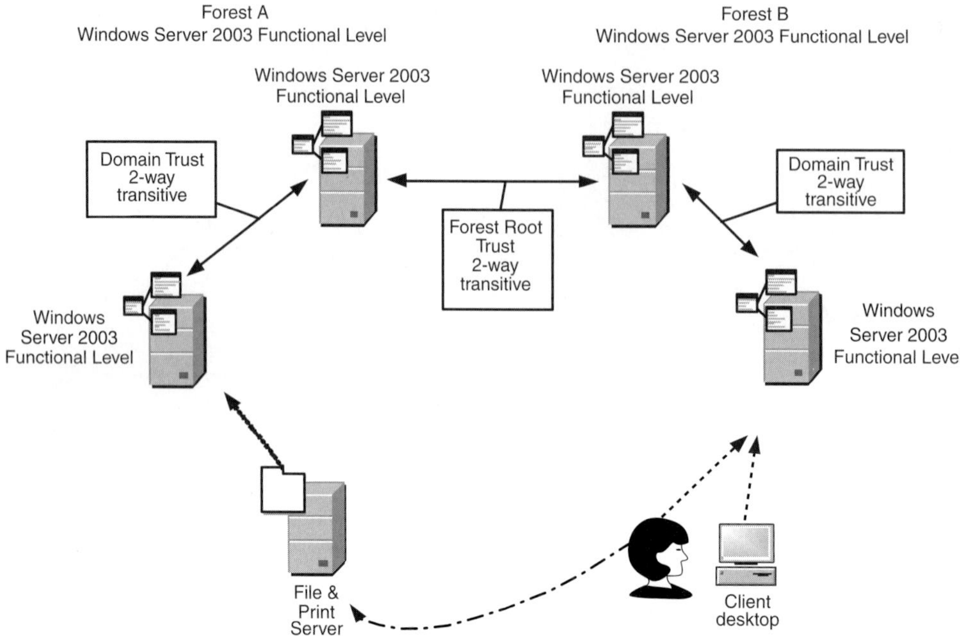

Figure 9.25 Final stage of Windows 2000 upgrade with all domain controllers upgraded to Windows Server 2003.

As with the root domain, you should start the upgrades with the PDC Emulator. When you've completed upgrading all Windows 2000 domain controllers, shift the domain functional level to Windows Server 2003 then shift the forest functional level to Windows Server 2003.

At this point, you can create a Forest trust between the forests. When this trust is in place, you can remove the External trust between the child domains. Verify that users can access resources in all domains through the Forest Root trust.

Migrating from NT and Windows 2000 Domains to Windows Server 2003

If you are unable to do a direct upgrade of your NT or Windows 2000 domain, you can create a new Windows Server 2003 domain and migrate users, computers, and groups into it from an existing domain. Microsoft provides several migration tools in the shrink-wrap for this purpose. The most rudimentary of these tools are a set of scripts for cloning security principals between domains. They are as follows:

- **Clonepr.** Copies a user account to the target domain.
- **Clonegg.** Copies Global groups to the target domain.
- **Clonelg.** Copies local groups to the target domain.
- **Cloneggu.** Copies Global groups and users to the target domain.
- **Sidhist.** Takes the SID of a user or group from one domain and assigns it to a user or group in the target domain. There will be more on SID History in a moment.

Using these scripts can get a little cumbersome in a large migration. They have very little in the way of error reporting and no testing capabilities. For more advanced migrations, Microsoft provides a suite of migration wizards it calls the *Active Directory Migration Tool*, or ADMT.

The technology in ADMT was originally licensed from NetIQ. The version that shipped in Windows 2000 was capable of doing small-scale migrations. Version 2 of ADMT in Windows Server 2003 has been extended and modified to permit migrating passwords, preserving user profiles, and simplifying the re-permissioning of file and print servers and user desktops. The documentation has been improved dramatically, as well.

It is entirely possible to handle a large-scale migration using just ADMTv2, but you may want to look at third-party offerings from vendors who make migration and consolidation tools. You may find that spending a few dollars on the right tool can save you hundreds of hours and lots of tedious work during the migration. Here are the major products in this area:

- **Controlled Migration Suite**. Aelita Software, `www.aelita.com`.
- **FastLane Migrator**. Quest Software (formerly FastLane Technologies), `www.quest.com`.
- **Domain Migration Administrator**. NetIQ, `www.netiq.com`.
- **bv-Admin for Windows 2000 Migration**. Bindview, `www.bindview.com`.

All of these tools handle the small details of migration equally well. They differentiate themselves primarily by their reporting capabilities, simplicity of use, and customizability. The vendors also offer additional tools that simplify domain management after you've completed the migration, so you might want to get a package deal if one of them looks attractive.

SID History

Figure 9.26 shows an example of a classic NT master/resource domain. The user is a member of the account domain. She logs on at a desktop that is a member of the resource domain. She accesses resources on a server that is a member of the same resource domain as the desktop.

A shared resource on the server is protected with an access control list that contains the SID of a Machine Local group. An administrator in the resource domain has nested a Global group from the account domain into the Machine Local group at the server. The user is a member of this Global group.

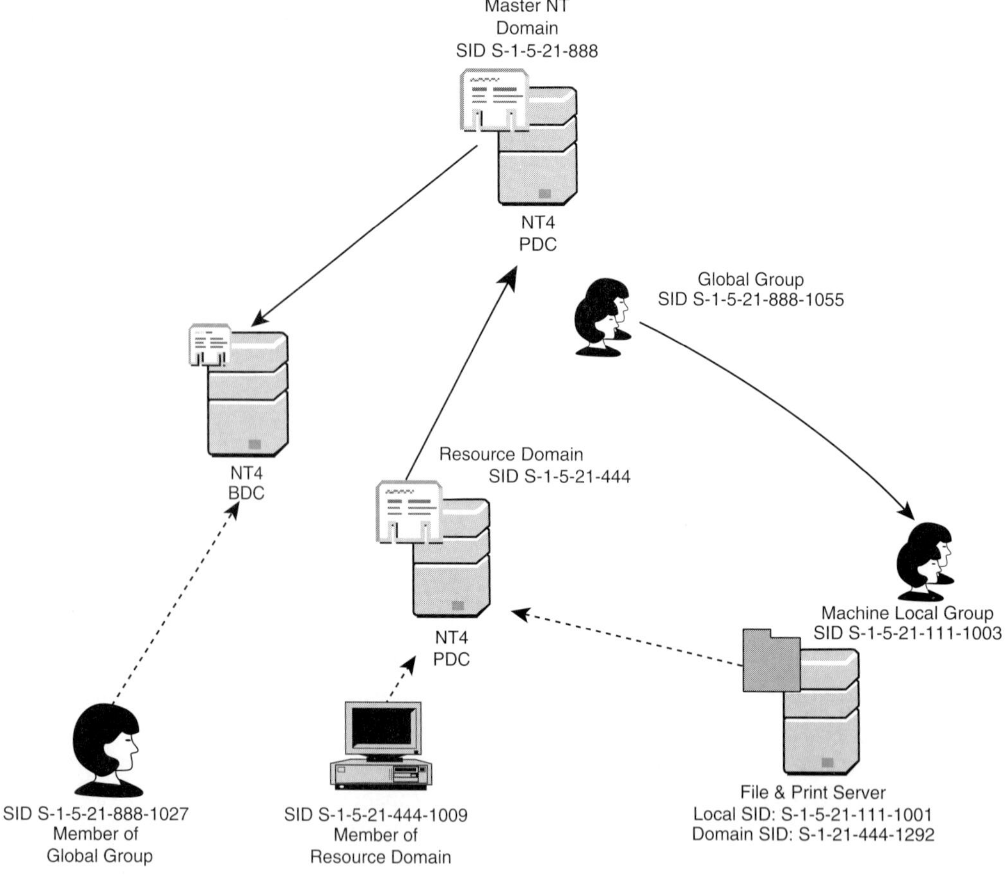

Figure 9.26 NT master/resource domains showing SIDs on various security principals.

Here's a quick synopsis of what happens when the user touches the shared resource. The server validates the user's credentials using classic NTLM pass-through authentication, then creates a local process thread for the user and attaches to it an access token. The token contains the user's SID, the SID of the Global group from the account domain, and the SID of the Machine Local group. This SID in the access token gives the user access to the shared resource.

If you create a new account for the user in the Windows Server 2003 domain, the user could log on but would get an entirely new SID with an entirely new set of group memberships. If you did nothing further to support the migration, the user would lose access to resources in the original domain. Sure, you could re-permission all the folders in the original domain with groups and users from the new domain, but that's a *lot* of work.

Microsoft provides a technology to resolve this problem, a technology that underlies all the migration tools, both from Microsoft and third parties. This is a function library called *SID History*. You'll also hear it called the SID History API.

SID History permits you to create an account for a security principal (user, group, or computer) in a target Windows Server 2003 or Windows 2000 domain then populate a special attribute called `SIDHistory` with the contents of the principal's original SID.

Figure 9.27 shows what happens when a freshly minted Windows Server 2003 user created using the SID History API touches a resource in the original domain.

The user logs on to the Windows Server 2003 domain using a new account that has been cloned into Active Directory from the original domain. The user touches a resource on a server in the original domain. The server validates the user using classic NTLM pass-through. The domain controller in the Windows Server 2003 domain provides a set of SIDs to the server. This list of SIDs includes the following:

- The user's SID from the Windows Server 2003 domain
- The user's SID from the original domain obtained via the `SIDHistory` attribute in the user's Active Directory object
- The Windows Server 2003 domain SID for the Global group to which the user belongs
- The original SID of the Global group obtained via the `SIDHistory` attribute of the Global group's Active Directory object

The local access token built by the server as part of this transaction contain those SIDs plus the SID for the Local Machine group that has the original domain Global group as a member. This local access token gives the user access to the resource even though the user logged on to a completely different domain.

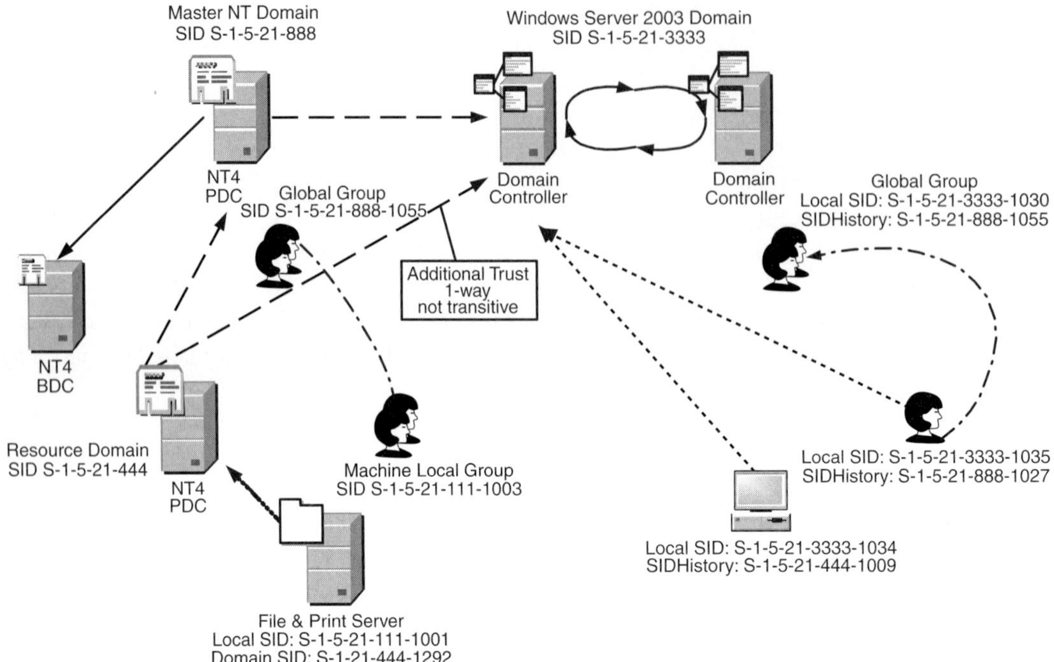

Figure 9.27 Security principals following migration from NT to Windows Server 2003.

Computer Account Migrations

The server and computer accounts in resource domains, such as those shown in Figure 9.27, present another sort of challenge for migration. The desktop is a member of a resource domain, whereas the user is a member of a trusted account domain. For the migration to work, the resource domain must trust the Windows Server 2003 domain or else the user will not be able to log on to the remote domain from the local desktop. Classic NT trust relationships are not transitive.

The permanent solution is to move the desktop to the new domain. This could be done by disjoining it manually from its resource domain and joining it to the Windows Server 2003 domain, but ADMT and the third-party migration tools have ways to automate the migration. As part of the process, the user's local profile and permissions to local NTFS files are transferred to the user's account in the remote domain.

ADMT has a security translation feature that can re-permission a member desktop or server, either by replacing the old user SIDS with their new SIDs or by using SID History to retain access for both accounts. This security translation feature is called up as part of a computer migration. Access to the user's original profile is maintained during this evolution. Figure 9.28 shows an example.

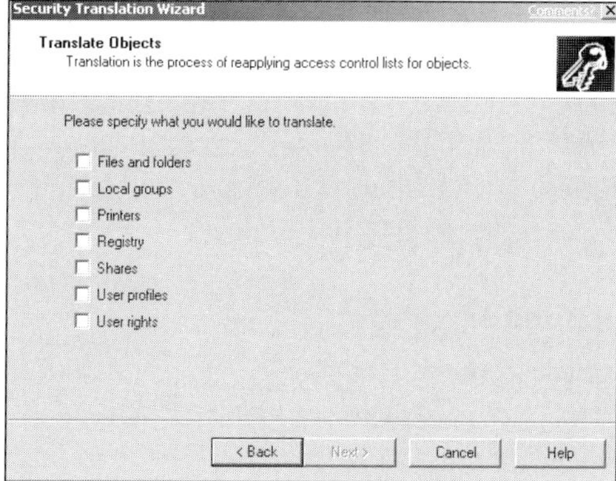

Figure 9.28 Computer Migration Wizard—Translate Objects window.

The Computer Migration Wizard also has options for renaming computers as part of the migration, which is helpful if you would like to add a prefix to indicate that the computer account is a member of the new domain.

The Computer Migration Wizard makes the changes to the local desktops and servers then dispatches an agent to restart the machine. For this to work, the Windows Server 2003 domain account you use to run ADMT must have administrator privileges on the desktops. You cannot put this account in the Domain Admins group of the NT or Windows 2000 domain because Global groups cannot have members from outside the domain. The simplest workaround is to use an account from the source domain that has been given sufficient privileges in the Windows Server 2003 domain to run ADMT.

You can also elect to run the security translation as a separate process after a migration to clean up permissions on desktops and servers and get rid of the old accounts. You should do this prior to decommissioning the NT domain to avoid lots of bare SIDs on the ACLs of your folders and files.

You can use ADMT to migrate IA64 desktops and servers to another domain, but the agent dispatched from an IA32 machine will fail to restart an IA64 machine. You must restart the IA64 machines manually.

Group Account Migrations

Migrating user accounts to the Windows Server 2003 domain only accomplishes half the work necessary to assure that users retain access to their resources in the original domain. On the other side of the equation lies the Machine Local and Global groups to which the user belongs.

When planning the user migration, start out by finding closed sets of users and groups. For example, you might want to migrate user Amcbeal, who is a member of the Legal group. But Jcage is also a member of this group, so you may decide to migrate him, as well. But Jcage is a member of the General_Partners group, so you want to migrate that group at the same time, but it has user Rfish as a member.

Tossing a lasso around all the interlocking users and groups in a domain can get a little complicated. Fortunately, ADMT has the capability to add migrated users into groups that have been previously migrated.

Preparing for Account Migration

As you can imagine, the ability to nab a user's SID from one domain and put it in a user account in another domain is a highly privileged operation. The SID History API has an *extensive* list of requirements. If you decide to migrate passwords along with the user accounts, there are even more items you must configure first before proceeding. Here are the prerequisites for performing an inter-forest migration (the next section contains the steps for including password migration):

- **Target domain functional level.** The target domain must be running in either Windows 2000 Native or Windows Server 2003 functional level. This is required because SID History cannot be stored in a classic SAM, so all BDCs must be off the wire.
- **Source domain affiliation.** If you are migrating from a Windows 2000 source domain, the domain cannot be in the same forest as the target domain.
- **Service packs.** An NT4 source domain controller must be running SP4 or later. A Windows 2000 source domain controller can be running any service pack.
- **Trust relationships.** The source domain must trust the target domain. This ensures that the ADMT agent has the proper security context.
- **Administrator privileges.** The account you use to perform the migration must have full administrator privileges in both the source and target domain. You can accomplish this by taking advantage of the trust relationship between the source and target domain. Place the Windows Server 2003 domain account you're using to perform the migration into the Administrators group in the source domain.
- **Resource domain trusts.** If you are migrating computer and server accounts out of a resource domain, the resource domain must have a direct trust to the Windows Server 2003 domain. You cannot use the trust between the account domain and the Windows Server 2003 domain because classic trusts are not transitive.
- **Migration tracking group.** The source domain must have a local group named `Domain$$$`, where `Domain` is the NetBIOS name of the domain—for example, `NT-DOM$$$`. This group cannot have any members. It is used to verify the identity of the source domain. ADMT will create this group automatically if it does not already exist. If you create it yourself, be sure to create a Domain Local group, not a Global group.

- **Network Connections.** Break all connections between the source and target domain controllers, including mapped drives and printers. The ADMT agent must have unambiguous control of the communication between the machines.
- **TCP/IP access to SAM.** Ordinarily, the SAM can only be accessed via RPC connections. For purposes of migration, ADMT needs access using TCP/IP connections. This requires a Registry change in the source domain. ADMT will make this change automatically, but here it is if you want to do the change manually:

```
Key:    HKLM | System | CurrentControlSet | Control | Lsa
Value:  TcpipClientSupport
Data:    1 (REG_DWORD)
```

- **Auditing.** Account management auditing must be enabled in both domains. This ensures that a record is kept of anyone who exercises the SID History API. See the sidebar, "Account Management Auditing," for details. Be sure to turn off auditing when migration is complete or you will fill the Security log.
- **Administrative shares.** The so-called dollar-sign (`$`) shares must be available on both the source and target domain controllers. Check this by running `NET SHARE` from the command line.
- **Target OU.** The migrated groups, users, and computers must be placed in an OU in the target domain. You can use existing OUs or create new ones for this purpose.

Password Migration

ADMT can preserve passwords by installing a password migration agent at the source domain controller that can respond to password dump requests from the target domain controller. For security reasons, the source DC must validate the identity of the target DC independently of the normal NTLM authentication. This is done using a password migration key.

You create the password migration key at the target DC by running a command-line version of ADMT. You then transport it by floppy to the source domain controller, where you run a Password Migration Wizard from the Windows Server 2003 CD. The wizard verifies that you have the password migration key prior to installing and initializing the migration agent on the source DC.

Account Management Auditing

Before you can use the SID History API, you must have auditing enabled in both domains.

In Windows Server 2003 and Windows 2000, account auditing is controlled by the `Audit Account Management` group policy in the `Default Domain Controllers Policy`. This policy is located under `Computer Configuration | Windows Settings | Security Settings | Local Policies | Audit Policy`. Enable the policy for success and failure.

In NT, account auditing is controlled by `User Manager for Domains`. Select POLICIES | AUDIT from the menu. Enable success and failure auditing for `User and Group Management` events.

The password migration agent at the source DC needs access to user accounts in Active Directory at the target DC. This requires support for null session access to Active Directory because the source DC is running NT and cannot perform a Kerberos logon. Part of the migration preparation, then, involves setting domain controller policies to permit null session access.

Perform the steps in Procedure 9.4 prior to running ADMT if you want to migrate passwords along with user accounts.

Procedure 9.4 Configuring the Password Migration Agent

1. Enable the Network Access: Let Everyone Permissions Apply To Anonymous Users group policy in the `Default Domain Controllers Policy` of the target domain. This policy is located in Computer Configuration | Windows Settings | Security Settings | Local Policies | Security Options.
2. Add the Everyone group to the Pre-Windows 2000 Compatible Access group in the target domain.
3. Create the password migration key and save it to a floppy using the ADMT command-line tool with the following syntax: `admt key` *`<source_domain_name> <drive letter> <password>`*. If you do not want to type the password in clear text on the screen, enter an asterisk (*) and you will be prompted to enter it. The password key will have a PES extension.
4. Transport the floppy containing the password to the source domain controller along with the Windows Server 2003 CD, which contains the password migration utility.
5. At the source domain controller, insert the floppy in the floppy drive and launch the password migration utility from the Windows Server 2003 CD in the `\Valueadd\Msft\Mgmt\Admt\Pwmig` folder.
6. The Password Migration Wizard finds the password file on the floppy and prompts you for the password to open it. The wizard then completes the installation of the migration utility to the source domain controller.

At this point, the password migration agent is installed on the source domain controller but it will not respond to dump requests until you toggle a Registry entry created by the setup wizard. Here is the Registry entry:

```
Key:   HKLM | System | CurrentControlSet | Control | Lsa
Value: AllowPasswordExport
Data:  0 (REG_DWORD)
```

Toggle the Data entry from 0 to 1. With this done, you're ready to begin the account migration.

Migrating User and Group Accounts

After the password migration agent is installed and properly configured on the source DC, and you've met the prerequisites for the account migration, you can run through a test migration using ADMT to verify that everything works as it should.

The example in Procedure 9.5 uses the Group Account Migration Wizard in ADMT to migrate groups and their users from an NT domain to a Windows Server 2003 domain. For me, it is simpler to select a single group to migrate than cherry-picking individual users from what might be a lengthy list. You may feel differently and want to migrate individual users. The end result is the same.

Procedure 9.5 Performing a User and Group Migration Using ADMT

1. Launch the ADMT utility from the ADMINISTRATIVE TOOLS menu.
2. Right-click top of the tree and select GROUP ACCOUNT MIGRATION from the flyout menu. This launches the Group Account Migration Wizard.
3. Click `Next`. The Test or Make Changes window opens. At this point, you only want to test the migration.
4. Click `Next`. The Domain Select window opens. Select the source and target domains from the pick lists. If the domain does not appear, you have a problem with WINS or DNS.
5. Click `Next`. The Group Selection window opens. Click `Add` to open the standard object chooser window. Select the groups you want to migrate from the source domain. You cannot migrate Builtin groups.
6. Click `Next`. The Organizational Unit selection window opens. Use the `Target OU` browser to select the OU where you want the groups to be migrated.
7. Click `Next`. The Group Options window opens (see Figure 9.29). Select all check blocks in this window except for `Update Previously Migrated Objects`.
8. Click `Next`. The wizard reports that you do not have a `TARGET$$$` local group in the source domain and offers to create it.
9. Click `Yes`. The wizard reports that you do not have the TCP/IP Registry support key in the source domain and offers to create it.
10. Click `Yes`. The wizard prompts whether you want to reboot the source domain controller to ensure the changes take effect. This is required for the Registry update.

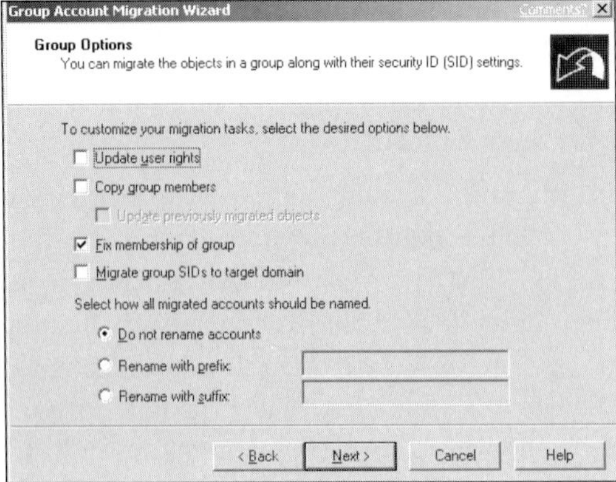

Figure 9.29 Group Migration Wizard—Group Options window.

11. Click `Yes`. While the source domain controller restarts, the wizard continues. The User Account window opens. Enter the credentials of an administrator in the source domain. Wait for the source domain controller to finish restarting before proceeding.
12. Click `Next`. The Naming Conflicts window opens (see Figure 9.30). Choose an option for handling situations where a group or username already exists. The safest option is `Ignore Conflicting Accounts And Don't Migrate`.
13. Click `Next`. The Group Member Password Options window opens. You can create passwords for the users or you can migrate their existing passwords. Select the `Migrate Passwords` radio button and select the source domain controller. If you did not install the password migration agent on the source domain controller, you will get a series of errors.

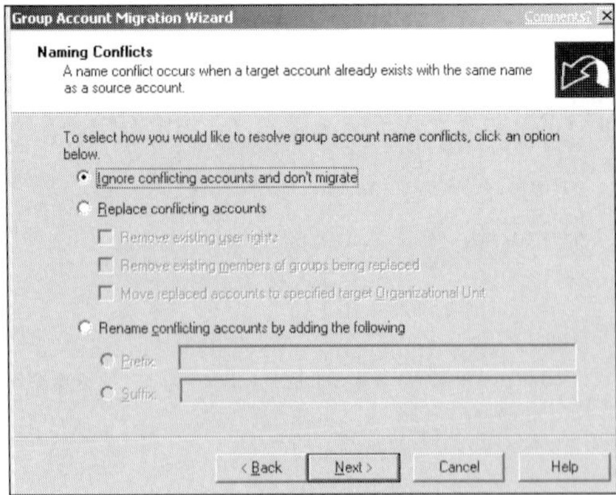

Figure 9.30 Group Migration Wizard—Naming Conflicts window.

14. Click `Next`. The Group Member Transition Options window opens. You can elect to enable the target accounts and disable the source accounts, but it's safer to leave both sets of accounts active in case something unexpected goes awry with the Windows Server 2003 logon. You can set an interval after which the source accounts are disabled automatically.
15. Click `Next`. A summary window opens.
16. Click `Finish`. The Group Migration Wizard walks through a trial migration and displays the results as it goes. This information is saved to a local Jet database where it can be referenced by later migrations.

If ADMT encounters any errors on the test migration, it lists them in the progress window with details in the Migration log. If there are no errors, you can proceed with the actual migration using the same steps.

When the actual migration is finished, verify the following:

- User and group accounts are in the correct OU.
- Group membership shows the correct users.
- Users can log on to the Windows Server 2003 domain using their original passwords.
- Users can log on to the Windows Server 2003 domain and access shared folders and printers on NT or Windows 2000 servers in the source domain.
- Users retained their original profiles with access to all share points.

A full migration of users, groups, and computers takes a long time. When the smoke clears, and you no longer need the source domains, take an afternoon and run through the ADMT Security Translation Wizard to remove the old accounts from the desktops and servers. This avoids having a bunch of bare SIDs that cannot be resolved to friendly names after the source domain controllers are no longer available.

You should also clear out the SID History entries from the security principal accounts in Active Directory. This speeds up performance somewhat and eliminates quite a bit of complexity when dealing with access rights issues.

Additional Domain Operations

This section discusses a few miscellaneous domain controller manipulations:

- Demoting a domain controller, including demoting the last domain controller in a domain
- Renaming a domain controller
- Renaming a domain

Demoting Domain Controller

Unlike NT PDCs and BDCs, Windows Server 2003 and Windows 2000 domain controllers can be demoted to become member servers. This demotion strips away the services involved with authenticating users and passing out group policies but does not affect the server's name or capability to support applications.

The domain controller must be able to communicate with its replication partners or it will refuse to accept demotion. If you pull the server off the wire then attempt to demote it, it will stubbornly refuse. In this situation, you are forced to reinstall Windows Server 2003 completely. Also, if the domain itself remains available, you must run metadata cleanup from the Ntdsutil utility to clean out the server name from Active Directory. See Chapter 10, "Active Directory Maintenance," for details.

Here is a checklist of domain-related services that the domain controller might be hosting:

- **Replication bridgehead.** Before demoting the bridgehead server for a site, you should assure yourself that another server is available for inter-site replication. The Inter-Site Topology Generator (ISTG) is responsible for determining the bridgehead server. If you down the ISTG, the remaining servers will realize after an hour that it is not available and they will determine which domain controller will become the new ISTG. See Chapter 7, "Managing Active Directory Replication," for details of the selection process. Determine the identity of the servers using the Replication Monitor, Replmon.
- **FSMOs.** Before demoting a domain controller that is also an operations master, you should first transfer the roles to another server. Use Replmon to determine the identity of the FSMOs.
- **Global Catalog.** Before demoting a Global Catalog server, be sure that another GC server is available in the site. If you leave a site without a GC, the clients will be forced to go across the WAN and that will hurt performance. Use Replmon to determine the GCs in a forest.
- **Application naming contexts.** If you delete the last domain controller in a domain, you must decide what to do with the Application naming contexts that contain DNS resource records. If you have no further need for the DNS zones that have been integrated into Active Directory, you can elect to remove the naming contexts along with the domain. If you want retain the DNS zones, though, you must take steps to configure another DNS server and make it the primary master for the zones.
- **DHCP.** Windows 2000 and Windows Server 2003 DHCP servers that are members of a domain rely on Active Directory to determine their authorization status. If you demote all domain controllers, the server will continue to show an `Authorized` status and continue to pass out addresses. If you want the server to behave otherwise, you must either manually de-authorize it or stop the service completely.

To demote the domain controller, launch `Dcpromo`. It will sense that Active Directory is loaded and offer you the option of demoting the server. If this is the last server in the domain, be sure to check that option so that the server will take additional steps to clean out the last vestiges of the domain from the Registry and make the server a standalone server in a workgroup.

Renaming Domains

You can now restructure forests by renaming domains and changing the domain hierarchy. The forest functional level must be at Windows Server 2003. The utility that does this trick is called RENDOM. It is not installed by default. You can find it on the Windows Server 2003 CD under `\Valueadd\Msft\Mgmt\Rendom`.

You cannot use RENDOM to separate a domain into a separate forest, nor can you merge a domain with an existing forest, so it is not the true prune-and-graft that Microsoft promised for this release, but it goes a long way towards simplifying internal restructurings.

Renaming Domain Controllers

If the domain functional level is set to Windows Server 2003, you can rename a domain controller using a new switch on the `NETDOM` command in the Support Tools. There are two options.

Rename Using Alternate Name

This option uses `NETDOM COMPUTERNAME` to add an alternate name, make that name the primary name, and then remove the original name. The sequence of events is described in Procedure 9.6.

Procedure 9.6 Renaming a Domain Controller Using *NETDOM COMPUTERNAME*

1. From a command prompt at the console of the domain controller you want to rename, issue the following command to assign an alternate name to the server (be sure to enter the fully qualified DNS name, not just the flat name):

   ```
   netdom computername <old-name> /add:<new-name>
   ```

2. Verify in DNS that the new name is registered.
3. Issue the following command to make the new name the primary name for the server:

   ```
   netdom computername <old-name> /makeprimary:<new-name>
   ```

4. Restart the server so that the new name will take effect.

5. Following the restart, open a command prompt once again and issue the following command to remove the old name:

```
netdom computername <new-name> /remove<old-name>
```

6. Verify that the server now has only one name using the following command:

```
netdom computername <new-name> /enumerate
```

At this point, if you look in DNS or in the Properties window for the server, you'll see only the new name.

Rename by Replacing Primary Name

This option uses NETDOM RENAMECOMPUTER to replace the primary name of the domain controller in one swoop. You can also use the command to reboot the server with a few seconds delay (configured at the command line) so that the new primary name takes effect. The syntax is as follows:

```
netdom renamecomputer <old-name> /newname:<new-name> /reb: 1
```

Following restart, the server registers its new name with DNS, which will be its primary name in Active Directory.

Moving Forward

This completes the deployment of Active Directory in the enterprise. In the next chapter, we'll see how to deal with any problems that might crop up, and then we'll veer away from Active Directory for a while to discuss how to deploy production servers for file and print access with special attention to security and reliability.

10 Active Directory Maintenance

Active Directory relies on a variety of services and features to function properly. If one of these services should fail, you are sure to get unusual or erratic behavior. This chapter covers the following failure scenarios and suggests recovery options for them:

- Loss of a DNS Server and its impact on clients and domain controllers
- Loss of a domain controller, including the loss of a Global Catalog server and Flexible Single Master Operations (FSMO) role masters
- Loss of key replication components, including bridgehead servers, Inter-Site Topology Generator (ISTG) servers, and WAN links
- Loss or corruption of the Active Directory database, including methods for backing up and restoring the database contents
- Performing Active Directory maintenance, including moving ESE files to alternate locations, defragmenting the AD database, and setting AD configuration parameters

By the time you finish this chapter, you'll have the basis for a set of best practices to use when planning for Active Directory recovery and for performing ongoing maintenance.

New Features in Windows Server 2003

The only new feature in Windows Server 2003 that affects Active Directory failure and recovery is the new capability of domain controllers that are not Global Catalog servers to cache Universal group membership. The GC holds the membership lists for Universal groups, and without this information, a domain controller refuses to let users authenticate. Ordinarily, a loss of connection to GC servers, such as might happen with a T1 cut, would result in users being unable to log on to the domain. By caching Universal group membership on standard domain controllers, the loss of access to GCs does not result in a loss of domain access.

Loss of a DNS Server

Losing a DNS server impacts Active Directory in several ways. First and foremost, a domain controller must be able to resolve host names and service locator (SRV) records to communicate and replicate with its fellow domain controllers. If the DNS server used by a domain controller fails, the domain controller cannot maintain full functionality for long.

You should design your DNS infrastructure so that the loss of a single DNS server does not result in a service interruption. You should always have at least two DNS servers that are authoritative for a zone, and your clients should point at both servers, one as a primary and one as a secondary. A Windows client falls back on its secondary DNS server when it gets no response from its primary DNS server.

Avoid the "Island" Effect

If you point a domain controller that is a DNS server with Active Directory integrated zones at itself for name resolution, you can become the victim of a subtle Catch-22 that Microsoft terms the *island effect*.

With an Active Directory integrated DNS zone, a domain controller updates its DNS records by replicating from another domain controller. The domain controller finds its replication partner by doing a DNS lookup. If the IP addresses change, the domain controller cannot find its replication partner and it cannot update DNS because it cannot replicate.

You can avoid this island effect by configuring the TCP/IP properties of a domain controller so that another domain controller is the primary DNS server. The DNS settings in the TCP/IP properties of the domain controller can point at the domain controller itself as a secondary DNS server on the assumption that the secondary entry will only be needed for a short time during an outage.

Impact of DNS Loss on Windows Clients

Without DNS, Active Directory clients cannot find the SRV records needed for locating domain controllers. Without these records, the clients cannot authenticate and perform LDAP lookups.

Initially, following a loss of access to DNS servers, clients will continue to function for a while using cached DNS records. The Start of Authority (SOA) record for the DNS domain determines the default time-to-live for DNS records issued by the name servers hosting the zone. The default Time-To-Live (TTL) for Windows DNS is 1 hour (3600 seconds).

After the `SRV` records expire, if the DNS server is still not available, the clients will be unable to locate their domain controllers. This causes them to fail to renew their Kerberos session tickets, so they lose the capability to connect to member servers.

When planning your DNS infrastructure, you should always have a fallback DNS server available in each location. This could be a standard secondary name server or a domain controller configured with an AD-integrated zone.

Loss of a Domain Controller

When a domain controller fails, the Kerberos service running at the clients will become aware of the loss when the locally cached Kerberos tickets time out and the Kerberos service attempts to renew them. When the client realizes that its logon server is not responding, it queries DNS for alternative domain controllers and uses one of them to reauthenticate. The user is none the wiser.

If the failed domain controller is the only domain controller in a site, the clients must reauthenticate across the WAN. This slows down the authentication, depending on the speed of the site link. During the period when a local domain controller is unavailable, LDAP queries such as searching for printers or using Outlook in an Exchange 2000 environment will be slow thanks to the latency across the WAN link.

If no other domain controllers are available for reauthentication, the client's Kerberos tickets will eventually expire and it will lose connection with member servers. If the clients log off, they can log back on with cached credentials but those credentials will not be sufficient to get access to member servers.

So, it is important to keep in mind that a cut WAN link can cause a loss of connection to local Windows servers if there are no local domain controllers. Your option would be to put a fallback WAN connection in place, such as an ISDN line that only goes hot when the primary connection goes down. Or, you can install a local domain controller. As we'll see in the next section, this domain controller either needs to be a Global Catalog server or it must be configured to cache Global Catalog records.

GC-Less Logons

Under normal circumstances, if a domain controller hosting a copy of the Global Catalog is not available, users are not permitted to log on to a domain. This is because the GC holds the membership list for Universal groups.

In addition, if users log on using their UPN (`user@company.com`), a GC is required to "crack" the UPN into its constituent parts. Windows XP will cache the cracked name after a user logs on the first time, but Windows 2000 needs a GC each time a user submits a UPN at logon.

In Windows Server 2003, a new feature has been added that permits standard domain controllers to cache Universal group membership information. This enables those domain controllers to authenticate users when a GC is unavailable. The

Universal group membership cache does *not* turn a domain controller into a GC. The caching domain controller does not listen for LDAP queries on port 3268 and it does not host objects from other domains apart from Universal group memberships.

Universal group caching does not require additional processors or memory on the part of the domain controllers in the site. When enabled, the Universal group cache is refreshed every eight hours. If a user is added to a Universal group after the last refresh, the permissions associated with that group (and any group to which that group belongs) will not be included in the user's PAC and therefore will not be included in any local access tokens created for the user on member servers. The Universal group membership cache holds about 500 groups.

You should enable Universal group membership caching for every site that does not have a Global Catalog server. Configure a site for GC-less logon caching by following Procedure 10.1.

Procedure 10.1 Enabling Universal Group Membership Caching

1. Open AD Sites and Services.
2. Highlight the site you want to configure.
3. In the right pane, open the Properties window for the `NTDS Site Settings` object. Figure 10.1 shows an example.

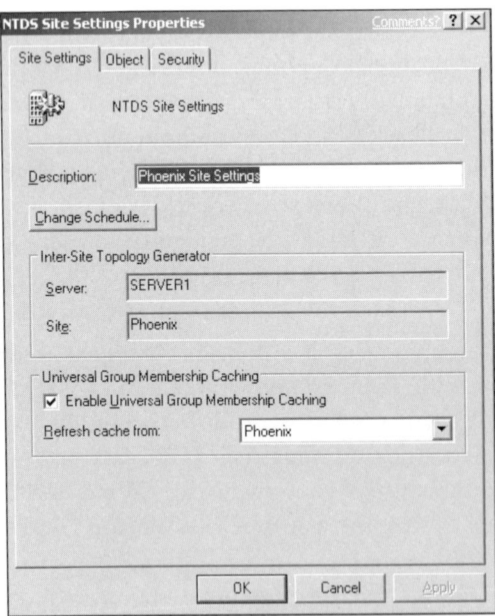

Figure 10.1 NTDS Settings Properties window showing `GC-Less Logon` option.

4. Select the option `Enable Universal Group Membership Caching`. Leave the `Refresh Cache From` pick list empty. The Knowledge Consistency Checker (KCC) will determine the closest site with a GC server.
5. Click `OK` to save the change and close the window.

Performing Metadata Cleanup on Failed Domain Controller

If you are unable to restore a failed domain controller, you must clean out references to it in Active Directory. This so-called *metadata* must be removed before you can promote another server with the same name to be a domain controller. If you lose an entire domain, you must also remove the metadata information for that domain before creating another domain by the same name.

The tool to perform this metadata cleanup is a text-based utility called Ntdsutil. The cleanup is done with Active Directory up and running. Follow Procedure 10.2.

Procedure 10.2 Performing Metadata Cleanup

1. Run `Ntdsutil`.
2. At the `ntdsutil:` prompt, enter `metadata cleanup`. This opens the `metadata cleanup:` prompt.
3. Enter `?` for an options list:

```
metadata cleanup: ?
 ?                                  - Show this help information
 Connections                        - Connect to a specific domain controller
 Help                               - Show this help information
 Quit                               - Return to the prior menu
 Remove selected domain             - Remove DS objects for selected domain
 Remove selected Naming Context    - Remove DS objects for selected Naming Context
 Remove selected server             - Remove DS objects for selected server
 Select operation target            - Select sites, servers, domains, roles and
                                        naming contexts
```

4. Enter `connections` and then enter `?` for an options list:

```
Clear creds                         - Clear prior connection credentials
Connect to domain %s                - Connect to DNS domain name
Connect to server %s                - Connect to server, DNS name or IP address
Help                                - Print this help information
Info                                - Show connection information
Quit                                - Return to the prior menu
Set creds %s %s %s                    - Set connection creds as domain, user, pwd
                                    ➥(Use "NULL" for null password)
```

5. If you are working from a member server and you are not logged on with administrator credentials, use the `set creds` command to define your binding credentials.

6. Enter `connect to server <dsa>` to bind to a server, where `<dsa>` is the fully qualified DNS name of the domain controller where you want to make the update to the Directory. Any functioning domain controller will do. The entries and transaction results so far look like this:

```
server connections: set creds company.com administrator pw
server connections: connect to server dc-01.company.com
Binding to dc-11.company.com as user(administrator) in domain(company.com) ...
Connected to dc-11.company.com as user(administrator) in domain(company.com) .
```

7. Enter `select operation target`. This opens the `select operation target:` prompt. Enter `?` for an options list:

```
Connections                      - Connect to a specific domain controller
Help                             - Print this help information
List current selections          - List the current site/domain/server
List domains                     - Lists all domains which have Cross-Refs
List domains in site             - Lists domains in the selected site
List roles for connected server  - Lists roles connected server knows about
List servers for domain in site  - Lists servers for selected domain and site
List servers in site             - Lists servers in selected site
List sites                       - List sites in the enterprise
Quit                             - Return to the prior menu
Select domain %d                 - Make domain %d the selected domain
Select server %d                 - Make server %d the selected server
Select site %d                     - Make site %d the selected site
```

8. Enter `list sites`. An example output looks like this:

```
select operation target: list sites
Found 4 site(s)
0 - CN=Phoenix,CN=Sites,CN=Configuration,DC=company,DC=com
1 - CN=Houston,CN=Sites,CN=Configuration,DC=company,DC=com
2 - CN=Albuquerque,CN=Sites,CN=Configuration,DC=company,DC=com
3 - CN=Salt_Lake,CN=Sites,CN=Configuration,DC=company,DC=com
```

9. Enter `select site <#>` where `<#>` is the number of the site containing the server you want to remove:

```
select operation target: select site 1
Site - CN=Salt_Lake,CN=Sites,CN=Configuration,DC=company,DC=com
No current domain
No current server
```

10. Enter `list domains in site`. An example output looks like this:

```
select operation target: list domains in site

Found 1 domain(s)
0 - DC=subsidiary,DC=com
1 - DC=company,DC=com
```

11. Enter `select domain <#>` where <#> is the number of the domain containing the server you want to remove:

```
select operation target: select domain 1

Site - CN=Salt_Lake,CN=Sites,CN=Configuration,DC=company,DC=com
Domain - DC=company,DC=com
No current server
```

12. Enter `list servers for domain in site`. An example output looks like this:

```
select operation target: list servers for domain in site

Found 1 server(s)
0 - CN=DC-11,CN=Servers,CN=Salt_Lake,CN=Sites,CN=Configuration,
➥DC=company,DC=com
```

13. Enter `select server <#>` where <#> is the number of the server you want to remove. An example output looks like this:

```
select operation target: select server 0

Site - CN=Salt_Lake,CN=Sites,CN=Configuration,DC=company,DC=com
Domain - DC=subsidiary,DC=com
Server - CN=DC-
11,CN=Servers,CN=Salt_Lake,CN=Sites,CN=Configuration,DC=company,DC=com
DSA object - CN=NTDS Settings,CN=DC-01,CN=Servers,CN=Salt_Lake,CN=Sites,
     CN=Configuration,DC=company,DC=com
DNS host name - DC-11.company.com
Computer object - CN=DC-11,OU=Domain Controllers,DC=company,DC=com
```

14. We've now targeted the server object we want to delete. Enter `q` to return to the `metadata cleanup:` prompt.
15. Enter `remove selected server`. A message window appears prompting you to verify your request.
16. Click `Yes` and the deed is done. An example output looks like this:

```
Metadata cleanup: remove selected server
"CN=DC-11,CN=Servers,CN=Salt_Lake,CN=Sites,CN=Configuration,DC=company,
➥DC=com" removed from server "dc-01.company.com"
```

17. Quit out of `Ntdsutil` and wait for the change to replicate.

You can use the same technique to remove a domain that was not fully deleted when the last domain controller was removed from service. Needless to say, be very careful that you don't delete any operational domains.

FSMO Loss

A few tasks are not suitable for multiple-master operation and must be handled by a single server. These tasks are called Flexible Single Master Operations (FSMOs). The server that is assigned a FSMO is called the *FSMO role master*. Chapter 8, "Designing Windows Server 2003 Domains," discussed the jobs assigned to FSMOs. The following is a quick overview:

- **Domain Naming Master**. This FSMO is responsible for ensuring the uniqueness of domain names in a forest. There is one Domain Naming Master in a forest.
- **Schema Master**. This FSMO holds the only read/write copy of the schema. There is one Schema Master in a forest.
- **PDC Emulator**. This FSMO replicates updates to classic NTbackup Domain Controllers (BDCs) while in Mixed. It also acts as a clearinghouse for password updates and a time standard for other domain controllers in a domain. There is one PDC Emulator in each domain.
- **RID Master**. This FSMO holds the master copy of the Relative ID number list. In Mixed, these RIDs are passed out sequentially. In Native, each domain controller gets a bank of RIDs from the RID Master. There is one RID Master in each domain.
- **Infrastructure Master**. This FSMO is responsible for the rapid transmission of name changes that affect inter-domain group memberships in a forest. There is one Infrastructure Master in each domain.

A short outage of a FSMO role master does not warrant special action, but if you plan on taking a role master down for an extended period, you should transfer its role or roles to another domain controller. This is especially true if the server is going under the knife with little hope of recovery.

If a FSMO role master crashes and cannot be recovered, you must seize its role or roles on behalf of another domain controller. In a normal transfer, the original role master must be online to accept the transfer request. In a seizure, the original role master is not online and the new role master simply takes the role.

After seizing a role, don't put the superceded role master back on the network. Treat it like Smokey Bear treats a campfire. Drown it, stir it, and drown it again. This prevents the old role master from passing out invalid information or providing a second means of updating controlled structures like the `Schema` or `Partition` container.

> **Role Master Designation**
>
> The item that designates a particular server as a FSMO role master takes the form of an attribute in the Active Directory object that controls a particular FSMO. For instance, the Domain object controls the PDC Emulator role. A FSMO attribute on this object contains the distinguished name of the server that has been designated as the PDC Emulator. When you transfer or seize a role, you change the distinguished name assigned to this role master attribute.

Recovering a Lost PDC Emulator

The only exception to the "don't bring back a superceded role master" rule is the PDC Emulator. If a superceded PDC Emulator is brought back online, it gets the name of the new PDC Emulator via replication and politely stops all of its role master activities.

In practice, the RID Master is usually placed on the same server as the PDC Emulator, so you would not put this server back in operation. Putting a superceded RID Master in operation can result in two objects having the same RID, which can cause security problems as well as database consistency errors. If the RID Master and PDC Emulator are on the same server and you must seize the role to another server, scrub the drive on the original sever and re-install Windows Server 2003.

Transferring a FSMO Role Master

When transferring a FSMO to a new role master, you have the option of using an MMC console or a command-line tool. The MMC console you use depends on the role you're transferring. Table 10.1 lists the FSMO roles and their associated MMC consoles along with precautions for placing the role.

Table 10.1 FSMO Transfer Information

FSMO Role	Console	Precautions
PDC Emulator	Users and Computers	Ensure the PDC Emulator stays in communication with all downlevel NT BDCs. In addition, because the PDC Emulator acts as a "court of last resort" for password validation, make sure it stays connected to make the WAN.
RID Master	Users and Computers	Put this role master on the same server as the PDC Emulator. If you absolutely must put the RID Master on a different domain controller, make sure it stays well connected to the PDC Emulator. In Mixed, the RID Master must be available to create each new user, computer, or group.
Infrastructure Master	Users and Computers	Put this role master on any domain controller that is not a Global Catalog server. See the side bar titled "Infrastructure Master Operation."
Domain Naming Master	Domains and Trusts	Keep this rolemaster and the Schema Master on the same domain controller. These two roles are unique in the forest, so make sure they stay connected to the WAN.
Schema Master	Schema Management	See Domain Naming Master instructions.

Infrastructure Master Operation

When you make a security principal (user, group, or computer) a member of a group, the distinguished name of the security principal is added to an attribute called `Members` for the group object in Active Directory. Active Directory maintains internal consistency by creating a *back-link* to the object representing the security principal. In this way, if the object name changes, the `Member` attribute in the group can be updated.

When you, as the administrator of a domain in a forest, add a security principal from another domain to a group in your domain, Active Directory is faced with a dilemma. It cannot create a back-link to an object in another Domain naming context. It solves this dilemma by creating a *phantom object*, which is essentially a listing in its Domain naming context consisting of the distinguished name of the object, its GUID (Globally Unique Identifier), and its SID.

The Infrastructure Master in a domain discovers name changes made to security principals represented by phantom records in its own domain. Without this service, the names displayed in group membership lists would not correspond to the new names in the source domains. This does not affect resource access because the SID has not changed, but it can be confusing for administrators.

The Infrastructure Master accomplishes its task by periodically perusing the list of phantom records and checking their names against names in the Global Catalog. If it finds a mismatch, it updates the phantom record to reflect the new name. This change is then replicated to other domain controllers in its domain that have a copy of the phantom record.

Global Catalog servers already have a copy of objects from other domains and therefore do not store phantom records. For this reason, it is important that the Infrastructure Master not be assigned to a Global Catalog server.

Transferring a Role Master Using an MMC Console

Refer to Table 10.1 to find the applicable console and then proceed with the transfer as directed in Procedure 10.3.

Procedure 10.3 Changing a Role Master Using an MMC Console

1. Open the applicable `MMC` console for the FSMO that you are going to transfer.
2. If you are not at the domain controller that will become the new role master, right-click the very top icon, the one with the same name as the console. Select CONNECT TO DOMAIN CONTROLLER from the flyout menu.
3. Select the name of the domain controller you want to be the new role master. This satisfies an LDAP requirement to bind to the server so that you can be authenticated.
4. Click `OK` to connect to the domain controller.
5. Right-click the top icon again. This time select OPERATIONS MASTER from the flyout menu. The Operations window appears.
6. Select the tab associated with the role you want to transfer.
7. Verify that the domain controller listed under `Current Focus` is the name of the server where you want the role to be transferred.
8. Click `Change`. You are prompted to verify.

9. Click OK. After a short wait, you'll be informed that the Operations Master was successfully transferred. The Operations tab now shows the new name under Current Operations Master.
10. Click OK to close the window.

At this point, you should wait for replication to fully converge so that all domain controllers know about the new role master. You can use the AD Sites and Services console or Replication Monitor (Replmon) from the Support Tools to force replication.

Transferring a Role Master Using Ntdsutil

If you prefer using a command-line tool (or you want to manage your servers via Telnet or SSH), you can use Ntdsutil to transfer role masters between domain controllers. Both the original role master and the target role master must be online (see Procedure 10.4).

Procedure 10.4 Transferring a Role Master Using Ntdsutil

1. Log on using an account with administrator privileges in the domain. If the transfer involves either of the enterprise roles, Schema Master or Domain Naming Master, you must also have administrator rights in the Configuration naming context.
2. Open a command session and run `ntdsutil`.
3. At the `ntdsutil:` prompt, enter `roles`. This opens the `FSMO maintenance:` prompt.
4. Enter **?** to get the options list:

```
fsmo maintenance: ?

 ?                                  - Print this help information
 Connections                        - Connect to a specific domain controller
 Help                               - Print this help information
 Quit                               - Return to the prior menu
 Seize domain naming master         - Overwrite domain role on connected server
 Seize infrastructure master        - Overwrite infrastructure role on connected server
 Seize PDC                          - Overwrite PDC role on connected server
 Seize RID master                   - Overwrite RID role on connected server
 Seize schema master                - Overwrite schema role on connected server
 Select operation target            - Select sites, servers, domains and roles
 Transfer domain naming master      - Make connected server the domain naming master
 Transfer infrastructure master     - Make connected server the infrastructure master
 Transfer PDC                       - Make connected server the PDC
 Transfer RID master                - Make connected server the RID master
 Transfer schema master               - Make connected server the schema master
```

5. Type `connections`. This opens the `server connections` prompt.

6. Type ? to get the options list:

```
server connections: ?
 ?                          - Print this help information
 Clear creds                - Clear prior connection credentials
 Connect to domain %s       - Connect to DNS domain name
 Connect to server %s       - Connect to server, DNS name or IP address
 Help                       - Print this help information
 Info                       - Show connection information
 Quit                       - Return to the prior menu
 Set creds %s %s %s           - Set connection creds as domain, user, pwd. Use
                            ➥"NULL" for null password
```

7. Enter connect to server %s where %s is the fully qualified DNS name of the domain controller where you want to transfer the role. For example, enter connect to server company.com. If successful, you get the following report:

```
server connections: connect to server dc-02.company.com.
Binding to \\DC-02.company.com ...
Connected to \\DC-02.company.com using credentials of locally logged on user
```

8. If you want to use another account, use the set creds command prior to issuing the connect to server command.
9. Enter q to exit the module and return to the FSMO maintenance prompt.
10. Select a role to transfer and enter the applicable command. For example, to transfer the PDC Emulator, enter transfer PDC.
11. A window appears requesting that you verify this operation. Click OK to initiate the role transfer.
12. If the transfer operation fails, you get an error message and the role remains with its original master. For example, if the target server is already the role master, you are notified of this. If the transfer operation proceeds without error, Ntdsutil responds with a list of the current role masters, indicating a successful end to the operation:

```
fsmo maintenance: transfer pdc
Server "dc-01.subsidiary.com." knows about 5 roles
Schema - CN=NTDS Settings,CN=DC-01,CN=Servers,CN=Phoenix,CN=Sites,
➥CN=Configuration,DC=company,DC=com
Domain - CN=NTDS Settings,CN=DC-01,CN=Servers,CN=Phoenix,CN=Sites,
➥CN=Configuration,DC=company,DC=com
PDC - CN=NTDS Settings,CN=DC-02,CN=Servers,CN=Phoenix,CN=Sites,
➥CN=Configuration,DC=company,DC=com
RID - CN=NTDS Settings,CN=DC-01,CN=Servers,CN=Phoenix,CN=Sites,
➥CN=Configuration,DC=company,DC=com
Infrastructure - CN=NTDS Settings,CN=DC-01,CN=Servers,CN=Phoenix,CN=Sites,
➥CN=Configuration,DC=company,DC=com
```

Shortcuts in Ntdsutil

You only need to enter enough of each word in an Ntdsutil entry to make it unambiguous. For instance, rather than typing out `connect to server`, you can enter `con t s`.

Seizing a FSMO Role Master

If the domain controller hosting a FSMO role master crashes or is otherwise permanently unavailable, you cannot use the management consoles to transfer roles. You must seize the role using Ntdsutil.

As a reminder, if you seize a FSMO from another domain controller, you must not reintroduce the superceded role master back onto the network. Formatting the hard drive is not too extreme.

Verify that the new target role master is online and follow Procedure 10.5.

Procedure 10.5 Seizing a FSMO Role

1. Log on using an account with administrator privileges in the domain. If the seizure involves either of the enterprise roles, Schema Master or Domain Naming Master, you must also have administrator rights for the Configuration naming context.
2. Open a command session and run `Ntdsutil`.
3. Select `roles` from the prompt. This opens the `FSMO maintenance` prompt.
4. Type `connections`. This opens the `server connections` prompt.
5. Enter `connect to server %s` where `%s` is the fully qualified DNS name of the domain controller where you want to transfer the role—for example, `connect to server company.com`. If successful, you get the following report:

   ```
   server connections: connect to server dc-03.company.com.
   Binding to \\DC-03.company.com ...
   Connected to \\DC-03.company.com using credentials of locally logged on user
   ```

6. Enter `q` to exit the module and return to `FSMO maintenance`.
7. Select a role to seize. For example, to seize the RID Master role you would enter `seize RID master`. A window appears requesting that you verify this operation. Click `OK`. (If the current role master is on the network, Ntdsutil will fall back and do a standard transfer.)
8. If the seizure fails, you get an error message and the role remains with its original master. If the transfer operation proceeds without error, Ntdsutil responds with a list of the current role masters.

Loss of Key Replication Components

When a domain controller fails, its replication partners realize that it has stopped responding to update requests. The partners notify their KCC service, which sets to work creating connection objects that bypass the failed DC, something like Department of Transportation workers directing traffic around an accident.

When the failed domain controller returns to service, its replication partners realize that it is available once again and they inform their KCC service. The KCC rebuilds the connection objects to the domain controller and tears down the bypass.

This work can take a little time, so be patient. You should eventually see a note in the Event log that the KCC was able to create the connection objects and the DRA was able to sync up the naming contexts.

The situation gets a little more complicated if the failed domain controller has special inter-site replication duties. This includes bridgehead servers and Inter-site Topology Generator servers.

Selecting a New Preferred Bridgehead Server

Replication between sites is performed by selected domain controllers called *bridgeheads*. Under normal circumstances, the KCC handles the loss of a bridgehead server with no administrator intervention. It sorts through the available domain controllers in order of their Globally Unique Identifier (GUID) and selects the server with the highest GUID.

You may want the KCC to select bridgeheads from a certain group of servers. For instance, it is best to have a Global Catalog server acting as a bridgehead so the partial naming contexts can be replicated in a single hop to the next site. You might want to limit the candidate list to GC servers.

Designate a domain controller as a preferred bridgehead server using the server properties in AD Sites and Services. Chapter 7, "Managing Active Directory Replication," has detailed steps for this operation. Figure 10.2 shows the bridgehead selection window from Active Directory Sites and Services.

Always designate at least two preferred bridgehead servers. If you select only one, and it fails, all replication will stop until you select another. If the last available bridgehead server goes down, you must select a new preferred bridgehead quickly so replication can recommence.

Selecting a New Inter-Site Topology Generator

The loss of an ISTG does not present an immediate problem. The only real chore the ISTG needs to do is create connections between bridgehead servers. This is not done very frequently. Still, you don't want the failure to go unhealed.

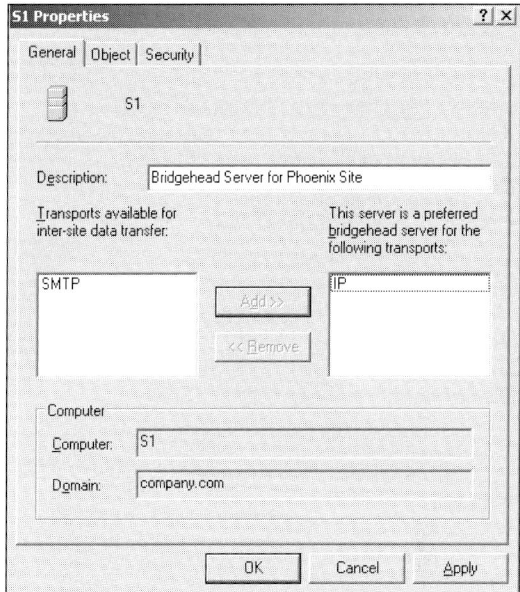

Figure 10.2 AD Sites and Services console showing server Properties window with preferred bridgehead selection for the IP transport.

The ISTG informs its replication partners of its presence by updating an attribute in its object every thirty minutes. If an hour goes by without an update, the KCC on the other domain controllers in the site realize that the ISTG is no longer available and they set to work selecting another.

The ISTG can be identified using the Properties window for the NTDS Site Settings objects in AD Sites and Services. Figure 10.3 shows an example.

The KCC uses the same algorithm to select a new ISTG as it does to select a new bridgehead. It selects the domain controller in the site with the highest GUID. In the case of the ISTG, however, there is no "preferred" domain controller setting.

Verifying Replicas with DSASTAT

After you get replication working, it's a good idea to ensure that the replicas on various domain controllers match. The simplest way to do this is by using the DSASTAT utility that comes in the Support Tools. Open a command console and run `dsastat -loglevel:info`. Depending on the speed of the links to the replication partners, the utility might take five to fifteen minutes to finish a run. At the end, you'll get a list of every object on the replicas and their sizes so you can compare object count and size.

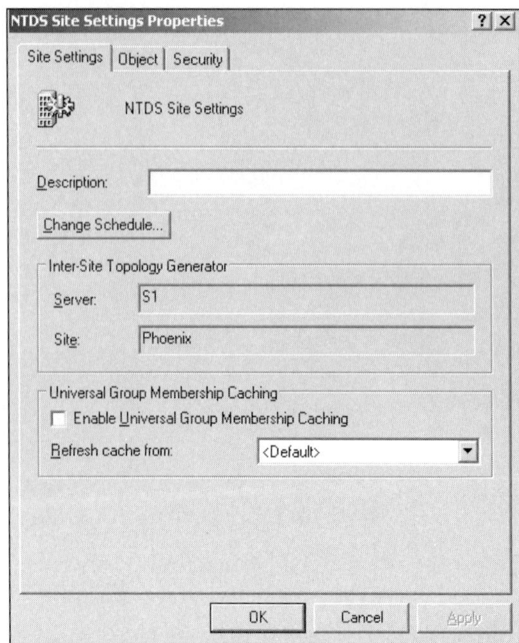

Figure 10.3 NTDS Site Settings object properties showing the ISTG server for the selected site.

Loss of a WAN Link

If a WAN link goes down, the bridgeheads on either side will realize that they cannot pull replication from their partner. If an alternate (but higher cost) connection exists to another site, the Directory Replication Agent (DRA) on the bridgeheads will use this connection automatically. The DRA also informs the ISTG, which tries to create new connections to other bridgeheads.

You should not need to intervene in the operation of the DRA and ISTG. If they are unable to come up with a suitable replication path due to the way your sites are configured and connected, you may have to live with disabled replication until you can re-establish communications.

Backing Up the Directory

In the good old days of classic NT, you could capture the Registry hives on a single Emergency Repair Disk in a smallish domain and on the hard drive using RDISK -S if the Security Account Manager (SAM) was too big to fit on a floppy. Those days are long gone. In fact, RDISK is no longer even available.

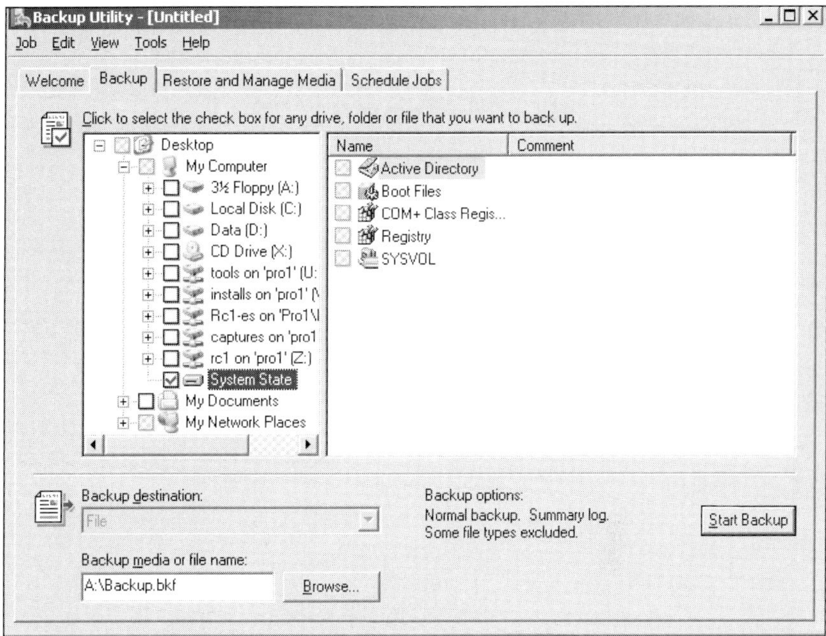

Figure 10.4 NTbackup management window showing the list of files backed up as part of System State.

Active Directory operations rely heavily on the Registry and many different system binaries, so you must back up and restore whole swatches of the system directory to retain integrity. Microsoft calls these files the *System State*. Figure 10.4 shows the list of System State files as they are displayed in NT backup. They include the following:

- All files protected by the Windows File Protection system (virtually everything in C:\Windows)
- The system files Ntdetect.com, Ntldr, and Bootsect.dat
- The Active Directory database, Ntds.dit, and its associated log and checkpoint files
- Selected Internet Explorer files and other shared files in the `Program File` directory
- All Registry hives from the `\Windows\System32\Config` directory (updated copies are placed in `\Windows\Repair`)
- The COM+ class registration database
- The contents of the Sysvol directory
- The Certificate service files (if installed)
- The Cluster service files (if installed)

Forcing you to back up all these files in one scoop does maintain consistency between the various data storehouses, but it means that if you make a minor mistake that affects a portion of the Registry out of reach of the Last Known Good Configuration rollback, you might be forced to restore all the System State files, including Active Directory.

This topic covers backing up and restoring the System State files using Ntbackup. This is a stripped-down version of Veritas Backup Exec. Third-party backup utilities are available that perform the same functions. This includes the full version of Backup Exec, Computer Associates ArcServe, Legato Networker, Tivoli Storage Manager, BEI Corporation UltraBac, CommVault Galaxy, and others. All of these vendors make backup utilities that are Windows Server 2003 compliant. Make sure you upgrade to the most current version, because a Windows 2000 backup utility may not be fully compatible with Windows Server 2003.

Why Active Directory Backups Are Necessary

You may be wondering why AD backups are required at all. After all, if you design your system correctly, you should always have at least three domain controllers in a domain. Each of these domain controllers has a full copy of Active Directory. If any of those servers crash, or even if two of them go down, you still have a third to fall back on. You can quickly promote another Windows member server to a domain controller and regain fault tolerance.

The most obvious answer to "why backup a domain controller" is that Mr. Murphy knows if you don't do backups and may arrange the universe so that all three of your domain controllers crash at the same time. Or, you may get a fire that takes your server room and you need a way to recover Active Directory at a remote site. You never want to be without a full backup in case the stars ever do align in a manner that is not in your best interests.

The more likely occurrence, though, is a mistake on the part of an administrator. I've done it. You'll do it. You get tired or distracted and you delete or modify the wrong object and well, needless to say, things can get a little ugly. If you accidentally delete an entire OU with thousands of user and computer and group objects in it, your mistake will merrily replicate to all the other domain controllers. The only way you'll get that information back is from tape.

You do not need to back up all your domain controllers. Select two or three from your domain and backup System State on those machines. Don't run applications on the domain controllers that would require them to be backed up by local administrators.

Performing a System State Backup

A System State backup is always performed with the machine online and operating normally. The Plug-and-Play Manager should find your tape drive and install the proper drivers for it. You may need to use the Removable Storage Manager to juggle your media pools. See Chapter 21, "Recovering from System Failures," for details.

To perform a System State backup using Ntbackup, follow Procedure 10.6.

Procedure 10.6 Performing a System State Backup

1. Mount a fresh tape in the tape drive.
2. Start Windows 2000 Backup via START | PROGRAMS | ACCESSORIES | SYSTEM TOOLS | BACKUP. The Backup window opens.
3. Click the `Advanced` button to avoid the backup wizard.
4. Select the `Backup` tab.
5. Expand the tree to reveal the `System State` option, which is the last option under the drive letters.
6. Place a check next to the `System State` option.
7. Under `Backup Destination`, select the tape unit you are using for the backup.
8. If you are backing up to a file, select `File` and then enter the path and filename under `Backup Media or File Name`. Be sure to save the files on reliable removable media or on a network drive that is sure to be available if you need to recover. Don't back up to the local hard drive.
9. From the menu, select TOOLS | OPTIONS. The Options window opens.
10. Select the `Backup Type` tab.
11. Under `Default Backup Type`, select the `Copy` option. This keeps the system from resetting the archive bit so that you'll be sure to capture the System State files on your normal nightly backup.
12. Select the `Backup Log` tab.
13. Select the `Detailed` radio button. This gives lots of information, including the name of every file included in the backup. Normally this gives too much information to be useful, but it is worth doing at least once to see exactly what is included in the System State backup.
14. Click `OK` to save the changes and return to the main Backup window.
15. We want to run this backup job interactively rather than scheduling it, so click `Start Backup`.

16. If this is the first time you've used this tape, you may get a message stating that `There is no unused media with the selected type, but unrecognized media is available.` You might also be prompted to confirm the overwrite of existing data if the tape is recognized. If you're sure you haven't inserted a tape with valuable data on it, click `OK`. Different tape systems have different formatting and retrieval schemes, so the messages may vary. Refer to your system documentation for specific instructions. Ntbackup uses the Microsoft Tape Format (MTF).
17. When the system can see the tape or the file location if you are using removable media, the backup begins. The Backup Progress window opens to show you what's happening.
18. When the backup is complete, you get a final window showing the statistics. The `Status` field will probably state that files were skipped. Click `Report` to view the backup log. The most likely culprit is the `DO_NOT_REMOVE_NtFrs_Preinstall_Directory` under Sysvol. This folder holds files that were copied as part of the initial migration of files and folders into the File Replication System database. It can be skipped.

Review the list of files in the log to see what is included. Note that the Active Directory files do not appear individually on the backup log. There is just a single line entry indicating that Active Directory was included in the backup.

The Registry files are first copied to a special folder called `\Registry` from their normal location in `\WindowsWindows\System32\Config`. The `\Registry` folder is a temporary, volatile folder used to capture a snapshot of the Registry for backup. This prevents a file lock during backup from blocking access to the Registry.

Restoring Active Directory

There are two basic scenarios requiring a recovery of the Active Directory database:

- A complete loss of a domain controller necessitating a full recovery from tape, including System State.
- A mistake on the part of an administrator that results in loss of or damage to a portion of Active Directory.

File-Based System State Backups Recommended

Although any Windows Server 2003 compliant backup utility can do a satisfactory backup and restore of System State, it is often impractical to do a quick restore. For example, you might have a big tape library with dozens or hundreds of servers in the backup catalog. Doing an across-the-wire restore of a large Ntds.dit file along with the other System State files can take time, and often requires repermissioning the agent on the domain controller because Active Directory is not available to authenticate the service.

To speed up the recovery, many organizations schedule a file-based backup of the System State files on their domain controller prior to doing the nightly tape backup. This puts a set of *.bkf files on a remote server where they can be captured to tape. Recovering a single file to a landing pad where it can be transferred to the domain controller for restoration is often simpler than doing the restore directly from tape.

In the first scenario, the tape restore of the System State files (which includes Active Directory) is done in conjunction with the restore of the operating system. When the newly restored domain controller comes back online, its replication partners update it with the changes that have occurred since the tape backup was run. For this reason, you should be able to restore from a relatively old tape (three or four days, even a week old) just in case you have problems with your tape library that prevent you from using last night's backup.

Directory Services Restore Mode Password

When restoring Active Directory at a domain controller, you must be able to log on to the server using the Administrator account in the local SAM. You may not know the password for this account.

To remedy this problem, Microsoft included a new feature in the Ntdsutil utility for resetting the local Administrator password. This feature is called Reset DSRM Administrator Password. If you have administrator privileges on a domain controller, you can use this feature to change the Administrator account in the SAM of the domain controller.

Ordinarily, non-administrators are not permitted to log on locally at a domain controller. If a non-administrator does succeed in getting access to a domain controller console and attempts to reset the DSRM password, this is the result:

```
Reset DSRM Administrator Password: reset pas on ser dotnet-rc-es
Please type password for DS Restore Mode Administrator Account:
Setting password failed.
        WIN32 Error Code: 0x6ba
        Error Message: The RPC server is unavailable.
```

Authoritative Restore

A standard System State restoration does "recover" objects you have deleted from Active Directory. When the newly restored domain controller replicates from its partners, any undeleted objects are promptly moved back to the `Deleted Objects` container and all your hard work goes for naught.

If you need to restore a portion of Active Directory (a single object, for instance, or an accidentally deleted OU), or the entire database in the event that it has become irresolutely corrupted, you must ensure that the objects and their properties on the tape replicate outward to the other domain controllers. This is accomplished with an authoritative restore.

An authoritative restore is not a restoration as such. It is performed after the actual tape restoration to mark the objects that will overwrite the replicas on other domain controllers. It does this by adding 100000 to the Property Version Number (PVN) of each property on the authoritatively restored objects.

The following is a REPADMIN listing showing how a sample object looks before and after an authoritative restore. The `ObjectClass` attribute is not touched by the authoritative restore because it is a special attribute used for indexing:

Before:

```
Loc.USN  Originating DSA     Org.USN  Org.Time/Date           Ver     Attribute
=======  ===============     =======  =============           ======  =========
   2562  Houston\HOU-DC-01    2562    2001-10-23 21:21.29     1       objectClass
   3112  Houston\HOU-DC-01    3112    2001-10-24 09:29.12     2       cn
   3112  Houston\HOU-DC-01    3112    2001-10-24 09:29.12     2       sn
   2562  Houston\HOU-DC-01    2562    2001-10-23 21:21.29     1       description
   2562  Houston\HOU-DC-01    2562    2001-10-23 21:21.29     1       givenName
   2562  Houston\HOU-DC-01    2562    2001-10-23 21:21.29     1       instanceType
...
```

After:

```
Loc.USN  Originating DSA     Org.USN  Org.Time/Date           Ver     Attribute
=======  ===============     =======  =============           ======  =========
   2562  Houston\HOU-DC-01   2562     2001-10-23 21:21.29     1       objectClass
  28905  Houston\HOU-DC-01   28905    2001-10-29 19:59.32     100002  cn
  28905  Houston\HOU-DC-01   28905    2001-10-29 19:59.32     100002  sn
  28905  Houston\HOU-DC-01   28905    2001-10-29 19:59.32     100001  description
  28905  Houston\HOU-DC-01   28905    2001-10-29 19:59.32     100001  givenName
  28905  Houston\HOU-DC-01   28905    2001-10-29 19:59.32     100001  instanceType
...
```

Use great caution when doing an authoritative restore of the Configuration naming context or of the entire Active Directory database. Make sure you understand the consequences of overwriting any system configuration parameters. This is especially true if you are running Exchange 2000 or other Active Directory-dependent applications. It is not necessary to restore the entire database to get back a single OU. Be selective.

Who Can Restore Active Directory

If you have a distributed IT organization with administrators in many regions, you may wonder who can perform a Directory restore. You may want to make sure that only qualified individuals do a tape restore on a domain controller. You may also want to find out if you can recover from a mistake without calling up the central IT staffers at headquarters to pull you out of a jam.

Performing a System State restore (which includes the Active Directory database) requires having the local Administrator password in the SAM on the domain controller. This is called the Directory Service Recovery password. If you know this password, you can also perform an authoritative restore of any or all of the Active Directory database, regardless of whether you have rights to a particular portion of the Directory tree. This is because the Active Directory service is not running when you do the authoritative restore, so the system has no way of collecting or validating your credentials.

Authoritative Restore and the Schema Naming Context

The Schema naming context cannot be authoritatively restored. If you want to recover a previous copy of the schema, you can do a standard System State restore on the Schema Master. Any changes made to the schema after the tape backup are lost.

For instance, let's say you install a new network monitoring application that makes changes to the Active Directory schema. You find a bug in the program that didn't show up in lab testing and you want to remove it from the schema. You should delete the new classes and attributes individually using the Schema Management console. You could also do a System State restore at the Schema Master using a tape taken before you installed the application. A System State restore done at the Schema Master will overwrite the schema for the entire forest.

Keep this operation of the Schema Master in mind when you do tape restores. If you do not want to restore the schema, do your System State restore on another domain controller.

You should guard the local Administrator password on domain controllers closely and change it frequently, but be aware that utilities such as ERD Commander permit anyone with physical access to a domain controller to set the local Administrator password to get full access. You should take the following actions to guard your Active Directory database:

- Never give anyone but highly trusted administrators the right to back up or restore System State on domain controllers.
- Only back up the System State on a few selected domain controllers. The administrators performing this backup should be among the most trusted administrators in the organization.
- Do not permit physical access to domain controllers in remote locations. You should make these headless servers without floppy or CD drives.

Explain to other administrators that domain controllers are like routers. They are appliances controlled by a certain cadre of administrators.

Time Limit for Using Backup Tapes

It happens in every IT organization at one time or another. You need to do a tape restore and last night's tapes are either unreadable or the backup didn't run. You go back into the library and find that some of the tapes are so old you can see daylight though the oxide layer. And some of the good tapes got jammed up in the library robot assembly and didn't actually get anything written to them. You will eventually find a mountable tape, but it might be a week or two old. You then wonder if you can safely restore Active Directory from that tape.

The good news is that you can restore System State from a somewhat older tape without compromising Active Directory. As soon as you finish the System State restoration and restart the domain controller, the restored copy of Active Directory will obtain updates from its replication partners and get caught up to date. If you perform an authoritative restore, on the other hand, you will lose any changes such as password resets, group membership changes, new domain trusts, and so forth that happened in the meantime. Be very careful when using an older tape for an authoritative restore.

Tombstone Lifetime

This ability to use an older copy of Active Directory has two limits. The first limit is tied to the *tombstone lifetime* for deleted objects in Active Directory.

When an AD object is deleted, the ESE engine does a little Dante number on it. The object is stripped of all but a couple of attributes and hurled into the depths of the `Deleted Objects` container where it sits and rots for 60 days. At the end of 60 days—the standard tombstone lifetime—the object is removed completely from the database by the garbage collection process.

This means that you must not restore System State (and by inference, Active Directory) from a tape that is more than 60 days old. Let me give an example to show the risk.

Let's say you delete an object from AD and then perform a System State restore from last night's backup. As long as you do not do an authoritative restore of that object, it will be redeleted as soon as the domain controller pulls updates from its replication partners. The updates say, in effect, "This object is in my `Deleted Objects` container. Move your copy of the object to the `Deleted Objects` container, as well."

But, if you restore from a tape that is more than 60 days old, the replication partners will have removed some of the tombstoned objects from the `Deleted Objects` container. They then have no way to tell the newly restored domain controller to delete the old objects. The newly restored go into limbo. They are deleted on all replicas of the naming context except for the restored machine. This corrupts Active Directory.

Keep this 60-day window in mind if you have disaster recovery procedures that could potentially introduce an older copy of Active Directory into your system. For instance, do not make images of domain controllers for use in disaster recovery. The CD that holds the image stops being your best friend and starts being your worst nightmare on day 61 after it was burned. If you want to use imaging as a recovery strategy, take an image *before* you promote a server to a domain controller. Restore the image then promote the machine to a domain controller. This replicates a fresh copy of the Directory from another domain controller.

If you lose all copies of Active Directory during a catastrophe of some sort, your only alternative is to restore from the most recent tape you can find and deal with any changes that have been made in the interim, such as password changes or group membership changes.

Tombstone Lifetime Interval

The 60-day interval for tombstone lifetime and the 12-hour garbage collection interval are default settings in Active Directory. You can change these default values by adding attributes to the `cn=Directory Service, cn=Windows NT,cn=Services,cn=Configuration,dc=<domain_name>,dc=<root>` object. The two attributes are as follows:

- **`Tombstone Lifetime.`** Minimum setting is 2 days.
- **`Garbage Collection Interval.`** Minimum setting is 1 hour.

Use great caution when changing the tombstone lifetime. The value must be long enough to accommodate using an older System State tape backup. *It is very important that you never restore Active Directory from a tape that is older than the tombstone lifetime.*

Active Directory Restores and Trust Relationships

A second time limit also affects your ability to do System State restores from older tapes. If you have external trust relationships to other forests or NT domains, these trust relationships have passwords that change every 7 days. When a new password is negotiated, the old password is retained. For this reason, if you restore from a tape that is older than 14 days, you will need to verify the external trust relationships and force a renegotiation of the password. In the worst case, you must remove and re-install the trust.

Authoritative Restoration and Sysvol

The File Replication Service, or FRS, replicates the contents of Sysvol among all domain controllers in a domain. If you authoritatively restore the Group Policy Container (GPC) objects in Active Directory without returning Sysvol to the condition that existed when the System State backup was obtained, you risk a mismatch between the GPC objects in AD and the GPT files in Sysvol.

There is no such thing as an authoritative restore of Sysvol. Instead, you must restore a copy of the System State files, including the Sysvol files, to an alternative location and then copy them over the Sysvol files after you restart following an authoritative restore of the AD. To see how it works, take a look at Procedure 10.7.

Procedure 10.7 Performing an Authoritative Restore of Sysvol

1. Perform a standard System State restore to the original location. *Do not restart.*
2. Do a second System State restore to an alternate location. This retains the older Sysvol files so you can use them following restart.
3. Perform an authoritative restore of the AD objects or containers you want to recover. This list should include group policy related objects, otherwise there is no reason to include Sysvol in your recovery plans.

4. Restart the domain controller and ensure that the Sysvol contents get updated from the replication partners. This is very important. The contents of Sysvol must fully converge on all domain controllers before proceeding.
5. At the domain controller where you did the authoritative restore, copy the contents of Sysvol from the alternate location to the standard Sysvol location. This overwrites the existing files. You can also delete the `Policies` and the `Scripts` folders and copy them from the alternate location if you want to remove any GPT files.
6. Wait for the contents of Sysvol to converge on all domain controllers.
7. Verify that clients receive the correct group policies.

Restoring System State

When you restore the System State files, you overwrite the existing files on the machine. Many of these files are databases that are normally locked when the server is operating. This includes the Active Directory database, the Registry hives, the Certificate database, and others.

To do a System State restoration, then, you must boot the machine into a configuration where these databases are not running. This is done using *Directory Service Restore Mode*, one of the safe mode options in Windows. Select this option from a menu by pressing F8 at the standard boot menu. If you do not see a boot menu, press F8 as soon as the machine completes POST. This puts the keystroke in the keyboard buffer where it will be seen when NTLDR is activated.

The Directory Service Restore Mode option loads the network drivers so you can do a tape restore across the network but does not start Active Directory and other critical databases. This mode also sets the environment variable `SAFEBOOT_OPTION` to `DSREPAIR`. This variable must be set or Ntdsutil will not perform an authoritative restore.

Because Active Directory is not available when booting to Directory Services Restore Mode, you must provide the password for the Administrator account in the local SAM. This is the password you entered when you promoted the server to be a domain controller.

Changing the Restore Mode Password

If you forget the Restore Mode password, or if you inherit a server and you do not know the password that was originally entered during DCPROMO, you can change the password using a utility from SysInternals (www.sysinternals.com) called ERD Commander. There are two versions of this utility. The free version does not allow you to change the Administrator password. The for-fee version does.

You might want to do what I do to remember these sorts of passwords. I jot them down on a slip of paper and lock them inside the server case. I also tape up a screen print of the Disk Management console inside the case, as well, if another administrator needs to know the original partition layout if the machine crashes.

When you have logged on to the Safe mode console, perform a System State restoration as shown in Procedure 10.8.

Procedure 10.8 Performing a System State Restore

1. At the domain controller where you want to restore Active Directory, start the system in Directory Services Repair mode.
2. Insert the backup tape with the System State files.
3. Open the Run window and enter `Ntbackup`.
4. Select the `Restore` tab.
5. Expand the tree to show the drive and list of previously submitted jobs. When you expand the tree at the tape icon, you might need to wait a while for the tape to rewind. If you have a catalog on the disk, the system will compare the signature in the catalog to the signature on the tape. If you do not have a catalog on the disk, you will need to catalog the tape. Right-click the media and select CATALOG.
6. In the tree displayed by the tape catalog, place a check next to the `System State` option.
7. Click `Restore Now`. You are prompted with a message warning that the System State files will always overwrite the existing files unless restoring to an alternate location. I do not recommend restoring to an alternate location because too many files and too many variables are involved if you try to copy them by hand. Hold your breath and enable the system to overwrite where it wants.
8. Click `Yes` to acknowledge the message and proceed. The Restore Progress window opens and the tape drive or removable media begins responding.
9. When the restore is complete, click `Report` and review the log to make sure that all files were restored without error.
10. Close Notepad and return to the Restore Progress window. Click `Close` to finish the restore. You are prompted to shut down the system. *Do not restart.* Instead, click `No` to bypass the restart option and close the Backup program.

At this point, you have completed the System State restoration. If you do not need to restore individual objects or containers, you can restart the domain controller and let it replicate any changes that have occurred since the backup was run. If you want to restore individual components of the Directory, proceed to the next section.

Performing an Authoritative Directory Restoration

Because the authoritatively restored properties have higher PVNs than the replicas on other domain controllers, the properties replicate outward and overwrite other replicas. For this reason, an authoritative restore can result in lots of replication traffic.

Schedule it for after hours and pay particular attention to domain controllers at the wrong end of slow WAN links. When you're ready to start, follow Procedure 10.9.

Procedure 10.9 Performing an Authoritative Restore

1. Open a command session.
2. Run `Ntdsutil`.
3. From the `Ntdsutil:` prompt, enter `authoritative restore`. This opens the `authoritative restore:` prompt:

```
authoritative restore: ?

 ?                             - Show this help information
 Help                          - Show this help information
 Quit                          - Return to the prior menu
 Restore database              - Authoritatively restore entire database
 Restore database verinc %d    - ... and override version increase
 Restore object %s             - Authoritatively restore an object
 Restore object %s verinc %d   - ... and override version increase
 Restore subtree %s            - Authoritatively restore a subtree
 Restore subtree %s verinc %d  - ... and override version increase
```

4. Enter the option corresponding to the item you want to restore. You'll need to know the distinguished name of the item. For instance, if you want to restore a single object, enter `restore object cn=BigBoss,ou=Executives,dc=Company,dc=com`.
5. A message window opens prompting you to verify the action. Click `Yes` to begin the authoritative restore. An example output looks like this:

```
Opening DIT database..............Done.
The current time is 2001-10-29 19:59.32.
Most recent database update occurred at 2001-10-29 14:27.52.
Increasing version numbers by 100000.

Counting records that need updating...
Records found: 000001
Done.

Found 000001 records to update.
Updating records...
Successfully updated 000001 records.
Authoritative Restore completed successfully.
```

   If the restore does not complete successfully, you may have a corrupted database. Try doing a soft restore and then a hard repair (as described later in this chapter). Next, retry the authoritative restore. If it still refuses to work, try restoring from tape one more time. Next, try restoring at a different domain controller. Next, call Microsoft Support Services for advice.

6. Quit out of Ntdsutil and restart the domain controller. When it comes back online, manually force replication.

When the changes converge at all the domain controllers, you should see the restored objects in their original locations.

Performing Directory Maintenance

Active Directory is like any other database when it comes to needing attention. Sometimes it gets filled with gaps and needs compacting. Sometimes it gets messy and needs reindexing. Sometimes it gets corrupted and needs repair. And sometimes it gets completely zonked and needs restoration. The tool for doing most of this work is the NT Directory Service Utility, Ntdsutil.

For some of its work, Ntdsutil uses a set of canned instructions from another utility, ESENTUTL, the grandchild of the ESEUTIL database utility designed for Exchange. ESENTUTL has a number of switches for setting and controlling restoration and integrity checks. Ntdsutil presents these options in a menu. The two most commonly used options are as follows:

- Compacting and reindexing Active Directory
- Repairing the Active Directory database

Compacting the Active Directory Database

If you are an experienced Exchange 5.5 administrator, you know how fragile the old ESE database can be. The new-and-improved ESE engine in Active Directory does not require much attention. Every 12 hours, a garbage collection process runs that removes objects that have been tombstoned longer than 60 days. The garbage collector then defrags and compacts the database. There is no need to perform an offline defrag or a reindex.

If you perform an offline defrag using Ntdsutil, the utility compacts the database by copying the contents to a new copy of Ntds.dit in a temporary directory of your naming. You then either copy the new file over the old file or point the system at the new directory. The log files are no longer valid and can be ignored.

The only time you should need to do an offline defrag is when you want to recover disk space using Ntds.dit. The online defrag packs the database but does not release the disk space. To do an offline defrag, follow Procedure 10.10.

Procedure 10.10 Performing an Offline Defragmentation of Active Directory

1. Boot the domain controller to `DS Repair mode` and run `Ntdsutil`.
2. At the `Ntdsutil:` prompt, enter `files`. This opens the `file maintenance` prompt.
3. Enter `compact to <directory>` where `<directory>` is the name of the temporary directory to store the compacted Ntds.dit. An example of the result follows:

```
file maintenance: compact to c:\ntdstemp
Opening database [Current].
```

```
Creating dir: c:\ntdstemp
Using Temporary Path: C:\
Executing Command: C:\WindowsWindows\system32\esentutl.exe /d
"e:\Windows\NTDS\ntds.dit" /8
 /o /l"e:\Windows\NTDS" /s"e:\WindowsWindows\NTDS" /t"c:\temp\ntds.dit" /!10240 /p


Initiating DEFRAGMENTATION mode...
Database: e:\WindowsWindows\NTDS\ntds.dit
Log files: e:\Windows\NTDS
System files: e:\Windows\NTDS
Temp. Database: c:\temp\ntds.dit

                Defragmentation Status  ( % complete )

          0    10   20   30   40   50   60   70   80   90  100
          |----|----|----|----|----|----|----|----|----|----|
          ...................................................

Note:
  It is recommended that you immediately perform a full backup
  of this database. If you restore a backup made before the
  defragmentation, the database will be rolled back to the state
  it was in at the time of that backup.

Operation completed successfully in 22.172 seconds.
Spawned Process Exit code 0x0(0)
```

4. Copy the new Ntds.dit file to the original NTDS directory. If you want, you can leave the new directory where it is and redirect the Directory pointers:

```
Set Path Backup <directory>
Set path DB <directory>
Set path logs <directory>
Set path working dir <directory>
```

If you normally keep your logs on a different drive, you can leave that pointer alone.

Repairing the Active Directory Database

If the ESE engine encounters a problem caused by corrupted pages in the database or a corrupt index file or a combination of the two, you may need to repair the database. Symptoms of this kind of problem are Event log entries, console errors, or the machine might reboot with errors from the Local Security Authority Subsystem (LSASS).

Active Directory repair has two stages:

- **Soft recovery.** This stage rebuilds the database entries using the logs and checkpoint file and then rebuilds the indexes.

- **Hard repair.** This stage covers the same ground as the soft recovery but also deletes any corrupted pages. This can cause loss of data, so don't do a hard repair unless you have no other alternative. You should always get a backup of the Directory prior to performing any database repair.

Both of these stages require that you restart in Directory Services Restore mode. When you're ready, proceed as follows in Procedure 10.11.

Procedure 10.11 Performing a Soft Recovery of Active Directory

1. Open a console session.
2. Run `Ntdsutil`.
3. At the prompt, enter `files`. This opens the `file maintenance:` prompt.
4. Enter `recover`. An example output looks like this:

```
Executing Command: C:\Windows\system32\esentutl.exe /r /8 /o /l"e:\Windows\NTDS"
/s" e:\Windows\NTDS" /!10240Initiating RECOVERY mode...Log files:
e:\Windows\NTDSSystem files: e:\Windows\NTDS

Performing soft recovery...
Operation completed successfully in 6.985 seconds.
Spawned Process Exit code 0x0(0)

If recovery was successful, it is recommended
 you run semantic database analysis to insure
 semantic database consistency as well.
```

As you can see, this operation proceeds relatively painlessly as long as nothing is wrong with the database. If a problem is discovered, the system will attempt to fix it. You should then perform a Semantic Database Analysis from Ntdsutil to verify and/or repair the internal name links in the database.

If the results of the soft recovery indicate that a problem persists, you may need to perform a hard repair. Consider contacting Microsoft Product Support Services before proceeding. They may have other suggestions that are not as drastic. When you do need to perform a hard repair, follow Procedure 10.12.

Procedure 10.12 Performing a Hard Repair of Active Directory

1. In Ntdsutil, from the `file maintenance:` prompt, enter `repair`. An example output looks like this:

```
Opening database [Current].
Executing Command: C:\Windows\system32\esentutl.exe /p "e:\Windows\NTDS\ntds.dit"
➥/! 10240 /8 /v /x /o

Initiating REPAIR mode...
```

```
Database: e:\Windows\NTDS\ntds.dit
Temp. Database: REPAIR.EDB
got 3910 buffers
checking database header
forcing database to consistent state

checking database integrity
<<result of integrity check deleted for brevity>>

integrity check completed.
Warning:
You MUST delete the logfiles for this database

Note:
  It is recommended that you immediately perform a full backup
  of this database. If you restore a backup made before the
  repair, the database will be rolled back to the state
  it was in at that time of that backup.

Operation completed successfully in 4.336 seconds.
Spawned Process Exit code 0x0(0)
```

If a problem is encountered during the repair, the error is written to the Repair.txt file in the `\WindowsWindows\NTDS` directory where the Ntds.dit file resides. You should also check the Event log for any errors.

2. Perform a full backup of the System State files using the procedure outlined in the "Backing Up the Directory" section earlier in this chapter.

Moving Active Directory Support Files

When you promote a domain controller, you select where you want the main Active Directory file, Ntds.dit, and the log files. You can change this location if you decide that you need to improve performance by putting the logs on a different spindle or you want to get the files off the system partition, where they go by default.

To move the files, you must boot into Active Directory Restore mode. This requires that you know the local Administrator password, also called the Active Directory Restore password. You should always put the files on an NTFS partition to get security and good random access performance. When you are ready to move the files, follow Procedure 10.13.

Procedure 10.13 Changing Active Directory File Locations

1. Boot to `AD Restore Mode`.
2. Open a console session.
3. Run `Ntdsutil`.
4. Enter `files` to get to the `files maintenance` prompt. Enter `?` to get an option list:

```
file maintenance: ?

 ?                              - Show this help information
 Compact to %s                  - Compact DB to specified directory
 Header                         - Dump the Jet database header
 Help                           - Show this help information
 Info                           - Return information about DS files
 Integrity                      - Perform Jet integrity check
 Move DB to %s                  - Move DB to specified directory
 Move logs to %s                - Move log files to specified directory
 Quit                           - Return to the prior menu
 Recover                        - Perform soft database recovery
 Set path backup %s             - Set online backup directory path
 Set path DB %s                 - Set DB file path
 Set path logs %s               - Set logging directory path
 Set path working dir %s          - Set NTDS working directory path
```

5. Use the `move db to %s` or `move logs to %s` options to move the database or the logs. Replace `%s` with the full path name, such as `D:\Windows\NTDS`.

Moving Forward

This completes the coverage of Active Directory. We've seen how to plan, replicate, deploy, manage, and fix Active Directory in a variety of circumstances. Now we're ready to put it to use. The next few chapters cover distributed security, group policies, and Public Key Infrastructure, all of which depend on Active Directory to do their job.

11 Understanding Network Access Security and Kerberos

I USED TO BE MIS DIRECTOR FOR A company that ran telesales call centers. Every once in a while, a sales agent would get a prospect on the line with a network security background. How would I know? The prospect would ask questions like, "How do I know beyond a shadow of a doubt that you are who you say you are?" and "How do I know beyond a shadow of a doubt that you're permitted to sell this to me?" and "Do you mind if I record this call?"

These questions indicate that the prospect was familiar with the three pillars of network security:

- Authentication
- Authorization
- Accountability (Auditing)

In case you're wondering, the sales agents would generally react to these types of questions by hanging up and moving on to a less sophisticated prospect, proving that IT training really does have practical uses in the real world.

This chapter covers how Windows Server 2003 achieves the three A's of network security. Chapter 18, "Managing a Public Key Infrastructure," covers advanced security topics associated with Public Key Infrastructure (PKI).

New Features in Windows Server 2003

The new security features in Windows Server 2003 improve functionality and shore up some traditionally vulnerable areas. They include the following:

- **New Standard Accounts.** New Local Service and Network Service accounts remove some services from the highly privileged Local System security context.

These accounts also benefit Internet Information Services (IIS) by permitting a web site to be assigned to a non-privileged account.

- **Anonymous logons.** New handling for anonymous logons limit the vulnerability of Windows Server 2003 to NetBIOS service scanners. The Everyone group is no longer assigned to the access token of an anonymous connection.
- **Credential caching.** It is now possible to store alternate names and passwords to use when accessing servers that are not on the domain. This simplifies managing servers in a DMZ section of a firewall and other standalone servers.
- **Reduced traffic to PDC Emulator.** If a DC that is not the PDC Emulator receives improper credentials from a user, it caches the result locally to reduce traffic to the PDC Emulator. By default, the user is limited to 10 forwarded requests. From that point forward, the user is denied access based on the cached information for a period of 10 minutes.
- **Password reset handling.** In Windows 2000, an unauthorized password reset results in gaining access to the cryptographic elements on a machine, compromising encrypted files and secure email. Windows Server 2003 protects cryptographic structures from unauthorized changes to passwords.
- **Lost password handling.** A new *Password Reset Disk* feature enables you to regain access to a standalone server if the local password has been forgotten.
- **Realm trust simplification.** Windows Server 2003 has new methods for building transitive trusts to MITv5 Kerberos realms that simplify the work necessary to integrate open source realms and Windows domains.

Windows Server 2003 Security Architecture

It pays to have a solid map in your mind of how the various components of the Windows Server 2003 security system work together. This helps you design a secure system and diagnose problems when they arise. Figure 11.1 shows the major components of the security system, called the *Local Security Authority*, or LSA.

Here are a few items of note in the figure:

- Authentication is achieved via password-based transactions involving Kerberos or classic NT LanMan (NTLM) Challenge-Response. The security system also directly supports third-party mechanisms that do not rely on passwords, such as smart cards, and permits add-on mechanisms such as biometrics.
- Authorization is achieved by protecting resources with special data structures called *security descriptors* that identify who can access a resource and what they can do. All processes are identified by *access tokens* that define the security context of the user.
- Auditing is handled by special functions in the security system designed to log access to secured objects.

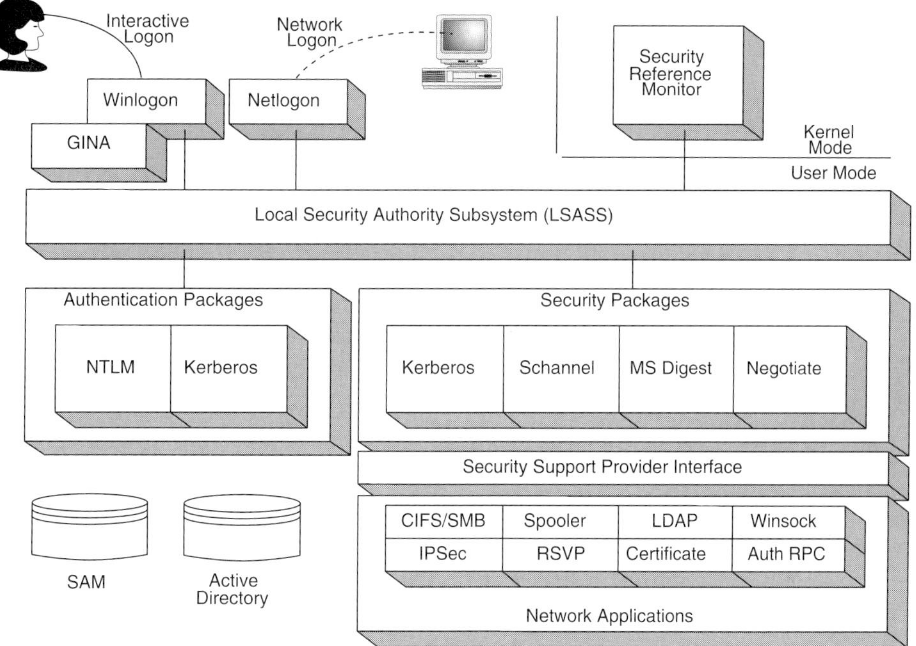

Figure 11.1 Local Security Authority functional diagram.

The LSA consists of kernel-mode services running as part of the Windows Executive and user-mode services that control client/server processes such as interactive logon and granting network access permissions. The user-mode security services in the LSA are contained in two executables: the *Local Security Authority Subsystem*, or LSASS, and Winlogon. LSASS hosts the following processes:

- **Kerberos KDC.** This service provides Kerberos authentication and ticket granting services. It uses Active Directory to store security credentials.
- **NTLM security support provider.** This service provides classic NT authentication and security management. It supports all downlevel clients and those modern Windows clients that are not members of a domain.
- **Security Account Manager.** This service is responsible for obtaining user credentials from the Security Account Manager (SAM) database in response to requests from the legacy NTLM provider.
- **Netlogon.** This service supports classic NT authentication by handling pass-through authentication from downlevel clients. Netlogon is not used to support Kerberos transactions. On Active Directory-based domain controllers, Netlogon is responsible for registering DNS records.

- **IPSec.** This service manages IP Security (IPSec) connection policies and IPSec Internet Key Exchange (IKE).
- **Protected Storage.** This service is responsible for encrypting and safely storing certificates associated with the PKI subsystem.

LSA Components

When you buy a stereo at Best Buy or Circuit City, you engage in a series of transactions with the sales clerk. The clerk takes your credit card, runs it through a machine that checks it against a database somewhere in the world, obtains your signature to document the sale, and bundles up your purchase for transport.

If you flowchart the little formalities of this purchase, you would identify the standard security elements: authentication, authorization, and auditing. Any one of these elements could be performed differently without affecting the others. For instance, if you present a check rather than a credit card, the authentication steps would expand to include a look at your driver's license.

When you access secure resources on a server, you encounter a similar set of security transactions. The services that manage these transactions are called *packages*. There are two package types: *authentication* packages and *security* packages.

Authentication Packages

As you might expect, an authentication package verifies your identity. Microsoft provides two authentication packages:

- **Kerberos.** A three-way authentication mechanism where a server uses a secret key issued by a trusted source to verify the identity of a client.
- **MSV1_0.** The legacy NT authentication package. This is often called a challenge-response authentication because it involves the transfer of an encrypted random number called a *challenge*. Windows Server 2003 supports LanMan (LM) Challenge-Response for DOS-origin clients (Windows 3.11, Windows 9x, and ME) and NT LanMan (NTLM) Challenge-Response for both NT clients and modern Windows clients that are not members of a domain.

Classic Security Databases

NTLM authentication stores security information in the Registry inside three databases:

- **Builtin.** This database contains the two default user accounts, Administrator and Guest, along with various default groups such as Domain Users for domains and Power User for workstations and standalone servers. The Administrator and Guest accounts cannot be deleted but they can be renamed. Builtin groups have special operating system privileges. They cannot be deleted or renamed. The Builtin accounts are contained in the SAM Registry hive.

- **Security Account Manager (SAM).** This database contains local user and group accounts. In classic NT, the SAM on a primary domain controller (PDC) defines the security entities in a domain. The SAM database is contained in the `SAM` Registry hive.
- **LSA.** This database contains the password rules, system policies, and trust accounts for the computer. The LSA database is contained in the `Security` Registry hive. This hive also contains a copy of the SAM database.

When you upgrade a classic PDC to Windows Server 2003, most of the contents of the Registry databases are migrated into Active Directory. System privileges and user rights defined by policies in the classic LSA database are replaced by a set of group policies stored in the Secedit.sdb database in `\Windows\Security\Database`.

Security Packages

A security package contains the protocols and features needed to manage credentials access, protect data, and secure message streams between clients and servers.

Security packages are also called a *Security Support Providers,* or SSPs. Applications that consume security services are not required to know the eccentricities of these providers. A single interface called the *Security Support Provider Interface*, or SSPI, abstracts the functions of the security providers. This is similar, in concept, to the way Open Database Connectivity (ODBC) abstracts access to databases and Network Device Interface Specification (NDIS) abstracts access to network cards.

Microsoft provides the following security packages in Windows Server 2003:

- **Kerberos.** Kerberos occupies a special position because it acts as both an authentication package and a security package. As a security package, it supports access by applications that are coded to present Kerberos tickets when they attempt access to resources. These are called *Kerberized* applications. An example would be the CIFS/SMB network file system service in Windows Server 2003 and Windows 2000. (SMB stands for Server Message Block, the command language used by Windows networking. CIFS stands for Common Internet File System, another term for SMB.)
- **NTLM.** This package supports connections by downlevel Windows clients and standalone Windows Server 2003, XP, and Windows 2000 machines.
- **Digest.** This is Microsoft's implementation of RFC 2617, "HTTP Authentication: Basic and Digest Access Authentication." The Digest package also includes support for the Digest authentication included in the *Simple Authentication and Security Layer* (SASL) protocol as defined in RFC 2831, "Using Digest Authentication as a SASL Mechanism." The new version of the Digest package in Windows Server 2003 permits using the MD4 password hash to encrypt the challenge, eliminating the need for reversible passwords.

- **Schannel.** This package contains the security protocols necessary to support private, protected web communications. This package contains the following security protocols: Transport Layer Security (TLS), Secure Sockets Layer (SSL), and Private Communications Technology (PCT).
- **Negotiate.** This pseudo-provider does not actually contain security protocols. Instead, it permits a client to discover the available security packages and to decide which one to use. For example, a Kerberized application calling Negotiate would be passed on to the Kerberos package.

In addition to the main security packages, Windows includes the following packages that are not included in Figure 11.1:

- Standard Digest authentication
- Clear text password authentication
- Distributed Password Authentication (for MSN support)
- Old-style MSN authentication

Winlogon

LSA needs some mechanism for obtaining logon credentials from users. The executable responsible for obtaining these credentials is Winlogon. You call up the services of Winlogon when you press `Ctrl+Alt+Del`, also known as the *Secure Attention Sequence (SAS)*.

This brings up a Security window, also controlled by Winlogon. If you have not yet logged on, the security window presents you with a place to enter your logon credentials. If you have already logged on, the Security window presents you with the option to logoff, shutdown, lock the computer, change your password, or open the Task Manager.

The windows presented by Winlogon come from a DLL called *Graphical Identification and Authentication* (GINA). Independent software vendors (ISVs) can write replacements or enhancements to the GINA to capture their own credentials. For example, Novell's Netware client installs a custom GINA that collects additional logon credentials for Novell Directory Services.

Security Reference Monitor (SRM)

If you think of a domain or a server as a castle that has authentication packages as gatekeepers, the Security Reference Monitor would be a contingent of bodyguards that protect individuals within the castle.

> **Registry Tip: Security Packages**
>
> The list of security support providers is located in `HKLM | System | CurrentControlSet | Control | SecurityProviders`.
>
> Control parameters for the LSA and its security support providers are contained in `HKLM | System | CurrentControlSet | Control | LSA`.

Windows provides discrete security for objects such as NTFS files/folders, Registry keys, Active Directory objects, printers, services, and kernel processes. It does so by linking each object to a special data structure called a *security descriptor*. The security descriptor contains an *access control list*, or ACL, that identifies the users, computers, and groups that are allowed access or denied access to the object.

When a user logs on, the LSASS builds an *access token* that represents the user to the security system. This token contains the user's security ID (SID) along with the SID for any groups that have the user as a member and a variety of security policy settings such as logon expiration time and password complexity requirements.

When a process owned by the user tries to touch a secure object, the Security Reference Monitor compares the SIDs in the security descriptor with the SIDs in the user's access token and derives a set of access permissions for the user.

Access tokens, like politics, are always local. They do not accompany users around the network. When a user connects to a server, the LSASS on that server must build a local access token representing the user so it can attach the token to the user's processes. The LSASS obtains the information it needs to build this local access token in one of two ways:

- For Kerberos authentication, it gets the information from the Authorization Data field inside the Kerberos session ticket presented by the client.
- For NTLM authentication, it gets the information from a domain controller as part of a pass-through authentication transaction.

It's important that the information used to build the access token be protected. If a bad guy could hijack an access token or otherwise compromise the mechanism that builds the access token, it doesn't matter if the authentication system is bulletproof; the bad guy still gets access.

Overview of LSA Operation

Let's pause here for a moment and take quick look at the cast of characters we've seen so far and how they fit into the three A's of authentication, authorization, and auditing:

1. Winlogon collects logon credentials from the user.
2. LSASS takes these credentials and uses them to validate the user's identity with the help of Kerberos or NTLM (via MSV1_0). This is the authentication stage.
3. LSASS builds an access token that defines the user's access permissions and system privileges.
4. The Security Reference Monitor (SRM) compares this token to the access control list (ACL) in an object's security descriptor to decide whether to give access to the user. This is the authorization stage.

5. Finally, LSASS and SRM work together to monitor access to security objects and build reports that record any or all of those access events. This is the auditing stage.

Now let's examine the fine points of these security components with an eye towards configuration options and potential vulnerabilities.

Security Components

Windows security relies on several fundamental elements. It's important to understand how each of these elements are derived and how they fit together. This gives you the basis for evaluating practical security options. This section covers these elements:

- Access tokens
- SIDs
- Security descriptors
- Access control lists
- Passwords

Access Tokens

The information in an access token essentially defines two P's:

- **Permissions.** The access token contains all necessary information for the system to evaluate which resources a user can touch and what the user can do with those resources.
- **Privileges.** The access token contains a list of rights that determine which core system functions the user can call upon. For instance, a user with `SeBackupPrivilege` is permitted to run processes that make use of the system backup functions.

Table 11.1 lists the contents of an access token. This gives you an idea of the information used by the system to make its security decisions.

Viewing Access Token Contents

If you want to know more about access tokens, I highly recommend the book *Programming Server-Side Applications for Windows 2000* by Jeffrey Richter and Jason D. Clark. Don't let the name fool you. Even if you never write a single line of code, this book is still worthwhile reading. The book comes with a CD that has several handy tools. One of these, Tokenmaster, displays the contents of the access token for any process running on a server.

Table 11.1 Access Token Contents and Functions

Content	Function
User's SID	The security system identifies users by number rather than by name, much the same as the Social Security Administration. The SID is a combination of the Relative ID (RID) assigned to the user and the SID of the domain or (in the case of local logons) the computer.
Group SIDs	The SID for each group that has the user as a member. This includes domain groups and groups on the local machine where the user logs on.
Logon SID	A unique and temporary SID that represents an individual logon session. If a user makes multiple connections to a server, such as from different machines, each session gets a different logon SID.
User privileges	These are system privileges such as the ability to change the system time, to do a backup, and so forth.
Default owner SID	This SID is used to mark the ownership of any security objects created by the user. Except for members of the Administrators group, this SID matches the user's SID. For members of the Administrators group, this SID matches the SID of the Administrators group.
Default group SID	Useful only for POSIX and Services for Macintosh (SFM), this SID matches the primary group SID selected in the user's account attributes.
Default DACL	Every system object has a security descriptor that contains a Discretionary ACL, or DACL. The DACL defines who can access the object and what they can do. If the process that creates an object does not specify the contents of the DACL, the system uses this default DACL.
Originating Process	The name of the system process that created the access token.
Token type	When a user logs on from the console, she gets a primary access token. A user logging on across the network gets an impersonation access token.
Impersonation level	There are four impersonation levels. Anonymous (no client information available), Identification (client identified but not impersonated), Impersonation (client identified and able to run local processes but not able to connect to other machines), and Delegation (client process can connect to other machines—requires Kerberos authentication).
Restrictive SIDs	This feature, introduced in Windows 2000, enables a developer to block a user's privileges without modifying the user's group membership.

Permissions

When a user process touches an object, the Security Reference Monitor matches up SIDs in the access token with SIDs in the object's Access Control List (ACL). There are two possibilities:

- If there is no match, the user is denied access. This is called *implicit deny*.
- If there is a match, the user is given the permissions associated with the entry in the ACL. This could be an `Allow` permission or a `Deny` permission.

For example, the `Allow Read` permission assigned to SID S-1-1-0 (Everyone) would give any user permission to read the contents of a security object. A `Deny Read` permission assigned to SID `S-1-5-2` (Network Users), on the other hand, would deny access to users who connect to the server across the network.

If a user were a member of both the Everyone and the Network Users groups in this example, the user would be denied Read access because `Deny` permissions take precedence over `Allow` permissions if both permissions have been directly assigned to the object. (Later, we'll see that inherited permissions are treated a little differently.)

SIDs

A typical user SID looks like this: `S-1-5-21-1683771067-1221355100-624655392-1001`. The format follows this pattern: `S-R-IA-SA-SA-RID`. Here are the terms and their functions:

- `S` represents a *SID identifier*. This flags the number as a SID rather than some other kind of long, obscure number.
- `R` represents the *Revision*. All SIDs generated by Windows use a revision level of `1`.
- `IA` represents the *issuing authority*. Nearly all SIDs in Windows specify the NT Authority, ID number `5`, as the issuing authority. Exceptions include SIDs that represent well-known groups and accounts.
- `SA` represents a *sub-authority*. The SA designates special groups or functions. For example, `21` indicates that the SID was issued by a domain controller or standalone machine. The long number, `1683771067-1221355100-624655392`, is the SA for the issuing domain or machine.
- `RID` is the *Relative ID*, a unique, sequential number assigned by the issuing SA to represent a security principal such as a user, computer, or group.

Functions of SIDs

If you're new to Windows system administration, this business of SIDs and RIDs might seem like geek-level stuff that no one really cares about. Nothing could be further from the truth. Understanding how SIDs are generated, stored, and manipulated is absolutely vital to managing a Windows system.

For instance, after you know that the system relies on the SID to uniquely identify a user, you won't be surprised that you can change a user's name without affecting the user's access permissions. You can take advantage of this in situations where a new user joins the company to replace a user who has left. You can simply rename the old user's account to the new user's name and retain the old account's access permissions and group memberships.

Knowing how the system uses SIDs also helps you to plan for moving accounts from one domain to another when you migrate an NT or Windows 2000 domain to a Windows Server 2003 domain. For example, when you copy a user account from one domain to another using the Active Directory Migration Tool (or a third-party equivalent), the user's SID in the classic NT domain is retained in a special `SID History` attribute so that the user can still access resources in the old domain when logged on to the new domain.

Well-Known SIDs

Not all SIDs represent specific user, group, and computer accounts. Certain SIDs have been set aside by Microsoft to represent standard accounts and groups. These are called *well-known SIDs*. For example, if you log on at the console of a Windows machine, your access token is assigned the SID `S-1-5-4`, which is the well-known SID for the Interactive group.

Table 11.2 lists the well-known SIDs and their functions. The UI displays accounts and groups represented by well-known SIDs with a special icon that includes a small red up-arrow.

New Well-Known SIDS

In classic NT and Windows 2000, the Local System account, SID `S-1-5-18`, provides the security context for nearly all services. This account is highly privileged and using it for common services represents a security vulnerability.

Windows Server 2003 attempts to minimize this vulnerability by introducing two additional well-known SIDS that provide a security context for services: *LocalService* and *NetworkService*.

There are two major advantages to using standard accounts to run services rather than Local System. First, these accounts have a SID and therefore can present Kerberos or NTLM credentials when accessing resources on other servers. The Local System account cannot do this and must use an anonymous logon session to access network resources.

The second advantage involves Public Key Infrastructure (PKI). The new service accounts each have a local profile and can therefore obtain PKI certificates. This helps identify the services if you implement digital signing in your system, such as for IPSec or secure email.

If you scan the list of services on Windows Server 2003 using Task Manager, you'll see that the two new service accounts own only a few of the background processes. Still, it's a start. They are especially valuable for IIS, where they are used to control access to the worker processes that own web sites.

Table 11.2 Well-Known SIDs and Their Functions

SID	Function
S-1-0-0	A memberless group used to represent an account with no known SID. This is also called a null session SID. Windows Server 2003 severely curtails the circumstances where a null session SID can be used to access resources.
S-1-1-0	This is the World SID, known in Windows as the Everyone group. All users except anonymous users get this SID in their access token.
S-1-2-0	The Local group. This group identifies users who have physically logged on to the console of a computer.
S-1-3-0	The Creator/Owner group. This acts as a placeholder in ACLs. It is replaced with the SID of the actual creator-owner when the security descriptor is enumerated. For instance, if user bbrown created a folder that has SID S-1-3-0 on the ACL, this entry would be replaced with bbrown's SID when she accesses the object.
S-1-3-1	The Primary group. This is another placeholder SID. It is replaced with the user's primary group when it appears on an ACL. Primary groups only have meaning to POSIX and Services for Macintosh. The default primary group for users of a standalone machine is Users. The default primary group for users in a domain is Domain Users.
S-1-5	The NT Authority.
S-1-5-1	Dial-up.
S-1-5-2	Network.
S-1-5-3	Batch.
S-1-5-4	Interactive.
S-1-5-5-#-#	Session Logon ID.
S-1-5-6	Service.
S-1-5-7	Anonymous Logon. Assigned to any user who does not present credentials when accessing a system.
S-1-5-8	Proxy (not used).
S-1-5-9	Enterprise Controllers. Includes all domain controllers in an Active Directory forest.
S-1-5-10	Self. A placeholder for a user identified by a specific SID in an access token.
S-1-5-11	Authenticated user. Added in NT4 SP3 to differentiate users who have received network authentication from the S-1-1-0 Everyone group.
S-1-5-12	Reserved for future use.
S-1-5-13	Terminal server users.

SID	Function
`S-1-5-18`	Local System. Provides a security context for system processes.
`S-1-5-19`	Local Service (new in Windows Server 2003). Provides a less privileged security context for services that control local processes.
`S-1-5-20`	Network Service (new in Windows Server 2003). Provides a less privileged security context for services that control network access.
`S-1-5-21`	Non-unique RIDs. Used as a prefix to domain and workstation SIDs.
`S-1-5-32`	Builtin Local groups. Identifies members of the Builtin database in the SAM (or Builtin container in Active Directory). This includes groups such as Administrators and Power Users.

Well-Known RIDs

RIDs assigned to users, computers, and groups start at 1000. A set of RIDs between 500 and 999 is set aside to represent accounts and groups that every Windows computer and domain have in common. These are called *well-known RIDs*.

Some well-known RIDs are appended to a domain SID to form a unique identifier. Others are appended to the Builtin SID, `S-1-5-32`, indicating that they are Builtin accounts that may have special privileges hard-coded into the operating system or assigned in the security database.

You can use these well-known accounts and groups to control access to resources. For instance, let's say a user who shares a computer wants to limit access to certain files on her local drive to users who share the computer. She could place the Network group on the ACL for the files with `Deny Full Control` permissions. This blocks access to any user who connects to her machine across the network while retaining access for users who log on at the console.

Table 11.3 lists the well-known RIDs and their functions. Domain SIDs are represented by an ellipsis `<...>`. The last few entries on the list are new well-known RIDs in Windows Server 2003.

Table 11.3 Well Known RIDs and Their Function

RID	Function
`S-1-5-<...>-500`	Administrator account.
`S-1-5-<...>-501`	Guest account.
`S-1-5-<...>-502`	KRBTGT, the account used to encrypt Kerberos ticket-granting tickets.
`S-1-5-<...>-512`	Domain admins.
`S-1-5-<...>-513`	Domain users.

continues ▸

Table 11.3 continued

RID	Function
S-1-5-<...>-514	Domain guests.
S-1-5-<...>-515	Domain computers.
S-1-5-<...>-516	Domain controllers.
S-1-5-<...>-517	Cert publishers.
S-1-5-<...>-518	Schema admins. This SID is on the ACL for the Schema container. Users assigned this SID have read/write/create permission for objects in the Schema.
S-1-5-<...>-519	Enterprise admins. This SID is on the ACL for the Configuration container and every Domain container in a forest. Users assigned this SID have full control permissions for all objects in those containers.
S-1-5-<...>-520	Group policy creator owners. This SID is on the ACL for the `cn=Policies,cn=System` container in each domain. Users assigned this SID have the ability to create new group policy containers.
S-1-5-<...>-533	RAS and IAS servers. This SID is on the RAS and IAS Servers Access Check container. Servers assigned this SID can verify user and group information in Active Directory.
S-1-5-32-544	Administrators.
S-1-5-32-545	Users.
S-1-5-32-546	Guests.
S-1-5-32-547	Power users.
S-1-5-32-548	Account operators.
S-1-5-32-549	Server operators.
S-1-5-32-550	Print operators.
S-1-5-32-551	Backup operators.
S-1-5-32-552	Replicators.
S-1-5-32-553	RAS servers.
S-1-5-32-554	Pre-Windows 2000 Compatible Access.
S-1-5-32-555	Remote desktop users (new in Windows Server 2003).
S-1-5-32-556	Network configuration operators (new in Windows Server 2003).
S-1-5-32-557	Incoming forest trust builders (new in Windows Server 2003).
S-1-5-32-558	Performance monitor users (new in Windows Server 2003).
S-1-5-32-559	Performance log users (new in Windows Server 2003).

Security Descriptors and Access Control Lists

As system administrators, we're faced every day with access management decisions. It's important to understand how the system implements our decisions so we can be sure that users don't get inappropriate permissions.

All NT-derived Windows platforms use a similar method for controlling access to security objects like files, folders, Registry keys, Active Directory objects, and services. Each of these security objects has a special data structure called a *security descriptor*. Figure 11.2 shows a block diagram of the six components of a security descriptor:

- **Header.** This describes the contents of the security descriptor. It also contains a control structure that defines whether the object can inherit permissions from the security descriptor of its parent.
- **Owner SID.** Except for administrators, the owner of an object is the user who created it. Objects created by any member of the Administrators Builtin group are assigned the Administrators group as the owner.
- **Primary group SID for the owner.** This identification is used for POSIX and Macintosh support only.

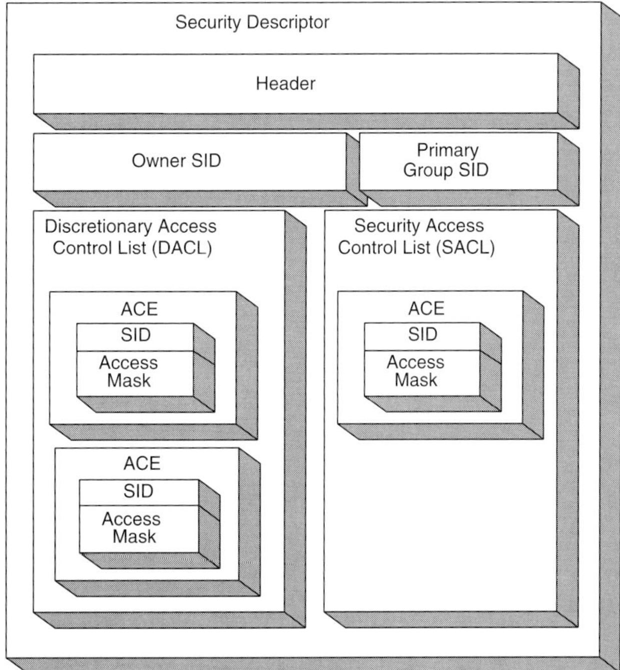

Figure 11.2 Block diagram of security descriptor.

- **Discretionary access control list (DACL).** This list defines the security principals who have been granted access or denied access to the object. The "discretionary" in DACL means that owners and administrators can make changes to the list.
- **System access control list (SACL).** This list defines users who will be logged by the auditing system when they access or fail to access an object. The ability to modify a SACL should be strictly controlled to prevent a bad guy from disabling auditing while he does dirty deeds.

Access Control Entries

An access control list contains one or more *access control entries* (ACEs). An ACE consists of two parts:

- A SID representing a security principal
- An access mask defining permissions for that security principal

Table 11.4 and Table 11.5 list the access permissions associated with each access mask entry. The system evaluates these bits differently depending on the type of security object. This information is important when you use tools or scripts that expose a security descriptor without interpreting the contents.

```
FILE_READ_DATA            0x1
FILE_WRITE_DATA           0x2
FILE_APPEND_DATA          0x4
FILE_READ_EA              0x8
FILE_WRITE_EA             0x10
FILE_EXECUTE              0x20
FILE_READ_ATTRIBUTES      0x80
FILE_WRITE_ATTRIBUTES     0x100
READ_CONTROL              0x20000
SYNCHRONIZE                 0x100000
```

Table 11.4 Access Masks and Their Functions

Generic Access Masks	
Mask	**Function**
0x10000	Delete (applies to entire object, including security descriptor)
0x20000	Read_Control (read security descriptor)
0x40000	Write_Dac (modify security descriptor)
0x80000	Write_Owner (change ownership)
0x100000	Synchronize (process level permission)

Table 11.5 Specialized Access Masks

Mask	File	Folders	Registry Keys	Active Directory Objects	Service Objects
0x1Read_Data	List_Directory	Query_Value	Create_Child	Query_Config	
0x2Write_Data	Add_File	Set_Value	Delete_Child	Change_Config	
0x4Append_Data	Add_Subdirectory	Create_Subkey	Actrl_DS_List	Query_Status	
0x8Read_EA	Read_EA	Enumerate_Subkey	Self	Enumerate_Dependencies	
0x10	Write_EA	Write_EA	Notify	Read_Properties	Start
0x20	Execute	Traverse	Create_Link	Write_Properties	Stop
0x40	N/A	Delete_Child	N/A	Delete_Tree	Pause/Continue
0x80	Read_Attributes	Read_Attributes	N/A	List_Object	Interrogate
0x100	Write_Attributes	Write_Attributes	N/A	Control_Access	User_Defined_Control

The access mask in an ACE is the sum of all the permissions assigned to the user identified in the ACE. Here's an example of how this works. Let's say you give the Administrators local group (SID `S-1-5-32-544`) permission to read and execute a file. The ACE mask associated with that entry would be the sum of these elements:

The access mask in the ACE for this entry would be `1021BF`. When the ACL Editor displays the entry, it calculates the constituent permissions and displays them to you.

Viewing and Modifying ACEs

The `Security` tab of an object's Properties window displays an *ACL Editor*. The ACL Editor shows several different views of the security descriptor. The first view, displayed in Figure 11.3, shows a consolidated list of ACEs and their generic access permissions.

If non-generic permissions have been assigned to an ACE, the permissions list shows a checkmark in the `Special Permissions` block.

If you click the `Advanced` button, you'll see a more detailed view of the security descriptor. Figure 11.4 shows an example.

This view lists each ACE on the DACL and the permissions assigned to it. If you highlight an entry and click `Edit`, the ACL Editor lists the full set of permissions for the ACE as shown in Figure 11.5. If an ACE has been assigned multiple individual permissions, you must use the Edit window to view the specific permissions.

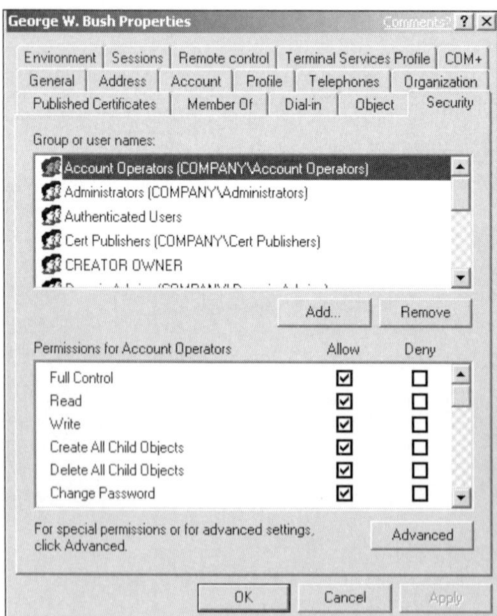

Figure 11.3 Security properties for a user object in Active Directory.

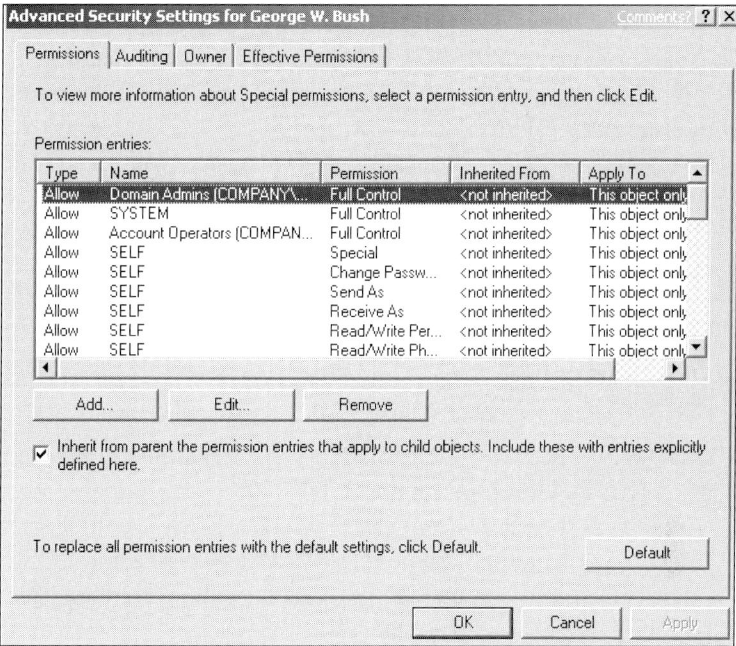

Figure 11.4 Advanced security descriptor view of an Active Directory user object.

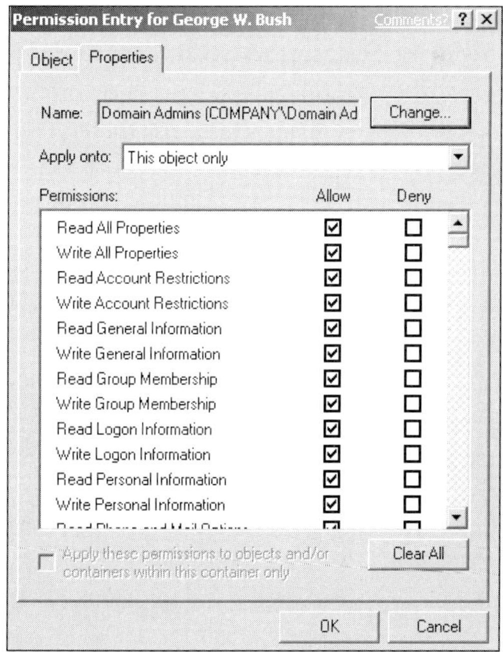

Figure 11.5 Properties view of a security descriptor.

Managing Object Ownership

The Advanced view of the ACL Editor has an Owner tab that displays the name of the user who created the object. Objects created by an administrator are assigned the Administrators local group as the owner.

If you have the Take Ownership system privilege, you can replace an object's current owner with your account. Because an object's owner has full access to any of the object's properties, the Take Ownership privilege should never be given to average users.

You cannot *transfer* ownership to another user using the ACL Editor. There are several command-line tools available for transferring ownership:

- **SUBINACL.** This tool is in the Resource Kit. The syntax for transferring ownership is: subinacl /file <*file_name*> /setowner=<*account_name*>.
- **CHOWN.** The Resource Kit has a CHOWN utility as part of the POSIX suite of tools. It requires running the POSIX subsystem, which is not supplied in Windows Server 2003. (You can purchase a POSIX-compliant package called Interix from Microsoft. Some references suggest avoiding POSIX because it was not included in the evaluation that certified the operating system's Common Criteria compliance.) The syntax is chown <*owner*> <*file*>. This utility does not permit transferring ownership to a group. If you need that function, take a look at the CHOWN utility that comes in the Services for UNIX (SFU) toolkit. SFU tools cost over $300, making it a fairly expensive option.

Managing Security Descriptors with Command-Line Tools

The ACL Editor is the most flexible way to view and modify the contents of a security descriptor, but there are many situations where a command-line tool is more useful. For instance, you may want to modify the permissions of an object using a script or a batch file or you may only have Telnet access or a remote shell connection to a server.

You have a variety of command-line tools at your disposal to view and modify the contents of a security descriptor. I've broken them down by object class: services, Active Directory objects, and NTFS files and folders.

Services

You can use SUBINACL to view and modify the security descriptor for a service. (The Resource Kit documentation lists a utility called SVCACLS for setting permissions on service security descriptors, but this utility was pulled from the product because the features were duplicated in SUBINACL.) Here is an example SUBINACL listing for the LanMan Workstation service:

```
C:\>subinacl /service lanmanworkstation

============================
```

```
+Service lanmanworkstation
===========================
/owner              =system
/primary group      =system
/audit ace count    =1
/aace =everyone          SYSTEM_AUDIT_ACE_TYPE-0x2
        FAILED_ACCESS_ACE_FLAG-0x80    FAILED_ACCESS_ACE_FLAG-0x0x80
        SERVICE_ALL_ACCESS
/perm. ace count    =4

/pace =authenticated users      ACCESS_ALLOWED_ACE_TYPE-0x0
        SERVICE_QUERY_CONFIG-0x1            SERVICE_QUERY_STATUS-0x4
        ➥SERVICE_ENUMERATE_DEPEND-0x8
        SERVICE_INTERROGATE-0x80            READ_CONTROL-0x20000
        ➥SERVICE_USER_DEFINED_CONTROL-0x0100

/pace =builtin\power users      ACCESS_ALLOWED_ACE_TYPE-0x0
        SERVICE_QUERY_CONFIG-0x1            SERVICE_QUERY_STATUS-0x4
        ➥SERVICE_ENUMERATE_DEPEND-0x8
        SERVICE_START-0x10                  SERVICE_INTERROGATE-0x80
        ➥READ_CONTROL-0x20000                 SERVICE_USER_DEFINED_CONTROL-0x0100

/pace =builtin\administrators   ACCESS_ALLOWED_ACE_TYPE-0x0
        SERVICE_ALL_ACCESS

/pace =system   ACCESS_ALLOWED_ACE_TYPE-0x0
        SERVICE_QUERY_CONFIG-0x1            SERVICE_QUERY_STATUS-0x4
        ➥SERVICE_ENUMERATE_DEPEND-0x8
        SERVICE_START-0x10                  SERVICE_STOP-0x20
        ➥SERVICE_PAUSE_CONTINUE-0x40          SERVICE_INTERROGATE-0x80
        READ_CONTROL-0x20000                  SERVICE_USER_DEFINED_CONTROL-0x0100
```

Active Directory Objects

For Active Directory objects, you can use a utility called DSACLS from the Resource Kit to view the contents of an Active Directory object's security descriptor. Here is partial DSACLS listing for the domain object `Company.com`:

```
C:\>dsacls dc=company,dc=com
Access list:
Effective Permissions on this object are:
Allow Everyone                                    SPECIAL ACCESS
                                                  READ PROPERTY
Allow NT AUTHORITY\Authenticated Users            SPECIAL ACCESS
                                                  READ PERMISSONS
                                                  LIST CONTENTS
                                                  READ PROPERTY
                                                  LIST OBJECT
Allow COMPANY\Domain Admins                       SPECIAL ACCESS
                                                  READ PERMISSONS
                                                  WRITE PERMISSIONS
                                                  CHANGE OWNERSHIP
```

```
                                                  CREATE CHILD
                                                  LIST CONTENTS
                                                  WRITE SELF
                                                  WRITE PROPERTY
                                                  READ PROPERTY
                                                  LIST OBJECT
                                                  CONTROL ACCESS
Allow BUILTIN\Administrators                      SPECIAL ACCESS
                                                  DELETE
                                                  READ PERMISSONS
                                                  WRITE PERMISSIONS
                                                  CHANGE OWNERSHIP
                                                  CREATE CHILD
                                                  LIST CONTENTS
                                                  WRITE SELF
                                                  WRITE PROPERTY
                                                  READ PROPERTY
                                                  LIST OBJECT
                                                  CONTROL ACCESS
Allow NT AUTHORITY\SYSTEM                         FULL CONTROL
Allow COMPANY\Enterprise Admins                      FULL CONTROL
```

NTFS File and Folders

To view the contents of the security descriptor for an NTFS file or folder, you can use the CACLS or XCACLS utilities. XCACLS has more options and comes in the Support Tools. You can also use the SUBINACL utility from the Resource Kit. Of the three utilities, XCACLS is the handiest but SUBINACL has the most features. For a read-only tool, there is also SHOWACLS from the Resource Kit.

Here is an example XCACLS listing for a file that has three ACEs—Authenticated Users, Administrators, and the well-known SID for the Interactive group:

```
C:\test>xcacls test.txt
C:\test\test.txt NT AUTHORITY\Authenticated Users:R

                 BUILTIN\Administrators:(OI)(CI)F

                 NT AUTHORITY\INTERACTIVE:(OI)(CI)(special access:)
                                                  READ_CONTROL
                                                  SYNCHRONIZE
                                                  FILE_GENERIC_READ
                                                  FILE_GENERIC_WRITE
                                                  FILE_GENERIC_EXECUTE
                                                  FILE_READ_DATA
                                                  FILE_WRITE_DATA
                                                  FILE_APPEND_DATA
                                                  FILE_READ_EA
                                                  FILE_WRITE_EA
                                                  FILE_EXECUTE
                                                  FILE_READ_ATTRIBUTES
                                                     FILE_WRITE_ATTRIBUTES
```

Here's a SUBINACL listing for the same file. As you can see, you get a lot more information, perhaps more than you really want:

```
C:\test>subinacl /file test3.txt

========================
+File C:\test\test.txt
========================
/owner             =builtin\administrators
/primary group     =cx612097-b\none
/audit ace count   =0
/perm. ace count   =3

/pace =builtin\administrators   ACCESS_ALLOWED_ACE_TYPE-0x0
        CONTAINER_INHERIT_ACE-0x2      OBJECT_INHERIT_ACE-0x1
    Type of access:
        Full Control
    Detailed Access Flags :
        FILE_READ_DATA-0x1           FILE_WRITE_DATA-0x2          FILE_APPEND_
        ➥DATA-0x4
        FILE_READ_EA-0x8             FILE_WRITE_EA-0x10           FILE_EXECUTE-0x20
        ➥FILE_DELETE_CHILD-0x40
        FILE_READ_ATTRIBUTES-0x80    FILE_WRITE_ATTRIBUTES-0x100 DELETE-0x10000
        ➥READ_CONTROL-0x20000
        WRITE_DAC-0x40000            WRITE_OWNER-0x80000          SYNCHRONIZE-
        ➥0x100000

/pace =authenticated users      ACCESS_ALLOWED_ACE_TYPE-0x0
    Type of access:
        Read
    Detailed Access Flags :
        FILE_READ_DATA-0x1           FILE_READ_EA-0x8             FILE_EXECUTE-0x20
        FILE_READ_ATTRIBUTES-0x80    READ_CONTROL-0x20000         SYNCHRONIZE-
        ➥0x100000

/pace =interactive      ACCESS_ALLOWED_ACE_TYPE-0x0
        CONTAINER_INHERIT_ACE-0x2      OBJECT_INHERIT_ACE-0x1
    Type of access:
        Special acccess :  -Read  -Write  -Execute
    Detailed Access Flags :
        FILE_READ_DATA-0x1           FILE_WRITE_DATA-0x2          FILE_APPEND_
        ➥DATA-0x4
        FILE_READ_EA-0x8             FILE_WRITE_EA-0x10           FILE_EXECUTE-0x20
        ➥FILE_READ_ATTRIBUTES-0x80
        FILE_WRITE_ATTRIBUTES-0x100 READ_CONTROL-0x20000          SYNCHRONIZE-
        ➥0x100000
```

Scripting and Security Descriptors

If you decide that you need to modify security descriptors in your scripts, you'll need lots of references and examples.

I highly recommend the book *ADSI Scripting for NT/Windows 2000 System Administrators* by Tom Eck for example scripts and a very clear explanation of security descriptor operations.

You should also consider purchasing third-party COM objects to simplify security descriptor operations. Take a look at the Ntsec library at `www.pedestalsoftware.com/ntsec`.

Windows Server 2003 includes new standard API calls that simplify security descriptor operations. Review the details on these new function calls in the Platform SDK, downloadable from `www.microsoft.com` or available in the MSDN library.

Access Permission Evaluation

We have finally arrived at the nitty-gritty of Windows authorization, the mechanism used by the system to determine whether or not to grant access for a particular object to a user. When a user process accesses a security object, the Security Reference Monitor (SRM) scans the DACL in the object's security descriptor looking for any SIDs that match SIDs in the user's access token.

When the SRM encounters a match, it evaluates the permissions in the ACE mask against the permissions requested by the process presenting the access token. If one of the permissions matches, the entire access mask is extracted from the ACE and added to a consolidated access mask for the user process.

If a user is granted permission by an ACE, that particular permission is not evaluated again. Keep this in mind as we trace an evaluation transaction. If a user is not explicitly granted access permissions by any ACE in a DACL, the user is denied access. This is called *implicit deny*.

Cumulative Allow Permissions

Permissions granted by Allow ACEs are cumulative—that is, permissions granted to the same user by different ACEs are collected together to form a single set of access permissions. Here's an example of how the system evaluates Allow ACEs to achieve this cumulative permission set.

Consider a process owned by user Jane. A thread from this process opens a file for `Read` and `Write` access. Jane has two ACEs in the DACL for the file, one with an `Allow Write` access mask and one with an `Allow Read` access mask. The thread has Jane's access token attached. When the thread attempts to access the file object, the SRM scans the file's DACL and finds an ACE containing Jane's SID.

Assigning `Allow` and `Deny` Permissions

Each ACE in a DACL is classified as an *Allow ACE* or a *Deny ACE*. This means you cannot mix `Allow` permissions and `Deny` permissions in the same access mask.

If you use the ACL Editor to check permissions in both the Allow and Deny columns for a single security principal, the editor creates two separate ACEs, one for the `Deny` permissions and one for the `Allow` permissions.

The SRM compares the permissions requested by the thread (`Read` and `Write`) with the permissions in the access mask of the ACE (`Read_Data`) and finds a match on the `Read` permission in the `Allow` ACE.

Because there is a SID match and a permissions match, the SRM adds the access mask in the ACE to a consolidated access mask for the thread and continues scanning the DACL.

It then encounters the second ACE with Jane's SID. During the permission comparison, it determines that the `Write` permission requested by the thread matches the `Write_Data` permission in the access mask for the `Allow` ACE. The SRM adds the access mask to the consolidated mask and continues scanning.

Because Jane has not been explicitly granted `Allow` permissions for any other permission, the final contents of the consolidated mask gives the thread `Write` and `Read` access to the file but nothing else.

Evaluation of Deny Permissions

`Deny` permissions take precedence over `Allow` permissions. Let's change the example a bit to see how. In the new example, a `Deny` ACE has been added for the `Write` permission.

When the thread owned by Jane touches the file, the SRM begins scanning the DACL and encounters an ACE containing Jane's SID. During the permission comparison, the SRM finds a match between the requested permissions (`Read` and `Write`) and the `Write_Data` permission in the access mask for the `Deny` ACE.

Because there is a SID match and a permissions match, the SRM adds the `Deny` access mask for `Write_Data` to a consolidated access mask for the thread and continues scanning the DACL.

The SRM then encounters a second ACE with Jane's SID. During the permissions comparison, it determines that the `Read` permission requested by the thread matches the `Read_Data` permission in the access mask for the `Allow` ACE. The SRM adds the `Read_Data` access mask to the consolidated mask and continues scanning.

The SRM then encounters a third ACE with Jane's SID. During the permissions comparison, it determines that the `Write` permission requested by the thread has already been evaluated in a previous ACE. It takes no further action and resumes scanning. Remember, once a permission has been assigned, it is not evaluated again.

Based on the final contents of the consolidated mask, the thread representing Jane gets `Read` access. She was explicitly denied `Write` access and all other permissions are implicitly denied.

It's important to note that the precedence of `Deny` over `Allow` relies on two key operational features:

- `Deny` ACEs are sorted to appear before `Allow` ACEs in a DACL. This is called *canonical sorting*.
- After the SRM has evaluated a permission, that particular permission is not evaluated again.

Windows automatically sorts ACEs in canonical order, but it plays favorites. Try an experiment. Open the Advanced view of the ACL Editor on a file object. This view lists the ACEs in the order they are evaluated by the SRM. Figure 11.6 shows an example of a user in an OU that sits three levels deep in Active Directory. Each OU has an administrative group assigned to it, so the user object ends up inheriting all three groups.

In the Advanced view of the ACL Editor, find a column labeled `Inherited From`. You'll notice that inherited ACEs are grouped below the directly applied ACEs in the list. This means that directly applied ACEs take precedence over inherited ACEs. The reason for this, and the mechanisms underlying permission inheritance, are explained in the next section.

Permissions inheritance makes it possible to quickly and easily modify the permissions of very large structures without actually modifying the security descriptor of every element in that structure. Inheritance also overcomes a problem in classic NT where an update to an ACL for a directory high in a structure would overwrite the ACLs in all the security descriptors underneath.

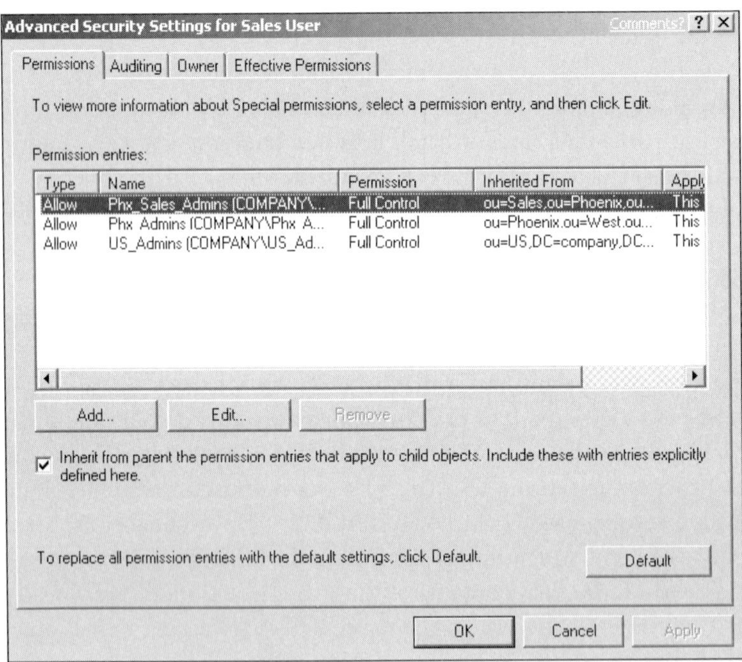

Figure 11.6 Advanced view of ACL Editor showing ACE groupings based on inheritance.

Exceptions to Canonical Sorting

It is possible to override canonical sorting of ACEs programmatically. This enables a developer to take advantage of the way the SRM evaluates individual permissions only once in an ACE scan.

For example, in Exchange 2000, the members of a distribution group can be hidden from view. This requires placing the Everyone group on the DACL in a `Deny Read` ACE.

If the DACL were subject to normal canonical sorting, this would block the Exchange service from seeing the contents. Access tokens for all accounts except Anonymous Logon automatically include the Everyone group. Exchange overcomes this problem by overriding the canonical sorting to give the Exchange service `Full Control` access before putting the `Deny` ACE for Everyone.

Because the SRM only evaluates permissions once, this non-canonical sorting gives full control to the Exchange service while denying access to everyone else. If you open the ACL Editor, you get a warning that the ACEs are not sorted in standard order.

Permissions Inheritance

Permissions inheritance takes advantage of a new way of managing security descriptors that was introduced in Windows 2000. The exact mechanism for this is covered in the section titled "Operational Description of Permission Inheritance" later in this chapter. Rather than place security descriptors on every object, the system maintains a separate database of security descriptors that the objects reference. (This is not true of Registry keys, though. Updating the DACL on an upper Registry key still involves changing the DACL on every child key.)

The ACL Editor has an option to block inheritance. Choosing this option creates a new security descriptor in the database and changes the pointers of the child descriptors. This mechanism retains the speed and efficiency of the classic NT SRM evaluation process with the flexibility of dynamic inheritance.

ACE Evaluation with Inheritance

ACEs that are directly applied to a DACL take precedence over ACEs that are inherited from a parent object. Also, ACEs applied at each tier of the file system or Active Directory take precedence of permissions applied higher in the tree. The system achieves this by sorting the ACEs based on their origin. Here is the sort order:

- **Directly applied `Deny` ACEs** are sorted to the top of the DACL.
- **Directly applied `Allow` ACEs** are placed next in line.
- **Inherited `Deny` ACEs**, if any, are placed here.
- **Inherited `Allow` ACEs** are evaluated last.

Blocking Permission Inheritance

When you choose to block permission inheritance at an object, the system prompts you to either `Copy` or `Remove` the inherited ACEs from the DACL. I recommend always copying the ACEs. You can then select which ACEs to remove and which to retain. This helps avoid accidentally disabling access to folders or objects further down the tree that might have been relying on an inherited ACE that you removed.

This means a directly applied `Allow` ACE takes precedence over an inherited `Deny` ACE. This is non-intuitive. Here's an example to demonstrate how it works.

Consider a user who is a member of two groups. Group A has been directly assigned to the DACL of a file with `Allow Read/Write/Execute` access permissions. Group B has been inherited from the parent folder with `Deny Read/Write` permissions.

The SRM only evaluates individual permissions once during an ACE scan. Because the first ACE in the scan has an access mask for `Read_Data`, `Write_Data`, and `Execute`, these permissions are not evaluated again when they appear in the `Deny` mask in the next ACE. The consolidated access mask assigned to the thread would have `Allow Read/Write/Execute` permissions.

Keep this behavior in mind as you define access permissions for security objects:

- **Don't assume that you block access to an entire subdirectory by assigning a `Deny` ACE at an upper folder.** Another administrator, or the owner of a subfolder, can block inheritance lower in the tree or directly apply an `Allow` ACE that overrides your `Deny` ACE. The same caution applies to Active Directory objects. An OU administrator can block permissions inheritance and stage a virtual coup.
- **Don't place an administrative group on a DACL with an `Access Denied` ACE.** You might accidentally lock yourself and your colleagues out of an important folder or container. Fortunately, the Administrators group owns all of the Directory objects, so you can change the ACL back if you make a mistake.
- **Don't associate an `Access Denied` ACE with the Everyone group.** If you lock out Everyone, you lock out yourself and your fellow administrators, as well. You even lock out the local system. This same caution applies to other well-known groups such as Interactive or Network or LocalService or NetworkService. If you don't want everyone to have access to an object, remove the Everyone group from the ACL and rely on implicit deny to keep out unwelcome intruders.

Operational Description of Permission Inheritance

Classic NT places a security descriptor in each object. If a change is made to the ACL in a parent object such as a file folder, the system has to open the security descriptor on each child object and update the ACL.

If you're an administrator on a classic NT file and print server and you've ever made a change to the root folder of a large NTFS volume, you know the time and resources that are involved in updating the ACLs on all the subfolders and files. The versions of NTFS that ship with Windows 2000, Windows Server 2003, and Windows XP handle permissions much more efficiently. Rather than put a security descriptor in each object, the file system maintains a table of security descriptors in a hidden database under the `$Secure` metadata folder. Each file and folder has a reference to a security descriptor in the table.

When you modify the DACL of a folder, all the child folders linked to that security descriptor get the new entry automatically. If you block inheritance at a folder, a new security descriptor is created in the database and the references in the subfolders are changed to point at the new security descriptor. This dramatically reduces the time and resources required to modify permissions. (For more information on NTFS security descriptor handling, see Chapter 16, "Managing Shared Resources.")

Assigning Inheritance Settings

The inheritance setting for each individual ACE in a DACL is separately flagged. You can configure the inheritance setting using the Advanced view of the ACL Editor.

When you click `Add` or `Edit` on an ACE in Advanced view, the Permission Entry window opens with an Apply Onto box that lists the inheritance options. Here are the options for NTFS objects:

- This folder only
- This folder and all subfolders and files
- This folder and subfolders
- This folder and files
- Subfolders and files only
- Subfolders only
- Files only

Here are the inheritance options for Active Directory objects:

- This object only
- This object and all child objects
- Child objects only

Active Directory objects have additional inheritance settings for selecting the class of objects that inherit a particular ACE. The Delegation Wizard simplifies the selection process. See Chapter 13, "Managing Active Directory Security," for details.

Viewing Consolidated Permissions

A user's access token contains the SID of every group that has the user as a member. It also contains the SID of every group that has those groups as members, and so on. It can sometimes be a challenge to determine the exact permissions a particular user has for a particular object.

You can view a resultant set of permissions for a specified user or group on a particular object using the ACL Editor. Figure 11.7 shows an example of an administrator who is in a group with Full Control permissions delegated to the OU containing a User object. The permissions can be viewed using the steps in Procedure 11.1.

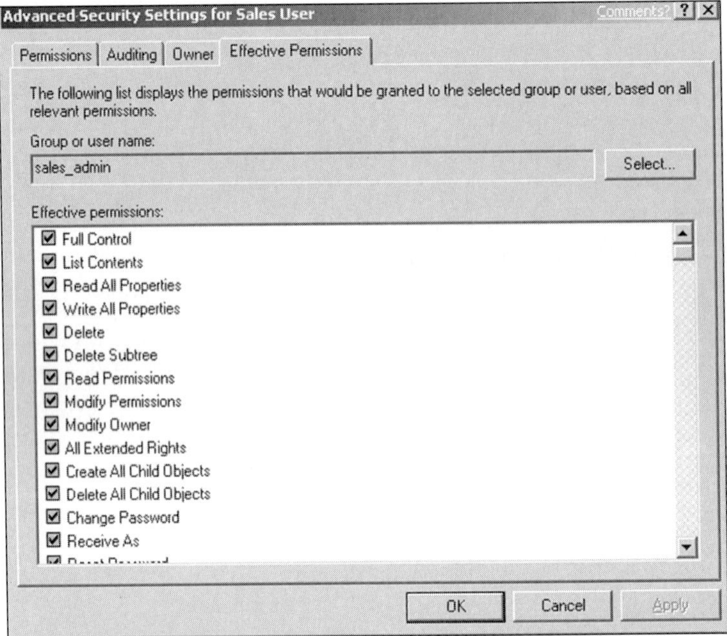

Figure 11.7 ACL Editor showing resultant set of permissions.

Procedure 11.1 Viewing a Resultant Set of Permissions

1. Open the Properties window for a security object.
2. Select the `Security` tab.
3. Click `Advanced`.
4. Select the `Effective Permissions` tab.
5. Click `Select`. The Select User, Computer, or Group window opens.
6. Enter the name of the user or group you want to evaluate.
7. Click `OK`. The Effective Permissions field populates with a checkmark for each permission available to the user.

System Privileges

So far, we've seen how the SRM controls access to security objects based on access tokens and security descriptors. There is an additional set of controls that define which users and groups can access basic system services such as the capability to perform a Backup/Restore or change the system time. These are called *system privileges*. Here is a quick list of the system privileges in Windows Server 2003 (privileges associated strictly with developers tools are not included):

- `Add workstations to domain`
- `Adjust memory quotas for a process`
- `Back up files and directories`
- `Bypass traverse checking`
- `Change the system time`
- `Create a paging file`
- `Debug programs`
- `Enable accounts to be trusted for delegation`
- `Force shutdown from a remote system`
- `Impersonate a client after authentication (new in Windows Server 2003)`
- `Increase scheduling priority`
- `Load and unload device drivers`
- `Manage auditing and security log`
- `Modify firmware environment values`
- `Perform volume maintenance tasks`
- `Profile single process`
- `Profile system performance`
- `Remove computer from docking station`
- `Replace a process level token`
- `Restore files and directories`
- `Shut down the system`
- `Take ownership of files or other objects`

These privileges are assigned via policies set either at a local machine or downloaded from a domain controller as part of a Group Policy Object (GPO):

- Local security policies are stored in the Secedit.sdb database. The database is located in `\Windows\Security\Database`. Local security policies are configured with the Group Policy Editor (Gpedit.msc), which can be launched from Start | Programs | Administrative Tools | Local Security Policy.
- Group security policies are linked to a particular Site, Domain, or OU in Active Directory. For example, domain controllers download their group security policies from the Default Domain Controller group policy object that is linked to the Domain Controllers OU. Group policies override local policies in the Secedit.sdb database. The group policies that control system privileges are located under `Computer Configuration | Windows Settings | Security Settings | Local Policies | User Rights Assignment`.

Security policies can be assigned directly to a user or to a group containing the user. In either case, the privileges associated with a user become part of the user's access token. They are evaluated whenever the user process attempts to perform a privileged system operation.

Viewing System Privileges

Several command-line utilities list the system privileges assigned to a user. These are useful when you are trying to troubleshoot why a particular user is not able to perform a certain task.

WHOAMI

The WHOAMI tool from the Resource Kit lists a user's groups and security privileges. Here's a sample listing (syntax: `whoami /all`):

```
C:\>whoami /all
[User]     = "COMPANY\Administrator"  S-1-5-21-2942328611-473866232-3689853989-500
[Group  1] = "COMPANY\Domain Users"  S-1-5-21-2942328611-473866232-3689853989-513
[Group  2] = "Everyone"  S-1-1-0
[Group  3] = "BUILTIN\Administrators"  S-1-5-32-544
[Group  4] = "BUILTIN\Users"  S-1-5-32-545
[Group  5] = "COMPANY\Schema Admins"  S-1-5-21-2942328611-473866232-3689853989-518
[Group  6] = "COMPANY\Domain Admins"  S-1-5-21-2942328611-473866232-3689853989-512
[Group  7] = "COMPANY\Group Policy Creator Owners"  S-1-5-21-2942328611-473866232-
➥3689853989-520
[Group  8] = "COMPANY\Enterprise Admins"  S-1-5-21-2942328611-473866232-
➥3689853989-519
[Group  9] = "LOCAL"  S-1-2-0
[Group 10] = "NT AUTHORITY\REMOTE INTERACTIVE LOGON"  S-1-5-14
[Group 11] = "NT AUTHORITY\INTERACTIVE"  S-1-5-4
[Group 12] = "NT AUTHORITY\Authenticated Users"  S-1-5-11


(X) SeChangeNotifyPrivilege          = Bypass traverse checking
(O) SeSecurityPrivilege              = Manage auditing and security log
(O) SeBackupPrivilege                = Back up files and directories
(O) SeRestorePrivilege               = Restore files and directories
(O) SeSystemtimePrivilege            = Change the system time
(O) SeShutdownPrivilege              = Shut down the system
(O) SeRemoteShutdownPrivilege        = Force shutdown from a remote system
(O) SeTakeOwnershipPrivilege         = Take ownership of files or other objects
(O) SeDebugPrivilege                 = Debug programs
(O) SeSystemEnvironmentPrivilege     = Modify firmware environment values
(O) SeSystemProfilePrivilege         = Profile system performance
(O) SeProfileSingleProcessPrivilege  = Profile single process
(O) SeIncreaseBasePriorityPrivilege  = Increase scheduling priority
(X) SeLoadDriverPrivilege            = Load and unload device drivers
(O) SeCreatePagefilePrivilege        = Create a pagefile
(O) SeIncreaseQuotaPrivilege         = Adjust memory quotas for a process
(X) SeUndockPrivilege                = Remove computer from docking station
(O) SeManageVolumePrivilege          = Perform volume maintenance tasks
(O) SeEnableDelegationPrivilege      = Enable accounts to be trusted for delegation
```

```
(0) SeAssignPrimaryTokenPrivilege   = Replace a process level token
(0) SeMachineAccountPrivilege        = Add workstations to domain
```

Notice that, according to WHOAMI, the Administrator account apparently does not have the `SeBackupPrivilege`, which is required to perform a backup. Yet, we know that the Administrator account can perform this function. This is because WHOAMI only reports on the privileges directly assigned to the user, not those assigned to groups that have the user as a member. The GPRESULT utility gives a more complete report.

GPRESULT (Standard Utility)

You'll get a more accurate picture of a user's true privileges using GPRESULT, which comes with a standard installation of Windows Server 2003 and XP. The listing includes all policies, not just system privileges. Here is an excerpt (syntax: `gpresult -v`):

```
GPO: Default Domain Controllers Policy
    Policy:             CreatePagefilePrivilege
    Computer Setting:   Administrators

GPO: Default Domain Controllers Policy
    Policy:             EnableDelegationPrivilege
    Computer Setting:   Administrators

GPO: Default Domain Controllers Policy
    Policy:             DebugPrivilege
    Computer Setting:   Administrators

GPO: Default Domain Controllers Policy
    Policy:             SystemTimePrivilege
    Computer Setting:   Server Operators
                        Administrators

GPO: Default Domain Controllers Policy
    Policy:             DenyBatchLogonRight
    Computer Setting:   N/A

GPO: Default Domain Controllers Policy
    Policy:             BackupPrivilege
    Computer Setting:   Server Operators
                        Backup Operators
                         Administrators
```

As you can see, this listing is more accurate than WHOAMI because it includes privileges obtained by dint of group membership, but the listing is not as easy to work with because you must sift though each privilege.

GPRESULT (Windows 2000 Resource Kit)

You can get a privilege list that is easier to scan with the GPRESULT tool from the old Windows 2000 Resource Kit. Here's a sample (syntax: `gpresult /v`):

```
User Group Policy results for:
CN=Administrator,CN=Users,DC=company,DC=com
Domain Name:            COMPANY
```

```
Domain Type:           Windows 2000
Site Name:             Default-First-Site-Name
Roaming profile:       (None)
Local profile:         C:\Documents and Settings\Administrator
The user is a member of the following security groups:

      COMPANY\Domain Users
      \Everyone
      BUILTIN\Administrators
      BUILTIN\Users
      COMPANY\Schema Admins
      COMPANY\Domain Admins
      COMPANY\Group Policy Creator Owners
      COMPANY\Enterprise Admins
      \LOCAL
      NT AUTHORITY\INTERACTIVE
      NT AUTHORITY\Authenticated Users

The user has the following security privileges:
      Bypass traverse checking
      Manage auditing and security log
      Back up files and directories
      Restore files and directories
      Change the system time
      Shut down the system
      Force shutdown from a remote system
      Take ownership of files or other objects
      Debug programs
      Modify firmware environment values
      Profile system performance
      Profile single process
      Increase scheduling priority
      Load and unload device drivers
      Create a pagefile
      Adjust memory quotas for a process
      Remove computer from docking station
      Perform volume maintenance tasks
      Enable computer and user accounts to be trusted for delegation
      Replace a process level token
      Add workstations to domain
```

SHOWPRIVS

If you want to see the users and groups that have been assigned a particular privileges, use the SHOWPRIVS utility from the Resource Kit. Here's a sample (syntax: `showprivs seshutdownprivilege`):

```
C:\>showpriv seshutdownprivilege
5 account(s) with the seshutdownprivilege user right:
BUILTIN\Backup Operators
BUILTIN\Print Operators new name
BUILTIN\Server Operators
BUILTIN\Account Operators
BUILTIN\Administrators
All accounts enumerated
```

Security Policies

In addition to group policies that affect fundamental system privileges, Windows has a long list of group policies that are used to manage security at a higher level. The policies affect Registry settings, not entries in the Secedit.sdb database. The policies are located in `Computer Configuration | Windows Settings | Security Settings | Local Policies | Security Options`.

Here is a list of the commonly used security policies along with their associated Registry keys and a description of the policy function:

- **Allow system to be shutdown without having to log on.** (`HKLM\Software\Microsoft\Windows NT\CurrentVersion\Winlogon\ShutdownWithoutLogon`) When you press `Ctrl+Alt+Delete` to log on, the Welcome to Windows window has a Shutdown button that permits shutting down the machine without logging on. For an XP desktop, this is acceptable, although it could result in data loss for other users if Fast User Switching is enabled. Servers should not be shut down from the logon window because users may have connections to the server. For this reason, running Windows Server 2003 have a local policy that disables `ShutdownWithoutLogon`.
- **Audit the access of global system objects.** (`HKLM | System | CurrentControlSet | Control | Lsa | AuditBaseObject`) The interior of Windows Server 2003 is a little like the Pentagon. Most of the secret places are fairly dull, even if you have the clearance to see them. For this reason, enabling auditing does not ordinarily reveal access to many obscure internal objects. Enabling this option adds the internal objects to the audit report. For the most part, this option is only useful to system-level programmers.
- **Audit the use of all user rights including backup and restore.** (`HKLM | System | CurrentControlSet | Control | Lsa | FullPrivilegeAuditing`) Under normal circumstances, if you enable auditing of access to privileged objects, the Security log would fill as soon as you performed your first backup. This is because you would be exercising your `Backup Operator` privilege over and over and over again. For this reason, backup and restore auditing is ordinarily bypassed. Only enable this option when you think someone is misusing his or her backup and restore privileges. Be sure to make the Security log very large to accommodate the entries and be prepared for a very slow backup.
- **Rename Administrator account [Guest Account].** (`Registry or Directory entry locked`) The Administrator account is like a J.R.R. Tolkien wizard. It wields powerful devices that are hidden to mere users. This makes the Administrator account a favorite object of hack attempts. This policy renames the Administrator (and Guest) account to help obfuscate the accounts. Unfortunately, there are some very simple API calls that reveal the identity of the Administrator account regardless of its name, so this policy will not trip up a sophisticated intruder.

- **Clear virtual memory pagefile when system shuts down.** (HKLM | System | CurrentControlSet | Control | Session Manager | Memory Management | ClearPageFileAtShutdown) Clearing out the paging file at each shutdown is a good way to enforce security by preventing storage of potentially sensitive information in the paging file. If you choose to deploy such a policy, the users will need this system privilege.
- **Shut down system immediately if unable to log security audits.** (HKLM | System | CurrentControlSet | Control | Lsa | CrashOnAuditFail) If you choose to audit a system, you may want to ensure that the auditing system catches every event you are monitoring. If the log fills, you will lose events. Therefore, you may want to force the system to shut down if the log gets full. An account with Administrator privileges can log on to save and clear the Security file.
- **Do not allow enumeration of account names and shares by anonymous users.** (HKLM | System | CurrentControlSet | Control | Lsa | RestrictAnonymous) This policy prevents users without credentials from getting the names of shares on a server. See the "Anonymous Logon" section for more information.
- **Disable Ctrl+Alt+Del requirement for logon.** (HKLM | Software | Microsoft | Windows NT | CurrentVersion | Winlogon | DisableCAD) This policy gives users who are not members of a domain the ability to get right to the Explorer shell without a logon. It should never be enabled.
- **Do not display last username in logon screen.** (HKLM | Software | Microsoft | Windows NT | CurrentVersion | Winlogon | DontDisplayLastUserName) It's handy to have your username displayed when you press Ctrl+Alt+Del to log on, but security-conscious administrators object to exposing a name so that all a bad guy needs to do is guess the password.
- **Secure channel: digitally sign secure channel.** (HKLM | System | CurrentControlSet | Services | Netlogon | Parameters | SealSecureChannel) This and the following two settings are designed to deal with a very specific potential security breach in Windows Server 2003. Member workstations and servers communicate to their domain controllers over a secure RPC link. This link is not checked for integrity, so a bright bad guy could conceivably impersonate a machine on the wire and divert secure traffic. The digital signing identifies each packet coming over the secure link. It slows down communications somewhat. (I do not have statistics.)
- **Secure channel: digitally encrypt all secure channel data.** (HKLM | System | CurrentControlSet | Services | Netlogon | Parameters | SignSecureChannel) Same as the preceding description, but with the addition of encryption for all traffic, not just passwords.

- **Secure channel: digitally encrypt or sign secure channel.** (HKLM | System | CurrentControlSet | Services | Netlogon | Parameters | RequireSignOrSeal) Same as preceding description, but forces secure traffic instead of letting the members auto-negotiate. Only set this option if every domain controller is set the same way.
- **Encrypt files in the offline folders cache.** (HKLM | Software | Microsoft | Windows | CurrentVersion | NetCache | EncryptEntireCache) Client-side caching speeds network communication by holding copies of executables and other read-only files at the local machine. A bad guy could conceivably nab these saved files and steal valuable secrets. Encrypting the files slows performance, but improves security. You may have noticed a trend.
- **Automatically log off users when logon time expires.** (HKLM | System | CurrentControlSet | Control | Session Manager | ProtectionMode) You can define a specific time of day after which a user or group of users is denied access. This is useful when you have a group of users who have specific duties from 8 to 5, but should not be messing around on the network after hours. This policy affects network access only, not the ability to log on to a local desktop.
- **Message text for users attempting to log on.** (HKLM | Software | Microsoft | Windows NT | CurrentVersion | Winlogon | LegalNoticeText) This and the next option define parameters for a special window that appears after the user presses `Ctrl+Alt+Del` but before the Winlogon credentials window. It is most often used to display boilerplate Human Resources text like "You are using COMPANY equipment and must obey COMPANY policies that are available in COMPANY offices."
- **Message title for users attempting to log on.** (HKLM | Software | Microsoft | Windows NT | CurrentVersion | Winlogon | LegalNoticeCaption) This option specifies the title bar text in the window configured by `LegalNoticeText`.
- **Number of previous logons to cache.** (HKLM | Software | Microsoft | Windows NT | CurrentVersion | Winlogon | CachedLogonsCount) If a workstation cannot contact its domain controller, a user can still be logged on via cached credentials. The cache is set for 10 by default. If you have a workstation at which many people log on, some of them may have been aged out of the cache. You can set this option to as many as 50 logons.
- **Restrict CD-ROM access to locally logged-on user only.** (HKLM | Software | Microsoft | Windows NT | CurrentVersion | Winlogon | AllocateCDRoms) C2 security requirements include a specification to exclude removable media from network access.
- **Restrict floppy access to locally logged-on user only.** (HKLM | Software | Microsoft | Windows NT | CurrentVersion | Winlogon | AllocateFloppies) See preceding item.

- **`Send unencrypted password to connect to third-party smb servers.`** (`HKLM | System | CurrentControlSet | Control | Lsa | LmCompatibilityLevel`) If you are using older Samba servers, they cannot use NTLMv2 password hashes. Setting this policy allows you to connect using LanMan (LM) password hashes. This policy should not be enabled. Instead, upgrade your Samba servers.

Password Security

It should be self evident that a password-protected computer system cannot be considered safe if it's possible to compromise the password database. Windows does not have a spectacular track record in this regard, so it's worth your time to understand how passwords are formatted, stored, and protected. You should also be as familiar as possible with the tools used by bad guys to get access to your system passwords.

This topic also covers two new password-related features in Windows Server 2003:

- **Credentials cache.** This feature permits storing alternate credentials for accessing standalone servers or servers that are on an outside domain.
- **Password Reset Disks.** This feature permits users who have forgotten their local password on a standalone machines to reset the password as part of the logon sequence.

Password Format and Storage

A user's clear-text password is never stored by Windows Server 2003 or any NT-based operating system. The password is converted into a *one-way function* or OWF, and it is this OWF that is stored, either in the SAM or in Active Directory. Another term for this OWF is a *hash* because it is obtained by running the user's password through a cryptographic process called a *hashing algorithm*. The system discards the clear-text password as soon as the hash is calculated.

Windows uses two different methods to hash a user's clear-text password:

- **DOS-derived Windows** (Windows 3.11, Windows 9x, and ME). These systems use an algorithm based on the *Data Encryption Standard* (DES). This hash is commonly called the *LanMan password* because it is used to perform LanMan Challenge-Response authentication.
- **NT-derived Windows** (classic NT, Windows 2000, Windows Server 2003, and Windows XP). These systems use the MD4 algorithm. MD stands for *message digest*. See Chapter 18, "Managing a Public Key Infrastructure," for more information. The MD4 password hash is commonly called the *NTLM password* because it is used to perform NT LanMan Challenge-Response authentication.

Each Windows platform stores the password hash in a different location:

- **DOS-derived Windows** stores the hash in a password (pwl) file in the Windows directory.

- **Classic NT** stores the hash in the SAM database in the Registry. The PDC stores the password hashes for a classic NT domain and replicates the contents to backup domain controllers (BDCs).
- **Modern Windows** stores the hash for local accounts in the local SAM. The hash for domain accounts is stored in Active Directory.

Password Vulnerabilities

Of the two password hashes, the legacy LM password hash is much more vulnerable. (For a detailed analysis, see `www.insecure.org/sploits/l0phtcrack.lanman.problems.html`. When you read this reference, pay particular attention to the ability of password crackers to derive the LM password hash by sniffing the contents of the LM Challenge-Response transactions. This makes it possible to get passwords without actually accessing the SAM or Active Directory.) Here is a quick rundown of the reasons:

- LM passwords are limited to 14 characters.
- The passwords are hashed in two, 7-byte units, making it simpler to attack each unit.
- The passwords use ASCII characters that must be uppercase. This severely limits the universe of possible characters.
- Only a limited number of special characters are permitted in the password.
- The algorithm used to create the LM one-way function is relatively rudimentary.

NTLM passwords are much more secure than LM passwords for the following reasons:

- The hashing algorithm uses 128-bit MD4, which is significantly stronger than the DES hashing method used on LM passwords.
- The passwords length limit is 128 characters, although normal users seldom use passwords longer than 8 to 10 characters.
- NT passwords use Unicode characters, not ASCII, which theoretically makes them more secure, although password crackers generally assume that the original password used ASCII characters, at least in Western countries. A single unusual character in a password dramatically decreases its vulnerability.

Password Storage in Active Directory

Active Directory stores passwords as hidden attributes of user and computer objects. These attributes are as follows:

- `DbcsPwd`. This is the LanMan password. DBCS stands for double-byte character set. The LanMan password history is stored in hashed form in `LmPwdHistory`.
- `UnicodePwd`. This is the non-reversible NT password used by Windows 2000, 2002, and XP. The password history is stored in hashed form in `NtPwdHistory`.

Starting with NT4 SP4, Microsoft improved the session negotiation and authentication transaction processing in NTLM Challenge-Response. The new version, NTLMv2, comes in Windows 2000, 2002, XP, and the Dsclient update available for Windows 9x/ME. By default, Windows Server 2003 negotiates down to older authentication methods unless local or group policy has been set to block this action.

Password Storage Vulnerabilities

Password-cracking programs work most efficiently when they have a copy of the password list from the SAM or Active Directory that they can pound away at.

There are password dump programs that can steal password hashes for later processing. The most popular of these dump utilities is PWDUMP3E. Using PWDUMP3E, an intruder with administrative privileges can save the password hashes to a file, transport the file to another machine, then use a password cracker such as l0phtcrack to break the passwords.

I highly recommend that you obtain a copy of PWDUMP3E and l0phtcrack to check the vulnerability of the passwords on your system. You'll probably be astonished at how fast and easy it is to find most of the passwords on your system.

Password Policies

You can take steps to improve your users' passwords by setting a variety of group policies. This section contains the most commonly implemented password policies.

Eliminate Weak LanMan Passwords

You can set a policy that prevents storing LanMan passwords in Active Directory. This significantly cripples password-cracking programs such as l0phtcrack. It is theoretically possible to find a collision with an NTLM hash, but the process is much more complex than with LM password hashes.

Password Crackers

Even though the algorithms used to hash LM and NTLM passwords cannot be reversed, it's possible to "guess" a password by looking for a known word with a hash that matches the password hash.

The algorithms that produce the LM and NTLM passwords are well known. It's possible to build a list of pre-hashed passwords to speed up a dictionary attack. If the original password is not a common word, the cracking program tries one combination of characters and numbers after another until it finds one that works.

The most notorious password-cracking program is l0phtcrack, although there are others. You can get details about l0phtcrack at `www.insecure.org/sploits/l0phtcrack.lanman.problems.html`. The most current version is LC3, available for purchase (a crippled time trial is available for download) from `www.atstake.com`.

You can find a tidy list of other popular password-cracking and system-scanning tools at `www.insecure.org/tools.html`.

The group policy that controls this setting is `Network security: Do not store Lan Manager level hash values on next password change`. The policy entry is set in the `Default Domain Controllers` policy. The item is located at `Computer Configuration | Windows Settings | Security Settings | Local Policies | Security Options`.

The legacy password will not be removed from Active Directory until the client changes the current password. With the default settings, this could take as many as 42 days. You can shorten the interval using the `Maximum Password Age` policy. This policy entry is set in the `Default Domain` policy. It is located at `Computer Configuration | Windows Settings | Security Settings | Account Policies | Password Policy`.

Finally, you should eliminate all legacy authentication mechanisms except for NTLMv2. This ensures that the non-Kerberos authentication transactions use the most secure password handling. The group policy that controls this setting is `Network Security: Lan Manager Authentication Level`. The policy entry is set in the `Default Domain Controllers` policy. The item is located at `Computer Configuration | Windows Settings | Security Settings | Local Policies | Security Options`.

Before setting these policies, you must enable your downlevel clients to use NTLMv2 authentication. For Windows 9x and ME clients, distribute the DSCLIENT patch from the Windows Server 2003 CD. For NT4 clients, make sure you are running SP4 or later.

You must also set an `Lmcompatibility` Registry entry at the Windows 9x and ME clients. This Registry entry prevents the clients from sending LanMan password requests.

Account Lockout Policies

You don't want to give a bad guy the opportunity to bang away at a logon window trying all sorts of possible passwords until one just happens to work. An account lockout policy discourages this behavior by disabling the user account after a given number of invalid logon attempts.

Account lockouts cost money because they result in Help Desk calls. You can minimize the impact by setting an interval after which the lockout clears automatically. The group policies that affect account lockout settings are located in `Computer Configuration | Windows Settings | Security Settings | Account Policies | Account Lockout Policy`. There are three parameters to set:

- **Lockout count.** The number of invalid logon attempts permitted before the account is locked out.

Standalone Servers

All of the policies discussed in these topics can also be set locally for a standalone server. This is important to remember if you are responsible for servers in a DMZ or some other situation that makes it difficult or impossible to create a domain.

- **Lockout reset time.** The interval between invalid attempts after which the lockout count is returned to zero. For example, a lockout reset time of 10 minutes would cause the lockout counter to continue incrementing for invalid logon attempts made every nine minutes.
- **Lockout duration.** The interval following a lockout after which the lockout is automatically cleared and the user can try to log on again.

The Local Security Authority imposes the lockout policy on any service that accepts network connections. This includes CIFS/SMB, FTP, telnet, and HTTP. Repeated invalid logon attempts using any combination of these services will also trip the lockout.

The lockout policy has very few exceptions. The Administrator account cannot be locked out, but this exception does not apply to accounts with administrative privileges. Computer accounts cannot be locked out. Neither can domain trust accounts.

Reversible Passwords

MD5-CHAP and Digest authentication require that the verifying server know the client's clear-text password. The same is true when authenticating Macintosh clients using the Random Number Exchange UAM in the AppleTalk File Protocol (AFP) or remote access via AppleTalk Remote Access Protocol (ARAP).

Neither the NTLMv2 password nor the legacy LanMan password can be used for these transactions because the system stores one-way functions that cannot be used to derive the original password. Active Directory can accommodate authentication mechanisms requiring clear-text passwords by storing a reversibly-encrypted password. When an MD5-CHAP or Digest client attempts access, the system decrypts the password and uses the result to verify the user's identity.

The group policy that controls this setting is `Store Password Using Reversible Encryption For All Users In The Domain`. The policy entry is set in the `Default Domain` policy. It is located at `Computer Configuration | Windows Settings | Security Settings | Account Policies | Password Policy`.

Computer Passwords

Now that we've seen some of the vulnerabilities of passwords and how to help overcome them (or at least limit our exposure), let's look at other places that Windows uses passwords.

Samba Clients and NTLMv2 Passwords

Clients running older Samba versions may not work with Windows without reversible password support. Newer Samba clients use NTLMv2 and can act as domain controllers in a Mixed domain.

Computers that are members of a domain have a password associated with their computer account. Active Directory stores the hash for this password in the computer's object, just as it does for user passwords. In addition to authentication and authorization, the computer password hash is used to encrypt data sent between the member computer and a domain controller. This is called a secure RPC connection. The data stream in the secure connection is encrypted using RC4 (a streaming encryption algorithm licensed from RSA Security) with the computer's password hash acting as the encryption key.

Diagnosing Computer Password Problems

Problems with the secure channel between a member computer and its domain controller can cause errors such as `Unable to contact domain controller...` when a user attempts to log on to the domain. If you think you are having problems with a computer's network authentication, test the secure channel with NLTEST as follows (the example uses a domain called `company.com`):

```
nltest /sc_query:company.com
```

DNS problems can also cause logon failures because the client cannot locate a domain controller to use as a logon server. If you get connection failures in NLTEST, you should look at network connectivity and name resolution.

The computer password used to set up the secure channel is changed every 30 days by default. Both the member computer and its logon server must be on the network for this transaction to occur. If a member computer (such as a laptop) is off the network at the time the password change is due, the client will change its password the next time it contacts the domain.

You can force a password change using NLTEST as follows:

```
nltest /sc_change_pwd:company.com
```

If a member server has lost its secure channel connection and cannot regain it, you can disjoin and rejoin the computer to the domain. The simplest and fastest way to do this is to log on at the member server using the local Administrator account then running the NETDOM utility from the Resource Kit as follows:

```
netdom remove server13 /domain:company.com
```

Then run the following:

```
netdom join server13 /domain:company.com
```

Restart the machine to let it complete the secure channel connection to the domain.

Credentials Cache

In modern Windows, a single domain password gives access to member servers throughout a forest thanks to transitive Kerberos trusts. Accessing servers outside the forest, such as standalone servers in a DMZ or servers in other domains, requires a separate authentication transaction with a separate password.

When you connect to a server outside your forest, you are prompted to enter a name and password for the target machine. When doing cross-domain authentications, you may need to specify a domain name in the format:

```
<domain_name>\<user_name> password
```

If you make this a persistent connection, the system reestablishes the session at the next logon and prompts once again for credentials.

Microsoft makes password management a little easier in Windows Server 2003 by including a new credentials database. This database is exposed via a Control Panel applet called Stored User Names and Passwords. You can store your username and password in the credentials cache and use them to automatically authenticate when reconnecting to the target server.

The credentials cache is stored in a file called Credentials in your profile under `Application Data\Microsoft\Credentials\<user_sid>`. The file is encrypted with your private key, which is itself encrypted with the Master crypto key. See Chapter 18, "Managing a Public Key Infrastructure," for more information about the PKI components of Windows Server 2003.

Names and passwords in the credentials cache are available at the command line for the `NET USE` command. For instance, let's say you create a drive mapping from the command line as follows: `net use * \\server13\shared_folder`. If you have an entry in the Credentials cache for Server13, the system will make the connection without the need to specify a username or password.

When using `NET USE` to make a connection, you can automatically save alternate credentials in the credentials cache via the `/savecred` switch. You'll be prompted for your username and password, which are then stored in the credentials cache if the logon is successful.

If you prefer to do all your credentials management from the command line, take a look at the new CMDKEY utility. This utility creates, displays, and deletes credentials in the credentials cache. For example, to add a new username and password to the cache, use `cmdkey /add:<server_name> /user:<user_name> /pass:<password>`. To see the contents of the credential cache, use `cmdkey /list`. Here is a sample listing:

```
C:\>cmdkey /list

Currently stored credentials:

    Target: laptop
    Type: Domain Password
    User: laptop\administrator
```

Windows Server 2003 only stores CIFS/SMB credentials in the credentials cache. Upcoming versions will store Internet Explorer credentials, as well. This will enable the system to store usernames and passwords for web sites.

Storing Names and Passwords

To store a set of credentials, proceed as directed in Procedure 11.2.

Procedure 11.2 Storing User Names and Passwords

1. Open the `Stored User Names and Passwords` applet in Control Panel.
2. Click `Add`. The Logon Information Properties window opens. Figure 11.8 shows and example.

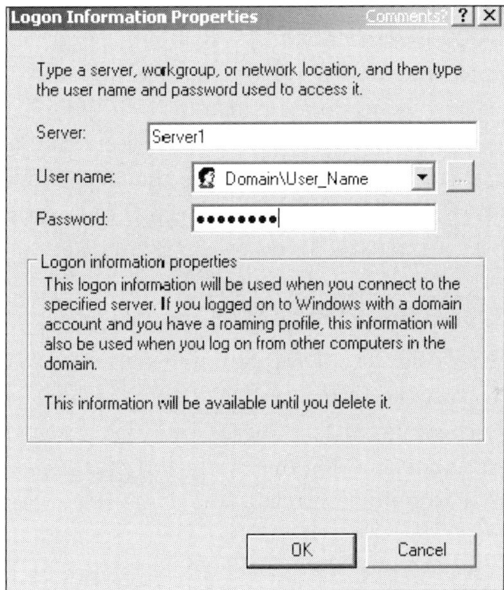

Figure 11.8 Logon Information Properties window of Stored User Names and Passwords applet.

3. Enter the fully qualified domain name of the server. The flat name would work, but you want to get accustomed to entries that don't rely on WINS.
4. Enter the username in the form *`<domain>\<name>`*. If you are connecting to a standalone machine, enter the flat name of the machine instead of the domain, as in `SERVER1\jjones`. (The name is not case-sensitive.)
5. Enter the password.
6. Click `OK` to save the change. The name of the server appears in the pick list.

Cached Logon Credentials

It is unfortunate that Microsoft chose to use the phrase *Credentials cache* for the new Stored User Names and Passwords feature because they already use a similar phrase in another context referring to logons when a domain controller is not available. In that context, the cached credentials are stored in a `Secrets` key in the `Security` hive in the Registry (often called LSA Secrets).

Password Resets

The ability to reset a password for another user is a highly privileged operation, as you might well imagine. If you can change a user's password, you can log on as that user and get access to the user's files and processes. The user's password also protects the Public Key Infrastructure (PKI) keys stored for the user, which protect the user's encrypted files, encrypted email, and secure web access, along with any other application that relies on the system's PKI providers.

Utilities are readily available that make changing a user's local password a trivial exercise. For example, the for-fee version of ERD Commander 2002 (`www.winternals.com`) makes it possible to boot a machine using the four Setup disks then change the password of any user in the local SAM database, including the Administrator account. (You cannot use this utility to change the passwords for Active Directory accounts.) Using a tool like ERD Commander, you can change a user's local password then log on as that user and get access to the user's data.

Password Reset Handling for Local Accounts

Windows 2000 had a significant shortcoming regarding password resets. When you reset a user's local password in Windows 2000, the system rebuilds the master crypto key using the new password. This means that you can use ERD Commander to change a user's password then log on locally and open any files that were encrypted with the user's local account. (This deficiency does not apply to files encrypted while the user is logged on to the domain.)

Windows Server 2003 and XP correct this deficiency by leaving the master crypto key in its original state unless the user changes the password using the `Change Password` option from the Windows Security window. If you reset a user's local password using any other mechanism, you will not get access to the user's encrypted files or any other PKI-protected information. You'll be warned about this if you use the password reset feature in the Users and Computers applet in Control Panel.

If you reset a user's local password and, later on, the user discovers that the reset caused a loss of access to encrypted files or email, the user can change the password back using `Ctrl+Alt+Del | Change Password`. This regains access to encrypted files and email. You may need to relax local password history requirements to permit the user to reuse a password.

Password Reset Disk

One of the most common support calls is the "forgotten password" call. In a domain, this problem can be quickly corrected by resetting the user's domain password. If you support standalone desktops or servers, though, a forgotten password becomes a nasty problem. If you cannot get physical access to the machine, you must walk the user through a local logon using the Administrator account. This compromises the password. (For some reason, users who cannot remember their own password for longer than five minutes will remember the local Administrator password for years.)

A new feature in Windows Server 2003 and XP called the *Password Reset Disk*, or PRD, helps alleviate this problem. The PRD is a floppy created by the user that contains a special key created by the system for the user. If the user forgets his local password, he can use the PRD to authorize a local password reset. Procedure 11.3 demonstrates how it works.

Procedure 11.3 Creating a Password Reset Disk

1. Log on using a local account. (The PRD does not apply to domain accounts because those passwords can be reset using `AD Users and Computers` or some other enterprise tool.)
2. Press `Ctrl+Alt+Del` and select `Change Password`.
3. Click `Backup`. The Forgotten Password Wizard opens.
4. Click `Next`. The Create Password Reset Disk window opens. Insert a blank, formatted floppy in Drive A.
5. Click `Next`. The Current User Account Password window opens. Enter your current password.
6. Click `Next`. The wizard writes the certificate information to the floppy.
7. Click `Finish`. The wizard closes. The floppy now contains a file with a PWS extension. This file contains a hash of the user's identification.

When a user forgets the local password, use the steps in Procedure 11.4 to reset the password using the PRD.

Procedure 11.4 Using a PRD to Change a Password

1. Press `Ctrl+Alt+Del` to log on.
2. Enter the correct username but an incorrect password. The system responds with an error asking if you want to reset your password.
3. Click `Reset`. This opens the Password Reset Wizard.

4. Click `Next`. The Insert Password Reset Disk window opens. Insert the floppy containing the PWS file into Drive A.
5. Click `Next`. The Reset the User Account Password window opens. Enter a new password and confirm it. This must be a different password than the one that currently exists in the SAM.
6. Enter a password hint. Hints are saved in clear text for each user under `HKLM | Software | Microsoft | Windows | Hints`. The hint should not indicate the password in any way. "My wife's name" is not a good hint because that information is easily obtained. "Third rock from the sun" has the same problem unless it's a hint for a password of "johnlithgow". The hint "e raised to pi*i" would be acceptably inscrutable except the answer, "-1", is too short for a good password.
7. Click `Next`. The password change is applied.
8. Click `Finish`. The Password Reset Wizard closes and you are returned to the logon window. Enter the new credentials and log on.

Password Reset Disk Contents

As you can see from the preceding section, if a user's PRD falls into a third party's hands, that third party can use the PRD to get access to the local system. Here are a few highlights about the file on the PRD:

- The PWS file contains a digital signature that identifies the user who created the file. It does not contain the user's password or any derivative of the password. It also does not use the user's PKI information to create the signature, so it is not tied to the user's profile.
- The signature contains information specific to the user's instance on a particular machine, so you cannot use the PRD to reset a user's password on another machine. Also, the information in the PSW file is not tied to the user's profile. You can delete the user's profile and the user can still use the Password Reset Disk to get logged on.
- You cannot use the PRD to change a password to the existing password, regardless of the local password history security setting. The password reset transaction must actually *change* the password. The new password must meet any complexity requirements in the local security settings.
- If you reset your password using the PRD, you will not lose access to encrypted files or any other component protected by the PKI subsystem. This includes encrypted email and access to protected web sites.
- After you've logged on with the new password, you can change your password back to the original (if you remember it) using `Ctrl+Alt+Del | Change Password`.

- If an administrator changes the user's local password, the user can still use the PRD to reset the password again.
- If you reset your password using the PRD, you will lose all entries in the credentials cache created by the Stored User Names and Passwords applet in Control Panel.
- If an administrator deletes a local user account and then makes another account with the same name, the PRD will not work for the new account.
- A user with accounts on several machines cannot use a PRD from one machine to reset a password on another.
- You can copy the PWS file to another floppy and use that floppy as the PRD.
- The same PSW file can be reused any number of times within the limitations listed in the preceding. The system keeps track of each use of the PRD by making entries in a history file (CREDHIST) in the user profile under `Application Data | Microsoft | Protect`.

Anonymous Logon

When a process owned by a user accesses a resource on a remote Windows server, the underlying network application (CIFS/SMB or Winsock, for example) handles authentication transparently to the user.

If the process is owned by the Local System account or some other account with no network security context, it cannot authenticate on the remote server. Instead, it attempts a *null session* connection with the remote server.

Only a few server processes in Windows are designed to accept null session connections. For example, when a client scans for shares on a server using Network Neighborhood, the network file system makes a null session connection to the server to obtain the share list.

Every process needs an access token, so when the local server builds an access token for a null session connection, it attaches the well-known SID of the Anonymous Logon account. For this reason, the terms *anonymous logon* and *null session* are more or less synonymous in Windows.

In classic NT and Windows 2000, the Anonymous Logon account was automatically made a member of the Everyone group. This permitted a thread running in a null session context to access quite a bit of information about a server. This spawned a set of utilities designed to scan for NetBIOS services and other resources that accept null session connections. An example is the LanGuard network scanner, a free download from `www.languard.com/languard/lanscan.htm`. Figure 11.9 shows an example of the kind of information collected by LanGuard when run against a classic NT4 BDC. Windows Server 2003 reveals much less information because of the additional restrictions put on null sessions.

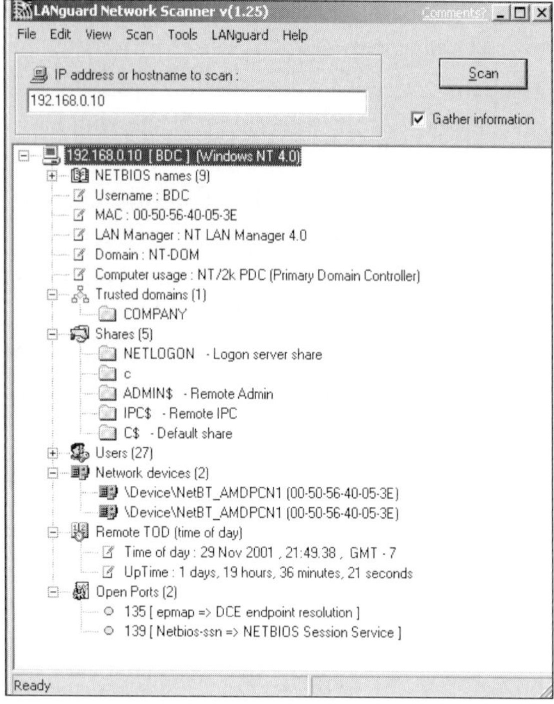

Figure 11.9 NetBIOS service and port scan results using LanGuard.

In Windows Server 2003, the Anonymous Logon account is not a member of the Everyone group. This helps restrict what a NetBIOS scanner can detect. It's still possible to get a lot of information, though, simply by doing a raw port scan.

If null session scanners are a concern for you, you should enable group policies to block anonymous enumeration of shares and account names. These policies are located in `Computer Configuration | Windows Settings | Security Settings | Local Policies | Security Policies`. Here are the policy names:

- `Network access: Do not allow enumeration of SAM accounts (Enable)`
- `Network access: Do not allow enumeration of SAM accounts and shares (Enable)`
- `Network access: Let Everyone permissions apply to anonymous users (Disable)`

You may have a share that absolutely must be accessed anonymously, such as a printer share. If so, you can add the share to the `Network Access: Shares that can be accessed anonymously` group policy.

Authentication

So far, we've met the supporting players in the pageant of network access security and we've seen how one part of the security triumvirate, authorization, functions to control access to resources. Now it's time to meet the star of the show, the process that controls authentication. Ladies and gentlemen, give it up for *Kerberos*.

Kerberos was developed at MIT as part of Project Athena. Windows Server 2003 implements Kerberos version 5, update 6, as defined by RFC 1510, "The Kerberos Network Authentication Service V5." All modern Windows platforms (Windows Server 2003, XP, and Windows 2000) use this version of Kerberos, making them fully interoperable. Windows Server 2003 Server also makes it fairly easy to build transitive trust relationships with classic MITv5 Kerberos systems. This is covered in detail later in this section.

Limitations of Classic NT Authentication

The first question you might have concerning Kerberos is, "Why change?" After all, classic NTLM Challenge-Response authentication seems to work pretty well. And the improved security in NTLMv2 went a long way toward blocking attacks.

In spite of the improvements in NTLMv2, classic authentication has several vulnerabilities and limitations. Here is a quick list:

- **Pass-through authentication.** When a client touches a resource on a classic member server, the server must negotiate a Challenge-Response transaction with a domain controller on behalf of the client to verify the client's identity. This slows down the authentication process and opens the door to denial-of-service attacks and potential hijacking of the client's credentials.
- **One-way authentication**. In NTLM, a domain controller or member server authenticates a client using pass-through authentication but the client never gets to verify the identity of the domain controller or member server. This raises the possibility of a man-in-the-middle attack.

Origin of the Name "Kerberos"

Kerberos takes its name from the mythological three-headed hound that guarded the gates of the underworld. This is because it uses three parties to carry out a transaction:

- A client (called a security principal)
- A target server (called a validating server)
- A central credentials repository (called a Key Distribution Center, or KDC)

If you're interested the spelling of the name Kerberos and details about the mythological origins of the name, take a look at the "Moron's Guide to Kerberos," `www.isi.edu/~brian/security/kerberos.html`.

- **Limitless logon time.** After a user has negotiated domain access via NTLM, the user is free to stay on the domain forever unless an administrator has imposed a specific logoff time. This means that a bad guy who manages to hijack a set of credentials can use them indefinitely.
- **No support for transitive trusts.** In a classic NT multi-master domain architecture, users from one domain can only access resources in a domain that directly trusts their domain. If Domain A trusts Domain B and Domain B trusts Domain C, users from Domain C cannot access resources in Domain A.
- **No support for delegation.** If a client initiates a process on a remote classic NT server, that process cannot reach out and access a resource on another server. This limits the capability of NT to support multi-tiered network applications. (An example of a multi-tiered application would be a database where one server holds the processes that implement the business rules while another holds the database.)

Authentication Methods Supported by Windows Server 2003

In spite of the limitations of NTLMv2, Windows Server 2003 continues to support it for backward compatibility. In an Active Directory domain, the default authentication mechanism is Kerberos. This is negotiated in the background and works completely transparently to the user.

Windows Server 2003 uses Kerberos authentication in the following instances:

- Authenticating modern Windows clients (Windows Server 2003 and XP, Windows 2000) when they log on to an Active Directory domain.
- Authenticating modern Windows clients when they access modern Windows servers that are members of an Active Directory domain.
- Authenticating modern Windows clients who access an Active Directory domain from another Active Directory domain in the same forest, from a different Active Directory forest via a Forest Root trust, or from an MIT v5 Kerberos realm via a Realm trust.

Windows Server 2003 uses NTLMv2 authentication in the following instances:

- Authenticating modern Windows clients logging on to a classic NT domain.
- Authenticating classic NT clients logging on to an Active Directory domain.
- Authenticating classic or modern Windows clients accessing servers in an Active Directory domain via an external trust.
- Authenticating users logging on to standalone modern Windows computers.
- Authenticating modern Windows clients accessing resources on standalone modern Windows servers.
- Authenticating downlevel clients accessing a modern Windows server if the client is configured with the Active Directory add-on.

Windows uses LM authentication to support Windows 9x clients that not been configured with the Active Directory add-on, Dsclient.exe.

You can verify the method used to authenticate a particular user by enabling logon/logoff auditing.

Overview of Kerberos Transactions

Kerberos uses three parties to authenticate users:

- A *security principal* who wants access to network resources. This could be a user or a service running on a computer.
- A *validating server* that receives the security principal's connection request and needs to verify the user's identity.
- A *Key Distribution Server* that holds the credentials for both the security principal and the validating server and issues special messages called *tickets* that the two parties use to verify each other's identity.

A Kerberos transaction resembles a scene from a John Le Carré spy novel. Imagine that a mole needs to contact her parent spy organization. She sends a prearranged signal and the parent organization agrees to send a runner to meet her. The mole has never seen the runner. The runner has never seen the mole. When they meet, how do they verify that they are genuine? Simple. They have a common acquaintance, the Chief back at headquarters. Procedure 11.5 shows how it works.

Procedure 11.5 High-Level Kerberos Example

1. The runner calls the Chief and says, "Give me a secret that only you and the mole know."
2. The Chief, always security conscious, verifies that the runner is genuine by verifying that the message was encrypted using the runner's secret encryption key.
3. The Chief then gets out the personnel files for the mole and the runner. The personnel files contain the secret encryption keys known only to the principals.
4. The Chief then builds a message to the mole. The message has two parts:
    - Part one contains a random number thought up by the Chief and encrypted with the runner's secret key.
    - Part two contains the same random number, the runner's name, and the time and date the chief wrote the note. This part is encrypted with the mole's secret key.
5. The runner uses his secret key to decode the random number in his portion of the message. If the result is gibberish, he assumes that someone has impersonated the Chief and given him a fake message. If the number looks right, he puts the mole's portion of the message in his wallet for safekeeping.

6. That afternoon, the mole and the runner meet. They exchange names and the runner gives the mole the second part of the Chief's message. They watch each other closely. We now have a Quentin Tarantino moment. (If you haven't seen the movie *Reservoir Dogs*, stop now and rent it.) Here's what happens:
   - If the mole cannot decode the Chief's message, the mole knows the runner is bogus and shoots him.
   - If the mole can decode the message, but the contents inside are scrambled, the mole knows the runner has fiddled with the message and she shoots him.
   - If the mole decodes the message and the runner's name in the message is different from the name he gave when they met, she shoots him.
   - If the mole has ever seen the random number before, she shoots him.
   - If the current time is later than the time the Chief wrote the note, the mole throws away the message and walks on.
7. If none of these unfortunate circumstances occur, the mole hands the runner a message. It contains her name, the current time, and the total number of letters in the message. This message is coded using the random number in the Chief's message as an encryption key.
8. The runner uses the random number he obtained from his part of the Chief's message to decode the mole's message. If the contents are garbled, the mole is an imposter and he shoots her. If the contents are clear but the timestamp is out of date, the mole is presenting an old message and he shoots her.
9. If the runner can decode the mole's message and the contents are acceptable, the authentication is complete and the two of them begin sharing information.

Extended metaphors make for slippery examples, but this game of *I Know A Secret, Do You?* parallels a Kerberos authentication fairly closely. The actual transactions are a bit more complicated only because the principals cannot meet face to face, so to speak. They send out their messages over a public network and so must assume that a bogeyman is out there capturing packets and using them to infiltrate the network.

Before examining the authentication transactions in detail, it's important to understand the terms and expressions used by Kerberos. They differ significantly from those used by classic NTLM.

Kerberos Vocabulary

Kerberos has existed in the public domain for years and has a colorful language all its own. The mix of this terminology with those used to describe classic NT authentication makes for a hodge-podge of lingo that is dense even by network systems standards. The following list of Kerberos terms explains their meaning and maps them to their classic NT counterparts.

Security Principal

An authentication mechanism verifies the identity of an entity who wants access to resources. The Kerberos term for such an entity is *security principal*, or often just *principal*. In Windows, *users* and *computers* are Kerberos security principals.

Realm

Every authentication system—Kerberos is no exception—requires a database to hold credentials. A Kerberos *realm* is defined by the contents of this database. The terms *domain* and *realm* are synonymous in Windows Server 2003. All objects in a domain, including those representing security principals, are contained in a single Active Directory database.

Ticket

The *ticket* is the fundamental unit of currency in Kerberos transactions. The ticket contains encrypted information that can only be read by the three parties involved in the transaction. It contains special features that prevent hijacking, replaying, or modifying the contents.

Key Distribution Center

The KDC is a central service that authenticates security principals and distributes tickets. (MIT Kerberos implementations can use separate servers for these two functions.)

Ticket-Granting Function

Whenever a security principal reaches out across the network to touch a server, it must present a Kerberos ticket for that server. The security principal obtains this ticket from the ticket-granting service of the KDC. In Windows Server 2003, the ticket-granting service is incorporated into the main Kerberos security package and does not appear as a separate item on a process list.

Authentication Function

Before security principals can obtain a Kerberos ticket, the KDC must verify their identity. The authentication service in a Kerberos KDC performs this function by checking the security principal's credentials against the contents of the security database.

When the KDC successfully authenticates a security principal at initial logon, it returns a special ticket called a *ticket-granting ticket*, or TGT. When the security principal needs to access a particular server, it must obtain a *session ticket* from the KDC specifically for the target server. It submits the TGT to speed up the process of issuing the session ticket.

This system of TGTs and session tickets resembles a county fair. You pay at the gate and you get a little stamp on your hand. That stamp doesn't give you permission to get on the midway rides. You have to buy individual tickets to get on the rides. When you do so, the attendant looks for the stamp on your hand to verify that you came through the front gate.

KRBTGT Account

When a KDC issues a ticket-granting ticket (TGT) to a security principal, it needs a way to assure that the contents of the TGT ticket haven't been modified when the principal returns the TGT to get a ticket to a server.

The KDC protects the TGT by encrypting the contents with a secret key known only to the KDC. This secret key comes in the form of a password hash that is an attribute of an account called KRBTGT. You can see this account in the Users container by using the AD Users and Computers console.

The KRBTGT account is built automatically when you promote or upgrade the first domain controller in a domain. The account cannot be deleted or renamed. You can change the password, but this is not recommended. If the KRBTGT password is known, you've compromised your entire authentication system. The KRBTGT password is long and complex. The system changes the password regularly.

Validating Server

A Kerberos validating server is equivalent to a Windows Server 2003 member server. A validating server forms the third leg of the three-way Kerberos transaction. When a client attempts to access a resource on a member server, the system at the client includes a Kerberos session ticket for the validating server. The validating server checks the ticket to see if it contains information placed there by the KDC and encrypted with the validating server's secret key.

A validating server must belong to the same Kerberos realm as the KDC that issued the session ticket. This is important to remember when we get to cross-realm authentication.

Kerberos Ticket Details

A Kerberos ticket is a highly important part of the authentication process, so it's worth taking a detailed look at its structure. Figure 11.10 shows a diagram of the ticket (or ticket-granting ticket) and the message that contains it.

Ports Used by Kerberos

If you're responsible for configuring firewalls, or communicating to those who do, you'll need to know the ports used by Kerberos. A Windows KDC listens on these ports:

- TCP and UDP port 88: authentication and ticket granting.
- TCP and UDP port 464: classic Kerberos kpasswd (password reset) protocol; not used by Windows.

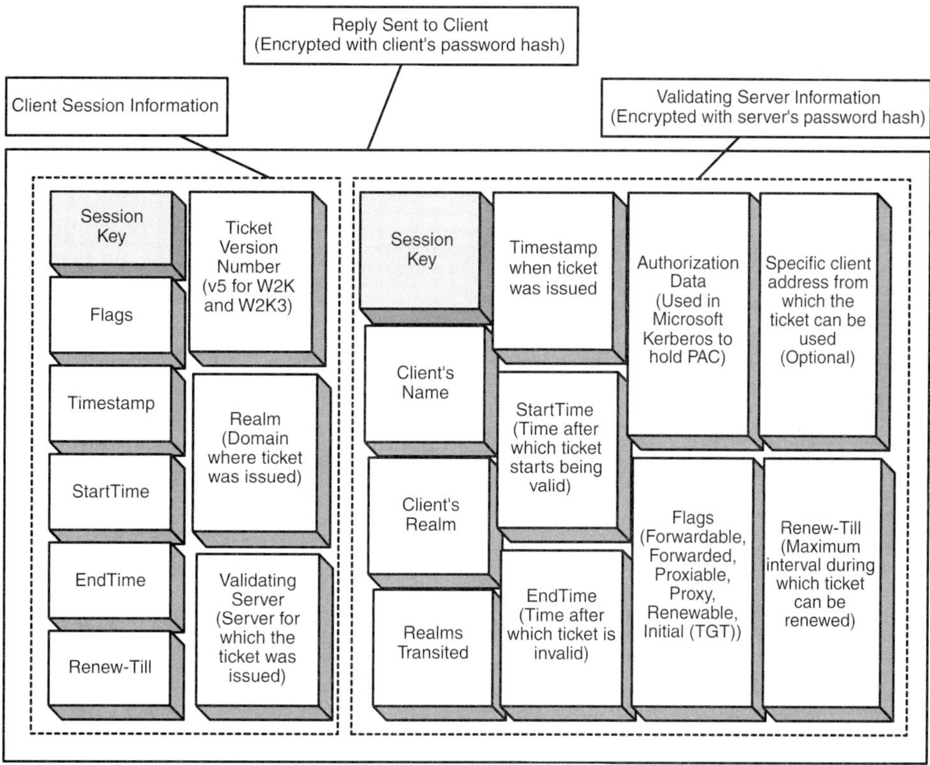

Figure 11.10 Kerberos reply containing ticket-granting ticket or session ticket.

When a client requests a TGT or a session ticket, the reply from the KDC contains two parts: a header that can be read by the client and the TGT or session ticket itself.

- The client information in the reply is encrypted with the client's password hash so it cannot be read by a bad guy on the network.
- A TGT is encrypted with the password hash of the KRBTGT account. The TGT can only be read by a domain controller because only domain controllers have the password hash of the KRBTGT account. This helps validates the authenticity and origin of the TGT.
- A session ticket is encrypted with the password hash of the member server, which is the Kerberos validating server. This helps validate the authenticity of the session ticket.

Here are the major elements of the reply message:

- **Session Key.** This important field contains a random number that uniquely identifies the TGT or session ticket. A copy of the session key is included in the TGT/session ticket. The session key becomes the shared secret that the security principal and validating server use when checking each other's identities.

- **Validating server name.** The name of the server that the user wants to access.
- **Realm name.** This is the Kerberos realm—Windows domain—of the KDC that issued the TGT or session ticket.
- **Flags.** A series of flags assigned by the KDC determine how the TGT or session ticket can be used. This includes permission to forward the ticket to another realm, which permits users in one domain to access servers in a trusted domain. A KDC can also put a flag on a ticket that authorizes a member server to use it as a proxy for the original client when accessing another server. Windows calls this *delegation of trust*.
- **Start time and end time.** This information determines an interval after which the TGT or session ticket is automatically invalid. After a ticket expires, the principal must obtain another. This limits the time that a bad guy who was able to compromise a ticket could do damage.
- **Ticket version number.** Windows uses Kerberos version 5.

The encrypted ticket or TGT includes the following major fields:

- **Session key**. This is a copy of the session key delivered to the client.
- **Client's name and realm**. This tells the validating server the identity of the client and the realm that holds the client's secret key. If the client declares an identity when submitting the ticket that does not match the ticket contents, the validating server knows that someone has hijacked the ticket.
- **Transited realms**. A user from one realm may want to get access to resources on a validating server in another realm. This is possible if there is a *trust* between the realms. This trust takes the form of a security principal in one realm that can be used to validate the identity of the security principal in the trusted realm. With the trust in place, a KDC can issue *cross-realm TGTs* to principals in other domains. When a client submits a cross-realm TGT, the KDC looks at the entries in the Transited Realms field to ensure that the client comes from a realm that has a set of cross-realm trusts with the KDC's realm. This helps implement transitive trusts that Windows relies on for building Active Directory trees and forests.
- **Timestamps**. A TGT or session ticket contains three different timestamps: The time the ticket was issued, the time it begins being valid (for postdated tickets), and the time it stops being valid. Windows does not use nor does it accept postdated tickets.

  The expiration time is determined by a Time-To-Live (TTL) value configured at the KDC. For Windows, the default TTL is 10 hours. For this timestamp to work correctly, all KDCs in a realm must have their times synchronized. Windows uses the W32Time service to synchronize time between domain controllers. The acceptable time skew is five minutes.

- **Authorization data.** This very important field has garnered a lot of attention in Microsoft's implementation of Kerberos.

Additional Kerberos Elements

Because it's a big, bad world out there, Kerberos takes pains to prevent likely attack scenarios. This includes hijacking tickets, denial-of-service attacks, and man-in-the-middle attacks.

Authenticator

If a bad guy can nab a session ticket out of a packet, it would be possible to impersonate a client and do lots of damage. To prevent this, a connection request between a security principal and a validating server includes a little piece of data called an *authenticator.*

The authenticator consists of the client's name and realm along with a timestamp. The client encrypts the authenticator with the *session key*, the random number assigned to the session ticket by the KDC. The client knows the value of the session key because it was included in the client portion of the session ticket reply.

When the validating server receives the access request, it decrypts the ticket with its own password hash. Now come a series of decision points:

- If the server cannot decrypt the ticket, or if the internals of the ticket have been changed, it rejects the connection attempt out of hand.
- If the server can decrypt the session ticket, it extracts the session key from the ticket and uses it to decrypt the authenticator. If the server cannot decrypt the authenticator, it has to assume that a bad guy has stitched together a ticket and an authenticator. It rejects the connection attempt.
- The server then compares the contents of the decrypted authenticator with the information in the connection request. If the client's name or realm does not match, the server assumes that a bad guy has fiddled with the authenticator. It rejects the connection attempt.
- If the user's credentials match but the timestamp is outside the acceptable five-minute skew, the server assumes that a bad guy has nabbed the authenticator for use at a later time. It rejects the connection attempt.
- If the timestamp exactly matches a timestamp in an earlier authenticator, the server assumes that a bad guy is replaying an earlier connection and it rejects the attempt. If the server should ever get confused about the connection requests from a client, it will reject *all* connection requests for the five-minute duration of the time skew.

If the session ticket and the authenticator survive the scrutiny of the validating server, the client is given access. Now let's see how Kerberos helps to stop man-in-the-middle attacks.

Preauthenticator

In the evolution of acronyms, DOS has now stopped being short for *Disk Operating System* and has become an acronym for *Denial Of Service*. One likely DOS attack for Kerberos consists of bombarding a KDC with invalid authentication requests in the hopes that the server would be so busy saying "No. No. No." that it would not have time to say, "Yes. Yes. Yes." to authentic requests.

To avoid this type of attack, a KDC has the option of accepting ticket-granting ticket requests only from clients that include a special data structure called a *preauthenticator* in their initial Kerberos TGT request. The preauthenticator is simply a timestamp that has been encrypted with the client's password hash.

When a KDC receives a TGT request, it retrieves the password hash from Active Directory and uses it to decrypt the preauthenticator.

If the preauthenticator decryption succeeds (the contents pass a cyclic redundancy check), the KDC begins processing the TGT request. If the decryption does not succeed, the KDC returns a bad name or password error to the client.

The KDC also verifies that the timestamp in the preauthenticator is within five minutes of the system time on the server just in case a bad guy is trying to submit a rigged TGT request.

It takes relatively few CPU cycles to process a preauthenticator, so even a moderately powerful KDC can withstand a fairly heavy DOS attack.

Mutual Authentication

A standard Kerberos transaction goes in one direction only. The client submits a ticket and the server accepts the ticket. But what if a bad guy puts up a server that pretends to be another server? This bogus server accepts Kerberos tickets but instead of giving back the requested files, it returns files filled with viruses and Trojan horse programs and other nasties.

A smart Kerberos client always makes sure that the server accepting the ticket is the real server. This is called *mutual authentication*. It's up to the client to request mutual authentication. All Windows clients do so.

A mutual authentication transaction is the mirror image of the session ticket submittal transaction. The validating server encrypts a timestamp with the session key from the ticket and returns the result to the client in a reply message. The client evaluates the authenticator and only continues with the connection transaction if the evaluation succeeds.

Negative Kerberos Caching

Starting with Windows 2000 SP2, if a DC that is not the PDC Emulator receives a set of bad credentials for a user, it caches the result locally to reduce traffic to the PDC Emulator. By default, the user is limited to 10 forwarded requests. From that point forward, the user is denied access based on the cached information for a period of 10 minutes.

Authorization Data

Kerberos is an authentication protocol, not an authorization protocol. The difference can be a bit subtle. Here's an example.

Back during our nation's adventure in managing Southeast Asian affairs, I opted for a tenure in the U.S. Navy on nuclear submarines with the (entirely valid) assumption that it was far safer sleeping next to a few tons of red-hot fissile material than boating along the Mekong.

In the military, you quickly learn the difference between authentication and authorization. When you come aboard a nuclear submarine, a topside watch checks your ID. If your face doesn't match the picture on your ID, or your name isn't on the submarine's access list, the topside watch shoots you. (Well, maybe not that drastic, but you *are* denied access.) This initial identity check is your *authentication*.

When on board the sub, you can visit the galley and the berthing areas, but without specialized clearance, you aren't allowed into sensitive areas like the torpedo room, the reactor area, or the wardroom wine cellar. This additional clearance constitutes your *authorization* to access the sensitive areas.

As we've seen, modern Windows uses Kerberos for its authentication mechanism and a combination of access tokens and security descriptors to control authorization. When Microsoft engineers developed their Kerberos implementation, they chose to fold part of the authorization function into the Kerberos transactions. They did this by taking advantage of a field in the Kerberos ticket called the *authorization data* field.

When the KDC is ready to build a ticket-granting ticket, it asks the LSASS for a special data structure called a *Privilege Access Certificate*, or PAC. This PAC contains the user information necessary to build a local access token for a user at a remote server. The PAC is digitally signed with both the domain controller's private key and the private key issued to the KDC service. This prevents a client or a bogus KDC from forging a PAC.

PAC Contents

A quick review of the PAC contents reveals many interesting items that relate directly to system administration. You'll recognize the parameters from group policies and user settings. Here is a list of the PAC elements:

- The time the user logged on and when the user's session expires, if that option is set. The PAC also defines if the user should be forcibly logged off when the session expires.

- The last time the user set her password and when she is allowed to change her password again (if a minimum password age policy is set). The password expiration date is also included.
- The user's flat logon name. This is the name stored in Active Directory as the `SamAccountName` and exposed in `AD Users and Computers` as the `Pre-Windows 2000 Logon Name`.
- The user's full name, stored as the Display Name in Active Directory. This name is not used for any security purposes.
- The name of the classic NT logon script assigned to the user's account, if any. The script must exist in the Netlogon share of the logon server.
- The UNC path to the user's roaming profile, if one has been assigned.
- The UNC path to the client's home directory, if one has been assigned, along with the drive letter to use when mapping the home drive to the directory path.
- The number of concurrent logon instances for the user. This number represents connections at the domain controller that constructs the PAC, not the entire domain, so it is *not* an accurate measure of concurrent logons.
- The number of unsuccessful logon attempts since the last successful attempt at the domain controller issuing the PAC.
- The user's Relative ID (RID). This number is combined with the domain SID to form a unique SID for the user.
- The RID of the user's primary group, used only in POSIX.
- The number of groups in the domain that have the user as a member and the RID for each of those groups.
- The well-known SIDs applicable to the user, such as `Authenticated User`, `Network User`, and `Everyone`.
- The name of the user's domain and name of the domain controller that authenticated the user.
- The SID of the domain, used in conjunction with the RIDs to create unique user and group SIDs.
- The SID of the resource domain, if the user logged on from a machine in a classic NT resource domain, and the SID of any groups in the resource domain that have the user as a member.

PAC Documentation

Documentation for the contents and format of a Privilege Access Certificate can be downloaded from `www.microsoft.com/Downloads/Release.asp?ReleaseID=20597`.

In addition, there is another data structure embedded in the PAC called `User Account Control`. This structure defines a number of user settings, many of which you'll recognize from check blocks in the `Account` tab of the user properties in `AD Users and Computers`. The User Account Control settings are as follows:

- Account Disabled
- Home Directory Required
- Password Not Required
- Temp Duplicate Account (no longer used)
- Normal Account
- MNS Logon Account (undocumented and unused)
- Interdomain Trust Account (represents a trust to another domain)
- Workstation Trust Account (represents a member computer in the domain)
- Server Trust Account (represents a classic backup domain controller)
- Don't Expire Password
- Account Auto Locked
- Encrypted Text Password Allowed
- Smart card Required
- Trusted For Delegation
- Not Delegated
- Use DES Key Only (LanMan authentication only)
- Don't Require Preauthentication

PAC Usage

Kerberos includes the PAC in the authorization data field of the ticket-granting ticket that it issues to a client. The Kerberos client caches the TGT and submits a copy each time it requests a session ticket from the KDC. When the KDC builds the session ticket, it extracts the PAC from the TGT and puts a copy in the authorization data field of the session ticket.

After the member server validates the session ticket, the Kerberos security package extracts the PAC from the ticket and delivers it to the LSASS, which uses the PAC to build a local access token for the client. This means that if you add a user to a group or change the user's security settings, the user must log off and then back on again to get a new TGT with a new PAC that contains the new group SIDs.

By eliminating separate transaction to obtain the user's PAC, Microsoft avoided additional steps in the access process. It also avoided potential vulnerabilities caused by passing the authorization information in a second, proprietary transaction. Unfortunately, this method for passing the PAC information was poorly documented at the release of Windows 2000, which angered many developers who wanted to port their applications to Windows Kerberos but did not have enough information about the PAC.

In the two years since Windows 2000 was released, Microsoft has documented the PAC but has not exactly gone out of its way to support efforts to incorporate the authorization data into third-party products. For example, Samba clients still must use NTLM rather than Kerberos because the developers of the advanced version of Samba are waiting to get a fuller understanding of how the PAC is processed.

At a much more esoteric level, the PAC also changed the way Microsoft implements Kerberos messages. Standard Kerberos requests and replies are small enough to fit into a single datagram and are therefore usually sent via UDP. A large PAC can exceed the size of a standard datagram, forcing the system to use TCP to guarantee sequential delivery of the entire session ticket. This can affect interoperability if a third-party Kerberos KDC is not coded to listen and respond on TCP port 88.

Summary of Kerberos Elements

Figure 11.11 shows the three corners of the Kerberos triangle and how information flows between the parties. Here's a capsulization before we look at the gory details:

- A Windows domain is a Kerberos realm.
- A Windows domain controller is also a Kerberos KDC.
- A Windows KDC performs both classic KDC functions: authentication and ticket-granting.

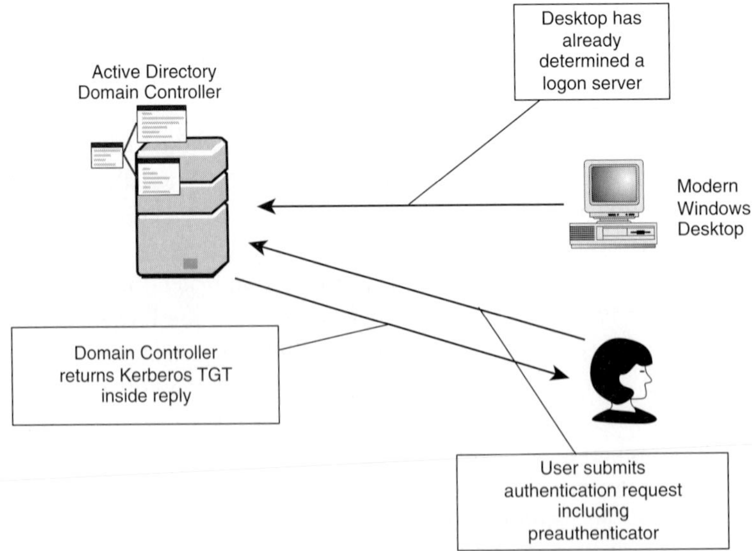

Figure 11.11 Kerberos components and transactions.

- Separate Windows domains in the same forest are connected via cross-realm Kerberos trusts. These trusts are two-way and transitive.
- A modern Windows computer that is a member of an Active Directory domain is also a Kerberos security principal. Services running on the computer that access resources on other servers obtain session tickets from the KDC.
- A modern Windows server that is a member of a Windows domain requires a Kerberos session ticket when being accessed by a modern Windows client. The server falls back to NTLM authentication for downlevel clients.
- A user logging on at the console of a modern Windows computer that is a member of an Active Directory domain will automatically authenticate in the domain using Kerberos. This is true even in a Mixed domain where a classic PDC or BDC is available for authentication.
- The authorization data field of TGTs and session tickets contain a Privilege Access Certificate (PAC) that details the information necessary to build local access tokens for users.

With all this in mind, it's time to see what happens when users log on via Kerberos and attempt to get access to resources.

Analysis of Kerberos Transactions

Modern Windows clients use Kerberos authentication in the following three situations:

- **Initial computer startup.** The client computer uses credentials stored in the LSA database to authenticate with an Active Directory domain controller. It then establishes a secure channel to that logon server.

Kerberos Authentication in Mixed Domains

A modern Windows computer that belongs to a Mixed domain will always authenticate with an Active Directory-based domain controller if one is available. This is true even if the computer must authenticate across the WAN to get to the AD-based domain controller.

Modern Windows clients check for service locator (SRV) records in DNS every time they start. As long as they don't see any indication of an AD-based domain, they're happy to use NTLM to authenticate. But after they see SRV records, they will insist on using Kerberos.

This behavior can come as a surprise if you've deployed hundreds or thousands of Windows 2000 and XP desktops while you are still running a classic NT4 domain. As soon as you upgrade your PDC to an AD-based domain controller, every modern Windows client will see the SRV records and go right to that AD-based domain controller to authenticate. They may come from all corners of the globe.

You can inhibit this behavior, but to do so you must put a Registry entry in place. See Chapter 9, "Deploying Windows Server 2003 Domains," for details.

- **Service account authentication.** Some services use Kerberos authentication when connecting to other servers. These so-called Kerberized applications register themselves as distinct security principals in Active Directory. Examples of Kerberized connections include LDAP connection to Active Directory, CIFS/SMB file access, and secure dynamic DNS updates.
- **Initial user logon.** A user logging on to an Active Directory domain from a modern Windows computer authenticates at the same domain controller as the computer.

Let's take a look at this last transaction, a user who logs on to an Active Directory domain from a modern Windows client. The transaction details are the same for Windows Server 2003, Windows XP, and Windows 2000.

Initial User Logon Authentication

Figure 11.12 shows a user logon in a single Active Directory domain. Here are the key points to watch for:

- The user must present domain credentials to get access to a domain member computer.
- The user's plain-text and encrypted password is never transmitted over the wire.
- The user is issued a ticket-granting ticket (TGT) during the initial domain authentication.

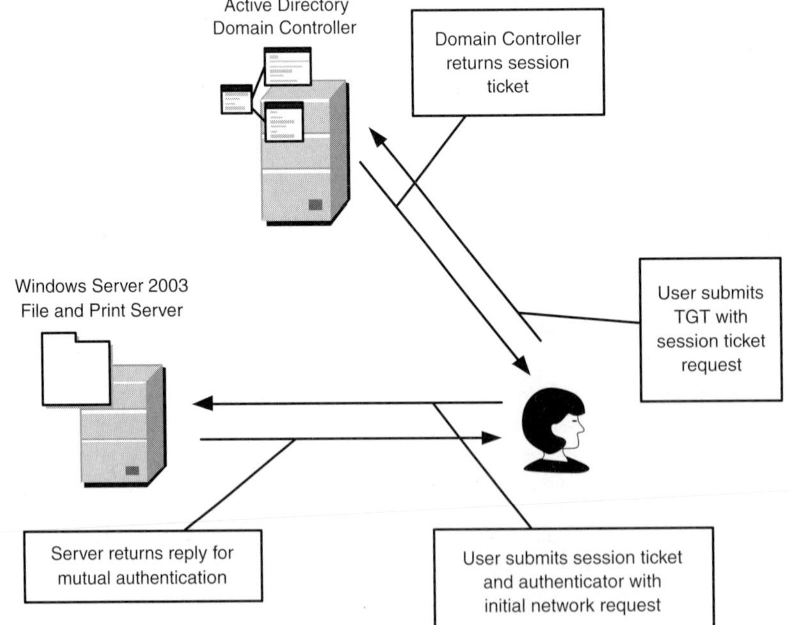

Figure 11.12 Logon transaction in a single AD-based domain.

Determining the Identity of the Logon Server

You can identify a user's logon server by opening a command prompt and running SET. Here's a partial listing. The LOGONSERVER variable is in bold:

```
C:\>set
ALLUSERSPROFILE=C:\Documents and Settings\All Users
APPDATA=C:\Documents and Settings\Administrator\Application Data
CommonProgramFiles=C:\Program Files\Common Files
COMPUTERNAME=SRV1
ComSpec=C:\WINDOWS\system32\cmd.exe
HOMEDRIVE=C:
HOMEPATH=\Documents and Settings\Administrator
LOGONSERVER=\\SERVER1
```

Procedure 11.6 traces the transaction starting from the initial logon.

Procedure 11.6 User Logon Transaction Using Kerberos

1. The user initiates logon by pressing `Ctrl+Alt+Del`. This is called the *Secure Attention Sequence*. It wakes up Winlogon and displays the logon credentials window defined in Gina.dll. This foils any Trojan horse programs that might get in ahead of the operating system and nab a user's password.
2. The user enters an account name and password and selects a domain in the Domain field of the logon window. As an alternative, the user could enter a User Principal Name (UPN) in the format *`user@domain.root`*. Either name format results in the same actions on the part of the security system.

UPN Versus Domain\Name Logon Format

A persistent rumor in the Windows administrator community asserts that entering a username and domain in Winlogon results in a classic NTLM authentication, whereas entering a UPN results in a Kerberos authentication. Unlike the protestations of a certain ex-president, there is absolutely no truth to this rumor. If the local computer has authenticated in an AD-based domain, the user will be authenticated using Kerberos regardless of the logon format. The only difference between using domain\name\password and a UPN is that the UPN requires a query to a Global Catalog server to extract the username and domain. Windows Server 2003 and XP clients cache the results of this query in case a GC server is not available.

3. Winlogon takes the user's credentials and passes them to the Local Security Authority Subsystem, LSASS, which hashes the user's password using MD4 and then works with the Kerberos package to authenticate the user.
4. The Kerberos package takes the user's password hash and uses it to construct a TGT request that contains the preauthenticator (a timestamp encrypted with the user's password hash). (This transaction does not require Netlogon at either the client or the domain controller.)

5. The KDC service at the domain controller receives the TGT request. If the user's name exists, the service obtains the user's password hash from Active Directory and uses it to decrypt the preauthenticator.
6. If the KDC fails to decrypt the preauthenticator, or if the timestamp indicates that it has been replayed or is out of the acceptable time skew, the authentication fails. The KDC sends a logon failure notification to the client.
7. If the KDC accepts the preauthenticator as genuine, it gets help from LSASS to create a PAC for the user. It places the PAC in the authentication data field of the TGT and returns it inside a reply message to the user. The TGT is encrypted with the password hash of the krbtgt account. The entire reply is encrypted with the user's password hash.
8. The Kerberos client decrypts the reply and caches the session key and TGT in memory, not on disk. It turns the PAC over to LSASS.
9. The LSASS uses the information in the PAC to build a local access token for the user. (It adds the SIDs of any machine local groups that have the user as a member and any local security policies that apply to the user.)
10. When the TGT expires (the default Time-To-Live is 10 hours), the client obtains a new TGT from the KDC. This happens transparently with no service interruption unless no domain controller is available, in which case the client loses access to the domain until a domain controller can be made available.

At this point, the console logon is complete. Winlogon passes control over to Userinit, which downloads and processes Registry-based group policies and then fires off the Explorer shell in the user's security context. Any subsequent processes spawned by the user get the user's access token.

Authentication When Accessing Member Servers

Following domain authentication, the user then accesses resources on member servers in the domain. Let's take a look at what happens. The key points to watch for are as follows:

- The client must go back to its logon server to get a session ticket for the target server.
- The client presents the session ticket to the member server inside the first connection transaction along with an authenticator and a mutual authentication request.
- The member server decrypts the ticket, validates the authenticator, and responds with an authenticator of its own. It also creates a local access token for the user.
- The client validates the server's authenticator.

Procedure 11.7 traces the transaction from the point where the user reaches out to touch a network resource.

Procedure 11.7 Server Access Transaction Using Kerberos

1. The user opens `My Network Places`, navigates to a server icon, and double-clicks the icon.
2. The network redirector calls on LSASS to get a Kerberos ticket for the target server. LSASS turns right around and calls on the Kerberos security package for help.
3. The Kerberos package gets a copy of the cached ticket-granting ticket (TGT) and uses it to build a *session ticket request* specifying the target server's name. The request is encrypted using the session key that came with the TGT.
4. The KDC receives the request and decrypts it with its copy of the session key. If the decryption fails, the KDC knows that someone has hijacked the ticket. If the contents do not pass CRC (Cyclic Redundancy Checking), the KDC knows that someone fiddled with the contents.
5. The KDC then builds a ticket for the target server. The ticket contains a new session key specific to this particular transaction. The KDC delivers the ticket to the client in a reply message. The ticket itself is encrypted with the target server's password hash. The entire reply is encrypted with the user's password hash.
6. The Kerberos package decrypts the reply and caches the session key and the ticket. It uses the session key to build an authenticator. It includes the authenticator and the ticket in an *access request* that it hands over to the network redirector.
7. The redirector builds a Server Message Block (SMB) message asking the server to create a session and to let the client connect using that session. It includes the Kerberos access request with that initial SMB message.
8. The target server extracts the access request from the SMB and passes it to LSASS, which calls on the local Kerberos package to decrypt the ticket and validate the authenticator.
9. When the client has been validated, the Kerberos package extracts a copy of the session key from the ticket and uses it to build an authenticator of its own, which it returns to the client in an access reply.

   At the same time, the server extracts the PAC from the authorization data field of the ticket and gives it to LSASS, which uses it to build a local access token for the user. (LSASS adds the SIDs of any machine local groups that have the user as a member and any local security policies that apply to the user.)
10. The client validates the authenticator returned by the server and then completes the SMB session setup.
11. When the session ticket expires (10 hours by default), the Kerberos package obtains another ticket from the KDC. It does this transparently to the user unless a domain controller is not available, in which case the user loses access to the member server.

Viewing Kerberos Tickets

You'll find two tools in the Resource Kit that help troubleshoot Kerberos transactions by listing the ticket-granting tickets and tickets obtained by a client:

- Kerbtray. This utility places an icon in the System Tray that you can double-click to view a list of tickets and details about the ticket contents. Figure 11.13 shows an example.

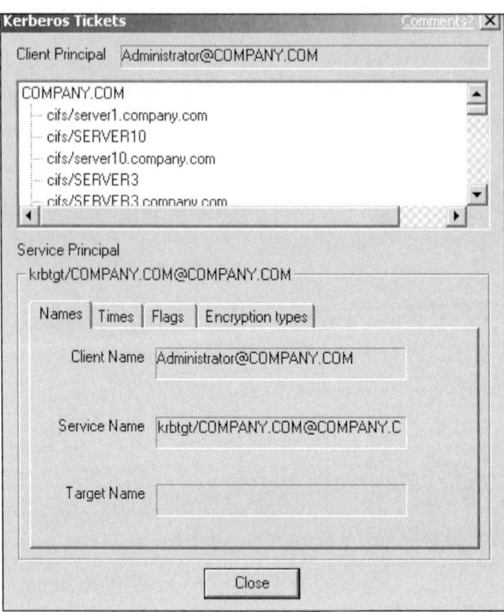

Figure 11.13 Kerbtray window showing ticket list.

- KLIST. This command-line utility is derived from the classic MITv5 Kerberos utility of the same name. Here is an example listing:

```
C:\>klist tickets
Cached Tickets: (2)
   Server: krbtgt/COMPANY.COM@COMPANY.COM
      KerbTicket Encryption Type: RSADSI RC4-HMAC(NT)
      End Time: 11/25/2001 19:55:37
      Renew Time: 12/2/2001 9:55:37


   Server: SERVER1@COMPANY.COM
      KerbTicket Encryption Type: RSADSI RC4-HMAC(NT)
      End Time: 11/25/2001 19:55:37
      Renew Time: 12/2/2001 9:55:37
```

Cross-Domain Authentication

One of the most powerful features of Kerberos is its capability to handle transitive cross-realm authentications. This means that a user in one domain can access a security object (NTFS file or folder, AD object, Service, or Registry key) in any other domain in a forest as long as an administrator has configured the object's security to authorize access.

Figure 11.14 shows an example of a cross-domain authentication transaction. In the example, a user in a child domain in one tree is trying to access a shared folder on a member server in a child domain in another tree. The roots of the two trees share a two-way trust.

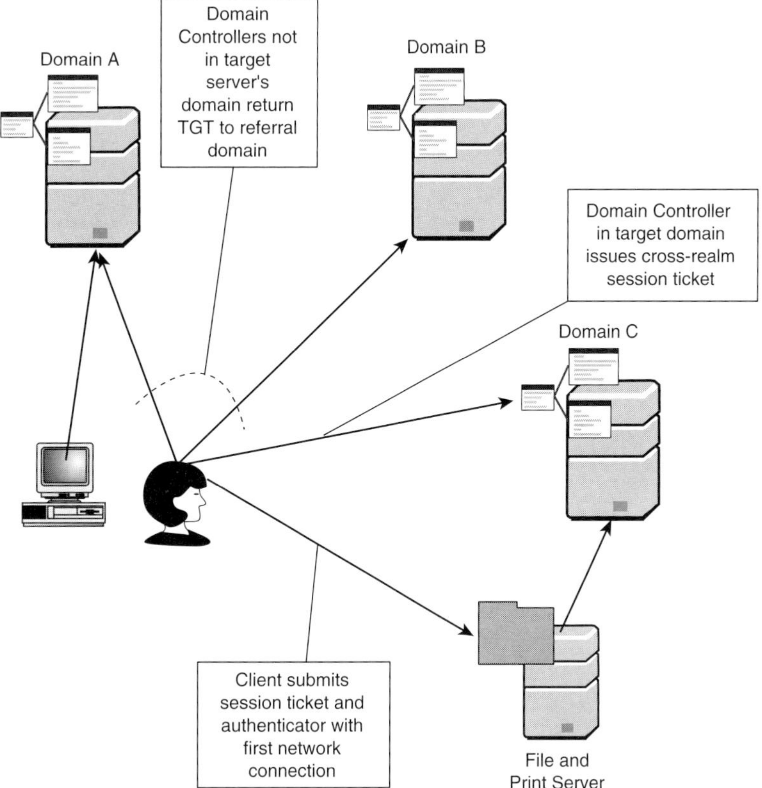

Figure 11.14 Forest of domains showing cross-domain authentication.

Domain controllers in one domain cannot issue session tickets for member servers in another domain. Recall that domains form separate naming contexts in Active Directory. A domain controller only has access to its own naming context. (A global catalog server has a partial replica of every Domain naming context, but the GC does not contain all the information necessary to build a session ticket.)

For the same reason, Kerberos clients from one domain cannot go directly to a KDC in a remote domain to obtain a session ticket to a server in that domain. The client has no credentials in the remote Domain naming context.

The local domain controller supports cross-domain access by obtaining a *cross-realm TGT* from its parent domain on behalf of the user. It returns this cross-realm TGT to the client along with a referral to the parent domain.

The domain controller can obtain the cross-domain TGT thanks to a Kerberos feature called *delegation*. Using delegation, a service on one machine can obtain TGTs or session tickets on behalf of a user on another machine. This is a powerful feature and one that represents a security vulnerability if it is not handled correctly. We'll take a closer look at delegation in the next topic.

The client follows up on the referral by submitting the cross-realm TGT to a domain controller in the parent domain and asking once again for a session ticket to the target server. If the server is not in that domain, the domain controller obtains a cross-realm TGT either to its own parent or to the top domain in the tree that contains the target domain.

Using this process, the client "walks the tree," asking each domain in its path for a ticket to the target server and obtaining a cross-realm TGT and a referral until it finally arrives at the domain that contains the target server. At this point, the client submits its cross-realm TGT to a domain controller in the target domain. The domain controller validates the TGT and issues a session ticket to the target server.

Part of the validation performed by the domain controller includes a determination that each domain transited (crossed by) by the client is trusted by domains on either side. The domain controller knows the domains transited by the client because that information is stored in the cross-realm TGT. The domain controller knows the forest structure based on partition information in Active Directory (also known as *knowledge*).

From this point, the transaction proceeds very much like a regular Kerberos transaction. The client submits the session ticket and an authenticator to the member server and is granted access. The PAC in the session ticket originated in a remote domain, so the user will only be authorized to access resources on the server if someone has added the user to the DACL on the resources.

Short-Cut Trusts

The example in the previous section demonstrated how transitive, two-way Kerberos trusts make it possible for a user to access resources anywhere in the forest by logging on to one domain.

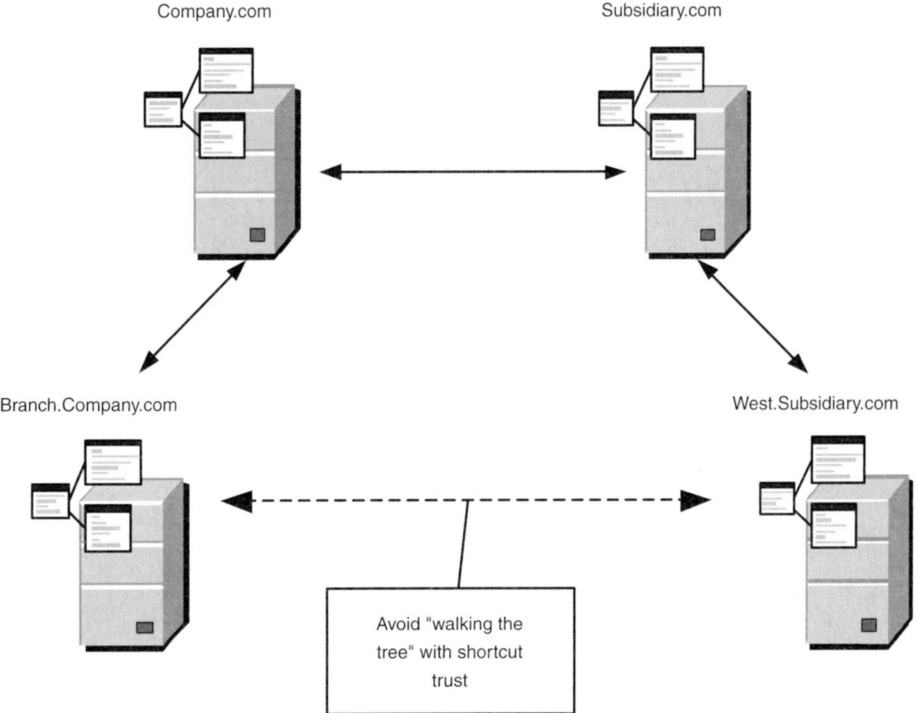

Figure 11.15 Forest showing short-cut trust between two child domains.

In an extensive, multi-domain environment, you may experience performance problems with cross-domain authentication. This slowdown is caused because the client is forced to communicate across the WAN when it walks the tree to get cross-realm authentication, as shown in Figure 11.15.

If the delays are too long and your users complain, you can shorten the process by creating a *short-cut trust* between one domain and another in a forest. The short-cut trust tells the KDC that it can go directly to the target domain for a cross-domain TGT and avoid walking the tree.

Kerberos Delegation

In the classic NTLM authentication shown in Figure 11.16, there is no support for pass-through authentication from one server to another server. This limits the ability of NT to support so-called *n-tier applications*. N-tier applications use a middle server to field user requests and then pass the request to one or more back-end servers.

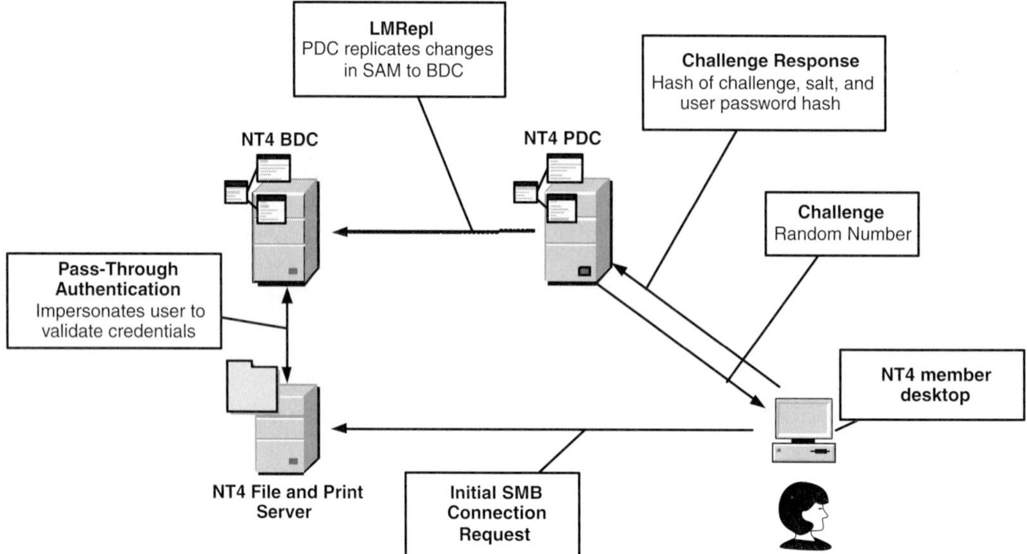

Figure 11.16 Forest showing short-cut trust between two child domains.

Because of the restrictions in NTLM, applications such as web front ends or Object Resource Brokers (ORBs) are required to log on to the back-end server using credentials stored at the middle server. This is commonly done using accounts and passwords embedded in ODBC connections or ActiveX Data Object (ADO) connections or third-party application data structures.

The problem with this sort of configuration is that all the user accounts essentially multiplex through the middle server into a single account that touches the backend servers. This creates a security problem if the application on the middle server is somehow compromised. You also lose accountability for user access to the back-end server.

Kerberos makes it possible for a middle server to obtain a user's credentials and to use those credentials when accessing a back-end server. This can be done in one of two ways:

- **Forwardable tickets.** In this configuration, the middle server asks the client to obtain a session ticket for the back-end server. The middle server then uses this ticket to make connection to the application running on the back-end server. The ticket must be flagged as *forwardable* for this trick to work.
- **Proxiable tickets.** In this configuration, the middle server asks the client to obtain a ticket-granting ticket for the domain and to give that TGT to the middle server. The middle server then uses the TGT to obtain a session ticket to the back-end server on behalf of the user. This TGT must be flagged as *proxiable*.

The difference between forwardable and proxiable tickets is the difference between lending a friend $10 for lunch and giving the friend a power of attorney and your checkbook.

The middle server can obtain Kerberos tickets to make it appear to be any user in the forest, so it occupies a highly secure position. For this reason, standard servers cannot obtain forwardable or proxiable tickets. A server must be flagged as "Trusted for Delegation" before it can obtain Kerberos tickets on behalf of a user.

Additional Kerberos Benefits

You might look at all these Kerberos features and say to yourself, "Fine. I like them. But we still have thousands of Windows 98 and NT4 workstations and hundreds of NT4 servers and we aren't going to be upgrading them overnight. I guess we'll have to forgo all those nifty features for a good, long while."

Fortunately, you don't have to wait as long as you might expect. As soon as you shift the domains in your forest to Native, the downlevel clients can participate in transitive trusts. In Native, domain controllers use transitive Kerberos trusts to obtain cross-domain TGTs and tickets on behalf of downlevel clients. Here's how it works.

When an LM or NTLM client attempts to touch an NT server in another Native domain, the server in the remote domain uses NTLM pass-through authentication to contact a domain controller in its domain.

The domain controller uses delegation to walk backward through the tree to obtain a cross-realm TGT on behalf of the client. This TGT is sufficient to authenticate the user in the remote domain.

The domain controller then completes the pass-through authentication and informs the member server that the user has been authenticated. It includes a classic NT data structure with the user's SIDs and security privileges that it obtained from the PAC in the cross-realm TGT.

Here's the bottom line. If you have Native domains in your forest, your NT, Windows 9x, and Samba clients get the following benefits:

- Domain Local groups can be placed on local ACLs.
- Users on the downlevel can access resources on any server in any domain (assuming they are on the local ACLs).

The reason this doesn't work in Mixed is because the Active Directory domains retain their classic NT limitations. After all, a client might authenticate on a classic BDC rather than an Active Directory domain controller and that eliminates the possibility of a cross-realm transaction.

Kerberos Policies

You can change certain Kerberos parameters by setting group policies. The policies are set in the Default Domain group policy. They are located under `Computer Configuration | Windows Settings | Security Settings | Account Policies | Kerberos Policies`. The polices are as follows:

- **`Enforce user logon restrictions.`** Each member server in a domain has a set of local account policy restrictions. These restrictions stipulate things like local logon permissions and who has permission to access the computer across the network. By default, the KDC validates that a user meets a server's local account restrictions prior to issuing the user a session ticket to the server. This adds more steps to the logon process but saves traffic by preventing the user from getting a session ticket that cannot be used anyway because of the local restriction.

- **`Maximum lifetime for service ticket.`** A *service ticket* is the same as a session ticket. Every session ticket has a default Time-To-Live of 10 hours. You can shorten this interval, but be careful not to make it too short or you will force the clients to obtain new tickets too often. The setting must be longer than 10 minutes and shorter than the `Maximum lifetime for user ticket` setting.
- **`Maximum lifetime for user ticket.`** A *user ticket* is the same as a ticket-granting ticket. By default, a TGT has a 10-hour lifetime, after which it must be renewed. The minimum setting is 10 minutes and should not be set lower than the `Maximum lifetime for service ticket` setting.
- **`Maximum lifetime for user ticket renewal.`** By default, TGTs can be renewed for a period of seven days. After that, the TGT expires and a new TGT must be obtained.
- **`Maximum tolerance for computer clock synchronization.`** By default, the maximum clock skew is five minutes. This value should not be changed.

MITv5 Kerberos Interoperability

If you have a network where you currently use MITv5 Kerberos for authentication, you are probably very interested in getting Windows Kerberos integrated into your system. By the same token, you may have an Active Directory domain where you want to use a Kerberos application that was coded to work in an MITv5 environment. In either case, you have a solid amount of work ahead of you to get the two systems to cooperate.

It is possible for a Kerberos realm and an Active Directory domain live side-by-side. Users from one side must access services and resources on the other side. Our job is to make that transition as seamless as possible. This section covers the general steps you would take to create a cross-realm trust that can accommodate Kerberos services and principals from both sides.

The Kerberos implementation in Windows follows RFC requirements that originated with MITv5 Kerberos, so the two versions can co-exist, but the operational details of the marriage vary widely depending on your platforms and applications.

Even if you do not use MITv5 Kerberos and have no plans to do so, it may be worth the exercise to go through this section. Each subsection outlines the differences in the way Windows implements the classic MITv5 components and spells out potential difficulties in making them work together.

MITv5 Kerberos References

Here are some excellent references you should consult when the time comes to set up a classic Kerberos MITv5 realm:

- **The Moron's Guide to Kerberos**, `www.isi.edu/~brian/security/kerberos.html`. Certainly not for a "moron," this well-written, concise overview from Brian Tung discusses how Kerberos operates and how it is implemented in a UNIX environment.
- **Kerberos: An Authentication Service for Computer Networks**, `www.isi.edu/gost/publications/kerberos-neuman-tso.html`. This seminal 1994 work by B. Clifford Neuman and Theodore Ts'o still stands as one of the best industrial-strength explanations of Kerberos operation. It does not contain implementation details, but you'll learn operational nitty-gritty that isn't spelled out anywhere else.
- **Kerberos FAQ**, `www.nrl.navy.mil/CCS/people/kenh/kerberos-faq.html`. Like most FAQs, this is a sprawling document. Fire up your search tools and be prepared to do some digging.
- **Kerberos V5 Installation Guide**, `www.lns.cornell.edu/public/COMP/krb5/install/install_toc.html` (among others). This authoritative reference describes exactly how to install UNIX-based MITv5 Kerberos in a diverse university environment. The document assumes you are running executables built from the MIT source code, but the steps are generally applicable to other implementations.
- **Step-by-Step Guide to Kerberos 5 Interoperability**, `www.microsoft.com/windows2000/techinfo/planning/security/kerbsteps.asp`. This guide came out in conjunction with the initial release of Windows 2000 in response to many queries from universities about how Microsoft Kerberos would work with MITv5 Kerberos. The working level detail in the paper is very good and can be applied to a variety of Kerberos implementations.
- **Red Hat v7.1 Reference Guide**, `www.redhat.com/support/manuals`. If you are interested in implementing Kerberos in a Red Hat Linux environment, this is a good place start. Don't take the instructions too literally because they are sometimes not quite up to date with the new features and changes in version 7.1.
- **Debian documentation**, `www.mit.edu/afs/sipb/project/debian/cvs/krb5/doc/krb5-install.info-1,v`. These documents are a lot more detailed than the Red Hat documentation, as you might expect from the Debian distro, but they tend not to be as current as you might like.
- **Services for UNIX (SFU)**, Microsoft Corp and Mortis Kerns Systems (MKS) partner together to produce SFU. The package has an extension that updates the AD schema to include UNIX attributes such as UID, GID, homedirectories, and so forth. This can be handy if you want to store and access UNIX information in Active Directory to support Kerberized applications.

Kerberized Applications

Before getting down to work, it's a good idea to define what we want to accomplish. It's not enough to say, "I want all my users to get authenticated with Kerberos," because that's only half of the challenge. The other half is to connect the users with services that take advantage of their Kerberos credentials.

A so-called Kerberized application generally consists of a client/server pair where the server side expects the client process to present a Kerberos session ticket when it attempts to access the application. The client side of the process is coded to obtain a session ticket from a KDC using the underlying functions of the operating system.

This means that for a Kerberized application to work on Windows, the developer must incorporate function calls with parameters that are compatible with Windows Kerberos. Kerberos clients that work fine in a classic MITv5 Kerberos environment may not work when run in a Windows Kerberos environment, and vice versa. For example, a Kerberized LDAP application running on a UNIX/Linux host might not connect correctly to Active Directory because the developer did not include function calls that the Kerberos security package on Windows expects to see.

In Windows Server 2003, the following applications depend on Kerberos for authentication:

- LDAP connections to Active Directory (SASL/GSSAPI)
- CIFS/SMB file access
- Secure dynamic DNS updates
- IPSec connections intermediated with Internet Key Exchange (IKE)
- Secure web services
- Enterprise Certification Authority (CA) certificate requests
- DCOM/RPC

Of these, the CIFS/SMB service probably garners the most attention because many organizations use Samba, the open source SMB protocol, to connect to Windows servers. Administrators in organizations that use Samba generally want to have a single Kerberos implementation, either MITv5 or Windows.

The news in this arena is not so good. A Kerberized version of Samba is available, but it does not enable a UNIX/Linux client to access CIFS/SMB services in a Windows domain using Kerberos credentials. The most current version of Samba that was available as of this writing was still limited to NTLMv2 authentication. See `us2.samba.org/samba/development.html` for information on the current state of development in this area.

Several other important applications in Windows are not Kerberized, meaning that UNIX/Linux clients must use some other form of authentication (NTLMv2, Digest, or clear text) to access these services running on a Windows server:

- **Telnet.** The Microsoft implementation of telnet does not use GSSAPI so there is no interface for Kerberos ticket implementation. As of this writing, Microsoft has no plans for reworking either their telnet client or the `Tlntsvc` service to use Kerberos. The only authentication supported by `Tlntsvc` is NTLMv2.
- **Ftp.** The Microsoft ftp service runs under the IIS framework. The fundamentals are in place for Microsoft ftp to use Kerberos, but the version that ships with Windows Server 2003 does not expose this functionality. The command-line ftp client in Windows Server 2003 and XP is largely unchanged from Windows 2000 and only supports NTLMv2, Digest, or clear-text authentication.
- **Transport Layer Security** (TLS). RFC 2712, "Addition of Kerberos Cipher Suites to Transport Layer Security (TLS)," describes a mechanism for incorporating Kerberos into TLS, but Microsoft did not incorporate this into either its Windows Server 2003 implementation of TLS or the IE client.
- **Internet Mail Access Protocol (IMAP).** The IMAP4 service in Windows Server 2003 runs as part of IIS. It does not support Kerberos authentication from clients such as Netscape Communicator and Eudora. The IMAP4 client in Outlook and Outlook Express does not support Kerberos authentication.
- **Secure Shell (SSH).** There is no native implementation of SSH in Windows Server 2003 or XP, Kerberos or otherwise. Commercial SSH servers for Windows are available from SSH Communications (`www.ssh.com`) and Pragma Systems (`www.pragmasys.com`). OpenSSH and its associated VNC tunnel are available at `www.cygwin.com`.

Cross-Realm Architecture

To start off, let's take a look at the components of MITv5 Kerberos and compare them to the Kerberos components in Windows Server 2003.

Kerberos Database

The Kerberos database holds the names and secret keys for security principals in the realm. The secret keys are used to encrypt various portions of the Kerberos tickets and ticket-granting tickets.

MITv5 Kerberos stores the Kerberos database in a file called Principal.db. (In Linux, the filename is simply Principal.) This file is typically stored in `/var/kerberos/krb5kdc`.

Administrative access to the Kerberos database is controlled by the Kadm5.acl file. This is a text file that is also stored in /var/kerberos/krb5kdc.

Other important files, from a security perspective, are the Kadm5.keytab file, which contains keys that authenticate the KDC, and the Kerberos stash file, .k5stash, that contains the master key that encrypts the Kerberos database. These files must be carefully guarded to prevent exposing the Kerberos database to attack.

An administrator creates the Kerberos database manually using the kdb5_util utility as follow:

```
[root@rhs1 sbin]# kdb5_util create -s
Initializing database '/var/kerberos/krb5kdc/principal' for realm 'RH.COM',
master key name 'K/M@RH.COM'
You will be prompted for the database Master Password.
It is important that you NOT FORGET this password.
Enter KDC database master key:
Re-enter KDC database master key to verify:
```

This process is automated in Windows. The DCPROMO Wizard creates the Active Directory database and populates it with security principals. The LDAP objects that represent these security principals contain password hashes that satisfy the same requirements as the entries in a classic Kerberos database.

The password hashes used in Windows Server 2003 are created using MD4. The algorithm used to encrypt Kerberos TGTs and session tickets in Windows is RC4-HMAC. This method was chosen because it is compatible with the password hashes used in Windows Server 2003 and previous versions of Windows.

RC4-HMAC is not one of the standard Kerberos encryption algorithms. Microsoft briefly proposed a change to the list of commonly approved algorithms in Kerberos, but that proposal has elapsed. For this reason, a UNIX/Linux Kerberos client authenticating in an Active Directory domain must maintain a separate local account. It is up to the administrator to provide a way to keep the local account password in sync with the domain password. This is typically done with a script that calls password change functions for the two platforms.

Kerberos Policies

A classic Kerberos realm has a short set of configuration parameters called *policies*. A realm can have multiple policies. Sets of principals can be assigned to each policy. You can list the available policies using kdadmin listpols. You can view the contents of a particular policy using kadmin getpol *<policy_name>*:

```
kadmin:  getpol Standard_Policy
Policy: Standard_Policy
Maximum password life: 31536000
Minimum password life: 0
Minimum password length: 1
Minimum number of password character classes: 2
Number of old keys kept: 5
Reference count: 20
```

The `password character class` entry defines how many different elements are required to be in a password. There are five choices: uppercase, lowercase, numbers, punctuation, and control characters. The more classes you require, the stronger the passwords will be, but the harder they will be to remember.

Windows defines these classic Kerberos policies as a subset of password policies. The Kerberos policies in Windows define parameters such as ticket lifetimes and permissible clock skew. In MITv5 Kerberos, these parameters are defined in the Krb5kdc.conf file. This file is generally found under `/var/kerberos/`.

Kerberos Services

Classic MITv5 Kerberos splits the Ticket Granting and Authentication functions between two daemons (services) called `krb5kdc` (ticket granting) and `kadmin` (authentication and database administration).

The `krb5kdc` daemon listens for ticket requests on UDP/TCP port 88. The `kadmin` daemon handles administration requests over UDP/TCP port 749 and handles password changes submitted via the `kpasswd` protocol over UDP port 464.

In Windows, Active Directory functions as the Kerberos database. There is no analog to the `kadmin` daemon. Windows does not listen on port 749. The `kdc` service in Windows runs as part of the Local Security Authority (LSA) and handles authentication and ticket granting over port 88 and classic Kerberos password changes over port 464. This is documented in draft-trostle-win2k-cat-kerberos-set-passwd-02.txt, "Windows 2000 Kerberos Change Password and Set Password Protocols."

Kerberos Clients

A UNIX Kerberos client obtains a ticket-granting ticket by running the `kinit` application. The user gives a password (used the validate the user's entry in the `principal` database) and if the credentials are valid, the user gets a TGT. The `kinit` utility caches the TGT so Kerberized applications on the machine can submit copies to the KDC when requesting session tickets to applications on specific servers. UNIX/Linux system administrators typically embed the `kinit` transaction into the initial logon routine.

When a UNIX/Linux user finishes up a work session and is ready to log off, she runs `kdestroy` to flush the ticket cache. Most system administrators incorporate `kdestroy` into a sign-off routine. If the user doesn't sign off, the cache stays populated until the tickets expire.

In Windows, the Kerberos security package handles ticket-granting ticket requests in conjunction with Winlogon. This is done transparently to the user. The TGTs and tickets are cached in memory, never on disk. When the user logs off, the tickets are wiped from memory.

Many Kerberos implementations also expose an API library described in RFC 1964, "The Kerberos Version 5 Generic Security Service Application Programming

Interface (GSS-API) Mechanism." Windows Kerberos does not expose the GSS API directly. Instead, it uses a similar set of function calls exposed by the Security Support Provider Interface (SSPI).

The reason this is important to system administrators is that you may have developers who are trying to get their applications to work on both Windows and UNIX/Linux. As you work with them to iron out the interoperability issues, you should keep in mind that some of the most basic mechanisms in the application might not work because of the difference in support for the GSS API.

Kerberos Service Location

UNIX/Linux Kerberos clients locate a KDC by reading a file called `/etc/krb5.conf`. This file also spells out supported encryption packages, library files, and log file locations. Here is an example for a realm called `RH.COM` and a KDC called `kerberos.rh.com`: (Uppercase names indicate realms and lowercase names indicate fully qualified DNS host names.)

```
 [logging]
 default = FILE:/var/log/krb5libs.log
 kdc = FILE:/var/log/krb5kdc.log
 admin_server = FILE:/var/log/kadmind.log

[libdefaults]
 ticket_lifetime = 24000
 default_realm = RH.COM
 dns_lookup_realm = false
 dns_lookup_kdc = false

[realms]
 RH.COM = {
  kdc = rhs1.rh.com:88
  admin_server = rhs1.rh.com:749
  default_domain = rh.com
 }

[domain_realm]
 .rh.com = RH.COM
 rh.com = RH.COM

[pam]
 debug = false
 ticket_lifetime = 36000
 renew_lifetime = 36000
 forwardable = true
 krb4_convert = false
```

Windows Kerberos clients do not need a Krb5.conf file. They use SRV records in DNS to locate domain controllers. The ticket lifetimes and other Kerberos configuration options are defined in group policies linked to the Domain object in Active Directory.

Kerberized Services

Both Windows and UNIX have Kerberized services (daemons) that must obtain session tickets (on the client side) and validate those tickets (on the server side). This means that client services must have Kerberos credentials that can be submitted to a KDC to obtain session tickets. On the flip side, a server-side service must have Kerberos credentials so it can decrypt the session tickets submitted by clients.

Classic MITv5 Kerberos stores the server credentials in a file called `/etc/krb5.keytab`. Windows stores the credentials in the Registry. See the "LSA Secrets" sidebar for more information.

LSA Secrets

Kerberized services in Windows store their local Kerberos credentials in the `Security` hive in the Registry. This hive is also called the Local Security Authority (LSA) database. The credentials are stored in a set of subkeys under a key called `Secrets`, so the contents of this key are often called LSA Secrets. Figure 11.17 shows a typical structure for keys in LSA Secrets.

Figure 11.17 `Security` hive showing LSA Secrets.

A surprising amount of secure information gets stored in LSA Secrets. Some of it is not as secure as you might think. A hacker tool called LSADUMP2 can show you some of the contents of many keys in LSA Secrets. For instance, it can show the dial-up passwords saved by users. Because users tend to use the same passwords for dialup and network authentication, this is a major security weakness.

As of this writing, LSADUMP2 does not run on Windows Server 2003 or XP. It's likely that by the time you read this, someone will have "fixed" the utility.

In a classic Kerberos environment, an administrator takes two actions to prepare a Kerberized application for authentication. Both of these actions are performed using the `kadmin` utility:

- Create an account in the Kerberos database representing the service and its host. The service account name uses a *Service Principal Name*, or SPN, format.
- Create an entry in the Krb5.keytab file on the server running the service. This keytab entry has the same secret key used to create the account in the Kerberos database. The entry is generated using a special function call that does not expose the secret key over the wire.

When the Kerberized service initializes, it authenticates at the KDC and obtains a TGT. When a client uses the service, it obtains a session ticket that is encrypted with service's secret key. The service uses its copy of the secret key stored in the keytab file to decrypt the session key and complete the authentication transaction.

Service Principal Names

Kerberos identifies services with an SPN, both in the Kerberos database and in the keytab file. For example, the SPN for the `ftp` service running on a host named `rhs1` in the `rh.com` DNS domain and `RH.COM` realm would have an SPN of `ftp/rhs1.rh.com@RH.COM`. The syntax elements are as follows:

```
<primary>/<instance>@<realm>
```

- **`<primary>`.** Identifies the service, such as `ftp` or `host` (used for telnet and rsh). The `<primary>` element can also identify a Kerberos role, such as `admin` or `changepw`. An SPN can also identify a user, although that format is generally called a *User Principal Name*, or UPN. A user named `mmantle` with the privilege to manage the Kerberos database in the RH.COM realm would have a UPN of `mmantle/admin@RH.COM`.
- **`<instance>`.** Identifies the fully qualified domain name of the host. In the case of services provided by a KDC, the `<instance>` element is the realm name. For example, the ticket-granting ticket service would have an SPN of `krbtgt/RH.COM@RH.COM`.
- **`<realm>`.** Identifies the name of the Kerberos realm. The uppercase letters differentiate it from the DNS domain. In Windows, the DNS name and realm name always match because a Windows domain must conform to a DNS namespace.

Windows stores SPNs in Active Directory as attributes of the associated computer object. For instance, the LanMan Server service on a server named `server1` in the

`Company.com` domain registers itself with the SPN `cifs/server1.company.com@COMPANY.COM`. (CIFS stands for Common Internet File System, another term for SMB.)

As we'll see in the next section, Windows also uses SPNs that diverge from the classic format. These can cause interoperability problems.

Some classic Kerberized services do not use specific service names in the `<primary>` element of their SPN. For instance, the `rlogin`, `rsh`, and `telnet` services all use `host` as a `<primary>` identifier, as in `host/rhs1.rh.com@RH.COM`. Microsoft uses the `host` identifier somewhat loosely to identify any machine running Kerberos.

You can enumerate the SPNs and UPNs in the Kerberos database using `kadmin getprincs`. Here is a sample listing. Notice that UPNs only specify the realm:

```
K/M@RH.COM
ftp/rhs1.rh.com@RH.COM
host/rhs1.rh.com@RH.COM
kadmin/admin@RH.COM
kadmin/changepw@RH.COM
kadmin/history@RH.COM
krbtgt/RH.COM@RH.COM
root/admin@RH.COM
root@RH.COM
```

The `K/M@realm` designator represents the master key used to encrypt the entire database. The administrator provides this key when the database is created.

Interoperability and SPNs

Microsoft made a few changes to the structure of the SPNs used in Windows to accommodate two situations that don't exist in classic MITv5 Kerberos:

- Windows-based domains
- Name resolution based on NetBIOS flat names

The best way to see the difference is to view the SPNs on a Windows computer using the SETSPN utility from the Resource Kit. As an alternative, you can use the ADSI Editor (Adsiedit.msc) from the Support Tools to view the Computer object for the domain controller. The SPNs are stored in the `ServicePrincipalName` attribute.

Here is a listing of the SPNs registered on an example Windows Server 2003 domain controller: (Each of these entries gets a @COMPANY.COM extension to form a full SPN.)

```
C:\>setspn -L server1.company.com
Registered ServicePrincipalNames for CN=SERVER1,OU=Domain
➥Controllers,DC=company,DC=com:
    SMTPSVC/SERVER1
    SMTPSVC/server1.company.com
```

```
NtFrs-88f6d2bd-b746-11d2-a6d3-00d04fc9b242/server1.company.com
DNS/server1.company.com
exchangeAB/SERVER1
GC/server1.company.com/company.com
HOST/server1.company.com/COMPANY
HOST/SERVER1
HOST/server1.company.com
HOST/server1.company.com/company.com
E3514235-4B06-11D1-AB04-00C04FC2DCD2/a54acff0-8185-4086-8d35-
➥d1cff06b1e09/company.com
LDAP/a54acff0-8185-4086-8d35-d1cff06b1e09._msdcs.company.com
LDAP/server1.company.com/COMPANY
LDAP/SERVER1
LDAP/server1.company.com
LDAP/server1.company.com/company.com
```

Notice that some SPNs represent hosts and domains by their flat NetBIOS names and others use hierarchical DNS names. Windows clients can use either name to get a session ticket for the service. The GUIDs represent domains uniquely in DNS so that clients can contain their service requests to their own domains.

This change to the SPN format in Windows creates an interoperability challenge. Programmers accustomed to working with classic Kerberos SPNs when they make well-known function calls are forced to change their code if they want to use Windows Kerberos for their authentications.

Name Mapping

SPN format has another subtle impact on system administration. Windows does not have a facility for creating classic multipart Kerberos *<primary>* elements. For example, you cannot create a Windows account called `jane/admin@COMPANY.COM`. Multipart usernames are recognized by MITv5 Kerberos, so a UNIX/Linux administrator might attempt to authenticate as `jane/admin`. This requires a little sleight-of-hand called *name mapping*.

An Active Directory user or computer object has an attribute called `AltSecurityIdentities` that can contain a multipart Kerberos name. You can populate this attribute by right-clicking a user object in `AD Users and Computer` and selecting NAME MAPPINGS from the flyout menu. Figure 11.18 shows an example.

Creating a Cross-Realm Trust

At this point, we have all the components we need to build a trust between a Windows Server 2003 domain and a classic Kerberos realm. Here's the sequence of events to build the trust:

- Create a two-way trust in the Windows domain that names the Kerberos realm as the trust partner. This creates the necessary Kerberos principals in Active Directory to support issuing cross-realm ticket-granting tickets.

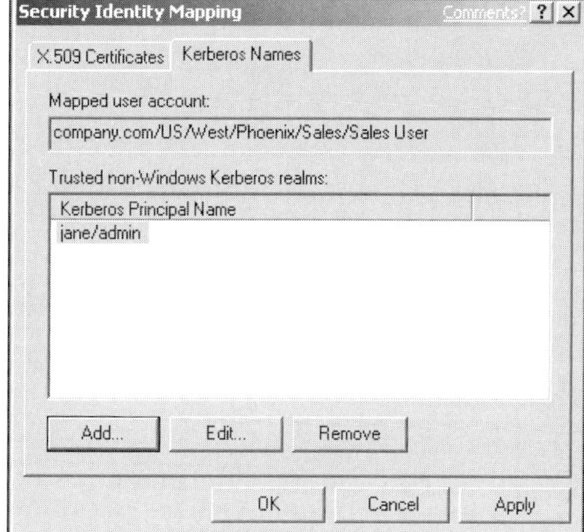

Figure 11.18 User object showing Name Mappings window.

- Create `krbtgt` principals in the Kerberos realm representing the Windows domain. These principals support the trust by permitting a KDC in the Kerberos realm to issue cross-realm TGTs to clients from the Windows domain.

In these examples, I'll use a Red Hat Linux 7.1 server as a MITv5 KDC. Detailed instructions are located at `www.redhat.com/support/manuals/RHL-7.1-Manual/ref-guide/s1-kerberos-server.html`. If you have an existing Kerberos realm, you can skip this section.

Install and Configure MITv5 Kerberos

Figure 11.19 shows a KDC and client configuration for a cross-realm trust. The MITv5 KDC is named `rhs1`. The name server is running BIND and hosts the zone table for `rh.com`. The realm name is RH.COM.

Here is a quick rundown of the steps to create the MITv5 realm; you must be logged on with an account that has administrator privileges, such as `root`:

1. Install the `krb5-workstation` and `krb5-server` packages.
2. Use `kedit` (or your favorite text editor) to make the `/etc/krb5.conf` file look like the following:

```
[logging]
default = FILE:/var/log/krb5libs.log
kdc = FILE:/var/log/krb5kdc.log
admin_server = FILE:/var/log/kadmind.log
```

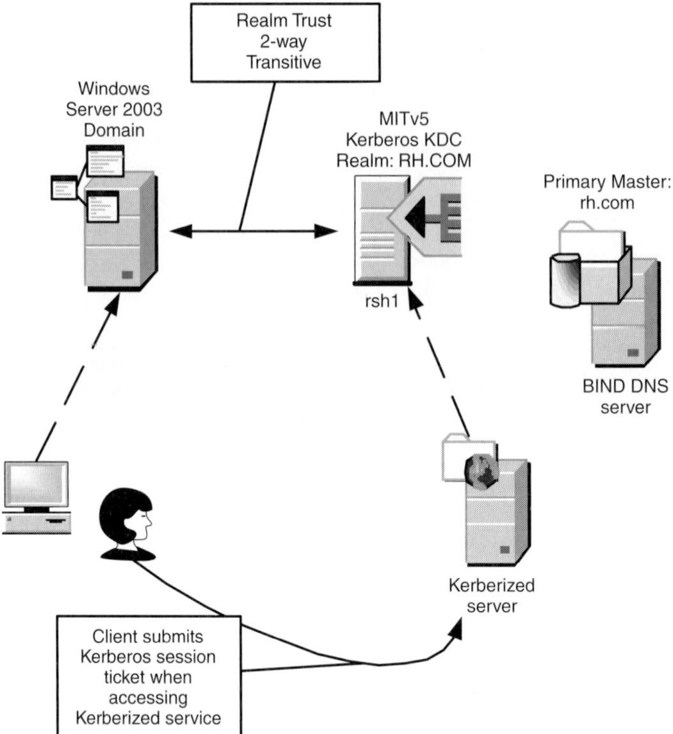

Figure 11.19 Cross-realm trust configuration.

```
[libdefaults]
 ticket_lifetime = 24000
 default_realm = RH.COM
 dns_lookup_realm = false
 dns_lookup_kdc = false

[realms]
 RH.COM = {
  kdc = rhs1.rh.com:88
  admin_server = rhs1.rh.com:749
  default_domain = rh.com
 }

[domain_realm]
 .rh.com = RH.COM
 rh.com = RH.COM

[kdc]
 profile = /var/kerberos/krb5kdc/kdc.conf

[pam]
 debug = false
 ticket_lifetime = 36000
 renew_lifetime = 36000
```

```
 forwardable = true
 krb4_convert = false
```

3. Edit the `/var/Kerberos/krb5kdc/kdc.conf` file to make it look like this:

```
[kdcdefaults]
 acl_file = /var/kerberos/krb5kdc/kadm5.acl
 dict_file = /usr/share/dict/words
 admin_keytab = /var/kerberos/krb5kdc/kadm5.keytab

[realms]
 RH.COM = {
  master_key_type = des-cbc-crc
  supported_enctypes = des-cbc-crc:normal des3-cbc-raw:normal des3-cbc-sha1:normal
des-cbc-crc:v4 des-cbc-crc:afs3
 }
```

4. Create the Kerberos database as follows (binaries located in `/usr/Kerberos/sbin`):

```
kdb5_util create -s
```

5. Edit the `/var/kerberos/krb5kdc/kadm5.acl` file to make it look like this:

```
*/admin@RH.COM *
```

6. Change directory to `/etc/rc.d/init.d` and start the Kerberos daemons as follows:

```
sh krb5kdc start
sh kadmin start
sh krb524 start
```

7. Run `gkadmin` to add principals to the Kerberos database. At a minimum, you need a principal for the root account and your own account. The account must already exist in Linux before you can add it to the Kerberos database. The passwords are not kept in sync automatically. The users can run `kpasswd` to change their Kerberos passwords.
8. Run `kinit` to issue yourself a ticket.
9. Run `klist` to check that the ticket was issued correctly. (The graphical tool is `krb5`.) Here's an example:

```
 [root@rhs1 Admin]# klist
Ticket cache: FILE:/tmp/krb5cc_p2722
Default principal: Admin@RH.COM

Valid starting     Expires            Service principal
10/05/01 13:47:51  10/05/01 23:47:51  krbtgt/RH.COM@RH.COM

Kerberos 4 ticket cache: /tmp/tkt0
klist: You have no tickets cached
```

Create the Cross-Realm Trust

At this point, we have a Windows domain and a classic Kerberos realm. We now want to create cross-realm trusts so that users authenticated in either the Kerberos realm or the Windows domain can access resources everywhere. Here are the major points of interest for creating the trust:

- The Windows domain controller where the trust is created must know the location of a KDC in the MITv5 realm. This is done using the Windows equivalent of a keytab entry. The entry is stored in the Registry. It is created using KSETUP.
- The Windows Trust Wizard creates an object in Active Directory with a secret key that is shared by security principals in the Kerberos realm. This object essentially "represents" the realm when it comes to distributing ticket-granting tickets. The object is under `cn=System,dc=<domain>,dc=<root>`. It has the same name as the Kerberos realm. You provide the secret key (a password) when you create the trust.
- You must create two krbtgt principals in the Kerberos realm that represent both sides of the two-way trust relationship. These security principals use the same password as the trust object. One of them issues ticket-granting tickets to users from the Windows domain. The other issues referral ticket-granting tickets to users from the Kerberos realm when they access the Windows domain.
- You must provide a "mapping" between principals in the Kerberos realm and users in the Windows Active Directory. This mapping permits generating a local access token for the classic Kerberos client.
- You must provide a way for Windows clients to locate classic Kerberos KDCs. This is because classic Kerberos doesn't register SRV records in DNS. Windows stores the realm name and fully qualified DNS names of classic MITv5 KDCs in the Registry. (This is the Windows equivalent of Krb5.conf file entries.)

With all this in mind, let's create a two-way, transitive trust between a Windows domain and a classic Kerberos realm. The example shown in Procedure 11.8 uses the principals and servers shown in Figure 11.19.

Procedure 11.8 Configuring a Cross-Realm Trust

1. Select a domain controller in the root domain of the Windows forest.
2. Log on with `Enterprise Administrator` permissions.
3. Install the Support Tools on the server. This installs the MITv5 Kerberos utilities.
4. Run this command at the console:

```
ksetup /addkdc RH.COM rhs1.rh.com
```

5. Open AD Domains and Trusts.
6. Right-click the root domain of the forest and open the Properties window.
7. Select the Trusts tab.
8. Click New Trust. The New Trust Wizard starts.
9. Click Next. The Trust Name and Password window opens.
10. Under Name, enter the name of the Kerberos realm. For example, RH.COM.
11. Under Trust Password, enter a strong password to use for negotiating the trust. You'll need this password when creating the security principals in the Kerberos realm.
12. Click Next. The Trust Type window opens. The Realm Trust option should be selected. If it is not, select it.
13. Click Next. The Transitivity of Trust window opens. Select the Transitive option to let other domains in the forest use the trust relationship.
14. Click Next. The Direction of Trust window opens. Select Two-Way to permit principals from either side to access resources in each other's domain/realm.
15. Click Next. The Trust Selections Complete window opens. Review the selections you made and change any that are incorrect.
16. Click Next. The Completing the New Trust Wizard window opens. Click Finish to save your changes and create the trust.

    At this point, you've built the Windows half of the trust. Now go to the KDC in the Kerberos realm and complete the job as follows:

17. Run kadmin and give Kerberos administrator credentials.
18. Add the following two security principals (replace the word password with the password you used to create the trust in Windows):

```
ank -pw password krbtgt/COMPANY.COM@RH.COM
ank -pw password krbtgt/RH.COM@COMPANY.COM
```

    The final steps create name mappings between security principals in the Kerberos realm and user accounts in Active Directory.

19. Open AD Users and Computers.
20. Create a user that corresponds to a security principal in the Kerberos realm.
21. Right-click the user object and select Name Mappings from the flyout menu.
22. Select the Name Mappings tab.
23. Click Add. The Add Kerberos Principal Name window opens.
24. Enter the Kerberos principal name corresponding to the user, such as root@RH.COM.

25. Click OK to save the change.

    The final step must be done at every workstation or server in the Windows domain where a user will log on to the Kerberos realm. This step tells the computer where to find a KDC in the classic Kerberos realm. This step requires the KSETUP utility from the Support Tools.

26. At the workstation or server, run the following (where rhs1 is the KDC in the RH.COM realm):

```
ksetup /addkdc RH.COM rhs1.rh.com
```

Testing Cross-Realm Trusts

After you've configured the cross-realm trust, test it to make sure users can get tickets. Follow the steps in Procedure 11.9 at the console of the workstation where you ran KSETUP.

Procedure 11.9 Testing Cross-Realm Kerberos Ticket Generation

1. Press Ctrl+Alt+Del to log on. Select the name of the Kerberos realm in the pick list of the Winlogon window.
2. Enter the name and password of the Kerberos principal that you configured with a name mapping.
3. Press Enter. The logon should succeed.
4. Open a command prompt.
5. Run `klist tgt` to see the contents of the ticket-granting ticket issued to the client. Here is an example:

```
C:\>klist tgt
Cached TGT:
ServiceName: krbtgt
TargetName: krbtgt
FullServiceName: root
DomainName: RH.COM
TargetDomainName: RH.COM
AltTargetDomainName: RH.COM
TicketFlags: 0x40c00000
KeyExpirationTime: 256/0/29920 0:102:8048
StartTime: 10/6/2001 13:19:02
EndTime: 10/6/2001 23:19:02
RenewUntil: 10/6/2001 13:19:02
TimeSkew: 10/6/2001 13:19:02
```

6. Run `klist tickets` to see the tickets issued to the user. Note that some come from the Windows domain (via the trust) and others come directly from the Kerberos realm. Here is an example:

```
C:\>klist tickets
```

```
Cached Tickets: (6)

   Server: krbtgt/RH.COM@RH.COM
      KerbTicket Encryption Type: Kerberos DES-CBC-CRC
      End Time: 10/6/2001 23:19:02
      Renew Time: 10/6/2001 13:19:02

   Server: krbtgt/COMPANY.COM@RH.COM
      KerbTicket Encryption Type: Kerberos DES-CBC-CRC
      End Time: 10/6/2001 23:19:02
      Renew Time: 10/6/2001 13:19:02

   Server: krbtgt/RH.COM@RH.COM
      KerbTicket Encryption Type: Kerberos DES-CBC-CRC
      End Time: 10/6/2001 23:19:02
      Renew Time: 10/6/2001 13:19:02

   Server: cifs/server1.company.com@COMPANY.COM
      KerbTicket Encryption Type: RSADSI RC4-HMAC(NT)
      End Time: 10/6/2001 23:19:02
      Renew Time: 10/6/2001 13:19:02

   Server: ldap/server1.company.com/company.com@COMPANY.COM
      KerbTicket Encryption Type: RSADSI RC4-HMAC(NT)
      End Time: 10/6/2001 23:19:02
      Renew Time: 10/6/2001 13:19:02

   Server: host/server1.company.com@COMPANY.COM
      KerbTicket Encryption Type: RSADSI RC4-HMAC(NT)
      End Time: 10/6/2001 23:19:02
      Renew Time: 10/6/2001 13:19:02
```

At this point, you should test access to Kerberized services on both sides of the trust. Some applications are not cross-platform compatible. For example, a Kerberized version of `rlogin` on a Windows platform may not be able to connect to the `klogin` or `eklogin` service on a UNIX/Linux host.

Security Auditing

As sanitation engineers and quantum physicists have long known, just because you can't see something doesn't mean it isn't there. Even if you have a small organization where everyone gets along with each other and no one would even *dream* of damaging the system, you need to take precautions.

This brings us to the final leg of the security triad, which is auditing. Any activity involving Windows security objects can be monitored and logged. This can require a lot of work on the part of your servers, so you should choose your auditing points carefully.

This section discusses how to configure auditing, what to audit, when to audit, how to interpret the audit logs, and how to set up systems to notify you in case of an audit warning so you don't constantly have to pore through the logs to see if something unusual happened. It also discusses various third-party products that can help you with auditing and event reporting.

Windows comes with an armada of auditing tools. The majority of these tools rely on monitoring access to security objects such as NTFS files/folders, Registry keys, Active Directory objects, printer objects, and services. As an administrator, you should understand that these monitoring tools look for *accesses*, not necessarily modifications.

Auditing is a little like putting a nanny monitor in your home. It will tell you that the nanny opened the refrigerator, but it won't tell you if she took any of the leftovers from Cheesecake Factory. Don't expect to use auditing as a compliance enforcement tool. Still, it's better than simply guessing about the origins of a security problem.

Audit Log

When you enable auditing, two services are involved. The Security Reference Monitor reports on events concerning security objects themselves and the LSASS reports on all other security events.

These services write their results into a log called Secevent.evt that is stored in `\Windows\System32\Config` along with the Registry hives. You can view the contents of the log with the Event Viewer, which can be launched from START | PROGRAMS | ADMINISTRATIVE TOOLS | EVENT VIEWER. You can also open the Event Viewer from the command line by simply typing `eventvwr`. The Event Viewer displays the log under the name Security.

The default size for an Event log is 512KB, which is too small if you audit many events. The default behavior of the log is to overwrite older entries when the log fills up, which might obscure old sins. You can change these and other log file settings as shown in Procedure 11.10.

Procedure 11.10 Changing Log File Settings

1. Open the `Event Viewer` console using START | PROGRAMS | ADMINISTRATIVE TOOLS | EVENT VIEWER.
2. Right-click the `Security Log` object and select PROPERTIES from the flyout menu. The Properties window opens.
3. Change the entry for `Maximum Log Size` to a value large enough to accommodate several days logging.
4. Under Event Log Wrapping, set the logging behavior when the log file gets full to `Do Not Overwrite Events`. You can set a system policy that causes the server to refuse connections if the Security log gets full. Don't forget to save the log and clear it manually every week or so.
5. Click `OK` to save any changes and close the Properties window.

Controlling Access to the Security Log

You should carefully manage who can access the Security log. A user who can clear the log essentially can wipe fingerprints from the crime scene. The system writes a log entry when someone clears the Security log, so you can ask the person what he was trying to hide, but you lose specifics of the transactions that were recorded.

You can modify Event log configurations as part of a group policy and push them out to member servers. This gives you a standard set of log parameters when you collect your audit information. The group policy can be set for a domain or for an OU containing the computer objects representing the servers. The policies are located under `Computer Configuration | Windows Settings | Security Settings | Event Log | Settings for Event Logs`. The policies include the following:

- **`Maximum log sizes.`** This sets the upper size of each of the Event logs. Be sure to set this at a size that is smaller than the free space available on the drives. Event logs were limited to 4GB in Windows 2000. The limit in Windows Server 2003 is extended to the maximum volume size under NTFS.
- **`Restrict Guest access.`** You should never need to enable this policy because you should never enable the Guest account.
- **`Retain logs.`** Enable this policy when you want to force administrators to periodically save copies of Event logs. It is of little real use in production because it does not automatically archive and empty Event logs.
- **`Retention methods.`** You should always retain your Security Event logs by selecting the `Do Not Overwrite Events` option for this policy. It is important that you archive your logs periodically or you will lose the events that occur after the logs fill up.
- **`Shutdown the computer when the Security log is full.`** For highly secure environments, you may want to enable this option. It will perform a standard shutdown when the log fills up and only an administrator can start up the server and log on to empty the log. Be *very* sure to empty the event log periodically if you enable this feature.

Enabling Auditing

Auditing can consume significant system resources so it is not enabled by default. You can enable auditing on a local server or you can set a policy to affect a set of servers in an OU or for an entire domain.

Audit policies are set in group policies under `Computer Configuration | Windows Settings | Security Settings | Local Policies | Audit Policy`. You can elect to audit for success or failure or both. The following events can be audited:

- **`Account Logon`**. This monitors *network* access to a computer via network logon and logoff. This contrasts to *local* access that is monitored with the `Logon Events` policy. Set this policy when you want a record of accounts that access a server and what privileges they have been assigned.

- **`Account Management`**. This records when an administrator adds, deletes, or modifies the attributes of a security principal. This is especially useful if you have delegated admin permissions to people outside your group and you want to monitor how they are getting along.
- **`Directory Services Access`**. This monitors access to Active Directory objects. See the section, "Enabling Object Access Auditing."
- **`Logon Events`**. This monitors *local* logon/logoff at the console of a machine. This contrasts with *network* access, which is monitored with the Account Logon policy. See the sidebar, "Logon/Logoff Audit Errors," for more information.
- **`Object Access`**. This monitors access to security objects such as NTFS files/folders and Registry keys. Auditing for Active Directory objects is controlled by the `Directory Services Access` policy. You must also configure auditing for each file/folder or key you want to monitor. See the section, "Enabling Object Access Auditing."
- **`Policy Change`**. This monitors for modifications to group policies. You should *always* enable this policy, because it gives you a record of who might have disabled a policy to hide certain activities.
- **`Privilege Use`**. This monitors privileged access to resources by the system or accounts that have system privileges. For example, only administrators can open the Security log. When you open the Security log, an entry is made in the log under Privilege Use that shows your account name and what you did that exercised a system privilege.
- **`Process Tracking`**. This monitors access to executable code such as EXE, DLL, and OCX files. This is handy for figuring out who is accessing a particular file. It can also help track down viruses, although most virus scanners offer better tools.
- **`System Events`**. This monitors the various system updates that occur during operation. If you're troubleshooting a pesky service that refuses to work for some inexplicable reason, this is a great trace to follow. Used in conjunction with `Process Tracking`, you can follow the service to see whether it performs an illegal or disallowed activity or asks the system to perform such an activity. The trace also shows you how the various security providers get initialized.

Managing the Event Log with AUDITPOL

The AUDITPOL utility permits you to modify audit settings on individual servers. It does not set Active Directory policies, so it is not as useful as it could be in an enterprise environment, but it is very handy for quickly managing audit policies via a command line.

AUDITPOL controls the following audit policies:

```
System
Logon
```

```
Object Access
Privilege Use
Process Tracking
Policy Change
Account Management
Directory Service Access
Account Logon
```

The syntax for the command is:

```
auditpol \\<server_name> /enable /logon:failure
```

Enabling Object Access Auditing

After Object Access or Directory Service Access auditing is enabled in a group policy, you must enable auditing for the objects you want to monitor. This is done by adding a user or group to the SACL (Security ACL) for the object or objects you're monitoring.

Audit entries are added via START | PROPERTIES | SECURITY | ADVANCED | AUDITING. For Active Directory objects, the Everyone group is added by default for all objects in a domain.

Use caution when enabling auditing because of permission inheritance. You may inadvertently apply the audit entry to the SACL of a large number of files and folders, minimizing the effectiveness of your monitoring and filling the Security log with unnecessary entries.

When you enable Object Access auditing, do so in a policy linked to an OU that contains the computer object you want to monitor. If you do not want to enable auditing on a large number of computers, you can add that specific computer to the ACLs for the policy itself.

When you enable Directory Service Access auditing, do so in a policy linked to the OU that contains the domain controllers.

Applying Group Policy Changes

After you change a security policy, you must refresh the security database so that the policy takes effect. This is done using the GPUPDATE utility. The update performed by GPUPDATE is the same as would happen automatically every five minutes on domain controllers and every 90 to 120 minutes on member computers. There is no need to restart.

After you refresh the audit policies, test them by performing an auditable activity. For example, if you enable Audit Account Logon Events and Audit Logon Events, log on at a member workstation and then access a domain controller via a share point. This should trigger two auditable events, one for the console logon and one for the network access.

Logon/Logoff Audit Errors

When you audit logon/logoff events, the log entry for a failed logon will be accompanied by an event code. In some instances, this code will not have a string explanation. Here are the potential errors:

```
528     Successful Logon
529     Logon Failure:  Reason:  Unknown user name or bad password
530     Logon Failure:  Reason:  Account logon time restriction violation
531     Logon Failure:  Reason:  Account currently disabled
532     Logon Failure:  Reason:  The specified user account has expired
533     Logon Failure:  Reason:  User not allowed to logon at this computer
534     Logon Failure:  Reason: The user has not been granted the requested logon
➥type at this machine
535     Logon Failure:  Reason:  The specified account's password has expired
536     Logon Failure:  Reason:  The NetLogon component is not active
537     Logon Failure:  Reason:  An unexpected error occurred during logon
538     User Logoff:
539     Logon Failure:  Reason:  Account locked out
540     Successful Network Logon
541     IPSec security association established.
542     IPSec security association ended.
        Mode: Data Protection (Quick mode)
543     IPSec security association ended.
        Mode: Key Exchange (Main mode)
544     IPSec security association establishment failed because peer could not
➥authenticate.
545     IPSec peer authentication failed.
546     IPSec security association establishment failed because peer sent invalid
➥proposal.
547     IPSec security association negotiation failed.
672     Authentication Ticket Granted
673     Service Ticket Granted
674     Ticket Granted Renewed
675     Pre-authentication failed
676     Authentication Ticket Request Failed
677     Service Ticket Request Failed
678     Account Mapped for Logon
679     Account could not be mapped for logon
680     Account Used for Logon
681     The logon to account: <client name> by: <source> from workstation:
➥<workstation> failed. The error code was: <error>
682     Session reconnected to winstation
683     Session disconnected from winstation
```

If you get a 681 error from the NTLM authentication package (MSV1_0), the potential causes for the error are as follows:

```
C0000064   User logon with misspelled or bad user account
C000006A   User logon with misspelled or bad password
C000006F   User logon outside authorized hours
C0000070   User logon from unauthorized workstation
C0000071   User logon with expired password
C0000072   User logon to account disabled by administrator
C0000193   User logon with expired account
C0000224   User logon with "Change Password at Next Logon" flagged
C0000234   User logon with account locked
```

If you don't see any entries in the Security log after enabling auditing and running GPUDATE, press F5 or select REFRESH from the console menu. If you still do not get entries, there might be a policy lower in the Active Directory tree that has a No Auditing option set. For more information about troubleshooting group policies, see Chapter 12, "Managing Group Policies."

Audit Recommendations

Before you enable auditing, you should determine exactly what you want to know. This eliminates extraneous log entries and unnecessary load on the servers that must write to the Security log. Here are a few examples of events that you may want to monitor for on a regular basis:

Unauthorized Folder Access

You're concerned that a certain user or group of users are trying to get unauthorized access to a certain folder. Follow the steps in Procedure 11.11.

Procedure 11.11 Monitoring for Unauthorized Folder Access

1. In AD Users and Computers, create a group called AccessCheck (use whatever group type you've decided to use for ACL entries) and add the suspected users to this group.
2. For the OU containing the member server, create a new policy called Unauthorized Folder Access Detection.
3. In the new policy, enable Audit Object Access for Failure.
4. In the ACLs for the policy, add the AccessCheck group and give it Apply Group Policy permissions. Remove all other groups except for the Administrators group. Give the Administrators Read-Write-Create-Delete but not Apply Group Policy.
5. Save the policy.
6. At the server containing the share, open the Properties window for the folder.
7. Select the Security tab; then, click Advanced and select the Auditing tab.
8. Add the AccessCheck group to the SACL for this object.
9. Click OK to save the change.
10. Run GPUDATE to apply the policy to the server containing the share.
11. Check the logs periodically to see if the suspected users have attempted to access the folder.

Unauthorized Directory Service Object Access

You're concerned that a certain user is poking around inside Active Directory and trying to make changes. The user does not have permission to make these changes, but you want to make sure he isn't attempting to do so anyway. Follow the steps in Procedure 11.12.

Procedure 11.12 Monitoring Access to Directory Service Objects

1. Open the Group Policy window for the Domain Controllers OU.
2. Create a new group policy called `Unauthorized DS Access Detection`.
3. In this policy, enable the `Audit Directory Service Access` policy for `Success` and `Failure`.
4. In the Properties for the policy, add the user's account and give it `Apply Group Policy` permissions.
5. Remove the other ACL entries except for Administrators and uncheck the `Apply Group Policy` from the Administrators group.
6. Apply the policy using GPUPDATE or wait five minutes for the background refresh.

Logon/Logoff Monitoring

You want a record of all user logon/logoffs in the domain and, in addition, you want a record of logon/logoff access to a particular server. Follow the steps in Procedure 11.13.

Procedure 11.13 Audit Monitor for Logon/Logoff

1. In the `Default Domain` policy, enable the `Account Logon` and `Logon Events` policies for `Success` and `Failure`.
2. In the OU that contains the server, create a new policy called `Logon Monitoring`.
3. In the new group policy, enable the `Account Logon` policy for `Success` and `Failure`.
4. In the Security properties for the new group policy, add the name for the server you want to monitor and set the `Apply Group Policy` permission. Clear the `Apply Group Policy` permission on all other entries.
5. Run GPUPDATE on the server or wait 90 to 120 minutes for the background refresh to apply the policy.

Printer Monitoring

Under most circumstances, you can get all the information you need about printing from the System log, which records each print event. You may find yourself wanting to monitor the management of the print queues themselves, though. For instance, you may have someone who is blocking print jobs or deleting the jobs or jockeying them around to get better position in the queue.

You may get a surprise if you use this auditing tool. When a user has a Printer window open, it communicates with the network printer every five seconds. This generates an *enormous* number of Object Access events on a production print server. Use this audit judiciously. Follow the steps in Procedure 11.14.

Procedure 11.14 Audit Monitoring for Printers

1. In the OU holding the computer object representing the print server, create a group policy called `Printer Monitoring`.
2. In the new policy, enable `Object Access` auditing for `Success` and `Failure`.
3. Open the Properties window for a printer; select `Security` and `Advanced` and then select the `Audit` tab.
4. Add the Everyone group to the ACL.
5. Save the changes and apply the policy using GPUPDATE.
6. Monitor the Security log on the server for a while to make sure no one left other objects with auditing enabled. This could fill your Security log with extraneous information.

Backup and Restore Monitoring

The ability to back up and restore files is a highly privileged operation. A user with these privileges could conceivably abscond with tons of sensitive information in a highly portable format. Windows 2000/Windows Server 2003 makes the backup privilege even more sensitive because the NTBACKUP utility makes it simple to backup to a file on portable media.

If you have reason to suspect that a user is exercising backup/restore privileges in an unauthorized manner, you can enable the `Audit use of backup and restore privilege` policy. You should enable this policy for an OU containing the machines you think are the target of this type of activity. The policy is located in `Computer Configuration | Windows Settings | Security Settings | Local Policies | Security Options`.

Additional System Monitoring

Here are additional recommendations for auditing policies. Remember to increase the size of your Security log to accommodate these entries:

- Always monitor for successful and failed logon/logoff activity for the domain and all servers.
- Always monitor for failed directory service access.
- Always monitor for failed account management events.
- Always monitor for failed privilege use.

Moving Forward

Security is too important a topic to cover in one chapter. So far we've seen how the security infrastructure works in Windows Server 2003 and how the operating system handles authentication, authorization, and auditing. In future chapters, we'll extend the security horizons to include specific ways to protect Active Directory, the Encrypting File System, and Public Key Infrastructure.

Kernel Object Auditing

It is possible to monitor access to kernel objects that control access to threads in the Windows Executive. I've never seen an instance where this type of auditing was needed for a production system. Developers interested in tracing problems with their code can use this type of auditing on test systems.

Kernel auditing is enabled via the Audit the access of global system objects policy, which should only be set in the local system policies. The policy is located in `Computer Configuration | Windows Settings | Security Settings | Local Policies | Security Options`.

12 Managing Group Policies

As a consultant, I'm constantly made aware of corporate policies. For instance, if I park too close to a building, someone hurries out to tell me, "Those spaces are reserved for employees. You contractors have to park over there." Or if I make a suggestion that veers too far out of a client's comfort zone, a manager usually points at a set of thick, three-ring binders and patiently explains that "things just don't work that way here."

I'm a child of the sixties, so I grouse at being bound by rules and policies, but I recognize their necessity. Any organization with more than two people needs policies to define roles and guide behavior. The same is true for computers. Users have certain expectations for their computers and we in IT can't meet those expectations unless we enforce a measure of uniformity on the desktops and servers that support those users.

Microsoft recognized this need and introduced policy-based desktop management way back in Windows 95 with a feature called *system policies*. These policies were essentially pre-packaged Registry updates. Clients downloaded a file containing the updates when they logged on and applied the updates to their local copy of the Registry. That was that.

Classic system policies were a step in the right direction, but they have several serious limitations:

- **System policies permanently change the local Registry on a client.** Microsoft calls this *tattooing*. If you've ever made a mistake in a system policy setting and unwittingly deployed the policy file, you know how difficult it can be to recover because of the changes made to the clients' Registries.

- **System policies can only manage a limited range of processes.** The number of Registry entries included in a standard set of system policies is very small, and system policies cannot be used to control processes that do not rely on Registry settings.
- **System policies can only be distributed from a single file.** For NT, the file is Ntconfig.pol. For Windows 9x, it is Config.pol. This requirement to package all changes into a single file makes system policies inflexible and difficult to manage. It's possible to target a specific group within a .pol file, but this creates a large file that is cumbersome to maintain and takes a while to download.

Starting with Windows 2000, Microsoft changed policy-based management considerably. It tossed out the clumsy, static, Registry-only system policies and introduced a new feature set called *group policies*. Windows Server 2003 includes all the group policies in Windows 2000 plus additional policies that help take advantage of the new features in servers running Windows Server 2003 and XP desktops.

This chapter explains how to create, distribute, and manage group policies. The focus is on operational features: How do policies do their work? What requirements must be met to use them? How could they break down in production, and how are they best fixed? For comprehensive coverage of group policies including lots of examples and specific recommendations for implementing individual policies, I highly recommend *Windows 2000: Group Policy, Profiles, and IntelliMirror* by Jeremy Moskowitz.

New Features in Windows Server 2003

Microsoft has added a considerable number of policies to Windows Server 2003 along with new policy features that improve flexibility and troubleshooting. Here are the specific enhancements:

- Over 160 new policies that help control dynamic DNS registration, roaming profiles, terminal servers, and Control Panel operation.
- A fully integrated Resultant Set of Policies (RSoP) calculator. This calculator simplifies planning and troubleshooting group policies in organizations that have many tiers of containers and many policies linked to those containers. The RSoP calculations can be done from the user interface (UI) via a wizard or from the command line.
- A complete log of the RSoP calculation performed at each computer when a user logs on. This log is stored in the same database that stores the hardware and operating system parameters accessed by Windows Management Instrumentation (WMI).
- The capability to filter Registry-based policies to show only those policies applicable to a particular Windows version. This reduces the clutter in the management console and helps target policies to the correct platforms.

- The capability to restrict running certain applications at the desktop. The restriction can be based on a particular executable, the path where the executable was launched, or the digital certificate attached to the executable.
- A new group policy update utility called GPUPDATE that replaces the obscure Secedit switches used in Windows 2000. Secedit is now used solely to apply and report on the contents of the security database.

Group Policy Operational Overview

Computer policies have a lot in common with corporate policies. As anyone from the HR department will tell you, a corporate policy can only be effective if it meets a few guidelines:

- The policy must be in a form that can be clearly and simply communicated to the recipient.
- The action required by the policy must fit the capabilities of the recipient.
- The recipient must be reminded frequently of the policy so that observance does not lapse.

The discussion in the next few sections examines how group policies in Windows Server 2003 meet these guidelines.

Purpose of Group Policies

At their simplest level, group policies provide a way to efficiently manage large numbers of computers. An exact definition of "manage" can be a little elusive. For example, business schools teach that people cannot truly be "managed." They may allow themselves to be guided, goaded, cajoled, or dragged in the direction of a particular goal, but they never lose their waywardness.

Computers are more malleable than people, but the principle remains the same. You don't manage computers; they *let* themselves be managed. As you'll see, each Windows Server 2003, Windows XP, and Windows 2000 client has a set of services that know how to process the instructions distributed in group policies. It is up to you as administrators to get the right instructions to the right clients at the right time.

In the next few sections, you'll see how group policies are generated, how clients know where to find them, how they are downloaded, and what happens when they are processed. Armed with this information, you'll then see how to implement each type of policy and how to troubleshoot them if they don't work as advertised.

Group Policy Components

Group policy deployment in an enterprise quickly becomes a maze of twisty little passages, all different. In my opinion, Microsoft made this adventure much harder than necessary by attaching a lot of highfalutin terminology to group policy components. I'll give a brief introduction to each one and then examine them in detail.

- **Group Policy Object (GPO).** Don't bother searching through Active Directory looking for an "object" with a name or class of GPO. Microsoft uses the term *Group Policy Object* as an umbrella to identify the two components of a group policy: the *Group Policy Container* and the *Group Policy Template*. Container objects in Active Directory such as sites, domains, and organizational units (OUs) can be *linked* to a GPO. This applies the GPO settings to user and computer objects under that container.
- **Group Policy Template (GPT).** A GPT is the set of instructions that implements a set of policies. For example, policies that update the Registry are stored in a GPT file called Registry.pol. File-based GPTs are stored in policy folders under the `Sysvol` folder on each domain controller. Figure 12.1 shows an example.
- **Group Policy Container (GPC).** A GPC is an Active Directory object that lists the names of the GPTs associated with a particular GPO. Windows clients use the information in a GPC to determine which GPTs to download and process. (Microsoft documentation sometimes uses the terms GPO and GPC interchangeably.)
- **Client-side extensions (CSE).** Various functions at a Windows client can be managed by group policies. These functions have services that know how to obtain and process group policies targeted at them. These services are called client-side extensions, or CSEs, and they come in the form of Dynamic Link Libraries, or DLLs. For example, folder redirection policies are processed by a CSE called Fdeploy.dll.

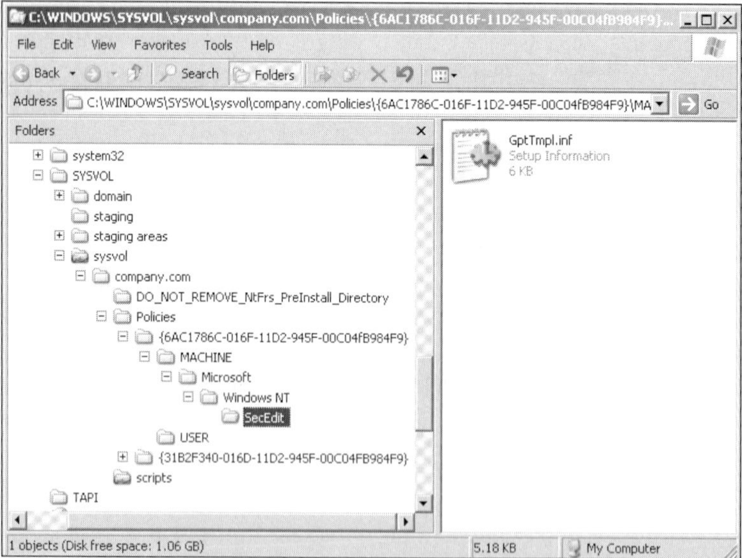

Figure 12.1 Typical `Sysvol` folder showing group policy folders and a Group Policy Template (GPT) file.

- **Group Policy Editor (GPE).** The GPE is an MMC (Microsoft management console) snap-in that creates and manages GPOs. Figure 12.2 shows the GPE for the Default Domain Policy, one of two GPOs installed in every domain.
- **Computer policies** and **user policies.** Policy settings in a GPO can apply to either computer objects or user objects. Computers download their policies when they start up. Users download their policies when they log on to the domain. Much of the complexity in deploying group policies comes from the dual nature of the GPO.
- **Group policies** and **local policies.** Not all policies are downloaded from the domain. Each client has its own stockpile of local policies that take effect when the machine is not a member of a domain or when a user logs on to the local SAM (Security Account Manager database) rather than logging on to a domain.

Now let's look at the operational details of these components to get a better idea of how they work together to support group policy creation, deployment, and management.

Group Policy Objects

The term *Group Policy Object* is an umbrella phrase that references the two constituents of a group policy: Group Policy Containers (GPCs) and Group Policy Templates (GPTs). It's convenient to think of a GPO as an independent entity simply because these two pieces should always be synchronized.

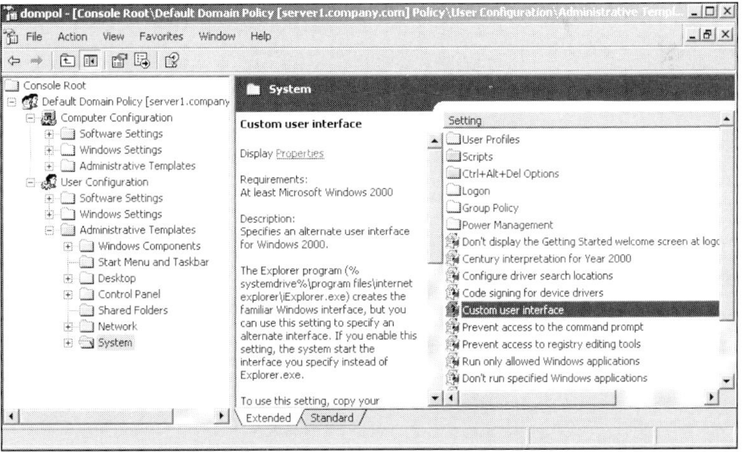

Figure 12.2 Group Policy Editor console showing the contents of the Default Domain Policy.

Viewing and Modifying GPOs

You can view the GPOs linked to a particular Active Directory container by opening the Properties window for the container in AD Users and Computers (or AD Sites and Services, in the case of site policies) and selecting the `Group Policy` tab. Figure 12.3 shows the GPO list for an example OU.

Every Active Directory domain has two default GPOs:

- **Default Domain GPO.** This GPO contains security settings that affect all the computers in a domain. The GPO is linked to the Domain object.
- **Default Domain Controller GPO.** This GPO contains security settings and configuration settings that affect domain controllers. The GPO is linked to the Domain Controllers OU.

Ordinarily, group policies affect only those objects in the container linked to the GPO (or any child containers, thanks to inheritance). The Default Domain Controller GPO policies work a little differently. This GPO contains many critical security policy settings that are vital to the proper operation of a domain controller. Therefore, the Default Domain Controller GPO policies literally chase down domain controller objects wherever they sit in Active Directory. The Domain Controller OU only acts as an anchor point for the GPO.

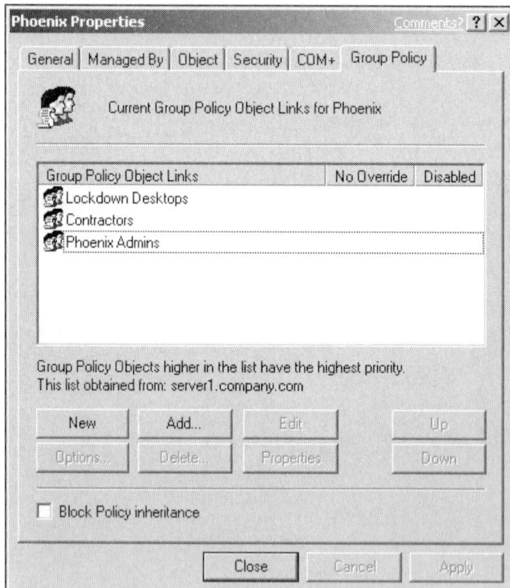

Figure 12.3 Properties window for an OU showing the group policy list.

Applying Group Policies with GPUPDATE

Ordinarily, a new User-side group policy does not take effect until the user logs off and back on, and a new Computer-side group policy does not take effect until you restart the computer. Group policies are also applied in the background as part of a periodic refresh.

If you want to apply a new group policy immediately, you can do so using the GPUPDATE utility. Just open a command prompt and enter **`gpupdate`**. This utility replaces the special `Secedit` switches used in Windows 2000 to apply group policies. You can specify User or Computer-side policies with the `/target` switch with the syntax `gpupdate /target:user` or `gpupdate /target:computer`.

If you apply a User-side group policy that requires a logoff/logon to actually see the policy take effect, you can use the `/logoff` switch with the syntax `gpupdate /target:user /logoff`. If the policies applied during this update do not affect a client-side extension that requires a logoff, then no logoff is performed.

If you apply a Computer-side group policy that requires a restart to actually see the policy take effect, you can use the `/boot` switch with the syntax `gpupdate /target:computer /boot`. If the policies applied during this update do not affect a client-side extension that requires a restart, then no restart is performed.

The GPUPDATE utility normally only downloads and applies group policies that have changed since the last download. This conserves bandwidth. If you want to download and apply all policies, use the `/force` switch with the syntax `gpupdate /force`.

GPO Version Numbers

The system tracks changes to a GPO by incrementing a *version number* attribute each time the GPO is changed. This version number has an interesting format because the system tracks updates to Computer Configuration policies separately from updates to User Configuration policies with the same version number. Here is the convention used to increment the GPO version number:

- When you make a change to a Computer Configuration policy setting, the GPO version number increments by 1.
- When you make a change to a User Configuration policy setting, the GPO version number increments by 65536.

The system identifies the two components of the GPO version number as a *revision level* for each component. When a client evaluates the GPO version number, it first divides the value by 65536. The result is the User revision level. The remainder is the Computer revision level. For example, a GPO version number of 131075 would yield a User revision level of 2 and a Computer revision level of 3.

You can view the revision levels associated with a GPO by opening the Properties window for a GPO. Figure 12.4 shows an example.

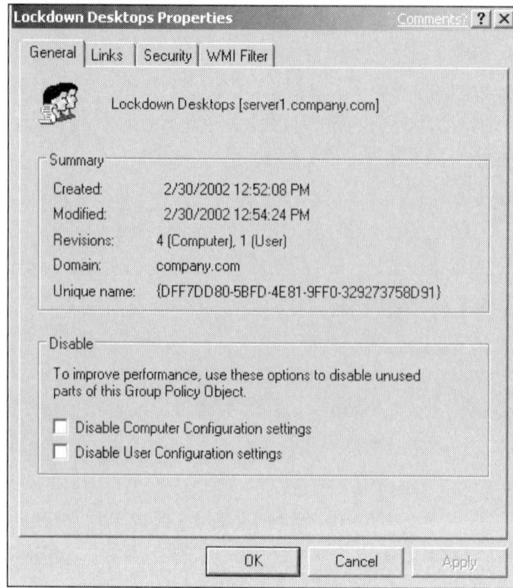

Figure 12.4 GPO Properties window showing revision levels for both parts of a GPO.

GPO Version Number Storage

There is no actual GPO to store the version number. A GPO consists of a GPC and a GPT, and a copy of the version number is stored in each as follows:

- The GPC object in Active Directory stores the version number in a `VersionNumber` attribute. Here is a partial attribute list from a GPC that shows this attribute:

```
versionNumber: 65538;
gPCFunctionalityVersion: 2;
gPCFileSysPath: \\company.com\SysVol\company.com\Policies\{5D769292-2424-4D93-
➥A8BC-3EDD73BC58FB};
gPCMachineExtensionNames: [{35378EAC-683F-11D2-A89A-00C04FBBCFA2}{0F6B957D-509E-
➥11D1-A7CC-0000F87571E3}];
gPCUserExtensionNames: [{35378EAC-683F-11D2-A89A-00C04FBBCFA2}{0F6B957E-509E-11D1-
➥A7CC-0000F87571E3}];
gPCWQLFilter: [company.com;{F76FB374-E3B3-434E-953D-0FDDFB634FCF};0];
```

- The GPT version number is stored in a Gpt.ini file at the root of the policy folder in `Sysvol`. Here is a sample listing:

```
[General]
Version=65538
displayName=TestGPO
```

Troubleshooting GPO Synchronization

The GPC and GPT version numbers should always be the same within the same GPO. And the contents of the two GPO components should always be the same on any given domain controller. Any persistent difference means that a replication error has occurred.

The GPT and GPC version numbers can differ for a short time thanks to the different replication methods used to propagate changes:

- GPC changes are replicated using the Active Directory (AD) replication engine. Updates take as much as 15 minutes to propagate within a site and up to 3 hours to propagate between sites.
- GPT changes in `Sysvol` are replicated using the File Replication Service (FRS). The FRS works much more quickly than AD replication. Under most circumstances, changes to `Sysvol` are replicated immediately.

To avoid problems caused by the slow GPC replication in relation to the GPT updates, a client downloads the contents of an updated GPT even if the version number does not match the associated GPC. This means there is no overt indication of a discrepancy between GPC and GPT version numbers. You need to check the version numbers periodically.

The best utility for tracking down version discrepancies between GPT and GPC, and discrepancies between the GPO contents of separate domain controllers, is GPOTOOL from the Resource Kit. You should run this utility each night using the Task Scheduler and save the results to a file that you review the next day.

For a quick consistency check of GPC and GPT version numbers, you can use the Replication Monitor (Replmon) utility from the Support Tools. Right-click the server icon and select SHOW GROUP POLICY OBJECT STATUS from the flyout menu. Figure 12.5 shows an example.

Diagnostic Logging for the File Replication Service

If you think your problems with maintaining consistency between GPT and GPC versions between domain controllers is due to a failure of the File Replication Service, try enabling debug logging for FRS. This requires a Registry change. Add the following value (a data entry of 5 imposes the most complete logging):

```
Key:   HKLM | System | CurrentControlSet | Services  NtFrs | Parameters
Value: DebugLogSeverity (REG_DWORD)
Data:  5
```

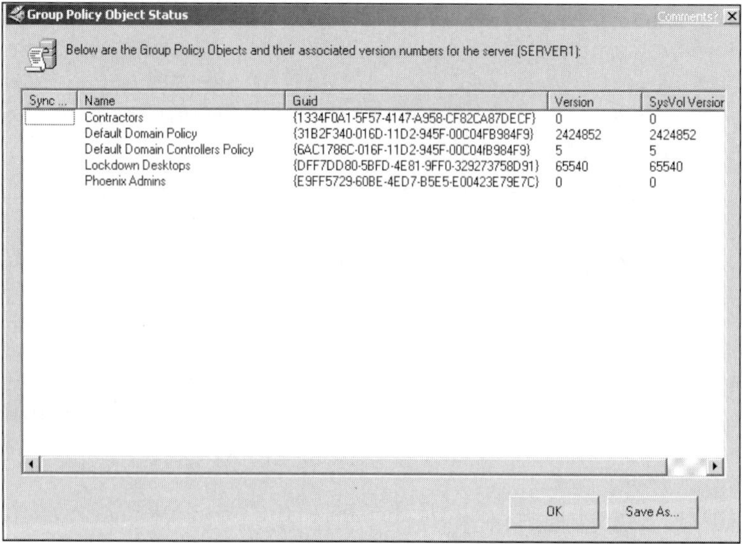

Figure 12.5 GPO synchronization status shown by Replmon.

Client-Side Extensions

If you're a parent or you were raised by a parent or you know a parent (did I miss anyone?), you have a pretty good idea of how group policies operate.

When you tell a five-year-old, "Don't scuff your shoes in the dirt," you expect the shoe-scuffing behavior to stop pretty darned quick. You don't need to explain how to lift the feet higher or how to maintain balance while one foot is farther from the ground than the other because the child already possesses these skills. Your short, simple directive should elicit the desired behavior. (See the troubleshooting topics scattered throughout this chapter for advice on what to do if your computers start behaving like *real* five-year-olds.)

Windows Server 2003 has 11 functions that are managed to some extent by group policies. With two exceptions, remote installation services (RIS) and software restrictions, each of these functions has a service running at the client that processes the group policies. These services are called client-side extensions, or CSEs. Each CSE runs as part of a Dynamic Link Library, or DLL. Table 12.1 lists the functions controlled by group policies and their associated CSEs.

Table 12.1 Group Policy Types and Client-Side Extensions

Group Policy Type	Implementing DLL
Administrative Templates (Registry)	Userenv.dll
Folder redirection	Fdeploy.dll
Logon/logoff (startup/shutdown) scripts	Gptext.dll
Security settings	Scecli.dll
Software Installation	Appmgmt.dll
Disk Quotas	Dskquota.dll
EFS Recovery and PKI	Scecli.dll
Internet Explorer Maintenance	Iedkcs32.dll
IP Security (IPSEC)	Gptext.dll
Remote Installation Services (RIS)	See Note 1
QoS Packet Scheduling	Gptext.dll
Software Restrictions	See Note 2
Wireless Networking	Gptext.dll

Note 1: RIS policies have no client-side extension. A RIS server obtains the contents of the policy when the Binary Negotiation Layer (BINL) service gets a connection request from a RIS client. The policy determines which OSC files the RIS server will include as part of the Client Installation Wizard.

Note 2: Software restrictions are implemented directly by the operating system in response to Registry entries put in place by the policy. There is no separate client-side extension.

You don't need to memorize the CSEs, but it is a good idea to remember that each one has certain special handling methods for the group policies it receives. These special handling methods include the following:

- Background refresh
- Synchronous processing
- Slow link processing
- Forced updates
- Script processing

Following are details about the special handling methods and how to configure them.

Registry Tip: Client-Side Extension List

The list of client-side extensions can be found at HKLM | Software | Microsoft | Windows NT | CurrentVersion | Winlogon | GPExtensions.

The list uses the ClassID (another term for GUID) to identify the CSEs. With one exception, the (Default) value of the CSE key contains the friendly name. The exception is the Administrative Templates policy, shown in bold in the list that follows, which has no default value for the key:

```
{25537BA6-77A8-11D2-9B6C-0000F8080861} = Folder Redirection
{35378EAC-683F-11D2-A89A-00C04FBBCFA2} = <Administrative Templates>
{3610eda5-77ef-11d2-8dc5-00c04fa31a66} = Microsoft Disk Quota
{426031c0-0b47-4852-b0ca-ac3d37bfcb39} = QoS Packet Scheduler
{42B5FAAE-6536-11d2-AE5A-0000F87571E3} = Scripts
{827D319E-6EAC-11D2-A4EA-00C04F79F83A} = Security
{A2E30F80-D7DE-11d2-BBDE-00C04F86AE3B} = Internet Explorer Branding
{B1BE8D72-6EAC-11D2-A4EA-00C04F79F83A} = EFS recovery
{c6dc5466-785a-11d2-84d0-00c04fb169f7} = Software Installation
{e437bc1c-aa7d-11d2-a382-00c04f991e27} = IP Security
{0ACDD40C-75AC-47ab-BAA0-BF6DE7E7FE63} = Wireless
```

Use this list when you enable debugging to trace a problem with group policies. Some of the debug traces identify a CSE by its ClassID rather than by its friendly name.

If you look through the CSE list in Regedit, you might notice that four of the CSEs are controlled by the same DLL. Gptext.dll contains the functions for QoS Packet Scheduler, IPSec, Wireless, and scripts. This has no operational impact, but it can be confusing when you review debug logs.

Background Refresh

Computer policies are applied when a computer starts up. User policies are applied when a user logs on. That seems pretty straightforward, but it's only half the story. Policies can change throughout the workday, and you don't want to force your users to log off or restart. For this reason, each CSE periodically requests updates to its group policies.

By default, domain controllers refresh their policies every 5 minutes, while member servers and desktops refresh their policies every 90 to 120 minutes. (The exact interval varies to prevent the clients from descending on their logon servers at the same time.) Two policy types do not refresh in the background because doing so would cause instability or confusion:

- Folder redirection
- Software distribution

Script policies are processed during a background refresh but do not take effect until the user logs off and back on again. (Or until he stops and restarts, in the case of computer scripts.)

Software restriction policies are refreshed in the background and take effect immediately. However, you may experience odd behavior due to the way the system implements software restrictions.

When a client process starts, it reads the software restrictions in the Registry. It caches the restrictions to speed up subsequent processing. This means that running process will not see a new restriction until the process re-initiates. Because most applications launch from Explorer, this re-initialization generally requires a logoff. (You can stop and restart Explorer from Task Manager, but this is not something your average user is likely to do.)

There is an exception to the logoff requirement for software restriction policies. The command-line (CMD) console works independently of Explorer, so when a new software restriction arrives in a background refresh transaction, it makes itself felt at the command line but not from the Explorer shell. This can lead to confusion, so prepare yourself for a few Help Desk calls from your power users if you implement software restriction policies.

Synchronous Processing

When the client-side extensions download and process their policies, they need time to do their work. Users see this as a delay in their morning logon, and one of the key design elements in Windows XP (and Windows Server 2003, though to a lesser extent) was to minimize those logon delays. To understand how Microsoft chose to minimize delays due to group policy processing, we need to take a look at the two processing alternatives:

- **Synchronous.** Using this processing alternative, all client-side extensions must finish their work before control is returned to the process that called them. In the case of Computer-side policies, the calling process is Winlogon. In the case of User-side policies, the calling process is Userenv. The term "synchronous" is a little counterintuitive because you typically think of synchronous as meaning "at the same time." In this context, synchronous means that processes occur in sequence.
- **Asynchronous.** Using this processing alternative, control is returned to the calling process as soon as all client-side extensions have been notified to begin processing.

Changing the Background Refresh Interval

You can change the default background refresh intervals with the following two group policies located under `Computer Configuration | Administrative Templates | System | Group Policy`:

- Group Policy Refresh Interval for Computers
- Group Policy Refresh Interval for Domain Controllers

In addition to the normal 90- to 120-minute refresh interval, clients also refresh their security policies every 16 hours. During this refresh, the client downloads all security policies regardless of whether they have changed.

Unlike the 5-minute and 90-minute background refreshes, which are controlled by values under the volatile Policies key in the Registry, the 16-hour (960-minute) refresh is hard-coded into the Registry under the `Winlogon | Parameters` key. The Registry entry that controls the interval is as follows:

```
Key:   HKLM | Software | Microsoft | Windows NT | CurrentVersion | Winlogon |
GPExtensions | {82...}
Data:  MaxNoGPOListChangesInterval
Value: 3c0 (960)
```

The end result of synchronous processing is that the user is not prompted with a logon window until all the Computer-side policies have finished processing and is not given a desktop until all User-side policies have finished processing. This is the default processing alternative for Windows 2000 except for User-side logon scripts, which are processed asynchronously.

The end result of asynchronous processing is that the user is given a logon window while Computer-side policies are still processing, and then is given a desktop while User-side policies are being processed. This speeds up access to the desktop and is the default processing alternative in Windows XP and Windows Server 2003.

Asynchronous processing can cause anomalous behavior if computer settings or items in the user environment rely on settings you've placed in group policies. For this reason, two policy types are singled out for special handling: folder redirection and software deployment. If you want your scripts to run in sequence, or you want them to finish before the users see their desktops, enable a group policy called `Run Logon Script Synchronously`.

Be sure to test your scripts thoroughly if you enable this policy. If a script hangs, the users get log-jammed out of their desktops. The maximum processing time for each individual script is 10 minutes, and all group policies must finish within 60 minutes. That's a long time to wait on a hung script.

The 60-minute limit cannot be modified by group policy or Registry hack. The 10-minute processing time for individual scripts can be modified with a group policy called `Maximum Wait Time For Group Policy Scripts`. The policy is located under `Computer Configuration | Administrative Templates | System | Scripts`.

Slow Link Processing

Just when you thought group policy deployment couldn't get more confusing, consider the plight of clients that make remote connections across a slow link such as a dial-up line or an ISDN/DSL line.

Group Policy Processing and Network Initialization

Another trick that Microsoft used to speed up logons was to deliver the desktop to a user prior to completely initializing the network. This significantly speeds up the logon process, but it has unfortunate side effects for group policies.

With delayed network initialization checking, for example, you must perform two logons to implement a software deployment policy. The first sets the policy, and the second downloads the software package.

Another example is using the advanced features in a folder redirection policy to select a particular group. In this configuration, you must perform three logons: one to set the policy, one to detect the group, and one to implement the folder redirection.

You can revert back to standard Windows 2000 network checking behavior with the `Always Wait For The Network At Computer Startup And Logon` policy. This policy is located in `Computer Settings | Administrative Templates | System | Logon`.

Each client-side extension has a different way of processing policies across a slow link. The following policy types are always processed regardless of the link speed:

- Security policies (including EFS and IPSec policies)
- Administrative Template (Registry) policies
- Software restrictions

The following policy types are not processed over a slow link unless specifically configured to do so:

- Quota settings
- Folder redirection
- Logon/logoff (startup/shutdown) scripts
- Internet Explorer Maintenance
- QoS Packet Scheduling
- Software Installation

You can override the slow link behavior of a CSE using the `Allow Processing Across A Slow Network Connection` setting for the associated policy under `Computer Configuration | Administrative Templates | System | Group Policy`.

Forced Updates

By default, a client conserves bandwidth and shortens logon time by downloading and processing only group policies that have changed since the last download.

A client determines if it has the most current GPO by checking the version number assigned to the two GPO components:

- The Gpt.ini file at the root of the policy folder in `Sysvol`
- The GPC object in Active Directory

Changing the Slow Link Processing Cutoff Speed

Windows Server 2003 defines a slow link as a connection running slower than 500Kbps. The system determines a connection speed by sending a series of ICMP (Internet Control Management Protocol) Echo Requests (pings) with a good-sized payload to the gateway, then measuring the return time of the Echo Reply.

If you have users who connect to the office using a VPN (Virtual Private Network) over a fast DSL line or with a cable modem, they may exceed a 500K connect speed and download group policies. You might not want this to happen for a variety of reasons. A 500K connection is pretty fast for Internet work but painfully slow for downloading software. Also you might also not want to implement new policies on users at home where they do not have ready access to the corporate Help Desk.

You can adjust the cutoff speed that defines a slow link using a group policy called `Group Policy Slow Link Detection`. The policy is located under `Computer Configuration | Administrative Templates | System | Group Policy`.

Each time a client downloads the contents of a GPO, it saves the version number from the GPC. The value is stored in the Registry under HKLM | Software | Microsoft | Windows | CurrentVersion | GroupPolicy | History.

The next time the client scans for GPOs, it examines the version number in both the Gpt.ini and the GPC. If either version number is higher than the last version number stored in the Registry, the client processes the GPO.

You can force a client to ignore version numbers when processing GPOs. This causes the client to download all policies even if they have not changed. This is done using a group policy called Process Even If The Group Policy Objects Have Not Changed. You must specify this policy for each individual CSE. The policies for the CSEs are located under Computer Configuration | Administrative Templates | System | Group Policy.

Script Processing

In Windows 2000, User-side logon scripts run asynchronously even though all other policies, including Computer-side startup scripts, run synchronously. In Windows Server 2003 and XP, as we've seen, all policies run asynchronously. If you want your User-side logon scripts to finish running before the users see their desktops, enable a group policy called Run Logon Script Synchronously. The policy is located under User Settings | Administrative Templates | System | Scripts.

Be sure to test your scripts thoroughly if you enable this policy. If a script hangs, the users will not get access to their desktops for a considerable amount of time. A script is given 10 minutes to finish. If it is still hung, the system stops processing it and continues on to the next script. If that script hangs as well, then there is another 10 minute delay.

All group policies must finish within 60 minutes. This time limit cannot be modified by group policy or direct Registry change. You can change the 10-minute processing time for individual scripts with a group policy called Maximum Wait Time For Group Policy Scripts. The policy is located under Computer Configuration | Administrative Templates | System | Scripts.

Group Policy Templates

The parameters that make up a specific policy are contained in one or more Group Policy Templates, or GPTs. Most GPTs come in the form of files that are downloaded and processed by the clients. There are two exceptions. PKI policies and IPSec policies are stored directly in Active Directory. The GPT files are stored in Sysvol on each domain controller.

Forcing Policy Processing Using the Command Line

If you enter gpupdate/force from the command line, the client ignores version numbers and downloads all policies regardless of the CSE setting.

With the exception of the binary .aas files used in software deployment, GPT files are simple text files. There is no rocket science at work here. Group policies do not use sophisticated client/server interactions. The client downloads a text file and does what the file says. In some ways, a Windows client is a little like Liza Dolittle in My Fair Lady when she sings

Words! Words! Words! I'm so sick of words!
I get words all day through;
First from HIM, now from you!
Is that all you blighters can do?

Table 12.2 lists each group policy type and its associated GPT.

Table 12.2 Group Policy Types and Their GPT Files

Group Policy Type	GPT File
Registry (Administrative Templates)	Registry.pol
Folder redirection	Fdeploy.ini
Logon/logoff (startup/shutdown) scripts	Script.ini and the script files themselves
Security settings	Gpttmpl.inf
Software deployment	*.aas files
Disk Quotas	Registry.pol (Note 1)
EFS Recovery and PKI	Certificates stored in Active Directory (AD)
IP Security (IPSec)	Policies stored in AD
Internet Explorer Maintenance	Install.ins
Remote Installation Services (RIS)	Oscfilter.ini
QoS Packet Scheduling	Not Applicable
Software restrictions	Registry.pol (see Note 1)

Note 1: Quota and Software restriction settings are distributed in Registry.pol, then processed separately.

GPT Creation

Here's an example to show how the Group Policy Editor creates GPT files. Let's say you create a GPO called `Desktop Lockdown` and you link this GPO to an OU called Phoenix. You define three policy settings in the GPO:

- A Registry setting that hides the `My Network Places` icon on the desktop.
- A security setting that gives authenticated users the ability to set the time on their local desktops.
- A folder redirection setting that moves everyone's `My Documents` folder into a folder with the user's name under a share called `\\Server\Docs`.

When you create this GPO, the GPE creates a GPC object in Active Directory and a policy folder under `Sysvol\<domain_name>\Policies`. It assigns the same name to the policy folder and the GPC. It derives the name using the same algorithm used to create Globally Unique Identifiers (GUIDs). This ensures that policies remain unique even if their friendly names change. The friendly name is just an attribute of the GPC object in Active Directory.

The policy folder in this example would contain three GPT files:

- A Registry.pol file containing a `NoNetHood` entry.
- A GptTempl.inf file containing an entry that assigns `SeSystemTimePrivilege` to well-known SID `S-1-5-11`.
- An Fdeploy.ini file with the following contents:

```
[FolderStatus]
My Documents=11
[My Documents]
s-1-1-0=\\server1\docs\%username%\My Documents
```

The new policy folder and its GPT files now replicate to the other domain controllers in the domain via the File Replication Service, or FRS. The FRS propagates changes to `Sysvol` immediately. It does not follow the 5-minute notification rules within a site or the polling frequencies defined for site links between bridgehead servers.

Group Policy Containers

A Group Policy Container (GPC) is an object in Active Directory. It has attributes that identify the GPT files associated with a particular policy and the CSEs required to process those GPTs. Here is a partial attribute list from the Default Domain Policy GPC:

```
cn: {31B2F340-016D-11D2-945F-00C04FB984F9};
displayName: Default Domain Policy;
gPCFileSysPath: \\company.com\sysvol\company.com\Policies\{31B2F340-016D-11D2-
➥945F-00C04FB984F9};
gPCFunctionalityVersion: 2;
gPCMachineExtensionNames: [{35378EAC-683F-11D2-A89A-00C04FBBCFA2}{53D6AB1B-2488-
➥11D1-A28C-00C04FB94F17}{53D6AB1D-2488-11D1-A28C-00C04FB94F17}][{827D319E-6EAC-
11D2-A4EA-00C04F79F83A}{803E14A0-B4FB-11D0-A0D0-00A0C90F574B}][{B1BE8D72-6EAC-
➥11D2-A4EA-00C04F79F83A}{53D6AB1B-2488-11D1-A28C-00C04FB94F17}{53D6AB1D-2488-11D1-
➥A28C-00C04FB94F17}];
gPCUserExtensionNames: [{3060E8D0-7020-11D2-842D-00C04FA372D4}{3060E8CE-7020-11D2-
➥842D-00C04FA372D4}];
gPCWQLFilter: [company.com;{F76FB374-E3B3-434E-953D-0FDDFB634FCF};0]; 1>
```

Following is an explanation of the attributes:

- The `GPCFileSysPath` attribute tells a client where to find the Group Policy Template files associated with the policy.

- The `GPCMachineExtensionNames` attribute specifies the ClassID of the client-side extensions the client will use to process the GPT files for computer policies.
- The `GPCUserExtensionNames` attribute specifies the ClassID of the client-side extensions the client will use to process the GPT files for user policies.
- The `GPCWQLFilter` attribute specifies details about any WMI filters that have been applied to the Group Policy Object.

GPC objects are stored in the Domain naming context under `cn=Policies, cn=System,dc=<domain_name>,dc=<root>`. It is important to keep in mind that separate domains in a forest maintain their own list of GPCs. The Domain naming context is not replicated to other domain controllers (except for global catalog servers, but those replicas are read-only). This imposes two operational restrictions when linking group policies with Active Directory containers:

- Avoid linking a GPO in one domain to a container in another domain.
- Avoid creating site policies in a multidomain forest.

The upcoming sections help explain why those configurations could cause you problems.

Cross-Domain GPO Links

GPT files associated with a GPO reside in `Sysvol` on domain controllers in the same domain as the GPC object in Active Directory.

If you link a GPO in one domain to a container in another domain, clients affected by the GPO must connect to a domain controller in the second domain to download the GPT files. This requires additional authentication. If the domain controller is at another location in the WAN, the transaction is slowed even further.

If you have a multidomain forest and you want to apply a consistent set of policies, you should create the policies in each domain. This increases the administrative workload because you must edit multiple GPOs each time you want to change a policy for the enterprise; but the alternative is to have your clients reach out across the WAN each morning to get their enterprise policies.

Site Policies in a Multidomain Forest

Site information is stored in Active Directory in a completely independent naming context from domain information. Site information is stored in the Configuration naming context, where it is replicated among all the domain controllers in a forest. Domain information, on the other hand, is stored in a Domain naming context where it is only replicated among domain controllers in the same domain.

Unfortunately, there are no provisions for storing site group policy information in the Configuration naming context. The GPC component of a group policy can only be stored in a Domain naming context. This has a couple of ramifications:

- Any number of domains in a forest can be present in any given site, so Microsoft chose to store GPCs for all site policies in one Domain naming context, the root domain. The root domain is the first domain in the forest.
- Because only domain controllers in the root domain store GPCs for site policies, the associated GPT files are only stored in `Sysvol` on domain controllers in the root domain.

The combination of these two engineering decisions restricts the functionality of site policies in a multidomain forest (see Figure 12.6). This diagram shows how site policies would be assigned in a forest with several domains.

The diagram shows two domains, NA and PACRIM, with domain controllers and users in two sites, LA and Tokyo, respectively. Both the LA and Tokyo sites have group policies. Remember that Group Policy Template (GPT) files for site group policies are stored in `Sysvol` on domain controllers in the root domain of the forest, regardless of the site location and the domains associated with the site.

When an NA domain client in the LA site logs on, the client downloads GPT files for the LA site policies from an NA domain controller. Because there is an NA domain controller in the LA site, it does not take long to download the GPT files.

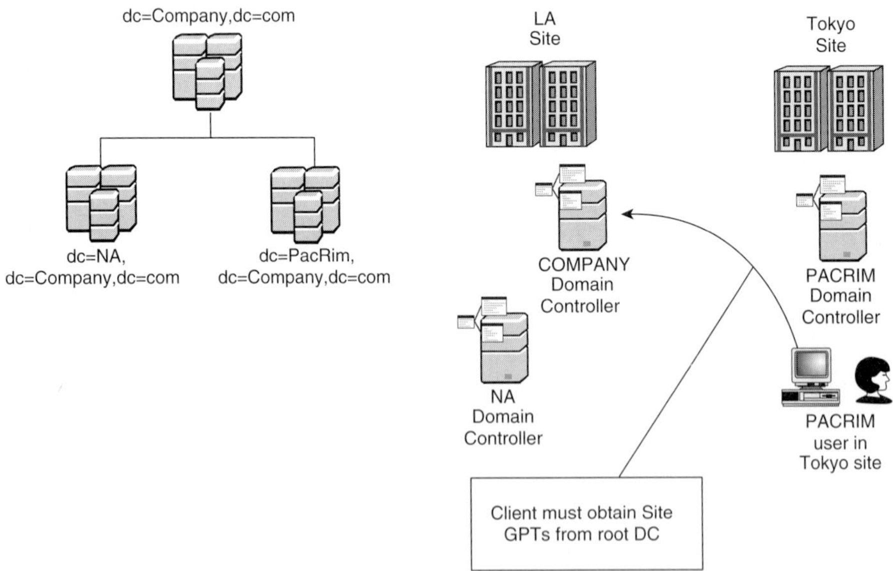

Figure 12.6 Site policies in a multidomain forest.

Life is not so sweet for a client in the PacRim domain who logs on in the Tokyo site. The GPT files for Tokyo site policy are stored on NA domain controllers, the root domain of the forest. The Tokyo client must reach out across the WAN to download the GPT files from an NA domain controller in the LA site. If the underlying WAN connection is a 56KB satellite leased line, users in Tokyo end up waiting quite a while for their logon requests to process.

So, if you have a multidomain forest and you want to implement site policies, put a domain controller from the root domain of the forest at each site with site policies or ensure that you have a fast WAN link to the closest site that contains a forest root domain controller. (Clients determine the closest site using referrals from domain controllers, which are able to check the site topology based on the IP addresses associated with the IP Subnet objects linked to each Site.)

Policy Hierarchy

GPOs are *linked* to container objects in Active Directory. This is how clients determine the list of group policies assigned to them. Only three container types in Active Directory can have links to GPOs:

- Sites
- Domains
- Organizational units (OUs)

Active Directory keeps track of these policy links with a GPLink attribute in the container object. Here is a partial attribute list for an OU named Phoenix that has two group policy links:

```
ou: OU=Phoenix,DC=Company,DC=com
gPLink: [LDAP://CN={91C0A3BC-141E-49BF-AD3B-2DA7905DBF09},CN=Policies,CN=System,
➥DC=Company,DC=com;0][LDAP://CN={205D4BEE-ACC2-465A-9ABA-D84575D72523},
➥CN=Policies,CN=System,DC=Company,DC=com;0];
gPOptions: 0;
```

- The GPLink attribute contains the distinguished name of any GPCs that have been linked to the container. Remember that policy names use a GUID format to ensure their uniqueness. A container can have links to multiple GPOs, and a GPO can be linked to multiple containers.
- The GPOptions attribute contains a setting for the *Block Policy Inheritance* option covered later in this chapter. (A value of 0 means that inherited policies are not blocked. A 1 means that blocking is enabled at this container.)

Clients know the containers in their distinguished name paths, so they can query Active Directory for any GPCLink attributes in those containers. Armed with that information, the clients assemble group policy settings from each GPO according to the following precedence (see Figure 12.7):

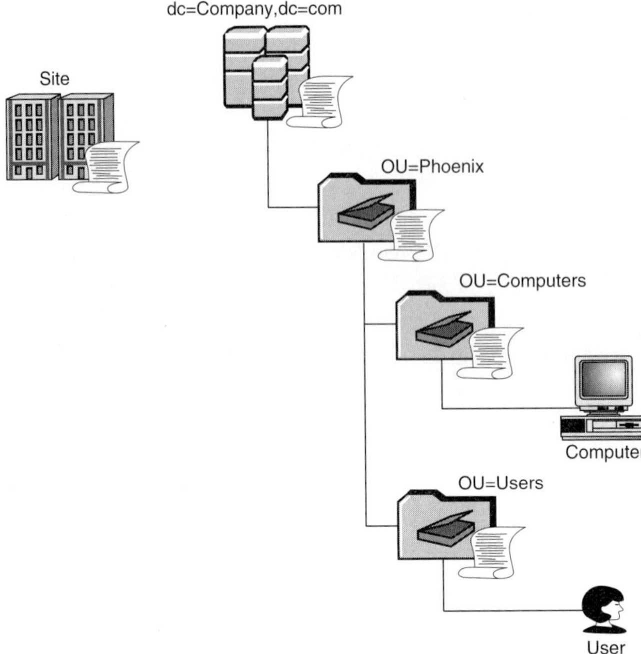

Figure 12.7 Diagram of policy inheritance.

- Local policies—that is, policies defined at the local computer—have the least precedence.
- GPOs linked to site containers are next in line.
- GPOs linked to a domain container take precedence over site and local policies.
- GPOs linked to an OU take precedence over everything that comes before.
- GPOs linked to the OU closest to the user or computer object have precedence over GPOs linked to OUs further up the tree.

The initials LSDOU are commonly used to represent this precedence. This policy preference order implements an *inheritance hierarchy*. You can override this hierarchy in one of two ways:

- You can set a policy setting that contravenes the same setting in a GPO linked to an OU higher in the tree.
- You can set an attribute in Active Directory that blocks the inheritance of all GPOs linked higher in the tree.

As you can imagine, both of these options have architectural and managerial ramifications. Let's see what they are.

Policy Tracking in the Registry

GPOs downloaded by a client are tracked in the local Registry under the key `HKLM | Software | Microsoft | Windows | CurrentVersion | Group Policy | Shadow`. Each policy is assigned a sequential number starting with zero. This sequence is determined by the precedence of the GPOs. The higher number has the higher precedence.

Records of all GPOs downloaded by a client are tracked in the Registry key `HKLM | Software | Microsoft | Windows | CurrentVersion | Group Policy | History`.

Overriding Policy Inheritance

It is possible to override policy inheritance at a particular OU. When this is done, objects in that OU (and any child OUs) stop receiving policy settings from containers higher in the tree.

Refer to Figure 12.7 in the last section. Let's say that you have created a GPO and linked it to the domain container. In this GPO, you define a security policy called `Message Text For Users Attempting To Logon`. This policy displays an informational message at logon. Your message includes a notification that all computing equipment belongs to the company and the company reserves the right to examine any and all data on the computer.

You link this GPO to the domain container because you want every user in the organization to see the message at each logon so they cannot claim they didn't know the restrictions.

Administrators in the Phoenix OU get tired of hearing their users complain about this message. They decide to block it for their OU. This small mutiny is relatively simple to accomplish. The administrators open the Properties window for their OU in AD Users and Computers and check the `Block Policy Inheritance` option in the Group Policy properties. Figure 12.8 shows an example.

After the Phoenix administrators make this change, the users in Phoenix stop getting the notice when they log on. This pleases the users but it does not please the company auditors when they pay a little visit the next week. The auditors report the infraction to management, and you, as a top-level administrator, are instructed to quell the mutiny. You use your privileges as Domain Administrator to uncheck the `Block Policy Inheritance` option in the Phoenix OU.

A few days later, after the brouhaha has died down, the Phoenix administrators sneak in early one morning and check the `Block Policy Inheritance` option once again. You notice their action a few days later and you uncheck the option. They check it. You uncheck it. This goes on for a while, then you notice that the Phoenix administrators appear to have finally capitulated. They make no changes to the `Block Policy Inheritance` option.

You take a closer look and discover that the Phoenix administrators have set a policy option in another GPO linked to the Phoenix OU that *disables* the `Message Text For Users Attempting To Logon` policy setting. Because this GPO is linked to an OU closer to the users than the domain container, it takes precedence and blocks the notification message.

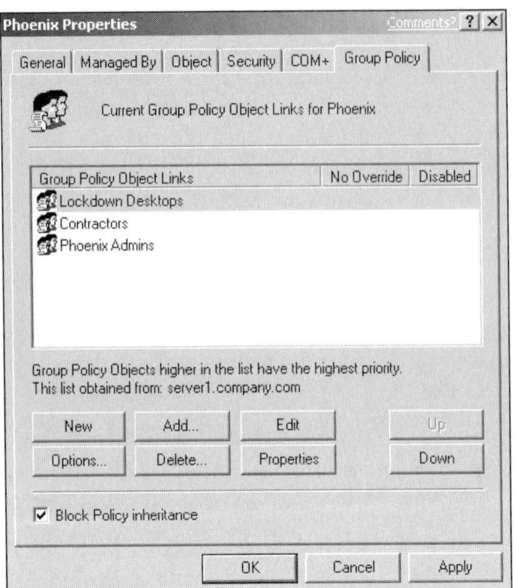

Figure 12.8 OU properties, Group Policy showing the `Block Policy Inheritance` option.

I don't know about where you come from, but in southern New Mexico we have a name for this kind of contest and we generally resolve it with six guns at high noon in front of the rowdiest saloon on Main Street. If you live in a more congenial climate, you might be interested in the following, less drastic, option.

Overriding Policy Blocks

You have the option, as a Domain or Enterprise Administrator, to set an option for a GPO high in the tree that overrides any policy inheritance blocks put in place farther down the tree. This is done as shown in Procedure 12.1.

Procedure 12.1 Overriding a Policy Block

1. Open the Properties window for a top-level container such as the domain container or an upper OU.
2. Select the `Group Policies` tab.
3. Highlight the GPO for which you want to force inheritance.
4. Click the `Options` button.
5. Select the `No Override` radio button as shown in Figure 12.9.
6. Click `OK` to save the change.

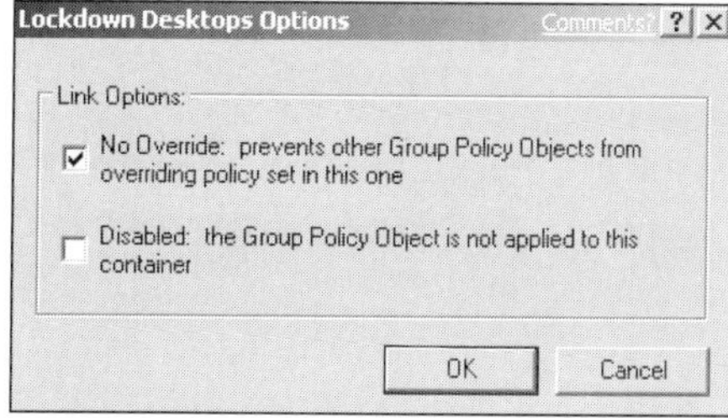

Figure 12.9 Options window for an OU container showing the `No Override` option for a particular group policy.

With the `No Override` option in place for a GPO, all policy settings defined by that GPO become mandatory for computers and users farther down the tree. Administrators can set the `Block Policy Inheritance` option, but it is ignored. And if the local administrators try to override a particular setting with one of their own, they'll discover that the various policy settings in your high-level GPO are dimmed in the Group Policy Editor so they cannot be modified.

Resultant Set of Policies (RSoP) Calculations

GPOs can be linked, filtered, blocked, and unblocked in myriad ways. Microsoft took a big step toward simplifying group policy management by including a tool in Windows Server 2003 that it licensed from Full Armor Software, `www.fullarmor.com`. The tool is called FAZAM, for Full Armor Zero Administration Management.

As with most third-party technology licensed by Microsoft, the RSoP features taken from FAZAM represent a subset of the commercial package. The portion of the FAZAM tool licensed by Microsoft permits calculating and logging a *Resultant Set Of Policies* (RSoP) based on the location of a particular user or computer object in Active Directory.

You can use RSoP calculations to see what happens with group policies if a specified user logs on to a specified computer. The calculation takes into account the location of the user's object, the computer's object, the site name, and any filters imposed based on group membership or hardware type.

Windows Server 2003 and XP also keep a log of the last set of RSoP calculations performed for any client who logs on at the computer. You can use the RSoP tool to view the contents of this log for any computer in the domain. The log is located in the CIM (Common Information Model) repository. See the upcoming section, "WMI Filtering," for more information.

RSoP Planning

The RSoP viewer can be launched in several ways. The simplest way is shown in Procedure 12.2.

Procedure 12.2 Running the RSoP Wizard in Planning Mode

1. Right-click a user or computer object in AD Users and Computers and select ALL TASKS | RSOP (PLANNING) from the flyout menu. This launches the RSoP Wizard starting with the Computer and User Selections window. Figure 12.10 offers an example.

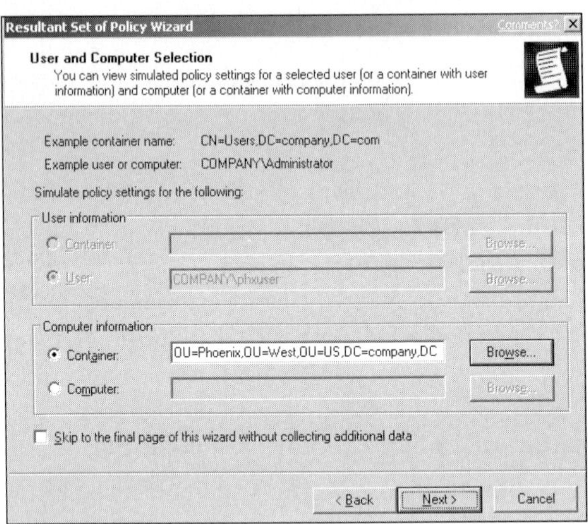

Figure 12.10 RSoP Wizard—Computer and User Selections window.

2. Under `Computer Information`, select the `Container` radio button, then click `Browse` and select the OU holding the user's account object.
3. At this point, the wizard has enough information to calculate an RSoP, so you could select the `Skip To The Final Page...` option and click `Next`. However, let's look at additional options that can help you diagnose potential problems.
4. Click `Next`. The Advanced Simulation Options window opens. You can select the following:
   - **`Slow Network Connection.`** This simulates the kind of GPO processing that would take place across a dial-up, ISDN, or DSL connection.
   - **`Loopback Processing.`** This simulates the Computer Configuration and User Configuration swaps that would take place if a loopback processing policy were in effect for the computer object.
   - **`Site.`** This selects the site where the user logs on.

5. Click `Next`. The Alternate Active Directory Paths window opens. This permits you to select a different OU for the user and computer account.
6. Click `Next`. The User Security Groups window opens. The window lists the groups that have the user as a member. You can select additional groups or remove groups for planning or diagnostic purposes.
7. Click `Next`. The Computer Security Groups window opens. The window lists the groups that have the computer as a member. You can select additional groups or remove groups for planning or diagnostic purposes.
8. Click `Next`. The WMI Filters for Users window opens. The window lists the linked WMI filters. You can select different filters for diagnostic purposes.
9. Click `Next`. The WMI Filters for Computers window opens. The window lists the linked WMI filters. You can select different filters for diagnostic purposes.
10. Click `Next`. The Summary Of Selections window opens. Use the `Back` button to change your selections, if necessary. You can also choose to process the selections on a different domain controller if you want to compare the results between DCs.
11. Click `Next`. When the wizard completes processing, a Finish window appears. Click `Finish` to see the RSoP window.

The RSoP viewer resembles a standard Group Policy Editor window except that it contains only the policy settings from GPOs that met the selection criteria. There is also an excellent RSoP viewer that comes as part of the Help and Support center. This gives a listing in XML that gives all the details of the group policies that have been applied to the computer. You must have local administrator privileges on the machine to run this tool.

GPRESULT

If you prefer the convenience of a command-line tool for viewing RSoP calculations, try the GPRESULT utility. Unlike the GPRESULT in the Windows 2000 Resource Kit, the Windows Server 2003 version performs the same calculations as those performed by the RSoP Wizard. You can also use it to view the contents of the RSoP log.

A GPRESULT listing is too long to show here, but it includes all the information necessary to trace each policy setting back to its originating GPO and linked container. You can run GPRESULT in planning or logging mode.

RSoP Logging

You can select the `(Logging)` option in the RSoP viewer to view the contents of the RSoP calculations performed for any client on any computer. You must have administrator rights on the computer where you are viewing the log. Proceed as shown in Procedure 12.3.

Procedure 12.3 Running the RSoP Wizard in Logging Mode

1. In AD Users and Computers, right-click a computer object and select RESULTANT SET OF POLICY (LOGGING) from the flyout menu. The RSoP Wizard opens with the Computer Selection window open.
2. Click `Next`. The User Selection window opens. Highlight the user name whose RSoP results you want to view.
3. Click `Next`. The Summary Of Selections window opens.
4. Click `Next`. The wizard retrieves the user's log entries from the selected computer and displays them in the RSoP viewer.

By comparing the RSoP results the client actually got to those that you get when you ran the user through the RSoP (Planning) calculations, you can see if there is a discrepancy and resolve it.

Additional Troubleshooting Tools

If you configure a group policy but it doesn't seem to work quite as you expected, check these items:

- **Event Viewer.** Look in the Application log for entries from the Userenv service. Warnings from this service are your first indication that something went wrong with group policy downloads.
- **Access rights.** One common problem with group policies is security access rights. Always make sure that the user has rights to the policy you're trying to apply. The easiest way to check this is to use the appropriate AD console to open the Group Policy properties for the associated container and then select the `Security` tab. The user should be a member of a group with `Read` and `Allow Group Policy` privileges.
- **Incorrect policy links.** Another common problem when configuring group policies is "losing the map," as they say in fighter pilot training. You may have linked the policy to one container but are testing it with a user account from another container. Or someone may have put another policy in place higher in the policy hierarchy than yours and is either overwriting your entry or blocking it completely.
- **GPOTOOL.** As I covered in the GPC topic, the GPOTOOL utility can help you trace inconsistencies between the version numbers of the GPTs and GPCs associated with a particular GPO.
- **Network problems.** Make sure the client is communicating with a domain controller, a global catalog server, and a DNS server. A failure to connect to any of these components can cause problems with group policy. You can run the NETDIAG utility to see if there are any errors.

- **Debug Userenv.** As a last-ditch effort to find the problem, you can enable group policy logging. Add a Registry value to the Winlogon key to enable logging:

```
Key:   HKLM | Software | Microsoft | Windows NT | CurrentVersion | Winlogon
Value: UserEnvDebugLevel
Data:  0x10002 (Hex) of type Reg_Dword
```

  Restart the computer after adding the value. The log file is located in `\Windows\Debug\Userenv.log`. Be prepared with a cup of coffee and some patience. The log contains a *lot* of information.

Computer Policies and User Policies

GPOs are divided into two parts:

- A Computer Configuration section that contains policy settings that apply to computer objects.
- A User Configuration section that contains policy settings that apply to user objects.

The Group Policy Editor displays these two sections as two top-level icons.

Some policy settings appear in both sections. When there is a conflict between settings for the same policy in the Computer Configuration and User Configuration sections, the Computer setting takes precedence. This is true even if the policy settings are in two different GPOs.

Consider an example where an OU named Phoenix contains both user and computer objects. There are two GPOs linked to the Phoenix OU:

- A GPO named Phx-Computers
- A GPO named Phx-Users

Each GPO contains a policy under `Task Scheduler` called `Prohibit New Task Creation`. When this policy is enabled, the Add Scheduled Task icon does not appear in the Scheduled Tasks applet in Control Panel.

The Phx-Users GPO has the policy under the `User Configuration` settings. The Phx-Computers GPO has the policy under the `Computer Configuration` settings. Here is how the policy is handled:

- In the Phx-Users GPO, the policy has been disabled, meaning it is possible to create new scheduled tasks.
- In the Phx-Computers GPO, the policy has been enabled, meaning it is not possible to create new scheduled tasks.

With this configuration, when a user in Phoenix logs on at a computer in Phoenix, the user would *not* see the `Add Scheduled Task` icon in the Scheduled Tasks applet. New task creation is disabled because the Computer Configuration policy takes precedence over the User Configuration policy.

If an administrator changes the policy setting in the Phx-Computers GPO from `Disabled` to `Not Configured`, as soon as a background refresh occurs at the desktop, the user will see the `Add Scheduled Task` icon.

Loopback Processing

The last section covered the situations where policy settings under Computer Configuration override the same policy settings applied under User configuration. There is another situation where the system must determine precedence based on the location of the policy setting.

Consider a scenario similar to the last example, but now there are two OUs under the Phoenix OU:

- The Users OU holds the user objects in Phoenix. It is linked to the Phx-Users GPO.
- The Computers OU holds the computer objects in Phoenix. It is linked to the Phx-Computers GPO.

The GPOs have a variety of settings. The specifics for the settings are not important in this example:

- The Phx-Users GPO has two policy settings: a security policy under Computer Configuration and a software distribution policy under User Configuration.
- The Phx-Computer GPO has two policy settings: an audit policy under Computer Configuration and a logon script policy under User Configuration.

When a user in the Users OU logs on to a computer in the Computers OU, the resultant set of policies would include the following:

- The software distribution policy from the Phx-Users GPO
- The audit policy from the Phx-Computers GPO

This makes sense under ordinary circumstances. But there are some situations when it makes sense to apply the User Configuration settings from GPOs linked to containers holding computer objects. The most common reasons are walk-up workstations, lab computers, or terminal servers where you want to maintain a consistent look-and-feel of the desktop and the software distributions regardless of who logs on.

In those situations, you can configure the system to apply the User Configuration settings from GPOs linked to containers holding computer objects. This is called *loopback processing*.

You can enable loopback processing using a group policy called `User Group Policy Loopback Processing Mode`. The policy is located under `Computer Configuration | Administrative Templates | System | Group Policy`. The default setting is `no loopback processing`.

You can enable loopback processing in two modes:

- **Replace mode.** This mode tells the client computer to ignore User Configuration policies coming from GPOs linked to the user's containers and apply User Configuration policies from GPOs linked to the computer's containers.
- **Merge mode.** This mode tells the client computer to first apply User Configuration policies from GPOs liked to the computer's containers, then apply User Configuration policies from GPOs linked to the user's containers. This gives precedence to the user's policy settings.

If loopback processing were enabled in Replace mode, the client would get this resultant set of policies:

- The audit policy from Phx-Computer
- The logon script policy from Phx-Computer

The User Configuration policy from the user's side is ignored because of loopback processing. The Computer Configuration policy from the user's side is ignored regardless of the loopback processing setting.

If loopback processing were enabled in Merge mode, the client would get this resultant set of policies:

- The audit policy from Phx-Computer
- The logon script policy from Phx-Computer
- The software distribution policy from the Phx-Users GPO

The Computer Configuration policy from the user's side is ignored regardless of the loopback processing setting.

You should avoid loopback processing except for specialized environments. They can make group policy troubleshooting very complex. Be sure to create separate OUs to hold the computer objects. You may want to physically identify computers affected by loopback processing (such as a sign on the monitor) so users are not surprised when they don't get their normal settings.

Group Policy Editor

The contents of Group Policy Objects are managed using the Group Policy Editor, or GPE. The GPE is an MMC snap-in that appears in a variety of locations.

The most common place you will see the GPE is when you open the Properties | Group Policy window for a site, domain, or OU object. When launched in this manner, the GPE displays only those GPOs linked to the container.

You can also build a custom MMC console and load the GPE snap-in into the console. When you do this, you'll be prompted for the name of the GPO you want to edit. Click `Browse` to open the Browse For A Group Policy window, then select the `All` tab to see a list of the GPOs in the domain. Figure 12.11 offers an example.

You can load the GPE snap-in multiple times into the same MMC console. Each time you load it, you can select a different GPO to manage. This is an ideal way to manage large numbers of GPOs from a single interface.

You can also point a custom console at a specific group policy or you can point it at a specific computer or both. These options use the `/gpcomputer` and `/gpobject` command-line switches. This is how Microsoft provides specialty consoles like the Local Security Settings console and the Domain Security Policy console. For example, here is the `Target` field from the shortcut that loads the Domain Security Policy console:

```
C:\WINDOWS\system32\dompol.msc /gpobject:"LDAP://CN={31B2F340-016D-11D2-945F-
00C04FB984F9},CN=Policies,CN=System,DC=company,DC=com"
```

As we'll see in the next section, the Dompol.msc console also takes advantage of an MMC feature that permits loading specific GPE extensions.

Special Configuration for Using Command-Line MSC Switches

If you want to use the `/gpcomputer` and `/gpobject` command-line switches to control an MMC console, you must set the following option for the group policy when you load the GPO into the console using the Add/Remove Snap-in window:

```
Allow The Focus Of The Group Policy Snap-In To Be Changed When Launching From The
Command Line
```

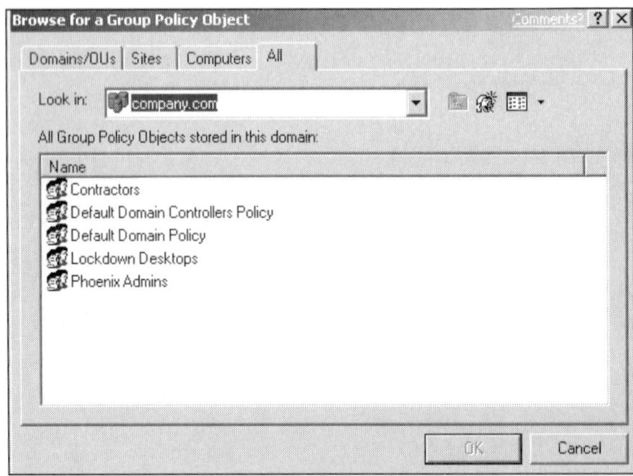

Figure 12.11 Browse For A Group Policy window showing the list of Group Policy Objects in the Company.com domain.

Selecting Group Policy Editor Extensions

The Group Policy Editor depends on several support files to supply editing capabilities for the various policy types. Table 12.3 lists the GPT files and their GPE extensions. If you get an error when opening a folder within a GPE, look for a problem with the respective editor or the files it tries to access.

Table 12.3 GPT Files and Their GPE Extensions

GPE Files	GPE Extension
Registry.pol	Gptext.dll
GptTmpl.inf	Wsecedit.dll
Script.ini	Gptext.dll
Fdeploy.ini	Fde.dll
*.aas (software deployment)	Appmgr.dll
Install.ins	Ieaksie.dll

If you build a custom MMC console for editing group policies as covered in the previous section, you can tailor the console by selecting individual editor extensions. Do this by selecting the `Extensions` tab in the Add/Remove Snap-In window, then uncheck all the extensions you don't want to load. Figure 12.12 shows an example for a custom console that only loads the Logon\Logoff Scripts extension.

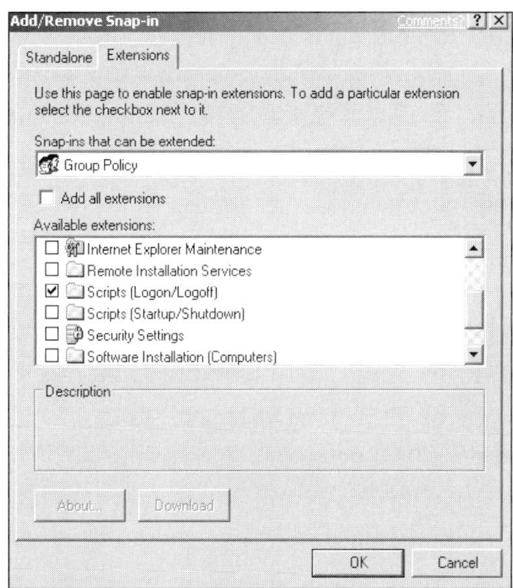

Figure 12.12 Add/Remove Snap-In window for a custom console showing a limited selection of policy editor extensions.

PDC Emulator and the Group Policy Editor

When you edit a GPO, the Group Policy Editor reads the GPC and GPT elements from a specific domain controller. By default, it selects the domain controller that holds the PDC Emulator role master token. This is true regardless of the focus of the AD Users and Computers (or AD Sites and Services) console when you open the GPE.

For instance, if you open AD Users and Computers at a workstation with a logon server of DC-37, the focus of the console will be at DC-37; but when you open the properties of a Group Policy Object for a container in the domain, the GPE will automatically read its information from the PDC Emulator, not from DC-37.

At first glance, this preference for modifying group policies at a single domain controller seems to violate the principle of multiple master replication. After all, changes to any replica of Active Directory or `Sysvol` will replicate to all other domain controllers, right?

The GPE prefers to work at a single domain controller in a domain because it is possible that two administrators could change policies in the same GPO during the same replication cycle. If this happens, changes made by one administrator will be overwritten during replication.

If you launch the GPE when the PDC Emulator is not available, you'll be prompted to select another domain controller or to wait until the PDC Emulator can be contacted. There's nothing wrong with modifying a GPO on another domain controller as long as you're sure that you are the only administrator working on that GPO. If you have any doubt, it's better to wait.

Changing the Default GPE Domain Controller

If you use domain controllers other than the PDC Emulator to modify GPOs, you can set a group policy to change the domain controller selection criteria. The policy name is `Group Policy Domain Controller Selection`. It is located under `User Configuration | Administrative Templates | System | Group Policy`.

This policy has three options:

- **`Use the Primary Domain Controller.`** This is the default option if the policy is not configured.
- **`Inherit From The Active Directory Snap-Ins.`** This puts the focus of the editor on the same domain controller used by the console, AD Users and Computers, or AD Sites and Services, that launched the editor.
- **`Use Any Available Domain Controller.`** This option permits the editor to use the first available domain controller. This is generally the logon server of the administrator using the tool.

You may have noticed that one seemingly obvious option is missing. You cannot simply select a different domain controller for everyone to use. If you want everyone to use the same domain controller, you must transfer the PDC Emulator role master to that server.

Group Policies and Local Policies

In addition to downloading group policies from a domain controller, servers running Windows Server 2003 and XP desktops have their own local store of policies in a hidden folder called `\Windows\System32\GroupPolicy`. The local computers also host the underlying data stores that group policies control, and local changes are often written directly to these data stores.

Policies overlay each other as they are applied, with the final set of policies getting the highest precedence. Local policies are always applied first, so they are like indigenous peoples who get overridden by marauding group policies as they sweep in from the domain.

If you manage a standalone desktop or server, you can change the local policies using the *Local Policy Editor* console, Gpedit.msc. The GPT files created by Gpedit.msc are stored in `\Windows\System32\GroupPolicy`.

Group policies downloaded from the domain are cached locally. For this reason, a user on a laptop that is disconnected from the network will continue to use the last set of group policies downloaded from the domain. This is important to remember because several group policies absolutely rely on cached information to function properly. An example is the Encrypting File System (EFS), which looks for a cached copy of the file recovery certificate from the domain Data Recovery Agent (DRA) when a user encrypts a file. If the domain DRA certificate is not available, the user cannot encrypt a file.

Because of group policy precedence, it is possible for local policies to become masked so that you forget they exist. They lie dormant in the Registry or the Secedit database and appear when the computer is disjoined from the domain or a user logs on to the local SAM instead of the domain.

Targeting Group Policies

In their default configuration, the settings in a GPO affect every user and computer object under the linked container. If you prefer a more tactical approach to assigning group policies, you'll appreciate being able to target policies by filtering out anyone who should not get the policy. Windows Server 2003 has two filter criteria:

- A user's or computer's group membership
- Hardware and operating system configurations exposed by Windows Management Instrumentation (WMI)

Filtering Group Policies Based on Security Groups

One of the most common misconceptions about group policies is that they are policies assigned to groups. Nothing is further from the truth, of course. Group policies are assigned to user and computer objects based on their location in Active Directory, never to groups.

You do have the option, though, of filtering a GPO so that it only takes effect if a computer or user is a member of a group. For instance, you may have a general set of desktop configuration policies in a GPO linked to a regional OU like Phoenix. The settings in this GPO suit most users, but the Sales Manager wants her people's desktops to be locked down severely so they stay focused on their quotas.

You could move the user objects for the salespeople to a separate OU under Phoenix and create a new GPO linked to that OU, but you might have restrictions that prevent you from taking this step. For instance, you might not have sufficient administrative privileges to create a new OU. Or, your organization might have AD design guidelines that do not permit you to create ad hoc OUs. Or, you might want to apply the group policies to users from a variety of OUs.

In these cases, you could create a new GPO and filter it so that only users in the Sales group apply the policy. This is done by modifying the security descriptor for the GPC object in Active Directory so that only certain groups have access to read and apply the group policy templates identified by the GPC. Figure 12.13 offers an example.

The simplest way to access the security descriptor for a GPC is shown in Procedure 12.4.

Procedure 12.4 Configuring a GPO Security Descriptor to Filter Policy Recipients

1. Right-click the site, domain, or OU linked to the Group Policy Object and select PROPERTIES from the flyout menu.
2. Select the `Group Policy` tab.
3. Highlight the group policy you want to filter and click `Properties`. The Properties window opens.
4. Select the `Security` tab.
5. Change the contents of the ACL to meet your filtering needs. Assign `Apply Group Policy` permissions to any groups you want to receive the policy.
6. Click `OK` to close the editor and save the changes.

If you elect to use filtering to target a GPO to a particular group or groups, keep in mind that the filter only applies if the objects representing the users in the group fall within the scope of the GPO. For instance, in the previous example, if you move a salesperson's user object out of the Phoenix OU and into the Atlanta OU, the user no longer gets the `Sales Lockdown` policy.

WMI Filtering

WMI, Windows Management Instrumentation, is Microsoft's implementation of the *Web-Based Enterprise Management* (WBEM) initiative of the *Desktop Management Task Force* (DMTF). Figure 12.14 shows a schematic diagram of the WMI components.

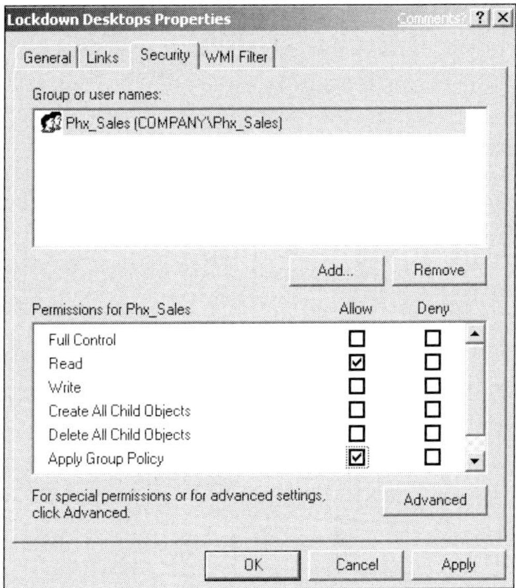

Figure 12.13 ACL Editor for a group policy showing a single security group assigned the `Apply Group Policy` permission.

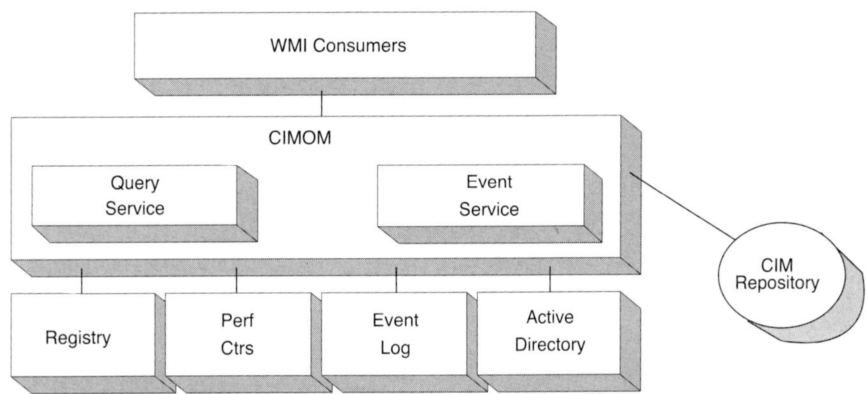

Figure 12.14 WMI components used in WMI filtering for group policies.

Here are the components:

- **Managed objects.** WMI collects information from a wide variety of devices and applications. Examples include hard drives and CPUs and memory and network adapters. These objects are abstracted by COM objects called *providers* that collect the information reported by the managed objects.

- **Common Information Model (CIM).** WMI stores information obtained from providers of managed objects in a repository called the *Common Information Model*, or CIM. This repository is less like a database and more like an auditorium where objects spit out information when they're called on. The top of the CIM repository is `\root\cimv2`.
- **Common Information Model Object Manager (CIMOM).** The CIM information repository is exposed by the CIM Object Manager, or CIMOM. CIMOM is responsible for processing input from the providers and communicating with applications that want information stored in the CIM repository.
- **WMI Query Language (WQL).** Because WMI is Microsoft's WBEM implementation, the information exposed by CIMOM is accessed via a language designed by Microsoft called the WMI Query Language, or WQL. The WQL provides read-only access to the CIMOM. Updates are done programmatically through the providers.
- **Event triggers.** In addition to responding passively to queries, the CIMOM can proactively send messages and take actions in response to events occurring in the CIM repository. Group policies do not make use of WMI events.

Windows Server 2003 uses WMI in a variety of ways. For group policies, you can use WMI to filter a GPO based on the results of a WQL statement.

WQL Statements

WQL syntax is a subset of SQL with extensions for specific classes in the CIM. The most common WQL statement used in WMI filters is a `Select` statement with `Where` modifiers that define a result set. Here are a few examples:

- Return the names of computers that have CPUs faster than 600MHz:

```
root\cimv2; SELECT * from Win32_Processor WHERE currentclockspeed < 600
```

- Return the names of computers that are running Windows 2000 Professional so you can deploy specific service packs or tools:

```
root\cimv2; SELECT * from Win32_OperatingSystem WHERE caption = ""Microsoft
➥Windows 2000 Professional"
```

- Return the names of computers that are running the Microsoft Client:

```
root\cimv2; SELECT * from Win32_NetworkClient WHERE name = ""Microsoft Windows
➥Network"
```

Notice the use of double quotes in the select statements. A double quote is a reserved symbol in WQL, so you must double-up the quotes if you need them to be included in the statement sent to CIMOM.

Rather than go on and on with examples, let me show you a great way to find interesting WMI classes so you can build your own WQL statements.

The WMI SDK comes with a web-based CIMOM browser called *CIM Studio*. You can download the WMI SDK from Microsoft at `msdn.microsoft.com/downloads`. Drill down through the tree to `Windows Development | Windows Management Instrumentation`.

CIM Studio is a browser-based utility. Figure 12.15 shows a sample page. You can use CIM Studio to find classes of interest to you by clicking the `Find` button (binoculars icon above the right pane) and entering a word like "network." This will return all the classes that contain the word "network."

Those classes that start with `Win32_` give access to providers of operating system information. Double-click one of the Win32_* entries in the pick list to display information about the class in the right pane.

To see what's stored in the CIM repository for a particular class, select the class, then click the `Instances` button (fourth button from the right, above the right pane). The pane fills with the results of a generic WQL query that essentially says, "Give me every instance of this class and all their attributes." You can use the column headings to develop your own WQL statements.

Configuring WMI Filters

WMI filters cannot be applied to individual elements of a GPO. For instance, you cannot filter just the Administrative Templates portion of a GPO. This means that you manage WMI filters as part of the properties of the GPO itself. Proceed as demonstrated in Procedure 12.5.

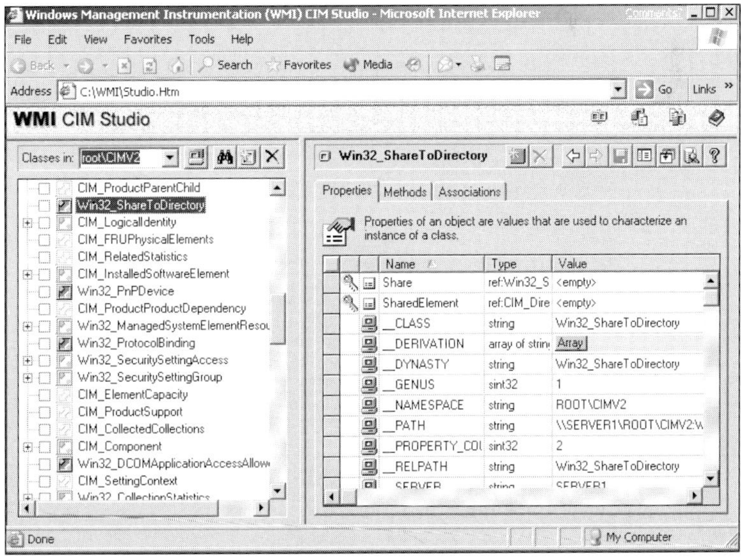

Figure 12.15 CIM Studio interface.

Procedure 12.5 Accessing the WMI Filter Interface

1. Open the Properties window for the GPO you want to filter.
2. Select the `WMI Filter` tab. Figure 12.16 shows an example.

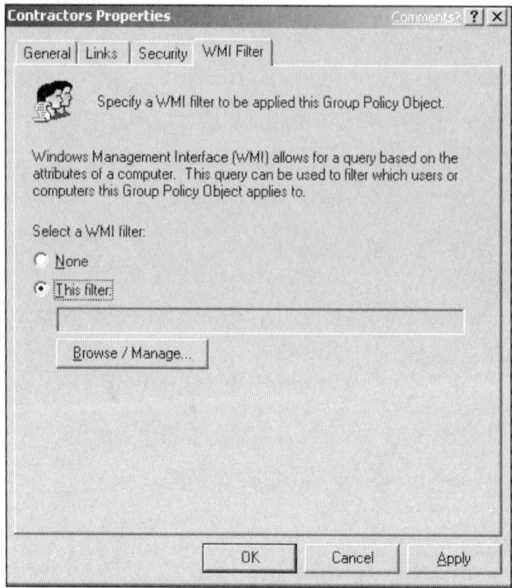

Figure 12.16 WMI `Filter` tab for a GPO.

3. Select the `This Filter` radio button, then click `Browse/Manage`. The Manage WMI Filters window opens.
4. Click `Advanced`. This exposes the `WMI Filter Editor` (see Figure 12.17).

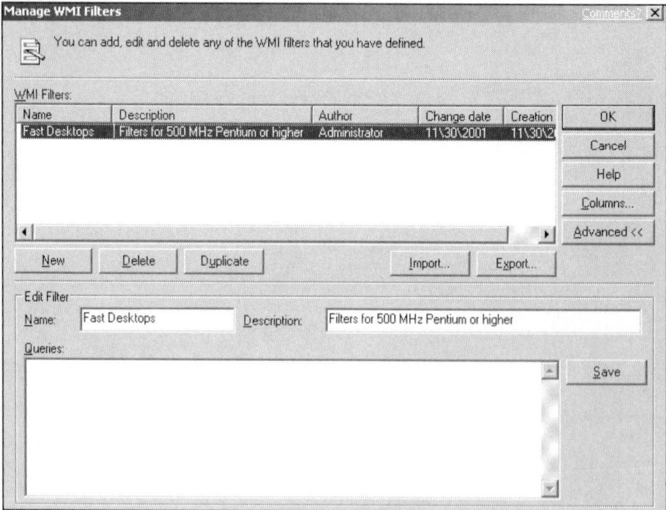

Figure 12.17 Advanced view of the Manage WMI Filters window showing the WMI Filter Editor.

5. Enter a WQL statement that you have designed to retrieve a set of computers or users that you want to get the policy settings in the GPO.
6. Click `Save` to save the WQL statement and then click `OK` to save the filter.
7. Test the filter by logging on from a computer that meets the filter requirements to see if you get the policy.

You can only select one WMI filter for any given GPO. The filter can be as complex as you like, but remember that the clients must execute the statement to its completion. Putting too many select criteria in the statement can negatively impact client logon time.

WMI Filter Storage

WMI filters are stored in Active Directory as MS-WMI-SOM object types. SOM stands for *Scope of Management*. The filter objects are stored under the SOM container, distinguished name `cn=SOM,cn=WMIPolicy,cn=System,dc=<domain_name>,dc=<root>`.

Here is a partial attribute list from a filter object that shows the attributes used to store and manage the filter:

```
cn: {C3BB1D85-D674-4568-B3BD-BBD4C6EC5A4D};
msWMI-Author: Administrator;
msWMI-ID: {C3BB1D85-D674-4568-B3BD-BBD4C6EC5A4D};
msWMI-Name: Phx-Filter-1;
msWMI-Parm1: Computers with CPUs faster than 600 MHz;
msWMI-Parm2: 1;3;10;60;WQL;root\cimv2; select * from Win32_Processor where
➥currentclockspeed > 600;;
```

Here are the items of note in the listing:

- `MSWMI-Author` stores the name of the user who created the filter. Keep this in mind if you cannot decipher the filter and you want to know the originator's intentions.
- `MSWMI-ID` stores the filter name. The name is derived using the GUID algorithm to ensure uniqueness.
- `MSWMI-Name` stores the friendly name for the filter.
- `MSWMI-Parm1` stores the filter description.
- `MSWMI-Parm2` stores the WQL statement for the filter.

Delegating Group Policy Management

One of the key strengths of Active Directory is the capability it offers to fine-tune the administrative rights you dole out. For instance, you can create an OU for a specific set of users and groups, then delegate admin rights over that OU to local administrators or experienced user representatives (sometimes called "department gurus").

Delegating the ability to create and manage GPOs is a little trickier than delegating the ability to manage users or computers or shared printers. The dual nature of a

GPO—the GPC and GPT components—means that the local administrator must have two privileges:

- The privilege to create and modify files in `Sysvol` on a domain controller
- The ability to create new GPC objects in Active Directory

These privileges are not given to users by default. You must assign them.

Assign GPT Access Permissions

GPTs are saved as files under policy folders in `Sysvol`. Assigning rights to these files involves setting NTFS permissions on the `\Sysvol\Sysvol\<domain_name>\Policies` folder.

This folder is actually a reparse point linked to the `\Sysvol\Domain\Policies` folder, so you can set permissions there, instead, if you want.

Start by creating a group for the local administrators. Then assign `Read, Write, Create, and Modify` permissions for the `Policies` folder to this group.

As an alternative, if you want the local administrators to manage a GPO but not create one, you can create the GPO first and then assign permissions on its policy folder.

These new NTFS permissions represent changes to the folders so they replicate to the other domain controllers via the File Replication Service.

Delegate GPC Access Permissions

After you've prepared the GPT permissions, give the admin group permission to create GPOs by adding it to the Group Policy Creator Owners group. This group has permission to create and modify objects in the Policies container in Active Directory, located at `cn=Policies,cn=System,dc=`*`<domain_name>`*`,dc=`*`<root>`*.

If you have not granted the admin group full control permission to the OU, you must also delegate it `Create Link` permission on the OU.

Managing Individual Group Policy Types

Now that we've seen how servers dole out the various group policies and how clients download and apply them, let's look at specific policy types to see how to use them to our advantage.

This topic covers the mechanics of implementing and troubleshooting the various policy types. For further information, refer to the following:

- Chapter 19, "Managing the User Operating Environment," has more information about using folder redirection and logon scripts to control the user environment.
- Chapter 11, "Understanding Network Access Security and Kerberos," covers specifics about using security policies.

- Chapter 17, "Managing File Encryption," and Chapter 18, "Managing a Public Key Infrastructure," cover specifics about EFS, PKI, and IPSec policies.
- Chapter 2, "Performing Upgrades and Automated Installations," covers how to use RIS policies to control the Client Installation Wizard.

Internet Explorer Maintenance policies fall outside the scope of this book.

Security Policies

The earlier part of this chapter covered the specifics of deploying security-related group policies in a domain. This section shows how the deployment mechanism works and how to configure security without the help of group policies.

Windows Server 2003, Windows XP, and Windows 2000 computers store their security settings in a local database called Secedit.sdb. This database is located in `\Windows\Security\Database`. Security-based group policies work by applying security settings to the Secedit.sdb database.

In addition to Secedit.sdb entries, security policies can also change the permission settings for NTFS files and folders, Registry keys, and local services.

Security-Related GPT Files

When you create security-related policy settings in a GPO using the Group Policy Editor, the GPE saves the settings to a GPT file called GptTmpl.inf.

Clients that are affected by the GPO download the GptTmpl.inf file and copy it to a local folder called `\Windows\Security\Templates\Policy`. If the client is affected by multiple GPOs that have security policy settings, it copies each GptTmpl.inf in sequence and gives them sequence numbers with an .inf extension. The sequence number matches the preference hierarchy of the GPO. The only exception is the Default Domain Policy, which is given a special .dom extension.

When a user logs on, the Winlogon process takes the contents of the .dom and .inf files and applies them to the local machine's security database and Registry. You can see the results of this transaction in the Winlogon.log file under `\Windows\Security\Log`. Security policies take effect immediately when they are downloaded.

Local clients also download security policy changes as part of their normal background refresh. The refresh occurs every 90 to 120 minutes for member computers and every 5 minutes for domain controllers. An additional background refresh of security settings only occurs every 16 hours. The standard background refresh only downloads policies that have changed. The 16-hour refresh downloads all security policies regardless of whether or not they have changed.

Special Handling for Account Policies

Account policies such as password policies, account lockout policies, and Kerberos policies can only be set in the Default Domain GPO. The policies appear in other GPOs, but setting them has no effect.

To view the security policies applied to a local server, launch the Local Security Settings console via `Start | Programs | Administrative Tools | Local Security Policy`. (Domain controllers have `Domain Controller Security Policy` and `Domain Security Policy` selections.) Figure 12.18 shows an example of the local security policies for a domain member server.

As you drill down through the policy settings, you'll notice that some have icons with little blue markings and some have icons that look like two little servers with a scroll of paper. The second icon type indicates that the policy settings originated in a group policy. The first icon type indicates that the policy originated in the local security database.

Default Security Templates

For domain controllers and domain member computers, group policies are the ideal way to manage security settings. However, you can also change security settings directly using the Secedit utility. Secedit relies on a template file to provide the settings that it applies to the Secedit.sdb database and other security objects.

There are two sets of security templates. The first are stored in `\Windows\INF`. The system uses these templates to do wholesales changes in security when a server changes its operating character. Here are the templates and their purposes:

- **DEFLTSV.INF.** Applied when a server is installed from scratch.
- **DEFLTDC.INF.** Applied when a server is promoted to a domain controller.
- **DSUP.INF.** Applied when a server is upgraded from Windows 2000 or NT4.
- **DCUP5.INF.** Applied when a domain controller is upgraded from a Windows 2000 domain controller.
- **DSUPT.INF.** Applied when a server is upgraded from NT4 Terminal Server Edition or a Windows 2000 server that was running in Application mode.
- **DCFIRST.INF.** Applied to the first server promoted to a domain controller in a domain. This template contains special Kerberos policies, account policies, restricted groups, and group membership.

Specialty Security Templates

In addition to the security templates applied during Setup and domain controller promotion, there are additional security templates stored under `\Windows\Security\Templates`. These templates contain prepackaged settings for basic, secure, and high security configurations for servers, workstations, and domain controllers. There is also a package for removing the Terminal Server User group from the NTFS permissions on a server.

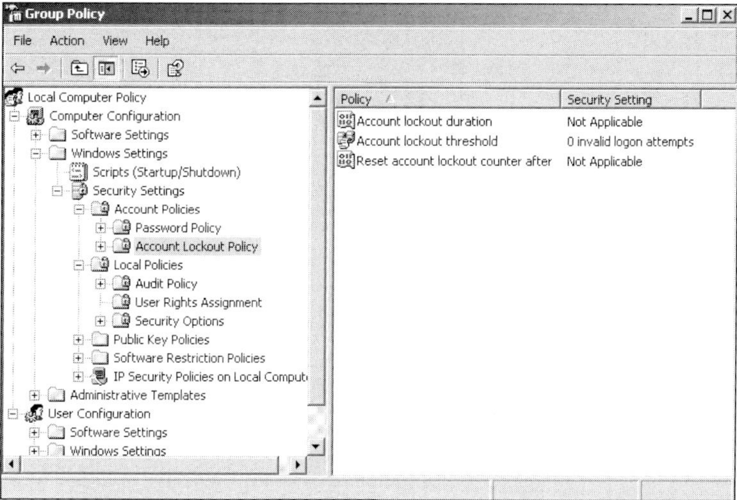

Figure 12.18 Local Security Settings console for a domain member server.

Registry Tip: Current Template File

The name of the security template applied by Setup or manually applied to the Secedit database is stored in the Registry under `HKLM | Software | Microsoft | Windows NT | CurrentVersion | Secedit | TemplateUsed`.

You can use these prepackaged security templates to analyze the settings on a system and to upgrade a system with new security settings. This should only be necessary if you manage a standalone server. A domain member should be managed using group policies.

Security Configuration and Analysis Snap-In

An MMC snap-in called Security Configuration and Analysis permits you to compare the current local security settings with the contents of a security template. You can also use this snap-in to apply the security settings in the template.

To use the snap-in, you must build a custom MMC console. After the console is built, you load a security template and use it as a benchmark for comparison with the current security settings. Any differences are identified for your attention with big red icons. Figure 12.19 shows an example. If you like the settings in the security template, you can choose to apply them. To perform these tasks, follow the steps listed in Procedure 12.6.

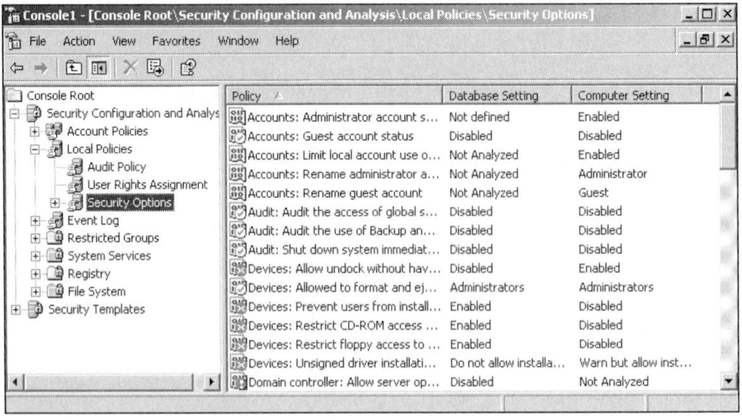

Figure 12.19 Security Configuration and Analysis console showing highlighted differences between security configuration template and computer settings.

Procedure 12.6 Using the Security Configuration and Analysis Snap-In

1. Open an empty MMC console by entering `MMC` at the Run window.
2. From the console menu, select `Console | Add/Remove Snap-in`. The Add/Remove Snap-in window opens.
3. Click `Add`. The Add Standalone Snap-in window opens.
4. Select both the Security Configuration and Analysis snap-in and the Security Templates snap-in.
5. Close the window to return to the Add/Remove Snap-in window. The two snap-ins are on the list. There are no extensions.
6. Click `OK` to save the additions and return to the MMC console.
7. Select `Console | Save As` and save the console with a descriptive name, such as Security Analysis.msc.
8. Expand the tree for both snap-ins. The `Security Templates` node displays a list of the security templates in `\Windows\Security\Templates`. The `Security Configuration and Analysis` node shows a set of instructions for performing an analysis.
9. Expand the tree under one of the templates and examine the settings under `Account Policies` and `Local Policies`. You can modify the template settings if you want to tailor it to your situation. You should save the result as a new template.
10. Right-click the `Security Configuration and Analysis` icon and select OPEN DATABASE from the flyout menu. The Open Database window opens.

11. Type in the name for a database that will store the result of your analysis. Do not try to open the existing Secedit.sdb database. You will get an *access denied* error if you try.
12. Right-click the `Security Configuration and Analysis` icon and select ANALYZE COMPUTER NOW from the flyout menu. The Perform Analysis window opens with a path for the analysis log.
13. Click `OK`. When the analysis is complete, expand the tree under `Security Configuration and Analysis` to show the security settings. Where there is a difference between the local settings and the template settings, you'll see a red icon.

Distributing Security Templates

If you have standalone servers—such as servers in a DMZ or application servers that you don't want to put in a domain or servers running Windows Server 2003 that are members of a classic NT domain—you can distribute security updates to these machines via the security templates and the Secedit utility.

The Secedit utility has four options, each implemented as a command-line parameter:

- **`Analyze.`** Compares the existing security settings with a template file and writes the output to an SDB database of your naming and a log file of your naming. The syntax is as follows:

  ```
  secedit /analyze /db somename.sdb /cfg template.inf /log somename.log
  ```

- **`Configure.`** Updates the existing security settings with the contents of a template file. You can select particular areas out of the template rather than applying the entire contents. The results are saved to a database file of your naming.

  Warning: Applying a template can make your machine either much too insecure or lock it down so severely that you cannot get in. Proceed with caution if you use this option. The syntax is as follows:

  ```
  secedit /configure /db somename.sdb /cfg template.inf /log somename.log /area
  ➥area1 area2
  ```

- **`Export.`** Takes the current security settings and writes them to a template file. This comes in handy when you want to configure a group of servers with the same security settings. Configure the security on one machine the way you want it, then clone off the settings into a security template and distribute the template along with Secedit. The syntax is as follows:

  ```
  secedit /export /cfg template.inf /log somename.log
  ```

- **`Validate.`** Takes the contents of a template and ensures that the syntax is correct for importing. The syntax to run this command is as follows:

  ```
  secedit /validate template.inf
  ```

You can use Secedit to deploy template files to Windows Server 2003 computers in a classic NT4 domain by placing the Secedit.exe file and the template in the `Netlogon` share on each domain controller, then adding a line to the logon script to apply the configuration. Be sure to set up your logon scripts so you only apply this command to servers running Windows Server 2003. (You could design multiple templates and use branching in your logon script to select the proper platform, but this is fairly difficult to do in standard batch files.)

Security Policy Highlights

Here are key points to remember about the way security policies are applied to local systems:

- Security policies for a local machine are stored in the Security Editor database, `\Windows\Security\Database\Secedit.sdb`.
- Security group policies are always downloaded regardless of the link connection speed.
- Account policies such as password history, password complexity, lockout policies, and so forth must be defined in the Default Domain policy. These policies are linked to the `Domain` container in Active Directory and cannot be altered by any other group policy.
- Local security policies are put in place by Setup and during domain controller promotion based on security templates stored in `\Windows\INF`.
- Local security policies can be modified with the SECEDIT utility using security templates stored in `\Windows\Security\Templates` as a reference.

Administrative Template Policies

The most obvious use for Administrative Templates is to hack the Registry on hundreds or thousands of machines at the same time. We've already seen most of the machinery involved with creating and managing Administrative Template policies. Here's a quick rundown of their operation before examining the details:

- The Group Policy Editor (GPE) displays Administrative Template settings based on the content of ADM template files. These ADM files are located in the `\Windows\INF` folder.
- When you enable or disable an Administrative Template policy, the GPE makes an entry in a GPT file called Registry.pol. This file resides in `Sysvol` under the policy folder. There are two copies of Registry.pol in each policy: one under the `Machine` folder that holds Computer Configuration policies and one under the `User` folder that holds User Configuration policies.

- Clients affected by a GPO containing Administrative Template entries download the Registry.pol files and process their contents into the special Policies keys in the Registry.
- Applications coded to look for parameters in the volatile Policies keys change their operation based on the contents of the group policy.

Let's see how this process works in a little more detail. You want to get very familiar with Administrative Template processing. Most of the distributed management features in Windows Server 2003 rely on Registry-based policies in one form or another.

Special Registry Keys Used for Policies

Administrative Template policies in Registry.pol are written to special locations in the Registry designed to accept volatile group policy entries. Four keys store these volatile policies. Computer Configuration policies are written to the HKLM keys, and User Configuration policies are written to the HKCU keys:

- `HKLM | Software | Policies`
- `HKLM | Software | Microsoft | Windows | CurrentVersion | Policies`
- `HKCU | Software | Policies`
- `HKCU | Software | Microsoft | Windows | CurrentVersion | Policies`

Values in these volatile Policies keys are refreshed each time the computer starts and users log on. If you remove an Administrative Template policy from a GPO or break the link to a GPO containing Administrative Template policies, the entries are removed from the local volatile Policies keys in the client's Registry. This eliminates the tattooing that plagued classic system policies.

Tattooing and Classic System Policies

Here's an example of system policy tattooing. Using classic NT system policies, it is possible to define a wallpaper bitmap for a group of users. If you make a user a member of the affected group, the policy is applied to the user's HKCU Registry hive and the wallpaper setting takes effect.

If you remove the user from the group, the wallpaper setting stays in place on the user's desktop. You would either need to visit the local desktop to remove the wallpaper or define another group with a system policy to remove the wallpaper and make the user a member of that group.

The situation is handled much more cleanly by group policies. First, you define the wallpaper policy by creating a GPO that has an Administrative Template policy called `Active Desktop Wallpaper` under `User Configuration | Administrative Templates | Desktop | Active Desktop`. You link this GPO to the OU containing the user accounts, and all the users get the wallpaper.

If you move a user out of the OU, the policy setting disappears and the wallpaper returns to the original setting that preceded the group policy (the *status quo ante*, to use a Washington, DC, beltway term).

Policies and Preferences

The flexibility and lack of permanence associated with Registry-based group policies makes them an attractive feature, but there's an important thing to remember about them. They only work if the application you're trying to manage is coded to look for Registry values in the correct location. In other words, you cannot manage application XYZ with volatile group policies if XYZ doesn't know to look in one of the four volatile Policies keys in the Registry for its parameters.

It is possible to use group policies to change Registry parameters outside of the volatile Policies keys. This creates hard-coded Registry entries similar to those created by classic NT system policies. Microsoft calls these non-volatile Registry entries *preferences* to contrast them with *policies* that can be added and removed freely.

Policies are much more flexible and simple to manage than preferences; but if you are trying to manage legacy applications, often you must resort to preferences to control the Registry entries. We'll see how to create a preference, but first let's see how the Group Policy Editor creates standard policies.

ADM Template Files

Administrative Template policies get their name because their settings are derived from entries in a set of text-based ADM template files. This sounds similar to classic NT system policies, but the structure of the ADM files and how they are used are significantly different.

The ADM template files are located in the `\Windows\INF` folder. The Group Policy Editor loads four of these templates by default:

- **System.adm.** A comprehensive set of policy settings that control most of the features exposed by the Explorer shell.
- **Inetres.adm**. Internet Explorer policies affecting components such as Internet Explorer, Control Panel, Offline Pages, Browser Menus, Persistence Behavior, and Administrator Approved Controls.
- **Conf.adm**. NetMeeting policies.
- **Wmplayer.adm**. Windows Media Player policies.

Legacy Templates

In addition to the standard ADM templates, Windows Server 2003 includes additional templates for backward compatibility with classic NT system policies. With one exception, these ADM templates cannot be loaded into the Group Policy Editor. They are accessed via the *System Policy Editor*, or Poledit. (The exception is Inetset.adm.) Following are the legacy templates you will find:

- **Inetset.adm**. This template contains preferences for controlling Internet Explorer settings (see the earlier section, "Policies and Preferences," for more information).

- **Inetcorp.adm**. System policies that control Internet Explorer languages, dialup restrictions, and caching.
- **Winnt.adm**. System policies for NT4.
- **Windows.adm**. System policies for Windows 9x.
- **Common.adm**. System policies common to both NT4 and Windows 9x computer settings.

Loading Additional ADM Templates

If you purchase an application that makes use of volatile group policies, such as Office 2000 or Office XP, you can load the ADM templates into the GPE as described in Procedure 12.7.

Procedure 12.7 Loading ADM Templates into the Group Policy Editor

1. Open the Group Policy Editor for the GPO where you want to use additional templates.
2. Expand the tree to the `Administrative Templates` icon (under either `Computer Configuration` or `User Configuration`—it doesn't matter.)
3. Right-click the `Administrative Templates` icon and select `Add/Remove Templates`.
4. Click `Add`. The list of templates from `\Windows\INF` appears.
5. Browse to the location where your templates are located and select the one you want to load.
6. Close the Add/Remove Templates window to save the selection and load the template. (The template selection is saved as part of the MMC console settings so the template will be loaded the next time the console is opened.)
7. Check to make sure that you can see the policies for the template you loaded. If the template is improperly formatted, you'll get an error when it loads.
8. If the template contains only classic system policies with no processing instructions, it will be placed under a foreign policy icon and the contents will not be accessible.

Poledit and Windows Server 2003

Windows Server 2003 includes a copy of Poledit that you can use for creating and managing Config.pol and Ntconfig.pol files for your downlevel clients.

Save the .pol files in `\Windows\Sysvol\Sysvol\<domain_name>\Scripts`. This folder is shared as `Netlogon`.

A modern Windows machine (Windows Server 2003, Windows XP, or Windows 2000) that is a member of an NT4 domain will download and use system policies. As soon as the domain is upgraded to Windows Server 2003 or Windows 2000, all modern Windows machines stop using system policies and start using group policies.

Group Policies and System Policies

Windows Server 2003 users and computers only process classic system policies if they are not exposed to group policies from an Active Directory domain. Here are some examples:

- A user in an Active Directory domain logs on to a Windows Server 2003 computer in an Active Directory domain: No system policies are processed.
- A user in an Active Directory domain logs on to a Windows Server 2003 computer in an NT4 domain: The system processes Ntconfig.pol computer policies.
- A user in an NT4 domain logs on to a Windows Server 2003 computer in an Active Directory domain: The system processes Ntconfig.pol user policies.

Registry.pol Files

When you enable Administrative Template policy settings in the Group Policy Editor (GPE), the GPE extracts the policy setting from the ADM template and uses it to create an entry in a file called Registry.pol. This file is a Unicode-based text file.

The GPE presents three alternatives for setting a group policy: `Enabled`, `Disabled`, or `Not Configured`. Here is what the GPE writes to Registry.pol based on these three options:

- **`Enabled`.** The GPE extracts a listing from the associated ADM template file and uses it to write an entry to Registry.pol. For instance, if you enable the `Hide My Network Places Icon On Desktop` policy, the GPE places the following entry in Registry.pol:

  ```
  [Software\Microsoft\Windows\CurrentVersion\Policies\Explorer ;NoNetHood  ; ; ; ]
  ```

- **`Disabled`.** The GPE writes an entry to Registry.pol that negates the listing from the ADM file. For instance, if you disable the `Hide My Network Places Icon On Desktop` policy, the GPE places the following entry in Registry.pol:

  ```
  [Software\Microsoft\Windows\CurrentVersion\Policies\Explorer ;**del.NoNetHood ; ; ;]
  ```

- **`Not Configured`.** The GPE removes all entries in Registry.pol related to the listing. This has no effect on other Registry.pol files, so that if the entry exists in another GPO, then the policy will be applied.

When a client downloads this Registry.pol file, the entries are written to the volatile Policies keys specified in the template. This is done by the client-side extension Userenv.dll and requires no intervention by an administrator.

ADM Listings Explained

The listings in the group policy ADM files are coded to write their entries to volatile Policies keys. Here is an excerpt from System.adm to show how this works:

```
CLASS USER
CATEGORY !!Desktop
    KEYNAME "Software\Microsoft\Windows\CurrentVersion\Policies\Explorer"
    POLICY !!NoNetHood
```

```
        #if version >= 4
           SUPPORTED !!SUPPORTED_Win2k
        #endif

        EXPLAIN !!NoNetHood_Help
        VALUENAME "NoNetHood"
     END POLICY
END CATEGORY

[strings]
Desktop="Desktop"
NoNetHood="Hide My Network Places icon on desktop"
NoNetHood_Help="Removes the My Network Places icon from the desktop.\n\nThis
➥setting only affects the desktop icon. It does not prevent users from connecting
➥to the network or browsing for shared computers on the network."
SUPPORTED_Win2k="At least Microsoft Windows 2000"
```

To make the ADM template more readable, Microsoft makes generous use of string tokens. When you see a double-bang (`!!`) next to a word, you know that it is a string token. The end of each ADM file has a list of the string tokens and their expanded versions.

Here is a quick explanation of the various elements of this ADM listing:

- **CLASS USER.** Identifies the listings that follow as sub-icons under the `User Configuration` icon in the Group Policy Editor.
- **CATEGORY.** Identifies the listings that follow as sub-icons under the icon name represented by the string token. In this case, the token `!!Desktop` expands to the same word, `"Desktop"`.
- **KEYNAME.** Identifies the listings that follow as having their Registry values in the identified Registry key. An individual listing can override this default `KEYNAME` entry with its own `KEYNAME` entry. Notice that the example shows a Registry value under one of the four volatile Policies keys, `Software\Microsoft\Windows\CurrentVersion\Policies`.
- **POLICY.** The listing will appear in the GPE with an icon name represented by the string token `!!NoNetHood`. This string token expands to `"Hide My Network Places icon on desktop"`.
- **SUPPORTED.** This new keyword in Windows Server 2003 identifies which platforms support the policy. This keyword is used by a GPE filter that displays only selected policies.
- **EXPLAIN.** This contains a help message that is displayed along with the policy listing in the GPE. The text is displayed on the `Explain` tab of the policy and in the sidebar of a web-enabled MMC console. The string token `!!NoNetHood_Help` expands to the full help text.
- **VALUENAME.** This contains the exact value that will be written to Registry.pol when this listing is enabled. The default value type is `REG_SZ`. An option `NUMERIC=` entry can identify the value as `REG_DWORD` or `REG_BINARY`.

When a client downloads a Registry.pol file containing this entry, the client-side extension will write the following Registry value:

```
Key: HKCU | Software | Microsoft | Windows | CurrentVersion | Policies | Explorer
Value: NoNetHood
```

The `My Network Places` icon will now be missing from the desktop (for Windows Server 2003) and the Start menu (for XP desktops). Remember that the only reason this works is because Explorer is coded to look for this particular Registry value when building the desktop interface for a user. There are literally hundreds of Registry entries used by Explorer but only a few dozen are coded to look at policy values.

Policies and Preferences

It's possible to create your own ADM template with listings that write to locations other than the volatile Policies keys. These entries will be processed by the client-side extension just like ordinary group policies, but the result will be an entry poked directly into the Registry.

Microsoft uses the term "preference" to describe a group policy that writes to the Registry outside of the volatile Policies keys. A preference is identified in the Group Policy Editor by a red dot in the icon. Standard group policies get a blue dot.

A convenient way to view red-dot preferences is to load the Inetres.adm template. This template contains listings that write to Registry keys other than the volatile Policies keys. The contents display as red-dot preferences.

A standard policy is also called a *managed* policy. By default, the GPE only displays managed policies. To display red-dot preferences, right-click the `Administrative Templates` icon and select FILTERING from the flyout menu. In the Filtering window, uncheck the `Only Show Policy Settings That Can Be Fully Managed` option and save the change.

At this point, you can view the red-dot preferences in the Inetres.adm template listings. They will show the following settings:

- If you `Enable` a red-dot preference, the Registry.pol entry lists the entire Registry path. The client-side extension puts the entry directly in the designated Registry key.
- If you `Disable` a red-dot preference, the Registry.pol file entry is changed to have a `**del` prefix, and the client-side extension removes the entry from the Registry.
- If you set the preference to `Not Configured`, the last setting you put in the Registry remains.

It's very important that you get rid of a preference by first disabling it and waiting for the clients to download the policy before changing the status to `Not Configured`.

Creating Custom ADM Templates

You can build your own ADM templates by cutting and pasting from existing templates. Before you do, check to make sure that the policy does not already exist somewhere. The Help and Support utility lists all policies. The Resource Kit has a group policy help file (Gp.chm) that lists them in a more concise way.

Remember: Writing a template entry that places a value in the Policies key only affects applications that are coded to look there. For the most part, all of these values have existing entries in the ADM templates. If you write a template entry that places a value in any other place in the Registry, the GPE will create a red-dot preference.

Software Deployment Policies

If you believe the hype in the trade press, the 21st century is the dawn of the Age of the Application Services Provider. Even if this is true, it's bound to be a long, long time before all the applications in your enterprise have migrated over to browser-based interfaces. Until that time arrives, if ever, we administrators dream of being able to wave a magic wand that can deploy desktop applications to the right user at the right computer in a configuration that works correctly right after being launched.

Software deployment in Windows Server 2003 isn't quite the stuff that dreams are made of, but it certainly beats walking from cubicle to cubicle with stacks of CDs. This topic covers the mechanisms for software deployment in Windows Server 2003 and the requirements for the deployment packages.

ADM Templates Can Be Unexpectedly Overwritten

Each time the Group Policy Editor opens a policy, it refreshes its local copy of the ADM templates with the master templates in `\Windows\INF`. For this reason, you should avoid modifying existing templates. Instead, create new ADM templates and keep them in a central location where they can be accessed by any administrator who modifies a GPO.

Alternative Software Deployment Tools

Policy-based software is good at distributing files, but that's about it. If your deployment needs are complex or you require extensive monitoring and reporting capabilities, I highly recommend that you look elsewhere for a tool. Candidates include:

- System Management Server (SMS) from Microsoft
- Tivoli from IBM
- ShipIT from Computer Associates
- InstallShield enterprise deployment products
- Mobile Automation

Software Deployment Functional Description

Like most policy-enabled features, software deployment depends on a confederation of components:

- **Windows Installer service.** A service that distributes the constituents of an application package and makes the proper Registry entries to support the installation. Versions are available for NT4, Windows 9x, and ME, but the policy-based software deployment in Windows Server 2003 requires Active Directory-aware clients. It cannot deploy to downlevel desktops such as Windows 9x or NT4.
- **Microsoft installer package (MSI).** An installation bundle consisting of the application's files along with a file catalog and instructions that tell Windows Installer how to perform the setup.
- **Software deployment package (AAS).** A group policy template file that contains the location of the MSI file and the instructions for how to deploy it. A Class Store object in Active Directory holds information about the software package.
- **Deployment server.** The server where the MSI file resides. It does not need to be a server running Windows Server 2003, or even a Windows server, but it does need to have a shared folder that can be accessed by clients who get the software deployment group policy.

Also, the deployed application must come bundled in an MSI file. (You can bundle legacy applications into a so-called ZAP file that is little more than a batch file for launching the application's setup program.)

Windows Installer Service

The Windows Installer service performs the following functions:

- Checks versions for each file and counts references to the files to minimize problems caused by one installation overwriting another. The Installer works in tandem with the Side-by-Side (SxS) features in Windows Server 2003.
- Performs a delayed installation by waiting until the user launches the program from the Start menu or double-clicks a data file with an associated extension.
- Maintains a transaction log of the installation so that the installation can be seamlessly restarted following an interruption. This includes the ability to roll back to a previous state even within the installation itself.
- Maintains a catalog of all installed components and Registry changes so the application can be thoroughly removed if it is de-installed. This feature supports a group policy option that removes an application when a user is taken out of the scope of the GPO containing the distribution policy.

- Supports self-healing applications by automatically downloading components that are accidentally deleted or overwritten.
- Can install applications using elevated permissions. This enables the user to install an application without local administrator privileges. (Did I hear you say, "*Hallelujah!*"?)

MSI Bundles

Policy-based software deployment depends on the Windows Installer service, and Windows Installer requires that an application be bundled into an MSI file.

All the components of the application need not be included directly in the MSI, but they must be present in a location that Windows Installer can find based on instructions in the MSI. Typically this means that the files and subfolders under the MSI need to be present in their standard configuration.

You can often tailor the installation of an MSI bundle with Microsoft Transform (MST) files. These files provide a *scripted installation* of the base MSI bundle. For example, the Office Resource Kit (ORK) has a tool for walking through the setup screens for Office 2000 or Office XP and saving the selections in an MST file.

Creating Roll-Your-Own Deployment Bundles

Any application bearing the Windows 2000 or Windows Server 2003 logo must have an MSI bundle. This excludes quite a variety of software, though. If you want to deploy 32-bit Windows applications that do not have an MSI, you can create your own using a variety of tools. Following is a list (in ascending order of expense but not necessarily of features) of what is available:

- **WinInstall 2000**. From Veritas, www.veritas.com. The Windows Server 2003 CD contains a light version of WinInstall.
- **Wise Installer**. From Wise Solutions, `www.wisesolutions.com`.
- **InstallShield Professional** (Installer Edition). From InstallShield, `www.installshield.com`.

Elevated Privileges for Software Installation

The capability of the Windows Installer to install an MSI package using elevated privileges eliminates a key source of desktop support calls.

By default, an installation with elevated privileges is only enabled when deploying an application with group policies. You can set a group policy that permits the Windows Installer to install all MSI packages with elevated permissions. This lets you use third-party tools, even email attachments, to distribute software that can be installed by average users.

The policy is called `Always Install With Elevated Privileges`. It is located under `Computer Configuration | Administrative Templates | Windows Components | Windows Installer`.

Only the process thread that performs the installation is given elevated permissions, so you don't need to worry that a user will obtain inappropriate permissions by breaking into an installation. However, enabling this policy does open the possibility of a Trojan Horse program masquerading as an MSI package to nab elevated permissions. Don't enable this policy without giving some thought to your vulnerabilities.

Software Deployment Package

The Group Policy Template (GPT) file for a software deployment package comes in the form of a binary file with an .aas extension. This file is stored on `Sysvol` under the policy folder associated with the GPO.

The deployment package tells the client-side extension where to find the MSI (usually via a network share identified by a UNC name) along with special handling instructions for the package. There are two ways a package can be deployed:

- **Published.** The application becomes a menu selection in the Add/Remove Programs applet in Control Panel. Users double-click entries for applications they want to install, and the Windows Installer service takes over to run the MSI bundle from the distribution server.

  If you publish many applications, you can help your users sort through them by assigning categories. To enter categories for published applications, open the Properties window for the `Software Distribution` icon and select the `Categories` tab.

- **Assigned.** The installation package places the appropriate shortcuts in the Start menu and registers the application in the Registry as if the application were actually installed. When the user selects the Start menu item or double-clicks a data file with the associated extension, the Windows Installer service takes over to run the MSI bundle from the distribution server.

In either case, the applications are installed so that the distribution server is not overwhelmed during peak logon hours. You can use the `Advanced` option of the software deployment policy to set an option that forces the installation of an Assigned package as soon as the user logs on. This is handy if you want to make sure that everyone has the most current version of a client frontend after you've upgraded the backend application.

The `Advanced` option also exposes these features:

- A support URL option for published application where users can click to get more information about the application.
- The option to uninstall the application if the user object is moved from the container linked to the GPO.
- The option to remove existing installations of an application that were not installed using group policies.
- Instructions for upgrading existing deployments of the application.
- The ability to designate MST (Microsoft Transform) files or other modifications to the base MSI bundle.

Software Deployment Troubleshooting

If you have problems getting a software deployment package to work, start by making sure that all other group policies in the same GPO are being applied. If so, check that the MSI file is accessible by the client and that you yourself can get the package if you put your own object into the linked container. If all of this looks right, break out the big guns: diagnostic logging and the ADDIAG utility.

Application Management Diagnostic Logging

The Appmgmt client-side extension is responsible for downloading and processing .aas deployment packages.You can enable diagnostic logging for Appmgmt so that you can trace its operations and find any errors or problems it encounters.

Enabling diagnostic logging requires a Registry change. Create the following key and value:

```
Key: HKLM\Software\Microsoft\Windows NT\CurrentVersion\Diagnostics
Data: AppMgmtDebugLevel (REG_DWORD)
Value: 4b
```

This creates a log called Appmgmt.log in the `\Windows\Debug\Usermode` folder.

Windows Installer Diagnostic Logging

After Appmgmt has downloaded and processed the .aas package, Windows Installer takes over to process the MSI bundle. Enabling diagnostic logging for the Windows Installer will tell you precisely what it tried to do to install an application along with any errors that occurred.This also requires a Registry change.Add the following value:

```
Key:   HKLM | Software | Policies | Microsoft | Windows | Installer
Data:  Logging (REG_SZ)
Value: voicewarmup
```

The letters in the `Value` field each have a meaning. They can be in any order. Following are their functions:

`I`—Status messages

`w`—Non-fatal warnings

`e`—All error messages

`a`—Startup of actions

`r`—Action-specific records

`u`—User requests

`c`—Initial UI parameters

`m`—Out-of-memory or fatal exit information

`o`—Out-of-disk-space messages

`p`—Terminal properties

`v`—Verbose output

`+`—Append to existing file

`!`—Flush each line to the log

`*`—Selects all options except v

`l*v`—Wildcard with verbose option

This creates a log in the default `%TEMP%` folder. The log name starts with MSI followed by a sequence number with a .log extension.

ADDIAG

The ADDIAG utility comes in the Support Tools. It gives information about what MSI packages are installed on a client and where they came from. Here's a listing that shows the report breakdown:

```
<Info>—Dumps general information
<TS>—Dumps Terminal Service information
<LocalApps>—Dumps local managed applications list
<ServerApps>—Dumps server deployed applications list
<MSIApps>—Dumps local mSI applications list
<GPOList>—Dumps local GPO list
<ScriptList>—Dumps local script application list
<ADHistory>—Dumps local AD policy history
<MSIFeatures>—Dumps local MSI features list
<MSILnks>—Dumps MSI shortcuts in the profile
<EventDump>—Dumps application log-related events
<Check>—Performs an AD integrity check
```

Here is an example ADDIAG listing that shows the information it collects:

```
Z:\Program Files\Support Tools>addiag /v
Microsoft (R) Software Installation Diagnostics. Version 1.00
Copyright  Microsoft Corp 1998-1999. All rights reserved.
Collecting info...
Initializing Remote DS Data...
Initializing Local AppMgmt Registry Data...
Initializing Local AppMgmt File Data...
Initializing Local Windows Installer Data...
Initializing Local Shell Data...
Initializing Local Event Data...

======================== General Info ========================

User -- NameSamCompatible: COMPANY\phxuser1
User -- NameFullyQualifiedDN: CN=phxuser1,OU=Phoenix,DC=company,DC=com
User -- Logon Server: \\SERVER1
User -- SID: S-1-5-21-2000478354-746137067-1957994488-1117
User -- Profile Type: LOCAL
User -- Locale: 1033
Processor Architecture: x86
System Locale: 1033

======================== TS Info ========================

Not running TS
```

```
========================= Managed Apps (Local List) =========================

No Managed applications were found.

========================= Managed Applications (Server) ========================

User dump for COMPANY.COM
Dumping GPO list (1 items)...
        GPO GUID: {B672BEFE-7815-44C4-9F28-E482AEC2CBAD}
        Name: Distro1
                Administration Tools Pack
                        Object GUID: {D34A6C2A-5D4D-4005-85F6-CBDBB5136C57}
                        Package Flags:
                                Published
                                PostBeta3
                                UserInstall
                                OnDemandInstall
                                OrphanOnPolicyRemoval
                        ProductCode: {5E076CF2-EFED-43A2-A623-13E0D62EC7E0}
                        UI Level: Full

========================= Windows Installer Apps =========================

Found 2 MSI application(s)
Easy CD Creator 5 Platinum
WebFldrs

========================= Local AD History =========================

Found 1 Applied GPO(s) in the history
Distro1
        GPO GUID: {B672BEFE-7815-44C4-9F28-E482AEC2CBAD}
        Version: 0xf000f

========================= Application log events =========================

EventID:  1004
Type: WARN
Date: 20:32:41.0000 - 2/02/2002
User: N/A
Computer: PRO10
Source: MsiInstaller
Description: Detection of product '{5E076CF2-EFED-43A2-A623-13E0D62EC7E0}', feat
ure 'FeDNSConsole', component '{455FE9A8-07D6-11D3-9C52-00A0C9F14522}' failed.
The resource 'D:\Windows\System32\dnsmgmt.msc' does not exist.
Data:
```

Folder Redirection Polices

When users save their files, the application generally offers them a default location. If the application carries the Windows 98, Windows 2000, Windows XP, or Windows Server 2003 logo, it is required to offer the `My Documents` folder by default. This standardization helps control the clutter of files on a user's desktop, but it does not go the extra step of putting the files on a server where they can be backed up and scanned for viruses.

This is also true of other folders in a user's profile. For example, the `Desktop` folder holds files and shortcuts that would be lost if the user's local drive died. The `Application Data` folder holds configuration information about programs loaded on the desktop along with other important data such as PKI keys. The ever-present Start menu holds shortcuts to every program loaded on the machine.

You can centralize the storage and management of these critical Explorer components by storing them on a server. This is most easily done using folder redirection policies.

A folder redirection policy takes the form of an Fdeploy.ini file that specifies the UNC name of the location where you want the system folder to reside. The client-side extension, fde.dll, processes the file by changing entries in the Registry associated with the Explorer shell folders. This changes the object namespace used by Explorer and other system components in Windows.

From the users' perspective, this redirection is seamless. The only time they'll know that their files are not being saved locally is when the network connection gets broken. This happens frequently to laptop users, of course. You might want to take a look at using offline folders to store local copies of files in redirected folders.

Script Policies

Classic NT had only one way to deliver a logon script to a user. You created a script and placed it in the `Netlogon` share of every domain controller. You then modified the users' profiles to point at that script. You could only run one script, and the script could not be in any other location.

Modern Windows changes this scripting situation considerably. Script policies permit you to run multiple scripts from any location. They also permit running logoff scripts for users and startup/shutdown scripts for computers.

The system continues to support classic scripts for downlevel clients. Active Directory includes an attribute in the user object for a logon script. Downlevel clients obtain this script name when they log on. The domain controllers continue to host a `Netlogon` share to hold classic scripts. The shared folder has changed, though. Modern Windows shares the `\Windows\Sysvol\Sysvol\<domain_name>\Scripts` folder as `Netlogon`. Classic NT shares the `\WINNT\System32\Repl\Import\Scripts` folder.

Classic Script Replication

Anything stored in the `Sysvol` folder is replicated to all domain controllers in a domain, and scripts are no exception. However, if you are running in Mixed with downlevel Backup Domain Controllers (BDCs), you face a challenge.

In classic NT, the contents of the `Netlogon` share on each domain controller were kept in sync using a service called LanMan Replication, or LMRepl. The LMRepl service replicated the contents of `\WINNT\System32\Repl\Export` on the PDC to the `Import` folder on the BDCs. It was this folder that was shared as `Netlogon`.

Windows Server 2003 does not support LMRepl. To keep your scripts in sync, then, you must set up a classic BDC as the LMRepl export server in lieu of a PDC. (The PDC Emulator must be running Windows Server 2003 in a Mixed domain.)

You must then use some method for copying the contents of the `Scripts` folder from the Windows Server 2003 PDC Emulator to the classic BDC export server. You can use Task Scheduler to kick off XCOPY or use one of the bulk copy utilities in the Resource Kit or a third-party tool. The LMBridge utility from the Resource Kit is especially useful.

Script Types

Scripts can take any form as long as the client is capable of interpreting the contents. This includes batch files (.bat) and command files (.cmd) along with more sophisticated scripting languages.

Windows Server 2003 and XP support VBScript and JavaScript natively as part of the Windows Script Host (WSH) framework. You can also run other scripting languages such as Perl and Python by deploying the interpreters to the desktops. (The most current versions of ActivePerl and ActivePython come with MSI bundles to simplify installation. See `www.activestate.com` for evaluation copies.)

VBScript and Viruses

You are probably aware that many email viruses take advantage of the ubiquitous nature of VBScript support in Windows to run exploits. The I-Love-You virus and the AnnaKornikova virus are two examples. To be fair, this is not a weakness of VBScript. If Microsoft had chosen to distribute ActivePerl on every Windows desktop instead of VBScript, then the exploits would use Perl.

You can set group policies in Windows Server 2003 to disable running VBScript attachments in email, but this does not preclude other vulnerabilities. Another solution, suggested by Jason Fossen from SANS, is to change the file association for *.vbs files from the native Cscript/Wscript engine to a benign application such as Notepad.

If you take this precaution, you can still use VBScript to code logon scripts. All you need to do is make the name of the script a parameter of the Cscript executable. Figure 12.20 shows what this would look like in the Edit Script window of the Group Policy Editor.

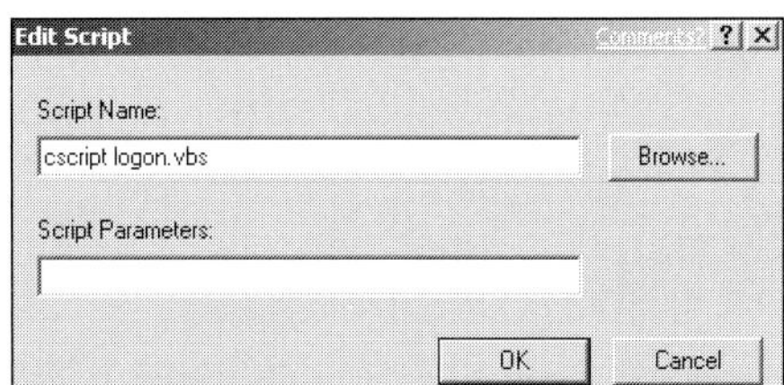

Figure 12.20 Edit Script window in the Group Policy Editor showing a VBScript as a parameter of Cscript.exe.

Deploying Scripts

Script policies rely on two constituents:

- A Script.ini file in the policy tells the client what scripts to run and where to find them.
- The scripts themselves. You should always store your scripts with the policy folder so that they will be replicated to all domain controllers. This prevents clients from going across the WAN to download their scripts.

To deploy a script, you must configure the Script.ini file using the Group Policy Editor. Do this by opening the Properties window for the script type you want to deploy. Figure 12.21 shows an example.

The `Show Files` option allows you to view the files in the `Scripts` folder. This is a quick and easy way to copy your scripts to the correct location in the policy folder. Otherwise, you have to drill down through `Sysvol` and guess at which of the GUID-named folders is the policy you want to update.

After you've placed the script file in the `Policies` folder, use the `Add` button to add the script to the Script.ini file.

Clients download the Script.ini file where the Gptext client-side extension processes it. The CSE then downloads scripts themselves, which run under a script engine based on their file association.

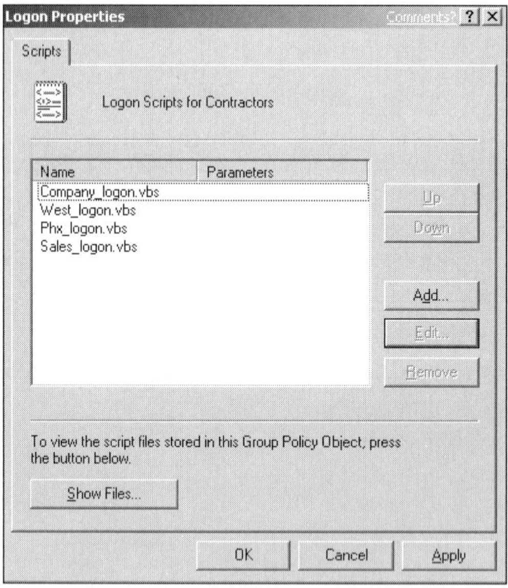

Figure 12.21 Logon Script Properties window showing selected scripts.

If a client downloads scripts from several GPOs, the scripts all run at the same time. For this reason, you should not put entries in one script that depend on actions taken by another.

Also, the users are presented with a desktop while their logon scripts run. This means you should not make shortcuts and other Explorer shell configurations that assume actions have been taken by logon scripts.

Many organizations like using tiered logon scripts. For instance, the top-level domain admins might issue a script that makes certain standard desktop settings such as mapping drives and running certain standard welcome applications. The OU administrators want to piggyback onto this main script but they cannot assume that the drive mappings are in place before their scripts run.

If you want to use tiered logon scripts, or if you want to block access to the desktop until all scripts have run, you can configure the system to run logon scripts synchronously rather than asynchronously. (See the earlier section in this chapter, "Synchronous Script Processing," for details.)

Moving Forward

At this point in our enterprise deployment of Windows Server 2003, we've gotten the system to where we can start accepting connections by users. Before we throw open the doors, though, we need to see how to configure data storage to make sure we provide a secure, reliable place for users to save their data.

13 Managing Active Directory Security

BIG PROJECTS LIKE OUR WINDOWS SERVER 2003 deployment generally go through several stages that more or less follow a musical theme. First comes the "Itsy-Bitsy Spider" stage where lots of good ideas rise up and get washed away. Then comes the Benny Goodman stage where everyone starts to get in the swing of things. We have now arrived at the Jerry Lee Lewis stage where there's a whole lot of shakin' going on.

During this stage, we need to come to terms with the security challenges in the Active Directory so that we can prepare for the final, Led Zeppelin stage where we climb our stairway to heaven and actually begin operating the network. (If we don't do things right, of course, we go to the Grateful Dead stage.)

The information in this chapter covers the following topics:

- Active Directory administration using permissions delegation.
- Using groups to manage Active Directory permissions, including step-by-step description of cross-domain group interactions.
- Secondary Logon Service (SLS) operation and how to use RunAs to avoid doing daily operations with your privileged administrator account.
- How to use WMI to automatically notify you if an Active Directory event occurs.

You may find some of the information in this chapter to be similar to that in Chapter 11, "Understanding Network Access Security and Kerberos." This is because the same security subsystem underlies many different structural components, such as Active Directory.

New Features in Windows Server 2003

Only a few Active Directory security features have changed in Windows Server 2003:

- **Permission sets.** Additional permission sets were added for delegating administration of Resultant Set of Policies (RSoP) and for managing InetOrgPerson object classes for interoperability with Novell Directory Services (NDS) and Netscape Directory Services (the other NDS).
- **Effective permission calculator.** The ACL Editor has a new Effective Permissions calculator that greatly simplifies management of overlapping inherited rights in Active Directory.
- **Smart card support.** The RunAs command now supports smart card authentication. The shell-based implementation of RunAs also includes special protection against misbehaving applications.

Overview of Active Directory Security

Just as a quick review of Chapter 11, "Understanding Network Access Security and Kerberos," let's go over the key elements of authentication and authorization in Window Server 2003:

- A security principal is a user, computer, or group that needs to access a resource either on a local computer or on a server.
- The primary means of authenticating a security principal is Kerberos. Legacy NTLMv2 (NT LanMan version 2) and LM (LanMan) authentication is available for supporting downlevel clients.
- Authenticated security principals receive a Privilege Access Certificate (PAC) that contains their security information. The PAC includes the principal's Security ID (SID) along with the SIDs for any groups that have the security principal as a member, the SIDs for groups having those groups as members, a list of system privileges assigned to the user, and a list of account restrictions assigned to the security principal.
- The Local Security Authority (LSA) uses the PAC to construct an access token that is attached to any processes initiated by the security principal.
- Key operating system objects are protected by a special data structure called a security descriptor. The security descriptor contains a Discretionary Access Control List (DACL) that defines who can access the object and what can be done with the object.
- When a process attempts to access a secured object, the Security Reference Monitor (SRM) compares the contents of the DACL with the contents of the access token and the type of access requested by the process and determines the effective permissions to assign to the process.

- Access permissions are evaluated in a canonical manner with `Deny` permissions evaluated prior to `Allow` permissions and explicit permissions evaluated prior to inherited permissions.

With all this in mind, let's see how Active Directory makes use of the security subsystem to assign administrative permissions and control access to objects.

Viewing Security Descriptor Contents

You can view the security descriptor for an Active Directory object by opening its Properties window from the associated Active Directory management console. For example, open the `AD Users and Groups` console and expand the tree to the `Users` container. Right-click on an object, select Properties from the flyout menu, and then select the `Security` tab. This opens the ACL Editor to view the security descriptor.

The initial view of the ACL Editor is a generic one showing the security principals that have been placed on the DACL. This list is in alphabetical order. A particular security principal might have several entries in the DACL. A cumulative permissions list is displayed in the lower part of the window when you highlight an entry. Figure 13.1 shows the ACL Editor generic view for a user object.

If additional permissions have been assigned, a listing called Special Permissions has a checkmark. This is your indication that you must use the Advanced view of the ACL Editor to see the full permissions for that security principal. Figure 13.2 shows the ACL Editor Advanced view for the same user object.

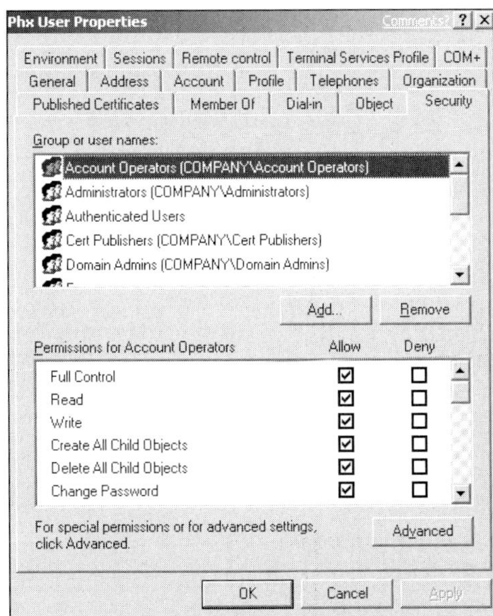

Figure 13.1 ACL Editor showing generic permissions for a user object.

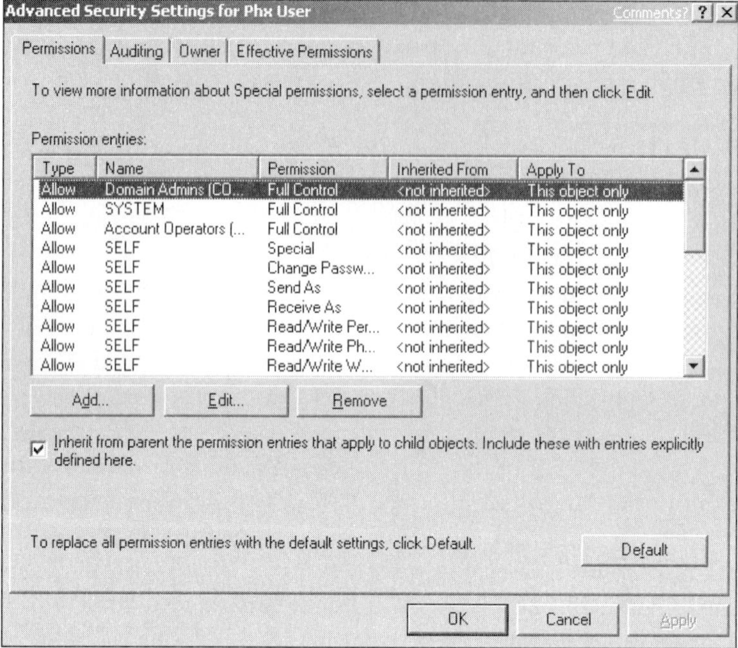

Figure 13.2 ACL Editor showing Advanced view listing specific permissions assigned to individual security principals.

The entries in the Advanced view are listed in the order that the SRM evaluates them when determining whether to permit access to a security object. Inherited permissions are identified to distinguish them from explicit permissions assigned directly to the security descriptor. The listing includes the identity of the source container for an inherited permission to aid in troubleshooting.

Effective Permissions Calculator

Windows Server 2003 has a new Effective Permissions calculator that displays the permissions a selected user would get when accessing an object. When you select the `Effective Permissions` tab and enter a name, the system performs a security evaluation and displays the result in a set of checkboxes. Figure 13.3 shows an example.

Types of Access Rights

In addition to the standard object permissions such as `Read`, `Write`, `Modify` permissions, and so forth, Windows Server 2003 has over 50 extended rights that can be assigned to Active Directory objects. Here are a few examples:

- **ChangePDC.** Gives permission to transfer the Flexible Single Master Operations (FSMO) role of the PDC Emulator.

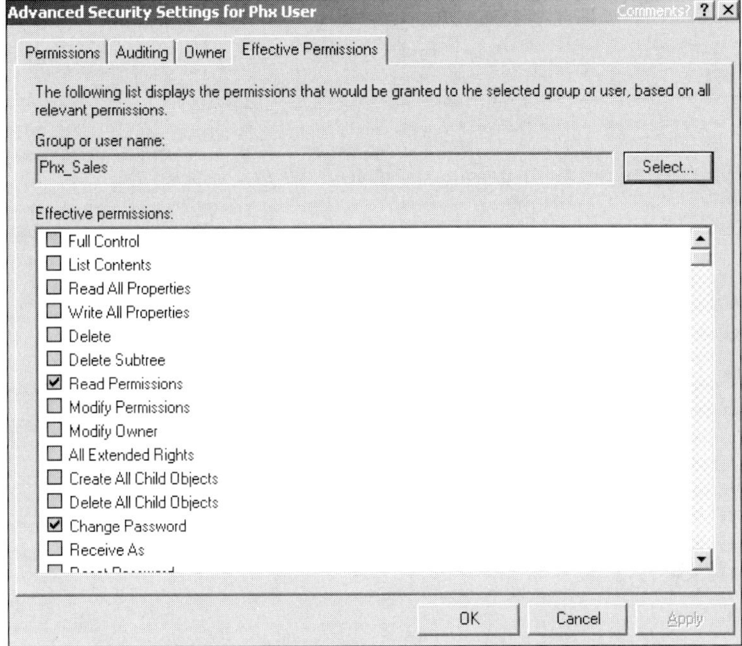

Figure 13.3 Effective Permissions calculator.

- **GenerateRSoPPlanning.** Gives permission to initiate a Resultant Set of Policies (Planning) calculation.
- **DomainPassword.** Gives permission to reset the password of a user object.

In addition to extended rights, you can assign permissions to individual properties of an object. For instance, let's say you have a developer who has coded an application for the Facilities department that updates certain attributes in Active Directory such as `TelephoneNumber` and `Location`. You can use property permissions to give Facilities personnel read/write access to the affected properties in User objects without letting them modify any other property in any other object type.

You can view the permissions assigned to individual properties in the Edit view of the ACL Editor. Figure 13.4 shows an example.

Access Control Inheritance

Inheritance determines whether the Access Control Entry (ACE) affects any child objects and what objects are affected. Normally, an ACE is inherited by all child objects in all subcontainers.

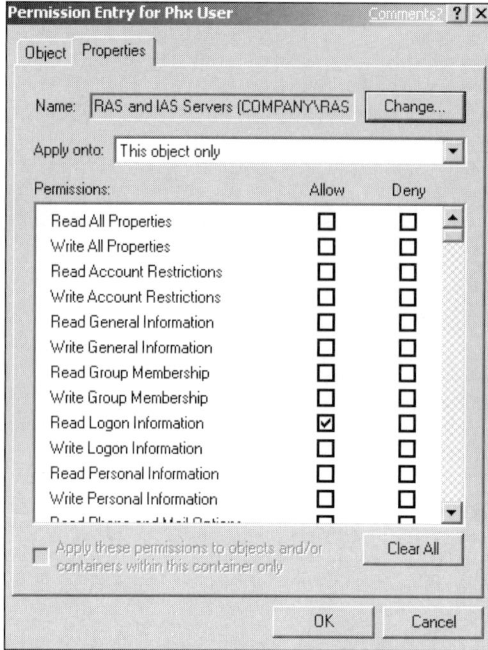

Figure 13.4 ACL Editor showing Edit view listing the individual properties permissions that can be assigned to a security principal.

The Edit view of the ACL Editor permits assigning special inheritance rules to an ACE. You have the option of controlling inheritance to an extremely granular level. For example, if you have a set of permissions that you only want inherited by Group objects in a specific container but not in any subcontainers, you can select an inheritance option that accomplishes that goal.

Needless to say, in normal day-to-day operations, you'll never drill down this deep into Active Directory permissions. But it is good to keep in mind that they are available to you if you need to resolve any sticky administrative problems.

Procedure 13.1 is an example that uses the Active Directory Users and Computers console to apply inheritable rights to a test Organizational Unit (OU).

Security Descriptors and Replication

Changing the DACL of an object high in the Active Directory tree causes updates to a lot of security descriptors thanks to inheritance. This does not initiate a storm of replication traffic, though. Only the object where you made the change is replicated. When the update arrives at a replication partner, the Active Directory database engine takes over to apply the change to the security descriptors of the child objects. This minimizes replication traffic caused by delegating security permissions.

Procedure 13.1 Applying Inheritable Rights to an Active Directory Container

1. Open the `AD Users and Computers` console.
2. From the menu, select VIEW | ADVANCED FEATURES. This exposes the `Security` tab for Active Directory objects.
3. Create a test OU to practice on. This prevents you from making an innocent mistake that mangles a production container. Create a couple of User objects under this OU. If this is a production server and your corporate policies prohibit creating user IDs, you can create contact objects. They act the same as User objects but they have no security rights.
4. Right-click the new OU and select PROPERTIES from the flyout menu.
5. Select the `Security` tab (see Figure 13.5). You'll see a list of access control entries.

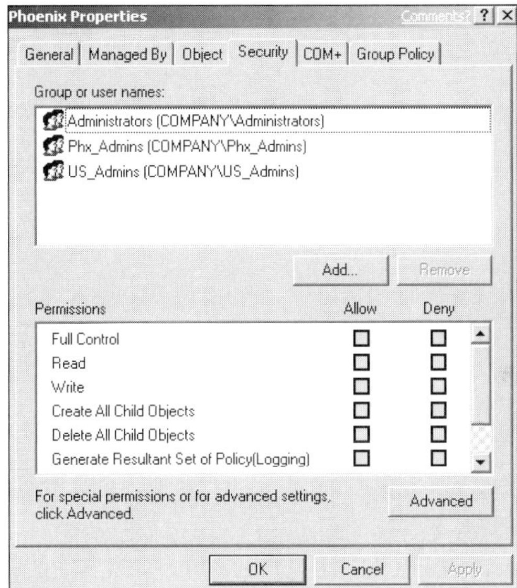

Figure 13.5 Properties page for an example OU showing the Security tab with access control entries.

6. Deselect `Allow Inheritable Permissions`. You'll be prompted to either copy the currently inherited ACE entries as permanent entries in the security descriptor or remove them.

7. Click `Remove`. The inherited entries disappear. In production, you should always use the `Copy Previously Inherited Permissions` option. This prevents you from accidentally removing a critical ACE. Having no ACE is the same as having a Deny ACE.
8. Click `Advanced`. The Access Control Settings window opens.

   Figure 13.6 shows a set of ACE settings for the example OU. Rights associated with Access Allowed ACE entries are cumulative, so a security principal with multiple ACEs gets each right assigned by the ACE after evaluating any Access Denied ACEs.

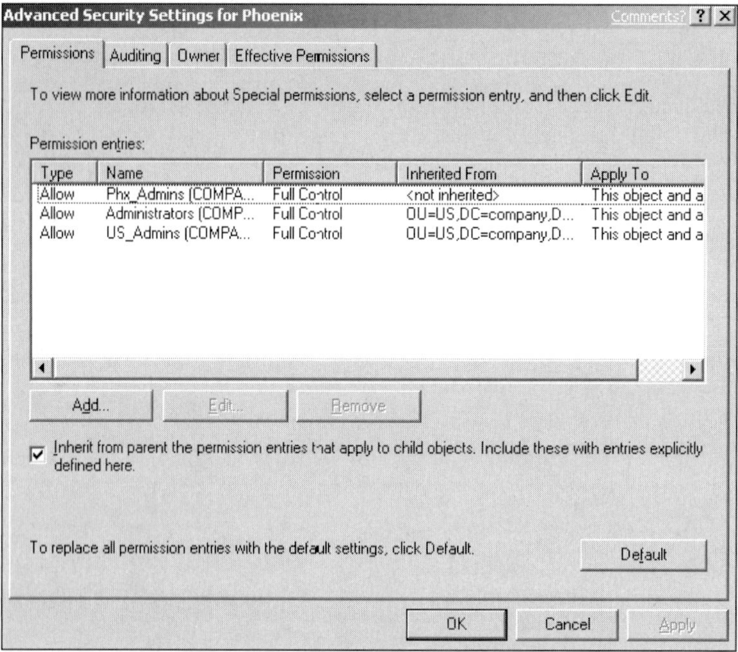

Figure 13.6 Access Control Settings window for OU showing the ACE type associated security principal, the type of permission, and the inheritance options.

9. Highlight one of the ACE listings and click `View/Edit`. The Permission Entry window opens. The `Apply Onto` drop-down box lists the inheritance options that can be associated with the ACE.
10. Close the windows you have open and return to the Active Directory Users and Groups console.

Access Rights Delegation

You can lose a good chunk of your youthful years trying to figure out exactly which set of granular permissions you need to apply to get a desired administrative result, not to mention all the inheritance options you'll have to consider when applying the new permissions.

Windows Server 2003 makes this process a lot simpler with a feature called *delegation*. This permits you to select from a menu of administrative options, then let the system decide which permissions to change.

There's a subtle difference between *inheritance* and *delegation*. Inheritance defines a mechanism for applying changes to child security descriptors based on the contents of a parent's security descriptor. Delegation involves selecting the access permissions that will be inherited. It's something like setting up a beach umbrella. The umbrella casts a shadow (delegation) and you sit in its shade (inheritance).

Delegation can have unexpected consequences. For example, in the novel *Catch 22*, Milo Minderbinder was able to use his delegated authority as a supply officer for a small Air Corps detachment to effectively take over the war effort in Italy. You could have a similar experience if you delegate administrative privileges indiscriminately.

Rather than trying to pick through the nearly 200 different properties associated with users, groups, and computers trying to figure out which ones to assign, and maybe getting some Milo Minderbinder-type consequences, it's much simpler to use the *Delegation of Control Wizard*. I'm not generally a fan of all the admin wizards in Windows Server 2003. For the most part, I think they complicate simple chores. But when it comes to assigning administrative rights in Active Directory, the Delegation of Control Wizard is my tool of choice. It consolidates the extensive range of object permissions, extended rights, and property permissions into a concise set of selection windows. You can also use the wizard to select granular permissions if you choose to use them.

Procedure 13.2 shows how the Delegation of Control Wizard works. The example uses an object in the AD Users and Groups console because this is where delegations are most commonly required, but you can delegate permissions on virtually any container in any console.

Procedure 13.2 Delegating Access Rights

1. In the AD Users and Groups console, right-click the test OU you created in the last procedure and select DELEGATE CONTROL from the flyout menu. The Delegation of Control Wizard starts.
2. Click `Next`. The Group or User Selection window opens.
3. Click `Add`. The Select Users, Computers, or Group window opens.

4. Enter the first few letters of the name of the security principal you want to add and then click `OK`. If more than one security principal meets the search criteria, select the desired name from the list.
5. Click `Next`. The Tasks to Delegate window opens (see Figure 13.7).

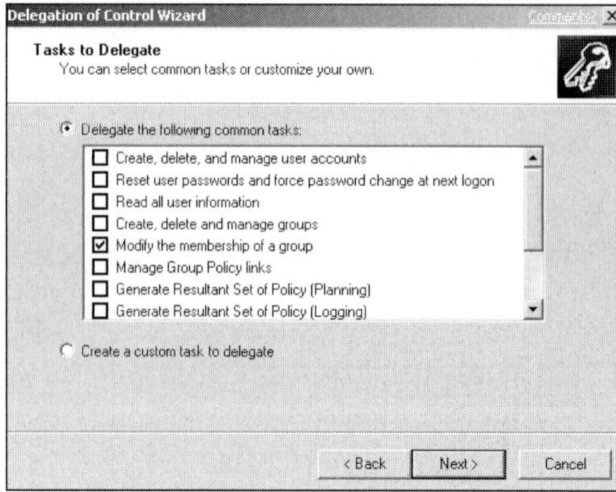

Figure 13.7 Delegation of Control Wizard—Tasks to Delegate window

6. You can select any or all of the options under `Predefined Tasks` or build a `Custom Task`. If you select a predefined task and click `Next`, you'll be presented with a summary window. Click `Finish` and the rights will be applied. Select `Custom Task` just to see what this option looks like.
7. Click `Next`. The Active Directory Object Type window opens (see Figure 13.8).

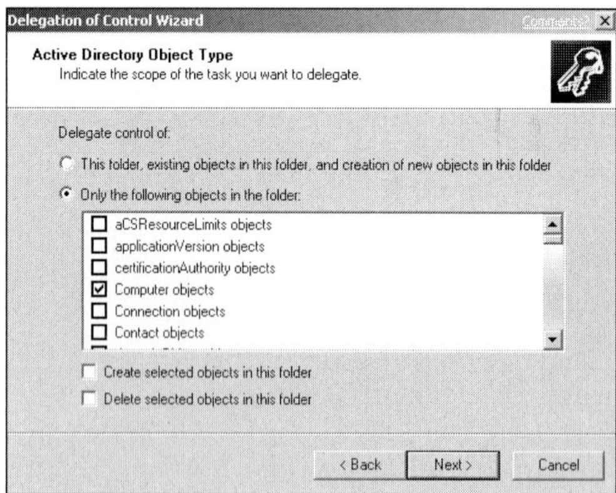

Figure 13.8 Delegation of Control Wizard—Active Directory Object Type window.

8. If you select `Entire Folder`, the rights you select in the next window will be assigned to all subordinate objects regardless of their type. If you select `Only the Following Objects in the Folder`, you can select one or more object types that will inherit the rights you assign.

   The `Create` and `Delete` checkbox options are handy if you want to give permission to add and remove instances of the selected object type.
9. Scroll down the list under `Object Types` and select `User Objects`.
10. Click `Next`. The Permissions window opens (see Figure 13.9). You can choose from the following:

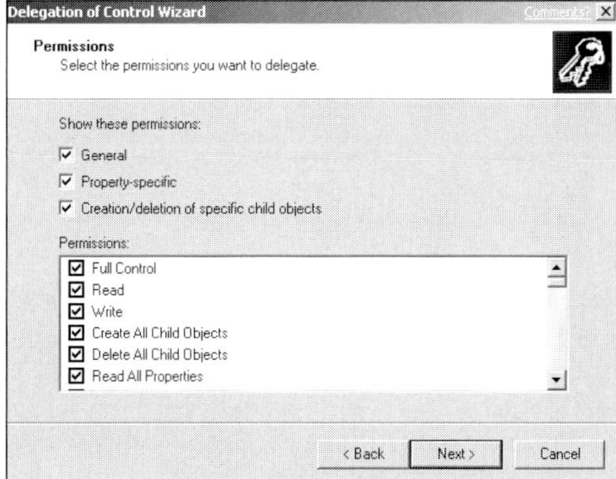

Figure 13.9 Delegation of Control Wizard—Permissions window.

- The `General` option includes standard object permissions along with any extended rights applicable to the object class.
- The `Property-Specific` option displays the properties associated with the object class with the option to permit or deny reading or writing to each property.
- The `Creation/Deletion of Specific Child Objects` option displays a list of object types so you can assign permission to add or remove instances of that class.

11. Select the permissions you want to grant and then click `Next`. The wizard displays a summary window. Click `Finish` to apply the changes. The update will be applied to every object of the type you selected.

Dssec.dat and Permission Displays

You'll notice if you edit individual properties on an object that the list of possible properties does not include all the possible properties of the object class.

This display list is controlled by a text file called Dssec.dat located in `\Windows\System32`. Here is a portion of the file for an example:

```
[user]
aCSPolicyName=7
adminCount=7
allowedAttributes=7
allowedAttributesEffective=7
allowedChildClasses=7
allowedChildClassesEffective=7
badPasswordTime=7
badPwdCount=7
bridgeheadServerListBL=7
c=7
canonicalName=7
cn=7
co=7
codePage=7
```

An entry of 7 means that the property will not be displayed. This prevents you from assigning permissions on properties that are controlled by the system.

If you want a particular property to be displayed, change the entry from `=7` to `=0`. You must log off and then log on to see the change.

Managing Access Lists with DSACLS

Up to now, I've used the AD Users and Computers console to manage permissions. If you prefer a command-line tool, the Support Tools includes a utility called DSACLS for managing Active Directory permissions.

The DSACLS syntax to view the contents of a security descriptor for an object called `cn=Average User` in the `Company.com` domain would be:

```
dscacls cn=average user,cn=users,dc=company,dc=com
```

Here is a sample DSACLS listing truncated for brevity to show a single ACE entry:

```
C:\>dsacls "cn=average user,cn=users,dc=company,dc=com"
Displaying ACTRL_ACCESS list: AccessList
        Entries: 1
                Flags: 1
                        cEntries: 3
                        Entry 0:
                                Trustee.Name: COMPANY\Domain Admins
                                fAccessFlags: 1
                                Access: 0x780001ff
                                ProvSpecificAccess: 0
                                Inheritance: 0x2
                                lpInheritProperty:
```

```
                        Entry 1:
                                Trustee.Name: NT AUTHORITY\SELF
                                fAccessFlags: 1
                                Access: 0x780001ff
                                ProvSpecificAccess: 0
                                Inheritance: 0x0
                                lpInheritProperty:
                        Entry 2:
                                Trustee.Name: NT AUTHORITY\SYSTEM
                                fAccessFlags: 1
                                Access: 0x780001ff
                                ProvSpecificAccess: 0
                                Inheritance: 0x0
                                lpInheritProperty:
DSACLS succeeded
```

The `Access` entry in each of the listings holds an eight-digit hex number called an *access mask*. Table 13.1 lists the standard access rights and their associated access mask. You may see these values in other command-line utilities and Event log entries.

Table 13.1 Directory Service Objects access mask types and mask numbers

Access Mask Type	Mask
Delete	08000000
Read Properties	00000010
Read Permissions	10000000
Modify Properties	00000020
Modify Permissions	20000000
Delete Subtree	00000040
Modify Owner	40000000
List Object	00000080
Generic Delete (inherited only)	80000000
Control Access	00000100
Create A Child Object	00000001
Delete A Child Object	00000002
List Contents	00000004
Add/Remove Self As Member	00000008

When you assign permissions to a security principal, the ACE mask contains the sum of the various permissions. If you assign access permissions to a particular property, the DSACLS listing includes the property name and its ACE mask. Here is an example:

```
Property: Change Password
        Flags: 1
                cEntries: 1
```

```
Entry 0:
        Trustee.Name: COMPANY\HelpDesk Admins
        fAccessFlags: 1
        Access: 0x100
        ProvSpecificAccess: 0
        Inheritance: 0x2
          lpInheritProperty:
```

In this instance, the HelpDesk Admins have been given Control Access rights (0x100) to the `Change Password` property for the object. This permits a member of that group to reset a user's password.

You can use DSACLS to modify rights as well as read them. For example, if you want to assign Full Control access rights to a group called Daily Operations for all objects in an OU called Sales and all subcontainers under Sales, you can do so with the following command:

```
dsacls ou=Sales,dc=Company,dc=com /s:co /g "Daily Operations":780001ff
```

For normal workday activities, DSACLS is probably too clumsy to use directly. But it can function as part of a script or batch file to simplify rights assignments or to pull quick scans of permissions for later analysis.

Using Groups to Manage Active Directory Objects

It is nearly always a good practice to aggregate users into groups based on common business functions or operational roles. Not only are groups easier to manage, but you also get a distinct performance improvement by using groups rather than individual users to control object security. It takes much longer to examine an access control list (ACL) with 3000 users on it than it does to check for a single SID that represents a group with 3000 members.

Properly creating and managing groups, then, is a critical task in Windows Server 2003. This section contains a description of each group type and guidelines of when to use each one. It also has step-by-step scenarios describing how the system uses group membership to evaluate Active Directory permissions. Understanding this process helps you architect your permissions and troubleshoot any problems.

Group Types

Here are the basic group types in Windows Server 2003:

- **Machine Local.** Defined in the Security Account Manager (SAM) of a non-domain controller. These group types exist for backward compatibility with NT and should not be used in Windows Server 2003.
- **Domain Local.** Defines a group that can have members from anywhere in the forest but can only be applied to ACLs in the local domain.
- **Global.** Defines a group that can have members only from the local domain but can be applied to ACLs anywhere in the forest.

- **Universal.** Defines a group that can have members from anywhere in the forest and can be applied to ACLs anywhere in the forest. This group type only exists in Native domains.
- **Builtin.** This is a special classification of Domain Local groups that exist for backward compatibility with NT. Local instances of these groups are contained in the SAM, similar to the way each system has a local Administrator and Guest account.

The purpose of having all these different group types is not to make system administrators turn to self-medication, although they sometimes have that effect. They exist for compatibility, flexibility, and to minimize replication traffic. Here is how they differ.

Builtin

In classic NT and in Windows Server 2003, certain groups have inherent system privileges. For example, the Backup Operators group has the necessary system permissions to transfer files to and from backup tape regardless of the file's ownership or access permissions. These groups exist in a key inside the SAM called Builtin. Figure 13.10 shows an example.

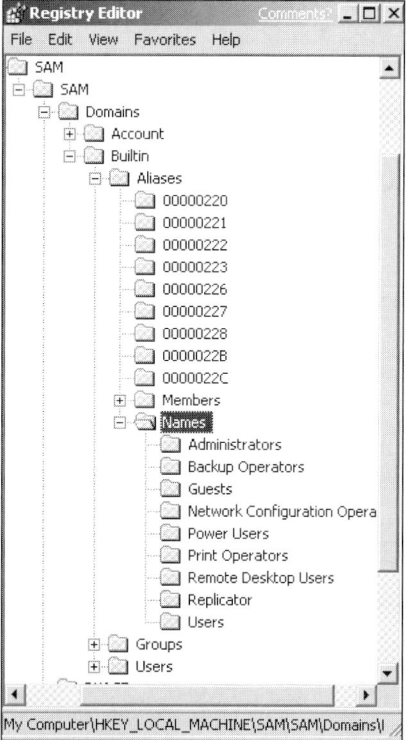

Figure 13.10 Regedit showing Builtin key inside the SAM hive.

Whenever you install Windows Server 2003 (or XP, for that matter), these groups are put in place. If you upgrade Windows Server 2003 to a domain controller, the existing SAM is deleted and a new SAM is put in its place that has the default Built-In groups.

Most of the system privileges granted to these groups are located in the Secedit database, but some are buried in the operating system deeper than the Batcave under Wayne Manor. You cannot delete or rename the Built-In groups. You should only assign administrators to these groups when they need highly privileged access to a local machine. The Built-In groups in Active Directory control access to domain controllers and Active Directory components.

Machine Local Groups (SAM-Based)

Distributed management of member servers and workstations in classic NT required a two-tier solution:

- The administrator responsible for the server was placed in the Builtin group called Server Operators at the local machine. This gave the administrator the ability to manage the contents of the local SAM without granting domain privileges.
- The designated server operator would then create machine local groups and place them on the ACL of local resources such as NTFS files and folders, Registry keys, and printers. The server operator would populate these machine local groups by plucking individual users and Global groups from the domain.

Using this server management method, each server ended up with a unique set of SAM entries that had to be backed up and preserved. If the operating system disk crashed and could not be recovered from tape, the data on the other disks survived but the ACLs were invalid.

Also, enforcing a uniform management policy on a diverse set of servers often taxed inter-collegiate affability. (Try explaining to highly independent and often cantankerous administrators that it is a bad thing to have eccentric sets of local groups. Go ahead. Try it.)

Windows Server 2003 attempts to resolve this problem by doing away with the need to have Machine Local groups. In Native, any of the three domain-based group types can be placed on the ACL of a local resource. Local server operators can be delegated permission to create groups in Active Directory. It is much easier to manage a central set of groups, and you don't need to worry as much about losing access rights on local data drives.

Domain Local Groups

Domain Local groups provide an ideal vehicle for delegating permissions in Active Directory because they can only be placed on the ACL of security objects in the local domain. This permits administrators in a domain to create the groups they need without worrying that the groups will be used inappropriately by administrators in another domain in the forest.

Domain Local groups can accept members from anywhere in the forest. This permits you to delegate permissions to administrators and users in other domains. For instance, you might have a central Help Desk that you want to give permission to reset passwords throughout your enterprise. Let's say you have five domains, one for each major continent. Here's what you do:

1. Create a Domain Local group in each domain. Call it Password Operators.
2. Delegate Password Reset permissions to the Password Operators group at the root of the domain.
3. Create a Universal group in the root domain called Help Desk Operators.
4. Nest the Help Desk Operators group from the root domain into the Password Operators group in the local domains.

Universal group membership replicates throughout the forest, so you need to evaluate the need for each Universal group. In this example, the makeup of the Help Desk Operators group would not change very often, so it is acceptable to place individual users in the group. In cases where group membership changes frequently, you should evaluate alternatives that do not involve putting individual users in the Universal group.

When you shift your forest to Functionality Level 2, individual Universal group members are replicated discretely. You do not need to be as concerned with Universal group placement, but you should still ask yourself whether the `AsiaPacific` domain controllers really need to have a replica of a group used exclusively by the `NorthAmerica` domain.

Global Groups

Global groups are intended to be repositories of user accounts or computer accounts in a domain. A Global group cannot have members from other domains, but it can be placed on ACLs in any domain in the forest. For Active Directory, the appeal of Global groups is their capability to limit outside membership. You can delegate permissions to a Global group with the assurance that another administrator cannot put an outside user in the group and thereby give the user inappropriate access.

You can nest Global groups into Domain Local groups, Universal groups, and other Global groups. You can use this capability to your advantage in many situations. For example, let's say your company has a group of internal auditors who belong to the same department but log on using accounts for domains on their continent. For instance, the Kyoto auditors log on to the `AsiaPacific` domain and so forth.

The auditors require `Audit` permissions on all Active Directory objects on every domain in the forest. Auditing is a highly privileged capability and you do not want unauthorized individuals to get it. You can create an Auditors Global group in each domain and delegate `Audit` permissions to this group.

However, the auditors tell you they want access to the Configuration and Schema naming contexts, as well. Because these naming contexts are assigned to the root domain in the forest, you can create a Domain Local group in the root domain called `Central Auditing`. Delegate `Audit` permission for the Configuration and Schema naming contexts to this group. Making it a Domain Local group assures you that it cannot be used on resources outside the root domain.

Then, nest the Auditors Global groups from each domain into the Central Auditing group. This gives the members permission to set auditing on the objects in the affected containers. Another advantage of using a Domain Local group is that administrators in the local domains cannot see the membership of the Central Auditing group.

Universal Groups

Universal groups can only be created after shifting a domain to Native. The appeal of Universal groups is their wide scope. Universal groups can accept members from any domain in the forest and they can be placed on the ACL of any Active Directory object in any domain in the forest.

You may wonder why you would ever use Global groups when Universal groups seem so much more flexible. The next section details the differences between Global and Universal groups and why two groups are necessary in a well-architected system.

Comparison of Global Groups and Universal Groups

To understand when to use Universal and when to use Global groups, we need to take a look at the way domain controllers use Kerberos to distribute group membership information to member servers and desktops.

Every group object in Active Directory has an attribute called `Member`. This attribute contains the distinguished name (DN) of each group member. User objects have an attribute called `MemberOf` that contains a back-link to the `Member` attribute in the associated group object. This back-link is used solely for referential integrity. It is not used to query for group membership. Group membership is determined by searching groups in Active Directory looking for the user's DN on the membership list.

For example, if user GWBush is a member of the Presidents group, the CmdrInChief group, the Republican group, and the Texans group, then the Local Security Authority (LSA) would assemble a Privilege Access Certificate (PAC) for him containing his SID and the SIDs of all four groups. In addition, LSA would scan Active Directory to determine if each of those four groups is a member of other groups. If so, those SIDs are included in the PAC. The user then gets local access based on the cumulative permissions assigned to each nested group.

Here is where the different types of groups come into play. Domain Local and Global group membership is stored in the local Domain naming context (NC) but not in the Global Catalog (GC). In contrast, Universal group membership *is* stored in the Global Catalog. This may seem like a small difference, but it has wide-ranging consequences. Here is a quick synopsis to use as a design guideline:

- Each domain controller hosts a replica of its own Domain naming context. This NC contains the membership for Domain Local groups and Global groups but not Universal groups.

  Therefore, an LDAP (Lightweight Directory Access Protocol) search for group membership directed at a standard domain controller returns only Domain Local and Global groups in the domain controller's own domain.

- A Global Catalog server hosts a full replica of its own Domain NC and a partial replica of every other Domain NC in the forest. The partial NC replicas contain the membership for Universal groups but not Domain Local groups and Global groups.

  Therefore, an LDAP search for group membership directed at a GC server returns Domain Local groups and Global groups in the GC's own domain plus Universal groups in the forest.

Any domain controller that is not itself a GC must query a GC before it can authorize access for a user. If a GC is not available, the LSA refuses to return a Kerberos ticket. Instead, it returns an Authentication Denied error with a code explaining that a Global Catalog server is not available. In Windows Server 2003, a standard DC can be configured cache copies of Universal group memberships. See Chapter 7, "Managing Active Directory Replication," for details.

Viewing Differences in Group Membership Lists

You can see the effect of the differences in membership storage by performing the following little experiment:

1. Create two different domains in the same forest in your lab. The domain controller in the first domain (the root domain of the forest) is a GC. The domain controller in the second domain is a standard DC.
2. Shift both domains to Native.
3. Create a Universal group in each domain.
4. Place the Administrator account from each domain in the Universal group of the opposite domain.
5. Open the `AD Users and Computers` console at the second domain controller while logged on as an administrator in the second domain.
6. Open the Properties window for the Administrator account and select the `Member Of` tab. Note that the membership in the Universal group in the root domain is not listed. This is because the domain controller is not a GC and therefore has no replica of the other domain's naming context containing the `Member` attribute of the Universal group. Without this information, it cannot calculate the `MemberOf` back-link.
7. Open the `AD Users and Computers` console at the first domain controller while logged on as an administrator in the root domain.
8. Open the Properties window for the Administrator account and select the `Member Of` tab. Note that the membership in the Universal group of the second domain is listed. This is because the domain controller is also a GC so it can resolve the Universal group membership in the opposite domain and create the back-link.

Keep this difference in group membership storage in mind as you go through the following three scenarios that show how group membership affects user access permissions in Active Directory. Here are the three scenarios:

- Protecting an Active Directory object using a Global group
- Protecting an Active Directory object using a Domain Local group
- Protecting an Active Directory object using a Universal group

Protecting an Active Directory Object Using a Global Group

In the diagram in Figure 13.11, an admin contractor by the name of Eager Temp has an account in the Phoenix OU under the `Company.com` domain. The contractor is a member of a Global group called `PhxContractors`.

Because of prior incidents involving admin contractors, the `PhxContractors` group has been placed on the ACL of the Phoenix OU with `Deny Create Child Object` permissions.

Eager Temp opens AD Users and Computers, right-clicks the `Phoenix OU`, and selects New | User from the flyout menu. The system responds with an `Access Denied` message. The steps in this section explain why this happened.

To summarize, a user in a domain attempts to create an object in an OU in the same domain. The user belongs to a Global group that has been denied permission to create new objects under that OU. Procedure 13.3 shows the sequence of events that block the user when he attempts to create the object.

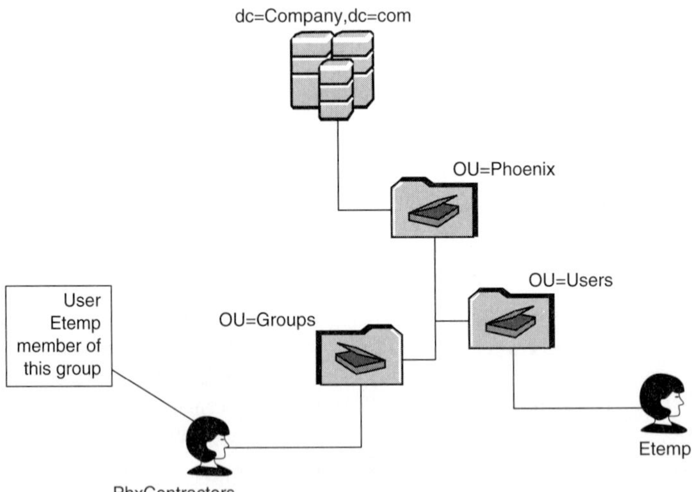

Figure 13.11 Active Directory diagram showing groups and managed objects.

Procedure 13.3 Functional Description of User and Group Validation Within a Single Domain

1. When Eager Temp logs on to the domain, the LSA on the domain controller handling the logon request first authenticates him and then starts compiling a PAC. To do so, it queries Active Directory to get Eager's SID. (In all these discussions, keep your eye on the PAC. It's like the little girl in the red dress in *Schindler's List*. You know it's important, you just don't know why yet.)
2. LSA then queries Active Directory for any groups that have Eager's distinguished name in their `Member` attribute. LSA finds one group, `PhxContractors`. It does a quick AD lookup to get the group's SID.
3. LSA then checks for membership in any Universal groups. It scans both for Eager and for the `PhxContractors` group. It performs this scan by submitting an LDAP search to a Global Catalog server. If the GC query returns a Universal group membership, the LSA obtains the SID for the group and queries for any groups that contain that Universal group as a member.
4. In this instance, user Eager Temp does not belong to any Universal groups so LSA finishes building the PAC by adding any privileges assigned to Eager along with applicable account restrictions.
5. LSA gives the PAC to the Key Distribution Center (KDC) service, which includes it in the `Authorization Data` field of the Kerberos Ticket-Granting Ticket (TGT) it issues to Eager. See Chapter 11, "Understanding Network Access Security and Kerberos," for information about Kerberos tickets and Ticket-Granting Tickets.
6. The network client at Eager's machine caches the TGT and then turns right around and uses it to get a session ticket to the domain controller. It needs this ticket to submit LDAP searches to Active Directory. The resulting ticket has a copy of the PAC from the original TGT.
7. When Eager Temp attempts to create a new user in the Phoenix OU, the AD Users and Computers console sends an `Create Object` command to the domain controller over a secure Remote Procedure Call (RPC) connection. This transaction contains the LDAP Kerberos ticket with its PAC payload.
8. When the domain controller gets the `Create Object` command and the accompanying Kerberos ticket, it extracts the PAC from the ticket and uses it to build a local access token for Eager. The LSA at the domain controller attaches this token to a thread representing the user.
9. The user's thread attempts to access Active Directory to create the User object under the Phoenix OU. The Security Reference Monitor compares the access token attached to the thread to the DACL in the security descriptor of the Phoenix OU. It

discovers that the SID for user Eager Temp matches the SID associated with a Deny Create Child Object ACE. It prevents the requested action from occurring.

10. This sets a complex series of actions in motion that eventually terminate with an `Access Denied` message being displayed in the AD Users and Computers console at Eager Temp's workstation.

In short, the ability of a user to access objects in Active Directory depends on the PAC in the Kerberos TGT issued when the user first authenticates in the domain. The PAC contains group SIDs based on a scan of the local Domain naming context and of the Global Catalog.

Now let's expand the scope a bit and see what happens when an administrator accesses an Active Directory object in another domain. This demonstrates how the LSA and KDC in the two domains exchange group information.

Protecting an Active Directory Object Using a Domain Local Group

Figure 13.12 shows two domains, `Company.com` and `Subsidiary.com`, that share a Tree Root trust. This means they also share a common Configuration and Schema naming context. (This contrasts to a Forest trust, where two domains have a transitive Kerberos relationship but separate Configuration and Schema naming contexts.)

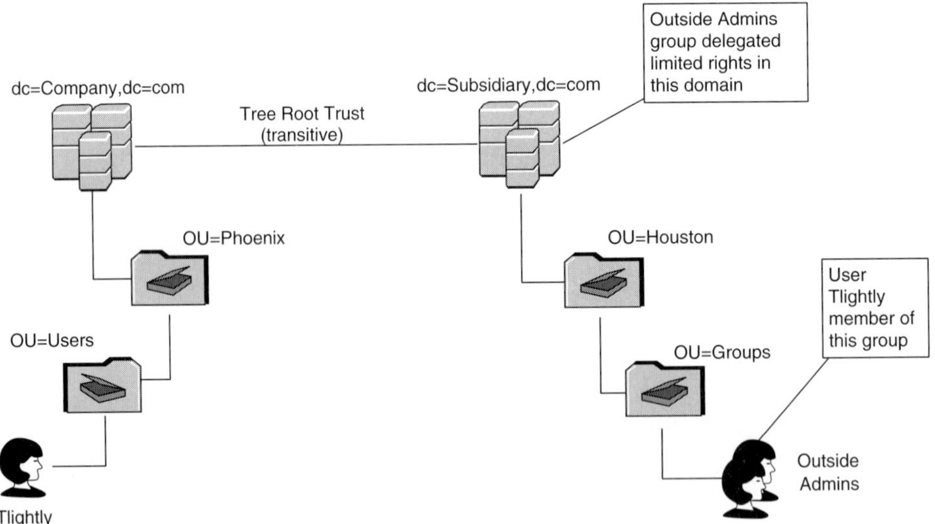

Figure 13.12 Two-domain forest with an administrator in one domain belonging to a group in the other domain.

In this scenario, management in both companies wants the IT staff to start sharing work. To this end, an administrator in the `Subsidiary` domain creates a Domain Local group called `Outside Admins` and delegates it a set of permissions at the root of the Subsidiary domain for creating and modifying objects.

The Subsidiary administrator places a Company administrator named Ted Lightly in the `Outside Admins` group. (The Subsidiary admin could not have done this with a Global group because Global groups cannot accept members from outside their domain.)

Ted tests out her new permissions by attempting to create a user object in Subsidiary. This attempt succeeds. The steps in this section describe why.

To summarize, a user from a trusted domain is placed in a group in another domain. The group has limited administrative permissions in the local domain. The user is able to exercise the permissions delegated to the group. Procedure 13.4 shows the sequence of events that occurs for this to happen.

Procedure 13.4 Functional Description of User and Group Validation Across Domains Using Domain Local Groups

1. When Ted logs on to the `Company` domain, the LSA on her logon server builds a PAC. It first scans its copy of the Company Domain naming context. It then scans the Global Catalog. Neither scan would find Ted's membership in the `Outside Admins` group in the `Subsidiary` domain. (The GC only holds Universal group membership.)
2. Ted opens AD Users and Computers and shifts the focus to the `Subsidiary` domain to create a user. The network client on her machine must obtain a ticket to the DC in Subsidiary. It attempts to get one from its logon server in the `Company` domain.
3. The Company DC cannot fulfill the ticket request because it does not have access to the Subsidiary naming context. It accommodates the user by obtaining a TGT to the `Subsidiary` domain on behalf of the user and returning it to the client.
4. When the Subsidiary DC gets the TGT request, it assembles a PAC for Ted by scanning its Domain naming context and the Global Catalog looking for group memberships. It finds Ted's membership in the `Outside Admins` Domain Local group. It adds the SID for this group to the original PAC along with any privileges and account restrictions applicable to Ted from the `Subsidiary` domain.
5. The KDC service on the Subsidiary DC adds the amended PAC to Ted's TGT and delivers it to the Company DC that requested it. The Company DC forwards the TGT to the Kerberos client at Ted's machine.
6. The client submits the Subsidiary TGT to the Subsidiary DC requesting an LDAP session ticket. The LSA on the Subsidiary DC extracts the PAC from the TGT and puts it in the ticket.

7. When Ted attempts to create the new user object, the AD Users and Computers console submits the Kerberos ticket along with the `Create Object` command. The Subsidiary DC extracts the PAC from the ticket and uses it to build an access token for Ted.
8. The PAC contains the SID of the `Outside Admins` group, which has been delegated permission to create child objects in the `Subsidiary` domain, so the Security Reference Monitor gives Ted the green light to create the new user account.

In short, users from one domain in a forest that are members of Domain Local groups in another domain obtain the access permissions delegated to the group because the PAC is amended as part of the cross-domain authentication.

It isn't necessary to go through any of these Kerberos machinations for Global groups because users from one domain cannot be added to Global groups in another domain. Also, Domain Local groups cannot be nested into Global groups because users from trusting domains might be members of the Domain Local group.

So, the stage is set to look at the complex scenario where a user who is a member of a Global group in one domain, a group that is nested into a Universal group in another domain, tries to access an Active Directory object protected by that Universal group. Ready? Here goes.

Protecting an Active Directory Object Using a Universal Groups

In the example shown in Figure 13.13, an administrator in the `Company` domain took advantage of several group management features to configure permissions on an OU in the `Subsidiary` domain. She performed the following evolutions:

- **Created Global groups in both domains to use for intra-domain administration.** The Company administrator can create groups in the `Subsidiary` domain if she belongs to the Enterprise Admins group (or a group nested in the Enterprise Admins group).
- **Created a Universal group in the `Subsidiary` domain.** Universal groups can be created in any domain that is running in Native.
- **Delegated `Create Child Objects` permission on the OU to the Universal group.** Universal groups can be used as security principals on any object anywhere in the forest.
- **Nested the Global groups from both domains into the Universal group in Subsidiary.** A domain running in Native has extensive capabilities to nest groups.

The example in Procedure 13.5 traces the sequence of events that validates an admin from the `Company` domain who tries to access the Subsidiary OU. The admin belongs to the Global group in Company that is nested in the Universal group in Subsidiary.

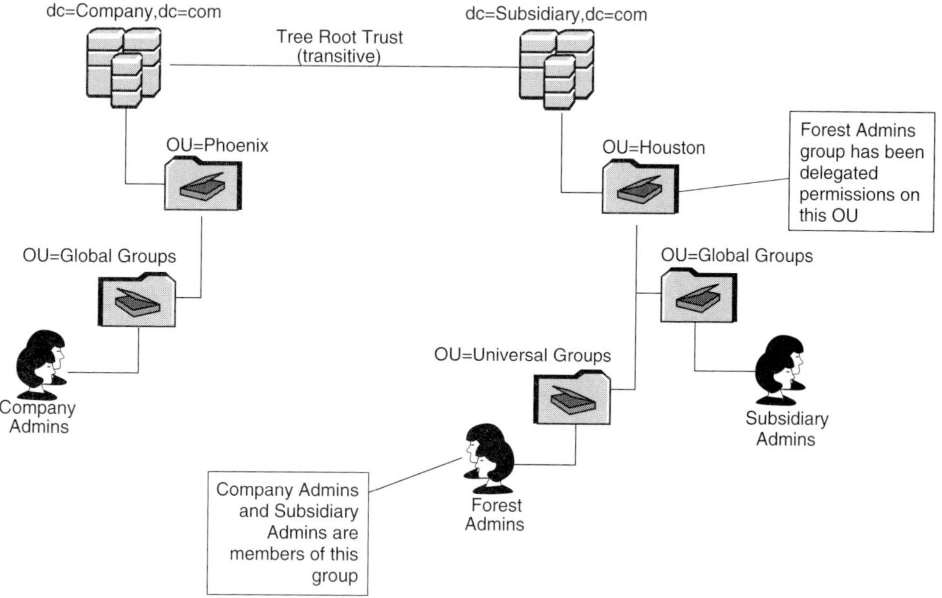

Figure 13.13 Diagram showing an OU in one domain being accessed by an administrator from another domain who belongs to a Universal group on the OU's ACL.

Procedure 13.5 Functional Description of User and Group Validation Across Domains Using Universal Group

1. When the admin logs on to the `Company` domain, the LSA on the `Company` domain controller scans for group membership in the local Domain naming context and the Global Catalog. It finds the Global group membership in the local Domain naming context. It discovers that the Global group is a member of the Universal group during the GC scan.
2. LSA bundles the SIDs for these groups into the PAC that it sends to the KDC service. The KDC puts the PAC into the TGT it sends to the client.
3. When the admin opens AD Users and Computers and sets the focus to the `Subsidiary` domain, the network client requests a ticket to the `Subsidiary` domain controller from its logon server in Company.
4. The Company DC cannot fulfill the ticket request so it obtains a TGT from Subsidiary on behalf of the user.
5. The LSA on the Subsidiary DC generates a PAC for the admin by scanning its own Domain Naming Context (NC) and the contents of the Global Catalog (GC). It does not find the Global group membership in either of these locations; therefore it does not discover the Universal group that is a member of the Global group. This doesn't

matter, though, because it retains the SIDs in the original PAC. It adds any local privileges and account restrictions and gives the PAC result to the KDC service.

6. The KDC returns the TGT to the client and the client uses it to get an LDAP session ticket to the `Subsidiary` domain controller. The LSA on the Subsidiary DC builds a local access token using the contents of the PAC. The Security Reference Monitor finds a match for the Universal group SID in the access token and the ACE on the DACL for the OU and grants access.

In short, if a user is a member of a Universal group in any domain, or a member of a group that is nested in a Universal group in any domain, the user gets the permissions assigned to that Universal group in any domain in the forest.

Summary of Group Functions

Windows Server 2003 can play Three Card Monte with Domain Local, Global, and Universal groups in ways that make W.C. Fields look like a Baptist preacher. Let's draw together the previous examples into a few general design principles:

- Protect AD objects accessed exclusively by users within a domain with Domain Local or Global groups from that domain.
- Protect AD objects accessed by users from other domains with Universal groups or with Domain Local groups that have Universal groups as members.
- Ensure that users have access to a Global Catalog server when logging on. This permits their Universal group membership to be fully evaluated. If a GC server is not available in a site, configure the standard domain controllers in the site as Universal group caching servers.
- Minimize group membership changes for Universal groups to limit forest-wide replication. This is less of a concern if you have shifted the forest to Functionality Level 2 to get discrete replication of group members.
- Don't expect to see cross-domain group membership in user properties. Expect different results when querying a GC compared to a DC.

If Thoreau were a systems administrator, he would urge us to simplify, simplify. It may seem that "simple information systems management" is an oxymoron, and you're probably right, but we can at least strive for elegance and economy. (We can also take lessons from Thoreau on burying the real costs of projects in budget reports.) Try to manage the Active Directory with as few groups as possible. Avoid using the Enterprise Admins group because its permissions are too wide sweeping. Create local OU admin groups and delegate only those permissions that the administrators require.

One final note: When adding users or groups from one domain into a group in another domain, the system maintains referential integrity by creating a *phantom object* in the local Domain naming context. This phantom object contains just a few attributes (SID, GUID, DN) from the outside security principal. Phantom objects appear in the AD Users and Computers console as entries in the Foreign Security Principals container.

If you change the distinguished name of the security principal (this happens if you move the object as well as rename it), the system must change the phantom object in the other domain to reflect the new distinguished name. Until this happens, the Member window for the group continues to show the old name. The icon is changed to one that has "gray hair" to indicate that the name is no longer valid.

Changing the contents of phantom objects is the job of the Infrastructure Master. Under Windows 2000, the Infrastructure Master did his chores very infrequently, so name changes often took several hours. Under Windows Server 2003, you can expect the new name to appear very quickly, depending on the replication intervals you have between sites.

I'll grant you that this is a small improvement in the wide scope of system operations, but it does eliminate a nagging problem.

Service Accounts

When a background service starts, it needs to run in the security context of an account. In classic NT, services typically run under the LocalSystem account. This causes security problems because processes running as LocalSystem have virtually unlimited privileges.

In Windows Server 2003, Microsoft tried to correct this vulnerability by including two new service accounts:

- **LocalService.** This account provides a security context for several services that access local system resources.
- **NetworkService.** This account provides a security context for several services that access network resources.

These two accounts have their own profiles under Documents and Settings so they can obtain public key certificates. This enables them to digitally sign files and network communications.

If you look at the service list in the Services.msc console, you'll notice that LocalSystem still owns the lion's share of the services. LocalService owns a few processes such as Alerter, Remote Registry, and the Web Client. NetworkService owns DNS client, RPC Locator, License Logging, and a few others. Look for an expansion of their roles in the future; but for now, don't expect the local service accounts to prevent too many attacks.

Using the Secondary Logon Service and RunAs

The examples throughout this chapter show local administrators going about their daily work while logged on using their Administrative accounts. This is generally not a good practice. Quite a few bad things can happen when logged on with full admin permissions. Viruses can get activated and make sweeping changes. Innocent mistakes can cause serious damage. Leaving your workstation open gives access to nefarious users. The list goes on and on.

Windows Server 2003 comes with a *Secondary Logon Service* (SLS) that makes it possible to log on as a standard user and then launch applications with alternative credentials to perform administrative tasks. This is philosophically similar to the `su` (superuser) command in UNIX, but is implemented somewhat differently.

The Secondary Logon Service is installed by default and starts at boot time. The service is hosted by Services.exe. The code is contained in Seclogon.dll.

RunAs Syntax

One of the easiest ways to use SLS is to open a command console window and launch an application using the RunAs command. Here is the syntax:

```
runas /u:administrator@company.com executable_name
runas /u:company\administrator executable_name
```

You can open a console in another security context by entering **`cmd`** as the executable name. You are prompted for a password and a second console window opens with a title bar that shows the alternate name you used. Applications launched from this console retain the alternate security context. For example, you can launch AD Users and Computers by typing **`dsa.msc`**. The console opens with your admin credentials so you can perform privileged operations.

If you prefer using the Explorer shell, you can specify alternate credentials by holding down the Shift key then right-clicking the icon for an executable or its shortcut. This adds a RunAs option to the flyout menu. Selecting this option opens a RunAs window where you can enter the alternate credentials. Figure 13.14 shows an example.

RunAs and Profiles

By default, RunAs opens an application with the profile of the user specified by the `/u:` switch. This differs from Windows 2000, which uses the Default User profile unless told otherwise. Opening the user's own profile ensures that applications making calls to standard shell elements such as My Documents open the user's elements, not the Default User elements.

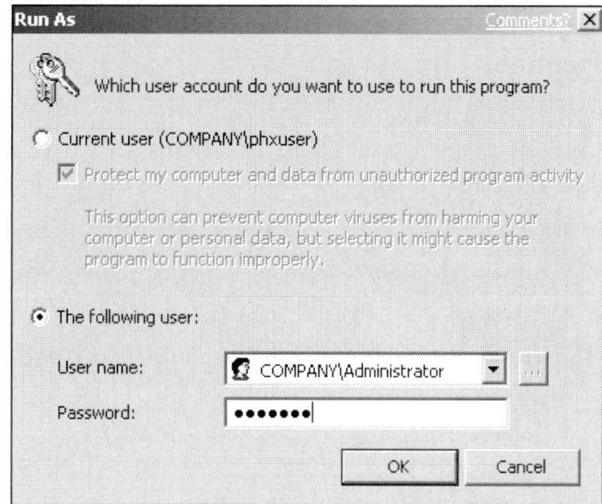

Figure 13.14 RunAs window when launching from the Explorer shell.

There is a `/noprofile` switch that loads the Default User profile rather than the user's profile. This speeds up an application launch if the designated user has no local profile on the machine, but can cause unexpected behavior if an application calls standard shell elements. Watch where you put your documents if you use the `/noprofile` switch.

RunAs Switches

The RunAs command has several other useful switches:

- **`/env.`** Uses the current environment variables rather than the variables for the alternate user. This helps troubleshooting application troubles at a local user's desktop.
- **`/savecred.`** Opens the window with the specified user's saved credentials, if any. This option helps when you are on a laptop that is not connected to the network and you need to launch a console using an Admin account with locally cached credentials.
- **`/smartcard.`** Uses smart card authentication instead of standard Kerberos or NTLMv2. This is a new feature in Windows Server 2003 that greatly simplifies network administration in organizations that use smart cards for logon authentication.
- **`/netonly.`** Uses the same credentials as those used to log on to the desktop. This helps avoid problems when running applications across the network using different credentials than those used to create the connection.

If you initiate a network connection from the console, you can access the connection through the console but not through the shell. For example, you can map a drive to an admin share at another server while you are at elevated permissions by entering `net use * \\server_name.company.com\c$`. The connection succeeds because you have sufficient credentials. If you go to a My Computer window and look at the drive you just mapped, however, it shows an `X` and denies access if you try to use it because the shell is still running with your logon permissions.

Use caution when launching interfaces that tie directly to the Explorer shell from a command console using RunAs. For example, if I'm working at a console prompt and I want to get a graphical view of the folder contents, I enter `start.` (`start` followed by a dot) on the command line. This opens the My Computer view of the current folder in Explorer. If I do this from RunAs, the window opens but the underlying security context is the same as my logon account.

If you want to run the shell at elevated permissions, too, you can shut down Explorer and then restart it using RunAs from the Task Manager. To do this, follow Procedure 13.6.

Procedure 13.6 Starting Explorer Shell Using RunAs

1. Open Task Manager by pressing `Ctrl+Alt+Del` and then clicking `Task Manager`.
2. Select the `Processes` tab.
3. Highlight `Explorer` and click `End Process`. Confirm when prompted.
4. When Explorer shuts down, select File, Run from the Task Manager menu and start Explorer as follows:

```
runas /u:administrator@company.com explorer.exe
```

After Explorer opens, some components such as the status bar and System Tray continue to run in the original logon context and are therefore unavailable to Explorer.

Using WMI for Active Directory Event Notification

Many Active Directory features signal problems by writing to the Event log. It can be handy to have the domain controller notify you when this happens rather than checking the logs all the time. This notification can be built fairly simply using Windows Management Instrumentation (WMI).

WMI permeates Windows Server 2003. You can discover virtually any fact about a computer, from the status of its network connections to the amount of free space on the drives to the temperature of the CPU, just by querying WMI.

WMI Reference

A full-blown explanation of WMI falls outside the scope of this book. For a great reference, see Windows Management Instrumentation (WMI) by Matthew Lavy and Ashley Meggitt.

WMI has an event handler that can initiate a trigger if a monitored element performs a selected operation or exceeds a threshold. You can query this event handler using a script. The code in the script "listens" for a designated event within the WMI event handler. Such a script is called an *event consumer*. By creating a custom event consumer, you can configure a server to notify you if an event occurs. This permits you to proactively monitor for problems.

Here is example code that establishes an event consumer for the Event log. The script uses MAPI to send a message if an entry is made to the Event log. (The `Set Events` statement in the script should be all on one line.) Here is the event consumer code:

```
Set Events = GetObject("WinMgmts:{(Security)}").ExecNotificationQuery("select *
from __InstanceCreationEvent where TargetInstance ISA 'Win32_NTLogEvent'")

Do
     Set NTEvent = Events.nextevent
     Notify(NTEvent.TargetInstance.Message)
Loop

Function Notify(Subject)
       Set objSession = CreateObject("mapi.session")
       objSession.Logon ("Microsoft Outlook Internet Settings")
       Set objMessage = objSession.Outbox.Messages.Add
       Set objRecipient = objMessage.Recipients.Add
       objMessage.subject = "An event has occured"
       objMessage.Text = Subject
       objRecipient.Name = "administrator@company.com"
       objRecipient.Type = 1
       objRecipient.Resolve
       objMessage.Send
       Wscript.Echo "Message sent successfully!"
       objSession.Logoff
End Function
```

Here are some items of interest in the script:

- The `WinMgmts:` entry calls the WMI interface, a COM provider.
- The `(Security)` entry enables the script to see changes in the Security log. (WMI demands that you announce that you'll use privileged operations, even if you are credentialed to do so already.) You can only view the Security log if you have administrator credentials, so you would need to initiate the script using RunAs if you are logged on with standard privileges.
- The `ExecNotificationQuery` entry submits the WMI Query Language (WQL) request to the WMI event handler. The event handler responds by creating a session for the consumer.
- The `.NextEvent` method tells the event handler to trigger if an event occurs.
- The `Notify` subroutine uses standard MAPI commands to formulate an email message.

This is just a simple example of the kind of things you can do with WMI to simplify your administrative chores. Experiment in your own environment to find ways to save time. You might even get to the point where you have a free weekend here and there.

Moving Forward

This completes the discussion of Active Directory, at least in a direct sense. Just about every feature in Windows Server 2003 ties to Active Directory in one form or another, so expect to see more about objects and LDAP and replication as we proceed to other topics.

In the saga of our enterprise Windows Server 2003 deployment, we are now ready to start configuring infrastructure items such as file systems, networks, and so forth. The next chapter kicks off the infrastructure topics with a discussion of data storage.

14 Configuring Data Storage

AT ITS MOST FUNDAMENTAL LEVEL, OUR JOB as system administrators is to serve up data, and to do so in just about any form our users demand. We are the Starbucks of the information age.

IBM recently celebrated the 25th anniversary of the IBM PC. The original PC model was capable of storing 128K of data on a 5-1/4 floppy and it could boot to a cassette tape. IBM then released the XT, which sported a massive 5MB hard disk drive that was as loud as a washing machine and cost about as much as an automobile.

Drive capacity has soared over the intervening years, and prices have plummeted. The server where I save my files has an array of 80GB drives that cost just over $200 apiece. Am I satisfied? No. The need for storage just grows and grows and grows.

Every time a professional takes on a new client, an engineering firm designs a new factory, a doctor scans a digital x-ray of a new patient, or an ad agency creates another multimedia presentation, another dollop of information goes into that huge maw that we call data storage.

A lot of data gets added. Not much goes away. Users treat the Delete key as if it were coated with contact explosive. They save and save and save until administrators simply refuse to store any more useless data and choke off the pipeline with quotas or by simply not buying more drives. Companies like EMC and Compaq and IBM vie in mythic battles to control just a portion of this huge market.

From a product perspective, data storage alternatives fall into these general categories (each embracing thousands of different offerings):

- **Fixed spinning storage.** This includes hard drives of any form on a bus that does not support simple removal such as IDE, ATA, and SCSI.

- **Detachable storage.** This includes hard drives on flexible buses such as Firewire, USB, and PCMCIA. It also includes solid-state storage.
- **Removable storage.** This includes drives with disks that can be removed from the unit such as CD-ROM, CD-RW, DVD-ROM, DVD-RAM, Zip, JAZ, Orb, and MO along with floppies, superfloppies, ultrafloppies, and pretty-darned-near-a-hard-drive-but-still-classified-as-a-floppy floppies.
- **Tape storage.** This includes just about any imaginable device where an engineer could figure a way to rub oxide-coated plastic against a magnetic head.

This chapter details the management of spinning storage with a focus on the operation of the *Logical Disk Manager*, or LDM. Microsoft licensed this technology from Veritas Software. LDM keeps track of the installed drives, their partitioning, and the required I/O methods. It also handles fault tolerance and data recovery.

Detachable and removable storage is managed by the *Removable Storage Management* service, or RSM. This service also handles tape storage units. For the most part, RSM has very little to do when managing spinning storage. It will get involved with CD jukeboxes and the like, but for day-to-day operation of removable spinning storage, you do not interface with RSM.

The topics covered in this chapter include:

- Functional description of LDM
- Disk changes made by LDM
- Upgrading from NT4 or Windows 2000
- Performing initial disk configurations
- Creating partitions and volumes
- Recovering failed fault tolerant disks

In addition, the 64-bit version of Windows Server 2003 and XP support a new disk management method on the Itanium platform called *GUID Partition Tables*, or GPTs. Chapter 2, "Performing Upgrades and Automated Installations," shows how to use the *Extensible Firmware Interface* (EFI) to set up storage on an Itanium machine. A section of this chapter is devoted to describing how to configure GPT-based storage after it has been initialized.

If you need more information about the hardware that underlies the storage subsystem, take a look at the Storage Review web site, `www.storagereview.com`. This site contains top-notch information about drives and storage alternatives along with excellent, independent technical reviews.

You may also want to pay a visit to `www.storage.ibm.com/hdd/support/download.htm` and download IBM's Drive Fitness Test utility. This is a quick way to test a wide range of features in your drives.

New Features in Windows Server 2003

The most significant difference between storage alternatives in Windows Server 2003 compared to its predecessors is the support for Itanium machines with their GUID-based partitioning system. There are also several feature enhancements that simplify IA32 operation. One of these enhancements, however, relinquishes a bit of backward compatibility. Here are the new features:

- **Expandable partitions.** In Windows 2000, it was necessary to convert a basic disk to a dynamic disk to add more space to an existing volume. In Windows Server 2003, Basic disk partitions can be extended. This is true even for the system partition.
- **Improved Dynamic disk upgrades.** The Master Boot Record is modified during dynamic disk conversion to remove all but the necessary partition table entries. This eliminates arbitrary restrictions on dynamic volume operations.
- **Diskpart.** A new utility, Diskpart, makes it possible to do all disk management from the command line. This feature has been a long time coming. With it, you can script an entire installation of Windows Server 2003 including the creation of additional partitions.
- **Dropped support for classic fault tolerant (FT) disk sets.** Here's some good news/bad news. The good news is that the underlying LDM code was modified extensively to improve performance. In benchmarks involving disk I/O, Windows Server 2003 handily outperforms Windows 2000, which itself outperformed Windows 9x. The bad news is that these changes relinquished backward compatibility with classic NT4 fault tolerant disk sets.

The last point bears further discussion. Under Windows 2000, you could upgrade a server with fault tolerant Ftdisk disk sets as long as one of them wasn't a mirror of the system partition. You would then convert the Ftdisk set to a dynamic volume after converting the disks to dynamic disks.

Under Windows Server 2003, if you have classic NT Ftdisk striped or volume sets, you must remove them prior to upgrading. To remove the Ftdisk set, you must back up and delete the FTdisk set, do the upgrade, then convert the disks to dynamic disks and configure the volume, then recover your data from tape.

If you use Ftdisk sets to mirror the operating system drive on a classic NT machine, you must break the mirror, do the upgrade, then make the disks into dynamic disks and recreate the mirror.

If you attempt to upgrade a system with Ftdisk sets, you will get an error message right at the start of Setup. The error is a little misleading, because it refers to NT4 basic disks when it should say NT4 fault tolerant disks. If the operating system is mirrored, the error is critical and you cannot upgrade. If data disks are mirrored, striped, or have volume spans, the error is simply a warning. If you go ahead and upgrade, though, you'll notice that the Ftdisk drive set appears in the Disk Management console with a drive letter, but it is inaccessible.

There is a workaround if you neglected to back up the data in the Ftdisk set prior to upgrading. The Support Tools on the Windows Server 2003 CD contains a utility called FTONLINE that you can use to mount the Ftdisk set in read-only mode so you can recover the data.

Functional Description of Windows Server 2003 Data Storage

The Windows Server 2003 storage system supports three different disk partitioning schemes, which Microsoft associates with three different disk types as follows:

- **Basic MBR disks.** This partitioning scheme uses the classic Intel *Master Boot Record* (MBR). The MBR contains a data structure called a *partition table* that defines up to four partitions that can be used to store data.
- **Basic GPT disks.** This partitioning scheme is available only on IA64 systems. It uses a new form of partition table that can define up to 128 partitions, each identified by a Globally Unique Identifier (GUID).
- **Dynamic disks.** This partitioning scheme is used on *dynamic disks* in Windows Server 2003, Windows XP, and Windows 2000. Partition information is stored in a database controlled by a service called the *Logical Disk Manager (LDM)*. Both IA32 and IA64 systems can have dynamic disks. On IA32 systems, a copy of the LDM database is stored in the final cylinder of each dynamic disk. On IA64 systems, the LDM database is stored in a Microsoft Reserved Partition near the beginning of the disk.

Logical Disk Manager Volume Configurations

The database managed by the Logical Disk Manager replaces Registry-based classic NT disk sets supported by Ftdisk. The Ftdisk driver has been relegated to middle management where it is responsible for handling basic MBR and GPT disks.

Under normal operation, with each disk holding its own discrete data, there is no need for anything other than basic disk with partition information stored in an IA32

MBR or IA64 GPT. The same is true for hardware RAID arrays, where the logical disk constructed by the RAID controller appears to the operating system as a single, large basic disk.

The Logical Disk Manager comes into play when you want more sophisticated disk configurations in software. This is when you would convert the basic disks to dynamic disk then use the LDM to create one or more of the following volume configurations:

- **Simple volume.** This is the equivalent of an MBR or GPT partition. When you create a simple volume, you set aside a certain portion of a disk for use by a file system. There is room in the LDM database for thousands of simple volumes, but it's not likely you'll want more than a handful.
- **Spanned volume.** This volume type links together free space on the same disk or from other disks to form a single logical drive. Spanned volumes are the equivalent of classic NT volume sets.
- **Striped volume.** This is a RAID 0 configuration. The data stream is divided into chunks that are written to separate disks. Striped volumes have performance advantages, especially when use with a high-speed data bus, but they increase the likelihood of data loss because a single drive failure disables the entire volume.
- **Mirrored volume.** This is a RAID 1 configuration. The same data stream is directed onto two disks simultaneously. The file systems on the mirrored volumes remain available if either disk fails. If the disks are on separate controllers, the volume is said to be *duplexed*. Mirrored volumes exhibit fast seek times because either disk can respond to a read request, but they are slower than single disks for writing because data must be written to two disks simultaneously.
- **RAID 5 volume.** In this configuration, the data stream is divided into chunks that are written to multiple disks along with parity information. See the sidebar "RAID 5 Operation" for more information. RAID 5 represents a compromise between performance, fault tolerance, and flexibility. It is slower than striping or spanned volumes but provides fault tolerance. It is slower than mirroring but makes more effective use of storage capacity.

LDM does not support more modern configurations such as RAID 0+1 (striping with mirroring) or RAID 10 (mirroring with striping).

Data Chunking and Performance

The underlying storage drivers in Windows Server 2003 (and NT and Windows 2000) move data to and from the disk subsystem in 64KB chunks. You can improve the performance of hardware RAID arrays by configuring the stripe size on the controller to match the 64KB data transfer value from the operating system.

RAID 5 Operation

If you've never experimented with fault tolerant drive configurations before, try setting up a three-disk RAID 5 array in your lab and then pulling the power plug on one of the drives. You'll get a small notification bubble message from a drive icon in the System Tray and that's about it. The logical drive is still available, albeit with slightly reduced performance.

RAID 5 accomplishes this magic by calculating and storing parity information that can be used to reconstitute the contents of a lost disk should one fail. This parity calculation uses a XOR, or exclusive OR, function. A XOR calculation works like a party game:

- If two values match, you get a logical 0.
- If two values don't match, you get a logical 1.

Table 14.1 shows a XOR truth table.

Table 14.1 XOR Truth Table

A	B	C
0	0	0
0	1	1
1	0	1
1	1	0

To see how XOR works to recover lost data, cover up any column in the truth table. You can quickly figure out the value of each hidden item based on the contents of the other two columns.

In the same way, if you remove a disk from a RAID 5 array, the system quickly calculates the value of the missing contents by doing a XOR on the data on the other disks (data XOR parity or data XOR data to get parity).

This is the reason you must have at least three disks to make a RAID 5 array. The system needs at least two chunks of data to calculate a parity chunk. Unlike some other RAID flavors, the parity chunks in RAID 5 are spread across the drives. This avoids a single point of failure.

Keep in mind with RAID 5 that you lose the equivalent of a drive's worth of capacity due to the parity information. If you have four drives of 20GB each, you would lose 25 percent of the total capacity, leaving 60GB of available storage.

Having more drives in the array makes RAID 5 more space-effective, but it can slow down overall performance if the SCSI bus becomes saturated. If you have an ultrawide SCSI 3 bus populated with fifteen drives, you would lose only 6.7 percent of the total capacity, but you might get very poor I/O results.

A regular striped volume does not calculate parity information, so its performance is dramatically better, but you lose fault tolerance.

LDM Database Structure

Let's avoid grunt-level detail here and just get a feel for how the LDM database is laid out on the disk. This information helps you to understand what you'll see if you use disk utilities. It will also help you avoid making changes that could render the LDM inoperable (and your data unavailable).

Figure 14.1 shows a block diagram of the LDM database structures stored on a disk. Here are the components:

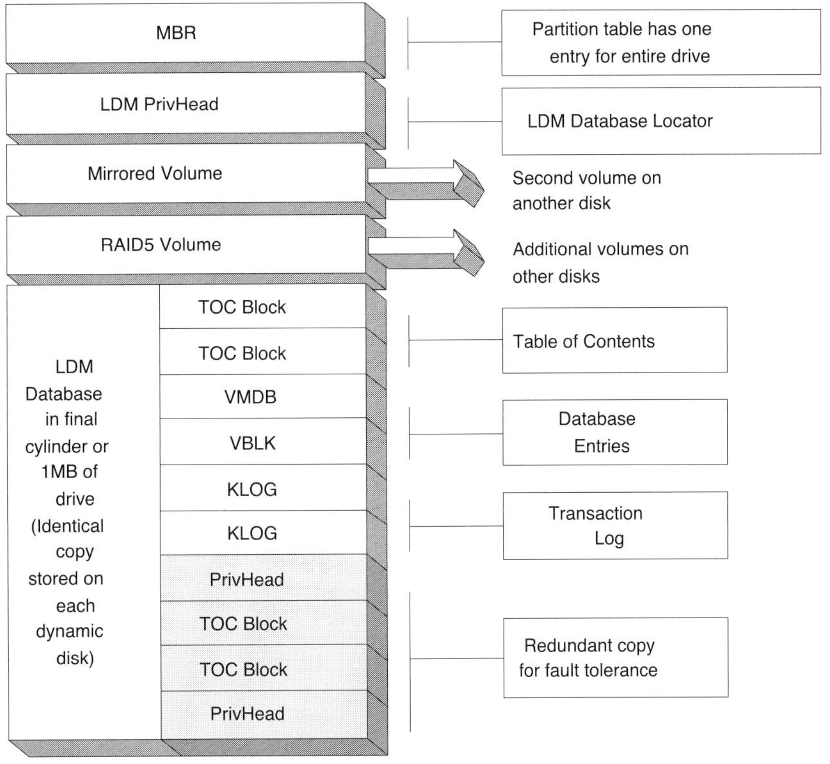

Figure 14.1 Diagram of Logical Disk Manager disk structures.

- **Private Header.** This has entries describing where to find the LDM database and generally defining what's inside. There are multiple copies of this header for fault tolerance.
- **Table of Contents.** This is a quick index of the database contents. Redundant copies are stored at the end of the disk for fault tolerance.
- **Volume Manager.** This is the database itself.
- **Virtual Blocks.** These are the database records, one for each partition, disk, and volume. At 256 bytes per record, there is enough space in the database for thousands of records. Microsoft recommends putting no more than 32 elements in the database. Personally, I think if you have more than one fault tolerant storage element in a server, you need to use hardware RAID.
- **Transaction Log.** This is a set of two sectors that hold uncommitted updates to the database to protect against a possible power loss or some other critical failure.

When you add a new dynamic disk to a system, either by promoting a basic disk or creating a new volume on an existing dynamic disk, the system adds a new Virtual Block to the Volume Manager. (This is the equivalent of adding a new record to the LDM database.) Each element (record) in the database is assigned a Globally Unique Identifier, or GUID. The GUID acts as a key for the record.

You can view a pile of details about the LDM database contents and structure by using the DMDIAG utility in the Support Tools. Here is a sample listing (the /v (verbose) switch gives ten times this amount of information):

```
C:\>dmdiag.exe

---------- Dynamic Disk Information -----------
 DiskGroup: S1Dg0
  Group-ID: e129db61-e6d5-4ff0-9d2e-660f570cc315

   Sub Disk  Rel Sec   Tot Sec   Tot Size  Plex         Vol Type  Col/Ord  DevName    State
   ========  =======   =======   ========  ====         ========  =======  =========  ======
   Disk1-01  0         10667097  0         Volume1-01   Simple    1/1                 MISSING
   Disk1-02  10667097  204800    0         Volume2-01   Simple    1/1                 MISSING
   Disk1-03  10871897  204800    0         Volume3-01   Simple    1/1                 MISSING
   Disk1-04  11076697  1042177   0         Volume4-01   Mirror    1/1                 MISSING
   Disk1-05  12118874  473088    0         Stripe1-01   Stripe    1/2                 MISSING
   LDM-DATA  0         0

   Disk2-01  63        8385867   12594960  Volume5-01   Simple    1/1      Harddisk0  ONLINE
   Disk2-03  10442250  2136645   12594960  Volume7-01   Simple    1/1      Harddisk0  ONLINE
   Disk2-04  8385930   1028160   12594960  Volume4-02   Mirror    1/2      Harddisk0  ONLINE
   Disk2-05  12578895  14017     12594960  Volume4-02   Mirror    1/2      Harddisk0  ONLINE
   Disk2-02  9414090   473088    12594960  Stripe1-01   Stripe    2/2      Harddisk0  ONLINE
   LDM-DATA  12592912  2048

 ---------- LDM Volume Information -----------

   Volume   Volume  Mnt  Subdisk   Plex        Physical    Size      Total     Col  Plex     Rel       Vol     Plex
   Name     Type    Nme  Name      Name        Disk        Sectors   Size      Ord  Offset   Sectors   State   State
   ======   ======  ===  ========  ==========  ==========  =======   =======   ===  ======   =======   ======  ======
   Volume1  Simple  C    Disk1-01  Volume1-01              10667097  10667097  1/1  0        0         ACTIVE  ACTIVE

   Volume2  Simple  R    Disk1-02  Volume2-01              204800    204800    1/1  0        10667097  ACTIVE  ACTIVE
   Volume3  Simple  S    Disk1-03  Volume3-01              204800    204800    1/1  0        10871897  ACTIVE  ACTIVE

   Volume5  Simple       Disk2-01  Volume5-01  Harddisk0   8385867   8385867   1/1  0        63        ACTIVE  ACTIVE

   Volume7  Simple       Disk2-03  Volume7-01  Harddisk0   2136645   2136645   1/1  0        10442250  ACTIVE  ACTIVE

   Volume4  Mirror  D    Disk1-04  Volume4-01              1042177   1042177   1/1  0        11076697  ACTIVE  ACTIVE

   Volume4  Mirror  D    Disk2-04  Volume4-02  Harddisk0   1042177   1028160   1/2  0        8385930   ACTIVE  ACTIVE
   Volume4  Mirror  D    Disk2-05  Volume4-02  Harddisk0   1042177   14017     1/2  1028160  12578895  ACTIVE  ACTIVE

   Stripe1  Stripe  E    Disk1-05  Stripe1-01              946176    473088    1/2  0        12118874  ACTIVE  ACTIVE
   Stripe1  Stripe  E    Disk2-02  Stripe1-01  Harddisk0   946176    473088    2/2  0         414090   ACTIVE  ACTIVE
```

LDM Group Names

Each dynamic disk is part of a *disk group*. Members of a disk group share the same LDM database. Windows Server 2003 can only have one disk group. (The commercial version of LDM from Veritas supports multiple disk groups.)

The disk group is given a name comprised of the computer name followed by the letters `Dg0`. For example, the dynamic disks on a server named SRV1 would have a group name of `Srv1Dg0`.

If you revert all dynamic disks in a server back to basic disks—this require removing all volumes, converting the drives, then restoring the data from tape—the next disk converted to a dynamic disk would start a new group named `Srv1Dg1`.

Group names play an important role when swapping dynamic disks between servers. If you put dynamic disks into a server, you can import the contents of the LDM database on those disks. When you do this, the disks are made part of the local disk group. For example, if you take disks out of server SRV1 and import them into the LDM database in SRV2, the disks would be given the new group name of `Srv2Dg0`.

The Registry keeps track of the disk groups in a machine. You cannot boot from a dynamic disk that is in a different disk group. For example, let's say the disk you imported into server SRV2 was a boot disk. During the import, the disk was added to `Srv2Dg0`. If you took this disk out and put it back into its original server, you would get a `0x0000007B, Inaccessible Boot Device`, blue screen stop as soon as the system compared the disk group name in the Registry with the name in the LDM database. There is no workaround for this, so use extreme caution when moving dynamic boot disks.

If you take dynamic disks from one server and put them in a server that has no dynamic disks of its own, the system behaves like a cubless she-wolf and adopts the new disks as if they were her own. The disks retain their original disk group name, which includes the name of the original server, not the server into which they were imported. The system assigns this name to any subsequent dynamic disks. If you find a system with a disk group name that doesn't match the computer name, this is the most likely cause.

Restrictions on Dynamic Volumes

A few restrictions apply when creating dynamic volumes:

- The Disk Management console only offers NTFS as the format option for a dynamic volume. You can create the volume and use the `FORMAT` command to create a FAT or FAT32 volume.
- Spanned volumes that include multiple disks cannot be mirrored.
- Striped and RAID 5 volumes cannot be mirrored.
- Only simple volumes can be spanned.
- The system and boot volumes can be mirrored but cannot be striped or spanned.

Barring these few restrictions, you can create as many different volumes on the dynamic disks in a system as you need. Keep in mind that the storage subsystem must respond to file system requests from all those volumes, so don't degrade performance by configuring lots and lots of volumes.

Also, avoid mixing IDE/ATA drives and SCSI drives in the same volume set. You put additional pressure on the storage subsystem to track data packets from two very different sources. The same is true of mixing radically different SCSI drives on the same bus or different SCSI host interface adapters in the same array.

For the most part, you can achieve acceptable performance and fault tolerance by mirroring a pair of drives for the operating system and then creating a RAID 5 volume set using at least three drives on another interface. Use SCSI drives to take advantage of the increased thread handling capabilities and more robust bus management subsystem.

XP and LDM

LDM in Windows XP does not permit creating fault tolerant volumes such as RAID 5 and mirrored drives. You can create simple volumes or striped volumes and you can span volumes. There is no architectural reason for this limitation; it merely differentiates the desktop product from the server product. This limitation has been present in all versions of classic NT and Windows 2000.

If you create a fault tolerant volume on a server, you can import the disks onto a desktop running XP. I do not recommend this practice because you never know when Microsoft might do something in the code to preclude this configuration.

It's worth noting here that the Home Edition of XP does not support dynamic disks of any form. You cannot install the Home Edition onto a dynamic disk and you cannot import a dynamic disk from another system into a system running Home Edition.

When to Use Dynamic Disks

Dynamic disks have one benefit: They permit you to smear data across multiple disks. There is no performance advantage to using a simple volume on a dynamic disk compared to a basic partition on the same disk. Performance is determined by the speed of the drives, the I/O path, and the file system. Dynamic disks are just as susceptible to viruses as basic disks because the executable code in the Master Boot Record and partition boot sector is unchanged.

This means you do not need a dynamic disk on a system with only one drive. Converting disks on laptops is restricted by a Registry setting because the laptop may connect to a docking station with an additional drive. It would cause problems for the LDM if the databases on the two drives were to get out of sync.

Many servers use hardware RAID. A RAID controller presents a virtual disk to the operating system. There is no benefit to converting this virtual disk from basic to dynamic. This was occasionally necessary under Window 2000 to permit expanding volumes by adding new storage to the array and then spanning to the unallocated space. Windows Server 2003 permits expanding basic disk partitions, so there is no need to convert.

If you decide to use the software-based RAID in Windows Server 2003, you'll like these features:

- Disk reconfigurations (other than the initial conversion of the system/boot disk) do not require rebooting.
- Dynamic volumes can be remotely managed, both from the Disk Management console and the command line using Diskpart.
- The LDM database is replicated to each dynamic disk, improving reliability.
- The database is on the drives themselves so you can move a drive assembly into another machine and quickly access the data.
- You can boot from a fault tolerant boot floppy to the secondary drive of a mirrored volume without breaking the mirror. This was not possible in classic NT using Ftdisk because the Registry on the mirrored disk was locked.
- You can move drives around within a server and retain their logical disk location within their volume sets. This added bit of flexibility is a significant improvement over classic NT Ftdisk sets.

Dynamic Disks and Laptops

You may notice that some laptops permit converting to dynamic disks. This is due to a mistake in the interpretation of the machine's BIOS.

There was an unpublished Registry hack in Windows 2000 that permitted running dynamic disks on a laptop. This hack does not work on Windows Server 2003 or XP (it causes the LDM service to fail) but here it is in case you want to know it:

```
Key:   HKLM | System | CurrentControlSet | Services | dmload
Value: Start
Data:  0 (REG_DWORD)
```

Dynamic Disks and Hardware RAID

The chief advantage to software RAID is its price. You can't get better than *free*. But even free has its price. Ask anyone who has attended a timeshare presentation just to get the free trip to Hawaii.

Dynamic disks do not provide the same kind of comprehensive feature sets found in hardware RAID controllers. This includes the following:

- No support for hot-swappable disks
- No hot-standby disks
- No dynamic growth when adding new disks
- No automatic partition management
- Not as capable of protecting data during some types of drive failure

In addition, hardware RAID is faster than software RAID, all other things being equal. If price is more important than performance, vendors such as Promise, IBM, Adaptec, and others now offer ATA RAID controllers at competitive prices.

Still, you can't beat free. If your budget is tight and your CIO or business owner or client can't or won't spend the money on hardware RAID, by all means make use of dynamic disks.

Basic Disk Conversion

LDM-based dynamic volumes have lots of advantages over classic MBR partitioning, but they have their eccentricities, most of which have to do with booting and backward compatibility. To understand these eccentricities, we need to get familiar with some of the basic structures on an MBR disk.

Figure 14.2 shows a diagram of a Master Boot Record. The MBR contains a few hundred bytes of executable code designed to scan a data structure called a *Partition Table*, which is also in the MBR. One of the entries in the Partition Table should be marked as "active," meaning that it can be used to boot the machine.

The MBR code then goes out to the location specified by the partition table entry and loads the sector at that location into memory. This sector, the partition boot sector, contains *bootstrap* code that is capable of finding and loading either an operating system or a secondary bootstrap loader. In the case of Windows Server 2003, the secondary bootstrap loader is Ntldr.

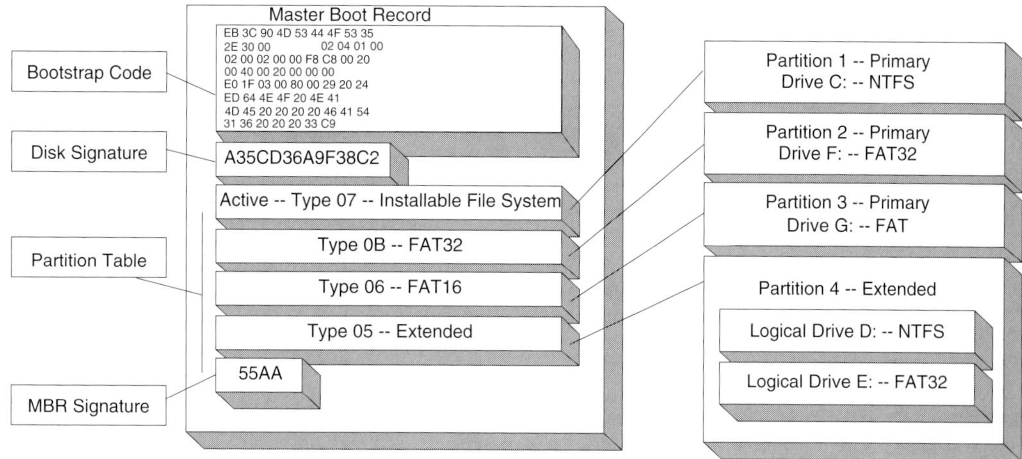

Figure 14.2 Diagram of key Master Boot Record elements and partitioning information.

This configuration changes somewhat when you convert the disk from a basic disk to a dynamic disk. Figure 14.3 shows the MBR and partition information following conversion to a dynamic disk. Several things happen during the conversion:

- An LDM partition is added to the end of the drive.
- The partition table entries from the MBR are added to the LDM database as simple volumes. Volumes are created for every primary partition and every logical drive within an extended partition.
- If the system already has dynamic disks, the new disk and its volumes are merged into the existing LDM database on those disks and the result is copied to the LDM database on the new disk.
- The logical drive letters assigned to the basic partitions by the Registry are retained for the newly created dynamic volumes.
- The partition table is modified to retain only the partitions required for INT13 access to the disk.

The user interface shows only a few changes. Explorer remains the same. The Disk Management console shows the disk status as `Dynamic` and `On-Line`. It identifies the volumes with a different color scheme. Unallocated space on the disk can now participate in dynamic volume structures such as spanning, mirroring, striping, and RAID 5.

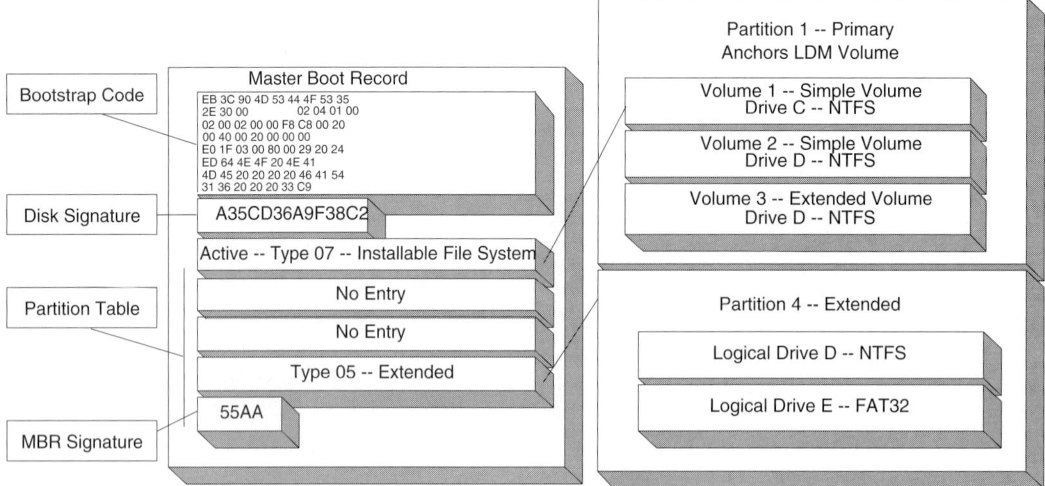

Figure 14.3 Diagram of Master Boot Record following conversion to a dynamic disk.

Conversions Requiring Restart

If you convert a basic disk that holds any of the following components, you must restart the system to complete the conversion:

- System files
- Boot files
- Paging files
- Crash dump files

The restart permits the system to create the necessary LDM database entries and Registry entries prior to mounting the file systems. Here is a quick rundown of the operations:

- An `Encapsulation Info` key is placed in the Registry under `HKLM | System | CurrentControlSet | Services | DMIO` with a binary value of `FDISK Data` showing the structure of the partitions on the disk.
- An `EncapsulationPending` key is put under `HKLM | System | CurrentControlSet | Services | DMLOAD` with no values. It acts as a flag to notify the system to make the change to the Master Boot Record and construct the LDM database using the information in the `Encapsulation Info` key.
- The system restarts, makes the change, and then you are prompted to restart again with the message that the system has found new hardware. This is because the dynamic disk participates differently in the Windows Server 2003 object namespace than a basic disk.

Prerequisites and Restrictions for Converting Basic Disks

Here is a quick checklist to use when planning a disk conversion. If one of the restrictions prevents you from doing the conversion, your only alternative is to remove the existing partitions (after backing up the data, of course), converting the disk, configuring the dynamic volumes, and then restoring the data to the new volumes:

- You cannot convert a disk with existing partitions if there is no room for the LDM database at the end of the disk. The database takes a minimum of 1MB but it must align to a cylinder boundary, so the actual size depends on the geometry of the disk.

  The system will resize any existing partitions to make room for the LDM partition. If this resizing fails, the disk cannot be converted. About the only time this would happen is if you have a foreign partition (third-party partition manager, Linux, and so on) as the final partition on the drive.

  If you have SCSI drives, the system will put the LDM database in the area of the disk set aside for sector sparing. This can dramatically reduce the cushion you have for handling sector failures. NTFS supports sector sparing in software, so this should not present a problem.
- You cannot convert detachable or removable disks to dynamic disks. Each dynamic disk has a copy of the LDM database. It would cause the LDM subsystem to become unstable if a copy of the database were on a removable platter.
- You can only read dynamic disks using Windows Server 2003, Windows XP, or Windows 2000.
- You cannot convert a dynamic disk back to a basic disk without first removing all volumes. This involves erasing all data, so it's vital to have a recoverable backup.
- The system files Ntdlr, Ntdetect.com, Boot.ini, Bootsect.dos, and Ntbootdd.sys can reside on a dynamic disk but they must be on a simple volume or a mirrored volume.

Booting and Dynamic Disks

When you boot an Intel computer, the system BIOS performs a series of INT13 calls to locate the bootstrap code for the operating system. (PCs built to PC97 specifications or later use extended INT13 calls that understand modern drive geometries.)

The INT13 service routines cannot read the LDM database. Without a standard partition table entry, the BIOS cannot locate an operating system partition. For this reason, when you convert a basic disk to a dynamic disk, the system retains the partition table entry for the system partition—that is, the partition that contains the bootstrap code. There are a couple of subtleties to this operation:

- It's possible that the system partition is not the first partition on the disk. If that is the case, sufficient partition table entries will be retained to permit INT13 to locate the system partition.
- It's possible to boot the operating system from a logical drive in an extended partition. For this reason, the partition table entries for all extended partitions are retained.

Keep in mind that you cannot boot to a drive that contains only dynamic volumes. If you mirror your system drive, be sure to partition the drive *first* and then delete the partition and mirror it. This creates a bootable partition in the MBR.

An INT13 call does not see the data boundaries created by the LDM database. For this reason, be very careful when using any disk utilities that run outside of the Windows operating system. This includes partition managers such as BootIt and Partition Magic, boot-time defragmentation features in Diskeeper and PerfectDisk. This also includes the Setup program and the Recovery Console, which relies on the drivers in Setup. See the next section for more details.

Setup and Dynamic Disks

You can install Windows Server 2003 onto a disk that has been previously configured as a dynamic disk. Before going over the inevitable restrictions and prerequisites, let's review what happens when you run Setup on a basic disk. (If you are new to Windows system administration, take a quick look at the sidebar "Boot and System Partitions." The nomenclature can be a little confusing.) Here's the review:

- If you elect to install both the system files and boot files into a single partition, Setup creates a single primary partition and gives it drive letter C. This is usually the first partition on the drive, although it does not have to be. Setup also marks this partition as "active," meaning that the BIOS boot routine will load the boot sector from that partition.

Creating a Bootable Drive

If you forget to pre-partition a mirrored drive and you lose the primary drive, you'll discover that the second drive in the mirrored set is not bootable because it has no Master Boot Record and no partition table. You can put a bootable partition in the MBR of the drive using the Diskpart utility, but first you need to boot the operating system. You can do this with a fault tolerant boot floppy. See section "Building a Fault Tolerant Boot Floppy" for instructions on creating the floppy.

When you've booted the operating system, load the Diskpart console and issue the following commands (the example assumes the disk is the first disk in the array and the volume is the first on the disk):

```
DISKPART> Select Disk 0
DISKPART> Select Volume 1
DISKPART> Retain
```

- If you elect to install the boot files and system files in separate partitions, Setup marks the partition containing the system files as "active" and gives it drive letter C. This is typically the first partition on the drive. The remaining partitions you specify in Setup become logical drives in a single extended partition. Setup will not create more than one primary partition.

The purpose of these rules is to ensure that the INT13 BIOS service routines can find the bootstrap code in the system partition and the operating system files in the boot partition.

If you install Windows Server 2003 onto a dynamic disk, the BIOS must still be able to find the bootstrap code and the operating system files. With this in mind, here are the prerequisites and restrictions:

- If the system or boot volume is mirrored, you must break the mirror before installing or upgrading to Windows Server 2003. You can remake the mirror later after installation.
- You must select a partition displayed by Setup. These represent volumes that are anchored to classic MBR partition table entries. Other dynamic volumes within these volumes are not displayed, so don't delete them unless you're sure they do not contain data.
- There will not be any unallocated space beyond the listed partitions. When you select a partition, Setup will probably find an existing Windows operating system. You can elect to overwrite that operating system.

To avoid data loss, you should avoid installing Windows Server 2003 onto a dynamic disk unless you are diagnosing a problem by installing a parallel version of the operating system.

Boot and System Partitions

In case you are not familiar with Microsoft's awkward and unintuitive definition of *boot* partitions and *system* partitions, here it is:

- The boot partition contains the Windows Server 2003 system files. By default, these files are located in the \Windows directory.
- The *system partition* contains the files that Windows Server 2003 uses to load the operating system: NTDLR, Ntdetect.com, Boot.ini, Bootsect.dos, and Ntbootdd.sys. These files reside at the root of the drive that is used to boot the system.

Confusing? You bet. Will it change? Not likely. If data storage and superstring theory ever merge so that a computer can store data in stasis between two infinitesimal instants of time, Microsoft would insist on the instant with bootstrap data the *system* instant.

The Recovery Console uses the underlying drivers in Setup, so don't make the mistake of running the MAP command in the Recovery Console and assuming that the drive letters you see are the only logical drives on the disks.

Partition and Volume Extensions

Growth is everywhere. 50 million years ago, horses were the size of a small dog. In 1930, the astronomer Edwin Hubbell proved beyond a shadow of a doubt that the universe is expanding. In 1965, Gordon Moore postulated that the rate of on-chip transistor density would double at a more or less steady rate. In 1999, Michael Dell made more money in one month than any person in history.

Still, nobody understands growth like a system administrator. And I'm not talking about the kind of growth that comes from eating too many chocolate donuts while troubleshooting a service outage. I'm talking about data growth. No matter how generously you size your storage systems, in a blink of an eye you're at a 90 percent loading factor. Let's see how we can use the LDM to respond to that kind of growth.

Basic Disk Partition Extensions

When you add more storage, you generally stuff more drives into an array of some sort, either a locally attached RAID controller or a Storage Attached Network (SAN) box of some sort. The additional storage appears in the operating system as unallocated space.

Under Windows 2000, if you wanted to expand an existing volume to encompass that new space without creating a new logical drive, you were forced to convert the virtual disk presented by the RAID controller to a dynamic disk so you could span volumes. Under Windows Server 2003, you can extend a basic partition without going through the hassle of a disk conversion. If you dual-boot between Windows Server 2003 and Windows 2000 or NT, the extended partition is accessible by the earlier operating systems.

Here are the restrictions for extending basic disk partitions:

- The partition must be formatted as NTFS. If it is currently formatted as FAT or FAT32, you can convert it using the CONVERT utility. The new CONVERT utility in Windows Server 2003 is fast and permits you to control the cluster size.
- The unallocated space must be on the same drive as the existing partition. You cannot span basic partitions across disks.
- The unallocated space must be contiguous to the basic partition you want to expand.

After you extend the partition, the space appears in Explorer as free space in the existing logical drive. See the section, "Performing Disk Operations on IA32 Systems," for the procedure to extend a basic partition.

Dynamic Disk Volume Extensions (Spanning)

You can add space to a dynamic volume by spanning to unallocated space elsewhere on the drive. You can also span across drives. This configuration has several restrictions:

- You can span a simple volume or an existing spanned volume. You cannot span striped, RAID 5, or mirrored volumes.
- You cannot span a system volume (the volume used to boot the operating system). This is because the BIOS locates the volume using INT13 calls, which rely on standard partition information in the MBR.
- You cannot span a boot volume (the volume that contains the operating system files) for the same reason as the system volume.
- You cannot span a volume that is anchored to a classic partition table entry. This was an issue under Windows 2000 because it retained the old partition table. Windows Server 2003 changes the structure of the partition table to eliminate most of the primary partitions.

The chief advantage of volume spanning using dynamic disks over partition extension using basic disks is the capability to span volumes across multiple disks. Ordinarily, you would avoid this configuration because it lacks fault tolerance. However, if you use a SAN for storage or some other fault-tolerance subsystem capable of presenting multiple virtual drives, you can span volumes across those virtual drives while retaining fault tolerance.

See the following section for the procedure to span a dynamic volume.

Performing Disk Operations on IA32 Systems

Now that we've seen how the LDM works, let's use it to configure storage alternatives. The primary means for converting and configuring spinning storage is the Disk Management console, Diskmgmt.msc.

The snap-in for this console is included in the Computer Management console. You can open the Computer Management console via START | PROGRAMS | ADMINISTRATIVE TOOLS | COMPUTER MANAGEMENT.

You can also open the Computer Management console by right-clicking the `My Computer` icon and selecting MANAGE from the flyout menu.

The Disk Management console does not manipulate the disk configuration directly. It communicates with the Logical Disk Server service via the Logical Disk Manager Administrator program, `Dmadmin`, which launches in concert with the Disk Management console. This means you can also manage disks on remote servers.

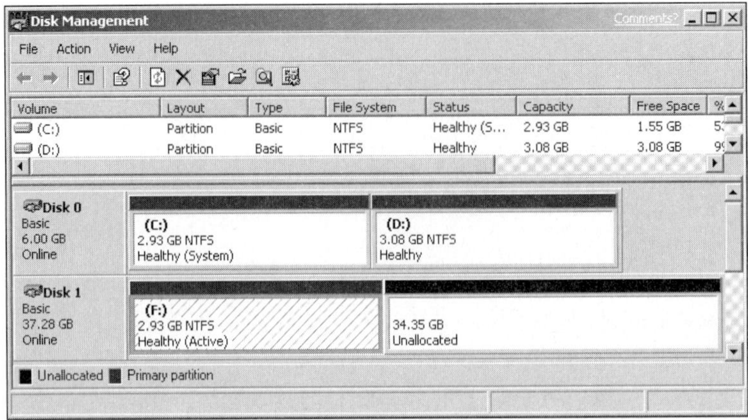

Figure 14.4 Disk Management console showing volumes and parameters.

Figure 14.4 shows the interface for the Disk Management console. The text portion at the top of the Disk Management console window shows information about each logical partition and/or volume. The graphical portion of the window shows a long bar for each disk with a status box to the left. If you right-click the graphical bar on an existing partition or volume, you'll get options to format it, assign or change a drive letter, or delete it. If you right-click unallocated space, you'll get options to create a partition or volume (basic or dynamic disk). You can also view the properties of the disk.

You can also perform just about any operation from the command line that you can perform using the Disk Management console. The Diskpart utility in the Support Tools provides a text-based console for this purpose. You can use this console for speed and convenience when managing remote servers, and you can script with it. See "Command-Line Disk Management," near the end of this section, for details.

Selecting the Correct Disk Configuration

Windows Server 2003 has a variety of disk configurations to choose from. For basic disks, you have two options:

- **Primary partition.** Use this option if you have a single disk that you want to divide into one or more logical drives. You may want multiple drives to keep the operating system separate from data, or to segregate data from different sources, or to limit the size of a partition. Creating a single partition for a 500GB array, for example, forces the file system to track a very large number of clusters and increases seek time.

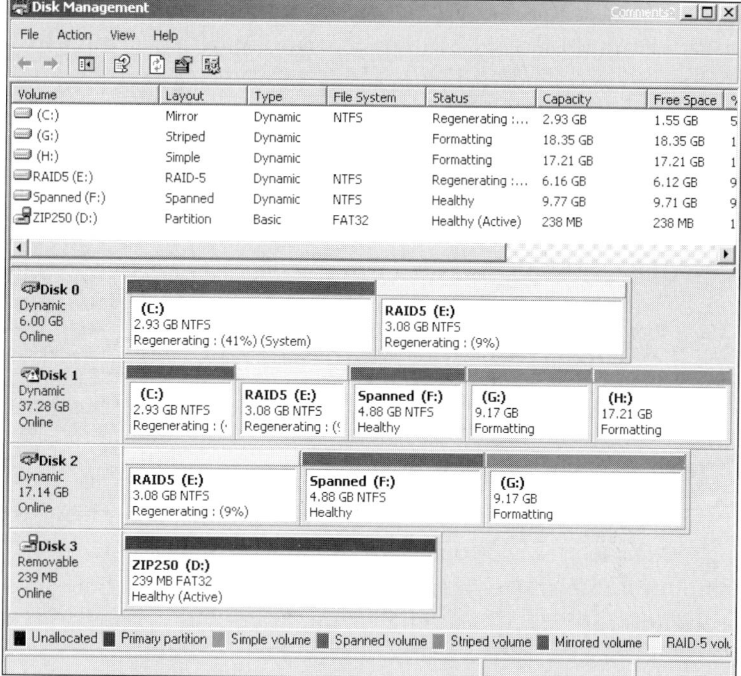

Figure 14.5 Disk Management console showing a system with nearly all dynamic disk configuration options.

- **Extended partition.** Use this option if you want to boot from DOS or Windows 9x and see files in a partition other than the primary partition that boots the operating system. If you use Windows 2000 or NT exclusively, you do not need extended partitions unless you want more than four logical drives.

If you use dynamic disks, you have many additional options. Figure 14.5 shows the Disk Management console for a system where just about all of these options have been selected:

- **Simple volume.** Use this option if you have a single dynamic disk that you want to divide into one or more logical drives.
- **Spanned volume.** Use this option if you have a hardware RAID array that you've expanded with additional drives and you want to keep the same volume name and drive letter. You should not span volumes between physical drives because it increases the likelihood of losing data.
- **Striped volume.** Use this option if you don't care about fault tolerance and want fast I/O. This is a popular configuration with CAD and multimedia workstations where work files are saved locally throughout the day and then copied to a file server at night for backup. You may not see much of a performance

improvement on IDE unless you use separate controllers. You can also improve performance on SCSI by using separate controllers if you have several drives in the striped volume.

- **Mirrored volume.** Use this option if you want good performance along with fault tolerance. Use separate controllers for maximum performance and to improve fault tolerance in the event of a controller failure. Mirroring is not available on XP Professional.
- **RAID 5 volume.** Use this option when you want fault tolerance and large logical drives where mirroring is not cost effective. This option is not available on XP Professional.

The next few sections contain the steps for creating these configurations.

Creating Primary Partitions on Basic Disks

If you create a second primary partition on a dual-boot machine, downlevel operating systems such as DOS and Win9x cannot see the partition. A disk can have a maximum of four primary partitions. To create primary partitions on basic disks, follow Procedure 14.1.

Procedure 14.1 Creating Primary Partitions on Basic Disks

1. Open the `Disk Management` console.
2. Right-click the graphic bar representing the disk you want to partition and select CREATE PARTITION from the flyout menu. The New Partition Wizard opens.
3. Click `Next`. The Select Partition Type window opens.
4. Select the `Primary Partition` radio button.
5. Click `Next`. The Specify Partition Size window opens. Enter a size for the partition in megabytes. The minimum size displayed in the window is only a guideline. You should not create very small partitions except for testing.
6. Click `Next`. The Assign Drive Letter or Path window opens.

   Normally, you would leave the selection at the next available drive letter and be done with it. The `Mount This Volume at an Empty Folder...` option makes use of *NTFS reparse points* to mount the partition at a folder in an existing NTFS drive.
7. Click `Next`. The Format Partition window opens. Select a file system to use for formatting.
8. Click `Next`. A window summarizes your selections.
9. Click `Finish` to create and format the partition.

The Disk Management console now displays information about the new partition.

Creating an Extended Partition and Logical Drives

A disk can have only one extended partition. The entire disk can be configured as an extended partition, if you desire, but only for data drives. The system files (those used to boot the system) must reside in a primary partition. Follow Procedure 14.2.

Procedure 14.2 Creating Extended Partitions and Logical Drives

1. Open the `Disk Management` console.
2. Right-click the unallocated space where you want to create the extended partition and select CREATE PARTITION from the flyout menu. The New Partition Wizard opens.
3. Click `Next`. The Select Partition Type window opens.
4. Select the `Extended Partition` radio button.
5. Click `Next`. The Specify Partition Size window opens. Enter a size for the partition in megabytes.
6. Click `Next`. A window summarizes your changes.
7. Click `Finish` to save the configuration and create the extended partition.
8. When the partition has been created, you must create at least one logical drive to get useful storage. Right-click the green area in the graphic representing the extended partition and select CREATE LOGICAL DRIVE from the flyout menu. The New Partition Wizard opens.
9. Click `Next`. The Select Partition Type window opens with the `Logical Drive` radio button selected by default.
10. Click `Next`. The Specify Partition Size window opens. Enter a size.
11. Click `Next`. The Assign Drive Letter or Path window opens. Assign a drive letter or select a volume and directory to use as a mount point.
12. Click `Next`. The Format Partition window opens.
13. Select a file system to format the partition.
14. Click `Next`. A window summarizes your selections.
15. Click `Finish` to accept the settings and create and format the logical drive.

The Disk Management console now displays the extended partition and its logical drive. You can create additional logical drives to the extent that you have free space available. The only limit to the number of logical drives is the number of drive letters that you have available, and even that isn't a limit if you use mount points without assigning drive letters.

Extending a Basic Disk Partition

You can increase the size of a basic disk partition as long as you have contiguous, unallocated space. You cannot use the Disk Management console, though. You must use the Diskpart command-line utility that comes in the Support Tools. The steps are listed in Procedure 14.3. The entries shown in each step are the commands you enter in the Diskpart console.

Procedure 14.3 Expanding a Basic Disk Partition Using Diskpart

1. Open a command console.
2. Launch `Diskpart`. This opens a text-based console.
3. List the disks in the machine: `list disk`.
4. Select the disk containing the partition you want to expand: `select disk 0`.
5. List the partitions on the disk: `list partition`.
6. Find the amount of free space on the disk: `detail volume`.
7. Find the order of the partitions and their size: `list volume`
8. Select the partition you want to expand: `select partition 1`

   The partition you want to expand must have unallocated space adjoining it. This is not possible to determine from Diskpart, so if you have reason to suspect that a disk might have non-contiguous unallocated space between partitions, you'll need to get a snapshot using the Disk Management console.
9. Expand the partition by specifying the amount of additional space you want to add in megabytes: `expand size=1024`.
10. Verify the new partition size using CHKDSK or Explorer.

Converting a Basic Disk to a Dynamic Disk

Review the checklist presented earlier in the chapter to ensure you meet the prerequisites and requirements for converting a basic disk, and then proceed as directed in Procedure 14.4.

Procedure 14.4 Converting a Basic Disk to a Dynamic Disk

1. Open the `Disk Management` console.
2. Right-click the disk status portion of the disk graphic and select CONVERT TO DYNAMIC DISK from the flyout menu. The Convert to Dynamic Disk window opens.
3. Verify that the disk you selected has been checkmarked.
4. Click `OK`. The Disks to Convert window opens. Verify that the proper disk is listed.

5. Click `Convert`. You'll be prompted to confirm.
6. Click `OK` to begin the conversion. If you are converting a disk that contains system, boot, paging, or crash dump files, you'll be prompted to restart.
7. After restart, if applicable, you'll be prompted to restart again because the Plug-and-Play Manager sees dynamic disks as a new device.

Following the second restart, you can create a new simple volume on the disk. If you have other dynamic disks in the machine, you can use the unallocated space on the disk to form volumes involving other disks.

Creating Simple Volumes on Dynamic Disks

You can create several simple volumes on a single dynamic disk, if you need to have multiple logical drives. You can also span the volume at a later time if it is not a system or boot volume. To do create simple volumes, follow Procedure 14.5.

Procedure 14.5 Creating Simple Volumes

1. Open the `Disk Management` console.
2. Right-click the unallocated space where you want to create the volume and select CREATE VOLUME from the flyout menu. The New Volume Wizard opens.
3. Click `Next`. The Select Volume Type window opens.
4. Select the `Simple Volume` radio button.
5. Click `Next`. The Select Disks window opens (see Figure 14.6). Enter the size of the volume.

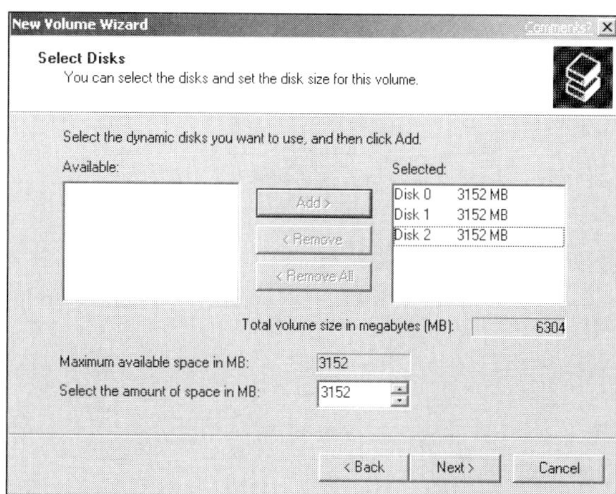

Figure 14.6 New Volume Wizard—Select Disks window.

6. Click `Next`. The Assign Drive Letter or Path window opens. Assign a drive letter or mount the volume at an empty folder on an NTFS drive.
7. Click `Next`. The Format Volume window opens. The only format offered is NTFS. You must use the `FORMAT` command to select another file system type.
8. Click `Next`. A window summarizes the options you selected.
9. Click `Finish`. The volume is created and formatted.

Extending (Spanning) Volumes Between Dynamic Disks

You can extend an existing simple volume by spanning it to unallocated space elsewhere on the disk or on another disk. You cannot span the boot volume or the system volume. Follow Procedure 14.6 to configure a spanned volume.

Procedure 14.6 Configuring a Spanned Volume

1. Open the `Disk Management` console.
2. Right-click the simple volume you want to extend and select EXTEND VOLUME from the flyout menu. The Extend Volume Wizard opens.
3. Click `Next`. The Select Disks window opens. Select the disk you want to include in the span. Only dynamic disks appear on the list. You can span to any dynamic disk that has free space.
4. Click `Next`. A window summarizes the options you selected.
5. Click `Finish`. The volume is created and formatted.

The Disk Management console displays the results. Note that when you extend a basic partition, the result is a new partition. When you extend a dynamic volume, even to contiguous space on the same drive, a new volume is created. This does not cause a fault tolerance issue unless the volumes are on different disks.

Creating Striped Volumes

If you want lots of storage space with great performance and you aren't concerned about fault tolerance, configure a striped volume. You must have at least two dynamic disks with unallocated space. Use separate controllers for maximum performance. To configure a striped volume, follow the steps in Procedure 14.7.

Procedure 14.7 Creating Striped Volumes

1. Open the `Disk Management` console.
2. Right-click the free space you want to include in the striped volume and select CREATE VOLUME from the flyout menu. The New Volume Wizard opens.

3. Click `Next`. The Select Volume Type window opens.
4. Select the `Striped` radio button.
5. Click `Next`. The Select Disks window opens. Select at least one other disk that you want to include in the volume. Only dynamic disks will appear on the list. You can stripe to any dynamic disk that has free space. The total space taken on any disk equals the smallest free space on any selected disk.
6. Click `Next`. The Assign Drive Letter or Path window opens.
7. Assign a drive letter or mount to an empty folder on an NTFS volume.
8. Click `Next`. The Format Volume window opens. The only option is NTFS.
9. Click `Next`. A window summarizes the options you selected.
10. Click `Finish`. The volume is created and formatted with the file system you selected.

Creating Mirrored Volumes

When mirroring drives, leave a little extra free space when you partition the first drive. Drives with the same specs, even drives from the same manufacturer, often have different useful capacities depending on manufacturing tolerances and the total number of bad sectors identified during low-level formatting. If the secondary disk is just one sector shy of the primary, the system will refuse to mirror. Procedure 14.8 shows how to create mirrored volumes.

Procedure 14.8 Creating Mirrored Volumes

1. Open the `Disk Management` console.
2. Right-click the volume you want to mirror and select ADD MIRROR from the flyout menu. The Add Mirror window opens.
3. Select the disk you want to use for a mirror and click `Add Mirror`.

   If you mirror the boot disk, the system sends a message prompting you to add a line to your Boot.ini file to enable booting from the mirrored disk. For example, here is a Boot.ini entry to boot to the second disk on the same SCSI controller as the primary drive (the text wording is mine. You can put anything you like):

   ```
   multi(0)disk(0)rdisk(1)partition(1)\Windows="Windows Server 2003 Mirrored
   ➥Secondary Disk" /fastdetect
   ```

   If the mirrored drive has never been configured with a classic bootable partition prior to the mirroring, you cannot use it to boot the system.
4. Click `OK` to acknowledge the message. The system begins building the mirror. This is indicated by a *Regenerating* status in the graphic for the two disks.

Regeneration copies the contents of the primary disk to the secondary disk sector by sector. This can take a long time for a big volume. You can allow users to access the file system while it is regenerating, but this slows down the regeneration. After the volume has regenerated, the status shows as `Healthy` in the Disk Management console.

Breaking a Mirrored Volume

If you need to break a mirrored volume, you have the choice of breaking the mirror or removing it. If you break the mirror, here's what happens:

- The file system is left intact on both volumes, yielding two exact replicas.
- The volume on the secondary disk is given the next available drive letter.
- If the primary volume was a boot volume, it retains the paging file.
- If another volume was mounted to a folder in the mirrored drive, the primary drive hosts the mount point.
- File shares on folders in the mirrored volume are retained by the primary volume.

If you choose to remove the mirror, you can delete the replica on either or both disks. The volume you retain keeps the same drive letter.

Breaking a mirror is the easy part. Recovering from the consequences can get a little tricky. If the mirror includes the boot volume, you may encounter a couple of problems after you break the mirror.

Procedure 14.9 shows the steps to break a mirror.

Procedure 14.9 Breaking a Mirrored Volume

1. Load the `Disk Management` console.
2. Right-click the mirrored volume and select Break Mirror from the flyout menu.
3. The system prompts for verification and reminds you that the volumes will no longer be fault tolerant. Click `Yes` to acknowledge.
4. If you break the mirror of the boot disk, the system also warns that the volume is in use and prompts for verification that you want to proceed. Click `Yes`.
5. The system breaks the mirror and assigns the next available drive letter to the volume on the secondary disk.

Now that the mirror is broken, try booting to the second disk. You may find that you get an `Inaccessible Boot Device` error. This is because the secondary drive had never been partitioned as a boot drive, so it lacks an entry in the partition table of the MBR. If this happens, use the Diskpart utility to put a partition on the drive.

First, boot to the mirrored drive using a fault tolerant boot floppy. Then load the Diskpart console and issue the following commands (the example assumes the disk is the first disk in the array and the volume is the first on the disk):

```
DISKPART> Select Disk 0
DISKPART> Select Volume 1
DISKPART> Retain
```

You may also experience a problem because the drive letter is incorrect. The system expects to boot to the C: drive. If you boot to the mirrored drive, the drive letter will be something other than C, which can cause strange problems.

You can avoid this problem, but it takes a little advanced planning. When you're ready to break the mirror, boot to the secondary volume using a fault tolerant boot floppy. Now, use the Disk Management console to break the mirror. In this case, the secondary volume will be assigned the C: drive and life is sweet.

Creating RAID 5 Volumes

If you have at least three dynamic disks with free space, you can configure them into a single RAID 5 volume. The volume size is limited by the available free space on the smallest disk. For example, if you have two 4GB disks and one 2GB disk, the resultant RAID 5 volume would be 6GB total space, 4GB effective space. To do this, follow Procedure 14.10.

Procedure 14.10 Creating RAID 5 Volumes

1. Open the `Disk Management` console.
2. Right-click the graphic for one of the disks you want to include in the striped volume and select CREATE VOLUME from the flyout menu. The New Volume Wizard opens.
3. Click `Next`. The Select Volume Type window opens.
4. Select the `RAID 5` radio button.
5. Click `Next`. The Select Disks window opens. Select at least two other disks you want to include in the volume.
6. Click `Next`. The Assign Drive Letter or Path window opens.
7. Assign a drive letter or an empty volume on an NTFS volume.
8. Click `Next`. The Format Volume window opens. The only option is NTFS.
9. Click `Next`. A window summarizes the options you selected.
10. Click `Finish`. The volume is created and formatted with the file system you selected.

Deleting Volumes Containing Mount Points

If you delete a volume that contains an NTFS mount point, the data in the mounted volume is not affected. You can go back later and mount the volume to another folder or give it a letter of its own.

It takes a while for the system to generate the volume (the interface shows the status as *regenerating*) and format it with a file system. If you have very large drives, plan on taking a long lunch.

Deleting a Volume

LDM does not permit changing the size of any volume other than a simple volume. If you want to change the size of a volume, you'll need to delete and recreate it. When you're sure you have a good backup, follow the steps in Procedure 14.11.

Procedure 14.11 Deleting a Volume

1. Open the `Disk Management` console.
2. Right-click the volume you want to remove and select DELETE VOLUME from the fly-out menu.
3. The system prompts to verify the action. Click `Yes`.
4. If you get an error saying that the volume is currently in use, you should cancel out of the action and locate the open files. If you don't spot anything obvious, look for processes in the Task List that might have a lock on the volume. Antivirus programs are notorious for this.
5. After the volume has been deleted, the Disk Management console shows free space on the disk.

Reverting a Dynamic Disk to a Basic Disk

You cannot revert a dynamic disk back to a basic disk after converting it. Unlike Windows 2000, the LDM in Windows Server 2003 makes permanent changes to the partition table. You must back up the data and remove all volumes first. This includes any participation in striped, spanned, mirrored, or RAID 5 volumes. Then, you can select the disk and convert it to a basic disk. If the operating system is on the disk, you'll need to re-install the operating system. During Setup, delete all existing partitions.

Changing Drive Letters

Windows has always been cantankerous in the way it assigns logical drive letters. Chapter 1, "Installing and Configuring Windows Server 2003," has a breakdown of the algorithm used by the system to assign drive letters. After installation, though, drive letters can change. This may come as a surprise to you if you are accustomed to working only with Windows 98 or ME.

In Windows Server 2003 and XP, drive letters change when detachable disks come on- and offline. The same is true for removable media drives. When media is in place during boot, the drive appears and gets a letter. When the media is not in place, the drive does not appear and *some other drive might get the same letter.*

You might also get awkward drive letter assignments because you forgot to disconnect network drives prior to creating a new partition or volume.

For fixed drives, once you assign a drive letter, it stays in place. This is true even if you upgrade a machine from an earlier version of Windows. This maintains storage access for applications that might have Registry entries that include a drive letter.

If you want to change the drive letter associated with a particular drive, you can do this in the Disk Management console. Consider a few precautions:

- You cannot change the letter of volumes or partitions containing boot or system files.
- Changing the letter of a drive can cause applications to fail. You may need to change Registry information for the application.
- Changing a drive letter causes all shared directories on that volume to fail. The Registry entries are stored as share names in the Registry key `HKLM | System | CurrentControlSet | Services | LanManServer | Shares`. *Write them down or take a screen shot before you change the drive letter.* Forgetting to replace a share can cause many irate Help Desk calls.
- If you have shortcuts to files and directories on NTFS volumes and partitions, the Distributed Link Tracking system automatically changes the shortcuts if the files are moved or renamed. If you change the drive letter, the link tracking system will not automatically update its database. However, link tracking clients fall back on a "best-guess" response that could include the new drive letter.
- Mount points (folders that contain symbolic links to file systems on other folders) are unaffected by drive letter changes. The internal database uses GUIDs, not drive letters.

The example in Procedure 14.12 shows how to change the drive letter of a CD-ROM drive. You can use the same technique to change the drive letter for a fixed disk or removable media disk.

Registry Tip: Mount Point Information

The Registry values containing mount point information are stored under `HKCU | Software | Microsoft | Windows | CurrentVersion | Explorer | MountPoints`.

Procedure 14.12 Changing Drive Letters

1. Open the `Disk Management` console.
2. Right-click the drive icon in the text section or the bar or the status block in the graphic section and select CHANGE DRIVE LETTER AND PATH from the flyout menu. The Drive Letter and Path window opens.
3. Click `Modify`. The Modify Drive Letter or Path window opens.
4. Select a new drive letter from the `Assign a Drive Letter` drop-down box.
5. Click `OK` to save the change. You'll be prompted to confirm. Click `Yes`. Changes are made to the Registry that appear in the Disk Management console.

Command-Line Disk Management

Windows Server 2003 includes a powerful and convenient tool for managing disk configurations. This is the Diskpart utility, which comes in the Support Tools on the Windows Server 2003 CD. Using Diskpart, you can create, configure, and delete all basic partitions and dynamic volumes both locally and on remote machines.

The utility is structured to be a text-based console with a set of namespaces that you navigate using interactive commands. You can string commands together to select operation targets, get a quick parameter listing, and perform operations. For example, to list all the partitions and volumes on a disk, the syntax would be the following:

```
DISKPART> select disk 0
Disk 0 is now the selected disk.

DISKPART> detail disk
Maxtor 90651U2
Disk ID: 30063005
Type   : IDE
Bus    : 0
Target : 0
LUN ID : 0

  Volume ###  Ltr  Label        Fs    Type        Size     Status     Info
  ----------  ---  -----------  ----  ----------  -------  ---------  ------
  Volume 1     C                NTFS  Partition   4103 MB  Healthy    System
  Volume 2     E                NTFS  Partition   196 MB   Healthy
  Volume 3     F                      Partition   502 MB   Healthy
```

Creating a Basic Disk Partition

Here are the Diskpart commands for creating a basic disk partition. You can format the partition from the command line using the FORMAT utility. The commands are the following:

```
DISKPART> Select Disk 0
DISKPART> Create Partition Primary Size=2048
```

```
DISKPART> Assign Letter=h
DISKPART> Exit
C:\>format h: /fs:ntfs
```

Note that you can use Diskpart to assign or change drive letters. If you hassle periodically with drive letter changes caused by removable or detachable media drives, you can create batch files to rearrange your drive letters for each configuration.

Creating a Dynamic Volume

You can use Diskpart to create striped and RAID 5 volumes and to mirror an existing simple volume. Here is an example for creating a RAID 5 volume:

```
DISKPART> List Disk
  Disk ###  Status      Size         Free     Dyn  Gpt
  --------  ----------  -------  -------  ---  ---
* Disk 0    Online       6142 MB  1341 MB   *
  Disk 1    Online      12288 MB  12288 MB  *
  Disk 2    Online      12288 MB  12288 MB  *
  Disk 3    Online      12288 MB  12288 MB  *

DISKPART> Create Volume Raid Disk=1,2,3
```

Extending a Basic Disk Partition

Diskpart can also extend basic partitions and dynamic volumes. The same restrictions that apply to the use of the Disk Management console also apply here. (Note: Diskpart uses the word *volume* to encompass both basic partitions and dynamic volumes.)

The following commands add 2GB onto an existing basic partition; it can be a system or boot partition:

```
DISKPART> list volume
DISKPART> select volume #
DISKPART> extend size=2048
```

You would use the same command to span an existing simple dynamic volume, but the volume cannot hold system or boot files.

Additional Diskpart Operations

In addition to the previous examples, you can use Diskpart to perform the following operations:

- Convert a basic disk to a dynamic disk and vice-versa.
- Perform operations on GPT disks.
- Delete volumes and partitions (with little or no verification, so be careful).
- Import foreign disks into the local LDM database.
- Create a partition table entry in the MBR corresponding to a volume in the LDM. This is used to make a dynamic disk bootable if it has never been a basic disk.

Recovering Failed Fault Tolerant Disks

If you have your data on a single drive or a non-fault tolerant volume such as a spanned volume or a striped volume, you expect to lose data if a drive fails. Because disk failure is an unavoidable fact of computer life, I assume that you have a good backup system and a plan for restoring data quickly. If a single disk in a striped volume fails, for example, you must delete the volume from the remaining disks, replace the disk, and rebuild the volume.

On the other hand, if you don't want to deal with masses of panicked users and their crazed managers who will gather outside the server room like enraged French revolutionaries looking for guillotine fodder, you'll want to put your data on a fault tolerant subsystem of one form or another. This topic covers putting a system back in a stable condition following a disk failure and then recovering the system to normal operation. This includes the following operations:

- Replacing a failed disk in a RAID 5 volume
- Building a fault tolerant boot floppy
- Replacing a failed disk in a mirrored volume
- Moving dynamic volumes between computers

Replacing a Failed Disk in a RAID 5 Volume

When a disk fails in a RAID 5 volume, you will get a very small and very temporary information balloon from a drive icon in the system tray. The message states `A disk that is part of a fault-tolerant volume can no longer be accessed.` The message comes from a process called `FT Orphan`. This is a special process that logically disconnects the drive from the system to eliminate the possibility of data corruption.

The file system on the volume with the failed disk continues to be active. Your only indication of the failure (unless you have installed a third-party utility to alert you of error log entries) is a slight decrease in I/O performance.

When you discover that you have a failed disk, open the `Disk Management` console. You'll get a display that looks something like that in Figure 14.7. Each disk for the volume shows a `Failed Redundancy` status and the failed drive shows a red `Stop` indicator.

Thanks to the fault tolerant nature of RAID 5, the system remains operational. However, you have now entered a statistical universe where the numbers are not in your favor. The next drive crash will cause data loss. If the drives were all manufactured in the same batch, your time might run out very quickly depending on the cause of the crash

Obtain a spare drive that has at least as much capacity as the drive you are replacing. It should be configured for the same SCSI ID to simplify installation, although this is not a requirement.

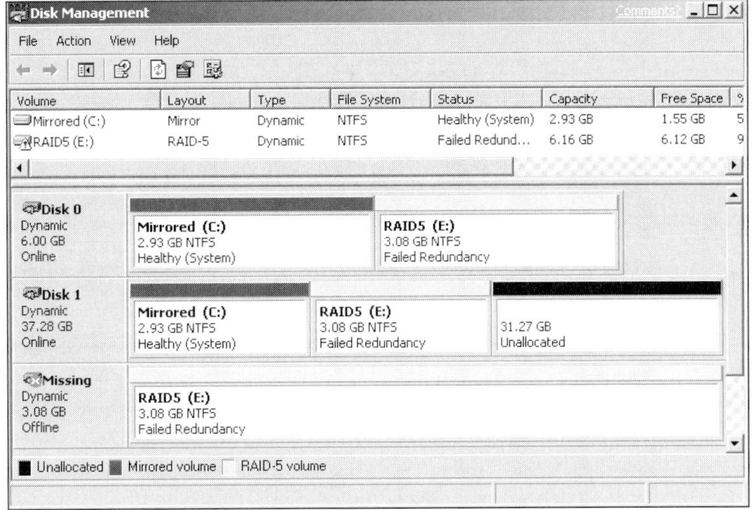

Figure 14.7 Disk Management console showing failed disk in RAID 5 volume.

Use the Disk Management console to check the SCSI ID assigned to the dead drive. Right-click the status block and select Properties from the flyout menu. The SCSI ID (called the Target ID) and *the Local Unit Number* (LUN) are listed. I recommend that you paste a screen print of this window on the server so that you have a reference when you replace the disk. The snarl of SCSI cables inside the machine can lead you astray unless you have a good map. Nothing is quite so embarrassing as replacing the wrong drive.

After you have the replacement drive in your hands and your users have left for the day, you're ready to get to work. Down the server and replace the drive. Test the drive operability using any IDE or SCSI hardware utilities you like.

Now restart and let the operating system load. The RAID 5 volume will initialize and the file system should mount. Open the `Disk Management` console. The display should look something like that in Figure 14.8.

The RAID 5 volume still shows a `Failed Redundancy` status. A status block for the missing disk opens because its information is contained in the LDM database on the other disks. The replacement disk is brand new, so it does not have a fault tolerant signature or a Master Boot Record. The system lists its status as `Unknown`. Follow Procedure 14.13.

Delays in Updating Disk Management Display

It sometimes happens that the LDM does not initialize correctly when loading the Disk Management console. The RAID 5 volume may show `Healthy` even though it is not. If this happens, select Action | Rescan Disks from the menu, close the `Disk Management` console, and open it again. You may need to do this a couple of times to get the display to show a `Failed Redundancy` status.

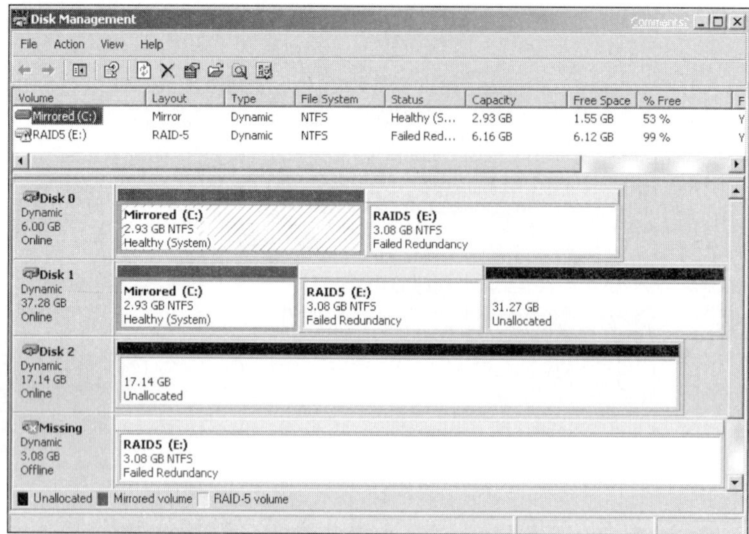

Figure 14.8 Disk Management console showing replacement disk with `Unknown` status and the RAID 5 array with a `Failed Redundancy` status.

Procedure 14.13 Replacing a Failed Disk in a RAID 5 Volume

1. Write a signature to the new disk by following the wizard instructions.
2. Upgrade the disk to a dynamic disk.
3. Right-click the RAID 5 volume and select REPAIR VOLUME from the flyout menu.
4. Select the new disk to use as a replacement for the failed disk. The new disk now becomes part of the RAID 5 volume and the system begins regenerating. This can take a long time, sometimes hours. It will take much longer if users access the drive.
5. While the regeneration is in progress, right-click the status block for the missing disk and select REMOVE DISK from the flyout menu. (Make absolutely sure you have the correct disk.) The status block disappears and the graphic display rearranges to show the new drive configuration.

Building a Fault Tolerant Boot Floppy

If you mirror your boot volume—the most popular fault tolerant choice—one of the most important tools you have for recovering from a failure is a fault tolerant boot floppy. The secondary drive is not necessarily bootable, so you need a way to boot the system to the mirrored volume on the secondary drive if the primary drive fails.

Even if the secondary drive is bootable, you or a colleague may have forgotten to modify the Boot.ini file to point at the secondary volume.

A fault tolerant boot floppy also comes in handy if you experience problems with the MBR or boot sector on a server that prevents the machine from booting. Viruses are one common cause for this problem.

A fault tolerant boot floppy does not boot Windows Server 2003 on a floppy. It uses the system files that are normally found at the root of the hard drive to bring up the
operating system.

Procedure 14.14 shows a brief set of steps for creating a fault tolerant boot floppy. Chapter 3, "Adding Hardware," contains information about ARC paths and Boot.ini entries.

Procedure 14.14 Building a Fault Tolerant Boot Floppy

1. Format a floppy. You cannot use a preformatted floppy because the boot sector must look for Ntldr. You can use a disk formatted on an NT4 machine.
2. Copy the system files to the root of the A: drive. These files are as follows:
   - Ntldr
   - Ntdetect.com
   - Boot.ini
   - Ntbootdd.sys (if required)
3. Use `ATTRIB` to remove the read-only attribute from Boot.ini.
4. Edit the Boot.ini file on the floppy to include the ARC path of the boot volume on the second drive. This would look something like this:

   ```
   multi(0)disk(0)rdisk(1)partition(1)\Windows="Windows Server 2003 Mirrored
   Secondary Disk" /fastdetect
   ```

   You might also want to change the time setting to `[ms]1`. This disables the counter.
5. Restart the computer and boot from the fault tolerant boot floppy.
6. When the Boot menu appears, select the second disk. The system will boot from the secondary disk. At this point, the floppy is no longer needed. Remove it from the drive.

Replacing a Failed Disk in a Mirrored Volume

If you lose a disk that is part of a mirrored volume, the system responds as it did for a failed disk in a RAID 5 volume. When the system attempts to write to the volume and fails to get a response from the disk, the `FT Orphan` process disconnects the system from the drive and announces this via a System Tray icon. The `FT Orphan` process locks the Registry on the failed drive, if possible, so that even if you get the drive back in service, the system will refuse to load the operating system from it.

When you open the Disk Management console following the drive failure, you'll get a display like that in Figure 14.9. The failed drive has a `Missing` status. The mirrored volume shows a `Failed Redundancy` status. The secondary drive moves to the top of the drive list. This may be different in your system, depending on your SCSI ID configuration.

As you can see by the figure, it can be difficult to determine exactly which drive failed. Keep careful records of the SCSI IDs or IDE controller numbers.

As with the RAID 5 failure, you do not need to take immediate corrective action. As many administrators will attest, however, you take a big chance if you wait too long.

Obtain a new disk that is at least the size of the one you're replacing. Configure it for the same SCSI ID or IDE master/slave configuration to simplify recovery. When you're ready to replace the drive, follow Procedure 14.15.

Procedure 14.15 Replacing a Failed Disk in a Mirrored Volume

1. Down the server and replace the drive.
2. Restart and boot using a fault tolerant boot floppy. If you replaced the drive using the same SCSI ID, pick the Boot.ini menu item corresponding to the original `rdisk()` value of the secondary drive. If you used a different SCSI ID, you need to figure out the `rdisk()` value based on the SCSI scan order. Use your SCSI adapter's configuration utility to see the scan order, then modify the Boot.ini file on the fault tolerant boot floppy accordingly.
3. After the operating system finishes loading, open the `Disk Management` console. The new drive does not have a fault tolerant signature or a copy of the LDM database, so an Initialize and Convert Disk Wizard opens to walk you through applying the signature and converting the disk to a dynamic disk.

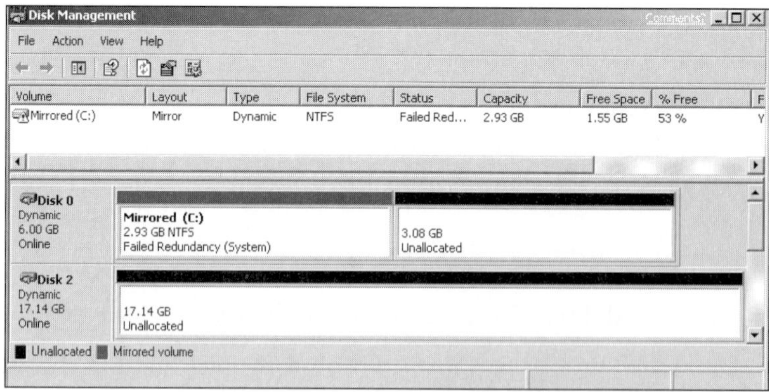

Figure 14.9 Disk Management console showing failed primary drive in a mirrored volume.

4. Once you've completed the Wizard, the Disk Management console is visible. You might be surprised to see that the old disk still appears in the display along with the new disk. This is to remind you of the original configuration. Figure 14.10 shows an example.
5. Right-click the mirrored volume and select REMOVE MIRROR from the flyout menu. The Remove Mirror window opens.
6. Select the missing disk from the list and click `Remove Mirror`. The system prompts for verification. Click `Yes`. The remaining disk now shows a `Healthy` status.
7. Right-click the status block for the missing disk and select REMOVE DISK from the flyout menu. The disk disappears immediately.
8. If you have verified that the new primary disk is bootable, remirror the volume to the new drive using the instructions in Procedure 14.8, "Creating Mirrored Volumes." If the new primary disk is not bootable, you'll need to get a good backup and then reinstall the operating system and recover from tape to get a bootable primary disk. After this is done, remirror the volume.

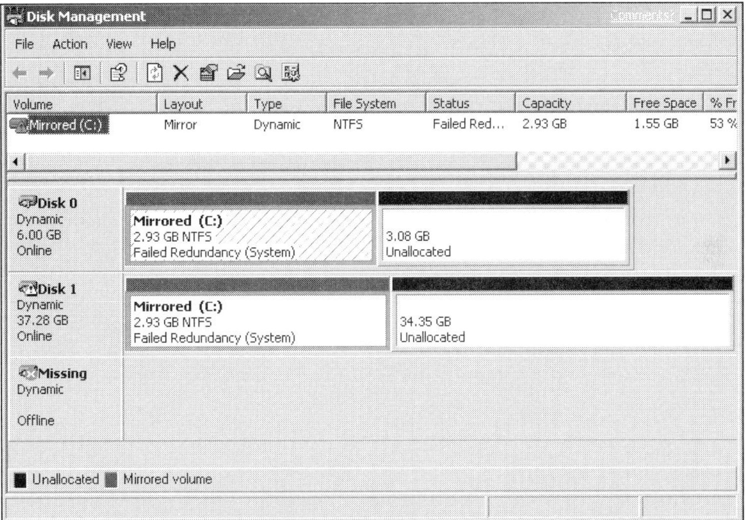

Figure 14.10 Disk Management console following disk replacement of a failed mirrored drive prior to regenerating the new disk.

Moving Dynamic Disks Between Computers

It sometimes happens that a server or workstation goes to that big byte bucket in the sky. (This usually happens about a half hour before your plane is due to leave on that vacation you've been planning for the past year.) If the problem is not with the storage system, one quick recovery method that might get you to the plane on time is to move the data disks to a new machine.

Moving disks between machines can cause other problems. Windows Server 2003 has a lot of information in the Registry that is hardware-dependent. If you move the boot disk (the disk with the operating system files) to a different platform, expect to see lots of Plug and Play (PnP) activity when you start the machine. You may need to supply hardware drivers. You may get blue screen stop errors if the memory management subsystem cannot interpret the chipset or memory configuration. You will certainly get a failure if the new server requires a different Hardware Abstraction Layer (HAL).

Moving data disks between machines is a much simpler matter. If the disk is a basic disk, the system sees the new disk, reads the partition table, and assigns the next available drive letters to any partitions it finds.

Moving dynamic disks, however, especially dynamic disks that contain volumes that span disks, is a bit more complicated. You'll need to merge the LDM database entries for the disks into the LDM database of the machine where you install them.

The operating system identifies disks with an outside disk group name as *foreign disks*. The purpose of the steps shown in Procedure 14.16 is to import the LDM information on those disks so that the disk group name can be changed and the system will accept the new entries.

Procedure 14.16 Moving a Fault Tolerant Volume to Another Computer

1. Down the two servers and transfer the drives. You might have to make room for new drives. You might need to rework the terminators and assign new SCSI IDs and so forth. The objective is to keep the drives together, if possible, although this is not absolutely necessary.
2. After the drives have been installed, test them to make sure that they are connected and that you know the order of their installation. The LDM permits the sequence of disks to be changed, but you make your job more difficult if the Disk Management console display has the foreign disks distributed willy-nilly.
3. Boot the operating system and make sure that the system loads. The data on the new drives will not be available until you import the disks. Also, any share points you have for directories on the drives will need to be recreated.
4. Open the `Disk Management` console. After initialization, the graphical display looks something like that in Figure 14.11. The disks from the other computer are flagged as `Foreign`.
5. Right-click the status block of the foreign disk or disks and select IMPORT FOREIGN DISKS from the flyout menu. The Import Foreign Disks window opens showing the name of the original server from where the disks came. This information comes from the LDM database at the end of the disks.

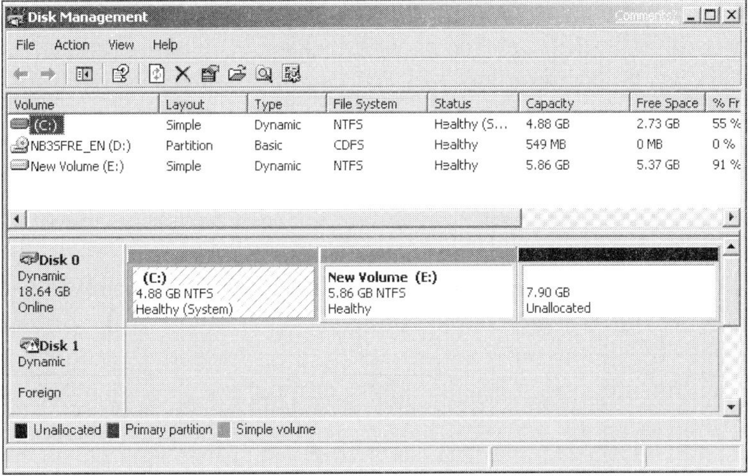

Figure 14.11 Disk Management console showing a dynamic disk moved from another machine and introduced into a new machine as a foreign disk.

6. Click `OK`. The system analyzes the disks, and then the Verify Volumes on Foreign Disks window opens.

   The system may report the `Data Condition` as `Data Incomplete`. This indicates that you did not move all the disks in the disk group. This is expected if the boot/system disk in the original server was a dynamic disk, or if there were other dynamic disks in the original server that you intentionally didn't move. Make sure that you have all the disks that are in the shared volume. You are permitted to move a subset of a disk group, but you'll need to do a few more steps.

7. Click `OK`. The system warns you that it might not be able to recover data if you had a `Data Incomplete` status in the preceding window.
8. Click `OK` to acknowledge the warning. The system imports the disks and then attempts to build the volumes and initialize the file system. The status may go to `Failed` on the disks. Don't worry (at least not yet). This is normal if you did not include all disks in the disk group in the transfer.
9. Right-click the status block for any of the new disks and select Reactivate Disk from the flyout menu. The system will think a long time and you'll hear lots of disk activity. If the reactivation is successful, a drive letter for the volume appears and the status changes to `Regenerating`. This regeneration takes a long time and consumes many CPU cycles. The file system is active during this time and you can access files, but this is not recommended because it slows down regeneration. After regeneration has completed, the new volumes show a status of `Healthy`.

10. There is a chance that any existing dynamic disks in the new machine will show an `Error` status after the import in the status block of the disk. This is because their copy of the LDM database has values that they cannot interpret. If this happens, right-click the status block for the disk and select REACTIVATE DISK from the fly-out menu. This should immediately correct the problem.

Working with GPT Disks

As I mentioned at the start of this chapter, the Itanium platform uses a new disk partitioning scheme called GUID Partition Tables, or GPTs. This new scheme was developed to address several shortcomings of the classic MBR approach:

- An MBR disk can have only four primary partitions.
- The maximum partition size is limited by a truncated Cylinder/Head/Sector geometry notation.
- There is no coordination between the various partition schemes. This causes a problem for disk utility vendors who must anticipate how a particular scheme will align with cylinder boundaries for both bare disks and virtual disks presented by RAID controllers.
- MBR disks have spawned a generation of utilities and operating systems that use hidden sectors containing critical storage parameters and components.
- A disk holds a single copy of the MBR, making it a single point of failure if the sector should go bad.

Chapter 1, "Installing and Configuring Windows Server 2003," tells how to use Setup to initially partition a GPT disk for Windows Server 2003, and Chapter 3, "Adding Hardware," contains the details for installing and configuring new GPT disks. This topic contains general information that compares GPT disk operation to MBR disks.

GPT Improvements

GPT disks address the classic MBR limitations by replacing the system entirely. A GPT disk does have a classic MBR on the first sector, but it is there purely as a protective measure. Standard disk utilities would interpret the lack of an MBR as a lack of partitioning and would possibly automatically repartition the drive, causing a loss of the GPT-based data.

In place of the classic MBR, a GPT disk uses a database to track partition identities and locations. The database identifies specific partition types by a Globally Unique Identifier, or GUID, hence the name. A vendor can define a new partition type by creating a GUID and be confident that the number has not been preempted by another vendor.

GPT disks have the following advantages over MBR disks:

- Partitions start at sector boundaries, not cylinder boundaries. This greatly simplifies interoperability between drives in the same machine.
- GPT disks can have 128 partitions.
- A single partition can be up to 18 exabytes, equivalent to having just under 19 million one-terabyte disk arrays connected together.
- Each GPT partition entry is copied for redundancy. In addition, a Cyclic Redundancy Check (CRC) value is stored along with the partition data to check for corruption.
- All data is stored in defined partitions. The operating system hides partitions used for purposes other than storing user data.

You can have MBR disks on an Itanium system, but you must boot to a GPT disk. The Extensible Firmware Interface (EFI) on an Itanium system expects to find OS loader information on the boot drive. Allowance was made in the EFI specification to permit storing this information on an MBR disk, but Windows Server 2003 and XP will only boot from an EFI disk.

You can convert an MBR disk to a GPT disk and vice-versa, but you must remove all existing partitioning, which causes a loss of data if you do not have a backup. Note that this operation is *not* the same as converting a basic disk to a dynamic disk. GPT partitions are not contained in the Logical Disk Manager database until the disk is converted to a dynamic disk.

GPT Format

Figure 14.12 shows the default partitions on a GPT boot disk. Here is a description of each element.

EFI System Partition (ESP)

The ESP holds the bootstrap files for any operating systems that are installed on the drive. The IA64 bootstrap files in Windows Server 2003 are Ia64ldr.efi and Fpswa.efi. The .efi extension designates executable code in the Extended Firmware Interface. The Fpswa.efi file contains floating-point information used by the operating system. Chapter 3, "Adding Hardware," has information on installing and formatting a GPT disk. Here are some points to remember about the ESP:

- If the ESP is created by Windows Server 2003 Setup, the ESP is given one percent of the disk size up to 100MB. The one-percent value is not recalculated if additional storage is added via hardware RAID.
- The ESP cannot be mirrored, striped, extended, or spanned.

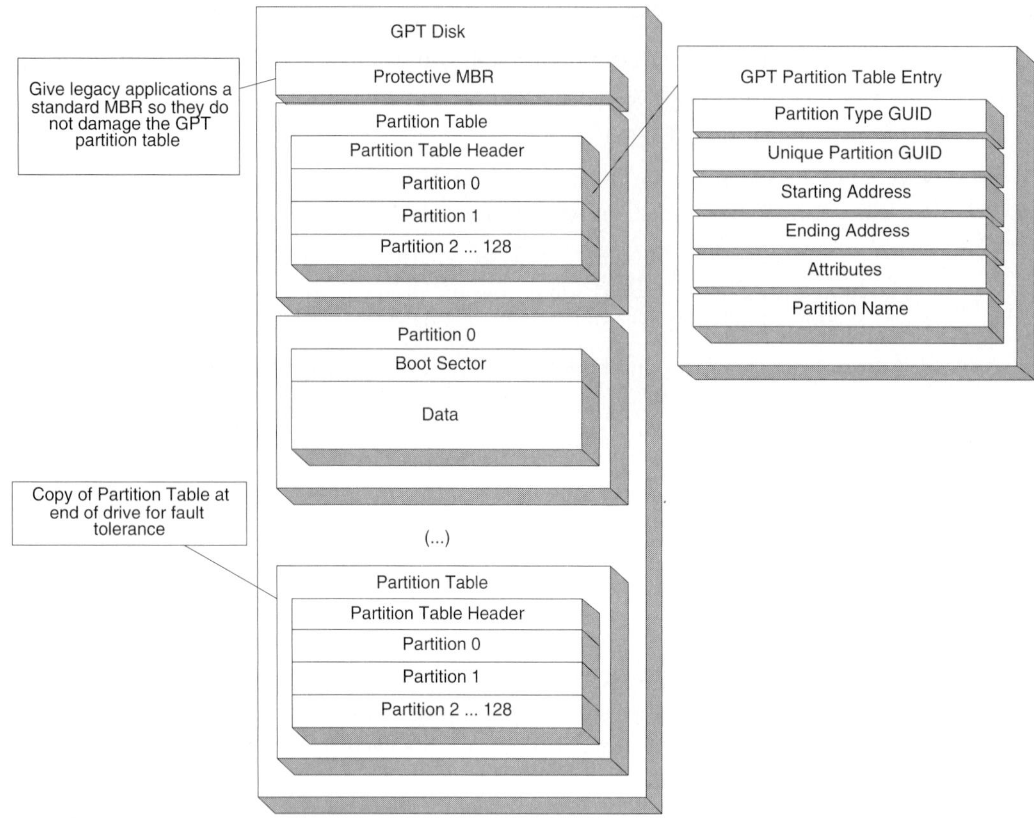

Figure 14.12 Diagram of GPT disk layout.

- The ESP should be the first partition so that it does not interfere with converting the disk to a dynamic disk. A GPT disk cannot be converted to a dynamic disk if the EFS is nestled between two data partitions.
- System vendors are encouraged to place their diagnostic and value-add files in their own partition, called an *OEM partition*, and not in the ESP. Microsoft is not a system vendor and places disk utilities in an MSUTIL folder at the root of the ESP.
- The ESP is formatted as FAT. Unlike other FAT-formatted partitions, the ESP is not given a drive letter by Windows and does not appear in the Disk Management console. However, you can view the contents of the ESP using the MOUNTVOL utility with the following command: `mountvol <drive_letter> /s`.

Microsoft Reserved Partition (MSR)

This partition sets aside space for Microsoft to use for specialized structures. For example, the Logical Disk Manager (LDM) database is put into the MSR. Other operating system vendors can create similar partitions. Here are the key points concerning MSR partitions:

- Like the ESP, the MSR should be created ahead of data partitions so that the disk can be converted to a dynamic disk, if desired. On a disk partitioned by Windows Server 2003 Setup, the MSR will be the second partition.
- The MSR is 32MB for disks less than 16GB and 128MB for [ge]16GB.
- The MSR does not use a recognizable file system. It contains data structures only understood by Windows Server 2003 system services.
- Users and administrators cannot view the MSR.

OEM Specific Partitions

A hardware vendor can create a partition to hold diagnostic and setup applications. This is similar to how Compaq handles their Smart Start suite of utilities.

The vendor is responsible for generating the GUID for its partitions and for creating and formatting its OEM partition on a GPT disk prior to shipment. Ordinarily, users and administrators cannot view the contents of an OEM partition. It is only accessible via tools supplied by the vendor.

Data Partitions

This partition type contains user data, which includes the operating system files. You can create additional data partitions. All data partitions must be contiguous for a GPT disk to be converted to a dynamic disk.

Microsoft data partitions can be formatted in Windows Server 2003 using any of the three supported formatting options: FAT, FAT32, or NTFS.

If you have operating systems other than Windows installed in other partitions, Windows might not be able to recognize the file systems. Partitions containing recognizable file systems are assigned drive letters.

GPT Requirements

The following restrictions apply when managing GPT disks:

- Only the IA64 version of Windows Server 2003 can read GPT disks.
- GPT disks can only be created on fixed spinning storage. You must use MBR partitioning for detachable disk drives and removable platter drives. For this reason, you cannot boot an Itanium machine to a Firewire drive as you can with an IA32 machine.

- You cannot use disk-imaging programs on GPT disks. This would result in a clone of the GUID. An OEM Preinstallation Kit (OPK) supplied by Microsoft supports cloning by zeroing out the GUIDs then initializing them during a mini-setup when the machine is first started.
- The boot disk for an IA64 system must be a GPT disk. Other disks in an IA64 system can be MBR or GPT.
- An MBR disk cannot be upgraded to a GPT disk. You must delete all legacy MBR partitions, then create a new GPT partition table.

Working with GPT Disks

Just like an IA32 system, the primary Windows Server 2003 tool for accessing and managing a GPT disk is the Disk Management console. The console is coded to create GPT partitions on a GPT disk and MBR partitions on an MBR disk. The Disk Management console on an IA32 system cannot be used to manage GPT disks across the network.

If you prefer a command-line tool, the IA64 version of the Diskpart utility in Windows Server 2003 can read and modify the configuration of a GPT disk. You can also use Diskpart to create an EPS and MSR partition on another drive. If you boot in to firmware, the EFI Shell has the ability to partition a GPT disk. Chapter 3, "Adding Hardware," provides the steps.

The big advantage of having a GPT disk over having an MBR disk is the partitioning flexibility afforded by the GPT partition table. You can create up to 128 partitions on a GPT basic disk. Figure 14.13 shows the Disk Management console for a basic GPT disk with over 40 partitions.

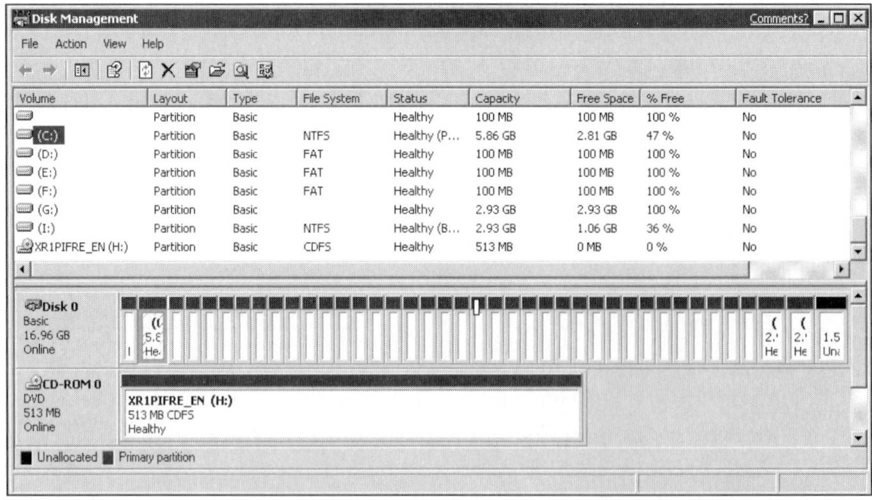

Figure 14.13 Disk Management console from an IA64 system showing how you can create many partitions on a basic disk.

If you want to have more sophisticated configurations with striping, RAID 5, or mirroring, you must convert the GPT basic disk to a dynamic disk. This replaces the GPT partition table with an LDM database stored in the Microsoft Reserved Partition. The LDM service operates the same on an IA64 system as it does on an IA32 system. The same fault tolerant configurations are permitted, and the same procedure is used to transfer disks between systems. The only LDM restrictions unique to a GPT disk are as follows:

- All basic data partitions must be contiguous.
- A GPT boot disk cannot be mirrored to an MBR disk.
- The EFI System Partition (ESP) cannot be mirrored.

Moving Forward

Now that the disk storage is in place, it's time to configure a file system. The next chapter covers how to configure and manage the three file systems in Windows Server 2003: FAT, FAT32, and NTFS. Subsequent chapters deal with standard file system security and the Encrypting File System (EFS).

15

Managing File Systems

IN THE LAST CHAPTER, WE SAW HOW to partition off raw storage on spinning media. This is a little like real estate developers who buy raw acreage out in sunny southern New Mexico. Sure, the acreage might have a beautiful view of the old Titan missile sites and dry alkali lakes, but the developers won't be able to convince Easterners to buy any property on this acreage until they section it off into plats and install some basic infrastructure like water and electricity and sewers and high-speed Internet connections.

For data storage, this sectioning and infrastructure development comes in the form of a file system. Windows Server 2003, like its predecessors, uses modular Installable File System (IFS) drivers to turn raw storage into an accessible data repository. Here are the file systems and their drivers:

- **NT File System (Ntfs.sys).** This is Microsoft's premier file system and the default file system on all Windows Server 2003 and XP platforms.
- **Encrypting File System (Efs.sys).** This driver sits above the NTFS driver and handles file encryption/decryption.
- **FAT and FAT32 (Fastfat.sys).** Windows Server 2003 supports both of these legacy file systems.
- **CD-ROM (Cdfs.sys).** This file system supports ISO 9660 disks, which includes CD-ROM, CD-R, and CD-RW disks. It can read both regular 700MB disks and extended 850MB disks.
- **Universal Disk Format (Udfs.sys).** This file system supports DVD drives. It can read Universal Data Format (UDF) formatted disks and FAT32 disks.
- **Remote Storage Services (RSS) driver (Rsfilter.sys).** This file system provides near-online access to files stored on tape as part of a hierarchical storage management system. The Rsfilter driver is only loaded if you install RSS.

- **File System Recognizer (Fs_rec.sys).** This driver figures out which file system to use when accessing a particular drive or media.

Network interfaces are also implemented as IFS file system drivers. This includes LanMan Server, LanMan Workstation, Microsoft's NetWare Client, the Mailslot and Named Pipe file systems, and the new WebDAV (Web-based Distributed Authoring and Versioning) redirector. These services are covered in Chapter 19, "Managing the User Operating Environment."

This chapter contains detailed functional and operational descriptions of the three core Windows Server 2003 file systems: FAT16, FAT32, and NTFS. This includes new features in the upgraded version of NTFS. (See the sidebar, "NTFS Versions.")

Operational topics at the end of the chapter contain step-by-step instructions for configuring and managing the following file system features:

- Converting from FAT/FAT32 to NTFS
- Compression
- Reparse points and mount points
- Distributed Link Tracking
- Disk Defragmentation
- Indexing
- Formatting and writing CD-R/RW and DVD-RAM media (a new feature in Windows Server 2003 and XP)

IFS References

For more information about file system design, I highly recommend *Developing Windows NT Device Drivers* by Edward Dekker and Joseph Newcomer.

NTFS Versions

For many years, most tech writers, myself included, used the same version number for NTFS as the associated NT version. This was done purely for convenience. The actual internal NTFS version number was generally of interest only to developers.

That changed in Windows Server 2003 because Microsoft included a new utility called Fsutil that shows lots of great information about the file system, including the internal NTFS version number.

So, at the risk of adding confusion to what is already a pretty confusing topic, I will use the internal version number throughout this chapter. Here are the internal NTFS version numbers broken down by NT/Windows version:

- NT 3.x – NTFS 1.0
- NT 4.0 – NTFS 1.2
- Windows 2000 – NTFS 3.0
- Windows Server 2003/XP – NTFS 3.1

New Features in Windows Server 2003

Version 3.1 of the NTFS file system changed the location of the Master File Table and two metadata files and modified the header information in the file records. This was done to improve performance.

When you upgrade a Windows 2000 or NT machine, any existing NTFS volumes are upgraded to NTFS 3.1. You are not asked for permission and there is no workaround. If you dual-boot between operating systems, make sure you are running NT4 SP6a or Windows 2000 SP1 or later. If you fail to take this precaution, you risk getting blue screen stops when attempting to boot in to the earlier operating system.

The following additional new file system features have been added or modified in Windows Server 2003:

- **Improved defragmentation.** There is now a command-line version of the defragmenter that can be scheduled. The new defragmenter can also defrag the Master File Table (MFT), which can dramatically improve performance.
- **Improved performance.** The system automatically places critical system files at strategic locations on the drive. It also periodically relocates commonly used files to improve performance.
- **Improved NTFS conversions.** The processes for creating and converting FAT and FAT32 partitions to NTFS have been reworked to minimize fragmentation and speed up conversion. Also, the conversion assigns restrictive permissions to the converted files rather than giving full access to the Everyone group. This enhances security for converted volumes.
- **File prefetch.** In Windows Server 2003 and XP, when an executable is opened, a record of the linked DLLs is stored in the `\Windows\Prefetch` folder inside a file with a .pf extension. The system also keeps track of how often the file is launched. Every three days, the system jockeys executable files around on the volume to pack the most commonly used files at the front. It also defrags them to make sure they load as quickly as possible.
- **Short file names preserved.** In previous versions of Windows, when you do a tape backup or a file copy, the short file names associated with the files and folders are not included in the backup. When you do a tape restore, the short names are regenerated. This can cause problems for applications that expect to see a particular file name. In Windows Server 2003, the backup API includes the original short name.
- **Writable CD/DVD support.** Microsoft licensed technology from Roxio (a spin-off from Adaptec) that permits writing data directly to CDs and DVDs. This is not a full-blown packet-writing engine, as you may be accustomed to seeing in third-party products, but it does make it fairly simple to drag and drop files onto a CD-R or CD-RW or DVD-RAM drive.

- **Posix support.** After being the red-headed stepchild of alternative Windows NT operating consoles for the longest time, Microsoft finally moved Posix completely out of the core operating system. Posix support is available for Windows Server 2003 as a fee-based add-on called Microsoft Interix. The current version of Interix is 2.2.
- **Improved WebDAV support.** Windows 2000 introduced the capability of doing network file transfers using HTTP rather than SMB. This implements an emerging set of technologies called *Web-based Distributed Authoring and Versioning*, or WebDAV. The WebDAV support in Windows Server 2003 and XP improved considerably thanks to the introduction of a dedicated redirector. Also, file property information used by WebDAV is now stored in named data streams inside the NTFS file record.

If you are currently an NT administrator, here is a list of NTFS 3.0 features introduced in Windows 2000 and covered in this chapter:

- **Consolidated security descriptors.** NTFS files and folders are protected by security descriptors that control access and define the operations that can be performed. Starting with NTFS 3.0, the security descriptors were moved from a resident attribute in the individual MFT records out to a separate database. This improved performance and simplified the file system operations required to support permission inheritance.
- **Distributed Link Tracking.** Files that are the object of shortcuts or other object linking and embedding (OLE) links are tracked down automatically if they are moved. This works both on the local system and if the file is moved to another computer in the domain.
- **Reparse points.** Enables mounting local volumes and devices regardless of their format, such as CD and DVD drives or even tape drives, as a folder on an existing volume. When you open the folder containing the reparse point, the system opens the target volume or device instead.
- **Quota Tracking.** Permits limiting the total space on a volume that a user can have when saving data.
- **Change Journal.** Provides a quick way for applications to find out if files have been modified. This feature is used by the Content Indexing service, the File Replication service, and the Volume Shadow Copy service.
- **Encrypting File System.** Allows encrypting files so that only the user who encrypted them and selected administrators can read them. See Chapter 17, "Managing File Encryption," for more information.
- **Sparse files.** This feature permits applications to keep large files while not actually using all of the requested space.
- **Content indexing.** This feature creates catalog files that speed up searches for words and phrases. The catalogs are available to network clients as well as local users.

Finally, if you have been working with FAT or FAT32 exclusively and Windows Server 2003 or XP is your first introduction to NTFS, this chapter covers these legacy NTFS features:

- **Short filename generation.** For backward compatibility with DOS applications and clients, the file system automatically generates a short (8.3) filename when a file or folder has a long name. The short-name algorithm is different than Windows 9x.
- **Compression.** In NTFS, individual files and folders can be selectively compressed. The system decompresses them on-the-fly when they are accessed.
- **Named data streams.** An NTFS file can store more than one discrete set of data in the same file record. The standard notion of "data" in a file is stored in a default, unnamed data stream. Additional data streams are identified by name. Many Windows Server 2003 features take advantage of this capability.
- **Journaling.** The NTFS file system protects critical system files by saving the changes to a log file first then committing them to the file system records at a later time.

Overview of Windows Server 2003 File Systems

A file system is a little like a commercial real estate agent. It acts as a broker between a lessor who has space available and a lessee who wants that space. In the case of a file system, the storage system determines what space is available, and applications are the lessees that want a piece of that space.

As administrators, we need to know enough about the elements of a file system transaction so we can spec out our storage needs and anticipate where problems might occur. This means we need to know details about certain disk structures that support file system operations:

- **Sectors.** These form the basic divisions of data on a disk. Sector location is determined by the disk geometry and is fixed by the manufacturer. Drives made for the U.S. market generally have 512-byte sectors.
- **Clusters.** The file system assigns addresses to clusters, which represent groups of sectors. By lumping sectors into clusters, the file system reduces the size of the address space it must track.
- **Partitions and volumes.** Raw storage on a drive is divided into partitions, each of which can be mounted by a separate file system. An IA32 system uses a Master Boot Record (MBR) to assign partitions on a basic disk. An IA64 system can use GUID Partition Table (GPT) or MBR partitioning for basic disks. Dynamic disks on either system are handled by the Logical Disk Manager (LDM), which uses a database to divide disk arrays into volumes. From the file system's perspective, these partitions and volumes all represent the same thing: a place to store files.

- **Partition boot sector.** This is the first sector of a partition. It contains information about the file system and a small amount of bootstrap code to start loading the file system.

To see how a file system turns raw storage into a data repository, we need to know a little about the structures that hold critical information. They are as follows:

- **Files.** These are addressable locations in a partition where discrete chunks of user data are stored. A file has a name and attributes that determine its contents.
- **Folders.** A folder is an index of filenames. Folders give structure to a file system, creating a hierarchy that makes it easier to locate individual files.
- **File Allocation Table (FAT).** This is a map of the clusters in a partition that has been formatted as FAT or FAT32. The file system uses the cluster map to locate files and folders.
- **Master File Table (MFT).** This is a database containing information about the file system elements stored in a partition that has been formatted as NTFS.
- **MFT metadata records.** These are special NTFS records that store information about the structure of the MFT itself and provide support for critical file system operations.

From an operational perspective, we need to know what each file system can do, what it can't do, and what to use as criteria when choosing between them. Let's start with storage details. (See the following sidebar, "More Information About File Systems.")

Sectors and Clusters

A hard drive stores data in concentric tracks that are divided into addressable units called *sectors* (see Figure 15.1). In most Western drives, a sector contains 512 bytes.

When a file system asks for data from a storage driver, it must specify the location of that data in relation to the start of the volume. The storage driver then works with the device controller to move the drive heads to the designated location, pick up the required information (plus a little extra for the cache), buffer the information, and deliver it to the file system driver.

A sector is the smallest addressable unit on a drive. Ideally, a file system would assign an address to every sector in a partition. This yields the best utilization, because any space left over between the end of a file and the end of the last sector holding the file is wasted.

At some point, though, a volume may contain so many sectors that the cost of maintaining addresses for all of them starts to become a burden and performance goes down. To improve performance, the file system clumps individual sectors into *allocation units*, or *clusters*.

More Information About File Systems

When I wrote about file systems for the predecessor to this book, *Inside Windows 2000 Server*, I did all of the investigative work myself. This involved many tedious hours studying hex dumps of disk structures. I was forced to do this because Microsoft has steadfastly refused to publish a specification for NTFS. Some information has dribbled out of Redmond over the years in the form of white papers and Resource Kit articles, but specific engineering details are tough to come by.

For this book, I benefited a great deal from work done in the Open Source community, specifically by the participants in the Linux-NTFS project. If you want to see details of NTFS data structures along with information about other exciting work in the cross-platform storage arena, visit `linux-ntfs.sourceforge.net`.

I also got great information about the on-disk structures of NTFS from the book *Windows NT/2000 Native API Reference* by Gary Nebbett. This is a great reference for anyone trying to understand the inner workings of Windows.

For details about the disk structures for FAT and FAT32, I recommend reading the Microsoft white paper, "FAT: General Overview of On-Disk Structure," available at `www.nondot.org/sabre/os/files/FileSystems`. This site is a good place to start when researching information about just about any file system.

For authoritative, high-level explanations of the workings of NTFS, I recommend reading "Inside Windows 2000" by David Solomon and Mark Russinovich, plus any of Mr. Russinovich's NTFS articles in *Windows 2000 Magazine* and other periodicals.

The Resource Kit also has a very good exposition on the Windows Server 2003 file systems. Someday perhaps Microsoft will allow the Resource Kit writers to include engineering specifications, as well.

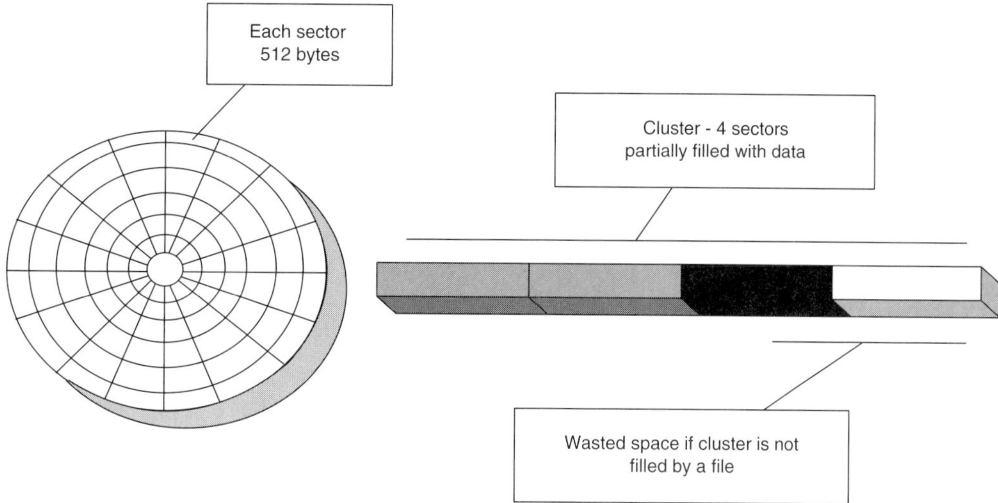

Figure 15.1 Diagram of sectors and clusters on a hard drive.

A cluster contains an even multiple of sectors. This is called the *cluster size*. Clusters come in increasing powers of 2, yielding cluster sizes of 512 bytes, 1K, 2K, 4K, 16K, 32K, and 64K. The maximum cluster size supported by any file system that ships with Windows Server 2003 is 64K.

If the end of a file does not completely fill its assigned cluster, the excess space is wasted. Windows does not provide sub-allocation of sectors within a cluster. This means cluster size has a direct impact on disk utilization. For example, I've seen instances where nearly 25 percent of the available space on a volume was reclaimed by converting a large, heavily loaded FAT volume formatted with 32K clusters into an NTFS volume with 512-byte clusters.

It is beneficial in some instances to match cluster size to average file size. A volume that holds hundreds of thousands of small files should have a small cluster size. That seems obvious. But a volume that holds a few, very large files (database files, for example) can benefit from the improved efficiencies of large cluster sizes. For the most part, though, letting Windows decide on a cluster size when formatting a volume usually yields optimal performance.

Changing cluster sizes requires reformatting. If you decide to increase the cluster size on a big array for a database server, you'll need to back up your data, reformat the array with a different cluster size, and then restore the data from tape.

Each of the three file systems in Windows Server 2003 uses 512-byte clusters up to a certain volume size. Beyond that, behavior differs. For FAT, cluster size doubles each time volume size doubles. FAT32 and NTFS keep cluster sizes at 4K for as long as possible. Table 15.1 lists the default cluster sizes for each file system based on volume size.

The 4K plateau on NTFS cluster sizes is there because the compression API does not work with cluster sizes above 4K. FAT32 is seen as an intermediate stage prior to converting to NTFS, so FAT32 cluster sizes are also constrained to 4K as long as possible.

Table 15.1 Cluster Sizes as a Function of File System and Volume Size

Volume Size	FAT	FAT32	NTFS
<32MB	512b	N/A	512b
64MB	1K	512b	512b
128MB	2K	1K	512b
256MB	4K	2K	512b
512MB	8K	4K	512b
1GB	16K	4K	1K
2GB	32K	4K	2K
4GB	64K	4K	4K
8GB	N/A	4K	4K
16GB	N/A	8K	4K
32GB	N/A	16K	4K
>32GB	N/A	N/A	4K

Cluster Size and Stripe Size

Cluster sizes are not related to the underlying data buffers used by Logical Disk Manager. This is often referred to as *stripe size* in hardware RAID. LDM always moves data to and from a drive in 64K chunks regardless of the cluster size.

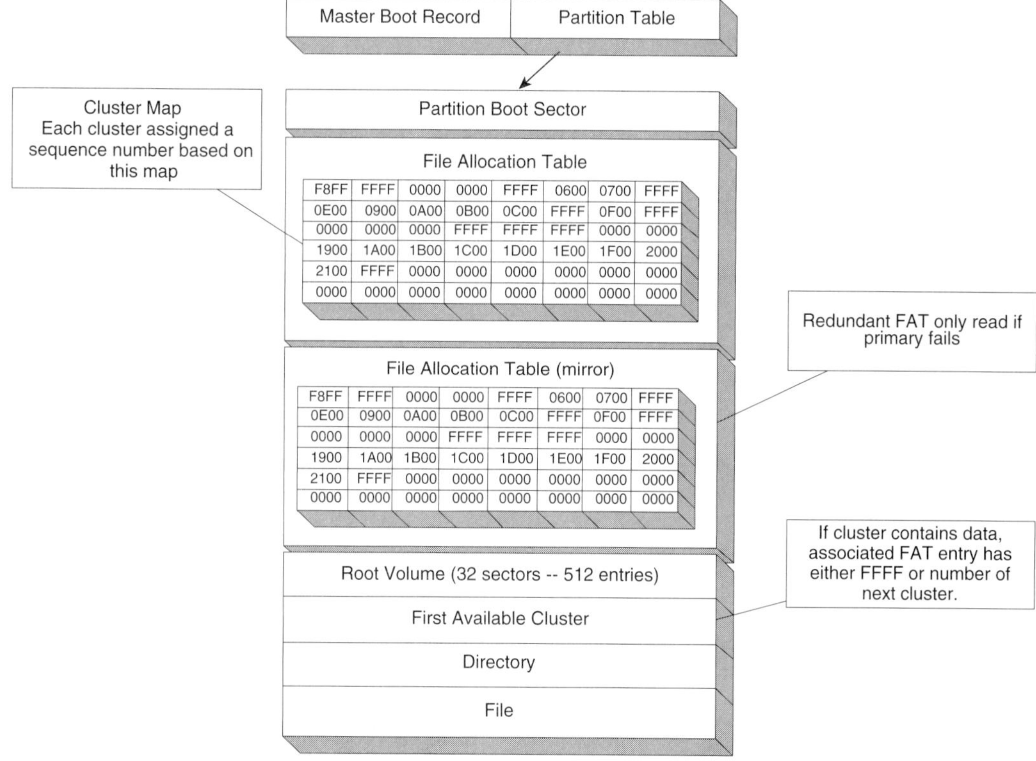

Figure 15.2 Diagram of FAT layout on a typical partition.

Historically, the defragmentation API was another reason for limiting the maximum NTFS cluster size to 4K. As we'll see in section, "Defragmentation," Windows Server 2003 and XP now permit defragmenting volumes with cluster sizes above 4K.

FAT File System Structure

Figure 15.2 shows the layout of the first few sectors on a disk that is formatted with FAT. The partition boot sector has an entry that identifies the format type and the location of the FAT and the mirrored FAT. Ordinarily, the FAT is located near the front of the disk to benefit from the fast read times there. (Tracks at the outside of a disk have a higher terminal velocity.)

The Fastfat.sys driver in Windows Server 2003 supports three cluster numbering schemes:

- **FAT12.** This format uses 12 bits to identify a cluster. This is the original FAT format. It is quite compact so it is used for formatting floppies and volumes smaller than 16MB.

- **FAT16.** This format uses 16 bits for numbering clusters, which pegs the maximum volume size at 2^{16} (0xFFFF) or 65,535 clusters. (The actual size is 1 cluster smaller than the maximum theoretical size of 65,536.) Windows Server 2003 supports a maximum 64K cluster size for FAT16, making the largest FAT volume 65535 * 64K or 4GB. (Windows 9x and DOS only support a 32K cluster size—a power of 2 less than the total number of clusters—for a maximum volume size of 2GB.)
- **FAT32.** This format uses a long integer (32 bits) for cluster numbering. This would ordinarily permit a very large volume, but Windows Server 2003 limits FAT32 volumes to 32GB. Standard Windows 95 and classic NT cannot read FAT32 partitions.

There is also a special version of FAT32 called *FAT32x* used by Windows 9x and ME when formatting drives larger than 8GB. FAT32x overcomes a limitation of traditional Cylinder/Head/Sector translation by forcing the operating system to use Logical Block Addressing (LBA), which assigns a number to each available sector reported by the drive. LBA ups the ante for partition sizes to whatever the file system can handle. For FAT32, that limit is 2TB (terabytes).

FAT32x volumes store their FAT tables at the end of the volume rather than the beginning. This signals the operating system to use LBA. Windows Server 2003 can read a FAT32x volume but does not use FAT32x formatting because the Fastfat driver always uses LBA unless specifically told not to. If you upgrade a Windows 9x/ME system to XP, there is no indication in any of the command-line utilities or in the Disk Management console that a volume is formatted as FAT32x rather than FAT2. For more information, visit `www.win98private.net/fat32x.htm`.

Location and Use of FAT Disk Structures

FAT12 and FAT16 file systems require the FAT to start at the first available sector following the boot sector. MBR partitions generally have a few hidden sectors between the partition boot sector and the start of the file system. These hidden sectors are often used for inscrutable purposes. GPT disks used on IA64 systems have no hidden sectors.

The mirrored copy of the FAT must follow immediately after the primary FAT. This fixed location of the FAT tables in FAT12 and FAT16 is a weakness. A failed sector can make the file system inaccessible. This weakness is overcome by FAT32, which can locate the FAT anywhere, although it is generally still located at the front of the disk right after the boot sector.

The first entry in the FAT represents the root directory of the partition. The root directory is special because it is exactly 32 sectors long, enough room for 512 entries. For this reason, you can only put about 500 files and directories at the root of a FAT partition. As you are no doubt aware, FAT and FAT32 support long filenames by robbing directory entries. This can quickly absorb many directory entries if you use long filenames in the root directory, greatly limiting the total number of files and folders you can store at root.

The size of the FAT table itself is determined by the number of clusters in the partition. The larger the partition, the more entries are needed in the FAT. For example, the FAT on a 2GB partition with the default 32K cluster size would take up 128K of disk space. The FAT mirror would also use 128K. This is a pretty efficient use of disk space when compared with FAT32 and NTFS, but the payoff comes in reduced reliability, slower performance for some drive operations, performance degradation in the face of even minimal fragmentation, and the lack of security and journaling features.

Cluster Maps

The FAT is actually just a big cluster map where each cluster in the partition is represented by a 16-bit (2-byte) entry. If there are 65,535 clusters in the volume, there would be 65,535 2-byte entries in the FAT. (FAT12 packs the bits for storage economy.) Figure 15.3 shows the layout of a few cluster entries in a FAT16 table.

The first two FAT entries are reserved and represent the root of the partition. The next entry represents the first file or folder created in the volume. In the diagram, this cluster is empty because the original file or folder has been deleted.

An empty cluster has a value of 0000. When you create a file or folder, the file system selects an empty cluster and writes data to the disk in that location. If the file or folder spills over into another cluster, the value of the FAT entry for the first cluster contains the number of the next cluster. This is called a *cluster chain*. The final cluster assigned to a file is identified with an end-of-file marker, FFFF.

Ideally, each cluster used by a file comes directly after the preceding cluster on the disk. Such a file is said to be *contiguous*. When you delete a file or folder, the FAT entry is set to 0000. This indicates that the cluster is available. As you add and delete files, the file system reuses empty clusters. This results in *fragmentation*.

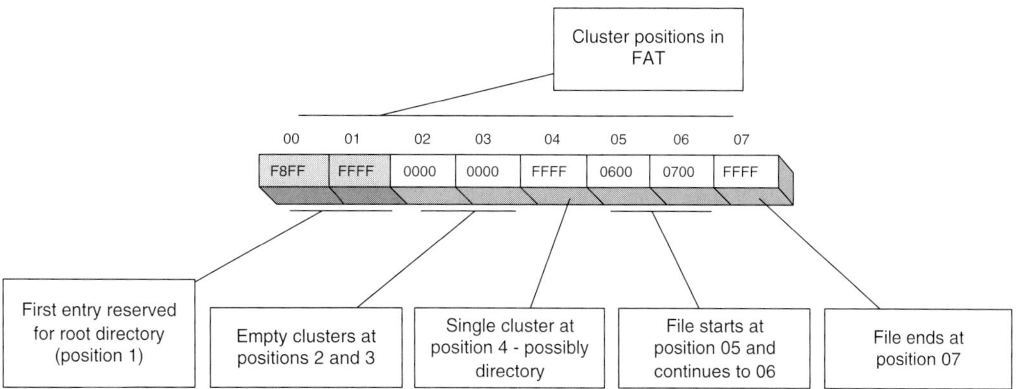

Figure 15.3 Diagram of typical FAT cluster mappings for a FAT16 file system.

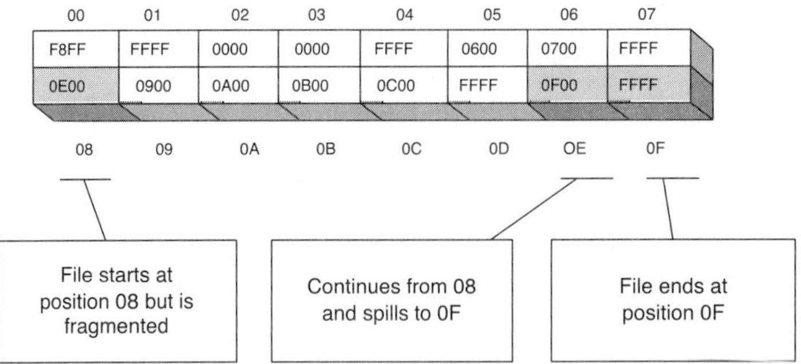

Figure 15.4 Cluster map for a fragmented file.

Figure 15.4 shows a portion of the FAT with a fragmented file. The cluster map shows a file that starts at cluster location 08. The file is too big to fit in one cluster and the next contiguous cluster already has a file in it. The file system driver selected the next available empty cluster and continued the file from there. Remember that the number in a FAT entry points at the next cluster in the chain, not the current cluster.

When the Fastfat driver delivers a file to the I/O Manager in the Windows Server 2003 Executive, it must "walk the chain" of FAT entries to locate all the cluster numbers associated with the file. The drive head must then travel out across the disk and buffer up the data, put it in order, then spool off the results to the guy upstairs. If the files and folders in the partition are heavily fragmented, it takes much more effort from the disk subsystem to collect the clusters. This impacts performance.

As we'll see, Windows Server 2003 and Windows 2000 have a built-in defragmentation utility that can put the FAT and the associated disk clusters back in apple-pie order. The same defragger is supplied in Windows Server 2003 and XP. You can schedule defragmentation in Windows Server 2003, something that required a third-party utility in Windows 2000.

FAT Directories

The file system cannot locate a file by its name simply by looking at the cluster map in the FAT. Finding a particular file by its name requires an index that shows the filename and the number of the first cluster in the file as listed in the FAT. That index is called a directory or a folder.

In addition to filenames, a FAT directory entry contains a single byte that defines the file's *attributes* (`Read-Only`, `Hidden`, `System`, and `Archive`) and a *timestamp* to show when the file was created. Directory entries are placed into a disk cluster just as if they were files. Figure 15.5 shows a diagram of disk clusters that contains a set of directory entries.

A directory entry can become fragmented like the example in the figure when the number of name entries exceeds the size of the cluster. This is another reason large FAT volumes need large cluster sizes.

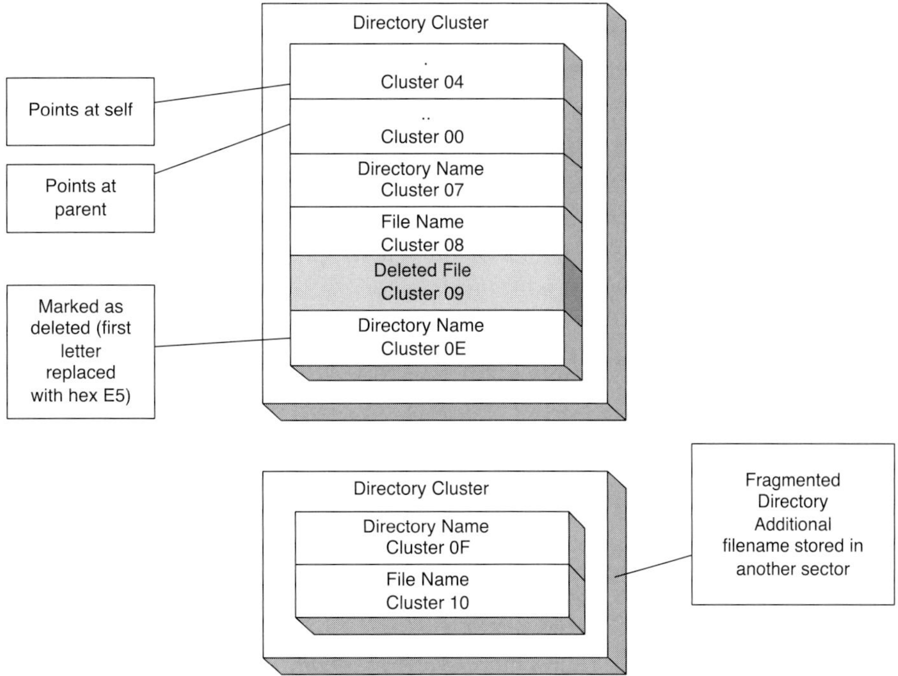

Figure 15.5 Disk clusters with fragmented directory entries.

If you add several files to a directory and the directory entry cannot grow into a contiguous cluster, the directory becomes fragmented. This significantly degrades performance. You can imagine the kind of work it takes for the file system to assemble fragmented directories and their linked files to display the results in Explorer.

FAT Partition and File Sizes

Due to real-mode memory limits, the cluster size for a FAT partition under DOS and Windows 9x is limited to a power of 2 less than the address limit. Therefore, the maximum cluster size is 2^{15} bytes, or 32KB. The maximum size of a FAT partition under DOS and Windows 95, then, is 65535 * 32KB, or about 2GB.

FAT under Windows Server 2003 (which boots into protected mode before the Fastfat file system driver loads) has a cluster size limit of 2^{16} bytes, or 64KB per cluster.

FAT supports 2^{16} clusters on a volume but it reserves 12 clusters for special use, leaving 65,534 clusters for storing files and folders. In practice, it is nearly impossible to select a partition size that would yield exactly the maximum size for a given cylinder alignment. Gaining a few clusters of theoretical capacity is not worth the effort.

The maximum partition size of a FAT partition on Windows Server 2003 (and any member of the NT family) is about 4GB (65,534 clusters at 64K per cluster). DOS and Windows 9x cannot access a partition with a cluster size larger than 32K, so avoid 64K clusters when running a dual-boot machine.

FAT file sizes are specified by a value in the directory entry. This value uses a 32-bit word, so file sizes are limited to 2^{32} bytes, or 4GB. The actual size is one byte shy of a full 4GB, or 4294967295 bytes, because a 32-bit word filled with 1s would be 0XFFFFFFFF.

You can verify this experimentally using Fsutil from the Support Tools. This utility permits you to create files of any length down to the nearest byte. In the experiment, create a FAT32 partition comfortably larger than 4GB. Issue the following command at the root of the partition:

```
fsutil file createnew 4294967296
```

You will get an error saying that insufficient disk space exists. Subtract one from the size and the file will be created with no errors.

FAT32

FAT32 was introduced to overcome some of the more glaring deficiencies in FAT. The most significant difference is the FAT32 cluster map, which uses 32-bit words to identify clusters rather than 16-bit words. This significantly increases the number of clusters that can be addressed. The first 4 bits of each 32-bit cluster address are reserved, so the maximum number of clusters is 2^{28}. Coupled with the maximum FAT32 cluster size under Windows Server 2003 of 64K, this yields a theoretical volume size of 4EB (exabytes).

Now for practicalities. The size of any MBR-based disk partition is defined by a Volume Size value in the partition table. This value specifies the number of sectors assigned to the partition without regard to the file system that formats the partition. This Volume Size value is a 32-bit word, so the maximum size of an MBR-based partition is 2^{32} sectors, or 2TB (terabytes).

If you use Dynamic disks in an IA32 system or GPT disks in an IA64 system, you avoid this partition table limit and a volume can grow to its theoretical limit. However, Windows Server 2003 will refuse to format a FAT32 volume larger than 32GB.

You can format a FAT32 volume under Windows 98 or ME to a size larger than 32GB and put it in a Windows Server 2003 machine, and the Fastfat driver can read and write to it. The maximum practical FAT32 volume size under ME is limited to 2TB because of the Volume Size entry in the boot sector.

FAT Size and Disk Efficiencies

The FAT itself is much, well, fatter under FAT32. The size of the FAT in FAT32 roughly doubles that of FAT16 because each cluster entry requires four bytes rather than two. Because the cluster chains in FAT are prone to breakage and corruption, a large FAT32 structure requires much care and maintenance. For the most part, you'll get equivalent performance and much better reliability using NTFS. If your previous experience with NTFS has been on older platforms, you should evaluate the performance improvements in NTFS 3.1. They are significant.

FAT and FAT32 Weaknesses

FAT and its cousin, FAT32, are kind of like a vaudeville act. They're notable for their longevity more than any remaining entertainment value they might have in them. Here are their primary weaknesses, most of which are corrected by NTFS:

- The FAT location is fixed in FAT12 and FAT16 partitions. If a sector containing a piece of the FAT fails, the system must fall back on the mirrored FAT. If both FAT tables become inoperable, which could happen because of their proximity, the entire file system becomes unmountable. FAT32 avoids this fixed location weakness.
- The number of files at the root of a FAT partition is limited to 512. The FAT32 limit is 65,534 files. Both FAT and FAT32 support long filenames by using additional directory entries, so you can exhaust the supply of root directory entries by using long filenames.
- The limited addressing space of FAT16 wastes drive space by forcing the use of large cluster sizes. FAT32 increases the cluster number but not as much as NTFS.
- The chain of FAT entries for a file or directory can become broken or corrupted. FAT also lends itself to truly stupendous fragmentation problems. This is also true for FAT32. NTFS deals with fragmentation more gracefully so the performance degradation is much less severe.
- The Fastfat driver is not as efficient as the NTFS driver for random file lookups and large files.
- FAT and FAT32 have no security. Anyone with access to the machine can access any of the files.
- The compression mechanism used for FAT and FAT32 partitions under Windows 9x is clumsy and a major source of support problems. DriveSpace volumes are not supported under Windows Server 2003. If you need to save space by compressing files on a Windows Server 2003 or XP machine, you'll need to convert to NTFS.

NTFS Cluster Addressing and Sizes

NTFS sets aside a 64-bit word for cluster numbering, but all implementations of NTFS limit the address to the first 32 bits. At the maximum cluster size of 64K, this yields a maximum partition size of 256EB (exabytes). The partition size limit for MBR disks remains at 2TB, even under NTFS, thanks to the maximum size specified in the partition table. This limit can be overcome with dynamic disks or by using GPT disks on IA64 machines.

The maximum default cluster size for NTFS is 4K, but if you have no need for compression, you can select a larger cluster size when formatting a partition.

The maximum NTFS file size is artificially constrained from the theoretical maximum of 2^{64} bytes to an actual maximum of 2^{44} bytes, or about 16TB. This was considered an outrageously large file when NTFS was first developed, but if you extrapolate out the growth of current storage solutions, it won't be long before some high-end Intel-based servers start to nibble at that 16TB limit. Microsoft has not stated what its strategy is for these types of files, but rumor has it that a future successor to Windows Server 2003 might sport a new file system capable of handling humongous files.

NTFS Structure

Unlike the cluster map used by FAT and FAT32 to locate files, NTFS uses a true database called the *Master File Table*, or MFT.

The MFT consists of a set of fixed-length records, 1KB apiece. Each record holds a set of attributes that, taken together, uniquely identify the location and contents of a corresponding file, folder, or file system component. (There are a few minor exceptions to this "one record, one file" rule, but they are encountered only when a file gets very large and very fragmented and are not typically a concern.)

There are three classes of MFT records:

- **File records.** These records store information typically thought of as "data" such as application files, driver files, system files, database files, and so forth.
- **Directory records.** These records store and index filenames. Directory records are also used to index other attributes such as reparse points, security descriptors, and link tracking information.
- **Metadata records.** These records control the structure and content of the Master File Table itself. Some of them use a file record structure. Others use a directory record structure. Still others use a unique set of attributes and a unique record structure.

Let's take a look at how each of these records is structured to get an idea of how the file system operates.

Metadata Records

Figure 15.6 shows the hierarchy of the metadata records, if you think of them as representing files and folders. The record names start with a dollar sign, `$`.

Metadata records are not exposed to the UI or to the command line. You can see the space set aside for them by running `CHKDSK`. Following is a sample listing. The bold entries show the space taking up by the metadata files:

```
635008 kilobytes total disk space.
535691 kilobytes in 8206 user files.
1894 kilobytes in 592 indexes.
14176 kilobytes in use by the system.
7647 kilobytes in use by the log file.
83247 kilobytes available on disk.
```

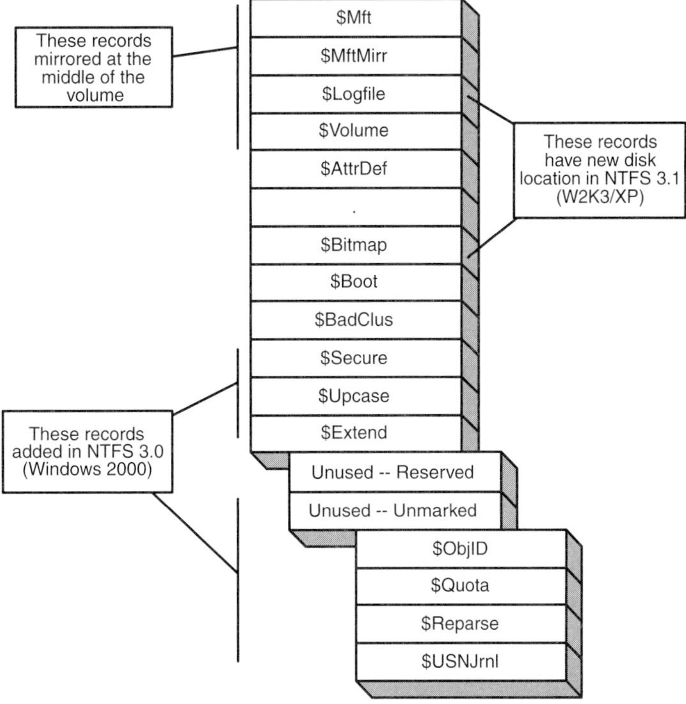

Figure 15.6 MFT metadata records.

As you can see, NTFS takes a significant chunk out of a small volume. On volumes in excess of 10GB or so, though, the percentage of total space consumed by NTFS is smaller than FAT32 when cluster sizes are equal.

The order and structure of the metadata records are rigorously controlled because of the impact their location has on performance and functionality. For example, the MFT contains a record representing the partition boot sector. The secondary bootstrap loader, Ntldr, loads the first few metadata records in the MFT and uses that information to locate and read the boot sector so it can mount the rest of the file system.

The MFT is a file, just like any other file. The first record in the MFT, then, is a file record representing the MFT itself. This is the `$MFT` metadata record. If the sector holding the $MFT record gets damaged or is otherwise unreadable, the operating system would fail to start. To prevent this from happening, the first four MFT records (`$MFT`, `$MFTMirr`, `$LogFile`, and `$Volume`) are copied to the middle of the volume. If Ntldr cannot open these records in their normal location, it loads the mirrored copies and uses information in the `$MFTMirr` record to learn the contents of the damaged sector so it can mount the file system.

NTFS 1.2, the version used in NT4, used the first 16 records of the MFT to hold metadata. Only the first 11 records actually contained any information, with the rest reserved for future use. NTFS 3.0 and later set aside the first 26 records for metadata and uses 15 of them.

You may encounter the names of these metadata records in a variety of scenarios. They appear most often in error messages, especially when the file system gets gravely ill. For the most part, though, knowing their names and functions is like knowing the names of the bones in your body. It helps you pinpoint problems where otherwise you would only be able to give vague references.

Here is a quick list of the metadata records and their functions, with more detail offered later in the chapter:

- **`$MFT`.** NTFS treats everything on the disk as a file, including the Master File Table itself. The `$MFT` record points at the MFT. The `$MFT` is a hybrid record type, containing both data and directory attributes. The directory attributes include a bitmap that lays out the MFT structure and shows which records are in use and which aren't.
- **`$MFTMirr`.** NTFS mirrors the first few MFT records at the halfway point of the volume. If the cluster holding the primary `$MFT` record goes bad, the system uses the mirror to find the remaining portions of the MFT. The `$MFTMirr` is a standard MFT file record with a pointer at the location of the mirrored `$MFT` record.
- **`$LogFile`.** This record contains the location of the log files used to support NTFS transaction tracking. NTFS writes updates to critical MFT records in a log prior to committing them to disk. The `$LogFile` record points at two log files, one primary and one mirror, located at the middle of the volume.
- **`$Volume`.** This record contains the name of the NTFS volume, its size, and the version of NTFS used to format it. The `$Volume` record uses a unique format with specialized attributes. It also contains a flag used to indicate if the file system shut down abnormally.
- **`$AttrDef`.** This record points at a file that lists the attributes supported by NTFS along with information about them, such as whether they must remain in the MFT or can be stored elsewhere on the disk. The `$AttrDef` record uses a standard file record format.
- **`$\`.** This record contains the root directory of the file system. The root directory is crucial to the integrity of the file system because all other directories refer to it. The `$\` record uses a standard directory record format.
- **`$BitMap`.** Just like FAT and FAT32, NTFS maintains a cluster map of a volume so that it can quickly determine the location of unused clusters. The NTFS cluster map uses individual bits rather than bytes, so huge volumes can be mapped in a compact structure. The `$BitMap` record uses a standard file record format. The section, "Performance Enhancements," found later in the chapter, describes changes made to this record in NTFS 3.1.

- **`$Boot`.** This file points at the partition boot sector at cluster 0. Ntldr uses this information to mount the file system. There are two data attributes in this record. One points at the main boot sector and one points at a mirrored boot sector at the end of the partition.
- **`$BadClus`.** This file contains the location of any bad clusters identified during initial formatting or subsequent operation. (If you choose the *quick format* option, the system does not scan for bad clusters and nothing is initially written to this record.) The `$BadClus` record uses a standard file record format.
- **`$Secure`.** This record was introduced in NTFS 3.0. It contains the security descriptors for all MFT records. Aggregating the security descriptors into one place rather than scattering them in the individual MFT records improves performance and enables features such as permission inheritance. The `$Secure` record uses a special format containing both data and index components.
- **`$UpCase`.** This file contains a map of lowercase Unicode characters to their uppercase equivalents. The `$UpCase` record uses a standard file record format.
- **`$Extend`.** This record was introduced in NTFS 3.0. It forms a folder that contains the additional metadata records added in NTFS 3.0: `$Quota`, `$ObjID`, `$Reparse`, and the Change Journal, `$UsnJrnl`. The `$Extend` record uses a standard directory record format.
- **`$Quota`.** The `$Quota` record is a directory that holds records for user SIDs and the files they own. It supports assigning space on a volume based on quotas. The `$Quota` record has existed in NTFS since its inception but was not implemented until NTFS 3.0 (Windows 2000). The `$Quota` record uses a standard directory structure.
- **`$ObjID`.** Another record introduced in NTFS 3.0, `$ObjID` contains an index of files and folders that contain Globally Unique Identifiers (GUIDs). This index is used by the Link Tracking Service to locate source files for OLE links such as shortcuts and compound documents.
- **`$Reparse`.** This record was also introduced in NTFS 3.0. It stores information about *reparse points*. A reparse point redirects a calling process to an alternate data repository such as another folder or file or even a separate file system such as a CD-ROM or DVD or tape drive.
- **`$UsnJrnl`.** Another new record in NTFS 3.0, this is a file record that contains the *Change Journal*. The Change Journal tracks when files are changed so that applications do not need to scan the entire file system. An example of an application that makes use of the Change Journal is the Content Indexing service.

The "Dirty" Flag

NTFS keeps a lot of data in cache waiting for convenient times to commit changes to disk. If you interrupt power (or if the system locks up), there is a possibility that some critical data might not have been saved. This missing data could conceivably compromise the file system.

When there are uncommitted pages in memory, NTFS toggles a flag in the `$Volume` record. This is commonly called the "dirty" flag. If the flag is set, the disk and the cache are not in a consistent state. When all uncommitted pages have been flushed to disk, NTFS toggles the dirty flag off.

If you start a system following a catastrophic event and the dirty flag is set, the system pauses before initializing the operating system and runs a special boot-time instance of CHKDSK called AUTOCHK. You can watch the results of this file system check in the console window. If the system finds errors, you'll be warned in the console and in the Event log, assuming that the system gets to the point where you can log on.

Bad Cluster Mapping

If NTFS tries to write to a cluster and fails, it marks the cluster as bad, maps the cluster number to a spare cluster somewhere else on the drive, and writes the data to the remapped cluster.

The cluster containing the bad sector is marked as bad by entering its Logical Cluster Number in the `$BadClus` metadata record. Each entry in `$BadClus` takes the form of a named data stream with a pointer to the bad cluster. In essence, the system blocks access to the cluster by assigning a file to it.

Bad cluster mapping is not required for SCSI drives, which are intrinsically self-repairing. If a sector goes bad (cannot be written) on a SCSI drive, the drive controller maps the sector address to one of a set of spare sectors set aside for this purpose. This *sector sparing* feature helps to keep the drive functioning normally as it ages. If NTFS is unable to write to a cluster on a SCSI drive, it first waits for the SCSI drive to handle the situation via sector sparing. If the drive runs out of spare sectors, NTFS uses bad cluster mapping. For IDE, USB, and FireWire drives, NTFS uses bad cluster mapping exclusively.

NTFS and Removable Drives

You can format a removable drive such as a ZIP, Jaz, or Orb drive using NTFS, but only if the drive itself has been configured to require safe removal instead of permitting it to be jerked from the system. This option is a property of the device driver, and you can set it using the Properties page for the device. Select the `Hardware` tab, then highlight the removable storage device and click `Properties` to open the Properties window for the device. Select the `Policies` tab. Figure 15.7 shows an example.

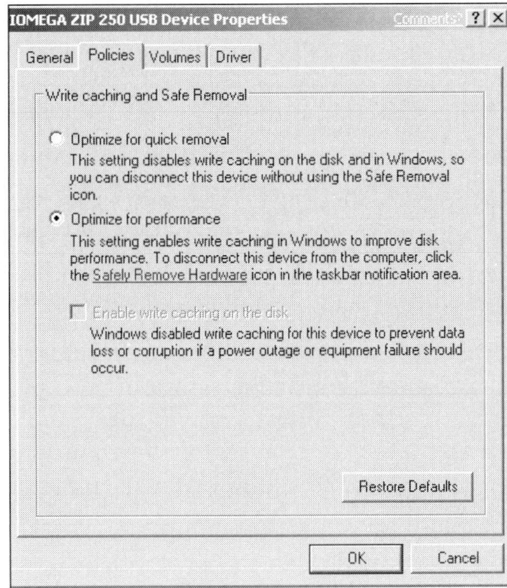

Figure 15.7 Properties window for a removable storage device showing the `Policies` tab where the write caching options are selected.

The `Write Caching and Safe Removal` field shows the caching setting for the device. The default setting is `Optimize for Quick Removal`. This disables write caching and permits you to snatch the drive from the system at any time. The `Optimize for Performance` option requires that you use the `Safe Removal` icon in the Notification area of the status bar to stop the device before removing it.

You're purely on the honor system, of course. If you jerk the USB or FireWire cable from the interface, how can the machine stop you? Still, this is a means of telling you to live by the rules. Write caching will be disabled by default to prevent unnecessary data loss.

Performance Enhancements

One of the advantages to merging the consumer and corporate code bases into Windows XP was that it forced Microsoft to confront performance issues head on, especially when it comes to disk I/O. Traditionally, NTFS has taken a back seat to FAT32 in raw performance. After all, with all the security and reliability overhead in NTFS, it's tough to compete against what is essentially a big table lookup engine.

To meet the performance expectations of FAT32 users while retaining the reliability of NTFS, Microsoft had to work on lots of little details. At a micro level, Microsoft reworked the MFT record headers to make them fit into even byte boundaries and reordered the information a little. This reduced the work necessary to read a record header. A small thing, to be sure, but the file system reads header information a bazillion times a day, so if you can shave a few clock ticks here and there, it adds up.

At a macro level, Microsoft modified the record location of two key metadata records: `$Bitmap` and `$Logfile`. Here are the modifications:

- The `$Bitmap` record essentially performs the same function as a FAT. It keeps a map of used clusters so that the NTFS driver can quickly locate empty space. The location of this record is critical because the hard drive heads have to pick up information from the record frequently.
- The `$Logfile` record is also critical because it supports file system journaling, a key reliability feature compared to non-journaled file systems such as FAT and FAT32.

Also, the MFT was moved from its traditional spot near the start of the volume to a location about one-third of the way in from the start of the volume. This gets it out of the way of application files, which NTFS 3.1 jockeys to the start of the volume to take advantage of the higher throughput. The MFT mirror remains at the middle of the drive.

If you format a partition as NTFS during Setup, or convert a FAT/FAT32 partition formatted by Windows Server 2003 or XP, these two critical metadata records are placed in their proper location. If you upgrade from a previous version of Windows and then convert, this performance enhancement is not applied.

Application file placement plays a role in perceived and actual performance. Windows Server 2003 monitors the applications run by the system and by the users. Every three days, the system defrags critical files and places them at the prime real estate near the start of the volume. This is done during idle times, so don't be surprised if you see a lot of commotion on a hard drive in the evening.

NTFS File Journaling

NTFS caches a considerable amount of data in memory while waiting for the opportunity to commit it to disk. If you've ever had the unfortunate experience of powering down a machine unexpectedly, you know what it's like to face a long and tedious wait at restart while the system runs AUTOCHK.

There is a possibility that AUTOCHK might be unable to reconstruct the contents of critical metadata records. If this were to happen, the file system would be unmountable and you would be spending a very long day restoring the volume from tape.

To prevent this from happening, the metadata files are *journaled*. That is, any changes made to MFT records are first written to a log file at the center of the disk. Then, at some later time, the entries are transferred from the log file to the main MFT.

This transfer from the log file to the MFT is handled by the *Log File Service*, or LFS. Each transfer is done as an *atomic transaction* so that if it is interrupted during the transfer, records are not left in an inconsistent state.

Journaling the file system makes it possible to recover the MFT quickly following an unexpected loss of power or a system lockup. All that AUTOCHK needs to do is verify the integrity of the MFT then replay the uncommitted journal entries.

NTFS Attributes

As I mentioned earlier, the MFT is a database. The records in this database contain attributes that describe elements of the file system such as files, directories, filenames, and so forth. These attributes are defined by the `$AttrDef` metadata record. Each attribute is given a code number that identifies it in the MFT records.

Following is a brief description of each attribute. If you would like to see this list in a production file system, the attributes are defined in the `$Attribute` metadata record. You can't see this record from the operating system shell, but you can scan the NTFS volume using a hex editor and search for any of the attribute names. Remember that they are prefixed with a dollar sign (`$`).

- **`Header.`** The first part of every MFT record consists of header information that does not have an attribute. This information includes the MFT record number, an increment counter for tracking changes to the record, and the MFT record number of the directory that contains the file or folder represented by the record.
- **`$Standard_Information.`** Contains the standard file attributes (`Read-only`, `Hidden`, `System`, and `Archive`) along with a set of timestamps. In addition, for NTFS 3.0 and later, `$Standard_Information` contains a pointer to a security descriptor in the `$Secure` metadata record. See section, "Security Descriptor," for more information.
- **`$File_Name.`** Contains the name of the MFT record. If a record has a long name, a second `$File_Name` attribute is added with the short, DOS-compatible name (unless short name generation has been disabled).
- **`$Security_Descriptor.`** This attribute is no longer used. Starting with NTFS 3.0, the `$Security_Descriptor` attribute was replaced by entries in the `$Secure` metadata record. The `$Standard_Information` attribute in an MFT record contains an index number for the `$Secure` entry that represents the security descriptor for the MFT record.
- **`$Data.`** This attribute stores what is commonly thought of as the contents of a file. An MFT record can have multiple `$Data` attributes. See the "Named Data Streams" section for more information.
- **`$Index_Root`, `$Index_Allocation`,** and **`$Bitmap`.** These attributes are used to index MFT attributes for quick access. They are primarily used by directory records to index filenames, but they are also used to index other attributes to support features such as link tracking and reparse points.

- **`$Reparse_Point`.** This attribute contains a pointer to a volume, folder record, or device. When the record containing this pointer is opened, the file system opens the target of the pointer instead. The `$Reparse_Point` attribute supports features such as mount points and Remote Storage Services.
- **`$Logged_Utility_Stream`.** This attribute is used by the Encrypting File System. See Chapter 17, "Managing File Encryption," for details.
- **`$Ea and $Ea_Information`.** These attributes were originally used to support the High-Performance File System (HPFS) used by the OS/2 subsystem. The OS/2 subsystem and HPFS are no longer supported by Windows 2000 or Windows Server 2003.

Security Descriptor

Before looking at the way NTFS 3.x deals with security descriptors, let's consider the handling of attributes in general.

NTFS attributes are classified by whether they reside completely in the MFT record (resident) or they sit somewhere else on the disk with a pointer in the MFT record (non-resident).

Timestamps

The `$Standard_Information` attribute in each MFT record contains four timestamps that show the following dates and times:

- Record Creation
- Attribute Modification
- Data or Index Modification
- Last Access

When you first create a file or folder, all four timestamps are set to the same value. The Record Creation timestamp remains at this original value.

When the `$Data` attribute of a file record or the `$Index_Root` attribute of a directory record are modified, the Data Modification timestamp is updated. When any other attribute in the MFT record is modified, the Attribute Modification timestamp is updated.

You would expect that the Last Access timestamp would get updated each time the record is opened, but this would put too great a load on the file system. Imagine how many updates would be necessary each time you open Explorer! Instead, the Last Access timestamp is updated only once in any one-hour period regardless of the number of times a file is touched. The last access time granularity for FAT32 is set for one day.

You can improve file system performance by eliminating the update to the Last Access timestamp completely. This might create auditing concerns, so do not make this change without some consideration for security. The Registry entry is as follows:

```
Key:    HKLM | System | CurrentControlSet | Control | FileSystem
Value:  NtfsDisableLastAccessUpdate
Data:   1 (REG_DWORD)
```

Some attributes, like `$Standard_Information` and `$File_Name`, must always remain resident. The system constantly needs information in those attributes and cannot be bothered to scratch around on the hard drive to find them. Other attributes, such as `$Data` or `$Index_Root`, can easily be moved somewhere else on the disk when they get too big to store directly in the MFT record.

When an attribute becomes non-resident, there is the possibility of fragmentation. This presented a problem for earlier versions of NTFS, where large security descriptors would be made non-resident. This forced the file system to go to some other place on the hard drive to check the security descriptor before it could allow access to the file or folder, which slowed file system performance considerably.

Windows 2000 also introduced permission inheritance. This made it possible to change the security descriptor of a parent folder and have the change "flow" down the tree to all files and subfolders. If Microsoft had implemented permission inheritance with the old resident/nonresident security descriptor paradigm, file system performance would have been truly pathetic.

Instead, NTFS 3.0 introduced a new MFT metadata record called `$Secure`. This record is essentially a hidden database containing all the security descriptors for the file system plus a couple of indexes to help find entries quickly. Figure 15.8 shows the layout of this database.

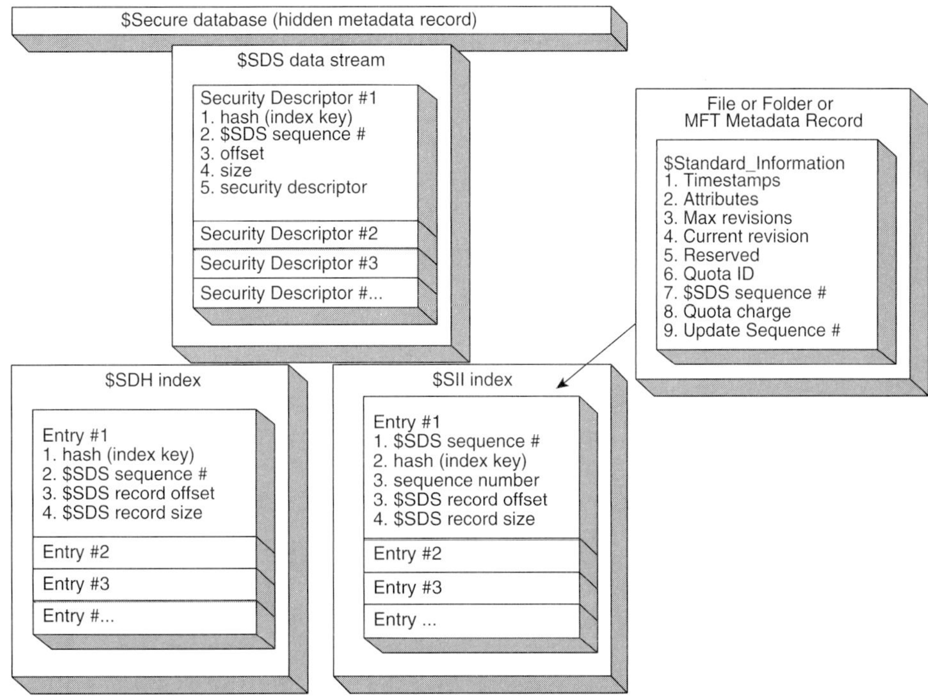

Figure 15.8 Layout of the `$Secure` database.

The security descriptors themselves are stored in a data attribute called `$SDS`. Along with the security descriptor itself, the system stores these additional values in each `$SDS` entry:

- A hash of the security descriptor to use as an index key.
- A sequence number assigned to each security descriptor to act as an identifier.
- The security descriptor size.
- The offset of the security descriptor from the start of the `$SDS` data stream.

These last two entries are important because security descriptors can be different sizes so that they can't be found by a simple fixed-record lookup algorithm.

Security Descriptor Links

The `$Standard_Information` attribute for each MFT record contains the sequence number of its assigned security descriptor. This makes it simple to implement inheritance. When a new file is created, NTFS links the MFT record to the same security descriptor as the other files in the folder by putting the same `$SDS` sequence number in the `$Standard_Information` attribute.

If you modify the security descriptor of a file or folder by adding entries to its access control list (ACL), or you select the `Don't Inherit` option in the ACL Editor to break the chain of inheritance, a new security descriptor is created in `$SDS` and the `$Standard_Information` attribute in the MFT record is updated to contain the sequence number assigned to the new security descriptor.

In practice, NTFS uses separate security descriptors for folders and files. So, if you do not make any changes to the security permissions for files or folders in an NFTS volume, there will be just two entries in `$SDS`, one for all the folders in the volume and one for all the files under those folders.

Security Descriptor Lookups

The `$Secure` record maintains two indexes named `$SDH` and `$SII`. These indexes are shown in Figure 15.8 and are described as follows:

- The `$SDH` index sorts the `$SDS` entries by their hash key.
- The `$SII` index sorts the contents of the `$SDH` index by the security descriptor sequence number.

The `$SDH` index helps to limit the number of security descriptors by recycling those that are already in `$SDS`. If you set the contents of a security descriptor for a file or folder to match those of another file or folder, including all the inherited permissions, the system uses the sequence number of the existing `$SDS` entry.

To make this trick work, the system needs a way to quickly scan for identical security descriptors. That is where the hash index in `$SDH` comes into play. The statistical likelihood of two security descriptors having an identical hash is vanishingly small, so the file system calculates the hash for a new security descriptor then scans for a match in `$SDH`. If it finds one, it uses the sequence number in the index to update the `$Standard_Information` attribute in the MFT record.

What is the end result? An NTFS volume has a compact set of security descriptors that is fully cross-indexed to use for controlling access permissions to files and folders. This improves performance and simplifies inheritance.

Security Descriptor Highlights

You don't need to remember the details of the various components of the `$Secure` database. Here is a quick checklist of the operational requirements based on how the `$Secure` database works:

- If you add ACE entries to the ACL of a file or folder while retaining inheritance, a new `$SDS` entry is created with a security descriptor that has an ACL reflecting the inherited and explicitly applied access control entries (ACEs).
- If you *move* a file to another location on the same volume, the MFT record location is not changed and neither is the `$SDS` index number. Therefore, the file retains its old security settings plus inherits the new settings from its new folder.
- If you *copy* a file to another location on the same volume, a new MFT record is created. This new record gets the same `$SDS` index number as its parent folder.
- If you move a file to a *different* volume, once again, a new MFT record is created. The record gets the `$SDS` index number from its parent folder.

If you use `xcopy /o` to copy a file to a new location while retaining its security permissions, the result depends on whether the file had explicitly assigned entries in its security descriptor:

- If the file had its own security descriptor in `$SDS`, the sequence number to that entry is copied to the new MFT record.
- If the file had explicitly assigned ACEs along with inherited ACEs, the system scans to see if another `$SDS` entry has the same combination. If not, it creates a new `$SDS` entry and puts the sequence number in the new MFT record.
- If the file had no explicitly assigned ACEs, the system uses the `$SDS` sequence number for the security descriptor used by the other files in the folder. (Remember that files use different security descriptor entries than folders.)

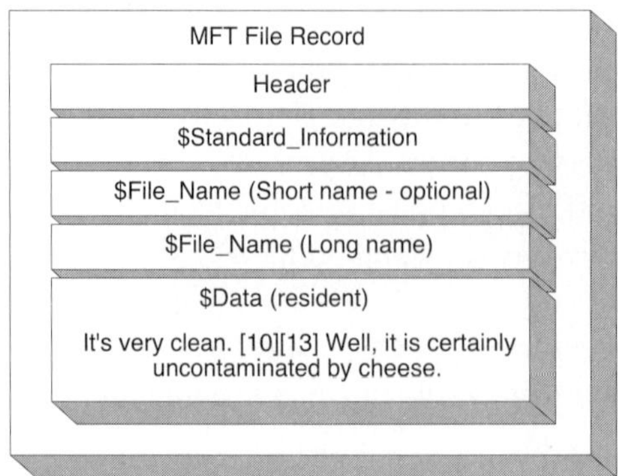

Figure 15.9 Attributes of a simple file record.

File Records

A file record is used to store data for access by the operating system or by user applications. A file record in the MFT also stores information about the file itself, such as the file's name and when it was created and how big it is and if it has any special attributes such as `Read-Only` or `Hidden` or `Compressed`.

Figure 15.9 shows the layout of a simple file record. It has a header and three attributes: `$Standard_Information`, `$File_Name`, and `$Data`.

Header Information

Some of the more important elements of the file header include the following:

- **MFT record number.** A sequential number assigned to the record that helps identify it. Indexes such as directories use this information to correlate a filename to an MFT record.
- **Record type flag.** Indicates whether this is a file record or a directory record. If this flag is set to 0, it indicates that the record has been flagged for deletion and can be overwritten. Other record types are 1, File, and 2, Directory.
- **Actual size** and **Allocated size.** The actual size is the true number of bytes in the file. The allocated size is the number of bytes in the clusters assigned to the file. The larger the clusters, the more likely it is to have large differences in these numbers.
- **Update Sequence Number**, or **USN.** This acts as a version number. Each time the file is modified, this number is incremented by one. If a file is deleted and the MFT record subsequently reused, this number is set to a starting value of 2. This indicates to the system that no references are being made to deleted files.

$Standard_Information Elements

This MFT attribute contains a set of timestamps, a pointer to the security descriptor for the MFT record, and a flag that is commonly referred to as the *file attributes*. Here are the important file attribute flag settings:

- Standard DOS file attributes: `Read-Only`, `Hidden`, `System`, and `Archive`
- Compressed
- Reparse Point
- Sparse file
- Not Indexed (Content Indexer flag)
- Encrypted

Keep in mind as you work with files and folders that these flags are kept in a separate attribute from the actual contents of the file, which are stored in the `$Data` attribute. For instance, if you *copy* a file to a new location, you build a new MFT record with a new `$Standard_Information` attribute and therefore new file attributes. But if you *move* a file, the MFT record remains the same and so does the setting of the attribute flags in `$Standard_Information`.

$File_Name

Every MFT record has at least one `$File_Name` attribute.The filename in this attribute can be 256 characters long, a limitation based on the single-byte Length field for the name entry.

A file can have more than one filename. For instance, if a name does not meet DOS 8.3 naming standards, the file system generates a short name and places it in a second `$File_Name` attribute. This supports DOS/Windows 3.x clients on the network plus any DOS applications at the console. See the following "Hard Links" sidebar for another example of multiple filenames.

Folder Attributes

If you set any of the `$Standard_Information` attribute flags on a folder rather than on a file, you tell the file system to apply the flag to any new files created in that folder. Explorer generally offers you the option of applying the flag to existing files, as well.

In Windows Server 2003 and XP, Microsoft changed the way Explorer displays the attribute setting in a folder from the traditional binary model (on or off) to a tri-state model (on, off, or content status indicator).

The status indicator for an attribute tells you if any files in the folder have that particular attribute set. For example, if you have a read-only file in a folder, the `Read-Only` attribute checkbox for the folder would be filled with color. Don't confuse this information setting with a checkmark, which indicates that the flag has been set on the folder and all new records will get that attribute.

Hard Links

I'm a big fan of an obscure 1970's comedy ensemble called Firesign Theater. If you like twisted, cerebral humor, their albums are now available on CD. One of my favorites is titled "How Can You Be in Two Places at Once When You're Not Anywhere at All?"

I bring this up because it relates to a long-dormant feature of NTFS called *hard links*. This feature permits you to create additional filename attributes and index them in different directories. In essence, you "create" multiple copies of the same file in different folders.

Prior to Windows Server 2003, the only way to create hard links was to use programming APIs. Windows Server 2003 introduces a new utility called Fsutil that makes it very easy to create hard links. The syntax is

```
fsutil hardlink create <target_file> <source_file>
```

where `target_file` represents the new name for the file you're creating and `source_file` is the name of the file that you're linking to. This file must be on the same volume as the target file.

When you use this command to create a hard link, NTFS adds the new filename attribute to the directory specified by the `<target_file>` entry. It also increments a hard link counter in the file header. When you delete an instance of the hard linked file, you only delete the filename attribute and the index entry in the directory. You cannot delete the file until all hard link instances have been deleted.

Short Name Generation

DOS compatibility is still important and will remain so for the next few years. (I'm sure that by 2020, the last lawyer who insists on using WordPerfect 5.1 will have retired.) DOS support requires 8.3 filenames. All the file systems in Windows Server 2003 will generate short, DOS-compliant filenames automatically when a long name is assigned. You can see the short names from the command line using `dir /x`.

Creating a short, 8.3 filename to represent a long 256-character name is not as straightforward as you might think. The system cannot simply take the first eight characters of the long name and the first three characters of the extension and call it a job well done. What if several files start with the same eight letters? Or how would you differentiate between .HTM files and .HTML files?

Windows Server 2003 uses two algorithms to generate short filenames. Both preserve the first letters of the long name for alphabetical sorting. The algorithm changes when five or more files in the same directory start with the same letters. Here's the algorithm for fewer than five files:

1. Delete all Unicode characters that do not map to standard ANSI characters.
2. Remove spaces, internal periods, and other illegal DOS characters. The name `Long.File.Name.Test` becomes `LongFileName.Test`.
3. Keep the first three characters after the last period as an extension. `LongFileName.Test` becomes `LongFileName.Tes`.
4. Drop all characters after the first six. `LongFileName.Tes` becomes `LongFi.Tes`.
5. Append a tilde (~) followed by a sequence numeral to the filename to prevent duplicate filenames. `LongFi.Tes` becomes `LongFi~1.Tes`.

6. Finally, convert the name to uppercase. The final short form of `Long.File.Name.Test` is `LONGFI~1.TES`.

The fifth and subsequent file with a long name that starts with the same six letters as other files in the folder is treated somewhat differently:

1. Drop Unicode characters, spaces, and extra periods (same process).
2. Keep the first three characters after the last period as an extension (same process).
3. Drop all characters after the first *two* instead of six. At this stage, `Long.File.Name.Test5` becomes `Lo.Tes`.
4. Append four hexadecimal numbers derived via an algorithm applied to the remaining characters in the long filename. `Long.File.Name.Test5` yields `D623` and `Long.File.Name.Test6` becomes `E623`. At this stage, the short name is `LoD623.Tes`.
5. Append a tilde (~) followed by a sequence numeral to the new filename just in case the algorithm comes up with duplicate names. `LoD623.Tes` becomes `LoD623~1.Tes`.
6. Finally, convert the name to uppercase. The final short form of `Long.File.Name.Test5` becomes `LOD623~1.TES`.

Long filenames have been around for years now, so I'm sure you are well aware of the standard pitfalls. Keep the following important items in mind:

- **Moving long-name files between machines.** The short name algorithm used by the NT family of Windows works differently than the 9x family, and these both use a different algorithm than the two long namespaces in NetWare—Os2.nam for version 3.x and Longname.nam for 4.1x and above.
- **Excessively long names slow performance.** It's a good idea to keep names shorter than 32 characters for optimal performance. If a directory gets heavily fragmented, the short and long name attributes can get separated, causing a dramatic increase in file lookup times.

Short Name Preservation

When you copy files from one place to another in Windows Server 2003, ordinarily the short filename is generated when the file is created in its new destination. If there is already another file in that location that has the same first six letters, the short name of the newly copied file will change. If you want to preserve the original short names when you copy, use the `/n` switch on the `COPY` or `XCOPY` command.

In Windows Server 2003, the backup API will also preserve the short names so that if you do a tape restore to a new location and there are already files that have the same first six letters, you must decide whether you want to overwrite those existing files.

- **Use caution in batch files.** The CMD.EXE command interpreter in Windows Server 2003 does not act the same as COMMAND.COM. For example, using CMD, you do not need to enclose long names with quotes when changing directories. You can enter `cd c:\dir one` and go right to the directory. This is not standard for all commands, however. If you enter `del dir one*`, you'll delete every file starting with `dir` and every file starting with `one`.
- **Special handling for file extensions.** File extensions also affect the operation of wildcards. Consider `Long.File.Name.Test1.htm` and `Long.File.Name.Test2.html` as examples. If you go to the command prompt and do a directory listing for *.htm, you get both files in the list instead of just the .HTM file. This seems like a fairly innocuous bug, but what if you enter `del *.htm`, thinking to get rid of only old .HTM files? You also delete the .HTML files, as well.
- **DOS applications delete long names.** If a DOS application changes a short name, the long name is deleted. This has the potential for upsetting Windows users.

$Data

A file record stores user data inside an attribute called `$Data`. The `$Data` attribute resembles a nestling. Although it's small, a few hundred bytes or so, it lives with the MFT record. When it gets too big for the nest, the file system locates some free space out on the disk and pushes the data out there. It becomes non-resident.

Data in a non-resident `$Data` attribute is stored in a contiguous set of clusters called a *run*. The portion of the `$Data` attribute remaining in the MFT contains a pointer to the location of this run. The pointer gives the following information:

- The number of the cluster that starts the run. This is called the *Logical Cluster Number*, or LCN. The LCN is measured from the start of the volume, so the 1500th cluster from the beginning of the volume would have an LCN of 1500.
- The length of the run in numbers of clusters. A 1024-byte file on a disk with 512-byte clusters would have a Run Length of 2.

If you add any data to the file, the file system simply appends the bytes onto the existing run and keeps expanding into new clusters as necessary.

Disabling 8.3 Filename Creation

You can eliminate the performance problems caused by short names by disabling 8.3 filename creation. This also reduces the disk space used to store index buffers. Do this only if you have no DOS/Win3.x clients. Use the following Registry entry:

```
Key:    HKLM | SYSTEM | CurrentControlSet | Control | FileSystem
Value:  NTFSDisable8dot3NameCreation
Data:   0
```

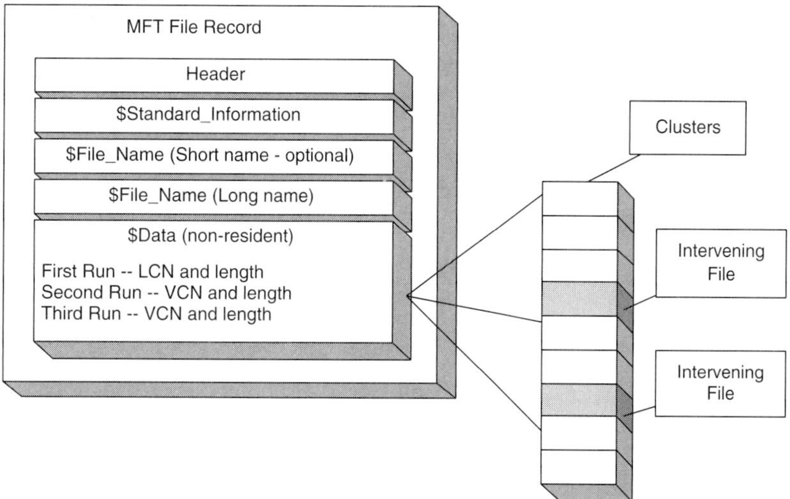

Figure 15.10 Fragmented `$Data` attribute.

As the file grows, the file system sometimes encounters a cluster that is already occupied by another file or folder. When this happens, the file system selects the next available empty cluster and starts another run. A second pointer is added to the `$Data` attribute in the MFT to identify the location of the second run. At this point, the `$Data` attribute is said to be *fragmented*. Figure 15.10 shows a diagram of a fragmented `$Data` attribute.

Unlike the pointer at the first run, which used a Logical Cluster Number to identify the start of the run, the pointer for the second and subsequent runs identifies the starting cluster in relation to the run before it. This is called a *Virtual Cluster Number*, or VCN. For instance, if Run 1 starts at cluster 100 and Run 2 starts at cluster 350, the VCN in the pointer to the second run would be 250.

As the file continues to grow and grow, it might encounter occupied clusters, forcing the file system to fragment the file even further. As the file becomes more and more fragmented, it requires more and more pointers in the MFT record.

At some point, the file becomes so fragmented that the pointers themselves will not fit in the 1K MFT record. When this happens, the file system creates another MFT record to hold the pointers. It leaves behind another type of pointer in an attribute called `$Attribute_List`. This pointer identifies the MFT record number that holds the additional pointers. This only happens when a file is severely fragmented.

MFT and Fragmentation

The MFT is a file, just like any other file in NTFS, and as such it can become fragmented if it is forced to grow into portions of the disk that already have clusters claimed by files.

MFT fragmentation can seriously degrade performance, so NTFS tries to prevent it if possible. The strategy used by NTFS to protect the MFT is the same strategy used by nations to protect their territory. NTFS sets up a defensive zone in front of the MFT and avoids this zone when assigning new data clusters on the drive.

By default, this MFT buffer zone takes up 12.5 percent of the volume size. On an 18GB volume, the MFT buffer would take up about 2.25GB. That is enough space for the MFT to hold more than 2 million files and directories without getting fragmented.

If the disk starts to get full, the file system behaves like a pirate nation and starts encroaching on the MFT buffer. At some point, if this encroachment continues, you are likely to get excessive MFT fragmentation. You should never let an NTFS volume get to less than 15 percent free space, with 25 percent free space being the optimal lower limit to allow room for defragmentation.

You can increase the MFT buffer size if you want, but the default should work fine as long as you don't overload your volumes. The following Registry entry controls the buffer size:

```
Key:     HKLM | System | CurrentControlSet | Control | FileSystem
Value:   NtfsMftZoneReservation
Data:    1-4 (REG_DWORD)
```

A setting of 1 represents the default 12.5 percent buffer allocation. Entering 2 carves out 25 percent. A 3 takes 50 percent, and a 4 takes 75 percent. The system works hard to keep the MFT buffer immaculate, so if you designate a bigger buffer, you should reduce your maximum volume loadings accordingly.

Named Data Streams

As we've seen, data saved to an NTFS file is stored in an attribute called `$Data`. As it turns out, an MFT record can have any number of `$Data` attributes. The default `$Data` attribute is like the star in an old-style spaghetti western. It has no name. When an application issues an API call to read from or write to a file, NTFS delivers the contents of this unnamed `$Data` attribute unless told otherwise.

MFT Buffer Zone Changes

In previous versions of NTFS, the MFT buffer zone could not be penetrated until all other space was used up. This put a serious crimp on defragmentation utilities because the buffer area might be the only free space left on the drive.

Under NTFS 3.1, Microsoft took a hint from the Bush administration's treatment of the Arctic National Wildlife Refuge. It degraded the MFT buffer zone somewhat, making it less of an absolute barrier and more of a helpful suggestion. This permits DEFRAG to use space inside the buffer zone for holding temporary clusters as it jockeys them around.

Any additional `$Data` attributes in a file must be identified by name. For this reason, they are commonly called *named data streams*. Here is an example of how to create named data streams:

1. Build a file named Superman.txt by echoing a few characters from the command prompt into a file as follows:

```
C:\>echo It's a bird. > Superman.txt
```

This creates a Master File Table record for a file named Superman.txt with an unnamed data attribute that contains the characters `It's a bird`.

2. Add a second data attribute by echoing text to a named stream in the same file as follows:

```
C:\>echo It's a plane. > superman.txt:stream1
```

3. Now, add a third data attribute with a different name:

```
C:\>echo It's SUPERMAN. > superman.txt:stream2
```

It can be something of a trick to view the contents of a named data stream. The application you use for viewing must be able to address the stream by name. Very few applications support this feature. In this simple example, let's use the `MORE` command to expose the named data streams:

```
C:\>more < superman.txt
It's a bird.

C:\>more < superman.txt:stream1
It's a plane.

C:\>more < superman.txt: stream2
It's SUPERMAN.
```

Implementations of Named Data Streams

Named data streams have more uses than just parlor tricks. Microsoft uses them to support several features, such as *Services for Macintosh* (SFM). An SFM volume uses named data streams to support dual-fork Macintosh files.

Another feature that makes use of named data streams is Summary Information. You can see this feature by opening the Properties window for a file and selecting the `Summary` tab. Figure 15.11 shows an example.

When you store information about a file using Summary Information, the data is stored in named data streams using the GUID for the file as the stream name. Because named data streams are supported by earlier versions of NTFS, you can copy files from Windows Server 2003 and Windows 2000 servers to NT servers without losing the summary information. You cannot access Summary Information from NT, though, because the interface is not coded to look for it.

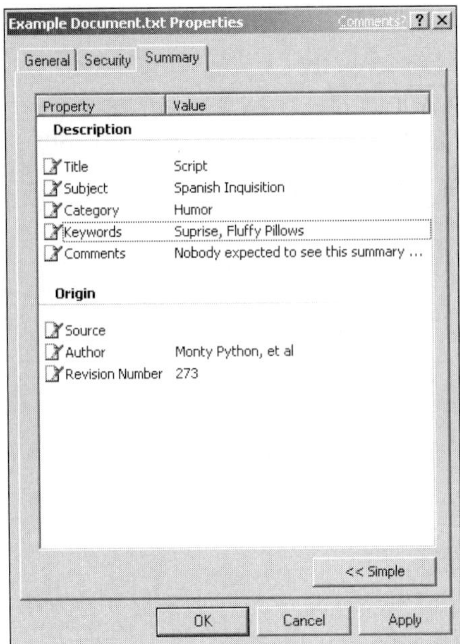

Figure 15.11 `Summary` tab for a typical file.

Named Data Streams and WebDAV

Another feature coming to prominence also makes use of named data streams. This feature is called *Web-based Distributed Authoring and Versioning*, or WebDAV.

WebDAV permits file manipulation using HTTP as the wire protocol. WebDAV is an open standard with lots of support from IETF (Internet Engineering Task Force), industry, and other movers and shakers. It will eventually replace FTP as the standard method for moving files around the Internet. WebDAV is discussed in detail in Chapter 16, "Managing Shared Resources."

The reason I bring up WebDAV at this point is because it uses named data streams in a way that may surprise you the first time you use the feature. To get an idea of how this works, set up a shared web folder on Windows Server 2003 that is running IIS. To do this, open the Properties window for a folder and select the `Web Sharing` tab. Click the `Share This Folder` radio button and accept the default options. This creates a virtual folder in the IIS metabase.

You must also configure IIS to publish WebDAV shares. It does not do this by default. Open the Internet `Information Services` console, right-click the server icon, and select SECURITY from the flyout menu. This launches a Security Lockdown wizard. Step through the wizard and in the Enable Request Handlers window, select `Enable WebDAV Publishing` under the `ISAPI Handlers` icon.

Instead of using a browser to connect to the web folder, use the new WebDAV redirector in Windows Server 2003 or XP by opening a command prompt and entering this command:

```
net use * http://<server_name>/<webshare_name>
```

You may be prompted for credentials. After the connection is established and the drive has been redirected, create a couple files in the network drive. If you were to take a look at the network traffic at this point, you would see that communications with this shared resource occur using HTTP rather than the Server Message Block (SMB) commands that would normally be used between Windows machines.

Open the Properties window for one of the files you created. You'll notice that there are only a few attributes you can change. They are `Read-Only`, `Hidden`, and `Archive`. You can also set the `Encryption` attribute, which will encrypt the temporary copy of the file on your machine and then copy the encrypted blob over the network to the web share. Read more about this functionality in Chapter 17, "Managing File Encryption."

If you set the `Read-only` or `Hidden` flags and click `OK`, you'll notice that the file shows these attributes in the Explorer window. Now go to the server and open the properties for the file. You'll notice that the attributes have not changed.

Here's the reason for this attribute duality. When you set an attribute via WebDAV, it is saved into a named data stream in the file. It does not touch the flags in the `$Standard_Information` attribute. This allows the system to manage WebDAV attributes via standard HTTP using methods such as `PropFind` and `PropSet`. It also means that WebDAV attributes must be managed separately from NTFS attributes. Keep this behavior in mind, because if you copy a WebDAV file to a location that is formatted with anything other than NTFS, you'll lose the WebDAV attributes.

Directory Records

Every database needs an index to locate records and speed lookups. NTFS is no exception. The most familiar attribute index is a directory, which indexes `$File_Name` attributes. The MFT permits indexing any attribute, though. Following are other attributes that also have indexes in NTFS:

- **Security Descriptors.** These attributes are stored in the `$Secure` metadata record and indexed by `$SDH` and `$SII`.
- **Globally Unique Identifiers (GUIDs).** If a file record is the target of an object linking and embedding (OLE) link, it is assigned a GUID. These GUIDs are stored in an `$Object_ID` attribute in the file's MFT record and they are indexed in the `$ObjID` metadata record.

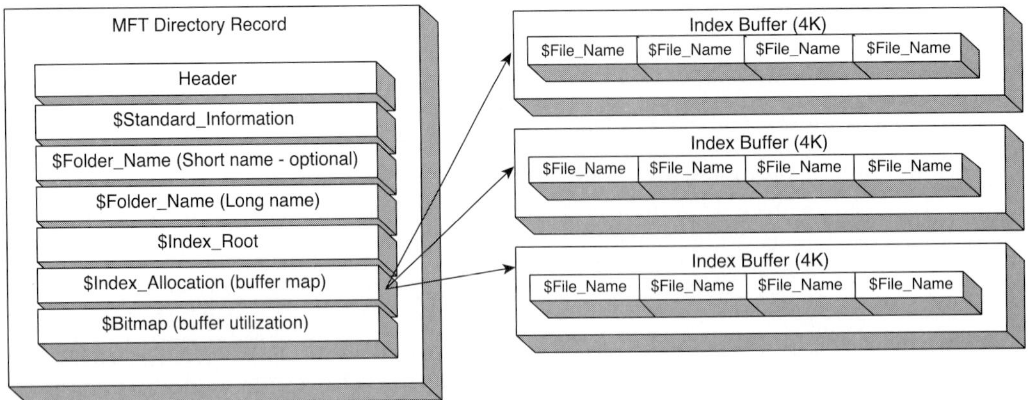

Figure 15.12 Example Directory record structure.

- **Quota charges.** A file record header contains quota information that is indexed in the `$Quota` metadata folder.
- **Reparse points.** Folders with symbolic links to other folders or volumes or devices contain a `$Reparse_Point` attribute. These attributes are indexed in the `$Reparse` metadata folder.

Directory Record Components

A directory record in the MFT is a special form of a file record. It has a header plus a `$Standard_Information` attribute and at least one `$File_Name` attribute. Instead of a `$Data` attribute, though, the MFT uses three additional attributes to store index information. Figure 15.12 shows how these attributes fit together in a typical directory:

- **`$Index_Root`.** This holds a copy of the indexed attribute. For example, in a Directory record, the `$Index_Root` attribute contains a copy of the `$File_Name` attributes from each file and folder in the directory. The `$Index_Root` attribute is always resident.
- **`$Index_Allocation`.** When the number of indexed entries grows to the point that the `$Index_Root` attribute cannot fit in its MFT record, the indexed entries are moved onto the disk into a set of 8K buffers. The `$Index_Root` attribute cannot be made non-resident, so the entries are put into a new attribute, `$Index_Allocation`, that contains the LCN of the start of the buffer run, the size of the buffer, and the length of the run.
- **`$Bitmap`.** This attribute assists in housekeeping by mapping out the free space in the index buffers.

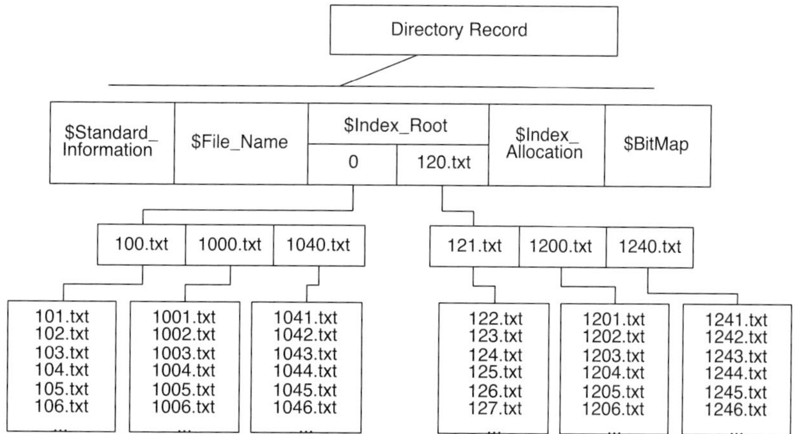

Figure 15.13 Directory record showing b-tree entries and several non-resident index buffers.

B-Tree Sorting

When index entries are made non-resident, the $Index_Root attribute retains the first entry of each buffer to act as a sorting mechanism. These root entries form a b-tree, a structured format that speeds sorting. Figure 15.13 shows the b-tree structure for a shallow directory. A b-tree lookup doesn't take much work on the part of the file system. In the example, if they system is searching for a filename that is lexicographically less than 120.txt, it goes down the left path. Otherwise, its goes to the right.

Short Names and B-Tree Sorting

Short filenames add complexity to the b-tree sorting scheme. Filename entries are placed in index buffers alphanumerically without distinguishing between short names and long names. For example, if you have three long names such as `Twilight of the Gods.txt`, `Twilight Double-Header.txt`, and `Twilight Zone.txt` in the same directory, the short names `TWILIG~1`, `TWILIG~2`, and `TWILIG~3` will sort to the top of the index buffer above the long filenames.

When you open a folder in Explorer or do a `DIR` from the command line, the file system retrieves both the short and long names. If you have many, many long filenames that all start with the same few letters, you can seriously degrade performance by forcing the system to do a full scan of all the index buffers looking for corresponding short names.

If you must continue to use short filenames to support downlevel clients or DOS applications, work hard to come up with naming schemes that do not use the same first letters. If that is not possible, consider breaking up your directory tree into many smaller folders to reduce the size of the index buffers.

Directory Fragmentation

Directories can become fragmented just like files. If a run of index buffers encounters a cluster owned by another file or folder, the file system is forced to start another run. This creates a second pointer in the `$Index_Allocation` attribute.

A heavily fragmented directory might fill the MFT record with pointers, at which time the system moves the pointers to another MFT record and leaves behind a pointer in an `$Attribute_List` attribute.

Fragmented directories slow performance as much or more than fragmented files because they force the file system to scrabble around on the drive collecting index buffers. Let's take a look at how NTFS handles defragmentation of files and directories.

Defragmentation

Like Windows 2000, Windows Server 2003 and XP include a defragmentation utility using code licensed from Executive Software. This code makes use of API calls created by Microsoft. These API calls are designed to safely move clusters without taking a chance of file system corruption should there be a power interruption or system lockup.

The defragmentation engine consists of two executables, Dfrgfat.exe and Dfrgntfs.exe. The Dfrgfat engine works with both FAT and FAT32. The management interface is the Disk Defragmenter console, Dfrg.msc. Figure 15.14 shows a typical defragmentation analysis graph for a volume.

For details on performing defragmentation, including how to use the new command-line defragger utility, see the "Defragmentation Operations" section later in this chapter.

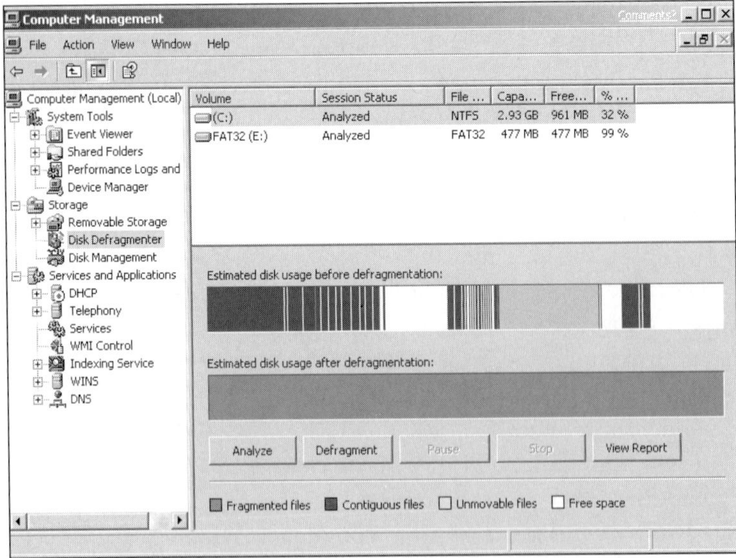

Figure 15.14 Defragmentation console showing typical fragmentation analysis graph.

Defragmentation in Windows Server 2003 has improved considerably compared to Windows 2000. Many of the nagging restrictions have been removed. Here is a quick list of the improvements:

- **MFT defrag.** The MFT can now be defragmented using the defrag API. Further, the MFT can be defragged while online. Earlier versions of Windows required running a commercial defragger at boot time to defrag the MFT. If you've ever sat through several nail-biting hours waiting for a boot-time defrag to finish so you could get a server back online, this is a welcome new feature.
- **Deeper defrag.** The defrag API has been tweaked to permit access to corners and cracks of the file system that were inaccessible in prior versions. For example, previous versions of the API were unable to defrag heavily fragmented files that used Attribute Lists. It was also unable to defragment extensive bitmaps or reparse points. All of these elements can be defragged using the new API.
- **Compressed file defrag.** Defragmentation now works with compressed files, but you still cannot completely defrag a heavily fragmented compressed volume. In production, compressed volumes tend to get very fragmented even when you defrag regularly. The only workaround is to get a backup, wipe the volume, and restore from tape.
- **Improved encrypted file security.** Encrypted files are defragged without being opened. This eliminates a potential vulnerability where temp files created during defrag could expose sensitive data.
- **Less intrusive defrag.** The same API fix that protects encrypted files also makes it possible to run the defragmenter with just `Read Attributes` and `Synchronize` permissions. This makes defragmentation less intrusive, but you still need Administrative permissions to defragment.
- **Flexible cluster sizes.** The defrag engine now works with any cluster size. Previous versions were limited to a maximum of a 4K cluster. This means that you can increase cluster size on volumes holding large database files without worrying that you cannot defrag the files.
- **Command-line operation.** A new command-line interface called DEFRAG makes it possible to use batch files to kick off a defrag. Using the batch file and Task Scheduler, you can schedule periodic defrags to run after hours.

In addition to these features, a performance tuning service runs every three days to jockey frequently used files into more advantageous locations on the drive. This tuning service does not perform a full defragmentation but it does a nice job of tidying up on a regular basis.

Two defrag limitations remain:

- **Paging file.** You cannot defrag the paging file.
- **Registry.** You cannot defrag the Registry.

You can prevent the paging file from becoming fragmented by defining the same value for the normal and maximum size. This prevents the file from growing and becoming fragmented. The simplest way to correct Registry fragmentation is to use the Pagedefrag utility from `www.sysinternals.com`.

Executive Software ships a commercial version of Diskeeper that has additional functionality and runs much faster than the engine included with Windows Server 2003. Other third-party defraggers include the following:

- PerfectDisk from Raxco Software, *`www.raxco.com`*
- SpeedDisk from Symantec, *`www.symantec.com`*
- Defrag Commander from Winternals, *`www.winternals.com`*

SpeedDisk uses a proprietary method for defragging that does not make use of the Microsoft APIs. This permits the product to defrag more thoroughly at each pass. Cautious administrators have expressed concern about this proprietary engine, but I have not heard of widespread problems. Make sure any defrag product you use has been certified for Windows Server 2003.

File Compression

When it comes to disk capacity, you can never have too much and it can never be too fast. As of this writing, 15,000 rpm UltraSCSI 160 drives cost about 1.6 cents a megabyte. By the time you read this, drives with double that capacity will probably sell for about the same price.

Even at those low prices, storage isn't free, and the time it takes to install and configure new drives certainly comes at a price. This is especially true of drives on user machines, which often contain data that must be backed up prior to replacing and imaging the drive. Compression helps to resolve storage problems quickly and cheaply, but it has its limitations.

Using NTFS, you can compress an individual file, all the files in a folder, or all files on a volume. The compression algorithm balances speed and disk storage. The compression engine has been improved in Windows Server 2003 to permit compressing files of any size as long as the `$Data` attribute is non-resident. Earlier versions of NTFS were limited to compressing files of 16 clusters or more.

The maximum cluster size that can be handled by the compression API is 4K. If you do not plan on using compression and you have applications that store data in large files, you can format a volume with larger cluster sizes to improve performance.

> **Registry Tip: Disk Defragmenter Keys**
>
> The controls for the Disk Defragmenter are located at the key `HKLM | Software | Microsoft | Dfrg`.
>
> The path to the Disk Defragmenter console, Dfrg.msc, is stored in `HKLM | Software | Microsoft | Windows | CurrentVersion | Explorer | MyComputer | DefragPath`.
>
> The default defrag path launches the console using the command `%systemroot%\System32\drfg.msc %c:`, which opens the console with the focus set for the C: drive.

A compressed file is identified by a flag in the `$Standard_Information` attribute, but it is actually controlled by a flag in the `$Data` attribute. This same flag is used for encryption and sparse files, so the three options are mutually exclusive.

When the compression flag is set, data is compressed and decompressed as it streams to and from the disk. This is also true for backups, so expect to widen your backup windows if you compress files on your servers.

If you set the compression flag on a folder, any new files created or copied to the folder are compressed. Existing files are not compressed unless you select that option when setting the flag on the folder.

See the "File Compression Operations" section later in this chapter for procedures to manage compressed files using Explorer and the command-line COMPACT utility.

File Compression and Performance

Compression exacts a significant performance penalty on file and print servers. Microsoft publishes numbers ranging from a 5 percent to 15 percent reduction in end-to-end data transfer times. My own experience points to much higher throughput degradation.

Exact numbers are difficult to quantify because busy production servers have hundreds of connected users doing who-knows-what with applications, personal databases, and data files from 1000 different vendors, and so on and so forth. Imposing compression on this mishmash generally makes you unpopular. Compressing personal files on a server makes better use of the feature than wholesale compression. Because users can compress their own files, take this into account when moving data.

You should never compress database files. The performance penalty of handling random file access into a compressed file is simply too high to be acceptable. Transfer the database files to a larger drive if you need more space.

File Compression Highlights

Working with compressed files in a production environment can result in some surprises. Here are some general operational guidelines:

- Compressed volumes can become heavily fragmented. The defragmenter does a poor job of defragging compressed volumes. Consider this before you enable compression on a server. You may be buying yourself a long weekend of scrubbing a volume to and from tape to get the volume defragmented.
- When copying or moving a file to another NTFS volume, a new file is created. The compression setting on the file is inherited from the new folder. This could result in decompressing a very large file into a tight volume. Use caution.
- The same compression algorithm is used in NTFS 1.2, 3.0. and 3.1, so compressed files are accessible from NT4, Windows 2000, and Windows Server 2003. Make sure as you have the most current service pack on the earlier versions to get the most current NTFS driver.

- Windows Server 2003 cannot read DriveSpace volumes. You must decompress any DriveSpace volumes prior to upgrading a Windows 9x or ME desktop.
- The compression flag stays set when a file is copied to tape. When you restore a compressed file to an NTFS volume, it is compressed as it is saved to disk regardless of the compression setting of the parent directory.
- Be careful when viewing the disk statistics reported by Explorer for compressed files. The file size parameter displayed in the UI shows the uncompressed size. You should always enable the `Show Compressed Files in Color` property in Folder Options.

Sparse Files

Database and imaging applications typically allocate large amounts of disk space that they don't necessarily fill right away. Windows Server 2003 supports an API that can build file structures called *sparse files*.

A sparse file specifies a certain size for itself but does not actually claim the disk space until the file begins to fill up. Because sparse files are handled at the application level, the disk savings come without the performance penalty of regular file compression.

You cannot create a sparse file simply by filling a text file with zeros. Nor do you necessarily get a sparse file when you build huge databases with lots of wasted space in the records. The database application must use the sparse file API. The only Windows Server 2003 application that uses sparse files is the Content Indexer, which stores its catalog information in sparse format. No special settings or Registry hacks are available for sparse file handling.

NTFS Conversion

You can convert a FAT or FAT32 partition to NTFS without losing data. That's the good news. The bad news is that you cannot change your mind and do the reverse. If want to go back to FAT or FAT32, you must back up your data, reformat the partition, then restore the data from tape.

Windows Server 2003 and XP contain many file system improvements that focus on NTFS conversion. That is because NTFS is available in XP Home Edition, making this the first time that NTFS has been available on a consumer product. Over the next few years, millions of Windows 9x and ME desktops will be upgraded to Windows XP. The conversion to NTFS needs to be a smooth one.

Conversion and Setup

One of the first improvements in NTFS conversion was to eliminate the need for conversion at all, at least in fresh installs of Windows Server 2003. The Setup program can now format an NTFS partition directly rather than going through an interim step of formatting with FAT/FAT32 and then converting. This means that the initial bulk file copy from CD puts the files directly into an NTFS file system, virtually eliminating the nasty MFT and system file fragmentation that normally occurs during Setup.

Still, not many shops do their server or desktop installations from CD. Most administrators prefer to install across the network to take advantage of scripted installations or Remote Installation Service (RIS).

If you install using the network, you must first format the system partition as FAT or FAT32 and then use WINNT to transfer the setup files to the local drive. Converting this partition to NTFS would normally cause fragmentation, but Windows Server 2003 improves the situation in two ways:

- A new utility called OFORMAT (the Irish cousin of FORMAT) is available in the Deployment Tools. This utility is designed to place the FAT/FAT32 cluster boundaries where they can smoothly convert to NTFS.
- New functionality was added to the CONVERT program to provide a "landing pad" that can hold the MFT during conversion. The MFT is copied to the converted volume only after all the other files have been converted. This all but eliminates MFT fragmentation.

There are also improvements in the conversion process itself. Conversion is much faster thanks to additional memory assigned to the task. Also, the existing FAT or FAT32 cluster size can be retained for cluster sizes up to 4K as long as the partition was formatted using Windows Server 2003 or XP. This is a big improvement over previous conversion programs, which insisted on using 512-byte cluster sizes regardless of the partition size.

The conversion can retain cluster sizes on volumes formatted by Windows 9x or NT only if the FAT/FAT32 cluster boundaries happen to fall at the required NTFS cluster boundaries. If this does not happen, conversion falls back to a 512-byte cluster size.

Conversion and Free Space

The conversion process preserves the integrity of the FAT right up until the last moment. All temporary writes are done to free space, so you need lots of elbow room on the volume to convert it. Use this rough computation as a guideline:

1. Multiply the number of files and directories on the volume by 1280.
2. Divide the volume size in bytes by 100. The lower limit is 1,048,576 and the upper limit is 4,194,304. Add this to the result of Step 1.
3. Divide the volume size in bytes by 803 and add to the result of Step 2.
4. Add 196,096 to the result of Step 3.

For example, the computation for a 4GB volume with 100,000 files looks like this:

```
100,000 * 1280 = 128,000,000
4GB * 1024 = 4096E6 / 100 = 40960000
4,096,000 + 128,000,000 = 132,096,000
4096E6 / 803 = 5,100,871 + 132,096,000 = 137,196,871
137,196,871 + 196,096 = 137,392,967
```

This volume needs approximately 134MB of free space to do the NTFS conversion. That represents less than 5 percent of the total space. You can get by with slim margins of free space, but for best results, give the conversion a lot more room than that. Otherwise, you will fragment the volume and spend lots of time defragging. You should also specify a conversion file in another partition for building the MFT to eliminate MFT fragmentation.

Conversion and File Security

Another weakness of previous conversion utilities was the way they left the file system completely open by putting the Everyone group on the security descriptor of every file and folder.

Windows 2000 improved the situation somewhat by making it easier to change the NTFS permissions at the top of the file system and letting inheritance take care of the rest, but you had to remember to do that extra step. Windows Server 2003 avoids the problem entirely by assigning the same default ACL to a newly converted partition that it assigns during the initial installation of the operating system. This consists of the following:

- Full control permissions for the LocalSystem account, Administrator account, the Creator/Owner, and the Administrators local group
- Generic `Read` permissions along with `Write_Data/Append_Data` special permissions for the local Users group

You can add other groups onto the permissions list after the volume has been converted.

Link Tracking Service

Do you spend days or weeks planning data moves because of the time it takes to coordinate with users who have shortcuts and compound documents linked to files buried deep in the directory structure under a share point? Relief is at hand in the form of the *Link Tracking Service*, or LTS. This feature was introduced in Windows 2000.

The LTS keeps track of the location of source files for shortcuts and OLE applications. An example of an OLE link is a compound document in Word that contains a link to an Excel spreadsheet. A file with a link to another file is called a *link client*. The target file for the link is called the *link source*.

Typically, if the link source file is moved, the link client will fail to find it and give an error to the user. In Windows Server 2003, the Link Tracking Service finds the link source file automatically and changes the link client pointer to reference the new location. This works even if the link source has been moved to another server in the domain.

Classic Link Source Location

In NT4 and Windows 9x, Explorer falls back on a relatively clumsy search algorithm if the link client cannot find the link source. Essentially, Explorer behaves like a gopher that has lost a carrot. It looks down, it looks up, it looks around, and then it gives up and goes for another carrot. The search pattern is shown in Procedure 15.1.

Procedure 15.1 Classic NT Link Search Pattern

1. Look down four levels.
2. Move up one level then look down four levels again from that vantage point.
3. Go to the desktop and look down four levels.
4. Go to the root of each drive and look down four levels.
5. Repeat without the four-level limit until the client application times out or the user loses patience.

Link Tracking Functional Description

The Link Tracking Service eliminates all this scrabbling around looking for the link source file. The LTS maintains an index of all link source files in an NTFS volume. If one of them is moved, the index tells LTS where it is so it can update the link client.

To do this magic, the LTS needs a way of identifying source files unambiguously in an enterprise. Once again, we meet the *Globally Unique Identifier*, or GUID. When a file or folder is specified as a link source by a link client, the system assigns the link source file a GUID.

The base portion of the GUID belongs to the host volume and is incremented for each new link source record. This enables the file system and Active Directory to index `$Object_ID` attributes by their source volume as well as their location in the MFT.

After the GUID is generated, it is stored in the file record of the link source using an attribute called `$Object_ID`. This attribute is indexed in the `$ObjID` metadata record. This record uses a standard directory format with the index store containing the GUID assigned to the link source and its MFT record number. Using this information, the system can find the any file record given its GUID.

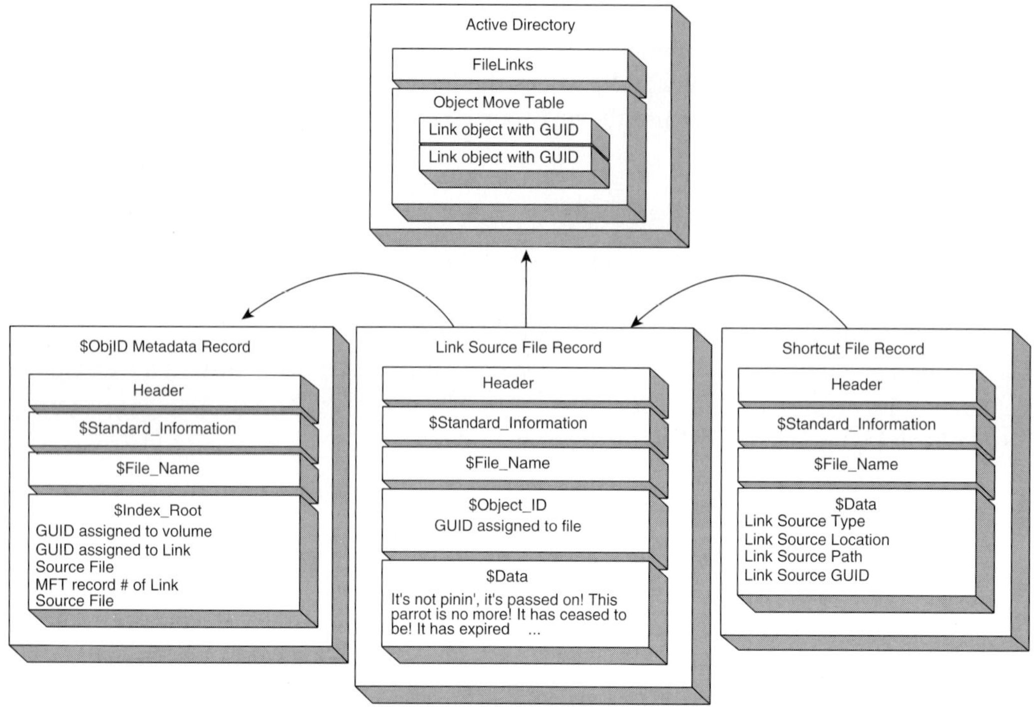

Figure 15.15 Link Tracking Service components.

Let's trace an example of how the LTS uses this index attribute to track down a link source file that has been moved. Figure 15.15 shows the components involved in a link tracking transaction. We'll create a link source/client pair by creating a shortcut in Explorer. A shortcut is an LNK file that defines an OLE link client, and the target file is the link source. Procedure 15.2 uses an experiment to demonstrate LTS functionality.

Procedure 15.2 Verifying Link Tracking Operation

1. Create a file on an NTFS volume.
2. Create a shortcut to the file on your desktop. When you do this, the file system creates a GUID for the file and puts it inside an `$Object_ID` attribute that is inserted into the file's MFT record.
3. The link client stores the GUID of the link source along with information about the link source itself such as its location, path, and type in the `$Data` attribute of the file.
4. Move the link source file to another directory on the same volume. This changes the file's directory, but the MFT record number remains the same. The `$ObjID` index entry does not change. However, the path to the link source file stored in the LNK file data is now incorrect.

5. Double-click the shortcut file. The link is invalid, so the link client cannot find the file. It puts in a frantic call to LTS, which does a lookup for the GUID in the `$ObjID` index. It uses the MFT record in the index to locate the file and then uses the back-link to the file's directory to determine the new directory path.
6. LTS reports the new path to NTFS, which updates the information in the shortcut file. The link client can now open the file.

If you move the file to another NTFS volume on the same machine, the lookup takes a little longer because LTS must search the `$ObjID` index on each volume looking for the source file's GUID. When it finds a match, it gets the necessary location information and path and updates the link client accordingly.

Link Tracking Across a Network

The situation gets a little more complex if you move the link source to an NTFS volume on another server. In this situation, the link tracking client needs help from a central repository of link information. This repository is in Active Directory.

Every Active Directory domain controller acts as an LTS Server. If you move a link source file to another server in an Active Directory domain, the LTS client on the originating member server sends an LDAP update to Active Directory.

Active Directory stores the update in a container called the Object Move Table. This container is located in `cn=FileLinks,cn=System,dc=<domain_name>,dc=<root>`. You can use the AD Users and Computers console to view this container, but first enable ADVANCED FEATURES from the VIEW menu.

Armed with the information it gleans from the LTS Server, an LTS client can update the MFT record of the link client with the UNC name of the new location for the link source. This assumes, of course, that a useful UNC path exists. One of the functions of LTS is to determine if a share point exists that exposes the new file location. If one does not, it uses the administrative ($) share for the volume. Users do not have access to ($) shares, but Help Desk technicians can be trained to recognize the error message and figure out where to request a new share.

Link Tracking Highlights

Here are some additional key points to remember about link tracking:

- LTS works only on Windows 2000, Windows Server 2003, and XP.
- Network Link Tracking works reliably only within a domain. You may get "episodes of success" with machines in different domains or workgroups, but not to the extent necessary to deploy it in production.
- When an LTS client finds a new path to the link source file and updates a shortcut, only the `Target` entry for the shortcut is updated. The `Start In` entry in the shortcut remains in its original value. This can cause problems for applications that use the `Start In` entry to find support files.

- If you copy a file rather than move it, the `$Object_ID` attribute and its associated GUID stay with the original file.
- When you restore a file that is the source file of a link, the `$Object_ID` attribute is restored, as well. If you restore to a separate location, you end up with two files of the same name with the same GUID in the same domain. This may cause problems if you end up with links to the two files and the tracking system gets them confused. Treat all restores with extreme care because of this.

Reparse Points

A reparse point acts like a miniature "redirector" inside an individual MFT record. The reparse point contains the name of a folder, volumes, or device such as a CD-ROM or DVD. When the MFT record containing the reparse point is opened, the target of the reparse point is opened instead. Using reparse points, it is possible to represent volumes and drives as folders, eliminating the need for additional drive letters and share points.

You have already encountered reparse points at least once in your deployment of Windows Server 2003. Every time you open the Sysvol folder on a domain controller and drill down through a folder with a domain name, you're going through a reparse point. The `\Windows\Sysvol\Sysvol\Domain_Name` folder actually mounts a folder at `\Windows\Sysvol\Domain`.

If you open a command prompt and pull a directory of the contents of the `\Windows\Sysvol\Sysvol` folder, you'll see that the file type shows up as `<JUNCTION>` rather than `<DIR>`. This is how the command shell identifies a reparse point. Another term is a *mount point*.

If you create a mount point that points at a device such as a CD-ROM or DVD, Explorer uses the icon representing the AutoRun executable on the media to give a hint about the nature of the device at the other end of the mount point.

Microsoft also uses reparse points to support the hierarchical storage management features in *Remote Storage Services*, or RSS. In RSS, a file physically resides on a tape library with a stub, in the form of a reparse point, left behind on the disk to act as a pointer.

Functional Description of Reparse Points

A reparse point is simply an attribute called `$Reparse_Point` inserted into a standard directory record in place of an `$Index_Allocation` attribute. The `$Reparse_Point` attribute contains an identifier that tells the system what is being mounted and a *symbolic link* to the target. A symbolic link is an operating system construct inside the *object namespace*. You can view the contents of the object namespace using WINOBJ from the Platform SDK or a utility of the same name (but more features) from `www.sysinternals.com`.

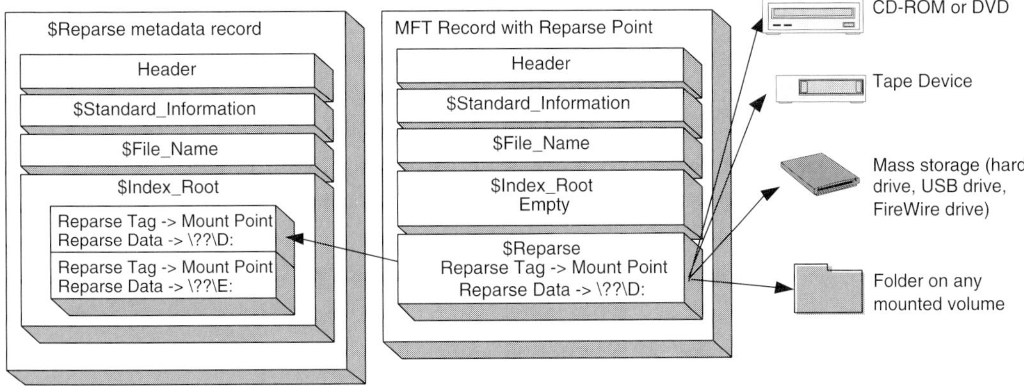

Figure 15.16 Reparse Point components.

Figure 15.16 shows a diagram of the components involved in reparse point transactions. The mount point is always a standard folder. The target, in this case, is a folder on another volume in the machine. Any local volume or device that has a mountable file system is fair game as the target of a reparse point. You cannot create reparse points for network file systems.

The target volume or device can be formatted with any file system supported by Windows Server 2003. This includes FAT, FAT32, NTFS, CDFS, UDFS, or RSS_FS. The volume can contain compressed files, encrypted files, and sparse files.

Information about the target file system is stored in a hidden database under the Root directory called `$RemoteMountManager`. Vendors can add file system filter drivers to this database for use when opening a particular device. The database is a named data stream in the `$Reparse` metadata record.

The `$Reparse` record also maintains an index that correlates the contents of the Remote Mount Manager database and any MFT records that contain a symbolic link reference in a `$Reparse_Point` attribute.

Using this information, when a user double-clicks on a mount point, the file system simply opens the MFT record for the mount point, makes note of the symbolic link, checks for filter drivers in the Remote Mount Manager database, then opens the volume or device and presents the contents as if they were part of the file system containing the mount point.

One use for this technology is CD-ROM towers. If you tire of creating a logical drive for every CD-ROM in a tower then mapping your users to those drives one by one, you can leave all that behind with a Madison Avenue flourish by creating mount points in an existing volume that point to each drive in the CD-ROM tower. Users access the CD-ROM drives via folders under a share point, just as if they were opening folders on a hard drive.

For step-by-step procedures to create and manage reparse points, see the "Reparse Point Operations" section later in this chapter.

Reparse Points Highlights

Here are some key points to remember about reparse points:

- If a folder record has any file or directory entries, it cannot be used as a mount point. The folder must be completely empty.
- Explorer does not add the capacity of the mounted volume to the capacity of the source volume when displaying drive utilization or free space. This means you can mount a 30GB drive from an existing 4GB volume, call it Drive D, but Explorer and the command line will continue to report the size of Drive D as 4GB.
- A search of the parent volume—or running a DOS utility such as TREE—includes the contents of any mounted volumes.
- A volume can be accessed by several mount points. Be careful if you do this. There is great potential for confusion and grief. Imagine the Help Desk call if you have two mount points under separate share points that link to the same target volume. The phone call goes something like this. "I copied all my files to my K:\MyData folder and then deleted my R:\MyData and now I can't see any files in K:\MyData. What happened?"
- Copying a folder with mounted volumes also copies the contents of the mounted volumes.
- Removing a mount point using the `RD` command only deletes the MFT record containing the reparse point, not the underlying volume. If, however, you delete a mount point using `DEL` or you use Explorer to send the mount point to the Recycle Bin or delete to it entirely, all the files and directories in the mounted volume are deleted.
- When backing up volumes with mount points, the backup includes files and directories on the mounted volumes. Keep this in mind when mounting a volume at multiple mount points. You could end up backing up the same volume several times. Ntbackup has the option to skip restoration from junction points and the files under those junction points.

File System Recovery and Fault Tolerance

The file system is the single most critical element of the operating system. If the file system gets corrupted, not only can data be lost entirely, it can be scrambled in ways that aren't immediately apparent. This can happen for a variety of reasons. A disk can crash or get large numbers of sector errors. You might lose power to the system thanks to a failed UPS (or no UPS at all) causing a total loss of cached data. A misbehaved driver might lock the system or run rampant over the file system metadata files. Or it might just be your time in the pit.

Recovering a consistent file system has the same urgency for a system administrator as recovering a stable pulse and vital signs has for an emergency care physician. This section covers several checks you should perform to ensure stable operations, discusses fault-tolerance features designed to save the day in case of catastrophe, and covers the operation of the Windows File Protection service. Let's start with periodic maintenance and a familiar face, CHKDSK.

CHKDSK and AUTOCHK

The first line of defense for preventing file system crashes is regular maintenance. The maintenance tool in Windows Server 2003 has a venerable name, CHKDSK. This utility analyzes the file system for corruption and consistency and repairs anything it finds that is broken.

The code that actually does the analysis associated with CHKDSK is contained in the file system drivers themselves—Ufat.dll for FAT and FAT32, and Untfs.dll for NTFS. This code can be initiated in several ways other than running CHKDSK. You can use Explorer by right-clicking a drive, selecting PROPERTIES from the flyout menu, selecting the `Tools` tab, and then clicking `Check Now` under Error-Checking. Or, you can initiate a consistency check at boot time using AUTOCHK.

Comparison of AUTOCHK and CHKDSK

AUTOCHK is designed to run in real mode during system startup to prevent locked files from blocking the consistency checks. AUTOCHK cannot be run after the operating system loads. The Registry entry that controls AUTOCHK is as follows:

```
Key:     HKLM | System | CurrentControlSet | Control | SessionManager
Value:   BootExecute
Data:    Autocheck AUTOCHK *
```

Under normal circumstances, AUTOCHK runs only if the so-called "dirty" flag is set in the `$Volume` record, indicating that that the system shut down abnormally. If AUTOCHK runs every time your server restarts, you have a very bad problem. Look for a caching RAID controller that is not Windows Server 2003 compatible or some other explanation, and do so in a hurry. Many administrators have watched perfectly good file systems turn into something that looks like the aftermath of a Chinese New Year celebration by ignoring consistent AUTOCHK initiations.

When AUTOCHK runs, it checks the disk in read-only mode and reports any problems to the Application log. Check the Event Viewer for details. If you get errors, you should restart again and run AUTOCHK in fixup mode (equivalent to `CHKDSK /f`) to correct the errors. This is covered in the next section.

Using CHKNTFS to Configure AUTOCHK

You can force AUTOCHK to run in fixup mode with the CHKNTFS utility. Here are the CHKNTFS settings and the syntax for setting AUTOCHK functions. In each case, `<volume>` can be a drive letter or a volume name:

- **`chkntfs <volume> /c`.** Sets AUTOCHK to run in fixup mode for the specified volume or drive letter. This switch adds `/m` to the AUTOCHK entry in the Registry.

- **chkntfs <*volume*> /d.** Returns the system to its default behavior of running AUTOCHK in read-only mode when the dirty flag is set.
- **chkntfs <*volume*> /t:time.** AUTOCHK can take a long time to finish. It runs in real mode, so very little memory exists to help it progress quickly. On a system with a big RAID array containing thousands of megabytes of files, AUTOCHK can take several hours to finish. By using this CHKNTFS option, you add a countdown to AUTOCHK so that you can bypass the check if you are reasonably certain that no file system corruption is present. For example, if you are going to down a server to install a new network card, you can use the `/t:time` option to bypass AUTOCHK, thereby avoiding the lengthy delay. This option adds an `AUTOCHKTimeOut` value to `HKLM | System | CurrentControlSet | Control |Session Manager`.
- **chkntfs <*volume*> /x.** Excludes a disk from AUTOCHK. Use this option with caution. If you forget you set this switch, the system does not do its necessary housekeeping checks at boot time. This option adds `/k:<volume>` to the AUTOCHK entry in the Registry.

Functional Description of CHKDSK (AUTOCHK)

When CHKDSK (or AUTOCHK) runs, it performs a series of consistency checks. The NTFS checks are as follows:

Pass 1

- Scans the MFT looking for active file and directory records and builds bitmaps of active MFT records and active clusters using the LCN information in the records.
- Uses the bitmaps to validate the `$Bitmap` file in metadata. If a record is unreadable or has an incorrect format, it is identified as a problem.

Pass 2

- Scans directory records to make sure that each file entry references an actual file record and agrees with the directory reference in the file record.
- Checks for circular references for subdirectories. A circular reference is a directory that thinks it is under itself as a subdirectory. Circular references are very rare but can result in the loss of a great deal of data by orphaning large chunks of the file system, so do not take them lightly.
- Checks for consistency between filename attributes in the file records and the filename entries in the associated directory index. This pass can take many minutes, even hours, depending on the number of entries in the MFT and the complexity of the directory structure. The speed has nothing to do with volume size. A 32GB volume with 1000 files finishes in the blink of an eye. A 3GB volume with 100,000 files takes a long time.

Pass 3

- Scans security descriptors to ensure that every record references a security descriptor and that the entry agrees with the reference in the security descriptor itself.
- If a Change Journal (also called a USN Journal) is associated with the volume, the system scans the log and verifies the index entries.

Pass 4

- Performs a disk scan and tries to read every sector that contains a file. Bad clusters are added to the `$BadClus` list. Data in the bad clusters is copied to a new cluster.

Pass 5

- Performs a disk scan of free space in the volume. Bad clusters are added to the `$BadClus` list.

CHKDSK Switches

Several CHKDSK switches affect how the scans are run. Two switches, `/i` and `/c`, were added in NT4 SP4 to speed up consistency checks by bypassing Passes 4 and 5. These switches also work for AUTOCHK:

- **`/f`.** Runs CHKDSK in fixup mode. (AUTOCHK uses `/p`.)
- **`/v`.** Displays cleanup messages.
- **`/r`.** Performs a full disk scan looking for bad clusters. Any that it finds are added to the `$BadClus` file.
- **`/l`.** Displays the size of the `$Logfile`. When paired with a `:size` parameter, such as `/L:4096`, changes the size of the `$Logfile` to the new value.
- **`/x`.** Forces a volume dismount. Any users with open files lose their data. Using this option also runs CHKDSK in fixup mode.
- **`/i`.** Skips internal consistency checks between the filename attributes in the file records and the associated filename listings in the directory index.
- **`/c`.** Skips the directory loop (cycle) checks.

An additional CHKDSK switch, `/p`, can only be used from the Recovery Console. This switch forces CHKDSK to run an exhaustive check.

Recommendations for Running CHKDSK

You should run CHKDSK periodically to find file system anomalies. You cannot run CHKDSK on a volume with active files, such as the system volume or a volume containing a database, because the files are locked. Use CHKNTFS to schedule AUTOCHK to run in fixup mode at boot time.

If you have users who keep getting corrupted files on their XP systems, you can break them of the habit of simply turning their machine off by configuring AUTOCHK to run in fixup mode at every boot. Make it clear that the extra boot time in the morning is necessary because they didn't down their machines correctly the night before. They'll take the hint eventually.

File System Logging

Under most circumstances, CHKDSK or AUTOCHK running in fixup mode can correct all file system anomalies. But what happens if the file system is in an unknown state caused by a system crash or a loss of power? NTFS keeps a great deal of data in cache to improve lookup times and to time disk writes for maximum effectiveness. This so-called *lazy write caching* dramatically improves system performance, but at the cost of a somewhat lessened file system reliability.

If the file system is put into an unknown state following a crash or lockup, AUTOCHK can rebuild the file system, but it goes about its work with painful slowness. This costs production time, not to mention the wear on the stomach linings and tempers of system administrators waiting to get their machines back online.

Servers crash on occasion. This is a fact of life, so it makes sense to plan for that eventuality by putting in place a way to recover a consistent file system more quickly. NTFS does this with the help of a kernel-mode service called the *Log File Service*, or LFS. The LFS is a general-purpose logging service. NTFS is currently its only client.

LFS Structure

The LFS keeps a record of all disk writes that affect the core file system. It stores these records in a file called `$Logfile`, one of the MFT metadata files. The `$Logfile` consists of a long run starting at a position on the disk chosen to get the maximum performance from the file system.

Most user data is not protected by the LFS. If you hit the big red switch on a server, data in the cache is lost. LFS will help get the critical files back to a consistent state, but you may need to wait for AUTOCHK to fix the user files.

LFS Functional Overview

The `$Logfile` consists of two parts: the *restart area* and the *infinite logging area*. The restart area (contained in buffers prefixed by `RSTR`) contains location information for data in the infinite logging area. A key component of the restart area is the checkpoint information. This tells the logging system those log entries that were flushed to the MFT and those that were not. The infinite logging area (contained in buffers prefixed by `RCRD`) works like an 8-track tape. When the log gets full, the log service starts at the beginning again, overwriting the oldest entries.

When an update to the core file system occurs, the disk write is handed to the LFS for recording in the `$Logfile`. These critical updates include changes to attribute headers, security attributes, directory locations, and modifications to the MFT metadata files.

Periodically, the log entries are flushed to the MFT and the checkpoint is moved. If the system crashes during this flushing operation, the LFS can recover a consistent file system very quickly, simply by finding the checkpoint and then walking through the last `$Logfile` entries. The LFS then works with the file system to purge any transactions that are not completely committed and recommit them again. The final condition of the MFT reflects the status of the file system at the time of the crash, excluding any commits that are in the lazy write cache waiting to go to the log file itself.

System recovery using the log file can take a while on large volumes but not nearly as long as a full file system rebuild using AUTOCHK. If the log recovery fails, the file system performs a full rebuild. If this fails, the only alternative is recovery from tape. No controls and no Registry hacks are available for the Log File Service.

The only index that is recovered by the LFS is the filename index in the directory records. Windows Server 2003 has several features that require special indexing of the MFT. Recovering these indexes with a full table scan is a tedious process. To help speed things up, the system has a new feature called the Change Journal, discussed in the next section.

Change Journal

Nobody likes to do a chore that doesn't need doing. For example, when the time comes to wash the dishes, do you unload your entire cupboard and scour everything you find? No. You only wash what's dirty, right? In our household, the definition of "dirty" is a dish that is in the sink. (Christine, my significant other, categorizes after-dinner dishes still on the table not as "dirty" but as "Bill's mess.")

When it comes to file system chores, you have to do backups and virus scans and quota evaluations and content indexing and on and on. Most of these chores don't need to be done for every single file in a volume. They involve opening files and scanning their contents, an expensive proposition both in terms of CPU cycles and I/O. If you can skip files that don't need work, you'll free resources for other, more useful chores.

This is the function of the *Change Journal*. It keeps track of changes to MFT records. Applications can use API calls to determine which records have been touched since the application last ran and only perform work on those files.

The applications in Windows Server 2003 that make use of the Change Journal are as follows:

- **Content Indexing Service (CISVC).** This service keeps a catalog of the contents of text files so they can be searched and retrieved quickly.
- **File Replication Service (FRS).** The FRS takes data from one server and copies it to another server automatically. By referring to the Change Journal, FRS only copies those items that have been modified since the last transfer.

- **Volume Shadow Copy Service (VSS).** This new service in Windows Server 2003 takes a snapshot of a volume for use in backups and in providing differential views of a shared folder.
- **Remote Storage Services (RSS).** This service moves files from disk to tape but makes them available as near-online storage when users select the files from disk. The Change log improves recovery time and substantially reduces the risk of data loss by simplifying consistency checks.

The Change Journal is a metadata record called `$UsnJrnl` stored under the `$Extend` metadata folder. Table 15.2 lists the events that trigger an entry in the Change Journal for indexed records.

Table 15.2 Events That Trigger a Change Journal Entry

Basic_Info_Change	Hard_Link_Change
Close	Indexable_Change
Compression_Change	Named_Data_Extend
Data_Extend	Named_Data_Overwrite
Data_Overwrite	Named_Data_Truncation
Data_Truncation	Object_Id_Change
Ea_Change	Rename_New_Name
Encryption_Change	Rename_Old_Name
File_Create	Reparse_Point_Change
File_Delete	Security_Change
Stream_Change	

The system keeps track of changes in the Change Journal using an *Update Sequence Number*, or USN. When an entry is made or updated in the journal, it gets the next available USN. This is similar to the way that the Active Directory tracks changes. The USN is a 64-bit number, so you have enough numbers to last billions of years.

No troubleshooting tips are involved with operating the Change Journal. Rather, the Change Journal is completely transparent, just like the Log File System. No UI settings or Registry hacks are available. If the journal becomes corrupted or is accidentally deleted, the applications that rely on it are forced to do a full scan of the MFT to reindex. This might take a while. Look in the Event log if you think restarts are taking inordinately long.

Windows File Protection

One insidious form of file corruption comes when an application overwrites a critical system file with its own copy of that file. The copy comes from the master platform used to compile the application, and there is no guarantee that this platform was running the same binaries as your server.

Nearly every system administrator has had a bad experience with applications that play games with core system services. You have a server that operated flawlessly for months and months. One day, you install a seemingly innocuous application and suddenly you enter Blue Screen purgatory.

It is the job of the *Windows File Protection* service, or WFP, to stop this rampant trampling of system files. It does so by comparing the digital signatures in the critical system files with a catalog of their signatures that was included in the original setup files.

If an application replaces one of the protected files, WFP checks the digital signature against the catalog. If the replacement file has the approved signature, WFP permits the file to remain. (This would happen if the developer built the installation package using a machine running the same operating system at the same service pack level as your system.)

If the digital signature does not match—that is, it is not in the catalog—or the replacement has no signature at all, WFP retrieves a copy of the original file from a cache folder and overwrites the intruder. It writes an information record to the Event log to notify you of its actions.

The following applications distribute executables signed by Microsoft:

- Service Pack installation using Update.exe
- Hotfix installation using Hotfix.exe
- Operating system upgrades using Winnt32.exe
- Windows Update service
- Device Manager/Class Installer

When you install a service pack, a new catalog file is added to those already on the system. The catalogs are stored in `\Windows\System32\Catroot`. The new catalog is given the name SP#.CAT, where # corresponds to the service pack number.

The WFP system keeps a copy of controlled files in a compressed folder under `\WINNT\System32\ DllCache`. This folder contains a copy of every file installed from the Windows Server 2003 CD during Setup. When one of these files is updated using one of the four approved methods, the cached file is replaced with the updated file.

Operational Description of WFP

You can test the operation of WFP as shown in Procedure 15.3.

Procedure 15.3 Verifying WFP Operation

1. Open Explorer and navigate to the `\WINNT\System32` directory. If Explorer is web-enabled, you are prompted to verify that you have business in `\WINNT` and in `\WINNT\System32`. This is your clue that the directories are on the list of "protected" directories in WFP.

2. Scroll down to one of the system files installed during Setup.
3. Right-click the icon for the file select DELETE from the flyout menu. Click `Yes` when asked to verify the deletion.
4. Don't do anything for a while. Just wait and watch. In a few seconds, the icon reappears. This is WFP at work.

WFP Elements

The WFP does not run as a separate service. Instead, it is a core feature of the operating system. The controls are kept in the Registry under `HKLM | Software | Microsoft | Windows NT | Current Version | Winlogon`. The values are as follows:

- **`SFCQuota.`** The amount of disk space allocated for the `DllCache` directory. The default value is `FFFFFFFF`, giving the `DllCache` folder a virtually limitless size of 4GB. You can get the same effect by entering –1.
- **`SFCDisable.`** If you set the value to 1, System File Protection is disabled for the next restart. It is enabled automatically on subsequent restarts. Use this switch to replace files with vendor-authorized versions or to use checked versions for debugging.
- **`SFCBugCheck.`** Under normal circumstances, if you attempt to replace or delete a protected file, the system warns you with a console message. If you set this value to 1, the system stops with a blue screen. This can be set on a desktop with a user who has a history of trying to change system files.
- **`SFCScan.`** Configures the WFP to scan the `DllCache` for missing files at boot time. A setting of 1 scans files at every boot. A setting of 2 scans files once.

Using the System File Checker, SFC

You do not need to hack the Registry to change the WFP settings. A command-line utility comes with Windows Server 2003 to set these values. Called the *System File Checker*, or SFC, the utility can also rebuild the `DllCache` directory if files are accidentally deleted. The switches for SFC are outlined in the following sections.

sfc /scanonce

This option scans the contents of the `DllCache` to verify that they match the signatures in the catalog and then scans the files in the protected directories. This scan does not commence until you log in.

While the scan is running, a message appears on the console asking you to wait. You can perform other tasks and run applications, but this slows the scan. If the system encounters a file that is missing in the cache or a system file that is the wrong version, it prompts you to insert the Windows Server 2003 CD so that the proper file can be restored.

If you installed Windows Server 2003 across the network or from an I386 directory on the local hard drive, you must still have the CD to do the file protection restore. If the machine does not have a CD-ROM drive, your only workaround is to compare the contents of the `DllCache` with that of another machine and copy the missing files manually.

sfc /scanboot

This option performs a protected file scan at every boot. On servers administered by professionals, this is seldom necessary. Desktops, on the other hand, might need more diligent care.

Use the `/scanboot` option if you have consistent problems with users who delete cached files and you want to make sure they go through the tedious process of correcting their own blunders. You can also use the `/SFCBugCheck` switch in the Registry to blue-screen the machine if the same users insist on playing with the protected files.

sfc /quiet

This option replaces missing files without asking for permission.

sfc /cancel

Use this option if you have the system to scan at the next boot, but then you change your mind.

WFP Highlights

The key points to remember about WFP are as follows:

- WFP protects system files loaded during setup.
- WFP only enables a few authorized executables to change system files.
- Deleted or corrupt system files are replaced from an on-disk cache.
- The SFC utility can manually scan system files and repair them.

Quotas

Windows 2000 came out with a file system feature that many administrators had waited a long time to see: the capability to limit the disk space assigned to a user based on a set of rules established by the administrator. In other words, quotas.

Unfortunately, this first attempt at quota management by Microsoft left a lot to be desired. It had several fundamental flaws:

- First, it charged file usage based solely on individual file ownership. Here's why this is a problem. It's quite common for one user to create a set of files for a group of users to fill with data. Legal pleadings are an example. Graphic designs and PC-based publications are another. A quota system based on ownership points the finger at the creator of the files, not the users who fattened them up.

- Second, the system tracks usage based on volumes, not individual folders. This makes it difficult to manage a big file server with several share points to the same array. "I got a 'Disk Full' error on my K drive so I tried to put the file in my M drive but it's full, too."
- Finally, the quota system lacks an enterprise management interface. The quota management console does permit you to copy individual quota settings from one volume to another, but there are no centralized tools that permit you to manage quotas for an entire system, perhaps with settings stored in Active Directory.

I would like very much to tell you that Microsoft resolved all these deficiencies in Windows Server 2003. Unfortunately, that is not the case. Rather than spend a lot of time covering quota management as it is implemented in Windows Server 2003, let me refer you to a few third-party Storage Resource Management (SRM) products that do a better job of managing disk space:

- **StorageCentral SRM** from Precise Software, `www.precise.com`. This is the leading quota management product for Windows 2000. It can define quota settings for users and groups, target limitations by file type, and has a raft of reports.
- **Quota Server** from Northern Software, `www.northernparklife.com`. This product has the most on-screen features but is a little more difficult to manage in an enterprise than the Wquinn product.
- **Quota and File Sentinel** from NTP Software, `www.ntpsoftware.com`. The interface of this product is more difficult than the others to use and manage. Look for an upgrade between when I'm writing this and when Windows Server 2003 is released.

These tools carry a fairly hefty price tag, but when you compare that to the cost of purchasing, installing, and backing up more storage, you may find them to be more than cost effective.

File System Operations

We're done with functional descriptions and checklists. It's now time to get some real work done. The next few topics contain operating procedures for the following:

- File compression
- Reparse points
- Defragmentation
- NTFS conversion
- Writing to CD-R/RW and DVD-RAM Devices

File Compression Operations

No controls are available in the UI or Registry hacks to change the compression mechanism. The only setting is to turn the compression bit on or off. This can be done using Explorer or a command-line utility called COMPACT. Procedure 15.4 shows how to turn compression on using Explorer.

Procedure 15.4 Enabling Compression

1. Open Explorer and navigate to the file or folder you want to compress.
2. Right-click the icon and select PROPERTIES from the flyout menu. The Properties window opens (see Figure 15.17).

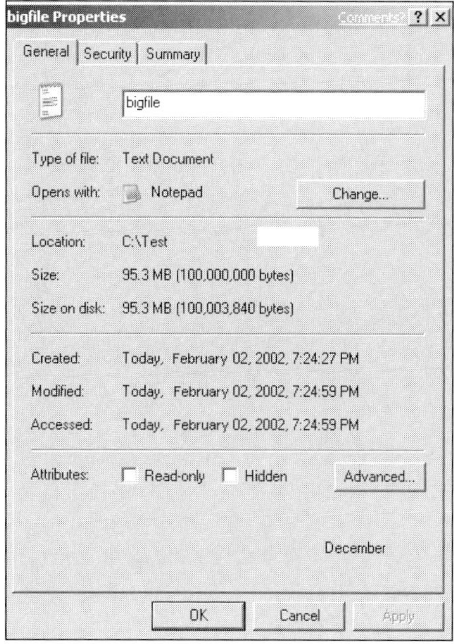

Figure 15.17 Properties window showing information about a big file in an uncompressed state.

3. In the Attributes field, click `Advanced`. The Advanced Attributes window opens. This window controls the various attribute bits in the MFT record. See the sidebar, "Using Advanced File Attributes," for more information.

Using Advanced File Attributes

The Advanced Attributes window for a file or folder, as shown in Figure 15.18, has several options that affect file storage. This is what they do:

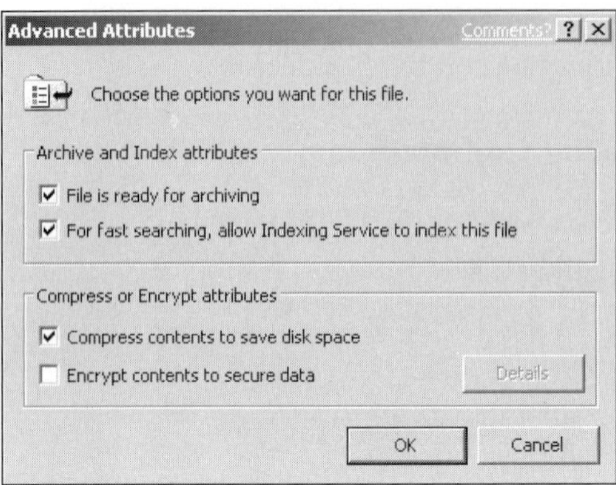

Figure 15.18 Advanced Attributes window showing status of file attributes such as compression and encryption.

- The `Archive` bit comes from classic NT and DOS. It signals that the file was changed but not backed up.
- The `Index` bit is new to Windows Server 2003 and indicates that the *Content Indexing Service*, or CISVC, should scan the file. This service began life as an add-on indexer for Internet Information Server and has now burrowed its way into the operating system. Fortunately, this option is turned off by default.
- The `Compress` attribute causes the system to compress the file.
- The `Encrypt` attribute causes the system to encrypt the file.

The `Compress` and `Encrypt` attributes are mutually exclusive. This happens for two reasons:

- Encrypted files have very few similar characters, so Microsoft does not consider them good candidates for compression.
- The system cannot restore compressed encrypted files from tape. The Restore process recovers a compressed file from tape by reading the header to find the starting cluster on the drive where the file was originally located. The Restore process, running in the context of a Backup Operator, cannot read the encrypted file to find the destination cluster.

4. Select `Compress Contents to Save Space` and then click `OK` to save the change and close the window.
5. Click `OK` to apply the change and close the Properties window. Depending on the size of the file, it may take a while to compress.
6. Close the Properties window and then open it again. The Size on Disk value shows you the new compressed size.

If you prefer command-line tools, use the COMPACT utility to compress and decompress files. To set the compression bit, run `compact /c`. To reset the bit, run `compact /u`.

If you want to set the compression bit on a directory and compress all the files in that directory and its subdirectories, run `compact /c /s`.

To list files and their compression information, run `compact` with no switches. For example, this is a list of the standard BMP files that come with Windows Server 2003 in their compressed state:

```
C:>\TestDir\compact
 Listing C:\TestDir\
 New files added to this directory will not be compressed.

     1272 :       1024 = 1.2 to 1 C Blue Lace 16.bmp
    17062 :      17062 = 1.0 to 1 C Coffee Bean.bmp
    16730 :      15872 = 1.1 to 1 C FeatherTexture.bmp
    17336 :      13312 = 1.3 to 1 C Gone Fishing.bmp

Of 4 files within 1 directories
4 are compressed and 0 are not compressed.
46,310 total bytes of data are stored in 32,430 bytes.
The compression ratio is 1.2 to 1.
```

Reparse Point Operations

You can create reparse points, also called *mount points*, using the Disk Management console or from the command line using LINKD. After it is created, you can manage and delete the reparse points using the Fsutil utility.

Using the Disk Management console, you can only mount an entire file system. LINKD makes it possible to mount a particular folder. You cannot mount a network file share or a device accessed via a UNC name.

Creating a Mount Point Using the Disk Management Console

Procedure 15.5 describes how to use the Disk Management console to create a mount point for another volume.

Procedure 15.5 Creating a Mount Point Using the Disk Management Console

1. Create an empty folder on an NTFS volume to act as a mount point. The folder can be in any subdirectory. If the folder has existing files or directory entries, it cannot be used as a mount point.
2. Open the `Computer Management` console using START | PROGRAMS | ADMINISTRATIVE TOOLS | COMPUTER MANAGEMENT.
3. Expand the tree to STORAGE | DISK MANAGEMENT.
4. Right-click the bar representing the CD-ROM drive and select CHANGE DRIVE LETTER AND PATH from the flyout menu. The Change Drive Letter and Path window opens (see Figure 15.19).
5. Click `Add`. The Add New Drive Letter or Path window opens.

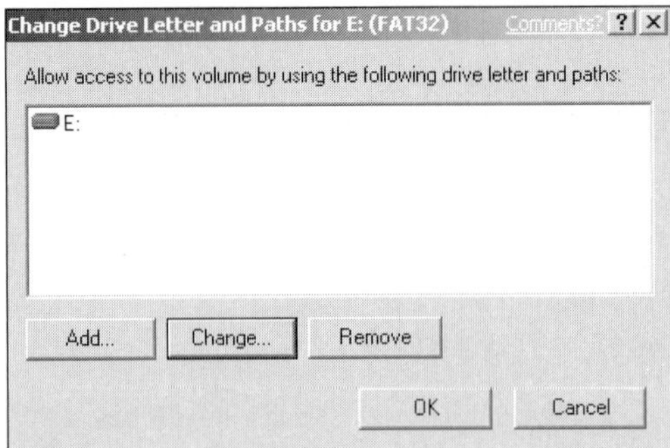

Figure 15.19 Change Drive Letter and Path window.

6. Select the Mount This Volume at an Empty Folder Which Supports Drive Paths radio button and click `Browse`. The Browse for Drive Path window opens.
7. Navigate to the NTFS volume where you created the folder for the mount point. You can also click `New Folder` to create a folder on any NTFS volume. Long names are permitted.
8. Click `OK` to accept the new folder and close the window.
9. At the Add New Drive Letter or Path window, click `OK` to mount the drive. The Disk Management console does not show that a volume is mounted on another volume.

Creating a Mount Point Using LINKD

The normal volume mounting process as described in the last section is limited to mounting an entire volume at a mount point. The Windows Server 2003 Resource Kit contains a utility called LINKD that can mount a folder to an empty folder as well as a volume or device. The syntax for LINKD is as follows:

```
linkd <empty_folder> <source_folder>
```

For example, to mount the `C:\Windows` folder at `D:\test` (an empty folder), enter the following:

```
linkd d:\test_dir c:\winnt
```

You cannot use LINKD to mount a folder on a network drive. Deleting the folder deletes only the link. The folder icons do not show a special mounted icon such as that used by regular volume mount points.

Managing Reparse Points Using Fsutil

The Fsutil console has a reparse point namespace for use in managing mount points and other junctions. For example, to check the contents of the reparse point entry in the mount point record, enter `fsutil reparsepoint query <name>`. Here is a sample listing:

```
C:\>fsutil reparsepoint query mountpointname
Reparse Tag Value : 0xa0000003
```

```
Tag value: Microsoft
Tag value: Name Surrogate
Tag value: Mount Point
GUID : {000E0000-0010-0006-5C00-3F003F005C00}
Data Length : 0x00000020
Reparse Data :
0000:  48 00 3a 00 5c 00 00 00 48 00 3a 00 5c 00 00 00  H.:.\...H.:.\...
0010:  00 00 00 00 00 00 00 00 00 00 00 00 00 00 00 00  ................
```

You can use Fsutil to delete the reparse point without touching the files behind it. Enter `fsutil reparsepoint delete <name>`. Unfortunately, there is no "create" command for Fsutil. You'll need to use LINKD from the Resource Kit.

Defragmentation Operations

There are two ways to initiate a defragmentation run for a volume. You can use the GUI-based console, Dfrg.msc, or you can use a new command-line utility, DEFRAG. The two interfaces execute the same code, so the choice is purely one of convenience. One advantage of the command-line version is that you can schedule it to run via the Task Scheduler.

The topics in this section give the procedures for cleaning up a disk prior to defragging, how to defrag a volume using the GUI, and how to schedule a defrag using the command line.

Cleaning up a Volume Prior to Defragmenting

Have you ever used the services of a housekeeper? What's the first thing you did before the housekeeper paid that first visit? You cleaned house, right? After all, you don't want a total stranger to think you're a slob, do you? The same rule applies to preparing a volume for defragmenting. It doesn't make sense to have lots of useless files on the disk that waste the defragger's time. So, do two things prior to defragging:

- Run `CHKDSK /f` on every volume you plan on defragging. If this means restarting to get AUTOCHK to run on the system/boot partition, it's worth doing. I have yet to see an instance where a system crashed or went blue-screen during defrag following a good CHKDSK.
- Get rid of deadweight files. Windows Server 2003 has a utility for this called *Disk Cleanup*. It comes in the form of an executable, Clnmgr.exe. Disk Cleanup scans a drive and identifies old Indexing catalogs, Temporary Internet files, temporary and superceded offline files, ActiveX and Java applet downloads, and Recycle Bin contents that can be deleted without causing problems.

Disk Cleanup is a quick and effective way to remove unwanted files. Run the utility as described in Procedure 15.6.

Procedure 15.6 Using Disk Cleanup

1. Launch Disk Cleanup using START | PROGRAMS | ACCESSORIES | SYSTEM TOOLS | DISK CLEANUP. The Disk Cleanup window opens.
2. Specify the drive letter for the volume you want to clean. The utility searches for files that are candidates for removal. If the disk has a mount point, the search includes the mounted volume. When finished, Disk Cleanup offers the results in a menu of options (see Figure 15.20).

   Choosing to delete `Temporary Internet Files` does not delete cookies. It does clear cached web pages, so you may experience delays when accessing web sites the next time you run Internet Explorer.

   Choosing to delete `Temporary Off-Line Files` is acceptable even if the user is offline or forgot to synchronize. Disk Cleanup only deletes offline files that are marked as synchronized with the source file.

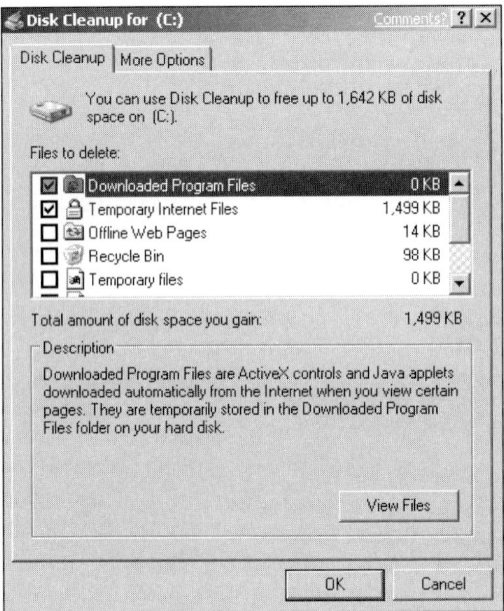

Figure 15.20 Disk Cleanup window showing menu options.

3. Click the options you want to use and then click `OK` to make the changes and delete the files. When Disk Cleanup finishes, it closes down without a final message.

Defragmenting an NTFS Volume Using the MMC Console

You can open the Disk Defragmenter console in several ways:

- Directly from the START menu: Start | Programs | Accessories | System Tools | Disk Defragmenter.
- From the Computer Management console: by expanding the tree to STORAGE | DISK DEFRAGMENTER.
- From Explorer or My Computer: by right-clicking a drive icon, opening the Properties window, and selecting TOOLS | DEFRAGMENT NOW.
- From the Run window: by entering **`dfrg.msc`**.

After you open the Disk Defragmenter console, you can run a fragmentation analysis of a volume or you can jump right in and defragment the volume. Start with an analysis (see Procedure 15.7). Don't be surprised to see lots and lots of files scattered all over the drive while the analysis tool reports that the volume does not require defragging. An NTFS volume is considered fragmented only when non-resident data attributes are split across multiple runs. The automatic system tune-up will move commonly-used files to strategic locations automatically.

Procedure 15.7 Performing a Defragmentation Analysis

1. Highlight the volume and click `Analyze`. The system looks for fragments and gives you a visual display and text report. Figure 15.21 shows an example.

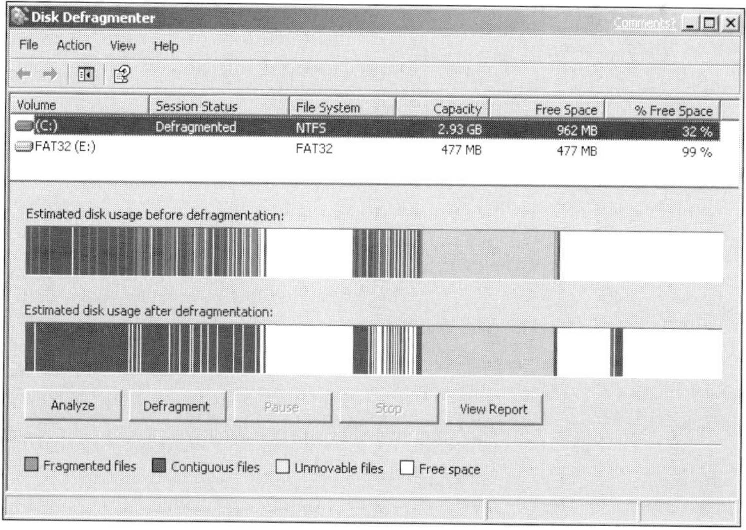

Figure 15.21 Disk Defragmenter window showing results of disk analysis.

2. Click `View Report`. The listing contains statistics for volume use, volume fragmentation, file fragmentation, pagefile fragmentation, directory fragmentation, and MFT fragmentation. Of this list, the defragger can correct file and directory fragmentation only. Expect to find nearly all the Registry hives near the top of the list for fragmentation.
3. Click `Defragment`. You can do this from the Report window or the main window. The system performs another analysis and then begins defragging. If it is a big volume with lots of fragmented files, the defragger may stay busy for hours. If you are defragging a server, you should do this after working hours. Not only is performance miserable, locked user files impedes the defragger from doing a thorough job. Times vary depending on I/O speed, CPU speed, and bus speed.
4. Following completion, Disk Defragmenter displays a new graphical fragmentation analysis and a new report. You may need to defrag several times if you have a heavily fragmented volume.

Defragmenting Using the DEFRAG Command-Line Utility

Windows Server 2003 corrects a deficiency in Windows defragmentation by supplying a command-line version of the defrag utility that can be scheduled using the Task Scheduler. The switches are for analyze only (`-a`) and verbose reporting (`-v`):

```
C:\>defrag d: -a -v
Windows Disk Defragmenter
Copyright  2001 Microsoft Corp. and Executive Software International, Inc.

Analysis Report

    Volume size                                 = 1.95 GB
    Cluster size                                = 2 KB
    Used space                                  = 1.87 GB
    Free space                                  = 89 MB
    Percent free space                          = 4 %

Volume fragmentation
    Total fragmentation                         = 28 %
    File fragmentation                          = 56 %
    Free space fragmentation                    = 0 %

File fragmentation
    Total files                                 = 3,516
    Average file size                           = 658 KB
    Total fragmented files                      = 40
    Total excess fragments                      = 753
    Average fragments per file                  = 1.21

Pagefile fragmentation
    Pagefile size                               = 0 bytes
    Total fragments                             = 0
```

```
Folder fragmentation
    Total folders                          = 283
    Fragmented folders                     = 21
    Excess folder fragments                = 72

Master File Table (MFT) fragmentation
    Total MFT size                         = 16 MB
    MFT record count                       = 3,820
    Percent MFT in use                     = 24
    Total MFT fragments                    = 2
```

If you have less than 15 percent free space on a drive, DEFRAG will give an error message and refuse to start. You can force the engine to use the MFT buffer area with the `-f` switch. The defragmentation will run a little more slowly, but it should succeed.

NTFS Conversion Operations

In spite of all the protections built into the conversion program, there is still the potential for wrecking your file system, so prudence dictates that you get a good backup before converting.

There are no conversion options in the Disk Management console. Conversion is done using a command-line utility called CONVERT. The syntax is as follows:

```
convert volume_name /fs:ntfs
```

You can specify a volume name, drive letter, or mount point as the conversion target. If you specify a drive letter, you are prompted for the volume name just to verify that you have the right volume. Run `VOL` if you need to verify the volume name.

The default cluster size is 512 bytes to make the most effective use of the volume during conversion. You cannot change the cluster size later without reformatting the volume.

The system must be able to get an exclusive lock on all files to do the conversion. If it cannot get exclusive access, you are asked whether you want to do the conversion at the next restart. If you answer `Yes`, the following entry is made to the Registry:

```
Key:     HKLM | System | CurrentControlSet | Control | SessionManager
Value:   BootExecute
Data:    AUTOCHK autoconv \??\c: /FS:ntfs
```

The `\??\c:` entry is the symbolic link in the Windows Server 2003 object namespace that represents the volume. If you change your mind and decide that you don't want to convert, you can edit this value to remove the `autoconv` entry and everything after it.

CD-RW and DVD-RAM Operations

The secret to having a pleasant experience with the CD writing features in Windows Server 2003 and XP is to tell yourself over and over, "This is not a CD copier. This is not a CD copier."

The reason for this mantra is that, although Microsoft licensed the code from Roxio (maker of Easy CD Creator), they did not license the packet writing engine that makes feats like CD duplication possible. Windows Server 2003 and XP use standard ISO9660/Joliet for structuring the disk contents, meaning that it treats the CD like a standard file repository.

If you want the features that come with a packet-engine CD writer, here are a few products to look at. Be sure to get the latest version to be confident that the product will run satisfactorily under Windows Server 2003:

- **Roxio** (www.roxio.com). Their flagship product is Easy CD Creator Platinum. (Roxio is a spinoff of Adaptec.)
- **CD Speed 2000** (www.cdspeed2000.com). Their product is Nero CD Burner. This is a popular program both for its price (very low) and features that simplify building audio CDs from ripped MP3s.
- **Golden Hawk Technologies** (www.goldenhawk.com). This is a German company with a product called CDRWIN, which has long held a niche for folks who want the fastest burner with minimal features. The documentation and interface could use some work, but it is solid technology.

You'll need to use one of these third-party products if you have a CD-R or CD-RW unit that is not fully MMC2-compliant. Look for the "Ready for Windows XP" logo or check the Hardware Compatibility List to make sure your unit will work with Windows Server 2003.

CD Writing Functional Description

To transfer files to a CD-R or CD-RW drive, drag and drop the files using Explorer onto the drive icon. This copies them into a temporary folder. From there, you instruct the system to burn the files to the CD. This can be done in one of several ways:

- Right-click the drive icon in My Computers and select `Write These Files To CD`.
- Double-click the drive icon to view the files that are already on the disk and those that are waiting to get burned to the disk. Under CD Writing Tasks in the side taskbar, select `Write These Files To CD`. If you do not see this taskbar, use TOOLS | FOLDER OPTIONS to enable the Show Common Tasks In Folders option.
- Eject the CD, either manually or from the flyout menu of the CD icon. This initializes a wizard that prompts you to either burn the files, save the temporary files, or forget about the whole thing and delete the temporary files.

Roxio DirectCD

Roxio has a product called DirectCD that burns directly from the files on a drive to CD-R, CD-RW, and DVD-RAM media. Ordinarily, the disk is formatted using a proprietary format that permits file compression. Only the Roxio driver can read this disk. Roxio has an option to use a non-proprietary format for this operation that does not include file compression.

This intermediate step that saves the temporary files is necessary to ensure a smooth transition of data to the burner. This avoids a dreaded *buffer underrun* condition where there is no more information for the laser to burn to the plastic. Any interruption to the process turns the CD from a data repository into a fancy throwing object.

Modern CD-R/RW units have very large buffers that can hold nearly all the contents of the CD in memory. This all but eliminates buffer underruns. The engine in Windows Server 2003 assumes a baseline model that has very little buffering. You cannot bypass the intermediate file copy step.

By default, the temporary file location is the C: drive. You can set this to an alternate volume if one is available. You'll need enough free space to hold all the files that a CD can hold. This is approximately 700MB for a standard CD and 850MB for an extended CD.

Although the files are burned to the CD, you should avoid initiating processes that might cause a break in data stream that is longer than the buffer on the CD-RW unit can accommodate.

As for sharing a CD-RW as a network resource, the network makes a poor connection for filling a write buffer, so the write engine is not exposed when transferring files to a shared CD-RW drive. You are limited to reading from a shared CD-RW device. (By the way, Windows Server 2003 does not install an administrative (dollar-sign) share on any CD, so if you want to test a shared connection, you'll need to create a share point.)

DVD-RAM Support

Windows Server 2003 and XP can read DVD-RAM disks formatted with Universal Disk Format (UDF) up through version 2.01 but it will not write to UDF disks.

The only writable format supported by Windows Server 2003 for DVD-RAM drives is FAT32. NTFS is not supported due to the continual writes to the file system journal.

As of this writing, Windows 2000 does not support reading DVD-RAM disks formatted with FAT32. You would need to install a third-party application to transport media between platforms.

To write files to a DVD-RAM device, you can use drag-and-drop or `COPY`/`XCOPY` from the command line or any other application that uses standard Win32 API file system calls. The system treats DVD-RAM as regular, albeit very slow, spinning media.

File writes to a DVD-RAM drive are buffered both in the file system driver and at the device. If you eject the media from the drive, either from the device or by selecting the option from the flyout menu, the file system will flush the cache to the buffer at the drive before releasing the device. The device will flush the buffer to the drive before letting the media spin down. Depending on how much information is in the cache and the speed of your unit, this operation might take a while.

If your current DVD-RAM device appears as two drive letters, this means the driver supplied by the vendor uses a special format that combines a FAT piece with a UDF piece. Windows Server 2003 interprets the report from such a driver as two different interfaces. You should not try to write to either of these two logical drives. Only use the software provided by the vendor.

If you need software that can read and write DVD-RAM drives in UDF format, try visiting the Software Architects web site at `www.softarch.com`. They are technology pioneers for UDF and do a good job of keeping up with various platforms.

Moving Forward

At this point in the enterprise deployment of our Windows Server 2003 servers, data storage and file systems are ready for users. The only thing left to do is to configure resource sharing. This is covered in the next chapter.

16 Managing Shared Resources

A SERVER IS A MACHINE THAT MAKES ITS local resources available on a network. A client is a machine that makes use of those resources. Servers give. Clients take. It is the ultimate symbiotic relationship.

This chapter covers network services and how to make them available to clients. In the creaky old OSI networking model, the services covered by this chapter reside at Layer 7, the application layer. The services fall into these general categories:

- File, print, fax, and desktop sharing services
- Universal Plug-and-Play services
- Internet services
- Telephony services, including web telephony
- Client/server applications

This chapter covers file, printer, and fax sharing. The first part of the chapter contains a functional overview of classic file and print sharing in a peer networking environment. The remaining topics cover new features in Windows Server 2003 along with those Windows 2000 services that continue to be useful.

New Features in Windows Server 2003

Windows Server 2003 includes enhancements for several resource sharing methods. They are as follows:

- **Fax Sharing.** This feature was incorporated from Small Business Server. It builds on the Windows 2000 Fax service, which was a standalone fax service. Fax sharing in Windows Server 2003 permits network clients to send faxes to a fax server just as they would send print jobs to a print server. Inbound faxes can be converted into email attachments and routed to an office administrator for distribution.

- **WebDAV.** This feature, which stands for Web-based Distributed Authoring and Versioning, was present in Windows 2000 but has been enhanced with a specialized network redirector. It permits opening files using HTTP as the wire protocol. You can use WebDAV over HTTP in place of classic LanMan Workstation over SMB or ftp.
- **Remote Desktop.** The two-node Administrator access via Terminal Services in Windows 2000 has been made a standard part of every server. The Remote Desktop Protocol (RDP) network provider has been enhanced with more features and improved performance, making Remote Desktop the preferred method for managing servers.

In addition, Windows Server 2003 incorporates several enhancements to resource sharing technologies:

- **File Replication Service topology management.** The topology of replicated links in a Distributed File System (Dfs) volume can be separately defined and managed. In Windows 2000, the replication topology was required to follow the Active Directory topology determined by the Knowledge Consistency Checker (KCC). This was often not efficient for large data transfers involved in replicated Dfs links.
- **Background Intelligent Transfer Service** (BITS). This is a new API that supports flow control for file transfers across the Internet. It knows when a user terminates a connection or shuts down the computer, and it restarts the download from the point it left off when the computer restarts. Windows Update uses BITS to control downloads. There are no management features in the user interface (UI) to control this.
- **Kernel-mode driver blocking.** This feature prevents loading legacy drivers on Windows Server 2003. Newer, miniport-based drivers are much less likely to cause stability problems and are preferred over the older, monolithic drivers.
- **New group policies.** Windows Server 2003 includes several new group policies to control Remote Desktop, printing, and file sharing.
- **Data Link Control (DLC) transport no longer supported.** If you use DLC to communicate with print server interface units, you may not consider this an enhancement, but by removing DLC from the product, Microsoft has eliminated a significant source of network traffic and router problems. Before you upgrade to Windows Server 2003, be sure to check that your print server devices support TCP/IP printing.
- **Simple Sharing.** A standalone XP desktop will not permit file and printer sharing by default. This helps prevent exposing files to the Internet inadvertently.

Although not strictly a server enhancement, this feature may surprise you so it is covered in this chapter.

- **Network Location Awareness** (NLA). The Winsock driver has been enhanced with a new set of routines that permit a developer to determine where a client is located based on the DNS domain name and network address. Developers can use this information to automate wireless device configuration, proxy determination, mapping, and other applications.
- **32-bit application support on IA64 servers.** An Itanium server can run 32-bit applications via a WOW64 subsystem. This is essentially a 32-bit emulator that intercepts Win32 API calls and maps them to their 32-bit equivalent.

Functional Description of Windows Resource Sharing

Figure 16.1 shows the general arrangement of network drivers in Windows Server 2003. The network stack consists of the following major elements:

- Network applications
- Network providers
- Redirectors
- Transports
- Network adapter interfaces

The applications at the top of the stack are not "applications" in the sense of spreadsheet or word processing programs. They are applications that make active network calls of one form or another. An email client application, for example, has a POP3 or an IMAP4 module that issues Winsock network calls to send and receive messages.

The network services that interact with network applications have two components:

- A *provider* that runs in the user memory space. The provider exposes network services to network applications. Network providers come in the form of Dynamic Link Libraries (DLLs) that are loaded and managed by the *Service Control Manager*, Services.exe.
- A *redirector* that runs in kernel space. This is a file system driver designed to communicate with a peer network service on another computer. The term *redirector* is a holdover from the early days of PC networking when network drivers intercepted DOS function calls and "redirected" them to the network interface. Network redirectors come in the form of SYS drivers running under the I/O Manager in the Windows Executive.

Providers and redirectors are paired together. For example, the LanMan Workstation provider is paired with the Mrxsmb.sys redirector driver.

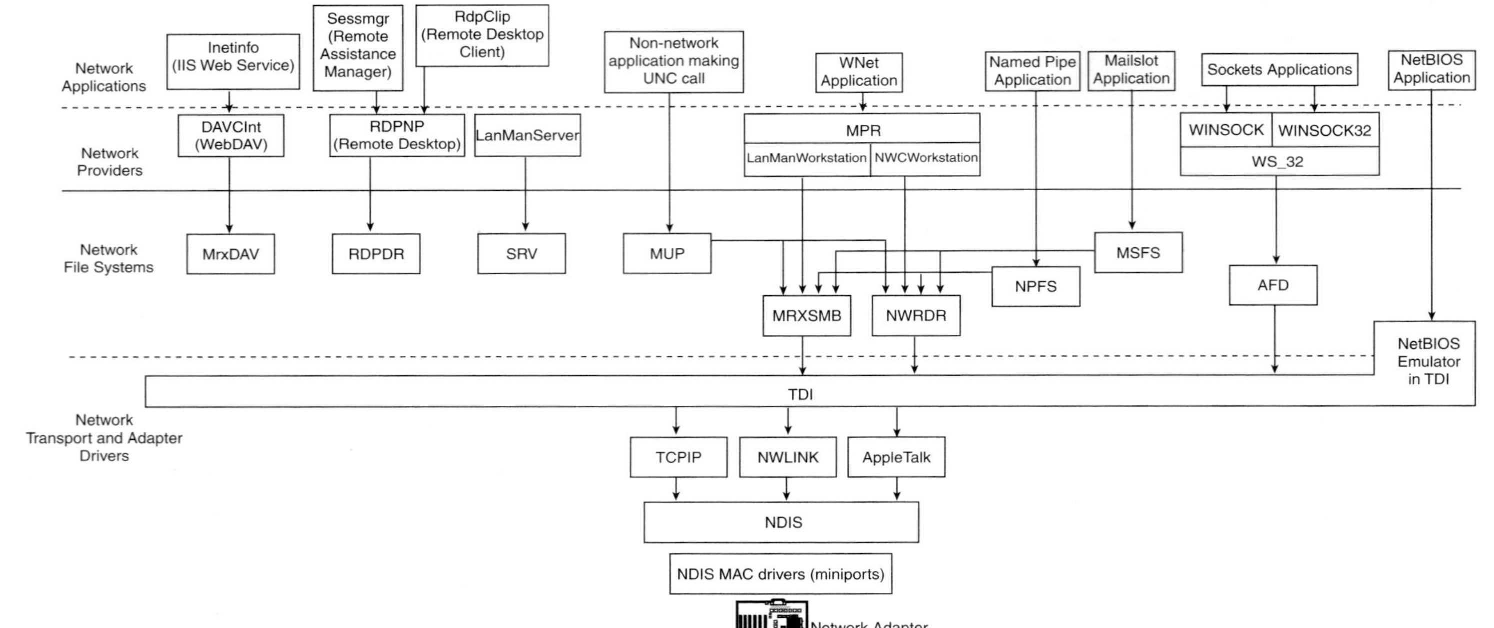

Figure 16.1 Network driver block diagram.

Redirectors communicate with transport drivers via the *Transport Driver Interface*, or TDI. The TDI layer acts like a United Nations translator. The redirectors don't need to know details about the transports and vice versa. They simply talk through the TDI to each other.

Just as the file system drivers do not communicate directly with the transport drivers, the transport drivers do not communicate directly with the network adapter drivers. Instead, they communicate via the *Network Driver Interface Specification* (NDIS) driver, Ndis.sys. The NDIS driver and its helpers present a networking face to the transport drivers and a hardware communications face to the network adapter.

The hardware face communicates with the adapter via an NDIS MAC driver supplied by the vendor. MAC stands for *Media Access Control*. NDIS also provides interfaces for asynchronous communications over modems and ISDN lines via the Telephony API, or TAPI.

Let's take a brief look at each of the components of the Windows network stack to see how they interface with each other. This information is useful when resolving problems that involve system integration, failures in network communication, or performance enhancements. For instance, if you have multiple network providers, you can improve performance by placing them in the correct binding order in the stack.

Network Applications

Most Windows-based network applications use one of four API libraries to access network services. The function calls for these network services are contained in the network provider DLLs, discussed in the next section:

- **Wnet.** Most network applications use the Wnet API within Win32 to communicate between servers and clients. For example, the `WnetAddConnection` function call connects a network client to a share point on a server.
- **Named pipes.** A pipe is an *Interprocess Connection* (IPC) method where two or more applications share the same memory and communicate with each other by manipulating the contents of that memory. A named pipe is a special form of pipe that contrasts with an anonymous pipe that has no name. Named pipes are commonly used by client/server applications such as database applications.
- **Mailslots.** A mailslot is also an IPC, but one that is unidirectional rather than connection-oriented like named pipes. Windows applications generally use mailslots when sending broadcasts or unicasts. For example, NetBIOS-over-TCP/IP name registration uses mailslots.
- **Winsock.** Winsock stands for *Windows Sockets*. A *socket* is a form of IPC first introduced in Berkeley Software Distribution (BSD) UNIX. A socket consists of an IP address, a port number, and a flag indicating whether the socket represents a datagram or a communications stream.

(A fifth networking method, NetBIOS, is still supported even though NetBIOS applications are becoming very rare. See the sidebar, "NetBIOS Support.")

Network Providers

Network applications require an interface that can convert their network API calls into commands that can be understood by the network file systems in the Windows Executive. That is the role of a network provider.

Windows Server 2003 includes several network providers in the shrink wrap. It's instructive to know their names and the source libraries because you will see this information in Event log entries when something goes wrong. Take note of these providers:

- **Windows provider.** For historical reasons, the Windows provider is called LanMan Workstation. The provider is part of Ntlanman.dll.
- **NetWare provider.** The NetWare provider is called NWCWorkstation. The provider code is contained in Nwwks.dll.
- **Remote Desktop provider.** This provider gives multiuser access to the server via the Remote Desktop Protocol (RDP). The provider code is contained in Rdpnp.dll. Citrix Metaframe loads an Integrated Computing Architecture (ICA) provider to support multiuser access from Citrix clients.
- **Web Client provider.** This is a new provider in Windows XP and Windows Server 2003. It is paired with the WebDAV redirector to give live file access (not just Puts and Gets) over HTTP. The provider code is contained in Davclnt.dll.
- **Winsock provider.** Windows provides both 16-bit (Winsock.dll) and 32-bit (Wsock32.dll) libraries that act as interfaces to the main 32-bit Winsock library, Ws_32.dll. This library supports both Winsock 1.1 and Winsock 2.0 applications.

NetBIOS Support

There is a lot of misinformation about NetBIOS floating around the world of Windows network administration. For instance, many administrators believe (or have been told) that Windows networking is NetBIOS-based. This is not the case now and has not been the case for at least a decade.

NetBIOS is a set of functions built into the hardware of a PC. A NetBIOS application works by building a data structure called a *Network Control Block* (NCB) in memory then issuing a BIOS-based interrupt—interrupt 5C to be specific—that essentially turns the contents of the NCB over to a network driver for delivery to the controller on the NIC.

In Windows, applications are not permitted to talk directly to the hardware. If you run an old NetBIOS application, the 5C interrupt is intercepted by the operating system and turned over to the NetBIOS Emulator, a part of TDI.

The NetBIOS Emulator converts the NetBIOS function calls into TDI calls that can be carried by any of the three native transport protocols.

For more details about NetBIOS, see `www.mcgrew.net/Training/NPS/nps-netbios.htm`.

The Windows server has a small user-mode service, LanMan Server, that acts something like a provider. Its job is to create shares, communicate management information to the server file system running in kernel space, and support the legacy Browser service by registering the server with the browser database. LanMan Server has no separate DLL.

The Named Pipe and Mailslot network file system drivers do not require separate providers. Win32 handles these API calls and establishes connection to the proper network file system.

Theoretically, an application could be coded to communicate directly to the TDI, or even directly to the transport drivers themselves. These are rare birds because coding them requires intimate knowledge of the core networking APIs, something that is very difficult to come by outside of Redmond.

Most third-party NOS vendors implement Windows clients in the form of network providers. Examples include Novell's *NetWare Core Protocol* (NCP) provider, Transarc's *Andrew File System* (AFS) provider, and Sun's *Network File System* (NFS) provider.

Print Providers

Figure 16.1 does not show the print providers, but they would occupy the same location as the file system providers. Print providers are network applications, similar to but much more limited than full-fledged file system providers, that know how to communicate to printer services running on a remote machine. Windows Server 2003 comes with a variety of print providers. The major ones are as follows:

- **LanMan print provider.** This supports print requests coming from Windows clients.
- **Internet print provider.** This supports HTTP-based print requests from Windows or non-Windows clients.
- **NetWare print provider.** This supports printing to NetWare print servers. A different provider, installed with Services for NetWare (SFN), enables a Windows server to accept print jobs directed at it from NetWare clients.
- **Macintosh print provider.** This supports printing to Macintosh hosts via AppleTalk.

There is no network print provider for UNIX. This service is part of the Line Printer Daemon (LPD), Lpdsvc, which is loaded as part of Print Services for Unix, an optional component in Windows Server 2003.

Multiple Provider Router

Each provider that supports the Wnet API is linked to the *Multiple Provider Router*, or MPR. This simplifies programming because MPR gives a consistent to network applications.

When presented with a function call to pass a message to a particular server, MPR must choose the correct network provider. It does this by polling the providers to determine which one speaks the proper command language to talk to the target server. It polls based on the network provider order stored in these Registry entries:

```
Key:   HKLM | System | CurrentControlSet | Control | NetworkProvider | Order
Value: ProviderOrder
Data:  NWCWorkstation,LanManWorkstation
```

For print providers, the Registry entries are as follows:

```
Key:   HKLM | System | CurrentControlSet | Control | Print | Providers
Value: Order
Data:  NetWare or Compatible Network, LanMan Print Services, Internet Print
➥Provider
```

If you have both a NetWare and Microsoft client loaded, you should always put the NetWare client at the top of the provider order. This is true even if the majority of your servers run Windows. The NetWare provider takes very little time to report back a failed connection. Microsoft providers, on the other hand, take their own sweet time thanks to all the browsing and name resolution that goes on in the background.

Multiple UNC Provider (MUP)

In addition to specific network client providers that interface directly with MPR, Windows Server 2003 has a general-purpose kernel-mode interface for applications that do not make network function calls but still need access to network resources. This access requires specifying the name and resource in *Universal Naming Convention* (UNC) format, so the general-purpose provider is called the *Multiple UNC Provider*, or MUP.

Here's how MUP works. If you use Notepad to open a file and you enter the path `\\srv2\data\textfile.txt`, Win32 recognizes this as a network path and passes the string to MUP, which parses the string to find the name of the server and the name of the shared folder then polls the network file system drivers, similar to the way MPR polled the providers, to find a driver that can contact the specified server.

Before polling the file system drivers, MUP checks the *Distributed File System* (Dfs) interface. If Dfs returns a positive response, it indicates that the UNC path is in a Dfs volume. At that point, MUP tests the link to the share at the host server. If the link is valid, MUP associates the UNC with the server that hosts the share. If there is no Dfs entry for the UNC, or MUP gets no response from the host server, it continues polling.

When MUP establishes an association between a UNC path and a network provider, it caches that association for subsequent transactions to the same server. For instance, if MUP determines that resource `\\bigred\folder_name` is a folder on a NetWare server, it will use the NetWare provider whenever the user connects to server `BIGRED`.

If a particular UNC path gets no traffic for 15 minutes, MUP removes it from the cache. The next connection request for that UNC causes MUP to poll again. Keep this behavior in mind when troubleshooting intermittent connection delays.

Installing Network Providers

The SMB provider, also called the *Microsoft Client*, is installed by default and cannot be removed. You can install additional providers using the Network Connections window. The following procedure uses the Microsoft *Client Services for Netware* as an example. Other providers can be obtained from third-party vendors.

Procedure 16.1 Installing Additional Network Clients

1. Right-click `My Network Places` and select PROPERTIES from the flyout menu. The Network Connections window opens.
2. Right-click the `Local Area Connection` icon and select PROPERTIES from the flyout menu. The Local Area Connection Properties window opens (see Figure 16.2). If you have more than one network adapter, it doesn't matter which one you choose. The client will be installed and linked to all network interfaces.

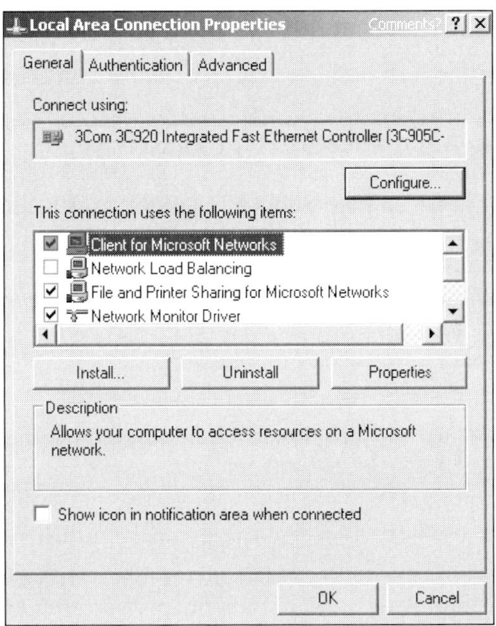

Figure 16.2 Local Area Connection Properties window.

3. Click `Install`. The Select Network Component Type window opens.
4. Highlight `Client` and click `Add`. The Select Network Client window opens. The default list has only `Client Services for NetWare`. If you need to install any other client, click `Have Disk` and point the system at the location of the drivers.
5. Highlight the provider and click `Add`. The system copies the files from the CD and returns to the Local Area Connection Properties window. Additional windows may open to set operating parameters.

Verify that the client is functioning properly by restarting and making connection with a server that is running the target protocol. In the case of the NetWare client, this involves authenticating either in Novell Directory Services (NDS) or a bindery-based NetWare server.

Changing the Network Provider Order

Both the Multi-Protocol Router (MPR) and the Multiple UNC Provider (MUP) poll the installed providers and network file systems looking for the correct one to use for a particular server. If a client has multiple network providers, you can improve initial connection performance by sorting the provider polling order so that the provider that is quickest to time out is listed first. This is generally the NetWare provider. Different networks respond differently, though, so you may need to fuss around with the sort order. Change the provider order as shown in Procedure 16.2.

Procedure 16.2 Changing the Network Provider Order

1. Right-click `My Network Places` and select PROPERTIES from the flyout menu. This opens the Network Connections window.
2. From the menu, select ADVANCED | ADVANCED SETTINGS. The Advanced Settings window opens.
3. Highlight the provider you want to reposition and click the up or down arrows to position it.
4. Click `OK` to save the changes and close the window. There is no need to restart.

Redirectors

The network client providers and MUP only provide an interface to the network. The real work is done by the network file system drivers, a.k.a. the *redirectors*. Redirectors are distinguished by the command language used to communicate to a server:

- **Windows Redirector** (Mrxsmb.sys). This driver communicates with Windows servers using the *Server Message Block* (SMB) command protocol.
- **NetWare Redirector** (Nwrdr.sys). This driver communicates with NetWare servers using *NetWare Core Protocol* (NCP).
- **RDP Redirector** (Rdpdr.sys). This driver communicates with Windows terminal servers using *Remote Desktop Protocol* (RDP).
- **WebDAV Redirector** (Mrxdav.sys). This driver communicates with WebDAV servers (Windows and others) using the WebDAV protocol.

The NetWare Redirector provided by Microsoft is NDS aware but does not support advanced NDS features such as *Zero Effort Networking* (ZENWorks) and *NetWare Application Launcher* (NAL).

In addition to accepting function calls from the Wnet client providers, the redirectors also handle network requests from other file system drivers. For example, both the Named Pipe File System (NPFS) and the Mailslot File System (MSFS) use the Mrxsmb redirector.

Server File Systems

The Server service also takes the form of a file system driver, Srv.sys. Like the Mrxsmb redirector, Srv.sys lives in kernel space as part of the I/O Manager. It is paired with LanMan Server service in user space. Client applications cannot make function calls directly to LanMan Server, so there is no need for it to link to MPR. Srv.sys depends on the Mrxsmb redirector to communicate with other servers.

Default Share Points

An SMB server exposes network resources in the form of *share points*. A share point can be a folder or a printer. A shared folder is often just called a *share*, as in "I need to create a share for that."

Registry Tip: Registry Keys for Redirectors

Parameters associated with the file system drivers and providers are located in the Registry under `HKLM | SYSTEM | CurrentControlSet | Services`. The file system keys have the same name as the drivers.

For example, the `HKLM | SYSTEM | CurrentControlSet | Services | Mrxsmb` key contains parameters and settings for the Windows file system redirector.

All Windows servers have default share points used to support network services and for administrative access. Some of these default shares have names that end with a dollar sign (`$`) to hide them from browsing interfaces such as My Network Places. These hidden shares are commonly called *dollar sign shares* or *administrative shares*, which are described as follows:

- **Administrative shares.** These shares provide access to the root of each drive on the server and to the system root folder, which is `\Windows` for Windows Server 2003. The permissions are set by the system to only permit access to members of the local Administrators group. The Domain Admins global group is nested in the Administrators group, giving domain administrators privileges to use the admin shares. See the sidebar, "Administrative Shares for CD-ROM Drives."
- **`IPC$`.** This share gives access to a symbolic link called *Interprocess Connection* (IPC). This share supports Remote Procedure Call (RPC) connections between Windows computers.
- **`Sysvol`.** This share is seen on domain controllers. It gives access to the `\Windows\Sysvol\Sysvol` folder, which contains group policies and classic logon scripts.
- **`Netlogon`.** This share gives access to the `\Windows\Sysvol\Sysvol\Scripts` folder. All domain member Windows clients (including Win3.11 and Win9x/ME) look for a `Netlogon` share on the domain controller where they authenticate. The share contains classic system policies and downlevel logon scripts.
- **`Print$`.** This share gives access to the `\Windows\System32\Spool\Drivers` folder. This folder contains the drivers for each printer loaded on the server. Clients who connect to a shared printer download the drivers from this share. This includes downlevel clients such as NT4 and Win9x/ME, if the drivers for those clients have been installed.
- **`FxsSrvCp$`.** This share is put in place when the Fax service is installed. It gives access to the folder holding the shared fax cover pages. By default, this folder is `\Documents and Settings\All Users\Application Data\Microsoft\Windows NT\MSFax\Common Coverpages`.
- **`RemInstall`.** This share is put in place when Remote Installation Service (RIS) is installed on a server. It gives PXE (Preboot Execution Environment) clients access to installation files.

You can get a quick list of the share points on a server by opening a command prompt and typing `net share`. Here is an example listing. This server is running Visual Studio, so the web root folder has been shared to permit collaborative work behind a firewall:

```
Share name   Resource                        Remark
-------------------------------------------------------------------------
C$           C:\                             Default share
IPC$                                         Remote IPC
X$           X:\                             Default share
ADMIN$       C:\WINDOWS                      Remote Admin
wwwroot$     c:\inetpub\wwwroot              Used for file share access to web
```

Administrative Shares for CD-ROM Drives

By default, Windows Server 2003, XP, and Windows 2000 do not create administrative shares for CD-ROM, CD-R/RW, DVD-ROM, and DVD-RAM drives. If you change the drive letter for one of these devices, at that point the system will create an administrative share for the new drive letter.

Configuring File Sharing

A share point represents a network path to a local file system. Windows never provides default share points that ordinary users can access. You must create shares at a server before users can map to the server.

There are several ways to create a share. You can use the Explorer shell, the Computer Management console, the command line via the `NET` command, or Resource Kit tools. This section covers all these methods:

File Sharing and XP

The primary focus of this book is on Windows Server 2003 products, but you should be aware that file sharing for standalone XP Professional desktops (not domain members) and XP Home Edition desktops works significantly differently than Windows Server 2003 or previous versions of Windows 2000 or NT.

First off, standalone XP desktops do not have network sharing enabled by default and NTFS permissions are not exposed to the Explorer shell. A feature called *simple file sharing* controls access to folders. This feature is enabled by default on all standalone XP Professional machines and is the only available option on XP Home machines.

You can view the settings for simple file sharing by opening any folder then selecting Tools | Folder Options from the folder menu. Select the `View` tab and scroll all the way to the end of the list to see the `Use Simple File Sharing` checkbox. Figure 16.3 shows an example.

Registry Tip: Shared Folders in the Registry

Shares are stored in the Registry under the following key: `HKLM | System | CurrentControlSet | Services | LanManServer | Shares`. Each share is represented by a value with several data properties in a `Reg_Multi_SZ` entry:

- **`CSCFlags`**. Client-side caching flags: 0 by default for manual caching, 16 for automatic document caching, 32 for automatic program caching, 48 for caching disabled.
- **`Max Uses`**. 4294967295 by default (all Fs for a long integer).
- **`Path`**. Local path to share point. If you change the path so that it does not match this Registry entry, the share no longer functions.
- **`Permissions`**. This entry supports downlevel clients who expect to see share-level security flags in the SMB representing a share point.
- **`Remark`**. Contains the comments for the share.
- **`Type`**. Always set to 0 in Windows Server 2003, XP, and 2000.

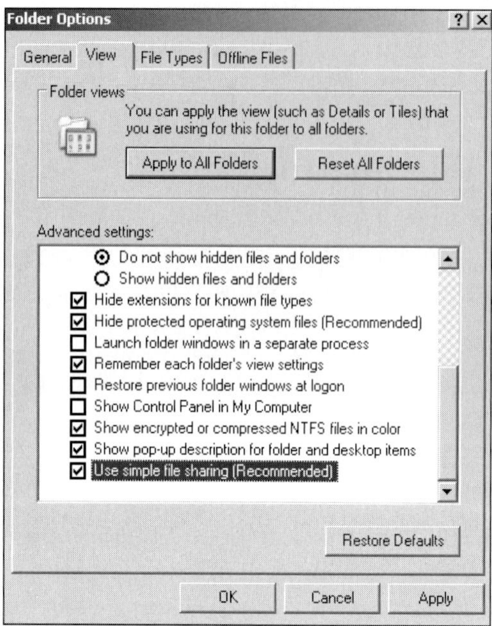

Figure 16.3 Folder Options window showing `Use Simple File Sharing` selection.

This option controls the following Registry entry:

```
Key:    HKLM | System | CurrentControlSet | Control | LSA
Value:  ForceGuest
Data:   1 (blocks access), 0 (permits access)
```

If ForceGuest is enabled (set to 1), the following simple file sharing restrictions apply:

- Files in the user's `My Documents` folder can be configured to be completely private (NTFS permissions set to `<User>:Full` and `System:Full`) or private with access by the local Administrators group (NTFS permissions include `Administrators:Full`.)
- The `All Users\Documents` folder is exposed to the shell as a `Shared Documents` folder. Users who want other users to see their documents can drag them to the `Shared Documents` folder. The NTFS permissions on this folder are set for `Users:Read,Write,Append`, `CreatorOwner:Full`, `Administrators:Full`, `System:Full`, and `Power Users:Change`.
- Folders can be shared on the network using the `Sharing` tab in the folder properties in Explorer. If the `Share This Folder On The Network` option is checked and the `Allow Network Users To Change My Files` option is cleared, an SMB share is created for the folder and the NTFS permissions are set to add `Everyone:Read` to the access list.

If the `Allow Network Users To Change My Files` option is checked, NTFS permissions are set to add `Everyone:Change` to the access list.

These restrictions only apply to SMB connections. A standalone XP Professional desktop running IIS can respond to HTTP and FTP connection requests even if simple file sharing is enabled but nothing is shared. The desktop can also respond to WebDAV connection requests. FTP and WebDAV requests may fail, however, if appropriate NTFS permissions are not set.

Simple file sharing is turned off when an XP Professional desktop joins a domain. (XP Home cannot join a domain.)

Share Permissions

In all previous versions of Windows, when a new share point was created, the Everyone group was placed on the permissions list for the share and granted Full Control access. Controlling access to the files and folders behind the share was given over to NTFS permissions.

In the new spirit of security that imbues Windows Server 2003, Microsoft changed the default permissions for a share point. The Everyone group is still the only entry on the access control list, but the default permissions are now `Read` rather than `Full Control`. This ensures that shares created on FAT and FAT32 volumes will not expose the file system to exploits.

You should always build servers with NTFS volumes so you can change the default share permissions back to `Everyone: Full Control`. This can be done from the Explorer interface or from the command line using new switches on the `NET SHARE` command as follows:

```
Net share <share_name>=<folder_path> /grant:everyone,full
```

By putting `Everyone:Full` on share permissions, you don't need to worry about someone in the future trying to resolve an access problem and forgetting about the share permissions.

If you do assign share permissions, keep in mind that they act as a filter that sits in front of the folder in the file system. If a user has `Full Control` access permissions in NTFS but `Read` permission at the share, the user can only read the files. By the same token, if a user has `Read` access permission in NTFS and `Full Control` in the share, the user can still only read the files.

Deciding Which Directories to Share

Share points multiply like bad rock bands if you aren't careful. When a server sends its resource list to a client, it includes the name of every share, even the hidden shares. If you create thousands of shares, you'll slow performance at the client.

Windows Server 2003 and Windows 2000 permit mapping a network drive to a folder underneath a share point. Use this feature to avoid excessive shares.

Also, avoid overlapping shares. This confuses users and can cause tragic Help Desk calls like this: "I deleted some extra files from my K drive but they also disappeared from my L drive. What happened?"

Creating a Share Using Explorer

The simplest way to share a folder is to use Explorer. The steps in Procedure 16.3 create a new folder and share it.

Procedure 16.3 Creating and Sharing a Folder

1. Log on at the console using an account with administrative privileges.
2. Open `Explorer` or `My Computer`.
3. Create a folder or select an existing folder. The example in Figure 16.4 shows a folder called `Sales`.
4. Right-click the folder icon and select SHARING AND SECURITY from the flyout menu. The Properties window for the folder opens with the `Sharing` tab selected.

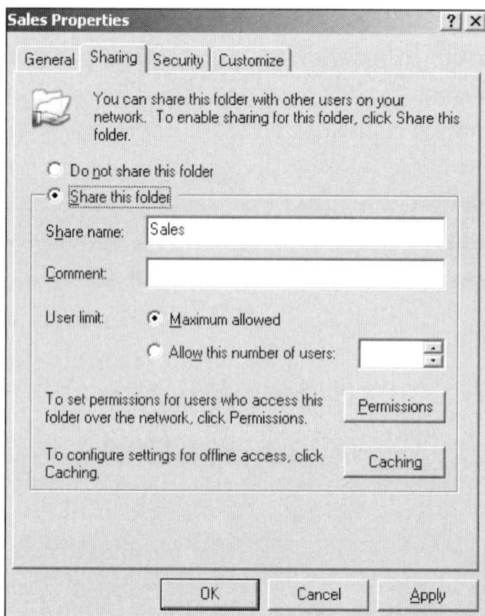

Figure 16.4 Properties window for `Sales` folder with `Sharing` tab selected.

5. Select the `Share This Folder` radio button. The system automatically inserts the folder name as the share name. If you already have a share by this name on the computer, the share name will be blank. You can select a different name.
6. Ordinarily you would leave the `Maximum Allowed` radio button selected. Set a value under `User Limit` only if you want to limit the maximum number of users who can access the share point. You can use this feature to meet licensing restrictions for executables inside the share.

Share Name Lengths

Select a share name that meets the allowable name length for the Windows clients in your network:

- Windows NT4 and later: 255 characters
- NT 3.51: 15 characters
- Windows 95: 12 characters
- Windows 3.x and DOS: 8 characters

If the share name exceeds the limit, the affected clients cannot see the share in a browse list or map a drive to it.

7. Click `Permissions` and set `Everyone` to `Full Control`, then click `OK`.
8. Click `OK` to create the share and close the Properties window. The `Caching` option is covered in Chapter 19, "Managing the User Operating Environment."

Note that the folder now has a little hand under it indicating that it is shared. If you issue the `NET SHARE` command from the command line, you see this folder listed as a share point.

Creating Shares on Remote Computers

The Explorer interface has no mechanism for creating shares on remote servers. You can create a share point on a remote computer using the Computer Management console as in Procedure 16.4.

Procedure 16.4 Creating Remote Shares Using the Computer Management Console

1. Open the `Computer Management` console using START | PROGRAMS | ADMINISTRATIVE TOOLS | COMPUTER MANAGEMENT.
2. Right-click the `Computer Management (local)` icon and select CONNECT TO ANOTHER COMPUTER from the flyout menu. The Select Computer window opens.
3. Click `Browse`. The standard object search window opens. Enter the first few letters of the server you're searching for then click `Check Names`. The search starts with an LDAP search of Active Directory then expands to search the browse list.
4. If more than one computer starts with the letters you entered, a Multiple Names Found window opens with a pick list. Double-click the name you want then click `OK` then `OK` again to select that machine.
5. Expand the tree under SYSTEM TOOLS | SHARED FOLDERS | SHARES. Figure 16.5 shows an example.
6. Right-click the `Shares` icon and select NEW FILE SHARE from the flyout menu. The Create Shared Folder window opens.

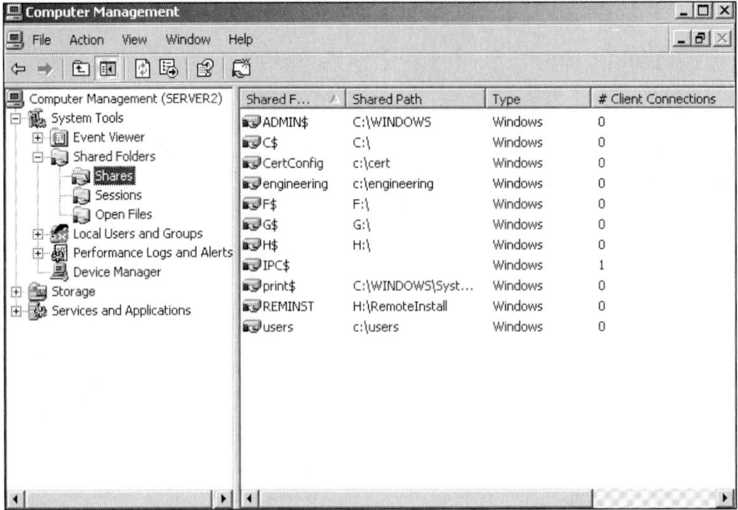

Figure 16.5 Computer Management console showing list of shares on a remote computer.

7. Click `Browse` to locate the folder you want to share. The Browse for Folder window appears (see Figure 16.6). The browse feature requires that you have functioning administrative shares (dollar sign shares) at the root of each volume on the remote computer. If you have deleted the administrative shares, you must enter the local path to the folder manually.

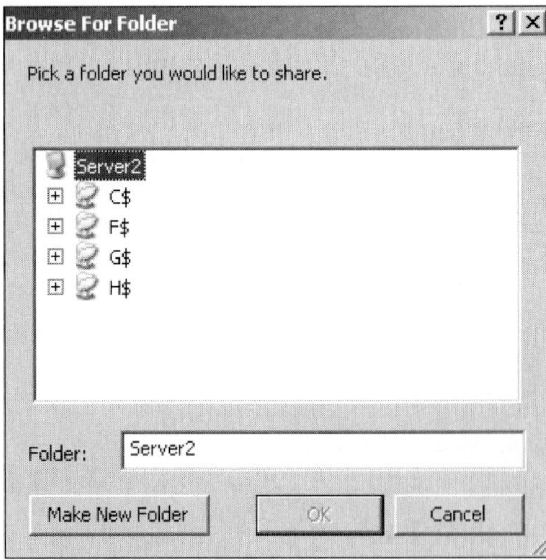

Figure 16.6 Browse For Folder window showing top-level folders represented by administrative shares at remote computer.

8. Select the folder you want to share or create a new folder.
9. Click OK to save the selection and return to the Create Shared Folder window.
10. Enter a Share Name and Share Description.
11. Click Next. Select a permissions option. The Custom button opens the Customize Permission window that contains a browse list to select users or groups to add to the list of authorized share users.
12. Click Finish to apply the changes and close the window.

The system responds with a notification that the share was successfully created. If it encounters a problem, you get an error message. The most common problem associated with creating remote shares is not having sufficient rights. The owner may have set restrictive NTFS permissions on the folder you're trying to share.

Creating Shares Using the Command Line

You can create a share from the command line using the NET SHARE command with the following syntax:

```
net share share_name=drive:\directory /grant:Everyone,Full
```

If you want to stop sharing a directory, use the /delete switch as follows:

```
net share share_name /delete
```

The NET SHARE command only works at the console of the server containing the directory you want to share. If you want to create a share on a remote directory from the command line, use a Resource Kit utility called RMTSHARE. The syntax for this command is as follows:

```
rmtshare  \\server_name\share_name=drive:path [/users:number | /unlimited]
                             [/remark:"text"]
                             [/grant user:perm]
                             [/remove user]
```

If you want to stop sharing a directory on a remote computer, use the /delete switch as follows:

```
rmtshare \\server_name\share_name /delete
```

Recreating Admin Shares

Access to the C$ and ADMIN$ shares (and other shares representing volumes on a server) is restricted to members of the Administrators group. If the shares are accidentally deleted, you can create a new share called C$, but it will not have the same permissions. You can replace deleted admin shares with their special permissions using the *Policy Editor* (Poledit). Follow Procedure 16.5.

Procedure 16.5 Restoring Deleted Administrative Shares with Poledit

1. Launch Poledit from the Run window.
2. From the menu, select FILE | OPEN REGISTRY.
3. Double-click the `Local Computer` icon. This opens the Local Computer Properties window.
4. Expand the tree under `Windows NT Network | Sharing`.
5. Select `Create Hidden Drive Shares (Server)`.
6. Click `OK` to save the change and return to the main Policy Editor window.
7. From the menu, select FILE | SAVE. This applies the change to the Registry.

This action places a value called `AutoShareServer` in the Registry key `HKLM | System | CurrentControlSet | Services | LanManServer | Parameters`.

Volume Shadow Copy

You've probably gotten this phone call: It starts off, "I was making changes to a macro in the spreadsheet that I use to calculate payroll and now my spreadsheet doesn't work. Can you restore it for me from last night's backup?" For some reason, the answer "I sure can and you'll have it next Wednesday" never seems to satisfy the user.

Tape backups are vitally important, but doing individual file restores imposes a signficant burden on IT staff and resources. Windows Server 2003 has a new feature, the Volume Shadow Copy service, that puts the user in charge of obtaining historical copies of data files. Volume Shadow Copy creates a database that holds changes to data files identified during periodic snapshots.

The operation of the Volume Shadow Copy database is controlled at the Properties window of a volume via the `Shadow Copies` tab. Figure 16.7 shows an example.

Using the Settings button, you can define the size of the database and the schedule for taking snapshots of the volume. The default schedule is two snapshots per day at 7:00 AM and 12:00 PM, Monday through Friday. The number of historical copies is controlled by the size of the database. The default database size is 10 percent of the volume size with a minimum of 100MB.

The Volume Shadow Copy database is stored in a hidden folder called `System Volume Information`, which is stored at the root of the volume. The database is encrypted to protect the file contents. The database cannot be defragged and there is no support for Volume Shadow Copy on the quorum drive of a cluster.

Volume Shadowing is enabled on a per-volume basis. It cannot be controlled by individual shares. For best results, Microsoft recommends putting the cache on a separate spindle or RAID array. You can choose whether or not to back up the historical files. The backup application must conform to the Windows Server 2003 backup API to avoid corrupting the database.

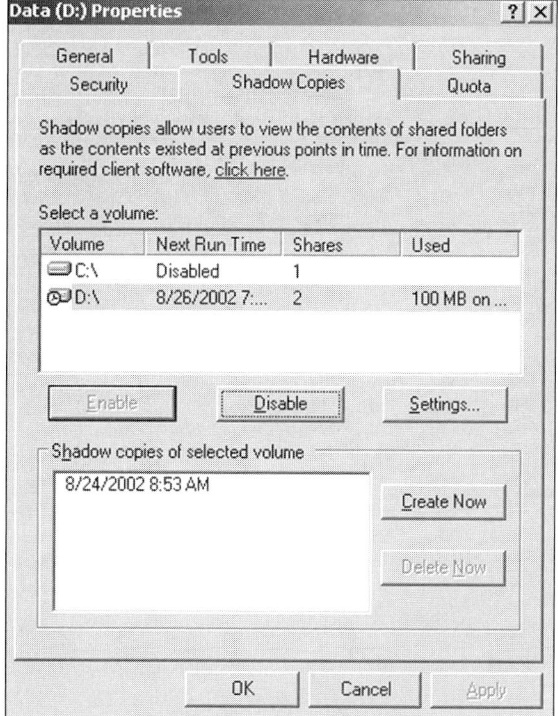

Figure 16.7 Properties window for an NTFS volume showing the `Shadow Copies` tab.

At clients, access to the Volume Shadow Copy database relies on an extension to the Explorer shell that must be installed separately. The client installation package is Twclient.msi and is stored in `\Windows\System32\Clients\Twclient`. You can deploy the package via group policies.

The Twclient extension only runs on Windows XP and Windows Server 2003. The extension exposes the content of the Volume Shadow Copy database via a `Previous Versions` tab to the Properties page for a file. Figure 16.8 shows an example.

The user can elect to view the previous versions and then either copy them to a new location or restore a copy if the original were accidentally deleted. There is a variety of safeguards to prevent users from accidentally overwriting their files.

If you use a SAN or NAS, the Volume Shadow Copy feature also supports taking snapshots of dynamic files such as databases so that they can be safely transferred to another location. Windows Server 2003 includes a new service called the *Virtual Disk Service*, or VDS, that exposes an API for accessing RAID and SAN/NAS configurations from the operating system. This permits changing hardware storage parameters from the console.

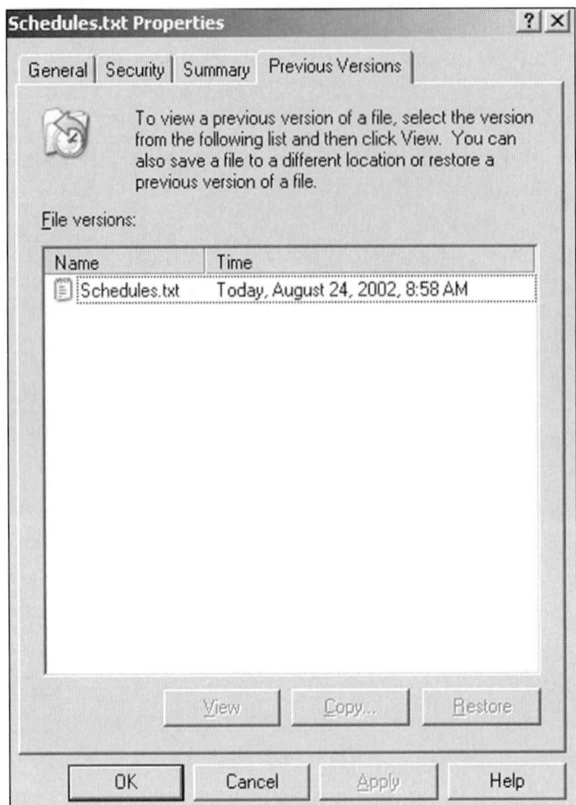

Figure 16.8 Properties page for a network file showing the `Previous Versions` tab.

Connecting to Shared Folders

You can share all the folders you want, but if users cannot find them with a minimum of fuss, you might as well be selling whiskey at a Methodist revival meeting.

Windows Server 2003 provides three ways to locate shared file resources: browsing, Active Directory publishing, and the Distributed File System (Dfs). The first two options are covered here. The Distributed File System is covered later in this chapter in section, "Resource Sharing with the Distributed File System."

Browsing

Browsing has been a feature of Windows networking for many years. It's a clumsy but serviceable way to locate servers and their shared resources.

Every network segment has at least one browser, called the *Subnet Master Browser*. Servers register their names with the Subnet Master Browser when they come onto the network. The database of server names maintained by the Subnet Master Browser is called a *Browse list*.

When a user opens My Network Places or views a resource list under Map Network Drive, the network client requests a copy of the Browse list from the Subnet Master Browser. The list of servers in the interface comes from that Browse list.

Any Windows computer with file sharing enabled can be a master browser or a backup browser. This includes Windows for Workgroups, Windows 9x/ME, all versions of NT, Windows 2000, XP, and Windows Server 2003. Master browsers are selected on the basis of a *browse election*. The results depend on a hierarchy designed to rig the election in favor of servers over desktops and domain controllers over servers and NT-based operating systems over Windows 9x/3.x operating systems.

It's possible that the Subnet Master Browser could get too busy to handle client requests. To get help, it behaves like a Revolutionary-era British merchant captain and presses other servers into action as *backup browsers*. The master browser replicates the latest Browse list to the backup browsers then refers client requests to them in round-robin fashion for load sharing.

Servers who toss their hat into the ring for the election to master browser are called *potential browsers*. If a potential browser loses the election, it becomes a candidate to be a backup browser. Each time 32 additional clients come on the wire, the master browser selects another backup browser.

In a routed TCP/IP environment, the Subnet Master Browsers replicate their Browse lists to the primary domain controller (PDC), which also acts as the *Domain Master Browser*. In an Active Directory domain, the PDC Emulator is the Domain Master Browser. The Domain Master Browser consolidates the Browse lists and redistributes the result to the Subnet Master Browsers, which in turn replicate them to the backup browsers.

Searching Instead of Browsing

In a large enterprise with hundreds or thousands of servers, it can take quite a while to open My Network Places to find a particular computer. It's much faster to use the Search utility from the Start menu. The Search feature searches the browse database, not DNS or Active Directory. Search for a computer as follows:

1. From the Search window, select the `Printers, Computers, or People` link in the left side of the window.
2. Click the `Computer on the Network` link.
3. Enter the flat name for the computer.
4. When and if the computer is found, double-click it to see the shared resources.

Troubleshooting Browsing Problems

Aside from printing and security, browsing is the network function that causes the most grief for system administrators. It's fairly straightforward to troubleshoot browsing failures, but it's important to keep the basic functionality in mind.

This is easy because most of the technology in legacy Windows parallels Dr. Seuss stories. Browsing was designed by someone who was raised on *Yertle the Turtle*. Remember Yertle's catch phrase? "I'm Yertle the Turtle, oh marvelous me. I am the *master* of all I can *see*, and nobody's head can see *higher* than me."

A Subnet Master Browser can see only the servers on its subnet, so its copy of the browse database only lists those servers. The Domain Master Browser can see all the Subnet Master Browsers, so his database contains all the servers, but only when he has obtained copies of the local browse databases. There is potentially a different master browser for each transport protocol, making it possible to have several Yertles in each local LAN or subnet.

Finally, If you try to put too many subnets into the same browsing database, the whole structure will come tumbling down and the browse master will become the master of mud, because that's all he can see.

Browsing, when it works, gives users a quick and convenient way to find servers and their resources. Browsing is much more complex than it first seems, though, and this complexity makes it somewhat confusing to users. Here is a list of browsing's most glaring deficiencies:

- Windows clients query the browse master for the first transport in the binding order. This often results in two machines sitting side by side that display different server lists.
- Browser registrations, browse elections, and Browse list queries cause a significant amount of broadcast traffic. Every network client in the subnet must process those broadcasts.
- Browse list replication has significant latency. It can take as much as 51 minutes for a downed server to disappear from a Browse list. During this time, the dead server continues to appear in My Network Places.
- Browsing in a TCP/IP network depends on Windows Internet Name Service (WINS), which is itself a little creaky at the joints. The Subnet Master Browsers locate the Domain Master Browser by querying WINS for the master browser record. In turn, the PDC locates the Subnet Master Browsers by their entries in WINS. If WINS gets unstable or is unavailable, browsing will soon suffer.

It is theoretically possible to eliminate browsing from your network by providing an alternate way of locating servers and their resources. One way to do this is by publishing the shares in Active Directory. As we'll see, this method leaves a bit to be desired, so a better solution is the Distributed File System.

Resource Sharing Using the Distributed File System (Dfs)

Networks are confusing places for the average end user. To tell users that their files are "on the network" is like telling them, "There's a $10 bill waiting for you somewhere in Chicago."

Figure 16.9 shows a typical set of network resources. Connecting to these shared resources requires mapping a network drive at the clients. Organizations spend lots of time and energy and ingenuity figuring out how to get a consistent set of drive mappings to their users. The users aren't knowledgeable enough about the network structure to correlate a drive mapping to a server, so these network drives *become* the servers in the user's mind. You hear this in conversation all the time. "My K drive went down again yesterday. Those IT people really need to get their act together, don't you think?" (UNIX administrators aren't free from this, either. Network File System (NFS) mount points take on a life of their own, as well.)

Another problem with this way of sharing resources is that you quickly run out of drive letters. Large organizations shuffle logical drive letters constantly. "If you're in Engineering, the H drive points at the Drawings share on server S23. If you're in Accounting, the H drive points at the Financials share on server S13."

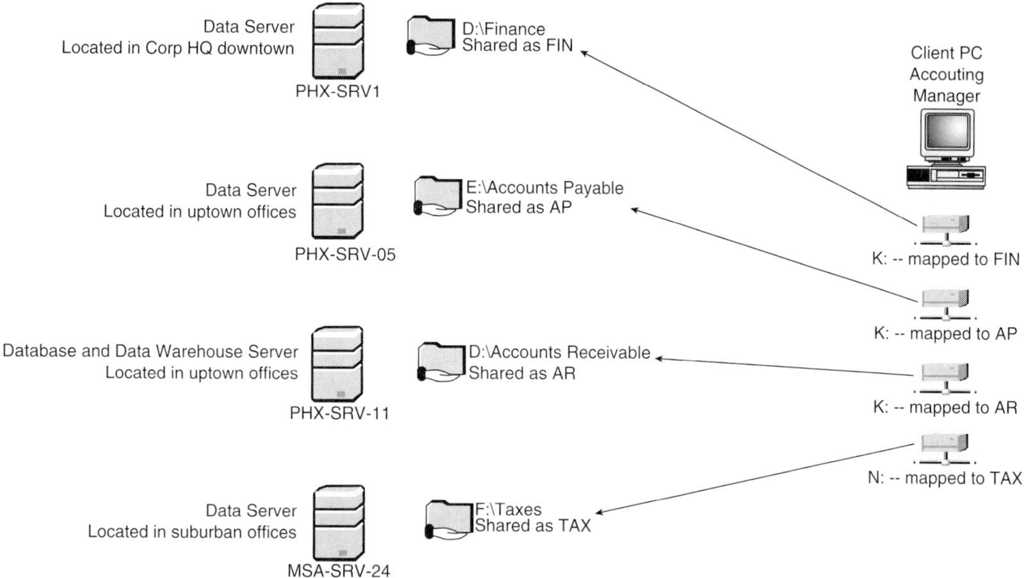

Figure 16.9 Standard shared folder structure. User must map to each shared resource.

What is needed is a structure where shared directories throughout the organization can be displayed in a single, logical format. A user who wants accounting information goes to an Accounting folder inside this virtual structure and not to some server in Cincinnati.

The technology to do this aggregation of share points is called the *Distributed File System*, or Dfs. (Microsoft uses a mix of upper- and lowercase letters to differentiate its product from IBM's Distributed File System, DFS.) This topic examines how Dfs works and how you can use it effectively in a production network to simplify resource access.

Dfs Structure

In a nutshell, Dfs defines a hierarchy of shared folders. The Dfs structure mimics a standard directory structure. You can think of Dfs as being a file system made up of share points instead of folders.

Figure 16.10 shows how the shares in Figure 16.10 would look under Dfs. A user enters the structure at the top via a single mapped drive and navigates through the folders just as if they were inside a big file system on a single server.

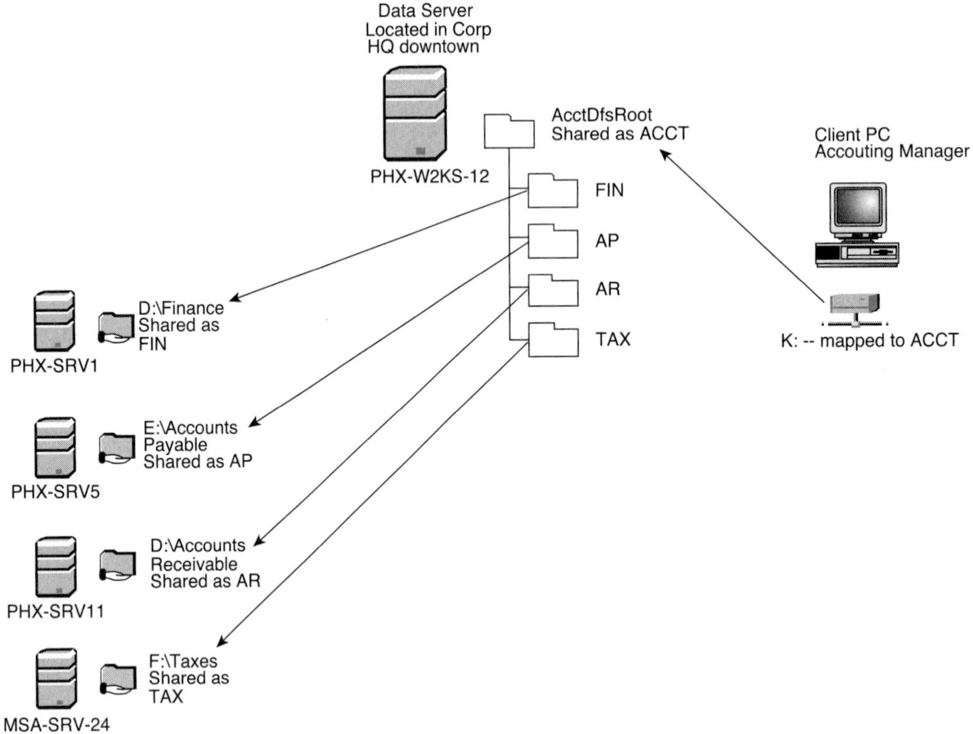

Figure 16.10 Dfs structure that replaces server-centric model.

Using Dfs, you can organize information in a way that complements the activities of your organization, not your IT department. For instance, a law firm can structure its Dfs by litigation type. An oil company can structure Dfs by business unit—Downstream and Upstream and Midstream and the like. None of the users know or care about the names of the servers or shares. They figure out where to find their information and they're happy.

Figure 16.11 shows a Dfs console window with the various architectural elements exposed. If Dfs were a real file system, you would call this structure a volume. Dfs refers to it as a *namespace*. Here are the major elements of a Dfs namespace:

- **Dfs Root**. Every file system needs a root. The root of a Dfs virtual file system resides at a shared folder on a server. In a domain Dfs, you can place copies of the Dfs root on multiple servers for fault tolerance.
- **Links**. The virtual file system represented by Dfs consists of a set of virtual folders that represent *links* to real share points at real servers. A link appears in Explorer as a standard folder.
- **Partition Knowledge Tables**. When a Dfs client connects to a Dfs link, it gets a *referral* to the real share point at a target server. This referral takes the form of a *Partition Knowledge Table*, or PKT, which contains the identity of the target server and its true share name. If a link has multiple target servers, the PKT sorts the servers in order by site then hands out the referral.
- **Dfs Targets.** This is a new term in Windows Server 2003 Dfs. It refers to the server or servers that host the shares that are the target of a Dfs link. A link containing multiple targets is said to be a *replicated* link. The File Replication Service is responsible for keeping the data in sync between the targets of a replicated link.

Let's take a closer look at these elements so we can get an idea how clients navigate through the Dfs structure.

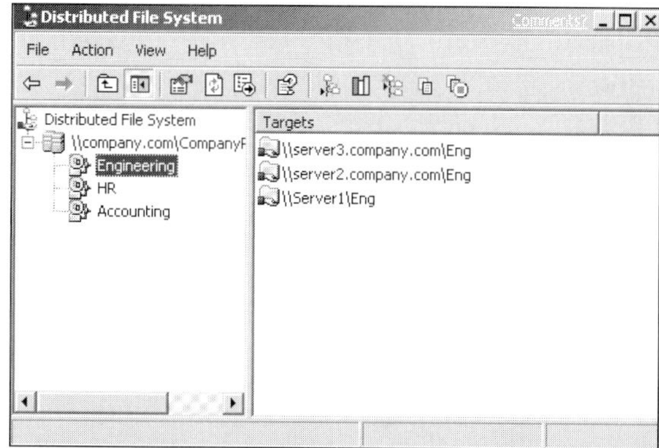

Figure 16.11 Dfs console showing architectural elements.

Dfs Root

The defining structure of a Dfs namespace takes the form of a set of folders on a Dfs root server. In addition, the root server has a Partition Knowledge Table, or PKT, that contains pointers to the folders in this structure along with the names and shares they represent. There are two types of Dfs roots, distinguished by where the root folder structure and PKT are stored:

- **Standalone root.** The folders representing the Dfs namespace reside on a single root server. The PKT information resides in the Registry of that server. If a standalone root server is unavailable, the Dfs structure it hosts is also unavailable.
- **Domain root.** The folders representing the Dfs namespace can reside on multiple servers. The PKT information resides in Active Directory where it is replicated to every domain controller in a domain. This provides fault tolerance because one root server can go down and the others can still pass out Dfs referrals to clients.

As you can probably guess, the domain root is preferred. To have a domain root, though, you need an Active Directory domain. The domain controllers can be running a mixture of Windows Server 2003 and Windows 2000. Dfs is fully compatible on both platforms. If you have a classic NT4 domain, or a simple workgroup, you must use a standalone root and take measures to protect it against downtime or network failures.

Dfs Root Limitations

Windows Server 2003 Dfs improves on Windows 2000 Dfs by permitting a server to host multiple domain Dfs roots. This is not true for standalone Dfs servers. A standalone Dfs server can only host one root.

A Dfs root must be hosted on an NTFS volume. Dfs links can point to shared FAT or FAT32 volumes, but this is not recommended due to security considerations.

Although this is not a root limitation, per se, it affects your naming scheme so I'll mention it here. Dfs is subject to the same maximum path length that affects all Windows operating systems. A path cannot be longer than 260 bytes. Keep your link names as short as possible so that the deepest link won't exceed this path length.

Registry Tip: Dfs Registry Information

Dfs information is stored in the Registry under these keys:

- `HKLM | Software | Microsoft | DfsHost`. This contains a flag indicating that the server hosts a Dfs root.
- `HKLM | Software | Microsoft | Dfs`. This contains the names of the roots, their logical shares, and in the case of standalone root servers, the binary information needed to build the PKT.
- `HKLM | System | CurrentControlSet | Services | Dfs`. This contains configuration and parameter information for the Dfs provider, Dfssvc.exe.
- `HKLM | System | CurrentControlSet | Services | DfsDriver`. This contains configuration and parameter information for the Dfs file system driver, Dfs.sys.

Dfs Links

When a Dfs client connects to a Dfs namespace, it sees a folder structure similar to a file structure. Figure 16.12 shows an example.

The "folders" are actually pointers, called *links*, to the shared folders hosted by servers around the enterprise. Think of Dfs as the 411 of networking. "Dfs Root, may I help you? Accounting files? Those are at the Acct shares on server S73."

When a Dfs client opens a Dfs folder, the client gets a *referral* to the target server hosting the shared resource. The client follows up on the referral and makes a connection directly to the target server. This keeps Dfs from becoming a bottleneck to network traffic. The client caches the referral locally so it does not need to go back to Dfs each time it connects to the same folder. The referral has a default timeout of 30 minutes. You can clear a referral manually from the Properties window in the Dfs tab. Click Clear History.

The user can map a drive to the root of the namespace and that is the only drive letter that needs to be expended. For standalone roots, the UNC path would be \\\<*server_name*>\\<*dfs_root_name*>. A domain Dfs, however, can use the name of the domain in the UNC path, such as \\\<*domain_name*>\\<*dfs_root_name*>. The client resolves the domain name into the name of a server hosting a replica of the root so it can read the folder structure.

For example, the UNC path to the top of the Dfs namespace in Figure 16.12 is \\company.com\dfsroot. You could include this as a drive mapping in a logon script, completely eliminating the need for the user to do any mapping. This makes them happy and your Help Desk happy.

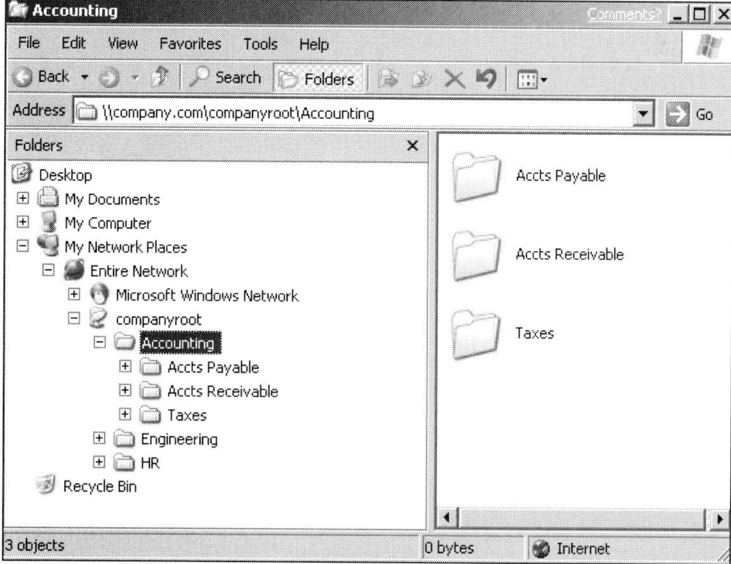

Figure 16.12 Explorer view of a Dfs namespace.

Because Dfs just gives a referral, not an actual connection, the target server does need not to be running Windows Server 2003. It doesn't even need to be a Windows server at all. If the client has the proper redirector, the target resource can be a NetWare volume, a Banyan drive, an NFS mount on a UNIX host, and on and on.

The exceptions to this are downlevel Windows 9x/ME clients. These clients can only accept a Dfs referral to an SMB server. To connect a downlevel client to a NetWare server, for example, you would need to use a Windows server as a NetWare gateway. Gateways are invariably slow and often finicky, so you should limit this kind of connection. NT4 clients can accept a non-SMB referral, and so do not need a gateway.

Dfs Link Limitations

The most significant limitation with links is that you cannot create child links from an existing link. For instance, if you have a link called `HR` that points at a target called `\\S23\HR`, you cannot create another link under `HR` that points at some other share. In essence, the basic Dfs namespace is one layer deep.

However, you can create a link from a Dfs root to another Dfs root or a folder in the Dfs namespace under another Dfs root. This permits you to create a master Dfs namespace that encompasses other Dfs namespaces. Figure 16.13 shows an example.

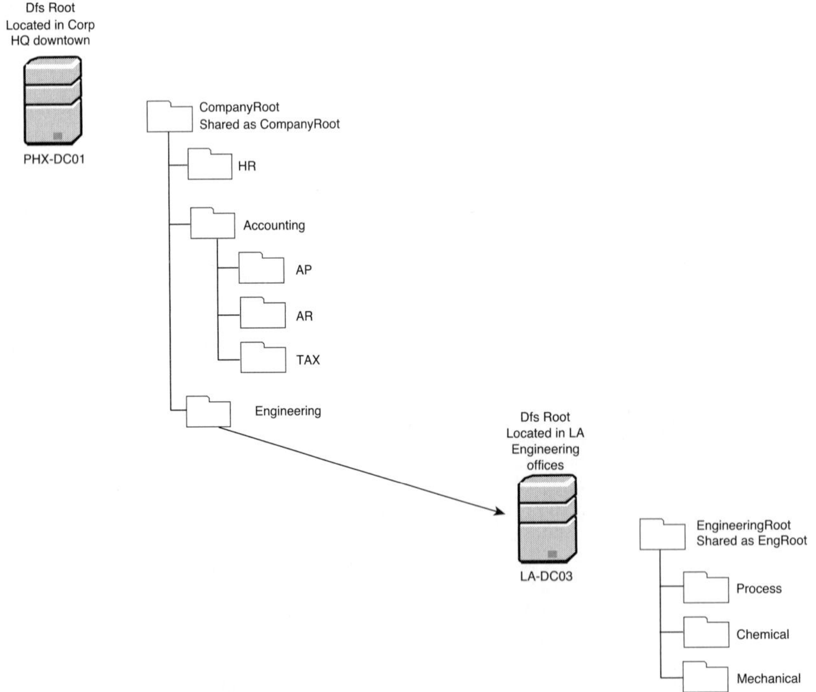

Figure 16.13 Using links to another Dfs root to create a multilevel Dfs namespace.

The figure shows a top-level Dfs root called `Dfsroot` rooted at server `S1`. A link called `Acct` points at another Dfs root called `Accounting` rooted at server `S20`. When a user connects to the `\\company.com\dfsroot` namespace, Explorer will display the `Accounting` root as a folder in the namespace. When the user double-clicks the `Accounting` folder, the Dfs client receives a referral to the root hosted by server `S20`.

This ability to link to other Dfs roots permits you to build hierarchy into your Dfs namespace. However, it also means that you'll need to design your roots carefully so that they mimic your organization. For instance, a university might have separate Dfs roots for Undergrad, Grad, Faculty, and Admin along with a master Dfs root that contains links to these specialized roots. Users could be given a logon script that maps to the top of the master Dfs namespace or to the specialized root, depending on their needs and circumstances.

Creative Namespace Structures

If you want to retain a single Dfs namespace (no alternate roots), you can finesse the single level naming limitation somewhat by creatively naming your links.

For instance, let's say you have an HR department with three divisions: Americas, Asia, and Europe. The three divisions have their files on separate servers and you want to aggregate the share points under a single Dfs folder called `HR`.

You can do this by assigning hierarchical names to the links. For instance, you could name the links as follows:

```
HR\Americas -> linked to -> \\S23\HR-Americas
HR\Asia -> linked to -> \\S372\HR-PacRim
HR\Europe -> linked to -> \\S105\HR-EU
```

When these links are displayed to the user, they will appear as one common parent folder called HR under the Dfs root with three subfolders.

This trick will not work to build a hierarchy that is three layers deep. In the example, you could not create a link with the name `HR\Americas\Contractors`. The system would error out, informing you that a link of that name already exists.

For this reason, you need to give lots and lots of thought to your naming scheme before implementing Dfs. It might take months to prepare for an afternoon's worth of actual configuration work. This will be time well spent, though, because users will love the new, streamlined file access points.

Partition Knowledge Table

The PKT contains the Dfs root name and the names of the root servers. It also contains a list of the Dfs links and their target servers. As you can imagine, this list can get fairly long if you have a lot of links and replicas. The information is stored in Unicode, so each entry takes double the number of bytes you would expect.

On a standalone Dfs root server, the PKT is stored in the Registry. A domain Dfs stores PKT information in Active Directory. Each Dfs root is represented by an FTDfs object that has a PKT attribute.

The size of a Dfs structure is limited by the maximum size of the PKT. For a domain Dfs, Microsoft recommends keeping the PKT attribute smaller than 5MB. This gives room for about 5000 links at the maximum path length. With reasonable path lengths, you can get a lot more links, but take it from me, having thousands and thousands of links is very difficult to manage. Just opening the Dfs console takes a long, long time.

A big Dfs structure can also cause replication headaches. Each time you make any change at all to Dfs that affects the PKT, Active Directory must replicate the entire PKT attribute. If the attribute is 3MB or 4MB because you have thousands of links and link replicas, the replication will take a considerable amount of bandwidth as it travels to every domain controller in the domain. It also takes a long time to start a Dfs root server when you have thousands of links.

The size of a standalone Dfs is limited by the space the PKT takes in the Registry. In previous versions of Windows, this limit was about 13MB based on the maximum System hive. The System hive cannot be larger than 16MB because of a limitation imposed by the nature of the Windows boot process. A 13MB size limit corresponds to about 10,000 links at the maximum path length.

In Windows Server 2003, the PKT information now resides in the Software hive. Microsoft still recommends a maximum of 10,000 links for a standalone root.

When a client connects to Dfs, the referral it gets comes from the PKT. The entire PKT is not transferred, just the portion referencing the link the client touched. The client caches this information to speed up subsequent connections to the same link.

You can view the contents of the PKT cache at a client using DFSUTIL from the Support Tools. The syntax is `dfsutil /pktinfo`. Here is a sample listing where the user has navigated to a Dfs link called Highways that has two replicas; the Active flag points at the replica the client is using:

```
C:\Program Files\Support Tools>dfsutil /pktinfo
—mup.sys—
1 entries...
Entry: \Company.com\Engineering\Highways
ShortEntry: \Company.com\Engineering\Highways
Expires in 300 seconds
UseCount: 0 Type:0x1 ( DFS )
   0:[\S2\highways] State:0x21 ( )
   1:[\S4\highways] State:0x31 ( ACTIVE )
```

You won't need this PKT information very often, but it is good to remember that it's there when you're troubleshooting. You might be able to resolve a Dfs problem quickly when others are scratching their heads because you can take a quick look at the PKT information and figure out that a client is not getting the information it needs, or has timed out a referral, or has some other problem getting link state information.

Multiple Dfs Targets

I said previously that Dfs acts like a directory assistance operator. In actuality, it acts more like a receptionist because it is able to decide where to route an incoming caller. "You want the Sales Vice President? That would be Ms. Proctor, but she isn't in. I'll give you the number of her assistant, Mr. Gamble." (Unlike a real receptionist, Dfs doesn't make the connection for the client. The client must follow up on the referral.)

The target information is stored in the PKT. If a particular link has more than one target, Dfs returns the PKT information for all the targets. It is up to the client to decide which to select. There are two versions of Dfs and they handle this differently. I'll give you more on this in a moment.

If a link points at multiple targets, this implies that each target has the same information. Dfs gives the chore of keeping the targets in sync to the *File Replication Service*, or FRS. You may recall that FRS is the service that keeps the contents of SYSVOL in sync between domain controllers in the same domain.

File Replication Service and Dfs

FRS is a general-purpose file synchronization service. Here are a few highlights of the service:

- The FRS engine is multithreaded. By default, eight files can be transferred at once between replication partners.
- Replication is based exclusively on notification. Replication partners do not poll each other looking for changes.
- FRS servers notify their replication partners immediately when a file changes. There is no five-minute delay as there is in Active Directory. Replication partners pull the change immediately upon being notified.
- An entire file is transferred if any part of the file is changed.
- FRS uses Remote Procedure Calls (RPCs) for both inter-site and intra-site replication. There is no SMTP option.

In Windows 2000, FRS was forced to use the same topology as Active Directory replication for all links, which was often not efficient for moving large volumes of data between Dfs replicas in different sites. Windows Server 2003 improved FRS considerably for use with Dfs. It is now possible to control replication topology for each Dfs link.

FRS topology can be configured in two ways. First, when you define additional targets for a link, the system automatically brings up a Configure Replication Wizard for FRS configuration. This wizard obtains two major pieces of information from you:

- The identity of the "master" server for the initial replication.
- Your desired replication topology.

The "master" server is the one from which the initial file replication will be pulled. After the files have been transferred, there is no subsequent "master" or "secondary" relationship. Changes made at any server are replicated to the remaining servers.

If the secondary server already has files in the target folder, you may get a surprise when you configure replication to that folder. To prevent the files from being overwritten, FRS moves them to a hidden folder called `NTFrs_PreExisting___See_EventLog`. Because this is a hidden folder, you may think that FRS has deleted your files. The files in `NTFrs_PreExisting___See_EventLog` are not staged for deletion, although the Event log entry makes it appear so. Figure 16.14 shows a sample Event log entry.

If you want to preserve the files that were originally on the secondary server, copy them into the main folder following initial replication. From there, FRS will replicate them to the master.

FRS Replication Topology

The second function of the Configure Replication Wizard is to select a replication topology. This is a new feature in Windows Server 2003. You can set a unique replication topology for every replicated link.

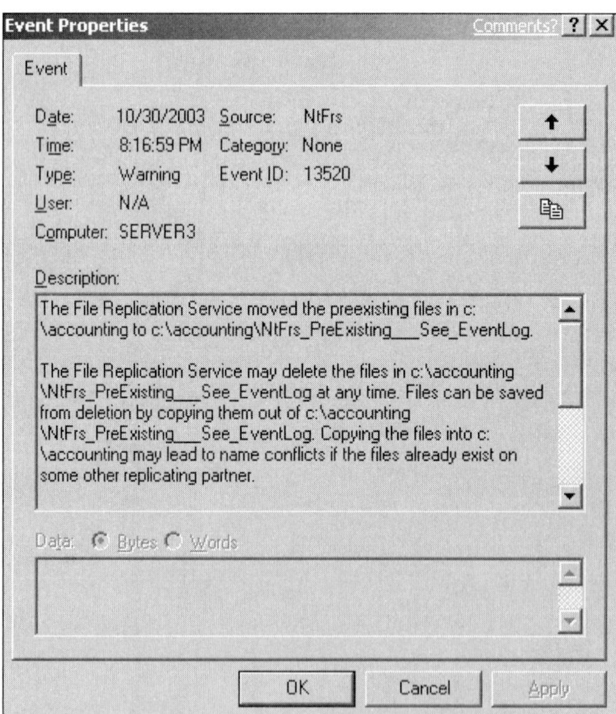

Figure 16.14 Event log entry documenting the move of existing files to the `NTFrs_PreExisting___See_EventLog` folder.

Like Active Directory replication, all FRS connections represent inbound data flows. A server *notifies* its partner that it has files waiting. The partner *pulls* the files during a replication transaction. Figure 16.15 shows the replication topology options from the Properties window of a multitargeted Dfs link. The options are as follows:

- **Ring.** This is the same topology used by Active Directory for intra-site replication, but the FRS connections may not match the KCC connections. Rings make efficient use of bandwidth with a slight delay in full convergence.
- **Full Mesh.** This topology minimizes convergence time at the expense of bandwidth. Use it only if you have connections that can handle the traffic.
- **Hub and spoke.** If you select this topology, you must identify one server as the "hub" server. The remaining servers replicate from this hub. Use this topology to make best use of WAN bandwidth. If the hub server goes down, though, replication fails throughout the system.
- **Custom.** This is the Burger King option. You can design your own topology based on your specific network layout. Be careful to build sufficient connections to prevent a downed link from disrupting too many servers.

Active Directory replication across a WAN is managed using sites. A site is an area of reliable, high-speed network connections. Connections between sites are defined by site links that manage bandwidth.

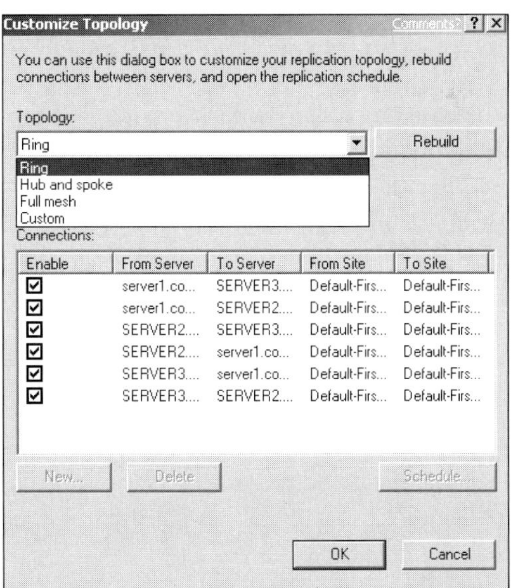

Figure 16.15 FRS replication topology options.

The topology you define for FRS understands when servers are in different sites, but it makes no allowances for them. If you define a fully meshed topology for a particular link, replication will propagate between all servers regardless of their site affiliation. FRS replication uses RPC for all replication.

Analysis of Dfs Target Server Failure

Having multiple copies of the same data on different target servers increases fault tolerance. If any server goes down, the Dfs clients are sent an alternate server with the same data.

The actual sequence of events that occurs when a target server goes down varies depending on the nature of the failure and what the client was doing at the time the server failed. Here's what happens:

- If the client has already connected to a server when the server fails, the system recognizes the problem immediately and selects a new target from the referral list in the cached PKT.
- If the client is navigating the Dfs namespace when the target failure occurs, the Dfs client waits for a timeout on the assumption that the delay is due to network latency. After the timeout occurs, the client selects another target from the PKT referral list.
- If a user has a data file open and attempts to save it when the target server fails, the system sets to work retargeting the client to an alternate server. During this period, the application shows an hourglass. After the client has been retargeted, the file is saved to the new location and the client behaves normally once again.

You can see the target server a Dfs client has selected for a particular Dfs link by opening the Properties window for the link in Explorer and selecting the `Dfs` tab. This tab is only exposed for Dfs links. Figure 16.16 shows an example.

If you want to change the target server, close all files, highlight the desired target in the Properties | Dfs window, then click `Clear History` followed by `Set Active`. The next file you open under the link will come from the new target.

Limitations of Multiple Dfs Targets

Before you get too excited at the possibilities of building huge, fully redundant network file systems based on Dfs, you need to know about a few limitations.

First, FRS only works between servers running Windows Server 2003 and/or Windows 2000. You cannot include a third-party server or a downlevel Windows server in an FRS topology.

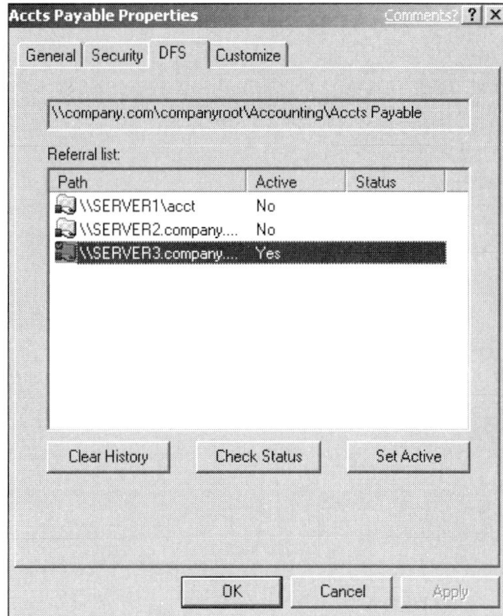

Figure 16.16 Dfs link properties in Explorer showing the Dfs tab.

Second, FRS keeps data in sync between replicas but it does not replicate the security descriptors. You must manage access permissions at each replica. This is generally done by establishing a set of permissions at the root folder. These are inherited by the child folders and files. Be sure to document your changes carefully because you must make the same changes at every replica.

Third, don't permit client-side caching at a Dfs folder. We'll get to details of client-side caching in Chapter 19, "Managing the User Operating Environment," but here's why it should be avoided with Dfs.

Using client-side caching, a user can "pin" files so they are cached locally and available when the user is offline. Let's say the user pins a few offline files from what appears to be a folder but is actually a Dfs link. The files originated at server S1 with a replica on S2. Now, assume server S1 goes down. A Synchronization Manager service running at the client sees that the connection has been lost and retargets the client to the local file cache. At the same time, the Dfs client sees that the connection has been lost and retargets the user to server S2.

When S1 finally comes back online again, the Synchronization Manager will replicate any local changes, so there is no data loss, but it is a confusing time for the user and the Help Desk technician who must soothe the user's fears.

The final and most important limitation when using replicated Dfs targets involves concurrent file use. FRS does a great job of keeping data in sync, but it is not designed to keep file *status* in sync. This means that file locks are not replicated between targets. Also, there is no central database of file locks or other file status information. This means that concurrent file use should be avoided. Users might have the same file open on different target servers. As they update their files, they overwrite each other's changes.

The lack of distributed file locks is a serious deficiency in Dfs only when you want to share files used by multiple users. For single-access files, or files that don't change (such as executables), replicated targets is a great tool for distributing files around your organization. You can even use Dfs to distribute RIS files to make sure each office has a consistent set of installations.

Designing Multiple Dfs Targets

As you decide what kind of data is right for use with multiple Dfs targets, try to ensure that users do not have concurrent access to the files. If that is not possible, keep the number of potential concurrent users down to a select minimum whom you can train about the eccentricities of the file locking limitations.

Here are some excellent candidates for multiple Dfs targets:

- Web pages (as long as they are controlled by a small group of webmasters)
- Executable files
- Company policies, standards, and procedures (with owners who understand the concurrent use limitations)
- User home directories, roaming profiles, and redirected folders (with the exception of laptop users and other users with offline files in their personal folders)

Here are items that should never be placed in Dfs links with multiple targets:

- Databases (unless it is a personal database only accessible by a single user)
- Collaborative files such as workflow documents and linked files in Lotus Notes or SharePoint Portal Server
- Data files accessed by multiple members of the same department or workgroup

Functional Overview of Dfs Referrals

When a network client touches a Dfs link, the Dfs service running on the host returns a referral to the client. The referral contains the Partition Knowledge Table entry for the link. The entry defines where the true target or targets reside. The client selects a target, if more than one are presented, and goes there to make the connection.

There are two versions of Dfs. NT4 and Window 9x/ME use Dfs revision 2. Windows 2000 and later use Dfs revision 3. The versions are backward compatible, so a Windows 2000 client can access a Dfs root hosted by an NT4 server and vice versa.

The Dfs version affects how clients initially access the Dfs volume. This can affect load sharing, as well. Here's how.

MUP Polling

When an SMB network client reaches out to touch a folder based on its UNC path, the Multiple UNC Provider (MUP) polls the network redirectors to see which one can communicate with the target server. This is the first place where the two versions of Dfs react differently. Here's how:

- **Windows Server 2003, XP, and 2000.** In Dfs revision 3 clients, MUP always polls the Dfs provider first to see whether the shared folder is linked to Dfs. If it is, the Dfs driver handles the referral containing the PKT information from the Dfs root server. If the share is not linked to Dfs, the Dfs provider times out and MUP continues on to the next provider in the binding order.
- **Classic Windows.** In Dfs revision 2 clients, MUP first polls the standard SMB provider with a query for the attributes of the target share. This query fails in the case of Dfs because Dfs links do not have share attributes. MUP then checks the UNC path on the assumption that the user gave the wrong server name. This also fails because a Dfs junction does not expose a standard path to a shared folder. MUP finally polls the Dfs provider in an attempt to get a Dfs referral. The host server returns the PKT information.

The main result of this difference is a longer delay in getting connected to a Dfs folder by older clients.

Target Selection

The second operational difference between Dfs versions affects load sharing by changing the way the client selects a target server:

- **Windows Server 2003, XP, and 2000.** Modern Windows servers, when queried by modern Windows clients, return a list of referrals with the local site servers sorted to the top. This is called a *managed list*. The Dfs client picks the server at the top of the referral list. If it cannot get a reply from that server, it proceeds to the next one on the list and so on.
- **Classic Windows.** NT4 and Win9X servers, and modern Windows servers queried by classic clients, return referrals in the order they exist in the Registry (or Active Directory). The client randomly chooses one of the referrals. This means that a classic client might get a referral to a replica in another site. You can avoid this by loading the DSCLIENT patch on the Win9x clients and the Active Directory hotfix for the NT4 clients.

A client also reports back to the Dfs server if it cannot find the host referenced in a referral. This `Report Dfs Inconsistency` SMB helps to keep the system free of broken links. Its use is optional, however, so you may encounter situations where the system doesn't realize that a link is broken.

After the client receives the PKT information in the referral from the host server, it caches this information for a period of time specified in the PKT information. This Time-to-Live (TTL) parameter is configurable in the Dfs console. Open the Properties window for a link and change the `Amount Of Time Clients Cache This Referral (in seconds)` option. Ordinarily, the default 30-minute (1800-second) cache interval is short enough to provide flexibility in moving around target servers while long enough to limit load on the Dfs server.

Dfs Namespace Design

When you lay out your proposed Dfs namespace, start with the name for the enterprise root. This is not a name users will see very often because you will map to it in a logon script. A common selection is `Dfsroot`.

Now decide how you will handle major information nodes in your enterprise. Ideally, the volume structure should match the logical organization of your enterprise so that users can navigate the Dfs as easily as they navigate an organizational chart.

A functional approach is to have a top-level link for major departments such as Accounting (`Acct`), Engineering (`Eng`), and `Sales` along with a top-level link with the company name for holding policies, standards, web pages, and other information of general interest. Remember to keep the names short so the paths don't exceed 260 characters.

You will also probably want links for IT operations—for example, a `SoftDistro` link for distributing applications, an `Apps` link for holding server-based applications, a `Web` link for Internet/intranet files, and a `Users` link for storing user home directories, roaming profiles, and redirected folders.

You can choose to have separate roots for these top-level items with links to them from the main Dfs root. There is no performance difference, although you may see some hesitation when clients negotiate the link from one Dfs to another.

Dfs roots should always be replicated to two or three additional servers for fault tolerance. You won't have many, if any, files at the root of the Dfs, so use a full mesh topology to shorten the convergence time.

Links containing files controlled by single users (or a small group of informed administrators) are candidates for multiple targets to get redundancy and site affiliation.

Dfs Deployment

You will get the most flexibility and reliability by using domain Dfs. If you elect to use a standalone root, the configuration options are similar except that you cannot have the following:

- Multiple root servers.
- Multiple target servers for a link.

- Site-based replica access.
- Domain-based central naming. (Clients must point directly at the standalone server.)

Here's a quick rundown of the steps involved in setting up a domain Dfs before looking at the procedures to do the work:

1. **Determine which servers will host Dfs roots.** These do not need to be domain controllers, but they must be members of the domain. The domain can be running in Mixed or Native.
2. **Create a shared folder on the Dfs server to act as the Dfs root**. Avoid placing files in this volume. Keep the files inside the linked shares. Some administrators like to put a brief text file or web page at the root of the Dfs with instructions on how to navigate.
3. **Create the Dfs root.** This can be any name because users won't see it very often.
4. **Assign additional root targets.** These servers become your fallback root servers.
5. **Create Dfs links to shared folders.** The Dfs volume starts out empty. You add links to shared folder on other servers to structure the volume according to your Dfs design plan.
6. **Assign additional link targets.** If you have identified shares as candidates for replicated links, create the shared folders on the additional servers then define the additional targets.

Create a Dfs Root Directory

You can use the Dfs console, Dfsgui.msc, to create and manage all roots and links. Launch the console from START | PROGRAMS | ADMINISTRATIVE TOOLS | DISTRIBUTED FILE SYSTEM. You can also use a command-line tool, DFSCMD.

When you've completed your namespace design and are ready to start deploying Dfs, follow the steps in Procedure 16.6.

Procedure 16.6 Creating a Dfs Root

1. Open the `Dfs` console.
2. Right-click the `Distributed File System` icon and select NEW ROOT from the flyout menu. The New Root Wizard opens.
3. Click `Next`. The Root Type window opens. Select the `Domain Root` radio button.
4. Click `Next`. The Host Domain window opens. Select the domain to host the Dfs PKT information. The root servers should be members of this domain.

5. Click `Next`. The Host Server window opens. Enter the fully qualified DNS name of the server that will host the Dfs root or click `Browse` to locate the server. This searches Active Directory. It does not use the browser. This ensures that you pick servers from the correct domain. The server need not be a domain controller.
6. Click `Next`. The Root Name window opens. Enter the name you selected for the Dfs root. The `Preview` field will show you the UNC name and the `Share To Be Used` field will show you the flat name of the share that will be created at the root server.
7. Click `Next`. If the share does not already exist on the root server, the Root Share window opens. Enter the full path to the folder. For example: `D:\Dfsroot`. If the folder does not already exist, it will be created.
8. Click `Finish`. The wizard shares the selected folder and creates the root. It makes the necessary entries in the local Registry and creates the FTDfs object in Active Directory.

Create Dfs Links

At this point, the Dfs namespace is like a freshly formatted disk. It has a root directory but no data. It's time to build links to share points in accordance with your design document. Open the `Dfs` console and follow the steps in Procedure 16.7.

Procedure 16.7 Creating Dfs Links

1. Right-click the Dfs root icon and select New Link from the flyout menu. The New Link window opens (see Figure 16.17).

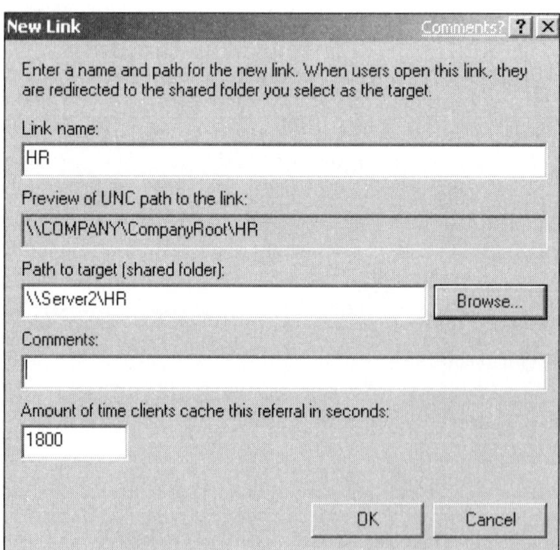

Figure 16.17 New Link window showing Dfs `Link Name` and share point used for referral.

2. Under `Link Name`, enter the name that you want the users to see when they browse Dfs.
3. Under `Path To Target`, enter the UNC path to the share point at the server or use the `Browse` button. This will search the `My Network Places` browse list. Remember that the target does not have to be a Windows server as long as you are running NT4 clients or later.
4. Click `OK` to save the change and add the link to Dfs.

Users can now browse the contents of the folder via Dfs. You can create additional links to other share points and those folders will automatically appear in the namespace.

If you decide you want to stop listing a shared folder in Dfs, you can delete the link. The data is not touched.

Assign Additional Link Targets

If you have a share that is a candidate for a replicated link, create a share on the secondary server then proceed as directed in Procedure 16.8. You'll be configuring FRS as part of this procedure.

Procedure 16.8 Designating Additional Dfs Link Targets

1. In the Dfs console, right-click the link you want to replicate and select New Target from the flyout menu. The New Target window opens.
2. Enter the UNC path to the shared folder on the secondary server or use `Browse` to locate the share. Make sure the `Add This Target To The Replication Set` option is checked.
3. Click `OK`. If the system finds the share point, you will get a message, `The target cannot be replicated until replication is configured. Do you want to configure it now?`
4. Click `Yes`. The Configure Replication Wizard opens.
5. Click Next. This window lists the UNC paths for the original link and the new target. Highlight the target you want to be the master. (Files will be copied from this server to the other.)
6. Click `Next`. Select a topology. The default topology is a ring.
7. Click `Finish`. The two targets are now listed in the right pane of the window. The link has an icon indicating that it has multiple targets.

Use this same procedure to add more targets to the link. The new targets will be added to the FRS replication topology you originally configured. The wizard will not reappear when you add more links.

Changing Replication Topology

If you decide after you create a set of multiple targets for a link that you want to change the replication topology, proceed as follows:

1. In the Dfs console, open the Properties window for the link you want to modify.
2. Select the `Replication` tab.
3. Click `Customize`. The Customize Topology window opens (see Figure 16.18).
4. Select a new topology. If you select a `Hub and Spoke` topology, select a server that will act as the master hub server.
5. Click `OK` to save the change. This updates the Active Directory object representing the Dfs root. As this object replicates to the rest of the domain controllers, the FRS on each server modifies its replication behavior.

You can also use the `Replication` tab to exclude certain file types from replication. By default, .bak and .tmp files are excluded. You can add others. You can also elect to exclude subfolders from replication.

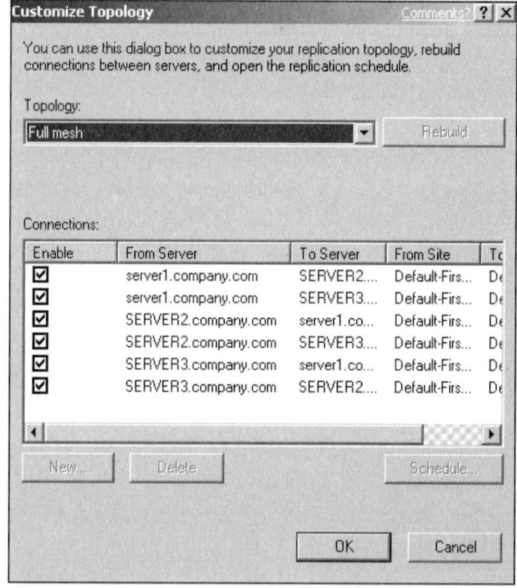

Figure 16.18 Customize Topology window showing the connections in a fully meshed topology.

Removing a Dfs Root

You can delete a Dfs root if it is no longer required. This requires a little surgery in the Registry of every root server and in Active Directory. Make sure users know that shortcuts to these folders will no longer work, then follow Procedure 16.9.

Procedure 16.9 Removing a Dfs Root

1. In the Dfs console, right-click the root icon and select DELETE from the flyout menu.
2. When prompted to confirm the decision, click `Yes` to complete the transaction.
3. In the Registry of each root server, delete the following subtree: `HKLM | Software | Microsoft | DfsHost`.
4. Open the `AD Users and Computers` console.
5. Enable the `Advanced View` option if it is not already set using VIEW | ADVANCED FEATURES.
6. Navigate to `System | Dfs-Configuration`.
7. Delete the `FTDfs` object representing the deleted root.
8. Restart Dfs by opening a command prompt and entering `Net Stop Dfs` then `Net Start Dfs`.

Managing Dfs from the Command Line

There are two utilities for managing Dfs from the command line. The DFSUTIL utility from the Support Tools is used to add and remove Dfs roots and to manage the contents of the PKT cache at the client and to display the structure of a Dfs. We've already seen the PKT information displayed by `dfsutil /pktinfo`. Here is a listing for the `/spcinfo` switch:

```
C:\Program Files\Support Tools>dfsutil /spcinfo
[*][s1.company.com]
[*][COMPANY]
[*][company.com]
[+][company.com]
        [+S1]
        [-NET-1]
[+][COMPANY]
        [+S1]
        [-NET-1]
```

If you're familiar with DFSUTIL from Windows 2000, you'll notice that the number of features has been trimmed quite a bit. The older DFSUTIL tool will work with Windows Server 2003.

The second utility, DFSCMD, cannot create or remove roots but it can do just about anything else, including creating and removing links, creating and removing replica targets, and viewing the Dfs structure.

A great feature in DFSCMD is the `/batch` switch, which creates a batch file that can recreate a Dfs structure should it be lost. This should not be necessary in a domain Dfs but it can be a lifesaver for a standalone Dfs root.

Printer Sharing

There's a high level of "print rage" among users. I think this is because users think that printing is a trivial thing that any numbskull should be able to get working. They don't realize that network printing involves a complicated set of technologies with devices and drivers and interface boxes from a myriad of vendors.

In this section, we'll take a look at how to configure network printing in Windows Server 2003 and how to avoid as much user wrath as possible by anticipating potential difficulties.

Functional Description of Network Printing

Figure 16.19 shows a diagram of a typical printing system layout. The fact that it resembles a game of Mousetrap is not coincidental. Rube Goldberg would have been astonished at the complexity of the transactions involved in turning a word on a screen to a word on a piece of paper.

Here is the sequence of events when a user sends a print job to a Windows print server:

- The user's application calls on Win32 to take the on-screen document and deliver it to the appropriate services for print rendering.
- Win32 works with the Graphics Rendering Engine to turn the document into an intermediate format called a metafile that can be transported quickly across the network. The job is spooled both before and after this rendering.
- The spooler hands the metafile to a network print provider, which then delivers it to the print processor service on a Windows print server.
- The print processor service renders the metafile into a set of printer commands and saves that to a file, which is spooled to disk.
- The spooler hands the file to a Printer Monitor service that delivers it to the print device.
- The print device applies toner/laser/sublimated dye to paper/emulsion/coffee mugs and, like an egotistical actor, takes credit for all the work done by the rest of the system.

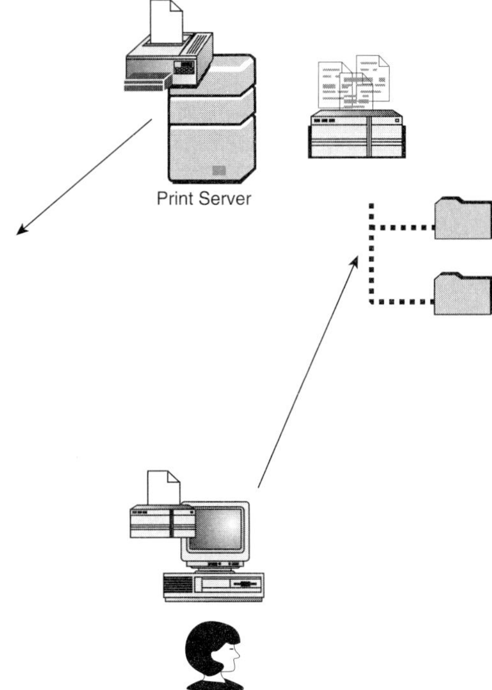

Figure 16.19 Block diagram of typical printing system arrangement.

Initial Job Rendering

The transactions in a network print job are set in motion when a user clicks the `Print` button inside an application. What happens at that point depends on the platform and the type of application:

- Native 32-bit Windows applications use Win32 API calls to render the page on-screen into a form that can be processed by a printer.
- 16-bit Windows applications use Win16 API calls that are interpreted by the Windows16-on-Windows32 subsystem, or WOW, that converts them into the equivalent Win32 API calls.

When Is a Printer Not a Printer?

If you are unfamiliar with Windows parlance, the term *printer* can trip you up. A physical printer is called a *print device*. In Windows, a "printer" is a logical object, not a physical one. You create a printer by configuring a set of drivers at a server or workstation. You would say, "I created a printer on this server using the HPLJ8000 driver."

The nomenclature becomes even more convoluted when you talk about devices such as the HP JetDirect or the Intel NetPro. These are often called "print servers," but in Windows, a print server is a Windows server that hosts a printer. Microsoft does not have a consistent term for a JetDirect or NetPro card. I will call them network printer interfaces.

- DOS applications issue raw print commands. These are converted to Win32 API calls by the Virtual DOS Machine (NTVDM) driver.
- UNIX/POSIX applications running under Interix in Windows Server 2003 issue shell commands that are converted into Win32 API calls.

Itanium machines use Win64 API calls and have an additional emulator layer, Win32-on-Win64, or WOW64, that handles native 32-bit Windows applications. WOW16 and the NTVDM run inside WOW64.

Because most of the system filenames were not changed when Microsoft wrote the IA64 version of Windows, it was necessary to put the 32-bit versions of the files in their own directory. WOW64 hides this directory using a file system redirector. When a 32-bit application accesses a system file, it is redirected to `\Windows\SysWOW64`.

The Win32 API calls initiate a set of routines inside the Windows Executive that call on the services of the *Graphic Device Interface*, or GDI. As you'd expect from its name, GDI controls all things graphical in Windows Server 2003, both on the screen and for printing. It is one of the three key components of the Win32 subsystem. User and kernel are the other two.

WOW64 maps the 8K memory pages used in the IA64 version of Windows Server 2003 to the 4K memory pages used by the IA32 version. This permits Win32 applications that do direct memory access to operate without compatibility issues. On multiprocessor servers with more than 32 processors, WOW64 also maps processor affinity for 32-bit application to maintain compatibility with the 32-processor limit of IA32 versions of Windows.

The printing engine wants to give control of the application back to the user as quickly as possible, so instead of taking the time to completely render the job into printer control commands, it renders the job into an intermediate format called an *Enhanced Metafile*, or EMF. Each new version of Windows has its own metafile format revision. Windows Server 2003 and XP are up to version 1.008.

Enhanced Metafiles

When GDI receives a print job, it *renders* the job into an EMF file. By first building an EMF file, the system can quickly return control of the system back to the user.

The EMF file is stored by the spooler while it waits for further processing. If the printer is located on a remote print server, the EMF file is sent across the network, not the fully rendered printer file. This conserves cycles at the client and bandwidth on the network.

The EMF file does not contain actual print commands. Instead, it consists of a series of native GDI commands that fully describes the printed page. Some printers are built to understand this native GDI language, but most have their own language so that vendors can add value and differentiate their products.

The EMF file is not completely independent of the printer driver. GDI needs general information about the printer so that it can design the page to match the printer's capabilities and specifications. For example, it would do no good to build a metafile with 1200dpi color output on an 11×17 page just to feed to a dot-matrix printer.

Microsoft Printer Drivers

A *printer driver* is required to convert an EMF file, which contains only raw GDI commands, into a print job containing printer control commands.

GDI resides in kernel space. Starting with NT4, print drivers were required to live in kernel space as well so GDI could access them directly. This made NT-style printer drivers highly privileged, something many administrators found to their dismay as they tried to implement cantankerous drivers and suffered through blue screen stops, erratic performance, and data corruption.

Windows Server 2003, XP, and 2000 finesse this problem by permitting a device driver to run in user space rather than kernel space. It took a long time for developers to learn the ins and outs of kernel mode writing, so they have not shown any particular eagerness to go back to user mode drivers. Microsoft dangles a carrot by offering more stack space, access to other device drivers, easier debugging, and better floating point performance in user space. It also wields a stick, warning that it may eventually stop supporting kernel-mode drivers.

You could potentially encounter a problem when connecting to printers hosted by the IA64 version of Windows Server 2003. The IA64 printer drivers will work on IA32 versions of Windows Server 2003 and XP but not with Windows 2000. You will need to configure Windows 2000 printer drivers at shared printers on IA64 servers.

Print Driver Group Policies

You can get a head start on Microsoft by implementing a group policy in Windows Server 2003 and XP called `Disallow Installation of Printers Using Kernel-Mode Drivers`. The policy is located under `Computer Configuration | Administrative Templates | Printers`. If you set this policy, users and administrators will be blocked from installing printer drivers that contain kernel-mode DLLs. The error will state this clearly and prompt the user to contact an administrator to get approved drivers.

Most printer drivers written by Microsoft and supplied with Windows Server 2003 have user-mode DLLs. The drivers are also digitally signed, indicating that they have been through logo certification. You can set a group policy to block drivers that do not have a digital signature. This also prevents Trojan horse programs from entering a system disguised as printer drivers. The policy is called `Code Signing For Device Drivers`. It is located in `User Configuration | System`. Enabling the policy blocks unsigned drivers.

Master Printer Drivers

The print driver design in Windows Server 2003 and Windows 2000 relieves a vendor of the majority of the coding work. Microsoft provides three master printer drivers:

- **"Universal" printer driver, Unidrv.dll.** This driver handles raster printers that use some derivation of the HP Printer Control Language (PCL).
- **Postscript printer driver, Pscript.dll.** This driver handles Postscript printers up to and including Postscript version 3 and Document Structuring Convention 3.1.
- **Plotter driver, Msplot.dll.** This driver handles pen plotters and plotter equivalent printers using inks or electrostatics.

These drivers are capable of handling just about any printer on the market. Vendors need only provide user interface plug-ins, rendering plug-ins, and one of the following types of printer data files:

- **Generic Printer Description (GPD) files.** These are text-based files that deliver configuration information to the Unidrv raster image processor.
- **Postscript Printer Description (PPD) files.** These are text-based files that deliver configuration information to the Pscript processor.
- **Plotter Characterization Data (PCD) files.** These are DLLs that deliver configuration information to the Msplot driver.

When you install a printer, the drivers are stored in the `\Windows\System32\Spool\Drivers` folder. This folder is shared so network clients can download their drivers directly from the print server.

Viewing Driver Details

You cannot look at the driver files and tell the drivers associated with each printer on a server. You also cannot determine the driver versions, which is important to know if you have a driver that is known to cause problems. You can view details about the suite of drivers loaded for a particular printer as shown in Procedure 16.10.

Procedure 16.10 Viewing Printer Driver Details

1. From the Printers and Faxes menu, select FILE | SERVER PROPERTIES.
2. Select the `Drivers` tab (see Figure 16.20).

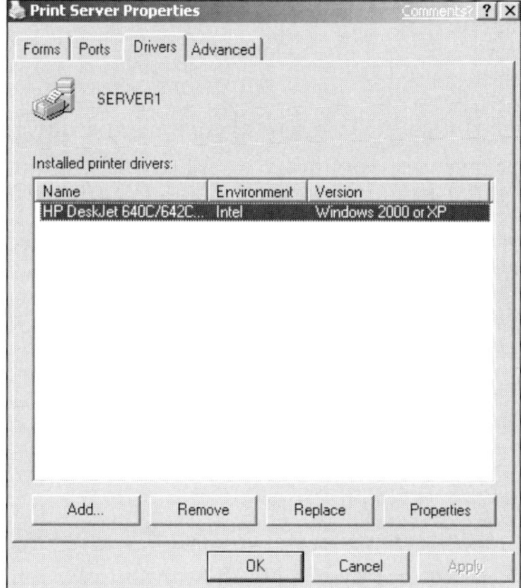

Figure 16.20 `Drivers` tab in print server Properties window showing the list of printers loaded on a print server.

3. Highlight a printer and click `Properties` to open the Driver Properties window (see Figure 16.21).

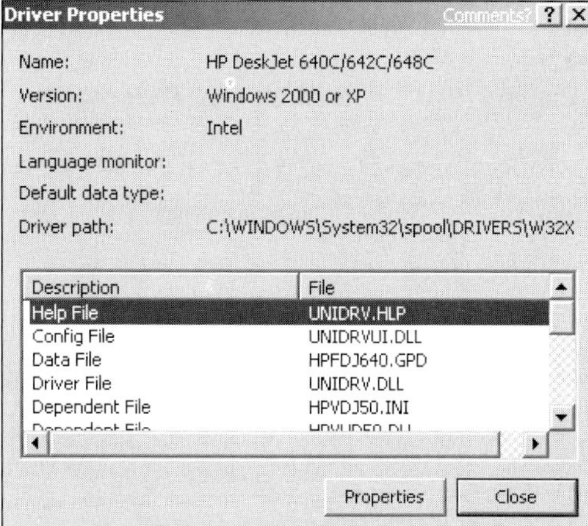

Figure 16.21 Printer Driver Properties window showing details about the drivers that are installed for a particular printer.

4. To see the version of a DLL, highlight it and then click `Properties` and select the `Version` tab.

You can also use this interface to remove a printer or change the driver.

Spooler

The Spooler service behaves like a school crossing guard watching over the hustle and bustle of print jobs going to and from the rendering engine, the disk, and the printer monitors on their way to the print devices.

Spooler is a client/server system. The client portion, Winspool.drv, takes a print job from an application and delivers it to the server portion of the spooler, Spoolsv.exe, which contains the core spooler code. Spooler also accepts jobs submitted across the network via Win32spl.dll.

You can stop and start this executable with the `NET` command. The syntax is `net stop spooler` and `net start spooler`.

Spooler stores pending jobs in the `\Windows\System32\Spool\Printers` folder. It saves two files for each print job:

- **Spool file.** These files have an .spl extension. They contain the contents of the print job itself, either the initial EMF file or the fully rendered job.
- **Shadow file.** These files have an .shd extension. They contain information and instructions concerning the job, such as the destination print device, print priority, and originating user.

Changing Spool File Location

You can change the location of the default spool directory by following Procedure 16.11.

Procedure 16.11 Relocating the Default Spool Directory

1. Open the Printers window using START | SETTINGS | PRINTERS AND FAXES.
2. From the menu, select FILE | SERVER PROPERTIES.
3. Select the `Advanced` tab (see Figure 16.22).
4. Under `Spool Folder`, enter the local path to the new spool directory. Ensure that proper access rights have been granted so that authenticated users can print.
5. Click `OK` to save the change.
6. Stop and start the Spooler service using `net stop spooler` then `net start spooler`.

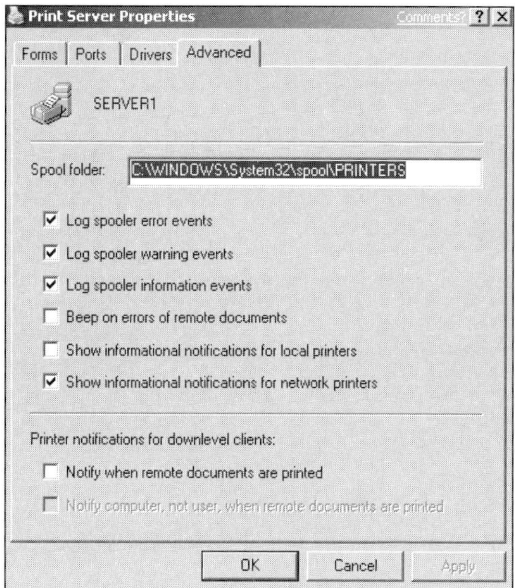

Figure 16.22 Print Server Properties window Advanced tab showing spool location.

Print Processor

Responsibility for generating a final print job based on the contents of the EMF file falls to the *Local Print Provider*, Localspl.dll. This driver combines the functions formerly performed by Winprint.dll, the print processor, and Localmon.dll, the local print monitor. (This change to the print architecture was made in Windows 2000 along with other changes designed to speed up booting.)

One of the key functions of Localspl is to assign a *data type* to a job. This defines how the job will be handled as it is converted into printer commands. Ordinarily, you never need to worry about the data types. They are handled in the background and that's that. But one day you will try to print to a print server running Windows Server 2003 using a non-Windows client and if you run into formatting problems, you'll need to know how the data types are assigned so you can change them, if necessary. Here are the data types:

- **Raw.** The print job has been fully rendered into native printer commands and requires no further processing.
- **Raw (FF appended).** A form-feed command is appended to the end of the rendered print job. This is useful for DOS applications that don't kick out the final page after they finish printing.

- **Raw (FF auto).** A form feed is appended to the rendered print job if one is not already present. Use this option if you get two blank pages at the end of every job. (The Help Desk call typically goes something like this: "We're printing a 300-page report and getting two blank pages at the end. We're tired of you IT people wasting paper.")
- **NT EMF 1.003, 1.006, 1.007, and 1.008 (Enhanced Metafile).** These are EMF versions for Windows Server 2003/Windows 2000, NT4 through several service packs, and Windows 98. Earlier versions of Windows and NT 3.5x use Journal files, which cannot be sent across the network.
- **Text.** This indicates a pure ANSI-compliant text job that contains no control codes. This data type should be assigned to Postscript jobs coming from UNIX clients.

Localspl assigns data types to the incoming byte stream based on the criteria in Table 16.1.

Print Providers

Spooler also contains a *router* component, Spoolss.dll. The router decides which *print provider* to use for communicating with the printer service that eventually prints the job. Local print jobs—that is, jobs destined for locally-attached printers—are handled by the Local Print Provider, Localspl.dll. This provider also handles print jobs destined for network print devices such as JetDirect and NetPro and Castelle boxes and cards.

Print jobs destined for network print servers are handed over to network print providers, which are as follows:

- **Windows (SMB) Network Print Provider** (Win32spl.dll). This provider handles print jobs destined for Windows-based print servers. For print servers running Windows Server 2003, XP, Windows 2000, or NT4, Win32spl sends the EMF file directly. Otherwise, it works with Localspl to fully render the job into printer commands prior to sending it to the server.
- **Internet Print Provider** (Inetpp.dll). This provider handles print jobs destined for Internet Printing Protocol (IPP) print servers.
- **NetWare Network Print Provider** (Nwprovau.dll). This provider gets jobs destined for NetWare print servers. The jobs get a RAW data type, meaning that the final rendering is done at the client.
- **UNIX print jobs.** Jobs intended for UNIX hosts are handled by the Line Printer Protocol (LPR) provider.

You can see both of these providers in the ADVANCED | ADVANCED SETTINGS properties window of the Network Connections window. Select the `Provider Order` tab.

Table 16.1 Print Processor Data Type Assignments

Job Source	Assigned Data Type
Windows Server 2003, XP, 2000, NT4, and Windows 98	Data type NT_EMF of the applicable revision.
NT 3.51, Windows 95, and Windows 3.1x	RAW.
DOS applications printing locally or across the network	RAW.
Macintosh clients printing to a Postscript printer on a server running Windows Server 2003	RAW.
Macintosh clients printing to a non-Postscript printer on a server running Windows Server 2003	PSCRIPT1. This calls up a second-level print processor to render the Postscript job for a non-Postscript device.
UNIX clients using l (as in Lima) parameter	RAW. The l parameter indicates job contains printer control codes.
UNIX clients using f parameter	TEXT. The f parameter indicates non-printing control characters have beenfiltered out. This includes the ESC character, which causes incorrect printing by PCL printers.

Port Monitors

After a job has been rendered into native printer commands, Spooler hands it over to a *port monitor*. This is a user-mode driver that communicates with the print device via a paired kernel-mode device driver.

For example, print jobs destined for a locally-attached printer on a parallel or serial port are sent to Localspl, which does double duty as a port monitor and the local print provider. If a job uses Printer Control Language (PCL), it is also sent through a *Language Monitor*, Pjlmon, for additional bidirectional print control. (PJL stands for Printer Job Language.)

NetWare CAPTURE Command

DOS applications often send print jobs that make certain formatting assumptions about tab length and end-of-page markers. In a Windows 9x environment when printing to a NetWare print server, these assumptions are handled by special options of the NetWare CAPTURE command.

Windows NT and later do not support NetWare CAPTURE. If you have legacy DOS applications that do gymnastics with graphics that ordinarily require CAPTURE settings on a Win9x machine, test them thoroughly on Windows Server 2003 or XP to make sure you can get them to work before deployment. Your only option if they don't is to leave the client on the older Windows platform or retire the application.

Print monitors are exposed to the UI as *ports*. For example, when you install a Universal Serial Bus (USB) printer, the Usbmon port monitor is activated and a virtual printer port is created at the USB interface.

There are print monitors for network print devices, as well. For example, the Tcpmon print monitor controls jobs destined for TCP/IP-based network print devices. This is the default printer monitor for network printing. (The older Hpmon interface for DLC printing has been eliminated. DLC is no longer supported in Windows Server 2003.) The Lprmon print monitor handles print jobs destined for the LPD service on a UNIX host. There are also print monitors for fax printers, Internet printing, and for bus interfaces such as IrDA and FireWire.

Final Print Job Delivery

After the print monitor finishes delivering a print job, Spooler deletes the .shl and .spd files from the spool folder unless the printer has been configured to retain print jobs.

During despool, Spooler keeps the SPL file locked but not the SHD file. If you kill a print job while it is printing, the SHD file may get deleted while the SPL file goes into limbo. From the printer window, you cannot delete the print job no matter how many times you click the `Cancel` option.

If this happens, stop the Spooler service (`net stop spooler`), delete the SPL file manually, then start Spooler again. Pending print jobs are not lost if you stop the spooler. Jobs that are actively despooling will be interrupted. They will restart from the beginning after you restart the spooler. This might irritate a user who was three pages away from finishing a 500-page end-of-year financial report, so check the status of the queues before stopping the spooler.

Configuring Windows Server 2003 Clients to Print

There are as many different ways to connect computers to printers as there are ways for people to communicate with each other. A Windows Server 2003 print communicates with these interfaces using a *print monitor*. In general, print topologies fall into these categories:

- **Printing to a local print device.** The print device is connected directly to the server via a parallel, serial, USB, infrared, FireWire, or PCMCIA interface.
- **Printing to a network print device.** The print device is connected to a network interface that the print server communicates with using a network print provider. Examples include HP JetDirect, Castelle LANpress, Intel NetPort, and the x-crowd: Lantronix, Xionics, Emulex, and Extended Systems.

> **Registry Tip: Printer Registry Entries**
>
> Registry entries affecting printing are contained in HKLM | `System` | `CurrentControlSet` | `Control` | `Print`.

- **Printing to a Windows server.** The print device is connected to a Windows server and is shared. The print server accepts print jobs from network clients, renders them, and despools them to the print device.
- **Printing to a UNIX server.** The print device is connected to a UNIX host or some other device that uses Line Printer Daemon (LPD) to control access to the print resource.
- **Printing to a third-party server.** The print device is connected to a third-party print server such as a NetWare server or a Macintosh host that requires special handling and protocols to deliver the print job.
- **Printing over the Internet.** The print device is connected to a server configured to accept print jobs via Internet Printing Protocol (IPP).
- **Printing to and from mainframe hosts.** The print device is connected to a mainframe or AS400 or some other host-based computing behemoth. This bit of arcanery falls beyond the scope of this book. It involves that most awful of marriages: APPN (Advanced Peer-to-Peer Networking) over SNA to SMB over IP. The acronyms themselves are enough to make you want to change professions. For specifics on mainframe printing in a Windows environment, look at the documentation that comes with Microsoft Host Integration Server (formerly SNA Server).

The following sections describe how to create a printer for each of the configurations in the preceding list.

Printing to a Local Print Device

For all but the parallel and serial ports, print driver installation in Windows Server 2003 is handled by Plug and Play (PnP). If the printer does not support Plug and Play, or it connects to a legacy port, you need to manually scan for the printer after connecting it to the computer. Do this by opening the `Device Manager` console, Devmgmt.msc, right-clicking the icon and the top of the tree, and selecting SCAN FOR NEW HARDWARE. If that doesn't work, follow Procedure 16.12 to manually load the drivers.

Procedure 16.12 Installing a Non-PnP-Compatible Printer

1. From the `Start` button, select SETTINGS | PRINTERS AND FAXES. The Printers and Faxes window opens.
2. Double-click the `Add Printer` icon. The Add Printer Wizard starts with the Select a Printer Port window open. In the `Use Following Port` drop-down box, select the `LPT` or `COM` port you want to use.
3. Click `Next`. The Install Printer Software window opens. Select the vendor and make/model of printer. If the printer is not listed, click `Have Disk` and provide the Windows Server 2003 drivers. Windows 2000 drivers will work, as well.

4. Click `Next`. The Name Your Printer window opens. Give the printer a name that isn't too long but clearly and uniquely identifies it. If this is the first printer, it will be selected as the default printer.
5. Click `Next`. The Printer Sharing window opens. If you want to share the printer on the network, give it a share name. Keep in mind that downlevel Windows 9x clients cannot read share names longer than 15 characters.
6. Click `Next`. The Location and Comment window opens. Enter information that helps the users differentiate between printers. This information is displayed in the Print windows of most 32-bit applications.
7. Click `Next`. The Print Test Page window opens. It is usually a good idea to print a test page because the information shows what drivers were loaded, their time and data and version, as well as other nice-to-know information about the printer. Keep the sheet in a file for future reference.
8. Click `Next`. A final completion window shows the selections you made. Click `Finish` to complete the installation.

If you install a printer manually that is actually a PnP printer, you may find that the system discovers the device the next time you reboot and insists on reinstalling it. Windows Server 2003 is much better about avoiding this scenario because it assigns unique names in the background to the printer, but mistakes still happen. If it does, you'll need to install the printer again. It doesn't take long now that the drivers have been installed.

Printing to a Network Print Device

The only real difference between printing to a network print device such as a JetDirect or NetPort card and a locally connected printer on a USB or FireWire interface is the complexity of the communications.

The print monitor works with a network *print provider* to send a print job to a network print device. There is no abstraction layer between the providers and the monitors. Each monitor is paired to its own provider and each provider handles one and only one protocol.

Windows Server 2003 and XP primarily rely on TCP/IP printing via Tcpmon when printing to network printer interfaces. Here are a few configuration issues that typically come up:

- **IP Address.** The print server needs to know the IP address of the print device. This is typically entered as a static address because most shops use fixed IP addressing for their printers. The reason is that historically, DHCP/BootP devices had no method for interacting with DNS so that if their address changed, the print servers would lose connection. With Dynamic DNS (Windows or BIND), the device can register its new IP address so this is not as much of an issue.

- **Multiple print hosts.** Many users hate to use print servers. They prefer to send their jobs directly to the print device. Sometimes this is a control issue and sometimes it's a reaction to an unreliable server. It is seldom a good idea to have users configure their local printers to print directly to a network printer interface. These devices have a limited buffer and they can become confused when confronted by many print jobs requests.
- **Simple Network Management Protocol (SNMP).** Network print devices that support SNMP are becoming more and more common. By spending an extra few dollars, you get a device that traps errors to a management console and can also be managed from a central console. This is a big win if you have the existing SNMP management infrastructure, but it's not worth the money if the only thing you're going to manage is printing.

Printing to a UNIX Host

You can print to a UNIX print server using the Line Printer protocol, or LPR. The UNIX host must be running the complementary service, Line Printer Daemon, or LPD. This service listens for LPR traffic and processes the jobs sent to it.

LPR is not loaded by default on Windows Server 2003. You must install Print Services for UNIX from the Add/Remove Programs applet in Control Panel. Look in the Other Network File and Print Services component.

With LPR installed, you will get an additional port in the Add Printer Wizard called the LPR Port. If you select this port, the system will present a window called Add LPR Compatible Printer to obtain the IP address and queue name of the LDP server and the print device.

Print Services for UNIX also adds an LPD service to the Windows server, making it possible for UNIX clients to print to the Windows server using LPR.

Printing to a Windows Server

A Windows Server 2003 client can print to any Windows print server —Windows 3.1x, Windows 9x, classic NT, Windows 2000, XP, and Windows Server 2003—if the user has sufficient access rights. The print jobs run a bit faster between modern Windows clients because the EMF file format is tighter, but you probably won't see a noticeable improvement.

Registry Tip: LPD Registry Entries

The Registry settings that control the LPD service are located in the following keys:

```
Key:    HKLM | System | CurrentControlSet | Services | LPDSVC | Parameters
Values:  AllowJobRemoval, AllowPrinterResume, and MaxConcurrentUsers (set for
64 by default)
```

There are several ways to connect a Windows client to a shared printer on a Windows server. The one used most often is the Add Printer Wizard. However, it is much easier to find the shared printer if you search Active Directory. This permits you to find the printers by location and by features. Figure 16.23 shows what the selection criteria looks like.

You can use these canned queries or you can create an advanced query to search from just about any attribute associated with the Printer object class. For instance, you could search for color printers capable of printing 11×17 on both sides and staple the results. For this to work, either you or the INF script for the printer driver must populate those attributes in Active Directory.

After you find the printer you want, right-click and select CONNECT from the flyout menu. This installs the printer driver and creates the local printer.

It's problematic whether you'll be able to train users to accept this search window. If you can't, you'll need to deliver the printer connections to them in some other way. That's covered in the next section.

Automating Client Printer Connections

You can relieve much of the user pain in creating connections to network print servers by doing it for them in a logon script.

Here is a three-line Visual Basic (VB) script that adds a printer connection to a Windows Server 2003, XP, 2000, or NT machine:

```
set obj = CreateObject("Wscript.Network")
PrinterShare = "\\<server_name>\<print_share>"
obj.AddWindowsPrinterConnection(PrinterShare)
```

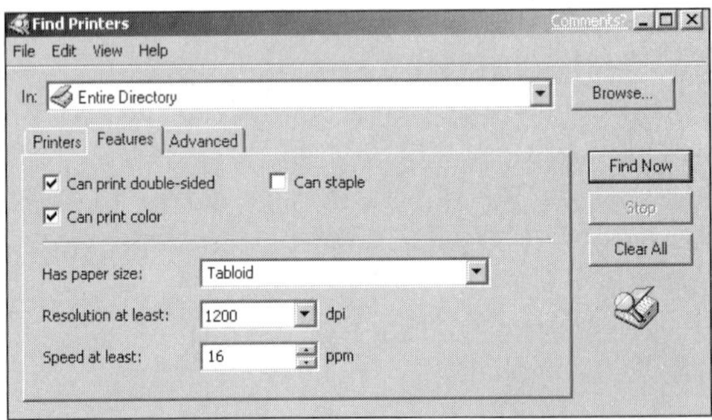

Figure 16.23 Find Printers window showing basic selection criteria.

This kind of scripting works when you want to automate the creation of a network printer connection. If you want to automate installing local printers as well, you can do this by calling the applicable switches on the PrintUI.dll function library. Do this using the Rundll32 utility. The syntax would be as follows:

```
rundll32 printui.dll,PrintUIEntry /ia /c\\s21 /m "HP Deskjet 640c" /h "Intel"
/v "Windows Server 2003" /f %windir%\inf\ntprint.inf
```

This command would install the HP Deskjet 640c printer on the computer named `S21` using the INF script stored locally on the machine. The word `PrintUIEntry` is case sensitive.

You can get a list of the `PrintUIEntry` switches by using the `/?` switch on the command line as follows:

```
rundll32 printui.dll,PrintUIEntry /?
```

There are around 50 different switches you can use for this function call. Those in the example are as follows:

- **`/ia`**. Install the printer using an INF script.
- **`/c`**. UNC path to the remote machine.
- **`/m`**. Printer driver name (typically a long string).
- **`/h`**. Printer driver type: Alpha, Intel, IA64.
- **`/v`**. Driver version: Windows NT 4.0, Windows XP or 2000, Windows XP.
- **`/f`**. Name of the INF file.

Troubleshooting Print Clients

Corrupted print drivers at the server will affect any new print clients that download the corrupted drivers. If you suspect you have a problem with corrupted printer drivers, try deleting the drivers at the desktop and then installing the drivers locally from CD. If this works but a subsequent reconnection to the server still fails, reinstall the printer at the server. You may need to delete the printer connection at the affected clients, remove the old driver files and reconnect to the printer server to download the fresh drivers.

Windows Server 2003, XP, and Windows 2000 client connection to a Windows printer server use Remote Procedure Calls. If you experience network problems, these RPC connections can break and cause client printing to fail. After a print client has lost RPC connection, it generally cannot regain it without rebooting the client.

If you have ongoing RPC problems, you may be tempted to let the clients print directly to the network print devices, if you have them installed. I would urge you to get to the bottom of your network problem because a network interface device just isn't built to handle dozens and dozens of concurrent print requests.

Printing to a Third-Party Server

If the third-party network client you install has a print provider, that provider and the third-party print monitor will work together to hand the rendered print job over to the associated server. Print jobs sent to non-Windows servers are always fully rendered locally, so this takes more horsepower at the client.

If you have multiple print providers, you will get some improvement in initial print performance by sorting the providers in the order they are most likely to be encountered on the network. This is done using the Advanced Settings window in Network Connections. Figure 16.24 shows an example of the print provider list. Use the up and down arrows to reposition the providers. There is no need to restart.

Printing Over the Internet

Windows Server 2003, XP, and Windows 2000 support *Internet Printing Protocol* (IPP) as outlined in a series of RFCs and Internet Drafts. Visit `www.normos.org` and search for IPP. There are at least a dozen papers on the subject.

IPP uses HTTP to communicate with a print server. Normal Windows printing uses RPC (Remote Procedure Call) over SMB. This is much faster than IPP but requires a solid network connection. IPP may be slow but it has the advantage of convenience and the capability to print over TCP port 80 through a firewall.

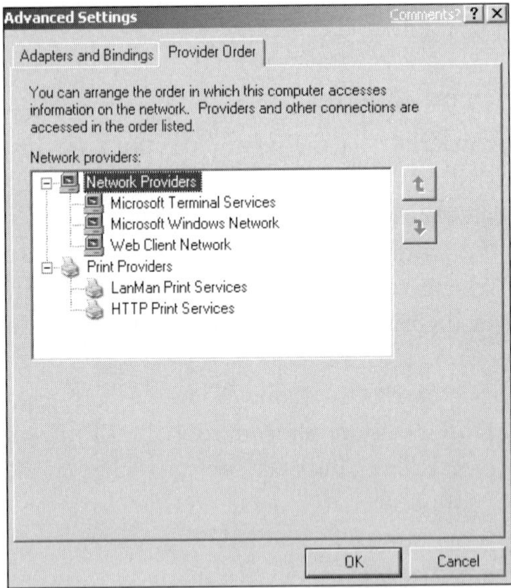

Figure 16.24 Network Connections Advanced Settings window showing print provider order.

IPP was developed as a replacement for LPR/LPD, which passes data in clear text. Because IPP uses HTTP, it can be used in conjunction with Transport Layer Security (TLS) to encrypt the data.

IPP Requirements

To use IPP on a Windows Server 2003 print server, the server must have *Internet Information Server* (IIS) service (Inetinfo) loaded. The printer support files are part of the default IIS configuration. They are placed in a virtual folder called `Printers` in the default web site (see Figure 16.25).

The ASP pages in the `Printers` folder contain code that queries for printer information then delivers it to the client via dynamic web pages. Click on a printer to see the current jobs in the queue and other information. Figure 16.26 shows an example.

Because these support files are installed automatically, delivering IPP functionality is simple for an administrator. The process is made even more automatic because Windows clients select the most efficient connection protocol for printing. Local Windows clients that are capable of making RPC connection to the print server use standard Windows printing protocols. Windows clients that come in through a firewall and find that they cannot make RPC connection will fall back on IPP over HTTP if TCP port 80 is open.

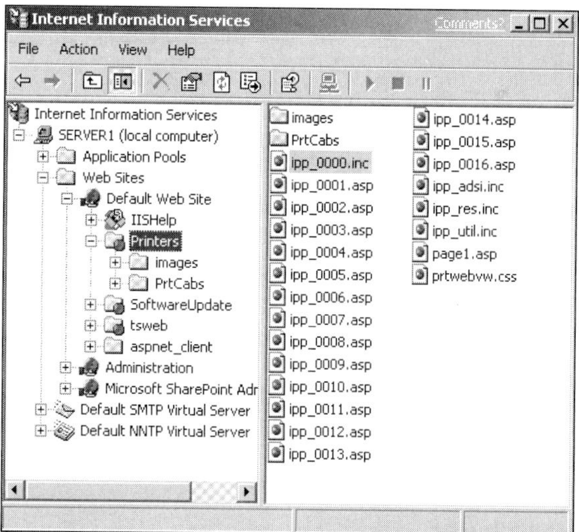

Figure 16.25 IIS Management console showing the `Printers` virtual folder in the default web site.

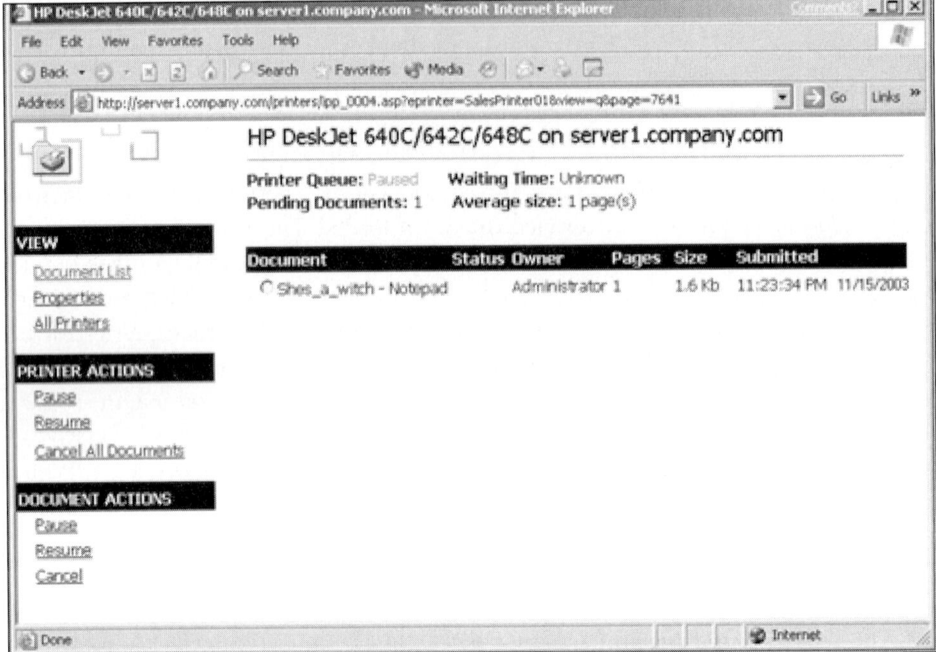

Figure 16.26 `Printers` web listing showing available printers on a print server.

Configuring Client for Internet Printing

A client can connect to a shared printer over IPP in two ways:

- The Add Printer Wizard, which requires the user to know the exact URL of the printer
- A default web page displayed with http://<print_server>/Printers

Of the two, the second option is probably the one your users will prefer.

If you insist that they use the Add Printer Wizard, they must enter the URL for the printer in the Locate Your Printer window. Figure 16.27 shows an example.

The syntax for the URL is as follows:

```
http://<server_name>/printers/<shared_printer_name>/.printer
```

The dot before the word `printer` at the end of the entry is important. Without it, the connection will fail.

It is much more convenient for a user to select a printer from a graphical listing. If the user is not authenticated on the same domain as the print server, the system prompts for credentials.

To connect to a particular printer, click the hyperlink for the name. This opens a page that displays the queued print jobs.

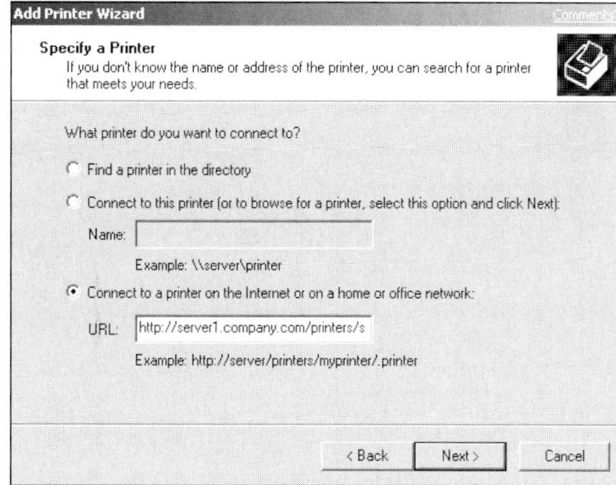

Figure 16.27 Add Printer Wizard—Locate Your Printer window showing URL entry.

Under the `Printer Actions` heading at the left edge of the window, click the `Connect` hyperlink. This downloads the printer drivers. This might take a while because of the slow HTTP protocol.

IPP Printer Properties

An IPP printer appears in the Printers and Faxes window of the local client just like a regular network printer. If the user elects to print to an IPP printer and the RPC connection is not available, the file is first fully rendered locally. The file is then passed the print server as raw text over HTTP.

When you look at the properties of an IPP printer, you'll see that it has these characteristics:

- The printer name is displayed in Printers and Faxes as *<printer>* on http://*<ip_address>*.
- The `Sharing` tab displays the message `Sharing is not supported for this type of printer.`
- The local port name will have the following structure:

```
http://<ip_address>/printers/<printer_name>/.printer
```

- The port configuration is essentially a credentials window where the user's name and password are entered. The name must be in the form *<domain>**<user_name>* so it can be properly interpreted at the IIS virtual folder.

Otherwise, the printer looks and behaves just like a standard network printer except that it is slower. Also, because the Printers and Faxes window tries to refresh the printer properties when it first initializes, you'll notice that it takes quite a bit longer for the window to open when you have IPP printers.

In the Printers and Faxes window, when you select a printer icon, the `See Also` header in the information bar at the left of the window includes an option to connect to the printer's web site. This makes it simple to select another printer from the same print server.

If you have several print servers on a campus, you can create an intranet web page with hyperlinks to the various print servers. By giving geographical information in the intranet page, you can give your users hints as to where to find their printers.

Fax Sharing

Windows 2000 contained a Fax service that permitted a user to send a document to a locally attached fax modem where it would be delivered just as if it were a standard fax. Windows Server 2003 includes a feature from Small Business Server 2000 that expands this Fax functionality by permitting a server to share its fax devices.

If you have a small- or medium-sized network, you can use this feature to give your users the ability to send documents as faxes without printing and loading them into the fax machine. It is not a replacement for a full-featured enterprise fax solution by any means, but you can't beat the price and convenience.

Fax Sharing supports both standard fax modems and intelligent fax boards such as the Brooktrout TruFax and TR114 and Intel/Dialogic Gammalink boards. These fax boards range in price from around $400 for a 1-port board to over $5000 for a board with a 24-port PRI (Primary Rate Interface) card and inbound routing features. The Fax service does not support high-end features such as Direct-Inbound-Dialing (DID) and other routing technology, and it is limited to a maximum of 4 ports, so you're best served with a less expensive fax board or fax modems.

The Fax service presents a shared fax modem as if it were a special kind of printer. Clients connect to this Fax printer using the Add Printers and Faxes window. There are drivers for Windows Server 2003, XP, and Windows 2000 clients.

The Windows Server 2003 Fax service is backward compatible with the local Windows 2000 fax client and with the Fax Sharing module in Small Business Server. The architecture has been extended considerably, though.

Fax Service Architecture

Figure 16.28 shows a diagram of the shared fax architecture used by Windows Server 2003. The fax service consists of a server executable, Fxssvc.exe, that exposes a client API for handling fax requests and a set of connections for delivering the faxes to a fax modem or a printer.

The Fax service uses the Telephony API (TAPI) to talk to a fax modem. This means it must interact with other TAPI clients such as networking, telephony, and routing clients. You can use the same modem for faxing as you do for networking, but this is not recommended for a production fax server. Stick to the "one function, one modem" rule.

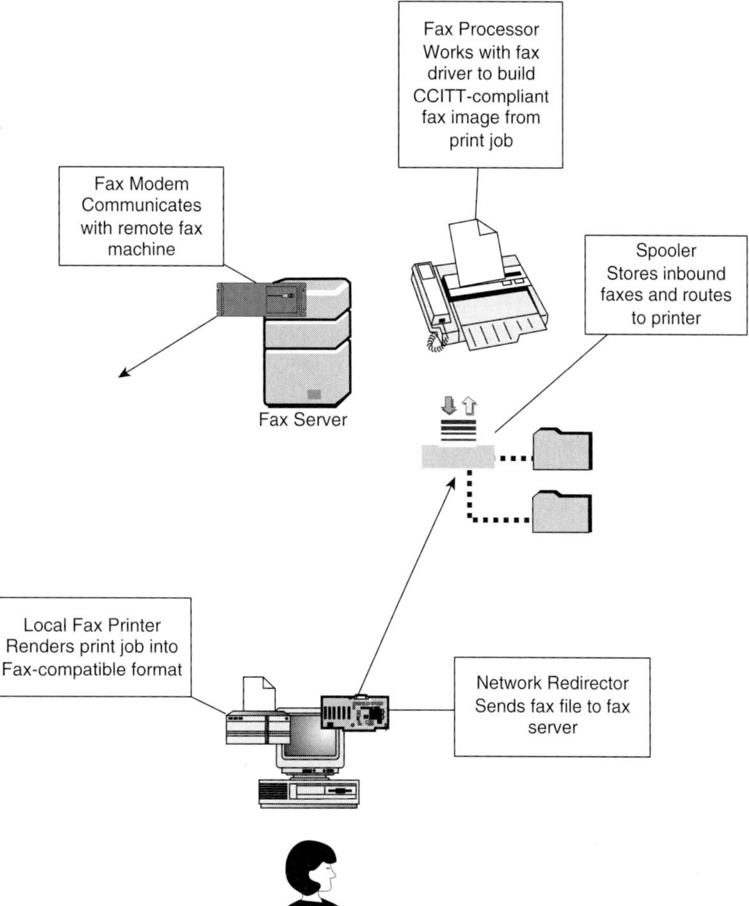

Figure 16.28 Shared fax architecture.

The Fax service can also send a fully rendered fax document to a print device via a special fax printer monitor. This monitor communicates either with the local spooler or a network print provider.

The Fax service also provides a simple set of routing alternatives for inbound faxes. It does not support automated routing based on Direct-Inbound-Dialing (DID) number, nor does it scan the fax header looking for the name of the recipient, as many commercial fax services do, but it can route the fax to a printer, to a file, and to a single user via email. This user can read the fax and forward the email to the designated recipient.

Fax Boards and Networking

If you work in a security-conscious environment that does not permit modems on servers because of the threat of back doors into your network, you'll like intelligent fax boards. They only receive calls from fax machines.

Installing the Fax Service

Unlike other network functions, the Fax service is not installed by default. Install it using the Add/Remove Programs applet in the Control Panel.

You'll also need to install either a fax modem or a fax board in the server. Spare yourself hours of teeth gnashing by using a fax modem that is on the Hardware Compatibility List (HCL) at `www.microsoft.com/hcl`. I'm not saying that other fax modems won't work. I'm just saying that digital communications across an analog phone line is a mysterious and arcane technology to begin with, and adding faxing to that mix only makes it more complex. It's best to have the odds in your favor.

If you have an internal modem or a USB modem, Plug and Play will discover the device and load the drivers. Check the Device Manager console, Devmgmt.msc, to make sure. If you install an external serial modem after starting the machine, it will not be enumerated automatically. You can force a bus scan by right-clicking the icon at the top of the device tree in `Device Manager` and selecting `Scan for Hardware Changes`. The modem should be discovered and the drivers loaded automatically. If not, you'll need to supply Windows Server 2003 or 2000 drivers.

Configuring the Fax Service

After the fax modem or board is installed and the Fax service is running, you can configure the server settings in one of three ways:

- Launch the `Fax` console from START | PROGRAMS | ACCESSORIES | COMMUNICATIONS | FAX. This starts the Fax Configuration Wizard, which walks you through the configuration.
- From the Printers and Faxes window, select the `Add A Local Fax Printer` hyperlink. After it is installed, open the Properties window to access the configuration settings.
- Launch the `Fax Service Manager` console, Fxsadmin.msc, from START | PROGRAMS | ACCESSORIES | COMMUNICATIONS | FAX and use it to configure the service.

The `Fax Service Manager` has more features, so it's the better choice, but it's more convenient to walk through the wizard. It will prompt you for the following:

- **`Sender information`**. This is used to populate fax cover pages.
- **`Modem configuration settings`**. These are used to set the dialing properties of the modem.
- **`Sending and receiving properties`**. This is used to set the Transmitting Service ID (TSID) and Client Service ID (CSID) that are included in fax and displayed on fax units.

- **Routing options.** These permit you to decide whether inbound faxes will be printed, stored in a file, routed to a select user by email, or all three.
- **Storage options.** You can select the folders for storing received faxes and sent faxes.

If you walk through the wizard and later want to change something, the sender information and fax storage folders can be modified in the Fax console. The remaining options can be modified in the Fax Service Manager console.

Setting Modem Properties

Set the properties of the fax modem or fax board by opening its Properties window in the Fax Service Manager console (see Figure 16.29).

If you want your business name and fax number to appear in the header of your outgoing faxes, enter it in the `Transmitting Station ID (TSID)` field.

By default, the modem is only configured to send faxes. This is for security reasons. If you want to receive faxes, select that option. If you want your business name and fax number to appear to be displayed at the sender when you receive faxes, enter it in the `Calling Station ID (CSID)` field.

Select the number of rings to wait before answering the line. This is set to 1 by default and should be left there unless you are configuring a server for a small business that shares a phone line for faxing and normal office business. In that case, you may want to delay fax pickup a few rings.

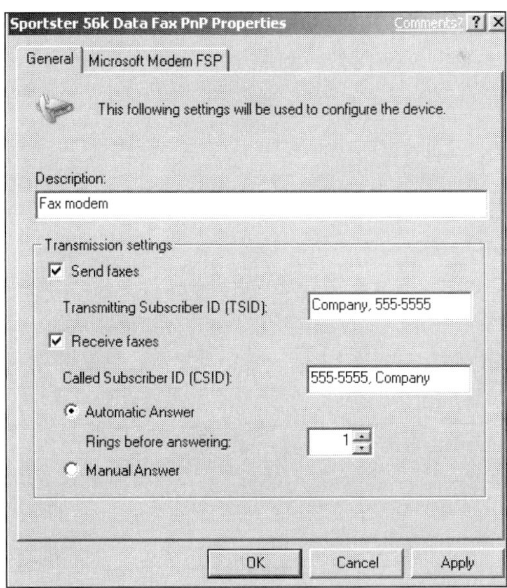

Figure 16.29 Fax modem Properties window showing TSID, CSID, and automatic answering options.

You can also configure the Fax service to pick up the modem when it hears fax modem at the other end of the line. This is called *Adaptive Answering* and is not supported by all modems. The Fax service makes no attempt to check for the feature on the modem. Check the documentation for your modem to determine if it's worthwhile setting this option.

Configuring Incoming Fax Handling

If you highlight the Incoming Methods icon under the fax modem icon, you'll see the three handling methods for incoming faxes. Configure them by opening the Properties window and selecting the tab of the same name. The options are as follows:

- **`Print.`** You can select the name of a printer from the list of printers that have been configured at the server. Any incoming faxes will be sent to that printer. You cannot select multiple printers, and you cannot select a fall-back printer.
- **`Store in a Folder.`** Enter the path to the folder where you want all incoming faxes to reside. This should be a volume with lots and lots of free space. You would be amazed at the rate inbound faxes can accumulate.
- **`Route Through E-mail.`** This option requires you to first perform a receipt setup preparation. See the sidebar, "Email Fax Routing."

After you configure the options you want to use, be sure to enable each one by right-clicking the icon and selecting ENABLE from the flyout menu.

Email Fax Routing

The Fax service does not have Direct-Inbound-Dialing (DID) routing capabilities, but you can choose to have inbound faxes converted into email attachments and sent to a single email address. This could be a special mailbox account like `faxadmin@company.com`. An office assistant or receptionist could get into this mailbox, glance at the fax, and forward it to the designated recipient.

For this to work, the Fax service must be set up for SMTP email receipts. Then, you can set up the incoming routing option. This is done via the Fax Service Manager console as follows:

1. Right-click the `Fax (Local)` icon at the top of the tree and select PROPERTIES from the flyout menu.
2. Select the `Receipts` tab (see Figure 16.30).
3. Select the `Enable SMTP E-mail Receipts Delivery` option.
4. Enter the email address of the intended recipient and the IP address or DNS name of the recipient's email server.
5. Check the Use This Configuration For The Microsoft Route Through E-Mail Incoming Routing Method option.
6. Click OK to save the change and close the window.
7. Open the Properties window for the Route Through E-mail Properties option under Devices and Providers | Devices | <device_name> | Incoming Methods (see Figure 16.31).
8. Enter the same email address in this window as you used in the SMTP E-mail Receipts Delivery window.
9. Click `OK` to save the change and close the window.

Test the configuration by sending a fax to the fax server and verifying that a copy of the fax is sent to the user via the specified email address.

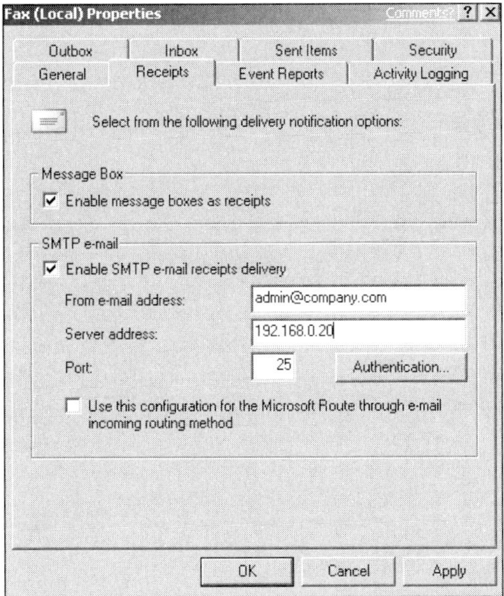

Figure 16.30 Fax Properties window showing the `Receipts` tab.

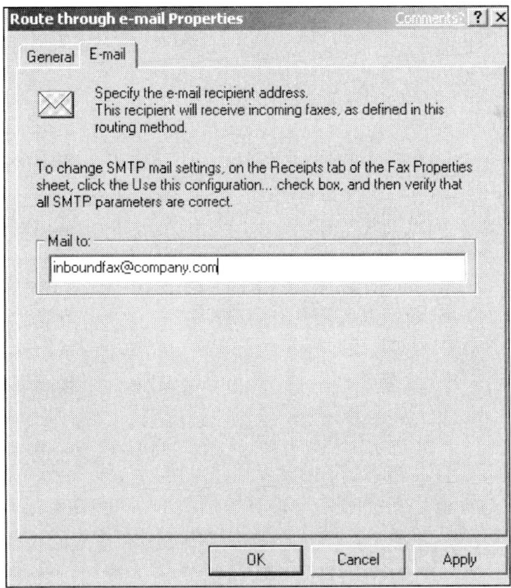

Figure 16.31 Route Through Email Properties window.

You can sort the order of the routing options based on how you would like them to occur. The routing methods are listed under `Incoming Routing | Global Methods`. Right-click the icon and select Move Up or Move Down to set its place in the order. The system will send the fax to any configured incoming method. The sort order simply sets which one will be done first.

Connecting a Client to a Fax Server

Clients can interact with the Fax service in two ways. The most common is to use it just like a print server. The client loads a driver designed to interact with the Fax service running on the server.

The fax printer drivers in Windows Server 2003 also work for XP and Windows 2000 clients, who will download them automatically.

The other method of sending a fax is to run an application that takes advantage of the Fax API built into Windows Server 2003. This bypasses the print driver and talks directly to the Fax service itself. Look for applications to start appearing soon after Windows Server 2003 ships.

Sending a Fax

A user sends a fax by printing to the Fax printer object or by selecting Start | Programs | Accessories | Communications | Fax | Send A Fax. In either case, the system launches a Send Fax Wizard, Fxssend.exe, that prompts for the recipient name and fax number (see Figure 16.32).

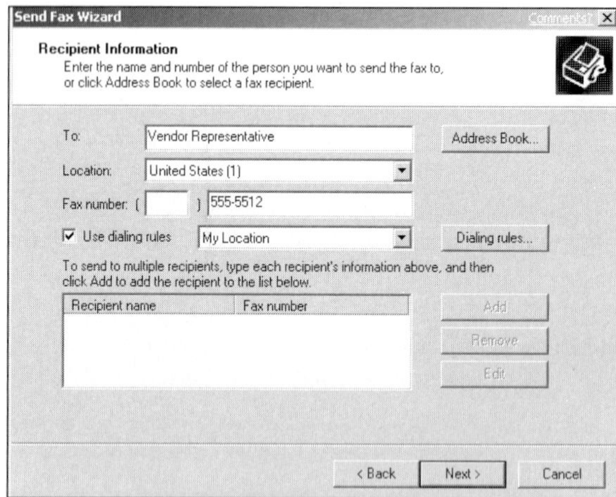

Figure 16.32 Send Fax Wizard showing Recipient Information window.

IPP and Fax Printing

You cannot print to a fax printer over HTTP. If you view the list of printers at `http://<server>/Printers`, you'll see the Fax printer on the list. However, if you select the hyperlink to the printer, you'll notice that the `Connect` option is missing.

The sender can enter the information directly or select contacts from the Windows Address Book, a database stored locally in user's profile under `Application Data\Microsoft\Address Book`. The user can add new entries in the address book via the Send Fax Wizard or by using the Windows Address Book utility, Wab.exe, launched from START | PROGRAMS | ACCESSORIES | ADDRESS BOOK.

The recipient information entered in the wizard is used to populate the fax cover page. The Fax service comes with a set of default cover pages stored in the All Users profile under `Application Data\Microsoft\Windows NT\MSFax\Common Coverpages`. This folder is shared with the share name `FxsSrvCp$` so that network clients can access the cover pages when they print to the fax server.

Cover pages use a special format with variables used to display information about the sender and recipient. See the next section for more information on cover pages.

You can use the Send Fax Wizard to schedule a fax to be sent immediately, at a specific time, or when discount rates apply. The discount rate schedule is set at the server via the Fax Service Manager console. Open the Properties window for the Fax (Local) icon and select the `Outbox` tab (see Figure 16.33). The user can also assign a priority to an outbound fax. Queued faxes are sorted in order of priority.

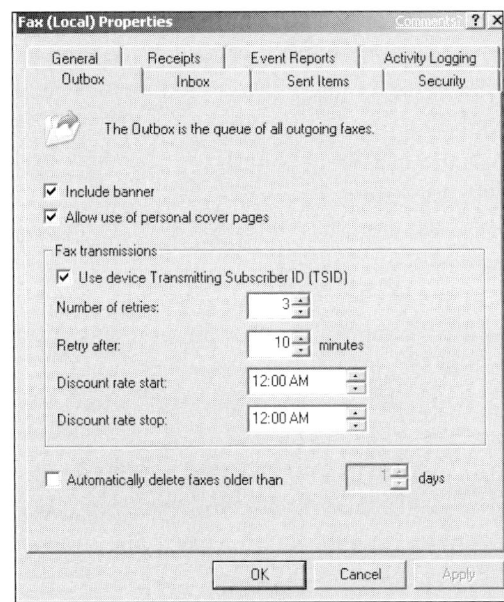

Figure 16.33 Fax service Properties window showing `Outbox` tab with dialing and discount rate settings.

Faxing to Exchange Contacts
If you are running Exchange, you can use the Global Address List (GAL) to select fax contacts by installing the Fax Transport in Outlook.

Finally, the user can select delivery notification options. This helps appease users who miss standing next to a physical fax machine and "really really really need to know" when an online fax is actually sent. The user can elect to get a pop-up notification, but this is only useful at the console. The user can also elect to get an email and even put a copy of the fax as an attachment. If the user is sending out a blast fax to multiple recipients, the user can elect to get a single notification.

The user has the option of viewing the fax before sending it. This launches the Windows Picture and Fax Viewer. This viewer consists of a DLL, Shimgvw.dll, opened under the auspices of Rundll32. When you double-click on a file with an extension registered with this viewer, the full command issued by the system is as follows:

```
rundll32 shimgvw.dll,ImageView_Fullscreen <image_file_path>
```

The viewer permits you to zoom and rotate and print and open an image editor for modifying the file. The viewer is capable of displaying multi-page documents, enabling you to riffle through a large fax. There are no OCR features to enable you to save the contents to a text file.

Also, this is a viewer, not an editor. You can launch an editor such as MS Paint from the menu.

Managing Cover Pages

Windows Server 2003 comes with a Cover Page Editor, Fxscover.exe, that is designed to create or modify cover pages that are compatible with the Fax service. The editor can be launched from START | PROGRAMS | ACCESSORIES | COMMUNICATION | FAX | FAX COVER PAGE EDITOR. Figure 16.34 shows an example of a cover page opened inside the editor.

The INSERT menu item has options for inserting fields into the cover page representing the sender's name and fax information, the recipient's name and fax information, and other general cover page information. The recipient information is obtained from the Send Fax Wizard or the Windows Address Book. The sender information is obtained from the Registry at the sender's desktop.

You can modify the sender information using the Fax Console, Fxsclnt.exe, launched from START | PROGRAMS | ACCESSORIES | COMMUNICATIONS | FAX. Select TOOLS | SENDER INFORMATION from the menu (see Figure 16.35).

You can also use the Fax console to create new cover pages, although it is much easier to copy one of the global cover pages and modify it.

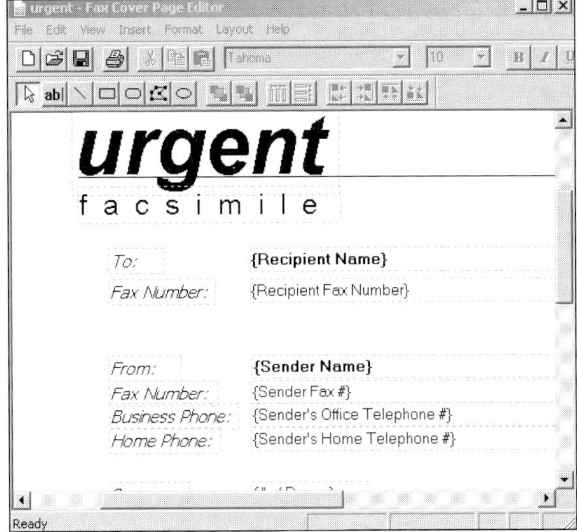

Figure 16.34 Fax cover page opened in the Cover Page Editor.

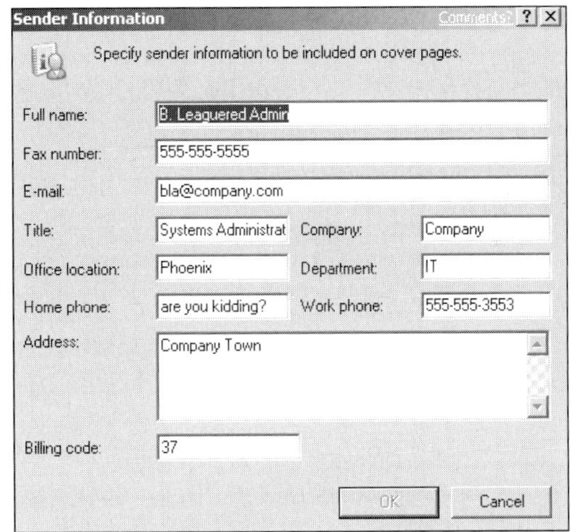

Figure 16.35 Fax console showing the Sender Information window.

Managing Fax Queues and Devices

The Fax Console configures inbound and outbound fax queues and fax devices. The queue interface in the Fax Console has four buckets that act as windows to the spooled contents on the drive:

- **Incoming.** These are faxes that have been received by the fax device but not yet processed.
- **Inbox.** These are faxes that have been processed. By default, files older than 90 days are deleted automatically.
- **Outgoing.** These are outbound faxes that are waiting for delivery to the recipient.
- **Sent Items.** These are copies of all outbound faxes. By default, files older than 1 day are deleted.

Faxes in the queues can be viewed using the Windows Picture and Fax Viewer. You can change the automatic deletion intervals using the Fax Service Manager console.

Fax Activity Monitoring

You can view the activity of a fax server via a program called the Fax Monitor, Fxsmntr.exe. Launch this utility from the main Fax Console menu via TOOLS | FAX MONITOR. A small graphic opens that shows pulses going back and forth between the fax server and fax clients.

Rather than watch this graphic all day long, you'll probably want to keep a log. The Fax service keeps two different logs:

- **Activity log.** This log records the sender, recipient, time, and filename of the rendered fax document. The Activity log is located in the All Users profile under `Application Data\Microsoft\Windows NT\MSFax\ActivityLog`. You can change this location using the `Fax Service Manager`.
- **Event log.** The Fax service places warnings, errors, and critical events in the Application log where they can be viewed by the Event Viewer.

That's about it for configuring and managing fax services. Let's turn our attention back to printing and see how to manage print services.

Managing Print Services

For all its complexity and snarl of protocols, a Windows Server 2003 print server has surprisingly few configurable components:

- **Print queues.** The queues are listed in the Faxes and Printers window. You must open each one individually to see the jobs inside.

- **Print server properties.** The server properties are accessed from the main menu of the Printers and Faxes window. You can also use this window to manage ports and drivers and configure notification and event logging.
- **Printer security.** These settings permit you to control who can print to a printer, who can manage the printer itself, and who can manage jobs in the print queues.

Managing Print Queues

You can use the `Printers and Faxes` window to check the status of documents in the queue and manage both the printer as a whole and individual documents in the print queue. You must have at least Print `Operator` privileges in a domain or `Power User` privileges on a standalone machine to manage a print queue.

When you double-click a printer icon, a window opens to display the jobs in the queue. Right-click a printer icon to see the available options. Most of them are self-explanatory. Here are a few items of note:

- **SET AS DEFAULT.** This flags the associated printer as the default for all print jobs. Many applications make a standard Win32 API call for the default printer. If one is not selected, this API call fails.
- **USE PRINTER OFFLINE.** This enables you to queue up jobs while the print device is unavailable. Otherwise, you will get errors about the inability to print to the device.
- **PAUSE PRINTING.** This halts all despool activity but the spooler continues to accept new jobs.

Right-click on a document in the print queue to see your options. Users with standard print privileges can see all queued jobs but can only pause and cancel their own jobs.

If you cancel a job, the .spl and .shd files are deleted from the spool area. If you pause a job then resume it, it picks up at the next page. If you select `Restart`, the job begins from page 1.

Open the Properties window for a document to see information about the print job (see Figure 16.36).

The `General` tab gives information about the job, including the number of pages, assigned data type, and the name of the print processor, which is always Winprint even though the print processor is now Localspl. If the job came from a Macintosh, the print processor will be Sfmpsprt. You can also see when the job was submitted and the job's owner.

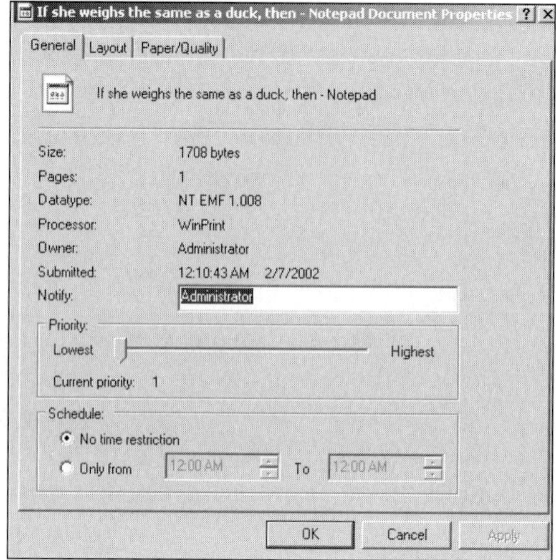

Figure 16.36 Print job properties.

The `Layout` tab controls orientation. An `Advanced` button shows specialized options for the device. These options come from the minidriver coded by the vendor. Examples of printers with a rich feature set include the Xerox DocuCenter printers, which have options that enable you to do everything including build entire saddle-stitched books with separate covers.

The `Paper/Quality` tab has options for selecting resolution, color matching, paper source, and so forth.

Managing Print Server Properties

You can configure parameters for the entire print server instead of individual printers by selecting Print | Print Server Properties from the Printers and Faxes menu. Use the `Advanced` tab to respond to user complaints about their jobs not being printed:

- The `Notify When Remote Documents Are Printed` option gives the user a pop-up when the job has finished despooling. This does not mean that it has printed successfully. Only the print device knows that.
- You may want to uncheck the `Log Spooler Information Events` option. It generally puts too much information in the Event log, hiding any real problems in a sea of successful print events.
- The `Beep On Errors Of Remote Documents` and `Show Informational Notifications for Local Printers` options are rarely of any use because you need to be standing right there at the print server when a user sends a problem job. They are useful for troubleshooting, though, so don't forget they're there.

The remaining notification items can normally be disabled except when troubleshooting.

Printer Security

Printer security is based on control of the printers themselves (the logical printers, not the physical devices), the documents in the print queues, and the ability to add documents to the queue. There are three basic rights required for this control:

- **Print.** The right to submit a print job to the printer.
- **Manage Printers.** The right to create and delete printers, pause and start the queues, and change printer properties.
- **Manage Documents.** The right to delete and change the properties of jobs in the queue other than the jobs submitted by that person.

Print jobs waiting in the queue are subject to NTFS permissions. The owner of the spooled files is the person who submitted the print job. The `Manage Documents` permission essentially gives the user the right to manage his own files in the `\Windows\System32\Spool\Printers` directory.

The ACL for a printer can be viewed by opening the Printer window, selecting PRINTER | PROPERTIES from the menu, then selecting the `Security` tab. The standard rights are as follows:

- **Administrators.** Full Control.
- **Creator/Owner.** Manage Documents.
- **Everyone.** Print.
- **Print Operators** (Power Users on standalone machine). Full Control.
- **Server Operators.** Full Control.

If you want to restrict access to a printer—for example, you don't want the whole company to print to the $150K IRIS color poster printer—you can assign users and groups to the ACL and give them appropriate rights.

The basic permissions for Fax are similar to the standard printer permissions. Additional permissions exposed by the Advanced view of the ACL Editor include permission to specify the fax priority and permission to view the fax archives.

Print Policies

Group policies make for a handy way to manage enterprise printing. There are nearly two dozen printer and fax policies that enable you to define who can print, what they can print, who is allowed to create and delete printers, and to define what a computer is supposed to do with any stored print jobs.

Here are printing policies I find very helpful:

- **`Custom Support URL in the Printers Folder's Left Pane.`** This policy has a very long name because it provides a very helpful service. The left pane of the Printers and Faxes window has a link called `Get Help With Printing`. This link normally points at the printer help at Microsoft's web site. You can specify your own internal web site using this group policy. This is a boon to the Help Desk.
- **`Browse a Common Web Site to Find Printers.`** When you enable this policy and give it an URL, the system puts a little `Browse The Intranet` link in the Specify A Printer window of the Add Printer Wizard. This link goes to the URL you specify, which would typically be the `Printers` virtual folder at a print server. This is a great way to give users a simple way to find their printers and download drivers.
- **`Default Active Directory Path When Searching For Printers.`** This is a nifty policy that focuses the Active Directory search in the Add Printer Wizard to a specified OU or domain rather than the entire Active Directory. It is not as nifty as it could be, however, because it does not affect the SEARCH FOR PRINTERS feature in the Start menu `Search` option.
- **`Prevent Addition of Printers.`** Administrators who really are tired of dealing with printer issues can use this policy to take total control of printer creation. Enabling this policy removes the `Add Printers` options from the UI. Sophisticated users can still map to a printer with the `NET USE` command or the Add Hardware Wizard, but users with that kind of knowledge are rare. As an administrator, you can add new printers using scripts.

Managing Printer Properties

The Properties window for a printer in Printers and Faxes contains configuration parameters for the following:

- Sharing
- Port management
- Security
- Print device settings

Print device settings are exposed by printer minidrivers and filters installed from the vendor's driver files. They expose parameters such as trays, collator, stapler, page size, and so on. The settings are too diverse to cover in this book. Here are the remaining settings.

Sharing

The `Sharing` tab exposes two features in addition to simply sharing the printer. `Additional Drivers` brings up a checkbox list of alternate clients that can download drivers when they connect to the shared printer. Some of these drivers are on the

Windows Server 2003 CD under the `\Printers` folder. The rest you'll need to download from the vendor's web site.

If you have the opposite situation, an NT4 print server with Windows Server 2003 or XP clients, you can install the updates drivers on the NT4 print server using the FIXPRNSV utility, located in the `\Printers` folder on the Windows Server 2003 CD.

You can also publish the shared printer in Active Directory using the `List in Directory` option. Publishing the printer helps users to find print resources quickly using the Search utility.

There are a few complexities associated with publishing printers in Active Directory. These complexities come from the capability of Active Directory to remove, or *prune*, published printers that no longer point at active printers. This might be because the print server has been decommissioned or the printer has been removed or the network connections are broken.

The pruning agent runs at the domain controller every 8 hours. During its run, it attempts to contact each printer that has a published share in Active Directory. If it is unable to contact a printer for 3 consecutive retries, it deletes the PrintQueue object from Active Directory.

A print server running Windows 2000 or Windows Server 2003 will republish its shared printers when it comes back online. If you publish printers from downlevel clients, you will need to republish them when the server becomes available.

You can change the pruning parameters using a set of group policies. The policies are located in `Computer Configuration | Administrative Templates | Printers`. Here is a list of the policies:

- **`Directory Pruning Interval.`** This tells the domain controller how often to check the status of printers with PrintQueue objects in Active Directory. By default, this interval is set to 8 hours.
- **`Directory Pruning Retry.`** This tells the domain controller how many times to try the connection before declaring it dead. This is 2 retries, by default.
- **`Directory Pruning Priority.`** This tells the system what priority to give the Printer Pruner. By default, this is normal priority.
- **`Check Published State.`** This tells print servers to constantly republish their shares printers in Active Directory rather than waiting for a restart of the print server. Only set this policy if you are having significant network instabilities that cause your published printer shares to disappear. This would have to be pretty severe to cause a 24-hour disruption.

Ports

The `Ports` tab of the printer Properties window lists the port that has been assigned to the printer along with the other available ports and their printer assignments. If you want to change the port assigned to the print device, or change the properties of the port itself, do it from here.

This is the place to go if you have changed the IP address on a network printer interface and you want to change the address assigned to the Tcpmon port monitor.

If you have a user workgroup that produces a lot of paper reports—for some reason, the Accounting department comes to mind—you can improve overall print throughput by installing multiple print devices that all despool from the same printer. This is called *printer pooling*. You won't speed up any individual print job with printer pooling, but it keeps jobs from piling up in the queue.

If you use printer pooling, make sure all the print devices you plan on putting in the pool will work with the printer driver associated with the printer. They do not need to be the exact same make/model, but they do need to recognize the same printer control codes. For example, don't mix Postscript Level 2 and 3 printers in a pool with a Postscript 3 driver.

Advanced Settings

The `Advanced` tab in the Properties window contain a variety of selections. Table 16.2 lists the options, their functions, and gives examples and cautions when selecting the options.

Table 16.2 Advanced Printer Options

Option	Function	Examples and Cautions
`Available From`	Assign the hours that the printer will despool to its print device. Print jobs submitted at other times are queued.	If your organization has a color printer that employees can use after hours, you can create a printer and set the `Available From` option so that jobs print at night.
`Priority`	If you have multiple printers that despool to the same print device, Spooler will ordinarily alternate between the two queues. If you want jobs in one queue to print in front of jobs in another queue, set the `Priority` value higher.	You may have a large-format printer owned by the Art depart ment but sometimes used by Technical Documentation. If the graphic designers grouse that they have to wait for the technical writers—I speak from experience on this subject—you can create a separate printer for the graphic designers with a higher priority.

Option	Function	Examples and Cautions
`Driver`	If you get a new driver for a printer, or you change the print device associated with a printer, use this button to load the new driver. If the printer is shared, users who connect to it automatically download the new drivers.	If you change drivers, the installation script may change the name of the printer. If this happens, the connected print clients can no longer use the shared printer even though the share name has not changed. Before installing a driver into an existing printer, copy the printer name to the Clipboard in case you need to reapply it.
`Spool Print Documents ... / Start Printing Immediately`	This tells Spooler to accept the incoming print job, render the byte stream as it comes, and despool it to the print device simultaneously.	This option speeds up printing large documents. If the job fails to print for some reason and Spooler is notified of this by the print monitor, the job is permitted to complete spooling, and then it is set to the print device again.
`Print Directly to Printer`	This tells Spooler to bypass local storage of the job. The job is rendered on-the-fly and sent directly to the print device.	If the printer is shared, this option is ignored.
`Hold Mismatched Documents`	This tells Spooler to make sure the printer setup matches the document setup.	If the printer uses a raster driver but the incoming print job is Postscript, this option holds the job. A job cannot be moved to another queue, so the only alternative is to cancel the job and print it again to the correct printer.
`Print Spooled Documents First`	Spooler favors spooled jobs over incoming jobs. If two jobs spool at once, Spooler favors the larger job. This option is used in conjunction with the `Start Printing Immediately` option.	Under normal circumstances, Spooler chooses the next job to print based solely on the assigned priority. This means a high-priority, 500-page job that might take an hour to print would get attention while a little 1-page job that has already spooled sits and waits. With this option, the spooled job prints first.

continues ▸

Table 16.2 continued

Option	Function	Examples and Cautions
`Keep Printed Documents`	This option holds the spool file after the document prints.	Sometimes it is important that a document print right the first time. For example, accounting packages print reports as part of the end-of-month and end-of-year closings. It is difficult to go back and print the report again if the job fails to complete. You can quickly run out of disk space if you leave it enabled for long.
`Enable Advanced Features`	With this option deselected, the Advanced options are not available.	If you experience compatibility problems when users take advantage of Advanced features exposed to the UI for their printer, you can deselect this option to disable certain of these features. The miniport driver must make explicit calls to this flag, however, so it might not resolve your problem.

Separator Pages

When many people use the same network printer, it can be difficult to sort through the jobs in the output tray. Separator pages (sometimes called *burst* pages as a holdover from the old green bar tractor paper days) identify the start of each print job with a page that can be seen easily by riffling through the paper stack.

There are four default separator pages. The files are stored in the `\Windows\System32` folder. They are as follows:

- **Pscript.sep.** Puts a dual-mode printer in Postscript mode but *does not print a separator page.*
- **Sysprint.sep.** Prints a separator page on a Postscript printer.
- **Sysprtj.sep.** Same as Sysprint.sep with the addition of special fonts that support Japanese language modules.
- **Pcl.sep.** Puts a dual-mode printer in PCL mode, and then prints the username, date, and job number of the print job.

The following is a sample separator file:

```
\
\H1B\L%-12345X@PJL ENTER LANGUAGE=PCL
\H1B\L&l1T\0
\M\B\S\N\U
\U\LJob : \I
\U\LDate: \D
\U\LTime: \T
\E
```

Table 16.3 lists the escape codes and their functions. If you want to switch a printer from Postscript to PCL without printing a separator page, for example, use the following separator file:

```
\
\H1B\L%-12345X@PJL ENTER LANGUAGE=PCL\0
```

Table 16.3 Separator File Escape Codes and Their Functions

Escape Code	Function
`\N`	Username of the submitter.
`\I`	Job number.
`\D\T`	Date and time.
`\Lxxxx`	This is an echo option. Prints the characters (*xxxx*) until another escape code is encountered. Use this to fill a line with characters to make the burst page distinctive.
`\Fpathname`	Prints contents of the specified file, starting on an empty line, without any processing. Use for printing custom informational messages.
`\Hnn`	Sets a printer-specific control sequence, where *nn* is a hexadecimal ASCII code. Refer to the printer manual for applicable codes.
`\Wnn`	Sets the width of the separator page. The default width is 80; the maximum width is 256. Any printable characters beyond this width are truncated.
`\B\S`	Prints text in single-width block characters.
`\E`	Page eject. Use to start a new separator page or to end the separator page file. If you get an extra blank separator page when you print, remove this code from your separator page file.
`\n`	Skips *n* number of lines (from zero through nine).
`\B\M`	Prints text in double-width block characters.
`\U`	Turns off block character printing.

Printing from DOS

A DOS application running inside an NT Virtual DOS Machine (NTVDM) is as oblivious to innovations such as Graphic Device Interface (GDI) and Windows Driver Model (WDM) and font libraries as a washboard maker is to Maytags. The DOS application expects to push bytes down an LPT port or bits down a COM port and nothing else is going to make it happy.

One of the functions of the NTVDM driver is to convert DOS hardware function calls into equivalent Win32 API calls. This works fine for well-behaved DOS applications that play by the rules. Many don't. The most common problems involve DOS applications that try to punch bytes directly to the printer port, either for reasons of control or performance. Those jobs will refuse to print.

Some DOS applications slam a print file closed without sending an `<EOF>` byte. The print processor thinks the application is still printing. There are several symptoms of this problem:

- Print job doesn't run until the application is closed.
- Last page of a print job stays in the printer, requiring a page feed to clear it.
- DOS jobs get mangled together with pages from different reports and documents mixed up in the same hopper. This is caused by applications that do calculations between pages of the report that are long enough to cause the LPT timer to time out and accept jobs from another source.

If you get these symptoms, try setting the default data type to `FF Appended`. If you are printing to a NetWare server, don't expect the `CAPTURE` command to solve the problem. The `CAPTURE` command is not supported on NT.

If you are trying to print to a nonstandard port, such as a network print device or an Infrared (IR) printer, or you are trying to print from DOS to a printer connected to a network print server, there is no LPT port to keep the DOS application happy. You must give it an LPT port using the `NET USE` command. This is true even if the machine itself is acting as the despool server for the printer.

Assume, for example, that you have a server running Windows Server 2003 that hosts a printer for a network print device such as an HP JetDirect card. The port for this device does not use LPT1 or LPT2; it uses a special port designed to print to the network device. If you want to print from a DOS application on this server, you must share the printer and redirect a printer port to the shared printer. If you do not want to share the printer, you won't be printing from DOS. The syntax for the printer port redirection is as follows:

```
net use lpt1: \\server_name\printer_share
```

The share name can be longer than eight characters. The DOS application prints to LPT1, just like it would on a DOS machine. You can use any LPT port number between one and nine, but most older DOS applications don't recognize anything above three. You don't need to put the colon on the port number. (I do it just to be consistent.)

Troubleshooting Printing Failures

When troubleshooting printing problems, start with the physical layer. Is the printer turned on? Is it plugged in? Is it connected to the computer? Does the serial printer have the right cable pinouts? I'm sure you know the drill. There are more subtle factors that can affect local printing after you've eliminated the common faults:

- **Bidirectional printing enabled.** The printer monitor for both PCL and Postscript printers expects to get status information back from the printer, which requires a bidirectional printer connection. An older parallel cable without a pinout for two-way communications will cause the system to either refuse to create the printer or print jobs will hang in the queue. Check CMOS for the printer port configuration. Often an EPP/ECP port is set to another configuration that does not support two-way communications.
- **Job in the wrong queue.** If you have a job in the queue that was supposed to be sent to another queue, you cannot drag and drop it to another printer. You must cancel the job and print it again to the correct printer. This is because the print job has already been rendered using the driver associated with the first queue. Moving it to another queue would mean it could possibly be incorrectly formatted for the target printer. It would be great to have an administrator's bypass on this so that jobs intended for the same type print device could be moved, but that's not in the product.
- **Jobs print partial pages or odd characters.** If the printed output includes control characters, Postscript code, lacks graphics characters that were in the document, or otherwise does not seem correct based on the screen display, look for a problem with the default data type. Open the Properties window for the printer, select the `Advanced` tab, click `Print Processor`, and select a different default data type. If you have UNIX clients who constantly complain that their jobs are getting fouled up in the print queue, for example, create a new printer for them and change the default data type for that printer to TEXT.
- **Slow or erratic printing performance.** If a user is printing locally and the jobs print very slowly, or performance gets erratic, you may need more memory or a faster processor or both. If the user demands fast printing but doesn't want to pay for hardware upgrades, try installing a separate print server to free the desktop from rendering the job.

- **Inadequate rights to spool directory.** If you set up a printer for a user and it worked fine, but now the user cannot get it to work, look at the NTFS permissions on the `\Windows\System32\Spool` directory. They might be restricting the user's access.
- **PnP error.** If the driver was installed automatically by PnP, check Device Manager to see if there is an error. The serial port might be sharing an IRQ with an add-on device. The parallel port might lack bidirectional capability or use a non-standard IOBase address. You do not ordinarily get IRQ problems with parallel ports, but watch out for add-on devices and security dongles that keep the port from working with a printer. If you have a second parallel port on a legacy machine, make sure that IRQ5 is enabled for legacy devices in BIOS and that this is the IRQ assigned by Device Manager.
- **Verify proper driver.** Windows Server 2003 uses Windows 2000 drivers with a preference for user-mode rather than kernel-mode drivers. Check the vendor's web site for the most current driver.

Command-Line Print Administration

Microsoft included several VBScript-based printer management utilities in Windows Server 2003. These scripts first made their appearance in the Windows 2000 Resource Kit. They use Windows Management Instrumentation (WMI) to display and manage printers, print jobs, and printer components such as ports, queues, and configuration.

Most of these scripts require you to have administrator, or at least printer admin, rights on the target server. Also, many of these tools require you to specify the printer name on the command line. This is a good reason to keep the names as short as possible.

There are six scripts; they correspond roughly to the tabs in the printer Properties window:

- **PrnPort.** This script enumerates, creates, configures, and deletes printer ports at a designated server. This is the functionality you would get in the `Ports` tab of the printer properties. Here is a sample listing:

```
C:\>prnport -l -s s1.company.com
Server name s1.company.com
Port name IP_10.1.1.81
Host address 192.168.0.81
Protocol RAW
Port number 9100
SNMP Disabled
Number of ports enumerated 1
```

- **PrnMngr.** This script adds and deletes printers and can be used to set a particular printer as the default. This is the functionality you would get from the Add Printer Wizard at the main Printers and Faxes window. Here is a sample listing:

```
C:\>prnmngr -l -s s1.company.com
Server name s1.company.com
Printer name testprn
Share name DeskJet648c
Driver name HP DeskJet 640C/642C/648C
Port name IP_10.1.1.81
Comment Standard letterhead paper
Location Bldg C, Floor 3, Cubicle 33C
Print processor WinPrint
Data type RAW
Parameters
Attributes 8776
Priority 1
Default priority 0
Status OK
Average pages per minute 0
```

- **PrnQctl.** This script can be used to view, stop, start, and manage the jobs in a print queue. You can also use PrnQctl to print a test page. This is the functionality you would get when you double-click the printer icon in the Printers and Faxes window and open the queue viewer.
- **PrnCnfg.** This script lists the configuration information for a printer that is normally displayed in the `Advanced` tab of the printer properties. Here is a sample listing:

```
C:\>prncnfg -s s1.company.com -p testprn -g
Server name s1.company.com
Printer name HP DeskJet 640C/642C/648C
Share name DeskJet648c
Driver name HP DeskJet 640C/642C/648C
Port name IP_10.1.1.51
Comment Standard letterhead paper
Location Bldg C, Floor 3, Cubicle 33C
Separator file
Print processor WinPrint
Data type RAW
Parameters
Priority 1
Default priority 0
Printer always available
Attributes local shared published do_complete_first
```

- **PrnJobs.** This script enumerates the jobs at a printer and gives the option of pausing a particular job, canceling it, or resuming it. This is the functionality you would get by right-clicking a job in the queue viewer. Here is an example listing:

```
C:\>prnjobs -s s1 -p testprn -l
Job id 14
Printer testprn
Document Test Page
Data type NT EMF 1.008
Driver name HP DeskJet 640C/642C/648C
Description newprn, 14
Elaspsed time 00:00:00
Machine name \\S1.company.com
Job status
Notify Administrator
Owner Administrator
Pages printed 0
Parameters
Size 75952
Status UNKNOWN
Status mask 0
Time submitted 12/16/2001 11:57:58
Total pages 1
Number of print jobs enumerated 1
```

- **PrnDrvr.** This script lists information about the print drivers that are loaded on a particular server. This helps to determine if the drivers are up-to-date. There is no UI window that gives information corresponding to this utility. Here is a sample listing:

```
C:\>prndrvr -s s1 -l
Server name s1
Driver name HP DeskJet 640C/642C/648C,3,Windows NT x86
Version 3
Environment Windows NT x86
Monitor name
Driver path C:\WINDOWS\System32\spool\DRIVERS\W32X86\3\UNIDRV.DLL
Data file C:\WINDOWS\System32\spool\DRIVERS\W32X86\3\HPFDJ640.GPD
Config file C:\WINDOWS\System32\spool\DRIVERS\W32X86\3\UNIDRVUI.DLL
Help file C:\WINDOWS\System32\spool\DRIVERS\W32X86\3\UNIDRV.HLP
Dependent files
 C:\WINDOWS\System32\spool\DRIVERS\W32X86\3\HPVDJ50.INI
 C:\WINDOWS\System32\spool\DRIVERS\W32X86\3\HPVUD50.DLL
 C:\WINDOWS\System32\spool\DRIVERS\W32X86\3\HPVUI50.DLL
 C:\WINDOWS\System32\spool\DRIVERS\W32X86\3\HPFIMG50.DLL
 C:\WINDOWS\System32\spool\DRIVERS\W32X86\3\HPV600AL.DLL
 C:\WINDOWS\System32\spool\DRIVERS\W32X86\3\HPFDJ6xx.GPD
 C:\WINDOWS\System32\spool\DRIVERS\W32X86\3\HPFDJ69x.GPD
 C:\WINDOWS\System32\spool\DRIVERS\W32X86\3\HPFDJ200.HLP
 C:\WINDOWS\System32\spool\DRIVERS\W32X86\3\HPFNAM50.GPD
 C:\WINDOWS\System32\spool\DRIVERS\W32X86\3\UNIRES.DLL
 C:\WINDOWS\System32\spool\DRIVERS\W32X86\3\STDNAMES.GPD
Number of printer drivers enumerated 1
```

An additional utility, PrintMig, is available in the Resource Kit. This is a standard executable that simplifies backup and restore of printer configurations out of the Registry. You can also use this utility to quickly and easily transport printer configurations to another server. This comes in handy in a business recovery scenario when your main print server goes down and you need to get the printers up on another server quickly. Figure 16.37 shows an example window that lists the printer elements installed on a server.

Printer Location Tracking

Each printer object in Active Directory has a `Location` attribute. Users who are searching for printers can limit the scope of their search based on the location information.

Sites form the search boundaries, so location tracking cannot be used if you have only one site. The location tracking option is in the Search utility.

When you select a site from the search list, the system automatically appends a forward slash (`/`) to the site name. To make location tracking work, then, you need to preface each location attribute with the site name, followed by a forward slash, followed by more specific location information such as building, floor, cubicle, and so forth.

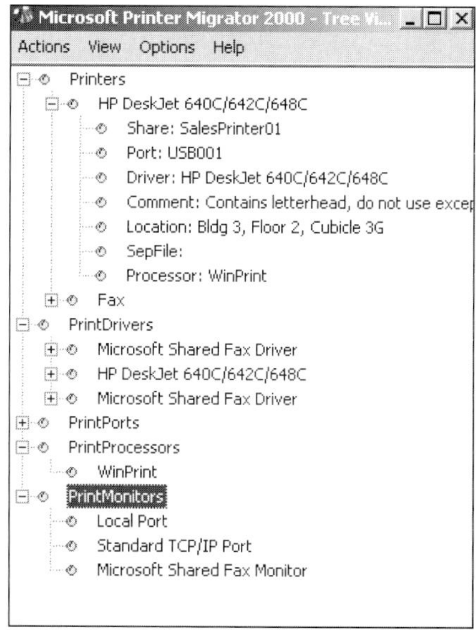

Figure 16.37 Printer Migration utility showing printer elements that can be backed up and restored elsewhere.

Moving Forward

It's time for a deep breath. If a Windows Server 2003 deployment were like the *Wizard of Oz*, at this point we'd be in front of the wizard for the first time, thinking that all we need to do is ask for our heart/brain/home/courage. Instead, we're about to face the most daunting part of the entire adventure. The next two chapters cover the Encrypting File System and Public Key Infrastructure.

After we've made it through that deep, dark place, we'll set up the user environment so everyone will be comfortable on the network, then configure dial-up services so everyone can be comfortable working from home, then plan for disaster recovery so we can go home, whether that's in Kansas or an apartment across town.

17 Managing File Encryption

IMAGINE THIS PHONE CALL. IT'S 1:30 on a Wednesday afternoon. The voice at the other end of the line belongs to the CFO. She is in New York making a series of presentations to potential investors. She has just arrived back from lunch to discover that someone took her laptop from a meeting room where she was assured that it would be "perfectly safe."

The CFO's most pressing concern is to get the files that she needs for her presentations, but your larger concern is for the data on the laptop's drive. If someone in the chain of criminals that handles the stolen laptop recognizes the nature of the data it holds, the machine takes on a whole new value. When the enormity of the vulnerability sinks in, company executives start getting interested in file encryption. (You've been suggesting it for a long time, of course.)

In response to situations like this, Microsoft developed an Encrypting File System (EFS) feature and included it in Windows 2000. Windows Server 2003 and XP have an enhanced version of EFS that corrects a couple of key deficiencies and adds features that make it more attractive for users and administrators. If you're making a list of reasons to upgrade your laptop fleet to XP, put EFS in the top five items for making the move as soon as possible.

This chapter covers the components involved in file encryption and a description of how they function together along with operational guidelines that help ensure the system does not become compromised and that files remain available for access by authorized personnel. The last section contains a set of step-by-step procedures for deploying and managing file encryption.

New Features in Windows Server 2003

If you have evaluated EFS in Windows 2000 and found critical features missing, it's worth taking a second look at EFS in Windows Server 2003 and XP. The changes include the following:

- **New and more cryptographically robust encryption methods.** You can now choose between DESX encryption (used by Windows 2000) and 3DES (Triple-DES), an algorithm that complies with government standards for handling of non-classified documents.
- **Offline file encryption.** This feature is one of the most significant improvements in Windows Server 2003 and XP. It enables users to use a highly convenient feature, offline file storage, while retaining the ability to protect their files with encryption.
- **Encrypted file transfer over WebDAV.** The Web-based Distributed Authorizing and Versioning redirector uses HTTP rather than SMB. Encrypted files are transferred in their encrypted state rather than being decrypted prior to transport as happens with SMB. Also, servers can store encrypted files using WebDAV without compromising security with Kerberos delegations.
- **More flexible group policy control.** EFS can now be disabled throughout a domain with a single click of the mouse in a group policy. This contrasts with Windows 2000, which requires removing and re-importing X.509 certificates to control encryption.
- **Shared encrypted files.** Users with encrypted files can assign access to other users. This enhances the use of EFS in a workgroup. Only individual users can be given access, not groups. Additional users can only be selected by users who already have access.
- **Copy warnings.** Explorer now warns users when they attempt to copy or move encrypted files to an unprotected location such as a Zip drive, floppy drive, or FAT partition. New switches in COPY and XCOPY permit overriding these protections, if necessary.
- **Visual cues.** The Explorer shell now shows the names of encrypted files and folders in a different color, similar to the way compressed files are displayed in Windows 2000.
- **Improved command-line administration.** The CIPHER command-line utility has been updated with several new features, including the ability to generate file recovery certificates, the ability to search for encrypted files on a volume, the ability to refresh certificates for all encrypted files on a volume, and the ability to wipe all unused disk space to remove temporary files. (The wipe feature was released in Windows 2000 SP3.)

- **Security improvements.** Although not strictly an EFS improvement, the handling of the crypto Master key has been changed so that it is not updated when a local user password is changed by anyone other than the user. This eliminates a serious deficiency for standalone laptops and desktops. Now a hacker cannot use utilities to change a user's password (or the Administrator password) on a standalone machine to gain access to encrypted files.

Not every change is a welcome one, however. In Windows 2000, files cannot be encrypted without the certificate of a Data Recovery Agent (DRA). This ensures that a user cannot encrypt files and then quit the company and leave you without a means of recovering the files. In Windows Server 2003 and XP, it is possible to encrypt files *without a DRA*. This "feature" has potentially serious consequences because users could encrypt their files and then lose the private key, thereby losing access to the files permanently.

File Encryption Functional Description

There's no getting around it. File encryption is a complex beast. EFS uses technologies that are only just now entering their maturity. You need to plan deployment carefully to ensure that files remain secure and available. EFS also requires a measure of insight and work from users, not always a key to success.

File Encryption Process Description

File encryption uses elements from a variety of Windows subsystems. To introduce the cast of characters, here is a summary of what happens when a file is encrypted. See Figure 17.1 for a block diagram of the components:

1. When a user sets the encryption flag on a file, the Encrypting File System driver calls upon the Microsoft Crypto Provider to issue a *File Encryption Key (FEK)*.
2. The Microsoft Crypto Provider uses the services of a Random Number Generator to produce a 128-bit cipher to use for the FEK. (Crypto providers use enhanced 128-bit services except when interfacing with legacy clients.)
3. EFS uses the FEK to encrypt the file. Only the data in the file is affected. All named data streams are encrypted as well. Other attributes such as filename, attributes, timestamps, and so forth remain in clear text. The pointer to the security descriptor that defines who can access the file also remains unchanged, although the file system does impose additional restrictions for handling encrypted files.
4. EFS hands the encrypted file over to NTFS, which saves the encrypted data stream just like any other data coming from an application. EFS does not bypass NTFS, it enhances NTFS.

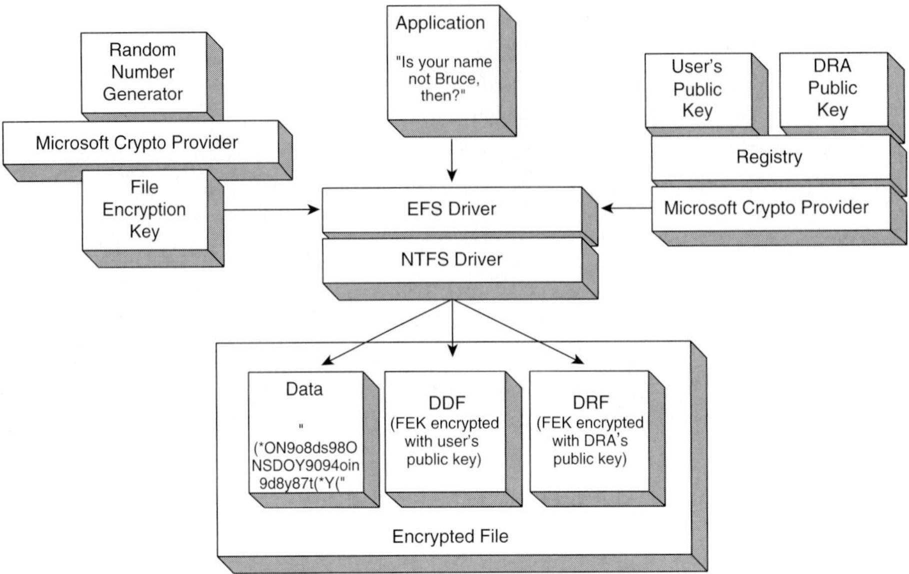

Figure 17.1 Data encryption elements.

5. EFS now turns to the Microsoft Crypto Provider once again, this time to obtain the user's public EFS key. It uses this key to encrypt a copy of the FEK to store along with the file in a *Data Decryption Field*, or DDF.
6. EFS encrypts another copy of the FEK with the public File Recovery (FR) key of the domain Administrator account and saves the result in a *Data Recovery Field*, or DRF, that also accompanies the file. The Administrator account is called the *Data Recovery Agent*, or DRA.
7. EFS hands the DDF and DRF to NTFS, which saves each one in the file record using a special attribute type called a `$Logged_Utility_Stream`.

The end result is an NTFS file with gibberish in the `$Data` attribute that can only be understood when decrypted using the FEK. Only the user who encrypted the file or the DRA can decrypt the file because only they have FEKs in the file record. (As we'll see, Windows Server 2003 and XP have a new feature that permits giving additional users access to the file.)

File Decryption Process Description

Here's a quick rundown of what the system does to decrypt an encrypted file when a user opens it (see Figure 17.2):

1. The user opens an encrypted file.
2. NTFS sees that the encryption attribute is set on the file and delivers the data stream to the EFS driver.

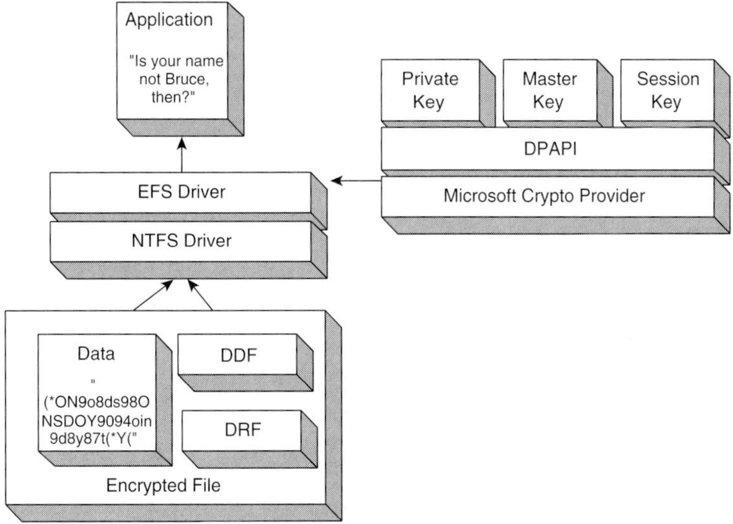

Figure 17.2 Data decryption elements.

3. EFS coordinates with the Microsoft Crypto Provider to get access to the user's private key. The Crypto Provider decrypts the private key using a Session key derived from the Master key managed by the Data Protection API (DPAPI).
4. EFS uses the private key to decrypt the FEK stored in the Data Decryption Field of the file.
5. EFS then uses the FEK to decrypt the data in the file, which it delivers to the application that asked for it.

Seem complicated? You bet it is. EFS has lots of moving parts. The remainder of this topic discusses how the parts work, how they mesh together, and what to expect if they don't interact as expected.

Data Encryption

When a user encrypts a file, the EFS driver works in concert with the NTFS driver in the Windows Executive to encrypt the `$Data` attribute of the file. Figure 17.3 shows a diagram of the Master File Table (MFT) record before and after encryption.

EFS converts the `$Data` attribute into a series of cipher blocks that it stores in the same location on the disk where the clear-text file originally resided. (If the `$Data` attribute is resident in the MFT record, it is made non-resident and placed out onto the disk.)

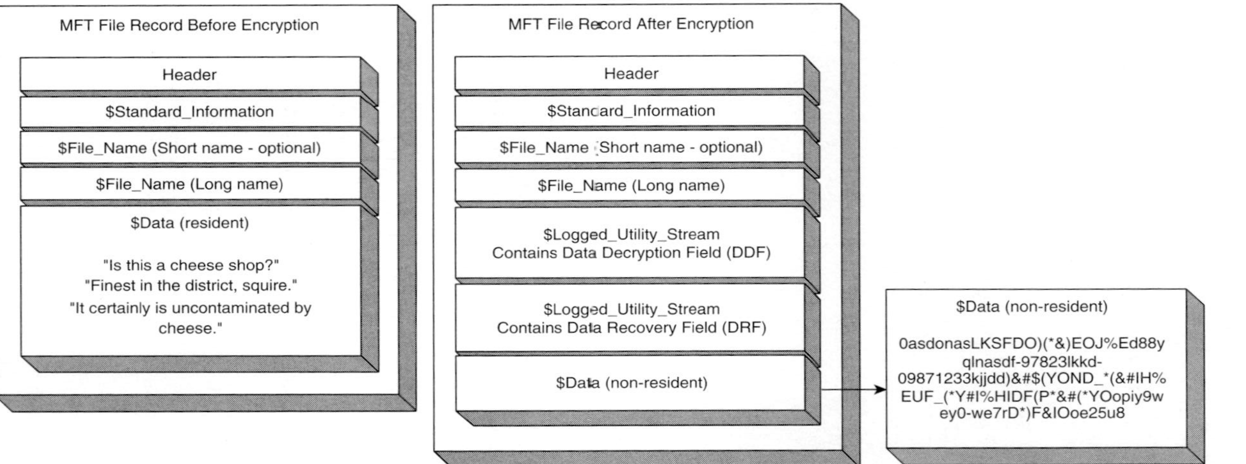

Figure 17.3 MFT record before and after encryption.

During this encryption transaction, a clear-text copy of the file is created. You can avoid this by setting an encryption flag on a folder and then saving files directly into the encrypted folder. This encrypts the data stream before it hits the disk and avoids temp files. See the following sidebar, "Wiping EFS Temp Files."

Data Encryption Algorithms

For many years, the only exportable encryption option was the Data Encryption Standard, or DES. Developed by IBM back in the 1970s, DES has just not been able to keep up with modern computing capabilities. A moderately priced machine can now break standard DES encryption handily.

To overcome this weakness, EFS uses one of two encryption mechanisms that are more secure than DES while retaining its exportability and most of its speed: DESX or 3DES (Triple-DES).

DESX

This is the encryption mechanism used by Windows 2000. DESX was formulated by Ronald Rivest at RSA Data Security in an effort to shore up DES by making it more resistant to brute-force dictionary attacks. In broad terms, DESX is a block cipher that uses a three-step process to encrypt a file:

- First, it encrypts each block with a 64-bit cipher using a simple XOR algorithm.
- Then, it uses a separate 56-bit cipher to encrypt the encrypted block again using standard DES encryption.
- Finally, it uses a different 64-bit cipher to perform yet another XOR encryption.

The combination of these three steps results in an encrypted file that is much less susceptible to key-search attack than DES. Unfortunately, DESX is not much better than standard DES when it comes to resisting sophisticated cryptanalysis.

Wiping EFS Temp Files

If you have reason to suspect that a user has created clear-text temp files by encrypting individual files, you can wipe the old temp files off the volume, along with any other unallocated clusters, using the `CIPHER` command.

The syntax is as follows:

```
cipher /w:<directory>
```

For example, `cipher /w:\e:\` would wipe all unallocated clusters on the E: drive of a machine. (The directory path is necessary because another file system could be mounted at the directory via a reparse point.)

`Cipher /w` overwrites unallocated clusters with 0s, then 1s, and then random numbers. The process takes awhile on a big drive. The user should not access the drive until all the unused clusters have been overwritten to ensure that no unprotected temp files are created.

Although it does a good job of scrubbing, `cipher /w` does *not* meet DoD 5220.22-M sanitizing requirements. If you need to meet these requirements, you must purchase a third-party product.

3DES

The crypto community, pragmatists to the core, reacted to the failure of DES with the same kind logic used by television producers:

- **Television.** "Last year's audience lost interest even though our episodes were lewd and loud, so this year we'll produce shows that are three times louder and three times lewder and that will get our audience back."
- **Cryptologists.** "Well, if a single DES encryption run is too easy to break, why don't we run DES three times? *That* should do the trick." (See the sidebar, "Advanced Encryption Standard," for the long-term fix.)

So, the basis of 3DES is to simply run the data through the engine three times, each time using a different one-third of a big master encryption key. The result is a cipher block that is a billion times more secure than DES alone, but performance is three times slower. DES isn't all that slow, though, and 3DES is still faster than many other alternatives.

A body called the *National Institute of Standards and Technology*, or NIST, decides on procedures and practices that companies must follow to do business with the government. Because *everyone* wants to do business with the government, many NIST recommendations become de-facto standards for industry.

NIST standards are published in a set of *Federal Information Processing Standards* (FIPS) publications. The FIPS publication that describes general requirements for computer security is FIPS-140-2, *Security Requirements for Cryptographic Modules*. This standard is also used by the Commerce Department to determine technologies that can be freely exported and those that require special handling.

Although 3DES is strong, it is subject to certain cryptanalytic attacks. To be fully FIPS-140-2 compliant, Microsoft changed the default EFS encryption algorithm in Windows Server 2003 and XP SP1 to the Advanced Encryption Standard (AES). This can cause interoperability problems with existing Windows 2000 and XP computers that still use DESX. You cannot transport an encrypted file from Windows Server 2003 to a Windows 2000 server and do a data recovery.

For backward compatibility, you can set a group policy to force Windows Server 2003 and XP SP1 to use DESX rather than AES until you have completed your migration. The group policy that controls encryption is System cryptography: Use FIPS compliant algorithms for encryption. The policy is located under Computer Configuration | Windows Settings | Security Settings | Security Options.

Advanced Encryption Standard

Even though it's fairly fast, 3DES is still too pokey to be acceptable for high-end encryption applications. In mid-2001, NIST selected a new encryption algorithm as a standard, calling it the *Advanced Encryption Standard*, or AES.

AES uses the Cipher Block Square algorithm, also called the Rijndael (pronounced "Rhine Doll" or "Rain Doll") algorithm, designed by Dr. Joan Daemen and Dr. Vincent Rijmen, both from Belgium. For more information on the Rijndael algorithm, see `www.ddj.com/articles/1997/9710/9710e/9710e.htm?topic=security`. For a FAQ on AES, see `www.nist.gov/public_affairs/releases/aesq&a.htm`.

File Encryption Key Protection

DESX, 3DES, and AES are symmetrical algorithms, meaning that the same cipher key is used for encryption and decryption. Longer keys are better than shorter ones, and the Microsoft Crypto Provider takes advantage of the loosening of export restrictions in 2000 to use a 128-bit random number as a cipher key. This is called the *File Encryption Key*.

Ordinarily, you would expect a security system to treat a cipher key like you would treat your house key. You do not leave your house key near your front door where someone could easily find it and break in. Unfortunately, the FEK must accompany a file because of portability considerations. For instance, if you do a tape restore of encrypted files to another location, you still want the capability of opening the files.

So, the FEK must accompany a file. But it must be adequately protected or else the entire encryption scheme would be compromised. What's needed is a separate encryption mechanism to protect the FEK. That's where Public Key Cryptography Services (PKCS) come into play.

PKCS is a system of public/private key pairs. Anything encrypted with one key in a public/private key pair can only be decrypted with the other key. EFS encrypts the FEK with the user's public key. Only the user's private key can decrypt the FEK, which is necessary to decrypt the file. The user's private key, then, is the sweet spot in making EFS work.

The private key is stored in the user's profile. The file holding the key is a hidden, system file. This keeps it from being encrypted by the Encrypting File System.

EFS does not use PKCS for encrypting an entire file because of poor performance. The encryption methods used by PKCS are impressively secure but very slow and processor-intensive. The combination of a moderately secure bulk file encryption mechanism and a highly secure PKCS key protection mechanism is fairly standard in the industry. S/MIME (Secure Multipurpose Internet Mail Extensions) uses it to protect email. IPSec (IP Security) uses it to protect data communications.

FEK Storage

The data structure used to hold the encrypted FEK is called a *Data Decryption Field*, or DDF. The DDF also contains a copy of the user's public key certificate for identification. The DDF is stored along with the file in a special NTFS attribute called `$Logged_Utility_Stream`.

EFS also makes provision for accessing a file if the user accidentally deletes the private key. When EFS encrypts a file, it includes another copy of the FEK encrypted with a File Recovery public key issued to the domain Administrator account. This account is called a *Data Recovery Agent*, or DRA. You can use the DRA's private key to decrypt its copy of the FEK, which then gives access to the file.

EFS stores the DRA's copy of the FEK in a data structure called a *Data Recovery Field*, or DRF, along with a copy of the DRA's public key certificate. The DRF is stored in its own `$Logged_Utility_Stream` attribute in the file record.

Encrypted File Sharing

Windows .NET/XP permits sharing access to encrypted files. It does this by encrypting another copy of the FEK with the public EFS key of any selected users. This gives the users the ability to decrypt the file, assuming that they have sufficient NTFS permissions to open it in the first place.

The user who first encrypts a file selects additional users to share the file via the file's Properties window. Click `Advanced` to see the encryption option, then click `Details` to see the list of users and DRAs assigned to the file. Figure 17.4 shows an example.

When a name is added to the list of authorized users for an encrypted file, EFS obtains the user's public key certificate either from the local certificate store (the Registry) or from Active Directory.

Any user with access to an encrypted file can add other names to the list of authorized users. Train your users to grant shared access only when absolutely necessary and then only to trusted colleagues.

EFSINFO

The Resource Kit includes a command-line tool called EFSINFO that can quickly display the name of the user who encrypted a file, any users who have been added to the file, and the DRA(s), if any, assigned to the file. Here is an example EFSINFO listing for a file on a standalone server without a local DRA:

```
E:\>efsinfo /u /r /c test.txt

test.txt: Encrypted
  Users who can decrypt:
    CX612097-B\Admin (Admin(Admin@localbox))
    Certificate thumbprint: 839E 9492 CF52 C280 6BB3 5EF5 1C60 B38A C464 5E8C
    Unknown (Bill(Bill@localbox))
    Certificate thumbprint: BEB0 795E 3F50 F36B 6357 C660 1164 C707 52F8 666B
  No recovery agent is found.
```

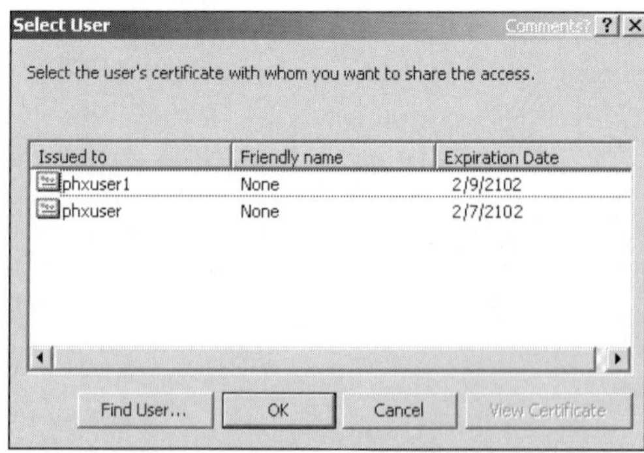

Figure 17.4 EFS Details for a file showing the users selected to access the encrypted file and the DRAs assigned to the file.

The thumbprint information comes in handy if you have a user with multiple EFS certificates. You can quickly identify which certificate was used to encrypt the file. You can find out the user's current certificate using `cipher /y`. Here is a sample listing:

```
E:\>efsinfo /y
Your current EFS certificate thumbnail information on the PC named localbox is:
  839E 9492 CF52 C280 6BB3 5EF5 1C60 B38A C464 5E8C
```

Private Key Protection

Have you ever seen the old 1970's television series *Get Smart*? At the start of each episode, Maxwell Smart (played by Don Adams) walks down a long corridor through a series of doors that leads to a phone booth where he dials a number and drops through a trapdoor. That pretty much sums up the way a user's private key is protected, one key after another key after another. Ready to see them in action? Here goes. . . .

The private key is stored in the user's profile under `\Application Data\Microsoft\Crypto\RSA\<User_SID>`. To protect the private key, the Microsoft Crypto Provider uses a Session key generated by the *Data Protection API*, or DPAPI.

The DPAPI generates this Session Key using a secret derived from the user's password hash. Details of how this secret is generated can be obtained from `www.microsoft.com/serviceproviders/whitepapers/security.asp`. In essence, the user's standard logon password hash is hashed again, this time using the 160-bit SHA-1 algorithm. It is then run through 4000 iterations of a password protection algorithm, PBKDF2, described in a document titled PKCS #5, "Password-Based Cryptography Standard." (See `www.rsalabs.com` for more information.) This creates a pseudo-random number based on the user's password hash. DPAPI refers to this as a *Master* key.

The Master Key is itself encrypted using a special function called an HMAC (or Hashed-based Message Authentication Code). An HMAC incorporates a secret key into a standard hashing function. The HMAC used to encrypt the Master key is a hash of the Master key itself with the user's password hash as the secret key. The encrypted Master key is stored in the user's profile under `\Application Data\Microsoft\Protect\<User_SID>`. So, as you can see, the reliability of the entire structure comes down to the security of the user's password. If I know your password, I can get access to your encrypted files. Simple as that. You can avoid this vulnerability by using smart card authentication. See Chapter 20, "Managing Remote Access and Internet Routing," for details about deploying smart cards.

When a user changes her password, DPAPI builds a new Master key and then uses it to generate a new Session key to re-encrypt the private keys when the user next logs on. If you as an administrator reset a user's password in Active Directory, DPAPI will build a new Master key the first time the user logs on with the new password. DPAPI then generates a new Session key derived from the new Master key and uses it to re-encrypt the private keys.

For machines that are members of a Windows Server 2003 or Windows 2000 domain, a backup copy of the Master key is stored at the local machine. This backup copy uses a public key stored in Active Directory as the secret key for the HMAC used to encrypt the Master key. This permits Master key recovery should the local copy get corrupted.

Private Key Protection on Standalone Machines

In a domain environment, the user password hash is stored in Active Directory. A copy of the hash is cached locally in the Registry under the Secrets key in the *Security* hive (often called LSA Secrets) but this copy cannot be changed as long as the user is off the network.

The same is not true for standalone machines, where the user password hash is stored in the local SAM. If a bad guy can get physical access to a standalone machine, he can use one of several utilities to change the user passwords stored in the SAM, including the Administrator password. Because the local Administrator account is the DRA for file encryption on a standalone machine, if you can log on as the Administrator, you stand a chance of compromising the user's encrypted files.

At least this was the situation in Windows 2000. The operation of the DPAPI has been changed in Windows Server 2003 and XP to eliminate this security flaw. In Windows Server 2003 and XP, if a user's password on a standalone machine is changed by any means other than one that includes DPAPI function calls, the Master key is not re-encrypted. Without access to the Master key, EFS cannot access encrypted files on behalf of the user. This keeps encrypted files safe from interlopers.

Windows Server 2003 and XP also have a new feature called a *Password Reset Disk*, or PRD. The PRD permits a user who has forgotten his password to change it at the logon window. DPAPI does not update the Master key if the user changes his password using the PRD. This means that the user loses access to encrypted files, which is especially nasty on XP because there is no requirement to have a DRA.

There is a workaround, however. The user can log on with the new password and then change the password back to what it was, if he can remember it. This will cause DPAPI to create a new Master key with the new user credentials. The Session key derived from this Master key will decrypt the user's private EFS key, giving the user access to encrypted files once again.

This change to the DPAPI does not prevent a bad guy from changing the Administrator account password then logging on and poking around trying to find clues for the original user passwords. For example, the bad guy might use a password cracker like L0phtcrack to derive the user passwords from the hashes stored in the SAM. It's possible that the user of the standalone laptop who was so concerned about protecting files with encryption was not as concerned about access security and used a simple password, or maybe even a blank password, for logon.

For this reason, users on standalone machines who want to encrypt files should always use long, complex passwords and should never save password hints or save dial-up passwords or save any application password if it is the same as their logon password. This potential vulnerability is only present on standalone machines.

EFS Key Storage

When a user first encrypts a file, the system obtains a set of EFS keys issued in the form of *certificates*. PKCS certificates are normally issued for specific reasons. In this instance, the certificate is issued for the express purpose of supporting the Encrypting File System. An EFS certificate cannot be used to digitally sign an email message, for instance.

If there is no Certification Authority (CA) available, the Microsoft Crypto Provider on the local machine issues the EFS certificate. This is called a *self-signed* certificate, meaning that it has no chain of authority leading to a CA. Self-signed certificates have security significance only on the local machine because other machines cannot check validity of the issuer.

If you have a Microsoft CA, a group policy informs the local clients of the CA's existence by distributing the CA's public key certificate. Clients use this public key to encrypt certificate requests that they send to the CA. When the CA gets a certificate request, it decrypts it with its private key, verifies the requestor's identity, then issues the certificate. It digitally signs the certificate with its own private key so the client can validate the certificate with the CA's public key.

After they are obtained, the EFS keys are stored in the user's local profile under a hidden folder called `Application Data`. Figure 17.5 shows the key locations.

- The user's public EFS key is stored in `System Certificates\My\Certificates`.
- The user's private EFS key is stored in `Crypto\RSA\`<*userSID*>.
- The crypto Master key and backup Master key are stored in `Protect\`<*userSID*>.

It is very important to train desktop technicians to treat profiles carefully after you deploy file encryption. *If you delete a user's profile, the user loses access to all encrypted files on that machine*.

As we'll see a bit later when we look at data recovery, the domain Administrator account is the default Data Recovery Agent for all member servers and desktops in a domain. A profile is created for this account on the first domain controller in the domain. The profile contains the File Recovery (FR) public and private keys used by the DRA. *If you delete the Administrator profile on the first domain controller in the domain, you cannot recover any encrypted files in the entire domain*.

You can and should export the Administrator's FR private key to a certificate so it can be safely stored away and used only when necessary. You can also designate other DRAs to use in addition to the domain Administrator.

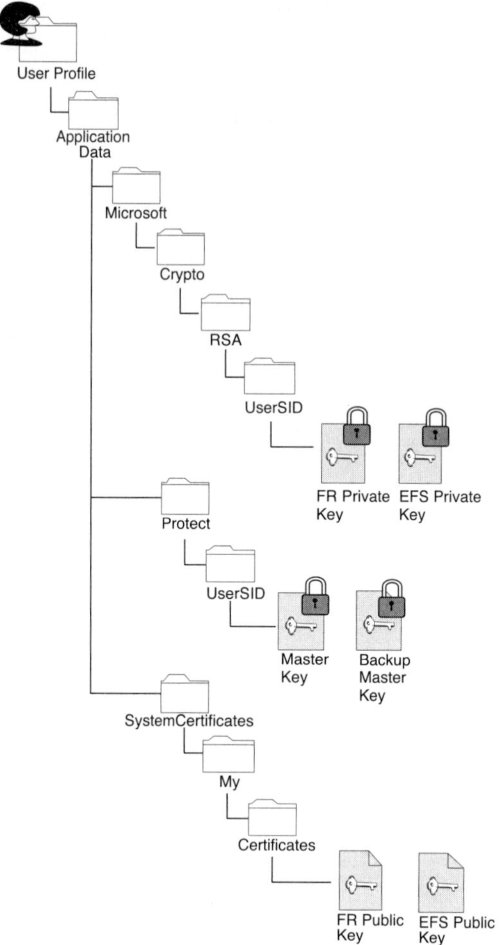

Figure 17.5 Key storage in the user profile.

EFS Keys and Roaming Profiles

The Application Data folder travels with a user who has a roaming profile. This is good news, because it means the same public key is used to encrypt files on different machines. This simplifies aggregating the files for the user, should that become necessary.

The bad news is that you cannot encrypt files within a roaming profile because of a Catch 22 in file handling. Let's say that you were able to encrypt a file in the My Documents folder of a roaming profile. When you log off, that encrypted file would be copied to a server.

When you log on the next time, the system downloads the contents of your roaming profile then uses it to initialize your local operating environment. But wait, there's an encrypted file in that roaming profile, and you can't open that encrypted file without your private key; but your private key is in your profile, which the system won't initialize until it has copied all the contents.

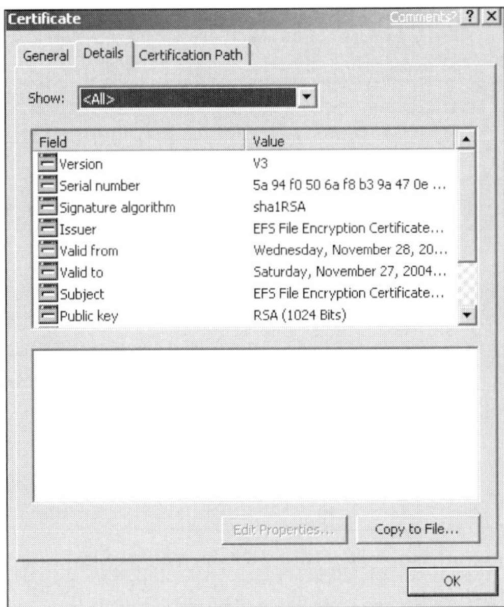

Figure 17.6 Contents of X.509 public key certificate.

To avoid this situation, Microsoft prevents users from storing encrypting in roaming profiles. If a user does encrypt a file inside a profile, the system gives an error at logoff stating that the file will not be copied to the server.

Users with roaming profiles who want to encrypt files in My Documents can do so this way: use folder redirection to place the My Documents folder on a server, enable offline folders, then encrypt the contents of the offline folder cache.

Certificate Management

A certificate is a data structure that contains a key, either public or private, along with information about the key and validation data for the key's issuer. If you build a mental picture of a valuable diamond accompanied by a gemologist's report and a certified pedigree with embossed signatures, you have a good idea of how a certificate is used.

The International Telecommunications Union (ITU) has promulgated a standard, X.509, that defines the content and structure of PKCS certificates. Figure 17.6 shows an example X.509 certificate.

There are other certificate types that enjoy wide acceptance in the marketplace but have not been incorporated into the ITU standard. RSA maintains a list of certificate types and documentation of their content and structure. Visit the RSA web site at `www.rsasecurity.com`.

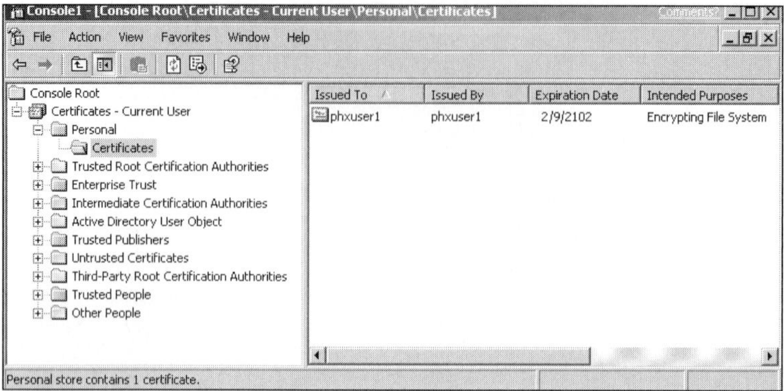

Figure 17.7 Custom console showing Certificates snap-in.

Certificates Snap-In

Certificates are stored in various locations depending on their use and whether they contain public or private keys. Windows has a "logical" certificate store that abstracts the physical locations. An MMC snap-in called Certificates permits you to view the contents of the logical store. Figure 17.7 shows the contents of the Certificates snap-in. You can view your own certificates and, if you have administrator privileges on the computer, you can view certificates issued either to the computer or to services running on the computer. You cannot view the contents of another user's certificate store.

There is no formal console that hosts the Certificates snap-in. You must load it into an MMC console manually. Use Procedure 17.1.

Procedure 17.1 Viewing Personal Certificates via the Certificates Snap-In

1. Open an empty MMC console using START | RUN | MMC.
2. From the console menu, select CONSOLE | ADD/REMOVE SNAP-IN. The Add/Remove Snap-in window opens.
3. Click `Add`. The Add Standalone Snap-in window opens.
4. Double-click `Certificates` to load the snap-in. If you are logged on with an account that does not have administrator privileges, the only option is to load the your own personal certificates. Otherwise, you get additional choices of computer and service certificates.
5. With the snap-in loaded, save the console with a descriptive name, such as Cert.msc. You may want to save it in `\WINNT\System32` along with the rest of the console files so that another administrator can use it. The console does not point at your specific certificate. It loads the certificates of the user who launches the console.
6. Expand the tree to `Certificates—Current User | Personal | Certificates.` Certificates issued to you are listed in the right pane. The `Intended Purposes` column

lists the certificate's function. If you have ever encrypted a file, you will have at least one EFS certificate. The domain Administrator account will have two certificates, one for EFS and one for File Recovery (FR).

7. Double-click a certificate to view the contents.

You can use the Certificates snap-in to obtain new certificates. This is not generally necessary for EFS certificates because the EFS service obtains the certificate automatically when you encrypt a file. If you want to designate more Data Recovery Agents, though, you'll need to obtain File Recovery (FR) certificates for them. You can request them using the Certificates snap-in.

EFS only issues one self-signed FR certificate. In a domain, it is issued to the domain Administrator account. For a local machine, it is issued to the first user who logs on to the machine following Setup. You'll need a Certification Authority (CA) to issue any further FR certificates.

Certificate Management

The keys stored in a user's profile are not in a transportable format. If you need to transfer a user's keys to another machine, the simplest way to do this is to configure a roaming profile for the user and then log on at the target desktop. This places a copy of the user's profile on the new machine with the EFS keys inside.

The FR public key is distributed via an X.509 certificate in group policies. Its security is not an issue. However, you should remove the certificate from group policies to disable file encryption on Windows 2000 clients until you are ready to deploy EFS in production.

The FR private key is another matter altogether. You most definitely do not want copies of the FR private key bandied about your network. One of the first steps you should take when deploying EFS is to copy the FR private key to a certificate, then remove it from any machines.

The Certificates snap-in is used to save keys in a certificate. Windows supports several certificate formats for this purpose:

- X.509 certificates (.CER) using Distinguished Encoding Rules (DER)
- X.509 certificates (.CER) using Base-64 encoding
- PKCS #7 Cryptographic Message Syntax Standard (.P7B)
- PKCS #12 Personal Information Exchange (PFX)

Of these four types, the first three are used to distribute public keys. Only the last type, the PFX certificate, can store a private key. The PFX format uses strong encryption to store the key without compromising it. For details about the PKCS #12 format, download the technical documentation from `ftp.rsasecurity.com/pub/pkcs/pkcs-12`.

Encrypted File Recovery

As we saw in the last topic, a long sequence of events fire off when a user opens an encrypted file. EFS must access the user's private key, which requires help from DPAPI to use the Session key derived from the Master key, which is itself protected by a key containing the user's password hash.

If the user leaves the company or goes on vacation or dies or just plain gets stubborn and refuses to open a file, you can reset the user's password in Active Directory and then log on as the user. The DPAPI will build a new Master key with the new password hash and use a Session key derived from this Master key to re-encrypt the private keys.

If commandeering a user's account is not an option, you can open the user's encrypted files using the credentials of the Data Recovery Agent, or DRA. This section discusses how the DRA public key is distributed around a domain, how to domain member clients use those certificates, and how a DRA account is used to read an encrypted file if the originating user is not available.

Encrypted File Recovery Group Policies

A file encrypted on a domain member computer contains a copy of the File Encryption Key (FEK) encrypted with the FR public key issued to a DRA. The default DRA is the domain Administrator account. You can and should install others.

EFS clients get a copy of the DRA's FR public key via an X.509 certificate stored in a group policy called `Encrypting File System`. The policy is located under `Computer Configuration | Windows Settings | Security Settings | Public Key Policies` (see Figure 17.8).

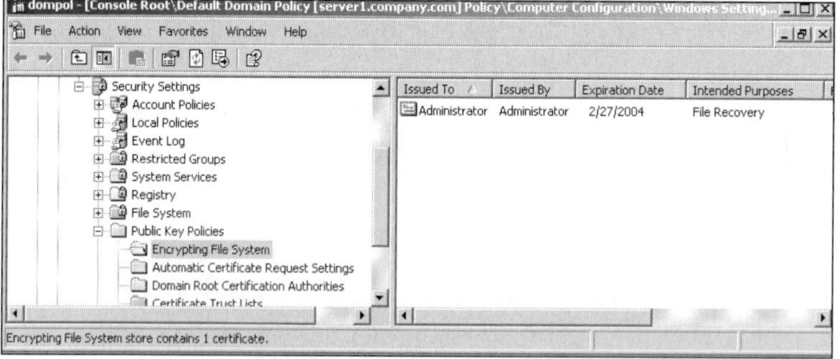

Figure 17.8 Default Domain GPO showing Administrator certificate under `Public Key | Encrypting File System Policies.`

When a domain member computer starts up, it downloads the DRA certificate as part of the group policies it gets from its logon server. The client caches the certificate in the local Registry. Thanks to this local cache, laptop users continue to use the DRA certificate when encrypting files, even when they are not on the network. This ensures that you can recover their files should there be a problem with their account.

Standalone Windows Server 2003 and XP clients either use a local account as a DRA or use no DRA at all. For this reason, it is very important that each and every desktop and laptop join an Active Directory-based domain, either a Windows Server 2003 domain or a Windows 2000 domain. If you try to manage file encryption on a hodgepodge of standalone servers and desktops, your job is *much* more difficult.

Because the EFS group policy that contains the DRA FR certificate is located in the `Computer Configuration` section of the group policy object, clients continue to use the certificate when encrypting files even if the user logs on to the local SAM instead of the domain. This is because the computer itself still belongs to the domain and will log on using cached credentials that include any cached group policies.

If a laptop is stolen, the bad guy can hack away at the accounts in the SAM without compromising the encrypted files. Only the DRA's public key is cached, not the private key, and exposing the public key does not represent a security vulnerability. Remember that the user has no local account that can be hacked, and the user's domain password hash is cached in LSA secrets where it cannot be modified.

The user's cached credentials are encrypted and stored in the `Security` hive of the Registry. As of this writing, the local credentials cache of any NT-based Windows platform has not been successfully hacked. This is not true of other Registry keys such as LSA Secrets, which have been the object of many successful hacks over the last few years.

Disabling EFS Group Policy Settings

A new feature in Windows Server 2003 permits you to turn off EFS in a domain or an OU with a single mouse click. Figure 17.9 shows the Properties window of the Encrypting File System policy that controls encryption in a domain.

By unchecking the `Allow Users To Encrypt Files Using Encrypting File System` option, you distribute a Registry update that turns off EFS. The Registry setting is as follows:

```
Key:    HKLM | Software | Policies | Windows NT | CurrentVersion | EFS
Value:  EFSConfiguration
Data:   1 to disable, 0 or removed to enable (REG_DWORD)
```

Windows Server 2003 and XP clients look for this entry in their group policies. If it is not there, the clients will encrypt files *even if a File Recovery certificate is not present in group policies*.

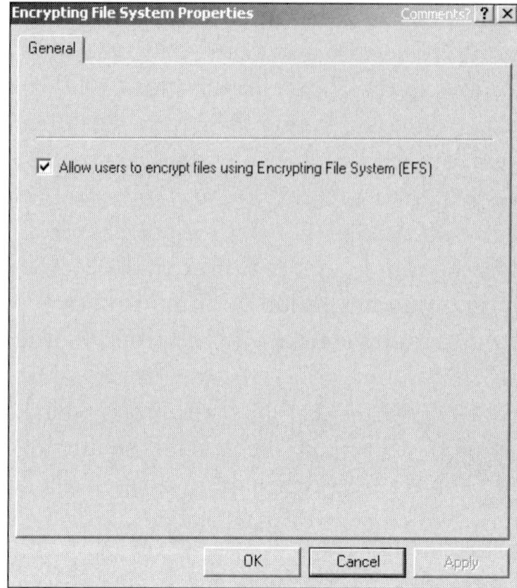

Figure 17.9 Properties window for `Encrypting File System Policies` showing the new Disable feature for domain file encryption.

This is exactly the opposite behavior that Windows 2000 clients exhibit and it will catch you by surprise if you aren't watching for it. Microsoft engineers should have made the clients look for a "1" in the `EFSConfiguration` setting to *enable* EFS, not disable it, but that's water under the proverbial bridge. The result, though, is that any XP desktops you deploy in a Windows 2000 domain will be perfectly content to let users encrypt files even though you have removed all certificates from the file recovery group policy.

The best course of action to take in this circumstance is to create a custom group policy in your Windows 2000 domain that distributes the `EFSConfiguration Registry` entry to your Windows Server 2003 and XP clients. Windows 2000 clients will ignore this Registry entry.

Opening Files as DRA

The term *encrypted file recovery* is a little misleading. You don't really "recover" an encrypted file. If you log on as the domain Administrator (or some other account that has been configured as a DRA) and your private key is available in your user profile on that machine, you'll be able to open any encrypted files on the machine. The act of opening the files is called *recovery*.

The secret to understanding the recovery process is to keep your eyes on the DRA's File Recovery private key. By default, this key resides in the Administrator profile on the first domain controller in the domain. If you log on at a client desktop as the domain Administrator, you cannot open encrypted files because there is no local copy of the Administrator's private key.

You can enable a roaming profile for the Administrator account, but this leaves copies of the private key everywhere. You might as well make 100 copies of your house key and give them to strangers. You have a couple of alternatives if you want to open a user's encrypted files without changing the user's password and essentially taking over the user's account:

- You can transport the DRA's private key to the user's desktop, either via a roaming profile or by exporting and then importing the key into the certificate store on the desktop. When you're done, you can delete the key and then wipe the unallocated space clean.
- A better solution is to transport the encrypted files to the machine where the DRA's private key resides. You cannot copy the files across the network, but you can roll them up into a backup file using Ntbackup and transport the backup file to the DRA's machine.

You must protect each DRA's private FR key to assure the reliability of your file encryption infrastructure. You should not leave copies of the FR private key on any machines in a normal production environment. Instead, you should export the key to transportable media that can be kept in a secure location and then import it only when required to perform a file recovery.

Encrypting Server-Based Files

File encryption and decryption requires the local presence of EFS keys at the machine where the files reside. This makes encrypting files on servers a little more difficult than you might first expect.

As we've seen several times, when a user encrypts a file on a local desktop or laptop, EFS works with the Microsoft Crypto Provider to create EFS keys and to place those keys in the user's local profile. If the user reaches out across the network to encrypt a file, EFS running at the server looks for the user's local profile *at the server*. EFS cannot access keys at a user's desktop because it does not have a security context anywhere except at the machine where it's running.

This means that the server must have a local profile for the user that contains both the EFS public key to encrypt the file and the EFS private key to open the encrypted file. To build the local private key, the Protected Storage service at the server must have a copy of the user's password hash so it can encrypt the Master key that protects the user's private key. It obtains this information by "impersonating" the user.

Impersonation and Kerberos

User impersonation by a server for purposes of EFS requires obtaining a Kerberos session ticket on behalf of the user to present when requesting the user's security credentials from a domain controller. A server has two ways of getting this session ticket:

- It can ask the Kerberos client at the user's desktop (this is done transparently to the user) to obtain the session ticket and pass it over to the server. Such a ticket would be marked as *forwardable*, meaning that the Kerberos client obtained it for the express purpose of giving it to another machine.
- The server can ask the Kerberos client for a ticket-granting ticket (TGT) that it can use to obtain its own session tickets as if the server were the user. The TGT would be flagged as *proxiable*.

The difference between a forwardable session ticket and a proxiable TGT is the difference between loaning a friend twenty dollars to pay for lunch and giving that friend a power of attorney and your checkbook. A server in possession of either one is in a position to do all sorts of mischief.

To prevent uncontrolled use of forwardable and proxiable Kerberos tickets and TGTs, a Windows domain controller will refuse to accept such tickets or TGTs unless the server submitting them has been *Trusted For Delegation*.

Trusted for Delegation

Before a server can create encrypted files for network users, it must be trusted for delegation. This option is configured in the server's Computer object in Active Directory. Figure 17.10 shows an example.

Windows Server 2003 has several delegation options. For the widest latitude, and to ensure that you get proper operation for EFS, select the `Trust This Computer For Delegation To Any Service (Kerberos Only)` option. The other options permit you to enable delegation for a tightly focused type of transaction.

After you configure a server to be trusted for delegation, it occupies a highly privileged position in your system. Be sure to physically secure the server and keep it away from possible sources of Trojan horse applications.

User Key Caching on Trusted EFS Servers

When you enable Windows Server 2003 to be trusted for delegation and users begin putting encrypted files on that server, the server will improve EFS performance by caching user private keys in memory. By default, the server will cache up to 15 keys. You can increase this number up to 30 using the following Registry value:

```
Key:    HKLM | SOFTWARE | Microsoft | Windows NT | CurrentVersion | EF
Value:  UserCacheSize
Data:   5 to 30 (REG_DWORD)
```

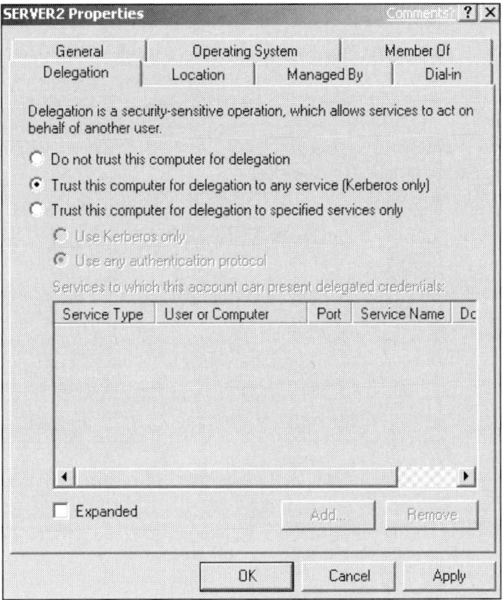

Figure 17.10 Property page for a server showing the various Trusted for Delegation options.

EFS File Transactions and WebDAV

Traditionally, Windows has used the SMB command language to manipulate files across the network. Windows Server 2003 and XP contain a new way of dynamically working with files on remote machines. It is called *Web-based Distributed Authoring and Versioning*, or WebDAV. For references on WebDAV, see RFC 2518, "HTTP Extensions for Distributed Authoring—WEBDAV," and the WebDAV working group's web site, `www.ietf.org/html.charters/webdav-charter.html`.

Chapter 16, "Managing Shared Resources," describes how to set up a shared web folder on a server or desktop. The host must be running Internet Information Services (IIS) because the shared folder is actually just a virtual folder in the default web site. Also, WebDAV publishing must be enabled in the IIS metabase. This is not done by default.

A network provider in Windows Server 2003, the WebDAV redirector, controls transactions to and from a web share. WebDAV uses HTTP as its wire protocol, making it possible to access files through a firewall using standard TCP port 80.

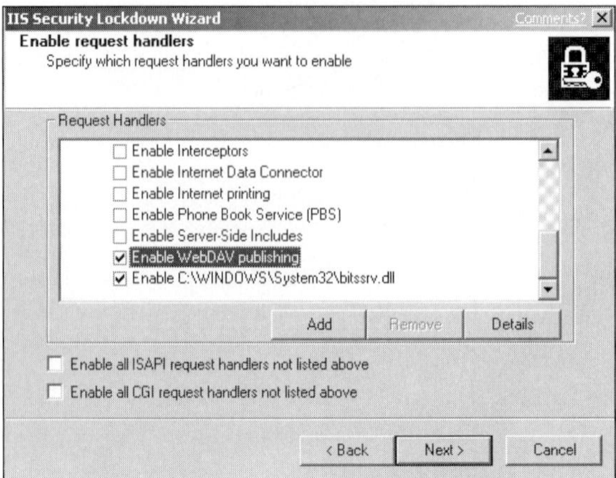

Figure 17.11 IIS Security Lockdown Wizard—Enable Request Handlers window showing the `Enable WebDAV Publishing` option.

To create a shared web folder, you must be running IIS on the server with security lockdown set to permit WebDAV publishing. Do this in the Internet Information Services console. Right-click the server icon, select SECURITY from the flyout menu, then walk through the IIS Security Lockdown Wizard. In the Enable Request Handlers window, select the `Enable WebDAV Publishing` option. Figure 17.11 shows an example.

Connecting to a WebDAV share is as simple as specifying the URL of the web share instead of a UNC name. For instance, you would map a drive to `http://server_name/ webshare` rather than `\\server_name\share`.

When you make a WebDAV connection and open a file, the WebDAV redirector issues an HTTP `Get` command to copy the file to the local Temporary Internet Files cache. The user makes changes to the local copy of the file. When the user saves the changes, the file is copied to the WebDAV share via an HTTP `Put`. This is not nearly as sophisticated as SMB, and much slower, but it is much handier than doing a series of FTP file transfers.

WebDAV Advantages for EFS

In addition to standard `Gets` and `Puts`, WebDAV also controls file locking and maintains version control on files using a special set of properties that are saved along with the data in the file. A WebDAV client accesses these properties via `GetProp` and `PostProp` commands. Figure 17.12 shows the WebDAV properties of a file.

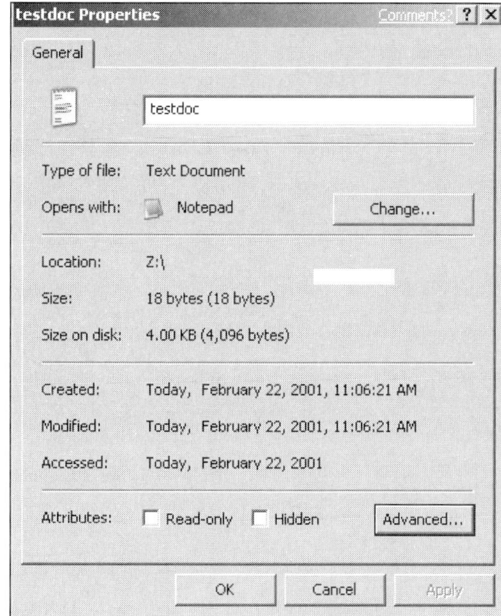

Figure 17.12 Properties of a file in a shared web folder.

Because WebDAV clients work on local copies of a file, they have a few advantages when working with encrypted files in an untrusted environment such as the Internet:

- **Encrypted file transfers.** Using WebDAV, the client encrypts the file locally in the Temporary Internet Files cache and then transfers the encrypted file across the network to the server. This contrasts to SMB, where the data stream going across the wire is unencrypted.
- **"Trusted for Delegation" option not required.** Using WebDAV, the client takes responsibility for file encryption, not the server. This means the server does not need the user's PKCS certificates and therefore does not need to be trusted for delegation. This relieves you of the chore of hardening the server against Trojan horse programs. Also, you will not see dozens or hundreds of user profiles proliferating in the Documents and Settings folder at the server.

Managing Encrypted File Transfer Over WebDAV

You need to be careful when manipulating encrypted files in a web share because there is no outside indication of a file's encryption status. The encryption bit is part of the WebDAV properties, which can only be seen when the file is viewed via the

WebDAV redirector. If you access an encrypted WebDAV file via Explorer or a standard SMB share, all you see is the gibberish of the encrypted contents. So, when a user encrypts a file on a WebDAV share, the only way the file can be opened again is through the WebDAV share.

This aspect of WebDAV has an interesting ramification. It makes encrypted file recovery very simple. To open an encrypted WebDAV file, all you need to do is log on at a server that holds the FR private key of a DRA and access the file via WebDAV. Because the file is first copied to a local file cache, you can open the file.

WebDAV transfer of encrypted files has its dark side, as well. Because the contents of the encrypted WebDAV file are completely opaque to file scanners, it permits users to bring unauthorized files into your system "under the radar" of any file scanners running at your firewall or proxy server. Layer 7 scanning has become popular as a block to viruses and other malicious code.

Because WebDAV uses port 80, there is virtually no way of stopping this file transfer other than establishing a policy in your file scanner that alerts you when files with encrypted contents traverse the firewall. You can then contact the user to determine what the file was for. This is a labor-intensive solution, I agree, but as WebDAV starts to get popular, some of the leading virus scanning vendors may figure out a way to automate the process.

Special EFS Guidelines

This section contains information about EFS limitations and special operational considerations for deploying EFS effectively.

Moving and Copying Encrypted Files

Files are like children growing up in rural communities. They rarely stay in the folder where they were created. When users move or copy encrypted files, they may get unexpected results, especially if they are unaware that the files were encrypted in the first place.

A user who encrypts a file (or whose name is on the list of additional users who can access an encrypted file) can copy the file contents anywhere. This is because the data stream is decrypted as it leaves the drive.

If a user attempts to copy or move an encrypted file to a location that does not support EFS, the Explorer shell will warn of the possibility of exposing the file's contents. The user can choose to ignore the warning and save the file anyway. If the user is working at the command line, the `COPY` and `XCOPY` commands will block operations involving insecure target volumes. There are new switches to override the block. The syntax is `copy /d` and `xcopy /g`.

If a user copies an unencrypted file into an encrypted folder, the new file is encrypted. If a user *moves* an unencrypted file into an encrypted folder, an action that ordinarily does not touch the file's data, the system takes over and encrypts the file anyway on the assumption that this is what the user would have wanted. This is not true if you work from the command line. The `MOVE` command leaves a file in clear text even if it is moved to an encrypted folder.

If a user copies an encrypted file to a server that has been trusted for delegation, the file is first decrypted at the client, then transmitted in clear text across the network, then encrypted again at the server using the public key in the user profile at the server. If you want files to traverse the wire in encrypted form, use WebDAV or implement IPSec (described in the next chapter).

A user who cannot access the data of an encrypted file can still *move* the file to another location on the same volume as long as he has sufficient NTFS permissions on the file. This is because moving the encrypted file does not touch the file's data, only the back-link to the parent directory. This ability to access the non-data portions of the file includes the ability to delete the file either by moving it to the Recycle Bin or removing it from the volume completely. Encryption is not a replacement for proper NTFS permissions.

If a user attaches an encrypted file to an email message, the file is first decrypted and then copied into the MIME attachment. This exposes the file unless the user has enabled S/MIME.

Files That Cannot Be Encrypted

Just about any file can be encrypted. This includes data files, executables and DLLs, temp files, and configuration files. Here are a few exceptions:

- **Compressed files.** Encrypted files cannot be compressed, and compressed files cannot be encrypted. The encryption algorithm scrambles a file to such an extent that there are no consecutive sets of characters to make compression worthwhile.
- **Mount points and reparse points.** Symbolic links to other file systems or folders cannot be encrypted. If you want to encrypt the files and folders behind a mount point, you can change directory into the mount point and then select the files from there. The mount point must contain a file system running NTFS 3.0 or later.
- **System files.** EFS will refuse to encrypt a file that has its system attribute set. The operating system may need to read a system file at boot time before EFS has had a chance to initialize. You can use this feature to your advantage by setting the system attribute on files you don't want users to encrypt.

In addition, if you have enabled the Content Indexing Service on a machine, any file that is encrypted is automatically removed from the index. This prevents giving away the contents of the file within the index catalog.

Temp Files, Paging Files, Hibernation Files, and Spool Files

If an application saves temp files, be sure to put the temp files in the same folder as the encrypted files—either that or encrypt the folder where the temp files are saved.

When encrypting temp folders, don't forget to include the `\Local Settings\Temp` folder in the user's profile. The simplest way to find this folder is to open a command prompt and run `cd /d %temp%`.

The contents of the paging file and hibernation file are not encrypted. You can enable policies to remove the paging file at logoff and disable hibernation. Erasing the paging file does not prevent someone from examining the contents with a hex editor, though it's a daunting task to search through 4KB pages looking for worthwhile information. Using XP, you can disable the paging file entirely. This eliminates the vulnerability, but you must ensure that you have sufficient memory in the machine to handle the applications loaded by the user.

If your laptop users threaten to mutiny if you disable hibernation, make a deal with them that you will leave hibernation enabled if they always close their data files before hibernating their machines. There's a big difference between "cross my heart" promises and full compliance, though, so let your auditing group know to be on the lookout for this problem.

If you want to protect the contents of files as they print, be sure to encrypt the spool files located in `\Windows\System32\Spool\Printers`.

Offline Files

If you enable offline files for laptop users, you should consider encrypting the offline folders cache. This encrypts the entire contents of the cache and does so without changing the encryption status of the files on the server.

The option to encrypt the files is set in the `Offline Files` tab of the Folder Options window. Figure 17.13 shows an example.

This feature is not available in Windows 2000. I recommend upgrading your laptops to XP as quickly as possible if you want to use Microsoft's file encryption services.

Virus Checking

Most virus scanners run in either the Local System security context or the new Local Service context. In that configuration, a scanner cannot open a user's encrypted files and therefore may miss a virus.

Unfortunately, there is not a clean workaround to this problem. Any solution that would permit a virus scanner to see a user's files could permit a bad guy to see the files, as well. The best solution is to have a real-time virus scanner running at the desktops and servers that can analyze files for virus signatures as they open. For some viruses, this might be too little, too late. Look for progress on this front from vendors of virus software.

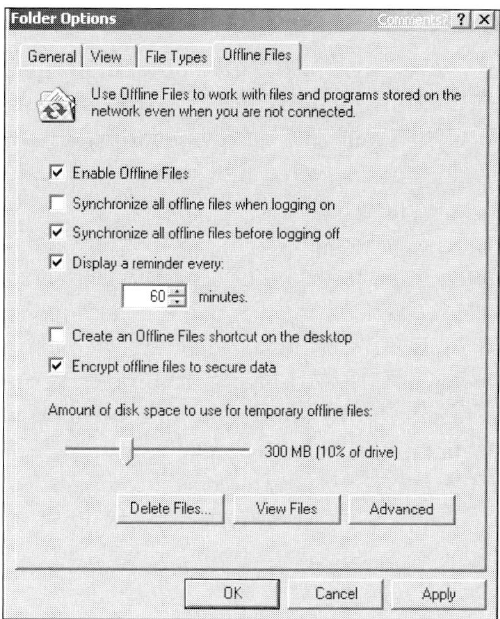

Figure 17.13 Folder Options window showing encryption option.

Encryption and System Restore

Windows XP sports a new feature called System Restore. This feature takes a snapshot of a system every so often and saves the settings to a cache file. This includes any software that's loaded along with drivers and system configuration settings. If a user installs an application that causes the system to become unstable, the user can return the system to the settings in a stored snapshot.

When System Restore rolls back a system to a previous configuration, you take the chance of exposing encrypted files. It has been my experience that System Restore does a good job of maintaining encryption status, but Microsoft warns of this possibility so it's worth taking seriously.

The System Restore service can be configured to exclude selected folders from the list of monitored folders and files. You can configure the service to avoid encrypted folders. In production, you may not be able to guarantee that the only encrypted files on a machine are in the designated folders. If you perform a system restore for a user, you may want to log on as the user and gather all encrypted files into a central location and then use Ntbackup to make a backup file of the encrypted files prior to running the system restore. Use `cipher /u /n` to scan for encrypted files.

EFS Procedures

At this point, you've probably had enough of the principles of operation of EFS and you're eager to put them into action. First, though, you need to buy yourself a little time while you plan your EFS deployment. You do not want to end up with hundreds or thousands of encrypted files scattered around your system without a clear plan for managing them.

The subsequent sections describe how to create additional DRAs and deploy their public keys, how to protect the DRA private keys, how to encrypt files and folders, and how to recover encrypted files if the user should be unavailable. You'll also see how to use the CIPHER command-line utility to perform many of these tasks.

Before deploying EFS, I highly recommend that you install at least one Certification Authority (CA) server in your organization. It does not need to be a Microsoft CA, but it does need to be able to issue EFS and FR certificates. If you have a third-party CA in place, it's usually easiest to install a Microsoft CA as a subordinate Enterprise Root so you get Active Directory certificate deployment and the full range of certificate purposes. The instructions for deploying a Microsoft CA are in Chapter 18, "Managing a Public Key Infrastructure."

When you're ready to deploy EFS, here is a quick checklist of items you'll need to perform:

1. Identify administrators who you want to become Data Recovery Agents for their local OUs. Have them obtain File Recovery certificates.
2. Import the FR public key certificates of the newly dubbed DRAs into the Encrypting File System group policy for GPOs linked to their local OUs.
3. Export and remove the FR private keys of the DRAs and save them in a secure location for use when a file must be recovered.
4. Import the FR public key certificate of the domain Administrator account. This enables EFS for Windows 2000 clients and sets up proper DRA certificate deployment for Windows Server 2003 and EFS clients.
5. Enable the EFS group policy for Windows Server 2003 and XP clients.
6. Encrypt folders and files at your laptops and desktops.
7. Set a group policy to encrypt the offline file cache at your laptops and possibly at your desktops.

In addition, you'll want to periodically test your ability to recover files as one of the local DRAs. The instructions for this are also included.

Disable Encryption

Windows Server 2003 and XP machines are capable of encrypting files without a DRA, which complicates the steps for disabling EFS in a mixed environment. You'll need to perform these three items to disable EFS on all your clients:

- For servers running Windows Server 2003 and XP desktops in a Windows Server 2003 domain, set the `Encrypting File System` group policy to disable EFS.
- For servers running Windows Server 2003 and XP desktops in a Windows 2000 domain, use a custom ADM (administrative) template to configure and distribute a group policy that will disable EFS.
- For Windows 2000 servers and desktops in a Windows Server 2003 or Windows 2000 domain, remove the DRA File Recovery public key certificate from the Encrypting File System policy (Windows Server 2003) or Encrypted Data Recovery Agent policy (Windows 2000).

If you have standalone servers running Windows Server 2003 or XP desktops, disable local file encryption via the `Encrypting File System` policy in the local security policies.

Disable EFS on Windows Server 2003 and XP Clients in a Windows Server 2003 Domain

You can disable file encryption at Windows Server 2003 and XP member computers in a Windows Server 2003 domain with a simple group policy option. Follow Procedure 17.2.

Procedure 17.2 Disabling EFS Using Windows Server 2003 Group Policies

1. Open the Group Policy Editor for the Default Domain GPO.
2. Navigate to `Computer Configuration | Windows Settings | Security Settings | Public Key Policies`.
3. Right-click the `Encrypting File System` icon and select PROPERTIES from the flyout menu.
4. Uncheck the `Allow Users To Encrypt Files Using Encrypting File System (EFS)` option.
5. Click `OK` to save the policy.

It will take 90 plus/minus 30 minutes for this policy to be felt at the desktops. You can force the update at a client by running `gpupdate` at a command prompt. Attempt to encrypt a test folder or file and verify that the action is blocked.

Disable EFS on Windows Server 2003 and XP Clients in a Windows 2000 Domain

Disabling EFS on Windows Server 2003 and XP clients in a Windows 2000 domain requires a little extra work on your part. Windows 2000 group policies do not contain the `EFSConfigure` policy used to control EFS in a Windows Server 2003 domain. You must create this policy yourself using a custom ADM template.

Use Notepad to build the custom ADM template in the `\Windows\INF` directory on the PDC Emulator. (The PDC Emulator is the default server for modifying group policies.) You can name the file anything you like as long as it has an ADM extension—for example, call it `Efs.adm`.

The contents of the file should look something like this. (Modify the double-quoted strings as you like, but leave the `SUPPORTED` string as it stands to be consistent with other policies.)

```
CLASS MACHINE

CATEGORY "Special EFS Handling"
     POLICY "Disable XP and Windows Server 2003 EFS"
                #if version >= 4
               SUPPORTED "At least Microsoft Windows XP Professional"
          #endif
          KEYNAME "Software\Policies\Microsoft\Windows NT\CurrentVersion\Efs"
          EXPLAIN     "This policy stops XP desktops from encrypting files in a
Windows 2000 domain. Enable the policy to disable EFS."
          VALUENAME "EfsConfiguration"
                VALUEON   NUMERIC 1
                VALUEOFF  NUMERIC 0
     END POLICY
END CATEGORY
```

After you've created the template, load it into the Group Policy Editor by right-clicking the `Administrative Templates` icon, selecting ADD/REMOTE TEMPLATES from the flyout menu, then double-clicking the name of the template to load it. You should see the Category listing directly under the Administrative Templates icon. Figure 17.14 shows an example.

When you enable the policy, it will not take effect for 90 plus/minus 30 minutes. You can force the update at a client by running `gpupdate` at a command prompt. When you attempt to create an encrypted file, you should get an `Access Denied` error. If not, run `gpresult /v` to see if you are getting the policy. Here is a snippet of the proper results:

```
Administrative Templates
------------------------
    GPO: Default Domain Policy
        Setting: Software\Policies\Microsoft\Windows NT\CurrentVersion\EFS
         State:   Enabled
```

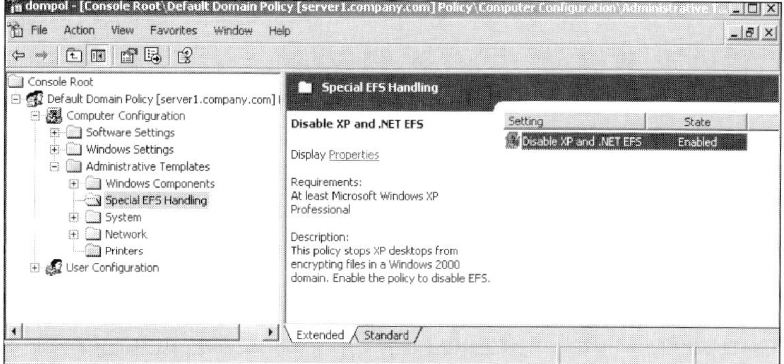

Figure 17.14 Group Policy Editor showing custom ADM template containing special EFS handling policy.

Be sure to put this policy in place before you begin deploying XP desktops. Identify any files that have been encrypted in the interim and decrypt them until you're ready to deploy file encryption on a production basis. Use `cipher /u /n` to search out encrypted files on a volume. You must be at the desktop (or take control via Remote Desktop) to run this utility.

Disable EFS on Windows 2000 Clients in a Windows Server 2003 Domain

To disable EFS on Windows 2000 clients, you must remove the FR public key certificate of the DRA from group policies. Without this certificate, the clients will refuse to encrypt files.

Export a copy of the certificate before you remove it so you can import it back when you're ready to deploy EFS. Even if you plan on deploying EFS immediately, it is a good practice to export the certificate and store a copy just in case someone accidentally deletes it from the group policy. The public key does not need special handling other than to be sure you have enough copies so that a single bad floppy doesn't cause a loss of the file. Follow Procedure 17.3.

Procedure 17.3 Exporting and Deleting the FR Public Key Certificate

1. Open the `AD Users and Computers` console.
2. Navigate to `Computer Configuration | Windows Settings | Security Settings | Public Key Policies | Encrypting File System`.
3. Right-click the `Administrator certificate` icon in the right pane and select All Tasks | Export from the flyout menu. The Certificate Export Wizard starts.
4. Click `Next`. The Export Private Key window opens. Select the `No, Do Not Export The Private Key` radio button.

5. Click `Next`. The Export File Format window opens. Select one of the certificate types. They are all cryptographically equivalent.
6. Click `Next`. The File To Export window opens. Enter or browse to a path and filename you want to assign to the certificate, such as `AdminPublicFR.cer`.
7. Click `Finish`. The wizard closes. Verify that the certificate file is in the location you designated.

After copying the file to different media, you can delete the certificate from the `Encrypting File System` group policy. Be sure to delete just the certificate, not the policy itself. If you delete the policy, Windows 2000 clients will encrypt their files using the local DRA.

Configure Additional DRAs

If you lose the FR private key issued to the Administrator account by deleting the profile at the first domain controller in the domain, you cannot recover files. For this reason, assigning additional DRAs should be high on your priority list before deploying EFS.

If you have geographically defined OUs, it is a good practice to create GPOs for each OU that contains the `Encrypting File System` policy for the DRA or DRAs in that OU. Said another way, you want a local administrator's pager to go off when a user cannot get access to an encrypted folder. For instance, you can create a GPO called PhxEFS, link it to the Phoenix OU, then load the FR public key certificate of the DRA in Phoenix into the `Encrypting File System` policy of the PhxEFS GPO.

Here is an important note. DRA certificates in cascaded GPOs are not cumulative. In other words, a client only gets the DRAs in the `Encrypting File System` policy closest to the computer object in Active Directory. All others are ignored. Therefore, don't expect to see the domain Administrator account on the list of DRAs if you assign DRAs in a GPO linked to an OU.

EFS obtains only one FR certificate automatically, that of the domain DRA. To obtain additional FR certificates, the administrator who you have designated to be a local DRA must obtain an FR certificate. The operation uses the Certificates snap-in. Obtain FR certificates as shown in Procedure 17.4.

Procedure 17.4 Obtaining FR Certificates for Additional DRAs

1. Log on as an administrator who has been designated as a DRA.
2. Load the Certificates snap-in into an MMC console.
3. Under Certificates - Current User, right-click the `Personal` folder and select REQUEST NEW CERTIFICATE from the flyout menu. This launches the Certificate Request Wizard.

4. Click `Next`. The Certificate Types window opens (see Figure 17.15). Select `EFS Recovery Agent` from the list of certificate types. (You will get an error if the client cannot contact a CA.)

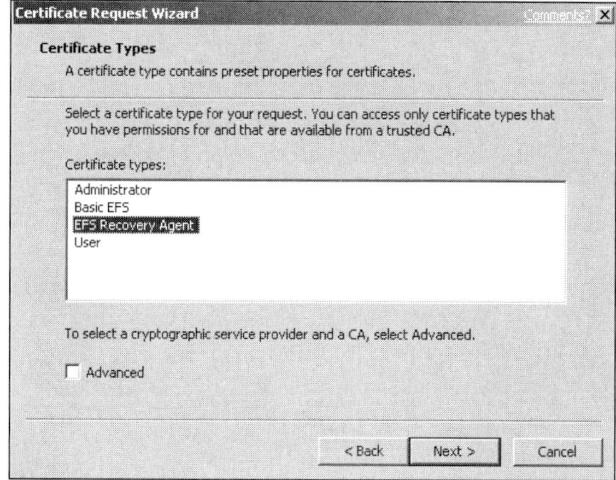

Figure 17.15 Certificate Request Wizard—Certificate Types window showing EFS Recovery Agent selection.

5. Click `Next`. The Certificate Friendly Name and Description window opens. Enter a short name for the Certificate and a description, if you desire. You can leave these fields blank, if you like.
6. Click `Next`. A summary window opens listing your selections.
7. Click `Finish` to request the certificate. You should get a `Certificate request was successful.` message when the transaction with the CA is complete.
8. Expand the tree under `Personal | Certificates` to see the new certificate. The Intended Purpose column lists File Recovery as the purpose.
9. Publish this certificate in Active Directory by dragging a copy to `Certificates | Active Directory User Object | Certificates`.

When you use the preceding steps to request an FR certificate, the CA issues two items:

- An X.509 certificate that contains the FR public key
- An FR private key delivered to the client via a secure channel

The local crypto provider puts the keys into the administrator's local profile. We'll see a little later how to export the FR private key to a certificate so it can be stored safely and the local copy deleted.

Load New DRAs into EFS Group Policies

Now that you have FR public key certificates for all your DRAs, you need to put their certificates into the GPOs linked to their OUs so clients in the OUs will download the certificates and use them when encrypting files. To do this, follow Procedure 17.5.

Procedure 17.5 Loading an FR Public Key into the EFS Group Policy

1. Open the `AD Users and Computers` console.
2. Open the Properties window for the OU where you want to have a new GPO.
3. Select the `Group Policy` tab.
4. Click `New` to add a new GPO. Give the GPO a name such as `PhxEFS`.
5. Click `Edit` to open the Group Policy Editor.
6. Navigate to `Computer Configuration | Windows Settings | Security Settings | Public Key Policies`.
7. Right-click `Encrypting File System` and select ADD DATA RECOVERY AGENT from the flyout menu. The Add Recovery Agent Wizard opens.
8. Click `Next`. The Select Recovery Agents window opens.
9. Click `Browse Directory`. The Find Users, Contacts, and Groups window opens. Use this window to locate the name of the DRA that you used to obtain an FR certificate in the previous steps. The user's distinguished name appears under Recovery Agents.
10. Click `Next`. A summary window opens.
11. Click `Finish` to load the certificate into the policy.

It will take 90 plus/minus 30 minutes for this policy to be felt at the desktops. You can force an update at a client by running `gpupdate` on a client in the OU. Encrypt a test file on an XP desktop and use Details to view the DRA list (or run `efsinfo /r` if you have the support tools loaded). The new DRA should be listed and the domain Administrator account will not appear on the list.

Export and Delete FR Private Keys

Without maintaining access control on the FR private keys, you cannot ensure the ongoing security of your EFS subsystem. Here are the general actions for securing an FR private key:

1. Export the FR private key to a certificate.
2. Save the FR certificate to several media and secure the media in a safe or vault.
3. Delete the FR certificate from the domain controller where it was originally located.

The steps in Procedure 17.6 describe how to perform these operations. Perform them at the machine where the DRA obtained the FR certificate.

Procedure 17.6 Exporting and Deleting an FR Private Key

1. Load the Certificates snap-in into an MMC console.
2. Expand the tree to `Certificates - Current User | Personal | Certificates`. If the icon is not there, you have logged on at the wrong machine.
3. Right-click the `File Recovery` certificate and select ALL TASKS | EXPORT from the flyout menu. This starts the Certificate Export Wizard. Use the Intended Purposes column to find the right certificate.
4. Click `Next`. The Export Private Key window opens. Select `Yes, Export The Private Key`.
5. Click `Next`. The Export File Format window opens (see Figure 17.16). The only available format for this operation is the PKCS #12 format, which encrypts the private key for additional protection.

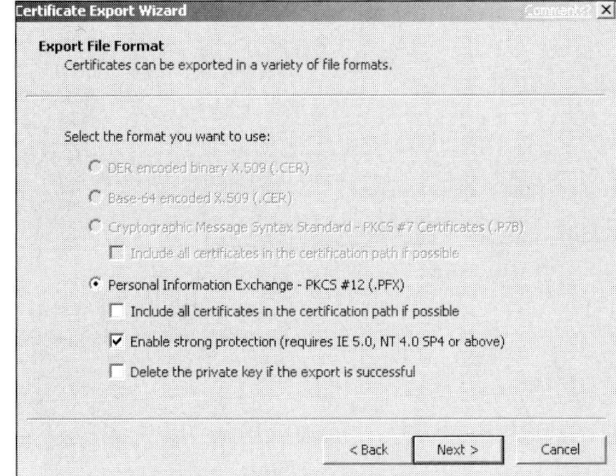

Figure 17.16 Certificate Export Wizard—Export File Format.

Leave the `Enable Strong Protection` option selected. This uses an advanced form of encryption that is not available for pre-SP4 versions of classic NT.

6. Click `Next`. The Password window opens. Enter a password and confirm. There are no complexity requirements, but long passwords are better than short ones, and the more non-alpha characters you use, the better.
7. Click `Next`. The File To Export window opens. Enter the name you want to give the exported certificate. The name has no cryptographic significance. Include something in the name that indicates the user it belongs to, such as PhxAdminPrivate.

8. Click `Next`. A summary window opens.
9. Click `Finish`. The wizard writes the certificate file and then informs you when the export has been successfully completed.
10. Close the `Certificates` console.

Be sure to save several copies of the exported certificate and lock the copies in a safe place.

Always test the private key certificate before deleting the private key from the server. Do so by importing the key from the certificate at another machine (server or desktop) and then verifying that you can open encrypted files at the desktop.

After you've verified the contents of the certificate, delete the FR private key from the server via the Certificates snap-in. This prevents unauthorized individuals from using the DRA's credentials to log on and then opening encrypted files.

Set Folder Encryption at Laptops

You're now ready to let your users encrypt their files. Encourage them to set encrypting on folders, not files, then save files in the encrypted folders. This avoids creating clear-text temp files.

If a user enables encryption on a folder that already contains files, the files will be encrypted. This leaves a temp file, so show the user how to run `cipher /w` afterwards to scrub away the temp file contents.

If EFS encounters a locked file when CIPHER tries to encrypt a file, a warning appears with the option to `Retry` or `Ignore`. Have the user make note of the locked file so she can encrypt it later after the lock has been released.

Encrypting Folders

To enable encryption for a folder, follow Procedure 17.7.

Managing Certificates Using CIPHER

You can obtain an FR certificate pair (X.509 public key certificate and PKCS #12 private key certificate) from the command line using CIPHER.

The syntax is `cipher /r:<file_name>`, where <*file_name*> is the name you want to assign to the certificate files.

After the files have been generated, double-click the file to launch the Certificate Import Wizard and import the key into your personal certificate store. Be sure to put them into your Personal store.

If you install a new DRA and you want to refresh existing encrypted files with the public key of the new DRA, enter `cipher /u`. This updates all encrypted files on the volume that can be accessed by the user running CIPHER. You can verify that the new DRA is in place by selecting the `Advanced` tab in the file Properties window and then clicking `Details`.

Procedure 17.7 Setting Folder Encryption

1. Open Explorer.
2. Navigate to the folder you want to encrypt. (Users with roaming profiles cannot encrypt the My Documents folder or any other component of their profiles.)
3. Open the Properties window for the folder.
4. Click `Advanced`. The Advanced Attributes window opens.
5. Select the `Encrypt Contents To Secure Data` option. You cannot select both this and the `Compress Contents` option.
6. Click `OK` to save the selection and return to the main Properties window.
7. Click `OK` to apply the change and encrypt the folder. The Confirm Attribute Changes window opens.
8. Select `Apply Changes To This Folder, Subfolders, and Files`. This ensures that all the contents of the folder and any subfolders the user may create are encrypted.

Show the user how to determine the encryption status by the color of the text for the folder or file. If the color does not change, enable the `Show Encrypted or Compressed NTFS Files in Color` option in the View tab of the Folder Options window. The user can also see the encryption status in the web content portion of the folder window.

Assigning Additional Users to an Encrypted File

A user who has encrypted a file can give access to additional users. This is done via the Properties window of the file by clicking `Advanced` under attributes and then `Details`. Figure 17.17 shows an example.

The selected user or users must have an EFS public key certificate either in a certificate store at the machine or in their Active Directory account. If the user has never encrypted a file before, you need to have him encrypt a file on a member computer in the domain to obtain an EFS certificate. The certificate will be copied to the user's Active Directory account automatically. You can also walk the user through loading the Certificates snap-in to request an EFS certificate from a CA. Personally, I think the first option is simpler.

Encrypting Individual Files

If users insist on encrypting individual files, you can simplify the operation for them by placing an ENCRYPT/DECRYPT option on the flyout menu. This requires a Registry change to add a new value. Here is the information:

```
Key:    HKLM | Software | Microsoft | Windows | CurrentVersion | Explorer |
Advanced
Value:  EncryptionContextMenu
Data:    1 (REG_DWORD)
```

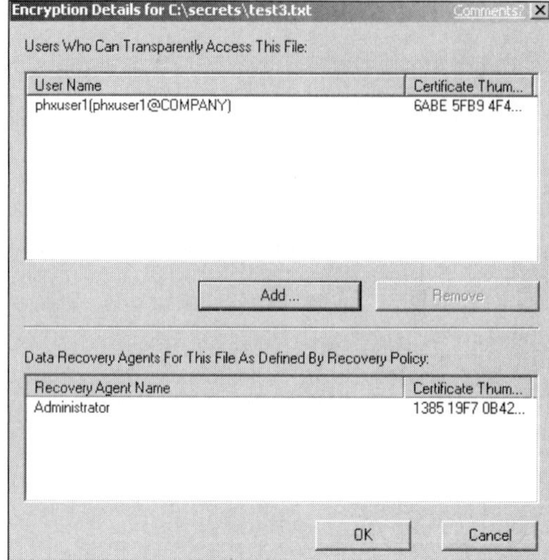

Figure 17.17 Detailed Encrypting File System properties showing the selection of additional users who can access an encrypted file.

Encrypting Files and Folders Using CIPHER

If you prefer a command-line alternative for manipulating encrypted files, use the CIPHER utility:

- To set the encryption flag on a folder, enter cipher /e /s:<folder_name>. This causes any new files in the folder to be encrypted, but does not encrypt existing files.
- To set the encryption flag on a folder and encrypt existing files, enter **cipher /e /a /i /s:<*folder_name*>*.***. The /i switch forces the encryption to continue even if it encounters a locked file. This operation generates a clear-text temp file and should be followed by cipher /w to wipe the unallocated space on the drive.
- To decrypt a folder, enter **cipher /d <folder_name>**. To decrypt the files underneath the folder, use **cipher /d /a /i /s:<*folder_name*>*.***.

Encrypted File Recovery

If a user is not unavailable to open an encrypted file, you can open it using the Data Recovery Agent's credentials as long as the file is on the machine hosting the DRA's private key. There are no special recovery mechanisms or recovery applications. The steps are as follows:

1. Import the DRA's FR private key from its saved certificate to a recovery machine. This machine does not need to be a server, but it should be running either Windows Server 2003 or XP and it must be a domain member.

2. Transport the encrypted files to the recovery machine using Ntbackup.
3. Open and decrypt the files using the DRA's credentials.
4. Delete the DRA's private key from the recovery machine.
5. Wipe the drive to remove vestiges of the private key.

The only step in this list that requires detailed instructions is importing the FR private key certificate. This is the PFX certificate you stashed on a floppy or CD in a safe. Follow Procedure 17.8.

Procedure 17.8 Importing an FR Private Key from a PFX Certificate

1. Copy the PFX file containing the FR private key to the hard drive of a machine running Windows Server 2003 or XP. I'll call this the Recovery machine.
2. Open Explorer and navigate to the folder containing the PFX file.
3. Double-click the file. The Certificate Import Wizard starts.
4. Click `Next`. The File To Import window opens. Make sure the filename is properly displayed.
5. Click `Next`. The Password window opens. Enter the password that was assigned to the PFX file when it was exported. Do not select the `Mark This Key As Exportable` option. You will be deleting this copy of the key as soon as you're done with it.
6. Click `Next`. The Certificate Store window opens. Select the `Place All Certificates In The Following Store` option and then click `Browse`.
7. Highlight the Personal folder in the logical certificate store hierarchy and click `OK` to return to the wizard.
8. Click `Next`. A summary window opens.
9. Click `Finish`. The key is extracted from the certificate and placed in the Personal store. The wizard notifies you with a `The import is successful.` message.
10. Now, open any encrypted files and recover them by copying the contents to another location, assigning another user to the file, or decrypting permanently.

Transporting Encrypted Files to New Machines

If a user changes laptops and wants to transfer encrypted files to the new machine, you face a bit of work. You cannot simply copy the encrypted files over the network to the new computer. You must do the following:

1. Back up the encrypted files to a backup file at the user's laptop (or a network drive).
2. Configure a roaming profile for the user.

3. Log the user on at the new machine with the roaming profile.
4. Copy the backup file to the new machine.
5. Restore the encrypted files on the disk of the new machine.
6. Verify that the user can open the files.

If you do not want to use a roaming profile, you can export the user's certificates using the Certificates snap-in and then import them at the new machine. Remember that you must be logged on with the user's credentials. Be sure to give the PFX certificate containing the private key a strong password and delete it off the old machine when you have completed the transfer. Wipe the deleted files with `cipher /w`.

Moving Forward

At this point, you may be thinking that EFS is just about as complex a system as you would ever want to deploy to users. But data communications security is just as important as data storage security, and that means you'll need to use several other Windows Server 2003 features that are even more intimidating. This includes IP Security (IPSec), Transport Layer Security (TLS), and support for applications such as email (S/MIME). All of these features require a solid Public Key Infrastructure (PKI) deployment. So let's take a deep breath and plunge ahead.

18 Managing a Public Key Infrastructure

REMEMBER THE OLD NEIGHBORHOOD? THE SHADE TREES where you played tag with your friends. The secret path to school where you could ditch your siblings. The grandmotherly lady who would give you fresh caramel apples on Halloween. Have you ever gone back? Are there bars on the windows and pit bulls in the backyards and LoJack stickers in the car windows?

That's the situation on the Internet nowadays. The once-friendly confines of virtual academia have deteriorated into a scary place where it's always midnight and somebody shot out the streetlights. You need a way to shield your data from bad guys and to ensure the integrity of your communications.

A set of technologies has evolved over the last decade that addresses the need for privacy and protection. Collectively, these technologies are called *Public Key Infrastructure*, or PKI. Windows Server 2003 includes support for the most popular of the current crop of PKI protocols. These services underlie a variety of features such as the Encrypting File System (EFS), IP Security (IPSec), Transport Layer Security (TLS), code signing, and smart cards.

Deploying PKI services can be dauntingly complex. Part of this is due to the nature of cryptography, but much of the complexity has come about because major elements of the technology were designed by disparate vendors and committees with independent and often conflicting agendas.

Take heart, though. If you can hack through the jargon and map out the concepts, the actual implementation of a Windows Server 2003 PKI takes very little effort. The real work lies in the planning. If you work for a small or medium-sized organization where you and a select group of your colleagues are the sole IT decision makers, this chapter will give you the necessary information to plan and implement a Windows Server 2003 PKI.

On the other hand, if you want to deploy a PKI in a large organization with a Byzantine decision structure, prepare yourself for an arduous couple of years filled with studies, product comparisons, requests for proposals, vendor presentations, white papers, and dozens of meetings with skeptical colleagues and confused managers. This chapter will at least give you a basis for starting the process and for evaluating Microsoft's contribution to the technology.

You'll need a working familiarity with these major PKI elements:

- **Cryptographic elements.** This includes the encryption and hashing technologies used to protect data and validate a sender's identity.
- **Public key elements.** There are a variety of technologies for generating and using public/private key pairs. Windows Server 2003 supports the most widely accepted methods. You need to know how they work to a sufficient extent to make sure you implement them correctly.
- **Certificates.** The core of a PKI is the secure exchange and storage of certificates. You'll need to understand the mechanisms used by Windows clients to request, validate, and store certificates.
- **Certification Authorities.** Any PKI entity is capable of generating public/private key pairs. The secret to making those keys a trustworthy medium for data exchange is to validate them with a Certification Authority, or CA. This chapter shows you how to establish a Windows Server 2003 CA hierarchy.
- **Certificate enrollment and revocation.** After you have your CA servers in place, you need to know how clients obtain certificates from them. Windows Server 2003 makes this as transparent as possible, but there are still places where administrative intervention is necessary.
- **Command-line tools.** Finally, you can streamline your operations by using command-line utilities in the Support Tools and Resource Kit for managing and troubleshooting your PKI.

New Features in Windows Server 2003

Windows 2000 was the first Microsoft product to contain a tightly integrated set of cryptography tools. Windows Server 2003 improves on these tools and incorporates changes and advancements promulgated in industry standards since the release of Windows 2000. These new features include the following:

- **Key recovery.** One of the more exciting new features in Windows Server 2003 is the ability to store and re-issue data encryption keys that users have lost or were erased.
- **User auto-enrollment.** This feature permits issuing User certificates as soon as a user logs on to the domain from an XP or Windows Server 2003 client. A User certificate can be used for EFS, S/MIME, and IPSec. This significantly reduces the complexity of deploying these applications.

- **3DES and AES support.** The Microsoft crypto provider in Windows Server 2003 now supports 3DES (Triple-DES) and the Advanced Encryption Standard (AES), making the system compliant with FIPS-140, a U.S. government standard for PC-based cryptography.
- **FIPS 180-2 support.** Windows Server 2003 supports the extended hashing algorithms specified in the new Secure Hash Standard, publication FIPS 180-2. You can get a copy of this standard at `csrc.nist.gov/encryption/shs/dfips-180-2.pdf`. The new algorithms are enhancements to the current 160-bit Secure Hashing Algorithm-1 (SHA1) standard. They are SHA-256, SHA-384, and SHA-512.
- **Delta CRLs.** To avoid lengthy, unmanageable Certificate Revocation Lists (CRL), the latest RFC provides for the periodic issuance of a base CRL with frequent updates, called *Delta CRLs*. Distributing Delta CRLs requires far fewer network and client resources than distributing a full CRL each time a change occurs.
- **Manageable certificate templates.** A new template version in Windows Server 2003 supports updated certificate extensions with the ability to set optional values for those extensions.
- **Smart card improvements.** With Windows Server 2003 and XP, you can now use smart cards to log on to a server via Remote Desktop. The NET and RUNAS utilities have also been improved to work with smart cards.
- **CA Root certificate updates.** When validating a certificate issued by an outside CA, an XP or Windows Server 2003 client will automatically use the Windows Update web site to check for a copy of the Root CA certificate. This simplifies deployment of solutions involving third-party PKIs.
- **Qualified Subordination.** Classic PKI implementations can be difficult to extend between organizations because of the unlimited nature of the cross-trusts. Windows Server 2003 takes advantage of RFC-compliant constraints to limit the range and types of certificates that can be trusted from outside hierarchies.

High Encryption Now Permitted for Export

For many years, the U.S. government only permitted export of encryption algorithms that incorporated 40-bit and 56-bit cipher keys. This changed on January 14, 2000, when the Commerce Department released a revision to the cryptographic export restrictions with an addendum issued on October 19, 2000. You can download copies of the new regulations and the addendum from these web sites:

- January 14 regulation: `www.bxa.doc.gov/Encryption/pdfs/Crypto.pdf`
- October 19 addendum: `www.bxa.doc.gov/Encryption/19Oct2KFactsheet.html`
- FAQ on October 19 addendum: `www.bxa.doc.gov/Encryption/Oct2KQandAs.html`

In spite of the loosened export restrictions in the U.S., some countries impose their own import restrictions that impose harsh penalties. Be sure to check the local laws before sending a user to a country with a laptop equipped with EFS or S/MIME or Pretty Good Privacy.

PKI Goals

The PKI services in Windows Server 2003 provide the underpinnings for applications that use cryptographic services. A properly designed PKI achieves the following goals:

- **Confidentiality.** The privacy of user transactions is protected by encrypting data streams and messages.
- **Authentication.** No transaction can be truly secure if the parties are completely unknown to each other. PKI provides a means for senders and recipients to validate each other's identities.
- **Integrity.** Transactions can be marked in such a way that any tampering is immediately apparent. This protection extends to preventing replays and detecting de-sequenced messages or datagrams.
- **Non-Repudiation.** It's one thing to authenticate the source of a message; it's quite another to keep the source from denying having sent the message. Digital signatures inextricably link senders to their messages.

A PKI uses standard elements to achieve these goals. Highly impenetrable encryption algorithms have been developed to achieve confidentiality. *Certificates* provide a secure transport to exchange the cipher keys used by these encryption algorithms. Authentication and integrity are assured by using *digital signatures* consisting of encrypted *hashes*. Non-repudiation is assured by applying digital signatures in such a way that senders always leave a mark on their communications.

Here are places to get additional information about the PKI components used in Windows Server 2003:

- RSA Labs, `www.rsalabs.com`
- Federal Information Processing Standards (FIPS) - `www.itl.nist.gov/fipspubs`
- PKI working group of the Internet Engineering Task Force (IETF), `www.ietf.org/html.charters/pkix-charter.html`
- Microsoft PKI documentation, `www.microsoft.com/security`
- PKI related RFCs, search `www.nexor.com`

There are quite a few vendors who sell PKI products that you can use in place of, or in conjunction with, a Windows Server 2003 PKI. Here are the major vendors:

- Verisign, `www.verisign.com`
- Thawte, `www.thawte.com`
- Schlumberger, `www.schlumberger.com`
- Digital Signature Trust, `www.dst.com`
- SecureNet, `www.securenet.com.au`

- Entrust, `www.entrust.com`
- Baltimore Technologies, `www.Baltimore.com`

Cryptographic Elements in Windows Server 2003

In 9th grade science class, my good buddy Mark Roff and I would exchange secret notes. Our code used a system of numerical letter displacements based on pages from the Bantam paperback edition of Lord of the Rings. We included the page numbers in the notes spelled out in High Elvish runes with the certain knowledge that we were the only two kids in the school capable of understanding them. We would fold the notes in a certain way so that we knew they came from each other and that no one else had opened them.

Needless to say, a seasoned cryptographer would not have puzzled long over our notes. (To be fair, Mark was capable of constructing a much more sophisticated system but he kept it simple for my benefit.) Despite their lack of sophistication, though, the notes contained all the elements of a modern PKI: an encryption algorithm, a unique cipher key, a way of exchanging the key in secrecy, and a way to validate the integrity of the process.

Encryption Methods

The cryptographic services in Windows Server 2003 use two general encryption methods:

- **Block.** A block cipher divides data into chunks, pads the last chunk if necessary, and then encrypts each chunk in its turn. The better ciphers use the output of one encrypted block as the basis for the key for encrypting the next block (cipher block chaining). Most encryption algorithms use block ciphers.
- **Streaming.** A streaming cipher uses a series of seemingly random numbers seeded with a cipher key to encrypt a stream of bits. The random number stream is actually a predetermined series of bits based on the cipher key seed, so the stream can be decrypted if the cipher is known. Streaming encryption is much faster than block encryption for bulk data transfers.

The default crypto providers in Windows Server 2003 support the following algorithms:

- **RC2 and RC5.** Ronald Rivest, one of the team of Rivest, Shamir, and Adleman that formed RSA Labs in the early 90s, developed these algorithms. They are block encryption algorithms with variable block and key sizes. This variability makes them difficult to break if the attacker does not know the original sizes when attempting to decrypt captured data.
- **RC4**. RC4, also from RSA, is a streaming encryption algorithm that also uses variable key sizes to thwart attacks.

- **DES.** The now-outdated Data Encryption Standard (DES) was co-developed by IBM and the U.S. Government. It uses a block algorithm with a 64-bit block and a 40- or 56-bit key. Its chief advantage was speed and exportability. DES was broken quite a while ago and is no longer use by any respectable encryption product.
- **DESX.** A modification of DES constructed by Rivest at RSA that sandwiches standard DES encryption between two XOR bit-wise replacement runs, all with different keys.
- **3DES.** Triple-DES is not so much a modification of DES as it is a way of strengthening the final output by running data through the DES engine three times.
- **AES.** The newly promulgated Advanced Encryption Standard (AES) uses the Rijndael (pronounced Rhine-doll) algorithm. This algorithm was developed by Joan Daemen and Vincent Rijmen of Belgium. AES will eventually displace DESX and 3DES.

Cipher Keys

In general, the longer and more complex the cipher key, the less likely it is that someone can deduce the contents of an encrypted message. This is not necessarily the case, of course. You could have an extraordinarily long key and an extraordinarily simple cipher, but what would be the point?

There are two types of cipher keys:

- **Symmetric**. In this kind of cipher, the same key is used to encrypt and decrypt data.
- **Asymmetric**. In this cipher, two keys are mathematically paired together. One is used for encryption, whereas the other is used for decryption.

Asymmetric keys are associated with slow algorithms that are generally unsuitable for encrypting large amounts of data. Bulk encryption algorithms tend to use symmetric keys, but this presents the challenge of exchanging the key in a secure manner. Most modern systems use a hybrid method with a short-lived symmetric key encrypted with asymmetric key technology. Protecting and validating the asymmetric keys is the job of a PKI.

Hashes

Encryption only fulfills two of the goals we set out to achieve, those of confidentiality and integrity. To get authentication and non-repudiation, PKI uses another form of data manipulation, the *hash*. (A hash is also called a *message digest*.)

In contrast to encryption, where the original input can be recovered, hashing scrambles the input with no chance of ever recovering it. If you've seen the last scene of the movie *Fargo*, you have an idea of how hashing works.

In its barest form, a hashing algorithm accepts a variable length input and produces a fixed-length output that is highly sensitive to the input. A single bit changed in the input produces dozens of changes to the output. The greater the number of bits in the hash, the more secure the algorithm. It takes longer to create a bigger hash, though, so there is a tradeoff between performance and security.

Digital signatures use hashing technology to verify a sender's identity. For example, the RSA digital signature method hashes a message (or TCP datagram) and then encrypts the hash with the sender's private key. The recipient hashes the message (or datagram) using the same algorithm and then decrypts the sender's hash using the sender's public key and compares the results. If the hashes match, the sender has been verified.

The Digital Signature Security Standard, or DSS, uses a similar signing method but generates the key pair using Digital Signature Algorithm (DSA) rather than RSA. DSA is slower but uses the more secure SHA-1 hashing algorithm, making it less likely that an attacker could generate an identical hash with different inputs.

Hashing is not a true cryptographic process but it is possible to add a cipher key to a hash to produce a kind of cryptographic mulligan stew. This technique is called *Hashed Message Authentication Code*, or HMAC. It is described in RFC 2104, "HMAC: Keyed-Hashing for Message Authentication." HMAC is used for digital signatures in S/MIME, IP Security (IPSec), and Secure Sockets Layer (SSL). It is also used for obfuscating passwords in Kerberos and NT LanMan (NTLM) Challenge-Response authentication.

It is theoretically possible to derive a hash by trial and error to produce a *collision*—that is, by producing a hash that has identical output for the same or dissimilar input. For example, Windows uses hashes to obfuscate passwords. Let's say you have a cleartext password of £oan$hark. The system hashes this password using RSA MD4 to produce a fixed, 128-bit hash that it stores in Active Directory. A password-cracking program can attempt to determine the password (or a substitute for the password) by hashing combinations of letters and numbers using MD4 until it gets a result that matches the hash in Active Directory.

Windows Server 2003 supports six hashing mechanisms:

- **MD4 and MD5**. (MD stands for message digest.) These are RSA algorithms. MD4 is used to hash user passwords in NT and Windows 2000 while MD5 is used to support third-party CHAP (Challenge Handshake Authentication Protocol) authentication for dial-in clients. Both algorithms process inputs in 512-bit blocks and produce a single 128-bit output block. MD5 is computationally more expensive but far more secure.

- **SHA-1** (pronounced Shah One). The Secure Hash Algorithm (SHA) was promulgated by the National Institute of Standards and Technology (NIST) to compliment the Digital Signature Standard (DSS). SHA-1 is based on MD4. It processes input in 512-bit blocks but produces a 160-bit output rather than 128-bit. This makes SHA-1 more secure than MD4 or MD5, all other things being equal. Also, SHA-1 is not as vulnerable to cryptanalysis thanks to the type of algorithm used to do the data scrambling. It is also faster than MD4 or MD5.
- **SHS (Secure Hash Standard).** This includes three extensions to the SHA-1 standard with larger digest sizes: SHA-256, SHA-384, and SHA-512. There is no Registry key to select a different algorithm. The application developer must select it from the function library.

Public/Private Key Services

Theoretically, users could exchange cipher keys with each user by copying the keys to a disk and transporting the disk using a secure courier. A PKI is a kind of electronic courier service that operates over a highly insecure network.

Public key technology got its start back in the late 1970's when a couple of guys, Whitfield Diffie and Martin Hellman, developed a way to exchange secret keys right out in the open, the cryptographic equivalent of passing your wallet to the beer guy at a basketball game without worrying that someone will reach in to take a fiver.

Soon after the introduction of the Diffie-Hellman key exchange method, the trio of Ron Rivest, Adi Shamir, and Len Adleman (founders of RSA Labs) took the idea of mathematically related keys and developed a more general-purpose encryption service using key pairs. Anything encrypted with one key can only be decrypted with the other key in the pair.

RSA identifies one of the keys as a *public* key. The public key can be freely distributed. You can spray paint it on the side of a building without fear of compromising your security system. (Here in Phoenix where I live, spray-painting buildings has very nearly replaced newspapers as the primary means of public communication.) The private key is another matter. The private key is heavily protected. PKI entities take another user's public key and use it to encrypt messages that can then only be read by the user with the private key.

RSA developed secure methods for validating and distributing public keys using *certificates*. A certificate contains a public key along with information about the key issuer, the key owner, and how long the key is valid.

RSA continues to be a major force in the development of PKI technology. Visit its web site at `www.rsalabs.com`.

Following the release of RSA public/private key exchange technologies, a computer programmer named Phil Zimmerman combined RSA asymmetric keys with a symmetric bulk encryption scheme to produce *Pretty Good Privacy* (PGP), still one of the most widely used mail encryption applications around. Visit the PGP web site, `www.pgp.com`. (PGP is now owned by Network Associates, `www.nai.com`.)

Network Associates has stopped all new development for their PGP tools and has stated that support will be dropped sometime in 2002. Phil Zimmerman is working to make NAI put the PGP code in the public domain. Refer to the OpenPGP web site at `www.openpgp.org` for developments in this area.

From its grassroots beginnings, public key technology has evolved into a systematic method for producing, acquiring, distributing, cataloging, and protecting cryptographic elements. The clearinghouse for PKI information is the PKIX Working Group, chartered by the IETF. For information, visit `www.ietf.org/html.charters/pkix-charter.html`.

Public Key Technologies in Windows Server 2003

Windows Server 2003 supports these public key exchange methods:

- Diffie-Hellman
- RSA
- Digital Signature Standard (DSS)

Diffie-Hellman

Diffie-Hellman (D-H) is the granddaddy of public key technologies. It is a way to share a secret key across an open network without actually passing the key or an encrypted form of the key. Windows Server 2003 uses D-H to support IP Security (IPSec), Secure Socket Layer (SSL), and Transport Layer Security (TLS).

In a D-H transaction, a sender and receiver use very large prime numbers and primitive roots of those prime numbers in an engine that produces secret keys. D-H relies on special features of prime numbers and logarithms of prime numbers in modulo algebra. Modulo is a Bizarro world where numbers are congruent if their remainders are equal after having been completely factored by the same number. The common divisor is called a *modulus*, hence the name. For example, 17/3 yields 5 remainder 2, so 17 mod 3 is 2. Because 23 mod 3 is also 2 (23/3 calculates out to 7 remainder 2), then 23 and 17 are congruent *modulo* 3.

In D-H, two entities independently generate a secret random number, *Ax* from one entity and *Bx* from the other entity. They each process their random numbers through the D-H engine to produce a public number, P_a and P_b. They exchange these public numbers and then run them through a second part of the D-H engine to produce a secret key. Here's where the magic of modulo algebra comes into play. The separate calculations performed at the two entities produce the same result.

The end result of this D-H transaction is a shared secret key that the entities can use for encrypting messages between each other. An attacker cannot reverse-calculate the D-H secret key without knowing the original secret random number at one of the entities.

RSA

Most of this topic concerns the generation and use of RSA keys, so I won't spend time discussing them now. Unlike Diffie-Hellman, where a key only exists during a particular session, RSA generates persistent keys that can be used for encryption, digital signatures, and so forth. Windows Server 2003 uses RSA for Kerberos. Exchange 2000 uses RSA for S/MIME.

Digital Signature Standard

In 1991, the National Institute of Standards and Technology (NIST) published standard 186, the *Digital Signature Standard*, or DSS. This standard incorporated a different method for generating public/private key pairs than the method used by RSA. The new method is called the *Digital Signature Algorithm*, or DSA.

NIST published DSA to address a perceived problem with the RSA method for producing digital signatures. (Only a cynic would think that avoiding the RSA license fees had anything to do with this decision.)

DSA uses session keys based on the difficulty of deriving discrete logarithms, just as Diffie-Hellman and RSA. The difference lies in the way the keys are used to apply and verify a digital signature. Using RSA, signing a message happens quickly, whereas verifying the signature is relatively CPU intensive. Using DSA, signing a message is the intensive step and the verification is simple. Windows Server 2003 supports both DSA and RSA. It's up to the application designer to decide which to use.

Windows Server 2003 Cryptographic Services

Windows Server 2003 uses a set of function libraries and executables to perform cryptographic chores such as generating cipher keys and handling certificates. In Windows 9x and NT, this library is called the *Crypto API*. In Windows 2000 and Windows Server 2003, it is called the *Data Protection API*, or DPAPI. The function calls in these libraries are common among all modern Windows platforms, although the underlying executable files are different. This ensures that encrypted and digitally signed data can be freely exchanged between all Windows clients.

Each discrete set of crypto functions is supported by a *Cryptographic Service Provider*, or CSP. Microsoft supplies a set of CSPs with Windows Server 2003 to provide core cryptographic services. Third parties add their own CPSs to support their hardware or independent cryptographic functions. Figure 18.1 shows the list of CSPs in the Registry under `HKLM | Software | Microsoft | Cryptography | Defaults | Provider`.

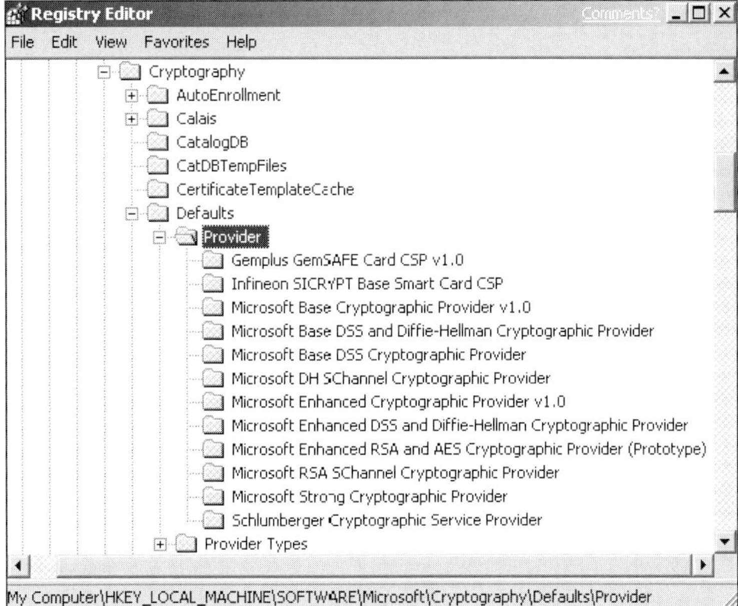

Figure 18.1 Registry showing location of keys for Cryptographic Service Providers (CSPs).

This list is actually more complex than necessary. Before export controls were lifted on cryptographic technology, it was necessary for Microsoft to divide CSPs into U.S.-only and exportable versions, typically using a Base and Enhanced moniker. Now that all cryptographic technology in Windows Server 2003 is exportable, there are now only two core CSPs and a few vendor add-ons:

- **RSAenh.** This CSP supports industry-standard RSA cryptographic functions along with U.S. Government cryptographic standards. These functions include key generation, certificate requests, hashing, and encryption. This CSP also supports Schannel services for secure web transactions.
- **Dssenh.** This CSP supports the U.S. Government's Digital Signature Standard and the more prevalent Diffie-Hellman key exchange transactions.
- **Smart card providers.** Windows Server 2003 includes generic interfaces for collecting tokens from smart cards and a set of drivers for Gemplus, Infineon (a spinoff of Siemens Semiconductors), and Schlumberger smart card readers.

Outlook 2000 and Outlook XP install another CSP, Exchcsp.dll, to support FIPS-140 compliant S/MIME. This provider is documented in a white paper available at `csrc.nist.gov/cryptval/140-1/140sp/140sp110.pdf`.

Key Storage

Windows Server 2003 and XP store a user's crypto keys in the user's profile. Figure 18.2 shows the locations.

- The user's private keys are stored under `Crypto\RSA`. The keys are encrypted with a Session key derived from a Master key generated by the *Data Protection API*, or DPAPI.
- The Master key is stored under `Protect\<userSID>`. It is encrypted using a special structure called an HMAC, which stands for *Hash-based Message Authentication Code*. An HMAC is a hash that combines a block of data with a secret key. The HMAC for the Master key consists of a SHA-1 hash of the Master key itself using the user's password hash as the secret key. This HMAC permits the Master key to be encrypted with a cryptographically strong key that is still derivable from the user's password.
- The user's public keys are stored under `System Certificates\My\Certificates`. Copies of the public key certificates are stored in the Registry. If a user is a member of a Windows Server 2003 or Windows 2000 domain, a copy of the user's public key can also be stored in Active Directory.

If you delete the user's profile, you lose the private keys that are paired with the public keys used to encrypt files and emails. The user then loses the ability to decrypt those files and emails. Be very careful when working with user profiles if you deploy a Windows-based PKI.

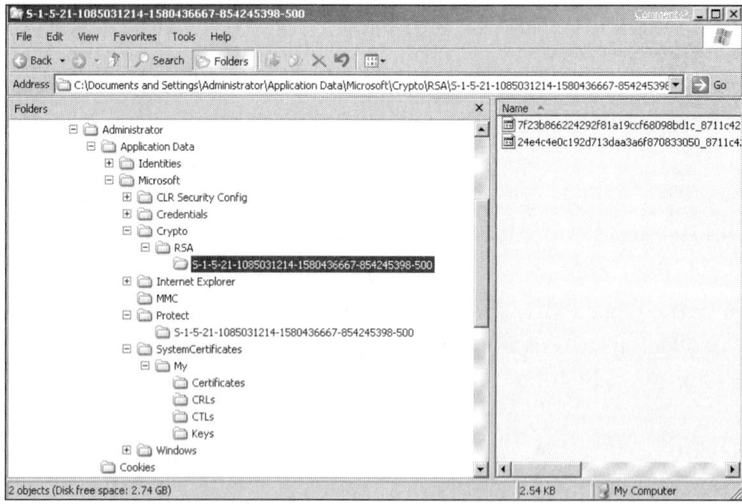

Figure 18.2 PKCS key locations in a user profile.

Certificates

In Diffie-Hellman and DSS key exchanges, a brand new cipher key is created for each session. This makes sense in applications like IPSec where a secure network communication link is established pretty much on an ad hoc basis. But what if you want to retain the key for later use, such as digital signatures? You need a way to transport the key securely and, just as importantly, you want to make sure that the key comes from an authorized issuer and has not been tampered with along the way.

The data structure used to transport and validate keys is called a *certificate*. A certificate acts as a strongbox that protects the key while guaranteeing the identity of the issuer, the identity of the owner, and the purposes for which the key can be used. The certificate also contains additional information called *extensions* that streamline the validation process.

A certificate cannot be forged because the issuing authority digitally signs it. The signature is applied to a hash of the certificate. This enables clients to validate the issuer's identity and check for tampering at the same time. The client decrypts the hash using the issuer's public key and then compares the result to a separate hash it performs on the certificate. If the results match, the certificate is valid.

In Windows Server 2003, Windows XP, and Windows 2000, certificates are handled by the Data Protection API. Certificates issued to a client are stored in the Registry and Active Directory. The keys are stored on disk. Certificates can also be stored in smart cards. This eliminates the vulnerability of on-disk key storage. You can view the certificates issued to you as a PKI client with the `Certificates` snap-in. There is no pre-built console for this snap-in, so you must load it into an empty console using the FILE | ADD/REMOVE SNAP-IN option in the MMC menu. Figure 18.3 shows the general details of a certificate.

A certificate contains the following items (some are optional):

- **`Issued By.`** The Certification Authority (CA) that issued the certificate. By default, a copy of the public-key certificate is stored in the CA database. A Windows Server 2003 CA can also retain private key certificates.
- **`Issued To.`** The entity that obtained the certificate. In a Windows Server 2003 PKI, computer names can be formatted with the computer's flat name or its fully qualified domain name. If the recipient is a user, the name can be the user's logon ID, User Principal Name (UPN), or Distinguished Name (DN).
- **`Intended Uses (OID).`** A certificate has one or more uses. You cannot issue a *carte blanche* certificate for every purpose. The issuing CA stipulates the purposes based on an *Object ID*, or OID. An OID uses a dotted-decimal notation to show a hierarchy. For example, the OID `1.3.6.1.4.1.311.20.2.1` refers to the Enrollment Agent function. The OID is rooted at the ISO in Geneva (1), issued to an ISO recognized organization, the U.S. Department of Defense (1.3.6), and controlled by the Internet Assigned Naming Authority (1.3.6.1).

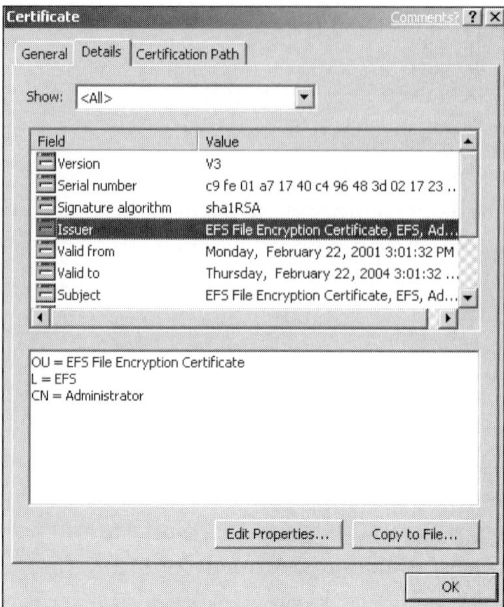

Figure 18.3 General details of a certificate viewed with the `Certificates` snap-in.

- **`Version.`** The certificate version. Windows CA servers issue X.509 Version 3 certificates.
- **`Serial Number.`** This is a sequential number assigned by the CA to the certificate. The number is unique and acts as a validity check.
- **`Signature Algorithm.`** The hashing algorithm used to do the digital signature for the certificate. This is typically either SHA-1 or MD5 (RSA).
- **`Issuer.`** This is the X.500 distinguished name of the issuing server—for example, `cn = ca-1, o = company, l = phoenix, s = az, c = us, e = administrator@company.com`.
- **`Valid From.`** This is the issue date of the certificate.
- **`Valid To.`** This important field defines the expiry date of the certificate. The CA determines how long to issue a certificate. Shorter intervals are more secure but require more work on the part of the clients.
- **`Subject.`** This is the X.500 distinguished name of the certificate's owner.
- **`Public Key.`** This data structure holds the public key itself.

- `CA Version.` This is the number of times the authorization certificate for a particular issuing server has been renewed.
- `Subject Key Identifier.` This important field contains an SHA-1 hash of the `Public Key` field used to uniquely identify the contents. This prevents tampering with the public key.
- `Certificate Template.` This is a unique Microsoft extension that contains name of the template used by the CA to generate this certificate.
- `Key Usage.` This field contains the OIDs of the purposes for the certificate.
- `Authority Key Identifier.` Contains an SHA-1 hash of the public key of the issuing CA along with the distinguished name of the CA.
- `CRL Distribution Points (CDPs).` Contains the identity of the CDPs listed by LDAP path, URL, and file share name.
- `Authority Information Access.` Tells a client where to find the certificate of the issuing CA.
- `Thumbprint.` A hash of the certificate used for positive identification.
- `Thumbprint Algorithm.` The algorithm used to obtain the certificate hash.

Certificate Documentation

The contents and structure of a standard PKI certificate is defined by the ITU (International Telecommunications Union) in the X.509 standard. The most current standard, Version 3, was defined in 1995.

The ITU works closely with the IETF (Internet Engineering Task Force) to make sure the standards match the current utilization. See RFC 2549, "Internet X.509 Public Key Infrastructure Certificate and CRL Profile," for IETF documentation of the certificate contents and structure.

Public key technology as it is used today was originally developed by RSA, and you can get documentation at its web site, `www.rsalabs.com`. The standard certificate structure is documented in PKCS#7 (P7B), "Cryptographic Message Syntax." RSA also documents certificate-handling mechanisms, including the following:

- **PKCS#10, Certification Request Syntax.** This is not a certificate, as such, but a way of obtaining a certificate from a Certification Authority.
- **PKCS#11, Cryptographic Token Interface Syntax.** This standard defines how to securely store certificates in hardware such as smart cards.
- **PKCS#12, Personal Information Exchange Syntax.** This certificate type is designed to securely store and transfer private keys.

Local Certificate Stores

The certificates and keys obtained by a PKI client are stored in various places at the local client depending on their function. Windows abstracts the physical locations behind a logical store that can be viewed with the `Certificates` snap-in (see Figure 18.4). The logical stores are as follows:

- **Personal.** This store holds certificates issued to the user, computer, and any services running on the computer. You can view computer and service certificates if you log on with administrator rights. The physical store is the Registry in `HKLM | Software | Microsoft | SystemCertificates`.
- **Trusted Root Certification Authorities.** Contains certificates for root CAs and third-party root CAs that have been preloaded or downloaded by Windows Update. The physical store is the Registry and in Group Policies.
- **Intermediate Certification Authorities.** Contains subordinate CA (and third-party subordinates) along with any Certificate Revocation Lists (CRLs).
- **Active Directory User Object.** Contains certificates that have been copied to Active Directory.
- **Request.** Shows submittals for certificates sent to a CA. Copies of the PKCS#10 requests are stored in the Registry.
- **Software Publishing Certificate (SPC).** Computer clients use this store to hold certificates from Authenticode and other digital signing software. The physical store for SPC is the Registry.

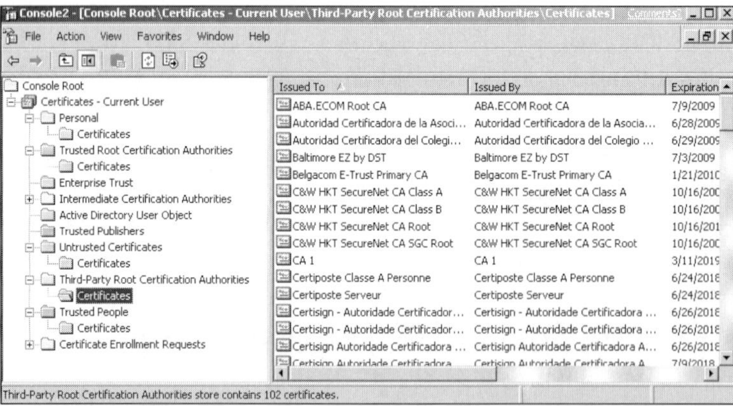

Figure 18.4 Certificate store shown in the `Certificates` snap-in.

Certification Authorities

A local PKI client generates its own public/private key pairs. It is free to send the public key to other entities, but there is no reason why the other entities should trust it because nothing validates the source of the certificate.

Turning self-generated public keys into something trustworthy requires the intervention of a *Certification Authority*, or CA. A CA acts like a notary public. It affixes its own signature to a client's public key, thereby proclaiming the key to be valid, at least to anyone who trusts the CA.

A CA is the ultimate entrepreneur. Anyone with administrative rights on a server running Windows Server 2003 or UNIX/Linux server can install the certificate services and go into the certificate issuance business. A new CA has no other CA to vouch for it, so it signs its own CA certificate and becomes a *root CA*.

Like any entrepreneurial concern, a CA can only survive if clients know where to find it and trust its integrity. Microsoft differentiates between CAs based on where they place their CA certificates:

- An *Enterprise CA* stores a copy of its CA certificate in Active Directory where clients can download it and place it in their local certificate store.
- A *Standalone CA* stores a copy of its CA certificate in a shared folder that can also be accessed via a web URL. Clients must be told the name of the CA so they can send it their certification requests and pick up their certificates at the designated location. (An Enterprise CA also uses fixed storage for clients that are not able to search Active Directory.)

An Enterprise Windows Server 2003 CA adds value to the certificate issuance process by using Kerberos or NTLM to validate the identity of an end-entity prior to issuing it a certificate. This provides additional assurance for PKI clients when they receive digital signatures from the entity.

By using a mixture of Enterprise and Standalone CAs, you can achieve a PKI that is both highly secure and highly scalable. As you plan your CA deployment, keep in mind that the name of the CA server and its distinguished name in Active Directory are incorporated into the X.509 certificates it issues, so a CA cannot be renamed or removed from a domain. Also, the Certificate service is not cluster-aware, so it cannot be run as a fail-over resource on a Windows Server 2003 Enterprise or Datacenter Edition cluster. It can, however, run on a single node of the cluster, if you desire.

CA Certificate Storage

Certificates issued by a CA are stored in a Jet database called <server_name>.edb under \Windows\System32\CertLog. This database contains the CA private key. Protect the database as carefully as you protect Active Directory. If you should lose the CA database, you lose the ability to audit certificates issued by the CA. The database is backed up as part of System State.

Enterprise CAs also place certificates in Active Directory in the Public Key Services container located under `cn=Services, cn=Configuration, dc=<domain>, dc=<root>`. This container holds the following subcontainers:

- **Enrollment Services.** This container holds PkiEnrollmentService objects representing CAs that are configured to issue certificates. These objects have a copy of the CA certificate, the DN (distinguished name) of the certificate, and the certificate templates advertised by the CA.
- **Certificate Templates.** This container holds PKICertificateTemplate objects. Attributes of these objects define the name, content, OID, and purpose of the certificate type the template was designed to produce. You must have a Windows Server 2003 domain to have Version 2 certificate templates in this container.
- **CRL Distribution Points (CDP).** These containers hold CRLDistributionPoint objects for each CA. Attributes of these objects hold the base CRL certificate and any Delta CRL certificates issued by the associated CA. Clients download these certificates and use them to perform local validation.
- **Authority Information Access (AIA).** This container holds copies of the CertificationAuthority objects also contained in the main Certification Authority container. Clients reference the AIA container when they need to retrieve the certificate of a CA in a trust chain.
- **Key Recovery Agent (KRA).** This container holds MsPKI-PrivateKeyRecoveryAgent objects for each CA. These objects have a `UserCertificate` attribute that lists the private keys stored by a CA that is configured as a Registration Authority.
- **Object Identification (OID).** This container holds MsPKI-Enterprise-Oid objects that define the name and OID of certificates issued by the CAs in the enterprise. OIDs are unique identifiers assigned to a certificate type by an issuing authority.

Certificate Templates

A Windows Server 2003 Enterprise CA uses *certificate templates* stored in Active Directory to generate certificates for users, computers, and other CAs. Standalone CAs do not use templates.

Certificate templates are managed via the `Certificate Templates` snap-in. The simplest way to access this snap-in is through the Certification Authority console. Right-click the `Certificate Templates` folder and select MANAGE from the flyout menu (see Figure 18.5).

Double-click a template to open its Properties window, which shows the purpose of the certificates issued with the help of the template and the extensions that will be included in the certificate (see Figure 18.6).

The snap-in displays two template types. The first type, shown in a dimmed color, is Version 1 templates. These templates contain fixed information that cannot be modified by an administrator. Windows 2000 uses Version 1 templates and they are included for backward compatibility. The second type, shown in full color in the console, is Version 2 templates. These templates contain configurable fields that provide much more flexibility in PKI design and deployment.

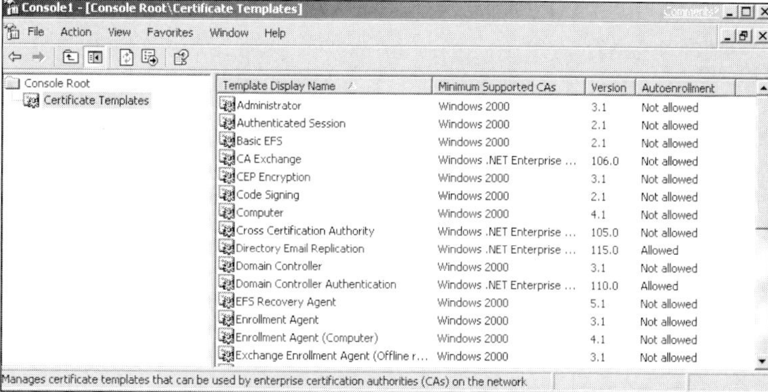

Figure 18.5 `Certificate Templates` snap-in showing the Version 1 and Version 2 templates available for distribution by a Windows Server 2003 CA.

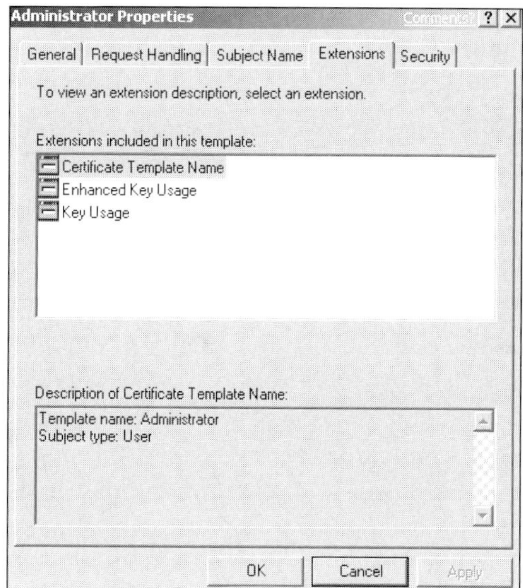

Figure 18.6 Certificate template properties showing the included extensions.

Armed with the new Version 2 templates, a Windows Server 2003 CA provides the following additional features compared to a Windows 2000 CA:

- **Key archive and recovery.** The CA can save copies of key pairs that can be recovered and re-issued to users who lose their keys. A CA providing this service is called a *Registration Authority*. Up until Windows Server 2003, the only Windows product that provided registration services was the Exchange Key Management Service (KMS). The next version of Exchange will hand KMS duties over to a Windows Server 2003 CA. If you currently use KMS in Exchange 5.5 or Exchange 2000, you can export the private keys to a Windows Server 2003 CA using the CERTUTIL utility in Windows Server 2003.

- **User auto-enrollment.** In Windows 2000, computers could be configured to auto-enroll for a Computer certificate. In Windows Server 2003, users can be configured to auto-enroll for a User certificate. The User certificate template supports the Encrypting File System, digital signatures, and client authentication for IPSec, SSL, and smart cards. User auto-enrollment is only available when logging on at an XP desktop or server running Windows Server 2003.
- **Qualified subordination.** This feature permits a CA to limit the type of certificates that can be issued by a subordinate CA.
- **Delta CRLs.** A large production PKI can have a very long Certificate Revocation List. This degrades performance because every client must check the CRL each time it is presented with a new certificate. Using a Delta CRL, the client only need download the changes to the base CRL, a significant savings in bandwidth.
- **Common Criteria requirements.** ISO standard 15408 defines an IT security evaluation checklist. The National Institute of Standards and Technology (NIST) refers to the 15408 standard the as the *Common Criteria*, or CC. The most current CC version is 2.1, which you can download from `csrc.nist.gov/cc/ccv20/ccv2list.htm#CCV21`. A properly implemented Windows Server 2003 CA hierarchy meets the Common Criteria requirements.

These are all great features and are welcome additions to Windows CA services, but the bad news is they are only available on Windows Server 2003, Enterprise Edition and Datacenter Edition. Windows Server 2003, Standard Edition, can only use legacy Version 1 templates and does not meet the Common Criteria standards due to lack of role-based management features. Also, you must have a Windows Server 2003 domain to use Version 2 templates because they require schema components that are not available in Windows 2000.

Certificate Revocation

A CA has another job that is equally as important as issuing certificates. It stands ready to revoke those certificates, if necessary. For instance, if a bad guy is able to compromise the private key of a user, you can revoke the user's public key certificate so that other users no longer trust it.

The CA maintains a Certificate Revocation List (CRL) containing the serial number of any revoked certificates. The serial number is a sequential integer assigned to a certificate by the issuing CA.

Use the Certification Authority console to revoke a certificate. Right-click the certificate and select All Tasks | Revoke Certificate from the flyout menu. This places the certificate in the Revoked Certificates container.

Use caution when revoking a certificate. There is no "un-revoke" feature. All digital signatures, encrypted messages, encrypted files, and other cryptographic applications that rely on the certificate become inoperable when the certificate is revoked. If you revoke the certificate of a subordinate CA, all certificates issued by that CA become invalid.

Certificate Revocation List

Certificates are like credit cards. A bank can revoke a card but it is nearly impossible to recall it. Instead, the bank adds the card to a revocation list. In a credit card infrastructure, each merchant is responsible for validating a card by dialing up a central clearinghouse and checking the revocation list. In a PKI, each CA issues a Certificate Revocation List (CRL) that identifies revoked certificates. Each PKI entity is responsible for checking the CRL when it validates a certificate.

When a CA creates a CRL, it places copies in strategic locations where clients can download it. These are called *CRL Distribution Points*, or CDPs. A CA certificate specifies the CDP locations. Figure 18.7 shows an example. If a client is unable to find the CRL at the specified CDP, it assumes that any certificate issued by the CA has been revoked.

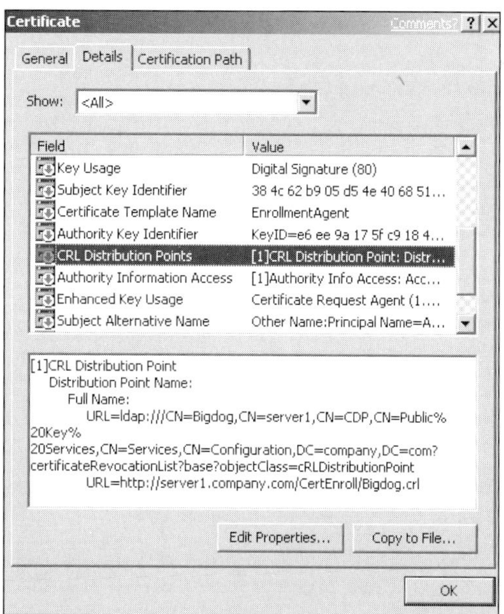

Figure 18.7 CDP listing in a CA certificate issued by an Enterprise Windows Server 2003 CA.

An Enterprise Windows Server 2003 CA publishes its CRL in Active Directory in a CRLDistributionPoint object under `cn=<server_name>, cn=CDP, cn=Public Key Services, cn=Services, cn=Configuration, dc=<domain>, dc=<root>`. A Standalone CA places the CRL on disk in `%systemroot%\system32\certsrv\CertEnroll`. This folder is also forms the root of a virtual web directory by the same name.

You can view the contents of a CRL from the Certification Authority console. Right-click the Revoked Certificates container, select PROPERTIES, and then click `View CRLs` (see Figure 18.8).

To prevent constant traffic to the CA, clients cache the CRL for a *publication period*. When the period expires, the client returns to the CDP to download an updated CRL. If one is not available, the client will assume that all certificates issued by the CA have been revoked.

A PKI client must be coded to do CRL checking when it receives a certificate. This is not a requirement. For example, Outlook does not perform automatic CRL checking because the client can function in offline mode. CRL checking must be done manually.

Clients learn the CDPs for a particular CA because the locations are included in a CDP extension entry in the CA certificate.

You can modify the CDP values in a CA certificate using the Properties window for the Certification Authority. Select the X.509 Extensions tab. Figure 18.9 shows an example.

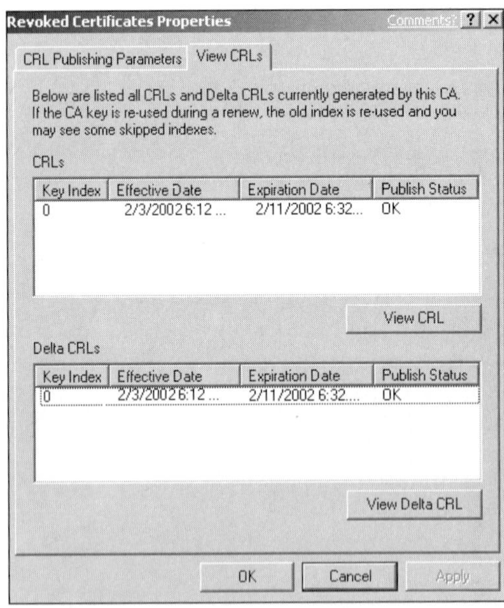

Figure 18.8 CRL certificate showing the revocation list.

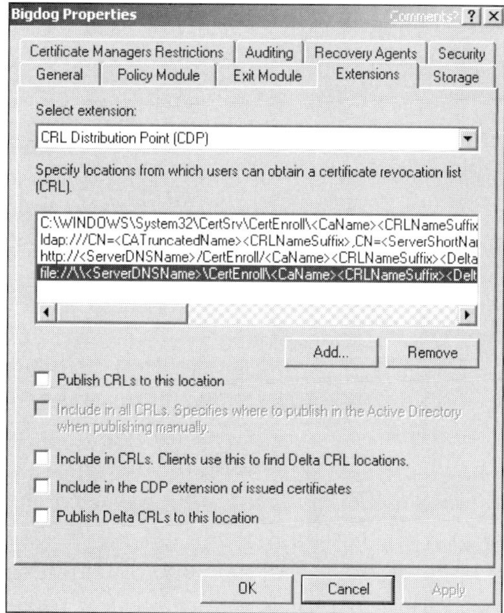

Figure 18.9 Certification Authority properties showing the CDP values used by the CA when storing CRLs.

CRL Publication

A CA *publishes* a CRL to make the list of revoked certificates available to clients. This consists of putting a copy of the CRL in the CDPs where clients can download it. Each CRL has a *publication interval*. Clients cache a CRL for its publication interval. This minimizes traffic to the CA.

You can manually publish a CRL in Windows Server 2003. This is done from the Certification Authority console. Right-click the `Revoked Certificates` container and select ALL TASKS | PUBLISH from the flyout menu. Figure 18.10 shows an example of the Publish CRL window.

A CRL can grow very large if you assign long expiration intervals on the issuing CAs. The most current PKIX RFCs allow for publishing *Delta CRLs*. These contain changes to the base CRL. Servers running Windows Server 2003, Windows Enterprise and Datacenter Editions support publishing Delta CRLs.

The default publication interval for base CRLs is one week. The interval for delta CRLs is one day. You can change the intervals using the Properties window of the `Revoked Certificates` folder. Figure 18.11 shows an example.

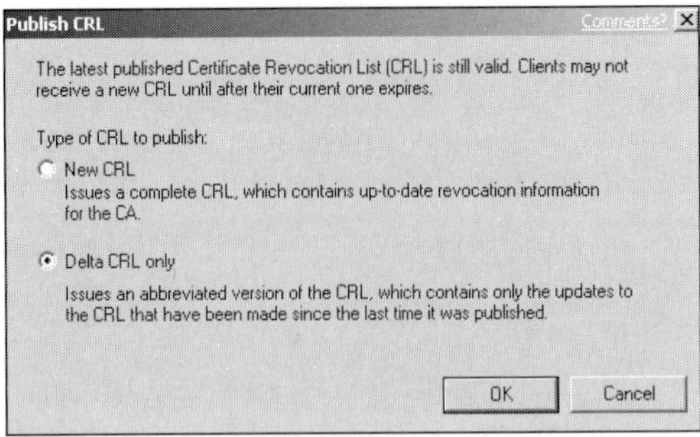

Figure 18.10 Publish CRL window showing full or Delta CRL options.

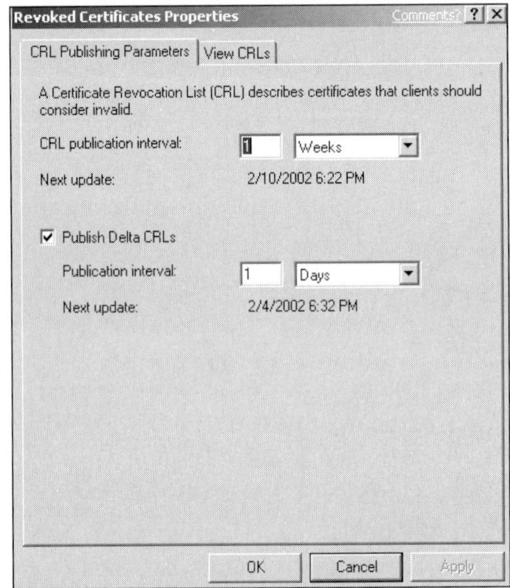

Figure 18.11 Revoked Certificates properties showing publication intervals for CRL and Delta CRL.

After a CRL expires, clients will refuse to honor any certificates issued by the CA until a new CRL is published. You should issue base CRLs infrequently with long publication intervals and then issue Delta CRLs as often as necessary to assure quick revocation of a certificate. For example, a small organization might get away with issuing the base CRL every quarter and Deltas every week. A large organization with thousands or tens of thousands of certificates might issue the base CRL every week and the Delta every day while manually publishing Deltas whenever a new certificate is revoked.

Obtaining CRLs via Windows Update

Microsoft accepts third-party CRLs at the Windows Update site, `windowsupdate.microsoft.com`. This permits PKI vendors to distribute their CRLs when they do not list their CDPs in their CA certificates. Figure 18.12 shows the Windows Update site with selections for software and driver updates.

If a user receives a certificate and the associated CA certificate is not in the client's trusted root store, the crypto system will go to the Windows Update site to check for a copy of the certificate and a copy of the CRL.

All downloads from the Windows Update site are digitally signed by Microsoft to validate their origin. This prevents a third party from redirecting clients to a bogus Windows Update server and fooling them into downloading malicious files.

CA Trusts

When two PKI entities exchange a piece of protected data, such as a digitally signed email message or an encrypted TCP datagram, the entities must have a copy of each other's public keys to decrypt the data or signature. The clients could simply exchange public key certificates, but how could they be sure that the certificate from the other entity is trustworthy?

For instance, picture me at a checkout line in an upscale menswear store. I give the clerk a document, signed by me, attesting to the fact I am shopping for the President of the United States and instructing anyone reading the document to accept my check. The clerk would laugh and call Security.

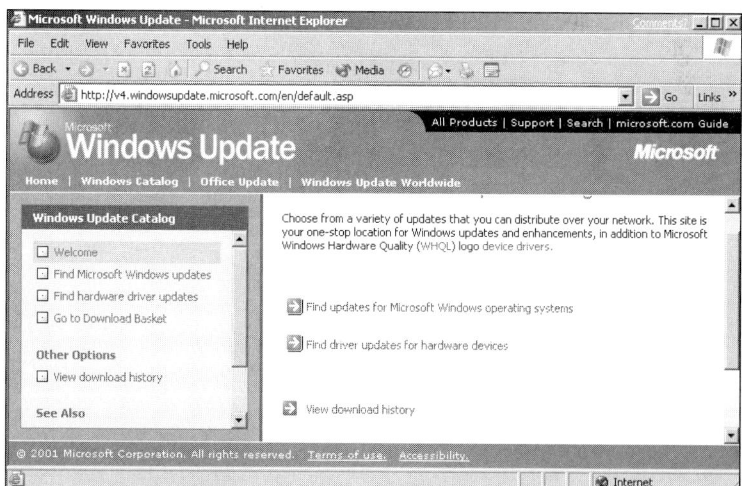

Figure 18.12 Windows Update web site showing various update options.

PKI entities do not implicitly trust certificates issued by end entities, or even by CAs. They must first *trust* the issuing CA. A PKI client trusts a CA if it has a copy of the CA's public key certificate in its local certificate store. It uses the public key in this certificate to verify the digital signature on the certificate offered by end entities.

There is no formal procedure in Windows Server 2003 or XP for obtaining the CA certificate from a trusted CA. Microsoft preloads certificates from quite a few third-party PKI vendors. Certificates can be downloaded via Windows Update. The certificates can be installed using the Signature Wizard when downloading an ActiveX control or installing some other form of digitally signed software. In an Active Directory domain, they can be obtained via group policy.

You can see the trusted certificates stored at a client by using the `Certificates` snap-in. The logical store is under `Trusted Root Certification Authorities | Certificates`. Figure 18.13 shows an example.

Because of the ad hoc nature of trusting CAs, it is important that users use caution when accepting certificates. For instance, when downloading an ActiveX or Java control, a Security Warning window appears to notify the user that the code has been signed and gives the user the opportunity to view the certificate before installing the control. If the user elects the `Always Trust Content From...` option, the CA certificate for the source is added to the trusted certificate store.

Just because code is digitally signed does not necessarily make it safe to install. For example, you may recall an incident in January 2001, when an untrusted party pretending to be a Microsoft engineer obtained two digital signing certificates from Verisign with the name "Microsoft Corporation" as the identifier.

The error was recognized quickly and the certificates were added to Verisign's CRL but unfortunately Verisign does not include a CDP in its certificates. Without a CDP, clients were unable to ascertain the contents of the CRL and would not block acceptance of the fraudulent certificates. Microsoft was forced to use other means to distribute a CRL containing the identifiers for the fraudulent certificates.

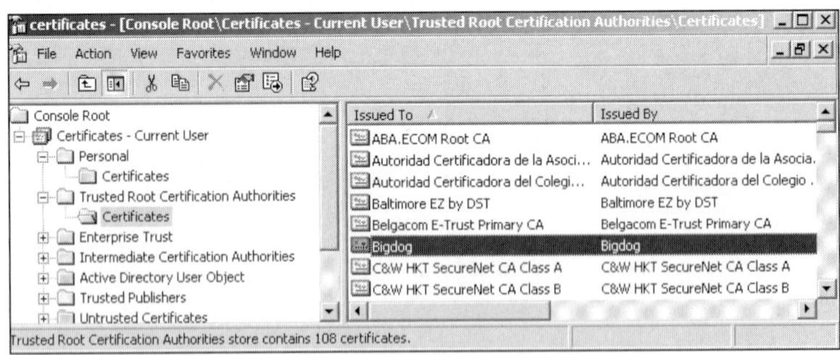

Figure 18.13 Trusted CAs shown in the `Certificates` snap-in.

By the time you read this, the fraudulent certificates will have expired, but this is just one example of a larger lesson. Digital security requires procedural security, as well. Windows Update provides a way for vendors to distribute Certificate Revocation Lists, and it is important to make these available to your clients, either by placing copies in Active Directory or permitting clients to contact the Update site directly.

CA Hierarchies

After a root CA is installed, it can issue CA certificates to other certificate servers, making them *subordinate* CAs. Subordinate CAs can issue CA certificates to other CAs, forming a hierarchy. Another term for this is a *chain of trust*.

The trust chain is included in every certificate issued by any of the CAs. You can view this hierarchy by selecting the `Certification Path` tab in the Certificate properties window (see Figure 18.14).

A strict hierarchy like that shown in the figure is satisfactory for a single organization with a single PKI. To support interaction with outside organizations, you need a way to include the root and subordinate CAs from that organization into your trust hierarchy so that your clients can validate the outside certificates.

This can be done by creating a *cross-trust*. In this configuration, a CA from one hierarchy issues a CA certificate to a CA in another hierarchy. In essence, it designates the outside CA as a subordinate in its own trust chain. Figure 18.15 shows an example of a cross-trust hierarchy.

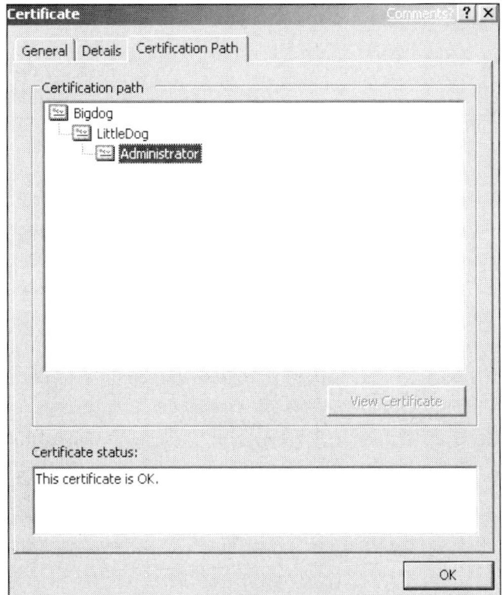

Figure 18.14 `Certificates` snap-in showing `Certification Path` of a subordinate CA.

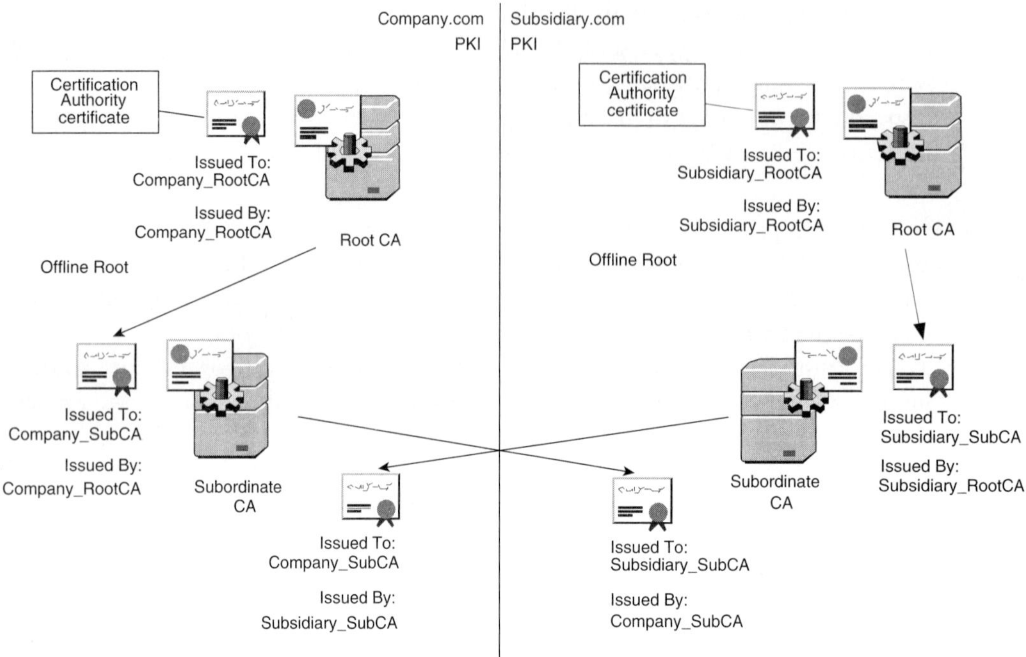

Figure 18.15 Cross-trust hierarchy.

Creating cross-trusts can turn into a complex affair. Any subordinate CA in one organization can create a cross-trust with any subordinate CA in another organization, forming a complex web of trusts and opening the possibility of circularities in the trust chain.

Microsoft and Entrust (Microsoft adopted its PKI from Entrust) once sought to simplify the trust process by the use of *Cross-Trust Lists*, or CTLs. A CTL is a signed set of CA certificate hashes that essentially acts like an electronic good old boy's club. "You can go ahead and trust this other CA," the CTL says. "I've checked him out. He knows the score." Clients who trust a CA would automatically trust a CTL issued by the CA.

Cross-trusts and CTLs share a common deficiency, though. Too much trust is placed on the CAs in the other organization. Any certificates issued by any subordinate CA below the point of the cross-trust would be trusted by entities in your organization.

To address this problem, Microsoft packages together constraints and policy usage extensions in the X.509 standard and uses them to support a feature called *Qualified Subordination*, or QS. Using QS, an administrator can limit the purpose of certificates that will be accepted from subordinate CAs in a cross-trust relationship and also limit the length of the trust chain so that no additional subordinate CAs would be trusted.

Designing a Trust Hierarchy

Figure 18.16 shows a diagram of a typical CA trust hierarchy. When designing a secure CA hierarchy, the first root CA should be an offline Standalone Root. By keeping the root CA off the network, you eliminate the possibility of someone compromising the PKI by obtaining the private key of the root CA. The offline root is used solely to issue CA certificates to subordinate CAs.

The offline root CA cannot be a domain controller, because domain controllers cannot be taken off the wire indefinitely, and it must not be an Enterprise Root because it has no way to communicate to Active Directory. It should be a member server so that it can validate the identity of servers selected to be subordinate CAs.

When you create a Standalone Root CA, elect to do a custom installation and set the key to a full 4096 bits. This takes a while to generate but it makes sure that the CA certificates issued by the root CA are as secure as possible. You won't be using this CA to do production signing, so the long key won't slow performance.

You must also be sure to store the CRL at a location that is not on the root CA itself. Remember that you will be taking the CA offline. Clients must be able to find the CDP to check for CRLs. Select a central location for the CDP and change the path in the Certification Authority properties. The same is true for AIA paths that point at fixed locations rather than Active Directory. Put the certificates in an accessible location and set the AIA paths before issuing any subordinate CA certificates.

The CA just under the offline root should be an Enterprise Subordinate. The subordinate is an Enterprise CA so it can publish its CA public key certificate in Active Directory. To enable this subordinate, you must either put the root CA on the network temporarily or save a PKCS #10 Certificate Request to a file, transport the file to the offline root, generate the CA certificate, and then transport the certificate to the subordinate.

When selecting key size for a subordinate, or issuing, CA, you should use a minimum of a 2048-bit key. A series of white papers published starting in 2002 have demonstrated possible crypto-analytic attacks on RSA keys that could make 1024-bit keys vulnerable over the next few years. Refer to Bruce Schneier's commentary at `www.counterpane.com/crypto-gram-0203.html#6`.

Because the standalone root does not publish its CA certificates in Active Directory, when you install a subordinate CA, you must request certificates from the standalone root via the Web Enrollment tools. For this reason, the standalone root must be running IIS and have a web share that holds the ActiveX controls that handle web enrollment. This web share, called CertSrv, is installed by default when you install Certificate Services.

At this point, you have a two-level hierarchy with root CA kept offline and one or more second-tier CAs. These are called *Issuing CAs*. Large organizations should consider using the second tier of CAs strictly to control policies and installing a third tier for the Issuing CAs. The Policy CAs can be kept offline, as well, for additional security.

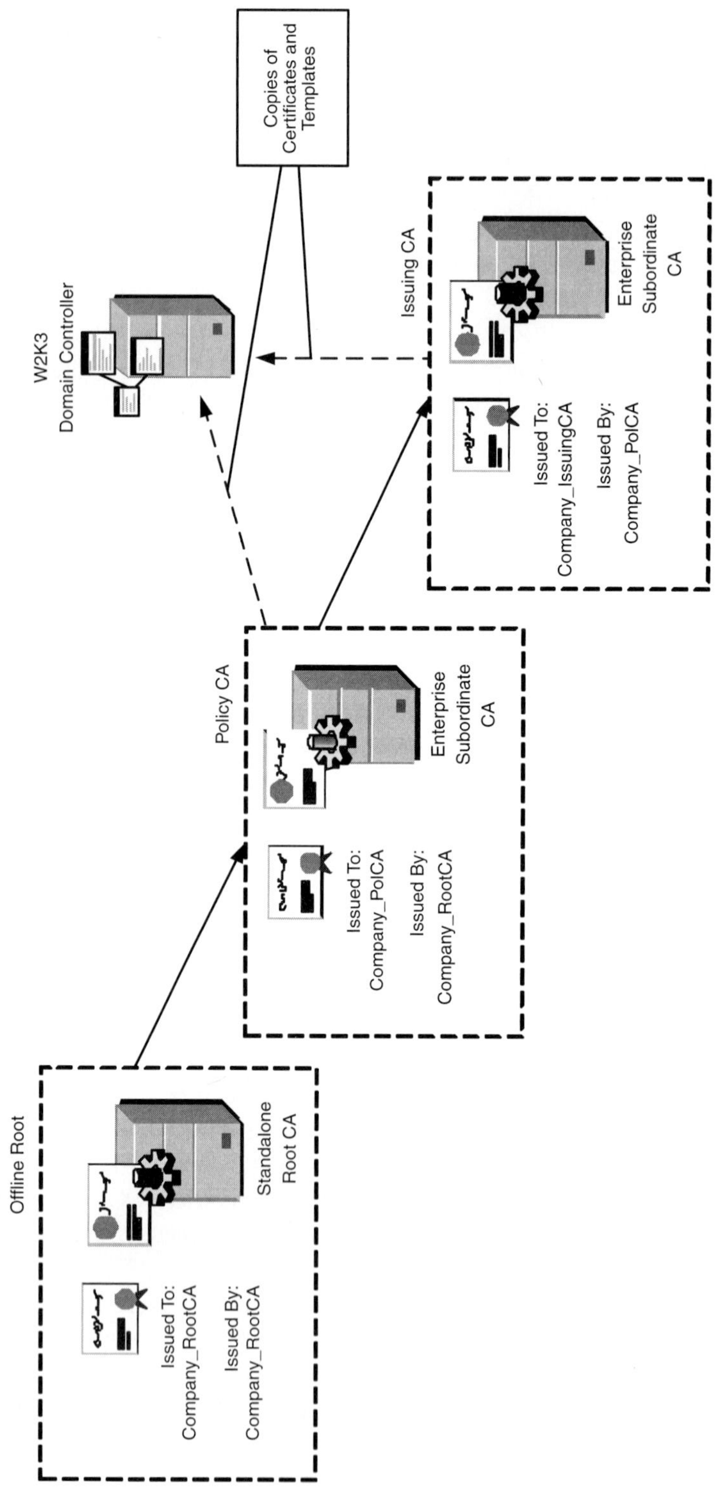

Figure 18.16 CA trust hierarchy.

Permissions Required to Install an Enterprise Subordinate CA

If you install an Enterprise Subordinate CA in a domain other than the root domain in the forest, you must either be a member of the Enterprise Admins group for the forest or you must have domain administrator privileges in the forest root domain.

If you have not logged on with forest administrator privileges, you will only get the option to create a Standalone Root or Standalone Subordinate CA, even though you are at the console of a domain controller in the child domain.

Each CA must be carefully backed up so that a server crash will not result in a loss of the CA. Remember that a CA's name and domain affiliation cannot change.

Installing a Certification Authority

When you've designed your PKI and determined where you want to locate your CA servers, it is time to install the Certificate service on the server that will be your Standalone Root CA. Follow Procedure 18.1.

Procedure 18.1 Installing a Standalone Root CA

1. Launch the `Add/Remove Programs` applet from the Control Panel.
2. Click `Add/Remove Windows Components`.
3. Select `Certificate Services`. You're prompted with a warning that the computer name and domain affiliation cannot change. Click `Yes`.
4. Click `Next`. The CA Type window opens. Select the `Standalone Root CA` radio button (see Figure 18.17).

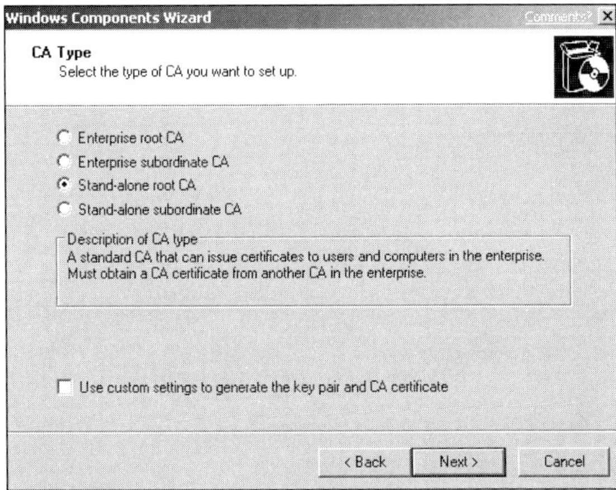

Figure 18.17 CA Type window showing selection of `Standalone Root CA`.

5. Click `Next`. The CA Identifying Information window opens (see Figure 18.18).

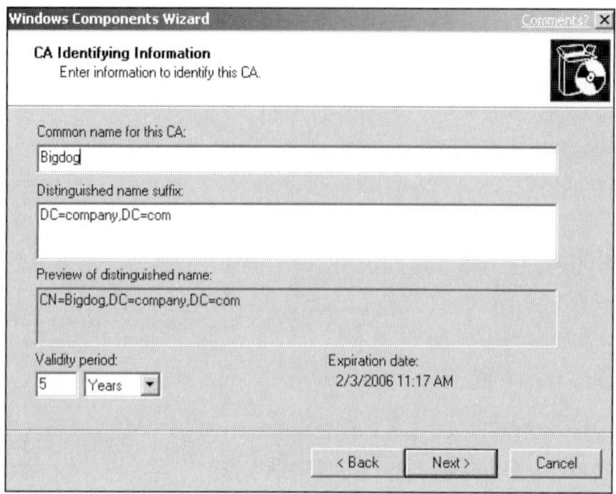

Figure 18.18 CA Identifying Information window.

6. Click `Next`. The Cryptographic Key window opens. The system generates a key and shows a progress bar.
7. After the key has finished generating, the Certificate Database Settings window opens. Ensure that the database and log files are stored on a drive that you can either remove from the machine to keep them offline or on the operating system partition if you will take that drive or the entire server offline.
8. Click `Next`. The system stops IIS temporarily and then installs the service, initializes the CA database, and restarts IIS.

After installing the service, you can use the Certification Authority console to manage the certificates it issues.

Validity Checks

Clients perform validity checks on certificates offered by other PKI entities. The validity checks consist of the following actions:

- **Format check.** The client verifies that the certificate is formatted in accordance with X.509 requirements.
- **Time check.** The client checks the expiration date of the certificate to ensure that it is still in force.

- **Integrity check.** Each certificate contains a hash of the certificate contents encrypted with the CA's private key. The X.509 standard calls this a *signature*; Microsoft (and Entrust) calls this a *thumbprint*. The terms are synonymous. The client performs an integrity check by decrypting the signature using the CA's public key obtained from the trusted CA certificate. The client then hashes the certificate using the same algorithm as the CA and, if the results match, the certificate's integrity is verified.
- **CA hierarchy check.** If the CA that signed a certificate is not directly trusted by the client, the client checks the chain of authority in each CA in the trust hierarchy.
- **Revocation check.** The client refers to Active Directory or a web site or a network share point to determine if an administrator has revoked the certificate of the root CA or any subordinate CAs in the trust list or of the end entity itself.

Of these checks, the most complex is the hierarchy check. This check requires the client to build a chain of trust leading up to the root CA. The simplest way for the client to build this chain is to reference two certificate elements, the *Authority Key Identifier*, or AKI, and the *Subject Key Identifier*, or SKI.

The AKI contains three important pieces of information about the certificate issuer:

- **Issuer's name.** This is the X.500 distinguished name or the UPN of the issuing CA.
- **KeyID.** This is a SHA-1 hash of the CA's public key. It acts as a cross-reference that uniquely identifies the certificate among any others that may have been issued by the same CA to the same end entity.
- **Certificate serial number.** This is a sequence number (usually a sequential integer) assigned by the issuing CA to the certificate.

The SKI designates the end entity to which the certificate was issued. Typically, this extension holds only the KeyID of the public key in the certificate, although it could hold other identifying information.

Authority Information Access (AIA)

When clients do their validity checks, they must be able to locate a copy of the certificate for each CA in the trust chain so they can check the digital signatures. Windows clients first check their local certificate store. If the certificate is not in the local store, they refer to an extension in the certificate called the *Authority Information Access*, or AIA. Figure 18.19 shows an example.

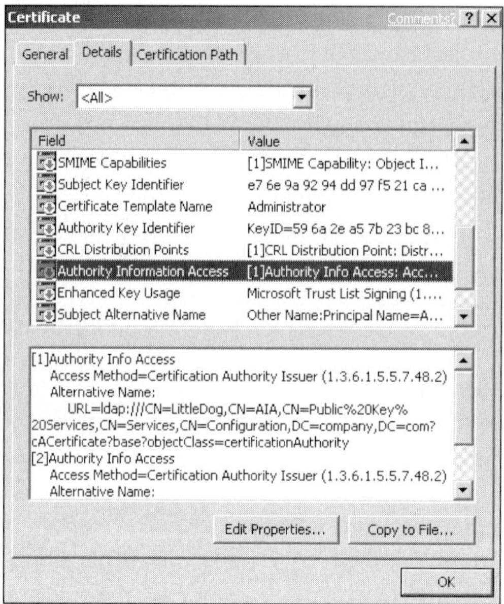

Figure 18.19 AIA contents for an Enterprise CA.

An AIA takes the form of an HTTP URL, ftp site, LDAP (Lightweight Directory Access Protocol) container, or file share where the CA certificate can be obtained. Here is an example entry:

```
[1]Authority Info Access
     Access Method=Certification Authority Issuer(1.3.6.1.5.5.7.48.2)
     Alternative Name:
          URL=ldap:///CN=CA-1,CN=AIA,CN=Public%20Key%20Services,
                      CN=Services,CN=Configuration,DC=company,DC=com

DC=net?cACertificate?base?objectclass=certificationAuthority
[2]Authority Info Access
     Access Method=Certification Authority Issuer(1.3.6.1.5.5.7.48.2)
     Alternative Name:URL=http://server1.company.com/CertEnroll/
                             server1.company.com_CA-1.crt
```

By default, an Enterprise CA puts copies of its CA certificate in a shared `CertEnroll` folder and in Active Directory under `cn=AIA,cn=Public Key Services, cn=Services, cn=Configuration, dc=<domain_name>, dc=<root>`. The `CertEnroll` folder forms a virtual web folder, as well, so clients can use HTTP to get a copy of the certificate.

When a CA is kept offline, the AIA must point at an URL on another server. For PKIs that involve users outside a domain, an AIA typically includes a location on a web server in the DMZ.

Online Certificate Status Protocol

One of the problems with a classic certificate validity check is that every client must hold copies of the certificates for all trusted CAs and intermediate CAs along with their CRLs and Delta CRLs.

You can simplify a PKI by offloading the validation process to a central server. A PKI client would ask this server to validate a certificate and the server would return a thumbs-up or thumbs-down (digitally signed, of course).

This server-based validation mechanism is one of the services provided by the *Online Certificate Status Protocol*, or OCSP. This protocol is documented in Internet Draft draft-ietf-pkix-ocspv2-02.txt, "Online Certificate Status Protocol, version 2." OCSP defines three services:

- **Online Revocation Status.** This check replaces a CRL lookup with a query to the OCSP server. The server must have a copy of the CRL, so this protocol does not eliminate the need for CDPs that are listed in the certificate extensions. It simply offloads the work to a limited number of servers.
- **Delegated Path Validation.** One of the more complex tasks now handled by a PKI client is to validate the path of a certificate. In a fully meshed PKI, it can take a long time to chase down all the potential chaining paths to determine if they are valid. The server performs this once and then stores the result, speeding up query responses to clients.
- **Delegated Path Discovery.** This is a subset of Delegated Path Validation in which the server simply returns the path and the client does the validation.

As you can tell by the lack of an RFC, OCSP is a relatively new protocol. Windows Server 2003 supports it in draft form.

Certificate Enrollment

A CA is a fussily bureaucratic beast. It will not issue certificates to just anyone. A client must submit its certificate request in a special format so that its identity can be quickly and reliably verified before its public key can be incorporated into a signed certificate. This process is called *enrollment*.

The most popular format for submitting enrollment requests is the *PKCS #10 Certification Request*. See RFC 2986, "PKCS #10: Certification Request Syntax Version 1.7," for details about the contents of the request. (Documentation is also available at the RSA web site, `www.rsalabs.com`.) A PKCS #10 certificate request contains the following information:

- **Client's public key.** This is the key the client wants the CA to countersign. Including the public key in clear text is not a problem because the public key was designed to be transmitted in the clear.

- **Client's distinguished name.** This is the client's name in X.500 or LDAP format. For example, the DN of the Verisign trust network is `OU = VeriSign Trust Network, OU = 1998 VeriSign, Inc. - For authorized use only, OU = Class 1 Public Primary Certification Authority - G2, O = VeriSign, Inc., C = US.` An example of a DN for an Active Directory user would be a much less imposing `cn=Jane User,ou=Phoenix,dc=Company,dc=com.`
- **Digital signature.** This is a hash of the certificate request encrypted with the client's private key. The private key itself is never transmitted on the wire. It stays securely situated in the user's local profile.
- **Hash method.** This is the hashing algorithm used to create the digital signature. Microsoft PKI using both MD5 and SHA-1.

When a CA receives a PKCS #10 certification request, it uses the public key in the request to decrypt the digital signature in the request. (Something encrypted with one half of a key pair can only be decrypted with the other half.) If the decryption fails, the CA is forced to assume that a bad guy has intervened and fiddled with the certificate request and the request is discarded.

If the CA can decrypt the digital signature, it then hashes the request using the same algorithm as that used by the client. If the resulting hash matches the hash in the decrypted signature, the user's identity is validated.

The CA then digitally signs the user's public key and incorporates it into an X.509 certificate, which it returns to the client. The client distributes copies of this certificate to other entities for use in encrypting data sent to the client. The other entities, when presented with client's X.509 certificate, validate it by checking the digita signature assigned by the CA.

Certificate Management Messages over CMS (CMC)

For a long time, RSA Security owned the intellectual property rights to PKCS technology, which caused the PKIX working group of the IETF to fork off a separate PKI standard called the *Certificate Management Protocol*, or CMP. This standard is documented in two RFCs: RFC 2510, "Internet X.509 Public Key Infrastructure Certificate Management Protocols," and RFC 2511, "Internet X.509 Certificate Request Message Format."

CMP is much more complex than the RSA key exchange method, but it also provides more features and corrects a couple of hypothetical vulnerabilities. The chief advantage of CMP, from a system administrator's perspective, is its support for the direct involvement of a Registration Authority that can hold copies of private keys in a secure form. In the event that a user loses his private keys, they can be re-issued.

From the vantage point of a crypto professional, CMP is an improvement over RSA because of the nature of the PKI protocols it uses. CMP uses the Cryptographic Message Syntax (CMS) as documented in RFC 2530, "Cryptographic Message Syntax."

Russ Housley and Tim Polk, the developers of CMS and CMP, have proposed a new protocol called *Certificate Management Messages over CMS (CMC)* that combines the best of RSA and CMP to produce a hybrid PKI solution. They document this protocol along with descriptions of the other major PKI components in RFC 2797 and in an outstanding book called *Planning For PKI.*

Windows Server 2003, Enterprise Edition and Datacenter Edition support CMC enrollment for XP and Windows Server 2003 clients and PKCS #10 enrollment for Windows 2000 and other downlevel clients. Windows Server 2003, Standard Edition supports only PKCS #10 enrollment.

Enrollment Functional Description

Windows Server 2003 and XP computers and users automatically enroll when they log on to a domain that contains a Windows Server 2003 Enterprise CA. Windows 2000 users transparently enroll for an EFS certificate when they encrypt a file in a domain with an Enterprise CA. Clients can also use an MMC-based snap-in called `Certificates` to request certificates. Clients that do not have direct access to a CA can enroll via the web. All these methods use an ActiveX control called Xenroll.dll to accomplish the enrollment. Here are details of the transactions.

Auto-Enrollment

Computers and users in a Windows Server 2003 domain are issued certificates automatically via group policies. This is configured using the `Automatic Certificate Request Settings` group policy located under `Computer Configuration | Windows Settings | Security Settings | Public Key Policies`.

The auto-enrollment feature is controlled by an Autoenrollment Settings object at the root of the `Public Key Policies` folder. Figure 18.20 shows the Properties window for this policy.

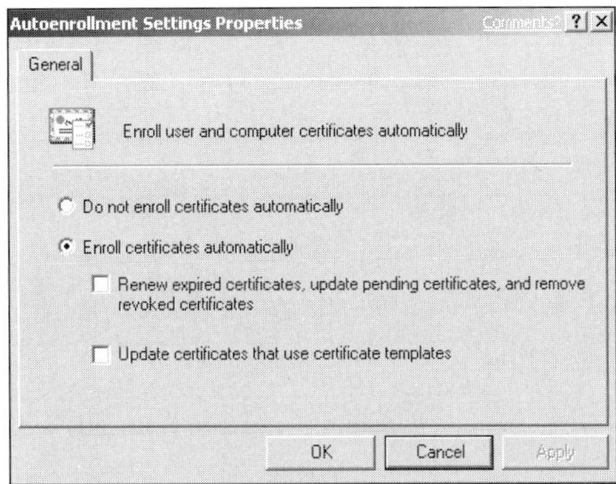

Figure 18.20 `Autoenrollment Settings` policy properties.

The main option for the policy is to `Enroll Certificates Automatically`. You can optionally choose to renew and revoke certificates automatically and you can choose to update certificate template types automatically. The option to update the template type is important in a mixed environment because Windows 2000 clients cannot obtain certificates derived from Version 2 templates through auto-enrollment.

Certificate Enrollment Using the *Certificates* Snap-In

Windows 2000 clients can enroll for a Version 1 certificate using the `Certificates` snap-in. Windows XP and Server 2003 clients can enroll for a Version 2 certificate directly using the `Certificates` snap-in.

For example, you can use the `Certificates` snap-in to obtain an Administrator certificate, which would permit you to do the following:

- Digitally sign a certificate trust list
- Encrypt data
- Encrypt email messages
- Digitally sign messages

To request a new certificate, right-click the `Personal | Certificates` icon in the `Certificates` snap-in and select REQUEST NEW CERTIFICATE from the flyout menu. This opens a Certificate Request Wizard. Select the certificate type from the pick list. Figure 18.21 shows an example.

When the CA issues the certificate, a copy will be stored locally in the user's Registry and another copy stored in the user's Active Directory object.

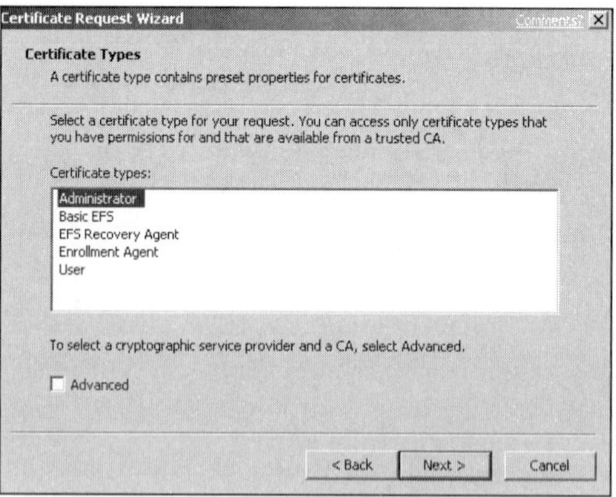

Figure 18.21 Certificate Request Wizard showing list of available certificates.

If you put the focus of the `Certificates` snap-in on the computer rather than the user account when you load it into an MMC console, you can request the domain controller and domain controller email replication certificates required to use SMTP for replication between sites.

Web Enrollment

Any client can request a certificate from a CA by using a web browser. You must be running IIS on your CA and you must install the web request feature. This installs a set of virtual directories that clients use to download the ActiveX control for enrollment, Xenroll, and manages the enrollment process using either classic RSA PKCS #10 or the PKIX standard CMC protocol.

Web enrollment uses a virtual directory called `CertSrv` that points at `Windows\System32\CertSrv`. This directory holds ASP pages and other support files to aid in obtaining a certificate along with copies of the CA certificate for the server. Pending enrollment requests and issued certificates are stored securely in the CA database.

Two other virtual directories support certificate enrollment: `CertEnroll` and `CertControl`. The `CertEnroll` directory holds the Certificate Revocation List (CRL), a digitally signed list of the certificates issued by the CA that are no longer in force. The `CertControl` directory holds the ActiveX controls used for enrolling web clients.

An Enterprise CA server requires users to present domain credentials before permitting them to connect to the CertSrv web site. Standalone servers permit anonymous requests unless specifically configured to disallow them.

An `Advanced` option in the web enrollment process permits you to submit an existing certificate for certification or to request a smart card certificate. To obtain a certificate from a web server, follow Procedure 18.2.

Procedure 18.2 Enrolling for a Certificate Using the Web

1. Connect to the CA via Internet Explorer 5.0 or later. Use the URL `http://<server_name>/certsrv`. You are greeted with a Welcome page that displays the request options (see Figure 18.22). The name of the CA server is displayed in the green bar at the top of the page.
2. Click `Request A Certificate`. The next page lists one certificate option, a User certificate, with an `Advanced Certificate Request` option for obtaining a smart card certificate.
3. Click `User Certificate`. The User Certificate - Identifying Information page opens.
4. Click `Submit`. The CA processes the request then returns a Certificate Issued page.

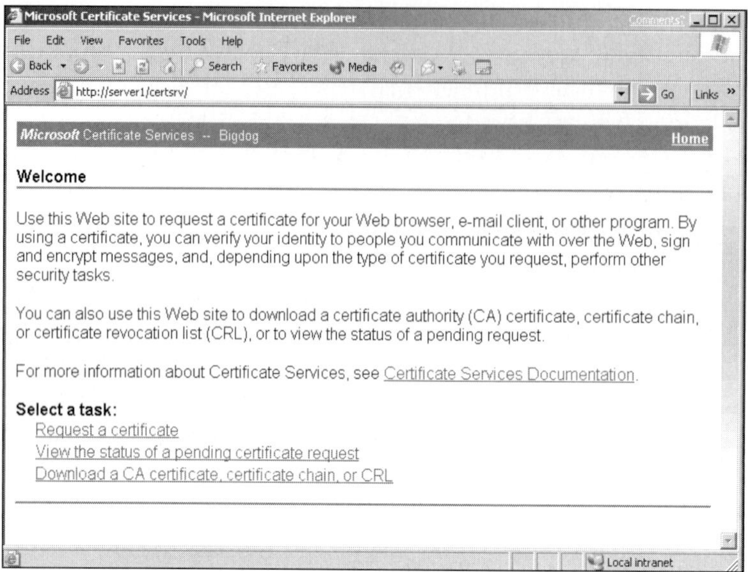

Figure 18.22 Web enrollment Welcome page.

5. Click `Install This Certificate`. When the certificate request has been processed, a Certificate Installed page opens. You can use the `Certificates` snap-in to check for the presence of the certificate.

Key Archival and Recovery

Any front desk clerk at a hotel will tell you that people cannot be totally trusted with keys. They get lost, washed, ironed, or simply left on the wrong side of a door with an automatic lock.

Providing a central repository for replacement keys is a tricky proposition. If this repository were to be compromised, the entire PKI would be useless. Worse than useless, actually, because it may still seem to be reliable as the bad guys plunder the encrypted files and email messages.

Still, the ability to maintain continued access to data in the face of user neglect or mistake makes a secure key repository a highly attractive feature. Standard PKI has defined such a creature. It is called a *Registration Authority*, or RA. For many years, Microsoft has provided a Registration Authority for Exchange users in the form of the Key Management Service, or KMS. This service stores copies of users' mail encryption keys where they can be re-issued, if necessary.

The KMS in Exchange 2000 is an add-on to a Windows 2000 CA. With Windows Server 2003, Microsoft includes a Registration Authority directly in the CA service.

The next version of Exchange will dispense with the KMS and use the Windows Server 2003 RA. In fact, there is even a migration utility to transfer the KMS database to a Windows Server 2003 CA.

The CA can only store encryption keys for re-issue. Digital signature keys cannot be re-issued because that defeats the non-repudiation feature of a signature. If you could store digital signature private keys, a sender accused of sending a malicious message could make the case that it was an administrator with access to the key repository that sent the message.

Key recovery requires the use of an enterprise-level certificate template called `Key Recovery Agent`. For this reason, you cannot do key recovery on a standalone CA. Only Enterprise CAs have access to templates. Also, by default, only Domain Admins or Enterprise Admins have access to the `Key Recovery Agent` template. This is controlled by permissions on the template in Active Directory. You can access the template via the AD Sites and Services console with the VIEW | SERVICES NODE option enabled. The template object is located in `Services | Public Key Services | Certificate Templates`. Change the permissions on the template to permit other administrative groups to issue Key Recovery certificates.

Key recovery is not enabled by default. In fact, enabling key recovery turns out to be a relatively complicated process, much more so than it should be. Here are the stages:

- Create a Key Recovery Agent. This account is issued a certificate authorizing it to generate and certify public/private key pairs on behalf of users. Recall that the normal key certification process requires that the user account generate the key pair then request certification for the public key.
- Configure a CA to archive keys and to permit key recovery.
- Issue a new template that will be used in lieu of the standard User template for generating archival certificates.

Create a Key Recovery Agent

Configuring a CA to issue Recovery Agent certificates involves loading the `Key Recovery Agent` template from the template cache in Active Directory into the template cache at the CA. You then use this template to issue a certificate to the Key Recovery account you have selected. Use the steps in Procedure 18.3 to create a Key Recovery Agent.

Procedure 18.3 Creating a Key Recovery Agent

1. Open the `Certification Authority` console.
2. Right-click `Certificate Templates` and select `New | Certificate Template to Issue`. The Enable Certificate Templates window opens (see Figure 18.23).

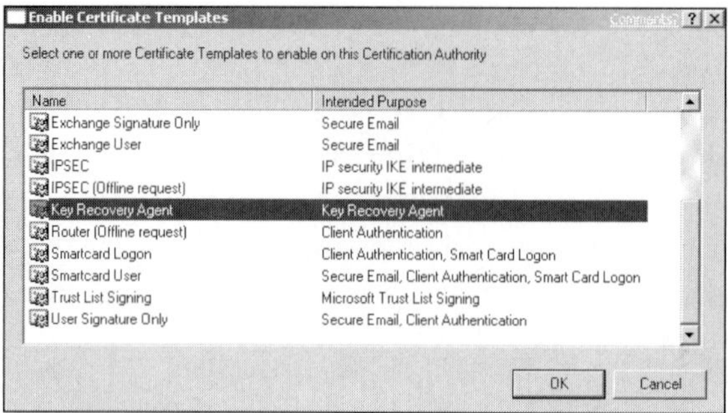

Figure 18.23 Enable Certificate Templates window showing the `Key Recovery Agent` template.

3. Click `OK` to load the template. It now appears in the right pane of the Certification Authority console.
4. Log on at the workstation you will use for Key Recovery using the account you have selected as the Key Recovery Agent.
5. Open the `Certificates` snap-in and expand the tree to Personal | Certificates.
6. Right-click the Certificates icon and select New | Request New Certificate from the flyout menu. The Certificate Request Wizard starts.
7. Click `Next`. The Certificate Types window opens. Select `Key Recovery Agent`.
8. Click `Next`. The Certificate Friendly Name and Description window opens.
9. Click `Next`. A summary window opens.
10. Click `Finish` to complete the transaction and close the wizard. You get a message that the request was received by the CA and the certificate will be issued when approved by the Certificate Manager.
11. In the Certification Authority console, select the `Pending Requests` icon. The certificate request is displayed in the right pane.
12. Right-click the certificate request icon and select All Tasks | Issue from the flyout menu. The certificate now appears under the Issued Certificates icon.

Configure a CA to Archive Certificates

The Key Recovery Agent is now prepared. The next stage is to configure the CA to archive certificates. Follow the steps in Procedure 18.4.

Procedure 18.4 Configuring a CA to Archive Certificates

1. In the Certification Authority console, right-click the server icon and select PROPERTIES from the flyout menu.
2. Select the `Recovery Agents` tab in the Properties window (see Figure 18.24).

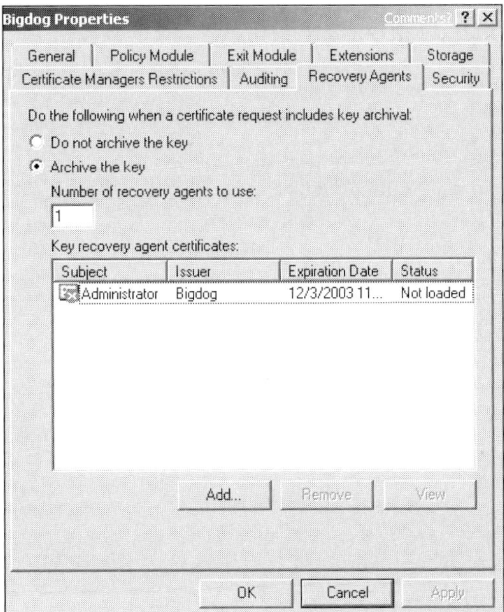

Figure 18.24 CA Properties window showing Recovery Agents tab.

3. Select the `Archive The Key` radio button.
4. Under the `Key Recovery Agents` field, click `Add`. The Key Recovery Agent Selection window opens, listing the account to whom you just issued a Key Recovery Agent certificate.
5. Click `OK` to load the agent into the list. The agent icon has a red X in it and the `Status` shows as `Not Loaded`.
6. Click `OK` to initialize key recovery. You'll be prompted to stop and restart the CA service. Do so.
7. When the service restarts, verify that the agent status shows `Valid`.

Create Archive Template

The CA is now ready to archive keys. The next stage is to create a template that can be used to issue archival keys and to load this template into the CA. Follow the steps in Procedure 18.5.

Procedure 18.5 Creating an Archive Template

1. In the Certification Authority console, load the `Certificate Templates` snap-in by right-clicking the `Certificate Template` icon and selecting MANAGE from the flyout menu.
2. Select the User template icon. At this point, the icon is dimmed.
3. Right-click the icon and select DUPLICATE TEMPLATE from the flyout menu. A Properties window opens for a copy of the `Recovery Agent` template (see Figure 18.25).

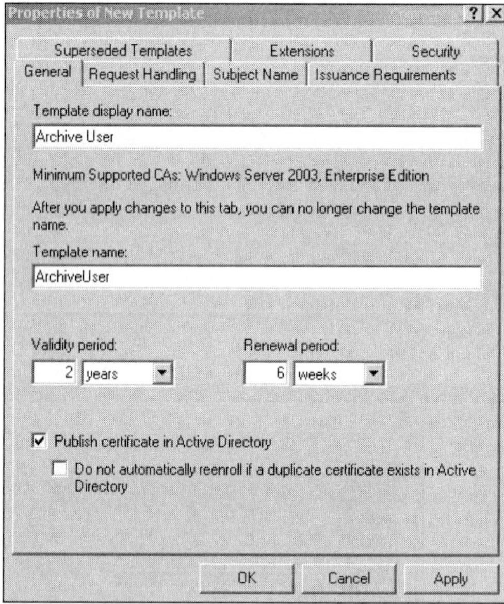

Figure 18.25 Properties window for copy of `User` template showing `General` tab.

4. Change the `Template Display Name` to `Archive User`. The `Template Name` will change automatically.
5. Select the `Publish Certificate In Active Directory` option.
6. Select the `Request Handling` tab (see Figure 18.26).

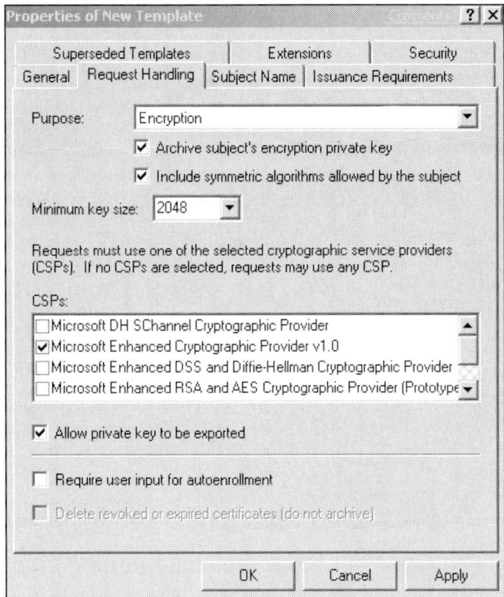

Figure 18.26 Properties window for copy of `User` template showing `Request Handling` tab.

7. Select the `Archive Subject's Encryption Private Key` option.
8. Select the `Allow Private Key to be Exported` option.
9. Select the `Issuance Requirements` tab.
10. De-select the `CA Certificate Manager Approval` option. This permits the CA to issue the certificate without the intervention of an administrator.
11. Click `OK` to initialize the new template. The icon appears in the Templates console in full color.
12. Close the `Templates` snap-in.
13. In the Certification Authority console, press F5 to refresh.
14. Right-click `Certificate Templates` and select NEW | CERTIFICATE TEMPLATE TO ISSUE from the flyout menu. The Enable Certificate Templates window opens.
15. Select the `Archive User` icon and click `OK`. The icon now appears in the list of available certificates.
16. To make sure you can tell the difference between standard certificates and archived certificates, enable the Archived Key column in the console by highlighting the `Issued Certificates` icon then selecting VIEW | ADD/REMOVE COLUMNS | ARCHIVED KEY from the main console menu.

At this point, you can request an Archive User certificate using the `Certificates` snap-in at a client desktop. Use the procedure in the section, "Certificate Enrollment Using the `Certificates` Snap-In."

Recover an Archived Certificate

If a user loses a private encryption key, recover the key from the CA using the steps in Procedure 18.6.

Procedure 18.6 Recovering a Lost Key

1. Open the `Certification Authority` console.
2. Under the `Issued Certificates` icon, locate the certificate for the key you want to re-issue. There should be a `Yes` in the Archive Key column, indicating that the certificate is recoverable.
3. Double-click the certificate icon to open the Properties window.
4. Select the `Details` tab and write down the serial number of the certificate (see Figure 18.27) or take a screen shot by using Alt+PrintScrn and then pasting into Mspaint and printing. There are 20 numerals in the serial number. Don't use spaces.
5. From a command prompt, use the CERTUTIL utility to extract the key to an output file, called a *blob* file, as follows:

```
certutil -getkey <serial_number> <blob_file>
```

Figure 18.27 Properties window for a certificate showing the `Details` tab that lists the serial number of the certificate.

6. This blob file contains the private key in PKCS #7 format. You must now convert this file to a PFX file (any name with a `.pfx` extension) so you can transport it to the user's desktop. Do this with the CERTUTIL utility as follows:

```
certutil -recoverkey -f <blob_file> <pfx_file>
```

7. When prompted for a password, assign a strong password to the file. You will need this password when importing the key at the user's desktop.
8. Transport the PFX file to the user's desktop then log on as the user and double-click the file in Explorer. This launches the Certificate Import Wizard.
9. Use the Wizard to place the key in the user's personal store. Verify using the `Certificates` snap-in that the key is in place.

This completes the recovery procedure.

Command-Line PKI Tools

The Certification Authority console provides the most convenient place to manage a CA trust hierarchy. There are several command-line tools in the Resource Kit that have functionality that is not present in the MMC console.

CERTUTIL

This utility allows you to dump, view, and manage certificates and CRLs issued by any CA over which you have administrative rights. You can also manage the CA database. Run `certutil /?` to get a list of switches and their functions.

For example:

```
C:\>certutil -verify server1.windomain.net_server1.crt
Issuer:
    CN=PolicyCA-1
    O=Windomain
    L=Phoenix
    S=AZ
    C=US
    E=administrator@windomain.ent
Subject:
    CN=Server1
    O=Windomain
    L=Phoenix
    S=AZ
    C=US
    E=administrator@windomain.net
Cert Serial Number: 611227e4000000000003
Revocation check passed
```

DSSTORE

This utility gives you a bit more control over the CA database than CERTUTIL. One particularly aggravating part of using DSSTORE is that some of the parameters are case sensitive. For example, here is a display listing of a CA root certificate. (The typeful name components—DN, CN, and DC—must be in upper case):

```
C:\>dsstore -display DC=windomain,DC=net
>>>>>>> CA Object # 0 <<<<<<<
DN: CN=EnterpriseRootCA,CN=Certification Authorities,CN=Public Key Services,
➥CN=Services,CN=Configuration,DC=windomain,DC=net

Cert #0
Issuer  :: EnterpriseRootCA
Subject :: EnterpriseRootCA
SHA5 HASH: A7180DE4 81036013 07F630F7 B1A3B8B5 DB1AA67B
```

Here is a DSSTORE listing of all the information for a CA:

```
C:\>dsstore -tcainfo
CA Name: EnterpriseRootCA ==============================
Machine Name: server4.windomain.net
DS Location: CN=EnterpriseRootCA,CN=Enrollment Services,CN=Public Key
➥Services,CN=Services,CN=Configuration,DC=windomain,DC=net
:: Supported Certificate Templates ::
EFSRecovery
EFS
DomainController
WebServer
Machine
User
SubCA
Administrator
::::::::::::::::::::::::::::::::::
CT #1    :   EFS Recovery Agent
CT #2    :   Basic EFS
CT #3    :   Domain Controller
CT #4    :   Web Server
CT #5    :   Computer
CT #6    :   User
CT #7    :   Subordinate Certification Authority
CT #8    :   Administrator
#CTs from enum: 8
Cert DN: CN=EnterpriseRootCA, O=Windomain, L=Phoenix, S=AZ, C=US,
➥E=administrator@windomain.net
```

Certmgr

This GUI-based utility from the Platform SDK is a different way to view the contents of certificate store than the `Certificates` snap-in. Run it at any machine where you want to see the certificates. Figure 18.28 shows an example of the selection window.

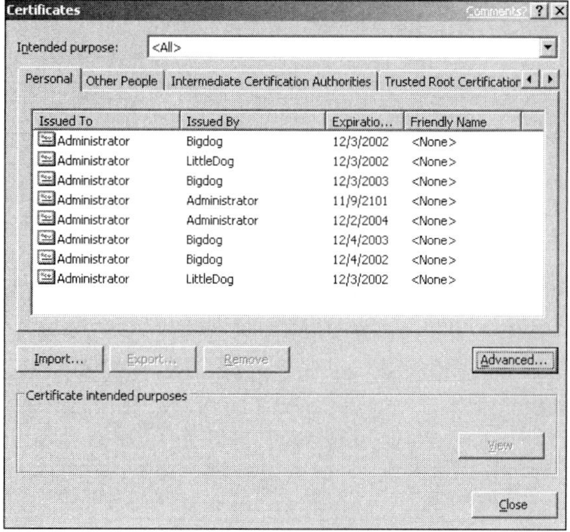

Figure 18.28 Certmgr utility showing selection window.

Signcode

This GUI-based utility from the Platform SDK lets you add a signing certificate to executables and DLLs. This is a great way to sign in-house applications as well as to prepare legacy drivers that do not have a digital signature as required to get the Windows 2000 logo.

Moving Forward

We're nearing the end of our enterprise deployment of Windows Server 2003. About all that's left to do is to configure the operating environment for our desktops and to accommodate our traveling users by providing dial-up and VPN solutions. Those operations are covered in the next two chapters.

19 Managing the User Operating Environment

THE DEFINING CHARACTERISTIC OF THE WINDOWS SERVER 2003 and XP operating environment is the new look-and-feel. Like a shape-changer in X Files, the Explorer shell has morphed into a lively but orderly place. The default desktop is clean except for the Recycle Bin. The Start menu has gained weight but the contents are more highly structured. The icons have changed from the silly-looking caricatures in Windows 2000 to attractive, modern graphics. Best yet, the entire interface can be replaced faster than Madonna changes singing styles.

You may find the new shell somewhat irritating because familiar items are in new places. If the new interface has no benefit for you, you can change it back to the classic interface with no loss of functionality.

The important changes run deeper than the glitzy façade of the new shell. There are new ways of handling executables and DLLs, new application migration and compatibility options, and a host of new terminal services features. Rather than spend a lot of time on the interface, this chapter covers elements of the operating environment that affect administration. The topics include the following:

- Side-by-Side assemblies
- User state migration
- Application compatibility
- Folder redirection and home directories
- Offline files
- Remote Desktop operations, including Remote Assistance

Classic Look and Help Files

The online Help utility, now called the Help and Support Center, often assumes that you have the new interface loaded, so the instructions can be a little difficult to follow in a classic environment. If necessary, you can shift to the new look, figure out what the Help file is trying to tell you, and then shift back to the classic look.

New Features in Windows Server 2003

From a server and desktop management point of view, Windows Server 2003 has several important new operational features:

- **Side-by-Side assemblies.** In an ongoing effort to avoid compatibility problems between different releases of the same DLL, Microsoft included a new feature in Windows Server 2003 and XP called *Side-by-Side assemblies*. This feature permits a single DLL name to represent multiple versions, a sort of Jekyll-and-Hyde approach to application management.
- **User profile migration.** Windows 2000 Service Pack 2 contained a feature called the User State Migration Toolkit, or USMT. An updated version of the toolkit ships with Windows Server 2003 and XP. This version enables you to transfer profile and application configuration settings between machines running any flavor of Explorer-based Windows. There is also a wizard-based tool for doing individual state migrations.
- **Remote Desktop Protocol (RDP) improvements.** The terminal services environment is now present in desktops as well as servers. A new version of RDP helps to make remote access quick and flexible. There is now support for 24-bit color depth, device redirection, hot key functionality within a session, and direct access to the console of a server or desktop.
- **Fast user switching.** This feature, an extension of terminal services, permits multiple users to run independent sessions at the console of a standalone XP desktop. This simplifies management of non-domain kiosk machines and small workgroup environments.
- **Remote Assistance.** A user can "invite" another user to share a console session, either to perform maintenance or to explain an operation. The invitation requirement prevents arbitrary prowling of user's desktops.
- **Unresponsive application handling.** If an application stops communicating with the operating system, the traditional way to kill it has been to use Task Manager or the KILL utility in the Resource Kit. In Windows Server 2003 and XP, the title bar menu for an application window remains responsive even if the application inside the window becomes autistic. This enables you to use the `Close` option from the title bar menu to kill the application.

- **User privileges.** The default NTFS permissions in Windows Server 2003 significantly restrict the ability of a user to access files in the system folder. This helps preserve the integrity of the operating system.

Side-by-Side Assemblies

RAM has historically been an expensive commodity, so Microsoft has always designed Windows to be frugal with memory. (Well, if not frugal, at least to gobble it with something less than the conspicuous consumption of a Roman Caesar.)

One way of conserving memory is to share the image of a DLL loaded by one process with other processes. This DLL sharing can cause no end of headaches, as I'm sure you're aware. For instance, a DLL installed by an application might be a version that lacks a function used by another application. If the second application launches after the first, it links to the DLL image that's already in memory. When it makes the ill-fated call to the missing function, the result is generally not pretty. It could be a "Dr. Watson" error or a general protection fault or even a bugcheck (Blue Screen of Death).

Nowadays, memory is much less expensive and reliability is much more important, so Microsoft is trying to reverse course on DLL handling to permit loading multiple versions of the same DLL. This uses more memory and disk space but it reduces compatibility errors.

Microsoft uses the term *assembly* to refer to common blocks of code such as DLLs. An assembly designed to run with multiple versions is called a *Side-by-Side (SxS) assembly*. Only two DLLs in Windows Server 2003 and XP are SxS assemblies:

- Shell Common Controls version 6.0 (Comctl32.dll)
- GDI Plus version 1.0 (Gdiplus.dll)

Two DLLs may not seem like much of a revolution, but these two are used by many applications and are potential sources of compatibility problems thanks to the use of *themes* in the new interface. By permitting a previous version of these two DLLs to run at the same time, applications are much less likely to experience compatibility issues. Look for an expansion of the number of SxS assemblies in future versions of Windows.

Local Images

An earlier multiple-version DLL workaround is still supported in Windows Server 2003. This workaround lets you flag an executable so that it loads its DLLs from its own directory instead of somewhere else in the path.

Local loading is enabled by building a zero-byte file with the same name as the executable but with a .local extension. For example, an executable with the name Zanzibar.exe would have a local DLL flag file of Zanzibar.exe.local.

When the operating system sees the .local extension, it loads any linked libraries from the same folder, if they reside there. Otherwise, it links to the images of the DLLs in memory, if they are already loaded.

An XML file called a *manifest* defines how an executable treats an SxS assembly. The manifest file sits in the same directory as the associated executable. It has the same name as the executable with a *.manifest* extension. The File Migration Wizard, Migwiz.exe, is an example of an application that uses an SxS assembly. It makes calls to the Common Controls library.

User State Migration

Users invest a lot of time and creative ingenuity in their local desktops. They also put quite a bit of effort into circumventing rules about where to save their files. When the time comes to migrate the user's desktops, the biggest challenge is to preserve their data and settings while implementing the new operating system and any new applications you're deploying at the same time.

Ordinarily, a deployment consists of three stages:

- Collect the user data and copy it to a server.
- Wipe the desktop drive and image it with the new operating system (OS).
- Transfer the user data back to the desktop.

Microsoft provides two tools that simplify the migration considerably:

- **Files and Settings Transfer Wizard (FSTW).** This tool consists of an executable, Migwiz, and a set of INF files that determine what is to be migrated and where to migrate it. FSTW is intended to be used for standalone machines or individual users.
- **User State Migration Toolkit (USMT).** This tool consists of two executables, Scanstate and Loadstate, and the same INF files used by FSTW. This tool is intended to be used in domain environments for migrating multiple users simultaneously.

Let's start by examining the INF scripts that are used to evaluate applications during a migration.

User Migration INF Files

Both the FSTW and the USMT use a suite of four INF files that act as migration scripts. Here's a quick list followed by a detailed look at the function of each file:

- Migapp.inf
- Miguser.inf
- Migsys.inf
- Sysfiles.inf

Migapp.inf

This script contains applications and their associated Registry entries and support files. It defines the following operations for a given application:

- The presence of the application in the Registry
- The prescribed environment for the application
- A set of instructions such as copying files to new locations and making new Registry entries

Table 19.1 lists the applications included in Migapp.inf. You can add more if you have third-party applications that aren't listed or in-house applications you want to automate during migration.

Table 19.1 Applications Included in Default Migapp.inf

Acrobat Reader 4.0	Acrobat Reader 5.0
Adobe Photoshop Suite 6	Adobe ImageReady 3
MM JukeBox 6	MSN Explorer 10
MS Netmeeting 3	MS MediaPlayer 7
MS Messenger 3.6	MS Money 2001
MS Movie Maker 1	CmdExe
CuteFTP 4	Yahoo Messenger
AIM	ICQ
GameVoice 1	RogerWilco
BattleCom	GoZilla
Microsoft Office	Office XP
Microsoft Office 97	NetscapeCommunicator
PSTPAB	Eudora 5
GetRight 4	Lotus Suitestart 99
Odigo	Prodigy Internet
Quicken 2001	QuickTime Player 5
RealJukebox 2 Basic	RealPlayer 8 Basic
Sonique	WinAmp
WinZip	Microsoft Works 2001
WordPerfect Office 2000	WsFTPLE5
MSN Zone 6	Quicken2001HAndB

Here is a listing of the entries for Quicken to give you an idea of what the script does:

```
[Quicken 2001.Environment]
QuickenDir=Registry, HKLM\SOFTWARE\Microsoft\Windows\CurrentVersion\App
➥Paths\QW.EXE [Path]

[Quicken 2001.Detect]
File, %QuickenDir%\QW.EXE, VERSION("ProductVersion","010.*")

[Quicken 2001.Instructions]
copyfilesex=Quicken 2001 CopyfilesEx
forcesrcfile=Quicken 2001 ForceSrcFile

[Quicken 2001 CopyfilesEx]
%QuickenDir%\QDATA.QSD,%QuickenDir%
%QuickenDir%\QW.CFG,%QuickenDir%
%QuickenDir%\QW.RMD,%QuickenDir%

[Quicken 2001 ForceSrcFile]
%QuickenDir%\QW.CFG
%QuickenDir%\QW.RMD
```

Miguser.inf

The Miguser.inf script includes user configuration settings in the Registry and the user profile that need to be copied to the new machine during the migration. Table 19.2 lists the default items in Miguser.inf.

Table 19.2 User Settings Included in Migration Scan

User Settings	Desktop Items
Shared Desktop Items	Start Menu Items
Shared Start Menu Items	My Documents
Shared Documents	My Pictures
Favorites	

Here is a sample of the actions taken on a portion of the user profile:

```
[Desktop Items.Detect]
Directory,%csidl_desktopdirectory%,EXISTS

[Desktop Items.Instructions]
ForceDestFile=ForceDestDesktop
CopyFilesFiltered=CopyDesktopFiles

[ForceDestDesktop]
%csidl_desktopdirectory%\desktop.ini

[CopyDesktopFiles]
dir=%csidl_desktopdirectory%\*
```

Migsys.inf

This script determines how to migrate operating system files and settings. Table 19.3 lists the system files that are included in the script. You can add others.

Table 19.3 System Files and Configuration Items Included in Migsys.inf

Fonts	Accessibility
Mouse and Keyboard	Internet Explorer
Favorites	Telephony
Ras Connections	International
Multimedia	Outlook Express
WAB	Screen Saver
Display	Task Bar
Folder Options	Wallpapers
Desktop Icons	
Appearance	

Here is a sample of the actions defined by the script for RAS connections to give you an idea of what the script does:

```
[Ras Connections]
AddReg = Ras.AddReg

[Ras.AddReg]
HKR\RemoteAccess\Profile\*

[Ras Connections.9X]
CopyFilesEx=RasCopy9X

[RasCopy9X]
%windir%\usmt.pbk,%CSIDL_APPDATA%\Microsoft\Network\Connections\Pbk,RasPhone.PBK

[Ras Connections.Environment.NT.Windows NT4]
RasUserFile = Registry, HKR\Software\Microsoft\RAS Phonebook [PersonalPhonebookFile]

[Ras Connections.NT.Windows NT4]
CopyFilesEx=RasCopyNT4
```

For the most part, there isn't much in this script that can be tailored. You may have specific settings in a system file that you want to migrate.

Sysfiles.inf

This script contains a list of operating system configuration files that require translation or special handling. Each operating system includes settings for all localized versions, such as French, Italian, German, Spanish, Chinese, Japanese, and so forth. The script also contains extensions for various files and their meanings and places to scan for them. Table 19.4 lists the operating systems included in the scan.

Table 19.4 Operating Systems Included in Sysfiles.inf

Windows 95	Windows 95 OSR2
Windows 95 OSR2.5	Windows 98
Windows 98 Second Edition	Microsoft Netmeeting
MMC 1.0 files	Windows ME
NT4	Windows 2000

Using the Files and Settings Transfer Wizard

The FSTW executable is Migwiz. The executable and support scripts are stored in `\Windows\System32\USMT`. The Windows Server 2003 CD has a copy of Migwiz and the support files that you can use to perform the data collection portion of FSTW at 9x/ME/NT4 machines. The Autorun screen on the CD lists the migration wizard under `Perform Additional Tasks` (see Figure 19.1).

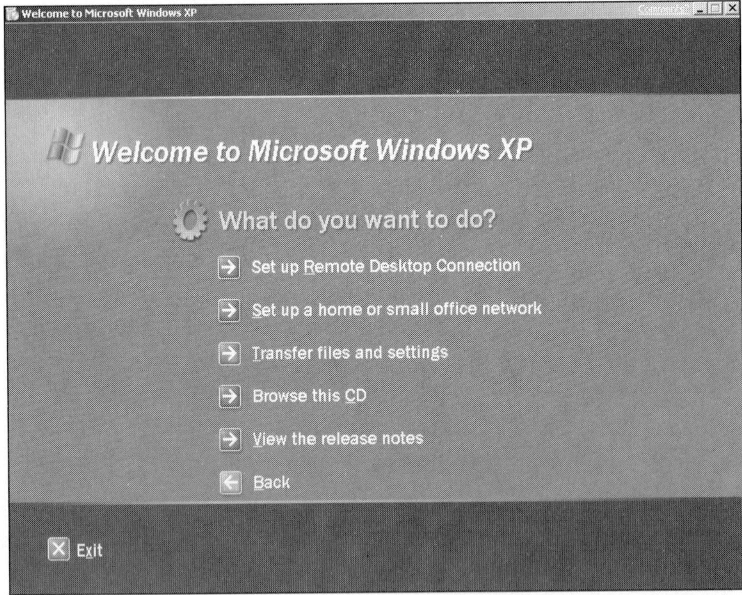

Figure 19.1 Additional options from the Windows Server 2003 CD.

The FSTW performs the migration in two phases. During Phase 1, you run the wizard at the existing machine to analyze and collect the Registry entries and files. This can take a long time, depending on the number of files you have. Plan on 30 to 90 minutes. The user should not access the machine during this time.

The wizard builds an enormous DAT file that contains the migration information. The wizard offers four ways to transfer the migration file to the new machine:

- **Home network.** This option permits you to transfer the files directly over the network. This option requires running the Home Networking Wizard to configure the machine. Most organizations with existing networks will not need to perform this evolution.
- **Other.** This saves the files to a folder where they can be transported by any means at your disposal, such as a Zip drive or by burning a CD or copying across the network. This is the option of choice for an organization with an existing network.
- **Floppy or removable media.** Users without a network can save the migration files to a floppy or Zip or Orb drive. Depending on the amount of user data on the drive, you might need a *lot* of floppies.
- **Direct Cable.** This is for users who do not have a network and do not want to use a stack of floppies for the transfer. The disadvantages of this method is its slowness and the fact that it calls for a certain degree of sophistication on the part of the user to choose the right type of serial cable and connect it correctly.

During Phase 2, you run the wizard at the new machine. When you are prompted with the message, `Do You Have a Windows XP CD?`, select `I Don't Need the Wizard Disk`. The wizard then knows you are in Phase 2 and prompts for the location of the migration files. Point the wizard at the file location and then sit back and wait for it to make the changes. This also takes a while.

If the wizard encounters a critical error, it will post an HTML page describing the nature of the problem. It also saves a log file in your user profile under `Local Settings\Application Data`. The `Local Settings` folder is hidden, so make sure you turn on hidden files before searching for it.

USMT

The User State Migration Toolkit (USMT) performs a similar function as the Files and Settings Transfer Wizard (FSTW) but it permits scripting the operations so you can run the migrations wholesale rather than retail. USMT only works with domain member computers. For standalone computers, use the FSTW.

USMT uses the same set of INF scripts used by the Files and Settings Transfer Wizard. Instead of the Migwiz executable, though, USMT uses two command-line executables:

- **Scanstate.** This compares the contents of the drive and Registry with settings in the INF scripts and builds a migration script.
- **Loadstate.** This takes the contents of the INF script built by Scanstate and applies it to a target machine.

There are several advantages to using USMT versus FSTW. One is the size of the migration file. Instead of building a big, unwieldy binary DAT file like FSTW, Scanstate builds a text-based INF script with folders that contain the files it needs to copy to the target machine. Scanstate also runs much, much faster than FSMW.

Here is the syntax for Scanstate. The entries should all be on one line:

```
scanstate <location> /c /v:7 /l:usmt.log /i:miguser.inf /i:migapp.inf
➥/i:migsys.inf /i:sysfiles.inf
```

Here are the meanings of the Scanstate switches:

- **`<location>`.** This is the location where you want Scanstate to save the migration files. You'll need 100MB to 150MB depending on how many user files are on the machine. This can be a network drive.
- **`/c`.** Skips errors involving long filenames. The skipped files are logged in Longfile.log.
- **`/v`.** This is a "verbose" switch. There are seven levels of verbosity, with 7 being the most verbose. I always use the 7 setting. If something goes wrong, I want to see everything about the failure in the logs.
- **`/l`.** The name of the log file to hold errors and other messages. I usually use the name Usmt.log.
- **`/i`.** Identifies the INF script to use for state collection. As you can see, you can specify more than one INF script. Specify all four INF scripts if you want to migrate system, application, and user settings.

Scanstate builds a fairly hefty INF file called Migration.inf plus a folder hierarchy that contains any files identified during the scan. Copy these files to the target machine and then run Loadstate with this syntax (the entries should be on one line):

```
loadstate <location> /v:7 /l:usmtload.log  /i:miguser.inf /i:migapp.inf
➥/i:migsys.inf /i:sysfiles.inf
```

In these command parameters, `<location>` is the location of the migration files saved by Scanstate. Don't put the full path to the INF file, just the path to the folder that contains the top folder of the migration hierarchy, which is Usmt2i.umc. For instance, if the path to `Migration.inf` is `D:\Usmtfiles\Usmt2i.umc\Migration.inf`, `<location>` would be `D:\Usmtfiles`.

After Loadstate finishes updating the machine, restart the machine to initialize the changes. If you get any errors, check the log for troubleshooting hints.

Managing Folder Redirection

In a perfect world, users would only use their PCs to run applications. All their files would be placed on servers where they could be backed up, scanned for viruses, and stored on fault-tolerant devices rather than local IDE hard drives. This avoids conversations such as the following:

User: You have to do something quickly. My computer made a loud, grinding noise and now when I turn it on, I get a message saying `Unable to load command interpreter. System halted.`

Administrator: We'll have someone up there in an hour to replace your hard drive.

User: What about payroll?

Administrator: I'll bite. What about payroll?

User: Today is Thursday. I need my spreadsheets so that I can calculate payroll.

Administrator: What server are they on?

User: I'm not sure. I think it's the C Drive server.

Trying to corral user data onto servers and other network-based storage is a never-ending chore. Users tend to save their files in convenient places, which usually means accepting whatever default location is offered by an application.

Many organizations use home directories to store user data. Unfortunately, very few applications default to a user's home directory. Starting with Windows 2000, Microsoft changed the logo standards so that applications are required to offer the `My Documents` folder as the default location for user files. Application developers either look for the *`%userprofile%`* variable, which points at the `My Documents` folder, or they make calls using the *`SHGetFolderPath`* function, which returns location information for all profile folders.

The default location of the `My Documents` folder is the local hard drive, but you can point it at a share point on a server either by manually entering a UNC path in the `My Documents` properties or by using a `Folder Redirection` group policy. In a purely Windows Server 2003, Windows XP, or Windows 2000 environment, folder redirection eliminates the need for classic home directories. If you need to support home directories for downlevel clients, or you prefer them to using group policies.

Folder Redirection Policies

The group policies that control folder redirection are located under `User Configuration | Windows Settings | Folder Redirection`. Here are the folders that can be redirected:

- **`My Documents.`** Contains user files, pictures, and sound clips.

- `Application Data.` Contains user configuration files, Public Key Infrastructure files, and user-specific data used by applications.
- `Desktop.` Contains the files and shortcuts displayed on the user's desktop in Explorer.
- `Start Menu.` Contains the files and shortcuts displayed on the Start menu.

When you enable a folder redirection policy, the files are transparently transferred to the target server. Users may not even realize their files are no longer on their local drives—that is, of course, until the network goes down or the server hosting the redirected folders crashes. Also, traveling users may notice slowness in opening and saving their files when they are in a remote office reaching out across the WAN to the server hosting their redirected folders.

You can mitigate these and other network issues by using Distributed File System (Dfs) to replicate the content of user folders to strategically placed servers around your organization. See Chapter 16, "Managing Shared Resources," for more information about Dfs.

Laptop users will also notice that their files are not stored locally when they leave the office and go on the road. See section, "Managing Offline Files," later in this chapter for ways to cache copies of their files locally.

Controlling Placement of Redirected Folders

When you enable a folder redirection policy in the Group Policy Editor, you are given two sets of options for placing the redirected folders: `Basic` and `Advanced`.

The `Basic` option specifies a single location for the folders for all users affected by the redirection policy. The files are separated underneath the share point based on usernames. There are four ways you can identify the folder location:

- Create a folder for each user under the root path.
- Redirect the folder to a specified location.
- Redirect the folder to the user's home directory.
- Redirect the folder to the user's local profile.

In addition, you can specify in the policy whether to copy existing files from the users' local folders to the server, what kind of access permissions to assign to the files on the server, and what to do if the policy is removed or the user moves outside the scope of the policy. Here are details about how these options function in production.

Create a Folder for Each User Under the Root Path

This is a new feature in Windows Server 2003 and is the preferred method for redirecting the `My Documents` folder. When you select this option, you enter a UNC path to the share point. The system automatically appends path with a *`<username>`* folder followed by a folder named `My Documents`. The Properties window displays an example of the path that will be assigned.

The user's redirected folders are created automatically at the server when the user logs on the first time after you enable the folder redirection policy. The permissions applied to the folder depend on the setting of the `Grant The User Exclusive Rights to My Documents` option, accessed via the `Settings` tab in the policy Properties window (see Figure 19.2).

If you select the `Grant The User Exclusive Rights to My Documents` option, a folder called `My Documents` is created and the user is given ownership. The access control list (ACL) for the folder includes only the user account and the System account, both of which have `Full Control` access permissions for the folder and all subfolders and files. Use this option when you want to assure privacy to the users. (Of course, it is always possible for someone with administrator privileges to take ownership of the folder and change the ACL. You can audit for this action.)

If you deselect the `Grant The User Exclusive Rights to My Documents` option, a folder called <*username*>`'s Documents` is created and the user is given ownership. The ACL for this folder is much different than the ACL with `Exclusive Rights` enabled.

First of all, the user account is given `Full Control` access only to the folder itself. The Creator Owner account is given `Full Control` access to the folder and all subfolders and files. This essentially gives the user full control rights, but if you ever transfer ownership, the access permissions shift to the new owner.

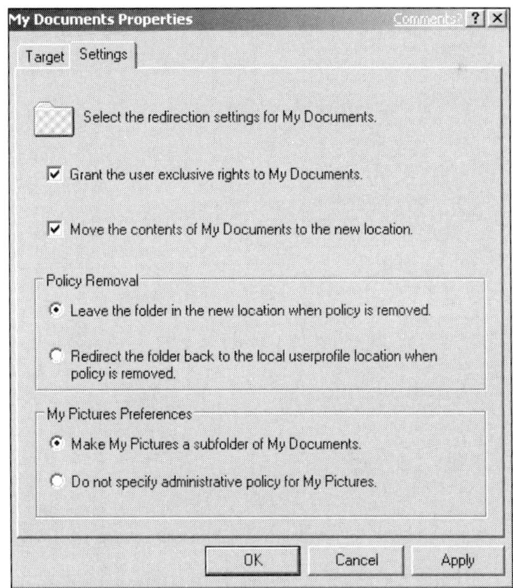

Figure 19.2 Folder Redirection Properties window showing the `Settings` tab.

In addition, the `<username>'s Documents` folder inherits permissions from the parent folder at the root of the share. It is important to limit NTFS permissions at the root folder. Otherwise, users will see each other's files, which generally causes a good deal of commotion.

Redirect to the Following Location

This option works similarly to Windows 2000 Basic redirection. Specify a UNC path to the shared folder and then add the `%username%` environment variable followed by `My Documents`. For example:

```
\\server1\user_docs\%username%\My Documents
```

This option has the advantage of backward compatibility. Use it if you have a mix of Windows Server 2003/XP and Windows 2000 machines.

This is the preferred option for `Start Menu` and `Desktop` folder redirection policies. If you point all the users at the same folder, you can maintain a uniform environment without imposing all the restrictions of a mandatory profile.

Any shortcuts you put in a redirected Start Menu appear "above the line" in the user's menu. They do not change the look, feel, or content of the new-format Start Menu. User permissions on the redirected folders are limited to `Read` and `Execute`.

Another use for the `Specify a Location` option is to point the `My Documents` folder at a different local drive. For example, some organizations just cannot convince their users to store files on a server. If the desktop team partitions the local drive into a "system" and "data" partition, you can use this option to redirect the `My Documents` folder to the data partition. Be sure to target this option only to users who have two partitions. You can do this with a Windows Management Instrumentation (WMI) filter that checks for the existence of a fixed disk with correct logical drive letter.

Redirect to the User's Home Folder

This is also a new option in Windows Server 2003. It comes in handy if you have a classic home directory infrastructure that you want to leverage.

If you select this option, the `Exclusive Rights` setting is ignored and the folders inherit their permissions from the root of the home directory. This ACL includes the Administrators group, by default.

This option is only available to Windows Server 2003 and XP clients. In a mixed domain, use the `Specify a Location` option with a UNC path to the share hosting the user home directories.

Redirect to the Local Userprofile Location

This is the equivalent of calling *olly olly oxen free* to the user's folders. Set this option to put the redirected folders back in their normal location in the users' local profiles. Leave this option in place long enough for all the desktops and laptops to get the setting then disable the policy entirely.

You can avoid this intermediate step by selecting the `Redirect the Folder Back to the Local Userprofile when the Policy is Removed` option when creating the policy. This option has the added benefit of automatically putting the user's data back on the local drive when the user object is moved out of the scope of the group policy. This happens when the user object is moved to another OU.

Specifying Folder Redirection Targets by Group

If you want to redirect folders based on group membership, select the `Advanced` option in the policy properties and identify the group name. After you select a group, you have the same location options as the `Basic` configuration. Figure 19.3 shows an example.

Folder Redirection Highlights

If you plan on implementing folder redirection, here are a few additional caveats to keep in mind:

- Avoid redirecting the `Application Data` folder if you use the Encrypting File System. This folder contains the user's PKI keys. If you redirect it to a server, laptop clients will not be able to encrypt or decrypt files when disconnected from the network. You cannot save Application Data in offline files.

Figure 19.3 Advanced folder redirection properties showing group-based redirection.

- If you host remote desktop users on a server running Application-mode Terminal Services, it's a good idea to enable a folder redirection policy for My Documents. This keeps the user data off your terminal server. You can also use Desktop and Start Menu redirection to provide a consistent look and feel to desktops in terminal service sessions.
- If users want to encrypt files in their redirected `My Documents` folder, the server hosting the folders must be trusted for delegation. This makes the server highly privileged. See Chapter 17, "Managing File Encryption," for more information and precautions when encrypting files on servers.

Creating and Managing Home Directories

If you don't want to use folder redirection policies but you still want to have users put their data on servers, you can use classic home directories. A home directory provides a convenient storage location that users seem to understand. You can say, "Put it in your U drive," and users generally know what you want them to do.

Preparing home directories for users is a two-step process:

1. Designate a home server and create a shared folder to host the user's home directories.
2. Configure each user's account in Active Directory to point at the shared folder on the home server.

Home directory information is stored in the User object in Active Directory in two attributes: `Home-Directory` and `Home-Drive`.

Any server can host home directories. It does not need to be a Windows server. If you have clients with multiple network providers, the home directory can be a NetWare or Banyan or UNIX box running NFS (Network File System).

If you use a Windows server, be sure to create the user home directory share on an NTFS volume so you can take advantage of file and folder permissions to keep users out of each other's personal data.

Assigning a Home Directory Using *AD Users and Computers*

You can create home directories in two ways. You can use the graphical user management tools in the AD Users and Computers console or you can use the command line. Let's start with the console. Assign a home directory to a user account as shown in Procedure 19.1.

Procedure 19.1 Assigning a User Home Directory with *AD Users and Computers*

1. Open the `AD Users and Computers` console and expand the tree to where the user objects are stored.
2. Double-click the user object to open the Properties window.
3. Select the `Profile` tab (see Figure 19.4).

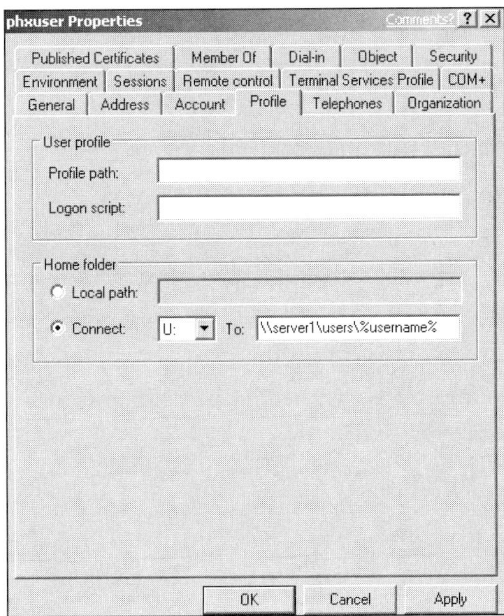

Figure 19.4 User Properties from AD Users and Computers console showing home directory setting under `Profile` tab.

4. Under Home Folder, select the `Connect` radio button.
5. Enter the drive letter you want to use for the home drive and the UNC path to the home directory.
6. Click `OK` to save the changes and close the Properties window. The system automatically creates a home directory at the specified shared directory. The ACLs are automatically configured to give the user and the Administrators group `Full Control` rights.

Creating Home Directories from the Command Line

If you don't like using a GUI for something as simple as creating a home directory, here are the actions for creating user home directories from the command line. Most of the tools come as standard utilities. A few tools come from the Resource Kit. The example shown in Procedure 19.2 creates a home directory for a Help Desk administrator named Rita Manuel.

Procedure 19.2 Assigning a Home Directory Using the Command Line

1. Open a command prompt and enter the following command to create the user account:

   ```
   net user rmanuel * /add /fullname:"Rita Manuel" /comment:"Help Desk Admin" /domain
   ```

   The `*` forces `Net` to prompt for a password and confirmation rather than entering the password on the command line.

   The `/domain` switch adds the user to the Active Directory. Without this switch, if you are at a member server or workstation instead of a domain controller, the `net user /add` command creates the account in the local Security Account Manager (SAM).

2. Create a home directory for Rita. This can be done at the console of the server or across the network as follows:

   ```
   MD e:\users\rmanuel
   ```

   Or:

   ```
   MD \\S1\users\rmanuel
   ```

3. If you choose to create individual shares for home directories, create a share point at the console of the server using the `Net Share` command as follows:

   ```
   net share rmanuel=c:\users\rmanuel
   ```

   To create a share across the network, use a tool in the Resource Kit called RMTSHARE. You must be logged onto the domain with administrator privileges to use RMTSHARE. The syntax for this utility is as follows:

   ```
   rmtshare \\S1\rmanuel=c:\users\rmanuel
   ```

4. Set Rita's user account to point at the home directory. This is also done with the `Net User` command. The default home drive letter is Z. No command-line option exists for setting a different drive letter. The syntax is as follows:

   ```
   net user rmanuel /homedir:\\S1\rmanuel
   ```

5. At this point, Rita's home directory inherits access permissions from its parent. This might include other users or inappropriate groups. Set the ACLs on the home directory so that only Rita can access it. The command-line utility for applying NTFS file permissions is Cacls.exe. You can use CACLS locally or across the network. This is the syntax for giving Rita and Administrator `Full Control` rights and removing everyone else from the ACL:

   ```
   cacls \\S1\users\rmanuel /t /g rmanuel:f /g administrator:f
   ```

   The `/t` option applies the change to the directory and all child directories and files.

   The `/g` option grants the specified permissions to the user.

   The `rmanuel:f` option grants `Full Control` access to Rita's account. The same is true for the Administrators local group.

6. When you enter this command, CACLS prompts for confirmation. Enter `Y` for Yes and the change is applied.
7. Finally, if you intend on using quotas, you need to set ownership of Rita's home directory to Rita. This cannot be done using tools from Microsoft. I recommend the CHOWN utility from Services for UNIX (SFU).

Armed with these commands, you can build a script to automate a user addition. Be sure to give the script file a .cmd extension. The following example shows a simple batch script that accepts the user's login ID, full name, and title as command-line arguments:

```
md \\S1\users\%1
net share %1=c:\users\%1 (or rmtshare \\S1\%1=c:\users\%1)
net user %1 * /add /domain /homedir:\\S1\users\%1   /fullname:%2 /comment:%3
cacls \\S1\users\%1 /t /g %1:f
chown \\S1\users\rmanuel rmanuel
```

You can use VBScript, JScript, or Perl to make more elaborate scripts. The person using the script must have sufficient administrative rights to add user accounts and modify ACLs.

Mapping Home Directories for Downlevel Clients

When you assign a home directory to a user at a modern Windows client, the home drive is mapped automatically when the user logs on. This is not true for users at downlevel clients such as Windows 3.1x and Windows 9x. Downlevel clients require that the home directory be mapped in a logon script. Here is the syntax:

```
net use u: \\S1\users /home
```

A limitation of classic Windows clients is that a network drive can only map to a share point, not a folder underneath.

For example, if you map the `U` drive for a downlevel client to `\\S1\users\dletterman`, the client maps only to the `users` share, so the `U` drive contains all the home directories, not just the files for `dletterman`.

The workaround is to create a share for each user home directory. You can hide the shares from the browser by giving them a dollar-sign ($) ending. For example, if the physical directory holding home directories is on the `E` drive of the server with the path `E:\Users\DLetterman`, the share point would be `Dletterman$` and the UNC path would be `\\S1\dletterman$`.

The dollar sign does not truly hide the share, so don't use it in place of tight NTFS security on the home directory folders.

Terminal Services and Home Directories

In the multiuser environment of terminal services, user configuration settings are saved to the user's home directory. If a user does not have a home directory, terminal services creates one in the user's local profile. This is done by a set of batch files that run each time a user logs on at a server running terminal services.

For example, Office 97 applications save user templates to `C:\Program Files\Office97\Templates`. If this is done in a terminal services environment, users would overwrite each other's templates. A set of scripts in the `\Windows\Application Compatibility Scripts` folder redirect common folders used by older applications to the individual user's home directory.

Managing Offline Files

Whether you use folder redirection or home directories, laptop users get upset when they cannot access their files. The answer to their dilemma is *offline files*. With this feature, a user can mirror his server-based files to his local laptop. When the user connects back to the network again, changes made to the offline files are synchronized with the copies on the server and civilization is saved.

Additional Uses for Offline Files

The names used by Microsoft for offline files varies depending on the perspective. At the server, the technology is called *client-side caching*. At the client, the technology is called *offline files*. But whatever you call it, the feature has applications in addition to helping laptop users. For example:

- **Local access to large files.** It can be difficult to work on huge files stored on a server. Graphic designers and CAD operators typically copy big files to their local hard drives to work on them during the day then copy them back in the evenings. Sometimes they forget, though, and you can help to automate the synchronization process by using offline files.

- **File availability during network outages.** Sporadic outages are darned near unavoidable, but users get cynical during prolonged periods of instability. They start keeping their files on their local drives. If your end users show reluctance to save their files on servers, offline files can be a way to lure them back onto the network again.
- **Application caching.** Users often want to run network-based applications while they're on the road. Instead of installing the applications on the laptops, you can use offline files to store cached copies of the executables.

Inappropriate Uses of Offline Files

Offline files are not the solution to every mobile user's problems. Here are instances where offline files are not a good solution:

- **Files accessed by multiple users.** Imagine files accessed by several different users who make modifications at their laptops while they are offline and then sync up. The last user to sync will overwrite all the other's changes. They won't be happy. You won't be happy.
- **Database files.** You definitely do not want to cache database files. The synchronization process may get the changed data file but miss a transaction log or a change to a support file.
- **Client/server application files.** Don't use offline files to save a local copy of client/server configuration files if the application makes its own caching provisions.
- **PST files.** If you run Microsoft Outlook in Corporate Workgroup mode, users can store offline folders and archives in a local PST (Personal Store) file. Outlook handles the synchronization between the Exchange information store and the local PST. Don't layer this synchronization with offline file synchronization. This will cause data corruption.

The system automatically filters for file types that meet the criteria listed above. This includes files with the following extensions:

.db (Foxpro)

.pst (Outlook)

.mdb, .mdw, .mde, and .ldb (Access)

.slm (Visual Sourcesafe)

If you have files with these extensions in a folder, the system will refuse to configure the folder for offline files. If a folder has been configured for offline files, the system will refuse to put a file with one of these extensions in the folder.

The extensions are hard-coded into the client-side caching service. You can override them with a group policy called `Files Not Cached`. This policy is in `Computer Configuration | Administrative Templates | Network | Offline Files`.

Use caution when enabling the `Files Not Cached` policy. It completely overrides the default extensions. If you have an extension that you want to add to the list, be sure to include all the rest from the preceding list.

Offline Files and Remote Desktop

Offline files are disabled on machines that have Remote Desktop enabled. This includes all servers running Windows Server 2003 because Remote Desktop is enabled by default. If you are running Windows Server 2003 on a laptop for testing, or you have some other reason for enabling offline folders on a server, you can disable remote desktop on the server as shown in Procedure 19.3.

Procedure 19.3 Disabling Remote Desktop

1. Right-click `My Computer` and select PROPERTIES from the flyout menu. This opens the Properties window.
2. Select the `Remote` tab.
3. Uncheck the `Allow Users To Connect Remotely To This Computer` option.
4. Click `OK` to save the change. This will not disconnect any current remote desktop users. You may need to log them off the server or restart before you get the offline file option.

You can enable Remote Desktop at any time by reselecting the `Allow Users To Connect Remotely To This Computer` option. If you have enabled offline files in the meantime, you must first disable it before enabling Remote Desktop connections.

The same restriction to offline files applies to standalone XP desktops with Fast User Switching enabled. This should not be a problem in a corporate environment because Fast User Switching is disabled when you join a desktop to a domain. If you have users at standalone XP desktops that connect to shared folders on servers running Windows Server 2003 or Windows 2000 and the users want to enable offline files, you must disable Fast User Switching. Select the `User Accounts` option in the new Control Panel interface and select `Change The Way Users Log On Or Off`. Uncheck the `Fast User Switching` option and save the change.

Configuring Client-Side Caching at the Server

Client-side caching is controlled at the server using parameters associated with the share point. In the `Sharing` tab of a shared folder, click `Caching`. This opens a Caching Settings window. Figure 19.5 shows an example.

There are three cache configuration options. They are differentiated by how the client selects items to be cached and how the server handles file changes.

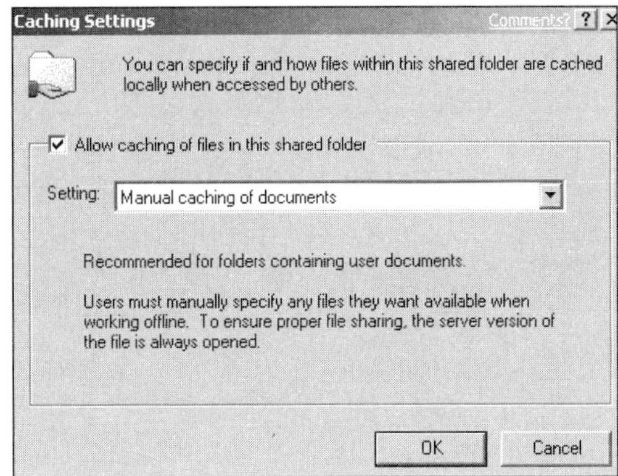

Figure 19.5 Caching Settings window for a shared folder showing the default caching option.

Manual Caching of Documents

This is the default caching option. In this option, the user must decide which files to save offline. This is called *pinning*. The name of this option is a little deceiving because a user can pin executables as well as data files.

A file or folder is pinned using the `Make Available Offline` option in the PROPERTIES menu of the file or folder. A pinned file or folder displays an icon with a blue, double-headed arrow.

When a user opens a pinned file, the system checks the server copy to see if any changes have occurred. If not, the local copy is opened. If changes have been made at the server, the server copy is downloaded into the local cache then the local copy is opened.

As long as the client keeps the local copy open, the server copy is kept locked. This prevents someone from modifying the server copy from another source. Unfortunately, it is up to the application to use locks and to look for locks. For example, Microsoft Word is a good neighbor and refuses to open a locked file. Notepad, on the other hand, ignores locks and opens any file you point it at.

Automatic Caching of Documents

With this option, the user is not required to pin a file to cache it. Local copies are cached whenever the user opens a file in the shared folder.

If a file has been automatically cached, the icon does not display any special insignia. If a user expects to see certain files when offline, the user should manually pin the files to make sure they will be available.

As with manually pinned files, when a user opens an automatically cached file, the server copy is checked first to see if it is different than the local copy. The locally cached copy is used for reading and any changes are made to both the local copy and the server copy. The server copy is kept locked.

When a user creates a new file in a share configured for automatic caching, the file is also cached locally. If a file is created at the server by someone else, it will appear in the file list in Explorer but it will only be cached if the user opens the file. Train your users with the following mantra, "To see the file later, open it now."

Automatic Caching of Programs and Documents

This option differs from the other automatic caching option only in the way it handles file locks. Data files are locked but executables are not. This is supposed to reduce network traffic, although eliminating a few Server Message Block (SMB) packets doesn't seem like much of a savings. For the most part, avoid this configuration and stick with `Use Automatic Caching of Documents`. Use this option only if you have a legacy application that does not behave well when multiple users access it.

Disabling Caching

There is a fourth option, of course. You can just say no to offline files and disable caching at the server. This must be done for each share point where you do not want to permit caching. For instance, if you have a share point that holds gigs and gigs of executables and you don't like the idea of users pinning all those files to their local cache, disable caching at the share.

You can also disable offline files at the clients. By default, offline files are enabled for XP desktops and disabled for servers running Windows Server 2003. The toggle is exposed in the TOOLS | FOLDER OPTIONS menu of any folder. Figure 19.6 shows an example. You can also configure the setting from `Appearance and Themes | Folder Options` in the new Control Panel interface.

When you select the `Enable Offline Files` option, the client becomes aware of any shares that have been configured for automatic caching, so be sure you have sufficient disk space. By default, the offline file cache can take up to 10 percent of the drive. Users are not warned if the cache gets full. Older files are pushed out of the cache when the cache size reaches its limit.

The default location of the offline file cache is a hidden folder called `\Windows\CSC`. If you prefer not to have this folder on the C drive, you can move it to another location using the Cachemov utility that comes in the Resource Kit. This is a GUI application that presents a pick list of the fixed disks on your system and their free space. You cannot move the cache to a removable media disk.

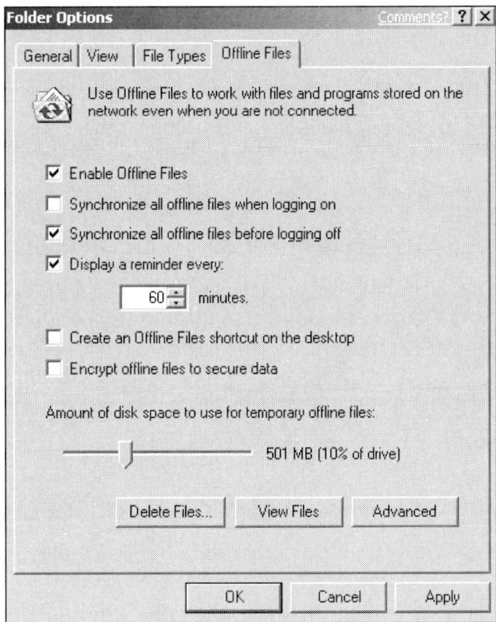

Figure 19.6 Folder Options showing the `Offline Files` tab.

Registry Tip: Client-Side Caching

The Registry entries that control client-side caching are as follows:

```
Key:    HKLM | Software | Microsoft | Windows | CurrentVersion | NetCache
Values: DefCacheSize (REG_DWORD) - Contains cache size in hex
  Enabled (Dword) - flag is 1 for enabled, 0 for disabled
  EncryptCache (Dword) - flag is 1 to encrypt entire cache, 0 to leave clear
```

Synchronization Manager

Keeping offline files at a client in sync with the files on a server, and doing so in a way that doesn't confuse a user, is a trick that took Microsoft years to master. After a series of almost-but-not-quite solutions, the job of keeping files in sync falls on the *Synchronization Manager*, or Mobsync.exe.

In addition to managing offline files, Synchronization Manager also handles offline web pages in Internet Explorer 5.0 and later. (You get a copy of Mobsync.exe when you install IE on a Win9x or NT machine.)

Synchronization Manager Registry Settings

You'll find the Registry settings for Synchronization Manager in the following:

```
Key:  HKLM | Software | Microsoft | Windows | CurrentVersion | SyncMgr
```

There are very few user-serviceable parameters. All known parameters have a setting in the User Interface (UI).

Synchronization Manager Options

Synchronization Manager does not run continuously. It performs its duties only when told to do so. By default, this is when the user logs on and off. You can configure it to synchronize at other times using one of three interfaces:

- Folder Options
- Synchronization Manager
- Group policies

We've already seen the Folder Options settings. Figure 19.7 shows the Synchronization Manager interface. Open this via START | PROGRAMS | ACCESSORIES | SYNCHRONIZE.

Click `Setup` to open the Synchronization Settings window shown in Figure 19.8.

The `When I Am Using This Network Connection` option will only list one LAN interface, even if you have multiple network cards in the machine. The remaining entries in the pick list, if any, represent dial-up connections. You can use these settings to configure special synchronization settings for slow connections. Ordinarily, no synchronization occurs for lines that run slower than 500Kbps.

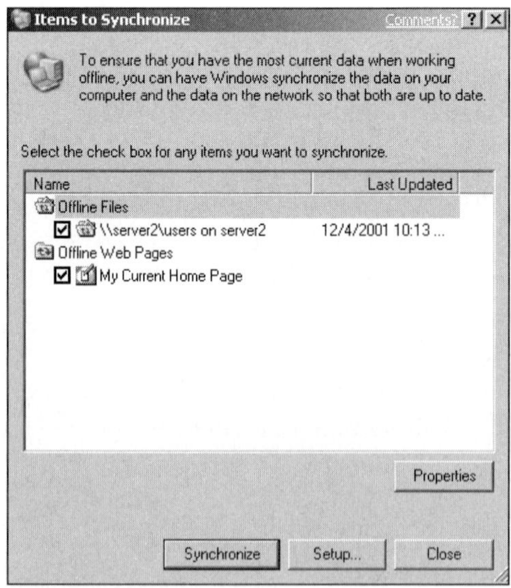

Figure 19.7 Synchronization Manager interface.

Client-Side Cache Database Corruption

Offline files stored at the client are cataloged in a CSC (Client-Side Caching) database. This database can become corrupted. Symptoms include inability to open files, files that appear only when offline, and Event log entries warning of corruption.

If these or other symptoms occur, you can try deleting files out of the client-side cache using the Folder Options | Offline Folders window then resynchronizing.

If this fails, initiate a full resync in the Folder Options | Offline Folders window by pressing the Ctrl+Shift keys then clicking `Delete`. This will cause a complete loss of any locally cached files, so make sure the server copies are up-to-date or make copies of the cached files. The computer must be restarted to complete this evolution.

Conflict Resolution

If the server copy of a file changes while a user is offline, Synchronization Manager must figure out what to do when the user reconnects. There are three potential scenarios:

- **Client copy did not change.** In this case, the server copy overwrites the local copy with no notice given to the user.
- **Server copy was deleted.** In this case, the local copy at the client is retained but only displayed when the user is offline. This "phantom" copy can be disconcerting to users. If the file is no longer needed, you can walk the user through deleting the file while offline. If the file is needed, make a copy of it into another location while offline and delete the original. Then, resync online and copy the file back into the folder.

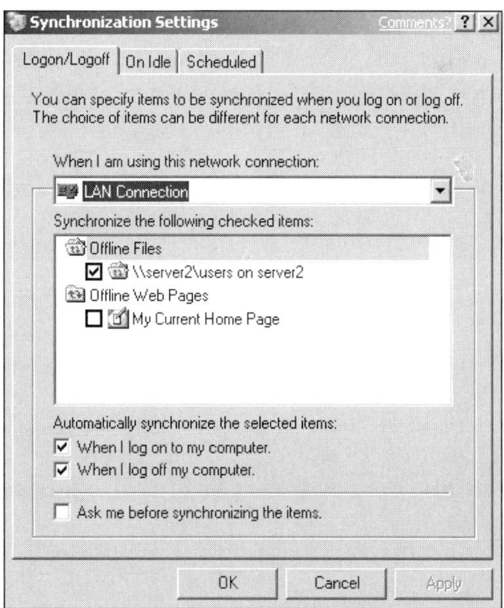

Figure 19.8 Synchronization Settings options.

- **Client copy also changed file changed.** In this scenario, the user is given a Resolve File Conflicts window to help Synchronization Manager decide what to do. Figure 19.9 shows an example.

The user resolves the conflict by selecting which copy to retain or by choosing to retain both copies by renaming the local copy. The user can view the files before making the decision. A savvy user can generally resolve a file conflict correctly. Less sophisticated users might be thrown off by the file location, which uses a UNC path. Don't be surprised if you get Help Desk calls with lots of forward-slash/back-slash conversations.

Offline Files and File Encryption

The files stored on a laptop often have more value than the laptop itself. Protecting those files with NTFS permissions won't stop a criminal. If the person who steals your laptop doesn't know how to hack the admin password, you can bet the fence knows how, or at least knows someone who knows how. The best protection is file encryption.

In Windows 2000, users were not able to encrypt the files in the offline file cache. This exposed server-based information to prying eyes. It was a critical deficiency and prevented many organizations from implementing offline folders.

In Windows Server 2003/XP, users can encrypt the contents of the offline cache. The local encryption status is completely independent of the encryption status at the server. This makes offline files a secure medium for transporting files on laptops.

To enable offline file encryption, select the `Offline Files` tab in the Folder Properties window and select `Encrypt Offline Files to Secure Data`. Make sure the laptop is a member of a domain and that you are logged on to the domain and not the local SAM. This ensures that the domain Administrator account is the Data Recovery Agent. See Chapter 17, "Managing File Encryption," for details.

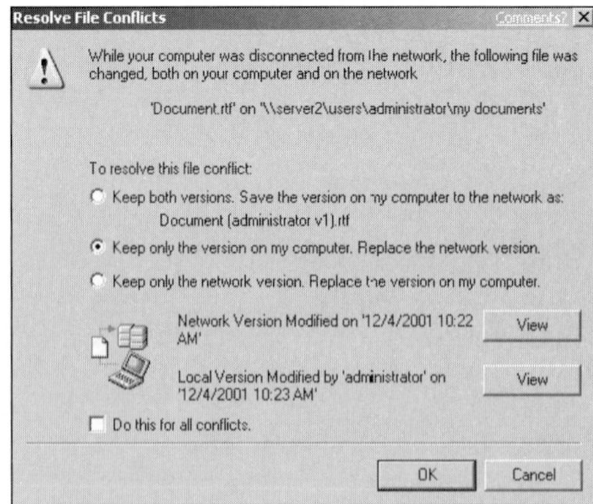

Figure 19.9 Resolve File Conflicts window.

Offline Files and Group Policies

Rather than configure the offline file settings at each client, you can use group policies. The policy settings are located under `Computer Configuration | Administrative Templates | Network | Offline Files`. In broad terms, these policies control the following:

- Enabling/disabling offline folders at clients and client-side caching at servers
- Setting synchronization events (logon/logoff/suspend)
- Disabling offline folder configuration items in Folder Options and Control Panel
- Disabling the user's ability to pin offline files
- Controlling the reminder balloons popped up by Synchronization Manager
- Encrypting offline files
- Set a different slow link speed (the default is 500Kbps)
- Set the default offline cache size (in percentage of disk space)
- Select file extensions that are not permitted to be stored in offline files

When setting group policies for offline files, keep in mind that your target audience uses laptops, which may not be online when you set the policy. Users who dial in from home receive Administrative Template policies and will see your policy changes but any new synchronization actions you prescribe will not take effect until the user connects to the network.

You may want to create a group called Laptop Users and target the group policy at that group. This avoids potentially creating offline file policies that affect desktop users.

Offline Files Operational Checklist

Here are a few key points to remember when working with offline files:

- All server-based shares are configured for `Manual Caching of Documents` by default. This requires the users to pin any files they want to keep offline.
- If you want to use automatic caching, select the `Automatic Caching for Documents` option rather than `Automatic Caching for Documents and Programs` to assure proper file locking.
- Files in a share point configured for automatic caching are not cached locally until they are opened. Train your users accordingly.
- When working with cached data files on the network, the local copy is always used for read access. Writes go to both copies at the same time.
- If a server file is modified and the user modifies the same file offline, a Resolve File Conflicts window walks the user through the corrective actions.

Managing Servers via Remote Desktop

You get the ultimate in server-based storage by eliminating the PC completely. Thin-client computing has been steadily gaining market share over the last few years as companies discover this and other benefits of hosting users directly on a server in a multiuser environment.

Multiuser Windows got its start in 1995 with Citrix WinFrame, a rework of the NT 3.51 base code. Citrix had already made its mark in the multiuser market with WinView, a rework of the OS/2 base code. The enabling technology in both WinView and WinFrame was Citrix's Integrated Computing Architecture (ICA) protocol, a highly efficient client/server mechanism for transmitting session information.

When NT4 came out, Microsoft decided that the multiuser code belonged in the core OS rather than an OEM version. Citrix and Microsoft worked out a licensing arrangement whereby Citrix retained control of the ICA protocol and Microsoft got everything else. The result: NT4 Terminal Server Edition, a mix of Microsoft and Citrix code.

In Windows 2000, Microsoft upped the ante by incorporating multiuser functionality into the base operating system rather than shipping it as a separate, layered product. This improved performance and stability. Windows 2000 terminal services had two operational modes:

- **Remote Administration mode.** This permitted two administrators to run sessions at a server at the same time.
- **Application mode.** This permitted any number of authorized users to run sessions concurrently, with each session getting discrete configuration parameters saved in the user's home directory.

Microsoft has now made terminal services ubiquitous throughout the product line. Both servers running Windows Server 2003 and XP desktops have terminal service capabilities. Microsoft also changed the terminology associated with terminal services. The ability to establish a terminal service session is now called *Remote Desktop*. The ability to host multiple, independent user sessions, similar to the Windows 2000 Application mode, is now simply called *Terminal Services*.

That's the good news. The bad news is that while the two-node concurrent access license is now standard on all servers running Windows Server 2003, true Terminal Services—that is, the ability to host multiple, concurrent, independent sessions—is only available on Enterprise Edition and Datacenter Edition. This adds at least a couple thousand dollars onto the cost of a terminal server, in addition to the client license costs.

Remote Desktop Protocol (RDP)

There are two ways to initiate a terminal services session on Windows Server 2003. One is Microsoft's proprietary Remote Desktop Protocol (RDP). Originally called T-Share, RDP is a rework of the international standard T.120 communications protocol. RDP is fast and permits multichannel communication, but up until Windows Server 2003 and XP, it was somewhat clunky and sported few features. RDP requires a Windows client.

The other interface is Citrix's ICA protocol. Using ICA requires loading the Citrix MetaFrame service and using an ICA client. There are ICA clients for virtually all non-Windows platforms, from Linux to HP-UX to Macintosh.

If you want to avoid the additional complexity and cost of MetaFrame to get non-Windows client support, there are a couple of alternatives. You can purchase a Java RDP client called HOBLink JWT that can connect to both W2K and Windows Server 2003 terminal services. Visit `www.hobsoft.com` for details. There is also an open-source RDP client. Download it from `www.rdesktop.org`.

Don't ignore MetaFrame completely, though. Citrix has worked hard over the last few years to add value to MetaFrame and ICA to make them worth the additional investment. For example, if you want to publish individual applications from a robust, centrally-managed server farm, you need MetaFrame. Visit the Citrix web site at `www.citrix.com` to see the new features in MetaFrame for Windows Server 2003. The product isn't free, not by a long shot, but the features are compelling and you'll get solid performance.

Still, you may not need MetaFrame after you see the features in the new version of RDP. Version 5.1 is not only faster and more reliable than earlier versions, it supports 24-bit color, a full suite of device redirection options, clipboard sharing, 128-bit encryption, and the ability to use keyboard shortcuts within the session. You can also use RDP to connect directly to the console of a server running Windows Server 2003 or XP desktop, something that required NetMeeting in earlier versions of Windows.

You can also run terminal services within a network load balancing (NLB) cluster. This feature was present in Windows 2000 but it was dogged with connection problems. Microsoft improved NLB cluster support in Windows Server 2003 with the addition of a Session Directory service. When a user connects to a server in the NLB cluster, the server notifies the Session Directory. If the user disconnects then reconnects, the server accepting the connection checks with the Session Directory then ushers the user back to the original server.

Remote Desktop

The Remote Desktop client (Mstsc.exe) is installed on every version of Windows Server 2003 as well as XP desktops. The shortcut is located in the classic Start menu under PROGRAMS | ACCESSORIES | COMMUNICATIONS | REMOTE DESKTOP CONNECTION.

The new Mstsc client differs from the Windows 2000 version by combining the RDP client with the connection manager, something that required two separate executables in Windows 2000. The configuration files saved by Mstsc are simple text files with an RDP extension. You can double-click one of these RDP files to open a session with the target server. This makes it simple to distribute links to clients.

The RDP 5.1 client will run on any 32-bit Windows platform. The Windows Server 2003 CD has an MSI package you can use to deploy the client to Windows 2000 desktops using group policies. You can push the client to your Windows NT/9x/ME clients using whatever deployment method you currently use. It requires the Windows Installer to run. Installation on downlevel clients requires a restart.

Advanced Client Features

As you are probably aware, Microsoft included "advanced" RDP clients in Windows 2000 SP1 and later:

- An MMC console-based client, Mstsmmc.msc, that supports simultaneous connections to multiple servers in the same window.
- A web-based client consisting of an ActiveX control, Msrdp.ocx, and an installation script, Msrdp.inf.

These clients are also in Windows Server 2003 under different packaging. The MMC-based client is installed by default on every Windows Server 2003. The shortcut is located under START | PROGRAMS | ADMINISTRATIVE TOOLS | REMOTE DESKTOP. The web-based client is a component of IIS along with a virtual folder, TSWeb, that contains an ASP page, Connect.asp, that collects credentials from users and routes them to whatever terminal server they select.

The RDP 5.1 client also has additional connection functionality exposed on the command line. Type **`mstsc /?`** to get a list of the options. Two of them are especially useful. You can specify a different port (RDP uses TCP port 3389 by default) if you need to get through a firewall. You can also connect directly to the console of a server rather than creating a new session.

RDP Client Connection Features

The Remote Desktop Connection application, Mstsc, contains the management options for the client. Launch it via START | PROGRAMS | ACCESSORIES | COMMUNICATION | REMOTE DESKTOP. (See Figures 19.10 and 19.11 for example windows.)

Here are the features that can be managed from the client interface:

- **Desktop size.** The session desktop can be any size up to and including the size of the base PC desktop. If launched as full screen, a navigational aid appears at the top of the screen to help remind the user that the screen displays a session and not the base desktop.

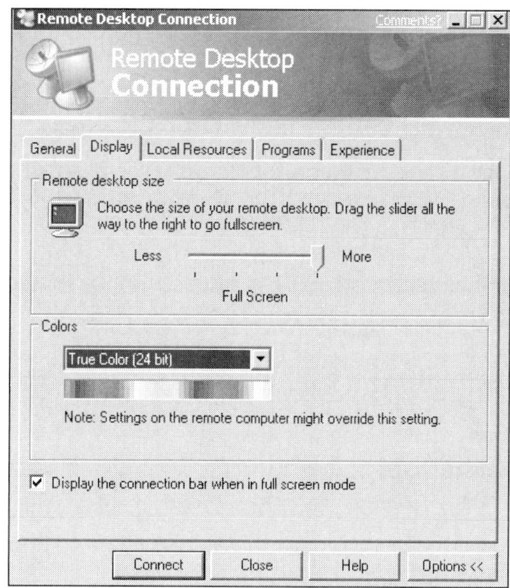

Figure 19.10 Remote Desktop Connection window showing the `Display` tab.

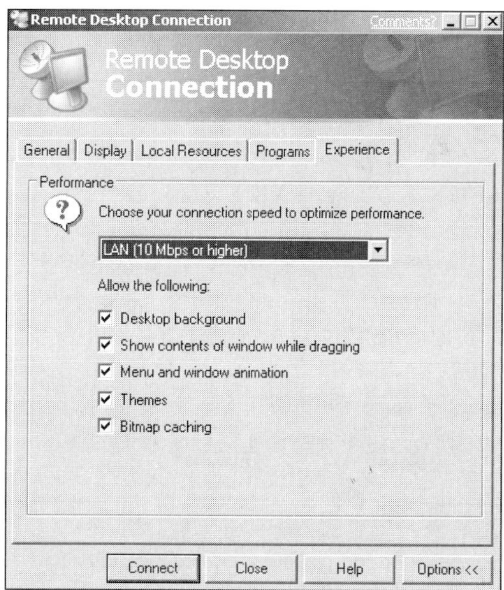

Figure 19.11 Remote Desktop Connection window showing the `Experience` tab.

- **Hot keys.** You can elect to use the Windows hot keyzs within the RDP session rather than on the base desktop. This is a big help for users who get confused when their favorite shortcut (like Ctrl+Alt+Del or the Window key) doesn't work as they would expect in the session.
- **Color depth.** Maximum color depth is 24 bits, but you'll get better performance without sacrificing much in the way of aesthetics by setting the color depth to 16 or 15 bits.
- **Local device redirection.** The user can choose not to redirect drives, printers, and serial ports. This protects local files. It does not affect performance.
- **Experience.** The user can select a connection speed and the client will automatically disable options that are not appropriate for the selected speed.

Console Redirection

The Terminal Service service (Termservice) is installed on every Windows Server 2003. The service supports both a standard client session and a direct connection to the console. This second option is essentially a remote control feature.

To connect to the console of a server, launch the Remote Desktop Connection executable, Mstsc, from the command line with the `/console` switch—`mstsc /console`—then select the server. When you make the connection, one of two things happens:

- If your account is currently logged on at the console of the server, your session takes over where the console left off and the console goes to a locked state.
- If someone else is logged on at the console and you have administrator privileges, you force the console user to log off and the console goes to a locked state.

The Remote Desktop feature on a server permits two concurrent users. The users share a common set of configuration parameters rather than the discrete settings maintained by true Terminal Services. This feature is intended for administrators to access servers for management purposes, but see section, "Controlling Remote Access Permission," for ways to give access to non-admins.

Remote Desktop and PocketPCs

The Windows Server 2003 CD comes with a Remote Desktop driver for handheld PCs (HPCs). This driver also works with PocketPCs such as the Compaq Ipaq. The ActiveSync product that comes with the handheld will not install this application. Copy the appropriate CAB file to the PocketPC then click on the CAB file and install it. For example, the RPC_SA1100.cab file works with the Ipaq handheld.

The client does not support 128-bit encryption, so be sure to set the terminal server encryption to `Client Compatible`. For more information, see `www.cewindows.net/faqs/terminalserver-citrix.htm`.

If your unit has a CDPD (Cellular Digital Packet Data) modem, you'll find that 9600 baud gives a slow but acceptable remote desktop connection.

Device Redirection

Past versions of Microsoft's terminal services and RDP gave scant support for device redirection. With NT4 Terminal Server Edition (TSE), you could include a NET USE command in a logon script to map a COM port back to a serial port at the client. This permitted using a modem or barcode scanner at the client. Starting with Windows 2000, printers could be redirected back to the client, as well, but an administrator was required to install printer drivers at the server.

The combination of an RDP 5.1 client and a Windows Server 2003 terminal server provides a suite of new device redirection features:

- Clipboard
- Drives
- Printers (with automatic printer redirection for Windows Server 2003, XP, and 2000 clients)
- LPT and COM ports (true redirection rather than NET USE)
- Audio mapping

All of these redirection options are enabled by default when a PC-based client makes an RDP 5.1 connection to a Windows Server 2003 terminal server. This includes downlevel clients such as NT4 and Windows 9x/ME. Here are details about the various redirection options.

Clipboard Mapping

This feature permits the user cut-and-paste information between an RDP session and the desktop or between different RDP sessions if you have a multisession thin-client device. This feature is available in Windows 2000 as an add-on package from the Resource Kit, Rdclip, but it is fairly clumsy to install.

The clipboard mapping feature is surprisingly useful. You can use it to grab screen shots, transfer document contents, even work at the command line. One thing to be careful of is inadvertently creating compound documents when you paste. If you build an OLE connection to an inserted object over an RDP connection, the pasted object will only be available inside an RDP session.

Drive Redirection

To see the behavior of client drive redirection, connect to a Server 2003 terminal server using an RDP 5.1 client. Open `My Computer` and look at the lower portion of the window under `Other`. The client drives are listed by their drive letter and the name of the client computer. Figure 19.12 shows an example.

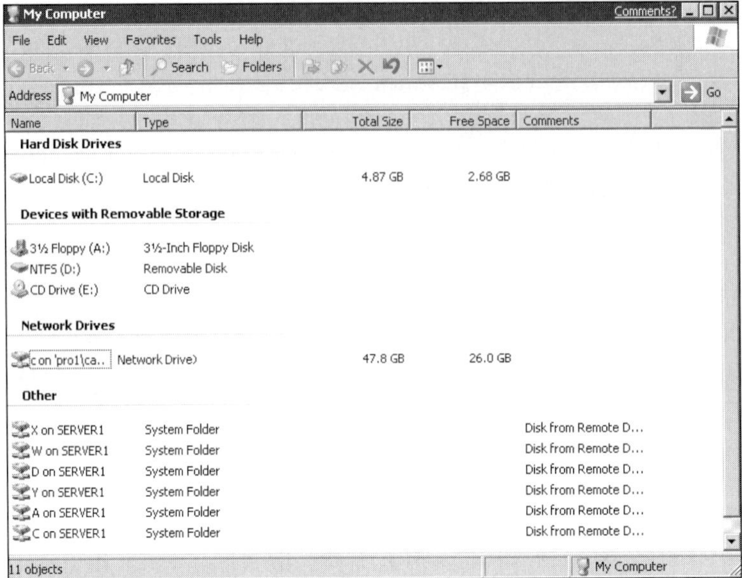

Figure 19.12 My Computer showing redirected client drives in an RDP 5.1 session.

Users can copy freely between server drives and client drives as long as they have appropriate NTFS permissions at the server. RDP is not as efficient as SMB for file transfers, so don't expect much in the way of performance. You can transfer files from the client drives to a network drive inside the client session at the server. The data stream is first sent to the server via RDP then it is handed over to the SMB redirector for delivery across the network. This transition takes time and CPU cycles.

Printer Redirection

To see the result of printer redirection, open the `Printers and Faxes` window within an RDP 5.1 client session. Do the same at the terminal server.

If you connect from a Windows 2000 or XP client, the RDP session will show each of the printers at your desktop plus the printers that are locally installed at the terminal server (see Figure 19.13). The Printers and Faxes window at the terminal server shows all printers from all active clients plus the locally install printers.

When the client logs off, the printers are removed from the printer list at the terminal server. The printers reappear when the user logs on again. The information for the printer settings comes from cached parameters for that client.

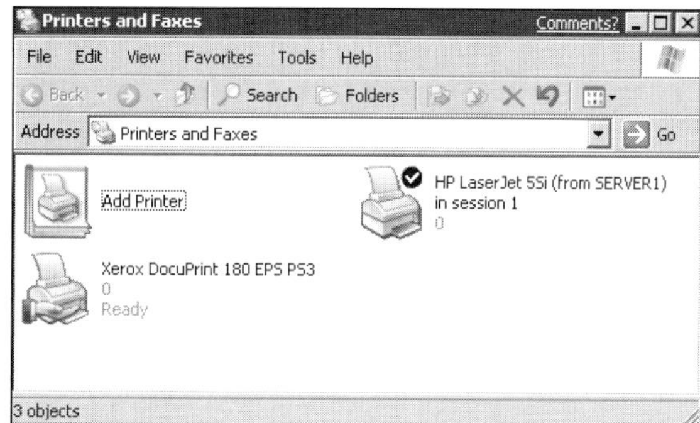

Figure 19.13 Printers and Faxes window showing printers that have been redirected from client PCs running RDP 5.1 client.

The redirected printers use RDP ports created dynamically at the terminal server that point back to the client PC. You can see the COM port redirections using the CHANGE PORT utility in the client session. Here is an example listing:

```
C:\>change port
AUX = \DosDevices\COM1
COM1 = \Device\RdpDr\;COM1:2\tsclient\COM1
COM2 = \Device\Serial1
```

Notice that COM2 redirects to the local COM1 (`Serial1`) interface, which then aggregates the ports (`COM1:2`) and sends them back to the terminal server via the Terminal Server director, Rdpdr. The parallel ports are redirected in the same way but do not appear in the port listing.

Redirected ports appear at the terminal server with names corresponding to the client session, such as `TS004, CLIENT1: LPT1`. Ports corresponding to redirected printers use the PRN device name, such as `TS011, CLIENT1: PRN1`. Figure 19.14 shows an example port list.

The terminal server automatically configures printers for Windows Server 2003, XP, and Windows 2000 clients by obtaining the drivers from the client. The permissions on the printers are set so that only administrators and the user who created the session has access. Users cannot see printers in other client sessions, but they do see printers created manually at the terminal server.

Printers for downlevel clients must be manually created and redirected at the terminal server. This is because the server is unable to obtain the proper driver from the downlevel client. Create the printer using the Add Printer Wizard as you normally would and select one of the client's redirected LPT or COM ports as the target port. The client must have an active session to see the port list.

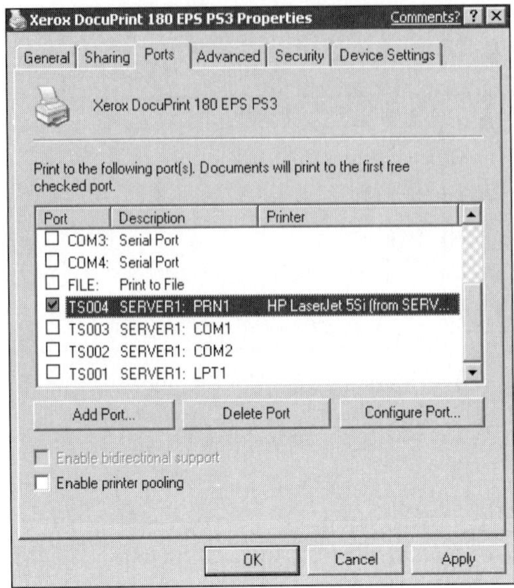

Figure 19.14 Port list at a terminal server showing redirected client ports.

The printer at the downlevel client must be installed on an LPT or COM port. You cannot redirect a terminal server printer to a USB port because the USB port does not "appear" until it is used, like an elementary particle appearing from nowhere around a black hole.

Print jobs are fully rendered at the terminal server then sent to the client's printer using RDP. This avoids driver conflicts. You'll need a Windows Server 2003/XP or Windows 2000 driver for the printer. This can be a challenge for less expensive printers that only have drivers for consumer desktops such as Windows 9x/ME. Driver availability should improve after XP makes inroads into the consumer market.

Audio Redirection

Many applications play sounds. Without audio redirection, the sounds would play at the terminal server, which only entertains/annoys the administrators in the server room. With audio redirection, the stream is processed at the client.

There are no codec compatibility issues because the stream is decoded at the server then packaged for delivery over RDP to the client. For example, as I write this, I'm listening to Monty Python's Dead Parrot sketch (`www.montypython.net/fullsketches.php`) streaming to an IE window in a remote desktop session and from there to my PC over RDP via audio redirection. A user could listen to an audio CD mounted at the terminal server if an administrator were crazy enough to put a disk in the player.

The audio stream uses User Datagram Protocol (UDP) for performance. If the bandwidth changes while the stream is playing, the client and server can automatically negotiate new stream capabilities.

Video playback is fairly poor via RDP. The frame rates are poor and you'll get a lot of dropped frames. Also, audio streams often become degraded on a busy terminal server. Use this feature only when necessary.

You can control the user's ability to redirect audio, video, and the other redirection features using the Properties window of the RDP connection in the Terminal Services Configuration console. The `Client Settings` tab has the options.

Terminal Server Security

Remote Desktop and terminal services security concerns generally focus in these areas:

- What protects the RDP data stream between the client and the server?
- How do I create an RDP connection through firewall?
- How do I prevent users in a terminal server session from messing with server files?
- How do I control who can get remote access to a server or desktop?

Let's start with the last item.

Controlling Remote Access Permission

As many administrators discovered in Windows 2000, the ability to connect to a terminal server depends on the security permissions assigned to the RDP-Tcp connection in the Terminal Services Connection console.

Here are the permissions associated with the RDP-Tcp connection:

- `Query Information`
- `Set Information`
- `Remote Control`
- `Logon/Logoff`
- `Message`
- `Connect/Disconnect`
- `Virtual Channels`

Windows Server 2003 has a new Built-In group called Remote Desktop Users. This group is on the RDP-Tcp connection ACL. Under the default Remote Desktop configuration, the group has `User Access` and `Guest Access` permissions. This represents only `Query`, `Logon`, `Message`, and `Connect` permissions. When full terminal services are installed, the Remote Desktop Users group gets `Full Control` permissions on the RDP-Tcp connection.

Windows Server 2003 has a new `User Rights Assignment` setting called `Allow Logon Through Terminal Services`. The Remote Desktop Users group is on the member list of this group. Membership gives users the ability to connect via an RDP session even though they have not been given explicit connection permissions at the console.

There is also a RemoteAssistant account with `Full Control` access to the RDP-Tcp connection. This account is used to provide access to individuals invited to participate in Remote Assistance at a desktop or server. This account is disabled by default. It is only used to intermediate the connection. If you delete this account at a local machine, you cannot connect to the machine via Remote Assistance, although you are still able to use Remote Desktop if that feature has been enabled.

The Remote Desktop feature has an additional security setting at XP desktops (not servers running Windows Server 2003). The account used to make the connection must have a password. By default, accounts with blank passwords are blocked from making any sort of network connection to an XP desktop.

System Configuration Lockdown

When you install Terminal Services on Windows Server 2003, Enterprise Edition, you'll be prompted to choose between `Full Security` and `Relaxed Security`. With the `Full Security` option, users are blocked from writing to or modifying system files and Registry entries.

This may present a problem for older applications that expect to get access to files in the system folder or to Registry entries that would be protected by the `Full Security` setting. If you have applications such as this, you may need to install with the `Relaxed Security` option.

You can shift back and forth between `Full Security` and `Relaxed Security` by toggling the setting in the Terminal Services Configuration Manager console. Highlight the `Server Settings` icon to reveal the settings in the right pane. Figure 19.15 shows an example.

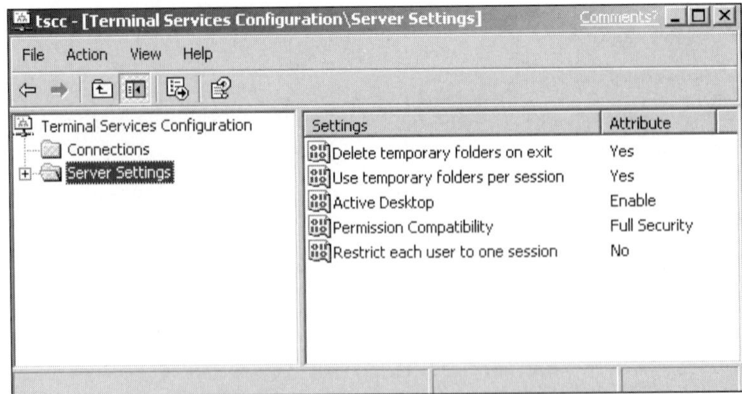

Figure 19.15 Terminal Server Configuration Manager console showing server settings.

The `Full Security` option in Server Settings is not, I repeat, *not*, a substitute for a full lockdown of the terminal server. It only protects the operating system files in `\Windows`, the common files in `\Program Files`, and critical `HKLM` Registry entries. You'll need to go through every folder outside those areas to determine how best to protect them from bored, negligent, or malicious users.

You should keep terminal server users off the Internet, if possible, or at least remove all rights to install software to keep them from installing applications from the Internet. Use the following group policies to your advantage:

- **`Set Path for Roaming TS Profiles.`** This option prevents roaming users from depositing their personal folders, which may contain executables, onto your terminal server. Specify a common location so that the users get a single profile for use when on the terminal server.
- **`Do Not Allow Drive Redirection.`** This option prevents users from copying files from their PC onto the terminal server. You may find that users keep executables in their home directories, so this is not a perfect solution.
- **`Loopback Processing.`** This policy applies the user policies in Group Policy Objects (GPOs) linked to Organizational Units (OUs) containing the computer object instead of the user policies in GPOs linked to OUs containing the user object. This prevents user policies from changing the configuration of the terminal server.
- **`Always Prompt Client for Password Upon Connection.`** This policy prevents an administrator from inadvertently removing the requirement in the RDP-Tcp configuration to require logon. Without this requirement, users can set their credentials in Remote Desktop Connection. Other users can use this RDP file to gain access.
- **`Allow Reconnection From Original Client Only.`** This prevents users from disconnecting from one machine, walking over to another machine, and reconnecting.
- **`Internet Explorer - Security Zones - Use Only Machine Settings.`** This prevents users from bypassing security zone settings and downloading ActiveX controls, Javabeans, Shockwave files, and other inappropriate material.
- **`Prohibit Access to the Control Panel.`** This keeps users from fussing with system settings.
- **`Prevent Access to the Command Prompt.`** This keeps users from bypassing Explorer limitations.
- **`Restrict These Programs From Being Launched From Help`**. Don't forget about back doors. The Help and Support Center is a mother lode of shortcuts to inappropriate programs.

- **`Remote Control Settings - View Session Without User's Permission.`** This is a controversial policy, I'll grant you, but nothing keeps people honest like knowing that someone might be looking over their shoulder without their knowledge. This one policy, combined with management's willingness to discipline folks who break the rules, is more effective than any lockdown setting.

This list is only the beginning of your adventure in TS user management. I cannot stress strongly enough that active support by management is essential to controlling the common workspace on a terminal server.

Terminal Servers and Firewalls

RDP uses TCP port 3389. Network administrators might refuse to open this port on the firewall. You cannot really blame them. After all, they're the ones who get blamed if a configuration change creates a vulnerability that some bad guy exploits to steal information or do damage.

If only certain ports are available in your firewall, you can configure both the terminal server and the RDP clients to use that port rather than port 3389.

First, change the RDP port in the Registry at the terminal server. Here is the setting:

```
Key:   HKLM | System | CurrentControlSet | Control | Terminal Server | Wds |
Rdpwd | Tds | TCP
Value: PortNumber
Data:  3389 (REG_DWORD)
```

Change the `PortNumber` data entry to a port available at the firewall. Be sure to select decimal, not hex.

Now change the port on this Registry key:

```
Key:   HKLM | System | CurrentControlSet | Control | Terminal Server | WinStations
Value: PortNumber
Data:  3389 (REG_DWORD)
```

Restart the server to initialize the new port. Verify using `netstat -a` that the server is listening on the new port.

To connect a remote desktop client to the server using the new port, launch the client using a command-line switch that specifies the port number:

```
mstsc /v:server1:6500
```

If you use the ActiveX control in the TSWeb interface to connect users to the terminal server through the firewall, configure the web page to redirect the user using a port other than 3389 by following the steps in Procedure 19.4.

Procedure 19.4 Changing Default RDP Port in the TSWeb Interface

1. Find the Connect.asp file under `\Windows\Web\TSWeb`.
2. Edit it with Notepad and look for entries starting with `MsTsc.AdvancedSettings2`.
3. Add a line right after these entries as follows:

```
MsTsc.AdvancedSettings2.RDPPort = 3389
```

4. Replace the `3389` with whatever port you've configured your terminal server to listen at.

This procedure does not work for Windows 2000 servers because the ActiveX control used by Windows 2000 does not export the `AdvancedSettings2` methods. You can work around this limitation by copying the `Tsweb` folder from a server running Windows Server 2003 to the server running Windows 2000 and creating a web share for the folder. If a client has already downloaded the Windows 2000 ActiveX control, you need to uninstall the control before the client connects to the updated share.

Data Stream Encryption

The RDP data stream is always encrypted. Windows Server 2003, XP, and Windows 2000 SP2 machines running the RDP 5.1 client use 128-bit encryption. Legacy clients that do not have the high encryption pack installed default to 56-bit in RDP 5.0 and 40-bit in RDP 4.0.

The security level is configurable in the Terminal Services Connection console. Open the `Properties` window for the RDP-Tcp icon. The `General` tab has an `Encryption Level` drop-down box. There are two options:

- **`Client Compatible.`** This permits a legacy client to request 56-bit or 40-bit encryption.
- **`High.`** This forces the encryption strength to 128-bit. Legacy clients will not be able to connect.

The 128-bit RC4 encryption stream is highly resistant to attack, but if you want a more secure environment for exchanging initial handshaking information, give Citrix SecureICA a try. It features Diffie-Hellman key exchange and 128-bit RC5 encryption.

Resource Management

Users tend to treat terminal server session connections rather cavalierly. They'll disconnect and reconnect rather than log on and off because of the speed. This is especially true in thin-client environments where the boot time of the client can be measured in tens of seconds.

If you permit disconnected sessions to pile up, you'll eventually run out of memory and other system resources. You can control session timeouts with the Terminal Services Configuration console. Open the `Properties` window for the RDP-Tcp connection and select the `Sessions` tab (see Figure 19.16).

The RDP client can request timeout values for disconnected session termination, active session limits, and idle session limits. These are generally requested as indefinite.

Select the `Override User Settings` option and set a time limit that allows users to reconnect soon after they disconnect to allow for dial-up failures and power failures but not so long that it encourages disconnects instead of logoffs. I've found 15 minutes to be satisfactory.

Be sure to select the `End Session` option for the default action when a timeout is reached. This prevents disconnected sessions from piling up.

If a user ends up with more than one session, he is presented with a pick list when he reconnects. You can use the TSCONS command-line utility (see the section later in this chapter) to swap into the other session to exit it gracefully. You can also use the Remote Control feature to break into the session if it is still active.

For security reasons, you may want to enable the `Allow Reconnection` feature and set the option for `From Previous Client`. This prevents the users from wandering around the floor reconnecting from various machines. This also potentially uses up licenses unnecessarily.

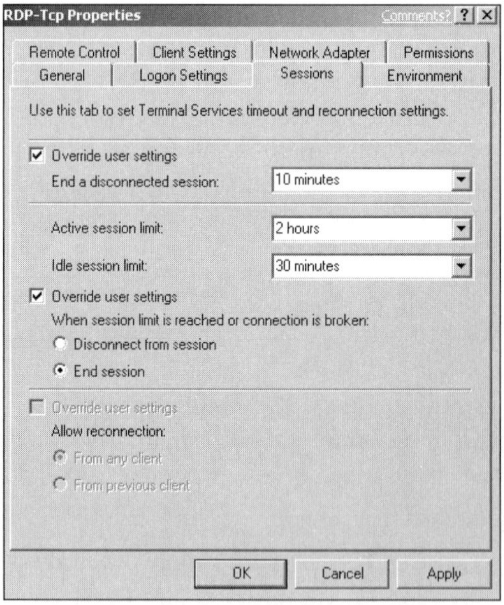

Figure 19.16 RDP-Tcp Properties window showing the `Sessions` tab.

Licensing

Terminal server licensing is a complex subject. The Microsoft Knowledgebase lists nearly two-dozen articles relating to TS licensing, and those are only the major articles. For the most current information, I suggest you talk over terms with a Microsoft VAR that has experience with terminal service products. Many Value-Added Resellers (VARs) do not understand the licensing jungle and you'll end up paying too much. Here is a synopsis.

First off, if you do not plan on using true terminal services to share applications in a multiuser environment, stop right here. You get two free licenses of Remote Desktop with each copy of Windows Server 2003. You can put anyone into the Remote Desktop Users group, not just administrators. Note: This is not a true multiuser environment. Configuration changes made by one administrative user will affect other users.

To connect to the terminal server, you'll need a TS Client Access License, or TS CAL. This CAL is essentially the same as a license of Windows XP, in so far as running a terminal service session is the same as running XP. You'll also need a standard CAL, which gives permission to make a network connection to the server.

If you connect to the terminal server from an XP desktop, you still need a TS CAL. This is a change from earlier versions of Terminal Services. You'll also still need the standard CAL. If you plan on installing Citrix MetaFrame, you must still purchase TS and standard CALs from Microsoft in addition to MetaFrame Server and ICA client CALs from Citrix. The total per-seat cost of all these client licenses, without volume discount, can easily total $400 or more. If you have 100 terminal server clients, you'll spend quite a bit of money just to have a few certificates in your file cabinet.

If you plan on using the terminal server only for anonymous, non-commercial Internet connections, you can purchase an Internet Connector license. The price for this license, which permits 200 concurrent connections, has historically hovered around $10,000. This may go up as Microsoft ramps up its pricing model. There is no per-user authentication permitted using this license. Purchasers of this license include large organizations that use terminal services to provide remote desktops to their mobile workforce.

License Servers

Within 120 days of installing Terminal Services, you must install the Terminal Services Licensing (TSL) service on at least one domain controller. Use the Add/Remove Programs applet in Control Panel. The TLS must be installed on an Active Directory domain controller because the other terminal servers use LDAP to find it. For stand-alone installations, install the service on the terminal server.

The license database is a standard Microsoft Jet database. The database location is selected during the licensing service installation. By default, it is `\Windows\System32\LServer`. The database name is TLSLic.edb.

Terminal servers discover the existence of TSLs by querying Active Directory. After a terminal server finds a TSL, it will use it exclusively to get licenses. The TSLs do not share or pool licenses. Stock a TSL in a high volume office with more licenses than a low volume office.

When you install a TSL, the installation wizard prompts you to decide between a Domain/Workgroup model and an Enterprise model.

If you select the Enterprise model, the TSL will pass out licenses to any client from any domain in a particular site. If you select the Domain/Workgroup model, the TSL will pass out licenses to any client in the domain regardless of the client's site affiliation.

If you have a multiple-domain forest, you'll be best served with the Enterprise model. However, this can make license distribution at remote sites a chore. Terminal servers will not search for a TSL in another site. Be sure you have at least one TSL in any site containing a terminal server.

The TSL must be activated either by connecting directly to the *Microsoft Clearinghouse* across the Internet or calling Customer Support for an initialization number. This activation does not contain any client licenses. It simply supplies a digital certificate to the TSL that uniquely identifies it to Microsoft. The TSL activation is not related to the Windows Product Activation (WPA) process other than it uses a similar methodology.

If you install MetaFrame, you'll also need to install a license server for the ICA client licenses. These licenses are a bit more flexible than TS CALs.

After the TSL is initialized, you must stock it with TS CALs. Obtain these from Microsoft or an authorized VAR. The CALs come in the form of a certificate with a 25-character number. You enter this number into the Licensing Manager console and it communicates to Microsoft across the Internet. After validating the CALs, the Microsoft server returns an authorization code, which is embedded into the TSL. License packs are available in a variety of programs, also called *agreements*. If you open the Properties window for the license server and select the `Licensing Program` tab, you can choose the agreement (see Figure 19.17).

You cannot change the name of the TSL or its domain affiliation or remove the license service from it. If you do, you sacrifice the licenses that are stored on the server. You can transfer the licenses to another TSL then change the server's status, if necessary.

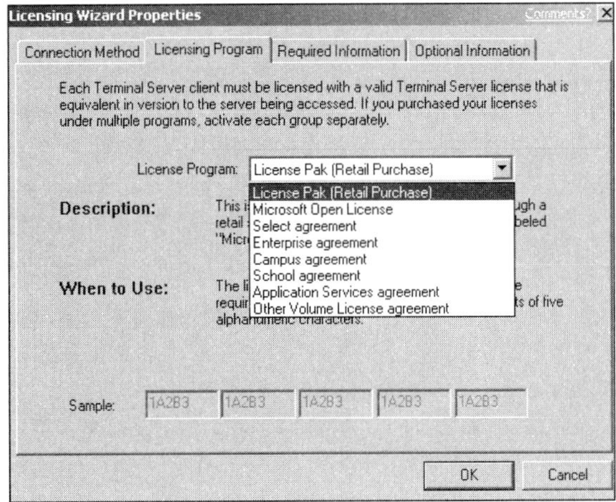

Figure 19.17 Terminal Services License Manager console showing Properties window for licensing server with the `Licensing Program` tab selected.

TS CAL Tokens

When a client connects to a terminal server, the license server issues a TS CAL *token*. This token is cached *at the client*. All TS CALs are issued on a per-seat basis. The token permits a licensed client to connect to any terminal server in the forest.

The per-seat nature of a TS CAL can come as a surprise if you aren't ready for it. For instance, if a TS user travels to branch offices in 20 cities and connects from a desktop in each city, you've just expended 20 TS CALs.

Per-seat TS CALs caused some problems in Windows 2000 that was fixed in Service Pack 3. The problems centered around devices that obtained a TS CAL token from a license server then never actually connected to a terminal server. The fix consisted of a two-stage licensing transaction.

The first stage consists of a temporary TS CAL token that expires in a random interval between 52 and 119 days. If a user actually logs on to a terminal server within that period, the token is changed to a permanent TS CAL token.

If a user does not log on to a terminal server from the device, the desktop client continues to get temporary tokens while the old tokens expire and are returned to the token pool. This prevent losing licenses to inappropriate devices.

If no one ever connects to a terminal server from those desktops again, you might think you've given away a lot of money, but the license agreement permits you to do a one-time transfer of the TS CAL to another device. You can also transfer the license if a device fails. This requires a phone call to a human being at the Terminal Services Licensing Clearinghouse operated by Microsoft. The process takes a few minutes.

TS CAL Token Storage and NT

The client PC stores its TS CAL token in the Registry under `HKLM | Software | Microsoft | MSLicensing | Store | License000 (or License001)`.

If there is more than one license listed, the TS CAL license has a Product ID of `41 00 30 00 32 00 00 00`.

An NT client might exhibit the problem of getting multiple TS CALs, one for each user who logs on to a terminal server from the desktop. This is because the user does not have sufficient rights to the `MSLicensing` Registry key. You can use Regedt32 to give the Authorized Users group `Full Control` permissions to the key.

You can remove the token from the client by deleting the entire `License###` key. Be sure to reclaim the token at the license server by calling Clearinghouse Customer Support.

If the TSL runs out of licenses, it issues 90-day temporary tokens to clients that do not already have a token. If you stock up the TSL with TS CALs within the 90-day interval, the clients will trade in their temporary token for a permanent one.

Automatic Licensing

As I said at the beginning of this section, you do not need to purchase a TS CAL to connect to a terminal server from an XP desktop. However, the TLS tracks these connections in a special built-in pool. The pool is unlimited and exists solely for administrative evaluation.

Automatic licensing can get a little tricky as you make the transition from Windows 2000 clients and servers to Windows Server 2003 and XP clients. Downlevel clients continue to use their TS CAL tokens, but modern clients will need specific TS CALs. By default, a TSL will issue an XP TS CAL to a Windows 2000 client if all the Windows 2000 TS CALs have been exhausted. This simplifies restocking your TSL.

You can block the automatic license upgrade if you want to maintain separate stores to avoid stocking upgrade licenses. The group policy is called `Prevent License Upgrade` and is located under `Computer Configuration | Administrative Templates | Windows Components | Terminal Services | Licensing`.

If you have a TS CAL token for a Windows 9x client then upgrade the client to Windows XP, you can reclaim the license for use by another downlevel client. This requires a call to Clearinghouse Customer Service.

If you are running TSL services on an evaluation version of Windows Server 2003, be sure to never install actual licenses on the server. You'll lose the licenses when the evaluation expires. Theoretically, you'll be able to get the licenses back by calling Clearinghouse Customer Service, but it's a hassle you don't need.

Remote Control

You can use the Terminal Services Manager console to remotely control, or shadow, a user session. This enables you or your Help Desk staff to troubleshoot or to demonstrate a feature to a user.

Determining Clearinghouse Customer Service Number

If you need to call Clearinghouse Customer Service, you can get its phone number for your area from the Licensing Manager console as follows:

1. Open the `Properties` window for the server.
2. Select the `Connection Method` tab.
3. Select your country and click **OK**.
4. Right-click the server icon and select INSTALL LICENSES from the flyout menu. The Licensing Wizard starts.
5. Click `Next`. The Obtain Client License Key Pack window opens. This window contains the telephone number and the 35-character TSL activation license.

Unlike ICA in Citrix MetaFrame, RDP does not permit shadowing a user directly at the console of the terminal server. You must connect to the terminal server using RDP then open the Terminal Services Manager console from within the session. Shadowing in RDP uses a T.120 feature that supports multicasting to selected devices.

Figure 19.18 shows the Terminal Services console with a list of users who have active sessions. To shadow a user, right-click the user's icon and select Remote Control from the flyout menu.

By default, the user's permission is required before you can shadow a session. After the user grants permission, your current session is disconnected and you get a copy of the user's session. You can interact with the session to show the user a step or fix a problem.

When you're done shadowing, press Ctrl+* from the numeric keypad to break out of the session and return to your own session.

You can also use the `SHADOW` command to break into a user session. See the "Managing Terminal Services from the Command Line" section for details.

If you want to shadow without asking permission, configure the RDP-Tcp connection in the Terminal Services Configuration console, proceed as shown in Procedure 19.5.

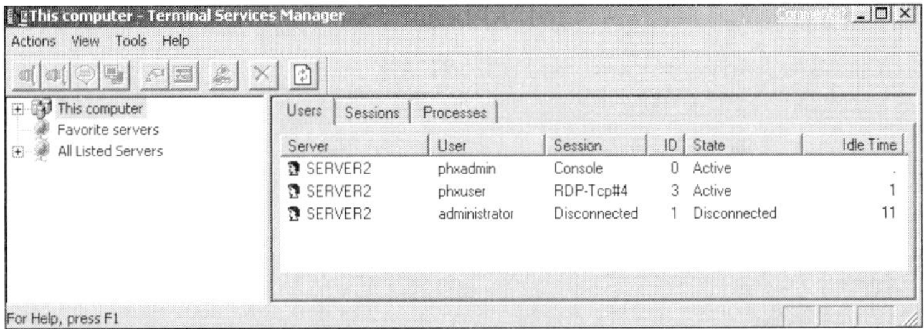

Figure 19.18 Terminal Services Manager console showing list of users.

Procedure 19.5 Permitting Unvalidated Shadowing

1. Open the `Properties` window for the RDP-Tcp connection and select the `Remote Control` tab (see Figure 19.19).

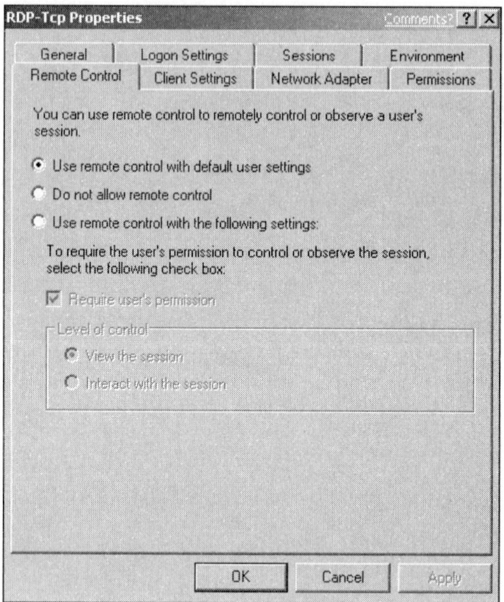

Figure 19.19 RDP-Tcp connection Properties window showing `Remote Control` tab.

2. Select the `Use Remote Control With The Following Settings` option and uncheck `Require User's Permission`.
3. Under `Level Of Control`, select whether you want to simply `View The Session` or you want to `Interact With The Session`.

Managing Terminal Services from the Command Line

There is a suite of command-line tools for use with terminal services. They run the gamut in functionality. Here is a quick list of the most commonly used utilities:

- CHANGE
- QUERY

- RESET
- MSG
- TSCON
- SHADOW
- TSKILL
- TSSHUTDN

CHANGE

The CHANGE utility has three options that call separate executables to perform the functions:

- `CHANGE USER` (CHGUSER)
- `CHANGE LOGON` (CHGLOGON)
- `CHANGE PORT` (CHGPORT)

CHANGE USER

The `CHANGE USER` option permits you to change the multiuser mode of the system. There are three switches for this option:

- **`EXECUTE.`** This mode maintains discrete application configuration files for each user. It is the default mode. For standard Remote Desktop servers, this mode has no effect.
- **`INSTALL.`** This mode permits you to install an application so that it can be run in multiuser mode. If you neglect to set this option during installation, the system treats the application as a single user application and does not store per-user configuration information.
- **`QUERY.`** Determines the current mode.

In previous versions of Windows and MetaFrame, you had to remember to shift to INSTALL mode when you installed applications. If you used the `Add Programs` option in Control Panel, the system automatically shifted to Install mode, but you had to remember to say `No` to automatic installations from an Autostart menu. Many administrators have found, to their dismay, that they forgot this step and were required to deinstall then reinstall their application in the correct mode.

A server running Windows Server 2003 automatically shifts to Install mode when you install an application. An After Installation window opens to guide you through shifting back to Execute mode when you've completed the installation.

CHANGE LOGON

This option is used to control RDP access to the terminal server. Use it to disable new session creation when you want to install an application or you are troubleshooting. The syntax is `change logon /disable` to stop new session creation and `change logon /enable` when you're ready once again for users.

CHANGE PORT

This option allows you to redirect a logical COM port outside the range understood by legacy applications to a lower port number. The syntax is `change port portx=porty`.

QUERY

This option consists of two elements, both of which are separate executables:

- **`QUERY PROCESS` (QAPPSRV.EXE).** This option lists the processes running on a terminal server by user. It includes the session name, session ID, program name, and process ID (PID). This is helpful when troubleshooting a process for a user.
- **`QUERY SESSION` (QPROCESS.EXE).** This option lists each session in a terminal server along with the associated user and device and the session status. The `/counter` switch tallies the active, disconnected, and reconnected sessions.
- **`QUERY TERMSERVER` (QWINSTA.EXE).** This option lists the known terminal servers in a domain. It obtains this information by querying Active Directory or by broadcasting.
- **`QUERY USER` (QUSER.EXE).** This option lists the users who have sessions at a terminal server along with the session ID, the session name, the idle time, and the logon time.
- **`QUERY WINSTA` (QWINSTA.EXE).** This option gives the same information as `QUERY SESSION`.

RESET

This command logs the user out of a session and reclaims the process. Don't use it unless you're sure the user has saved all data because it does not exit gracefully.

TSCON

This utility allows you to connect to an active or disconnected terminal server session. TSCON is an invaluable tool for recovering users' sessions when they have been disconnected and cannot reconnect, or when they reconnect and get a new session. Without this tool, the old session becomes an orphan that is eventually removed when the disconnected session timeout is reached. Using TSCON, you can swap into the session and close it down gracefully, saving the user's data in any running programs at the same time.

You must issue this command within a session. It will not work from the console. You'll need to know the ID or name of the session to which you want to connect. Determine this information using the `QUERY SESSION` command. After you know the session information, the syntax to connect to that session is `tscon <session_id>`.

When you issue this command, it disconnects you from your current session and disconnects the user from the session (you both can connect up later) then connects you to the user's session, which is still running in the user's security context. You must have administrator privileges on the terminal server.

SHADOW

This utility is related to TSCON. You can use it to initiate a remote control session with a terminal server client. Instead of swapping out a session like TSCON, the SHADOW utility creates a second instance of the session that includes both you and the user. This is the same as selecting the Remote Control feature for a user session in the TS Management console.

Like TSCON, you can only use this utility from inside a session on the same terminal server. Run `QUERY SESSION` to determine the user's Session ID then take remote control of the session using the following syntax: `shadow <id>`.

When you issue this command, you are disconnected from your session and the user is prompted to give you permission to take remote control of the user's session. You can then use this shadowed session for troubleshooting. The command line takes the place of taking remote control of a session from the Terminal Services console.

As soon as you exit out of the client's session (using Ctrl+* from the numeric keypad), you are reconnected to your session.

Thin-Client Products

To get the most benefit out of terminal services, especially when it comes to reducing that all-important Total Cost of Ownership, you should consider deploying thin-client devices. These are simple, CE-based units that link up to a terminal server via RDP or ICA. Most units come with a local serial and printer port along with a USB. Some legacy-free units have strictly USB connections. Be sure you get the most current models that support RDP 5.1.

The advantage to a thin client is flexibility and simplicity. Don't look for ultra-low prices. Quality units range in price from $400-$600 depending on speed, video, and extra features such as a web browser, local CD, or even a local hard drive. A few not-so-thin clients are essentially XP-based desktops in a tight enclosure. Some even run embedded NT4.

Thin-client vendors typically build lots of margin into their retail prices, much more than for PCs, so bargain hard, especially if you are purchasing quite a few units. Also, not all devices are created equal even though their specs might look the same.

Insist on fast video with lots of memory, 100MB Ethernet, and enough system memory to support multiple concurrent sessions.

For a great web site that has an up-to-date list of thin-client solutions, visit `www.thinplanet.com`. You can get product guides, pricing, and feature comparisons.

Remote Assistance

XP desktops run the same Terminal Service service, Termservice, that Windows Server 2003 runs. However, a desktop cannot host virtual sessions, only a single console session.

For reasons of security, an administrator or average user cannot simply connect to the console of an XP desktop. The user must "invite" another user to connect to the console, either for troubleshooting or demonstration purposes. This *Remote Assistance* feature resembles many "over-the-shoulder" products that permit a Help Desk administrator to work at a user's desktop remotely.

Windows Server 2003 also has the Remote Assistance feature, but it's not likely that you'll use it much with the standard 2-node connection feature available.

XP desktops also permit multiple-user sessions at the physical console. This feature is called *Fast User Switching*. This feature is only enabled on standalone desktops. It requires a special logon window (called a GINA, for Graphical Identification and Authentication). It is possible to produce a custom GINA, but as of this writing, only Microsoft has a GINA that supports Fast User Switching. If you install the NetWare Client or a remote control program such as PC Anywhere that replaces the GINA, you will lose Fast User Switching capabilities.

Enabling Remote Assistance

The Remote Assistance feature is enabled by default on XP desktops. The setting is in the new interface Control Panel under `Network and Internet Connections`. Click the `Remote Desktop` link in the left pane.

You can also enable Remote Desktop connection to an XP desktop. With this feature enabled, an administrator can connect to a desktop without being invited. In this situation, though, the administrator takes over the console session and the console is locked. Console sharing is only enabled via Remote Assistance.

Remote Assistance is initiated via an "invitation" from the user. This invitation takes the form of a digitally signed file delivered in one of three ways:

- Instant Messenger
- Email
- File

Remote Assistance via Messenger

As you might expect, this feature only works with Microsoft Instant Messenger, not with IM clients from Yahoo or AOL. The invitation recipient must be running Windows XP or Windows Server 2003 to get the most current version of Instant Messenger, the RDP client, and the Remote Assistance application.

Right-click an entry in your "buddy" list and select ASK FOR REMOTE ASSISTANCE from the flyout menu. This sends an invitation to the recipient. The recipient accepts the invitation and creates an RDP session.

Before the RDP session can make the final connection to the user's desktop, the user must click `Yes` when asked, "Do you want to let this person view your screen and chat with you?"

With the amenities out of the way, the person receiving the invitation gets a Remote Assistance window that shows a view-only rendition of the user's desktop. They can chat with each other in text or by voice (see Figure 19.20).

The invitee can click TAKE CONTROL from the top menu to share control of the console session with the user.

This session requires TCP port 3389 open through any intervening firewalls. For the most part, you would not want users to expose their desktops to the outside world, so you can leave this for internal use only by not opening up port 3389.

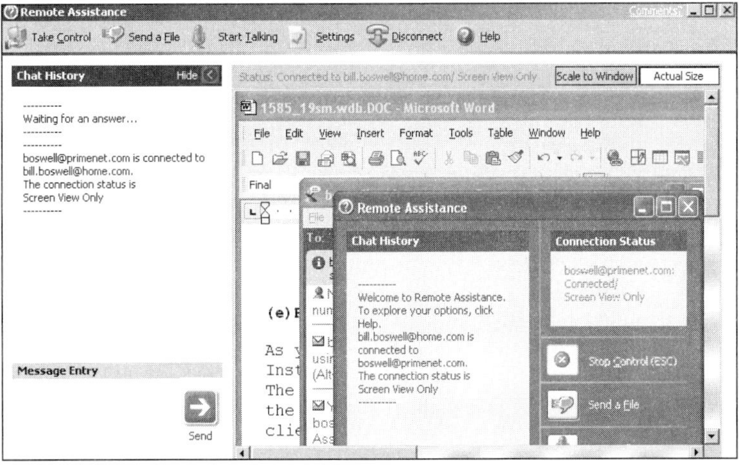

Figure 19.20 Remote Assistance window.

Remote Assistance via Email or File

You can send an invitation via email. The invitation takes the form of a MsRcIncident file that is delivered as an email attachment. You also have the option of saving the file and delivering it another way if the email option is not available.

Both of these options are only available in the Help and Support Center. Click `Invite a Friend to Connect to Your Computer`. This opens a little wizard that walks you through sending the invitation via email or saving it to a file. Figure 19.21 shows what this interface looks like.

The MsRcIncident file is an XML file that contains the following elements:

```
<?xml version="1.0" encoding="Unicode" ?>
<UPLOADINFO TYPE="Escalated">
<UPLOADDATA USERNAME="bboswell"
RCTICKET="65538,1,222.222.222.222:3389;
xp-boswell.company.com:3389,
DyujDzxhdao46uOGBJ0=,
wVcu/xeOrJp73FloZ7+SFYht2CKrKJbYXElZcD8szM8=,
```

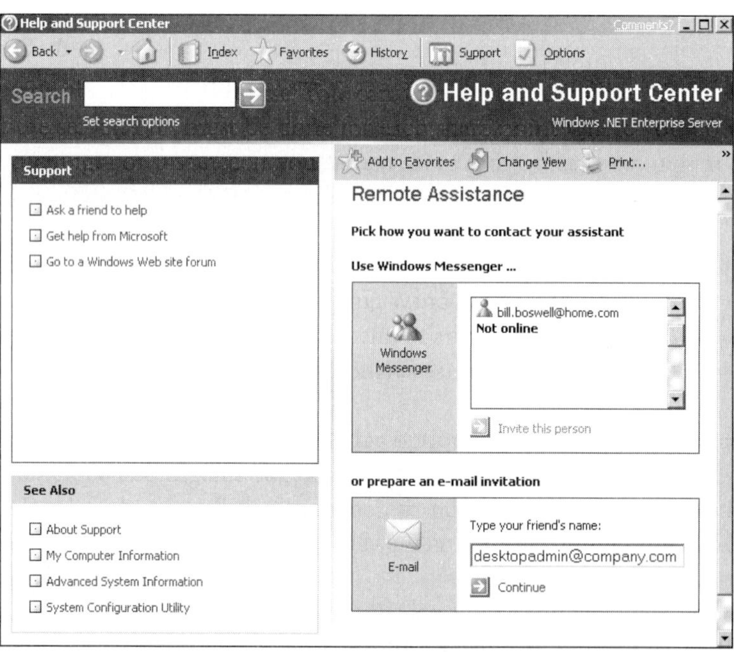

Figure 19.21 Help and Support Center interface to Remote Assistance options.

```
SolicitedHelp,
LCrBVQ19e6Al7Z3GWZY9xz/DYtD4po/4jour9/cJG4b5yZZoT3viOw==,
gQ09tB5A6qNglkeSwXNb0omFRC8="
RCTICKETENCRYPTED="1"
DtStart="999091377"
DtLength="60"
PassStub="UP!9Udt*cemT4h" L="1" />
</UPLOADINFO>
```

The sensitive portion of the contents are encrypted and digitally signed. The recipient can be required to know a password to use the file. The sender must communicate the password to the sender in some fashion.

The MsRcIncident extension is associated with the Help and Support Center. You can double-click the file to view the rendered contents. Figure 19.22 shows an example.

Disabling Remote Desktop

If you want to protect a server by disabling Remote Desktop access, follow Procedure 19.6.

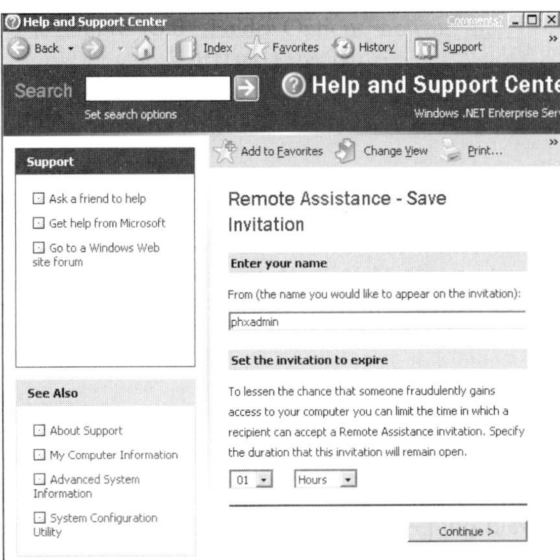

Figure 19.22 Remote Assistance file message displayed by Help and Support Center.

Procedure 19.6 Disabling Remote Desktop on Windows Server 2003

1. Right-click the `My Computers` icon and select PROPERTIES from the flyout menu.
2. Select the `Remote` tab (see Figure 19.23).

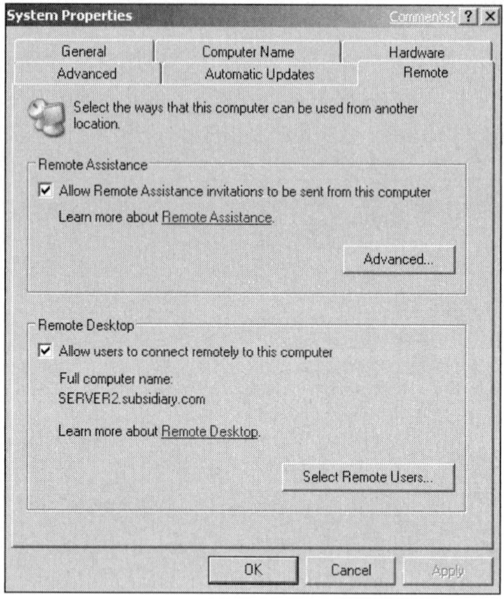

Figure 19.23 System Properties showing the `Remote` tab.

3. Under `Remote Desktop`, uncheck the `Allow Users To Connect Remotely To Your Computer` option.
4. Click `OK` to save the change.

Moving Forward

We're getting close to that magic moment when the system is ready for full production. In the next chapter, we'll see how to make preparations for dial-up users, Internet connections via Virtual Private Networks, and outbound Internet connections via Network Address Translation.

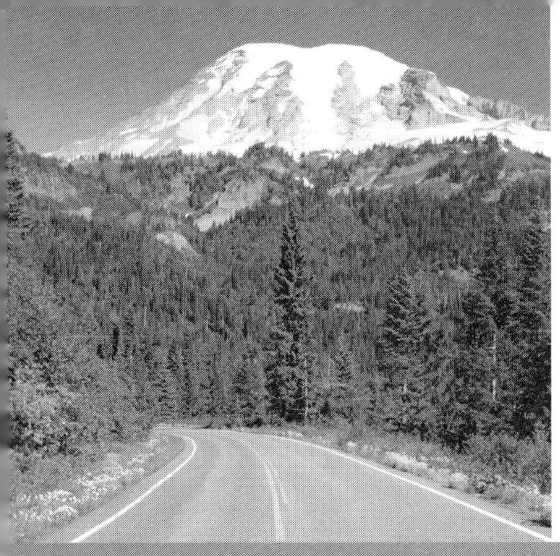

20 Managing Remote Access and Internet Routing

EVERY GENERATION HAS ITS FAVORITE TOYS FOR building complex and fanciful structures. Tinker Toys gave way to Erector Sets, which gave way to LEGOs, now yield ground to K'Nex. Personally, I'm convinced that the toys we play with as children have a profound impact on the engineered structures we design as adults. This is especially apparent in data communications topologies. First point-to-point, then hub-and-spoke, then full mesh, and now three-dimensional neural structures.

As system administrators, we live inside these data communications structures just as surely as if they were made of glass and concrete. If you work in a large organization with a sizeable IT budget, it's safe to say that the components making up this structure were purchased specifically for particular functions. If you need to route traffic, you buy a router. If you need to provide dial-in services, you buy a network access point. If you need to provide secure Internet communications, you buy firewalls and Virtual Private Networks (VPNs).

But medium and small organizations, or cash-starved elements within a large organization, often need infrastructure services without spending money on specialized equipment that may or may not be in their realm of expertise. This is where a general-purpose server can come into the picture.

The IP infrastructure services in Windows Server 2003 are more than capable of supporting a moderate number of users in a production environment. The exact number of users depends on what they are doing and their performance expectations. For instance, a group of 30 thin-client users in a call center boiler room can use a server running Windows Server 2003 as a router to the main office where the terminal server resides. If the WAN connection is fast enough, the performance will be acceptable. But if that same server supported the same number of users but was required to use a Layer 2 Tunneling Protocol (L2TP) VPN with IPSec encryption, it might start to falter. You have to experiment to find the line for your situation.

This chapter covers the design and deployment of routing and remote access services in Windows Server 2003. It starts with an operational overview of the wide area networking services available in the various server packages and in XP desktops. It includes specific details on authentication methods so you can design proper security into your system. Then it covers the steps you'll need to perform to provide the following services to your users:

- **Connect dial-up users directly to your private network.** Windows Server 2003 equipped with modems or ISDN interfaces can be configured to accept inbound calls and route traffic directly onto the network. Dial-in clients provide credentials to make connections and these credentials are validated using information in Active Directory. Connections can be managed to require callbacks and to control bandwidth.
- **Connect dial-up users to servers outside the firewall.** Windows Server 2003 configured as a remote access server can be located outside a firewall for additional security. Users can be authenticated using RADIUS (Remote Access Dial-In User Services). Windows Server 2003 inside the firewall running Internet Authentication Service (IAS) acts as the RADIUS interface to Active Directory.
- **Connect users over the Internet via Virtual Private Networks (VPNs).** Windows Server 2003 can be configured with virtual network adapters capable of accepting encrypted connections using Point-to-Point Tunneling Protocol (PPTP) or Layer 2 Tunneling Protocol (L2TP). The L2TP option relies on IPSec for data encryption, and IPSec requires a Public Key Infrastructure (PKI) for the distribution of computer certificates to use for encryption keys and digital signatures.
- **Authenticate users using smart cards.** An extra measure of security can be included in any of the remote access configurations by the use of smart cards, which contain certified key pairs that can be used to validate a user's identity prior to permitting connection to the remote access server.
- **Connect users to the Internet.** Windows Server 2003 can act as a secure router between a local private network and the Internet. The server uses Network Address Translation (NAT) so that all users share the same public IP address. The server has an integrated firewall to prevent access to ports that would otherwise be exposed on the public interface.
- **Connect users on segments with different network media.** Ethernet networks often must connect to 802.11b wireless networks and HomePNA Phoneline networks. (PNA stands for Phoneline Networking Association.) Windows Server 2003 equipped with appropriate adapters can route or bridge between any or all of these network types.

New Features in Windows Server 2003

Here is the list of new routing and remote access features covered in this chapter:

- **PPPoE Support.** Broadband has become the Internet access connection of choice for many business, organizations, and home users. Service providers take a hard look at their bottom line and demand per-user fees for traffic across the connection. Point-to-Point Protocol over Ethernet (PPPoE) provides a way to connect individual client computers to a service provider over a single broadband connection. Windows Server 2003 and XP have built-in support for making PPPoE connections.
- **Integrated Firewall.** Any computer connected to the public network needs a way to secure itself from bad guys. Servers running Windows Server 2003 and XP desktops have an integrated firewall that can be put in place when the server is configured as an Internet gateway.
- **Mixed Media Bridging.** Any modern Windows machine can route between different network segments, but routing requires separate subnets, which can complicate network setup, especially in a SOHO environment. Windows Server 2003, Standard or Enterprise Edition, or an XP desktop can bridge between disparate segments, merging them into a single interface with a single IP address.
- **Integrated 802.1x wireless security support.** The crop of wireless access points that have been released over the last few years depend on *Wired Equivalent Privacy*, or WEP, to protect user data. Unfortunately, WEP depends on static 40-bit or 128-bit encryption keys that can be easily cracked by wireless packet sniffers. The 802.1x standard addresses this problem by enabling dynamic keys that are exchanged using Transport Layer Security (TLS). This feature supports using either Extensible Authentication Protocol (EAP) or Protected EAP (PEAP).
- **IPv6 support.** Windows Server 2003 includes an IPv6 stack but the user interface has not been modified to include 128-bit addressing. The stack installs as a new protocol in the Properties window for an interface in Network Connections. This also installs two virtual interfaces for Toredo tunneling through NAT as described in `draft-ietf-ngtrans-shipworm-05.txt`. IPv6 addresses and routes are accessed via the Netsh utility. The syntax is `netsh interface ipv6`. New /ipv6 switches for ping and tracert and netstat will list any IPv6, TCPv6, and UDPv6 connections.
- **IAS Proxy.** This feature permits the Internet Authentication Service (IAS) to forward Remote Access Dial-In User Services (RADIUS) requests to another IAS or RADIUS server. This feature permits using RADIUS for dial-in, VPN, and 802.1x wireless authentication throughout a federation of forests.

Many of the new Routing and Remote Access Services (RRAS) features in Windows Server 2003 involve improvements to existing services rather than the creation of new services. Here is a list of the major improvements covered in this chapter:

- **Improved smart card support.** Windows 2000 is capable of supporting smart card logons, but many of the administrative tools, especially the command line tools, still require a password. Windows Server 2003 includes smart card support for the `RUNAS` and `NET USE` commands. It also supports smart card logon in terminal server sessions, which simplifies remote administration in a smart card environment.
- **Simplified support for multiple RADIUS clients.** This enhancement permits you to specify an address range for RADIUS clients rather than identify each RADIUS client by IP address. With this feature, you can quickly configure a large number of Extensible Authentication Protocol (EAP) switches to use the same RADIUS server for authentication.
- **NetBIOS name resolution over dial-in connections.** As much as we as IT professionals would like to see the end of NetBIOS name resolution, broadcast resolution is still a suitable and effective method in small networks. A Windows Server 2003 remote access server can forward NetBIOS name broadcasts from dial-in clients to support name resolution. This feature is disabled by default.
- **Dynamic Host Configuration Protocol (DHCP) configuration for XP dial-in clients.** Historically, Windows servers that obtain addresses for dial-in clients from DHCP have been unable to redistribute the DHCP configuration settings to the clients. This continues to be the case in Windows Server 2003, but XP clients overcome this limitation by obtaining configuration information using DHCPINFORM packets. A Windows Server 2003 remote access server will route the DHCPINFORM packet to a selected network segment where it can find a DHCP server.

Functional Description of WAN Device Support

Outside the confines of PC networks, which run for the most part over a limited set of compatible Ethernet technologies, lies the wide world of WAN communications across the *Public Switched Telephone Network*, or PSTN. This is a world where flat satin cables lead to corroded punchdown blocks that connect to 30-year-old signal aggregators that tie to ATM interconnects that interface with multimillion-dollar switches that communicate over fiber optic networks designed and built by hundreds of different vendors and operated by thousands of corporate and government entities, all of whom never seem talk to each other over the very networks they control.

Apparently the only person in the last 50 years who has not had any say at all in the structure of the public switched telephone network was my grandmother, and that's only because her complaints to AT&T always got lost in the only system that is even more complex than the PSTN: the public mail service.

Figuring out how to patch PC data communications into the hodgepodge of the PSTN has absorbed the talents of some of the finest engineers and scientists this generation has produced. I try hard to recognize and respect the complexity of their task while I spend days and days trying to get a simple DSL connection into an apartment so that a travel-challenged client can work from home without hassling with a modem.

From the point of view of connecting a Windows user in one location in the world to a server running Windows Server 2003 in another location in the same world, the available alternatives fall into these general categories:

- **Circuit-switched networks.** Interfacing with these networks generally involves the familiar analog dial-up connections used by modems. You can also use switched digital connections via ISDN devices.
- **Packet-switched networks.** Interfacing with these networks is done via X.25 PADs (Packet Assembler/Disassemblers) and Frame Relay Access Devices (FRADS) of one form or another. Connections across packet-switched networks either involve a Permanent Virtual Circuit (PVC) or the much less common Switched Virtual Circuit (SVC). Individual devices can make direct connection to each other via Point-to-Point Protocol (PPP) over Frame Relay.
- **Cell-switched networks.** These networks primarily consist of Asynchronous Transfer Mode (ATM) devices. Although ATM typically makes up the backbone of a network, PCs can access each other directly over ATM using LANE (LAN Emulation) interfaces. Devices can make direct connection to each other over a cell-switched network via PPPoA (Point-to-Point over ATM).
- **Dedicated networks.** This is a generic term for interfaces that have a full-time connection to the PSTN. Most organizations use full or fractional T-1 (DS-1) lines, although some use DS-3 and faster if their budget allows.
- **Broadband.** This is a generic term for technologies that use high-bandwidth signaling to connect customer premise equipment to a special interface either at a PSTN central office or a digital network service center. Broadband includes a myriad of DSL flavors along with digital cable.

WAN Support and NDIS

The day-to-day business of running a communications server involves very little interaction with the devices that interface with the WAN. However, getting the server properly configured, or fixing it when it decides to take a small vacation, can involve a variety of challenges directly related to how the devices communicate with each other inside the Windows Executive. Figure 20.1 shows a diagram of the network drivers used to support WAN communications.

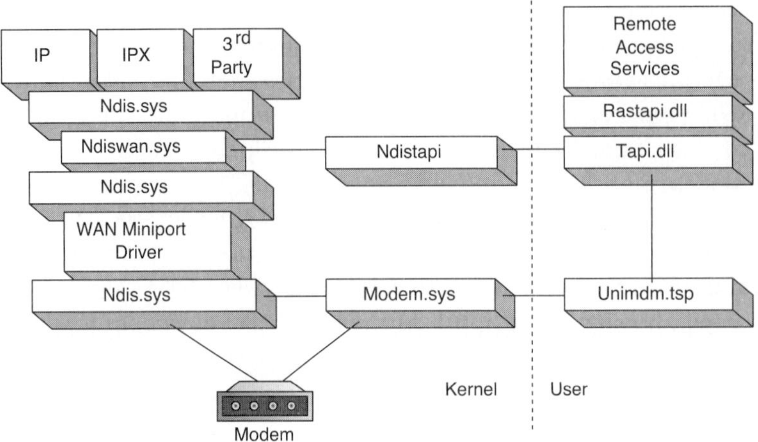

Figure 20.1 WAN driver diagram.

Windows supports WAN interfaces by making them appear to be standard network adapters. This permits the upper level protocols to go about their business without concern for the way data is getting shoveled around the network. Data link and media access control services that communicate to these devices are managed by the *Network Device Interface Specification* (NDIS) drivers.

Because of their special nature, circuit-switched devices such as modems and ISDN terminal adapters are separately managed by *Telephony API* (TAPI) drivers that then interface with NDIS. The details of this connection do not normally help configuration and troubleshooting, but it is a good idea to remember that a particular modem might work fine when making serial connection that is handled solely by TAPI but fail miserably when called upon to do networking services.

NDIS communicates with network adapters via miniport drivers. The generic miniport for WAN communications is the RAS Async Adapter driver, Asyncmac.sys. The INF file Netrasa.inf in `\Windows\INF` contains the setup information for this and other virtual WAN miniport drivers, such as the Layer 2 Tunneling Protocol (L2TP) interface, Point-to-Point Tunneling Protocol (PPTP) interface, and the direct parallel interface (PTI).

NDIS works with the adapter minidriver to build a frame that conforms to the appropriate IEEE 802 specification for the interface. For example, an Ethernet frame conforms to IEEE 802.2, whereas a frame suitable for wireless Ethernet conforms to 802.11b. For WAN interfaces, NDIS uses an intermediate driver, Ndiswan.sys, to construct a communications frame that conforms to the requirements of the underlying PPP connection. The format for the framing is defined in RFC 1662, "PPP in HDLC-like Framing."

Modem Registry Entries

Modem configuration information is stored in the Registry under the Class ID (CLSID) for modems, `4D36E96D-E325-11CE-BFC1-08002BE10318`. The configuration entries are kept in the following Registry entry:

```
HKLM | System | CurrentControlSet | Control | Class | {4D36E96D-E325-11CE-BFC1-08002BE10318}
```

Each modem is given a separate key that is a sequential number starting at 0000. Figure 20.2 shows the entries for a typical modem.

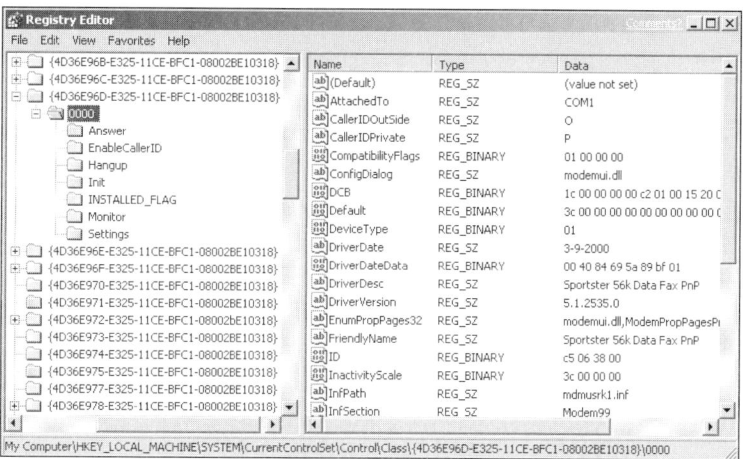

Figure 20.2 Modem parameters stored under the Modem class in the Registry.

These Registry entries come from INF scripts found in a hidden folder called `\Windows\INF`. If you encounter a modem setup problem that is resolved with a Registry change, make a corresponding change to the modem's INF file in the event that you install the same modem again.

Point-to-Point Protocol (PPP)

When it comes to data communications, a LAN is like the stock exchange. There's lots of shouting and signaling and tallying and somehow, in the end, transactions are completed. PC communications over a WAN are more deliberate and more focused. One box talks to another box over a link the two of them work step-by-step to create. The protocol used to create that communications link is called the *Point-to-Point Protocol*, or PPP.

PPP has a lot of duties and it uses a suite of helper protocols to accomplish those duties. The protocols are defined in RFC 1661, "Point-to-Point Protocol." Here is a quick list of the stages involved in a PPP transaction followed by a description of the protocols used at each stage:

- **Link Establishment.** During this stage, two physical devices must establish a data link connection that defines who they are, what size and type of frame to use, and what authentication protocol will follow.

- **Authentication.** In this stage, the remote access server takes credentials supplied by the user who initiated the connection and uses them to validate the user's identity. This dial-in authentication is independent of any network authentication that might be required after the PPP connection is made.
- **Network Layer Establishment.** After the user has been authenticated, the client interface is given an IP address and additional configuration settings, such as compression and encryption. It might also be required to hang up and wait for a callback to verify the actual source of the call.

Link Establishment

A PPP transaction begins with a negotiation performed using the *Link Control Protocol*, or LCP. This protocol is responsible for defining the data link parameters for the underlying network connection. These parameters include the following:

- **Maximum Received Reconstructed Unit (MRRU).** This is the maximum frame size that will be transmitted over the connection. Messages larger than this frame size are dissected then reassembled. The MRRU is defined in RFC 1717, "PPP Multilink Protocol," and is set to 1614 bytes by default. (See the "PPPoE" section later in this chapter for additional constraints on the frame size.)
- **Asynchronous-Control-Character-Map (ACCM).** The first 32 ASCII characters can act as control characters in an asynchronous serial connection. They are also potentially part of the data stream if that stream contains binary files. The ACCM option represents control characters as discrete bits in a 32-bit sequence. For example, Ctrl+L (`^L`) would be represented by bit 12. If the mask is set to all 0s, this indicates that no mapping is required.
- **Authentication Type.** This option determines the authentication method that will be used in the next phase of the connection. The method depends on the configuration of the client and server. There are five options: EAP (0xC2-27), MS-CHAPv1 (0xC2-23-80), MS-CHAPv2 (0xC2-23-81), CHAP (0xC2-23-05), SPAP (0xC0-27), and PAP (0xC0-23).
- **Magic Number.** A magic number is a random number that validates the packet source. If a host sees its own magic number in a packet, it knows there has been a loopback. It then discards the packet and re-establishes the link.
- **Protocol Field Compression.** This option permits compression of the protocol field in the PPP frame. Both parties must agree to set this option before it can be used. The option is set ON by default.
- **Address and Control Field Compression.** This option permits compression of the 1-byte `Address` field and the 1-byte control field in the PPP header. This option is set ON by default.

Authentication

PPP entities agree on an authentication method during the LCP phase of the connection. The selected method is implemented during this phase. This is the most complex part of the PPP transaction, and is detailed in the "PPP Authentication" section.

Network Layer Establishment

After the user has been authenticated, PPP gives the helm to the *Network Control Protocol*, or NCP. This protocol is responsible for establishing the network link over the top of the data link built by LCP.

NCP employs several additional protocols. These include the following:

- Callback control
- Compression control
- Encryption control
- Transport control

Callback Control Protocol (CBCP)

This protocol determines the callback options, if any, that have been set for the user. In Windows Server 2003, the user's callback options are contained in one of two places. For standalone dial-up servers, the information is stored in the user's SAM account. For domains, the information is stored in the user's Active Directory object in the `MSRADIUS-Callback-Number` attribute. CBCP provides three options for setting callbacks:

- **`No Callback`.** If this option is set, CBCP immediately returns control back to NCP.
- **`Callback Set by Caller`.** If this option is set, CBCP tells the dial-in client that a callback is required and requests a callback number. The user enters a phone number then CBCP terminates the connection. The client waits for a callback from the server. The number entered by the user is recorded in the Event log. This option is commonly used to support overseas callers because an outbound call from the States is much cheaper than an inbound call from overseas.
- **`Callback Preset To`.** If this option is set, CBCP tells the dial-up client that a preset callback number has been defined. The client acknowledges then terminates the call and waits for a callback from the server. The server dials the preset number, re-establishes the link, and turns control back to NCP. This option is used when you want to make absolutely certain that a particular user is making the connection.

Compression Control Protocol (CCP)

This protocol negotiates a data compression method. Windows uses a variation of CCP called *Microsoft Point-to-Point Compression*, or MPPC. It is documented in informational RFC 2118. MPPC can negotiate additional features with Windows clients while still supporting standard CCP for non-Windows clients. MPPC uses options set by the dial-up client and server to determine the compression setting.

By default, Windows PPP uses software compression. Unfortunately, TAPI exposes a feature that enables hardware compression, as well. You should not use both simultaneously. This wastes cycles compressing frames that will just get compressed again by the modem. Software compression is usually faster, so if you want to disable hardware compression, the option is available at `Control Panel | Phone and Modem | Modem Configuration Properties`.

With Windows 98 clients, always leave software compression enabled. The PPP connection transaction will fail if software compression is not selected.

Encryption Control

Standard PPP assumes that higher-level application protocols will encrypt the data stream if encryption is desired. Microsoft added encryption negotiation in the network establishment phase of PPP. The option is selected in Dial-Up Properties under the `Security` tab. Figure 20.3 shows an example from an XP client. Windows 9x uses a similar configuration window in Dial-Up Networking.

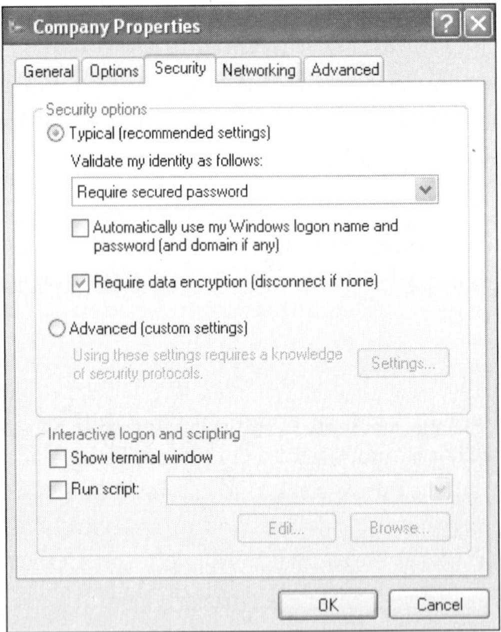

Figure 20.3 Dial-Up Properties window, `Security` tab showing the `Require Data Encryption` option.

When you select the encryption option, the client and server and encrypt the data stream using *Microsoft Point-to-Point Encryption* protocol, or MPPE, as documented in RFC 3078, "Microsoft Point-To-Point Encryption (MPPE) Protocol," and RFC 3079, "Deriving Keys for use with Microsoft Point-to-Point Encryption (MPPE)."

MPPE uses RC4 streaming encryption with a 128-bit cipher key now that export controls on strong encryption have been relaxed. Bruce Schneier from Counterpane Systems (`www.counterpane.com`) points out that although a 128-bit key sounds secure, it is ultimately derived from the user's password, which is artificially limited to 14 characters and often contains far fewer, so the long key does not make MPPE significantly more resistant to attack than the older 56-bit key.

PPP encryption only protects the data stream between the two end-point entities. If a client makes a PPP connection to an RRAS server then maps a drive to a server other than the RRAS server, the data stream will be unencrypted between the RRAS server and the destination server.

If your data is secure enough to warrant encryption, you should consider implementing a VPN using L2TP and IPSec rather than using PPP encryption. See "Configuring Virtual Private Network Connections" for details.

Control Protocols

After compression and encryption protocols have been defined, NCP turns its attention to the control protocols that configure the interface to the networking protocols used by the system. Each network transport supported by Windows Server 2003 has a corresponding control protocol. They are as follows:

- **IPCP (Internet Protocol Control Protocol).** This protocol is defined in RFC 1332, "The PPP Internet Protocol Control Protocol (IPCP)." IPCP sets parameters such as the client's IP address, primary and secondary DNS servers, primary and secondary WINS servers, and the option to use Van Jacobson compression for the IP header.
- **IPXCP (IPX Control Protocol).** This protocol is used to control NetWare's Internetwork Packet Exchange (IPX) over a dial-in connection as defined in RFC 1552, "The PPP Internetwork Packet Exchange Control Protocol (IPXCP)." IPXCP sets parameters such as the IPX Network Number, the IPX Node Number, the IPX Compression Protocol, the IPX Routing Protocol, and the IPX Router Name.
- **NBFCP (NetBIOS Frame Control Protocol).** This protocol is defined in RFC 2097, "The PPP NetBIOS Frames Control Protocol (NBFCP)." NBFCP sets parameters such as NetBIOS Name Projection that lists the names of the servers to add to the NetBIOS Name table at the client and Peer Information that declares whether the client is an end-point or a gateway. There is also an `IEEE MAC Address Required` option to specify whether transmitted frames include MAC addresses to facilitate communication on the other side of a gateway and a `Multicast Filtering` option to control NetBIOS broadcasts through the gateway.

At the conclusion of the IPCP negotiation phase, PPP is finished and the link is established. NDIS takes over and begins sending data to the interface.

PPPoE

PPP is not limited to connections between circuit-switched interfaces such as modems and ISDN terminal adapters. Windows can use PPP to establish a direct data link connection between two entities over a number of underlying WAN protocols.

One increasingly common example of this ability is the use of PPP to authenticate and connect a DSL user to a DSL provider network over an existing full-time broadband connection. This link uses a variation of PPP called *PPP over Ethernet,* or PPPoE, documented in RFC 2516, "A Method for Transmitting PPP Over Ethernet (PPPoE)."

Purportedly, the reason for using PPPoE lies with security. In early DSL implementations, each DSL interface was assigned a fixed IP address and was "always on" the network. A server or workstation with a DSL interface could route users onto the Internet using NAT, or the user could get an inexpensive hardware gateway to do the same thing. DSL providers saw this as a security vulnerability because users could do mischief from the anonymity of a NAT connection.

The real purpose for PPPoE, though, lies with revenue generation rather than security. A single DSL line can handle dozens of users, and the customer gets those connections for the cost of a single Digital Subscriber Line (DSL) interface. This is common practice over dedicated connections like a T-1, but the revenue model for T-1 networking is much different than for DSL, which is far less expensive.

The industry wrangled over this for a while and came up with PPPoE as way to manage user accounts individually over the same DSL interface. Each PPPoE request is separately authenticated and separately logged and billed. Servers running Windows Server 2003 and XP desktops have PPPoE support built in, so there is no need to install separate authentication software.

One important limitation imposed by PPPoE is a reduction of the maximum frame size that can be transmitted by clients through a server that has a PPPoE-enabled connection. A standard Ethernet frame has a useful payload of 1500 bytes (octets). This is termed the *Maximum Transmission Unit,* or MTU. The PPPoE header takes 6 octets with an additional 2 octets for the PPP protocol ID. This leaves an MTU of 1492.

When a TCP/IP client negotiates a connection to a server, the two entities negotiate an MTU. This is ordinarily 1500 octets. If the client sits behind a server with a PPPoE connection, the PPPoE server will drop the frame and return an Internet Control Management Protocol (ICMP) message to the server telling it that the MTU is 1492. If the web server has been configured to refuse ICMP, and many are, the web page will not load completely.

A handy diagnostic technique to check for this situation is to ping the web server from the client with the `-l` switch to specify a payload size and the `-f` switch to prevent fragmentation. The syntax would be as follows:

```
ping -f -l 1492 <internet_host>
```

If you get an error saying `Packet needs to be fragmented but DF set`, you'll know that you've exceeded the MTU of the web server or one of the intervening routers.

You can avoid these sorts of problems by reducing the MTU at clients that sit behind a server that uses a PPPoE device. You can do this for each client or you can make the change at one client then export the change using Regedit into to a file that can be applied to the remaining clients in a logon script. Here are the changes:

```
Key:    HKLM | System | CurrentControlSet | Services | Ndiswan | Parameters |
Protocols | 0

Values: ProtocolType
Data: 0x0800 (REG_DWORD)

Values:  PPPProtocolType
Data: 0x0021 (REG_DWORD)

Values:  ProtocolMTU
Data: <MTU size> (REG_DWORD)
```

PPP Authentication

PPP requires that the user present a set of credentials that are then validated by the remote access server. Security of outside connections is supremely important, so it is worth taking a long look at the details of each authentication method. This information helps you to decide which protocol to use and how to troubleshoot if the protocol gets misconfigured.

PPP itself has no preferred authentication protocol. The authentication method is negotiated during the Link Control Protocol stage of the connection transaction. Windows Server 2003 supports a variety of authentication methods for use within PPP. Here is a short summary of each followed by a detailed analysis:

- **Password Authentication Protocol (PAP).** The client transmits a clear-text password to the server, where it is compared to the user's password stored in a database of some form. PAP is unsuitable for all but the most trivial dial-up transactions.
- **Shiva PAP (SPAP).** This proprietary form of PAP is used by Shiva LANRover and other products. It transmits a reversibly encrypted password to the server, which is better than PAP, but still unsuitable when there is potential for impersonation of the remote access server.

- **Challenge Handshake Authentication Protocol (CHAP).** This industry-standard authentication method is used by nearly all Internet Service Providers (ISPs). CHAP does not transmit passwords over the wire. Instead, it uses a *challenge-response* methodology where the user's password is used to hash a response to the server, which compares the result to a hash performed using the same password.
- **Microsoft CHAP (MS-CHAP).** This is a proprietary version of CHAP that uses a hashed version of a user's password to respond to the challenge rather than the password itself. This method is used by Windows 3.1x and the original Windows 95.
- **Microsoft CHAPv2 (MS-CHAPv2).** This is an improved version of MS-CHAP that eliminates several weaknesses by including mutual authentication between the client and server, a longer challenge, and a more secure means of changing an expired password.
- **Extensible Authentication Protocol (EAP).** This is not an authentication protocol, as such, but rather a mechanism for using an alternate authentication protocol. The primary use of EAP in Windows is to support smart card authentication. Vendors can add more EAP methods.

Now let's take a close look each authentication protocol and examine its strengths and weaknesses.

Password Authentication Protocol (PAP)

PAP authenticates a user by collecting the user's logon credentials (name and password) and sending them to the server in clear text. Figure 20.4 shows how this looks in a packet capture.

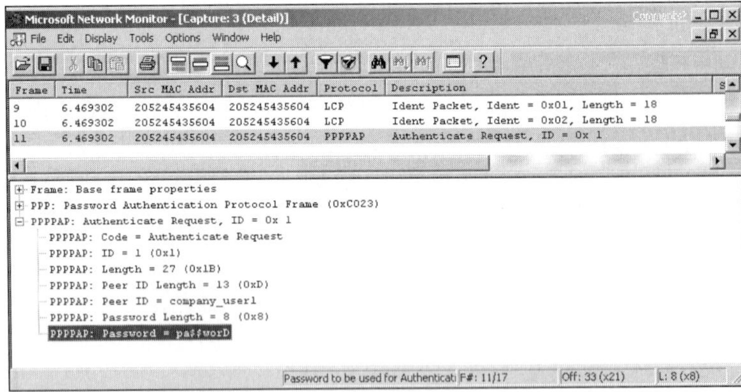

Figure 20.4 Captured PAP logon packet showing clear-text credentials.

A Windows remote access server obtains a copy of the user's password via a secure, encrypted channel to a domain controller. It uses this copy of the user's password to validate the authentication request.

Active Directory does not store clear-text versions of user passwords. You can, however, enable the storage of passwords that are encrypted with a reversible key. The domain controller can decrypt the password and send the result to the remote access server to support PAP authentication. See the sidebar, "Reversible Passwords," for details.

PAP is only acceptable when connecting a trusted client to a trusted server over a trusted phone line. Even then, the ability to view user passwords via packet captures is simply too much of a temptation. It's best to avoid PAP by disabling it at the server.

Reversible Passwords

If you have non-Windows clients that use PAP, SPAP, or CHAP authentication, you must configure the domain controllers to store reversible passwords. This is required because the remote access server needs a clear-text copy of the password to validate the responses coming back from clients who use these authentication methods.

There are two general ways to enable reversible passwords, one for individual users and one for the entire domain (after setting either one of these options, the users must change their existing passwords to generate reversible passwords):

- **Individual users.** Enable the `Store Password Using Reversible Encryption` option in the user's Active Directory account (see Figure 20.5).

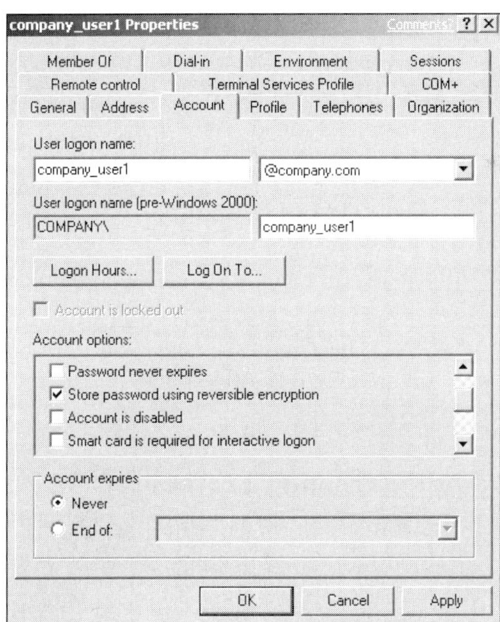

Figure 20.5 User account properties showing the `Store Password Using Reversible Encryption` option.

- **All domain users.** Enable the group policy `Store Passwords Using Reversible Encryption for All Users In The Domain` (see Figure 20.6). This policy is located under `Computer Configuration | Windows Settings | Security Settings | Account Policies | Password Policy`.

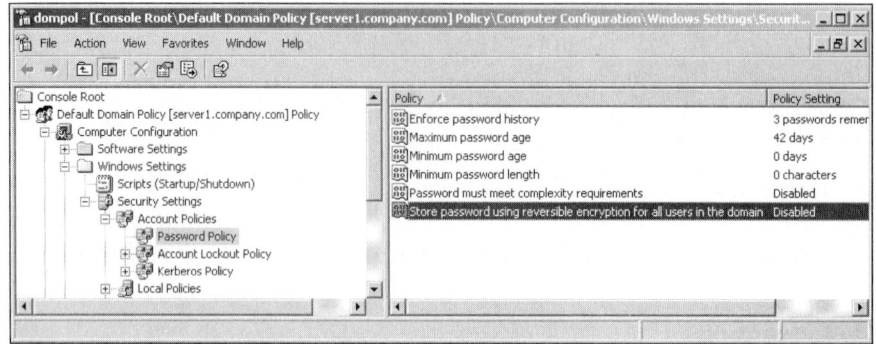

Figure 20.6 Password Policy list showing the `Store Passwords Using Reversible Encryption for All Users In The Domain` enabled.

Reversible passwords represent a security vulnerability, so only enable this feature if you absolutely must support clients who use CHAP, PAP, or SPAP.

Shiva Password Authentication Protocol (SPAP)

SPAP is used by Shiva's LANRover products and Shiva-compatible remote access servers. SPAP is supported by RAS both to permit a Shiva client to dial into a Windows RAS server and to permit a Windows client to dial into a LANRover device.

Unlike PAP, SPAP transmits passwords in encrypted form, not clear text. This is a scant improvement because the passwords are reversible, simple to break, and not coupled with information to keep them from getting shanghaied and used for impersonation.

SPAP should never be enabled as a dial-up authentication protocol at an RRAS server. It should only be used by dial-up clients connecting to a LANRover remote access server.

Challenge Handshake Authentication Protocol (CHAP)

Standard CHAP is defined by RFC 1994, "PPP Challenge Handshake Authentication Protocol (CHAP)." Windows remote access servers use CHAP to support non-Windows clients. Windows clients use CHAP when connecting to non-Windows remote access servers, such as those at an ISP.

The advantage of CHAP compared to PAP or SPAP is that the password, or a derivation of the password, never travels along the wire. Procedure 20.1 shows an outline of a CHAP authentication transaction.

Procedure 20.1 CHAP Authentication Transaction

1. The user enters a name and password and initiates the dial-up connection.
2. At the start of the Authentication phase of the PPP transaction, the remote access server sends a challenge to the client in the form of a random number and a session number.
3. The dial-in client combines the challenge, the user's password, and the session number, and then hashes them using the RSA MD5 algorithm, which creates a 128-bit message digest.
4. The client returns the hashed challenge to the server along with the user's logon ID. Figure 20.7 shows a packet capture of the challenge-response.

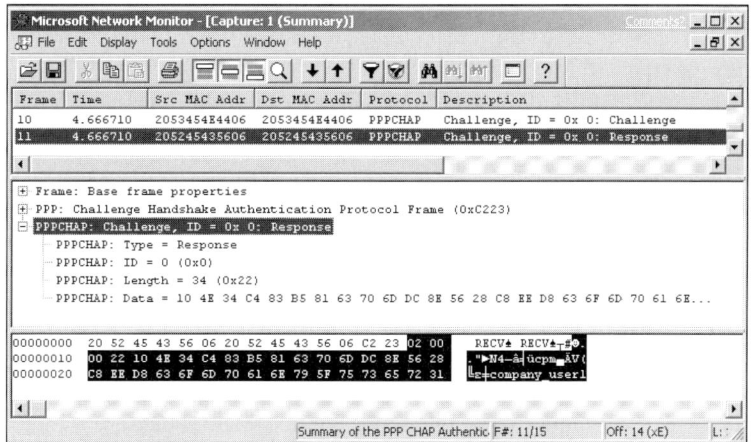

Figure 20.7 Packet capture of a CHAP transaction showing challenge-response from client.

5. The remote access server establishes a secure connection to its logon server (either an Active Directory domain controller or a classic primary domain controller/backup domain controller (PDC/BDC)) and obtains a copy of the user's clear-text password. (See the sidebar, "Reversible Passwords.")
6. The remote access server then takes the user's password and performs the same hash routine as the client. If the results match, the server sends the client a `Success` message.
7. CHAP also re-authenticates the user periodically, limiting the time that an impersonator could do damage.

By default, CHAP is disabled at a Windows Server 2003 RRAS server. If you need to support third-party clients, you must enable it manually along with enabling reversible passwords.

Microsoft Challenge Handshake Authentication Protocol (MS-CHAPv1 and v2)

A Windows client authenticating against a Windows RRAS server has an advantage over a third-party client because both the client and the server have a copy of the same password hash used for network logons. This permits the two entities to substitute the user's password hash for the clear-text password during the challenge-response transaction. This avoids storing reversible passwords.

Microsoft terms this alternate authentication protocol MS-CHAP. There are two versions of MS-CHAP. The original version is documented in informational RFC 2488, "Microsoft PPP CHAP Extensions." This version exposed some fairly notorious security vulnerabilities, including the use of the very weak LanMan (LM) Data Encryption Standard (DES) password hash in the challenge-response, the potential for man-in-the-middle attacks, a password change procedure that exposes accounts to simple exploits, and an implementation of streaming encryption that made it fairly simple to extract the secret key.

These MS-CHAP vulnerabilities are documented in a white paper called "Cryptanalysis of Microsoft's Point-to-Point Tunneling Protocol," co-authored by Bruce Schneier at Counterpane Systems and Mudge from L0pht Heavy Industries (now @Stake). A copy of this white paper is available at `www.counterpane.com`.

In response to these vulnerabilities, Microsoft replaced MS-CHAP with a second version, MS-CHAPv2. This protocol is documented in informational RFC 2759, "Microsoft PPP CHAP Extensions, Version 2." This new version incorporates the following improvements:

- LanMan DES password hashes are no longer used in challenge-response transactions, only NT LanMan (NTLM) MD4 password hashes. MD stands for Message Digest.
- Longer challenges (16 bytes vice 8 bytes).
- Mutual authentication between client and server to eliminate man-in-the-middle vulnerabilities.
- A new change password transaction that avoids documented exploits.
- Changes to the way RC4 encryption keys are generated for streaming encryption to make it more difficult to extract the keys.

Mr. Schneier and Mudge along with David Wagner from UC Berkeley have documented vulnerabilities peculiar to MS-CHAPv2 in an update to their original PPTP white paper. (The updated white paper is also available at the Counterpane web site.) Paul Leach from Microsoft has disputed several of the assertions in the white paper in a message posted on Bugtraq. (Search for Mr. Leach's name and MS-CHAPv2.)

At the end of the day, we as system administrators need to come to a conclusion about what technology to implement. It is fair to say that MS-CHAPv2 is the most secure of the password-based authentication protocols natively supported on Windows Server 2003. (RADIUS does not replace MS-CHAPv2, it merely designates a different location to go for credentials.) If security is a high priority—and when shouldn't it be?—you should consider using smart cards for remote access authentication. See the "Deploying Smart Cards for Remote Access" section for details.

Extensible Authentication Protocol (EAP)

EAP is not an authentication protocol in and of itself. It provides a way to use alternate authentication methods not directly supported by PPP. Windows Server 2003 comes with two EAP packages:

- **MD5-CHAP.** This method uses the same transactions as standard CHAP but initiates them as part of EAP for testing purposes.
- **Certificate or Smart card.** This method uses an X.509 certificate issued to a user and stored in a smart card to affect the authentication.

The MD5-CHAP package is included in EAP purely as a diagnostic tool. If you are having trouble getting a smart card deployment to work and you want to see if there is a problem in EAP itself, you can enable reversible passwords, change a test user's password to get a reversible copy, then use MD5-CHAP to validate the EAP mechanism. Do not use MD5-CHAP for production authentication.

Using smart cards for authentication requires a PKI in which an administrator enrolls a smart card user and obtains an X.509 certificate from a trusted Certification Authority (CA) that is stored in the memory of the smart card. The user inserts the smart card in a reader when initiating the dial-in connection. See "Deploying Smart Cards for Remote Access" for details about generating certificates and saving them to smart cards.

The dial-in client software must be configured to use smart card authentication. For Windows clients, this configuration is done in the `Security` tab of the Properties window of the dial-in connection. Figure 20.8 shows an example.

Procedure 20.2 shows a rundown of a smart card authentication transaction.

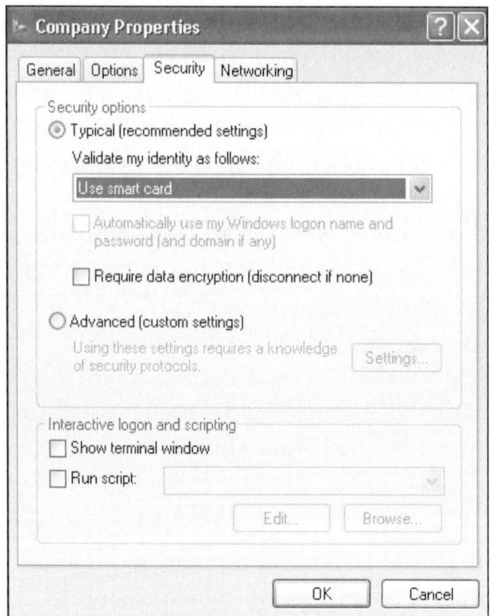

Figure 20.8 Properties window of a dial-in connection showing the `Security` tab where a smart card authentication has been selected.

Procedure 20.2 EAP Smart Card Authentication Transaction

1. When the user initiates the dial-in connection, the local Cryptographic (Crypto) Service Provider (CSP) prompts the user to insert a smart card in the card reader and collects the user's PIN. The PIN is not part of the PPP transaction. It is used by the CSP to gain access to the tokens in the smart card.
2. During the Link Control Protocol (LCP) phase, the client and server negotiate an EAP authentication method.
3. At the start of the Authentication phase, the client sends an EAP packet containing the user's User Principal Name (UPN), which has the format `user@domain.root`.
4. The RRAS server makes a secure connection to a domain controller and verifies that a user with the submitted UPN actually exists. This UPN check requires access to Active Directory, so standalone remote access servers do not support smart card authentication.
5. If the user's UPN exists in Active Directory, the remote access server returns a copy of its X.509 certificate and a list of trusted root CAs from its local trusted root store.
6. The client validates the server's certificate using standard Public Key Cryptography Services (PKCS) trust and revocation checks. It then compares the CA that signed its own smart card certificate with the list of trusted CAs returned by the server. If there is a match, the client returns a copy of its certificate to the server.

7. The server and client use each other's public keys, extracted from their respective X.509 certificates, to validate a digital signature applied to a final exchange of data. If this succeeds, the authentication transaction succeeds.

Just as with a standard PPP CHAP transaction, smart card authentication is only used to create the data connection. The user still needs to authenticate on the network. You can elect to also use a smart card for the network logon or you can fall back on a password. The best route is to use the smart card for network access, as well. This is done using the `Logon Using Dial-Up Connection` option in Winlogon.

If you use a smart card for network logons, the users do not know their passwords. If they choose to log on to their machines without doing a dial-up connection, they can insert the card and get local access. The system caches their smart card-based credentials just as it would their password-based credentials. (The public-private key pair and PIN are not cached, just the user's UPN and a data structure that includes the user's SID.)

If you decide to use smart cards for LAN authentication as well as remote logon, you might be interested in a few new features in Windows Server 2003/XP that make life easier for administrators in a smart card environment:

- You can use the `RUNAS` command with a smart card. The syntax is `runas /u:`*`user@domain.root`* `/smartcard`. The same is not true for the GUI RunAs window. There, you must select alternate credentials by password.
- You can use a smart card with the `NET USE` command. The syntax is `net use * \\`*`server`*`\`*`share`* `/smartcard`. The same is not true for the GUI Map Network Drive window. There you must select alternate credentials by password.
- You can use a smart card to authenticate in a Terminal Server session. This simplifies management via Remote Desktop.

Smart Card Limitations

Even with all the additional smart card functionality in Windows Server 2003 and XP, there are still some holes. For instance, you cannot store a user's Encrypting File System (EFS) credentials in a smart card. This feature would avoid storing the user's private key in the local profile.

Also, the system will insist on storing a password for a smart card user even though the user should never need it. You can minimize the security impact of having passwords by setting a group policy to enforce long/strong passwords and setting them yourself for the user. This is most simply done via the NET USER command, although it is possible to use Active Directory Services Interface (ADSI) functions, as well. To change a password, log on with administrative privileges and enter `net user` *`username password`* at the command line.

If you force passwords to be the full 14 characters permitted by Windows with a mix of uppercase/lowercase letters, numbers, and special characters, you can be pretty much assured that a brute force attack on them has scant chance of succeeding.

You can then set a group policy to reject all but smart card logons, but be sure to exempt certain administrators from this policy to ensure you can always access the domain should something go wrong with your PKI.

RADIUS Authentication

If you have a remote access server that is not a member of a domain but you want to authenticate users based on their domain credentials, you can make use of the same authentication method used by most ISPs: *Remote Authentication Dial-In User Services*, or RADIUS.

RADIUS originated with Livingston Systems and is now an open standard described in RFC 2138, "Remote Authentication Dial-In User Service (RADIUS)," and RFC 2139, "RADIUS Accounting." Microsoft has published extensions to the standard RADIUS attributes in informational RFC 2548, "Microsoft Vendor-specific RADIUS Attributes," and Nortel has done the same in informational RFC 2882, "Network Access Servers Requirements: Extended RADIUS Practices."

RADIUS is both an authentication mechanism and a way to implement policies based on the user's identity, platform, connection method, and other attributes. ISPs use RADIUS policies to do tricks such as, "This is user X. She is calling from the 623 area code into the Albuquerque network access server. Grant user X the IP address `24.3.28.201` and route her to the least privileged router."

Internet Authentication Service

The Windows service that implements RADIUS goes by the name *Internet Authentication Service,* or IAS. The primary advantage of using IAS service, compared to a third-party RADIUS service, is that IAS can obtain user credentials directly from Active Directory. This eliminates the need for dual databases and dual passwords that must be kept in sync. It also means you can set up an IAS server in any convenient location as long as a domain controller is available. You can even run the IAS service directly on a domain controller for maximum throughput.

Figure 20.9 shows a simple Windows Server 2003 RADIUS configuration. The dial-up clients make connection to a remote access server that has been configured to use RADIUS as an authentication mechanism. The IAS server has been configured to accept authentication requests coming from the remote access server. The IAS server accepts the RADIUS packets from the remote access server then collects the user's credentials using a secure channel to a Windows Server 2003 or Windows 2000 domain controller.

An IAS server can handle RADIUS requests from any RFC-compliant RADIUS device, not just Windows Server 2003 RRAS servers. This includes most remote access concentrators, terminal servers, and boundary routers sold by major vendors. Multiple IAS servers can be used for fault tolerance. See "Configuring Internet Authentication Services (IAS)" for details on setting up an IAS server and configuring a Windows Server 2003 remote access server to use IAS for RADIUS authentication.

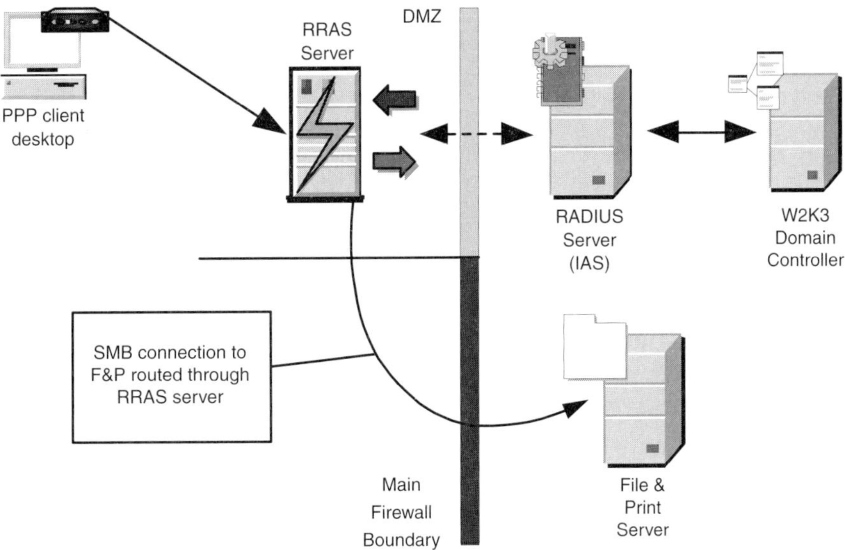

Figure 20.9 Diagram of RADIUS implementation using a Windows Server 2003 remote access server and a Windows Server 2003 IAS server.

Configuring Remote Access Profiles

If you do not use IAS, the RADIUS policies assigned to a particular set of dial-in users are configured using the RRAS console under the Remote Access Policies icon. The default policy is configured to permit 24 × 7 access after it has been set to `Grant` from `Deny`.

Each RADIUS policy has an underlying profile. The terminology is a little confusing because the two terms are used in several other contexts. Think of a RADIUS policy as defining *who* will get a particular setting, whereas the profile determines *what* the setting will do.

For instance, the default RADIUS policy defines a logon time range of Monday through Sunday from midnight to midnight. This policy will apply to anyone who makes a dial-in connection to the server. The profile underlying this policy stipulates the authentication and IP address settings that will apply to dial-in users who fall under the policy, which in this case would be everyone.

The authentication settings in a RADIUS profile essentially mirror the settings in the RRAS server properties, but the two are not automatically kept in sync. Keep this in mind, because you can spend a lot of diagnostic time poking around in the RRAS configuration when your problem lies in RADIUS.

The profile options under the `Encryption` tab determine how data will be encrypted between dial-in clients and the remote access server. Figure 20.10 shows an example.

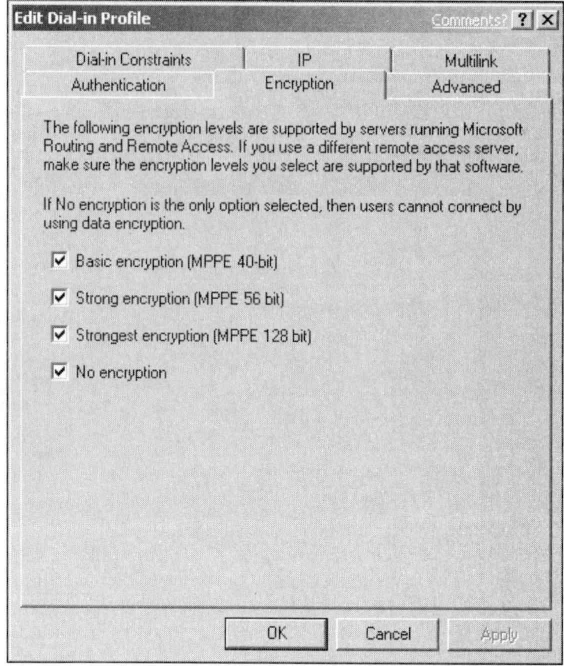

Figure 20.10 RADIUS profile underlying a remote access policy.

There are four encryption options:

- `Basic` uses either 40-bit MPPE RC4 streaming encryption or DES block encryption, depending on the connection type.
- `Stronger` uses 56-bit MPPE RC4 or DES.
- `Strongest` uses 128-bit MPPE RC4 or 3DES.

Selecting `No Encryption` with no other options prevents all forms of encryption. Selecting `No Encryption` in conjunction with one or more other options permits a client to negotiate that setting.

The remaining tabs define policies that refine and control the configuration of the dial-in clients that are permitted to access the system. Many of these options are redundant to options that can be configured at the Windows clients and in the server properties in RRAS. This is because IAS can be used by any RADIUS server, not just Windows Server 2003 RRAS servers.

Dial-Up Authentication and Domain Authentication

Two authentication transactions occur when a user makes a connection to a remote access server. One authentication takes place during the PPP transaction and the other takes place when the user touches a shared resource on a member server after the PPP connection has been made. The mechanism for obtaining credentials in the remote domain varies depending on the user's operating system.

When users on Win9x-based machines are not connected to the network, they typically escape past the first domain logon window to get to their desktop. They then use Dial-Up Networking to make connection to the remote access server. When the connection completes, a domain logon window appears and the user enters credentials to get authenticated. If the user does not authenticate at this point, no network permissions are granted. Because the user has been authenticated on the domain, each time the user touches a member server through the dial up connection, the server is able to authenticate the user via classic pass-through authentication.

Users on NT-based machines have two alternatives. The first is that they make the PPP connection prior to logging on to the desktop. The Graphical Identification and Authentication (GINA) window used by Winlogon has an option `Log On Using Dial-up Connection` to use for this purpose. If the user selects this option, the system makes PPP connection to the remote access server then Winlogon takes over to perform a domain logon, just as if the user were on the local network. Modern Windows clients use Kerberos for this transaction. Post-SP3 NT4 uses NTLMv2.

As an alternative, the user could log on to the local machine using cached credentials then make PPP connection to the remote access server. In this circumstance, the user is not immediately given domain access. When the user touches a member server for the first time, she is prompted for credentials. If the server is running Windows Server 2003 or Windows 2000, the Local Security Authority at the client takes over and obtains a Kerberos ticket-granting ticket (TGT) for the user's domain followed by Kerberos session tickets for each server that the user touches. (This succeeds only if the client is able to find a DNS server through the dial-up connection.)

The client caches the TGT and session tickets from the same domain as the user. Session tickets for servers in remote domains are not cached unless the user's domain and the remote access server's domain are both running in Native. You can see the contents of the ticket cache using Kerbtray or Klist from the Resource Kit. From this point forward, the user has been authenticated in the domain and is no longer prompted for credentials.

If the member server hosting the resource touched by the user is running NT4, the user is prompted for credentials and the server performs classic NTLM pass-through authentication to validate the user's identity. The user does not get Kerberos tickets and will be prompted for credentials again when touching another server.

This is an important point to remember for troubleshooting. XP and Windows 2000 clients participate in Kerberos transactions in an Active Directory domain even if the user does not initially log on to the domain. This minimizes hassle for the user and speeds up access to servers, especially in a WAN where classic pass-through authentication works very slowly.

The only real difference between this situation and logging on to the domain right away using the `Log On Using Dial-up Connection` option is the effect on group policies.

When the user logs on to the domain from the main Winlogon window, group policies are downloaded. That actual set of policies obtained by the client depends on the `Slow Link` setting in group policy. The default for this setting is 500 Kbps. Administrative templates and security settings are downloaded regardless of the link speed.

Multidomain Authentication

If you have a multidomain forest, you will probably want users from any domain to use remote access servers in any other domain. This includes access by direct dial-up and VPN. After all, if a user from Brussels stays overnight in Tokyo, why would she need to dial long distance to Europe if there is a perfectly good remote access server in Japan?

When a user from one domain makes a PPP connection to a dial-in server that belongs to another domain, the dial-in server must obtain the user's credentials from a domain controller in the user's domain. That's because only a domain controller in the user's domain has a full copy of the naming context for that domain. The Global Catalog (GC) does not contain sufficient information to authenticate a PPP user.

This presents a problem. The RRAS service runs in the Local System security context. When it touches Active Directory, it uses Kerberos tickets obtained by the local machine. The machine account in one domain does not have privileges to read user information from Active Directory in another domain. You can encounter a similar problem if the dial-in user belongs to a domain in one forest in a federation and the RRAS or IAS server is a member of a domain in another forest.

For RRAS server in different domains in the same forest, this problem is resolved by making the RRAS server a member of the RAS and IAS Servers group in each domain in the forest. This group has the following access permissions for User-class objects in its local domain:

- `Logon Information`
- `Group Membership`
- `Account Restrictions`
- `Remote Access Information`

The net effect of these permissions permits servers in the RAS and IAS Servers group to obtain the critical Active Directory user information needed to complete PPP authentication transactions.

Registry Tip: Persistent Dial-In Connections

Ordinarily, when a user logs off, any dial-up connections are automatically broken. You can keep a dial-in connection alive between logons by making the following Registry change:

```
Key:    HKLM\SOFTWARE\Microsoft\Windows Windows Server 2003\CurrentVersion\Winlogon
Value:  KeepRASConnections
Data:   REG_SZ (This is not a misprint. This value uses a String data type.)
Data:   1
```

In addition, the RAS and IAS Servers group has `Read/Write` permissions on the RAS and IAS Servers Access Check object under `cn=System,dc=`*`<domain>`*`,dc=`*`<root>`*. This object serves as a touchstone. If a server cannot read the contents of this object, it knows it doesn't have access to the rest of the naming context and immediately returns an error to the client.

When you first initialize the remote access service, the wizard automatically adds the server to the RAS and IAS Servers group in the local domain. You must add the server manually to the RAS and IAS Servers group in the other domains. If you forget to do this, users will get an error when they attempt a PPP connection stating that the authentication server did not respond in a timely fashion. This is the same error you will get if the IPSec portion of L2TP is not configured correctly; so don't go down a long diagnostic path for what is otherwise a simple problem to fix.

For RRAS servers in different forests, you can take advantage of the new proxy feature in IAS. This feature permits an IAS server to forward authentication requests to an IAS server in another forest.

Standard PPP Authentication Transaction

Before we dive into the various authentication methods used by PPP, it is instructive to follow through the details of a relatively straightforward sample transaction. Figure 20.11 shows a dial-up configuration with an XP client and a Windows Server 2003 remote access server. The server is a member of one domain and the user is a member of another domain. Procedure 20.3 shows the sequence of events that occurs when the client uses a modem to connect directly to the server.

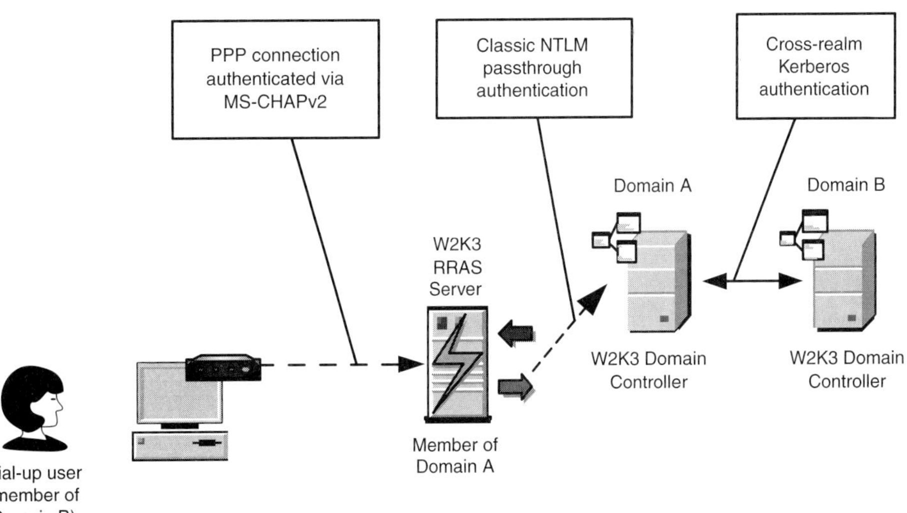

Figure 20.11 Diagram of dial-in connection with XP dial-up client and a Windows Server 2003 RRAS server in a multi-domain forest.

Procedure 20.3 Standard PPP Transaction Details

1. After the modems complete the physical connection, the PPP transaction begins. The first action involves the Link Control Protocol. Among the items negotiated during LCP is the authentication method. By default, this is MS-CHAPv2. If a suitable method cannot be negotiated, LCP exits and the user gets an `Unable to connect` error.
2. After LCP is finished, a PPP CHAP negotiation begins. For MS-CHAPv2, the server sends the client a 16-byte random number as a challenge.
3. The client generates a challenge-response consisting of an MD4 hash of three elements: the server's challenge, a 16-byte random number generated at the client, and the MD4 hash of the user's logon name.
4. The client sends the challenge-response to the remote access server along with the user's name and domain.
5. The server creates a secure (encrypted Remote Procedure Call, or RPC) channel to its logon server, which in this example is a Windows Server 2003 domain controller. (For variations on this authentication connection based on domain version, see "Authentication Limitations in NT4 and Mixed Domains" later in the chapter.)
6. The remote access server uses the secure channel to its domain controller to verify that the user name exists in the specified domain. If it does, the remote access server requests a copy of the user's MD4 password hash, a list of security settings pertaining to the user, and a flag indicating whether or not the user has dial-in permission.
7. In this example, the domain controller is unable to fulfill the request because the user is in another domain. The domain controller contacts a domain controller in the user's domain and obtains a Kerberos ticket-granting ticket on behalf of the remote access server. It returns this TGT to the remote access server.
8. The remote access server uses the TGT to establish a secure connection with a domain controller in the user's domain. It uses this connection to obtain the user's credentials and dial-in permissions. This requires access to the user's Active Directory account, which is why the remote access server must be in the RAS and IAS Servers group.
9. Armed with the user's password hash, the remote access server validates the dial-up client's challenge by hashing the same elements that the client hashed. If the results match, the user is valid. The RRAS server returns a `Success` message to the client.
10. This completes the PPP CHAP portion of the PPP transaction. The client and server now execute the CBCP (Callback Control Protocol) and perform a hang-up and callback, if specified.
11. The client and server then execute the IP Control Protocol (IPCP) and the CCP (Configuration Control Protocol) simultaneously. This is where the WAN interface obtains its IP address and negotiates any encryption options selected by the client or server.

This completes the PPP transaction. Traffic from the client is now routed through the RRAS server onto the main network, where the client is authenticated if the `Logon Using Dial-Up Connection` option was selected.

Comparison of Dial-Up Authentication for Various Clients

This section examines PPP and domain authentication used by various client platforms. This helps you to categorize connection problems based on whether they are PPP-related or they are related to domain authentication.

The examples in this section use the network configuration shown in Figure 20.12. In this figure, the remote access server is running Windows Server 2003. There are two domains in the forest. The remote access server is a member of the parent domain, although the results would not differ if it were a member of the other domain. As far as dial-in permissions are concerned, there is nothing special about the root domain of a forest.

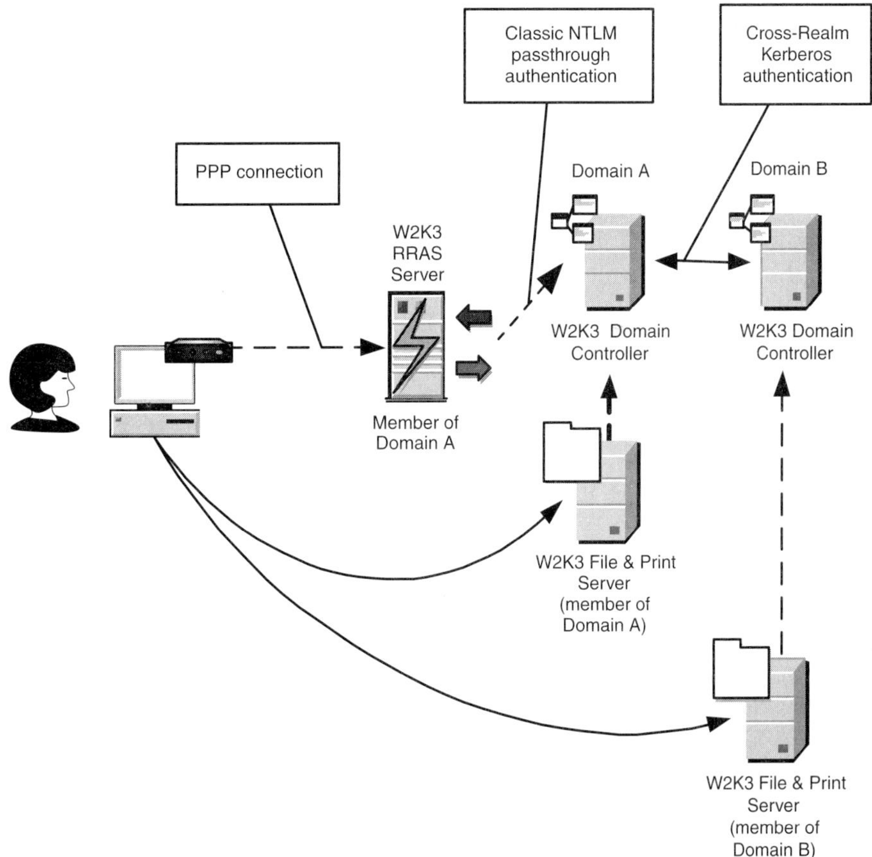

Figure 20.12 Diagram illustrating authentication methods used in various dial-up situations.

The forest and the two domains in it have been set to full Windows Server 2003 functionality, although the results would be the same if the functionality level were left at Windows 2000 Native. A Mixed functionality level would affect the outcome only if NT4 Emulation is enabled at the domain controllers. See Chapter 9, "Deploying Windows Server 2003 Domains," for details.

Scenario 1: Dial-In User on a Standalone XP/Windows 2000 Pro Machine

The client makes a PPP connection and is authenticated via MS-CHAPv2, the highest default security level. For this authentication to succeed, the user must have credentials in one of the domains in the forest. The name of the domain must be stipulated at the client. This is true even for XP Home Edition clients, even though they cannot join the domain. At this point, it is the user being authenticated, not the desktop.

If the user is a member of a domain other than the home domain of the remote access server, the server must be a member of the RAS and IAS Servers group in the user's domain. This permits the server to obtain user credentials.

After the PPP connection is made, when the user touches a shared resource on a server in one of the domains, the server prompts for credentials. Recall that the user's machine is not a member of a domain (standalone workstation) and therefore cannot participate in a Kerberos transaction. The target server performs an NTLM pass-through authentication to its logon server to validate the challenge-response performed by the user.

The end result is that the user can access resources in any domain in the forest. This is true even if the domains are running in Mixed. The user is prompted for credentials each time a server is touched.

Scenario 2: Dial-Up User on a Non-Windows Platform

The initial PPP connection is authenticated via CHAP unless the machine is configured with a PPP package that supports MS-CHAPv2. CHAP authentication requires reversible passwords in Active Directory, so this option must be enabled in group policy.

After the PPP connection has completed, the subsequent transactions are the same as for Windows clients. For example, if the third-party machine is running Linux with the most current version of Samba, the client will present NTLMv2 credentials when challenged by member servers and the server will validate the challenge via classic pass-through.

Scenario 3: Dial-In User at a Windows 9x Machine

The initial PPP connection is authenticated via MS-CHAPv2. (Only original Windows 95 uses MS-CHAPv1.) The user is prompted to perform a Windows domain logon after the dial-up connection has completed. This transaction uses classic LanMan Challenge-Response (DES password hash).

When the user touches a shared resource on a member server, the server authenticates the user via LanMan pass-through to its logon server. The user is not prompted for credentials because domain logon has already been completed. The user has access to resources in any domain as long as the intervening domains are running in Native or higher.

A group policy called `Do Not Store LAN Manager Hash Value On Next Password Change` affects this transaction. This policy prevents storing the highly vulnerable LanMan DES password hash in Active Directory. This prevents utilities such as L0phtcrack from using the weak password to gain access to the system.

Enabling this policy prevents Windows 9x clients from logging on to an Active Directory domain unless they have been configured with the Dsclient patch from the Windows Server 2003 or Windows 2000 Server CD. This patch upgrades the client to NTLMv2 authentication. See Chapter 11, "Understanding Network Access Security and Kerberos," for details.

If you set this group policy then attempt a dial-up connection from a Windows 9x client that has not been patched with Dsclient, here is the result: The initial PPP connection *succeeds* but the subsequent logon to the domain fails. The failure of the domain logon is something you should expect with no LanMan password hash in Active Directory, but the success of the initial PPP connection might be a surprise. It reveals how the RRAS server obtains user credentials from its logon server.

The reason the initial PPP connection succeeds is that RRAS always uses NTLM pass-through to obtain user credentials for MS-CHAP authentication transactions. The use of NTLM results in the return of the user's NT password hash regardless of the platform used by the dial-in user. See the sidebar, "NTLM and RRAS" for more information.

If you attempt a PPP connection from a classic Windows 95 client using MS-CHAPv1, the PPP connection will appear to fail during the authentication phase, but it actually fails during the IPCP phase when the client attempts to negotiate encryption and there is no LanMan password available at the server. The encryption used by MS-CHAPv2 relies on the NT password hash so the encryption negotiation succeeds.

The end result is that users at Windows 9x machines can make dial-in connection to any remote access server and access resources in any domain in the forest. If LanMan passwords have been disabled in group policy, the clients must be running the Dsclient patch.

NTLM and RRAS

There is a group policy called `Network Security: LAN Manager Authentication` that can be used to control the authentication methods offered and accepted in a domain. This policy controls the Registry key `HKLM | System | CurrentControlSet | Control | LSA | LMCompatibilityLevel`. There are six possible settings:

- `Send LM and NTLM responses`
- `Send LM and NTLM responses - Use NLTMv2 session security if negotiated`
- `Send NTLM response only`
- `Send NTLMv2 response only`
- `Send NTLMv2 response only \ refuse LM`
- `Send NTLMv2 response only \ refuse LM and NTLM`

The most secure of these settings is the last because it prevents the domain controller from responding to anything other than NTLMv2 transaction requests. This prevents transmitting weakly hashed challenge-responses on the wire.

If you select the highest setting, it causes PPP connections to fail on remote access servers throughout the domain. This is because remote access servers use NTLM, not NTLMv2, to retrieve user credentials from their logon servers. When you set a policy that rejects NTLM authentication, the remote access servers have no mechanism to obtain user password hashes and PPP authentication fails. When this happens, dial-in users are asked several times for a correct password then the connection is broken. This happens for Windows 9x, Windows 2000, and XP clients.

If you decide to improve security by enabling the `Network Security: LAN Manager Authentication` group policy, be sure to set the level to reject LM but not to reject NTLM authentication requests.

Authentication Limitations in NT4 and Mixed Domains

The presence of classic NT BDCs inhibits full remote access authentication functionality in Windows Server 2003 and Windows 2000. As long as there is a possibility that a remote access server could try to validate a dial-in user via pass-through to a classic BDC, the following features cannot be implemented:

- Connection control with remote access policies
- Caller ID verification
- Assignment of static IP addresses and static routes

These options are available in the Properties window of a user account in AD Users and Computers on the `Dial-In` tab (see Figure 20.13). The options remain dimmed until you shift to Native. At that point, all classic BDCs should be off the network.

The shift to Native might catch your support staff off-guard because of the change in the default dial-in permission setting for users. In Mixed, a new user is denied dial-in permissions by default. In Native, the permissions are controlled by remote access policy, which is set to `Grant Access` by default.

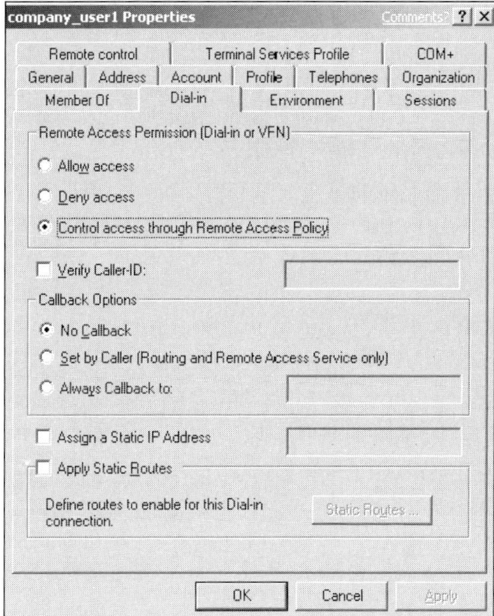

Figure 20.13 User Properties window showing `Dial-In` tab.

NT4 RAS Servers and Active Directory Domains

There's one more item of business left to cover before starting to deploy Windows Server 2003 remote access servers, and that's how to deal with any classic NT4 RAS servers that might be still be in production. Unless you make special accommodations for these RAS servers, they will not be able to authenticate dial-up users in an Active Directory domain. The reason for this harkens back to the origins of Windows networking in LanMan Server.

As we've seen, MS-CHAPv2 requires that the remote access server obtain the user's NT password hash to complete the authentication transaction. The NT4 RAS server makes its call to the domain controller to get the user's credentials, but the domain controller says, "Not so fast, buddy. Let me see some Kerberos credentials, first, before I let you touch Active Directory."

Well, NT4 doesn't know diddly about Active Directory and it keeps submitting its tried-and-true connection request until it finally gives up and returns an `Access Denied` message to the user.

Null Sessions

It's a little mystifying at first to figure out why this happens because a user at an NT4 server is able to access Active Directory without a hitch. The problem lies with the security context of the RAS service, which runs under the aegis of the Local System account. The Local System account on a Windows computer has no SID and therefore it cannot make a normal connection to a domain controller.

In an NT4 domain, this lack of security context is not a problem because the RAS service can make a *null session* connection to the domain controller. A null session is a special type of connection in which a connecting entity that presents no credentials whatsoever is given limited access permissions on a server. The NT4 RAS server uses a null session connection to perform an *impersonation* of the user to the extent necessary to look up the user's credentials and dial-up permissions in the SAM and LSA databases.

Windows Server 2003 and Windows 2000 domain controllers do not permit null session connections to touch Active Directory. This avoids certain notorious exploits that have plagued (and continue to plague) classic NT. A Kerberos-enabled remote access server is able to access Active Directory by using the Kerberos credentials obtained by the underlying computer account. The RAS service on an NT4 server is not that fortunate because the underlying computer has no means of obtaining Kerberos credentials.

So we have a stalemate of sorts. The workaround involves a group with the long but appropriate name of *Pre-Windows 2000 Compatible Access*. This group has `Read` access to the following User attributes in Active Directory:

- `Remote Access Information`
- `General Information`
- `Logon Information`
- `Group Membership`
- `Account Restrictions`

The group also has the following permissions for Group objects:

- `Read All Properties`
- `List Contents`
- `Read Permissions`

What is the net result? These permissions give members of the Pre-Windows 2000 Compatible Access group the ability to obtain a user's logon credentials, account restrictions, and group membership, all the information needed to validate an MS-CHAPv2 authentication.

Anonymous Access

Now comes the ugly part. Because NT4 RAS servers have no Kerberos identity, you cannot simply put their computer objects in the Pre-Windows 2000 Compatible Access group and expect dial-in authentication to work. You must open the door to null session connections across the board by making the Anonymous Logon group a member of the Pre-Windows 2000 Compatible Access group.

This is a change from Windows 2000, where it was necessary to add the Everyone group rather than the Anonymous Logon group to the Pre-Windows 2000 Compatible Access group. This is due to a change in the way Windows Server 2003 handles null session connections. In legacy Windows, including Windows 2000, the null session connection was assigned membership in the Everyone group by default. This was accomplished by putting the well-known SID representing Everyone into the access token that was auto-generated for null session connections.

In Windows Server 2003, null sessions are not put in the Everyone group. This stymies many of the null session port scanners that circulate around the Internet for use in hacking Windows networks. The Anonymous Logon group is a new well-known RID in Windows Server 2003 that is tied to the domain, as contrasted with the Everyone group SID, which is the same for any domain.

During Dcpromo, the utility that promotes a server running Windows Server 2003 to a domain controller, there is an option that asks whether or not to maintain Windows 2000 compatibility. This option controls whether the Anonymous Logon group is added to the Pre-Windows 2000 Compatible Access group. (The Everyone group is also added for backward compatibility with Windows 2000.)

Additionally, because the NT4 RAS server must query for specific attributes in user and group objects rather than the entire object itself, as is done in classic NT, the NT4 RAS server must be running Service Pack 4 or later. This service pack contains changes to RLOGON and other functions that permit NT to read specific attributes.

Anonymous Access and Active Directory Security

Leaving a null session connection capable of reading Active Directory, even for the limited number of attributes controlled by the Pre-Windows 2000 Compatible Access group, represents a vulnerability that you should avoid. For this reason, you should upgrade your NT4 RAS servers to Windows Server 2003 or Windows 2000 prior to migrating your domain to Active Directory.

If you should choose to retain Windows 2000 compatibility for sake of your NT4 RAS servers then later upgrade those servers to Windows Server 2003, you can eliminate the null session vulnerability by removing the Anonymous Logon and Everyone groups from the Pre-Windows 2000 Compatible Access group.

IMPORTANT: You must *restart every domain controller* after you've made this change to stop Anonymous Logon from reading Active Directory.

Deploying Smart Cards for Remote Access

Passwords of one form or another have been used for computer-based authentication for over a half a century. The day is coming quickly, though, when password-based authentication will seem as antiquated as crank-starting an automobile or having a television without a remote control. Oh, passwords will never go away completely, but they are fundamentally insecure, and that makes them increasingly dangerous as the computing climate changes.

The most obvious challenger to passwords is biometrics. The problem with biometric logons is deciding what characteristics to use for user recognition and how to analyze those characteristics quickly and with as little error as possible using technology that is relatively inexpensive. Faced with these requirements, it may be several years before biologons become common.

There is a compromise between biometrics, which uniquely identify an individual, and passwords, which only identify a user who knows a secret. That compromise uses *smart cards*. A smart card contains PKI key pairs issued to a user along with a small processor that can deliver those keys when called upon by a properly coded driver. Used in conjunction with a PIN, which is really just a fancy term for a password, the smart card links a unique commodity, the PKI tokens in the smart card, with a user who knows a secret, the PIN for the card.

The PIN is used solely by the Crypto Service Provider to give access to the tokens on the card. The PIN is not used in any logon function. When the user logs on to the domain, the public key certificate is sent to the domain controller as part of the Kerberos transaction.

You may doubt that your organization needs the level of security that smart cards offer, at least at the local desktop, but you should definitely consider them for remote users. Remote access opens your network to all sorts of nefarious galoots. By using smart cards to validate external logon requests, you have better protection against someone pounding away at your system looking for password vulnerabilities.

Form Factors

Smart cards come with sufficient memory to store tokens for a variety of purposes, such as logon, secure email (S/MIME), secure web access, and so forth. Many organizations put a picture on the card, as well, making them a physical access pass along with a virtual one.

Smart cards come in a variety of packages. Most look like credit cards with gold contacts on the outside for connection to the reader. (More advanced cards use magnetics and therefore do not have external contacts.) The reader connects to the computer via USB or the serial port. It is managed by a Cryptographic Service Provider (CSP).

Another popular form factor is a small dongle that can fit on a key chain. The dongle slides right into a USB port where it can be accessed by the CSP. The advantage is that no special reader is required. The disadvantage is the cost of the dongle, which is 3 or 4 times more expensive than a smart card.

SecurID Cards

The SecurID smart card from RSA does not incorporate a PKI token. Instead, it uses a two-part PIN consisting of a fixed portion known by the user and a dynamic portion that is generated and displayed by the card. The dynamic portion of the PIN (call the *authenticator*) changes every 60 seconds and is synchronized with a master server on the network. When the user logs on, she enters her static portion of the PIN and the dynamic portion of the PIN from the card along with her logon name.

If you want to avoid the need for a user to enter a PIN, you might want to take a look at the Sony FIU-710, also called the "puppy." This unit combines a fingerprint scanner and a smart card reader. The fingerprint takes the place of a PIN. The fingerprint scanner resists common exploits such as copper-sulphate coated gelatin impressions of fingerprints.

Selecting Smart Cards

Installing the infrastructure for smart cards looks complicated at first, but the steps are fairly straightforward. The hardest part is deciding which vendor to use. There are dozens to choose from. Visit the Hot List web site at `www.andreae.com/hotlist.htm` to start your search.

Driver Support

Two obvious candidates are products from Gemplus and Schlumberger because their drivers are built into the operating system. (Infineon - formerly Siemens - also ships a CSP in the shrink-wrap, but their chips are typically OEM'd in other solutions that might not use the same CSP.)

Even the two built-in vendors have elements that must be distributed. For example, the drivers for the Schlumberger USB reader are included in XP but the INF script isn't, so you must copy the INF script to the `\Windows\INF` folder on each desktop before inserting the reader in the USB port. The Gemplus reader requires a full setup to install the most recent drivers.

Here are additional vendors that have smart card solutions with support for Windows Server 2003 and XP and their products:

- **Aladdin Knowledge Systems—eToken.** (`www.aks.com`)
- **Rainbow Software—iKey.** (`www.rainbow.com`)
- **Dallas Semiconductor—iButton.** (`www.ibutton.com`)
- **Spyrus—Rosetta USB.** (`www.spyrus.com`)

Active Directory Integration

Active Directory integration is important to avoid maintaining dual databases of user accounts. Some smart card vendors maintain a separate database that may or may not be coupled to Active Directory. This includes SecurID from RSA and ActivCard. There is nothing inherently wrong with a solution that is not fully AD integrated, but it adds complexity.

Kerberos Integration

I prefer smart cards that use the existing Windows Kerberos authentication rather than their own proprietary certificate validation mechanism. This marries the certificates in the cards with a proven methodology for transporting them rather than a proprietary method that might have as-yet-unknown holes in it.

Here's how Kerberos integration works. When you use a Kerberos integrated smart card solution, the timestamp used as an authenticator, which is normally encrypted with the user's password hash, is instead digitally signed using the private key in the smart card. A copy of the public key certificate is included in the ticket-granting ticket request sent to the domain controller. The DC validates the public key certificate then uses the key to check the digital signature on the authenticator. If that succeeds, the remaining portion of the Kerberos transaction proceeds as it would with a password.

Token Management Utilies

Finally, during your evaluation, look closely at the utilities that ship with the card to set the PIN and format the cards. Make sure the vendor is keeping up with Windows XP and Windows Server 2003 support for these utilities. Often you'll find that the tools only run on Windows 2000 because the vendor hasn't adjusted the tool to run with the new Crypto Service Providers in Windows XP and Windows Server 2003.

Deployment Methods

A final checkpoint on your evaluation list should be ease of deployment. USB smart card readers are an ideal choice if your desktops have USB ports. You can use serial port readers for the older machines, although they are a bit slower and somewhat fussy to install, especially if you have modems and scanners and other paraphernalia stuffed onto the serial ports already.

Preparing the PKI for Smart Cards

While you're evaluating potential smart card vendors, you may want to start deploying a PKI and making preparations to issue certificates to smart card users. You must have at least one CA capable of issuing Smart Card User and Smart Card Logon certificates. Ideally, you would have multiple CAs for fault tolerance and security. See Chapter 18, "Managing a Public Key Infrastructure," for details on deploying a Windows Server 2003 PKI. If you choose to deploy a third-party PKI, be absolutely sure that you test the mechanisms for enrolling users and certifying the key pairs generated by the cards. Some vendors make this simple. Others don't.

As you deploy the PKI, keep in mind that you will need to have certain workstations dedicated to initializing the smart cards and certain individuals with administrative rights to burn tokens into the cards. The security of your smart card deployment is only as good as your processes for managing the cards. If Sally's admin assistant can call you on the phone and obtain a smart card for her boss, you don't have sufficient controls on your processes.

Also, remember that you may someday need to revoke a user's smart card certificate as well as disable his logon account. It is extremely important that you verify the functionality of the Certificate Revocation List (CRL) distribution in your PKI prior to beginning your smart card deployment.

You will also need to obtain Computer certificates for all remote access servers that accept smart card logons. The certificate is used to digitally sign the authentication responses so the client can verify the server's identity.

When you have selected your vendor, deployed the reader hardware, set up the PKI, and you have secure processes in place to enroll users, you're ready to proceed. Here are the basic steps:

- Configure an enrollment station.
- Prepare certificate templates in the CA and Active Directory.
- Designate enrollment agents who can issue smart cards.
- Prepare the cards using the vendor prep utility.
- Issue certificates to the smart card on behalf of a user (enrollment) and test the result.
- Configure remote access servers to accept smart card authentication and enroll the servers for Computer certificates.
- Test the smart card authentication from various client types.

Configuring Smart Cards

Start by designating a particular workstation as an enrollment station. This should be a secure workstation with a smart card reader installed along with the vendor's card configuration utility. You'll need the utility to set the user's and the administrator's PINs on the cards and to unblock the card should the user exceed the maximum number of PIN attempts (typically three tries).

The enrollment station should be running XP or Windows 2000, depending on the vendor. If you are using a Windows Server 2003 PKI, you will need IE5 or later to interact with the Certification Authority via the web.

Prepare the Certificate Templates

The templates used for smart card logons are not installed by default on a Windows Server 2003 CA. Neither is the template for Enrollment certificates, which the administrators responsible for user enrollment will need. You must install these templates manually using the Certification Authority console (see Procedure 20.4). Figure 20.14 shows the default template list in the CA console.

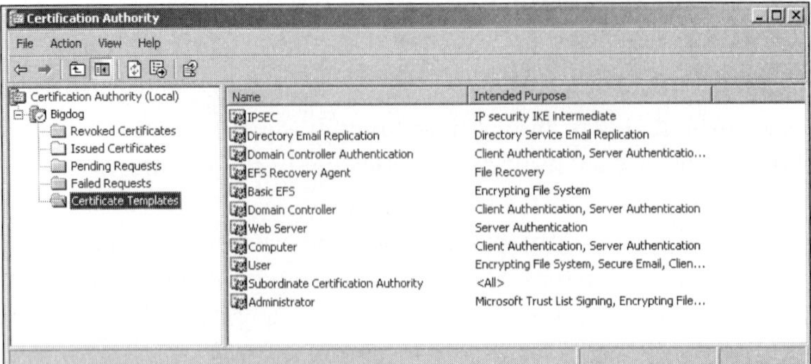

Figure 20.14 Certification Authority console showing default list of certificate templates.

Procedure 20.4 Enabling the Smart Card User Template

1. Right-click `Certificate Templates` and select NEW | CERTIFICATE TEMPLATE TO ISSUE from the flyout menu. The Enable Certificate Templates window opens (see Figure 20.15).

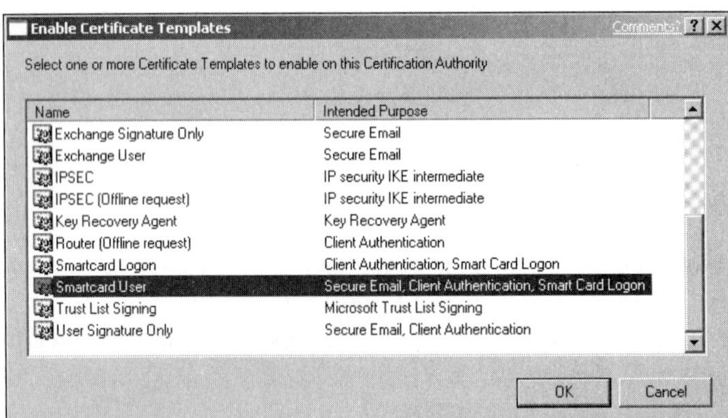

Figure 20.15 Enable Certificate Templates window showing a list of templates that have not yet been enabled.

2. Select `Smartcard User` from the list and click `OK`.
3. Do the same for the Smartcard Logon template if you want to deploy only the logon features.
4. Do the same procedure again and this time select the `Enrollment Agent` template.
5. Verify that the templates are now listed in the main window of the console.
6. Close the console.

At this point, the certificate templates are ready for use in enrollment. Copies of the templates are placed in Active Directory where they are available to all Enterprise CA servers. (Standalone CAs do not use templates.)

The next stage is to issue Enrollment Agent certificates to the administrators who will be running the enrollment station.

Issuing an Enrollment Agent Certificate

A Windows Server 2003 CA will not issue a Smart Card User or Smart Card Logon certificate unless the administrator making the request has an Enrollment Agent (EA) certificate to use for digitally signing the request. The administrator's EA certificate must be physically present on the enrollment workstation.

The simplest way to obtain an EA certificate is to request it via the `Certificates` snap-in while logged on at the console of the enrollment workstation. Alternatively, you can obtain the certificate at the administrator's home workstation then make a copy of the certificate and put the copy on the enrollment workstation.

For security purposes, the CA will not issue an EA certificate to someone unless they have access permission to the associated template in Active Directory. By default, only the Domain Admins group and the Enterprise Admins group is on the access list for this template. To avoid giving your EA administrators such wide-ranging privileges, create a new group called Enrollment Agents and put this group on the access control list (ACL) for the Enrollment Agent certificate with `Read` and `Enroll` permission. This is explained in Procedure 20.5.

Procedure 20.5 Issuing Enrollment Agent Certificates to Operations Administrators

1. Log on at the console of the enrollment station as a Domain Admin or Enterprise Admin.
2. Use the AD Users and Computers console to create a new group called Enrollment Agents (or some other name you prefer).
3. Make the Operations administrator responsible for issuing smart cards a member of this group.
4. Open the `AD Sites and Services` console.
5. From the menu, select View | Show Services Node to display the Services container. (If that option is not in the View menu, make sure the very top icon in the tree is highlighted then try again.)
6. Expand the tree to `Services | Public Key Services | Certificate Templates` and locate the Enrollment Agent icon in the right pane (see Figure 20.16).

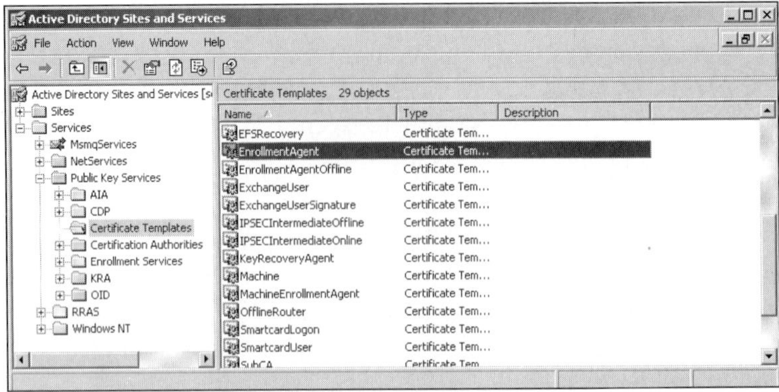

Figure 20.16 AD Sites and Services console showing Certificate Templates container holding the Enrollment Agent certificate.

7. Open the Properties window for the Enrollment Agent template and select the `Security` tab.
8. Add the Enrollment Agents group to the access list and give the group `Read` and `Enroll` permissions.
9. Close the console.
10. Open an empty console by entering `MMC` at the Run window.
11. From the menu, select FILE | ADD/REMOVE SNAP-IN.
12. Click `Add` to open the Add Standalone Snap-In window.
13. Select `Certificate` from the pick list and click `OK`. The Certificates Snap-In window opens.
14. Select `My User Account` and click `Finish`.
15. Click `Close` to close the Add Standalone Snap-In window.
16. Click `OK` to close the Add/Remove Snap-In window. The Certificates tree for the current user is now listed in the main window.
17. Expand the tree to `Personal | Certificates`.
18. Right-click `Certificates` and select ALL TASKS | REQUEST NEW CERTIFICATE from the flyout menu. The Certificate Request Wizard starts. If the wizard does not start, you either do not have sufficient rights to select *any* certificate (unlikely) or the workstation is not a member of the domain or it is unable to communicate with a domain controller to retrieve a list of certificate templates.
19. Click `Next`. The Certificate Types window opens (see Figure 20.17).

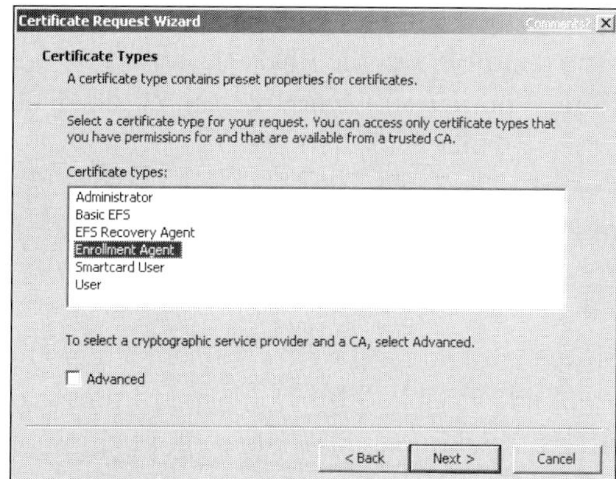

Figure 20.17 Certificate Types window showing list of certificate templates for which the user has `Enroll` permissions.

20. Highlight `Enrollment Agent` and click `Next`. The Certificate Friendly Name and Description window opens. Leave this blank.
21. Click `Next`. A summary window opens. Click `Finish` to save the changes and obtain the certificate. A message will notify you when the certificate has been successfully issued.

At this point, the administrator holding the EA certificate is ready to prepare smart cards for users at the enrollment workstation.

Enrolling a Smart Card User

The process called *enrollment* consists of obtaining a certificate for the public key generated as part of a public/private key pair by an engine on the smart card. This is done using a web interface rather than the `Certificates` snap-in because the web interface includes an ActiveX control for transferring the certificate securely to the smart card's memory.

To perform this procedure, you'll need a card that is compatible with the smart card reader. You can prep the card with a new PIN using the vendor utility, or you can assign the PIN during the enrollment process. For vendors other than Gemplus and Schlumberger, you will need to install the vendor's CSP in the enrollment station and all workstations using that vendor's smart card. There may also be additional components to install in Active Directory and the enrollment station.

You can only issue smart card certificates to users in the same forest as the CA. This ensures that domain controllers in the forest can validate the certificate when it is presented during logon. When you have the prerequisites in place, you're ready to begin. To enroll a user, follow Procedure 20.6.

Procedure 20.6 Enrolling a Smart Card User

1. At the enrollment station, point the web browser at the CA by entering its fully qualified name with a `/certsrv` tacked on—for example, `server1.company.com/certsrv`. A Welcome page like that shown in Figure 20.18 opens.

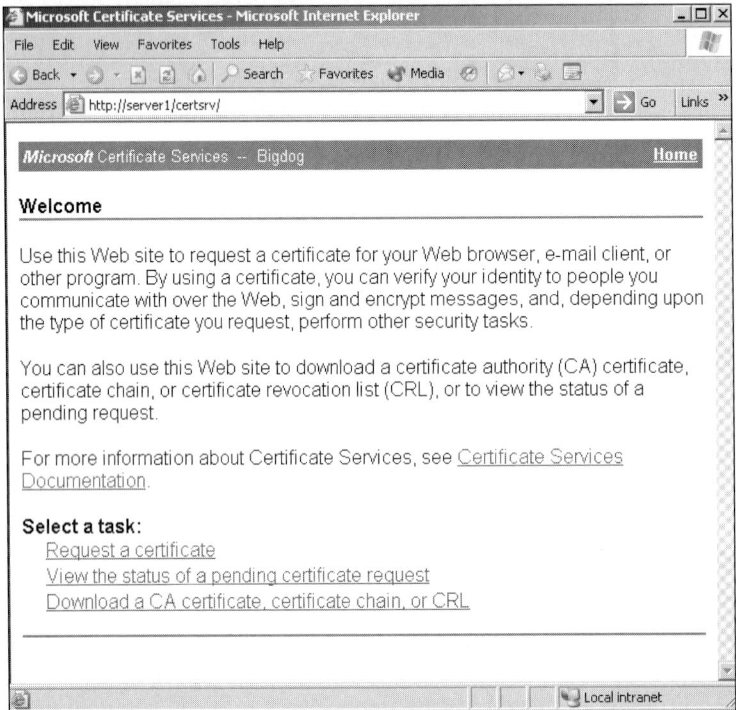

Figure 20.18 Welcome page from the Certificate Services web site running on a Windows Server 2003 CA.

2. Click `Request a Certificate`. The Request a Certificate page opens.
3. Click `Advanced Certificate Request`. The Advanced Certificate Request page opens (see Figure 20.19).

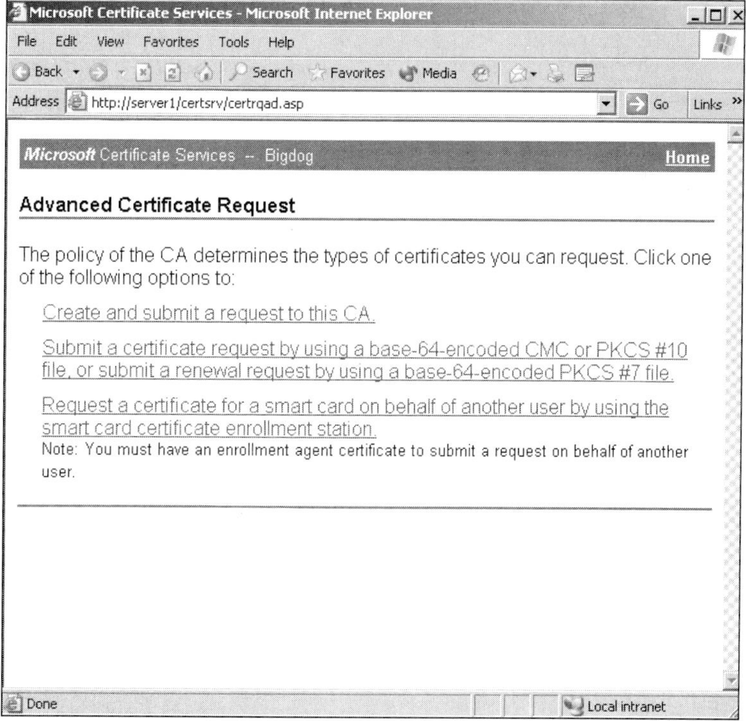

Figure 20.19 Certificate Services—Advanced Certificate Request page.

4. Click the option that starts out `Request a Certificate for a Smart Card...` The Smart Card Certificate Enrollment Station page opens (see Figure 20.20).

   If the field next to `Administrator Signing Certificate` is empty, you did not obtain an Enrollment Agent certificate or you did not transfer the certificate to this computer.

5. Next to `Certificate Template`, select `Smartcard User`. This certificate type includes the Smart Card Logon usage, so there is no need to issue a separate certificate for the logon function.

   If the `Certificate Authority` field does not now list a CA, you forgot to enable the associated template in the Certification Authority console.

6. Next to `Cryptographic Service Provider`, select the name of the vendor you're using for your smart cards.

   If the vendor name does not appear on the list, you have not installed the vendor's CSP on the enrollment workstation.

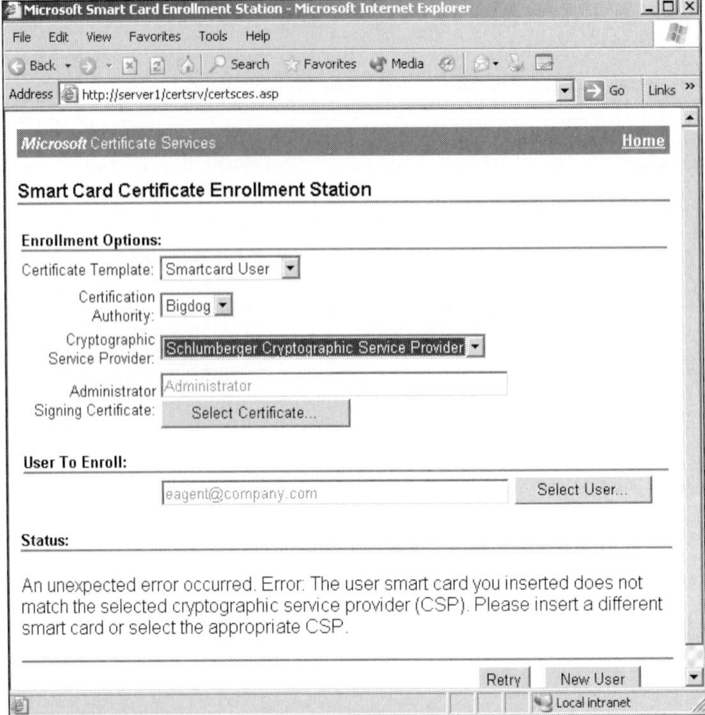

Figure 20.20 Certificate Services—Smart Card Certificate Enrollment Station page.

7. Click `Select User` and find the user's name in the Active Directory search window. The user must have domain credentials. For testing, it's best to enroll yourself so you can immediately check the results.
8. Place the smart card in the reader and click `Enroll`.
9. If you've done everything right, the CSP will take over and display a window for entering the PIN assigned to the card. (Figure 20.21 shows example from the Schlumberger CSP.)

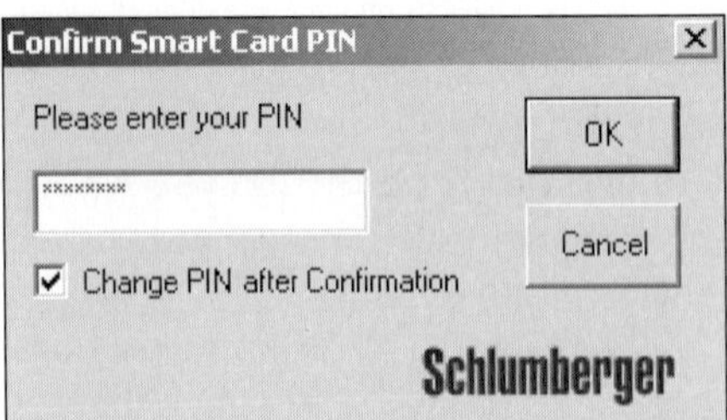

Figure 20.21 Confirm Smart Card PIN window.

10. The default PIN for a Schlumberger card is 00000000 (8 zeros). The default PIN for a Gemplus card is 1234. *Never leave the card with the default PIN.*
11. When the certificate has been stored in the card, the Enrollment Station page updates with a completion status message. Click `View Certificate` to make sure the certificate was issued to the proper user (see Figure 20.22). This is extremely important. You do not want to accidentally enroll one user then give the card to another user.

Figure 20.22 Certificate contents for a newly issued smart card user.

This completes the enrollment process. Now test the card to make sure it gives access.

Testing the Certificate

Any Windows Server 2003 or XP machine will accept a smart card logon request if the appropriate reader for the card has been installed. When the reader is found by the system, the window displayed by Winlogon is modified to show an icon of a reader and a prompt for the user to either enter a password or insert a smart card.

When you insert the card, you are prompted for a PIN. Enter the PIN that was assigned during enrollment. The only reason the logon should fail is if the user no longer exists in Active Directory or a domain controller and Global Catalog (GC) server are not available. (Like standard logons, a GC is required to obtain the user's Universal group memberships and to crack the UPN into the name\domain components.)

You should also perform at least one test of certificate revocation handling. Do this using the Certification Authority console to revoke a card issued to a test user. Publish a Delta CRL then validate that the user cannot log on using the smart card. The user should get a notification that the card has been revoked. See Chapter 18, "Managing a Public Key Infrastructure," for details on revocation publishing.

Now that the smart card infrastructure is in place, you're ready to configure the remote access server to accept smart card authentication at logon.

Configuring RRAS to Accept Smart Cards

Any Windows Server 2003 or Windows 2000 remote access server is capable of accepting smart card logons. You only need to configure the RRAS service to use Extensible Authentication Protocol (EAP) and to select smart card logons as the EAP method.

What makes the process a little more complicated than you would otherwise expect is that you must also configure the remote access policies if you are in Native. Don't forget to do this, because the RRAS server will refuse the connection even though you think that you've done everything correctly. Procedure 20.7 contains the details for preparing the server to accept smart card logons.

Procedure 20.7 Preparing a Remote Access Server for Smart Card Logons

1. Open the `RRAS` console.
2. Open the `Properties` window for the server.
3. Select the `Security` tab.
4. Select `Windows Authentication` then click `Authentication Methods`.
5. Select the `Extensible Authentication Protocol (EAP)` option then click `EAP Methods`.
6. From the selection list, double-click `Smart Card or Other Certificate` and click `OK`.
7. Uncheck all other authentication options then click `OK` to return to the Properties window.
8. Click `OK` to save the changes, close the window, and return to the main RRAS console.
9. Navigate down the tree to `Remote Access Policies`. You can create a new policy for smart card logons or you can modify the existing policy. In this instance, let's modify the existing policy.
10. Double-click the `Allow Access If Dial-In Permission Is Enabled` icon to open its Properties window.
11. Click `Edit Profile`.
12. Select the `Authentication` tab (see Figure 20.23).

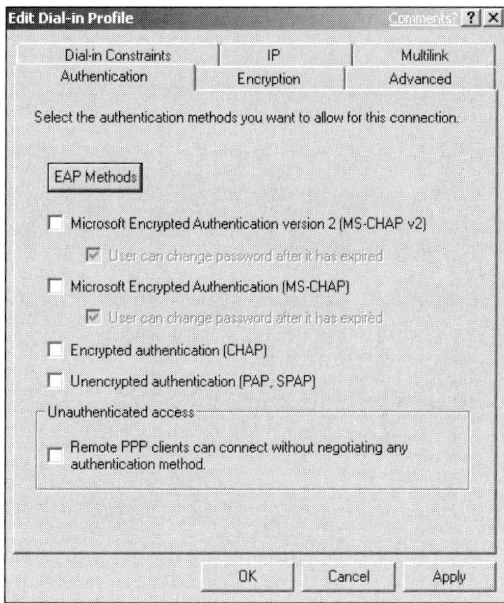

Figure 20.23 Edit Dial-In Profile window showing `Authentication` tab with all options other than `EAP` deselected.

13. Click `EAP Methods`. The Select EAP Providers window opens.
14. Click `Add`. The Add EAP window opens.
15. Select the `Smart Card or Other Certificate` option and click `OK` to return to the Select EAP Providers window.
16. Click `Edit`. The Smart Card or Other Certificate Properties window opens.
17. In the `Certificate Issued To` field, select the Computer certificate issued to the server (see Figure 20.24).

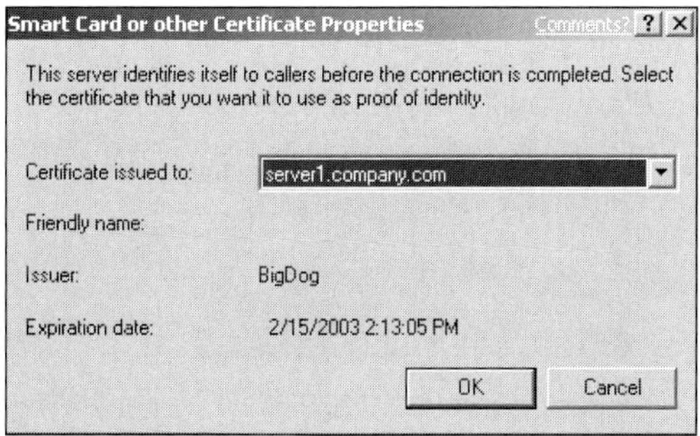

Figure 20.24 Smart Card or Other Certificate Properties window showing the selection of the computer certificate issued to the RRAS server.

18. Click `OK` then `OK` again and `OK` once more to close all the windows and return to the main RRAS console.

The remote access server is now ready to accept smart card authentication. Now test to make sure it works.

Smart Card Remote Logon Testing

Configure a dial-in client to use smart card authentication. The exact procedure for doing this varies depending on the platform. Figure 20.25 shows the configuration settings for an XP client.

After the client has been configured to use smart card logons, double-click the dial-in connection icon to initiate the connection and insert a smart card into the reader when prompted. (You can also insert the card first to avoid the first prompt.) A pop-up window collects your PIN then the system makes the dial-in connection.

If the CSP refuses to read the card because of an improper PIN, use the vendor prep utility to reset the PIN. The authentication transaction to the remote access server does not involve the PIN in any fashion.

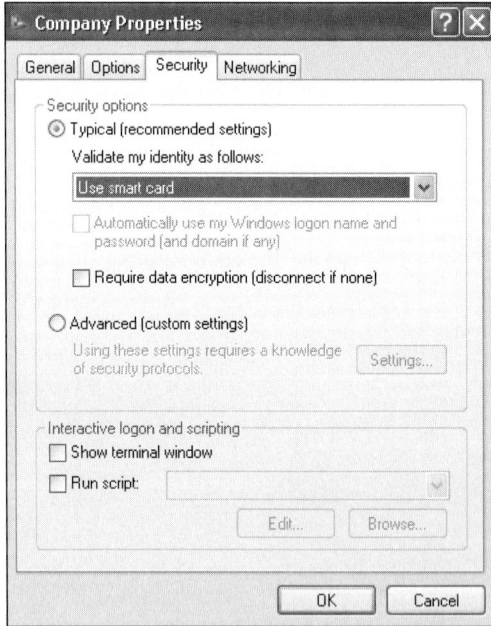

Figure 20.25 XP dial-in connection properties showing smart card settings in the `Security` tab.

If the system accepts the PIN and reads the card but you get an `Access Denied - Unknown User or Password` error, verify once again that you can use the card to log on to the domain from the console of a computer that is on the network. If this works, you may have a situation where the remote access server cannot resolve the user's UPN. The server must have access to a domain controller and a Global Catalog server.

At the completion of a successful test, you're ready to begin production deployment. All you need now is time and budget.

Installing and Configuring Modems

Plug and Play takes a lot of the pain out of modem installation. Ideally, you should be able to install a new modem by putting it in a PCI slot, booting the machine, and watching for a balloon in the Notification area of the status bar as PnP does its thing. If you have a laptop, you can install a PC Card modem while the computer is running and the PnP Manager will find it and install the drivers. Installing USB modems is just that easy, as well.

Installing legacy modems is a bit more problematical. The PnP Manager uses a driver called Serenum.sys to enumerate serial devices. It should find any legacy and plug-and-play modems connected to the RS-232 ports or attached to the PCI bus. In the Windows Driver Model (WDM), Serenum is considered both a bus driver, because it enumerates components on the bus, and a filter driver, because it builds a virtual device that represents the modem. See Chapter 3, "Adding Hardware," for details on WDM drivers.

When Serenum finds a modem, it calls on a modem class installer to locate the correct driver. The class installer queries the modem for its make and model then searches for a corresponding INF file in the `\Windows\INF` folder. Windows Server 2003 has over 350 modem-related INF scripts, each one containing configuration instructions for multiple modems, so it's rare to come across a modem that doesn't have a driver. Each INF script is paired with a PNF file, which is a precompiled version of the INF that can be read more quickly by the PnP class installer.

If the class installer cannot find an INF for a modem but the modem responds correctly to a standard Hayes command set, the installer uses a generic INF, Mdmgen.inf to obtain basic functionality. Certain features in the modem may not be available using the standard settings. Also, the modem may fail to operate satisfactorily because the initialization string is improperly formatted.

If you have an external PnP modem and you don't want to restart your computer to install it, open the `Device Manager` console (Devmgmt.msc), right-click the computer icon at the top of the tree, and select SCAN FOR HARDWARE CHANGES from the flyout menu. The modem lights should flash and the modem should appear in the device tree.

If a modem does not use Plug and Play, you must install it manually. Use the Phone and Modem Options applet in the Control Panel to launch the Add New Hardware Wizard. Just in case the installation hangs, the installation is handled by Rundll32 with the help of the modem class installer, Mdminst.dll. Kill the process in Task Manager and try again.

Testing and Troubleshooting Modem Connections

If a modem does not work properly after installation, check the device properties in Device Manager to make sure you do not have a resource conflict or an improper driver. One way to open the Device Manager console is by right-clicking `My Computer` and selecting PROPERTIES from the flyout menu. Select the `Hardware` tab and click `Device Manager`.

Figure 20.26 shows an example device tree with a problem modem as indicated by a big question mark next to the modem name. This indicates either a resource conflict of some sort or the driver could not be found.

Normally, if the system is not able to locate an INF script containing a driver for the modem, the Found New Hardware Wizard launches automatically to walk you through loading the vendor's drivers. If the vendor does not supply drivers for that particular modem model, try one that is similar in speed and feature set. You can also try one of the Standard Modem selections that match the speed of the modem you are installing. Figure 20.27 shows this selection.

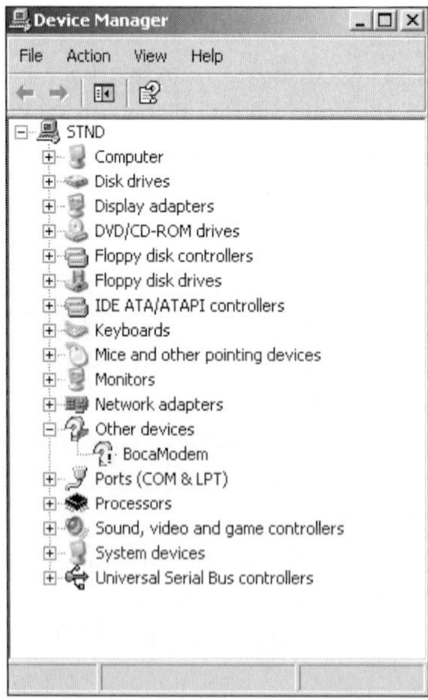

Figure 20.26 Device Manager console showing device tree with a problem modem.

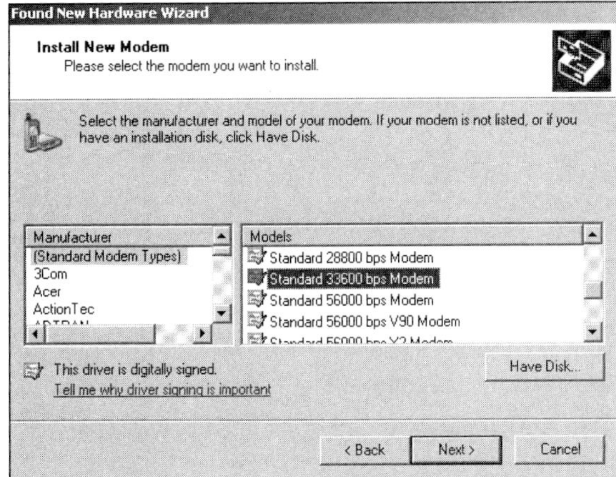

Figure 20.27 Found New Hardware Wizard—Install New Modem window showing selection of a `Standard Modem` option for an unsupported modem make/model.

If the correct driver is installed, select the `Resources` tab for the modem in the Device Manager console. All resource settings should be dimmed for PnP modems. If you can select specific resource settings, the system has detected the modem as a legacy device. If the modem is supposed to be a PnP device, you may need to move a jumper or change the software configuration.

Now look for listings in the `Conflicts` field. This tells you if the system was unable to distribute IRQs in a fashion that permits the modem to run without conflict with another device. External modems rarely have a conflict problem, but internal modems sometimes conflict with other serial devices.

Here is list of other things to try if a modem seems to be installed correctly but still refuses to work:

- Save yourself wasted hours by checking the Hardware Compatibility List at `www.microsoft.com/hcl`. If your modem is not on the HCL, check to see if the vendor supplies updated Windows Server 2003, XP, or Windows 2000 drivers. If not, consider getting a more current modem. Life is short and modems aren't that expensive.
- Check CMOS to make sure the COM port is enabled.
- For internal ISA modems, make sure the ISA slot is set to recognize PnP devices. Some internal modems have dual personalities, one for ISA and one for PnP.

Table 20.1 Standard COM Port I/O Base and IRQ Settings

COM Port	I/O Base	IRQ
COM1	3F8	4
COM2	2F8	3
COM3	3E8	4
COM4	2E8	3

- You can sometimes resolve erratic performance by making a change to the initialization string ("init string") for the modem. Check the vendor's knowledgebase for possible changes in the settings. Select the `Advanced` tab then make entries in `Extra Initialization Commands`. Settings entered here override the same setting in the INF script.
- For external modems, check to make sure the associated COM port is enabled and uses a standard I/O Base address and IRQ. Older laptops are notorious for having non-standard configurations. Table 20.1 shows the standard COM port configurations.
- If you are installing an external modem, you can verify that is connected to a functional serial port by opening a command session and entering `atdt > com#:`. Look for lights on the modem to flicker. If they do not, the serial cable may have the wrong pinouts. Table 20.2 shows the correct pinouts.
- For PC Card modems, verify that the card does not require legacy card and socket drivers. These are not supported by Windows Server 2003. Only APM and ACPI compatible PC Cards are likely to work correctly, if at all.
- Check the Microsoft Knowledgebase for known issues with the modem.
- Winmodems do their processing using the computer's CPU. These modems can be clumsy to configure and require special attention because of the resources they consume. *Winmodems should never be used in a remote access server.*
- Some modems come as part of a multifunction card such as a PC Card combo Ethernet/modem or a combo adapter for MIDI/modem. The card itself may be plug-and-play compatible, but the laptop may use a flavor of APM or PnP BIOS or an older version of ACPI so that the modem component is not recognized. You may need to configure resources manually.
- If none of this does the trick, see "Troubleshooting Using Modem Logs" for additional diagnostic aids.

Even if the modem seems to work, your job may not be finished. Many seemingly unrelated problems can arise when using an incompatible modem. If a system becomes erratic soon after installing a new modem, expect the worst. NDIS treats a serial device like a network connection, and this often exposes design inadequacies.

Table 20.2 Serial Cable Pinouts for Connection to Modems

25-Pin Straight-Through

Male	Female	Function
1	1	Chassis Ground
2	2	Transmit Data
3	3	Receive Data
4	4	Request to Send
5	5	Clear to Send
6	6	Data Set Ready
7	7	Signal Ground
8	8	Carrier Detect
20	20	Data Terminal Ready

25-pin to 9-pin

Male	Female	Function
8	1	Carrier Detect
3	2	Receive Data
2	3	Transmit Data
20	4	Data Terminal Ready
7	5	Signal Ground
6	6	Data Set Ready
4	7	Request to Send
5	8	Clear to Send
22	9	Ring Indicator (optional)

Also, a modem can behave just fine in a standard terminal connection but fail miserably when used for remote access. This is especially true when the root cause of the problem is poor line conditions. It's worth the money to pay for modems that have top-quality error correcting circuitry. You can also request the telco (local telephone company) test the line conditioning to make sure it is suitable for 56k modem connections. Do the same of your internal telephone support folks in case the problem is with premise wiring.

Suggested Lab Setup for Dial-In Testing

You may (and probably will) encounter problems that are due to server configuration rather than modem configuration. You may want to build a small test bed to use for configuring remote access servers. You will need a way to connect modems together. You cannot simply connect a piece of standard straight-through telephone cable between the two units. Modems require ringback and other special signaling from a phone switch.

Table 20.3 Pinouts for 9-Pin Null Modem Cable

Signal	Remote	Local
Transmit Data (TD)	3	2
Receive Data (RD)	2	3
Request to Send (RTS)	7	8
Clear to Send	8	7
Data Set Ready and Carrier Detect (DSR and CD)	6, 1	4
Signal Ground	5	5
Data Terminal Ready (DTR)	4	6, 1

Table 20.4 Pinouts for 25-Pin Null Modem Cable

Signal	Remote	Local
Transmit Data (TD)	2	3
Receive Data (RD)	3	2
Request to Send (RTS)	4	5
Clear to Send	5	4
Data Set Ready and Carrier Detect (DSR and CD)	6, 8	20
Signal Ground	7	7
Data Terminal Ready (DTR)	20	6, 8

You can buy a modem eliminator, which permits connecting two phone or modems together, but these are relatively pricey items and highly specific in their functions. You may find that your modems don't work with the type of eliminator you purchase.

A more flexible solution is to contact several phone installers in your area and ask if they have an old Public Branch Exchange (PBX) unit they will sell you. You can often find a used but serviceable unit for a couple of hundred dollars plus another hundred dollars for the programming phone. Such a unit permits you to do end-to-end testing with the same type of modems you use in production.

If you just want to test serial line communications, you can make a direct connection between two Windows computers using serial cables. It is important to use a special null-modem cable that has the proper pinouts. Don't make the mistake of getting LapLink cables. Null-modem cables are getting harder and harder to find as USB gadgets replace serial devices. Tables 20.3 through 20.5 show the pinouts for null-modem serial cables.

Table 20.5 Pinouts for 25-Pin to 9-Pin Null Modem Cable

Signal	25-pin	9-pin
Transmit Data (TD)	2	2
Receive Data (RD)	3	3
Request to Send (RTS)	4	9
Clear to Send	5	7
Data Set Ready and Carrier Detect (DSR and CD)	6, 8	4
Signal Ground	7	5
Data Terminal Ready (DTR)	20	6, 1

After you have the null-modem cable connected between serial ports on two machines, follow Procedure 20.8 to enable dial-up connections.

Procedure 20.8 Installing a Direct Serial Line Connection

1. Open the `Phone and Modem Options` applet in the Control Panel.
2. Select the `Modems` tab.
3. Click `Add`. The Add Hardware Wizard starts and opens the Install New Modem window.
4. Select `Don't Detect My Modem` and click `Next`.
5. The system pauses for a while to build a list of modems then displays the list.
6. Under `Manufacturer`, select `Standard Modem Types` and under `Models`, select `Communication Cable Between Two Computers`.
7. Click `Next`. The Install New Modem window now prompts you to select a port.
8. Select the COM port used by the modem then click `Next`.
9. A summary window opens. Click `Finish` to close the wizard.

At this point, you can use the cable connection for a dial-up connection just as if it were a modem by walking through the New Connection Wizard in Network Connections.

Monitoring Dial-Up Sessions Using Protocol Tracing

Remote Access has an extensive tracing capability that permits monitoring any or all of the protocols involved in WAN communications. The trace must be configured manually in the Registry in `HKLM | Software | Microsoft | Tracing`.

The key contains a long list of traceable protocols. You can enable tracing on as many protocols as you wish. Each protocol has two tracing possibilities, `Log tracing` and `Console tracing`, but only the `Log Tracing` option actually works. `Console Tracing` is no longer supported.

The logs are saved under `\Windows\Tracing` using a file name that corresponds to the item name in the Registry. Here is a list of the traceable protocols and what their acronyms mean:

- **BAP.** Bandwidth Allocation Protocol.
- **CONFMSP.** NetMeeting media service provider.
- **CONFTSP.** NetMeeting TAPI service provider.
- **EAPOL.** EAP-over-LAN—an 802.11b protocol.
- **H323MSP.** Internet conferencing protocol H.323 media services provider.
- **IASHLPR.** Internet Authentication Services helper.
- **IASRAD.** IAS Radius interface.
- **IASRECST.** IAS Record Storage.
- **IASSAM.** IAS Security Account Manager interface.
- **IGMPv2.** Internet Group Membership Protocol version 2.
- **IPBOOTTP.** IP Bootstrap Transfer Protocol, also used for DHCP.
- **IPRIP2.** IP Routing Information Protocol, release 2.
- **IPRouterManager.** IP component of the RAS multiprotocol router.
- **IPXAutonet.** IPX frame detection.
- **IPX Traffic Filter Logging.** IPX traffic filter log.
- **IPXCP.** PPP control protocol for IPX.
- **IPXRIP.** IPX Routing Information Protocol.
- **IPXRouterManager.** IPX component of the RAS multiprotocol router.
- **IPXSAP.** IPX Service Advertising Protocol.
- **IPXWAN.** IPX Wide Area Network control component.
- **KMDDSP.** Kernel-mode mapper, one of the two main TAPI service providers. (The other is NDPTSP.)
- **NAPMMC.** The IAS snap-in.
- **NDPTSP.** NDIS Proxy TAPI Service Provider, one of the two main TAPI service providers (the other is KMDDSP).
- **NTAUTH.** NT LanMan Challenge-Response user authentication.
- **OSPF.** Open Shortest Path First.
- **OSPFMIB.** OSPF Management Information Block information used for SNMP (Simple Network Management Protocol).

- **PPP.** Point-to-Point Protocol.
- **RASADHLP.** RAS Automatic Dialer helper.
- **RASAPI32.** RAS 32-bit Application Programming Interface.
- **RASAUTO.** RAS Automatic Dialer service trace.
- **RASBACP.** Bandwidth Allocation Control Protocol.
- **RASCHAP.** RAS Challenge Handshake Authentication Protocol.
- **RASCPL.** RAS Control Panel applet trace—not applicable to Windows Server 2003.
- **RASDLG.** RAS helper DLL trace.
- **RASEAP.** Extensible Authentication Protocol for RAS.
- **RASIPCP.** Internet Protocol Control Protocol.
- **RASIPHLP.** RAS Internet Protocol helper DLL trace.
- **RASMAN.** RAS Management service, Rasadmin.exe.
- **RASMON.** RAS Monitor service.
- **RASNBFCP.** NetBIOS Frame Control Protocol.
- **RASPAP.** RAS Password Authentication Protocol authentication service.
- **RASPHONE.** RAS Phonebook service.
- **RASSCRIPT.** RAS script service.
- **RASSPAP.** RAS Shiva Password Authentication Protocol.
- **RASTAPI.** RAS Telephony API driver.
- **RASTLS.** RAS Transport Layer Security, used for monitoring smart card, RADIUS, and MD5-CHAP.
- **RASTLSUI.** RAS TLS User Interface.
- **RASUSER.** The main RAS GUI module.
- **RCAMSP.** Streaming video media services provider.
- **Router.** Traces activity of the multiprotocol router service.
- **RTM.** Response Time Monitor, used in SNA.
- **TermMgr.** Terminal services manager.
- **Various TAPI drivers.** The TAPI3 and TAPI32 are the client-side interfaces to the main TAPISRV module.
- **WaveMsp.** Wave audio media services provider.

You can view the contents of a log by double-clicking on the log file to launch Notepad. This does not block updates to the file, but you must close and reopen Notepad to view any changes. Also, the captured data is flushed to the file infrequently to improve performance, so the file sizes displayed for the log files may be smaller than the actual file size. If you refresh Explorer, the file size will update.

Troubleshooting Using Modem Logs

When a modem goes into trauma, the fix can be frustrating because of the difficulty in figuring out the exact nature of the problem. I've often thought that veterinarians would make great data communications technicians because they are good at diagnosing patients who cannot talk.

Windows Server 2003 has two places to get information about a modem: the Modem Detection log, `ModemDet.txt`, and the Modem log, `ModemLog_<modem-name>.txt`.

ModemDet.txt

The ModemDet.txt log records the interrogations (`AT` commands) sent to the modem by the class installer when the modem is installed. The log is only written during plug-and-play detection. Here is an example listing for an external non-PnP modem:

```
A modem was found on COM1:
ATI0<cr> = <cr><lf>3362
ATI0<cr> = <cr><lf>3362
ATI1<cr> = <cr><lf>221C
ATI1<cr> = <cr><lf>
ATI2<cr> = <cr><lf>OK
ATI2<cr> = <cr><lf>OK
ATI3<cr> = <cr><lf>Sportster 33600/Fax V2.31
ATI3<cr> = <cr><lf>Sportster33600/Fax
ATI4<cr> = <cr><lf>USRobotics Sportster 33600 Fax Settings...
ATI4<cr> = <cr><lf>USRoboticsSportster33600FaxSettings
ATI5<cr> = <cr><lf>USRobotics Sportster 33600 Fax NVRAM Settings...
ATI5<cr> = <cr><lf>USRoboticsSportster33600FaxNVRAMSettings
ATI6<cr> = <cr><lf>USRobotics Sportster 33600 Fax Link Diagnostics...
ATI6<cr> = <cr><lf>USRoboticsSportster33600FaxLinkDiagnostics
ATI7<cr> = <cr><lf>Configuration Profile...
ATI7<cr> = <cr><lf>ConfigurationProfile
ATI8<cr> = <cr><lf>OK
ATI8<cr> = <cr><lf>OK
ATI9<cr> = <cr><lf>(1.0USR0003\\Modem\PNPC107\Sportster 33.6 FAX EXT)FF
ATI9<cr> = <cr><lf>(USR\\Modem\PNPC\Sportster33.6FAXEXT)
ATI10<cr> = <cr><lf>ERROR
ATI10<cr> = <cr><lf>ERROR
AT%V<cr> = <cr><lf>ERROR
AT%V<cr> = <cr><lf>ERROR
Modem ID = UNIMODEM7ABE8C8F.
A modem was not found on COM2.
```

The responses to these queries tell the class installer what to look for in the INF files. When the installer finds the right file, it assigns a Unimodem ID number to the device. This identifies it in the Registry. In the preceding listing, `UNIMODEM7ABE8C8F` is the identifier.

ModemLog Files

The `Diagnostics` tab in a modem's Properties window has an option called `Record A Log File`. This option records commands sent to a modem after it is installed. The file is saved to the `\Windows` directory. The filename starts with `ModemLog_` followed by the name of the modem as recorded in the Registry.

The listing is relatively lengthy. It contains every preliminary test performed on the modem, the test results, the messages sent to the remote modem, the names and versions of the drivers used, and so forth. This gives invaluable clues about the modem's operation. Don't leave logging enabled for an extended period of time, though. The file gets large pretty quickly.

Configuring a Remote Access Server

With the preliminaries and theory out of the way, it's time to prepare a server for dial-in access. The Routing and Remote Access Services (RRAS) service is installed by default but it is kept in a disabled state until needed.

The RRAS service is managed via the Routing and Remote Access Services console, Rrasmgmt.msc. You can manage all servers running RRAS from a single console as long as you have administrator rights on the servers themselves. You cannot manage desktop connections from the RRAS console. You can also manage NT4 RRAS servers but several of the router options are not available. Your best option is to copy the classic NT4 RAS management utility, Rasadmin.exe, to your desktop. When you add the legacy server to the RRAS console and click the icon, the console automatically launches Rasadmin.

Initial RRAS Service Setup

Figure 20.28 shows a relatively simple remote access configuration. The remote access server has been placed outside the firewall in a De-Militarized Zone (DMZ) to improve security. The server routes dial-in client traffic onto the main network through the DMZ interface, which is trusted but provides a higher level of control than simply dialing into the server behind the firewall. Because a standalone RRAS server can only authenticate users in its local SAM, it has been configured to use RADIUS and paired with an IAS server inside the firewall.

Here are the general steps involved in building this configuration:

- Install a modem or modem bank or T-1 card or ISDN BRI or PRI adapter in the remote access server. You'll need drivers designed either for Windows Server 2003/XP or Windows 2000.
- Configure the RRAS service for remote access.
- Configure remote access to accept dial-in connections and to use RADIUS for authentication.

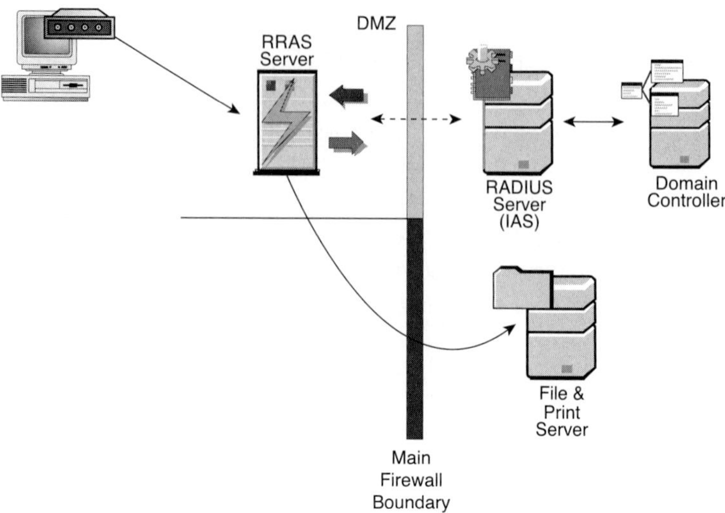

Figure 20.28 Simple dial-up configuration that permits domain users to connect directly to an RRAS server then be routed onto the main network after being authenticated via RADIUS.

- Configure the IAS server to accept authentication requests from the remote access server.
- If the domain is in Mixed, configure the individual user accounts in Active Directory to permit dial-in access. If the domain is in Native, use the remote access policies in RRAS to control dial-in permissions.
- Add the remote access server to the RAS and IAS Servers group in other domains in the forest, if there are any.

There is no need for special configuration at the dial-in clients. The clients use their default authentication method, which is MS-CHAPv2 for Windows clients.

Like most setup operations in Windows Server 2003, the RRAS setup uses a wizard. The configuration options you select in the wizard are not quite as simple as they appear. Let's use the wizard to initialize the service then walk through some details on the settings. Follow Procedure 20.9.

Procedure 20.9 Initializing the RRAS Service to Support Remote Access

1. Open the `Routing and Remote Access` console using START | PROGRAMS | ADMINISTRATIVE TOOLS | ROUTING AND REMOTE ACCESS. The icon representing the local server has a red down-arrow, indicating that the service has not yet been started.

2. Right-click the local server icon and select CONFIGURE AND ENABLE ROUTING AND REMOTE ACCESS from the flyout menu. This launches the Routing and Remote Access Server Setup Wizard. The Configurations window opens first (see Figure 20.29).

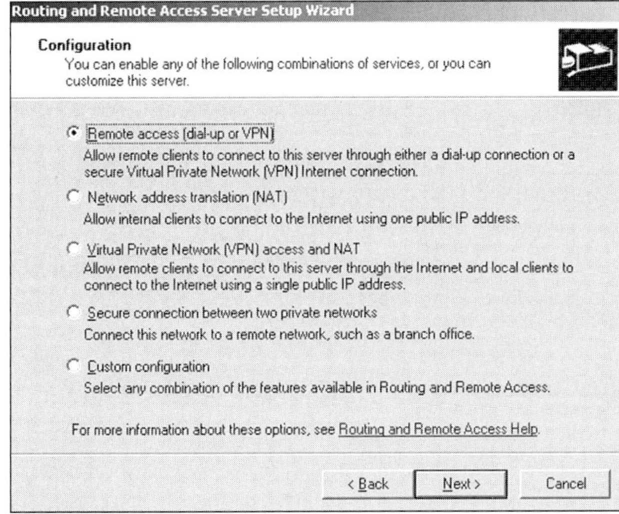

Figure 20.29 RRAS Setup Wizard—Configurations window showing options for wizard-based configuration.

3. Select `Remote Access` and click `Next`. The Remote Access window opens.
4. You can select either Dial-up or VPN or both. For now, select `Dial-up`.
5. Click `Next`. The Network Selection window opens (see Figure 20.30). This is where you select the interface that the server will use for assigning IP configuration settings. On a multihomed server, be sure to select the interface connected to the main network.

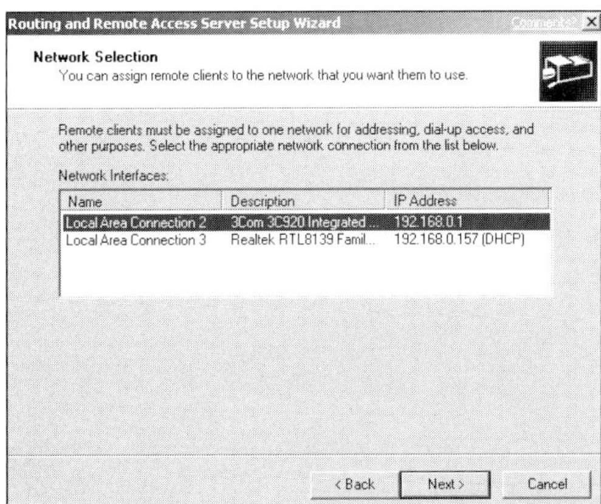

Figure 20.30 RRAS Setup Wizard—Network Selection window showing list of available interfaces.

6. Click Next. The IP Address Assignment window opens. You can elect to use DHCP or a static address range. See the section, "Configuring Dial-In IP Settings," for details about what to select here based on your IP infrastructure.
7. Click Next. The Managing Multiple Remote Access Servers window opens. This window gives you the option of using RADIUS for authentication. When you select this option, the wizard steps you through selecting a RADIUS server and a shared secret. See the "Configuring Internet Authentication Services (IAS)" section for details.
8. Click Next. A summary window opens. Click Finish to start the service.
9. If the domain is in Mixed, make sure the user accounts have dial-in permission in Active Directory. If the domain is in Native, use the RRAS console to change the setting of the Allow Access If Dial-in Permission Is Enabled policy under Remote Access Policies to Grant Access. This gives access to authorized users.

Checking Dial-In Connections Using Remote Access Logging

The server is now ready to accept dial-in users. Test by making a connection from a client desktop using credentials from an Active Directory account. If you encounter problems that are related to remote access, not the modem connection, you may want to enable one of the Logging options in RRAS.

The first logging option is enabled for the server itself via the RRAS server Properties window (see Figure 20.31).

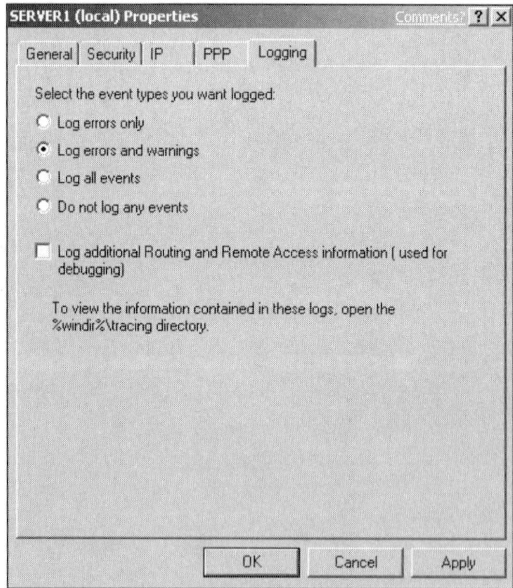

Figure 20.31 RRAS server Properties window showing Logging tab.

This option places information about the server operation in the Event log. The second logging option is available in the Remote Access Logging icon in the RRAS management console. This option tracks activity at each dial-in interface. It is a valuable analytical tool, but it takes a little patience to interpret.

The log is a comma-delimited file with each line representing one record. The first line is a header that contains information about the dial-in user who accessed the server:

```
10.4.1.1 - IP address
testuser - logon name
02/15/2002 - access date
22:24:5 - access time
RAS - access method
DC-01 - target domain controller
```

The next fields are number pairs. The first number is the attribute designator and the second number is the value for the attribute. Here is a brief example for a user who was denied access:

```
4121,0x00453D36343920523D3020563D33 - CHAP error
4127,4 - authentication type
4130,SUBSIDIARY\testuser - Fully qualified user name
4136,3 - packet type (accept-reject)
4142,48 - rejection reason (incomplete accounting-request packet received.)
```

If you want more information about the attributes and constraints that are listed in the log entries, search the online help for "Interpreting IAS-Formatted Log Files." This contains an exhaustive list of the attribute types and meanings. Also check out RFC 2138, "Remote Authentication Dial In User Service (RADIUS)" with Microsoft extensions documented in RFC 2548, "Microsoft Vendor-Specific RADIUS Attributes."

The vendor attributes associated with each interface are stored in Active Directory in an object called Identity-Dictionary. This object is located in `cn=RRAS, cn=Services,cn=Configuration,dc=<domain>,dc=<root>`. You can view the contents of this attribute using with the ADSI Editor from the Support Tools.

Configuring Dial-In IP Settings

From the perspective of NDIS, the network interface represented by a modem or ISDN terminal adapter is no different than that of an Ethernet adapter. You'll see terms in the interface such as *PPP adapter* and *virtual WAN interface* assigned to these connections. In actuality, NDIS sees all network interfaces as virtual adapters, not just remote access connections. One of the functions of the NDIS wrapper is to hide underlying physical hardware behind a virtual shroud of access logic.

If you were to run `ipconfig /all` on any of the machines shown in the figure, you'd see a PPP adapter listed along with the network adapter. Here's an example listing:

```
Windows IP Configuration
        Host Name . . . . . . . . . . . . : pro1
        Primary Dns Suffix  . . . . . . . :
        Node Type . . . . . . . . . . . . : Mixed
        IP Routing Enabled. . . . . . . . : No
        WINS Proxy Enabled. . . . . . . . : No

Ethernet adapter Local Area Connection:
        Connection-specific DNS Suffix  . :
        Description . . . . . . . . . . . : 3Com XL 10/100 PCI NIC (3C905C-TX)
        Physical Address. . . . . . . . . : 00-14-39-3C-6B-2D
        Dhcp Enabled. . . . . . . . . . . : No
        IP Address. . . . . . . . . . . . : 192.168.0.3
        Subnet Mask . . . . . . . . . . . : 255.255.255.0
        Default Gateway . . . . . . . . . : 192.168.0.254
        DNS Servers . . . . . . . . . . . : 192.168.0.15

PPP adapter Company VPN:
        Connection-specific DNS Suffix  . :
        Description . . . . . . . . . . . : WAN (PPP/SLIP) Interface
        Physical Address. . . . . . . . . : 00-13-25-00-00-00
        Dhcp Enabled. . . . . . . . . . . : No
        IP Address. . . . . . . . . . . . : 192.168.10.23
        Subnet Mask . . . . . . . . . . . : 255.255.255.255
        Default Gateway . . . . . . . . . : 192.168.10.23
        DNS Servers . . . . . . . . . . . : 192.168.10.100
```

The default gateway for the PPP adapter is the same as the IP address assigned to the interface by the RRAS server. This is an old routing trick that says, in essence, "If you want an exit path off this machine, I'm your guy." You can confirm this by running `route print`. Here's an example with the dial-in connection shown in bold:

```
===========================================================================
Interface List
0x1 ........................... MS TCP Loopback interface
0x2 ... 00 14 39 3C 6B 2D ........ 3Com 10/100 PCI NIC (3C905C-TX)
0x20006 ...00 13 25 00 00 00 ...... WAN (PPP/SLIP) Interface

===========================================================================
Active Routes:
Network Destination        Netmask          Gateway       Interface  Metric
          0.0.0.0          0.0.0.0      192.168.0.1    192.168.0.253     21
          0.0.0.0          0.0.0.0    192.168.10.23    192.168.10.23      1
        127.0.0.0        255.0.0.0        127.0.0.1        127.0.0.1      1
      192.168.0.0    255.255.255.0    192.168.0.253    192.168.0.253     20
      192.168.0.2  255.255.255.255        127.0.0.1        127.0.0.1     20
    192.168.0.255  255.255.255.255    192.168.0.253    192.168.0.253     20
     192.168.10.3  255.255.255.255        127.0.0.1        127.0.0.1     50
   192.168.10.255  255.255.255.255    192.168.10.23    192.168.10.23     50
```

```
        224.0.0.0        240.0.0.0     192.168.0.253   192.168.0.253      20
        224.0.0.0        240.0.0.0     192.168.10.23   192.168.10.23       1
  255.255.255.255  255.255.255.255     192.168.0.253     192.168.0.2       1
Default Gateway:        192.168.10.23
===========================================================================
Persistent Routes:
  None
```

The end result of this maneuvering is to route non-local IP traffic from the client to the RRAS server and from there onto the network. A single virtual WAN adapter at the RRAS server handles all incoming traffic. The interface appears in the Network Connections as an Incoming Connections icon.

The IP settings assigned to the PPP adapters come from the RRAS server unless the system has been configured to permit dial-in clients to use static addresses assigned at the client. The IP options for RRAS are located on the `IP` tab of the Properties window for the server in the RRAS console. Figure 20.32 shows an example.

Assigning Client IP Addresses

The IP Address Assignment window has two options for assigning addresses to dial-in clients and to the PPP interface on the RRAS server.

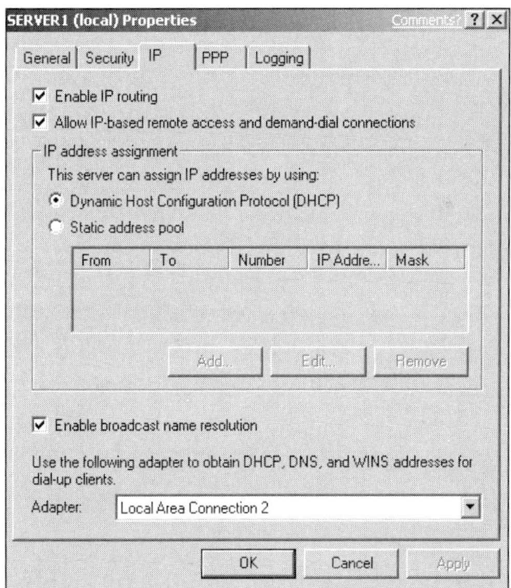

Figure 20.32 Properties window for an RRAS server showing the `IP` tab for configuring routing, address assignments, and name resolution settings.

One option specifies a static range of IP addresses. This option is for use if you do not have a DHCP server or you do not want to obtain dial-in addresses from DHCP. When you specify the address range, select a range in a different subnet than the main interface on the RRAS server. The server will route traffic between the two subnets. See the sidebar, "Routing Protocols."

The other option is to use DHCP. When you make this selection, the RRAS server locates the DHCP server for its subnet and leases IP addresses for its dial-up interfaces from that DHCP server. The key word here is *interfaces*, not *clients*. The RRAS server does not wait for the client to connect to lease the address. It grabs the addresses immediately.

In NT4, this could cause problems if you had a rack with 20 or 30 modems or you configured a few dozen Point-to-Point Tunneling Protocol (PPTP) interfaces. The RRAS server would reach out and nab addresses for all the interfaces plus one for it-self. This could exhaust the supply of addresses in the DHCP address pool.

Starting with Windows 2000, RRAS was modified to lease only 10 addresses at a time. If you have 10 modems and 30 VPN interfaces but normally only have 18 con-current logons, you would lose only 20 addresses from the DHCP address pool.

Configuring Name Resolution

A dial-in client needs to resolve names to IP addresses just like every other PC on the network. Getting the DNS and WINS settings to the client, though, is not as straight-forward as you might think.

PPP clients obtain their configuration settings during the IPCP phase of the con-nection transaction. The remote access server determines where to obtain the values for these settings based on the IP addressing options discussed in the previous section.

Static IP Addressing

If the remote access server is configured to use a static range of addresses, the DNS and WINS settings are obtained from the LAN adapter settings.

If the LAN adapter is configured to use DHCP, the settings given to the dial-in clients are taken from the dynamic settings on the LAN adapter.

If the LAN adapter uses DHCP but also has static configurations for DNS and WINS, the static configurations take precedence and are the only settings delivered to the dial-in clients.

Routing Protocols

If you have a remote access server that uses a separate IP subnet for the dial-in clients along with various LAN segments connected to different servers, it can be a hassle keeping the routing tables up to date. Also, you might have standard routers that also need to know about the subnets.

In these situations, you can enable *Routing Information Protocol* (RIP) in the RRAS console. RIP uses broadcasts to keep its fellow routers updated with new routes. If your existing routers use OSPF (Open Shortest Path First), you can enable OSPF at the RRAS server. Work carefully with the network engineers to ensure you do not create a routing circularity or propagate inappropriate OSPF information. The last thing you want is to have 5000 network clients routed through your RRAS server just because it advertised its routing metrics incorrectly.

If the remote access server has more than one LAN adapter, you can select which one will be used to obtain IP configuration settings. The option is located in the `IP` tab of the RRAS server Properties window.

If you leave the selection in the default setting of `Allow RAS to Select Adapter`, the server will select the first adapter listed under the Routing Interfaces icon of the main RRAS console. This is typically the first interface installed on the server. If this adapter is not available, the second one on the list is used.

DHCP-Based IP Addressing

If the remote access server is configured to use DHCP to lease addresses for the dial-in client, the situation gets a little more complex.

As discussed in the last section, the IP addresses assigned to the dial-in clients come from a set of addresses leased from DHCP and cached locally by the remote access server. However, the IP configuration settings delivered to the dial-in clients during IPCP come from the LAN interface, not from DHCP. There is not enough time during IPCP to stop and get current configurations from DHCP.

You can effectively deliver current DHCP configuration settings, though, by enabling DHCP on the LAN interface of the remote access server. The DNS and WINS settings obtained from DHCP become the settings that will be delivered to the dial-in clients. If you statically assign different DNS or WINS settings to the LAN adapter, those take precedence.

DHCPINFORM

Many IT shops prefer to statically assign IP settings to servers. If the statically assigned DNS and WINS settings on the LAN adapter are suitable for the dial-in clients, this is not a problem. In cases where those settings are not appropriate, a modern Windows client can take over and obtain different settings from DHCP.

This trick depends on a relatively new DHCP feature called DHCPINFORM. One of the functions of DHCPINFORM is to permit a non-DHCP client to obtain configuration settings from a DHCP server.

Windows Server 2003, XP, and Windows 2000 clients take advantage of this feature by broadcasting a DHCPINFORM packet after the PPP transaction has been completed. The DHCP Relay Agent service on the remote access server passes the DHCPINFORM packet to a DHCP server, which responds with a configuration packet. The client assigns the settings in the configuration packet to its dial-up interface in addition to those it obtained during IPCP.

You do not need a packet sniffer to follow this transaction. At a dial-in client, disable the Ethernet interface then run `ipconfig /all` at a command prompt. You will get no listings. Now, initiate a dial-in connection to the remote access server. As soon as the modem finishes squealing, start repeating the `ipconfig /all` entry. You'll first see a single set of configuration settings that match the LAN interface at the remote access server. Then, in a few seconds, the listing changes to include the configuration settings from the DHCP server.

You'll end up with at least two entries for DNS and WINS. This is your indication that the DHCPINFORM process completed successfully. Here's a sample listing. The bold entries were obtained via DHCPINFORM. The secondary entries came from the LAN interface:

```
C:\>ipconfig/all
Windows IP Configuration
        Host Name . . . . . . . . . . . . : xp-pro1
        Primary Dns Suffix  . . . . . . . : subsidiary.com
        Node Type . . . . . . . . . . . . : Unknown
        IP Routing Enabled. . . . . . . . : No
        WINS Proxy Enabled. . . . . . . . : Yes
        DNS Suffix Search List. . . . . . : subsidiary.com

PPP adapter server3:
        Connection-specific DNS Suffix  . :
        Description . . . . . . . . . . . : WAN (PPP/SLIP) Interface
        Physical Address. . . . . . . . . : 00-53-45-00-00-00
        Dhcp Enabled. . . . . . . . . . . : No
        IP Address. . . . . . . . . . . . : 192.168.10.19
        Subnet Mask . . . . . . . . . . . : 255.255.255.255
        Default Gateway . . . . . . . . . : 192.168.10.19
        DNS Servers . . . . . . . . . . . : 192.168.10.200
                                            192.168.0.100
        Primary WINS Server . . . . . . . : 192.168.10.200
        Secondary WINS Server . . . . . . : 192.168.0.100
```

As you can see from the listing, the DHCPINFORM settings become the primary settings for the client. This permits the client to use DNS and WINS servers that are appropriate for its IP subnet.

Remember to enable the DHCP Relay Agent service in the RRAS console. You'll need to specify an interface on which to listen for DHCPINFORM broadcasts and you'll need to enter the IP address of at least one DHCP server.

If you have NT4 and Windows 9x clients, you will need to configure a different workaround because those clients do not use DHCPINFORM. The most straightforward method is to statically configure DNS and WINS settings in the dial-up connection. These settings will take effect even though the client obtains an address from the remote access server.

Flat Name Resolution

The `Enable Broadcast Name Resolution` option in the `IP` tab of the remote access Property window is a new feature in Windows Server 2003 and one that is not enabled by default. Its purpose is to simplify name resolution on small networks where DNS and WINS services are not installed.

An example would be a small manufacturing firm where the computer names were assigned by the owner's teenage children when they installed the network. When a dial-up user at a laptop named `Blink_182` attempts to connect to a server named `DMX` over a mapped drive, the laptop needs a way to resolve the name into an IP address.

On the local network, this would be done with broadcasts. By enabling broadcasts through the dial-up connection, the name can still be resolved.

Broadcast name resolution is not a welcome feature in large networks, but for a few dozen nodes in a single subnet, it works well and should not be avoided simply because of the traffic. If you are going to install Windows Server 2003 in this office, though, you might as well install DNS and WINS and avoid the broadcasts.

Configuring Miscellaneous IP Options

The `Enable IP Routing` option in the `IP` tab of the remote access server Properties window is set by default. This option controls access to the main network. This is a handy way to block network access when you want to change settings but you do not want to bring down the server. You do not need to stop and restart the service if you change this option. It takes effect immediately.

The `Allow IP-Based Remote Access and Demand-Dial Connections` option acts as an on-off toggle for remote access. This is a useful option when you are troubleshooting a problem and you want to leave the RRAS service up but you want to block access. Unfortunately, the users get a `Cannot connect to remote network` error rather than an error such as `Remote network temporarily unavailable`.

RRAS Command-Line Management

Windows Server 2003 includes a general-purpose, text-based tool for managing network settings, including the settings in RRAS. The tool is called the *Network Shell*, or Netsh.

The Netsh utility provides a text-based interface with a variety of options. If you run the utility on one of your servers, you may not see some of these options listed. They are only displayed if the associated service is enabled.

To go to a particular context in the namespace, enter the name of the context at the prompt. For example, enter `ras` to go to the `netsh ras>` context.

You can move from one context to another without navigating up and down the namespace. For example, from the `netsh ras>` context, you can enter `interface` to go directly to the `netsh interface>` context. You can navigate up to a parent context using a double dot (`..`), just like navigating in a directory tree. Type `bye`, `exit`, or `quit` to exit the shell.

To see the available commands at each level of the namespace, type `?` at the `netsh>` prompt. Some commands have additional parameters. Enter the command followed by a question mark to see them. For example, the `show ?` command lists the parameters of the current context:

```
netsh ras>show ?
show tracing        - Shows whether extended tracing is enabled for components.
show user           - Displays RAS properties for a user(s).
show authmode       - Shows the authentication mode.
show authtype       - Displays the authentication types currently enabled.
show link           - Shows the link properties PPP will negotiate
```

```
show multilink          - Shows the multilink types PPP will negotiate
show registeredserver   - Displays whether a computer is registered as a RAS
                        ➥server in the Active Directory of the given domain.
show domainaccess       - Displays whether NT4 RAS servers or Windows Server 2003
                        ➥RAS servers in trusted NT4 domains have been enabled in
                        ➥the Active Directory of the given domain.
show activeservers      - Listens for RAS server advertisements.
show client             - Shows RAS clients connected to this machine.
show alias              - Lists all defined aliases.
show mode               - Shows the current mode.
```

Enter the command with the correct syntax and the results are listed in the console:

```
ras>show registeredserver domain=company.com
The following RAS server is registered:
     RAS Server:     DC-01
     Domain:            company.com
```

To change a parameter, substitute the word `set` for `show`. The Network Shell has two modes: online and offline. You can shift back and forth between them by entering online or offline at the `netsh>` prompt. In the online mode, any changes you make are implemented immediately. In the offline mode, changes are saved but not implemented. Implement them using the `commit` command or discard them using the `abort` command.

One of the most useful Network Shell features is its capability to dump the current configuration to a script so you can replay the script and get back your original configuration. The command to show the running configuration is `dump`. You can type `dump` at the shell prompt to see the results on the screen, but to save the output to file, you must run it from a command prompt and redirect the output to a file. For example, enter `c:\>netsh dump > netsh.scr`.

If you want to limit the dump to a particular context, put the context on the command line. Here is an example:

```
c:\>netsh ras ip dump > netshrasip.scr

# -----------------------------------------
# RAS IP Configuration
# -----------------------------------------

pushd ras ip

set negotiation mode = allow
set access mode = all
set addrreq mode = deny
set pool addr = 10.1.2.0  mask = 255.255.255.240
set addrassign method = auto

popd

# End of RAS IP configuration.
```

To apply the settings you saved in the script, enter `netsh -f <filename>`. For example:

```
c:\>netsh -f netshrasip.scr.
```

You can use Netsh to control other servers either by executing the script remotely using a remote shell or by putting the script in the Windows Scheduler at the remote server for execution at a later time.

Managing Client Remote Access Connections with Group Policies

There are a variety of group policies available for managing remote access connections at the client desktops. These policies are available in the Group Policy Editor under `Administrative Templates | Network | Network Connections`. There is a short set of policies for Computers and a longer set for Users.

The Computer-side policies permit you to disable the following services at the desktops:

- Internet Connection Sharing (ICS)
- Internet Connection Firewall (ICF)
- Network Bridge
- Certificate-based authentication of wireless connections

Of these, you may want to consider disabling ICS very soon after you begin deploying Windows 2000 and XP desktops. This prevents users with local admin rights from creating back doors out of your network.

The User-side policies restrict users from changing or even viewing the contents of their remote access connections. This is a handy set of policies to implement if you want to avoid constant calls to the Help Desk from users who think they know enough to change the connection settings. Because group policies remain in effect even when a machine is off the network, you may want to ease up on the restrictions for users who might need to change phone numbers for connecting to their ISPs as they travel.

Making Dial-In Connections from the Command Line

You do not need to use the graphical user interface to initiate a dial-up session. An executable to handle the connection, Rasdial.exe, can be called from the command line or a batch file.

Using Rasdial, you can configure an unattended workstation to use the Task Scheduler to make dial-up connections, transfer files, pick up email, or do other periodic chores. Do this by configuring the batch file to give Rasdial the name of a phonebook entry. The name of the entry is the same as the name assigned to the Connection icon in the Networking and Dial-up Connections window. For example, if you have a connection named Home Office, the syntax would be as follows:

```
rasdial "home office"
```

During the time that the system is making the connection, the console displays the same status information that you would see from the graphical interface. When you are ready to hang up, enter the following:

```
rasdial /disconnect
```

Unfortunately, you cannot use Rasdial in conjunction with a smart card. You must use passwords. If you do not cache your passwords when you use dial-up connections, or you want to provide a different set of credentials than those stored in the phonebook, you can provide this information on the command line. Here's the syntax: (The parameters are not case sensitive.)

```
rasdial "home office" username * /DOMAIN:domain /PHONE:phonenumber
/CALLBACK:callbacknumber /PREFIXSUFFIX
```

The `*` causes Rasdial to prompt for a password. You can enter the password on the command line, if you prefer. The `/prefixsuffix` switch tells Rasdial to use the TAPI settings for the modem interface.

You can also modify the phonebook from the command line by entering `rasphone` on the command line. This opens the standard graphical interface, but at least it's faster than going through all the mouse-clicks to get to the Connection icons. If you enter `rasphone -a`, you are taken directly to the Network Connection Wizard.

Configuring a Demand-Dial Router

Broadband is becoming available in most metropolitan areas, but DSL is highly sensitive to the distance from the central office and digital cable is only just now being offered to businesses. Other full-time connection alternatives, such as fractional T-1s, are pricey even in an area with reasonable tariffs.

Often, the only affordable solution for branch-office or SOHO connectivity is a circuit-switched connection using modems or ISDN lines. There is no difference, at least conceptually, between routing over a circuit-switched connection or a leased line. The only practical difference is the speed and the delay as the connections are made and broken. For ISDN, this is a matter of a few hundred milliseconds. For modems, it should be no more than 15 to 20 seconds.

A Windows Server 2003 RRAS server can be configured to make and maintain a circuit-switched connection that can function as a tolerably good point-to-point solution. By using multiple modems, you can often achieve faster throughput than with ISDN and low-cost dedicated circuits.

Many ISDN routers have demand-dial routing built in, but you can get an attractive price for a simple ISDN terminal adapter that does not do "B" channel (bearer channel) bonding or demand-dial routing, then let RRAS do the chores. This section describes how to initialize routing services in an RRAS server and configure demand-dial connections to the Internet, either by using public IP addresses or NAT and a firewall.

Initializing Routing Services

To use any of the demand-dial alternatives, it is necessary to enable both Remote Access and Routing features in RRAS. Enabling routing in an existing remote access server involves restarting the service, so perform these steps after working hours, if necessary. You will not lose any existing remote access settings. Proceed as directed in Procedure 20.10.

Procedure 20.10 Initial Configuration of Routing Services

1. Open the `Routing and Remote Access` console.
2. Select the `Remote Access Clients` icon and verify that no users are connected to the server.
3. Right-click the local server name and select DISABLE ROUTING AND REMOTE ACCESS from the flyout menu. A warning appears informing you that disabling the service requires reconfiguration when it is re-enabled. Click `Yes` to acknowledge the warning and disable the service.
4. After the service stops—and this might take a while—the icon associated with the server changes to a red down-arrow. After the service has stopped, reinitialize RRAS using the instructions in Procedure 20.9 with the following additional steps.
5. At the Routing and Remote Access window, select `Enable Server as a Router` and select the `Local and Remote Routing (LAN and WAN)` radio button.
6. At the Dial-in or Demand Dial Interfaces window, select the `Enable All Devices For Both Routing and Remote Access` radio button.
7. The remaining steps are the same. When the RRAS service restarts, the Routing and Remote Access console contains an additional icon called `Routing Interfaces`.

After you have enabled routing, you can configure the server to be a demand-dial router to another office, a demand-dial Internet router, or a demand-dial Internet NAT gateway. The next two sections describe how to configure a demand-dial Internet router and an Internet NAT gateway. Demand-dial routing between offices is not covered because it is becoming increasingly rare as organizations move their commerce to the Internet.

Configuring a Demand-Dial Internet Router

If you want to retain public addresses in your network, then you will need a routed interface to the Internet. If this is a dial-up connection, then you need to configure the RRAS sever to automatically make a connection whenever a client attempts to touch an Internet host. Here are the prerequisites for configuring a demand-dial Internet connection:

- Windows Server 2003 equipped with a modem or ISDN adapter. If you have multiple modems or bearer channels, you can use multilink to bundle them together after the interface has been created.
- Routing must be enabled on the server. See "Initializing Routing Services."
- Assign the LAN interface on the demand-dial server a static address and do not assign a gateway. Configure the clients on the network to use the demand-dial server as their default gateway.
- You must have a valid PPP account at the ISP. The ISP must agree to let you connect to its network using a router. This generally involves an agreement to filter all unacceptable traffic. This includes NETBEUI, IPX, and any other transport protocols other than IP. You must also block broadcasts, although ISPs are good about doing that for you at their boundary routers.
- The ISP must also agree to add your network to the routing tables on its routers. This usually comes as part of the fee for the IP addresses. If you provide your own addresses, an extra fee is added. ISPs generally charge fees at the top of the market for this service because they know that without their routers, you cannot connect to the Internet. The routing fee often comes bundled with a service package that includes DNS and email. You may or may not want this package.
- Your network must use an IP subnet with sufficient public addresses to support all IP devices, including those that might never access the Internet. Getting those addresses might cost quite a bit of money.

Installing a Demand-Dial Interface

With the prerequisites in place, you're ready to install the demand-dial interface, configure it to route to the Internet, and configure automatic connection pickup. Start with installing the interface by following Procedure 20.11.

Procedure 20.11 Installing a Demand-Dial Interface

1. Open the `Routing and Remote Access` console.
2. Each communications device must be configured for demand-dial routing. Right-click the `Ports` icon and select PROPERTIES from the flyout menu. The Port Properties window opens.
3. Double-click a device that will be used for the demand-dial interface to open its Configure Device window.
4. Select the `Demand-Dial Routing Connections` option and click `OK`.

5. Repeat for each device that will be used for demand-dial routing then close the Ports Properties window.
6. At the RRAS console window, right-click the `Routing Interfaces` icon and select NEW DEMAND-DIAL INTERFACE from the flyout menu. The Demand Dial Interface Wizard starts.
7. Click `Next`. The Interface Name window opens. Enter a name that describes the destination of the router. For example, use a name like `ISP_rtr`.
8. Click `Next`. The Connection Type window opens. Select the `Connect Using a Modem, ISDN Adapter` unless you are using a VPN. If you select the VPN option, the wizard presents an additional window for `VPN Type` (set to Automatic by default) and the IP address or host name of the VPN server.
9. Click `Next`. If you have multiple circuit-switched devices, the `Select A Device` list appears. Select the device you want to associate with the demand-dial interface. If you want to use more than one device and multilink them together, you can do that after creating the demand-dial interface.

   If the device you want to use does not appear on the list but it does appear on the `Port` list, make sure you configured it for demand-dial routing.
10. Click `Next`. The Phone Number window opens. Enter the phone number of the modem or ISDN line at the remote location. The `Alternate` option permits adding more numbers to call if the first is busy.
11. Click `Next`. The Protocols and Security window opens. Leave the `Route IP Packets On This Interface` selected. If you normally need to use login scripts when connecting to the ISP, select the `Use Scripting` option. The wizard presents you with a Router Scripting window to select a script.
12. Click `Next`. The Dial Out Credentials window opens. Enter the `Name` and `Password` for the account that will make the dial-up connection. Because this is a connection to the Internet, you should not need a domain unless your ISP uses NT or Windows Server 2003 to perform authentications.
13. Click `Next`. The final wizard window opens. Click `Finish` to add the interface and return to the Routing and Remote Access console.

Configuring the Demand-Dial Router

Now that the interface is in place, it must be configured to connect to the Internet Service Provider's access server (see Procedure 20.12).

Procedure 20.12 Configuring a Demand-Dial Router

1. Highlight the `Routing Interfaces` icon. The new demand-dial interface is listed in the right pane with a status of `Enabled`.
2. Right-click the demand-dial icon and select PROPERTIES from the flyout menu to open a properties window. At the `General` tab, under `Connect Using`, you can select additional modems or ISDN adapters if your ISP supports multilink.
3. Select the `Options` tab. Use the `Connection Type` option to set an inactivity time for the interface. You can choose to make this a `Persistent Connection`, but this generally violates the ISPs fair use agreement unless you have contracted for a full-time connection.

   The default value for `Redial Attempts` is set to 0. The value you set depends on how often you need to retry the ISP line during the busiest time of the day.
4. Select the `Networking` tab then open the Properties window for `Internet Protocol`.

   You must obtain a fixed IP address for the WAN interface from the ISP. This is the address that the ISP will put in its routing tables to get to your network. Some ISPs assign a fixed address automatically based your logon ID. In this case, you can leave the `Obtain An Address Automatically` radio button selected.
5. Click `OK` to save the changes and return to the RRAS console.

Test the connection by right-clicking the demand-dial interface icon and selecting CONNECT from the flyout menu. When the connection is made and the interface status changes to `Connected`, ping a few Internet addresses and names to make sure you have connectivity and proper DNS operation.

If the connection does not work, test using a standard dial-up connection. If that works, check the name and password you're using by right-clicking the demand-dial interface icon under `Routing Interfaces` and selecting CREDENTIALS from the flyout menu.

Configuring Automatic Connection Pickup

Now that the ISP connection is made, you must add a routing table entry so that traffic from clients in the local LAN is routed to the Internet interface. It is impossible to define a routing table that contains all the different IP addresses on the Internet, so the alternative is to configure a gateway that routes all non-local traffic to the demand-dial interface.

The default gateway is defined by a single routing table entry consisting of zeros for network destination and subnet mask. Default gateways are configured automatically for dial-up clients but you must enter the route manually for demand-dial interfaces.

You have already removed the default gateway from the LAN interface as part of the prerequisites for demand-dial routing. At this point, before configuring a default gateway, verify that one does not already exist. Run `route print` from the command line. There should be no `0.0.0.0` entries, meaning that there is no default gateway for the router. Here is an example routing table before adding a gateway entry:

```
C:\>route print
===========================================================================
Interface List
0x1 ........................... MS TCP Loopback interface
0xe000004 ...00 53 45 00 00 00 ...... WAN (PPP/SLIP) Interface
0x11000002 ...00 c0 4f 53 6a f2 ......3Com 3C918
===========================================================================
===========================================================================
Active Routes:
Network Destination        Netmask          Gateway       Interface  Metric
         10.1.0.0      255.255.0.0         10.1.1.1        10.1.1.1       1
         10.1.1.1  255.255.255.255        127.0.0.1       127.0.0.1       1
   10.255.255.255  255.255.255.255         10.1.1.1        10.1.1.1       1
        127.0.0.0        255.0.0.0        127.0.0.1       127.0.0.1       1
        127.0.0.1  255.255.255.255        127.0.0.1       127.0.0.1       1
    206.132.49.94  255.255.255.255        127.0.0.1       127.0.0.1       1
   206.132.49.255  255.255.255.255    206.132.49.94   206.132.49.94       1
        224.0.0.0        240.0.0.0         10.1.1.1        10.1.1.1       1
        224.0.0.0        240.0.0.0    206.132.49.94   206.132.49.94       1
  255.255.255.255  255.255.255.255         10.1.1.1        10.1.1.1       1
  255.255.255.255  255.255.255.255    206.132.49.94   206.132.49.94       1
===========================================================================
Persistent Routes:
  None
```

Addresses with host octets of 255 represent subnet broadcasts. Addresses of `255.255.255.255` represent general broadcasts. Addresses starting with `224.0.0.0` represent multicast subnets. Procedure 20.13 shows how to configure the interface for automatic pickup.

Procedure 20.13 Configuring Automatic Connection Pickup

1. From the RRAS console, expand the tree under the `Local Server` icon to show the IP Routing icon.
2. Right-click `Static Routes` and select Create a New Static Route from the flyout menu. The Static Route window opens (see Figure 20.33).
3. Under `Interface`, select the new ISP demand-dial interface you just created.
4. Under `Destination` and `Network Mask`, enter all zeros (0). This designates the demand-dial interface as the default gateway for the router. The `Gateway` entry itself is dimmed because demand-dial connections have no gateways.

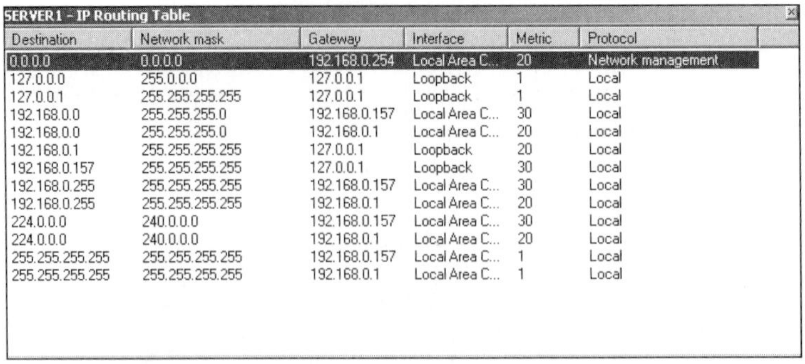

SERVER1 - IP Routing Table

Destination	Network mask	Gateway	Interface	Metric	Protocol
0.0.0.0	0.0.0.0	192.168.0.254	Local Area C...	20	Network management
127.0.0.0	255.0.0.0	127.0.0.1	Loopback	1	Local
127.0.0.1	255.255.255.255	127.0.0.1	Loopback	1	Local
192.168.0.0	255.255.255.0	192.168.0.157	Local Area C...	30	Local
192.168.0.0	255.255.255.0	192.168.0.1	Local Area C...	20	Local
192.168.0.1	255.255.255.255	127.0.0.1	Loopback	20	Local
192.168.0.157	255.255.255.255	127.0.0.1	Loopback	30	Local
192.168.0.255	255.255.255.255	192.168.0.157	Local Area C...	30	Local
192.168.0.255	255.255.255.255	192.168.0.1	Local Area C...	20	Local
224.0.0.0	240.0.0.0	192.168.0.157	Local Area C...	30	Local
224.0.0.0	240.0.0.0	192.168.0.1	Local Area C...	20	Local
255.255.255.255	255.255.255.255	192.168.0.157	Local Area C...	1	Local
255.255.255.255	255.255.255.255	192.168.0.1	Local Area C...	1	Local

Figure 20.33 Static Route window showing default gateway route.

5. Leave `Metric` set for 1.
6. Verify that `Use This Route To Initiate Demand-dial Connections` is selected. This tells RRAS to pick up the demand-dial circuit when any traffic arrives that is not bound for an address on the local subnet.
7. Click `OK` to save the changes and return to the RRAS console. The new static route appears in the right pane.

Now test the connection. From a client that is configured to use the demand-dial router as a gateway, ping the WAN interface on the server. When that ping succeeds, start a continuous ping to an Internet address, such as `ping -t 192.80.3.105`. Wait for the demand-dial connection to the ISP to pick up.

At that point, the ping succeeds. If either ping fails, use TRACERT or PATHPING to see where the connection is failing. If you get an Internet Control Management Protocol (ICMP) echo from the demand-dial router but not from the Internet, check that you correctly configured the routing table at the ISP router. Make sure to keep connection up while you troubleshoot.

Unless you select the `Persistent Connection` option, the demand-dial connection will eventually time out and disconnect. If you are using a modem, you need to educate your users to wait for a few seconds after they fire off their browsers while the modem picks up. For ISDN links, you have the opposite problem. You do not want the ISDN line to stay hot continuously. Ask anyone who has gotten a $2000 phone bill the month after installing his spanking new ISDN line. Stay aware of the traffic patterns at the demand-dial router until you're sure that you won't get any surprises.

One note of caution: In this demand-dial router configuration, your network is bare to the Internet. The NAT option in the next section includes the ability to enable the Internet Connection Firewall (ICF) in Windows Server 2003. This is preferable than the simple demand-dial routing configuration outlined in this section. If you do not want to use NAT, you should install a firewall in front of the demand-dial router.

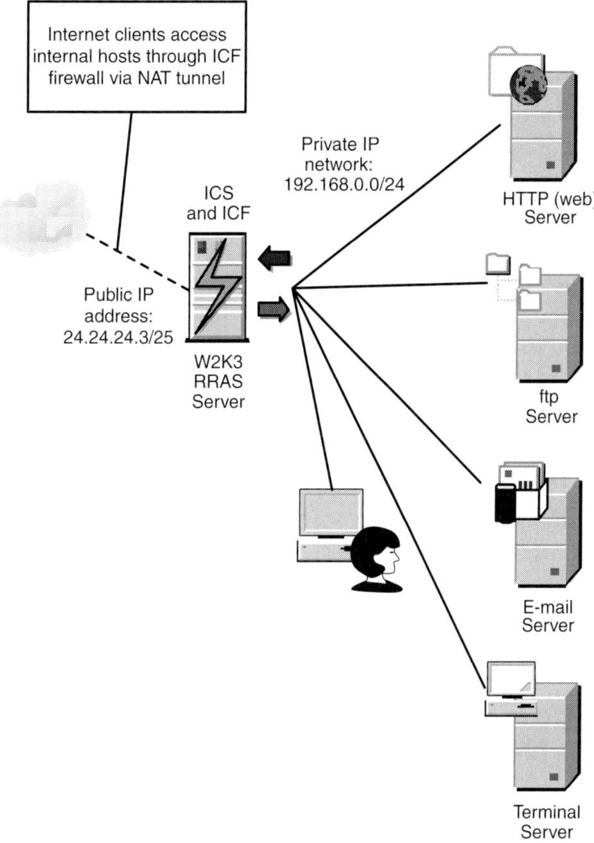

Figure 20.34 Typical SOHO network with a Windows Server 2003 server running RRAS as a gateway.

Configuring an Internet Gateway Using NAT

Figure 20.34 shows a typical SOHO network configuration. In this example, a single server running Windows Server 2003 supports all network services, including acting as a gateway to the Internet.

You may look at this diagram and wonder why the vendor who set up the system didn't simply use a low-cost SOHO appliance as the gateway. Part of the reason is money. The additional equipment isn't free and many SOHO installations are *extremely* price sensitive. A better reason, technologically speaking, is the generous feature set supported by Windows Server 2003. This feature set includes a firewall, flexible inbound port forwarding, the ability to have multiple public IP addresses, and virtually unlimited client connections.

Using a single server for file-and-print and network services isn't the most fault tolerant solution, of course, but small business owners are accustomed to thinking in terms of bottom line rather than business recovery. This same business probably has critical machines on the operations floor and rolling stock in the parking lot that do not have redundancy, either. Most small business owners measure risk against cost and decide to have a single server. You can mitigate the impact of a downed server by designating one or more XP desktops as alternate Internet gateways. An XP desktop functions tolerably well in these circumstances and it only takes a second to make the configuration change as long as you already have a second network adapter in the desktop.

Setting up a Windows Server 2003 as an Internet gateway involves installing an additional network interface that connects to the Internet (this could be a network cable connected to a cable modem, a DSL adapter, or a demand-dial connection) then configuring the following RRAS components:

- Routing service
- Network Address Translation (NAT) service
- Firewall service

If the public interface connects to a DSL provider that requires individual connections, setting up the gateway also involves configuring the integrated *Point-to-Point Protocol over Ethernet* (PPPoE) support in Windows Server 2003. See the previous section, "PPPoE," for details.

Functional Description of Network Address Translation

If the server in Figure 20.34 were configured as a standard router, each client in the office would need a public IP address. This presents two problems. One involves security. The clients would be exposed to the Internet where all the bad guys can find them and do nasty things to them.

The other problem involves architecture. The supply of available IP addresses is dwindling rapidly. IPv6 will alleviate this problem, and the security problem as well, but it will take many years for the deployment of IPv6-capable devices and hosts to reach the point where address availability is not an issue.

For the time being, NAT solves both problems by a trick that any teenager would love. NAT translates one IP address into another IP address, permitting a client to be something different on a private network and a public network. NAT is documented in RFC 1597, "Address Allocation for Private Internets," and RFC 1631, "Network Address Translation (NAT)."

Address Mapping

To take advantage of NAT, you need to deploy IP addresses from one of the reserved ranges set aside for private use. Internet routers are configured to block any traffic from these reserved ranges. They are as follows:

Class A: `10.0.0.0` to `10.255.255.255`

Class B: `172.16.0.0` to `172.31.255.255`

Class C: `192.168.0.0` to `192.168.255.255`

Broadband Performance

To get the latest updates on tweaks that can improve performance over broadband connections, visit `www.speedguide.net`.

As an administrator thinking about how to implement NAT, you are free to choose any of the private address ranges that fit your needs. The most flexible is the Class A because of the large number of networks and hosts it can support, but the Class C range is simpler to manage for a small network.

Here's how NAT works. Consider a client on the private side of a NAT device. The client makes an HTTP connection to a web server on the public side. The client sends HTTP traffic to the web server via well-known Transport Control Protocol (TCP) port 80. The client selects an unused TCP port on which to listen for a response. This source port is included in the datagram sent to the web server so the server knows where to reply.

When the HTTP packet from the client arrives at the NAT device, the NAT device modifies the IP header by substituting its own public IP address for the client's address then sends the packet on its way.

The web server responds to that IP address, which returns the traffic to the public interface on the NAT device. The NAT service swaps back the client's IP address and sends the packet into the private network where it is routed to the client.

Port Mapping

True NAT uses a one-to-one mapping between a private address and a public address. This protects the client's identity, but it does very little to minimize the use of public IP addresses. That is the job of another feature called *Port Address Translation*, or PAT. The NAT service in Windows Server 2003 implements both NAT and PAT.

Here's now PAT differs from NAT. When a private client sends traffic to a host on the public side of the NAT device, the NAT device not only substitutes its public IP address, it substitutes a random TCP port number for the port on which the client is listening for a response. It keeps the original IP address and port number in a lookup table.

When the web server responds, it returns an HTTP packet to the public interface on the NAT device using the number of the substituted port. The NAT device swaps the client's information back into the packet then sends it onto the private network where it is routed to the client.

So, the difference between NAT and PAT lies in the way they use the public address. With pure NAT, you would need a public address for each client on the private side. With PAT, you essentially multiplex the private clients onto one public IP address.

Windows Server 2003 RRAS, like most NAT devices, uses a combination of NAT and PAT. You can see the address and port mappings used by the Windows Server 2003 NAT service by opening the RRAS console, right-clicking the NAT interface, and selecting the `Show Mappings` option.

If the public interface of the RRAS server has more than one IP address, the NAT service maps private clients one-to-one with the public addresses until it arrives at the last available address. It then shifts to PAT for the remainder of the clients. This is sometimes called *NAT overloading*. There is no performance difference between NAT and PAT.

NAT Editors

In addition to simply translating IP header addresses, NAT may need to peer inside the TCP or User Datagram Protocol (UDP) packet itself to find source IP addresses put there by an application.

For example, when you ping a host, the ICMP packet contains the IP addresses of the source and destination hosts. The same is true for the FTP `port` command and other applications. In addition, there are instances when source addressing is used outside of the TCP or UDP payload. This occurs in Point-to-Point Tunneling Protocol (PPTP), where the Generic Routing Encapsulation (GRE) protocol handles IP communication with the TCP and UDP datagrams and their port number tunneled inside the packet. (The embedded IP addresses in L2TP over IPSec are encrypted, making them impervious to NAT translation.) Windows Server 2003 NAT uses information stored in special configuration files called *NAT Editors* to determine the location of IP address information in an application packet. Each application requires its own NAT Editor. Windows Server 2003 has NAT Editors for FTP, ICMP, and PPTP. NAT Editors are not included for Simple network Management Protocol (SNMP), Lightweight Directory Access Protocol (LDAP), Microsoft COM, and Remote Procedure Call (RPC).

Inbound Connections Through NAT

As long as a connection to a public host originates from a client in the private network, the NAT service will permit inbound traffic from the public side. If the connection request originates on the public side, however, NAT blocks the request.

There may be situations when you want clients on the public side of the NAT to connect to a server on the private side. Linux calls this *port forwarding*.

Routing inbound traffic backwards through NAT is a little like taking a guest to a State Department dinner. Admittance is strictly by invitation only. Inbound mapping through NAT is done on a port-by-port basis. For instance, if you have a web server in the private network that you want to make available to public clients, you can configure the NAT router to accept inbound connections directed at port 80 and route them to the selected web server. A user on the public side who points a browser at the IP address of the NAT would see web pages returned by the server on the private side.

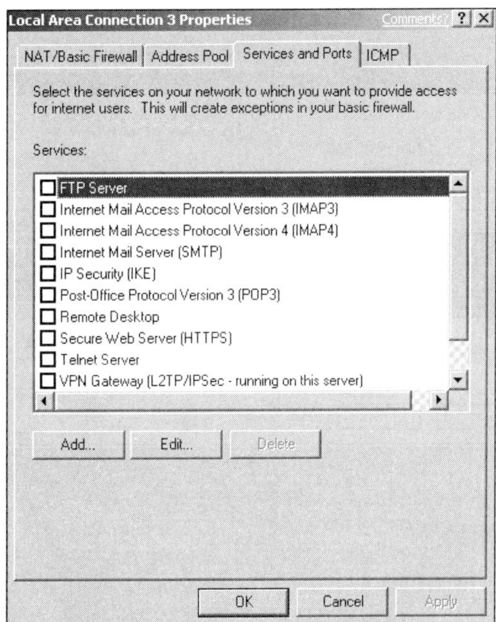

Figure 20.35 Properties window of public NAT interface showing the services that can be configured to map between a public address and a private address.

RRAS has two ways to configure port forwarding through NAT. The simplest way is to associate a port on the public side with a server and a port on the private side. This is done using the `Services and Ports` tab in the Properties window of the public interface. Figure 20.35 shows an example.

If you want to publish a private web server on the public side, select the `Web Server` option. This opens an Edit Service window where you can define the private address and ports.

This one-to-one mapping of external well-known ports to internal servers works fine so long as you have only one server on the private side hosting a particular service. But what if you have three web servers on the private side that you want to publish on the public side? You could use different ports on the public side, but this would require using non-standard ports, which complicates the connection for clients.

A better solution is to obtain a pool of addresses from your ISP then configure the public interface to use this pool for inbound NAT mapping. You can then select an IP address and port number on the public side to represent each server and service on the private side.

You can assign addresses to the public interface using the `Address Pool` tab of the Properties window for the public interface.

Controlling ICMP Responses

Internet Control Message Protocol (ICMP) is used for communicating between clients and hosts for a variety of purposes. Unfortunately, bad guys often "Shanghai" this protocol to crash servers or initiate denial-of-service attacks. Windows Server 2003 has a new option for selecting the ICMP message types to which the public interface will respond. The Properties window for the public interface has an `ICMP` tab that lists the messages and their function. Figure 20.36 shows the selection list.

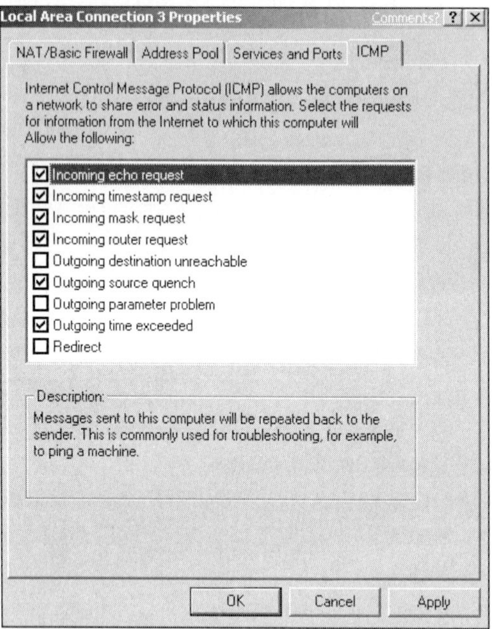

Figure 20.36 Public interface Properties window showing the `ICMP` tab that lists the various messages you can elect to enable or disable.

If you have cannot obtain a contiguous set of addresses from your ISP, you can enter the addresses one at a time as separate address ranges with a range of 1 address. There is no need to stop and start the RRAS service after making a new port mapping.

NAT Deployment Checklist

Here are the key points to remember about NAT before installing and configuring the service:

- NAT requires a separate IP network for the local LAN that either uses a private IP address space (preferred) or public addresses that are unique in your organization.
- NAT maintains a volatile mapping of TCP/UDP ports and private IP addresses. If you down the server, this map is lost and clients must reconnect to the public hosts to get new mappings.

- NAT can use multiple public IP addresses for inbound port forwarding if you have several servers hosting the same service.
- If you have a unique application that inserts IP addresses into the payload of a TCP or UDP packet, or puts IP address information into another protocol, you must configure a NAT Editor to translate the addresses properly or the application will not work through NAT.
- Network clients must be configured to use the NAT router as a gateway to the Internet. This is most easily done using DHCP, but you can manually configure the IP stack on the clients, if you prefer.

Internet Connection Sharing (ICS)

Creating an Internet gateway using the NAT service available in RRAS requires some fairly sophisticated skills. You need to know how to set up RRAS as a router, how to configure NAT and the interfaces within NAT, how to set up clients to use the NAT server as a gateway, and how to handle DNS requests from clients on the private side of the NAT server.

For a small office with a single server running Windows Server 2003, there is a much simpler way to configure the gateway. You can click two selections and restart the clients and call it a day. This convenience comes to you in the form of *Internet Connection Sharing*, or ICS. ICS is also available in XP desktops, Windows 2000 servers and desktops, Windows ME and Windows 98 Second Edition.

ICS is enabled via the Network Connections window as an option in the `Advanced` tab of the Properties window of the public interface (see Figure 20.37).

ICS is a suite of services that automates the creation of an Internet gateway. Here is what happens automatically when you enable ICS on the public interface:

- The IP address of the private interface is automatically changed to `192.168.0.1`. This address cannot be changed, bypassed, or overridden. (There is a Registry hack for ICS in Windows 98/ME, but not for Windows Server 2003/XP.) If you have already configured the network with a different private address, you will have to change your selection.
- Then, if the public interface is a circuit-switched device, it is reconfigured as a demand-dial router.
- A small DHCP service is initialized to pass out addresses in the `192.168.0.0/24` network. This service is controlled by the Ipnathlpr.dll. It is not a full-blown installation of DHCP.
- A small DNS proxy service is installed, also controlled by Ipnathlpr.dll. This proxy passes DNS queries to the DNS server configured on the public interface. This generally comes from the service provider via DHCP.

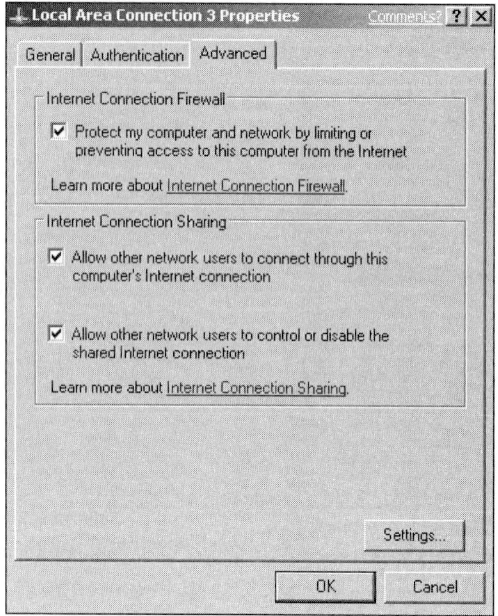

Figure 20.37 Properties window of the public interface on a multihomed server showing the ICS and ICF options in the `Advanced` tab.

Internet Connection Firewall (ICF)

Although NAT is a key component of a firewall, NAT in and of itself is *not* a firewall. In other words, NAT takes no active part in blocking traffic directed at ports on the public side of an RRAS server. Microsoft responded to the presence of an integrated firewall in Linux with a new feature in Windows Server 2003 and XP called the *Internet Connection Firewall*, or ICF.

Compared to more sophisticated (and costlier) firewall solutions, such as Microsoft's Internet Security and Acceleration (ISA) Server or CheckPoint Firewall, ICF looks relatively pale. It lacks the enterprise controls and extensive reporting you'd expect from an enterprise firewall solution; but for its niche, which is to act as a firewall for ICS, it performs very well.

ICS and DHCP

You might be concerned that the indiscriminate use of ICS in your network could result in rogue DHCP servers passing out `192.168` IP addresses. To avoid this, an ICS server or desktop uses DHCPINFORM packets to discover the presence of other DHCP servers on the wire. If it finds any, it disables itself and makes an Event log entry.

Also, the DHCP feature in ICS does not respond to requests from the DHCP allocator in RRAS. This prevents dial-up clients from obtaining addresses from the ICS server.

As of this writing, there have been no tactical or strategic weaknesses identified (or at least reported) in ICF. The service lacks many of the features you would expect in a commercial firewall, but as a way of blocking access to the Internet-facing side of a server, it seems to do the trick. With ICF in place, all ports resisted probing by the typical tools used to do such things. For instance, the public interface came up negative when probed by Legion and LanGuard and the ShieldsUp page at the Gibson Research web site, `www.grc.com`.

ICF is enabled in one of two ways. If you use NAT, it is an option on the private interface under NAT in the RRAS console. If you use ICS, it is an option on the same properties page where you enable ICS.

Configuring NAT in RRAS

Setting up NAT on an Internet gateway is much simpler than configuring a standard routed connection because there is no need for additional services from your ISP. Here is a quick checklist to use for your preparations:

- If you have a DNS server that is the Start of Authority (SOA) for your public DNS namespace, you'll need to either keep the server in the public network or map port 53 in NAT to point at the DNS server. If you move the DNS server into the private address space and do not map the original address to the public interface for NAT, you will need to contact your ISP or the operator of your top-level domain (TLD) to change the address of the name server at the TLD servers. Do the same for any other servers that are moved to the private side, such as your email server (which uses an MX record in DNS).
- The gateway needs at least two network interfaces: one for the private side and one for the public side. The public interface can be a circuit-switched interface (modem or ISDN) or a dedicated interface.
- Do not use a domain controller as a NAT router. You will get erratic results, especially with DNS and LDAP.
- RRAS must be configured to support routing.
- The circuit-switched interface, if any, must be configured for demand-dial routing. This is done from the RRAS console by opening the Port Properties window, double-clicking the device to open the Configure Device window, then selecting the `Demand-Dial Routing Connections` option.
- Some ISPs have fair use policies barring NAT connections to their systems. Check to make sure so you won't get your service disconnected.

With these prerequisites in place, you're ready to set up the gateway.

Configuring NAT and ICF

Start by making sure that the connection to the Internet at the gateway server is fully functional. Then load interfaces into NAT and configure them as directed in Procedure 20.14.

Procedure 20.14 Configuring NAT and ICF

1. Open the `Routing and Remote Access` console.
2. Expand the tree under the IP Routing icon to show the Network Address Translation icon.
3. Right-click the `Network Address Translation` icon and select NEW INTERFACE from the flyout menu. The New Interface For Network Address Translation window opens.

Double-click the public interface. A Properties window opens for the interface.

5. Select the `Public Interface` radio button then check the `Translate TCP/UDP Headers` option and the `Enable Firewall On This Interface` option. Click `OK` to save the change.
6. Double-click the private interface. A Properties window opens for the interface. Select the `Private Interface` radio button and click `OK`.

If you use DHCP, change the configuration settings to point your clients at the IP address of the NAT server. If you do not currently use DHCP but would like to start because of NAT, you can simplify your DHCP setup by using the DHCP Allocator in NAT. You can also use NAT to configure a DNS proxy.

Open the Properties window for the NAT service and select the `Address Assignment` tab (see Figure 20.38).

The simplest configuration is to check the `Automatically Assign` checkbox and leave the address range at `192.168.0.0/24`. This is the same range that would be allocated by ICS.

Select the `Name Resolution` tab and select `Resolve IP Addresses for Clients Requesting DNS`. This configures NAT to forward DNS requests to the DNS server assigned to the public interface. Make sure one the DNS server is available before you make this change.

Enabling ICS and ICF

After verifying that you have a reliable Internet connection on a public interface, enable ICS by following the steps in Procedure 20.15.

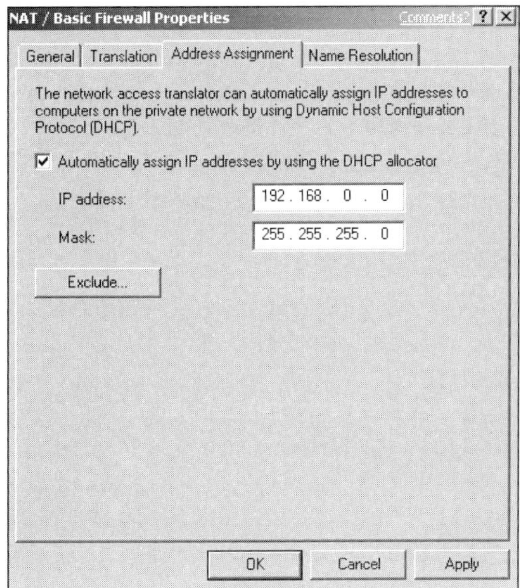

Figure 20.38 NAT properties showing the `Address Assignment` tab for configuring the DHCP Allocator.

Procedure 20.15 Enabling Internet Connection Sharing and Internet Connection Firewall

1. Check that no users have open files or connections on the server. This is necessary because the next steps result in a change of the server's private IP address. Use the Computer Management console, Compmgmt.msc, to check for live sessions.
2. Open the `Network Connections` window.
3. Open the `Properties` window for the public interface.
4. Select the `Advanced` tab.
5. Under `Internet Connection Firewall`, select the `Protect My Computer` option.
6. Under `Internet Connection Sharing`, select the `Allow Other Network Users to Connect` option.
7. Click `OK` to save the changes. The system presents a warning that the IP address of the local area connection will be changed to `192.168.0.1` and that this may cause loss of connection to the local network. Click `Yes` to acknowledge the warning and proceed with the ICS installation. The loss of network connection is temporary until the clients acquire a new network address using DHCP.

It only takes a few seconds for the updates to take effect. Use `ipconfig` to verify that the IP address of the LAN interface has changed to `192.168.0.1`.

At each DHCP client, do an `ipconfig /release` and `ipconfig /renew` (or the `winipcfg` equivalent for Windows 9x clients) to obtain a new DHCP address in the `192.168` network. Verify with Ping that you can touch the gateway and the Internet from the client. Open `Network Connections` at an XP desktop and verify that you have an Internet Gateway icon.

If you are using an ISDN line to connect to the Internet, keep an eye on usage for a while. The ICS features should not keep the line hot, but you never know what the clients might do after they get access to the Internet. Use Network Monitor at the server to sniff for traffic if the line never goes down.

Configuring a Network Bridge

If you install a wireless card into a laptop or a Phoneline segment in your office, you will want to connect these devices into your main network. Figure 20.39 shows an example.

With Windows Server 2003, Standard Edition, or XP desktop, you have the option of either routing or bridging between the segments. The problem with routing in a SOHO network is that you need to configure multiple IP subnets. This can get a little complicated in what is supposed to be a simple networking environment. For simplicity, bridging is a better solution.

Both Windows Server 2003, Standard Edition, and XP have a Network Bridge feature that can be used in place of routing to connect interfaces in different network segments. (Bridging is not available in the Enterprise or Datacenter Edition packages.) Windows treats a Network Bridge as a distinct device with its own interface and IP address. This eliminates the complexity of running a multihomed server.

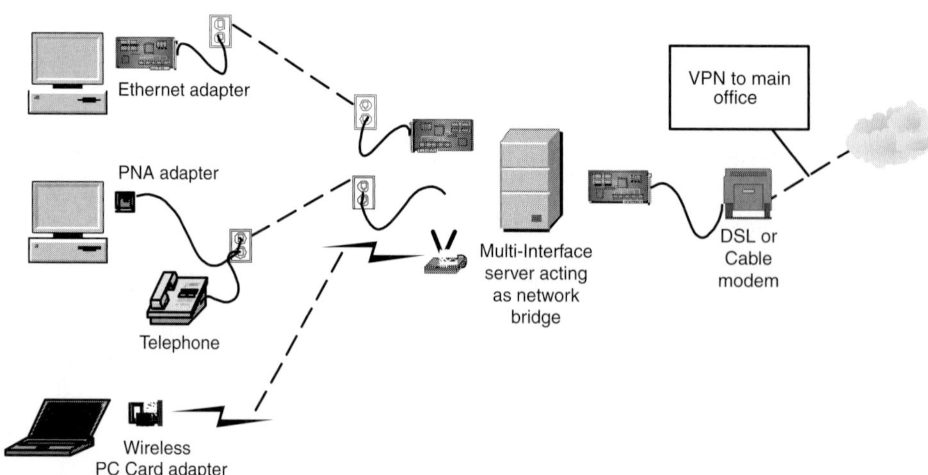

Figure 20.39 Office with a mix of physical network devices bridged at a server running Windows Server 2003.

XP and Routing

An XP desktop is capable of routing, also called IP forwarding, but the feature is not exposed in the User Interface (UI). You can make a Registry change to enable the feature. Here is the setting:

```
Key:   HKLM | System | CurrentControlSet | Services | Tcpip | Parameters
Value: IPEnableRouter
Data:  1 (REG_DWORD)
```

Bridging Overview

As I'm sure you know, bridging connects interfaces at the data link layer of the OSI networking model. At this layer, only the physical MAC addresses assigned to the interfaces matter. Bridging uses a spanning tree algorithm to sort out where the frames should be sent.

A spanning tree is essentially a big lookup table. The bridge service builds the spanning tree table by looking at the MAC address of any frames that arrive at each interface. It makes a little note that says, "Device 00-b3-a9-37-ef-1a came in on the Phoneline adapter." If, at some later time, a frame destined for that MAC address arrives on another segment, the bridge shuttles the frame onto the interface for that segment and sends it on its way.

The disadvantage of bridging over routing is its limited scalability. MAC address lookups are not a particularly sophisticated way to shovel traffic around a network. A spanning tree table does not do a good job of handling segments with large numbers of hosts. You have to be careful about accidentally creating spanning tree loops by interconnecting segments in two different places. Also, bridges do not block broadcasts or multicasts.

Still, for a small office where only a few users have alternate media devices, using a bridge to connect disparate network segments works quite well.

Configuring a Network Bridge

A Network Bridge is configured in the Network Connections window. There is really only one step to the process. You need at least two network adapters in the server.

Hold the `Control` key down and select the interfaces you want to bridge together. Then, right-click and select BRIDGE CONNECTIONS from the flyout menu. The system thinks about this for a while then creates a new icon that represents the bridge. Figure 20.40 shows the results.

After the bridge is up, the underlying connections are abstracted behind it. Utilities such as IPCONFIG only show the bridge, not the actual adapters. This can take a little getting used to. Still, after the bridge is in place, you can pretty much forget it is there until you have to do maintenance on the server.

If you have several LAN segments in your office, be especially careful not to bridge in more than one place unless you map our your topology carefully. If you create a loop, the spanning tree will crash and all interconnections will cease.

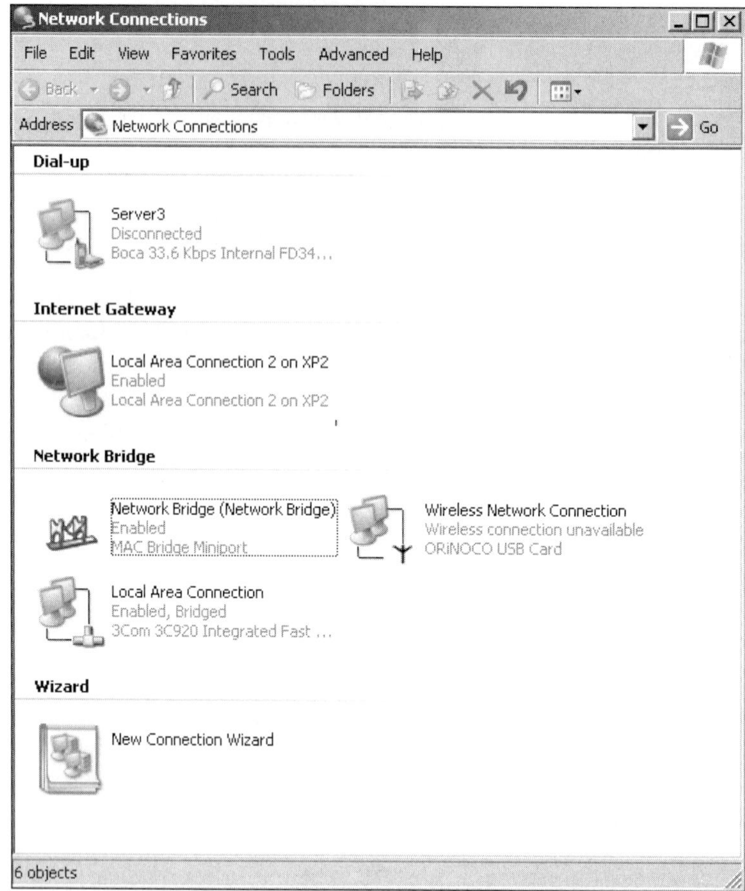

Figure 20.40 Network Connections window showing a Network Bridge.

Configuring Virtual Private Network Connections

In the book *A Gift From Earth*, author Larry Niven introduced a character with an unusual talent. It seems that whenever this character got nervous, folks would just start looking away from him. They didn't realize they were doing this, and were surprised when it was pointed out to them. All the same, they never failed to look away if the character were nervous or scared enough to trigger the effect. He might as well have been invisible. Niven called this phenomenon "Plateau Eyes" because the book was set on top of a plateau miles above the surface of a planet.

I bring up this example for two reasons. First, I've always thought that working in IT is like being on top of a miles-high plateau where every fall is a long, long fall. Second, in the cruel world of the Internet, it would be nice if your data could induce "Plateau Eyes" on all the nasty folks out there who want to see your secrets. That's the premise of a *Virtual Private Network*, or VPN.

In a VPN, two entities exchange data over a public network but the data and the identity of its end-points are encrypted so that they cannot be read by someone sniffing the wire. The encrypted packets are assembled at each end and decrypted using cipher keys known only to the end entities.

This process of encrypting data from one pair of entities and stuffing it into the payload of packets handled by another set of entities is called *tunneling*. Windows Server 2003 supports two tunneling methods: *Point-to-Point Tunneling Protocol* (PPTP) and *Layer 2 Tunneling Protocol* (L2TP). Deciding which one to use, and configuring it to get the security you expect, requires knowing some details about their operation.

PPTP

PPTP encapsulates encrypted messages into a standard PPP frame using a special protocol called *Generic Routing Encapsulation*, or GRE.

PPTP requires two data streams: a *control channel* negotiated over TCP port 1723 for setting up and tearing down the VPN connection and a *tunnel channel* negotiated over IP using protocol 47, which contains the encrypted data inside the GRE packets.

PPTP Transaction

A PPTP connection mimics a PPP dial-up transaction except that the client already has a network connection to the RRAS server. The client sends its PPTP connection request to the RRAS server and is authenticated using MS-CHAPv2 by default, although you can elect to use EAP with smart cards for greater security.

After the PPTP link has been established, all traffic passing to and from the client and the RRAS server is encrypted within GRE packets. This uses a great deal of overhead. For instance, using a simple `TYPE` command to look at the contents of a 10-byte file across a PPTP connection generates nearly a dozen frames carrying GRE packets. This is because the SMB and TCP preliminaries are encrypted right along with the data.

The end-point of a PPTP connection at the RRAS server requires no special configuration. When you enable remote access at the server, five PPTP virtual WAN interfaces are created by default. You can increase this number if you need more concurrent connections. The setting is in the Properties window of the Ports icon in the RRAS console. Highlight the `PPTP` protocol and click `Configure` to open a configuration window. The `Maximum Ports` setting controls the concurrent connection limit.

PPTP Weaknesses

Data in PPTP is encrypted using the same Microsoft Point-to-Point Encryption (MPPE) protocol used by PPP encryption. The underlying encryption algorithm is streaming RC4 with a cipher key refresh every 256 frames.

As discussed in the "PPP Authentication" section earlier, the original MPPE protocol was significantly flawed. Windows Server 2003 (and every other current Windows remote access service) uses PPTPv2, which has been strengthened considerably but is still the object of criticism.

As it turns out, the similarity of PPTP to standard PPP turns out to be its greatest weakness. This is because the authentication phase occurs outside of the encrypted tunnel, so it's possible for a bad guy to devise an exploit to shanghai the transaction before the encryption phase begins. This is one reason for implementing smart cards if you decide on using PPTP for your VPN.

L2TP avoids the weaknesses in PPTP by embedding the authentication phase into the encrypted transactions and by digitally signing all message traffic. If PPTP is like a bonded courier service, L2TP is like a Brinks armored courier.

Still, PPTP is not exactly a sieve, and it does have the advantage of simplicity. All you need for building a PPTP-based VPN is two Windows entities (or Linux, if you install the PoPToP package) that can see each other on a network. A Windows 98 desktop can set up a PPTP VPN to an XP desktop, although the reverse is a little trickier to set up. This is not true of L2TP, which is only supported on modern Windows platforms and requires a PKI because it uses certificates.

L2TP

As you might have guessed from the name, L2TP works at Layer 2 of the OSI stack, as opposed to PPTP, which is an application-layer protocol. L2TP works in concert with IPSec to encrypt and digitally sign traffic between the client and the RRAS server.

L2TP works by packaging an entire packet into the payload of another packet. It is theoretically possible to use L2TP simply to package traffic into a stream of anonymous UDP datagrams. Marrying IPSec with L2TP results in an end-to-end system that meets the fundamental security requirements of privacy, authentication, integrity, and non-repudiation.

IPSec encrypts an entire packet and digitally signs it to prevent man-in-the-middle and spoof attacks. The protocol used to create the encrypted packet is called *Encapsulating Security Payload*, or ESP. This protocol supports several encryption protocols, including DES, 3DES, and Advanced Encryption Standard (AES). By default, Windows Server 2003 and XP uses 3DES, although this might change to AES after the new standard achieves wide support.

L2TP takes the ESP packet and makes it the payload of an otherwise anonymous UDP packet. This is how it "tunnels." The tunnel is initiated by an exchange of X.509

certificates between the end-point computers before the client name is even announced on the wire. This avoids exposing the authentication stage of the connection, which can use MS-CHAPv2, RADIUS, or EAP with smart cards.

Figure 20.41 shows a packet trace that highlights the various components of an L2TP frame. The SPI designator you see in the trace stands for *Security Parameter Index*, a number that uniquely ties the contents of the encrypted payload with a clear-text header. This prevents spoofing.

The IP header parser identifies the packet as `Encap Security Payload (ESP) for IPv6`. This is because IPSec was initially developed with IPv6 support. ESP will accept IPv4 packets.

The ESP sequence number is important because L2TP does not use TCP so it has no means of guaranteeing sequential delivery. IPSec must keep track of its own sequence numbers and request resends if there are gaps.

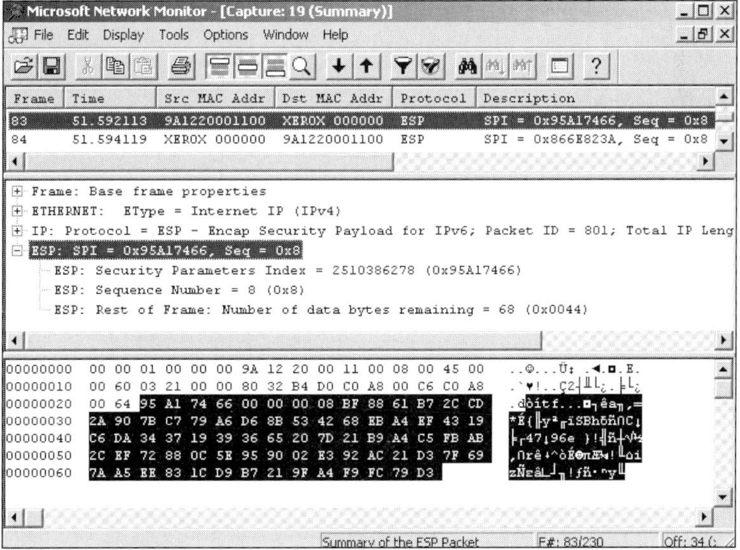

Figure 20.41 Packet trace of L2TP frame containing ESP payload.

Deploying Computer Certificates

The most difficult part of deploying IPSec is distributing certificates to the computers that participate as end entities. The simplest way to do this in a Windows Server 2003 PKI is to use group policies.

There is a policy called `Automatic Certificate Request` that defines what certificates will be assigned to a computer. By defining this policy to require Computer certificates, machines that fall under the influence of the policy will auto-enroll without any intervention on the part of an administrator. This policy is located in `Computer Configuration | Windows Settings | Security Settings | Public Key Policies`.

Group policies can only enforce Computer auto-enrollment for Windows Server 2003, XP, and Windows 2000 machines. These are the only Windows platforms that support L2TP, so the limitation is moot.

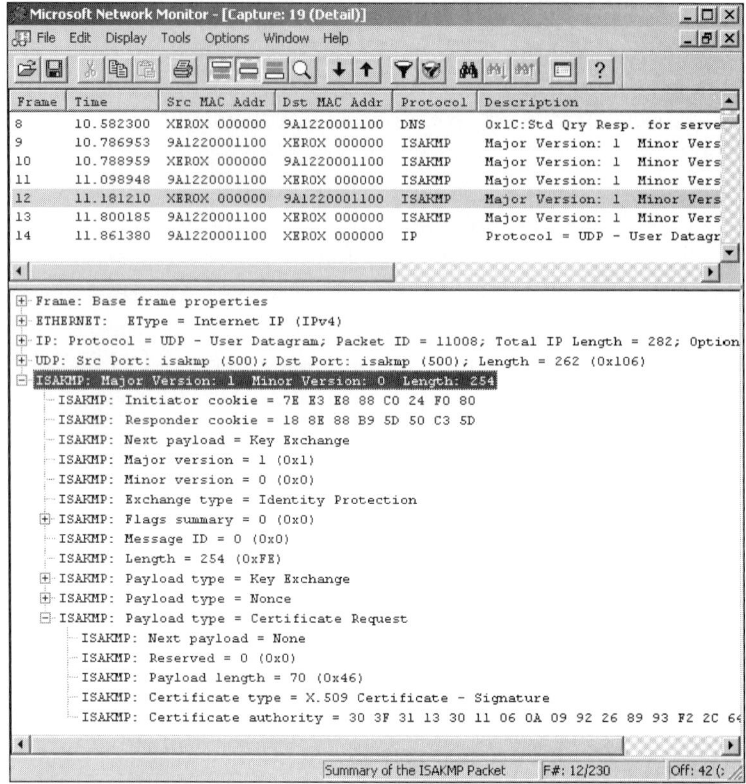

Figure 20.42 Packet trace of frame containing an ISAKMP packet.

L2TP Transactions and IPSec

An L2TP connection transaction uses a protocol called ISAKMP, which stands for *Internet Security Association and Key Management Protocol.* This protocol resembles a meeting between two neurosurgeons. They identify themselves, agree on terms of the meeting, and then begin speaking in an incomprehensible jargon. Figure 20.42 shows a packet trace of a frame containing an ISAKMP packet.

It is worth noting that this packet contains the initial connection transaction from an L2TP client to an RRAS server. This packet starts the negotiation for a mutually acceptable *Security Association*, or SA. An IPSec SA defines policies under which the two entities can exchange information. An SA is defined in an IPSec policy. An L2TP SA policy file is available by default on all Windows Server 2003, XP, and Windows 2000 computers.

After the entities agree on an SA, they authenticate each other by engaging in a key exchange. ISAKMP supports exchanging X.509 certificates or creating dynamic session keys using Diffie-Hellman. Windows L2TP only uses certificate exchange.

The SA negotiation and certificate exchange are the only bits of clear text sent between the two entities. After they have validated each other's certificates, the entities encrypt all messages. This means that the remaining portion of the authentication phase occurs within the tunnel.

IPSec uses UDP port 1701 and requires only one channel for both data and control. This avoids the separate control channel in PPTP.

L2TP Weaknesses

L2TP is by far the more secure of the two tunneling protocols supported by Windows Server 2003, but it has a few deployment challenges.

First of all, you need an enterprise PKI with Certification Authorities available to any computers engaging in an L2TP transaction. It does not need to be a Microsoft PKI, but if you use a third-party PKI, you will need to arrange for obtaining computer certificates without the convenience of auto-enrollment.

Second, L2TP is very processor intensive, much more so that PPTP. This is because the 3DES encryption used by IPSec is more complex than the MPPE encryption used in PPTP, and the system must check the digital signature of each packet. You can improve IPSec performance significantly by installing network adapters that have on-board IPSec co-processors. Every major network card vendor makes such a card.

Finally, and probably most important, IPSec is not "firewall-friendly" because ESP exposes no port information that can be used by NAT. There are ways to "tunnel" IPSec through a NAT firewall, but the complexity of this workaround gets out of hand pretty quickly. Check references from your particular firewall vendor and be sure to have its tech support number handy as you try to implement the instructions. Windows Server 2003 includes support for the latest RFCs that are designed to implement IPSec tunneling through firewalls; however, this technology is still in its infancy, and you'll need to do a lot of tweaking to get any results.

You can avoid firewall problems with IPSec by terminating the L2TP tunnel at an RRAS server in a DMZ. Figure 20.43 shows an example of this configuration. This has the added benefit of permitting the firewall to do a stateful inspection of the unencrypted traffic as it enters the main network. This avoids stealth viruses that might come in under the radar inside an encrypted payload.

Setting Up VPN Connections

PPTP and L2TP virtual adapters are created automatically when you enable the remote access portion of RRAS. No additional configuration is required to accept a PPTP connection. For L2TP, the RRAS server and the client both need a computer certificate. If you do not want to enable auto-enrollment for these certificates, obtain one as follows in Procedure 20.16 (the steps assume you have a Windows Server 2003 or Windows 2000 CA available).

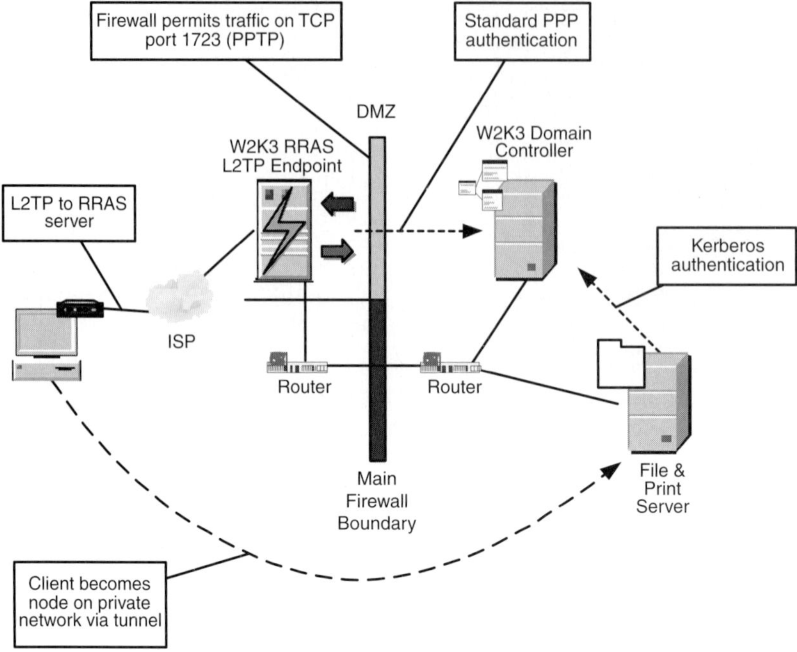

Figure 20.43 L2TP-based VPN terminating at RRAS server in DMZ.

Procedure 20.16 Manually Obtaining a Computer Certificate

1. Log on to the machine using an account with administrator privileges.
2. Open an empty MMC console.
3. Load the `Certificates` snap-in using FILE | ADD/REMOVE SNAP-INS from the main menu. Select the `Computer Account` option rather than `My User Account`.
4. Expand the tree to `Certificates | Personal`.
5. Right-click the `Personal` icon and select REQUEST NEW CERTIFICATE from the flyout menu. The Certificate Request Wizard opens.
6. Click `Next`. The Certificate Types window opens. Select `Computer`.
7. Click `Next`. The Certificate Friendly Name and Description window opens. Leave these blank.
8. Click `Next`. A summary window opens. Click `Finish` to obtain the certificate.

After you have obtained Computer certificates at the RRAS server and the client, you can configure the client to make a VPN connection. This configuration varies depending on the platform. The key item is to have network connection available to the RRAS server and to specify the IP address of the RRAS server in the client configuration.

Configuring Internet Authentication Services (IAS)

Windows Server 2003 IAS is fully compatible with Windows 2000, so you can mix and match components as you upgrade your system.

If you have an existing third-party RADIUS implementation, you need to check the UDP ports used by the RRAS servers and the RADIUS servers. The current RADIUS standard uses UDP port 1812 for authentication and UDP port 1813 for accounting. Older RADIUS implementations used port 1645 for authentication and 1646 for accounting. If you have existing RADIUS servers or network access servers, they may use the old port number. You can configure IAS to use the old port number if the port conflict does not impact your current operations.

A server meeting the minimum memory and CPU requirements for Windows Server 2003 can handle tens of thousands of users. Ordinarily, you should install IAS on a domain controller. This eliminates any network delays in the transactions between the IAS service and Active Directory. This is not a requirement, however. IAS can process a large number of authentication requests per second regardless of whether it is running on a domain controller or as a standalone server. A Global Catalog (GC) server should be available in the same site as the IAS server.

Installing IAS

When you've chosen the server to act as the IAS server, install the IAS service using the Add or Remove Programs applet in Control Panel. There is no need to restart. After the service is running, you can configure logging and remote access policies, register the server with Active Directory so it can perform authentication transactions, and configure it to accept RADIUS requests from the RRAS server.

Configuring IAS Logging and Remote Access Policies

Figure 20.44 shows the default configuration of the IAS management console, Ias.msc. This console is listed under ADMINISTRATIVE TOOLS in the START menu.

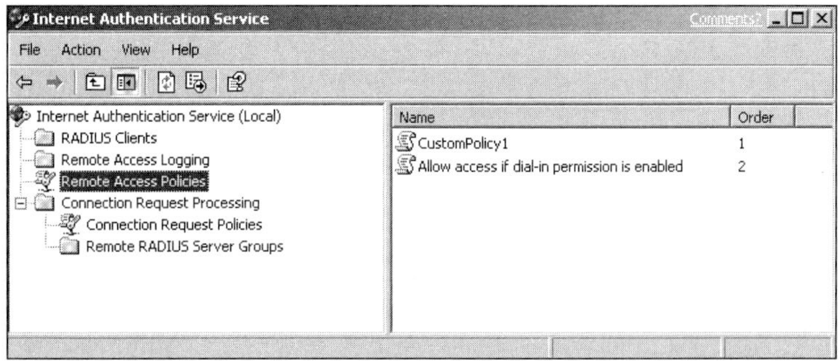

Figure 20.44 IAS management console.

The `RADIUS Clients` folder is used to configure relationships between the IAS server and RRAS servers. This is covered in the next section.

The `Remote Access Logging` folder contains the configuration interface for the RADIUS accounting feature. This takes the form of a Local File icon. The log file controlled by the accounting feature is stored under `\Windows\System32\Logfiles`. The configuration settings for the logging feature are exposed in the Properties window.

Ordinarily, you would want to select all logging options. This ensures that you have a record if someone abuses her dial-up privileges or if an exploit occurs. The IAS log file can grow fairly large. The `Local File` tab has an option for changing the file's location and for creating new logs periodically, such as every day or week or month depending on the number of users and the size of the logs.

When it comes to configuring remote access policies, you may be taken back a little by the large number of configuration possibilities in RADIUS. The standard was designed for ISPs that handle millions of users and need lots and lots of policies.

Under normal circumstances, you only need a policy that grants dial-in access to users. This policy is created by default and resides in the `Remote Access Policies` folder.

The default setting for this policy is to `Deny Remote Access Permission`. Change this to `Grant` when you are ready to permit dial-in connections. Before this policy takes effect, though, the user account in Active Directory must be configured to use remote access policies. This option is only available in Native.

Registering an IAS Server with Active Directory

An IAS server cannot use Active Directory to authenticate users until the IAS service has been "registered" in Active Directory. This registration consists of adding the computer account for the IAS server into the RAS and IAS Servers group.

You can add the IAS server to the RAS and IAS Servers group manually, but you may find it more convenient to use the server registration feature in the IAS console. This only adds the server into the RAS and IAS Servers group in its own domain. If you have IAS servers in several domains and users need to cross-authenticate, you must manually add the IAS servers to the RAS and IAS Servers groups in all domains. Use the steps in Procedure 20.17 to register an IAS server in Active Directory.

Procedure 20.17 Registering an IAS Server with Active Directory

1. Right-click the `Internet Authentication Service` icon and select REGISTER SERVICE IN ACTIVE DIRECTORY from the flyout menu.
2. A message appears notifying you that the computers that are running IAS must be authorized to read users' dial-in properties and prompting you to confirm that you want to do this. Click `OK` to confirm.

3. A notice appears informing you that the server has been registered. You are also reminded that it must be added to the RAS and IAS Servers group in any trusted domains to authenticate users from those domains.

At this point, the IAS server is ready to process authentications. Now, configure the RRAS server to be a client of the IAS server.

Configuring IAS and RRAS to Support RADIUS Authentication

Before an IAS server will accept RADIUS authentication requests from an RRAS server, there must be a trust relationship between servers. Like a classic NT trust, this trust has a secret password that the two machines share. This permits the IAS server to validate the identity of the RRAS server to prevent man-in-the-middle exploits. To configure an RRAS server as an IAS client, follow Procedure 20.18.

Procedure 20.18 Configuring an RRAS Server as an IAS Client

1. In the IAS console, right-click the `Clients` icon and select ADD CLIENT. The Add Client window opens.
2. Enter the name of the RRAS server in the `Friendly Name` field. (This is used only for display.) The only available protocol is RADIUS.
3. Click `Next`. The Client Information window opens. Under `Client Address`, enter the fully qualified DNS name or IP address of the RRAS server.
4. Under `Client-Vendor`, select `Microsoft`. This tells the IAS server to use a Windows domain controller for handling incoming RADIUS authentication requests.
5. Under `Shared Secret`, enter a password that the IAS and RRAS servers will share. This password is not changed dynamically, so make sure it is long and complex to prevent someone from setting up an RRAS server at the same IP address to spoof authentication requests.
6. Click `Next` to save the changes.

Now, configure the RRAS server to use RADIUS and point it at the IAS server by following Procedure 20.19.

Procedure 20.19 Configuring RRAS to Use RADIUS Authentication

1. In the Routing and Remote Access console, open the Properties window for the server icon.
2. Select the `Security` tab.

3. Under Authentication Provider and Accounting Provider, select the RADIUS options.
4. Next to the Authentication Provider field, click Configure to open the RADIUS Authentication window. This holds a list of the RADIUS servers that will be used by this RRAS server.
5. Click Add. The Add RADIUS Server window opens.
6. Under Server Name, enter the fully qualified DNS name or IP address of the IAS server.
7. Next to the Secret field, click Change to open the Change Secret window.
8. Enter the password you entered in the client configuration at the IAS server and click OK.
9. Click OK to add the IAS server to the list of RADIUS servers. The Initial Score column shows the default score of 30. The RRAS server will change this score based on how quickly it gets responses back from the RADIUS servers. There is seldom a need to set this value manually.
10. Perform the same actions for the Accounting Provider.
11. Stop and start the RRAS service to initialize the new providers.

At this point, the RRAS server is ready to accept client connections. You can test the configuration by making a standard dial-in connection using a domain account. The RRAS server will authenticate using the domain credentials supplied by the IAS server.

Moving Forward

Now that we have remote access and Internet connectivity, we've completed our deployment of Windows Server 2003. We can now act a little like farmers and sit back on the stoop in front of the homestead to admire our work. I think you'll agree that it was a heck of a lot of work.

We can't get too comfortable, though. Even as we relax for a few moments, there are weeds pushing up through the sod and pests flying in from the prairie and the weather forecaster's talking about a drought. We need to get prepared for disaster, and that brings us to the last chapter.

21 Recovering from System Failures

IN THIS, THE FINAL CHAPTER IN THE SAGA of deploying Windows Server 2003 throughout an enterprise, the time has come to talk about the inevitability of disaster. Throughout the book we've seen how to deal with problems, big and small, that can crop up when implementing the functions and features in Windows Server 2003, but in this chapter we'll look at how to handle serious problems that cause a system to crash and crash hard. We'll see how to figure out what happened and how to take steps to keep it from happening again.

The chapter covers the following:

- Backing up and restoring system and data files
- Using Safe Mode to restore stable operations
- Recovering from Blue Screen stops
- Out-of-band server management
- Using Safe Mode
- Restoring functionality with the Last Known Good Configuration
- Working with the Recovery Console

New Features in Windows Server 2003

Where I come from in southern New Mexico, folks like giving nicknames to their friends. Well, if Windows Server 2003 were from New Mexico, it might very well earn the nickname "Bring 'em back alive" because so many new features are focused on maintaining continuity of access to data. Here are some of the new features:

- **Automated System Recovery (ASR).** This feature simplifies the restoration of the operating system partition.

- **Goodbye, Emergency Repair Disk.** There is no more ERD in Windows Server 2003. The only repair options are the Recovery Console or ASR.
- **Emergency Management Services (EMS).** If a server cannot be reached via the network, EMS provides an out-of-band connection to the server via a serial port.
- **Online Crash Analysis.** The kernel-mode debugging utilities in Windows Server 2003 can now run on the same machine as the operating system they are monitoring. This permits running a variety of debugging chores at the console.
- **Volume Shadow.** Locked files create problems for backup programs. Users get irate when you tell them that you can't restore a file because it was locked during the backup while they were working from home. The Volume Shadow service takes a snapshot of a locked file so that the backup program can save the snapshot.
- **System Restore.** This feature, only present on XP, periodically takes snapshots of the system configuration that you can use as checkpoints for rolling back the system to a previous configuration.
- **Online event tracking.** If an application fails or otherwise causes a system error, the system collects information about the failure and sends that information to Microsoft, where it is compiled and analyzed for trends.
- **Shutdown Event Tracker.** This "feature," if you want to call it that, requires that you specify a reason each time you shut down a system. This reason is put in the Event log. If the system crashes, you must specify a reason when the system restarts.

Functional Description Ntbackup

Like all Windows products starting with NT 3.51, Windows Server 2003 comes with a backup utility, Ntbackup, that is a stripped-down version of a commercial package called Backup Exec from Veritas Software, `www.veritas.com`. Data backups performed with earlier versions of Ntbackup can be restored using the Windows Server 2003 version because they use the same Microsoft Tape Format (MTF).

Ntbackup does not incorporate a tape handler. Tape handling is done by the Removable Storage Management (RSM) service. The RSM service can handle individual tape drives as well as robotic libraries. It also is responsible for handling CD-ROM, CD-R, CD-RW, DVD-ROM, DVD-RAM, Zip, Jaz, Orb, and magneto-optical drives.

Unlike most other administrative tools in Windows Server 2003, Ntbackup is managed by an executable, not by an MMC console. This enables it to retain a command-line interface that can be used for scheduling backup jobs to run in the background.

Launch Ntbackup using START | PROGRAMS | ACCESSORIES | BACKUP. The first time you run the program, it starts in a Wizard mode. I'm as much of a Harry Potter fan as the next guy, but when it comes to data recovery, I prefer to avoid wizards. There is an option in the launch window to shift to an Advanced view that does not use a wizard. All examples in this chapter use the Advanced view except for scheduling a backup, which requires the use of a wizard.

The Advanced view of Ntbackup uses a familiar tabbed control to show the features. Figure 21.1 shows an example of the Ntbackup window with the `Backup` tab selected.

The directory tree in the left pane of the Ntbackup window uses the standard Explorer namespace, rooted at `Desktop` and descending through `My Computer`, `My Documents`, and `My Network Places`. When selecting items to back up, you have the option of selecting an entire drive or individual folders or files. A blue checkmark indicates that you have selected an item. If you select an individual file, the folders above it get gray checkmarks indicating that the directory structure will be included in the backup.

You can back up network files either by selecting a mapped drive or by expanding the tree under `My Network Neighborhood` and selecting a share from the server's resource list. Ntbackup does not use agents on remote machines so it is unable to handle sophisticated transactions such as database locking or data compression.

The `Backup Destination` selected for a particular backup job can be a local tape drive or a file on a local or network drive. The target can be a removable media hard drive such as a Zip or Jaz drive or a DVD-RAM. It cannot be a CD-RW drive unless you use a third-party packet writing engine. If you use file-based backup, the target file can be in an NTFS or FAT/FAT32 volume.

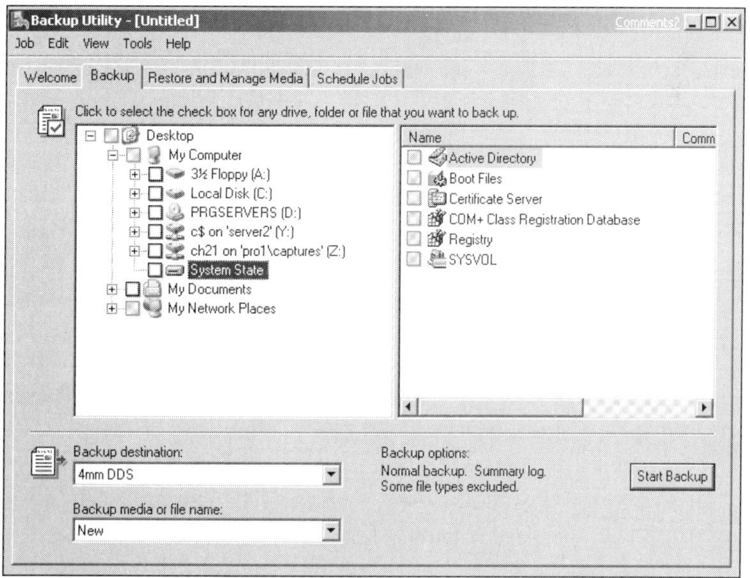

Figure 21.1 Ntbackup window showing `Backup` tab.

Agent-Based Network Backups

Network backups using Ntbackup are limited to files you can reach using a network client redirector. When Ntbackup runs, it works in conjunction with the Local System account to access locked system files. Locked system files cannot be backed up via a network client redirector. It requires an agent running on the server.

A backup agent provides a client/server link between the server being backed up and the server running the backup. The agent runs in the security context of a user with `Backup Operator` privileges so it can access locked system files. The agent sends copies of the files to the backup server where they are put on tape. Agents typically encrypt files that are sent across the network.

Backup Types

When a file is modified, the file system toggles the archive bit on the file attributes. This tells a backup program that the file needs to be backed up. Ntbackup supports five different backup types classified by the way they handle the archive bit.

To view the backup type options, launch `Ntbackup` in Advanced mode and select TOOLS | OPTIONS from the main menu. The Options window opens with the focus set to the `Backup Type` tab. Figure 21.2 shows an example. Here are the options to choose from:

- **`Normal.`** This option backs up the selected files and clears the archive bit if it is set.
- **`Copy.`** This option backs up the selected files and does not clear the archive bit.
- **`Differential.`** This option backs up only the selected files where the archive bit is set. It does not clear the archive bit.

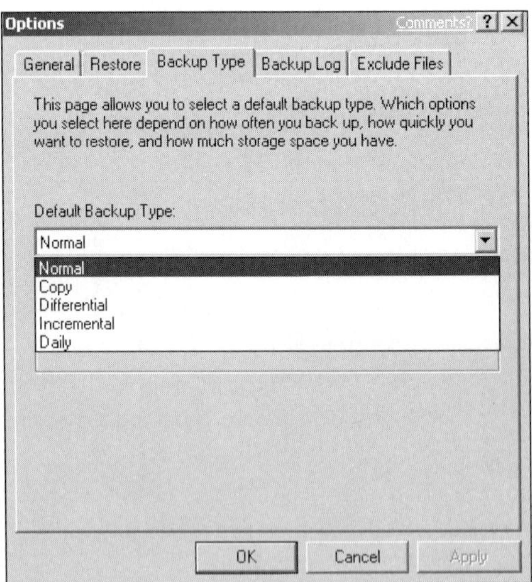

Figure 21.2 Backup Options window showing `Backup Type` tab.

- `Incremental.` This option backs up only the selected files where the archive bit is set. It clears the archive bit.
- `Daily.` This option does not use the archive bit. It backs up files with a Modified timestamp that matches the backup date.

The `Copy` option is primarily used for transferring files to another system and not for scheduled backups. Here are details about the other options along with criteria to use when choosing one over the other.

Normal Backups

Running a normal backup every night makes restoration easy. All the files you need to restore a system to its most current configuration are right on one tape (or set of tapes). Normal backups take time, though, so you have to measure their usefulness against the size of your backup window.

Differential Backups

Because differential backups only capture files with the archive bit set, they shorten the nightly backup considerably. As time goes by, though, a differential backup takes longer and longer because it does not reset the archive bit. For example, if File_A changed on Monday, each night's differential backup will include File_A.

Restoration from differential backups is a two-step process. First, you must restore the last normal backup; then, you restore the latest differential backup.

Differential backups simplify requests for individual file restores because you only need to go to one of two tapes—the last normal backup or the last differential backup—to find the file.

Be sure to design your tape rotations so that the normal and its associated differential tapes are stored together. It can be embarrassing to overlay the normal backup from one week with a differential backup from another week.

Incremental Backups

Incremental backups avoid the ever-increasing backup duration caused by differential backups because it resets the archive bit. In this way, any incremental backup only captures files that changed since the last incremental or full backup.

The problem with incremental backups is that they make recovery much more complex. To restore a volume, you must first restore the last normal backup then restore each of the incremental backups in sequence. If any particular tape fails to restore, this can cause problems with data consistency.

Incremental backups also complicate individual file restores because you must search through several different tapes. If the user is a little fuzzy about the date when the file was lost, you have a chore in front of you.

Daily Backups

Both differential and incremental backups rely on the archive bit. If you run other utilities that change the archive bit, you may end up missing files in your nightly backups. A daily backup avoids this problem by reading the timestamp on the files rather than the archive bit.

The same caveats apply to daily backups that apply to incremental backups. You must keep them in order and apply them in order after first applying the last normal backup.

Backup Logs

Ntbackup keeps a log of each backup and restore job. You can access the log from the Ntbackup menu by selecting TOOLS | REPORT. Logging is a critical element of a backup strategy. Without a log, you could be unaware of a problem that puts your data at risk. For example, if you back up files across the network, a problem with the network connection can cause the files to be skipped. Without checking the log regularly, you won't know this happened.

Backup logs are saved to the local profile of the user who runs the backup. The path is `\Documents and Settings\<logonID>\Local Settings\Application Data\Microsoft\Windows NT\NTBackup\Data`. This path is fixed. There is no Registry parameter that can be set to change it. Each backup job creates a new backup log. The logs are numbered sequentially and renumbered automatically after reaching 10, so the oldest log is overwritten.

The Backup Options window, accessed via TOOLS | OPTIONS, controls the type of log that is saved. Figure 21.3 shows an example. Ntbackup has two logging options:

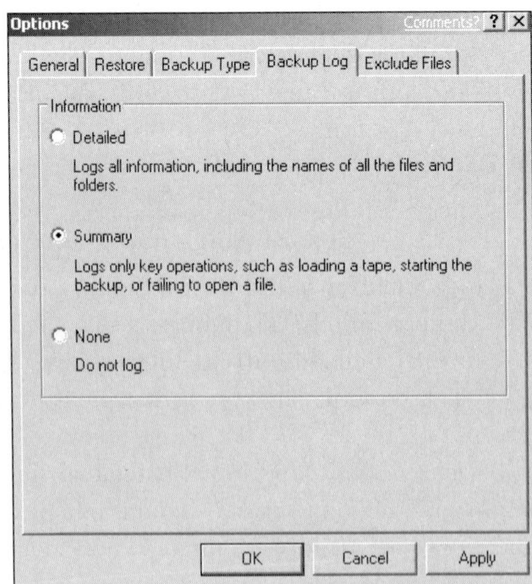

Figure 21.3 Options window showing `Backup log` options.

- The `Detailed` option logs include the name and path of every file in the backup.
- The `Summary` option logs include a file count and tell you if any files were skipped.

Summary logs are the better choice for standard daily backups because you stand less of a chance of missing a problem buried in a long, detailed report. If you are troubleshooting a backup problem involving missed files, enable the `Detailed` option and scan the report for clues on why they were missed.

File Exclusions

The Backup Options window has an `Exclude Files` tab. Figure 21.4 shows an example.

The `Files Excluded For All Users` field lists file extensions and individual files that are deliberately left out of all backup jobs.

The default list of excluded files includes the paging file, temp files, the client-side cache for offline files, contents of the debug folder, the File Replication System (FRS) database and any FRS cache folders on volumes containing replicated files (such as `\Windows\Sysvol`), the Windows registration files, the Distributed Transaction Coordinator log, and the local cryptographic certificate database.

Adding File Exclusions

You can add file classifications to the exclusion list and narrow the focus to individual folders. You can do this for all backup jobs or jobs run by the current user. Add a new exclusion as shown in Procedure 21.1.

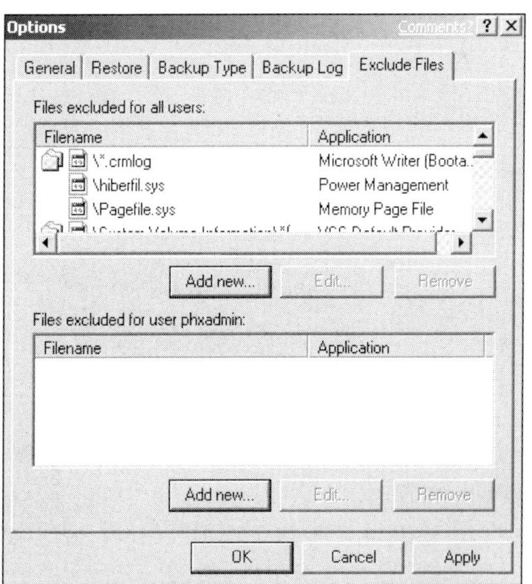

Figure 21.4 Options window showing `Exclude Files`. The `Add New` button can be used to exclude other file types.

Procedure 21.1 Adding File Types to the File Exclusion List

1. Click `Add New` under the `All Users` field or the `Current User` field. The Add Excluded Files window opens.
2. Select the class of file you want to exclude. Use the `Applies To Path` field to narrow the scope to a particular folder.
3. Click `OK` to save the selection and return to the Options window.
4. Click `OK` to save the setting and close the window.

Registering File Types for Exclusion

If you back up a volume across the network and you have a file type on the source machine that you want to exclude but it is not on the local extension list, you must register the file locally on the machine running Ntbackup. The easiest way to do this is shown in Procedure 21.2.

Procedure 21.2 Registering File Types for Backup Exclusions

1. Open the network drive in Explorer.
2. Right-click one of the files of the type you want to exclude and select OPEN WITH from the flyout menu.
3. Double-click the executable you want to associate with the file type. This closes the window and adds the application to the list in the Open With window.
4. Select the `Always Use This Program to Open These Files` option.
5. Click `OK` to save the change and make the association in the Registry.

Now that the file type is registered, you can exclude it using the steps mentioned earlier in Procedure 21.1.

General Backup Options

From the Ntbackup menu, select TOOLS | OPTIONS then select the `General` tab. Figure 21.5 shows an example. Most of the options are self-explanatory and are selected by default.

`Compute Selection Information Before Backup and Restore` delays the backup and restore long enough to calculate the total number of files and bytes. This calculation takes a while, sometimes a long while, and unless you need to check for sufficient storage capacity prior to initiating a backup or restore, you can deselect this option.

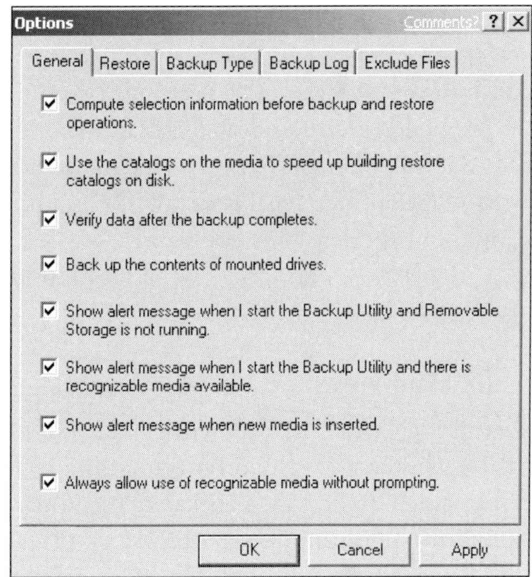

Figure 21.5 Backup Options window showing `General` options.

`Use the Catalogs on the Media to Speed Up Building Restore Catalogs on Disk` is a highly recommended option. In backup parlance, a *catalog* is an index of the files that were included in the backup and their locations. Ntbackup (and every other backup program) uses catalogs to determine where to place files and folders during a restore. Ordinarily, when you run Ntbackup, a copy of the catalog is saved to the local drive in the profile of the user who submits the job. For example, if the local Administrator submits a job, the catalog is stored under `\Documents and Settings\Administrator\Local Settings\Application Data\Microsoft\Windows NT\NTBackup\Catalog`. The catalogs are assigned hexadecimal sequence numbers with a .v01 extension. An index file with an .sm extension defines the members of the catalog.

By putting a copy of the catalog on the tape, you quickly recover it during a restore if your restoration server does not have a local copy of the catalog. Without the on-tape copy of the catalog, Ntbackup must scan the entire tape to build a catalog prior to performing a restore. This can take hours and hours, which can be a wrenching experience if the data is critically needed.

`Verify Data After The Backup Completes` adds an extra measure of assurance to your backup. After the backup has completed, each tape entry is read to assure that it is not corrupt. This verification does not touch the file system.

`Back Up The Contents Of Mounted Drives` is a default option. A mounted drive (mounted volume, really) consists of an NTFS reparse point that redirects a process to a remote file system such as another volume or folder or CD-ROM. If the target volume of the reparse point also has a drive letter that you are backing up, you will get two identical backups. There is no performance penalty for backing up via a mount point. If you have a mounted CD-ROM that you do not want to include in the backup, de-select this option.

`Always Allow Use of Recognizable Media Without Prompting` is the default option if you have never opened the Removable Storage Manager console. For the most part, if a tape drive is the only removable media that requires administrator intervention on a server, select this option. This lets Ntbackup communicate with RSM to obtain and manage tapes without the need for you to give any input. Without this option, each time you put a fresh tape in the drive, you'll be responsible for preparing it for the Backup pool.

Locked Files and the Volume Shadow Service

Ntbackup runs in the Local System security context so it is able to back up system files such as the Registry and Active Directory and the other databases that support system operations such as DHCP, WINS, and so forth. But even with a privileged system account, Ntbackup cannot override a lock placed on a file by a user process.

Applications like Word or Access that lock their files stymie just about any backup program. Locked files are getting to be more and more common as users connect from home using dial-in and VPNs. It can cause users discomfort to find out that they cannot restore a critical file because they've been working on it every night for the last week during your backups. Here is a short listing from an Ntbackup log that demonstrates this problem:

```
Backup Status
Operation: Backup
Active backup destination: 4mm DDS
Media name: "TestBackup"

Backup of "C: "
Backup set #1 on media #1
Backup description: "Test"
Media name: "TestMedia"

Backup Type: Normal

Backup started on 2/15/2002 at 3:35 AM.
Warning: Unable to open "C:\Test\LiveDocument.doc" - skipped.
Reason: The process cannot access the file because it is being used by another
➥process.
```

Windows Server 2003 fixes this problem using a service called *Volume Shadow*, or VS. The VS service takes a snapshot of a locked file so that Ntbackup can save the snapshot rather than the original. Here is a listing that shows the Ntbackup log with Volume Shadow enabled:

```
Backup (via shadow copy) of "C: "
Backup set #1 on media #1
Backup description: "Test"
Media name: "TestMedia"
```

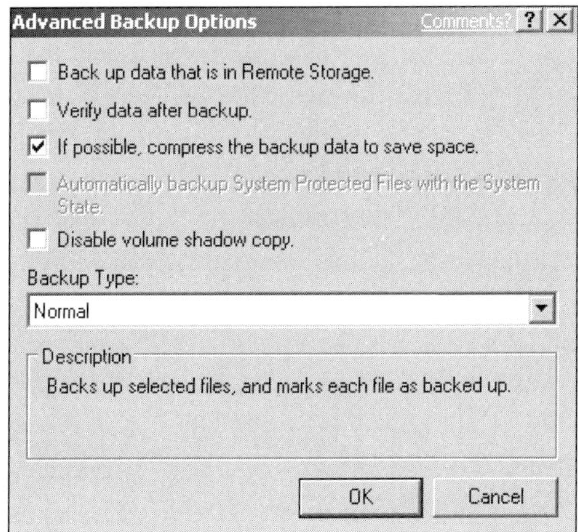

Figure 21.6 Advanced backup options showing the `Volume Shadow Copy` selection.

```
Backup Type: Normal

Backup started on 2/25/2002 at 3:39 AM.
Backup completed on 2/25/2002 at 3:39 AM.
Directories: 2
Files: 2
Bytes: 4,437
Time:  4 seconds
```

The Volume Shadow service, Vssvc.exe, only takes snapshots of files in NTFS partitions and it uses NTFS partitions to store its temp files, so you must have sufficient free space to hold the largest locked file.

If a system lacks NTFS volumes, or those volumes lack free space, Ntbackup proceeds with standard locked file handling, which consists of 30 seconds of retries then the file is skipped.

You can elect to run Ntbackup without shadow copies. This avoids taking snapshots of large database files that you do not want backed up. The option is part of the Advanced backup selections. Figure 21.6 shows an example.

System Restore on XP Desktops

The System Restore feature is only available on XP. It takes periodic snapshots of a system configuration that can be used for rollback. Snapshots are taken daily and whenever you install applications or make major changes to the system configuration. These snapshots are called *restore points*.

To take a manual snapshot or roll back to a previous restore point, access the System Restore features from the Help and Support Center (HSC). Look for the `System Restore` option on the HSC home page. Click the link to open a page for selecting either to create a restore point or to roll back to an existing restore point. If you choose to roll back, the system displays a window with a calendar that allows you to select a day and view the restore points that were saved for that day. Figure 21.7 shows a restore point taken prior to installing Microsoft Office XP.

If you elect to roll back to an earlier restore point, only system executables that were modified in the interim are rolled back, not data files. This means users will not lose data as a result of a System Restore rollback, but they may lose critical links within their application. The further you reach back, the more likely you are to have a consistency problem.

Rollbacks do not affect encrypted files. You cannot unencrypt a file simply by rolling back to a time when the file was in plain text.

Security Considerations

When you place an account in the Backup Operators group, or otherwise assign `SeBackupPermission` and `SeRestorePermission` to an account, this gives the user permission to back up any file on the machine regardless of its security descriptor or encryption status. Backup operators can also strip security permissions from files during restoration. In short, it's hard to imagine a more serious security breach than the frivolous granting of backup operator privileges.

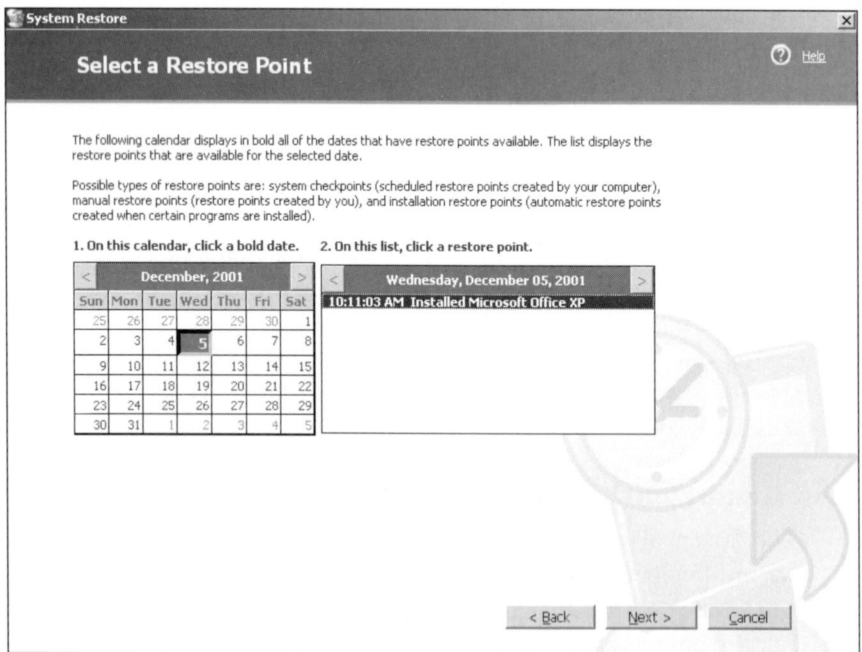

Figure 21.7 System Restore page showing Restore Point calendar with details about an earlier restore point.

A similar problem exists for third-party backup applications that use client-based backup agents. These agents run in the security context of an account with `Backup Operator` permissions. Because of their privileged nature, backup agent accounts are often used for other purposes. It is common to find virtually every administrator logged on with the backup account.

If you want to run the nightly Ntbackup jobs using an account other than the Administrator account, you can create a special account that is a member of the Backup Operators group then assign this account to the job via the Task Scheduler. Figure 21.8 shows an example. Access the Task Scheduler via the Control Panel.

Physical control of backup tapes is also important. It is common to find shops where unauthorized users aren't allowed within 100 yards of a production server, but backup tapes are routinely put in the custody of unbonded couriers and temporary contractors. You need secure off-site storage with a known and licensed chain of custody for the tapes.

Finally, don't forget about the possibility of data loss due to theft. This is emphatically true for small businesses in strip malls and office parks with easy access from the street. It only takes a few seconds to toss a rock through a window and snatch a computer. Servers look impressive, so thieves often spend a few extra minutes looking for them. Don't multiply your loss by leaving your backup tapes where they can be scooped up, too.

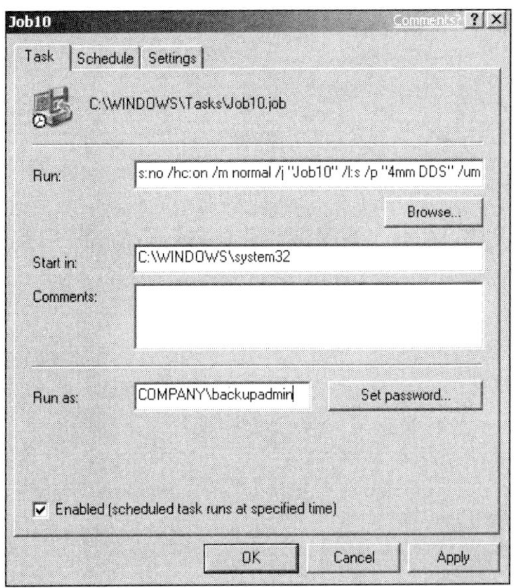

Figure 21.8 Task Scheduler job properties showing alternative credentials entered in the `Run as` field.

Backing Up System State Files

In Windows Server 2003 and Windows 2000, Microsoft groups a large number of files under an umbrella term called *System State*. These files must be backed up and restored as a unit to maintain data and operational consistency. The System State files include the following:

- Active Directory database, NTDS.DIT, and its associated log and checkpoint files in the `\Windows\NTDS` folder
- Registry hives from the `\Windows\System32\Config` directory
- COM+ class registration database
- Files protected by the Windows File Protection service (This includes most of the files in `\Windows` and many of the Microsoft files in `\Program Files`.)
- System files from the root of the boot drive: Ntdetect.com, Ntldr, Boot.ini, Bootsect.dos, and Ntbootdd.sys
- Certification Authority database files (if the Certification Service is installed)
- Contents of the `\Windows\Sysvol` folder, which contains group policies and scripts
- IIS metabase (if IIS is installed)
- Cluster database (if the Cluster service is installed)

You cannot use Ntbackup to back up System State files from another machine across the network. And don't make the mistake of thinking that doing a backup of the `Admin$` share is the same as a System State backup. Many of the files are locked if you merely run Ntbackup across the network. If you want to do central backups of System State, you must purchase a commercial backup package.

Backing Up to a File

One of the nicer features of Ntbackup is its capability to send a backup job to a file rather than to tape. This makes it possible to do quick backups of local desktops saved to removable media or network drives. File-based backups are also an essential component of encrypted file management. To move encrypted files from one machine to another, you must back them up to a file, transport the backup file, then restore the encrypted files inside at their new location.

File-based backups have their downside. Desktop users with local `Backup Operator` privileges can use Ntbackup to run a backup of their entire hard drive to a file on a server. Consider establishing a group policy limiting access to Ntbackup.

Automated System Recovery (ASR)

Restoring a failed operating system partition has always been a tedious affair. Ordinarily, you have to format the partition, reinstall the operating system, mount the backup tape, catalog the tape, and then run a full restore.

As the name implies, the Automated System Recovery (ASR) feature makes this process much simpler. An ASR backup takes a standard backup of the operating system partition then saves the catalog and other configuration information to a floppy. If you need to restore the operating system partition using ASR, all you need to do is boot to the Windows Server 2003 CD with the backup tape mounted in the tape drive, press F2 when prompted to select the ASR option, and watch the process take off. ASR installs the operating system from CD then mounts the tape and does the restore. Remember to take the floppy out of the drive after the initial text-based portion of the restore has completed, and then come back in an hour to have a server that is up and running, good as new.

To create an ASR backup, use the ASR Wizard in Ntbackup. The only option is to do an interactive backup. You cannot use Task Scheduler to schedule an ASR backup. The wizard consists of just one window that asks the target backup device and media label (or backup file and filename). The only other time the wizard prompts for input is to ask for a blank, formatted floppy on which to store the Setup Information Files (SIFs).

ASR retains the original partitioning, so it should not disturb data volumes that are on the same spindle as the operating system. If the boot drive is mirrored, you will need to break the mirror prior to running ASR.

One challenge that can come up when using ASR is loading third-party device drivers that are required for the initial setup phase. These are generally mass storage device drivers that you would press F6 to load during a normal interactive Setup. To load these additional drivers automatically, you must make a modification to the Asr.sif file that scripts ASR to include an `[InstallFiles]` section in the following format:

```
[InstallFiles]

[Installfile-Key]=[System-Key],[Source-Media-Label], [Source-Device],
➥[Source-File-Path], [Destination-File-Path], [Vendor-Name], [Flags]
```

Here is a guide to the components of the `[InstallFiles]` section. The double-quotes in some examples are part of the entry you would put in the Asr.sif file:

- **`[Installfile-Key]=[System-Key]`**. `Installfile-Key` is a unique sequence number assigned to each entry. `System-Key` is the index entry under the `[System]` section that designates the operating system partition you are installing. Example: The first entry in the [InstallFiles] section with a reference to the first entry in the `[System]` section would be listed as `1=1`.
- **`[Source-Media-Label]`**. This is the label assigned to the floppy that contains the additional files. Example: If you want to load a SCSI driver from a floppy, give the floppy a label such as `SCSIFiles`. Then put an entry of "SCSIFiles" in the Asr.sif file. During ASR, you will be prompted to insert a disk with this label.
- **`[Source-Device]`**. This entry defines the device path of the media holding the file. The path is specified in object namespace format, such as `"\Device\Floppy0"` or `"\Device\CdRom0"`.

- **[Source-File-Path]**. This is the source path and filename for the driver you are installing. If you need to install more than one file, you must make multiple entries under `[InstallFiles]`. Do not start the path string with a backslash. Example: `"Scsidrvr.sys"` is the path to the file at the root of the floppy.
- **[Destination-File-Path]**. This is where you want the file to be copied. Do not start the string with a backslash. Example: `"%systemroot%\System32\Drivers\Scsidrvr.sys"`.
- **[Vendor-Name]**. This is the name of the vendor that created the driver. It is just used for a display string, so you can enter anything you want. Example: `"Additional SCSI Driver"`.
- **[Flags]**. These are flags that tell ASR how to prompt for the floppy. The options are listed in the next list. Example: `"0x00000001"`.

Here is a list of the flags that can be used in the `[InstallFiles]` section:

- **0x00000001**. Always prompt. This gives the installer a chance to insert the media right at the end of the file copy phase of Setup.
- **0x00000006**. Prompt for required files. Same as `0x00000001` except ASR will not proceed without the file.
- **0x00000010**. Overwrite the file if it already exists.
- **0x00000020**. Prompt before overwriting a file that already exists.

With these settings in mind, here is an example entry that prompts the user for an additional SCSI driver:

```
[Install Files]
  1=1,"SCSIFiles","\Device\Floppy0","Scsidrvr.sys","%Systemroot%\System32\
  ➥Drivers\Scsidriver.sys","Adaptec", 0x00000001
```

Removable Storage

You should be able to manage all tape backup functions from within Ntbackup, but the tape handling is actually done by the *Removable Storage Management* (RSM) service.

RSM is managed with an MMC snap-in called `Removable Storage`. The snap-in is part of the Computer Management console (see Figure 21.9). A command-line utility, Rsm.exe, can be used instead of the snap-in to perform many functions such as mounting and dismounting media and allocating media to a specific service. The Help and Support Center contains the command syntax for the Rsm utility.

> **Recovering from a Loss of an ASR Floppy**
>
> The floppy configured by the ASR wizard contains two System Information Files, Asr.sif and Asrpnp.sif, along with a copy of the Setup.log file. Copies of these files are saved to tape, as well. You can extract them from the tape and put them on a formatted floppy. The files are located in the `\Windows\Repair` folder.

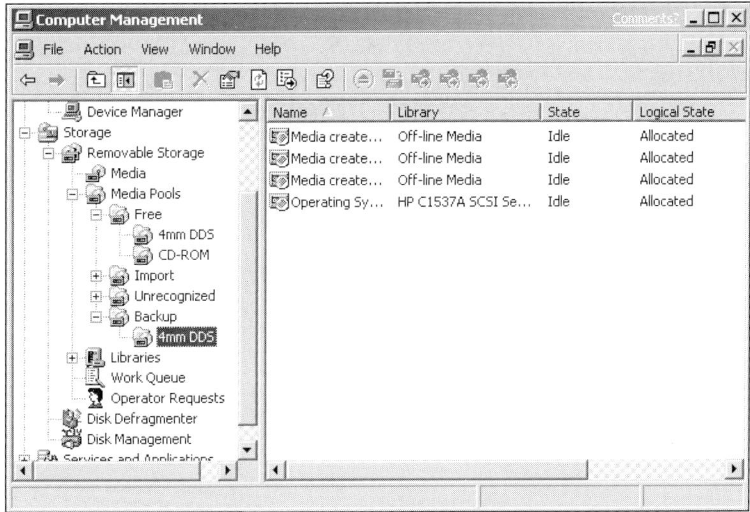

Figure 21.9 Computer Management console with `Removable Storage` snap-in expanded.

RSM handles all removable media in a system, from single-drive tape devices and CD-ROM players all the way up to 100-disk CD jukeboxes and robotic tape libraries. RSM assigns media to one of four *media pools*. They are as follows:

- **Free.** This pool contains media that has been marked with a `Free` media label and are available for allocation.
- **Import.** This pool contains tape media that were formatted using Microsoft Tape Format (MTF) and have a recognizable tape label but have not yet been allocated to a particular device. This includes backup tapes created by classic NT.
- **Unrecognized.** This pool contains tape media that are blank or formatted in a foreign format.

The `Removable Storage` snap-in permits you to select users who can access particular devices and media. It does this using standard access control lists (ACL) exposed by a `Security` tab on the device properties. Figure 21.10 shows an example for a tape backup device.

There are three sets of permissions that can be applied to a Removable Storage object:

- **`Use.`** Permits a user to mount and dismount media loaded in the device.
- **`Modify.`** Permits a user to create and delete media pools and to allocate and deallocate media to and from those pools.
- **`Control.`** Permits a user to send commands to the library that controls its physical operation.

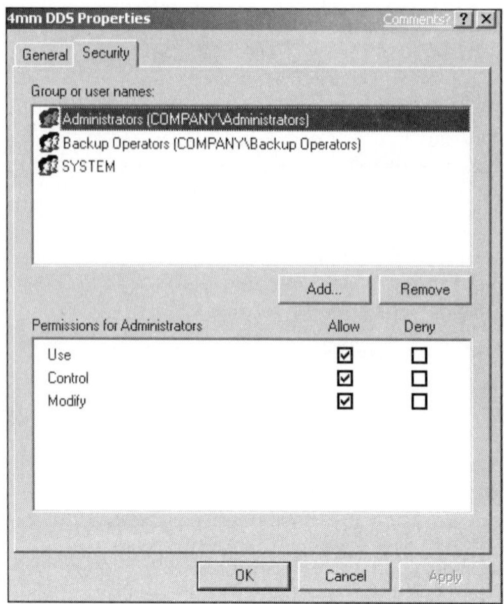

Figure 21.10 Security properties for a tape device in the Removable Storage snap-in.

Tape Names and Ntbackup

The Removable Storage service abstracts much of the tape handling from Ntbackup and other backup products. This is a good thing, because it frees the backup applications from the need to contain proprietary tape handling functions, but it can also be downright irritating because the backup program has no real control over the tapes themselves. All tape handling is done by the Removable Storage service.

One source of irritation caused by this marriage of Ntbackup and Removable Storage service is the way tape names are managed. Ntbackup has no way to know if the Removable Storage service has mounted a tape in a single drive unit or a big multi-tape, multi-headed robotic tape library. Because libraries need special handling, Ntbackup is forced to assume the existence of a robotic library. This means that each tape must have a definite name that Ntbackup can use when requesting a tape from the library. When Ntbackup overwrites a tape, it applies a name that it can use in case you need the tape for a restore.

This puts you into something of a loop when you configure backup tape rotations. Ntbackup looks for a particular tape name and it writes a tape name as part of an overwrite job. If you use the default media label of Media Created On *<date>*, you cannot easily configure a backup job to look for that date each day or each week.

Unmanaged Backups

Ordinarily, when you run Ntbackup as part of a scheduled job, you must specify the name of the target tape. This requirement prevents you from accidentally overwriting a tape in a tape library. If you have a single tape unit, you usually don't care too much about tape names. You want the backup job to run regardless of the tape that is in the drive.

There is an undocumented Ntbackup command-line switch called `/um`, for Unmanaged, that tells Ntbackup to ignore the tape name and simply use whatever tape is mounted in the drive. Add the `/um` switch to the job description in Task Scheduler.

If you use the `/um` switch, you must include the `/p` switch, for Pool, to specify the name of the tape pool you want to use—for example, "4mm DAT". You can get the pool name from the RSM console display.

This workaround is not appropriate if you have a robotic tape library. You do not want the library to randomly select a tape and overwrite it. Always use specific tape names when configuring backup jobs for an automated tape library.

When configuring tapes for a rotating system, you must establish a separate job for each day of the week with a tape label that matches the job. For example, for a weekly tape rotation, you can configure a Monday backup job that writes a media label of `Monday` to the tape. The job looks for a tape labeled `Monday` when it runs. If a tape labeled `Friday` is still in the drive when the Monday job runs, the backup fails.

To work a blank tape into this configuration, you must write the correct label to the tape. Microsoft *should* provide a utility for this, but it doesn't. You must do a little manual backup job to write the label. See the sidebar, "Unmanaged Backups," for a way to avoid the need for specific tape labels.

Third-Party Backup Options

There are many players in the Windows backup game. Table 21.1 shows the names of the major vendors and their products. Their feature sets change constantly, so check their web sites for the latest updates.

Table 21.1 Third-Party Backup Packages

Product	Company	Web address
ArcServe	Computer Associates	`www.cai.com`
Backup Exec	Veritas	`www.veritas.com`
Networker	Legato	`www.legato.com`
ADSM	IBM	`www.pc.ibm.com`
Novastor	Novastor	`www.novastor.com`
Ultrabac	BEI Corporation	`www.ultrabac.com`

Backup and Restore Operations

This section gives step-by-step procedures for performing interactive backups, scheduling backups, and restoring files.

Performing an Interactive Backup

You can run backup jobs interactively from the Ntbackup window or you can schedule them to run in the background. Unlike NT, you can use Ntbackup to both configure and schedule backup jobs. The steps in this section assume that you have a blank tape. If the tape already has backup files on it, you'll be prompted in several places to confirm overwriting the tape name and its contents and whether you want to import the tape into the RSM Free media pool.

The steps in Procedure 21.3 describe how to configure and run an interactive backup job using the Advanced view of Ntbackup.

Procedure 21.3 Performing an Interactive Backup

1. Start Ntbackup using START | PROGRAMS | ACCESSORIES | SYSTEM TOOLS | BACKUP. Shift to `Advanced` mode if prompted with the Wizard window.
2. Select the `Backup` tab. Figure 21.11 shows an example. Select the drives and/or folders you want to include in the backup job. You can use My Network Places to select shared folders on other servers, as well.
3. From the NTBACKUP menu, select TOOLS | OPTIONS. The Options window opens. Select the `Backup Type` tab. Select a `Default Backup Type` for the job.

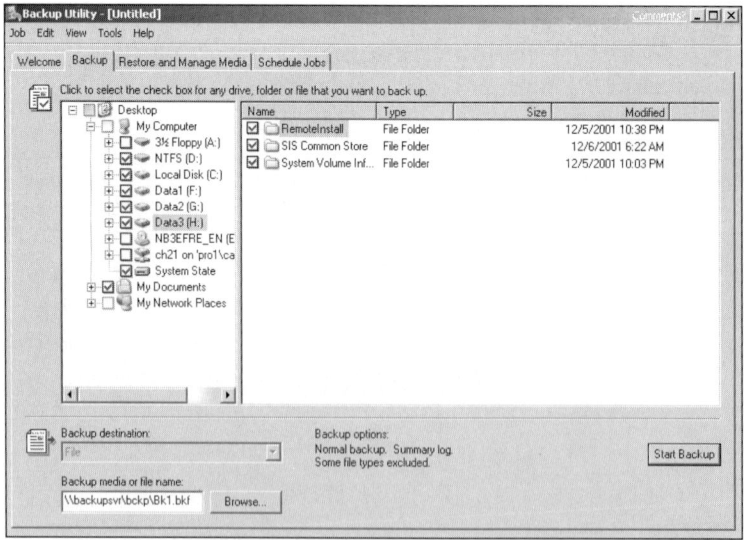

Figure 21.11 Backup window showing file and folder selections.

4. Select the `Backup Log` tab. Under `Information`, select either `Detailed` or `Summary`. The `Summary` option is selected by default.
5. Click `OK` to save your configuration and return to the main Backup window.
6. Under `Backup Destination`, select the tape backup unit.
7. Under `Backup Media or File Name`, select `New`. This tells Ntbackup to take the blank tape from the Free media pool in RSM.
8. Click `Start Backup`. The Backup Job Information window opens (see Figure 21.12). The field labeled `If The Media Is Overwritten...` is very important. It determines the name applied to the tape when it is overwritten.
9. Click `Advanced`. The Advanced Backup Options window opens (see Figure 21.13).

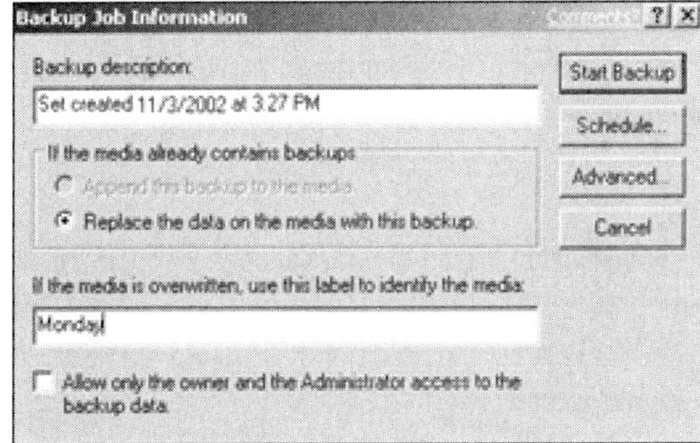

Figure 21.12 Backup Job Information window showing default entries for Backup Description and media labeling.

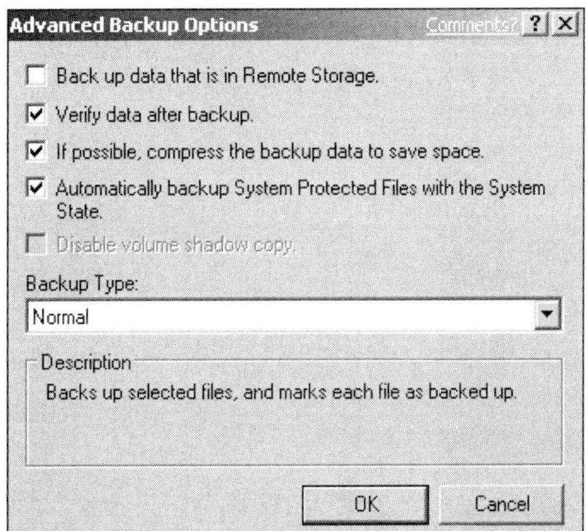

Figure 21.13 Advanced Backup Options window showing default backup options.

10. Select the `Verify Data After Backup` option and the `If Possible, Compress the Backup Data to Save Space` options and then click `OK` to save the settings and return to the Backup Job Information window.
11. Click `Start Backup`. If there is media in the Free pool but it has not been prepared with a `Free` media label, RSM gives you an informational message and prompts you to confirm the tape overwrite.
12. After the backup job commences, the Backup Progress window opens and the files begin to flow to the tape. If you cancel out of the job, Ntbackup prompts you to complete backing up the current file. You have the option of bypassing this and canceling the job immediately.
13. When the backup has completed, the Backup Progress window informs you of the status. Click `Report` to open Notepad and view the backup log. Here is an example log for a job that backed up one file:

```
Backup Status
Operation: Backup
Active backup destination: 4mm DDS
Media name: "New"

Backup of "C: "
Backup set #1 on media #1
Backup description: "Monday"
Backup Type: Normal

Backup started on 2/27/2002 at 10:22 AM.
Folder C:\
Backup completed on 2/27/2002 at 10:46 AM.
Directories: 38
Files: 239
Bytes: 1,208,708
Time:  45 seconds
```

At the completion of the backup, you can close the Backup Progress window. Be sure to label the tape and store it safely.

Scheduling a Backup Job

After you have verified (using an interactive job) that your backup system is working, you can schedule jobs to run in the evening. Be sure to coordinate backups around your virus scans. You can configure and schedule a job from within Ntbackup as described in Procedure 21.4.

Procedure 21.4 Configuring and Scheduling a Backup Job

1. In Ntbackup, select the `Schedule Jobs` tab. This displays a calendar.
2. Double-click the day you want to start the job. This launches the Backup Wizard. (You have to use the wizard for this configuration.)
3. Click `Next`. The Items to Back Up window opens. Select the drives you want to include in the backup job. Be sure to select `System State` as one of your options.
4. Click `Next`. The Backup Type, Destination, and Name window opens. Select the tape drive and a tape name that the job will look for.
5. Click `Next`. The Type of Backup window opens. Select a `Normal` backup type. You can use this procedure to create differential or incremental jobs as a follow-on to this normal job.
6. Click `Next`. The How to Back Up window opens. Select the `Verify Data After Backup` and `Use Hardware Compression` options.
7. Click `Next`. The Backup Options window opens. The `Replace Existing Backups` option is selected by default for normal backups. As an additional security precaution, you can select the `Allow The Owner...` option.
8. Click `Next`. The Backup Label window opens. Enter the name that the job will apply to the tape under `Media Label`. Enter the name you want displayed in the catalog under `Backup Label`.
9. Click `Next`. The When to Back Up window opens. Select the `Later` radio button and enter a job name then click `Set Schedule`. The Schedule Job window opens.
10. Use the `Schedule Task` option to select a repetition option such as `Daily` or `Weekly` then select a `Start Time`.
11. Click `OK` to return to the main wizard then click `Next` to open the Set Account Information window. Enter the credentials of the account you've created to run backups.
12. Click `OK` to save the credentials. A summary window opens. Click `Finish` to save the changes as a scheduled task. The job icon will appear in the calendar on each day it is scheduled to run.

All you need to do now is make sure you have the right tapes in the drive depending on how you configured the job. The next section covers performing this same task using the Backup Wizard.

Backup Job Structure

When a scheduled job comes due, the Task Scheduler launches Ntbackup in the background with command-line switches that were set based on your selections in the Backup Wizard. Here is an example of a backup job listing:

```
C:\Windows\system32\ntbackup.exe backup "@C:\Documents and Settings\Administrator\
➥Local Settings\Application Data\Microsoft\Windows NT\NTBackup\data\Monday.bks"
➥/n "Monday" /d "Monday" /v:yes /r:no /rs:no /hc:on /m normal /j:"Monday Backup"
➥/p "4mm DDS"
```

The entry is long because the path to the backup file is buried deep in the Administrator's user profile. Here are the switches and their functions:

- **`/n.`** The name of the tape specified for the job. A tape by that name *must* be in the drive or the job will abort.
- **`/d.`** The name applied to the tape when it is overwritten. This should be the same name specified in `/d` so the same tape can be used the next time.
- **`/v.`** This sets the `Verify` option.
- **`/r.`** This sets the `Restriction` option. If set, only members of the Administrators group can access the tape.
- **`/rs.`** This sets the `Remote Storage backup` option.
- **`/hc.`** This sets the `Hardware Compression` option.
- **`/m.`** This sets the backup type.
- **`/j.`** This defines the job name.
- **`/p.`** This specifies the backup device.

If you have a single tape device and don't want to mess around with tape names, add the `/um` switch. For details on other command-line options, type `ntbackup /?` at a command prompt.

Restoring Files

The best backup rotation system in the world won't help you if you can't get files off a tape and back onto a disk when you need them. This section describes how to do individual file restores because that's the source of the majority of restore requests. Full restores of a data volume works the same—there are just more files involved. Full restores of an operating system volume are described under "Automated System Recovery (ASR)" earlier in this chapter.

When you configure a Restore job, you'll be given the following three choices for placing the restored files:

- `Original Location`. If you select this option, Restore puts the files in the same directory that they came from. If the directory structure is no longer present, it is recreated. This option is most appropriate for restoring entire volumes. Under normal circumstances, you do not want to restore individual user files back to their original location because the user may have placed changes in the target file that is currently on disk and you don't want to overwrite them.

- `Alternate Location`. This option brings up a path field and `Browse` button. Use these to find a folder to hold the restored files. This writes the original directory structure to the target folder. This option is most appropriate for restoring an entire subtree rather than an individual file.
- `Single Folder`. This option also brings up a path and `Browse` button. Use these to find a folder to hold the restored files. This does not preserve the original directory structure. This option is most appropriate when restoring individual files. If you elect to restore an entire directory using the `Single Folder` option, the files are plucked out of the directory and put at the root of the specified folder.

During the configuration, you will also be asked to set the security option for the restored files. The options are as follows:

- `Restore Security`. This option applies the original permissions to the newly restored files. This is the default selection and the one most appropriate for the majority of file restores. If you have a situation where the original security descriptors are no longer valid—you may be restoring data after reinstalling the operating system—or you want to scrub the old descriptors and replace them with the defaults in the restoration folder, deselect this option.
- `Restore Removable Storage Database`. Use this option to restore the media settings in the Removable Storage database along with the data.
- `Restore Junction Points, Not The Folders And File Data They Reference`. This option permits you to restore one volume without reaching through a mount point to the files in another file system. If you are not sure if a particular volume has mount points, select this option just to be on the safe side. You can restore the mounted volume separately, if necessary.
- `When Restoring Replicated Data Sets[el]`. This option is used when restoring files to a volume that is replicated using the File Replication System. This option is only available when restoring System State files. By selecting this option, the timestamps and date stamps on the replicated files are made current so they become the files that will propagate outward to other server holding a replica of the volume.

When you are ready to restore a file, use the steps in Procedure 21.5.

Procedure 21.5 Restoring a File Manually Using Ntbackup

1. Insert the tape that contains the files you want to restore into the tape device. It can take up to a minute for the Removable Storage Management system to make the tape available to Ntbackup.
2. Launch `Ntbackup`.

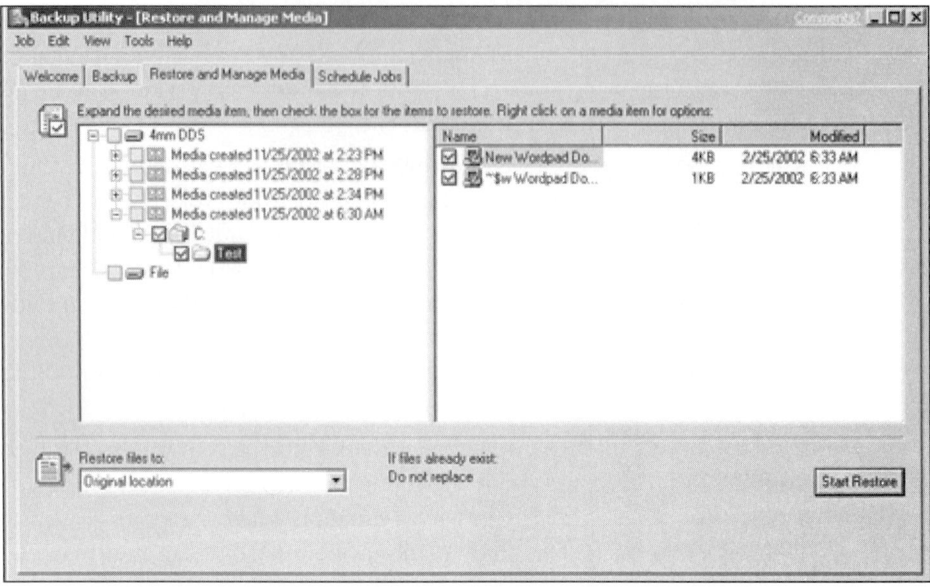

Figure 21.14 Ntbackup window showing `Restore and Manage Media` tab.

3. Select the `Restore and Manage Media` tab and highlight the tape device icon (see Figure 21.14).
4. In the right pane, look for the catalog entry with a `Media Location` that indicates it is mounted. The other catalog entries will show `Offline`.
5. Select the files or folder you want to restore.
6. Under `Restore Files To`, select one of the three location options.
7. Click `Start Restore`. In the Confirm Restore window, click `Advanced`. The Advanced Restore Options window opens (see Figure 21.15).

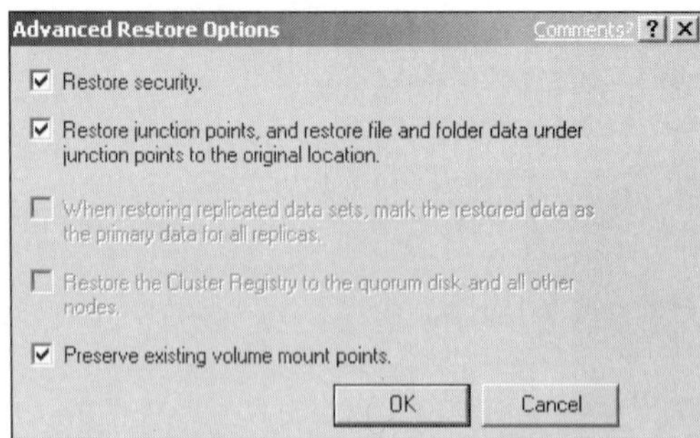

Figure 21.15 Advanced Restore Options window showing default options.

8. Select the appropriate security, junction point, and mount point options. Click `OK` to return to the Confirm Restore window.
9. Click `OK` to begin the restore job. The Restore Progress window keeps you apprised of the job status and tells you when it is complete.
10. When the restore has finished, close the Restore Progress window.

Check the report to confirm that there were no problems noted during the restore, and then put the user's file back where it belongs.

Cataloging a Tape

When Ntbackup writes a backup file to tape, it includes a copy of the catalog entry for that job. If you have a tape that contains backup files but no on-disk catalog, you can restore the catalog from tape then restore the files on the tape using the restored catalog (see Procedure 21.6).

Procedure 21.6 Cataloging a Tape

1. Insert the tape in the tape drive and wait about a minute for RSM to mount it and read the label.
2. Launch `Ntbackup` and select the `Restore and Manage Media` tab.
3. In the right pane, look for the catalog entry with a `Media Location` that indicates it is mounted. The other catalog entries will show `Offline`.
4. Right-click the media name in the right pane and select CATALOG from the flyout menu.
5. When the tape has finished cataloging, the structure will be added to the catalog entries in the tree under the tape device in the left pane.

You can now do a restore from the tape.

Recovering from Blue Screen Stops

There are two varieties of executables in Windows Server 2003:

- Kernel services that run in a privileged memory space inside the Windows Executive
- User applications that run in unprivileged memory

For the most part, it should be nearly impossible for a User-side application to crash a system. Oh, a user app can load the system outrageously or cause it to become autistic, but it should not cause a complete loss of system services.

Kernel services, on the other hand, are fully capable of causing drastic malfunctions. Rather than risk widespread memory and file corruption, when a kernel service misbehaves, the system is brought to a stop and information about the crash is displayed. This kernel-mode stop is commonly called a *Blue Screen Of Death*, or BSOD, due to the background color of the informational display. This blue screen display is handled by a kernel-mode routine called `KeBugCheckEx`, so it is often called a bugcheck.

Online Event Tracking

If a server crashes due to a bugcheck, or an application hangs and must be killed from Task Manager or by DrWatson, the system assembles a set of XML files that contain the names of the processes that were running at the time of the crash or hang and system information about memory contents and CPU register contents, similar to what you see at the blue screen.

These XML files are sent to Microsoft where they are added to a repository of failure information used to determine causes and help identify solutions for crashes. For example, if thousands of error reports flood into Microsoft that identify a particular driver as the culprit in a crash, Microsoft will work with the vendor to determine the cause of the instabilities.

You may not want this information to be transmitted to Microsoft. There is a set of group policies under `Computer Settings | Administrative Templates | System | Error Reporting` that control the online error report settings. You can elect to block reporting completely, to report on selected applications, or to report only unplanned shutdown events.

Bugcheck Codes

The top lines of the blue screen contain *bugcheck codes* that identify the source of the stop, information about the stop that differs depending on the stop code, and oftentimes the name of the culprit. The information looks like this:

```
*** STOP: 0x0000001E (0xC0000005, 0x8041E9FB, 0x00000000, 0x00000030)
KMODE_EXCEPTION_NOT_HANDLED
*** Address 8041E9FB base at 80400000, DateStamp 377509d0 - ntoskrnl.exe
```

The bugcheck codes are your best bet for quickly finding the cause of the crash. The rest of the stop screen usually (but not always) contains stack dump information listing the processes that were in memory at the time of the crash and what they were doing. Here's a brief explanation of the bugcheck information:

- The first entry after `STOP` is the hex ID of the stop code. This corresponds to the name on the second line. If there is no name, the exception was so severe that the system was not able to refer to the lookup table to generate the name.
- The next four entries are parameters that were passed to `KeBugCheckEx` when the `STOP` error was issued. The meaning and origin of these parameters vary depending on the type of error.

- The line following the bugcheck code specifies the base address of the image that caused the exception, a hex representation of the date stamp on the image, and its name. In this case, the exception was thrown by the kernel driver, Ntoskrnl.exe.

The fact that a particular executable is implicated by bugcheck does not necessarily mean that it was the actual perpetrator. In this game of blue screen Clue, you have to search through all the rooms to find out who killed Mr. Server. The name at the top of the bugcheck list might have just been a dupe used by the real culprit.

The Microsoft Knowledgebase is your best source for information about bugcheck codes. Start by searching for `Q103059`, which lists the stop codes and their names. Then check out `Q192463` for ways to collect information without doing full-blown kernel debugging. For a full list of stop codes, download the Windows DDK from `msdn.microsoft.com` and take a look at the include file, bugcodes.h.

Online Error Reporting

In an effort to find and correct common sources of system hangs and bugchecks, Windows Server 2003 has an Error Reporting service, Ersvc, that collects kernel information from bugcheck and application information from Dr. Watson and sends them to Microsoft where they are cataloged and analyzed. Chapter 3, "Adding Hardware," discusses this feature in detail.

Common Stop Errors

Of the more than 200 kernel-mode stop codes, only a few are especially common. Here they are:

- **`Kmode_Exception_Not_Handled (0x0000001E).`** This error says that an exception occurred in the kernel for which there was no error handler. In most cases, bugcheck can tell you the name of the misbehaving driver. This will be listed in the third line of the display.
- **`Irql_Not_Less_Or_Equal (0x0000000A).`** When a thread issues a software interrupt, it does so at a particular interrupt request level (IRQL). There are 32 IRQLs, with higher numbers having higher priority. An `0A` error occurs when a driver running at one IRQL tries to access memory that is owned by a process at a higher IRQL.
- **`Unexpected_Kernel_Mode_Trap (0x0000007F).`** This is generally a hardware problem. Refer to KnowledgeBase article Q137539 for a list of common culprits.
- **`Ntfs_File_System (0x00000024).`** This is commonly caused by a virus, or sometimes an overly aggressive virus checker. It is also commonly cause by file system utilities that attempt to reach around the APIs to access the file system directly. It can also be caused by file system corruption.

- **`Page_Fault_In_Nonpaged_Area (0x00000050)`.** This is also commonly caused by virus checkers. It has also been tied to many TCP/IP problems, as well. Some fairly notorious denial-of-service attacks result in a `0x50` stop error, so if you start getting this on your DMZ machines, you might try enabling auditing and applying a packet sniffer to see if you can capture the source of the problem.
- **`Inaccessible_Boot_Device (0x0000007B)`.** If this occurs when starting a system that has been in operation a while, it almost always indicates a failed drive, drive controller, or a boot sector virus. If it occurs on a new installation, you may have drive sector translation problems or an improver host adapter driver. This error also occurs if you restart a system following a failure of the primary drive in a mirrored set.

Memory Dumps

There are a variety of steps you can take to assess the cause of a bugcheck and try to prevent another like it:

- If you get a stop error after installing a new piece of hardware, a driver upgrade, or a new application, your first step should be to restart and select the `Last Known Good Configuration` option. See "Restoring Functionality with the Last Known Good Configuration" for details.
- If that doesn't work, boot to a Recovery console and delete or rename the offending driver.
- If you can't physically get to the server, you can set it up for out-of-band (OOB) access to see the bugcheck codes and restart. See "Using Emergency Management Services."

If you try all of these and are still unable to restore normal operation, you can capture the contents of memory at the time of the stop and send it off to Microsoft Product Support Services (PSS) to analyze. PSS charges a few hundred dollars per incident for this service, but when you compare that against the losses incurred from server downtime, it's often worth the expense.

Configuring Memory Dumps

By default, as part of the bugcheck, the contents of RAM are dumped to the paging file. After restart, the paging file is copied to a file called Memory.dmp in the `\Windows` folder.

For this full memory dump to succeed, the paging file must be at least the size of RAM plus 1MB for header information. The paging file must be in the root of the boot drive. (Microsoft calls this the System partition.) This is because the bugcheck routine cannot mount a file system, so it is limited to using bare INT13 calls. You can have other paging files on other drives, but they will not be used for the memory dump.

If you have a fire-breathing server with many, many gigabytes of RAM, you probably don't want to give up gigabytes and gigabytes of real estate in your system partition for the paging file. Also, a multi-gigabyte dump file is not likely to have useful content unless the misbehaving driver leaves a known footprint. To avoid large memory dumps, you have two options:

- **Small memory dumps.** This dumps just that portion of RAM owned by the operating system. This is rarely over 1GB and cannot be more than 2GB, at least on IA32 systems. IA64 systems can have a larger footprint. You'll have to check Task Manager to find out how much dump space to set aside.
- **Kernel memory dumps.** This dumps just the stack space. This can be useful only if the offending driver leaves a very clear indication. Otherwise, it does not include sufficient information for a full diagnosis.

Memory dump options are controlled by System properties. Right-click the `My Computer` icon and select PROPERTIES from the flyout menu. The `Advanced` tab has a `Startup and Recovery` button that opens a window to access the memory dump settings. Figure 21.16 shows an example.

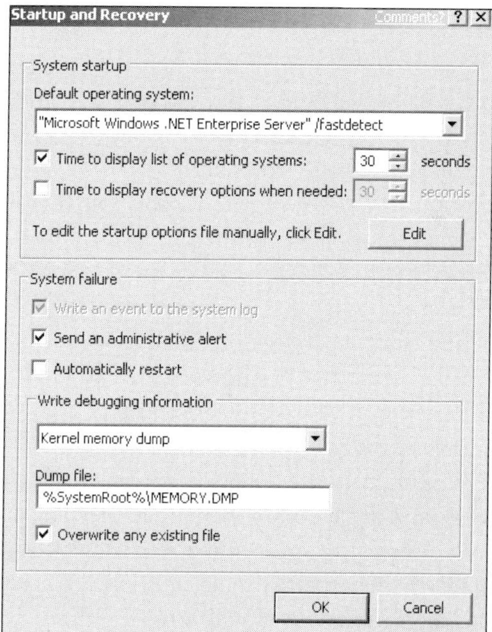

Figure 21.16 Startup and Recovery window showing default Recovery settings for handling system stop errors.

Several recovery options in this window are worth your attention. They are as follows:

- `Send an Administrative Alert` uses the Alerter service, if it is still functioning after the crash, to put out a network broadcast to members of the Administrators domain local group to notify them of the stop error. If you have a trap management console of some sort (HP Openview, for example), you should also load an SNMP agent on the server so it can trap when the failure occurs.
- `Write Debugging Information To` specifies the name of a file that will hold the memory contents after the system reboots. The dump stays in the paging file until the system restarts successfully.
- `Write Kernel Information Only` saves hard drive space that would go to waste if you have lots of RAM in a server. You can size the paging file by opening `Task Manager`, selecting the `Performance` tab, and looking at the total memory value under `Kernel Memory`.
- `Automatically Reboot`. This option restarts the system after the memory dump has completed. It has the potential of causing a continuous loop if the cause of the blue screen stop doesn't go away after restart. For this reason, it is a good idea to monitor your servers with some sort of SNMP tool that will notify you when the server crashes.

Examining Memory Dumps

In production, if you have a server that is crashing regularly and you cannot figure out the problem, it's probably a good idea to spend the money to call Microsoft's Product Support Services. They may want a copy of the memory dump file. Before you burn a huge dump onto a CD for the overnight pouch to PSS, it's a good idea to make sure there is useful information in the dump file. The Windows Server 2003 CD has a utility called DUMPCHK that verifies the integrity of the file contents.

If you'd like to do your own poking around in the dump file, you'll need a tool. The simplest and most flexible dump analysis tool is the *Windows Debugger*, Windbg. You can get this tool on the Windows Server 2003 CD, which comes in Technet or can be downloaded from the MSDN web site.

The Windows Server 2003 CD also has a fairly hefty *symbols file* that you need to install. These symbols help the debugger interpret what it sees in the dump file. There are two sets of symbol files, one for the retail version of the product and one for the debug version. Unless you are running the debug version of Windows Server 2003 from the MSDN library, use the retail symbols.

When you install Windbg, it will look for the symbols in the `\Windows\Symbols` folder. If you did not install the symbols into that default location, you must configure Windbg with the actual location. This is in done in View | Options | Symbols.

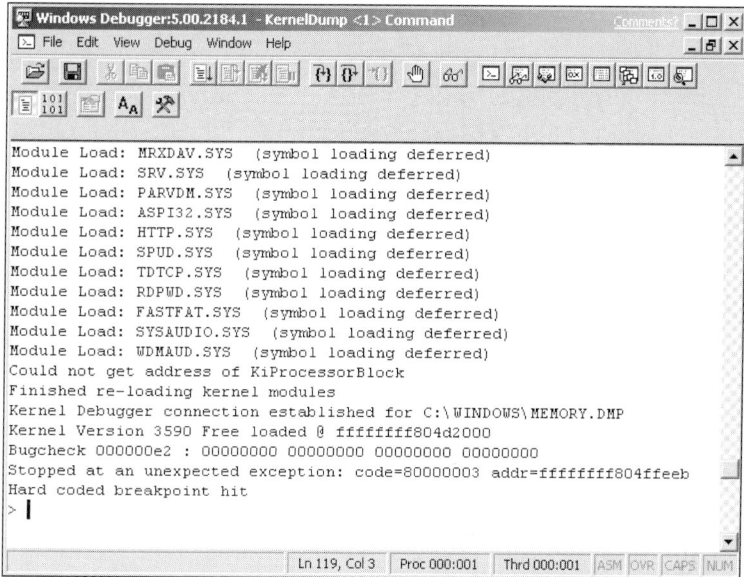

Figure 21.17 Windbg Debugger window showing results of loading a crash dump file.

Windbg has a huge number of uses and switches, all of which lie outside the scope of this book. The feature that can help with crash dump analysis, though, is pretty straightforward. Simply point the program at the crash dump file, `\Windows\Memory.dmp`, using FILE | OPEN CRASH DUMP. Figure 21.17 shows an example following a crash. I generated the crash in this example using a diagnostic feature in Windows. (If you sneered just now, you're a cynic.) To enable this feature, make the following Registry change to the keyboard driver:

```
Key:    HKLM | System | CurrentControlSet | Services | i8042prt | Parameters
Value:  CrashOnCtrlScroll
Data:   1 (REG_DWORD)
```

After restarting with this setting, you can crash the system by pressing the right `Ctrl` key (not the left) and then pressing the `Scroll Lock` key twice.

The debugger will point right at the source of the crash if it can get a clear picture from the dump file about the events that led up to the bugcheck.

Following the restart, the Error Reporting Service will want to send Microsoft information about the crash. A notification window gives you the opportunity to decide whether or not to send the information. A hyperlink takes you to the details of what will be sent. Figure 21.18 shows an example.

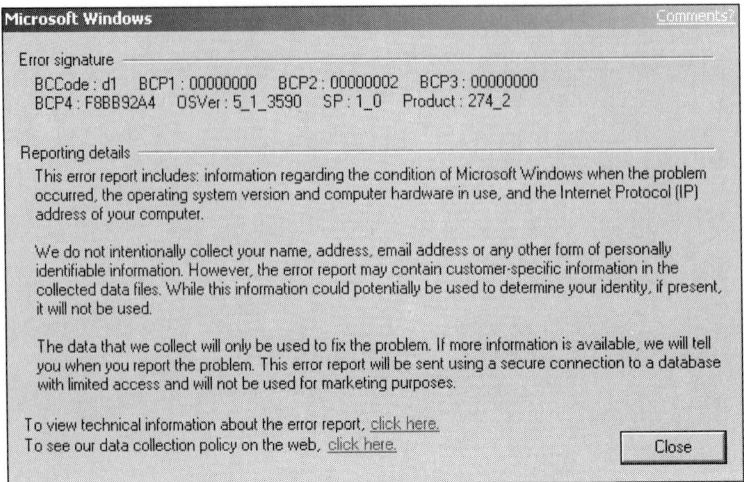

Figure 21.18 Error Reporting window following a system crash.

Using Emergency Management Services (EMS)

It is often handy to access a server outside of the normal network connection. For example, the network interface at the server might not be functioning. Or, something has broken the connection between you and the server. Or, the server refuses to respond and you want to check out the problem.

Windows Server 2003 provides a way to access a server via a serial line connection. This feature is called *Emergency Management Services*, or EMS. The name is a little misleading because there really isn't a service called Emergency Management. Instead, EMS represents a base functionality that can be enabled using a switch in Boot.ini. This switch redirects output to a serial port and listens for responses.

The simplest way to configure EMS port redirection is to use the BOOTCFG utility. Run the utility at a command prompt at the server where you want run EMS. Here is the syntax to redirect the first ARC path in a Boot.ini file to COM1 at 115200bps:

```
bootcfg /ems on /port com1 /baud 115200 /id 1
```

Here is the listing of the Boot.ini file that shows the changes in bold:

```
[boot loader]
timeout=0
default=multi(0)disk(0)rdisk(0)partition(1)\WINDOWS
redirect=COM1
redirectbaudrate=115200
[operating systems]
multi(0)disk(0)rdisk(0)partition(1)\WINDOWS="Microsoft Windows XP
➥Professional" /fastdetect /redirect
```

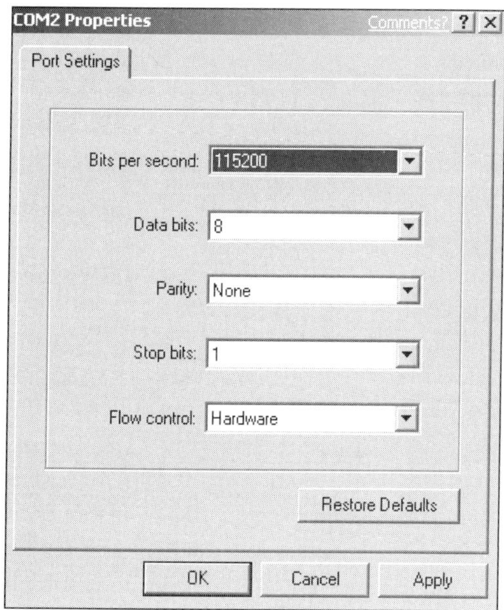

Figure 21.19 Hyperterm COM port configuration properties.

When you boot the server with this configuration, EMS is enabled and you can pick up the output from the serial port. To make a serial-line connection to the server, you'll need a null-modem cable. Look for a serial cable with female DB-9 connections at each end. Don't use a LapLink data transfer cable. It won't work for this application.

Also, you'll need a terminal emulator running at a client on the other end of that serial line. A convenient terminal emulator comes in all 32-bit versions of Windows. It is Hyperterm, loaded from ACCESSORIES | COMMUNICATIONS. Configure Hyperterm to use a COM port rather than a modem and configure the properties for the COM port at 8n1 with a 115200bps connection speed and hardware flow control (see Figure 21.19).

If you want to configure out-of-band connections to many servers in a server room, take a look at serial-port concentrators from vendors such as Muxmaster and Cyclades. These concentrators give you both a network and a dial-up connection to the serial ports and they incorporate logon security, a feature missing from standard EMS. You should never connect a modem directly to the serial port of a production server. Some 14-year-old kid will find it using a demon-dialer and you'll end up with all sorts of strange things happening to your system.

Special Administration Console (SAC)

When you make a serial-line connection to a server running EMS, you are presented with a text screen called the Special Administration Console, or SAC. This console has a short list of functions shown in Figure 21.20.

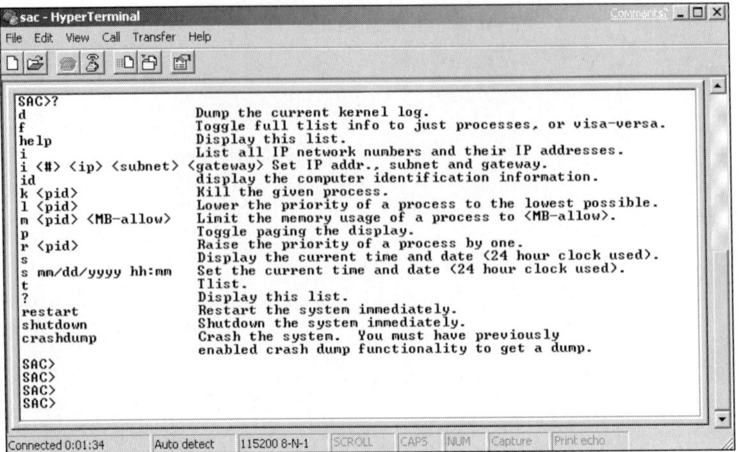

Figure 21.20 EMS Special Administration Console.

For the most part, the SAC functions are self-explanatory. For example, the `t` function mimics the Tlist utility in the Resource Kit by giving a list of the running executables and their Process IDs, or PIDs. You can use this information to find the PID for a hung process and then use the `k` function to kill the process. The `restart` function is handy for bouncing a hung server.

If, for some reason, SAC is unavailable, the system falls back on an emergency SAC called !SAC. This console has only four options:

- **`Restart`**. Performs an immediate restart.
- **`D`**. Displays Event log entries.
- **`ID`**. Displays server identification information.
- **`Q`**. Returns the serial port to normal operation.

EMS and Bugcheck

If a system crashes as the result of a kernel-mode stop error, EMS redirects the bugcheck screen to the serial port. Figure 21.21 shows an example.

Unless you have the server configured to not restart following the memory dump, this bugcheck window will disappear in a few minutes to be replaced with the SAC as soon as the server restarts.

If you configure your terminal emulator to capture all input, you'll be able to scroll up and see the bugcheck window. This gives you an idea where to look for problems following the restart.

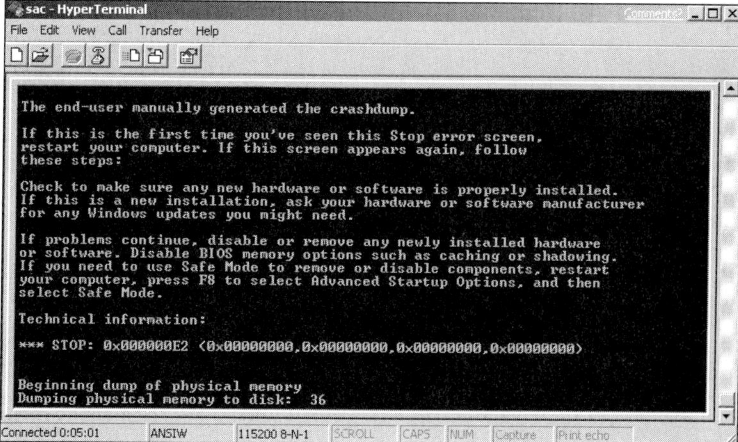

Figure 21.21 EMS connection showing bugcheck results displayed in Hyperterm console.

Using Safe Mode

When a driver decides to do bad things that cause a system to crash or behave erratically, you can try booting with a set of critical system drivers and nothing else. This is called *Safe Mode.* There are various flavors of Safe Mode. Access them by pressing `F8` at the boot menu. Here is a list of the options in this menu:

- **`Safe Mode.`** This mode loads a bare set of peripheral drivers, 16-color VGA video, SCSI and IDE interfaces for mass storage, floppy interface, and a few system services. Safe Mode does not load network services. When you select this option, an environment variable called `SAFEBOOT_OPTION=MINIMAL` is set.
- **`Safe Mode with Networking.`** This option loads the same drivers as standard Safe Mode with the addition of network drivers. This mode is useful when you want to restore files across the network or run a third-party backup agent to do a tape restore. This mode sets the `SAFEBOOT_OPTION=NETWORK` environment variable.
- **`Safe Mode with Command Prompt.`** This is the same as Safe Mode except that the Explorer shell does not start. All you get is a bare command window. Use this mode if corruption in the Explorer files or abnormal Registry entries cause the machine to bugcheck in graphics mode. Avoid running graphical programs in the command window because they automatically launch Explorer, which could crash the machine. This mode sets `SAFEBOOT_OPTION=MINIMAL` in the environment.
- **`Enable Boot Logging.`** This is not a Safe Mode option. Use this option if you want a log of the kernel service drivers as they load. The output goes to a file called Ntbtlog.txt in the `\Windows` directory. The system boots with its normal contingent of drivers and services.

Special Logon Considerations in Directory Services Restore Mode

When booting to DS Restore Mode, Active Directory does not start. This means the Kerberos security provider is not available. The MSV1_0 security provider is the only source of authentication for local logon, and MSV1_0 uses the SAM to validate logon credentials.

When a server is promoted to domain controller, the old SAM is deleted and a new SAM put in place with a new Administrator account. The promotion wizard collects a password for this new Administrator account. When you boot to DS Repair Mode, you must log on using this password. I recommend writing it down and keeping the note in a secure place. One trick used by some administrators is to put the note inside the locked server.

- **`Enable VGA Mode`.** This is not a Safe Mode option. It replaces the currently loaded video drivers with standard 16-color VGA drivers. This is useful for troubleshooting video problems, although it can be a pain because you must manually reload the correct drivers after selecting this option. If you aren't sure of the correct drivers, you might find yourself searching around for the driver disk or downloading them again from the vendor's web site.
- **`Last Known Good Configuration`.** A troubleshooting option designed to return the `System` hive to a previously stable condition.
- **`Debugging Mode`.** This option sets up the system for kernel-mode debugging. See the Microsoft Knowledgebase for a description of kernel-mode debugging.
- **`Directory Service Restore Mode (Domain controllers only)`.** This is a special version of Safe Mode used to correct Active Directory database problems and to recover the System State files on a domain controller. This mode sets `SAFEBOOT_OPTION=DSREPAIR` in the environment.

You'll notice while you are in Safe Mode that the Desktop displays the Windows Server 2003 version number and build number along with the term *free*. This indicates that you're running a build that is free of debug symbols. A *checked* build consists of system files that contain the debug symbols used for kernel-mode debugging. A checked build runs more slowly and takes more memory.

While in Safe Mode, you can replace a problem driver or disable a service or install a different driver to correct a problem. You can run Jet repair utilities against any of the support databases. If you think your problem is more fundamental, you can use CHKNTFS to schedule a full disk scan at boot time.

Restoring Functionality with the Last Known Good Configuration

It's happened to me, and I'm sure it's happened to you, as well. You pop in a CD to install a driver for a snazzy new piece of hardware and *blam*, the system comes to a grinding halt and the bugcheck screen appears. After a few minutes, the system restarts and you watch as *blam*, the system crashes again.

It doesn't take a diagnostic genius to figure out that the driver you just installed made some change in the deep recesses of the machine that is giving Mr. Computer indigestion. The problem now becomes restoring the system back to functionality.

The obvious first step is to keep the bad driver from loading. Drivers are loaded by Registry entries in a top-level key in the `System` hive called a *control set*. If you could just use a copy of the old control set that doesn't have the entry for the new driver, life would be good. This is the philosophy behind the `Last Known Good Configuration` option in the Safe Mode menu.

Structure of Control Sets

Launch the Registry Editor and expand the tree under the `HKLM | System` hive to a key called `Current Control Set`. This control set holds four high-level keys that have the parameters for controlling services and drivers. These keys are as follows:

- **`Control.`** This key contains the parameters that the operating system kernel needs to boot the system. This includes settings for software classes, device classes, load sequencing for device drivers, and security settings. `Control` also contains parameters used by the Configuration Manager so it can access the Registry. This leads to a Catch-22 situation. The Configuration Manager needs parameters in the `Control` key to tell it how to read transaction tracking logs. If an update to the `Control` key is in the transaction tracking log, the system could fail to start. For this reason, the system stores a complete backup of the `System` hive in a file called `System.alt`.
- **`Enum.`** This key stores the results of Plug-and-Play enumeration. When you open the Device Management console and see the list of devices and their associated parameters and resources, you are looking at a graphical representation of the `Enum` key contents.
- **`Hardware Profiles.`** This key is like a miniature control set that sets special parameters for Docked or Undocked conditions. Hardware profiles are rarely needed thanks to Plug-and-Play, but if you define profiles, the special configuration settings associated with that profile are saved here. If multiple hardware profiles exist, then Ntldr presents a selection menu right after the standard boot menu.
- **`Services.`** This key contains the operating parameters for all services and drivers.

You'll notice that there are three control set keys: the `Current Control Set` and `Control Set 1` and `Control Set 2`. Highlight the `Select` key, which sits outside the control sets. This key has three values:

- **`Current.`** This points to the control set that was used to boot the machine. This entry points at `Control Set 1`.
- **`Default.`** This points to the control set that will be used during the next normal boot. This entry also points at `Control Set 1`.

- **`Failed.`** If this entry has a value, it's because a control set has been marked as `Failed` following the selection of a new default control set. The normal entry is 0, meaning that no control sets have been marked as failed.
- **`LastKnownGood.`** This entry points at the control set that last successfully booted the machine. This entry points at `Control Set 2`.

Recovering the Last Known Good Configuration

With this information in mind, Procedure 21.7 shows the sequence of events when a machine boots and the user selects the `Last Known Good Configuration` option.

Procedure 21.7 Booting with the Last Known Good Configuration

1. The machine POSTs then loads the boot sector image. This image loads the NT bootstrap loader, Ntldr.
2. One of Ntldr's duties is to check `HKLM | System | Select` to find the identity of the `Default` control set. It passes the number of this control set to the NT kernel driver, Ntoskrnl.
3. If the user interrupts the standard boot process by pressing `F8` at the boot menu, Ntldr displays the `Advanced Options Menu`. One of the options is `Last Known Good Configuration`.
4. Highlight the `Last Known Good Configuration` option and press `Enter`. The system returns to the boot menu with a red message across the bottom of the screen saying `Last Known Good Configuration`. At this point, two things happen in the `Select` key. The original `Default` control set, which was `Control Set 1`, is now marked as `Failed`. Also, the `LastKnownGood` control set, `Control Set 2`, is set as `Default`.
5. Select the standard boot menu item, which should say `Microsoft Windows Server 2003`, and press `Enter`. NTLDR starts loading drivers then displays the Hardware Profile/Configuration Recovery Menu.
6. The Recovery Menu is a combination of the hardware profile selection menu and a control set selection window. This window is a holdover from classic NT. No action should be taken.
7. Press `Enter` to continue or let the counter do it for you. The Windows Executive loads, shifts to graphics mode, then initializes the system based on the contents of the `Default` control set, which at this time is `Control Set 2`. In other words, `Control Set 2` becomes the `Current` control set.
8. If the system boots successfully, defined as all services starting, all drivers loading, and a user logging on successfully at the console, then a value of 1 is set in the `ReportBootOK` value under the Winlogon key in `HKLM | Software | Microsoft | Windows NT | CurrentVersion`.

9. A `ReportBootOK` of 1 indicates that the current control set successfully booted the system. The contents of the current control set, which is now `Control Set 2`, is copied to a new control set, `Control Set 3`, which becomes the `LastKnownGood` control set.

After this procedure, the resulting control set assignments in the `Select` key would be the following:

- **`Current`**—`Control Set 2`
- **`Default`**—`Control Set 2`
- **`Failed`**—`Control Set 1`
- **`LastKnownGood`**—`Control Set 3`

As you can see, this game of musical control sets only resolves a blue screen problem if it is caused by an entry in a control set subkey. If the problem is caused by an entry in some other hive, such as `Software`, the system will continue to be unstable.

Recovery Console

The Recovery Console uses a miniature version of Windows Server 2003 built by the Windows Server 2003 CD to access files on the system partition. Using this operating environment, you can run a small set of diagnostic utilities, disable drivers and services, replace driver files, and do other surgical procedures to recover a failed system. The Repair Console can be loaded in one of two ways:

- Boot from the Windows Server 2003 CD and select the `Repair` option.
- Install the console files on the local drive, which makes the Recovery Console part of the boot menu.

There is no option for booting the Recovery Console from floppies because Windows Server 2003 has no floppy Setup option. Let's install the Recovery Console files on the hard drive then see how it works.

Installing a Bootable Copy of the Recovery Console

The steps in Procedure 21.8 copy the boot files from the Windows Server 2003 CD to the boot drive of the server and configures a boot menu option that loads the Recovery Console. You'll need the Windows Server 2003 CD.

Dynamic Volumes and the Recovery Console

Because the Recovery Console does not load a full-fledged copy of the Logical Disk Manager, it is unable to determine the content of dynamic volumes that are soft-linked to the LDM database. See Microsoft Knowledgebase article Q227364 for more information.

Procedure 21.8 Installing the Recovery Console

1. Insert the Windows Server 2003 CD in the CD-ROM drive.
2. Open a command session and navigate to the `\I386` directory on the CD.
3. Run `winnt32 /cmdcons`. After a fairly long pause, the Windows Server 2003 Setup window opens with a `Recovery Console` warning.
4. Click `Yes` to acknowledge the warning and install the console.
5. After Setup installs the recovery console files, it displays a `Successful Completion` message then exits.

This Recovery Console installation makes the following changes to the drive:

- Creates a hidden folder, `\cmdcons`, in the root directory. This folder contains the same files that are in the boot environment of the Windows Server 2003 CD. Essentially, when you boot using files in the `\cmdcons` folder, you're booting to the Windows Server 2003 CD.
- Copies the Partition Boot Sector from the Windows Server 2003 system volume to the `\cmdcons` folder into a file called Bootsect.dat.
- Puts an alternative bootstrap loader, Cmldr, at the root of the boot partition.
- Modifies the Boot.ini file to include the alternative for booting to the Recovery Console.

Using Bootsect.dat to launch an alternative operating system is a standard Windows trick. This same workaround is used to boot Windows 9x using the Windows Server 2003 bootstrap loader. The Boot.ini file is modified as follows, with the new line in bold:

```
[boot loader]
timeout=30
default=multi(0)disk(0)rdisk(0)partition(1)\Windows
[operating systems]
multi(0)disk(0)rdisk(0)partition(1)\Windows="Windows Server 2003 Standard Edition"
➥/fastdetect
C:\CMDCONS\BOOTSECT.DAT="Windows Server 2003 Recovery Console" /cmdcons
```

When you select the `Recovery Console` option from the boot menu, Ntldr shifts the computer back to Real mode and loads the contents of the Bootsect file into memory at location `0x700h` just as if it had been loaded by a standard INT13 call. Ntldr then turns control over to the executable code in the boot sector image.

The executable code points at an alternative bootstrap loader called Cmldr. This bootstrap loader brings up an alternate command interpreter that has just enough versatility to do file checks, copy drivers, and diagnose a few errors.

Whether you boot to the Windows Server 2003 CD or the `cmdcons` option on the hard drive, the steps to load the Recovery Console are the same. At the Welcome to

Setup screen, select `R` to load the Recovery Console (see Figure 21.22). Notice that there is no longer an Emergency Repair option. So long, Emergency Repair Disk.

The Recovery Console searches for installations of Windows NT, Windows 2000, and Windows Server 2003 and displays them to you for selection. Be careful, because the instructions say `ENTER` in capital letters, but you have to select a partition number first or you will exit out of the Recovery Console and you'll have to boot all over again.

The Recovery Console then prompts you for logon credentials. The only option is to log on using the local Administrator account. If this is a domain controller, you would use the password you gave when you promoted the machine to a domain controller.

If you do not know the Administrator password, you can use one of several utilities to hack a change into the SAM:

- ERD Commander 2000 from `www.winternals.com` ($350 US)
- NTAccess from `www.sunbelt-software.com` ($70 US)
- Windows XP/2000/NT Key from `www.lostpassword.com` ($195 US)

Also, if you have access to any utility that can mount an NTFS partition, or you want to install Windows Server 2003 into a separate partition, you can delete or rename the `SAM` hive file from `\Windows\System32\Config`. The system will build a new SAM with a blank Administrator password. Do not do this if there is the possibility of having unique accounts in that copy of the SAM.

To exit from the Recovery Console and restart the machine, enter `exit` at the console prompt. Pressing `Ctrl+Alt+Del` will not do anything.

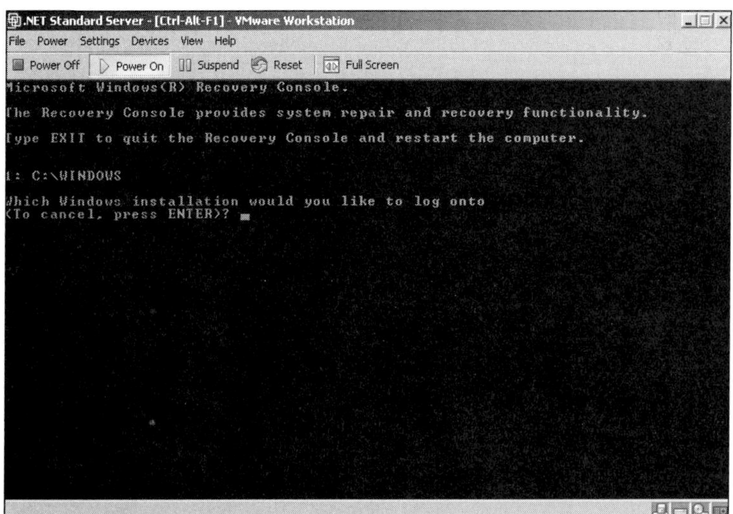

Figure 21.22 Recovery Console welcome and logon screen.

Recovery Console Options

After you've booted into the Recovery Console, if you type `help` at the console prompt, you'll get a list of the available command options. Figure 21.23 shows some examples.

Most have standard functions you would expect from their DOS counterparts. Others are specific to the Recovery Console. Here is a list of the commands with special functionality:

- **`Attrib.`** Changes the attributes of a file but does not display them. Use `Dir` to see attributes.
- **`Batch`**. Runs the contents of a designated text file as a batch file—for example, `batch script1.txt`. Only commands that are part of the Recovery Console command interpreter can be part of the script.
- **`Enable/Disable`**. Use pair of commands to control service entries in the Registry. You can turn off a service that is the source of your troubles. This lets you restart and figure out what happened.
- **`Diskpart`**. Brings up a partition manager very similar to that used in the text-based portion of Setup. You can use this utility to create the partition and then use the `Format` command to install a file system.
- **`Fixboot`**. Replaces the partition boot sector. This is a useful way to remove a boot sector virus.
- **`Fixmbr`**. This writes a new Master Boot Record while leaving the partition table intact. This is similar to using `fdisk /mbr` and has the same potential for making the machine unbootable if the Master Boot Record is non-standard.

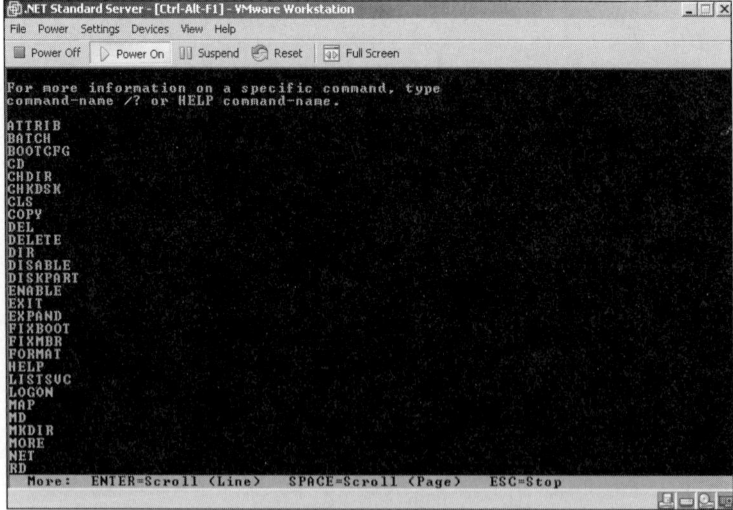

Figure 21.23 Recovery Console command list.

- `Listsvc`. This command lists the services that are in the Registry along with their status setting. Use this command in conjunction with `Enable/Disable`. It's a handy way to look up the short name for the service.
- `Logon`. This initiates the same logon routine that you encountered when the Recovery Console first loaded. You can use it to log on to another instance of Windows on the local system.
- `Map`. This lists the symbolic links under `\Device` in the Object Namespace. These links represent drive partitions.
- `Systemroot`. This option takes you to the system root for the Windows instance that you logged on to. For Windows Server 2003, this is `\Windows`.
- `Exit`. As you would guess, this exits the console and restarts the machine.

Recovery Console Limitations

The default configuration of the Recovery Console imposes several limitations:

- **Directory limits.** You can only view files in the root directory, `\Windows` directory, and the `\cmdcons` directory, if there is one. Attempting to enter other directories gives an `Access Denied` error. This is a security measure to prevent hacking around in user data.
- **File copy limits.** You can only copy files *onto* the hard drive, not off of it. This prevents stealing files.
- **Wild card limits.** To prevent accidental damage to large numbers of files, the Recovery Console does not permit the use of wild cards when deleting files. You cannot run `del *.htm`, for example.
- **Administrator logon.** You must give the Administrator account password to log on to the Recovery Console.

You can remove these security limitations using group policies or direct Registry entries. The group policies are located in `Computer Configuration | Windows Settings | Security Settings | Local Policies | Security Options`. They are as follows:

- **`Allow Automatic Administrative Logon.`** This option uses the local Administrator password to create an automatic logon.
- **`Allow Floppy Copy and Access to All Drives and All Folders.`** This option removes the limitations on copying files *from* the hard drive and it permits you to roam at will on all the drives.
- **`Copy prompts.`** To preserve file integrity, you are prompted when overwriting a file using the `Copy` command.

I'm not necessarily recommending that you enable these policies; I'm just telling you that the options are available. After the second policy is in place, as an additional layer of protection, you must use the `Set` command to specify environment variables in the Recovery Console that enable the expanded functionality. Here are the environment variables (be sure to include the spaces around the equal sign in your `Set` command):

- `AllowWildCards = true`
- `AllowAllPaths = true`
- `AllowRemovableMedia = true`
- `NoCopyPrompt = true`

Loading the Recovery Console from RIS

You can configure a Remote Installation Services (RIS) server to distribute Recovery Console images. This can simplify using the Recovery Console on machines that do not have CD-ROM drives.

You must already have a "flat" RIS image on the RIS server. See Chapter 2, "Performing Upgrades and Automated Installations," for details on installing this image. At the RIS server, create a System Information File (SIF) using a text editor. Give the file an 8.3-compliant name with an `.sif` extension, such as `cmdcons.sif`. The file contents are as follows:

```
[data]
floppyless = "1"
msdosinitiated = "1"
OriSrc = "\\%SERVERNAME%\RemInst\%INSTALLPATH%"
OriTyp = "4"
LocalSourceOnCD = 1

[SetupData]
OsLoadOptions = "/noguiboot /fastdetect"
SetupSourceDevice ="\Device\LanmanRedirector\%SERVERNAME%\RemInst\%INSTALLPATH%"

[UserData]
FullName = "%USERFULLNAME%"
OrgName = "%ORGNAME%"
ComputerName = %MACHINENAME%

[RemoteInstall]
Repartition = no
[OSChooser]
Description ="Windows Server 2003 Recovery Console"
Help ="Loads a Windows Server 2003 Recovery Console."
LaunchFile = "%INSTALLPATH%\%MACHINETYPE%\templates\startrom.com"
ImageType =Flat
Version="5.0"
```

The most important line in this file is the one I've put in bold: `Repartition=no`. If you neglect to include this line, RIS will reformat your hard drive. That can be tough to explain to Management.

Place this SIF file in the following folder under the `\Remoteinstall` folder that holds the RIS image files: `\Remoteinstall\Setup\English\Images\Windows\i386\templates`. Test by booting a PXE (Pre-boot eXecution Environment) client and verifying that it loads the Setup files and can initialize the Recovery Console. From this point forward, you can use the Recovery Console just as you would if you had booted from the Windows Server 2003 CD or from the `\cmdcons` folder.

Moving Forward

Well, you made it. It was a long road to get here to the end of a full deployment of Windows Server 2003. You can now sit back and trade war stories with your colleagues. If you are still besieged with problems and you're getting discouraged and you wish all this Windows Server 2003 stuff were just a tad bit easier, keep these sage words of Orson Welles in mind:

> Italy had thirty years of warfare, terror, murder, and bloodshed under the Borgias and they produced Michelangelo, Leonardo da Vinci and the Renaissance. Switzerland had five hundred years of brotherly love and democracy and peace and what did they produce? The cuckoo clock.

Just remember to have fun.

Index

A

B

C

D

E

G

H

I

J

K

L

M

N

O

P

Q

R

S

T

V

W

X

Z

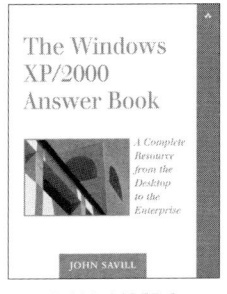

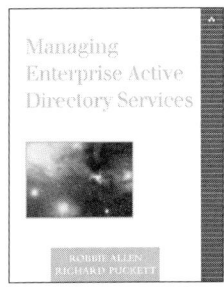

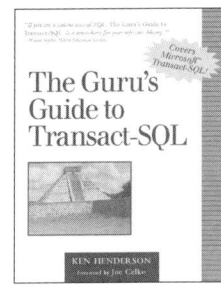

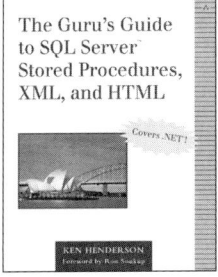

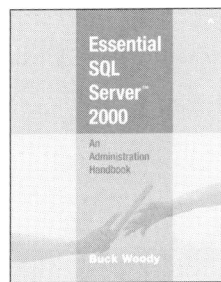

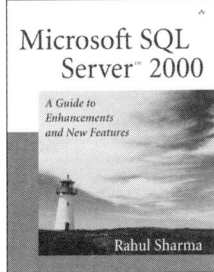

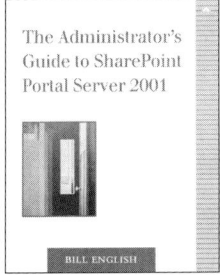

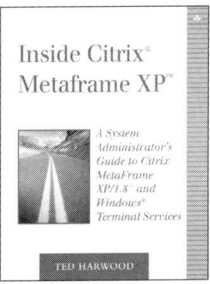

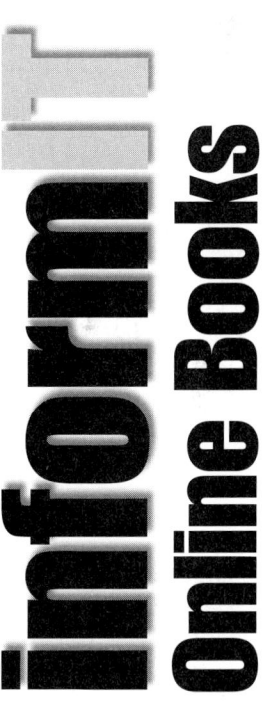